ENVIRONMENTAL LAW

ENVIRONMENTAL LAW

SECOND EDITION

Editors

DAVID WOOLLEY QC
JOHN PUGH-SMITH
RICHARD LANGHAM
WILLIAM UPTON

Contributors

SASHA BLACKMORE
NOÉMI BYRD
MATTHEW REED
JONATHAN WILLS
KATRINA YATES

OXFORD
UNIVERSITY PRESS

OXFORD
UNIVERSITY PRESS

Great Clarendon Street, Oxford OX2 6DP

Oxford University Press is a department of the University of Oxford.
It furthers the University's objective of excellence in research, scholarship,
and education by publishing worldwide in

Oxford New York

Auckland Cape Town Dar es Salaam Hong Kong Karachi
Kuala Lumpur Madrid Melbourne Mexico City Nairobi
New Delhi Shanghai Taipei Toronto

With offices in

Argentina Austria Brazil Chile Czech Republic France Greece
Guatemala Hungary Italy Japan Poland Portugal Singapore
South Korea Switzerland Thailand Turkey Ukraine Vietnam

Oxford is a registered trade mark of Oxford University Press
in the UK and in certain other countries

Published in the United States
by Oxford University Press Inc., New York

British Library Cataloguing in Publication Data

Data available

Library of Congress Cataloging in Publication Data

Data available

Typeset by Cepha Imaging Private Ltd, Bangalore, India
Printed in Great Britain
on acid-free paper by
CPI Antony Rowe, Chippenham, Wiltshire

ISBN 978-0-19-923280-2

1 3 5 7 9 10 8 6 4 2

PREFACE TO THE SECOND EDITION

The editors were as surprised as they were gratified when asked by the publisher to prepare a second edition of this work. Successive royalty statements generated by the first showed over the years that sales, never more than modest, had dwindled to near invisibility. In the world of legal textbooks, however, the numbers, while not rivalling those of Harry Potter, were deemed at least respectable and, in overseas countries, encouraging. Intriguingly, they had been remarkable in China and India, given the reputations, apparently undeserved, of those nations for indifference to environmental protection.

During the last eight years English and Welsh courts have had to address problems raised by the ceaseless grinding of legislative mills in Brussels, Westminster, and Whitehall. This edition tries to cover all these sources of law, up to 1 August 2008.

The editors wish to thank those readers who, with much courtesy and forbearance, pointed out shortcomings in the first edition. Particular thanks are due to Bill Brewer, Jan Stewer, and Peter Gurney. Thanks are also due to all our friends, family, and colleagues. The editors are much obliged to Stephen Tromans and Richard Banwell for their valuable assistance in the preparation of this edition. We hope that the mistakes have been cured, even if replaced by others of which we are ignorant. We must also offer heartfelt thanks to the publishers. Their knowledge and expertise are matched only by their pained tolerance, followed by correction, of grammatical error, syntactical solecism, and missed deadlines.

London EC4

August 2008

CONTENTS—SUMMARY

Detailed Contents	vii
Table of Cases	xxxvii
Table of Statutes	lvii
Table of Statutory Instruments	lxxvii

PART 1: THE FRAMEWORK

1. The History of Environmental Law	3
2. The Structure of Environmental Legislation and Regulation	25
3. International Environmental Law	87
4. European Environmental Law	117
5. Environmental Information	159

PART 2: THE UK REGULATORY FRAMEWORK

6. Environmental Permitting and Integrated Pollution Control	203
7. Waste Management	289
8. Radioactive and Hazardous Substances, and Genetically Modified Organisms	349
9. Water Resources	399
10. The Water Industry	461
11. Nature Conservation	519
12. Contaminated Land	587
13. Miscellaneous Environmental Controls	623

PART 3: THE ROLE OF TOWN AND COUNTRY PLANNING

14. The Relationship between Planning and Pollution Control	661
15. Environmental Impact Assessment	705

PART 4: THE COMMON LAW

16. Common Law Liability for Environmental Damage   745

Index   795

CONTENTS

Table of Cases   xxxvii
Table of Statutes   lvii
Table of Statutory Instruments   lxxvii

PART 1: THE FRAMEWORK

1. The History of Environmental Law   3

   A. Introduction   1.01

   B. The Cholera Epidemic of 1831   1.02
      Conclusions of the report into the cholera epidemic 1.03
            Sanitary conditions   1.03
            Overcrowding   1.04
            Expectation of life   1.05
            Administrative reform   1.06

   C. The Public Health Act 1848   1.07
      Boards of health   1.08
      Drains and sewers   1.09
      Street and house cleansing   1.10
      Rivers and sewers   1.12
      Sanitation and overcrowding   1.13

   D. The Public Health Act 1875   1.14
      The scheme of the Act   1.14
      Drainage of buildings   1.16
      Disposal and treatment of sewage   1.17
      Refuse and sewage collection   1.18
      Water supplies   1.19
      Cellars and lodging houses   1.21
      Statutory nuisances   1.22
      Slums   1.25

Diseases and hospitals 1.26
Burial of the dead 1.29

E. Water Pollution 1.31
Introduction 1.31
Refuse in watercourses 1.32
Prosecutions 1.34
Defences 1.36

F. Unfit Housing 1.38

G. Housing Act 1890 1.42
Introduction 1.42
Procedure under the Act 1.43
Clearing the slums 1.46
Compulsory purchase 1.48
Unfit houses 1.49

H. Town and Country Planning 1.53
Introduction 1.53
The mechanism of the Act of 1909 1.54
Enforcement 1.57
Social changes 1918–1939 1.58
Town and Country Planning Act 1932 1.59
Development control—development
  orders 1.62
Buildings of architectural or historic interest 1.65
Compensation for planning decisions 1.66

I. Modern Developments in Environ mental Law 1.67
Introduction 1.67
Town and Country Planning Act 1947 1.70
The National Parks and Access to the Countryside Act 1949 1.71
The Clean Air Acts 1.74
Wastes 1.76
Noise 1.83
Air pollution 1.84

J. The Integrated Approach—Modern Legislation 1.85

2. **The Structure of Environmental Legislation and Regulation** 25

A. Introduction 2.01

B. The Regulatory Framework 2.05
Environmental statutes 2.05
Environmental Protection Act 1990
  (EPA 1990) 2.06

The Water Resources Act 1991 and the Water Industry Act 1991   2.07
Environment Act 1995   2.08
Public health laws   2.10
Health and safety at work   2.11
Alternatives to regulation   2.12

C. The Different Jurisdictions of the UK   2.16
     England and Wales   2.16
     Scotland   2.18
     Northern Ireland   2.22
     The influence of other common law jurisdictions   2.24

D. The Responsible Public Authorities   2.26
     The role of central government   2.26
     Central government guidance   2.27
         The crown and the royal prerogative   2.32
     The local authorities   2.34
     Other public bodies and executive agencies   2.36
         Statutory undertakers   2.38
         The Royal Commission on Environmental Pollution   2.39
         Other research bodies   2.41

E. The Environment Agency   2.42
     The establishment of the Agency   2.42
         The legal structure of the Agency   2.44
         The regional structure of the Agency   2.46
     The specific responsibilities inherited by the Environment Agency   2.47
         Her Majesty's Inspectorate of Pollution (HMIP)   2.48
         The National Rivers Authority (NRA)   2.49
         Waste and the waste regulation authorities   2.50
     The Environment Agency's principal aims and objectives   2.52
         The principal aim of the Agency   2.53
     The Environment Agency's general functions   2.55
         General functions with respect to pollution control   2.55
         General provisions with respect to water   2.56
         General environmental and recreational duties   2.57
         Incidental powers   2.59
         Environment Agency guidance   2.60
     The financial constraints on decisions made by the Environment
         Agency   2.62

F. Prosecution and Enforcement of Environmental Offences   2.65
     Regulatory reform and risk-based regulation   2.67
         Prosecutions   2.71
         The Environment Agency as prosecutor   2.72
     The decision to prosecute for an environmental offence   2.74

The Agency's enforcement and prosecution policy   2.75
Categorization of incidents   2.76
Other prosecution authorities and the Code for
    Crown Prosecutors   2.79
Environmental sentencing   2.83

G. Holding Public Bodies to Account—Judicial Review   2.88

H. Holding Public Bodies to Account—Complaints to the
    Ombudsman   2.96

3. International Environmental Law   87

A. Introduction   3.01

B. International Law and the Environment   3.02
The relevance of international law within the UK   3.04
    Future legislation   3.05
    Interpretation of legislation   3.06
European policy initiatives   3.09
National policy   3.10
Sustainable development and climate change   3.11
    Sustainable development   3.11
    Climate change   3.13
    The precautionary principle   3.18

C. International Environmental Agreements   3.20
International trade and the environment   3.23
Marine pollution   3.25
Air pollution   3.26
Trans-frontier trade in waste   3.28
Nature conservation and the protection of wildlife   3.29
The Aarhus Convention and access to justice   3.31

D. Human Rights Law and the Environment   3.35
International human rights law and the environment   3.35
The European Convention on Human Rights   3.36
    Human Rights Act 1998   3.37
    The Convention rights   3.40
    Article 8   3.42
    Property rights   3.47
    Procedural rights   3.49

4. European Environmental Law   117

A. Introduction   4.01
The structure of the European Community and its institutions   4.02

The European court of justice 4.06
  The ECJ and the purposive approach 4.09
  The ECJ and proportionality 4.12
The current framework and aims of European environmental policy 4.13
  The precautionary principle 4.17
European policy documents on the environment 4.18
  Action programmes 4.18
  Communications 4.21
The different types of European environmental legislation 4.24
  Regulations 4.25
  Directives 4.26
  Directives and the doctrine of 'direct effect' 4.30
  Decisions, recommendations, and opinions 4.40
The European Union and human rights 4.41

B. The implementation of European Law in the UK 4.43
The constitutional status of European law 4.43
The need for national courts to refer questions to the ECJ
  under Article 234 4.47
The use of the principles of European law in the UK courts 4.49
  The precautionary principle 4.51
  The 'polluter pays' principle 4.53
  Environmental liability 4.54

C. European Remedies for Individual Litigants 4.56
Individual remedies—Judicial review 4.58
Individual remedies—Damages against the state 4.63
Individual remedies—Defence in criminal proceedings 4.69
Infraction proceedings against the UK 4.72
Challenging community legislation—Direct actions 4.73

5. Environmental Information 159

A. The Royal Commission on Environmental Protection 5.01
Introduction 5.01
Public apprehension 5.12
The public interest 5.13
Progress—The change of climate 5.15

B. Nuclear Waste 5.19
The Royal Society 5.20

C. Environmental Information—General Provisions 5.22
Introduction 5.22
The Environmental Information Regulations 5.23

Code of practice and historical records   5.36
Appeals and enforcement   5.38
The Local Government (Access to Information) Act 1985   5.40

D. Environmental Information about Land   5.50
Town and country planning   5.50
Environmental impact   5.59
Appeals under the Town and Country Planning Acts   5.80
Waste   5.84
Contamination   5.93
Registers of contaminated land   5.98

E. Information about Air Pollution   5.121

F. Information about Water   5.125
The registers   5.125
The content of the registers   5.126
Integrated pollution control publicity   5.134
Gathering information   5.138
Publicity   5.148

G. Information about Radioactivity   5.153
Nuclear installations   5.153
Other premises   5.158

H. Information on Miscellaneous Matters   5.163

I. The Powers of Inspectors   5.165
Environment Agency inspectors   5.165
Obstruction of inspectors   5.167
Powers of entry   5.169
Emergencies   5.174
Immunity of inspectors   5.175

PART 2: THE UK REGULATORY FRAMEWORK

6. Environmental Permitting and Integrated Pollution Control   203

A. Introduction   6.01
A short history of industrial pollution control and its future   6.01
The current system   6.04

B. Part A(1) Installations and mobile plant   6.08
The regulatory bodies   6.08
The 'regulator'   6.08
The Secretary of State   6.09
The regulation of facilities   6.10

The person   6.10
The subject matter of IPPC: 'regulated facilities' and 'activities'   6.11
    Regulated facilities   6.11
    Activities   6.20
The interpretation of IPPC categorizations   6.25
The limits of IPPC   6.27
    Insignificant processes and low level activities   6.27
    Waste management   6.30
    Mobile plant   6.36
    Noise   6.38
    Radioactivity and GMOs   6.39
The changeover from the 2000 Regulations to the 2007
    Regulations—transitional provisions   6.40
The regulator's exercise of its functions   6.41
    A(1) Installations and mobile plant   6.41
Best available technique ('BAT')   6.56
Waste operations   6.65
Landfill installations   6.70
Waste motor vehicles   6.72
Waste electrical and electronic equipment   6.73
Waste incineration   6.74
Solvent emissions installations and plant   6.77
Combustion plants, asbestos, titanium dioxide, and
    petrol vapour recovery   6.78

C. The Environmental Permit Procedure   6.79
The application   6.79
Operator competence   6.90
Charges   6.95
Alternative forms of application   6.96
    The staged application   6.96
    Composite applications   6.99
Consultation and public participation   6.103
    Public consultees   6.103
    Other European Member States   6.108
Timing of application, including novel applications
    and where planning permission is required   6.109
The determining body   6.113
    Generally   6.113
The manner of exercising   6.114
    The framework for the decision   6.114
The permit—specific requirements   6.120
The permit—the conditions   6.122
The permit—standard rules   6.129

Conflicts between permits 6.136
The time limits for determination of an
   application 6.137
The effect of a grant 6.139
Determination by the Secretary of State 6.140

D. Review, Variation, Transfer, Revocation, Remediation, and
   Surrender of Environmental Permits 6.144
Review and inspection 6.144
Variations of environmental permits 6.147
Transfer of environmental permits 6.153
Revocation of environmental permits 6.156
Remediation 6.158
Surrender of environmental permits 6.160

E. Appeals 6.167
The right of appeal 6.167
The date for appealing 6.169
The effect of an appeal 6.171
Appeal procedure 6.172
   Making the appeal 6.172
   Notification 6.175
   Other procedural requirements 6.176
   Hearings 6.177
   Written representations 6.181
   Call in and recovery of cases 6.183
   The decision 6.184
   Costs 6.185
   Further appeals 6.186

F. Enforcement of Environmental Permit Regime 6.188
Introduction 6.188
The Environment Agency's
   enforcement policy 6.189
The enforcing authority's
   investigative powers 6.190
Prohibitory notices 6.194
   Enforcement notices 6.194
   Suspension notices 6.196
Landfill closure notices 6.199
Direct action 6.200
Offences 6.201
   The Agency's prosecution policy 6.202
   Corporate offences 6.208

Contents

Operating a regulated facility without or in contravention
of an environmental permit or prohibitory notices   6.209
Other offences   6.215
Offences under the Environment Act 1995   6.222
Court orders   6.226
Statutory orders   6.226
Crown immunity   6.235

G. Local Authority Control of Installations and Mobile Plant   6.236
Local authority control—general
matters   6.236
The role of the local authority
in LAPPC and LA-IPPC   6.237

H. The Responsibilities of the Local Authority   6.242
Part A(2) Installations and mobile plant   6.243
Part B Installations and mobile plant   6.244
Waste operations   6.253
Contaminated land   6.254
Determination of LAPPC and LA-IPPC applications   6.255
The authorization framework   6.256
LA-IPPC (Part A(2))   6.261
LAPPC (Part B)   6.276
Water consent issues   6.277
Transfer, variation, review, and revocation   6.278
Enforcement   6.283

I. Registers   6.286
The information on the public register   6.286
Form and content of registers   6.293
The exclusion from the public register of information affecting
national security   6.295
The exclusion of confidential information from the public register   6.298
The result of exclusion from the public register   6.306

7. Waste Management   289

A. Introduction   7.01

B. Waste—The Definitions   7.05
Controlled Waste   7.09
The Controlled Waste Regulations—household waste   7.16
Removal of household waste   7.23
Holiday houses and caravans   7.29
Recyclable and non-recyclable waste   7.31

Schools, colleges, and racing stables	7.33
Miscellaneous waste and removal charges	7.35
Industrial waste	7.37
Sewage	7.40
Clinical waste	7.42
Waste from aircraft, vehicles, and vessels	7.44
Offensive waste	7.45
Oil, solvents, and scrap metal	7.47
Commercial waste	7.48
Exemption for public bodies	7.51
C. Special Waste	7.53
Special waste—compounds	7.60
Explosives	7.62
Directive waste	7.63
Hazardous waste	7.70
Specific types of waste	7.76
Packaging	7.77
Motor vehicles	7.78
D. A National Strategy for Waste	7.85
Introduction	7.85
The strategy	7.86
The import and export of waste	7.88
Rationing landfill	7.89
Strategy	7.93
E. Waste Management—The Duty of Care	7.95
Introduction	7.95
Persons under the duty of care	7.96
Exemptions from the duty of care	7.105
F. Waste Licensing	7.110
The previous regime	7.110
The present regime	7.111
G. Enforcement	7.122
Introduction	7.122
The machinery of enforcement	7.123
Registers	7.128
H. Obtaining a Waste Management Licence	7.131
Introduction—the deposit of controlled waste	7.131
'Causing or permitting'	7.133
Pollution of the environment and harm to health	7.136
Defences	7.139

Household waste	7.143
Exemptions for incineration and burning	7.164
Miscellaneous exemptions	7.167
Fly-tipping	7.168
The right to a licence	7.170
The relationship to town and country planning	7.173
The functions of the Environment Agency	7.174
Fitness to hold a licence	7.177
Conditions of a licence	7.188
Appeals	7.193
I. The Duty of Care	7.197
Introduction	7.197
Transfer notes	7.201
The Code of Practice	7.203
Carriers	7.207
Breach of the duty of care	7.209
Variation, transfer, surrender, and revocation of licences	7.211
Transfers	7.217
Revocation	7.225
Surrender	7.229
Mobile plant licences	7.234
Closed landfill sites	7.235
J. Waste Collection and Disposal	7.236
Collection	7.236
Disposal	7.246
Landfill	7.257
8. Radioactive and Hazardous Substances, and Genetically Modified Organisms	**349**
A. Introduction	8.01
B. Radioactive Substances	8.02
Introduction	8.02
Nuclear installations	8.06
Nuclear installations—licensing	8.07
Conditions of a licence	8.11
The currency of the licence	8.12
Surrender and revocation	8.17
Compensation for breach of duty under the NIA	8.18
Restrictions on the right to compensation	8.20
Jurisdiction over claims to compensation	8.28

Additional sanctions	8.34
Radioactivity and congenital disease	8.36
C. Radioactive Materials and Waste	8.38
Introduction	8.38
Exemptions from registration	8.41
Registration procedure	8.43
Appeals	8.45
Mobile radioactive apparatus	8.47
Cancellation and variation of registration	8.49
Radioactive waste	8.50
Enforcement	8.56
Transport of radioactive material	8.61
D. Hazardous Substances—The Planning (Hazardous Substances) Act 1990	8.65
Introduction	8.65
Definitions	8.67
Keeping hazardous substances	8.70
Exemptions from consent	8.72
Deemed consent	8.77
Applying for hazardous substances consent—hazardous substances authorities	8.80
Consultation	8.84
Determining the application	8.86
Appeals	8.90
Amendment and termination of consents	8.91
Revocation and modification of consents	8.97
Compensation	8.100
The powers of the Secretary of State	8.105
Enforcement of hazardous substances control	8.110
Hazardous substances contravention notices	8.117
Appeals against contravention notices	8.121
Other sanctions against breaches of control	8.129
Miscellaneous provisions	8.132
Accidents involving hazardous substances	8.140
Lead shot	8.149
PCBs	8.151
E. Genetically Modified Organisms	8.154
Introduction	8.154
The uses of genetic modification	8.157
GMOs—the definition	8.160
GMOs—the system of control	8.172

Importation, acquisition, release, and marketing of GMOs   8.176
Notification   8.182
Policing the control of GMOs   8.187
Sanctions   8.195
GMOs—miscellaneous provisions   8.200
GMOs—health and safety at work   8.202
Containment of GMOs   8.203
Release and marketing of GMOs   8.210
Traceability and labelling of GMOs   8.212

9. **Water Resources**   399

A. Water Resources—An Introduction   9.01
   The main Acts   9.01
   European law   9.04
   The public authorities   9.06
   The Environment Agency and its duties and powers   9.07
       The Agency's relationship with the Water Industry   9.12

B. Water Resources Management   9.15
   The strategic policy framework   9.15
       Water Framework Directive   9.16
   River Basin Management Plans   9.18
       The potential to set minimum acceptable flows   9.21
   Groundwater   9.22
       Oil storage   9.25
       Nitrate vulnerability zones   9.28
   Abstraction licensing   9.32
       The requirement for an abstraction licence   9.33
       General exemption for small quantities   9.34
       Potential enforcement and offences   9.35
       Restriction on who can apply for an abstraction licence   9.37
       Types of abstraction licence   9.38
       The application process for an abstraction licence   9.41
       The Secretary of State's role in abstraction licencing   9.45
       Appeals regarding an abstraction licence   9.46
       The contents of an abstraction licence   9.47
       Other abstraction licence exemptions   9.49
   Damage from abstraction   9.50
   Impounding licences   9.51
   Modification and revocation of licences   9.55
       Agency proposals to revoke or modify   9.56
       Modifications on the application of the owner of fishing rights   9.57

Water rights trading   9.59
    Charges for licences   9.60
Compensation provisions   9.61

C. Drought   9.62
Ordinary drought order   9.62
Emergency drought order   9.67
    Restricting the use of water   9.69
    Effect on inland navigations   9.70
    Power to carry out works   9.71
    Compensation   9.72
Drought permits   9.73
Offences   9.76
Drought plans   9.77

D. Control of Pollution of Water Resources   9.78
Water quality   9.78
Water pollution offences   9.81
    The common elements of Section 85 offences   9.87
    Controlled waters   9.89
    Causing or knowingly permitting—acts and omissions   9.90
Causing   9.93
Liability due to an act or default   9.98
    Poisonous, noxious, or polluting matter   9.100
    Waste matter   9.102
    Trade effluent or sewage effluent   9.103
    Entry or discharge   9.106
    A prohibition imposed under Section 86   9.107
Statutory defences   9.108
    Discharge consents   9.109
    Emergency   9.115
    Vessels   9.119
    Crown immunity   9.120
    Highway authorities   9.121
    Abandoned mines   9.122
    Anti-pollution works notices   9.125

E. Land Drainage and Flood Control   9.128
Introduction   9.128
    Flood controls   9.129
Riparian owners   9.132
Regional flood defence committees   9.133
Internal drainage boards   9.134
Drainage powers   9.137
Standards of flood defence   9.143
Financial provisions   9.144

10. The Water Industry   461

  A. Organization of the Water Industry   10.02
      Historical background   10.02
      The privatized water industry   10.09
          Water and sewerage undertakers   10.09
          Licensed water suppliers   10.11
          The Secretary of State and the Authority   10.12
          The Council   10.14
          Local authorities   10.15

  B. General Duties Under the WIA   10.16
      Section 2—General service duties of the Secretary of State/NAW
          and the Authority   10.17
      Sections 3 and 4—General environmental and recreational
          duties of the Secretary of State/NAW, the Authority,
          and undertakers   10.19

  C. Appointment of Water and Sewerage Undertakers   10.25
      Introduction   10.25
      Conditions of appointment   10.28
      Modification of conditions   10.32
          Modification with agreement of the undertaker and the
             Authority   10.33
          Modification following reference to the Competition
             Commission   10.34
          Modification under the Enterprise Act 2002   10.39
      Variation and termination of appointments   10.40
      Mergers and disposal of land   10.44
          Mergers   10.44
          Disposal of protected land   10.46

  D. Water Undertakers   10.49
      General duty on water undertakers under Section 37   10.50
      Regulations   10.52
      Duties of water undertakers in relation to domestic supply   10.57
          Duty on water undertaker to provide and maintain
          domestic supplies   10.58
          Demand for a domestic supply   10.61
          Enforcement   10.63
      Duty on water undertaker to provide a new water main for domestic
          purposes   10.65
          Enforcement   10.68
      Duty of water undertaker to provide connection to water main for
          domestic purposes   10.69
          Enforcement   10.74

Duty on water undertaker to maintain constancy and pressure
   of domestic supplies   10.75
   Enforcement   10.79
Duties of water undertakers with regard to non-domestic supplies   10.80
   Duty of water undertakers to maintain existing non-domestic
     supplies   10.80
   Requests to water undertakers for new non-domestic supplies   10.81
   Fire hydrants   10.84
   Cleansing sewers etc   10.85
   Bulk supplies   10.86
Disconnections   10.89
Obligations on water undertakers in respect of the quality of
   domestic supply   10.95
   Duty on water undertakers and licensed water suppliers under
     Section 68   10.95
   Water unfit for human consumption   10.102
Quality of non-domestic supply   10.105
Contamination, waste and droughts   10.106
   Contamination and waste   10.106
   Hosepipe bans   10.108
   Drought orders   10.109
   Water resources management plans   10.110
   Drought plans   10.111

E. Licensed Water Suppliers   10.112
   Rights conferred by a water supply licence   10.116

F. Water Supply Functions of Local Authorities   10.122

G. Sewerage Undertakers   10.127
   General duty   10.128
   Regulations   10.131
   Drainage of premises   10.136
     Right of occupiers/owners of premises to utilize undertaker's
       sewerage system   10.136
     New connections to existing sewers   10.139
     Requisitions of new sewers for domestic purposes   10.143
     Sewers to premises erected before 1995   10.146
     Other powers with respect to the sewerage system   10.148
     Compensation following exercise of powers under Sections
       101A–116   10.152
   Trade Effluent   10.153
     Introduction   10.153
     Discharge consent under Section 119   10.159
     Variation of discharge consents   10.162

Agreements under Section 129   10.165
Special category effluent   10.168
Reference to the Environment Agency   10.169
Review by Environment Agency   10.171
Procedure   10.173
Processes regulated under Section 2 of the Pollution
Prevention and Control Act 1999   10.175
Treatment   10.176
Discharges of treated sewage   10.181

H. Sewerage Functions of Local Authorities   10.182

I. Undertakers' Works etc   10.184
Powers to lay pipes in streets and private land   10.184
Pipe laying in streets   10.187
Pipe laying in private land   10.189
Discharges by water undertakers in the course of pipe laying   10.191
Restrictions on interference with other water-related
infrastructure   10.193
Compensation for pipe laying in private land   10.194
Code of Practice and complaints   10.195
Compulsory purchase of land by water and sewerage undertakers   10.198
Compulsory works orders of water undertakers   10.199
Adoption of apparatus   10.200
Water undertakers—agreements to adopt domestic water
mains etc at a future date   10.201
Sewerage undertakers—adoption of existing apparatus at
insistence of undertaker   10.208
Sewerage undertakers—adoption of proposed apparatus at
insistence of owner   10.209
The mining code   10.211
Maps of underground apparatus   10.214
Right of landowners to require removal of undertaker's apparatus 10.217

J. Powers of Entry of Water and Sewerage Undertakers   10.219

K. Charges   10.222
Charges schemes and agreements   10.222
Metered supply of water   10.227

L. Enforcement   10.230
Introduction   10.230
Enforcement orders   10.232
Duties enforceable under Section 18 and responsibility for
enforcement   10.233
Obligation to make enforcement order   10.236

Final and provisional enforcement orders 10.237
Procedure for confirming provisional enforcement
orders and making final enforcement orders 10.242
Compliance with enforcement orders 10.244
Financial penalties 10.245
Special administration orders 10.250
Power to require information in connection with
enforcement action 10.253

M. Complaints Against Undertakers and Licensed Water Suppliers 10.255

N. Review and Information Provided by the Secretary
of State and the Authority 10.259
Review and reports 10.259
Information 10.260

11. Nature Conservation 519

A. Introduction 11.01

B. The Organization of Nature Conservation 11.02
Governmental organizations 11.02
Central Government 11.02
Local Government 11.03
The UK Conservation Bodies 11.04
The Environment Agency 11.06
The Forestry Commission 11.07
The Crown Estate Commissioners 11.09
The Natural Environment Research Council (NERC) 11.10
The European Community 11.11
Non-Governmental organizations 11.12
ARG UK (Amphibian and Reptile Groups of the UK) 11.13
The Bat Conservation Trust (BCT) 11.14
Bird Life International 11.15
Botanical Society of the British Isles (BSBI) 11.16
British Herpetological Society (BHS) 11.17
British Trust for Conservation Volunteers (BTCV) 11.18
British Trust for Ornithology (BTO) 11.19
Buglife—the Invertebrate Conservation Trust 11.20
Butterfly Conservation 11.21
Fauna and Flora International (FFI) 11.22
Froglife 11.23
IUCN—The World Conservation Union (IUCN) 11.24
The Mammal Society 11.25
Marine Conservation Society (MCS) 11.26
National Federation of Badger Groups (NFBG) 11.27
The National Trust 11.28

Plantlife International   11.29
People's Trust for Endangered Species (PTES)   11.30
Royal Society for the Prevention of Cruelty to Animals (RSPCA)
  11.31
Royal Society for the Protection of Birds (RSPB)   11.32
Wildfowl and Wetlands Trust (WWT)   11.33
The Wildlife Trusts   11.34
The Woodland Trust   11.35
World Conservation Monitoring Centre (WCMC)   11.36
WWF UK (World Wide Fund for Nature)   11.37
Other groups   11.38

C. International Obligations   11.40
The Convention concerning the protection of the World
   Cultural and Natural Heritage ('World Heritage Sites')   11.41
The Ramsar Convention on wetlands of international importance
   ('The Ramsar Convention')   11.42
The Convention on international trade in endangered species
   ('The CITES Convention')   11.43
The Bern Convention on the conservation of European wildlife
   and natural habitats ('The Bern Convention')   11.44
The Bonn Convention on the conservation of migratory species
   of wild animals   11.45
EC Council Directive on the conservation of wild birds
   ('The Birds Directive')   11.46
EC Council Directive on the assessment of the effects of certain
   public and private projects on the environment
   ('The EIA Directive')   11.47
EC Council Directive on the conservation of natural habitats and
   of wild flora and fauna ('The Habitats Directive')   11.49
The Rio Convention on biological diversity ('The Biodiversity
   Convention')   11.50
The Convention for the Protection of the marine environment
   of the North-East Atlantic (OSPAR)   11.55
EC Council Directive on the environmental assessment of plans
   and programmes (The SEA Directive)   11.56
Convention on access to information, public participation in
   decision-making and access to justice in environmental matters
   ('The Aarhus Convention')   11.57
EC Water Framework Directive ('The Water
   Framework Directive')   11.58

D. Habitat Conservation   11.59
Introduction   11.59
Biogenetic Reserves   11.63
Biosphere Reserves   11.64

Ramsar sites	11.65
Special Protection Areas (SPAs)	11.67
Special Areas of Conservation (SACs)	11.68
The Habitats Regulations	11.69
National Nature Reserves (NNRs)	11.73
Marine Nature Reserves (MNRs)	11.77
Sites of Special Scientific Interest (SSSIs)	11.78
Limestone pavements	11.83
Areas of Special Protection (AOSPs)	11.84
Local Nature Reserves (LNRs)	11.85
Sites of Nature Conservation Interest or Importance (SNCIs and SINCs)	11.86
Environmentally Sensitive Areas (ESAs)	11.87
National Parks	11.88
The Norfolk and Suffolk Broads	11.89
Areas of Outstanding Natural Beauty (AONBs)	11.90
Green belts	11.91
Country Parks	11.92

E. Species Protection — 11.93

Introduction	11.93
Evaluation procedures	11.94
Conservation of birds	11.96
Protection of other wild animals	11.103
Protection of fish	11.115
Protection of individual wild plants	11.118
Trees and woodlands	11.121
Important hedgerows	11.130
Protection of endangered species	11.133

12. Contaminated Land — 587

A. Introduction — 12.01

Control over development	12.03
Building regulations	12.04
Power to abate the condition of a vacant site/open land which is seriously injuring the amenity of the locality	12.05
Statutory nuisance	12.07
Water	12.11
Activities regulated under the Environmental Permitting Regulations 2007	12.15
Civil liability	12.17

B. Part IIA of the EPA — 12.23

Contents

'Contaminated land'   12.27
  Pollution linkage   12.31
  'Significant harm'   12.32
  'Significant possibility' of significant harm   12.33
  Harm caused by facilities regulated under the Environmental
  Permitting Regulations   12.34
  'Pollution of controlled waters'   12.35
Identification of contaminated land   12.37
  Duty to inspect   12.37
  Notification and consultation   12.40
  Special sites   12.43
    Remediation started before land is designated as a special site 12.48
    Termination of designation   12.50
The duty to serve a remediation notice   12.51
  Introduction   12.51
  Restrictions   12.53
    Section 78YB—overlap with other controls   12.54
    Section 78H(5)—unreasonable cost, voluntary
      remediation etc   12.55
    Measure would cause hardship to appropriate person if
      required by a remediation notice   12.57
Remediation   12.60
  Test of reasonableness   12.64
The 'appropriate person' for a measure   12.65
  Class A and B liability groups   12.65
  Class A liability group   12.68
    'Person'   12.68
    'Caused'   12.69
    'Knowingly permitted'   12.70
    'To any extent referable'   12.73
    Chemical reactions etc   12.74
    Mines abandoned before 31 December 1999   12.75
  Residual liability of owner/occupier   12.76
    Land which is only contaminated land because
      it is causing pollution of controlled waters 12.76
  The appropriate person in the case of escapes   12.77
    Person who causes or knowingly permits the contaminants
      to be in the original site   12.79
    Subsequent owners of the original site   12.80
    Owner/occupier of the second site, where the second site
      threatens harm   12.81
    Owner/occupier of the second site where the third
      site threatens harm   12.82
  Insolvency practitioners   12.84

Exclusion and apportionment of liability where there are several
    appropriate persons for a particular remediation measure   12.85
    Exclusion of persons within Class A liability group   12.88
    Apportionment between remaining members of the Class A
        liability group   12.89
    Exclusion of members of a Class B liability group   12.90
    Apportionment between remaining members of the Class B
        liability group   12.91
Remediation measure attributable to two or more linkages   12.92
    Limits on duly apportioned costs to be borne by
        the appropriate person   12.95
The remediation notice   12.96
    Consultation   12.96
    Contents   12.100
    Other permission   12.102
    Measures affecting rights of third parties   12.103
    Appeals against remediation notices   12.105
    Offences of non-compliance   12.107
Remediation by enforcing authority   12.110
    Recovery of expenses   12.113
    Charging notices   12.117
Information and reports   12.119
    National security   12.122
    Confidential information   12.123
    Reports   12.128
Guidance   12.129

13. Miscellaneous Environmental Controls   623

A. Introduction   13.01

B. Pollution of the Air   13.02
  Alkali works   13.02
  Clean Air Acts   13.05
  The Ringelmann Chart   13.06
  Prevention measures—Industrial furnaces   13.10
  Prevention measures—Domestic furnaces   13.14
  Monitoring   13.15
  The height of chimneys   13.19
  Smoke control areas   13.26
  Creating a smoke control area   13.31
  Smoke control areas—Offences   13.38
  Burning unauthorized fuels   13.39
  Adaptation of existing furnaces and fireplaces   13.43

Motor fuel and air pollution   13.49
The lead content of petrol   13.52
The lead content of diesel   13.54
Cable burning   13.57
Research into air pollution   13.58
Records and returns   13.60
Notices connected with research and
    publicity   13.65
Mines and quarries   13.70
Railway engines   13.71
Vessels   13.72
Research establishments   13.73
The Crown   13.74
Administration   13.75
Corporations, occupiers of premises,
    and powers of entry   13.77
Conclusion   13.78

C. Noise Pollution—Construction Sites   13.79
Control of works   13.79
Sanctions   13.83
Section 61 consent   13.85

D. Loudspeakers in Streets   13.88
The controls   13.88
Relaxation of control   13.91
Relaxation of control—Procedure   13.94

E. Noise Abatement Zones   13.96
Introduction—Declaring a noise abatement
    zone   13.96
The controls   13.98
The register of noise levels   13.101
Reductions in noise levels   13.103
Anti-Social behaviour   13.108

F. Noise from Plant or Machinery   13.112

G. Aircraft Noise   13.122
Introduction   13.122
Control by the Secretary of State for Transport   13.124
Short take-off and landing (STOL) aircraft   13.133

H. Noise—Road Traffic   13.137
The mischief   13.137
Exemptions from control   13.141

MOT test certificates   13.143

I. Burglar Alarms   13.145

J. Implementation of EU Directives
on Noise   13.151

PART 3: THE ROLE OF TOWN AND COUNTRY PLANNING

14. The Relationship between Planning and Pollution Control   661

A. Introduction   14.01

B. The Relationship Between Planning
And Pollution Controls   14.04
The legal overlap   14.04
Development and the requirement for environmental
impact assessment   14.07
PPS 23 and the Policy Approach to the Overlapping Controls   14.09
The court's approach to the overlapping controls   14.12
Sustainable development and the planning system   14.16

C. An Outline of the Town and Country Planning Regime   14.21
The statutory framework of town and country planning law   14.21
The planning authorities   14.22
The requirement to obtain planning permission   14.25
The meaning of 'development'   14.25
Material changes of use   14.28
Permitted development rights   14.30
The determination of applications for planning permission   14.32
The statutory test and the role of the development plan   14.32
Outline applications   14.35
Material considerations   14.38
Conditions   14.41
Planning obligations   14.47
The location and need for a development   14.50
Risk assessment   14.52
Public opposition as a material consideration   14.55
Planning appeals   14.58
Court challenges   14.59
The role of third parties in the planning process   14.61
Planning enforcement powers   14.63
Special considerations and regimes   14.67
Listed buildings and conservation areas   14.67

Conservation areas 14.71
Archaeology and historical monuments 14.73
Nature conservation constraints 14.75
Trees and hedgerows 14.77

D. The Environment and Development Plans 14.79

E. Planning Considerations for Specific Types of Development 14.84
Industrial pollution and development control 14.84
Waste management and development control 14.87
Nuisance and the effect of planning permission 14.92
Noise and development control 14.93
Flood risk areas 14.97

15. Environmental Impact Assessment 705

A. Introduction 15.01
What is Environmental Impact Assessment? 15.05
What is Strategic Environmental Assessment? 15.07

B. The Legislative Framework 15.10
The purpose of Environmental Impact Assessment 15.10
The implementation of the Directive in UK law 15.14
The 1985 Environmental Assessment Directive 15.14
The 1997 Environmental Assessment Directive 15.17
Directive 2003 amendment 15.19
The effect of the reforms on existing applications 15.20
The relationship between the Directives and UK law 15.21

C. When is Environmental Impact Assessment required? 15.22
The 'project' to be assessed 15.22
The general definition 15.22
Are outline applications still possible? 15.24
Defining the project in relation to future development 15.29
Identifying a project as 'EIA development' 15.31
The EIA regulations 1999 15.32
Schedule 1 development 15.33
Schedule 2 development 15.34
Exclusive thresholds 15.36
Development in a 'sensitive area' 15.38
Further development, changes and modifications to
development projects 15.39
Schedule 2: general selection criteria 15.41
Government guidance on Schedule 2 15.43
Guidance on the use of indicative criteria and thresholds 15.44

D. Deciding Whether an Environmental Impact
Assessment is Required   15.45
The initial screening   15.45
The environmental effects on other countries   15.51

E. The Contents of the Environmental Statement   15.52
The prescribed contents   15.52
The required level of detail   15.54
Requests for further information   15.55
Limiting the scope of the assessment   15.57

F. The Use of the Environmental Statement in the
Consent Decision   15.59

G. Possible Challenges   15.63
Public participation   15.63
The requirement to provide a non-technical summary   15.65
Reasons for the decision   15.66
Challenges through the courts   15.67

PART 4: THE COMMON LAW

16. Common Law Liability for Environmental Damage   745

A. Introduction   16.01

B. Nuisance   16.04
Introduction   16.04
Types of private nuisance   16.05
Nuisance by physical damage or encroachment   16.06
Nuisance by interference with the enjoyment of land   16.08
Who may sue in private nuisance?   16.11
Responsibility for the nuisance   16.12
The wrongdoer   16.12
The occupier   16.13
The landlord   16.15
The concept of the reasonable user   16.17
Foreseeability in nuisance   16.21
Public nuisance   16.30
Defences to nuisance   16.34
Statutory authorization   16.35
Prescription   16.39
Unsuccessful defences   16.41

C. The Rule In *Rylands v Fletcher*   16.45

Contents

D. Negligence	16.54
Duty of care	16.55
Foreseeability in negligence	16.59
Breach of duty	16.62
The defendant's reliance on common practice	16.65
The defendant's reliance on regulatory standards	16.66
E. Trespass	16.67
F. Breach Of Statutory Duty	16.71
The Occupiers' Liability Acts	16.71
Breaches of general statutory duties	16.72
G. Liability For Breach of Contractual or Property Rights	16.74
Breaches of covenants	16.74
Rights to water	16.75
Contractual liabilities	16.76
H. Civil Liability of the Regulatory Authorities	16.77
General considerations	16.77
Damages for maladministration	16.78
Liability in negligence	16.79
Liability for negligent operational or policy decisions	16.81
Liability for negligent inspection and regulation	16.82
Liability for the public authority's decision not to act	16.85
Nuisances created by public authorities	16.86
I. Causation	16.88
J. Practical Considerations	16.93
Civil litigation: the costs and risks	16.93
Limitation of actions	16.94
Latent damage and limitation periods	16.97
K. The Measure Of Damages	16.98
Introduction	16.98
Damages for personal injury	16.99
Damage to property	16.100
The assessment of property damages	16.102
Damage caused to part of a property	16.103
Recovering the costs of repair	16.104
Damages for nuisance	16.106
The problem of economic losses	16.107
Loss due to hidden defects and fear of future damage	16.109
Damages for negligent advice	16.111
Exemplary damages	16.112
Index	795

TABLE OF CASES

United Kingdom

AB v South Western Water Services Ltd [1993] 1 All ER 609, CA 4.33
Abbahall v Smee [2003] 1 All ER 465 . . . . 16.28
Adams v Ursell [1913] 1 Ch 269 . . . . 16.10
ADT Auctions Ltd v SSETR [2000] JPL 115 . . . . 11.71
Agricultural Training Board v Aylesbury Mushrooms Ltd [1972] 3
    All ER 280 . . . . 13.37
Alconbury and others v Secretary of State for the Environment, Transport and the Regions [2001]
    2 WLR 1389; [2001] UKHL 23 . . . . 3.38, 3.49, 4.50
Alford v Department for Environment, Food & Rural Affairs
[2005] EWHC 808 (Admin) 15.14
Allen v Gulf Oil Refining Ltd [1981] AC 1001;
    [1996] 1 All ER482 . . . . 16.32, 16.35, 16.36, 16.38, 16.86
Alphacell v Woodward [1972] AC 824 . . . . 2.24, 9.87, 9.90
American Cyanamid v Ethicon Ltd [1975] AC 396 . . . . 6.223
AMF International Ltd v Magnet Bowling Ltd [1968] 1 WLR 1028, QBD 16.71
Anderson v Alnwick District Council [1993] 1 WLR 1156 . . . . 11.117
Andreae v Selfridge & Co [1938] Ch 1 . . . . 16.106
Andrews (Geoffrey Wallace) v Reading Borough Council [2005]
    EWHC 256 . . . . 3.46, 16.44
Anglian Water Services v H G Thurston & Co Ltd [1993] EGCS 162, CA 16.24
Anns v Merton LBC [1978] AC 728 . . . . 16.72, 16.84, 16.85
Anthony v Coal Authority [2006] Env LR 17 . . . . 16.14, 16.28
Anufrijeva v Southwark LBC [2003] EWCA Civ 1406 . . . . 3.39
Armstrong v British Coal Corp (1998) 31 July, CA; The Times 6 December 1996, CA 16.61
Arscott and others v Coal Authority and another [2005]
    Env LR 6, CA 9.132, 16.18, 16.52, 16.53
Ashcroft v Cambro Waste Products [1981] 3 All ER 699;
    [1981] 1 WLR 1349 . . . . 7.135, 9.107
Associated Provincial Picture Houses v Wednesbury Corpn
[1948] 1 KB 223 . . . . 5.109
Attorney-General v Copeland [1902] 1 KB 690 . . . . 16.40
Attorney-General v de Keyser's Royal Hotel Ltd [1920] AC 508 . . . . 2.32
Attorney-General v Emerson [1891] AC 649 . . . . 11.78
Attorney-General v PYA Quarries [1957] 2 QB 169 . . . . 16.30, 16.33
Attorney-General's Reference (No 2, 1988) [1990] 1 QB 77, CA 14.87
Attorney-General's Reference (No 1, 1994) [1995] 1 WLR 599 . . . . 9.92
Attorney-General's Reference (No 5, 2000) [2001] EWCA Crim 1077;
    [2002] Env LR 139 . . . . 4.08, 7.08
BAA Plc v Secretary of State for Transport, Local Government and the Regions [2002]
    EWHC 1920; [2003] JPL 610 . . . . 15.45
Bainbridge v Chertsey UDC [1915] 84 LJ Ch 6 . . . . 16.10

Ballard v Tomlinson (1885) 29 ChD 115 .... 16.75
Barclays Bank plc v Fairclough Building Ltd (No 2) The Times
    15 February 1995, CA 16.61
Barnes v Irwell Valley Water Board [1939] 1 KB 21, CA 16.84
Barnet v Kensington and Chelsea Hospital Management Committee [1960]
    1 AC 428 .... 16.88
Barnet London Borough Council v Eastern Electricity Board [1973]
    1 WLR 430 .... 11.126
Barrett v Enfield London Borough Council [2001] 2 AC 550, HL. 16.79, 16.81
Bateman v Poplar District Board of Works (1887) 37 ChD 272. .... 16.87
Baxter v Camden LBC (No 2) [1999] Env LR 561; (1999) 3 WLR 93 HL 16.16, 16.18
Beckett v Newalls Insulation Co [1953] 1 WLR 8, CA 16.63
Bedwell Park Quarry Co v Hertfordshire CC [1993] JPL 349, CA. 16.74
Bellcross Co Ltd v Mid-Bedfordshire DC (1988) 15 EG 106. .... 11.123
Benjamin v Storr [1874] LR 9 CP 400 .... 16.72
Berkeley v Secretary of State for the Environment (2000) 81 P & CR 492; [2001]
    2 AC 603, CA; 4.11, 14.62, 15.12, 15.31, 15.52, 15.63, 15.64, 15.67
Berkeley v Secretary of State for the Environment and another [1998] Env LR 741 .... 15.49
Berkeley v Secretary of State for the Environment Transport and the Regions
    and another [2001] EWCA Civ 1012 .... 15.36
Blair v Deakin (1887) 57 LT 522 .... 16.90
Blue Circle Industries v Ministry of Defence [1997] Env LR 341;
    [1998] 3 All ER 385 .... 3.07, 8.15, 16.101–16.103, 16.105
Blyth v Birmingham Waterworks (1856) 11 Ex 781 .... 16.62
Bocardo SA v Star Energy UK Onshore Ltd and another [2008]
    EWHC 1756 (Ch) 16.69
Bolam v Friern Hospital Management Committee [1957] 1 WLR 582 .... 16.62
Bolitho v City and Hackney Health Authority [1998] AC 232 .... 16.62
Bolton MBC v Secretary of State for the Environment [1991] JPL 241 .... 14.38
Bolton MBC v Secretary of State for the Environment [1995] JPL 1043, HL 14.60
Bolton MBC v Secretary of State for the Environment and Greater Manchester
    Waste Disposal Authority (1990) 61 P & CR 343 .... 2.92
Bone v Seale [1975] 1 WLR 797. .... 16.106
Bonnington Castings v Wardlaw [1956] AC 613. .... 16.89, 16.92
Bourgoin SA v MAFF [1986] QB 716, CA. 4.63
Bowden v South West Water Services Ltd [1999] Env LR 438. .... 4.66
Brew Bros Ltd v Snax (Ross) Ltd [1970] 1 QB 612 .... 16.16
Bridlington Relay v Yorkshire Electricity Board [1965] Ch 436 .... 16.10
British Celanese Ltd v A H Hunt (Capacitors) Ltd [1969] 1 WLR 959 .... 16.32, 16.51
British Railways Board v Secretary of State for the Environment and Hounslow LBC
    [1993] JPL 342, HL. 14.46
Bromley LBC v GLC [1983] 1 AC 768, HL 2.88
Broome v Cassell & Co [1972] AC 1027, HL. 16.112
Budden v BP [1980] JPL 586, CA. 16.66
Bullock v Secretary of State for the Environment (1980) 40 P & CR 246. .... 11.124
Bulmer Ltd v Bollinger SA [1974] Ch 401, CA. 4.47, 4.49
Burgoine v Waltham Forest LBC The Times 7 November 1996. .... 16.77
Business Environment Group Ltd v Wembley Fair (Wembley) Ltd
    [2005] EWCA Civ 1230. .... 16.32
Butler v Standard Telephone and Cables Ltd [1940] 1 KB 339 .... 16.07
Bux v Slough Metals Ltd [1973] 1 WLR 1358. .... 16.65
Bybrook Barn Centre Ltd v Kent County Council [2001] BLR 55 .... 9.143, 16.04, 16.37

Cambridge Water Company v Eastern Counties Leather [1994] 2 AC 264, CA; [1994]
   1 All ER 53, HL 2.03, 2.04, 12.20, 16.01, 16.17,
                16.18, 16.47–49, 16.52–16.54, 16.59, 16.75, 16.100, 16.101, 16.105
Campaign for Nuclear Disarmament v Prime Minister of the UK and others
   [2002] EWHC 2777 (QB) 3.04
Caparo Industries v Dickman [1990] 2 AC 605 . . . . 16.55, 16.56, 16.58, 16.79
Capital and Counties plc v Hampshire CC [1997]
   QB 1004, CA. 9.143, 16.64, 16.79, 16.80
Cargill v Gotts [1981] 1 WLR 441 . . . . 16.40
Carltona v Commissioners of Works [1943] 2 All ER 560 . . . . 15.45
Carpets of Worth v Wyre Forest District Council (1992) 62 P & CR 334 . . . . 11.91
Cave v Robinson Jarvis & Rolf [2002] UKHL 18; [2003] 1 AC 384 . . . . 16.96
Cemex UK Cement Ltd v Defra, DTI and others [2006] EWHC 3207 (Admin);
   (2007) Env LR 21. . . . . 2.13
Charing Cross Electricity Supply Co v Hydraulic Power Co [1914] 3 KB 772 . . . . 16.49
Church of Jesus Christ of Latter Day Saints v Price [2004] EWHC 3245. . . . . 16.04
Church of Jesus Christ of Latter Day Saints (GB) v West Yorkshire FCDA
   The Times 9 May 1996. . . . . 16.80
Circular Facilities (London) Ltd v Sevenoaks District Council [2005] JPL 1624 . . . . 12.71
City Equitable Fire Insurance Co, Re [1925] Ch 407 . . . . 2.75
City of Edinburgh v Secretary of State for Scotland [1997] 1 WLR 1447. . . . . 14.33
City of London Corporation v Bovis Construction Ltd [1992]
   3 All ER 697. . . . . 2.35, 13.84
Coats Paton (Retail) Ltd v Birmingham Corpn (1971) 69 LGR 356 . . . . 16.81
Collin v Duke of Westminster [1985] QB 581 . . . . 16.51, 16.95
Cooper (Stephen) v HM Attorney General [2008] EWHC 2178 . . . . 4.68
Council of Civil Service Unions (CCSU) v Minister for the
   Civil Service (GCHQ case) [1985] AC 374. . . . . 2.32, 2.39, 2.88, 4.58
Cox v Paddington Vestry (1891) 64 LT 586 . . . . 16.87
Crake v Supplementary Benefits Commission [1982] 1 All ER 498 . . . . 2.88
Crehan (Bernard) v (1) Inntrepreneur Pub Company (CPC) (2) Brewman Group
   Limited [2004] EWCA Civ 637 . . . . 4.66
Crown River Cruises Ltd v Kimbolton Fireworks Ltd and London Fire and Civil Defence
   Authority [1996] 2 Lloyd's Rep 533 . . . . 16.79
Crumbie v Wallsend Local Board [1891] 1 QB 503. . . . . 16.96
Cunliffe v Bankes [1945] 1 All ER 459 . . . . 16.25
Curran v Northern Ireland Co-Ownership Housing Association Ltd
   [1987] AC 718. . . . . 16.79, 16.85
Cushing v Peter Walker & Sons Ltd [1941] 2 All ER 693 . . . . 16.29
Customs and Excise Commissioners v Samex [1983] 1 All ER 1042 . . . . 4.47
D & F Estates Ltd v Church Commissioners [1989] AC 117. . . . . 16.109
Davies v Ilieff [2000] WL 33201551. . . . . 16.102
Dean v Ainley [1988] 1 WLR 1729, CA. 16.104
Dear v Thames Water and others (1993) 33 Con LR43; (1994) 4 Water Law 116 . . . . 16.87
Defra v ASDA Stores Ltd The Times 27 June 2002, DC 4.25
Delaware Mansions Ltd v Westminster City Council [2001] 1 AC 321 . . . . 16.11, 16.27
Delyn BC v Solitaire (Liverpool) Ltd [1995] EGCS 11 . . . . 16.38
Dennis v Ministry of Defence [2003] Env LR 34 . . . . 16.44
Department of Transport v North West Water [1983] 3 All ER 273. . . . . 16.86
Derbyshire Waste Ltd and another v The Secretary of State for the Environment,
   Food and Rural Affairs [2004] EWCA Civ 1508 . . . . 14.88, 14.91
Dillingham Construction v Downs (1972) 13 Build LR 97 . . . . 16.111

Dimmock v Secretary of State for Children, Schools & Families [2007]
    EWHC 2288 (Admin) 3.13
Dimsdale Developments (South East) Ltd v Secretary of State for the Environment
    and Hounslow LBC [1986] JPL 276. . . . . 2.30
Dobson (Hanifa) and others v Thames Water Utilities Ltd
    (OfWAT as Intervenors) [2007] EWHC 2021 (TCC). 2.38
Dodd Properties (Kent) v Canterbury City Council [1980] 1 WLR 433 . . . . 16.104
Donoghue v Stevenson [1932] AC 562. . . . . 2.18
DPP, ex p C [1995] 1 Cr App R 136 . . . . 2.73
Drane v Evangelou [1978] 2All ER 437, CA. 16.112
Dunne v North Western Gas Board [1964] 2 QB 806, CA 16.49, 16.87
Dunlop v Woollahra Municipal Council [1982] AC 159, PC 16.78
Dutton v Bognor Regis UDC [1972] 1 QB 373 . . . . 16.84
Earl of Lonsdale v Attorney-General [1982] 1 WLR 887 . . . . 11.78
Eastern Counties Leather plc v Eastern Counties Leather Group Limited [2002]
    EWHC 494 (Ch); [2002] EWCA Civ 1636 . . . . 2.04
East Dorset District Council v Eaglebeam [2006] EWHC 2378 (QB). 16.31
East Suffolk Rivers Catchment Board v Kent [1941] AC 74. . . . . 9.143, 16.85
Eckersley v Binnie & Partners 8 Feb 1988, CA 16.100
Ellis v Loftus Iron Co (1878) LR 10 CP 10 . . . . 16.68
Ellis and Ruislip-Northwood UDC, re [1920] 1 KB 343. . . . . 11.123
Elmbridge BC and others v Secretary of State for the Environment, Transport and
    the Regions (2000) unreported, 10 November 15.25
Emms v Polya (1973) 227 EG 1659 . . . . 16.106
Empress Car Company (Abertillery) Ltd v National Rivers Authority
    [1999] 2 AC 22 . . . . 9.92, 9.95, 9.96, 12.69
Envirocor Waste Holdings v Secretary of State for the Environment
    [1996] Env LR D42 . . . . 14.54
Environment Agency v BIFFA Waste Services and another [2006] EWHC 1102 (Admin). . . 9.97
Environment Agency v Stanford (1999) Env LR 286. . . . . 2.73
Esso Petroleum v Kingswood Motors [1974] QB 142 . . . . 4.44
Esso Petroleum v Southport Corporation [1956] AC 218 . . . . 16.07, 16.70
Evans v Godber [1974] 1 WLR 1317 . . . . 11.73
Ewing v ODPM [2005] 1 WLR 1260. . . . . 2.94
Express Dairies Distribution v Environment Agency [2003] EWHC 448 (Admin);
    [2004] 1 WLR 579. . . . . 9.118
Express Ltd v Environment Agency [2004] EWHC 1710 (Admin) 9.99, 9.101
Factortame cases *see* R v Secretary of State for Transport, ex p Factortame
Fairchild v Glenhaven Funeral Services Ltd [2003] 1 AC 32, HL. 16.89
Fardon v Harcourt-Rivington (1932) 146 LT 391. . . . . 16.63
Farmer Giles v Wessex Water Authority [1990] 1 EGLR 177, CA 16.104
Feakins (Robert) v Secretary of State for the Environment, Food & Rural Affairs
    [2002] EWHC 2574 (Admin); (2004) 1 WLR 1761, CA 2.33
Ferguson v Welch [1987] 3 All ER 777, HL 16.71
Fernback and others v Harrow LBC [2001] EWHC 278 (Admin). 15.48
Fisher and another v English Nature [2004] EWCA Civ 663. 3.49
Fitzpatrick Developments Ltd v MHLG (1965) 194 EG 911 . . . . 14.92
Friends of the Earth, Re [1988] JPL 93, CA 8.15
Friends of the Earth Incorporated v Laidlaw Environmental Services
    [2000] 120 S Ct 693. . . . . 2.25
Gafford v Graham (1998) 77 P & CR 73, CA. 16.106
Garden Cottage Foods v Milk Marketing Board [1984] AC 130 . . . . 4.63
Gateshead MBC v SOS for the Environment (1994) 71 P & CR 350;
    [1994] JEL 93 . . . . 14.03–14.06, 14.12

Gateshead MBC v Secretary of State for the Environment [1995]
    JPL 432, CA. 14.57, 14.84, 14.91
Geddis v Proprietors of Bann Reservoir (1878) 3 App Cas 430 . . . . 16.35
Gillick v West Norfolk AHA [1986] 1 AC 112, HL. 2.31
Gillespie v First Secretary of State and Bellway Urban Renewal [2003]
    EWCA Civ 400; (2003) Env LR 30 . . . . .15.45, 15.47
Gillingham BC v Medway (Chatham) Dock Co Ltd [1992]
    3 All ER 923. . . . . .16.31, 16.38
Glasgow Corpn v Muir [1943] AC 448. . . . . .16.59, 16.63
GLC v Secretary of State for the Environment and LDDC and another
    [1986] 52 P&CR 158, CA 14.51
Goldman v Hargrave [1967] 1 AC 645, PC 16.25
Gorringe v Calderdale Metropolitan Borough Council [2004] UKHL 15;
    [2004] 1 WLR 1057. . . . . 16.85
Graham and Graham v Rechem International Ltd [1996] Env LR 158 . . . . .2.18, 16.93
Grampian Regional Council v City of Aberdeen [1984] JPL 590. 14.45
Gransden v Secretary of State (1985) 54 P & CR 86 . . . . 14.24
Greater Nottingham Co-operative Society v Cementation Piling and
    Foundation Ltd [1989] 1 QB 71, CA 16.107
Green v Lord Somerleyton [2003] 1 P & CR 33 . . . . 16.28
Griffin and others v South West Water Services Ltd [1995] IRLR 15, QBD. 4.33
Grigsby v Melville [1973] 3 All ER455 . . . . 11.107
Guildford BC v Hein [2005] EWCA Civ 979. . . . . 2.35
Guppys (Bridport) Ltd v Brookling [1983] 14 HLR 1. . . . . 16.112
Haley v London Electricity Board [1965] AC 778. . . . . 16.60
Halsey v Esso Petroleum [1961] 1 WLR683 . . . . 16.10, 16.40, 16.106
Hampshire CC v Beer (t/a Hammer Trout Farm) (2003) 21/7/2003, CA 3.38
Hampshire Waste Services Ltd v Intending trespassers upon Chineham Incinerator
    Site [2003] EWHC 1738 (Ch); [2004] Env LR 9 . . . . 16.68
Hanrahan v Merck, Sharpe and Dohme [1988] IRLM 629 . . . . 2.24
Harris v Evans and another [1998] 1 WLR 1285, CA 16.82
Harris v James (1876) 45 LJQB 545 . . . . 16.15
Harris v First Secretary of State and others [2007] EWHC 1847 . . . . 4.51
Hatton and others v UK (2003) 37 EHRR 28. . . . . .3.44, 3.45
Hedley Byrne v Heller [1963] 2 All ER 575. . . . . 16.83, 16.108, 16.109, 16.111
Henderson v Merrett Syndicates Ltd [1995] 2 AC 145, HL. 16.111
Hilda's Montessori Nursery Ltd v Tesco Stores Ltd [2006] EWHC 1054 . . . . 16.07
Hill v Chief Constable of West Yorkshire [1989] AC 53, HL. 16.79
Hillen v ICI (Alkali) Ltd [1936] AC 35. . . . . .16.69, 16.71
Hills v Ellis [1983] QB 680. . . . . 5.167
Hill Samuel Bank Ltd v Frederick Brand Partnership (1994) 10 Const LJ 72. . . . . 16.107
Hoare & Co v McAlpine [1923] 1 Ch 167 . . . . 16.07
Hodden v Chief Constable of Lancashire [1987] QB 380, CA. 16.112
Holbeck Hall Hotel Ltd v Scarborough BC The Times 15 October 1997
    QBD (OR); (1997) EGLR 213. . . . . 16.28
Holmes v Wilson [1839] 10 A & E 5. . . . . 16.96
Holtby v Brigham Cowan (Hull) Ltd [2000] 3 All ER 421 . . . . 16.89
Hooper v Rogers [1975] Ch 43. . . . . 16.110
Hopkins Developments Ltd v Secretary of State [2006] EWHC Admin 2823 . . . . 14.15
Horton's Estate Ltd v James Beattie Ltd [1927] 1 Ch 75 . . . . 16.06
Hubbard v Pitt [1976] QB 142. . . . . 16.04
Huckerby v Elliott [1970] 1 All ER 189 . . . . 2.75
Hughes v Riley [2006] 1 P & CR 29. . . . . 16.17

Hulley v Silversprings Bleaching Co [1922] 2 Ch 268 . . . . 16.40
Humber Sea Terminal Ltd v Secretary of State for Transport
    [2005] EWHC 1289 (Admin) 11.71
Hunter v Canary Wharf Ltd [1997]
    2 WLR 684, HL 16.10, 16.11, 16.38, 16.50, 16.100, 16.106, 16.108
Ilford UDC v Beal and Judd [1925] 1 KB 671 . . . . 16.24
Impress (Worcester) Ltd v Rees [1971] 2 All ER 357 . . . . 9.95
Invercargill City Council v Hamlin [1996] AC 624 . . . . 2.24, 16.84
Islington LBC v UCL Hospital NHS Trust [2006] PIQR P29 . . . . 16.56
J H Rayner (Mincing Lane) Limited v Department of Trade and Industry
    [1990] 2 AC 418 (the International Tin Council case) 3.04
John Munroe (Acrylics) Ltd v London Fire and Civil Defence Authority and others
    The Times 22 May 1996 . . . . 16.79
John Young & Co v Bankier Distillery [1893] AC 691 . . . . 16.75
Jones v Department of Employment [1989] 1 QB 1 . . . . 16.80
Jones v Llanwrst UDC [1911] 1 Ch 393 . . . . 16.75
Jones v Mersey River Board [1948] 1 QB 143 . . . . 9.137
Jones v Pritchard [1908] 1 Ch 630 . . . . 16.40
Jones (Insurance Brokers) Ltd v Portsmouth City Council [2003] 1 WLR 247 . . . . 16.26
Junior Books v Veitchi Co [1983] 1 AC 520, HL 16.97
Kane v New Forest DC (No 1) [2001] EWCA Civ 878 . . . . 16.79
Ken Lane Transport v North Yorkshire County Council The Times 22 May 1995,
    DC; [1995] 1 WLR 1416 . . . . 4.69
Kennaway v Thompson [1981] QB 88, CA 16.42, 16.43, 16.106
Kent v Griffiths The Times 23 December 1998, CA 16.79
Kent v Griffiths (No 3) [2001] QB 36, CA 16.81
Kent CC v Batchelor (No 1) (1976) 33 P & CR 185 . . . . 11.124
Kent CC v Batchelor (No 2) [1978] 3 All ER 980; [1979] 1 WLR 213 . . . . 11.127
Kent CC v Queenborough Rolling Mill Co (1990) 89 LGR 306 . . . . 7.07
King v Liverpool City Council [1986] 1 WLR 890, CA 16.29
King v Victor Parsons & Co [1973] 1 WLR 29, CA 16.96
Kirkland v Robinson [1987] Crim LR 643 . . . . 11.99
Kirklees BC v Wickes Building Supplies Ltd [1990] 1 WLR 1137;
    [1993] AC 227, HL 4.59, 4.63, 4.66
Knightly v Johns [1982] 1 WLR 349 . . . . 16.79
Kuddus v Chief Constable of Leicestershire [2001] UKHL 29; [2002] 2 AC 122 . . . . 16.112
Kynoch Ltd v Rowlands [1912] 1 C 527 (CA) 16.69
Lam v Brennan (t/a Namesakes of Torbay) and Torbay Borough Council
    [1998] PLCR 30, CA 16.79, 16.83
Lambert v West Devon BC [1997] JPL 735 . . . . 16.83
Lambton v Mellish [1894] 3 Ch 163 . . . . 16.90
Larner v British Steel [1993] 4 All ER 102, CA 16.72
Lavis v Kent County Council (1994) 90 LGR 416, CA 16.81
Leakey v National Trust [1980] QB 485 . . . . 16.07, 16.25, 16.27–16.29
Lemmon v Webb [1895] AC 1 . . . . 16.07, 16.40
Levy v EA (2002) July 30, EWHC 2.91
Lewin v End [1906] AC 299 . . . . 11.107
Lidl Properties v Clarke Bond Partnership [1998] Env LR 602 . . . . 16.111
Liverpool Corpn v Coghill [1918] 1 Ch 307 . . . . 16.40
Livingstone v The Rawyards Coal Company (1879–80) LR 5 App Cas 25 (HL) 16.74
LMS International Ltd v Styrene Packaging & Insulation Ltd [2005]
    EWHC 2065 . . . . 16.53
Loftus-Brigham v Ealing LBC [2003] EWCA Civ 1490 . . . . 16.07

London Borough of Hillingdon v Secretary of State for the Environment and
    Hillingdon Hospital NHS Trust and others 30/7/99 . . . . 2.33
Lord Advocate v Dumbarton District Council [1990] 2 AC 580, HL 2.32
Lough (David) and others v First Secretary of State and
    Bankside Developments [2004] 1 WLR 2557 . . . . 3.46
Louis v Saddiq (1997) 74 P& CR 324, CA 16.105
M v Home Office, sub nom M, re [1993] 3 WLR 433, HL 2.32
McCarthys Ltd v Smith [1979] 3 All ER 325 . . . . 4.44
McFarlane v EE Caledonia [1994] 2 All ER 1 . . . . 16.64
McKenna v British Aluminium Ltd [2002] Env LR 30 . . . . 16.50
McKinnon Industries Ltd v Walker [1951] 3 DLR 577 . . . . 16.08
McLeod v Buchanan [1940] 2 All ER 179 . . . . 7.133
Magnohard v UKAEA Sc Ct of Session (Outer House) 15 August 2003;
    [2004] Env LR 19 . . . . 8.15, 16.108
Maidstone Borough Council v Mortimer [1980] 3 All ER 522 . . . . 11.126
Main v Swansea Corp (1984) 49 P & CR 26 . . . . 5.53
Manchester Corpn v Farnworth [1930] AC 171 . . . . 16.10, 16.35, 16.38
Marchiori v Environment Agency and others [2002] EWCA Civ 03 . . . . 3.04, 8.52
Marcic v Thames Water Utilities Limited [2002] EWCA Civ 64, CA;
    [2003] UKHL 66; [2004] AC 42, HL 2.38, 3.45, 16.37
Margereson v J W Roberts The Times 17 April 1996, CA 16.61
Matania v National Provincial Bank Ltd [1936] 2 All ER 633 . . . . 16.18
Mayer Parry Recycling Ltd v The Environment Agency [1999] Env LR 489 . . . . 4.08
Mayor and Burgesses of the London Borough of Bromley v Susanna (a female)
    [1999] Env LR D13 (CA) 16.68
Mayor and Commonalty of the City of London v Bovis Construction [1989] JPL 263 . . . . 16.31
Mayor of London v Enfield London Borough Council [2008] EWCA Civ 202 . . . . 14.23
Merlin v British Nuclear Fuels [1990] 3 All ER 711 . . . . 8.15, 16.105, 16.108
Metropolitan Asylum District v Hill (1881) 6 App Cas 193 . . . . 16.35
Metropolitan Properties Ltd v Jones [1939] 2 All ER 202 . . . . 16.18
Milford v Hughes [1846] 16 M&W 174 . . . . 7.102
Miller v Jackson [1977] QB 966, CA 16.43, 16.98
Ministry of Defence v Blue Circle Industries Plc [1999]
    Ch 289 . . . . 16.105, 16.108, 16.110
Monsanto v Tilly [2000] Env LR 313 . . . . 16.68
Morgan Crucible v Hill Samuel [1991] Ch 295 . . . . 16.63
Morrell v Owen The Times 14 December 1993 . . . . 16.60
Mourton v Poulter [1930] 2 KB 183 . . . . 16.60
Murphy v Bradford DC The Times 11 February 1991, CA 16.71, 16.72
Murphy v Brentwood DC [1991] 1 AC 398;
    [1990] 2 All ER 908 . . . . 2.24, 16.47, 16.84, 16.108–16.110
MWB v London, Brighton and South Coast Rly [1910] 2 KB 890 . . . . 10.59
Nash v Eli Lilly [1993] 1 WLR782, CA 16.96
National Coal Board v Neath BC [1976] 2 All ER 478 . . . . 16.04
National Provident Institution v Avon CC (1992) EGCS 56, ChD 16.100
National Rivers Authority v Biffa [1996] Env LR 227 . . . . 9.101
National Rivers Authority v Coal Products Ltd ENDS Dec 1993,
    Vol 227, 45 . . . . 9.106, 9.108
National Rivers Authority v McAlpine [1994] 4 All ER 286 . . . . 12.69
National Rivers Authority v Yorkshire Water Services
    [1995] 1 AC 444 . . . . 9.92, 9.94, 9.105, 12.69
Newbury DC v SoS for the Environment [1981]
    AC 578, HL 7.189, 8.87, 8.181, 14.42

Newcastle under Lyme Corp v Wolstanton Ltd [1947] Ch 92 . . . . 10.200
Newham LBC v SSE and East London Housing Association (1987)
    53 P & CR 98. . . . . .14.93, 14.96
Newport County BC v Secretary of State for Wales [1998] JPL 377, CA 14.56
Nitrigin Eireann Teoranta v Inco Alloy Ltd [1992] 1 WLR 498 . . . . 16.97
Northampton Borough Council v Perrin [2007] EWCA Civ 1353 . . . . 11.125
North Wiltshire DC v Secretary of State for the Environment and Clover
    [1992] JPL 955. . . . . 2.30
O'Fee v Copeland Borough Council [1996] Env LR 66, CA 13.06
OLL Ltd v Secretary of State for Transport [1997] 3 All ER 897, QBD 16.79
O'Reilly v Mackman [1983] 2 AC 237, HL 2.18
Orjula, The, Re [1995] 2 Lloyd's Rep 395 . . . . 16.101
Pacific Associates v Baxter [1990] 1 QB 993 . . . . 16.111
Padfield v MAFF [1968] AC 997 . . . . .2.32, 7.189
Payne v Rogers (1794) 2 HBl 350 . . . . 16.16
Pearce v Croydon RDC (1910) 74 JP 429 . . . . 16.70
Pehrsson v Secretary of State for the Environment [1990] JPL 764 . . . . 11.91
Perry v Kendricks Transport Ltd [1956] 1 WLR 85 . . . . 16.53
Perry v Sidney Phillips & Son [1982] 1 WLR 1297, CA 16.111
Persey and others v SoS EFRA [2002] EWHC 371 (Admin) 3.40
Petition of Kincardine and Deeside District Council (1992) 4 JEL 289;
    [1993] Env LR 151. . . . . 4.33
Phelps v Hillingdon LBC [2001] 2 AC 619. . . . . 16.79
Phillips v First Secretary of State [2004] JPL 6. . . . . 14.51
Pidgeon v Great Yarmouth Waterworks Co [1902] 1 KB 310 . . . . 10.59
Pirelli General Cable Works Ltd v Oscar Faber and Partners [1983] 1 AC 1 . . . . 16.97
Polymeric Treatments Ltd v Walsall MBC [1993] Env LR 427. 5.167
Price v Cromack [1975] 1 WLR 988. . . . . 9.92
Pride of Derby and Derbyshire Angling Association v British Celanese [1952]
    1 All ER 1326; [1953] 1 All ER 179, CA. 16.37, 16.86, 16.87, 16.90
Pwllbach Colliery Co v Woodman [1915] AC 634, HL. 16.10
Pyx Granite v MHLG [1960] AC 260. . . . . 8.87
R v Advertising Standards Authority, ex p Insurance Services plc [1990]
    2 Admin LR 77. . . . . 2.37
R v Alath Construction Ltd [1991] 1 PLR 25 . . . . 11.126
R v Anglian Water Services Ltd The Times 18 August 2003;
    [2003] EWCA Crim 2243 . . . . 2.83
R v Associated Octel [1996] EWCA Crim 1237 . . . . 2.84
R v Board of Trustees of the Science Museum [1993] 1 WLR 1171, CA. 2.11
R v Bolton MBC, ex p Kirkman [1998] JPL 787 . . . . 14.06, 14.12, 14.24, 14.91
R v Caldwell [1982] AC 341. . . . . 5.53
R v Canterbury Council, ex p Springimage [1993] 3 PLR 58. . . . . 2.92
R v Cemex Cement Ltd [2007] EWCA Crim 1759. . . . . 2.85
R v Chief Constable of Sussex, ex p International Traders' Ferry Ltd [1995]
    4 All ER 364, DC; [1997] 3 WLR 132; Independent 31 January 1997, CA. 2.88
R v Clifton Steel Ltd [2007] EWCA Crim 1537 . . . . 2.85
R v Commissioner for Local Administration, ex p Eastleigh [1988] 1 QB 855, CA 2.98
R v Cornwall County Council, ex p Hardy [2001] Env LR 473. 15.61
R v Cross [1812] 3 Camp 224. . . . . 16.40
R v Daventry District Council, ex p Thornby Farms Ltd [2003] QB 503. . . . . 6.270
R v Deputy Governor of Parkhurst Prison, ex p Hague
    [1992] 1 AC 58 . . . . .2.39, 16.80
R v Dovermoss (1995) 159 JP 448, CA. 9.100

R v Durham County Council, ex p Lowther [2001] EWCA Civ 781 . . . . 15.40
R v Durham County Council, Sherburn Stone and Secretary of State for the
    Environment, ex p Huddleston [2000] 1 WLR 1484. . . . . 4.37
R v Dyfed County Council, ex p Manson [1995] Env LR 83 . . . . 11.88
R v Environment Agency, ex p Gibson and Learn [1999]
    Env LR 73, QBD 2.89, 15.40
R v Environment Agency ex p Mayer Parry Recycling Ltd (No.2)
    [2001] Env LR 35. . . . . 4.59
R v Environment Agency, ex p Petrus Oils Ltd [1999] Env LR 732, QB 2.90
R v Ettrick Trout Company [1994] Env LR 1G5 . . . . 9.114
R v Exeter City Council ex p J L Thomas [1991] 1 QB 471; [1990] 1 All ER 413;
    [1990] JPL 129. . . . . 14.92
R v F Howe and Son [1999] 2 All ER 249; [1999]
    2 Cr App R(S) 37 . . . . .2.83, 2.85
R v Friskies Petcare UK Ltd (2000) 2 Cr App R(S) 401 . . . . 2.86
R v Goldstein [2006] 1 AC 459 . . . . .16.31, 16.33
R v Hall [1982] 4 Cr App R 153 . . . . 5.152
R v Henn and Darby [1981] AC 850 . . . . 4.69
R v HM Inspector of Pollution, ex p Chapman [1996] COD 154, DC 2.88, 2.89
R v HM Treasury, ex p British Telecommunications
    The Times 2 December 1993, CA. 4.59
R v Hertfordshire CC, ex p Green Environmental Industries and another
    [1997] Env LR 114 . . . . 5.145
R v Home Secretary, ex p Brind [1991] 1 AC 696; [1991]
    1 All ER 720, HL 2.88, 4.50
R v Hounslow LBC, ex p Williamson [1996] EGCS 27, QBD 16.80, 16.82
R v Kennet DC, ex p Somerfield Property Co [1999] JPL 361, QBD 14.96
R v Kenneth George Davis [2007] EWHC 1730 (Admin). 2.71
R v Knowsley MBC, ex p Macguire The Times 26 June 1992 . . . . 16.78
R v Leicestershire County Council and others ex p Blackfordby & Boothorpe
    Action Group Ltd (2001) Env LR 2 . . . . 2.93
R v Leominster District Council, ex p Pothecary [1998] JPL 335, CA 14.33
R v Lincoln Justices, ex p Wickes Building Supplies The Times 6 August 1993, CA 4.69
R v Local Administration Commissioner, ex p Doy (2002) Env LR 11;
    [2001] EWCA Admin 361 . . . . 2.99
R v London Borough of Hammersmith and Fulham [2000] Env LR 549. . . . . 4.60
R v London Borough Transport Committee, ex p Freight Transport
    Association Ltd [1991] RTR 13, CA; [1991] 3 All ER 915, [1991]
    1 WLR 828, HL 4.15, 4.33, 4.35
R v Lord Chancellor, ex p Child Poverty Action Group [1999] 1 WLR 347 . . . . 2.94
R v Lyons [2002] 3 WLR 1562 . . . . 3.04
R v Manchester Metropolitan University, ex p Nolan [1994] ELR 380, DC. 2.88
R v Metropolitan Stipendiary Magistrate, ex p London WRA The Times
    14 January 1993; [1993] 3 All ER 113 . . . . 7.101
R v Milford Haven Port Authority (*Sea Empress case*) [2000]
    2 Cr App R(S) 423; (2000) Env LR 632 . . . . .2.83, 9.86, 9.87, 9.98, 9.99
R v Ministry of Agriculture, Fisheries and Food, ex p Bell Lines [1984] 2 CMLR 502 . . . . . . 4.60
R v MAFF, ex p Monsanto [1999] 2 WLR 599 . . . . 4.59
R v Nature Conservancy Council, ex p London Brick Property Ltd
    [1996] JPL 227. . . . . 11.80
R v Newton (1982) 4 Cr App R(S) 388 . . . . .2.86, 6.229
R v North Somerset District Council, ex p Garnett [1998] Env LR 91;
    [1998] EGCS 48, QBD 14.74

R v Northumberland National Park Authority, ex p Secretary of
State for Defence (1998) 77 P & CR 120 . . . . 11.88
R v North West Thames RHA, ex p Daniels The Times 22 June 1993, DC 2.92
R v North Yorkshire County Council, ex p Brown [1998] Env LR 385, CA;
[1999] JPL 616, HL 15.21, 15.39
R v Nottingham City Council, ex p Nottinghamshire CC [1988] RVR 151. . . . . 2.88
R v O'Brien and Enkel [2000] 2 Cr App R 358; [2000] Env LR 653 . . . . 2.84
R v Panel on Takeovers and Mergers, ex p Datafin plc [1987] QB 815 . . . . 2.37
R v Parliamentary Commissioner for Administration, ex p Balchin
[1996] EGCS 166 . . . . 2.97
R v Parliamentary Commissioner for Administration, ex p Dyer [1994]
1 WLR 621, DC. 2.97
R v Peak District National Park Authority, ex p Blacklow Industries Ltd
[1999] EGCS 58 . . . . 15.39
R v Pharmaceutical Society of Great Britain, ex p Association of
Pharmaceutical Importers (API) [1987] 3 CMLR 951. . . . . 4.47
R v Plymouth Justices, ex p Rogers [1982] QB 863 . . . . 4.69
R v Pollution Inspectorate, ex p Greenpeace (No 2) [1994] 4 All ER 329 . . . . 8.53
R v Richmond upon Thames LBC, ex p McCarthy and Stone [1992]
2 AC 48, HL 2.59
R v Rochdale MBC, ex p Brown [1997] Env LR 100. . . . . 5.109
R v Rochdale MBC, ex p Milne [2001]
Env LR 22 . . . . 11.48, 15.25, 15.27, 15.28
R v Rochdale MBC, ex p Tew [2000] Env LR 1 . . . . 11.48, 15.25, 15.26
R v Ruffell (David) (1992) 12 Cr App R(S) 204, CA 16.33
R v St Edmondsbury BC, ex p Walton [1999] 3 PLR 51; [1999] ELR 869. . . . . 15.45
R v Searle The Times 27 February 1995, CA 4.69
R v Secretary of State, ex p Greenwich LBC The Times 17 May 1989 . . . . 2.39
R v Secretary of State for Employment, ex p EOC [1995] AC 1, HL;
[1994] 1 All ER 910 . . . . 4.62
R v Secretary of State for Health, ex p Eastside Cheese Co [1999] COD 321, CA 2.88, 3.47
R v Secretary of State for the Environment, ex p Factortame (No 5)
The Times 3 November 1999, HL 4.65, 4.67
R v Secretary of State for the Environment, ex p Friends of the Earth Ltd
[1996] Env LR 198, CA 4.61
R v Secretary of State for the Environment, ex p Greenpeace [1994]
4 All ER 352; Independent 8 March 1994. . . . . 8.52
R v Secretary of State for the Environment, ex p Kingston-upon-Hull City
Council [1996] Env LR 248, QBD. 4.60
R v Secretary of State for the Environment, ex p National & Local Government
Officers' Assocn (NALGO) (1993) 5 Admin LR 785, CA 2.88
R v Secretary of State for the Environment, ex p RSPB [1997] Env LR 431, The Times 10
February 1995 HL; [1997] Env LR 442, ECJ 2.25, 4.49, 4.59, 11.67, 11.68, 14.75
R v Secretary of State for the Environment, ex p Surrey Heath BC (1987)
56 P & CR 250. . . . . 2.30
R v Secretary of State for the Environment, ex p Watson The Times 31
August 1998. . . . . 2.92
R v Secretary of State for the Environment, Transport and the Regions,
ex p Marson [1998] JPL 869, CA 15.45
R v Secretary of State for the Home Department, ex p Adan [2001] 1 All ER 593 . . . . 3.06
R v Secretary of State for Social Services, ex p Hincks (1973) 123 SJ 436 . . . . 16.81
R v Secretary of State for Trade and Industry, ex p Duddridge
[1995] Env LR 131, QBD 3.19, 4.51, 16.91

R v Secretary of State for Trade and Industry, ex p Greenpeace (No.2)
[2000] Env LR 221. . . . . 3.07
R v Secretary of State for Transport, ex p Factortame [1990] 2 AC 85. . . . . 2.32
R v Secretary of State for Transport, ex p Factortame (No 2)
[1991] 1 AC 603, HL. 4.44, 4.56, 4.59, 4.62
R v Secretary of State for Transport, ex p Richmond LBC and others [1994]
1 All ER 577; [1994] 1 WLR 74; The Times 11 May 1995 . . . . 13.125, 14.24
R v Shorrock (Peter) [1994] QB 279, CA 16.33
R v Somerset County Council (2000) Env LR 582 . . . . 4.37
R v Swale Borough Council, ex p Royal Society for the Protection of Birds
(1991) 1 PLR 6. . . . . 4.10, 4.59
R v Tower Hamlets LBC ex p Chetnik Developments Ltd [1988] AC 858. . . . . 2.88
R v Waveney District Council, ex p Bell [2001] Env LR 465 . . . . 15.25, 15.67
R v Weymouth and Portland Borough Council ex p Portland Port
Limited and another [2001] EWHC 1171 (Admin) 15.27, 15.30
R v Wicks [1998] AC 92, HL 9.114
R v Yorkshire Water Services Ltd [2001] EWCA Crim 2635 . . . . 9.85
R (Aggregate Industries UK Ltd) v English Nature and Secretary of
State for the Environment, Food and Rural Affairs [2002]
EWHC 908 (Admin) 3.49, 11.80
R (AMVAC) v Secretary of State EFRA [2001] EWHC Admin 1011 . . . . 3.47
R (Anderson) v Bradford MDC [2006] EWHC 3344 (Admin). 15.16
R (Anti-Waste Ltd) v Environment Agency
(2007) EWCA Civ 1377. . . . . 6.13, 6.14
R (Barker) v Bromley LBC [2006] 3 WLR 1209;
[2006] UKHL 52. . . . . 5.79, 15.16, 15.21, 15.61
R (Brennon) v Bromsgrove District Council [2003]
EWHC 752 (Admin) 3.41, 11.122
R (Blewett) v Derbyshire County Council [2004] Env LR 29 . . . . 15.60
R (Buglife – the Invertebrate Conservation Trust) v Thurrock Thames
Gateway Development Corporation and Rosemound Developments
Ltd [2008] EWHC 475 . . . . 11.20
R (Candlish) v Hastings Borough Council, ex p RSPB [2005] EWHC 1539. . . . . 15.29
R (Catt) v Brighton BC [2007] EWCA Civ 2 . . . . 15.47
R (Chelmsford Car & Commercial Ltd) v Chelmsford Borough Council [2005]
EWHC 1705 (Admin) 14.51
R (Christopher Mellor) v Secretary of State for Communities and Local Government
[2008] All ER (D) 98 (Jan), CA 15.45
R (Corner House Research) v Secretary of State for Trade and Industry
[2005] 1 WLR 2600. . . . . 2.94
R (Cummins) v Camden LBC [2001] EWHC Admin 1116 . . . . 14.33
R (Davey) v Aylesbury Vale DC [2007] 1 WLR 878 . . . . 2.94
R (Edwards) v Environment Agency and others [2005]
EWHC 657 (Admin); [2006] EWCA Civ 877; [2007] Env LR 9,
CA; [2008] UKHL 22 . . . . 2.92, 6.44, 15.40, 15.67
R (Enfield London Borough Council) v Mayor of London [2007]
EWHC 1795 (Admin) 2.34
R (Fisher) v English Nature [2004] EWCA Civ 663 . . . . 11.80
R (Friends of the Earth) v Environment Agency [2004] Env LR 31 . . . . 11.72
R (Friends of the Earth Ltd and another) v Secretary of State for the Environment,
Food and Rural Affairs and others [2002] Env LR 612, CA. 8.52
R (Friends Provident) v Secretary of State for the Environment, Transport and
the Regions and Norwich City Council [2002] 1 WLR 1450 . . . . 3.49

R (Furness and Guildford BC v Environment Agency & Thames Water
   Services Ltd (Interested Party) [2001] EWHC Admin 1058 . . . . 3.46
R (Goodman) v Lewisham LBC [2003] EWCA Civ 140. .11.48, 15.46
R (Greenpeace) v Secretary of State for Trade & Industry [2007]
   EWHC 311 (Admin), (2007) Env LR 29 . . . . 2.31, 2.89, 4.57
R (Hart DC) v SSCLG [2008] EWHC 1204 (Admin) 11.72
R (Horner) v Lancashire County Council and Castle Cement Ltd [2005] EWHC 2273 . . . 15.36
R (Howsmoor Developments Ltd and others) v South Gloucestershire
   County Council [2008] EWHC 262 (Admin) 15.08
R (JHM Newsum) v Welsh Assembly Government [2004] EWCA Civ 1565. . . . . 11.68
R (Jones) v Mansfield Borough Council [2004] Env LR 391 . . . . .15.02, 15.54
R (Lebus) v South Cambridgeshire DC [2003] 2 PLR 5 . . . . 15.47
R (Lewis) v Redcar & Cleveland BC & Persimmon Homes
   Teeside Limited [2008] EWCA Civ 746 . . . . 11.72
R (Littlewood) v Bassetlaw District Council [2008] All ER (D) 268 (Jun) 15.47
R (Malster) v Ipswich Borough Council [2002] PLCR 251, CA 15.46
R (Middleton) HM Coroner for the Western District of Somerset and
   another [2004] UKHL 10. . . . . 3.38
R (Mount Cook Land Ltd) v Westminster District Council [2003]
   EWCA Civ 1346; [2004] 2 P & CR 405. . . . . .2.94, 14.51
R (National Grid Gas Plc) v Environment Agency [2007] UKHL 30;
   [2007] 1 WLR 1280. . . . . 4.53
R (NFU and others) v Secretary of State for the EFRA and Secretary of
   State for Wales [2003] 6/3/2003 . . . . 3.47
R (Pridmore) v Salisbury District Council and another [2004] EWHC 2511 (Admin) 5.53
R (Richardson) v North Yorkshire CC (2004) JPL 911 . . . . 15.67
R (Rockware Glass Ltd) v Chester City Council [2005]
   EWHC 2250 (Admin) 4.60, 6.44, 6.48
R (SPCMA SA and others) v Secretary of State for Environment, Food and
   Rural Affairs [2007] EWHC 2610 (Admin) 4.48
R (Tree and Wildlife Action Committee Ltd) v Forestry Commission
   [2007] EWHC 1623 (Admin) 11.08
R (Trailer & Marina (Leven) Ltd) v Secretary of State for the Environment
   Food & Rural Affairs & English Nature [2005] 1 WLR 1267 . . . . 3.49
R (Vetterlein) v Hampshire County Council [2002] JPL 289 . . . . 3.46
R (Villa Ria Trading) v First Secretary of State and another [2006]
   EWHC 3326 (Admin) 4.52
R (Wembley Fields Ltd) v Brent LBC [2005] EWHC 2978 (Admin). 15.67
R (Western Power Distribution Investments Ltd) v Countryside
   Council for Wales [2007] EWHC 50 (Admin) 2.91, 11.80
R (Wilson) v Wychavon District Council and another [2007] 2 WLR 798 . . . . 3.41
Racz v Home Office [1994] 2 AC 45, HL. 16.78
Radford v de Froberville [1977] 1 WLR 1262. . . . . 16.104
Rainham Chemical Works v Belvedere Fish Guano Co
   [1921] 2 AC 465 . . . . .16.49, 16.50
Ratcliff v McConnell The Times 3 December 1998, CA 16.71
Read v Croydon Corp [1938] 4 All ER 631;
   (1937) 37 LGR 53 . . . . 10.101, 16.80, 16.84
Read v J Lyons & Co Ltd [1947] AC 156, HL. 16.04
Reay and Hope v BNFL [1994] Water Law 22-23; 5 Med LR 1. 16.92
Residents Against Waste Site Ltd v Lancashire County Council and another
   [2007] EWHC 2558 (Admin) 14.87
Reynolds v Clarke (1725) 2 Ld Ray 1399 . . . . 16.70

Rickards v Lothian [1913] AC 263 . . . . 16.51
Ricketts and Fletcher v Secretary of State for the Environment [1988] JPL 768 . . . . 14.92
Rigby v Chief Constable of Nottinghamshire [1985] 1 WLR 1242 . . . . 16.81
Rimmer v Liverpool City Council [1985] QB 1 . . . . 16.16
Riverstone Meat v Lancashire Shipping [1961] AC 807. . . . . 8.197
RMC Management Services Ltd v SSE (1972) 222 EG 1593. 14.92
Robinson v East Riding of Yorkshire Council [2002] EWCA Civ 1660 . . . . 11.122
Robinson v Everett [1988] Crim LR 699. . . . . .11.98, 11.104
Robinson v Kilvert (1889) 41 ChD 88 . . . . 16.08
Robinson v Post Office [1974] 2 All ER 737 . . . . 16.88
Roe v Ministry of Health [1954] 2 QB 66, CA 16.61, 16.90
Rollo v Minister of Town and Country Planning [1948] 1 All ER 13. . . . . 13.37
Rookes v Barnard [1964] AC 1129, HL 16.112
Roswell v Prior (1701) 12 Mod 635 . . . . 16.12
Rouse v Gravelworks Ltd [194011 KB 489, CA 16.51
Rowland (Josie) v Environment Agency [2003] EWCA Civ 1885;
[2003] TLR 20/1/2004, CA 3.47
Rushmer v Polsue & Alfieri [1906] Ch 234. . . . . 16.09
Ruxley Electronics and Construction Ltd v Forsyth [1996] AC 344, HL 16.106
Ryeford Homes v Sevenoaks DC [1989] JPPL 36;
      The Times 15 February 1989 . . . . .16.82, 16.96
Rylands v Fletcher (1866) LR 1 Ex 265; affirmed (1868)
      LR 3 HL 330 . . . . 2.04, 2.18, 12.19, 12.20, 12.21, 16.03, 16.07,
      . . . . .16.45, 16.47, 16.49, 16.50, 16.53, 16.87, 16.93
St Anne's Well Brewery Co v Roberts (1929) 140 LT 1 . . . . 16.16
St Helen's Smelting Co v Tipping (1865) 11 HLC G42. . . . . 16.06, 16.09, 16.103
Salvin v North Brauncepath Coal Co [1874] 9 Ch App 705 . . . . 16.10
Sampson v Hodgson-Pressinger [1981] 3A11 ER 710. . . . . 16.16
Savage v Fairclough [2000] Env LR 183 . . . . 12.21
Scott-Whitehead v National Coal Board (1987)
      53 P & CR 263, QBD 16.40, 16.75, 16.84, 16.102
Seaport Investments Ltd and others v Department of the Environment
      for Northern Ireland [2007] NIQB 62; [2007] NIQB 103 . . . . 15.08
Secretary of State for Transport v Haughian (1996)
      73 P & CR 85, CA 15.20, 15.67
Sedleigh-Denfield v O'Callaghan [1940]
      AC 880, HL. 16.08, 16.13, 16.24, 16.29, 16.33
Severn Trent River Authority v Express Food Group (1989)
      153 JP 126. . . . . 9.114
Shelfer v City of London Electric Co [1895] 1 Ch 287 . . . . 16.42, 16.43, 16.106
Simaan Contracting Co v Pilkington Ltd [1988] 1 QB 758. . . . . 16.108
Skandia Property (UK) Ltd v Thames Water Utilities Ltd The Times
      7 September 1999, CA 16.104
Skinner v Secretary of State for Transport The Times 3 January 1996, QBD 16.79
Smeaton v Ilford Corpn [1954] Ch 450 . . . . .10.139, 16.87
Smedley, ex p [1985] 1 QB 657. . . . . 16.49
Smith v East Elloe RDC [1956] AC 736 . . . . 16.78
Smith v Littlewoods Organisation [1987] AC 241;
      [1987] 2 WLR 480. . . . . .16.29, 16.57
Smith v Secretary of State [2003] 2 P & CR 11 . . . . .14.13, 14.14
Smith (Maureen) v Secretary of State for the Environment, Transport and Regions
      and others [2003] EWCA Civ 262; (2003) Env LR 32 . . . . 15.12, 15.61, 15.62
Sochacki v Sas [1947] 1 All ER 344. . . . . 16.51

Somerset CC v Fewings [1995] 1 All ER 513 . . . . 2.88
Southport Corpn v Esso Petroleum [1954] 2 QB 182, CA. 16.31
South Shropshire Disrtict Council v First Secretary of State
    and another [2003] EWHC 1351 (Admin). 3.10
Southwark LBC v Mills The Times 28 August 1998, CA. 16.16
Spring v Guardian Assurance plc [1994] 3 All ER 129. . . . . 16.111
Stephens v Anglian Water Authority [1987] 1 WLR 1381, CA 9.50
Stockdale v Haringey LBC (1990) 88 LGR 7 . . . . 2.88
Stoke on Trent Council v B & Q Ltd [1984] Ch 1, CA; [1984] AC 754. . . . . 2.35
Stokes v Guest, Keen and Nettlefold (Bolts and Nuts) Ltd [1968] 1 WLR 1776. . . . . 16.65
Stovin v Wise [1996] AC 923, [1996]
    3 WLR 388 HL 16.77, 16.80, 16.85, 16.86
Strable v Dartford BC [1984] JPL 329 . . . . 16.82
Stringer v Minister of Housing and Local Government [1971]
    1 All ER 65; [1970] 1 WLR 1281 . . . . 14.04, 14.38, 14.92
Sturges v Bridgman (1879) 11 Ch D 852 . . . . .16.09, 16.41
Sutradhar v Natural Environment Research Council [2007] Env LR 10. . . . . 16.58
Swale Borough Council and Medway Ports Authority, ex p Royal Society for
    the Protection of Birds [1991] JPL 39 . . . . 15.29
Sweet v Secretary of State for the Environment and the Nature Conservancy
    Council [1989] JPL 927. . . . . .11.80, 11.81
Swordheath Properties v Tabet [1979] 1 All ER 240 . . . . 16.102
SW Suburban Waterworks Co v St Marylebone Union [1904] 2 KB 174. . . . . 10.59
Tate & Lyle Ltd v GLC [1983] 2 AC 509 . . . . 16.35
Taylor Woodrow Property Management Ltd v NRA [1995] Env LR 52. . . . . 9.114
Tesco Stores v Secretary of State for the Environment [1995] 1 WLR 759;
    (1995) 70 P & CR 184, HL 2.30, 14.33, 14.38, 14.47
Tetley v Chitty [198G] 1 All ER 663. . . . . .16.16, 16.65
Thompson v Brown [1981] 1 WLR 744 . . . . 16.95
Thompson v Gibson (1841) 7 M&W 45G 16.12
Thompson v Smith Shiprepairers (North Shields) Ltd [1984] QB 405 . . . . 16.65
Thompson-Schwab v Costaki [1956] 1 WLR 335. . . . . 16.04
Thornby Farms Ltd v Daventry District Council; David Murray v Derbyshire
    County Council [2002] EWCA Civ 31; (2002) Env LR 687, CA 14.91
Thorpe v Brumfit (1873) 8 Ch App 650 . . . . 16.90
3C Waste Ltd v Mersey Waste Holdings Ltd [2006] EWHC 2598 (Comm) 7.261
Tidman v Reading BC The Times 10 November 1994 . . . . 16.82
Tito v Waddell (No 2) [1972] AC 425. . . . . .11.78, 16.104
T-Mobile UK Ltd and others v First Secretary of State and another
    [2004] EWCA Civ 1763. . . . . .4.51, 14.52
Tomlinson v Congleton Borough Council [2003] UKHL 47; [2004] 1 AC. 16.71
Tower Hamlets LBC v Creitzman [1984] JP 630 DC 13.88
Trailer & Marina (Leven) Ltd v Secretary of State for the Environment,
    Food and Rural Affairs [2007] EWCA Civ 1580. . . . . 11.80
Transco v Stockport Metropolitan District Council
    [2004] 2 AC 1 . . . . 12.20, 16.02, 16.48, 16.49, 16.50, 16.53
Trusthouse Forte Hotels v Secretary of State for the
    Environment (1986) 279 EG 680. . . . . 14.51
Twyford Parish Council v Secretary of State for Transport
    [1992] Env LR 37. . . . . 15.20
United Utilities Water Plc v Environment Agency [2006] Env LR 42;
    The Times 26 October 2007; [2007] UKHL 41 . . . . .6.12, 7.08
Vacwell Engineering Co Ltd v BDH Chemicals Ltd [1971] 1 QB 11. . . . . 16.57

Vibroplant v Holland (Inspector of Taxes) (1982) 126 SJ 182 . . . . 7.99
Vyner v Waldenburg Bros [1946] KB 50 . . . . 16.92
Wagon Mound, The (No 2) [1967] 1 AC G17 . . . . 16.18
Wallington v Secretary of State for the Environment and
    Montgomeryshire [1990] JPL 278 . . . . 14.93
Wallis v Vale of Glamorgan Council [2006] 14.88
Ward v Cannock Chase DC [1986] Ch 546 . . . . 16.104, 16.106
Ward v Ritz Hotel (London) Ltd [1992] PIQR P315, CA 16.65
Waste Recycling Group PLC [2003] 28/7/03, Ch.D 3.47
Watt v Kesteven CC [1955] 1 QB 408 . . . . 16.81
Watts v Morrow [1991] 4 All ER 937, CA. 16.111
Welton v North Cornwall DC [1997] 1 WLR 570, CA. 16.77, 16.82, 16.83
West v Secretary of State for Scotland (1992) SLT 636. . . . . 2.18
West Leigh Colliery v Tunnicliffe [1908] AC 27 . . . . 16.110
West Midlands Probation Committee v Secretary of State for
    the Environment [1998] JPL 388, CA 14.55
Westminster City Council v French Connection Retail Ltd [2005] EWHC 933 . . . . 13.89
Wheat v E Lacon & Co Ltd [1966] AC 552, HL. 16.71
Wheeler v JJ Saunders [1995] 2 All ER 697; [1995] 3 WLR 466, CA 16.38
White v Chief Constable of South Yorkshire Police [1999] 2 AC 455, HL 16.77
White v St Albans City and DC The Times 12 March 1990, CA 16.71
Whitmores Ltd v Stanford [1909] 1 Ch 427 . . . . 16.50
Wilmott Trading (No 2), Re, The Times 16 June 1999 . . . . 7.229
Wilsher v Essex AHA [1987] QB 730 . . . . 16.64
Wood v Conway Corp [1914] 2 Ch 47 . . . . 16.10
Wychavon DC v National Rivers Authority [1993] 1 WLR 125 . . . . 9.92
X (Minors) v Bedfordshire CC and others [1995] 3 WLR 152, HL 16.79
Younger Homes (Northern) Ltd v First Secretary of State and Calderdale
    Metropolitan District Council [2004] EWCA Civ 1060, CA 15.67

European Community

European Court of Justice

Aannemersbedrijf PK Kraaijveld BV and others v Gedeputeerde
    Staten van Zuid-Holland ('the Dutch Dykes' case) C-72/95 [1996]
    ECR I-05403 (1997) Env LR 265. . . . . 4.08, 4.10, 4.38, 4.39, 15.21, 15.40, 15.44
Aher-Waggon GmbH v Germany Case C-389/96 (1998) ECR I-04473 . . . . 4.12
Amministrazione delle Finanze dello Stato v Simmenthal SPA Case
    C-106/77 [1978] ECR I-629 . . . . 4.02, 4.25, 4.56
Arco Chemie Nederland Ltd v Minister van Volkshuisvesting, Ruimtelijke
    Ordening en Milieubeheer (Case C-418/97) and Vereniging Dorpsbelang Hees,
    Stichting Werkgroep Weurt+ and Vereniging Stedelijk Leefmilieu
    Nijmegen v Directeur van de dienst Milieu en Water van de provincie
    Gelderland (Case C-419/97) [2000] ECR I-04475 . . . . 4.08
ATRAL SA v Belgian State Case C-14/02 [2003] ECR I-04431 . . . . 4.27
Auer v Ministère Public [1983] ECR 2727, ECJ 4.32
Barra v Belgian State and City of Liège Case C-309/85 [1998] ECR 355 . . . . 4.62
Bettati (Gianni) v Safety Hi-Tech Srl Case 341/95 [1998] ECR I-04355 . . . . 4.51
Bozetti v Invenizzi SPA Case C-179/84 [1985] ECR I-2301 . . . . 4.56
Brasserie du Pêcheur SA v Germany; R v Secretary of State for Transport, ex p
    Factortame (No 4) Cases C 46/93 & C-48/93 [1996] ECR I-1029 . . . . 4.63, 16.78
Bresciani Case C-87/75 (1976) ECR 129 . . . . 3.09

Bund Naturschutz Bayern and others v Freistaat Bayern (Bavarian Roads Case)
Case C-396/92 [1994] ECR I-3717 . . . . 15.20

Burgemeester en wethouders van Haarlemmerliede en Spaarnwoude
and others v Gedeputeerde Staten van Noord-Holland Case C-81/96
[1998] ECR I-03923 . . . . 15.39

Cassis de Dijon case *see* Rewe-Zentrale Attorney-General v Bundesmonopolverwaltung fur
Branntwein

Chemische Afvalstoffen Dusseldorp BV and others v Minister van
Volkshuisvesting, Ruimtelijke Ordening en Milieubeheer
Case C-203/96 [2001] ECR I-2099 . . . . 4.12

Comet BV v Produktchap voor Siergewassen Case C-45/76 [1976]
ECR I-2043 . . . . 4.56

Comitato di Coordinamento per la Difesa della Cava v Regione
Lombardia Case C-236/92 [1994] ECR I-483 . . . . 4.35

Commission v Austria Case 320/03 [2005] ECR I-09871 . . . . 4.50

Commission v Belgium Case 77/69 [1970] ECR 237 . . . . 4.66

Commission v Belgium Case C-134/86 [1987] ECR I-2415 . . . . 4.60

Commission v Belgium Case C-376/90 [1992] ECR I-6153 . . . . 4.15

Commission v Denmark (Danish Bottles case) Case C-302/86 [1990]
ECR I-2143; [1989] 54 CMLR 619; (1988) ECR 4607 . . . . 4.12, 4.50

Commission v France Case C-38/99 [2000] ECR I-10941 . . . . 4.72

Commission v Germany Case C-57/89R [1989] ECR 2849 . . . . 4.72

Commission v Germany Case C-195/90R [1990] ECR I-2715 . . . . 4.72

Commission v Germany Case C-431/92 (Dortmund Power Station case)
[1995] ECR I-2189 . . . . 15.20, 15.64

Commission v Greece Case C-45/91 [1992] ECR I-2509 . . . . 4.60

Commission v Greece Case C-420/02 [2004] ECR I-11175 . . . . 4.35

Commission v Hellenic Republic Case C-103/00 [2002] ECR I-01147 . . . . 4.72

Commission v Ireland Case C-392/96 [1999] ECR I-05901 . . . . 15.42

Commission v Ireland Case C-459/03 [2006] ECR I-04635 . . . . 3.08

Commission v Ireland Case C-216/05 (2006) ECR I-10787 . . . . 4.29

Commission v Italy Joined Cases 30-34/81 [1981] ECR 3379 . . . . 4.60

Commission v Italy Case C-365/97 [1999] ECR I-7773 . . . . 4.35

Commission v Spain Case C-58/02 [2004] ECR I-00621 . . . . 4.28

Commission v Spain, Intervener: United Kingdom Case C-416/02
[2005] ECR I-7487 . . . . 9.28

Commission v UK Case C-337/89 (Drinking Water)
[1992] ECR I-6103 . . . . 4.61, 4.66

Commission v UK Case C-56190 (Blackpool Beaches) [1993] ECR 1-4109 . . . . 4.66

Commission v UK Case C-340/96 The Times 30 April 1996; ECR I-02023 . . . . 4.61

Commission v UK Case C-69/99 [2000] ECR I-10979 . . . . 9.29

Commission v UK Case C-508/03 [2006] ECR I-03969 . . . . 11.47

Commission v UK C-6/04 (Re Conservation of Natural
Habitats Directive) [2005] ECR I-09017 . . . . 4.28, 11.11, 11.72

Commission v UK Case C-508/3 [2006] ECR I-3969;
[2006] QB 764 . . . . 4.68, 15.16, 15.32

Commission v UK Case C-37/05 [2006] ECR I-00006 . . . . 15.04

Commune de Brain-le-Chateau and Michel Tilleut and others v
Region Wallonee (Joined cases C-53/02 and C217/02) 14.88

Costa v ENEL Case 6/64 [1964] ECR 585 . . . . 4.47, 4.56

Enichem Base v Commune di Cinisello Balsamo C-380/87 [1989]
ECR 2491; [1991] 1 CMLR 313 . . . . 4.34

Faccini Dori v Recreb Case C-91/92 [1995] All ER (EC) 1; The Times
    4 August 1994 .... 4.66
Farrell v Minister for the Environment (Ireland) and Motor Insurer's Bureau of
    Ireland (MIBI) Case C-365/05 [2007] ECR I-03067 .... 4.32
Foster v British Gas plc Case C-188/89 [1991] 1 QB 405, ECJ 4.32, 4.33
France v UK [1979] ECR 2923. .... 4.72
Francovich and Bonifaci v Italy Cases C-6/90 & C-9/90
    [1991] ECR I-05357 .... 4.28, 4.63, 4.65, 4.66, 4.67, 16.78
Fratelli v Costanzo SpA v Commune di Milano Case C-103/88 [1989]
    CMLR 239, ECJ 4.33
Frontini v Ministerodelle Finanze [1974] CMLR 372 .... 4.02
Garland v British Rail Engineering Ltd Case 12/81 [1983] 2 AC 751;
    [1982] 2 All ER 402 .... 3.06
Gaston Schul Case C-461/03 [2005] ECR I-10513 .... 4.48
Grau Gomis Case C-458/93 [1995] All ER (EC) 668, ECJ 4.47
Greenpeace and others v Commission C-321/95 [1998] ECR-I-1651 .... 4.74
Inter-Environnement Wallonie ABSL v Region Wallonie Case C-129/96
    [1997] ECR I-07411; [1998] 1 All ER (EC) 155. .... 4.27
Internationale Handelsgesellschaft v EVGF Case 11/70 [1970] ECR 1125;
    [1972] CMLR 255. .... 4.02
International Fruit Company NV v Commission Joined Cases 41-44/70
    [1971] ECR 411. .... 4.74
Johnston v Chief Constable of the RUC Case C-222/84 [1987] QB 129, ECJ. 4.33
Köbler v Republic of Austria Case C-224/01 [2003] ECR I-10239 .... 4.68
Kupfberg Case C-104/81 (1982) ECR 3641 .... 3.09
Landelijke Vereniging tot Behoud van de Waddenzee v Staatssecretaris
    van Landbouw, Natuurbeheer en Visserij [2004] ECR I-07405 .... 11.72
Luciano Arcaro Case C-168/95 [1997] All ER (EC) 82. .... 4.69
Marks & Spencer plc v Commissioners of Customs & Excise Case
    C-62/00 [2002] ECR I-06325 .... 4.62
Marleasing SA v La Commercial Internacional de Alimentation
    SA Case C-106/89 [1990] ECR I-4135. .... 4.69
Marshall v Southampton and South West Hampshire Area Health
    Authority Case C-152/84 [1986] 2 WLR 780, ECJ. 4.33, 4.63, 15.21
National Park Authority v Secretary of State for Transport, Local
    Government and the Regions [2003] EWHC 236 Admin. 3.10
Opinion 2/94 European Convention on Human Rights 12 Mar 1996. .... 4.41
Peralta Case C-379/92 [1994] ECR I-3453. .... 3.19, 4.51
Pfeiffer Case C-397/01 [2004] ECR I-8835 .... 4.56
Pfizer Animal Health SA v Council of the European Union Case T-13/99
    [2002] ECR II-3305. .... 4.08, 4.17
Plaumann v Commission [1963] ECR 95 .... 4.74
PreussenElektra AG v Schhleswag AG Case C-379/98 (2001) I-02099 .... 4.12
Procureur de la Republique v Association de Defense des
    Bruleurs d'Huiles Usagees Case C-240/83 [1985] ECR 531 .... 4.09
Pubblico Ministero v Ratti Case C-148/78 [1979] ECR 1-1629 .... 4.69
R v HM Treasury, ex p British Telecommunications plc Case C–392/93 [1996]
    ECR I–1631; The Times 16 April 1996, ECJ 4.63
R v Minister of Agriculture, Fisheries and Food, ex p Hedley Lomas (Ireland)
    Ltd Case C-5/94 [1996] ECR I-2553; [1997] QB 139;
    The Times 6 June 1996. .... 4.62, 4.65
R v Secretary of State for the Environment, ex p RSPB (the Lappel Bank)
    Case C-44/95 [1996] 3 CMLR 411, ECJ 4.59

R (Barker) v Bromley LBC and the FSS Case C-290/03 [2006]
    ECR I-03949 . . . . 11.47, 15.16, 15.21, 15.32
R (Thames Water Utilities Ltd) v South East London Division, Bromley
    Magistrates' Court (Environment Agency, interested party)
    Case C-252/05 [2007] ECR I-03883; [2007] 1 WLR 1945 . . . . 4.48, 9.104
R (Wells) v Secretary of State for Transport, Local Government and the
    Regions Case C-201/02 [2004] ECR I-00723. . . . . 4.39, 15.29, 15.61
Reiser Internationale Transporte GMBH v Asfinag Autobahnen
    Und Schnellstrassen Finanzierungs-Aktiengesellschaft Case
    C-157/02 [2004] ECR I-1477 . . . . 4.33
Saddick Case C-458/93 [1995] All ER (EC) 664, ECJ 4.47
Safety Hi-tech Srl v S & T SrI Case C-284/95 [1998] ECR I-04301 . . . . 4.51
Schmidberger v Austria Case C-112/00 [2003] ECR I-5659 . . . . 4.41
Simmenthal Case C-106/77, see Amminstrazione delle Finanze dello Stato v
    Simmenthal SpA
Traghetti del Mediterraneo SpA v Repubblica italiana C173/03 [2006]
    ECR I-05177 . . . . 4.48, 4.68
TWD Textilwerke Deggendorf GmbH v Germany Case C-188/92 [1994] ECR I-833 . . . . . 4.40
Unión de Pequeños Agricultores v Council of the European Union
    Case C-50/00P [2002] ECR I-06677 . . . . 4.74
Van den Burg Case C-169/89 [1990] ECR I-2143 . . . . 4.69
Van Duyn v Home Office Case C-41/74 [1974] ECR 1337 . . . . 4.30
Van Gend en Loos v Netherlandse Tarief Commissie Case
    C-26/62 [1963] ECR 1. . . . . 4.30, 4.56
Von Colson and Kamann v Land Nordrhein-Westfalen Case C-14/83
    [1984] ECR I-1891 . . . . 4.26
Zuckerfabrik Suderdithmarschen Case C-143/88 & C-92/89
    [1991] ECR I-415 . . . . 4.59
Zuckerfabrik Wadenstedt GmbH v Council Case 6/68 [1968] ECR 409. . . . . 4.74

Court of First Instance

Campo Ebro Industrial SA v Commission Case T-472/93 [1995] ECR II-421 . . . . 4.74
Jégo-Quéré & Cie SA v Commission of the European Communities Case
    T-177/01 [2002] ECR II-2365. . . . . 4.74
Sweden v Commission Case T-229/04 [2007] ECR II-02437 . . . . 4.72
WWF-UK Ltd v Council of the European Union Case T-91/07
    Order of 2 June 2008 . . . . 4.75

Other Jurisdictions

Canada

Gresten v Municipality of MC [1974] 41 DLR (3rd) 646 . . . . 16.100
Shuttleworth v Vancouver Hospital [1927] 2 DLR 573. . . . . 16.110
Trail Smelter Arbitration (Canada/USA) 33 AJIL 182(1939); 35 AJIL (1941). 3.21

European Court of Human Rights

Athanassoglou and others v Switzerland (2001) 31 EHRR 13 . . . . 3.46
Balmer-Schafroth v Switzerland (1998) 25 EHRR 598 . . . . 3.46, 3.49
Bryan v UK (1996) JPL 386; (1995) 21 EHRR 342 . . . . 3.49

Buckley v UK [1996] JPL 1018; 23 EHRR 101 ....3.40, 3.43
Fadeyeva v Russia (55723/00) [2007] EHRR 10 .... 3.44
Guerra v Italy [1998] 4 BHRC 63; 26 EHRR 357 .... 3.40, 3.43, 3.44, 4.66
Hans Gaida v Germany (Application No. 9355/03
    European Court of Human Rights 3/7/2007) 4.51
Holding and Barnes PLC v UK application no. 2352/02, 12 March 2002 .... 3.49
James v UK Series A No 52, 24, (1986) 8 EHRR 123 .... 3.47
Lithgow and others v UK (1986) 8 EHRR 329 .... 3.47
Lopez Ostria v Spain 8 July 1992, application no. 16798/90;
    [1995] 20 EHRR 277 .... 3.42–3.44
Matos & Silva LDA v Portugal (1997) 24 EHRR 573 .... 3.48
Ortenberg v Austria [1995] 19 EHRR 524 .... 3.46, 3.49
Osman v United Kingdom (1998) 29 EHRR 245 .... 16.79
Pine Valley Developments and others v Ireland [1992] 14 EHRR 319 .... 3.40
S v France (1990) 25 DR 250 .... 3.47
Sporrong and Lonnroth Series A No 52, (1982) 5 EHRR 35 .... 3.47, 3.48
Tauira and others v France [1995] DR 83-B112 .... 3.39
Tre Traktorer Aktiebohg Series A No 159, (1989) 13 EHRR 309 .... 3.48

International Court of Justice

Gabc˘ikovo-Nagymaros Project Judgment of 25 September 1997 .... 3.11

United States of America

Massachusetts, et al v Environmental Protection Agency, 549 US [2007];
    127 S Ct 1438 (reversing 415 F 3d 50, DC Cir 2005) 2.25, 4.74
Tennessee Valley Authority v Hill 437 US 153 (1978) 2.25
United States v Fleet Factors Corp 901 F 2d 1550 (1990) 2.25

World Trade Organisation

Shrimp/Turtle case 3.11

TABLE OF STATUTES

Acquisition of Land
    Act 1981 . . . . 6.126, 10.198
    s 18 . . . . 11.28
Act of Union 1707 . . . . 2.18
Agriculture Act 1947 . . . . 9.25
    s 98 . . . . 11.99, 11.113
Agriculture Act 1986 . . . . 11.87
    s 18(3), (4) 11.87
Alkali Act 1874. . . . . 6.01
Alkali & Works Act 1863 . . . . 2.48, 6.01
Alkali & Works Regulation
    Act 1906 . . . .6.01, 13.02–13.04, 14.21
Ancient Monuments and Archaeological Areas
    Act 1979 . . . . 14.22
    s 33 . . . . 14.73
    Sch 1 . . . . 14.73
Animal Health Act 1981. . . . . . . 2.91, 11.99
    Parts 1–3 . . . . .2.91
Animal Health Act 2002. . . . . .2.91
Anti-Social Behaviour Act 2003—
    Part V. 13.108
    s 40 . . . . 13.109
    s 41 . . . . 13.111
Armed Forces Act 1991—
    s 30 . . . . 12.44
Asylum and Immigration Act 1996. . . . .3.06
Atomic Weapons Establishment
    Act 1991 . . . . 12.44
Badger Act 1973. . . . . 11.111
Badger Act 1991. . . . . 11.111
Building Act 1984 . . . . 2.10, 10.183
    s 76 . . . . 12.10
Birds (Registration Charges) Act 1997 11.101
    s 25 . . . . 10.126
    s 59 . . . . 10.183
Civil Aviation Act 1982 . . . . 13.122, 13.125
    ss 76, 77 . . . . 13.123
    s 78(3) 13.124
Civil Liability (Contribution) Act 1978 16.90
Clean Air Act 1956. . . . . 1.68, 1.74,
        5.43, 13.05, 13.07, 13.16, 13.19, 13.26,
              13.29, 13.43, 13.59, 14.21
    Part I 13.05

s 1 . . . . 1.74
s 6 . . . . 1.75
s 11 . . . . 1.75
s 23 . . . . 1.75
s 79 . . . . 5.13
Clean Air Act 1968. . . . . 13.11, 13.19, 14.21
Clean Air
    Act 1993 . . . . .2.06, 2.20, 5.43,
        7.181, 13.05, 13.10, 13.15, 13.19,
        13.21, 13.26, 13.41, 13.43, 13.59,
            13.68, 13.72–13.78
Part I 13.26
s 1(1) 13.06
s 2 . . . . 13.06, 13.08
s 3 . . . . 13.07
Part II. 13.26
s 6(1) 13.10
s 7 . . . . 13.11
s 7(2), (3) 13.12
s 7(5) 13.13
ss 8, 9 . . . . 13.14
s 10 . . . . 13.15
s 11 . . . . 13.17
ss 12, 13 . . . . 13.18
s 14 . . . . 13.20
s 15(1) 13.22
s 15(4), 95). 13.23
s 15(8), (9) 13.24
s 16 . . . . 13.25
Part III 13.28
s 18 . . . . 13.32
s 19(1) 13.35
s 19(3), (4) 13.36
s 20(1), (2) 13.27, 13.38
s 20(4) 13.28
s 20(5) 13.38
s 21 . . . . 13.39
s 22 . . . . 13.40
s 23(1), (2) 13.41
s 23(4)-(6) 13.42
s 24(1)-(3) 13.45
s 25 . . . . 13.45
s 26 . . . . 13.47

Clean Air Act 1993 (*cont.*)
s 27 . . . . 13.45
s 28 . . . . 13.48
Part IV 13.57, 13.70
s 30 . . . . 13.50
s 33 . . . . 13.57
Part V. 13.58
s 34 . . . . 13.59
s 35 . . . . 13.64
s 35(2) 13.64
s 36 . . . . 13.60, 13.63
s 37 . . . . 13.63, 13.65
s 38 . . . . 13.65
s 39 . . . . 13.69
s 42 . . . . 13.70
s 43 . . . . 13.71
s 44 . . . . 13.72
s 45 . . . . 13.73
s 46 . . . . 13.74
ss 47, 48 . . . . 3.75
ss 49–51 . . . . 13.76
ss 52–55 . . . . 13.77
s 56 . . . . 13.64, 13.77
ss 57–61 . . . . 13.77
Sch 1 . . . . 13.34
Sch 2 . . . . 13.45
Sch 5, para 7 . . . . 13.21
Clean Neighbourhoods and Environment
Act 2005 . . . . 2.05, 2.87, 13.150
Part 7 . . . . 13.149
Climate Change and Sustainable Energy
Act 2006 . . . . 3.13
Companies Act 1985 . . . . 2.75
Competition Act 1998 . . . . 10.236
Competition and Service (Utilities)
Act 1992 . . . . 10.07
s 46(1), (3) 9.105
Compulsory Purchase Act 1965 . . . . . 10.198
Congenital Disabilities (Civil Liability)
Act 1976 . . . . 8.37
s 3(2) 8.37
s 4(1) 8.37
s 4(4) 8.37
Conservation of Seals Act 1970. . . . . . 11.114
ss 1–6 . . . . 11.114
ss 9, 10 . . . . 11.114
Constitutional Reform Act 2005. . 2.17, 2.22
Consumer Protection Act 1987. . . . . . 10.101
Control of Pollution
Act 1974 . . . . 1.80–1.82, 1.84,
2.48, 2.51, 7.07, 7.51, 7.53, 7.101, 7.108,
7.134, 7.181, 7.198, 7.217, 13.50, 13.59,
13.79, 13.80, 13.81, 13.85, 13.107,
13.112, 13.122, 14.21, 16.66

Part I 6.163
s 1 . . . . 1.81
ss 3–10. . . . . 1.82
s 5 . . . . 14.87
s 17 . . . . 7.53, 7.54
ss 11–28 . . . . 1.82
Part II. 9.01
s 42 . . . . 5.13
s 52(1) 13.88
Part III 1.83, 13.81
ss 58, 59 . . . . 13.123
s 60 . . . . 13.81, 13.84, 13.87
s 60(1), (2) 13.80
s 60(3) 13.81
s 60(4) 13.82
s 60(7), (8) 13.83
s 61 . . . . 13.85
s 61(4)–(7) 13.86
s 61(8), (9) 13.87
s 62(1A), (1B). 13.91
s 62(2) 13.91
s 62(3) 13.93
s 62(3A) 13.91
s 63 . . . . 1.82, 13.96
s 64 . . . . 1.82
s 64(1)–(3) 13.98
s 64(4) 13.99
s 65 . . . . 1.82, 13.102
s 66 . . . . 1.82, 13.105
s 68 . . . . 13.112
Control of Pollution (Amendment)
Act 1989 . . . . 2.06
Countryside Act 1968 . . . . 1.72, 3.29, 11.02
s 7 . . . . 11.92
s 11 . . . . 11.02
s 15 . . . . 11.82
s 15(2) 11.75
s 49(4) 11.02
ss 75, 76 . . . . 1.84
s 78 . . . . 1.84
Countryside and Rights of Way
Act 2000 . . . . . 2.14, 2.58, 11.60, 11.78
s 74 . . . . 2.58
Countryside (Scotland) Act 1967 . . . . . 11.92
Crime and Disorder Act 1998—
s 80(2) 2.83
Criminal Justice Act 1982—
s 37 . . . . 6.223
Criminal Justice Act 2003—
s 154(1) 6.213
Crown Estates Act 1961—
s 1 . . . . 11.09
Crown Proceedings Act 1947—
s 21(1)(a) 2.32

Sch 2 . . . . 2.33
Data Protection Act 1998 . . . . 5.28
　s 4 　. . . . . 5.28
　Schs 1, 2 . . . . 5.28
　Sch 6 . . . . 5.38
　Deer Act 1991 . . . . 11.113
　s 1 . . . . 11.113
　s 1(1), (2) 11.113
　ss 2–4 . . . . 11.113
　s 4(1), (4) 11.113
　s 5 　. . . . . 11.113
　s 7 . . . . 11.113
　s 7(1) 11.113
　s 7(3), (4) 11.113
　s 8 　. . . . . 11.113
　s 8(3) 11.113
　s 9(1), (2) 11.113
　s 10(1) 11.113
　ss 11, 12 . . . . 11.113
　s 13(1) 11.113
　s 14(1) 11.113
　s 16 . . . . 11.113
　Schs 1, 2 . . . . 11.113
Deer (Scotland) Act 1959 . . . . 11.113
Deer (Scotland) Act 1982 . . . . 11.113
Deer (Scotland) Act 1996 . . . . 11.113
Defective Premises Act 1972 . . . . 16.47
　s 1 　. . . . . 16.109
Deposit of Poisonous Wastes
　　　Act 1972 . . . . . . 1.69, 1.76, 2.51, 14.21
　s 1 　. . . . . 1.76
　s 4 　. . . . . 1.78
Drought Act 19976 . . . . 9.62
Dumping at Sea Act 1974 . . . . 1.79
　s 1 　. . . . . 1.79
　ss 34–40 . . . . 1.80
Electricity Act 1989 . . . . 11.70
Endangered Species (Import and Export)
　　　Act 1976 . . . . 11.43, 11.133
　s 1(1)–(3) 11.133
　s 4(1), (1A), (2), (3) 11.133
　Schs 4, 5 . . . . 11.133
Energy Act 2004 . . . . 3.139
Enterprise Act 2002 . . . . 10.39, 10.44
Environment
　　　Act 1995 . . . . 1.88, 2.04, 2.06,
　2.08, 2.20, 2.33, 2.42–2.44, 2.48–2.52, 2.54,
　　　2.71, 5.40, 5.85, 5.93, 5.165, 5.173,
　　　6.222, 7.02, 7.85, 7.110, 7.235, 9.07,
　　　9.19, 9.62, 9.73, 9.125, 10.106, 10.146,
　　　　　11.06, 11.117, 11.132, 14.21
　s 1 　. . . . . 2.44
　s 1(1) 2.42

s 1(5) 2.45
s 2 　. . . . . 9.07
s 4 　. . . . . 2.62, 9.08, 9.129
s 4(1) 2.53
s 4(2) 2.54
s 4(3) 2.53, 2.54
s 5 　. . . . . 2.55
s 5(1) 9.09
s 5(5) 9.09
s 6 　. . . . . 2.56, 9.08
s 6(1) 9.08, 11.06
s 6(2) 9.09, 9.14
s 6(4) 9.09, 9.129
s 6(6) 2.56, 9.09
s 7 　. . . . . 2.55, 2.57, 11.06
s 7(1)(a) 2.57
s 7(1)(c) 2.57
s 7(2)–(4) 2.57
s 8 　. . . . . 2.57, 11.06
s 9 　. . . . . 11.06
ss 11–13 . . . . 2.46
ss 14–19 . . . . 2.44, 2.46, 9.133
s 20 . . . . 11.06
s 38 . . . . 2.45
s 39 . . . . 2.62, 16.81
s 39(2) 2.62
s 40 . . . . 2.45
s 40(2) 9.22
s 41 . . . . 6.95, 9.60
s 41(6), (10) 9.60
s 42 . . . . 9.60
s 46 . . . . 2.44
s 52 . . . . 2.44
s 56 . . . . 9.07
s 56(1) 2.62
s 65 . . . . 11.88
Part IV 6.271
s 80 . . . . 3.26
s 92 . . . . 2.50, 7.86
ss 93–95 . . . . 2.14
s 97 . . . . 11.93, 11.124, 11.130, 14.78
s 97(2), (3) 11.130
s 108 . . . . 5.168, 6.224, 12.39
s 108(1) 5.165, 6.190
s 108(4) 5.171, 6.191
s 108(4)(j) 5.172
s 108(6) 5.169, 6.192
s 108(11) 6.191
s 108(13) 5.173
s 108(15) 5.174
s 109 . . . . 5.174, 6.193, 6.223
s 110(1) 5.166, 6.222
s 110(2) 5.168

Environment Act 1995 (*cont.*)
s 110(4) 6.223
s 110(5) 6.225
s 120(1) 9.78
Sch 1, para 6. . . . . 2.44
Sch 3 . . . . 2.46
Schs 4, 5. . . . . 2.44
Sch 6 . . . . 11.06
Sch 9, para 3. . . . . 11.85
Sch 18 . . . . 6.192
Sch 21, para 2. . . . . 9.120
    para 6(4). 5.175
Sch 22 . . . . 9.130
    para 233(1). 9.78
Sch 23, para 16. . . . . 2.50
Environmental Assessment (Scotland)
    Act 1995 . . . . 11.56
Environmental Protection
    Act 1990 . . . . .1.81, 1.82, 1.88,
    2.05, 2.06, 3.05, 4.53, 4.54, 5.85, 6.01,
    6.163, 6.236, 7.02, 7.03, 7.06, 7.14,
    7.32, 7.40, 7.52, 7.85, 7.96–7.100,
    7.102, 7.106, 7.110, 7.111, 7.115, 7.121,
    7.122, 7.134, 7.136, 7.155, 7.168, 7.169,
    7.172, 7.187, 7.198, 7.217, 7.221, 7.234,
    7.235, 7.240, 7.253–7.255, 8.160,
    8.165, 8.172, 8.173, 8.180, 8.186, 8.195,
    8.197, 10.181, 11.04, 11.70, 13.73,
    13.79, 14.57, 14.65, 14.85, 16.33
    Part I 2.06, 2.20, 2.34,
    2.62, 3.05, 3.26, 6.190, 7.107, 7.147,
    11.70, 13.57, 14.84, 14.89, 16.72
s 1(5) 7.97
s 1(6) 7.98
s 4(2) 2.55
s 7 . . . . 16.72
Part II. 2.06, 2.35, 2.37,
    3.05, 5.84, 5.90, 5.143–5.145, 7.40, 7.65,
    7.68, 7.69, 7.98, 7.167, 7.169, 9.104,
    11.70, 14.87, 14.89
s 29 . . . . 9.101
s 29(3) 7.137
s 29(6) 7.97, 7.100, 7.132, 7.138
s 32 . . . . 7.248
s 32(2) 7.249
s 33 . . . . .7.105, 7.132, 7.139,
    7.197, 7.200, 9.104
s 33(1) 7.131, 7.140, 12.17
s 33(1)(c) 6.34, 7.136
s 33(1)(b) 7.131
s 33(1B) 6.34
s 33(2) 7.19, 7.143
s 33(3), (4) 7.143

s 33(5) 7.168
s 33(6) 7.131
s 33(7) 7.139
s 34 . . . . 7.99, 7.102, 7.114
s 34(1) 7.95–7.97, 7.114, 7.197
s 34(2) 7.40, 7.95
s 34(3) 7.198
s 34(4) 7.199
s 34(5) 7.200
s 34(6) 7.209
s 34(7) 7.203
s 34(10) 7.203
s 35 . . . . 7.111
s 35(1) 7.111
s 35(2) 7.171
s 35(3) 7.188
s 35(6)–(8) 7.113
s 36 . . . . 14.87
s 36(1) 7.171
s 36(2) 7.173, 14.87
s 36(3) 7.176, 7.189, 14.87
s 36(3)(c) 7.187
s 36(4), (5) 7.174
s 36(7) 7.175
s 36(9) 7.190
s 37 . . . . 5.88
s 37(1), (2) 7.212
s 37(5) 7.214
s 37(6) 7.215
s 38(1) 7.226
s 38(2) 7.227
s 38(3) 7.226, 7.227
s 38(4) 7.227
s 38(6) 7.222
s 38(9)–(11) 7.224
s 39(1) 7.229
s 39(4) 7.115, 7.232
s 39(5) 7.232
s 39(6), (7) 7.233
s 39(9) 7.233
s 40(1), (2) 7.218
s 40(4)–(6) 7.221
s 42(1), (2) 7.116
s 42(3), (4) 7.117
s 43 . . . . 7.215, 7.228
s 43(1), (2) 7.193
s 43(4)–(6) 7.194, 7.216, 7.221
s 43(7) 7.195, 7.216
s 44A 2.50, 2.52, 7.86
s 44A(5), (6). 7.86
s 45(1) 7.236
s 45(2) 7.242
s 45(3) 7.237

s 45(4)	7.242
s 45(5)	7.239
s 46	7.24, 7.31
s 46(1), (2)	7.240
s 46(3)–(9)	7.241
s 47	7.28, 7.243
s 47(2)	7.244
s 47(6)	7.244
s 47(9)	7.244
s 48(1)	7.246
s 48(3)–(5)	7.246
s 48(6)	7.247
s 48(8)	7.247
s 49	7.245
s 49(3)	7.245
s 49(5), (6)	7.245
s 50	7.119
s 50(1)	7.248, 7.251
s 50(3)	7.120
s 50(4)	7.251
s 50(5)	7.121
s 50(7)	7.121
s 51(1)	7.252
s 51(2)	7.253
s 52	2.13
s 52(3)	7.254
s 59	7.117, 7.122, 7.123, 7.255, 13.87
s 59(1)	12,54
s 59(2), (3)	7.123
s 59(4)	7.123, 7.256
s 59(5), (6)	7.256
s 59(7)	7.124, 7.256, 12.54
s 59(8)	7.124, 7.256
s 59(9)	7.118, 7.256
s 61	7.125, 7.235
s 61(1)	7.125
s 61(8)	7.126
s 61(10)	7.126
s 62	7.54
s 62(2)(e)	5.85
s 63(2)	12.17
s 64	5.86, 7.128
s 65	7.129
s 67	7.130
s 73(6)	7.210, 12.17
s 74	7.177, 7.185
s 74(3)	7.177
s 74(3)(c)	7.185
s 74(4)	7.182
s 74(3)(b)	7.183
s 75	7.05, 7.09
s 75(2)	7.05, 7.06
s 75(4)	7.09
s 75(5)	7.10
s 75(6)	7.11, 7.12
s 75(7)	7.13
s 75(8)	7.14
s 78(2)	12.76
s 78(2)(b)	12.75, 12.76
s 78(3)	12.76
s 78(5)	12.60
Part IIA (ss 78A–78YC)	2.06, 2.34, 5.93, 5.121, 6.254, 9.19, 12.01–12.03, 12.07, 12.14, 12.16, 12.23, 12.25–12.27, 12.34, 12.35, 12.54, 12.75, 14.11
s 78A(2)	12.27, 12.29, 12.30, 12.130
s 78A(4)	12.32
s 78A(5)	12.30, 12.130
s 78A(7)	12.60
s 78A(9)	5.98, 12.35
s 78B	12.37, 12.41
s 78B(1)	12.97
s 78B(2)	12.38, 12.130
s 78B(3)	12.40
s 78B(4)	12.41
s 78C(1)–(3)	12.45
s 78C(4), (5)	12.47
s 78C(6), (7)	12.46
s 78C(8)–(10)	12.43
s 78D	12.47
s 78D(1)	12.45
s 78E	12.41
s 78E(1), (2)	12.100
s 78E(4)	12.55, 12.57, 12.64, 12.111
s 78F	4.53, 12.65
s 78F(2)	12.66–12.68
s 78F(3)	12.66, 12.67, 12.73
s 78F(4)	12.67
s 78F(6), (7)	12.130
s 78F(9)	12.74
s 78F(10)	12.73
s 78G	12.104
s 78G(2)–(4)	12.103
s 78G(5)	12.105
s 78H	12.42
s 78H(1)	12.96
s 78H(2)	12.96, 12.97
s 78H(3)(a)–(c)	12.97
s 78H(4)	12.99
s 78H(5)	12.53, 12.55, 12.57, 12.59
s 78H(5)(a)	12.77
s 78H(5)(b)	12.55, 14.11
s 78H(5)(c)	12.55
s 78H(5)(d)	12.55, 12.110

Environmental Protection Act 1990 (*cont.*)

s 78H(6), (7) 12.56
s 78J. 12.110
s 78J(3). .12.75
s 78K 12.77, 12.110
s 78K(3) .12.81
s 78K(4) .12.82
s 78K(5) .12.80
s 78K(6) .12.83
s 78L 12.105
s 78L(2), (3) 12.105
s 78M(1),(2). 12.107
s 78M(3), (4) 12.108
s 78M(5) .12.109
s 78N 12.49, 12.55, 12.59,
                 12.83, 12.110, 12.111, 12.113
s 78N(2). .12.112
s 78N(3). .12.57
s 78N(3)(a)–(d) 12.110
s 78N(3)(e). 12.57, 12.110
s 78N(3)(f). 12.110
s 78P(1) 12.113
s 78P(2) 12.57, 12.58, 12.115
s 78P(3), (4) 12.117
s 78P(8) 12.118
s 78P(9) 12.118, 12.122
s 78Q(1). 12.48, 12.49
s 78Q(4). .12.50
s 78R 12.119, 12.123
s 78R(1). 5.99
s 78R(3). 5.101, 12.120
s 78R(4), (5). 5.102, 12.121
s 78R(6). 5.103, 12.121
s 78R(7). 5.103, 12.121, 12.125
s 78R(8). 5.104
s 78R(9). 5.106
s 78S 12.122
s 78S(1) 5.112
s 78S(3) 5.114
s 78S(4) 5.113, 5.114
s 78T 12.123, 12.125
s 78T(1). 5.115, 12.124
s 78T(2). 5.116, 12.126
s 78T(3), (4). 5.118, 12.126
s 78T(8). 5.118, 12.127
s 78T(10). 5.115, 12.124
s 78T(11). .12.124
s 78U 5.120, 12.128
s 78V(1), (2). 12.129
s 78X(1). 12.29
s 78X(3), (4). 12.84
s 78YA(1). .12.131
s 78YA(2). .12.130

s 78YB 12.54, 12.112
s 78YB(1). 12.16, 12.34, 12.54
s 78YB(3). 12.14, 12.54
s 78YB(4). .12.14
Part III 2.06, 2.34, 6.272
s 79 . . . . .12.07
s 79(1)(a) .12.07
s 79(1)(e) .12.07
s 79(1A), (1B). 12.07
s 79(7) 12.08
s 80 . . . . .12.07
s 82 . . . . .12.09
Part IV 2.06
s 89(1)(f) 7.33
Part V. 2.06
Part VI 3.05, 8.160, 8.165,
        8.166, 8.185, 8.186, 8.195, 8.197, 8.200
s 106 . . . . 8.162, 8.164
s 106(1) 8.160
s 106(2), (3) 8.161
s 106(4) 8.162
s 106(5) 8.163
s 107(2) 8.165
s 107(3) 8.166
s 108(1) 8.173
s 109 . . . . 8.174, 8.196
s 110 . . . . .8.175
s 111 . . . . 8.174, 8.196
s 111(1) 8.176
s 111(6), (7) 8.178
s 111 . . . . .8.168
s 112(1) 8.180
s 112(2) 8.182, 8.185
s 112(3)–(5) 8.185
s 122(7) 8.185
s 113 . . . . .8.186
s 115 . . . . .8.191
s 116 . . . . .8.192
s 117 . . . . .8.194
s 118 . . . . 8.196, 8.197
s 119 . . . . .8.198
ss 120, 121 . . . . .8.199
ss 122, 123 . . . . .8.201
s 130(2) 11.05
s 130(2)(a) 11.05
ss 140–142. . . . . .3.05
s 143 . . . . 12.01, 12.02
s 152 . . . . .2.06
s 156 . . . . .3.05
s 157 . . . . .2.75
Sch 2 . . . . .15.29
Part II. 7.250
para 5 . . . . .7.249

Sch 2A 2.52
Sch 3 . . . . 7.160, 7.164, 7.167
para 17(2). 7.159
paras 27, 28 . . . . 7.163
para 30 . . . . 7.165
para 31 . . . . 7.166
para 32 . . . . 7.167
Sch 21, paras 1, 2 . . . . 2.33
European Communities Act 1972. 3.07, 4.43,
    4.44, 5.22, 8.63, 9.19, 13.151, 15.14
s 2 . . . . 4.43
s 2(1) 4.25, 4.44
s 2(3) 4.26
Sch 2 . . . . 4.43
European Communities Act 1986. . . . . . 4.43
European Communities Act 1993. . . . . . 4.43
European Communities Act 1998. . . . . . 4.43
Factories Act 1961 . . . . 2.11, 7.11
s 29(1) 16.72
Factories Act 1971 . . . . 2.11, 7.39
Finance Act 1996 . . . . 2.13
Finance Act 2000 . . . . 2.13
Financial Services Act 1986. . . . . 5.150
Fires Prevention (Metropolis)
    Act 1774 . . . . 16.53
Food and Environment Protection
    Act 1985 . . . . 2.34, 5.122, 5.164, 7.109
Part II. 3.25, 6.31
Food Safety Act 1990 . . . . 2.10
Food Standards Act 2000 . . . . 2.10
Forestry Act 1967 . . . . 11.93
s 1(2) 11.07
s 1(3A) 11.07
s 9(1) 11.08
s 9(2)–(4) 11.129
ss 10–12 . . . . 11.129
s 15 . . . . 11.129
s 17 . . . . 11.129
ss 17A–17C 11.129
Sch 2 . . . . 11.129
Freedom of Information
    Act 2000 . . . . 5.27, 5.39
Part V (ss 57–61) 5.38
Game Act 1831 . . . . 11.113
Game Licences Act 1860. . . . . 11.113
Government of Wales Act 1998 . 2.17, 14.22
s 121 . . . . 2.17, 2.28
Sch 2 . . . . 11.02
Government of Wales
    Act 2006 . . . . 2.17, 11.02
s 107(1) 3.38
Greater London Authority
    Act 1999 . . . . 2.34, 14.23

s 356 . . . . 14.23
Greater London Authority Act 2007 . . . . 2.34
s 31 . . . . 14.23
Green Belt (London and Home Counties)
    Act 1938 . . . . 11.91
Health and Safety at Work etc
    Act 1974 . . . . 2.06, 2.11, 2.85,
    6.01, 7.142, 8.75, 8.114, 8.134, 8.202,
                    8.204, 9.108, 1.302
Part I 13.03
s 1 . . . . 13.03
ss 3, 4 . . . . 2.11
s 5 . . . . 13.03
Health Protection Act 2004 . . . . 2.10
Highways Act 1980 . . . . 13.40, 15.21
s 41 . . . . 9.121
s 100 . . . . 9.121
s 105A 15.14, 15.18
ss 105B, 105C 15.18
Housing Act 1890 . . . . 1.38, 1.42, 1.43,
    1.48, 1.51, 1.52, 1.54, 1.59
Part III 1.52
s 4 . . . . 1.44, 1.45
s 5 . . . . 1.44
s 6 . . . . 1.45
ss 13, 14 . . . . 1.47
ss 21–23 . . . . 1.48
s 35 . . . . 1.50
ss 38–40 . . . . 1.51
Housing Act 1985 . . . . 2.10
Housing and Local Government Act 1989—
    Schs 11, 12. . . . . 2.96
Housing and Planning Act 1986. . . . . . 8.65
Housing, Town Planning etc
    Act 1909 . . . . 1.54, 1.58, 1.70
Part I 1.54
s 54(1), (2) 1.55
s 55 . . . . 1.56
s 57 . . . . 1.57
Sch 4 . . . . 1.56
Human Rights Act 1998. . . . . 3.37–3.40,
                    3.45, 4.50, 6.228, 16.78
s 3 . . . . 3.38
s 3(1) 3.38
s 4 . . . . 3.38
s 6 . . . . 3.38
s 6(3)(b) 3.38
s 7(1) 3.39
s 8 . . . . 3.39
s 11 . . . . 3.38
Hunting Act 2004
Insolvency Act 1986 . . . . 5.150, 10.252
ss 25, 26 . . . . 10.252

Interpretation Act 1987—
  ss 22, 23 . . . . 2.16
Justice (Northern Ireland) Act 2002 . . . . 2.22
Land Clauses Act 1845 . . . . 1.48
Land Compensation Act 1961—
  s 5 . . . . 6.128, 8.102
Land Compensation Act 1965—
  s 5 . . . . 10.194
Land Drainage Act 1930 . . . . . . 9.128, 9.137
Land Drainage Act 1991 . . . . 9.07, 9.128,
        9.130, 9.144, 11.06, 11.65, 11.132
  Part 1 . . . . 9.134
  s 1(1)–(3) 9.134
  ss 2–4 . . . . 9.134
  s 7 . . . . 9.134
  ss 9, 10 . . . . 9.135
  s 12 . . . . 9.136
  s 13 . . . . 9.136, 11.88
  s 14, 15 . . . . 9.137
  s 18 . . . . 9.138, 9.139
  ss 19–21 . . . . 9.139
  ss 23, 24 . . . . 9.140
  s 25 . . . . 9.141
  s 27 . . . . 9.141
  ss 28–30 . . . . 9.142
  ss 32–34 . . . . 9.144
  Part IV, Chapter I 9.145
  ss 37, 38 . . . . 9.145
  Part IV, Chapter II 9.146
  s 61A 9.136
  s 61C 9.136
  s 72 . . . . 9.130
  s 72(1) 9.134
  s 72920 . . . . 9.145
Land Drainage Act 1994—
  s 2 . . . . 9.136
Landlord and Tenant Act 1927—
  s 18(1) 16.74
Latent Damage Act 1986 . . . . 16.95
Law of Property Act 1925—
  s 84 . . . . 16.74
Laws in Wales Act 1535 . . . . 2.16
Legislative and Regulatory
        Reform Act 2006 . . . . 2.67
  ss 22, 23 . . . . 2.67
Limitation Act 1980 . . . . 16.95
  s 11 . . . . 16.95
  s 14 . . . . 16.95
  s 14B 16.95
  s 32 . . . . 16.96
  s 32(2) 16.96
  s 33 . . . . 16.96
Local Government Act 1972 . . . . 5.40

s 71(1) 11.79
s 72(1) 11.79
ss 100A–100I 11.86
s 100A 5.41
s 100A(2), (3) 5.42
s 100B(1) 5.44
s 100B(5) 5.46
ss 100C, 100D 5.47
s 100H 5.47
s 100I 5.43
s 106 . . . . 5.40
s 111 . . . . 2.59
s 111A 11.85
s 250 . . . . 6.179, 6.185
s 250(2)–(4) 6.179
s 250(5) 6.179, 14.58
s 222 . . . . . 2.35, 2.59, 4.62, 13.83, 16.31
Sch 17, para 34 . . . . 11.85
Local Government Act 1974—
  s 4(3) 2.98
  Part III 2.96
  s 25 . . . . 2.96
  s 26(2) 2.97
  s 26(6) 2.98
  s 34(1) 2.96
  Sch 5 . . . . 2.98
Local Government Act 1988 . . . . 2.96
  Sch 3 . . . . 2.96
Local Government Act 2001—
  Part I 2.35
  s 2(4) 2.35
  s 3 . . . . 2.35
Local Government (Access to Information)
        Act 1985 . . . . 5.40–5.48, 11.86
Local Government and Housing Act 1989—
  s 68 . . . . 7.249
Magistrates Courts Act 1980 . . . . 8.31
Merchant Shipping Act 1979 . . . . 3.25
Merchant Shipping Act 1985—
  s 129 . . . . 3.25
Merchant Shipping Act 1995—
  s 128 . . . . 3.05
  ss 153, 154 . . . . 16.73
Merchant Shipping (Oil Pollution)
        Act 1971 . . . . 3.25
Motor Cycle Noise Act 1987 . . . . 13.138
  s 1 . . . . 13.139
National Parks and Access to the Countryside
        Act 1947—
  s 6(1) 11.05
  s 11A 11.05
National Parks and Access to the Countryside
        Act 1949 . . . . . 1.71, 1.73, 11.49, 11.78

Part 1 . . . . 1.72
s 5(1), (2) 11.88
s 11A 11.88
s 15(1), (2) 11.74
s 15(2)(a) 11.73
s 15(3) 11.74
s 15A(1) 11.74
s 16 . . . . 11.85
s 16(1) 11.73, 11.85
s 16(3)(a), (c) 11.74
s 17 . . . . 11.75, 11.85
s 17(1) 11.85
s 18 . . . . 11.75
s 20(2) 11.75
s 20(2)(c) 11.75
s 20(3) 11.75
s 21 . . . . 11.85
s 21(4) 11.85
Part III 1.73
s 87 . . . . 11.90
s 88(1) 11.90
s 90(1) 11.88, 11.90
s 114(1) 11.74, 11.78
National Parks (Scotland) Act 2000 . . . 11.87
National Trust Act 1907 . . . . 11.28
s 4(1) 11.28
National Trust Act 1937 . . . . 11.28
s 8 . . . . 11.28
National Trust Act 1939 . . . . 11.28
National Trust Act 1953 . . . . 11.28
National Trust Act 1971 . . . . 11.28
s 24 . . . . 11.28
National Trust Charity Scheme
    Confirmation Act 1991 . . . . 11.28
National Trust for Scotland Order
    Confirmation Act 1935 . . . . 11.28
Natural Environment and Rural Communities
    Act 2006 . . . . . 2.37, 3.13, 11.04, 11.60
s 2(1) 3.12, 11.04
s 2(2)(a) 11.04
s 2(2)(b)–(e) 11.05
s 7(2)(c), (e) 11.74
s 22(3) 11.04
s 32(1), (2) 11.04
s 34(2) 11.04
s 37 . . . . 2.59
s 37(3)–(8) 2.59
s 40 . . . . 2.58, 11.05
s 40(1) 11.53
s 40(2)–(4) 2.58
s 41(1) 11.54
s 42(1) 11.54
s 74 . . . . 11.54

s 99 . . . . 11.05
Sch 4 . . . . 11.04
Natural Heritage (Scotland) Act 1991 . . 11.90
Nature Conservation (Scotland)
    Act 2004 . . . . 11.78
New Roads and Street Works Act 1991—
    Part III 10.188
Noise Act 1996 . . . . 16.33
Noise and Statutory Nuisance
    Act 1993 . . . . 13.145, 13.150
s 8 . . . . 13.95
s 9 . . . . 13.148
s 69 . . . . 13.149
Sch 2 . . . . 13.91, 13.95
Sch 3 . . . . 13.145, 13.148
Sch 4 . . . . 13.144
Norfolk and Suffolk Broads
    Act 1988 . . . . 11.89
s 1 . . . . 11.89
s 4(1) 11.89
s 5 . . . . 11.82
s 5(1)(a) 11.89
s 5(2) 11.89
s 6 . . . . 11.89
s 9 . . . . 11.89
s 11 . . . . 11.89
s 24 . . . . 11.89
Nuclear Installations
    Act 1965 . . . . .3.07, 5.154, 5.158,
        8.06, 8.11, 8.14, 8.18, 8.21, 8.32–8.35,
                                    8.38, 16.108
s 1(1), (2) 8.07
s 2 . . . . 8.08
s 2(1B) 8.10
s 3(1), (2) 8.10
s 4(1) 8.11
s 4(4), (5) 8.12
s 4(6) 8.13
s 5(1) 8.17
s 6 . . . . 5.154, 8.14
s 7 . . . . 8.15, 8.18, 16.73
s 7(1) 8.14
s 7(2)–(4) 8.17
ss 8, 9 . . . . 8.16, 8.18, 16.73
s 10 . . . . 8.18, 16.73
s 11 . . . . 8.61
s 12 . . . . 8.22, 8.23, 16.102
s 12(1), (2) 8.18
s 12(3A) 8.19
s 13(1), (2) 8.20
s 13(3) 8.21
s 13(4) 8.22
s 13(5), (5A) 8.23

Nuclear Installations Act 1965 (*cont.*)
s 13(6) 8.24
s 14 . . . . 8.25
s 15 . . . . 8.26
s 15(1) 8.26
s 15(2) 8.26, 8.31
s 16 . . . . 8.23, 8.25
s 16(1) 8.27, 8.31
s 16(2)–(4) 8.27
s 17 . . . . 8.28
s 17(1), (2) 8.28
s 17(3) 8.29
s 17(5), (6) 8.30
s 18(1), (2) 8.31
s 19(1) 8.31
s 19(5) 8.31
s 20(1) 8.32
s 22 . . . . 8.33
s 22(1) 5.156
s 22(2) 5.156, 8.33
s 22(4), (5) 5.157
s 25(1), (2) 8.33
Sch 1 . . . . 8.10
Occupier's Liability Act 1957 . . 12.22, 16.71
s 1(1) 16.71
s 2(2) 16.71
s 2(4)(a) 16.71
Occupier's Liability Act 1984 . . . . 16.71
Official Secrets Act 1989. . . . . 8.09
Parliamentary and Health Commissioners
Act 1987 . . . . 2.32
Parliamentary Commissioner
Act 1967 . . . . 2.32, 2.96
s 5(1)(a) 2.97
s 5(2) 2.98
s 12(3) 2.98
Sch 2 . . . . 2.96
Sch 3 . . . . 2.98
Petroleum Consolidation Act 1928 2.34, 9.25
Pipelines Act 1962 . . . . 11.70
Planning and Compensation
Act 1991 . . . . 1.88, 14.21, 14.48
s 22 . . . . 4.37, 14.20
Planning and Compulsory
Purchase Act 2004 . . . . . . 14.01, 14.22,
14.49, 14.79, 14.80
Part 1 . . . . 14.22, 14.79
Part 2 . . . . 11.86, 14.79
s 17(3) 14.81
s 19(2) 14.81
s 19(5) 14.82
s 24 . . . . 14.81
s 38 . . . . 14.80
s 38(5) 14.79

s 38(6) 14.32, 14.33
s 38(8) 14.79
s 39 . . . . 14.82
s 39(3) 14.82
Part 4 . . . . 14.64
s 60 . . . . 2.17, 14.22
Part 6 . . . . 14.22, 14.79
s 62(6) 14.82
Part 7 . . . . 2.33
Planning (Consequential Provisions)
Act 1990 . . . . 14.21
Planning (Hazardous Substances)
Act 1990 . . . . .8.65, 8.66, 8.68,
8.70, 8.74–8.76, 8.87, 8.95, 8.99, 8.104–
8.110, 8.117, 8.131, 8.134, 8.137, 14.21
s 1 . . . . 8.80
s 3 . . . . 8.81
s 4 . . . . 8.73
s 4(1) 8.68
s 4(2), (3) 8.72
s 4(4) 8.73
s 10 . . . . 8.87
s 11(1) 8.74, 8.86
s 11(2) 8.75, 8.86
s 11(3) 8.76, 8.86
s 11(4), (5) 8.76, 8.88
s 11(6) 8.76
s 11(7) 8.77
s 11(7)(b) 8.78
s 11(8) 8.77
s 12 . . . . 8.88
s 13 . . . . 8.90
s 13(1) 8.91
s 13(2) 8.92
s 13(3) 8.92, 8.93
s 13(4)–(7) 8.93
s 14 . . . . 8.98
s 14(1) 8.97
s 14(2) 8.98
s 15 . . . . 8.99
s 16 . . . . 8.101
s 16(1) 8.97, 8.98
s 16(5) 8.102
s 17(1) 8.94
s 18 . . . . 8.104
s 20 . . . . 8.106
s 22 . . . . 8.109
s 22(1), (2) 8.107
s 23(1) 8.70
s 23(2), (3) 8.70, 8.112
s 23(4) 8.70, 8.116
s 23(5)–(7) 8.116
s 24(1) 8.118
s 24(3) 8.118

s 24(5)–(7) .8.120
s 26A 8.126
s 26AA 8.131
s 26B 8.139
s 27 . . . . 8.132
s 28 . . . . 8.133
s 29 . . . . 8.134
ss 30–32 . . . . 8.135
s 34 . . . . 8.136
s 36 . . . . 8.138
s 36A 8.139
s 40 . . . . .8.67
s 112 . . . . .8.79
Police and Criminal Evidence
        Act 1984 . . . . 5.166, 5.170
    PACE Codes. 5.166
Pollution Prevention and Control
        Act 1999 . . . . .2.05, 2.06, 5.134,
            6.01, 6.188, 10.175, 13.61, 14.21
s 2 . . . . 10.175
Prescription Act 1832—
    ss 1, 2 . . . . 16.39
Prevention of Oil Pollution Act 1971 . . . 3.25
Prosecution of Offences Act 1985—
    s 3(2)(a) 2.71
    s 6(2) 2.71
    s 23 . . . . .2.71
Protection of Animals Act 1911 . . . . . 11.109
Protection of Animals (Scotland)
        Act 1912 . . . . 11.109
Protection of Badgers Act 1992. . . . . . 11.111
    ss 1–5 . . . . .11.111
    s 1(1) 11.111
    s 1(3) 11.111
    s 2(1) 11.111
    s 3 . . . . 11.111
    s 6 . . . . 11.112
    s 8(4)–(9) .11.112
    s 10(1)(d), (e) 11.112
    s 10(2), (3) 11.112
    s 10(8) 11.111, 11.112
    s 12(4) 11.111
    s 13(1) 11.111
    s 14 . . . . 11.111
Protection of Birds Act 1954. . . 11.84, 11.99
Protection of Birds Act 1967. . . . . .11.99
Protection of Seals Act 1970 . . . . .11.110
Public Health Act 1845. . . . . 1.21, 7.181
    s 12 . . . . .1.08
    s 54 . . . . .1.09
    s 55 . . . . .1.10
    s 57 . . . . .1.11
    s 58 . . . . .1.12

Public Health Act 1848. . . . .1.07, 1.14, 1.16,
                                    7.181, 9.01
Public Health Act 1875. . . . . 1.14, 1.17,
    1.19, 1.22, 1.25, 1.28, 7.181, 9.01, 10.02
    ss 5, 6 . . . . .1.14
    s 13 . . . . .1.14
    s 15 . . . . .1.15
    s 19 . . . . .1.15
    s 21 . . . . .1.16
    s 23 . . . . .1.16
    s 27 . . . . .1.17
    s 41 . . . . .1.17
    s 42 . . . . .1.18
    ss 51, 52 . . . . .1.19
    s 58 . . . . .1.12
    ss 69, 70 . . . . .1.20
    ss 71–90 . . . . .1.21
    ss 92–96 . . . . .1.24
    ss 97–99 . . . . .1.25
    ss 120, 121 .1.26
    ss 131, 132 .1.27
Public Health Act 1936. . . . . 2.51, 7.181,
                                    10.02, 14.21
    ss 72, 73 . . . . .2.51
    s 76(1)(b) 2.51
Part XII 13.45
Public Health Act 1961—
    s 17 . . . . .10.183
Public Health (Control of Disease)
        Act 1984 . . . . 2.10, 2.35
Public Health (Drainage of Trade Premises)
        Act 1937 . . . . .14.21
Radioactive Material (Road Transport)
        Act 1991 . . . . .8.61
Radioactive Substances Act 1960 . . . .16.101
Radioactive Substances Act 1993 . . . . 5.159,
    5.162, 7.167, 8.38, 8.40, 8.47, 8.48,
            8.50, 8.56, 8.57, 15.33
    s 1(1) 8.39
    s 1(4), (5) 8.39
    s 6 . . . . 5.159
    s 6(1) 8.38
    s 7 . . . . 5.160, 8.40, 8.44
    s 7(1), (2) 8.40
    s 7(3), (4) 5.160, 5.162
    s 7(6) 5.161
    s 7(8) 5.162
    s 8 . . . . 8.47
    s 8(1) 5.162, 8.41
    s 8(2) 8.41
    s 8(4), (5) 8.42
    s 8(6) 5.162
    ss 10, 11 . . . . 8.47

Radioactive Substances Act 1993 (*cont.*)
s 12 . . . . 8.49
ss 13, 14 . . . . 8.50
s 14(3) 8.50
s 15(1), (2) 8.50
s 16 . . . . 8.51
s 18 . . . . 8.50, 8.55
ss 19, 20 . . . . 8.57
s 21 . . . . 8.58
s 22 . . . . 8.60
s 26 . . . . 5.160, 8.50
s 26(1) 8.45, 8.49
s 26(2) 8.45, 8.60
s 26(3)–(5) 8.45
s 32 . . . . 8.58
s 33 . . . . 8.57, 8.60
Sch 1 . . . . 8.39
Regional Development Agencies
Act 1998 . . . . 14.22
Rehabilitation of Offenders
Act 1974 . . . . 6.94, 6.287, 7.182
Rivers Pollution Prevention
Act 1876 . . . . 14.21, 16.40
Rivers Pollution Prevention
Act 1987 . . . . 1.31, 9.01
s 2 . . . . 1.32
s 3 . . . . 1.33
s 11 . . . . 1.37
s 13 . . . . 1.37
Rivers (Prevention of Pollution)
Act 1951 . . . . 9.87, 14.21
s 2(1)(a) 9.90
Road Traffic Regulation Act 1984—
s 22 . . . . 11.88, 11.90
Salmon and Freshwater Fisheries
Act 1975 . . . . 9.19, 11.110, 11.115
s 1(1) 11.115
s 2(1)–(4) 11.115
s 3(1) 11.115
s 4(1), (3) 11.115
s 4(5) 11.115
s 5(1), (2) 11.115
ss 6–9 . . . . 11.115
ss 13, 14 . . . . 11.115
s 16(1) 11.115
ss 19–23 . . . . 11.115
ss 25–40 . . . . 11.115
Sch 1 . . . . 11.115
Sch 2 . . . . 11.115
Salmon and Freshwater Fisheries
(Consolidation) (Scotland)
Act 2003 . . . . 11.115
Science and Technology Act 1965 . . . . . 11.10

s 1(3) 11.10
Scotland Act 1998 . . . . 2.19
Sch 5 . . . . 11.02
Sea Fish (Conservation) Act 1967 . . . . 11.116
s 1 . . . . 11.117
Sea Fish (Conservation) Act 1992 . . . . 11.116
Sea Fisheries Regulation
Act 1966 . . . . 11.97, 11.116
Sea Fisheries (Shellfish) Act 1967 . . . . 11.116
ss 1–3 . . . . 11.117
ss 16, 17 . . . . 11.117
Sea Fisheries (Wildlife Conservation)
Act 1992 . . . . 11.116
Statute of Proclamations 1539 . . . . 2.05
Statutory Water Companies
Act 1991 . . . . 10.08
Supreme Court Act 1981—
s 31 . . . . 4.56
s 31(4) 4.58
s 31(6) 4.62
s 32A 16.99
s 51 . . . . 16.44
Theft Act 1968—
s 1 . . . . 11.119
s 4(3) 11.119
Town and Country Planning
Act 1932 . . . . 1.58, 1.59, 1.61,
1.62, 1.65, 1.66, 1.70, 8.65, 8.66, 8.87,
8.97, 8.105, 8.107, 8.121, 9.140
s 1 . . . . 1.59
s 10 . . . . 1.61, 1.62
s 14 . . . . 1.63
s 18 . . . . 1.66
s 21 . . . . 1.66
Town and Country Planning
Act 1947 . . . . 1.70, 2.51, 8.65,
8.66, 8.87, 8.97, 8.105, 8.107, 8.121,
9.140, 14.04, 14.21
Town and Country Planning
Act 1971 . . . . 14.04
s 52 14.48 . . . .
Town and Country Planning
Act 1990 . . . . 1.88, 2.17, 2.33,
8.46, 8.65, 8.66, 8.71, 8.87, 8.97, 8.105,
8.107, 8.121, 8.122, 9.140, 11.70,
11.121, 11.122, 11.124, 11.129, 11.132,
14.01, 14.04, 14.21, 14.22, 14.63, 14.65,
14.80, 14.81, 14.88, 15.35, 15.55
s 2A 14.23
Part II 11.86
s 11 . . . . 11.86
s 12(6) 14.81
ss 17, 18 . . . . 8.102

s 30 . . . . 11.86
ss 37, 38 . . . . 14.83
s 39(2) 8.71
s 52 . . . . 16.74
s 54A 14.32
s 55 . . . . 14.25
s 55(1A) 14.26
s 55(2)(a) 14.28
s 55(2)(e) 11.08, 11.122, 15.14
s 65(2) 5.52
s 65(6) 5.53
s 65(8) 5.52
s 69 . . . . 5.54
s 69(5) 5.54
s 70 . . . . 14.32, 14.41
s 71 . . . . 14.61
s 71A 15.35
s 72(1)(a) 14.41
s 75(2), (3) 14.28
s 77 . . . . 11.02
s 78 . . . . .5.74, 11.02, 11.125, 14.58
s 79 . . . . 11.125
s 79(2) 5.81
s 91 . . . . 14.21, 14.41
s 92 . . . . 14.35
s 97 . . . . 11.70
s 102 . . . . 11.70
s 106 . . . . .14.48, 14.49, 15.27, 15.47
ss 106A, 106B 14.48
s 107 . . . . 11.70
s 115 . . . . 11.70
Part VII 11.70
s 171B 14.66
s 171C 14.64
ss 171E–171H 14.64
s 172 . . . . 14.65
s 174 . . . . 8.121, 14.58
s 183 . . . . 2.64, 14.64
s 183(4) 3.41
s 186 . . . . 2.64, 14.64
ss 187A, 187B 14.64
s 191(1) 14.66
s 192 . . . . 14.66
Part VIII 11.93
s 197 . . . . 11.122, 14.77
s 198 . . . . 14.78
s 198(1)–(3) 11.123
s 198(6) 11.125, 11.126
s 198(6)(b) 11.125
s 199(1) 11.123
s 201(1) 11.123
ss 202A–202G 11.122
ss 203, 204 . . . . 11.125

s 206 . . . . 11.128
s 207(5) 11.128
ss 208, 209 . . . . 11.128
s 210(1) 11.126
s 210(1)(a), (b) 11.126
s 210(2), (3) 11.127
s 211 . . . . 14.78
s 211(1) 11.123
s 211(3) 11.123, 11.126
s 212 . . . . 14.78
s 213 . . . . 11.128
s 214A 11.127
s 215 . . . . 12.05
Part XI 2.58
s 284 . . . . 14.59
s 284(1)(e) 11.123
s 285 . . . . 14.59
s 288 . . . . 14.59, 14.60
s 288(1) 11.123
s 288(5) 11.123
s 289 . . . . 14.59, 14.60
s 320 . . . . 14.58
s 330 . . . . 14.64
s 336(1) 8.71, 8.97, 14.88
Town and Country Planning (Listed
    Buildings and Conservation Areas)
    Act 1990 . . . . 14.21, 14.67, 14.69
s 1(5) 14.69
s 3(1), (2) 14.70
s 4 . . . . 14.71
s 10 . . . . 14.69
s 20 . . . . 14.69
s 21(3) 14.69
s 66(1) 14.70
s 67(1) 14.71
s 72(1) 14.71
s 74(1) 14.72
Transport Act 1968 . . . . 7.207
Transport and Works
    Act 1992 . . . . 8.79, 11.70, 15.14
Tribunals and Inquiries Act 1958 . . . . . 8.108
Tribunals and Inquiries
    Act 1971 . . . . 7.196, 8.46, 8.108
Tribunals and Inquiries
    Act 1992 . . . . 7.196, 8.46
Waste and Emissions Trading
    Act 2003 . . . . 7.89
ss 1–4 . . . . 7.89
s 6 . . . . 7.90, 7.91
s 7 . . . . 7.91
ss 8–13 . . . . 7.92
ss 17–20 . . . . 7.93
ss 29, 30 . . . . 7.94

Waste and Emissions Trading Act 2003 (*cont.*)
s 33 ....7.94
s 66 ....9.133
s 68 ....9.133
Water Act 1945—
s 31 ....16.80
Water Act 1973 ....2.03, 2.49, 7.181,
10.03, 10.04
Water Act 1989 ....2.04, 2.07, 2.49,
7.181, 9.01, 9.80, 9.82, 10.06,
10.07, 10.73
Water Act 2003 ....2.07, 2.37, 2.38,
2.68, 7.181, 9.06, 9.13, 9.14, 9.32, 9.34,
9.35, 9.38–9.40, 9.42, 9.44, 9.49, 9.56,
9.62, 9.77, 9.133, 10.07, 10.245
s 2 ....9.53
s 3 ....9.54
s 4 ....9.54
s 5 ....9.49
s 8 ....9.49
s 21 ....9.53
s 27 ....9.36
s 30 ....9.36
ss 62–64.......................9.14
ss 81–83.......................9.14
s 100 ....2.07
s 102 ....9.39
s 131 ....9.66
Water Environment and Water Services
(Scotland) Act 2003 ....11.58
Water Industry Act 1991 ....1.88, 2.05,
2.07, 2.38, 3.45, 5.150, 9.01, 9.03,
9.06, 9.11–9.14, 10.01, 10.07, 10.11,
10.80, 10.106, 10.127, 10.182,
11.65, 16.37, 16.73
s 1A..........................10.12
s 2 ....10.12, 10.16, 10.17,
10.19, 10.20, 10.29, 10.34, 10.43, 10.236
s 2(2A)........................10.17
s 2(2C)........................10.17
s 2(3) 10.18
s 3 ....10.12, 10.16, 10.19,
10.22, 10.24, 10.29, 10.34, 10.43, 10.46,
10.48, 10.236
s 3(2) 10.20
s 3(2)(a) 9.14
s 3(3) 10.21
s 3(5) 10.22
s 4 ....10.12, 10.16, 10.19,
10.22–10.24, 10.46, 10.236, 11.88
s 5 ....10.24
s 6(1) 10.26
s 6(2) 10.25

s 7 ....10.40
s 7(1) 10.27
s 7(3) 10.41
s 7(4)(a)–(bb).................10.40
s 7(4)(c) 10.29, 10.40, 10.252
s 7(5) 10.40
s 8 ....10.42
s 8(7) 10.42
s 9(3) 10.40
s 9(4) 10.43
s 11(1) 10.29
s 11(2) 10.30
s 12(1) 10.29
s 13(1) 10.33
s 13(4), (5) 10.33
s 14 ....10.34
s 14(6) 10.34
s 14B 10.35
s 15(1) 9.12, 10.36
s 15(2) 9.12
s 16 ....10.33
s 16(1) 10.34, 10.36
s 16(2) 10.36
s 16(5) 10.38
s 16A(3), (4)...................10.37
s 17 ....10.39
s 17(3) 10.112
s 17A(2), (5)...................10.113
ss 17F–17H 10.114
ss 18–22F....................10.230
s 18 ....10.23, 10.51, 10.63,
10.68, 10.79, 10.84, 10.85, 10.101,
10.115, 10.123, 10.130, 10.145,
10.146, 10.195, 10.207, 10.210,
10.216, 10.218, 10.230, 10.232–
10.236, 10.241, 10.246, 10.253,
10.255, 10.262
s 18(2) 10.236, 10.238
s 18(3) 10.238
s 18(4) 10.239
s 18(6)(b) 10.234
s 18(8) 10.231
s 19 .....10.236, 10.243, 10.252, 10.260
s 19(1)(a)–(c) 10.236
s 19(1A).......................10.236
s 19(2) 10.236
s 19(3) 10.243, 10.252
s 20 ....10.242
s 20(1) 10.241
s 20(3)–(5)....................10.242
s 20(6)–(8)....................10.240
s 21 ....10.241, 10.242
s 22 ....10.244

s 22(3), (4) 10.244
ss 22A, 22B 10.245
s 22C 10.245, 10.248
s 22D 10.245
s 22E 10.245, 10.248
s 22F 10.245
s 23(4) 10.251
s 24(2) 10.252
s 24(2)(a)–(e) 10.252
s 27(1), (2) 10.259
s 27A 10.14
s 27H 10.258
s 29(10) 10.258
ss 32, 33 . . . . 10.44
Parts III, IV 10.10
ss 37–93 . . . . 10.50
s 37 . . . . 10.50–10.53, 10.111,
10.234, 10.252
s 37(2) 10.51
s 37A 10.110
s 37B 10.110, 10.111
ss 37C, 37D 10.110
s 38 . . . . 10.56
s 38(1) 10.52
s 38(1)(b) 10.56
s 38(2) 10.52, 10.56
s 38A 10.56
s 39(1)–(3) 10.54
s 39(4), (5) 10.55
s 39(7) 10.55, 10.135
s 39A 10.56
s 39B 10.111
s 39B(1) 10.111
s 40(1) 10.86
s 40A 10.88
s 41 . . . . 10.65
s 41(3), (4) 10.68
s 42 . . . . 10.66, 10.67, 10.74
s 43(4), (5) 10.66
s 44 . . . . 10.67
s 45 . . . . 10.69, 10.70
s 45(2) 10.71
s 45(4), (5) 10.74
s 45(6), (6A) 10.72
ss 46–51 . . . . 10.69
s 51A 10.202
s 51A(2) 10.206
s 51B 10.202, 10.203
s 51C 10.202, 10.205
s 51D 10.201, 10.202
s 51E 10.202
s 52 . . . . 10.58
s 52(2) 10.59

s 52(3) 10.60
s 52(5) 10.62
s 54(1), (2) 10.63
s 55 . . . . 10.81, 10.82
s 55(3), (4) 10.81
s 56(1), (2) 10.81
s 56(5) 10.83
s 56(7) 10.82
s 57 . . . . 10.84
s 57(7) 10.84
s 58 . . . . 10.84
s 59 . . . . 10.85, 10.234
s 60 . . . . 10.89, 10.91
s 61 . . . . 10.89, 10.90
s 62 . . . . 10.89, 10.92
s 63 . . . . 10.89
s 63(3) 10.80, 10.94
ss 63AA–63AC 10.121
s 64(4) 10.220
s 65 . . . . 10.75, 10.79
s 66 . . . . 10.78
s 66(3) 10.220
s 66A 10.116
s 66B 10.117
s 66D 10.118, 10.119
s 66E 10.120
s 67 . . . . 10.105, 10.111
s 68 . . . . 10.95, 10.96, 10.99,
10.102, 10.111, 10.115
s 68(1) 10.96, 16.80
s 68(1)(a) 10.244
s 68(1A) 10.98, 10.115
s 68(1A)(a) 10.244
s 69 . . . . 10.99, 10.111
s 70 . . . . 10.102
s 70(1A) 10.102
s 70(3), (4) 10.104
s 71 . . . . 10.106
s 72 . . . . 10.106, 10.220
s 73 . . . . 10.106
s 74 . . . . 10.62, 10.81, 10.106,
10.116, 10.124, 10.220
s 74(3)(a) 10.107, 10.124
s 75 . . . . 10.62, 10.93, 10.107, 10.220
s 75(2) 10.107
s 76 . . . . 10.108
s 77 . . . . 10.122
s 77(1) 10.122
s 78 . . . . 10.64, 10.122
s 78(1), (2) 10.122
s 79 . . . . 10.123
s 79(2) 10.123
ss 80–83 . . . . 10.125

Water Industry Act 1991 (*cont.*)

s 86A 10.255, 10.255
s 93(1) 10.63
ss 93A–93D 10.106
s 94 . . . . .10.128, 10.131, 10.132,
10.176, 10.234, 10.252
s 94(1) 16.87
s 94(2) 10.129
s 94(3) 10.130
s 95(1) 10.131
s 95(2) 10.132
s 95A 10.133
s 96(3) 10.134
s 96(4), (5) 10.135
s 96A 10.133
s 97 . . . . 10.15, 10.182
ss 98–117 . . . . 10.131
s 98 . . . . 10.143, 10.185
s 98(3), (4) 10.145
s 101 . . . . 10.145
ss 101A–116 . . . . 10.152
s 101A 10.146, 10.150, 10.152
s 101A(7) 10.146
s 101B 10.185
s 102 . . . . . .10.208, 10.221, 10.225, 16.87
s 102(5) 10.208
s 103 . . . . 10.221, 10.225, 16.87
s 104 . . . . 10.209, 10.221, 16.87
s 104(5) 10.210
s 105 . . . . 10.221, 16.87
s 105(2) 10.209
s 105A 10.208
s 106 . . . .10.136–10.139, 10.156, 10.221
s 106(1) 10.136
s 106(2)(a) 10.137
s 106(2)(b) 10.138
s 106(4) 10.139
s 106(4A) 10.140
s 107 . . . . 10.140, 10.221
s 107(3) 10.140
s 108 . . . . 10.141, 10.221
s 109 . . . . 10.142, 10.221
s 111 . . . . 10.221
s 111(1) 10.137
s 111(1)(a), (b) 10.156
s 112 . . . . 10.148, 10.221, 16.87
s 113 . . . . 10.149, 10.150, 10.221
s 114 . . . . 10.149, 10.221
s 115 . . . . 10.221, 16.87
s 116 . . . . 10.151, 10.221, 16.87
s 116A 10.255, 10.255
s 117 . . . . 10.181
s 117(6) 16.87

ss 118–141 . . . . 10.131, 10.221
s 118 . . . . 10.169
s 118(3), (4) 10.156
s 119 . . . . 10.156, 10.159
s 119(1) 10.159
s 120(1)–(3) 10.169
s 120(4) 10.170
s 120(9), (10) 10.170
s 122 . . . . 10.161, 10.166
s 122(2)(e) 10.224
s 124 . . . . 10.162
s 125(1) 10.164
s 125(2), (5) 10.164
s 126 . . . . 10.163
s 127 . . . . 10.171
s 127(2), (3) 10.172
s 129 . . . .10.156, 10.165, 10.169, 10.224
s 130(1) 10.169
s 130(2) 10.170
s 130(7) 10.170
s 130(9) 10.170
s 131(2), (3) 10.172
s 132 . . . . 10.173
s 133(1) 10.174
s 133(6) 10.173
s 135(2) 10.161
s 139(1) 10.158
s 141(1) 10.154
s 142 . . . . 10.222
s 143 . . . . 10.83, 10.161, 10.222
s 143(6), (7) 10.222
s 143A 10.222
s 144A 10.228
s 144A(3), (5) 10.228
s 144B 10.229
s 146(2) 10.73, 10.139
s 146(4) 10.225
s 147 . . . . 10.226
ss 155–192 . . . . 10.184
s 155 . . . . 10.198
s 156 . . . . .10.47, 10.48, 11.82, 11.88
s 156(7) 10.48
s 158 . . . . .10.141, 10.185, 10.187,
10.191, 10.193, 10.198, 10.219
s 158(7) 10.185
s 159 . . . . .10.185, 10.189, 10.191,
10.193, 10.198, 10.219
s 159(5) 10.189
s 161(1) 10.141, 10.187, 10.191,
10.193, 10.219
s 161(2) 10.190, 10.191, 10.219
s 162 . . . . 10.187
s 163 . . . . 10.191, 10.193, 10.219

s 165 . . . . 9.108, 10.193, 10.219
s 165(1) 10.191
s 165(3) 10.192
s 166 . . . . 10.191
s 167 . . . . 10.199
s 168 . . . . 10.219
s 169 . . . . 10.220
s 170(1)–(4) 10.220
s 171 . . . . 10.221
s 181 . . . . 10.195, 10.196, 10.256
s 181(3) 10.234
s 182 . . . . 10.195
s 185 . . . . 10.217, 10.218, 10.234
ss 186, 187 . . . . 10.193
s 192(5) 10.184
s 195 . . . . 10.242, 10.260
s 196 . . . . 10.234
ss 198, 199 . . . . 10.214
Part IV 3.25
s 201(1), (2) 10.261
s 202 . . . . 2.45
s 202(1) 10.262
s 203 . . . . 10.253
s 203(1), (3) 10.253
s 209 . . . . 16.73
s 218 . . . . 10.59
s 219 . . . . 10.221
s 219(1) 10.47
s 221 . . . . 2.33
Sch 2 . . . . 10.43, 10.252
Sch 4A 10.89
Sch 9 . . . . 10.198
Sch 11 . . . . 10.199
Sch 12 . . . . 10.152, 10.196
    para 1 . . . . 10.188
    paras 2, 3 . . . . 10.194
    para 6 . . . . 10.192
Sch 14 . . . . 10.211, 10.212
Water Industry Act 1999 . . . . 10.07
Water Resources Act 1963 . . . . . . 2.04, 2.07,
                              2.49, 10.02
Water Resources Act 1991 . . . . . . 1.88, 2.05,
2.07, 2.38, 2.60, 4.54, 5.125, 5.138, 5.147,
    5.149, 5.150, 7.108, 9.01, 9.03, 9.07,
    9.11, 9.32, 9.41, 9.43, 9.49, 9.78, 9.79,
    9.108, 9.120, 9.127, 9.134, 10.181,
    11.06, 11.70, 11.132, 12.11, 12.13,
            12.54, 12.75, 16.72
s 2 . . . . 9.133
ss 6, 7 . . . . 2.46
s 17 . . . . 11.88
s 18 . . . . 9.68
s 18A 9.133

s 21 . . . . 9.21
s 21(4), (5) 9.43
s 24 . . . . 9.33
s 24(1)–(5) 9.35
s 24A 9.38
s 25 . . . . 9.50, 9.53, 9.119
s 25(2) 9.52
s 25(8) 9.51
s 25C 9.36
s 25C(3), (4) 9.36
s 26 . . . . 9.49
s 26(2) 9.49
s 27 . . . . 9.34
s 27A 9.06, 9.34
s 29 . . . . 9.49
s 29(1) 9.49
ss 30, 31 . . . . 9.49
s 32(1)–(3) 9.49
s 33 . . . . 9.49
s 33(1) 16.73
s 33A 9.49
s 35 . . . . 9.37
s 35(4) 9.37
s 37 . . . . 9.14
ss 37A–37D 9.14
s 38(2)(a), (b) 9.42
s 38(3)(a), (b) 9.42
s 39 . . . . 9.42
s 39B 9.14, 9.34, 9.77
s 39C 9.14, 9.77
s 41 . . . . 9.45
s 42(5) 9.45
s 43(1) 9.46
s 44(6) 9.46
s 46(2)–(5) 9.47
s 46(6), (7) 9.48
s 48(1) 9.42
s 48A 9.50
s 48A(6) 9.50
s 51 . . . . 9.53
s 51(1) 9.55
s 51(1C–1G) 9.53
s 51(2)–(4) 9.55
s 52(2) 9.56
s 53 . . . . 9.61
s 53(4) 9.56
s 54 . . . . 9.36, 9.56
s 55 . . . . 9.57
s 55(5) 9.57
s 56 . . . . 9.36
s 57 . . . . 9.69
ss 59A–59D 9.40
s 60 . . . . 9.42

Water Resources Act 1991 (*cont.*)
s 60(3) 9.45
s 61 . . . . .9.61
s 61(4) 9.56, 9.61
s 62(3) 9.58
s 63 . . . . .9.61
s 63(2) 16.73
s 69 . . . . .9.46
s 70 . . . . 16.72
Part II, Chapter III (ss 73–81). 9.62
s 73(1) 9.64
s 73(2) 9.67
s 73(3)(b) 9.64
s 73(6) 16.73
s 74 . . . . .9.63
s 74(1) 9.65
s 74(2) 9.66
s 74(3), (4) .9.63
s 75 . . . . .9.67
s 75(2)(c) 9.68
s 75(3), (4) .9.68
s 76(1)(a) 9.69
s 77(1) 9.70
s 78 . . . . .9.71
s 79A 9.73
s 80 . . . . .9.76
s 80(4) 9.76
Part III 6.31, 9.08
s 82 . . . . .9.79
s 83 . . . . 5.125, 9.79
s 83(3), (4) .9.79
s 84 . . . . 9.78, 9.109
s 85 . . . . 2.04, 9.01, 9.81, 9.85,
9.87, 9.94, 9.101, 9.102, 9.105, 9.108,
9.115, 9.119, 9.121, 9.123, 12.11,
12.35, 12.69
s 85(1) 9.83, 9.87, 9.90, 9.91,
9.94–9.96, 9.99, 9.100
s 85(2) 9.106, 9.107
s 85(3) 9.105, 9.106
s 85(4) 9.105, 9.107
s 85(6) 9.84, 9.110, 9.113
s 85(7) 9.102
s 86 . . . . .9.83, 9.107, 9.110, 9.121
s 86(6) 9.107
s 87(1) 9.105
s 87(1A)–(1C) 9.105
s 87(2) 9.94, 9.105
s 88 . . . . 12.11
s 88(1) 9.108
s 88(1)(c) 9.108
s 88(2) 9.109
s 89(1) 9.115, 9.118

s 89(2) 9.119
s 89(3) 9.123
s 89(3A) 9.124
s 92 . . . . .9.11
s 100 . . . . 12.18, 16.72
s 104 . . . . 9.02, 9.89
Part IV 9.134
s 105 . . . . .5.130
s 106 . . . . 2.44, 9.129
s 110A 9.105
s 113 . . . . .9.134
s 161 . . . . .2.04, 9.08, 9.125, 12.12
s 161A 9.08, 9.125, 9.126
s 161A(4) 9.126
s 161B 9.08, 9.127
s 161B(3) 9.126
s 161C 9.08
s 161D 9.08, 9.126
s 161D(3) 9.126
s 163 . . . . .9.108
ss 165, 166 .9.133
s 190(1) 5.125
s 191 . . . . .5.164
s 192 . . . . .9.89
s 195 . . . . .5.164
s 195A 9.44
s 198 . . . . .5.164
s 199 . . . . .9.49
s 199A 9.49
s 202 . . . . .5.145
s 202(1), (2) 5.139
s 202(3) 5.140
s 202(4) 5.141
s 203(1) 5.148
s 203(3)–(6) 5.148
s 204 . . . . .5.164
s 204(1) 5.149
s 204(2) 5.151
s 204(4), (5) 5.151
s 205(6) 5.152
s 206 . . . . .5.152
s 217(3) 9.98, 9.99
s 221 . . . . 9.33, 9.84, 9.103
s 221(1), (3) 9.33
s 222 . . . . 2.33, 16.31
s 221(1) 9.113
s 222(2) 9.25
s 222 . . . . .9.120
Sch 4 . . . . .9.133
Sch 8 . . . . .9.62
para 2 . . . . .9.63
Sch 9 . . . . .9.72
Sch 10 . . . . .9.109

para 3(2). 9.109
para 3(4). 9.109
para 5. . . . . .9.109
para 6. . . . . .9.110
para 7. . . . . .9.111
para 7(4), (5) 9.112
para 8. . . . . .9.111
Sch 25, para 5 . . . . .9.133
Welsh Language Act 1993. . . . . .2.17
Wild Mammals (Protection)
   Act 1996 . . . . .11.93
ss 1–3. . . . . .11.109
s 5 . . . . .11.109
s 6(1) 11.109
Wildlife and Countryside
   Act 1981 . . . . .2.14, 3.29, 4.54,
   7.175, 10.47, 11.04, 11.11, 11.70, 11.73,
        11.78, 11.80, 11.97, 11.99
Part I 11.44–11.46, 11.93,
               11.96, 11.102
Part II. 11.46, 11.49, 11.60,
               11.61, 11.66
s 1 . . . . .11.84
s 1(1) 11.96
s 1(2)(a), (b) 11.98
s 1(3) 11.99
s 1(5) 11.84, 11.98
s 1(6) 11.97
s 2 . . . . 11.84, 11.97
s 2(4) 11.97
s 3 . . . . 11.84, 11.100
s 4 . . . . 11.99, 11.106
s 4(1) 11.99
s 4(2)(a)–(c) 11.99
s 4(3) 11.99
s 5 . . . . .11.107
s 5(1) 11.100
s 5(4), (5) 11.100
s 6 . . . . .11.101
s 6(1)–(3) 11.101
s 6(3)(b) .11.101
s 6(4) 11.101
s 6(8), (8A). 11.101
s 7(1) 11.102
s 7(2A) 11.102
s 7(3), (4) 11.102
s 8(1)–(3) 11.102
s 9 . . . . 11.104, 11.106, 11.110
s 9(1) 11.104, 11.105
s 9(2)–(4) 11.104
s 9(5) 11.104, 11.105
s 10 . . . . 11.104, 11.106, 11.110
s 10(1) 11.106

s 10(2) 11.107
s 10(3), (4) 11.106
s 10(5) 11.106, 11.107
s 10(6) 11.106
s 11 . . . . 11.107, 11.110
s 11(1), (2) 11.108
s 11(6) 11.108
s 13 . . . . .11.118
s 13(1)(b) .11.119
s 13(2), (3) 11.119
s 14 . . . . .11.97
s 14(1) 11.105
s 14(2) 11.119
s 14ZA(1). 11.104, 11.119
s 15 . . . . .11.133
s 16(1), (2) 11.99
s 16(3) 11.106
s 21(6) 11.108
s 22 . . . . .11.93
s 24(1) 11.04, 11.93
s 27(1) 11.96–11.98, 1.100,
              11.103, 11.118
s 27(3) 11.103
s 27AA 11.78, 11.79
ss 28–34. . . . . .11.78
s 28 . . . . .11.80
s 28(1) 11.78, 11.79, 11.80, 11.81
s 28(3) 11.81
s 28(4) 11.81
s 28(4)(b) .11.81
s 28(5), (6) 11.81
ss 28B–28D 11.81
s 28E(1) 11.81
s 28E(3) 11.81
s 28E(3)(a) 11.81
s 28F(1), (10) 11.81
s 28G 11.81, 11.82
ss 28J, 28K 11.82
s 28L(1), (12) 11.82
s 28M(1) 11.81
s 28M(2) 11.82
s 28N 11.82
s 28P 11.81
s 29 . . . . .3.29
s 31 . . . . .11.04
s 31(1) 11.81
s 34 . . . . .11.83
s 34(1), (2) 11.83
s 34(4), (5) 11.83
s 35(1) 11.73
s 36(1) 11.77
s 37(1)–(3) 11.77
s 37A(2) 11.65

Wildlife and Countryside Act 1981 (*cont.*)
s 39 .... 11.88, 11.89
s 42(3)–(5) 11.88, 11.89
s 42(7) 11.88
s 50(3) 11.88
s 67(2) 11.77, 11.83
Sch 1 ....11.93
   Part I 11.98
   Part II......................11.97
Sch 2 ....11.93
   Part I 11.97
   Part II.............. 1.100, 11.102
Sch 3 ....11.93
   Part I 11.100, 11.101
   para 31(2)...................11.89
Sch 4 .... 11.93, 11.102
Sch 5 .... 11.93, 11.103–11.105
Sch 6 ....11.93
Sch 7 ....11.93
Sch 8 .... 11.93, 11.118, 11.120
Sch 9 ....11.93

   Part I 11.97, 11.105
   Part II.....................11.120
Sch 11 ....11.83
Sch 12 ....11.77
Sch ZA1......................11.93
Wildlife and Countryside (Amendment)
   Act 1991 ....11.100
Wildlife and Countryside (Scotland)
   Act 1981 ....11.92

New Zealand

Resource Management Act 1991.......2.24

USA

Clean Air Act 1970, 42 USC 7604 .....2.25
Endangered Species Act 1973 ....2.25

TABLE OF STATUTORY INSTRUMENTS

Act of Sederunt (Fees of Solicitors in the Sheriff Court) 1989 (SI 1989/434) 5.163

Action Programme for Nitrate Vulnerable Zones (England and Wales) Regulations 1998 (SI 1998/1202) 9.30

Advisory Committee for Wales (Environment Agency) Abolition Order 2002 (SI 2002/784). 2.46

Aerodromes (Noise Restrictions etc) Regulations 2003 (SI 2003/1742) 13.133
reg 3 . . . . 13.133
reg 6 . . . . 13.134
Sch 2 . . . . 13.134

Aeroplane Noise Regulations 1999 (SI 1999/1452). 13.127
reg 2 . . . . 13.134
regs 4, 5 . . . . 13.127
reg 6 . . . . 13.131
reg 7 . . . . 13.134
reg 8, 9 . . . . 13.127, 13.135
reg 12 . . . . 13.136
reg 13 . . . . 13.129
regs 15, 16 . . . . 13.128
regs 20–24 . . . . 13.129
reg 25 . . . . 13.131
regs 27, 28 . . . . 13.132
Sch 1 . . . . 13.129

Agricultural or Forestry Tractors and Tractor Components (Type Approval) Regulations 1988 (SI 1988/1567) 13.151

Air Navigation Order 1989 (SI 1989/2116). 13.123

Air Navigation Order (Noise Certification) 1990 (SI 1990/1514) 13.123

Ancient Monuments (Applications for Scheduled Monument Consent) Regulations 1981 (SI 1981/1301). 14.73

Animal By-Products Order 1999 (SI 1999/646). 2.33

Anti-Pollution Works Regulations 1999 (SI 1999/1006). 5.133, 9.36, 9.54, 9.109, 9.125

reg 7 . . . . 9.127
reg 28 . . . . 9.36
reg 30 . . . . 9.36

Bathing Waters (Classification) Regulations 1991 (SI 1991/1597) 9.78

Bathing Waters (Classification) (England) Regulations 2003 (SI 2003/1238). 9.78

Building Regulations 2000 (SI 2000/2531). 12.04, 16.72
Sch 1 . . . . 12.04

Carriage of Radioactive Material by Rail Regulations 1996 (SI 1996/2090). 8.64

Clean Air (Arrestment Plant) (Exemption) Regulations 1969 (SI 1969/1262). 13.11

Clean Air (Height of Chimneys) (Exemption) Regulations 1969 (SI 1969/411). 13.21

Clean Air (Measurement of Grit and Dust from Furnaces) Regulations 1971 (SI 1971/161). . 131.6

Conservation (Natural Habitats, &c) (Amendment) Regulations 1994 (SI 1994/2716). 9.62, 11.05, 11.11, 11.45, 11.46, 11.49, 11.66–11.71, 11.73, 11.77, 11.83, 11.93, 11.103, 11.107, 11.110, 14.82
reg 2 . . . . 11.67
reg 3(2). 11.73, 11.77, 11.83
regs 7, 8 . . . . 11.68
reg 10(1). 11.67, 11.68
reg 10(1)(c) 11.67, 11.68
reg 10(2). 11.67, 11.68
regs 16, 17 . . . . 11.69, 11.74
regs 18–27 . . . . 11.69
reg 20 . . . . 11.71
reg 24 . . . . 11.71
reg 23(3). 11.69
reg 26 . . . . 11.69

Conservation (Natural Habitats, &c)
    (Amendment) Regulations 1994
    (SI 1994/2716) (*cont.*)
    regs 28–31 . . . . 11.69
    reg 37 . . . . 14.82
    regs 38–41B 11.107
    reg 39 . . . . 11.110
    reg 39(1). 11.69
    reg 39(6). 11.69
    regs 40, 41 . . . . 11.110
    reg 41(1). 11.69
    reg 41(6). 11.69
    reg 43(1). 11.69, 11.120
    reg 43(2). 11.120
    reg 43(7). 11.69
    regs 44, 45 . . . . 11.110, 11.120
    reg 48 . . . . 11.71
    reg 48(1). 11.72
    reg 48(1)(a), (b) 11.71
    reg 48(5). 11.71
    reg 49 . . . . 11.71
    reg 49(1). 11.71
    reg 49(5). 11.71
    regs 50–52 . . . . 11.70
    regs 53, 54 . . . . 11.71
    regs 55, 56 . . . . 11.70
    reg 57(1), (3) 11.70
    reg 60 . . . . 11.70, 11.71
    reg 62 . . . . 11.70
    regs 64–66 . . . . 11.70
    regs 71–82 . . . . 11.70
    regs 83–85 . . . . 11.70
    Part 4A (regs 85A–85E) 11.11
    regs 94–96 . . . . 11.69
    regs 98, 99 . . . . 11.69
    reg 100 . . . . 11.69
    regs 101–101F 11.69
    reg 103 . . . . 11.69
    Sch 1 . . . . 11.69
    Schs 2, 3 . . . . 11.110
    Sch 4 . . . . 11.120
Conservation (Natural Habitats, &c)
    (Amendment) Regulations 2007
    (SI 2007/1843). 11.11
Conservation (Natural Habitats, &c)
    (Northern Ireland) Regulations 1995
    (SI 1995/380). 11.49
Conservation of Seals (England) Order 1996
    (SI 1996/2905). 11.114
Construction Plant and Equipment
    (Harmonisation of Noise Emission
    Standards) Regulations 1985
    (SI 1985/1968). 13.151

Contaminated Land Regulations 2006
    (SI 2006/1380). 5.94, 12.25
    reg 8 . . . . 5.94
    reg 9 . . . . 5.95
    reg 10 . . . . 5.96
    reg 11 . . . . 5.97
    reg 13 . . . . 5.99
    Sch 3 . . . . 5.100
Control of Atmospheric Pollution (Appeals)
    Regulations 1977 (SI 1977/17). . . . 13.63
Control of Atmospheric Pollution
    (Exempted Premises) Regulations 1977
    (SI 1977/18). 13.62
Control of Atmospheric Pollution (Research
    and Publicity) Regulations 1977
    (SI 1977/19). 13.65, 13.68
    reg 3 . . . . 13.65
    reg 4 . . . . 13.67
    regs 5, 6 . . . . 13.68
Control of Major Accidents Regulations
    1999 (SI 1999/743) 4.54, 6.80,
                                   6.83, 8.140
    reg 1 . . . . 8.142
    reg 3 . . . . 8.140
    reg 6 . . . . 8.142–8.144
    reg 7 . . . . 8.144
    regs 8–11 . . . . 8.144
    reg 14 . . . . 8.145
    reg 15 . . . . 8.147
    regs 17, 18 . . . . 8.144
    reg 19 . . . . 8.148
    reg 21 . . . . 8.148
    Sch 1 . . . . 8.140
    Sch 2 . . . . 8.141
    Sch 3 . . . . 8.142
    Sch 4 . . . . 8.144
    Sch 6 . . . . 8.146
Control of Noise (Appeals) Regulations 1975
    (SI 1975/2116). 13.83, 13.100
    reg 5 . . . . 13.83
    Part II 13.106
    Part III 13.105
Control of Noise (Codes of Practice for
    Construction and Open Sites) Order
    1984 (SI 1984/1992) 13.81
Control of Noise (Measurement and
    Registers) Regulations 1976
    (SI 1976/37). 13.101
Control of Pesticides Regulations 1986
    (SI 1986/1510). 2.34, 5.122–5.124
    reg 8 . . . . 5.122
    reg 8(4). 5.124
    Sch 4 . . . . 5.124

Control of Pollution (Applications,
    Appeals and Registers) Regulations 1996
    (SI 1996/2971)......... 5.126, 5.130,
                                    5.132, 9.109
  reg 2..........................5.127
  reg 3.................... 5.126, 5.127
  reg 4............... 5.127, 5.130
  reg 5............... 5.128, 5.130
  reg 6......................5.130
  reg 7......................5.131
  regs 9, 10 ....5.129
  regs 12, 13 ....5.129
  reg 15.....................5.132
Control of Pollution (Channel Tunnel
    Rail Link) Regulations 1998
    (SI 1998/1649)...............9.109
Control of Pollution (Oil Storage)
    (England) Regulations 2001
    SI 2001/2954) 9.25–9.27
  regs 2–4 ....9.26
Control of Pollution (Silage Slurry and
    Agricultural Fuel Oil) Regulations
    1991 (SI 1991/324) 9.25
Control of Pollution (Special Waste)
    Regulations 1980
    (SI 1980/1709).......... 5.61, 7.54
  reg 2.................... 7.55, 7.58
  Sch 1 .... 7.55, 7.59
  Part I 7.57
  Part II—
    para 1................ 7.55, 7.56
    para 2.....................7.56
    para 4.....................7.55
Control of Substances Hazardous to
    Health Regulations 2002
    (SI 2002/2677)................2.11
Control of Trade in Endangered Species
    (Enforcement) Regulations 1997
    (SI 1997/1372)........ 11.43, 11.133
Control of Trade in Endangered Species
    (Enforcement) (Amendment)
    Regulations 2005
    (SI 2005/1674)........ 11.43, 11.133
Controlled Waste (Regulation of Carriers and
    Seizure of Vehicles) Regulations 1991
    (SI 1991/1624)........ 7.207, 7.209
  reg 5(1)......................7.207
  reg 6(1)(f) 7.207
Controlled Waste Regulations 1992
    (SI 1992/588).......... 6.31, 7.14,
            7.16–7.28, 7.34, 7.52, 7.237
  reg 1.......................7.20
  reg 2.......................7.24

reg 2(1).....................7.16
reg 3........................7.19
reg 7........................7.41
Sch 1 ....7.16
  para 2.....................7.50
Sch 2 .... 7.23, 7.237, 7.238
  para 4.....................7.42
  para 6.....................7.29
  para 9.....................7.33
  para 10....................7.28
  paras 11, 12 ....7.34
  para 13....................7.29
  paras 16–18 ....7.36
Sch 3 ....7.37
  para 3.....................7.38
  paras 5, 6 ....7.39
  para 7............... 7.40, 7.41
  para 8........7.31, 7.32, 7.42, 7.43
  para 8(a)..................7.42
  paras 9, 10 ....7.44
  paras 12, 13 ....7.45
  para 15....................7.47
Sch 4 .... 7.48, 7.52
  paras 1–4 ....7.49
  para 5.....................7.50
  para 6.....................7.51
  para 7.....................7.52
Crop Residues (Burning) Regulations
    1993 (SI 1993/1366) 2.06

Dangerous Substances (Conveyance by
    Road in Road Tankers and Tank
    Containers) Regulations 1981
    (SI 1981/1059)...............7.207
Dark Smoke (Permitted Periods)
    Regulations 1958
    (SI 1958/498)......... 13.08, 13.09
Drought Plan Regulations 2005
    (SI 2005/1905)................9.77

Electricity and Pipe-line Works (Assessment
    of Environmental Effects) Regulations
    1990 (SI 1990/442) 5.163
Electricity Works (Environmental Impact
    Assessment) (England and Wales)
    Regulations 2000
    (SI 2000/1927)...............15.14
End of Life Vehicles Regulations 2003
    (SI 2003/2635)................7.78
End of Life Vehicles (Producer
    Responsibility) Regulations 2005
    (SI 2005/263).................7.78
  reg 2.......................7.78

End of Life Vehicles (Producer
Responsibility) Regulations 2005
(SI 2005/263) (*cont.*)
regs 6, 7 . . . . 7.79
reg 9 . . . . 7.79
regs 10, 11 . . . . 7.81
reg 12 . . . . 7.79–7.81, 7.83
regs 14–16 . . . . 7.79
reg 17 . . . . 7.79, 7.81
reg 18 . . . . 7.79, 7.82
regs 19–21 . . . . 7.79
reg 23 . . . . 7.84
reg 27 . . . . 7.83
reg 29 . . . . 7.83
reg 48 . . . . 7.83
Environment Act 1995 (Commencement No
9 and Transitional Provisions) Order
1997 (SI 1997/1626) 2.33
Environment (Northern Ireland) Order
2002 (NI 2002/3153) 11.78
Environmental Assessment
(Afforestation) Regulations 1988
(SI 1988/1207) 5.163, 15.14
Environmental Assessment
(Forestry) Regulations 1998
(SI 1998/1731) 11.07
Environmental Assessment of Plans and
Programmes Regulations 2004
(SI 2004/1633) 11.56, 14.07,
14.82, 15.07
Environmental Assessment of Plans and
Programmes Regulations
(Northern Ireland) 2004
(SR 2004/280) 11.56
Environmental Assessment of Plans and
Programmes (Wales) Regulations 2004
(SI 2004/1656) 11.56, 14.82
Environmental Assessment (Salmon Farming
in Marine Waters) Regulations 1988
(SI 1988/1218) 5.163, 15.14
Environmental Impact Assessment
(Agriculture) (England)
(No 2) Regulations 2006
(SI 2006/2522) 11.47
Environmental Impact Assessment (Fish
Farming in Marine Waters) Regulations
1999 (SI 1999/367) 15.14
Environmental Impact Assessment (Forestry)
(England and Wales) Regulations 1999
(SI 1999/2228) 11.08, 15.14
Environmental Impact Assessment
(Forestry) (England and Wales)
(Amendment) Regulations 2006
(SI 2006/3106) 15.14

Environmental Impact Assessment
(Land Drainage Improvement
Works) Regulations 1999
(SI 1999/1783) 15.14
Environmental Impact Assessment (Land
Drainage Improvement Works)
(Amendment) Regulations 2005
(SI 2005/1399) 15.14
Environmental Impact Assessment (Land
Drainage Improvement Works)
(Amendment) Regulations 2006
(SI 2006/618) 15.14
Environmental Impact Assessment
(Uncultivated Land and Semi-Natural
Areas) (England) Regulations 2001
(SI 2001/3966) 15.14
reg 2(1) 15.14
Environmental Information Regulations 1992
(SI 1992/3240) 4.33, 5.36
Environmental Information Regulations 2004
(SI 2004/3391) 3.34, 5.22–5.39
reg 3 . . . . 5.23
reg 4 . . . . 5.24
reg 5(1)–(3) 5.25
reg 5(5) 5.26
reg 6 . . . . 5.31
reg 7 . . . . 5.32
reg 8 . . . . 5.33
reg 10 . . . . 5.34
reg 12(4), (5) 5.30
reg 13 . . . . 5.28
reg 13(3) 5.29
reg 13(5) 5.28
regs 14, 15 . . . . 5.35
reg 16 . . . . 5.36
reg 17 . . . . 5.37
reg 18 . . . . 5.39
reg 19(1) 5.39
reg 19(4) 5.39
Environmental Licences (Suspension and
Revocation) Regulations 1996
(SI 1996/508) 9.60
Environmental Permitting (England
and Wales) Regulations 2007
(SI 2007/3538) 2.06, 6.01,
6.04–6.07, 6.13, 6.14, 6.25, 6.26, 6.30,
6.34, 6.40, 6.65, 6.70, 6.76– 6.78, 6.87,
6.110, 6.188, 6.201, 6.206, 6.209,
6.235, 6.237, 6.242, 6.254, 6.302,
6.303, 9.102, 9.108, 12.11, 12.15,
12.34, 14.87, 14.89, 14.91
reg 2 . . . . 12.44
reg 2(1) 6.12, 6.20, 6.36, 6.38
reg 3 . . . . 12.44

reg 3(3). 6.37
reg 4. . . . . .12.100
reg 5. . . . . .6.32
regs 7–12 .12.106
reg 8. . . . . .6.36
reg 8(3). 6.33
reg 9. . . . . 6.41, 6.42, 6.247
reg 11 . . . . .6.235
reg 11(1). 6.10
reg 12 . . . . 6.210, 12.15
reg 14 . . . . .6.120
reg 15 . . . . 6.125, 6.137
reg 16 . . . . 6.136, 6.287
reg 16(2). 6.57
regs 17, 18 . . . . .6.99
reg 19(4). .6.305
reg 20. . . . . .14.08
reg 20(1)–(3) 6.147
reg 21(3). .6.155
reg 22. . . . . .6.156
reg 22(1). 6.156, 6.280
reg 22(2)–(4) 6.156
reg 23. . . . . .6.157
reg 23(1). .6.280
reg 23(2). .6.281
reg 23(6)(c) 6.157
reg 24. . . . . 6.160, 6.278
reg 25. . . . . .6.160
reg 26. . . . . .6.274
reg 26(1), (2) 6.130
reg 27(3). .6.131
reg 28. . . . . .6.134
reg 30(3). .6.135
reg 31. . . . . .6.167
reg 31(3). 6.95, 6.167
reg 31(5), (6) 6.184
reg 31(8). .6.171
reg 31(9). 6.156, 6.171
reg 32(1). 6.08, 6.24
reg 32(20 .6.237
reg 33. . . . . .6.100
reg 33(1). 6.08, 6.239
reg 34(2). .6.144
reg 36. . . . . .6.194, 12.15, 12.16,
                              12.34, 12.54
reg 37. . . . . 12.16, 12.34, 12.54
reg 37(1), (2) 6.196
reg 37(3). .6.197
reg 37(4). .6.196
reg 37(5). .6.198
reg 38(1)(a) 6.200, 6.210, 6.226,
                              6.228, 12.16
reg 38(1)(b) 6.157, 6.200, 6.211,
                              6.226, 6.228

reg 38(1)(c) 6.200, 6.212, 6.226,
                              6.228, 6.231
reg 38(1)(d) 6.216, 6.219
reg 38(1)(e) 6.217
reg 38(1)(f) 6.218
reg 38(2)(a) 6.220
reg 38(3). .6.214
reg 39. . . . . .6.227
reg 39(1). .6.213
reg 40. . . . . .6.206
reg 41. . . . . .6.208
reg 42. . . . . . . .6.231, 12.16, 12.34, 12.54
reg 44. . . . . 6.227, 6.229
reg 44(3). .6.227
reg 45. . . . . .6.299
reg 46(1). .6.286
reg 46(2). .6.287
reg 46(4). .6.290
reg 46(5). .6.291
reg 46(8)(a), (b) 6.292
reg 46(9). .6.293
reg 47(1)–(3) 6.295
reg 47(4). .6.296
reg 48. . . . . .6.298
regs 50, 51 . . . . 6.287, 6.300
reg 51(2)(b) 6.302
reg 51(3). .6.303
reg 51(4). .6.304
reg 52. . . . . 6.287, 6.300
reg 53. . . . . 6.300, 6.300
reg 53(1). .6.169
reg 53(2). .6.301
reg 53(4), (5) 6.301
reg 55(1), (2) 6.306
reg 56. . . . . .6.298
reg 57. . . . . .6.158
reg 57(1)–(3) 6.200
reg 58. . . . . 6.147, 6.277
reg 60. . . . . .6.287
reg 60(2). .6.216
reg 62. . . . . 6.09, 6.140
reg 64. . . . . .6.07
reg 65. . . . . 6.95, 6.288
reg 65(5). .6.95
reg 68. . . . . 14.89, 14.90
reg 69. . . . . .12.15
reg 69(1). .6.40
reg 70(1). .6.40
reg 72(1). .6.40
reg 73. . . . . .9.102
Sch 1 . . . . 6.04, 6.20, 6.39
Part 1—
para 2. . . . . .6.25
para 3 . . . . .6.29

Environmental Permitting (England
and Wales) Regulations 2007
(SI 2007/3538) (*cont.*)

para 4 . . . . .6.26
para 5 . . . . .6.27
paras 45(1), (3) 6.35
Part 2 . . . . 6.21, 6.26, 6.53
   Section 5.1 . . . . .6.74
Sch 2—
para 2 . . . . .6.32
para 2(3) 6.32
para 4 . . . . .6.32
para 4(1) 6.235
para 4(2)(a) 6.235
para 5 . . . . 6.32, 6.257
para 6 . . . . .6.35
para 8 . . . . .6.32
para 8(2) 6.32
para 9 . . . . .6.220
paras 10, 11 . . . . .6.35
para 12(3) 6.221
para 13 . . . . 6.32, 6.144
Sch 3 . . . . .12.119
Part 1 . . . . .6.32
Sch 4—
para 2(2)(b) 6.235
paras 3, 4 . . . . .6.235
Sch 5 . . . . 6.79, 6.153
Part 1 . . . . .6.114
para 1 . . . . .6.114
para 3 . . . . .6.89
para 4 . . . . 6.82, 6.257
para 4(2) 6.169
para 5 . . . . .6.103
para 5(1)(b) 6.133
para 6 . . . . 6.103, 6.104
para 6(2) 6.297
para 6(3) 6.301
para 7 . . . . .6.103
para 8 . . . . .6.150
para 10 . . . . .6.108
para 12 . . . . .6.114
para 12(2) 6.118
para 12(3) 6.151
para 13 . . . . 6.90, 6.263
para 15 . . . . .6.138
para 15(2) 6.137
para 17 . . . . .6.119
para 18(3) 6.154
para 23 . . . . 6.127, 6.128
paras 24–27 . . . . .6.128
Sch 6—
para 2(1), (2) 6.172
para 2(3) 6.173

para 3 . . . . .6.169
para 3(2) 6.170
para 4(1), (2) 6.175
para 4(3) 6.176
para 4(4) 6.174
para 5(1) 6.177
para 5(3), (4) 6.178
para 5(5) 6.179
para 5(6) 6.179, 6.185
para 6 . . . . .6.180
para 7(1) 6.186
para 7(1)(c) 6.187
para 7(2), (3) 6.187
Sch 7 . . . . 6.41, 6.116
para 3 . . . . .6.117
para 4 . . . . .6.80
para 5 . . . . .6.41
para 5(1)(a) 6.42, 6.44
para 5(1)(b) 6.44–6.47, 6.121
para 5(1)(c) 6.44, 6.48, 6.250
para 5(1)(d) 6.49, 6.251
para 5(1)(e) 6.49, 6.251
para 5(2)(f) .6.49
para 5(5) 6.50
para 6 . . . . 6.104, 6.107, 6.251
para 8 . . . . .6.117
Sch 8 . . . . .6.251
para 3 . . . . .6.245
para 5(1)(a) 6.247, 6.248
para 5(1)(b) 6.248, 6.249
para 5(1)(c) 6.248, 6.250
para 5(2)(b) 6.248
para 5(2)(e) 6.251
para 5(2)(f) .6.249
para 7(1) 6.252
Sch 9—
para 2 . . . . 6.112, 14.87
para 3 . . . . .6.67
para 4 . . . . .6.69
Sch 10—
para 1(b) 6.70
para 5(1)(a)–(g) 6.71
para 5(1)(h) 6.71, 6.199
para 5(1)(i), (j) 6.71
para 5(3) 6.71
paras 7–9 . . . . .6.71
para 10 . . . . .6.199
para 10(1), (2) 6.199
para 11 . . . . .6.166
Sch 11—
para 3(1) 6.72
Sch 12—
para 3(1) 6.73
Sch 13 . . . . .6.287

para 2(1). 6.74
para 3 . . . . .6.74
paras 4–13 . . . . .6.75
Sch 14—
para 3 . . . . .6.77
Schs 15–17. .6.78
Sch 19 . . . . 6.287, 6.294
para 1 . . . . .6.287
para 1(2). 6.287
para 1(2)(c) .6.288
para 1(3). 6.287
para 2 . . . . .6.289
para 3 . . . . .6.287
Sch 20—
para 3 . . . . .14.89
para 3(1). 6.67
para 4 . . . . 6.69, 14.90
para 6 . . . . 14.90, 14.91
para 6(2). 14.90
Sch 21, Pt I, para 21 . . . . .9.102
Environmental Protection (Amendment
    of Regulations) Regulations 1991
    (SI 1991/836). 7.106
Sch 1, Chap 5, para 5.1. . . . . .7.107
Environmental Protection (Disposal of
    PCBs and other Dangerous
    Substances) Regulations 2000
    (SI 2000/1043). 8.152
regs 2, 3 . . . . .8.152
reg 4 . . . . .8.153
regs 6–8 . . . . .8.153
reg 13 . . . . .8.153
Environmental Protection (Duty of Care)
    Regulations 1991
    (SI 1991/2839). 7.201
Environmental Protection (Prescribed
    Processes and Substances) Regulations
    1991 (SI 1991/472) 7.106
Sch 1, Part A. 7.106
Environmental Protection (Restriction on
    the Use of Lead Shot)
    (England) Regulations 1999
    (SI 1999/2170). 8.149
reg 3. . . . . .8.150
Schs 1, 2. . . . . .8.150

Forestry (Felling of Trees) Regulations
    1979 (SI 1979/791) 11.129
Sch 2 . . . . .11.129

Gas Transporter Pipe-Line Works
    (Environmental Impact Assessment)
    Regulations 1999
    (SI 1999/1672). 15.14

Genetically Modified Organisms
    (Contained Use) Regulations 2000
    (SI 2000/2831). 8.202, 8.211
reg 3 . . . . .8.203
regs 4–8 . . . . .8.204
reg 9 . . . . .8.205
regs 10, 11 . . . . .8.206
reg 14 . . . . .8.207
reg 14 (3), (4) 8.207
reg 16 . . . . .8.208
regs 20, 21 . . . . .8.208
regs 24, 24A .8.207
reg 29 . . . . .8.209
Sch 8 . . . . .8.208
Genetically Modified Organisms (Deliberate
    Release) Regulations 2002
    (SI 2002/2443). 3.05, 8.162,
                                            8.169, 8.210
reg 2 . . . . .8.176
reg 4 . . . . .8.169
reg 5 . . . . .8.176
Part II. 8.178
reg 11 . . . . .8.179
reg 14 . . . . .8.210
Sch 1 . . . . .8.178
Genetically Modified Organisms (Traceability
    and Labelling) Regulations 2004
    (SI 2004/2412). 8.212
regs 3–6 . . . . .8.213
Sch 8.213
Gibraltar Point (Area of Special Protection)
    Order 1995 (SI 1995/2876) 11.84
Greenhouse Gas Emissions Trading
    Scheme Regulations 2003
    (SI 2003/3311). 2.13
Sch 1 . . . . .2.13
Groundwater (England and Wales) Regulations
    1998 (SI 1998/2746) 6.83, 6.146,
                                            9.22, 9.23, 9.25
regs 2–13 . . . . .9.23
reg 18. . . . . .6.31

Harbour Works (Assessment of
    Environmental Effects) Regulations
    1988 (SI 1988/1336) 5.163
Hazardous Waste (England and Wales)
    Regulations 2005
    (SI 2005/894). 7.70, 7.71, 7.258
regs 8–10 . . . . .7.72
reg 13. . . . . .7.72
regs 15–17 . . . . .7.72
reg 21(1). 7.71
reg 23. . . . . .7.71
regs 38–41 . . . . .7.73

Hazardous Waste (England and Wales)
Regulations 2005
(SI 2005/894) (*cont.*)
regs 56–60 . . . . 7.71
reg 62 . . . . 7.74
reg 66 . . . . 7.75
Schs 1–3 . . . . 7.70
Health and Safety (Enforcing Authority)
Regulations 1989
(SI 1989/1902) 2.11
Hedgerows Regulations 1997
(SI 1997/1160) 11.36, 11.93,
11.130, 11.131
reg 3(1) 11.131
reg 3(3) 11.130, 11.131
reg 3(4) 11.132
reg 5(1) 11.132
reg 5(1)(b)(i), (ii) 11.132
reg 5(1)(c), (d) 11.132
reg 5(6) 11.132
reg 6(1) 11.132
reg 7(1) 11.132
reg 8 . . . . 11.132
reg 8(4) 11.132
reg 9 . . . . 11.132
regs 11–15 . . . . 11.132
Sch 1, Pt II, paras 6(3)(B), 6(4) 11.94
Sch 4 . . . . 11.132
High Hedges (Appeal) (England) Regulations
2005 (SI 2005/711) 11.130
Highways (Assessment of Environmental
Effects) Regulations 1988
(SI 1988/1241) 5.163, 15.14
Highways (Assessment of Environmental
Effects) Regulations 1999
(SI 1999/369) 15.14, 15.18
Highways (Environmental Impact
Assessment) Regulations 2007
(SI 2007/1062) 15.14

Landfill Allowances and Trading Scheme
(England) Regulations 2004
(SI 2004/3212) 7.272
Landfill (England and Wales)
Regulations 2002
(SI 2002/1599) 4.25, 7.257, 7.258
reg 1 . . . . 7.269
regs 2, 3 . . . . 7.268
reg 4 . . . . 7.260, 7.269
reg 5 . . . . 7.268, 7.269, 7.272
reg 6 . . . . 7.265, 7.273
reg 7 . . . . 7.273
reg 7(1) 7.258

reg 7(2), (3) 7.259
erg 8 . . . . 7.273
reg 8(1), (2) 7.260
reg 9 . . . . 7.260, 7.274
reg 11 . . . . 7.261
regs 13–15 . . . . 7.262
reg 17 . . . . 7.263
Sch 1—
paras 1, 3 . . . . 7.264
para 5 . . . . 7.264
paras 10, 11 . . . . 7.266
paras 14–16 . . . . 7.267
Part 3 . . . . 7.266
Sch 2 . . . . 7.268
Sch 3 . . . . 7.269
Sch 4 . . . . 7.270
Landfill (Scheme Year and Maximum Landfill
Amount) Regulations 2004
(SI 2004/1936) 7.271, 7.272
Lawnmowers (Harmonisation of Noise
Emission Standards) Regulations 1992
(SI 1992/168) 13.151
List of Wastes (England) Regulations 2005 (SI
2005/895) 7.15
Local Authorities (Access to Meetings and
Documents) (Period of Notice)
(England) Order 2002
(SI 2002/715) 5.41

Marine Works (Environmental Impact
Assessment) Regulations 2007 (SI
2007/1518) 15.14
Marketing of Gas Oil (Sulpher Content)
Regulations 1994 (SI 1994/2249) . 13.51
Merchant Shipping (Prevention of Pollution)
(Intervention) Order 1980 (SI
1980/1093) 3.25
Merchant Shipping (Prevention of Pollution)
(Law of the Sea Convention) Order 1996
(SI 1996/282) 3.25
Motor Cycle Silencer and Exhaust
Systems Regulations 1995
(SI 1995/2370) 13.140
Motor Cycles (Sound Level Measurement
Certificates) Regulations 1980
(SI 1980/765) 13.151
Motor Fuel (Composition and
Content) Regulations 1994
(SI 1994/2295) 13.52
reg 5 . . . . 13.53
reg 6 . . . . 13.53, 13.54
reg 6(1) 13.52
reg 8 . . . . 13.55

reg 8(3). 13.56

Motor Vehicles (Approval) Regulations 2001
   (SI 2001/25). 13.143

Motor Vehicles (EC Type Approval)
   Regulations 1992
   (SI 1992/3107). 13.151

Motor Vehicles (Type Approval for Goods
   Vehicles) (Great Britain) Regulations
   1982 (SI 1982/1271) 13.151

National Assembly for Wales (Transfer of
   Functions) Order 1999 (SI 1999/672,
   11.02) 2.07, 2.17, 11.02

Nature Conservation and Amenity Lands
   (Northern Ireland) Order 1985
   (NI 1985/1) 11.77, 11.78, 11.87

Nitrate Vulnerable Zones (Additional
   Designations) (England) (No. 2)
   Regulations 2002
   (SI 2002/2614). 9.29

Noise Emissions in the Environment by
   Equipment for Use Outdoors Regulations
   2001 (SI 2001/1701) 13.113

regs 4, 5 . . . . 13.114
reg 6. . . . . 13.117
regs 7–9 . . . . 13.115
reg 18. . . . . 13.116
regs 20, 21 . . . . 13.116
Sch 1 . . . . 13.117
Sch 2 . . . . 13.118
Sch 3 . . . . 13.115
Sch 6 . . . . 13.119
Sch 13 . . . . 13.119
   paras 1–3 . . . . 13.120
   para 6. . . . . 13.120
   paras 12, 13 . . . . 13.121

Notification of Installations Handling
   Hazardous Substances Regulations 1982
   (SI 1982/1357). 8.75, 8.77
Sch 1 . . . . 8.76

Nuclear Installations (Dangerous
   Occurrences) Regulations 1965 (SI
   1965/1824) 5.156, 8.33

Nuclear Installations (Increase in Operator's
   Limits of Liability) Order 1994 (SI
   1994/909) 8.27

Nuclear Installations Regulations 1971
   (SI 1971/1823)—
reg 3. . . . . 8.97

Off-Shore Marine (Natural Habitats & etc)
   Regulations 2007
   (SI 2007/1842). 11.46, 11.49

Packaging (Essential Requirements)
   Regulations 2003
   (SI 2003/1941). 7.77

Petroleum Consolidation Act
   (Enforcement) Regulations 1979
   (SI 1979/427). 2.34

Pipe-Line Works (Environmental Impact
   Assessment) Regulations 2000
   (SI 2000/1928). 15.14

Planning (Hazardous Substances) Regulations
   1992 (SI 1992/656) 8.67, 8.70,
                   8.73, 8.111, 8.122
Part 3 (regs 5–13) 8.82
reg 5 . . . . 8.82
reg 5(3). 8.96
regs 6, 7 . . . . 8.83, 8.91
reg 8 . . . . 8.83
reg 10 . . . . 8.84
reg 14 . . . . 8.75
reg 17(2). 8.119
reg 17(3). 8.120
regs 18, 19 . . . . 8.121
reg 22 . . . . 8.127
reg 23 . . . . 8.135
Sch 1 . . . . 8.67, 8.68, 8.76
   Part D 8.69
Sch 2 . . . . 8.96
Sch 3 . . . . 8.78
Sch 4—
   Parts 1–4 . . . . 8.122
   Part 5 . . . . 8.122, 8.124, 8.130

Pollution Prevention and Control Regulations
   2000 (SI 2000/1973) 5.135, 6.01
reg 28. . . . . 5.134, 5.135
reg 29. . . . . 5.134, 5.136
regs 30, 31 . . . . 5.134
Sch 2 . . . . 5.136
Sch 9, paras 4, 5 . . . . 5.137

Prison (Amendment) Rules 1992
   (SI 1992/514). 7.106

Private Water Supply Regulations 1991
   (SI 1991/2790). 5.164, 10.99,
                       10.125, 12.44

Producer Responsibility Obligations
   (Packaging Waste) Regulations 1997
   (SI 1997/648). 2.14

Protection of Water Against Agricultural Nitrate
   Pollution (England and Wales) Regulations
   1996 (SI 1996/888) 9.29

Protection of Water Against Agricultural
   Nitrate Pollution (England and Wales)
   (Amendment) Regulations 2006 (SI
   2006/1289) 9.30

Radioactive Contaminated Land (Modification
   of Enactments) (England) Regulations
   2006 (SI 2006/1379) 12.26
Radioactive Material (Road Transport)
   Regulations 2002
   (SI 2002/1735). 8.61
Radioactive Substances (Appeals) Regulations
   1969 (SI 1990/2504) 8.45
Radioactive Substances (Electronic Valves)
   Exemption Order 1967
   (SI 1967 /1797) 8.42, 8.48
Radioactive Substances (Exhibitions)
   Exemption Order 1962
   (SI 1962/2645). 5.162, 8.42
Radioactive Substances (Gaseous Tritium
   Light Devices) Exemption Order 1985
   (SI 1985/1049). 5.162, 8.42,
                       8.48, 8.50
Radioactive Substances (Geological Specialism)
   Exemption Order 1962
   (SI 1962/2712). 8.50
Radioactive Substances (Hospitals) Exemption
   Order 1990 (SI 1990/2512) 8.42
Radioactive Substances (Phosphatic
   Substances, Rare Earths etc) Exemption
   Order 1962 (SI 1962/2648) 5.162
Radioactive Substances (Precipitated
   Phosphate) Exemption Order 1963
   (SI 1963/1836). 8.42
Radioactive Substances (Schools etc)
   Exemption Order 1963 (SI No
   1963/1832) 8.42
Radioactive Substances (Smoke Detectors)
   Exemption Order 1980
   (SI 1980/953). 5.162, 8.42, 8.50
Radioactive Substances (Substances of Low
   Activity) Exemption Order 1986
   (SI 1986/1002). 8.42
Radioactive Substances (Testing Instruments
   etc) Order 2006
   (SI 2006/1500). 8.38
Regulatory Reform (Deer) (England
   and Wales) Order 2007
   (SI 2007/2183). 11.113
Road Vehicles (Construction and Use)
   Regulations 1986
   (SI 1986/1078). 13.151
Rules of the Supreme Court 1965 (SI
   1965/1776) 4.58
  Ord 53—
  r 3(2)(a)(ii). 4.58
  r 4   4.62
  Ord 54. . . . . 7.196

Scotland Act (Commencement) Order 1998
   (SI 1998/3178). 11.02
Sludge (Use in Agriculture) Regulations
   1989 (SI 1989/1263) 7.152
Smoke Control Areas (Authorized Fuels)
   Regulations 1991
   (SI 1991/1282). 13.29
  reg 2. . . . . 13.29
  Sch 1, para 7. . . . . 13.29
Smoke Control Areas (Exempted Fireplaces)
   Order 1993 (SI 1993/2277) 13.39
Special Waste Regulations 2005
   (SI 2005/894). 4.25
Surface Waters (Abstraction for Drinking
   Water) (Classification) Regulations 1996
   (SI 1996/2001). 9.78
Surface Waters (Classification) Regulations
   1989 (SI 1989/1148) 9.78
Surface Waters (Dangerous Substances)
   (Classification) Regulations 1989 (SI
   1989/2286) 9.78, 12.44
Surface Waters (Dangerous Substances)
   (Classification) Regulations 1992
   (SI 1992/337). 9.78, 12.44
Surface Waters (Dangerous Substances)
   (Classification) Regulations 1997
   (SI 1997/2560). 9.78, 12.44
Surface Waters (Dangerous Substances)
   (Classification) Regulations 1998
   (SI 1998/389). 9.78, 12.44
Surface Waters (Fish Life) (Classification)
   Regulations 1997 (SI 1997/1331). . 9.78
Surface Waters (Fishlife) (Classification)
   (Amendment) Regulations 2003
   (SI 2003/1953). 9.78
Surface Waters (River Ecosystem)
   (Classification) Regulations 1994
   (SI 1994/1057). 9.78
Surface Waters (Shellfish)
   (Classification) Regulations 1997
   (SI 1997/1332). 9.79

Town and Country Planning (Application of
   Subordinate Legislation to the
   Crown) Order 2006
   (SI 2006/1286). 2.33
Town and Country Planning (Assessment of
   Environmental Effects) Regulations 1988
   (SI 1988/1199). 5.59, 5.60, 11.47,
         14.08, 15.04, 15.12, 15.14, 15.18,
           15.25, 15.32–15.36, 15.57
  reg 2(1). 5.60
  reg 4. . . . . 5.70

reg 4(2)........................15.04
reg 5..........................15.48
reg 7...........................5.74
reg 8...........................5.75
reg 9...........................5.74
reg 10..........................5.71
regs 13, 14 ....5.72
regs 16, 17 ....5.72
regs 20, 21 ....5.73
Sch 1 ....5.60, 5.61
Sch 2 ....5.60, 5.62–5.64, 5.69
Sch 4 ....5.76
Town and Country Planning (Determination
    of Appeals by Inspectors) (Inquiries
    Procedure) Rules 2000
    (SI 2000/1625)................5.82
rr 14, 15.......................5.82
Town and Country Planning (Development
    Plan) (England) Regulations 1999
    (SI 1999/3280)—
reg 20(2)......................14.81
Town and Country Planning (Environmental
    Assessment and Unauthorized
    Development) Regulations 1995
    (SI 1995/2258)......... 15.15, 15.18
Town and Country Planning (Environmental
    Impact Assessment) (England
    and Wales) Regulations
    1999 (SI 1999/293) 5.59,
        11.02, 11.47, 14.08, 15.03, 15.04,
        15.08, 15.12, 15.14, 15.15, 15.18,
        15.19, 15.25, 15.31, 15.32,
        15.34, 15.38, 15.50, 15.52,
        15.55, 15.57, 15.66
reg 2..........................11.48
reg 2(1)...... 15.04, 15.32, 15.34, 15.36,
        15.38, 15.52, 15.58, 15.59
reg 2(2).......................15.32
reg 2(3).......................15.31
reg 3.................... 14.08, 15.55
reg 3(2)................. 15.04, 15.59
reg 4(2)(a) 15.45
reg 4(3).......................15.45
reg 4(4).......................15.32
reg 4(5)................. 11.48, 15.41
reg 4(6).......................15.45
reg 4(8).......................15.37
reg 5..........................15.48
reg 5(1), (2) 15.48
reg 5(6).......................15.48
reg 7..........................15.45
regs 8, 9 ....15.49
reg 10.........................15.57

reg 10(7)......................15.58
regs 13, 14 ....15.64
regs 16–18 ....15.64
reg 19.........................15.55
reg 19(7)......................15.55
reg 19(10).....................15.55
reg 20.........................15.45
reg 20(1), (2) 15.64
reg 21(1)(c) 15.66
reg 21(2)......................15.66
reg 22................... 15.04, 15.53
regs 23–25 ....15.04
reg 26................... 15.04, 15.51
reg 26B........................15.16
regs 27, 28 ....15.51
reg 32.........................14.08
reg 32(2)......................15.04
reg 34(2)......................15.18
reg 35(2)......................14.29
reg 35(3)......................15.48
reg 35(8)......................15.49
Sch 1 ....11.48, 14.08, 15.06,
        15.13, 15.32–15.35, 15.40,
        15.45, 15.46, 15.48
para 1(d)......................15.35
paras 9–11 ....15.33
para 17(a).....................15.33
para 19.......................15.33
Sch 2 .... 11.48, 14.08, 15.06, 15.13,
        15.29, 15.32–15.41, 15.43–15.46,
        15.48, 15.49, 15.61
para 3(g)......................15.33
para 3(i) 15.35
para 4.........................15.35
para 6(a)......................15.40
para 10........................15.35
para 11(b).....................15.35
para 12........................15.35
para 13........................15.40
para 13(ii).....................15.40
Sch 3 .... 11.48, 15.36, 15.40, 15.41,
        15.42, 15.52
Sch 4 ....11.48, 15.25, 15.52, 15.57
Part I 15.52, 15.53
Part II................ 15.52, 15.54
Town and Country Planning (Environmental
    Impact Assessment) (England and
    Wales) (Amendment) Regulations 2000
    (SI 2000/2867)...............15.32
Town and Country Planning
    (Environmental Impact Assessment)
    (Amendment) Regulations 2006
    (SI 2006/3295)......... 15.19, 15.32

Town and Country Planning (Environmental
  Impact Assessment) (Wales)
  (Amendment) Regulations 2006
  (SI 2006/3099). 15.19, 15.32
Town and Country Planning (General
  Permitted Development) Order 1995
  (SI 1995/418). 2.38, 11.82, 14.30
  art 1(5). 11.88, 11.89, 14.31
  art 1(5)(b) 11.90
  art 1(6). 11.89, 14.31
  art 3 . . . . 14.35, 14.36
  art 3(1). .14.31
  art 3(10). .15.15
  art 4(1). .14.31
  art 8 . . . . .14.61
  art 19 . . . . .14.61
  art 22 . . . . .14.31
  Sch 2—
  Part 1 . . . . 11.88–11.90, 14.30
  Part 2 . . . . .14.30
  Part 3 . . . . .14.28
  Part 4 . . . . .14.30
    Class B .11.70
  Part 6 . . . . 11.132, 14.30
    Class A 11.88, 11.89
  Part 7 . . . . 11.88, 14.30, 15.14
    Class A 11.88, 11.89
  Part 8 . . . . 11.88–11.90, 14.30
  Parts 12–16 . . . . .14.30
  Part 17 . . . . .9.71, 11.88–11.90
  Part 18 . . . . .14.30
  Parts 19–23 . . . . .14.30
  Part 24 . . . . 11.88–11.90, 11.132,
                                   14.30, 14.52
  Part 25 . . . . 11.88–11.90, 14.30
Town and Country Planning (General
  Development Procedure) Order 1995
  (SI 1995/419). 5.52, 5.80, 11.82,
                                 14.100–14.102
  art 1(2), (6). 5.52
  art 3(2). 15.55
  art 7 . . . . .5.52
  art 8 . . . . .5.55
  art 8(3). 5.56
  art 8(4), (5). 5.58
  art 9 . . . . .5.80
  art 10 . . . . .14.100
  art 10(1)(u) 11.71, 11.82
  art 19(zd), (ze) 14.100
  art 14(2). .15.49
  art 25 . . . . .5.54
Town and Country Planning (Inquiries
  Procedure) Rules 2000
  (SI 2000/1624). 5.82

Town and Country Planning (Listed
  Buildings and Conservation Areas)
  Regulations 1990
  (SI 1990/1519). 14.69, 14.72
Town and Country Planning (Local
  Development) (England) Regulations
  2004 (SI 2004/2204)—
  reg 15. . . . . .14.81
Town and Country Planning (Mayor of
  London) Order 2000
  (SI 2000/1493). 14.23
Town and Country Planning (Mayor of
  London) Order 2008
  (SI 2008/580). 14.23
Town and Country Planning (Trees)
  Regulations 1999
  (SI 1999/1892). 11.123, 11.124
  reg 2(1)–(3) 11.123
  reg 3(1), (2) 11.123
  reg 4(1). .11.123
  reg 6. . . . . .11.123
  reg 10(2). 11.124
  Sch 11.123, 11.124
    para 5(1). 11.125
    para 5(1)(b) 11.124
    para 5(1)(d) 11.125
Town and Country Planning
  (Use Classes) Order 1987
  (SI 1987/764). 14.28, 14.29
  Art 3(6) 14.29
  Art 3(6)(g) 14.29
Trade Effluents (Prescribed Processes and
  Substances) Regulations 1989
  (SI 1989/1156). 10.168
Trade Effluents (Prescribed Processes and
  Substances) Regulations 1992
  (SI 1989/339). 10.168
Trans-frontier Shipment of Waste
  Regulations 1993
  (SI 1993/3031). 8.63
Trans-frontier Shipment of Waste Regulations
  1994 (SI 1994/1137) 7.88, 7.208
  reg 11. . . . . .7.88
Trans-frontier Shipment of Waste
  Regulations 2007
  (SI 2007/1711). 3.07, 3.28
Transport and Works (Assessment of
  Environmental Effects) Regulations 1995
  (SI 1995/1541). 15.14, 15.15
Under-sized Lobsters Order 1993 (SI
  1993/1178) 11.117
United Utilities Water plc (Ullswater)
  (Drought) Order 2003
  (SI 2003/3341). 9.62

Urban Waste Water Treatment (England and
    Wales) Regulations 1994
    (SI 1994/2481). 9.109, 10.176,
                        10.177, 10.178
  reg 5. . . . . .10.178
  reg 7. . . . . .10.179
  reg 8. . . . . 10.179, 10.180
  Sch 4. . . . . .10.179
Urban Waste Water Treatment (England and
    Wales) (Amendment) Regulations 2003
    (SI 2003 No 1788) 9.109, 10.176,
                        10.177, 10.178

Waste Management Licensing Regulations
    1994 (SI 1994/1056) 5.86, 7.63,
    7.64, 7.67, 7.69, 7.95, 7.96, 7.104,
    7.144, 7.198, 7.213, 7.218, 7.230,
                        9.25, 14.12
  reg 2. . . . . .7.230
  reg 2(1). 7.172
  reg 3. . . . . .7.181
  reg 4. . . . . .7.183
  reg 4(1), (2) 7.184
  reg 6. . . . . .7.193
  reg 6(2). 7.193
  reg 7. . . . . .7.193
  reg 9. . . . . .7.196
  reg 10(1). 5.90
  reg 10(1)(a) 5.86
  reg 10(3). 5.91
  reg 10(4). 5.87
  reg 11(1), (2) 5.92
  reg 14. . . . . .7.191
  reg 15. . . . . 7.191, 9.22
  reg 16. . . . . .7.105
  reg 17(2), (3) 7.144
  reg 17(4). 7.145
  reg 17(5). 7.148
  reg 19. . . . . .14.89
  Sch 1 . . . . .7.230
  Sch 3 . . . . .7.146
    para 1. . . . . .7.146
  Sch 4 . . . . 7.64, 14.89
    para 2(2). 14.91
    para 4. . . . . .7.65
    para 9(7). 7.187
    para 4(1). 7.145
    para 9. . . . . .7.65
    Part II. 7.65
  Annex 1, para 1.5 . . . . .7.96
Water Act 2003 (Commencement No 6,
    Transitional Provisions and Savings)
    Order 2006 (SI 2006/984) 9.32

Water and Sewerage (Conservation,
    Access and Recreation) (Code of
    Practice) Order 2000
    (SI 2000/477). 2.60, 9.11
Water Environment (Oil Storage)
    (Scotland) Regulations 2006
    (SI 2006/133). 9.25
Water Environment (Water Framework
    Directive) (England and Wales)
    Regulations 2003
    (SI 2003/3242). 9.05, 9.16,
                        9.18, 11.58
  reg 2(2). 9.19
  reg 4. . . . . .9.18
  regs 5, 6 . . . . .9.20
  reg 8. . . . . .9.20
  reg 10. . . . . .9.18
  reg 11. . . . . 9.18, 9.20
  regs 12–16 .9.18
  reg 17. . . . . .9.19
Water Environment (Water Framework
    Directive) (Northern Ireland)
    Regulations 2003 . . . . .11.58
Water Environment (Water Framework
    Directive) (Northumbria River Basin
    District) Regulations 2003
    (SI 2003/3245). 9.16
Water Industry (Charges) (Vulnerable
    Groups) Regulations 1999
    SI 1999/3441. . . . . .10.222
Water Industry (Charges) (Vulnerable
    Groups) (Amendment) Regulations
    2000 (SI 2000/519) 10.222
Water Industry (Charges) (Vulnerable
    Groups) (Amendment) Regulations
    2003 (SI 2003/552) 10.222
Water Industry (Charges) (Vulnerable
    Groups) (Amendment) Regulations
    2005 (SI 2005/59) 10.222
Water (Prevention of Pollution)
    (Code of Practice) Order 1998
    (SI 1998/3084). 2.60, 9.11
Water Resources (Abstraction and
    Impounding) Regulations 2006
    (SI 2006/641). 9.36, 9.41,
                        9.46, 9.52
  regs 3, 4 . . . . .9.41
  regs 6–10 . . . . .9.41
  reg 12. . . . . 9.41, 9.46
  reg 13. . . . . .9.41
  reg 31. . . . . .9.56
  reg 33. . . . . .9.54
  reg 34. . . . . .9.41
  reg 37. . . . . .9.41

Water Resources (Abstraction and Impounding)
    Regulations 2006 (SI 2006/641) (*cont.*)
    Sch 2 . . . . 9.41
    Part 3 . . . . 9.41
Water Resources (Environmental Impact
    Assessment) (England and Wales)
    Regulations 2006
    (SI 2006/3124). 15.14
Water Resources (Licences) Regulations
    1965 (SI 1965/534) 9.41
Water Supply and Sewerage Services
    (Customer Service Standards)
    Regulations 1993
    (SI 1993/500). 10.53, 10.132
Water Supply and Sewerage Services
    (Customer Service Standards)
    (Amendment) Regulations 1996
    (SI 1996/3065). 10.53
Water Supply and Sewerage Services
    (Customer Service Standards)
    (Amendment) Regulations 2000
    (SI 2000/2301). 10.53, 10.132
Water Supply Licence (Applications)
    Regulations 2005
    (SI 2005/1638). 10.114
Water Supply Licence (Prescribed Water
    Fittings Requirements) Regulations
    2005 (SI 2005/3077) 10.106
Water Supply (Water Fittings) Regulations
    1999 (SI 1999/1148) 10.106
Water Supply (Water Fittings)
    (Amendment) Regulations 1999
    (SI 1999/1506). 10.106
Water Supply (Water Quality) Regulations
    1989 (SI 1989/1147) 5.164
Water Supply (Water Quality)
    (Amendment) Regulations 1989
    (SI 1989/1384). 5.164
Water Supply (Water Quality)
    Regulations 2000
    (SI 2000/3184). 9.78, 10.99, 12.44
Water Supply (Water Quality)
    Regulations 2001
    (SI 2001/3911). 9.78, 10.99
Water Supply (Water Quality)
    (Amendment) Regulations 2001
    (SI 2001/2885). 10.99
Wildlife and Countryside Act 1981
    (Variation of Schedule) Order 1988
    (SI 1988/288). 11.93

Wildlife and Countryside Act 1981
    (Variation of Schedule) Order 1989
    (SI 1989/906). 11.93
Wildlife and Countryside Act 1981
    (Variation of Schedule) Order 1991
    (SI 1991/367). 11.93
Wildlife and Countryside Act 1992
    (Variation of Schedule) Order 1992
    (SI 1992/320). 11.93
Wildlife and Countryside Act 1981
    (Variation of Schedule) Order 1992
    (SI 1992/2350). 11.93
Wildlife and Countryside Act 1981
    (Variation of Schedule) Order 1992
    (SI 1992/2674). 11.93
Wildlife and Countryside Act 1981
    (Variation of Schedule) Order 1992
    (SI 1992/3010). 11.93
Wildlife and Countryside Act 1981
    (Variation of Schedule) Order 1994
    (SI 1994/1151). 11.93
Wildlife and Countryside Act 1981
    (Variation of Schedule) Order 1997
    (SI 1997/226). 11.93
Wildlife and Countryside Act 1981
    (Variation of Schedule) Order 1998
    (SI 1998/878). 11.93
Wildlife and Countryside Act 1981
    (Variation of Schedule) Order 2007
    (SI 2007/1843). 11.93
Wildlife and Countryside (Registration and
    Ringing of Certain Captive Birds)
    Regulations 1982
    (SI 1982/1221). 11.102
Wildlife and Countryside (Registration to
    Sell Certain Dead Birds)
    (Amendment) Regulations 1982
    (SI 1982/1219). 11.101
Wildlife and Countryside (Registration to
    Sell Certain Dead Birds)
    (Amendment) Regulations 1991
    (SI 1991/479). 11.101
Wildlife and Countryside (Ringing of
    Certain Birds) Regulations 1982
    (SI 1982/1220). 11.101
Wildlife (Northern Ireland) Order 1985
    (NI 1985/761) 11.84

PART 1

THE FRAMEWORK

1

THE HISTORY OF ENVIRONMENTAL LAW

A. **Introduction**	1.01	
B. **The Cholera Epidemic of 1831**	1.02	
Conclusions of the report into		
the cholera epidemic	1.03	
Sanitary conditions	1.03	
Overcrowding	1.04	
Expectation of life	1.05	
Administrative reform	1.06	
C. **The Public Health Act 1848**	1.07	
Boards of health	1.08	
Drains and sewers	1.09	
Street and house cleansing	1.10	
Rivers and sewers	1.12	
Sanitation and overcrowding	1.13	
D. **The Public Health Act 1875**	1.14	
The scheme of the Act	1.14	
Drainage of buildings	1.16	
Disposal and treatment of sewage	1.17	
Refuse and sewage collection	1.18	
Water supplies	1.19	
Cellars and lodging houses	1.21	
Statutory nuisances	1.22	
Slums	1.25	
Diseases and hospitals	1.26	
Burial of the dead	1.29	
E. **Water Pollution**	1.31	
Introduction	1.31	
Refuse in watercourses	1.32	
Prosecutions	1.34	
Defences	1.36	

F. **Unfit Housing**	1.38	
G. **Housing Act 1890**	1.42	
Introduction	1.42	
Procedure under the Act	1.43	
Clearing the slums	1.46	
Compulsory purchase	1.48	
Unfit houses	1.49	
H. **Town and Country Planning**	1.53	
Introduction	1.53	
The mechanism of the Act of 1909	1.54	
Enforcement	1.57	
Social changes 1918–1939	1.58	
Town and Country Planning Act 1932	1.59	
Development control—development		
orders	1.62	
Buildings of architectural or		
historic interest	1.65	
Compensation for planning decisions	1.66	
I. **Modern Developments in**		
Environmental Law	1.67	
Introduction	1.67	
Town and Country Planning Act 1947	1.70	
The National Parks and Access to the		
Countryside Act 1949	1.71	
The Clean Air Acts	1.74	
Wastes	1.76	
Noise	1.83	
Air pollution	1.84	
J. **The Integrated Approach—**		
Modern Legislation	1.85	

A. Introduction

There is an occasional temptation to think of the nineteenth-century English **1.01** countryside as a landscape by Constable or Turner made real, and of the towns as nothing but the backdrop to a scene from *Pickwick Papers*. A reading of two or three pages of Sir Edwin Chadwick's *Report into the Sanitary Conditions of the Poor* removes such temptation, peremptorily and permanently. Its publication in 1842 can legitimately be seen as the birth, or at any rate the conception, of environmental law in England and Wales. As often happens, it took something approaching disaster to bring action from those in high places.

B. The Cholera Epidemic of 1831

1.02 In 1831, a cholera epidemic began to make its way across Europe from the east. It reached the British Isles in 1832, and continued for many months. Cholera is a water-borne disease, not one which is the result of malnutrition or of living in insanitary or inadequate conditions. The alarm which the epidemic generated was enough to galvanize Ministers into requiring the Poor Law Commissioners to investigate the causes of the spread of the disease and to recommend how it should be prevented or controlled in future.

Conclusions of the report into the cholera epidemic

Sanitary conditions

1.03 First, the authors perceived that there was a direct relationship between the insanitary conditions in which many people lived, the defective or non-existent drainage of their houses, the contaminated water which they drank, and overcrowding in their dwellings, on the one hand, and disease, shortened expectation of life, and antisocial behaviour, on the other. The examples, of which there were dozens, showed that just as there was no real distinction between town and country, so there was none between north and south, or east and west. Things were as bad in Dorchester as in Durham.

Overcrowding

1.04 The second, and not altogether separate point, urged on Parliament in the report was that the gross overcrowding led the poor, even the deserving ones, into temptations which were virtually irresistible. At Mottisfont, near Romsey in Hampshire, the Medical Officer of the union described how 14 members of one family slept in one room, where the mother was in labour at the time, two of the sleepers being a boy and girl of 18. The results were as might be expected.[1]

---

[1] Chadwick, *Report into the Sanitary Conditions of the Poor*, 191.

Expectation of life

The Commissioners directed their third main proposition at the pockets of the **1.05**
politicians and their supporters whose votes would be needed if the suggested
reforms were to become law. One witness told how the daughters of the agricultural workers in his area became the mothers of bastards and filled the workhouses,
so becoming a burden on the ratepayers. The boys were drunks and layabouts, and
petty criminals who burdened the rates whenever they were prosecuted for poaching and theft.[2] In short, early Victorian England was more Hogarth than
Constable.

Administrative reform

The fourth and last recommendation was that the administration of any legisla- **1.06**
tion which might be passed to address the obvious horrors which had been
described should be conducted by experts, preferably in Whitehall. The Courts
Leet, and other medieval hangovers, should be replaced by professionals.

C. The Public Health Act 1848

Eventually, Parliament passed the first modern statute which bore upon the topic, **1.07**
the Public Health Act 1848. The machinery of the Act exemplified the two main
defects of the statute as a whole—it was largely permissive, and did not compel
those potentially responsible to take action; secondly, it left the initiative to the
ratepayers who all too clearly had a financial interest in letting matters lie, since to
take action would cost them money.

Boards of health

If the ratepayers decided to bring the Act into force in their area, the local Town or **1.08**
Borough Council became the Local Board of Health, with the functions which
this status involved.[3] The franchise was narrow, with residential, property, and
sexual restrictions (women, almost inevitably, had no votes in council elections).

Drains and sewers

The Act, for the first time, distinguished public from private sewers, and vested **1.09**
the former in the Boards of Health. It also, again for the first time, required new
buildings to be connected to one or the other type of drain or sewer.

---

[2] Ibid, 324–325.
[3] *Public Health Act 1848*, s 12.

There was, of course, little point in requiring decent sanitation to be provided, if there were no powers to police the regulatory code. The Act conferred these powers on Local Boards in two ways. First, no new building could be erected without the Local Board's consent. Secondly, Local Boards were under a duty to ensure that all private drains, water closets, privies, cesspools, and ash-pits did not become nuisances. In order to discharge that duty they had power to enter and lay open the drains or other facilities, and to require that any nuisance should be ended. Failure to comply with that requirement, the precursor of the nuisance order and abatement notice, was a criminal offence, punishable with a fine.[4]

Street and house cleansing

1.10 Local Boards were given the duty of ensuring that the streets in their areas were kept swept and cleansed. Secondly, so that the ratepayers should not be burdened with the no doubt substantial cost of discharging that duty, the Boards were given power to make bye-laws requiring the occupiers of property to clean refuse from their premises and from the streets.[5]

1.11 Another of these residual powers given to Local Boards was to provide public conveniences.[6] It is ironic that, while Parliament perceived a need for these humdrum but welcome facilities in the first half of the nineteenth century, the last decade of the twentieth, which one might have taken to be more enlightened, has seen them virtually disappear from the major cities of the kingdom.

Rivers and sewers

1.12 The next enactment imposed a duty on Local Boards to clean or to cover open drains, streams, and sewers.[7] Since these had been a major source of cholera infection, it is no surprise that this measure was passed.

Sanitation and overcrowding

1.13 Miscellaneous controls over what would now be called special industrial uses, such as slaughterhouses, were introduced. Local Boards were also empowered to regulate the letting of cellars for human habitation, and to provide baths, wash houses, and mortuaries.

---

[4] Ibid, s 54.
[5] Ibid, s 55.
[6] Ibid, s 57.
[7] Ibid, s 58.

D. The Public Health Act 1875

The scheme of the Act

The Public Health Act 1875 ran to 343 sections and five schedules. Its main **1.14**
purpose was to strengthen and elaborate the controls introduced by the Act of 1848.
It began this by establishing urban and rural sanitary districts, administered by borough councils and Local Boards in urban areas, and by rural sanitary authorities
elsewhere.[8] These authorities became the owners of all sewers except private sewers
(echoing the Act of 1848 in this), land drains, and sewers under the authority of the
Crown.[9]

Sanitary authorities were made subject to a duty to maintain their sewers, and to **1.15**
a further duty to build such sewers as were needed to drain their districts effectu-
ally. The sewers had also to be kept so as not to be a nuisance or injurious to
health.[10] The Act expressly prohibited the building or use of sewers so as to
discharge untreated sewage into a stream or watercourse, canal, pond, or lake.

Drainage of buildings

A new provision, which was based on the Act of 1848, but extended it, entitled the **1.16**
owner or occupier of any premises to connect his drains with any public sewer,
on giving notice and complying with the authority's bye-laws.[11] The converse
of this right was that the local authority had power to require owners and occupiers
to make a covered drain or drains to connect with a public sewer, provided
that the latter was within 100 feet of the house in question. If no such sewer existed,
then the authority could require the drains to connect to a cesspool or other place.[12]

Disposal and treatment of sewage

The Act empowered, without requiring, local authorities to construct sewage **1.17**
works within their districts, and to make arrangements with other authorities for
the treatment of the sewage arising in each other's areas.[13] By contrast, the powers
of the earlier Act over factories were extended significantly, in that local authorities
were enabled to require the provision of lavatory accommodation for both sexes
without restriction on the number of employees in the premises. Another example

---

[8] Public Health Act 1875, ss 5 and 6.
[9] Ibid, s 13.
[10] Ibid, ss 15 and 19.
[11] Ibid, s 21.
[12] Ibid, s 23.
[13] Ibid, s 27.

of the rise in general standards and change of attitude was the requirement that all new or rebuilt dwellings should have water closets or other sanitary provision as a matter of course.

The public became involved in the policing of the 1875 Act. Any person could complain in writing to the local authority that any drain or privy, but not a sewer, was a nuisance or injurious to health. The local authority could then empower a surveyor or inspector to enter private premises and inspect the offending equipment, if necessary opening the ground. If the nuisance or injury to health was found to be substantiated, the authority could require the owner or occupier of the premises to do the necessary works, upon penalty of a fine in case of failure to comply.[14]

Refuse and sewage collection

1.18 Another step forward was the extension of the powers and duties which resulted in improved provision for the collection of refuse and sewage from earth closets and privies, and the cleansing of streets. Local authorities were given the power and, if required by the Local Government Board, put under a duty, to remove house refuse from dwellings; to cleanse earth closets and other sanitary facilities other than water closets; and to clean the streets in their areas.[15]

Water supplies

1.19 The absence of a guaranteed supply of pure water had, as will be recalled, been a major source of disease in the 1840s. The Act of 1875 attempted to deal with this problem also, by giving local authorities power to supply water within their districts. If the power was exercised, the authority was put under a duty to keep the water pure and wholesome.[16]

1.20 Pollution in general was attacked by giving local authorities power to take proceedings by bill in Chancery (the predecessor of the injunction) to protect any watercourse within their jurisdictions from sewage pollution, and to close polluted wells, tanks, and cisterns, on application to a magistrates' court.[17]

Cellars and lodging houses

1.21 Cellar dwellings and common lodging houses, as has been seen, figured prominently in the Act of 1845. The controls were elaborated and extended. Common lodging houses were made subject to a system of registration and their owners

---

[14] Ibid, s 41.
[15] Public Health Act 1875, s 42.
[16] Ibid, ss 51 and 55.
[17] Ibid, ss 69 and 70.

required to meet not very exacting standards of maintenance, such as an obligation to limewash the internal walls and ceilings twice a year.[18]

Statutory nuisances

A major change introduced by the Act of 1875 was the creation of the notion of a statutory nuisance, which has remained a feature of public health law ever since. The definition of a statutory nuisance has changed little with the passing of time, and is discussed more fully elsewhere. Prophetically, Parliament made a defence available to industrialists that any accumulation or deposit necessary for the conduct of the business had not been kept longer than necessary, and that the best available means had been taken for preventing injury to health.   **1.22**

Local authorities were placed under a duty to inspect their districts with a view to teasing out the existence of statutory nuisances, and enforcing the requirements of private Acts in force in their districts requiring domestic fireplaces to consume their own smoke; commercial and industrial fireplaces and furnaces which failed to do so being defined as statutory nuisances.   **1.23**

Once satisfied of the existence of a nuisance, the authority was under a further duty to serve an abatement notice, failure to comply with which would make the offender liable to prosecution before a magistrates' court, and to an order requiring compliance with the demands of the abatement notice.[19] This procedure has survived with its essentials virtually unaltered.   **1.24**

Slums

The Act of 1875 also introduced the forerunner of the slum clearance legislation. For the first time, it enabled a house deemed to be unfit for human habitation to be vacated. The order for closure, which later became a closing order made under the Housing Acts, had to be made by a magistrates' court, with a right of appeal to Quarter Sessions.[20]   **1.25**

Diseases and hospitals

An entirely new area of regulation was introduced by a part of the Act dealing with infectious diseases and hospitals. A duty was imposed on local authorities, where their medical officers had represented that a house was in such a condition that it needed disinfecting in order to prevent or check infectious disease, to require the   **1.26**

---

[18] Ibid, ss 71–90.
[19] Ibid, ss 92–96.
[20] Ibid, ss 97–99.

owner or occupier to cleanse and disinfect the premises. This could include an order for the destruction of infected bedding, clothing, and other articles.[21]

1.27 Local authorities, for the first time, acquired power to build hospitals, to contract for the use of hospitals built by other bodies, and to recover the costs of treatment and the stay in hospital from the patient, unless he or she was a pauper.[22] A subsidiary power, to provide temporary supplies of medicine for the 'poorer inhabitants' of a district, was also conferred.

1.28 The same underlying purpose informed the part of the Act of 1875 which was expressly directed at the control of epidemic diseases, and which was also unprecedented.

Burial of the dead

1.29 The Local Government Board was given power to make regulations for the purposes of achieving the speedy interment of the dead; visiting houses in order to investigate the health of the occupiers; and providing medical aid and accommodation, cleansing, ventilating, disinfection, and guarding against the spread of disease 'whenever any part of England . . . appears to be threatened with or is affected by any formidable epidemic endemic or infectious disease'.

1.30 The remainder of the Act was not directly concerned with public health or environmental matters, but with the administrative arrangements of local authorities. It is, therefore, outside the scope of this book.

E. Water Pollution

Introduction

1.31 The early attempts to control pollution of watercourses and standing waters were, as has been seen, more or less perfunctory. Their inadequacy was recognized, at least by implication, when the Rivers Pollution Prevention Act became law in 1876. This was the first statute specifically targeted at pollution of water, rather than one where water contamination was treated as one of several factors relevant to public health in general. In essence the Act re-enacted the earlier provisions designed to stop the pollution of waters, and extended the pre-existing controls.

---

[21] Ibid, ss 120 and 121.
[22] Ibid, ss 131 and 132.

Refuse in watercourses

The Act began by making it a criminal offence to put or knowingly permit another 1.32
person to put solid refuse from a factory or quarry, rubbish or cinders, waste, or
'solid putrid matter' into a stream, so as to interfere with its flow or pollute the
water.[23]

The discharge of sewage into a watercourse was dealt with separately, but in the 1.33
same way, save that there was a defence that the best practicable and available
means of treating the sewage so that it was harmless had been taken before the discharge or escape.[24]

Prosecutions

The ultimate ineffectiveness of the Act was guaranteed by the restrictions which it 1.34
contained on taking proceedings against polluters. Sanitary authorities alone were
able to bring prosecutions under the Act, and then only with the consent of the
Local Government Board. Even then, there was no obligation to prosecute.

Given the complexity of these arrangements, which would have been remarkable 1.35
in Byzantium itself, the fact that the Act proved to be largely unworkable is hardly
surprising.

Defences

Where a sanitary authority was minded to bring a prosecution, the putative 1.36
defendant had a right to object in writing, and to demand a hearing by the sanitary authority at which he could try to persuade them not to prosecute, calling
witnesses and appearing in person or by agents.[25] Procedurally, therefore, the
number of bites at a variety of cherries which an ingenious defendant could take
was almost unlimited.

A further opportunity for procrastination and delay was given by the grant of a 1.37
right of appeal by way of case stated to the High Court from a county court order
under the Act.[26] Finally, and as if defendants needed yet more protection from the
consequences of their polluting actions, no prosecution could be brought unless
two months' written notice had previously been given.[27]

---

[23] Rivers Pollution Prevention Act 1876, s 2.
[24] Ibid, s 3.
[25] Ibid.
[26] Ibid, s 11.
[27] Ibid, s 13.

F. Unfit Housing

1.38 The growing power of officialdom was to be embodied in the enactment of the Housing Act 1890, which, for the first time, gave powers with teeth to bite landlords and others who allowed the conditions which had prevailed throughout living memory to continue.

1.39 In the towns, where the cost of providing running water and drainage was less and the returns greater, more progress in the improvement of housing had been made than had occurred in the country.

1.40 Even moderately prosperous townsfolk led lives which were hardly sybaritic. One tap and one lavatory to serve the needs of a whole family, the latter a windswept journey away from the house across a back yard, do not strike the late twentieth-century mind as excessively luxurious. Bathing was ceremonious, involving zinc baths filled with laboriously heated water.

1.41 Any temptation to view these arrangements as unduly primitive or insanitary should be resisted. As recently as the 1950s the bathing arrangements of at least one leading boys' public school were for all practical purposes identical. The more austere boarding houses there required that the water in the zinc baths should be cold—all year round.

G. Housing Act 1890

Introduction

1.42 As has been noted, Parliament responded to the continuing and widespread shortcomings in the nation's housing by passing the Housing Act 1890. This introduced a regime for dealing with slum housing which has proved enduring and survives in its essentials today.

Procedure under the Act

1.43 The machinery of the Act of 1890 could be started by twelve ratepayers or two Justices of the Peace. They could complain to the Medical Officer of Health for the area concerned (or to any Medical Officer of Health in London) that any houses, courts, or alleys were unfit for human habitation; or that the narrowness, closeness, and bad arrangement, or the bad condition of the streets and houses or groups of houses within the relevant area, or the want of light, air, ventilation, or proper conveniences, or any other sanitary defects, were dangerous or injurious to the health of the inhabitants of the buildings in question or of other buildings.

Thereafter the Medical Officer of Health was under a duty to inspect the area, and **1.44** make a report stating whether or not the area or a part of it was unhealthy or not. Alternatively, and this was the more common procedure in practice, the Medical Officer could make a report on his own behalf to the effect that the buildings or areas were unfit for human habitation, dangerous, or injurious to health.[28]

If the Medical Officer recommended that the defects in the houses or the area **1.45** could not be remedied other than by an improvement scheme for the rearrangement and reconstruction of the streets and houses or some of them, then the authority was bound to take the representation into consideration and to make a scheme if satisfied that the Medical Officer's opinion was correct, and that it had sufficient resources to carry out the scheme.[29] There was power to exclude parts of the area from the scheme, to house those displaced by the work, to provide proper sanitary arrangements, to identify land to be acquired compulsorily, and to provide for the improvements to be carried out by the freeholder of land within the area of the scheme under the local authority's supervision and control.[30]

Clearing the slums

Once Parliament had authorized an improvement scheme by statute, the author- **1.46** ity became under a duty to buy any land needed to bring the scheme into effect, and to take whatever other steps were necessary to implement it. This could be done by selling or letting the land included in the scheme, if necessary by granting a building lease which obliged the tenant to build, maintain, or repair the relevant buildings.

Private enterprise was given additional opportunities to participate in slum clear- **1.47** ance by a provision which required that any land which had been acquired under the Act and had not been sold or let to the private sector within five years of acquisition, should be sold by auction, and its future left to the open market, subject to its being redeveloped in accordance with the requirements of the relevant central government authority.[31]

Compulsory purchase

The compulsory purchase code enshrined in the Lands Clauses Acts applied to **1.48** the acquisition of land for the purpose of implementing the Act of 1890, with important exceptions. Where the premises were used for illegal purposes such as gaming or prostitution, any enhancement in value was to be ignored. Similarly,

---

[28] Ibid, ss 4 and 5.
[29] Ibid, s 4.
[30] Ibid, s 6.
[31] Ibid, ss 13 and 14.

if the premises were in such a state as to be a nuisance, in a state of defective sanitation, or dangerous to health, the compensation was to reflect the cost of remedying these defects, the amount being deducted from the arbitrator's award. Thirdly, and here the 1890 Act showed the shape of things to come, if the dwelling was unfit for human habitation, the compensation was to be the value of the land and of the materials of the buildings—what later came to be known as site value.[32]

Unfit houses

1.49 Similar provisions enabled local authorities, acting on representations from their Medical Officers, to close or demolish houses which were unfit for human habitation.

1.50 The owner had what now seems to be an inappropriate right of appeal to Quarter Sessions against a closing or demolition order.[33]

1.51 As is still true, the local authority had power under the Act of 1890 to promote redevelopment schemes of land declared to be the site of unfit housing—without such powers that land would have been no more than waste for an indefinite period.[34]

1.52 Common lodging houses evidently remained a cause of concern, because they were also the subject of attention in the Act of 1890. Part III gave local authorities powers to build, acquire, and manage these establishments. This, together with changes in the circumstances and expectations of the public, seems to have cured the problem, because lodging houses played little part in the deliberations of Parliament and in environmental legislation from then on.

H. Town and Country Planning

Introduction

1.53 The late nineteenth-century was a time of rapid spread of urban development coinciding with a period when architectural taste was, at least in the opinion of the aesthetically inclined, singularly unfortunate, and eventually it became apparent that some sort of check on the efforts of speculative builders was needed in the interests of the countryside and its appearance.

---

[32] Ibid, ss 21–23.
[33] Ibid, s 35.
[34] Ibid, ss 38–40.

The mechanism of the Act of 1909

This momentous step was taken, almost apologetically, by tacking 14 sections **1.54** onto an Act of which Part I, consisting of 53 sections, dealt with the related but separate topic of unfit housing. Part I of the Act of 1909 made a large number of individually insignificant amendments to the Housing Act 1890, but the main object of the Act of 1909 was plainly to adjust the law governing the improvement and removal of unfit housing.

If a local authority was able to satisfy the Local Government Board that there was **1.55** a prima facie case for making a scheme, then the latter could authorize the authority to prepare a town planning scheme, where the land involved was in the course of development or appeared likely to be used for building purposes. Land not likely to be used for building could also be included in the scheme if it was appropriate to do so, and buildings standing on such land could be demolished or altered in accordance with the scheme. The scheme had to be prepared with the general objects of securing proper sanitary conditions, and amenity and convenience in the laying out and use of land.[35]

The Local Government Board retained strict control over the way in which local **1.56** authorities dealt with their planning schemes. It could make regulations prescribing the way in which highways were built and stopped up or diverted; the erection of buildings and other structures; preservation of objects of historical interest or natural beauty; sewerage, lighting, and water supply; the dealing with or disposal of land by local authorities; their powers to enter into contracts with landowners and with other authorities; enforcement; and the time limits within which the scheme was to remain operative.[36]

Enforcement

The local authority was given power to remove, pull down, or alter any building **1.57** or other work in the area covered by the scheme where these contravened the scheme.[37] There was an additional power to carry out any work which the scheme required should be undertaken and which had not been executed, if the authority was of opinion that delay in doing the work would prejudice the operation of the scheme.[38]

---

[35] Housing, Town Planning etc Act 1909, s 54(1) and (2).
[36] Ibid.
[37] Ibid, s 57.
[38] Ibid.

Social changes 1918–1939

1.58 A mere five years after the 1909 Act became law, and before it had had time to make any real impact on the problems which it was designed to address, the country descended into the Armageddon of the 1914–18 war, and the control of development naturally assumed a low position in the nation's priorities. When life returned to normal in the 1920s, three features of social behaviour became particularly marked. First, there was a drift of population from north to south; second, a move from the city centres to the suburbs, especially in London and the Home Counties; and, third, steep rise in ownership and use of private motor cars. The response was the Town and Country Planning Act 1932.

Town and Country Planning Act 1932

1.59 Like its predecessor of 1909, the Act of 1932 relied heavily on the notion of the planning scheme, but, again, as with the Act of 1909, the function of drawing up a scheme was made permissive, rather than obligatory. The objects of a scheme were the securing of proper sanitary conditions, amenity and convenience, and (for the first time) preserving existing buildings or other objects of architectural, historic, or artistic interest and places of natural beauty.[39] For the first time, the influence of the heritage and conservation movements had made itself felt.

1.60 The fundamental principle, that local authorities were the architects of planning schemes, subject to the control of central government (in this instance the Minister of Health, who had taken over the functions of the Board of Works), was maintained.

1.61 Under the Act of 1932 a planning scheme could prohibit or regulate the development of land, prescribe the number of buildings in the area which it covered, and the space around them, their height, size, and design. The planning authority could impose restrictions on the way that the buildings were used, even to the extent of prohibiting the letting in separate 'tenements'.[40] Building operations could be regulated, or prohibited altogether.

Development control—development orders

1.62 The mechanics of development control under the Act of 1932 turned on the device of the interim development and supplementary orders, and direct action by the planning authority. An interim development order, like its successors, had to be made so as to apply pto all areas where resolutions to prepare schemes had

---

[39] Town and Country Planning Act 1932, s 1.
[40] Ibid, s 10. 'Tenement' is not defined, but appears to have referred to the letting of dwelling-houses in multiple occupation. Strictly, of course, 'tenement'means any holding in land, but the echoes of the nineteenth-century legislation regulating the overcrowding of dwelling-houses had not, apparently, died away by 1932.

been made but the scheme had not been approved, and the Minister also had power to make special orders applying to specific areas. The interim development orders either themselves permitted development or empowered the authorities to permit the development in question. Where an order prescribed that permission was required for the carrying out of development, then the authority could grant or refuse consent, but was deemed to have given unconditional consent if it had not given notice of its decision within two months.[41]

The supplementary order was designed to enable landowners to remedy omissions discovered in a scheme. If the scheme provided for making supplementary orders, owners of land could propose that such orders could be made adding to the contents of a scheme. The procedure for approval of the original scheme had to be followed, and if it survived this process the supplementary order became part of the scheme.[42]   **1.63**

The principal mechanism for enforcing control of development was action by the planning authority. Before taking action the authority was obliged to give six months' prior notice to any owner and occupier of the relevant building or land who would be affected by the action proposed. The authority could, on expiry of the notice, demolish or alter any building or work which did not conform with the scheme, whether erected before the scheme came into effect or afterwards.   **1.64**

Buildings of architectural or historic interest

The Act of 1932 also contained provisions calculated to protect buildings of special architectural or historic interest. After resolving to prepare a scheme, the planning authority could submit to the Minister an order directing that a building of such interest should not be demolished without its consent. There was no equivalent provision regulating the alteration of historic or beautiful buildings.   **1.65**

Compensation for planning decisions

The Act of 1932 contained a relatively simple code of compensation and betterment for owners of property affected by planning decisions. Where property was damaged or injuriously affected by the operation of a scheme, or a person suffered damage in consequence of enforcement action, or where expenditure was made abortive by a variation or revocation of a scheme, the loss was compensatable. Conversely, where a scheme, or the carrying out of enforcement action by an authority under a scheme, increased the value of property, the betterment was recoverable from the owner.[43] In several instances, for example, restrictions on the   **1.66**

---

[41] Ibid, s 10.
[42] Ibid, s 14.
[43] Ibid, ss 18 and 21.

height of buildings, or on use of buildings, or those made in the interests of health and safety, no compensation was payable.[44]

I. Modern Developments in Environmental Law

Introduction

1.67 Since the end of the Second World War, the development of the law in this field has been marked by two discernible trends. First, and this will cause no surprise to anyone who reads a newspaper or can switch on a television, continuously increasing awareness of environmental issues in the widest sense, as exemplified by the sustained interest in the activities of pressure groups such as Greenpeace, Friends of the Earth, and the Green Party (the latter being, like all political parties, in effect a pressure group).

1.68 Secondly, legislation until the 1990s tended to be enacted piecemeal and often in response to major disasters, actual or potential. Thus the Clean Air Act 1956 was the legislative consequence of a long period of thick fog in London (a genuine and nearly the last ever 'London Particular'), where the fog was green or yellow in colour, with a palpable and nauseating taste of sulphur. The fog led to widespread respiratory problems and several deaths, and it was realized that the uncontrolled use of coal fires in private houses and the discharge of large quantities of polluted smoke from commercial boilers had to come to an end.

1.69 Another example was the Deposit of Poisonous Wastes Act 1972, passed because Parliament was roused to activity by the discovery of poisonous waste which had been fly-tipped in Essex near a children's playground.

Town and Country Planning Act 1947

1.70 The first landmark piece of legislation of the modern era was the Town and Country Planning Act 1947. Where the Acts of 1909 and 1932 had been permissive, imposing control on building and development only where the local authority resolved to adopt and exercise the powers given them by statute, the Act of 1947 was obligatory. It required that planning controls should come into force automatically throughout England and Wales. It was in fact the basis of the system of planning control which survives 50 years later, and which is described fully elsewhere.

---

[44] Ibid, s 19.

The National Parks and Access to the Countryside Act 1949

As things returned to normal after the Second World War, people, and especially **1.71**
town dwellers, found themselves with more leisure and more disposable income.
They began, in increasing numbers, to spend their leisure in the countryside,
travelling there to an ever-increasing extent in private motor cars. It soon became
clear that the beauty of the most popular and attractive areas had to be protected
from violation by the numbers of people who wanted to visit and enjoy them in
their different ways. At the same time the interests of land owners had, if
possible, to be reconciled with the wishes of the many who wanted to make use of
land in which they had no direct interest. The National Parks and Access to the
Countryside Act 1949 was the response.

It established the concept of a National Park, administered at national level by an **1.72**
authority, the National Parks Commission, and locally by a Board responsible for
the park (as in the Lake District). Where the Park covered several local authority
areas, as in the Peak District National Park, which impinged on six countries, a
Joint Planning Board was the planning authority.[45] The concept was that public
access to a National Park was to be encouraged to an extent reconcilable with the
interests of the owners of land in the area, and the preservation of its natural
beauty.

The second achievement of the National Parks Act was to establish procedures for **1.73**
the identification of footpaths, bridleways, and other essentially recreational rights
of way in the countryside.[46] This created the system of definitive maps showing
the network of footpaths, bridleways, and other highways on maps prepared and
kept by county councils. It also provided for inquiries by which the existence or
non-existence of these rights of way could be established.[47]

The Clean Air Acts

The Clean Air Act 1956 was passed to deal with the problems of air pollution **1.74**
already described, and was conspicuously successful. The fundamental concept
was simple—it became a criminal offence to emit 'dark smoke' (an expression
which was not defined, and which was left to be determined by the courts as a
question of fact) from any chimney, subject to certain defences, as to which the
burden of proof, on the balance of probabilities, was laid on the defendant. For
example, the defence could escape liability if the smoke was emitted solely because

---

[45] National Parks and Access to the Countryside Act 1949, Part I. The National Parks
Commission was later replaced by the Nature Conservancy Council under the provisions of the
Countryside Act 1968. Its current name is 'Natural England' (see Natural Environment and Rural
Communities Act 2006).
[46] Ibid, Part III.
[47] Ibid.

a cold furnace was being lit up; or because it was impossible to obtain suitable fuel at the time of the emission.[48]

1.75 New furnaces were required to be fitted with plant which arrested grit and dust (what later came to be known as 'scrubbers').[49] Local authorities were given power to declare areas to be smoke control areas, in which it was an offence to emit smoke of any kind, dark or otherwise, from a chimney.[50] A consultative Clean Air Council was established to advise the Minister of Housing and Local Government about the progress made in abating the pollution of the air in England and Wales.[51]

Wastes

1.76 The Deposit of Poisonous Wastes Act 1972 was a vivid example, both of the way in which the development of environmental law occurred by way of reaction to events, and, consequently, of the fact that it was no more than patchy in its coverage of environmental concerns. The Act was short, consisting of no more than six sections, and, unusually, with no schedules. It created the criminal offence of depositing poisonous or other dangerous waste, without providing for a licensing system or identifying methods by which such wastes could be legitimately disposed of.[52]

1.77 In addition, the Act gave the right to claim damages in a civil action to any person who suffered damage due to the commission of an offence except where the damage was wholly due to the fault of the victim.

1.78 Prophetically, the Act recognized the contribution which operators of commercial tips (or waste disposal sites as they came, prolixly, to be called) could make to solving the problem of what to do with toxic waste, by providing that they were to be outside the Act, provided that the responsible local authority had been notified that the waste was to be dealt with by them.[53]

1.79 The growing concern of the public and politicians with all environmental matters was attested by two statutes passed in 1974. The Dumping at Sea Act was passed to bring into law the provisions of a Convention, to which the UK was a party, signed in 1972. It prohibited dumping of any substances or articles at sea unless a licence to do so was in force.[54]

---

[48] Clean Air Act 1956, s 1.
[49] Ibid, s 6.
[50] Ibid, s 11.
[51] Ibid, s 23. This is an early example of a quango.
[52] Deposit of Poisonous Wastes Act 1972, s 1.
[53] Ibid, s 4.
[54] Dumping at Sea Act 1974, s 1.

The concern to prevent dumping at sea was complemented by similar prohibi-   **1.80**
tions on pollution of inland waters, estuaries, and coastal waters contained in Part
II of the Control of Pollution Act 1974. This made it an offence to discharge sewage, trade effluent, or water from working mines into such waters, and empowered the Secretary of State for the Environment to make regulations specifying the
precautions to be taken for preventing the escape of pollutants into watercourses
and coastal waters.[55]

The Act also concerned itself with pollution by the dumping of waste on land,   **1.81**
noise, and burning of fuel so as to pollute the air. The provisions as to waste were
the forerunners of the duty of care legislation introduced into the corpus of environmental law by the Environmental Protection Act 1990. Without creating anything remotely as demanding as the duty of care under the Act of 1990, the
Control of Pollution Act 1974 required waste disposal authorities (a title reproduced in the Act of 1990) to prepare what were in effect waste disposal plans.[56]

The Act of 1974 also set up a code of licensing for waste disposal sites. It did not   **1.82**
impose responsibility for the sites upon owners after closure, as did the Act of
1990, but established a system under which waste licensing authorities were
bound to regulate waste disposal sites, and could impose conditions on the
licences, designed to ensure that the operation of the sites was well conducted. It
also continued the offence of depositing waste except on a licensed site and in
accordance with the licence and its conditions.[57] Other sections of the Act dealt
with refuse collection, the removal of waste from unlicensed sites, the handling
and disposal of toxic and hazardous waste, and specific sources of waste such as
coal mines and sewage works.[58]

Noise

Noise pollution was the subject of Part III of the Act of 1974. It gave local authori-   **1.83**
ties power to control noise from construction sites, which they had not previously
possessed, and enabled them to designate noise abatement zones, where noise
from premises could be controlled by measurement and recording of noise levels
within the zone. Noise in excess of the recorded level was not to be exceeded
except with the consent of the authority, and, if it was, a reduction notice, similar
to a noise abatement notice, could be served requiring the noise level to be reduced.
There was a right of appeal to a magistrates' court against a noise reduction notice,
and contravention of the notice was a criminal offence.[59]

---

[55] Ibid, ss 34–40.
[56] Control of PollutionAct 1974, s 1.
[57] Ibid, ss 3–10.
[58] Ibid, ss 11–28.
[59] Ibid, ss 63–66.

Air pollution

1.84 Its attempt to control atmospheric pollution was one of the less adventurous parts of the Control of Pollution Act. It did no more than empower the Secretary of State to make regulations governing the composition and contents of fuel used in motor vehicles, and limiting the amount of sulphur in fuels used in furnaces and engines.[60] There was also a section which made it an offence to burn insulation from a cable with a view to recovering metal from the cable. This hardly justified the parliamentary time spent in enacting it.[61]

J. The Integrated Approach—Modern Legislation

1.85 A child born at the turn of the twentieth-century, who in infancy saw a stagecoach drawn by horses pass his front door, could live to see television pictures of men walking on the moon, and that without reaching more than late middle age. The technical advances which made that possible were matched by increased knowledge of the effects of advances in civilization, if that is the correct word. As the UK Government put it:

> Ever since the Age of Enlightenment, we have had an almost boundless faith in our own intelligence and in the benign consequences of our actions. Whatever the discoveries of science, whatever the advances of commerce and industry, whatever the rate at which we multiplied as a species, whatever the rate at which we destroyed other species, whatever the changes we made to our seas and landscape, we have believed that the world would stay the same in all its fundamentals. We now know that this is no longer true.[62]

1.86 The realization described in that passage was the product of several separate influences.

1.87 The discovery of the greenhouse effect and the perforations in the ozone layer (a natural phenomenon of which no one outside the scientific community had even heard until about 1980); pollution of rivers and beaches; the effects on the health, particularly of children, of motor traffic; and, above all, the consciousness of the dire consequences of misuse or mishandling of nuclear power, highlighted by the Windscale fire in the 1950s and Chernobyl disaster in 1985, all combined to persuade government that an integrated attack on all types of environmental

---

[60] Ibid, ss 75 and 76.
[61] Ibid, s 78.
[62] White Paper *This Common Inheritance* Cmd 1200 (London HMSO, 1990). The passage quoted has power and impact not normally associated with such prosaic publications.
   141 See, for example, Environmental Information Regulations 2004 Planning Policy Statement 23 *Planning and Pollution Control* (ODPM 2005)

impact was required. All these have combined to bring about great and widespread public concern with all aspects of environmental protection.

The initial response was the flurry of legislation of the 1990s. The main statute **1.88** was the Environmental Protection Act 1990, which is covered in depth elsewhere. At the same time, the planning legislation was consolidated, re-enacted, and modernized in the Town and Country Planning Act 1990 and the Planning and Compensation Act 1991.The law regulating the administration of the water industry and the pollution of water was overhauled by the Water Resources Act 1991 and the Water Industry Act 1991. The Environment Act 1995 notably established the Environment Agency, which has power to control most types of pollution, in contrast to the multiplicity of enforcement authorities which it replaced. As has been observed above more than once, a notable and regrettable exception is pollution by motor vehicles. Even this omission is in the process of being remedied by the imposition of increasingly strict requirements upon the manufacturers of motor vehicles and upon drivers by traffic legislation which is outside the scope of this work.

The trend has continued into the new millennium. Central government policy **1.89** documents have increasingly concentrated on the control of pollution in the planning process. Quantities of European and UK primary legislation have been passed which emphasize the importance given to environmental matters, and will undoubtedly come forth for the foreseeable future.

There are even grounds for optimism. In recent years salmon have been reported **1.90** in the Rivers Thames and Tyne. In April 1996 there were accounts of the discovery of evidence that an otter was present on the banks of the Thames at Reading, where no otter had been seen for decades. The new laws may have been passed just in time.

2

THE STRUCTURE OF ENVIRONMENTAL LEGISLATION AND REGULATION

A. **Introduction**	2.01
B. **The Regulatory Framework**	2.05
Environmental statutes	2.05
Environmental Protection Act 1990 (EPA 1990)	2.06
The Water Resources Act 1991 and the Water Industry Act 1991	2.07
Environment Act 1995	2.08
Public health laws	2.10
Health and safety at work	2.11
Alternatives to regulation	2.12
C. **The Different Jurisdictions of the UK**	2.16
England and Wales	2.16
Scotland	2.18
Northern Ireland	2.22
The influence of other common law jurisdictions	2.24
D. **The Responsible Public Authorities**	2.26
The role of central government	2.26
Central government guidance	2.27
The crown and the royal prerogative	2.32
The local authorities	2.34
Other public bodies and executive agencies	2.36
Statutory undertakers	2.38
The Royal Commission on Environmental Pollution	2.39
Other research bodies	2.41
E. **The Environment Agency**	2.42
The establishment of the Agency	2.42
The legal structure of the Agency	2.44
The regional structure of the Agency	2.46

The specific responsibilities inherited by the Environment Agency	2.47
Her Majesty's Inspectorate of Pollution (HMIP)	2.48
The National Rivers Authority (NRA)	2.49
Waste and the waste regulation authorities	2.50
The Environment Agency's principal aims and objectives	2.52
The principal aim of the agency	2.53
The Environment Agency's general functions	2.55
General functions with respect to pollution control	2.55
General provisions with respect to water	2.56
General environmental and recreational duties	2.57
Incidental powers	2.59
Environment Agency guidance	2.60
The financial constraints on decisions made by the Environment Agency	2.62
F. **Prosecution and Enforcement of Environmental Offences**	2.65
Regulatory reform and risk-based regulation	2.67
Prosecutions	2.71
The Environment Agency as prosecutor	2.72
The decision to prosecute for an environmental offence	2.74
The Agency's enforcement and prosecution policy	2.75

Categorization of incidents	2.76	G. Holding Public Bodies to	
Other prosecution authorities		Account—Judicial Review	2.88
and the Code for Crown		H. Holding Public Bodies to	
Prosecutors	2.78	Account—Complaints to the	
Environmental sentencing	2.83	Ombudsman	2.96

A. Introduction

2.01 The structure of environmental law in the UK is becoming clearer. Large areas have been consolidated and modernized, and an increased emphasis is now placed on using an integrated approach to the different regimes and rules. But it is still necessary to analyse the huge subject of environmental law one topic at a time. Whilst this is partly in the interests of clarity, this also reflects the complex response adopted by lawyers and legislators to the growing concerns about the state of our environment. The history of this response has been described in the introductory chapter. The heart of this book analyses the main regimes which exist today to protect the environment, and which are intended to prevent, minimize, or render harmless any pollution. Whilst the focus of this book is necessarily on England and Wales, some useful legal parallels can be drawn from the other jurisdictions in the UK as well as from abroad.

2.02 There are important differences between the powers and duties of the various public authorities who administer the regulatory regimes. Whilst the central government departments set the main policy agenda, the main enforcement role lies with a standalone statutory authority, the Environment Agency, and the local authorities. Most people's contact will be them and the Environment Agency continues to play the dominant role. The continuing development of environmental law is intimately bound up with the way in which the Agency is able to operate.

2.03 It should be noted that it will often be necessary to refer to several chapters of this book over what might otherwise appear to be one incident. A good example of this overlap between the topics covered can be seen in the different ways in which the law was used to deal with the pollution incident at the heart of the *Cambridge Water Company* case.[1] The court case concerned the private property right to abstract water from the ground and was fought through the civil courts, relying on principles of common law and not statute law. But the whole context of the dispute was that damage had occurred to the water environment, namely the aquifer underneath the plaintiff's site. The pollution of this water by chemicals meant

---

[1] *Cambridge Water Company v Eastern Counties Leather* [1994] 2 AC 264, CA and HL. See, in particular, Chapter 16 Common Law Liability for further discussion of this important case.

that there had been a breach of the new UK water quality standards, which had been introduced as a result of European demands.[2] The pollution was therefore of concern to the regulatory authorities. Indeed, counsel for both parties to the civil action each submitted policy arguments in support of their respective causes.[3] The defendant was concerned to demonstrate that modern legislation, in regard to both the management of resources and the control of pollution, no longer made it either just or convenient that the common law should intervene to impose strict liability for the pollution of an aquifer. The plaintiff relied on the maxim 'the polluter should pay', which is embodied in the EEC Treaty, to support its claim. These principles provided the background to the courts' decisions.[4]

The practical results of the overlapping common law and statutory rights of action   **2.04** in the *Cambridge Water Company* case are instructive. After a prolonged and complex investigation, both the Water Authority[5] and the plaintiff company surmised that the defendant company's tannery was at least materially responsible for the pollution. The plaintiff company[6] brought an action against the defendant in negligence, nuisance, and under the rule in *Rylands v Fletcher*, claiming damages of about £1 million as well as injunctive relief. The Water Authority considered using its statutory powers to ensure that the pollution was cleaned up. It could choose either to prosecute the defendant company or to carry out certain remedial works at the company's expense.[7] The civil case did not succeed. The House of Lords ultimately dismissed the plaintiff's nuisance action, on the main ground that it had not been able to establish that the pollution of its water supply by the

---

[2] In 1982, the UK for the first time fixed specific parameters for such water, in order to implement the Directive relating to the Quality of Water intended for Human Consumption (80/778/EEC). Before, the dispute would have been whether or not the water was 'wholesome' as required under the statutory obligations then contained in the Water Act 1973.

[3] Summarized by Mann LJ [1994] 2 AC 264 at 276h.

[4] For instance, the remarks of Lord Goff in the House of Lords [1994] 2 AC 264 at 305e–h and 307c–d. It is notable that Lord Goff considered the broad approach to strict liability for hazardous operations of the Council of Europe, as well as the European Union, and the law in the USA.

[5] At the time, the public body responsible for regulating both water quality and water pollution, and for most water supplies in the area was the Anglian Water Authority. In the wake of the privatization of the water industry in 1989, this mix of responsibilities was seen as undesirable. Responsibility for water quality passed to the Drinking Water Inspectorate. Responsibility for water pollution passed to the National Rivers Authority in 1989, and is now part of the new Environment Agency's powers.

[6] At the time, the Cambridge Water Company was a statutory water supply company, licensed under the Water Act 1989, and charged with providing a public water supply in the Cambridge area. They abstracted groundwater from the borehole under a licence issued under the (then current) Water Resources Act 1963. Neither of these Acts gave them a statutory cause of action or enforcement powers.

[7] Under the Water Resources Act 1991 ss 85 and 161—see Chapter 9. The regulator did not then have the power to serve a 'Works Notice' on the offending party to carry out the works themselves (a power added to the 1991 Act by the Environment Act 1995). Note that although the contaminated land regime under the Environment Act 1995 had not then been enacted, it would have made little difference to the regulatory decisions.

defendant's actions was foreseeable in the circumstances. The plaintiff not only had to pay the substantial legal costs of the action but also did not recover its own substantial losses. By contrast, the regulatory authority was able to persuade the defendant company to arrange for a clean-up operation in the area around its tannery.[8] Although an indirect benefit of this operation is that the plaintiff may be able to use its borehole again at some stage in the future, it will not otherwise benefit from the regulatory authority's actions. It is likely that such contrasting results will continue to occur.

B. The Regulatory Framework

Environmental statutes

2.05   The main period of consolidation and modernization of the statutory regimes in England and Wales occurred in the 1990s. Those who advise on environmental law should be familiar with the workings in particular of the Environmental Protection Act 1990, the Water Resources Act 1991, the Water Industry Act 1991, and the Environment Act 1995.[9] Whilst these main Acts have been further amended since then,[10] the major changes that have occurred have been mainly through amending the secondary legislation. Indeed, the wide powers to introduce statutory instruments granted under the Pollution Prevention and Control Act 1999 has enabled reforms, such as Environmental Permitting, to be carried out without detailed Parliamentary processes.[11]

Environmental Protection Act 1990 (EPA 1990)

2.06   The Environmental Protection Act 1990 (EPA 1990) is as close to codification of environmental law as the law of England and Wales has got, and it has had to be

---

[8] By this time, the National Rivers Authority had taken over the responsibilities. The clean-up operation is reported in ENDS No 233, p 7: the NRA agreed a plan with Eastern Counties Leather costing £50,000, given the company's limited resources, rather than a possible plan costing £2 million. There are now also concerns about vapours (ENDS No 293, p 6). The issue of whether these costs were covered by the contractual indemnities made on the transfer of the business were settled in ECL's favour in *Eastern Counties Leather plc v Eastern Counties Leather Group Limited* [2002] EWHC 494 (Ch); [2002] EWCA Civ 1636, see case commentary Payne, 'Clean Up and Indemnity: A Postscript to *Cambridge Water*' [2003] 15 JEL 202.

[9] These are reproduced in the main encyclopedias, with the various amendments that have been made; a free internet source is <http://www.statutelaw.gov.uk.>, which also includes the amendments.

[10] For instance, whilst the Clean Neighbourhoods and Environment Act 2005 brings together many of the powers that dealt with litter, graffiti, dog control and abandoned vehicles, it was also used to amend the EPA 1990 on waste, litter and nuisance.

[11] Whilst this does enable reform to be introduced more quickly, the power to use secondary legislation to amend principal Acts does cause constitutional qualms as the level of Parliamentary scrutiny is limited. It has been likened to a 'Henry VIII clause'—in reference to the Statute of Proclamations 1539, which was seen as a mark of Tudor despotism.

heavily amended over the intervening years. It is split into several Parts dealing with the different areas. Part I of the EPA 1990 dealt with Integrated Pollution Control (IPC), and Air Pollution Control by local authorities. This was repealed and replaced with the IPPC regime,[12] which itself has now been superseded by Environmental Permitting.[13] Part II of the EPA 1990 deals with the controls over waste on land, including waste management licensing and the general duty of care placed on those who deal with waste. The regime is supplemented by a system of registering all waste brokers and carriers under the separate Control of Pollution (Amendment) Act 1989. Part II has also been subject to considerable amendment, and the introduction in 2008 of Environmental Permitting has replaced waste management licences. [14] A new Part IIA on the remediation of contaminated land has been squeezed into the EPA 1990 by the Environment Act 1995.[15] Part III of the EPA 1990 represents a consolidation of the old law on statutory nuisances. But, notably, any smoke pollution which does not amount to a nuisance remains covered by the Clean Air Act 1993. Other parts of the EPA 1990 cover litter (Part IV), genetically modified organisms (GMOs, under Part VI),[16] straw and stubble burning,[17] and miscellaneous amendments to matters such as nature conservation.

The Water Resources Act 1991 and the Water Industry Act 1991

The aquatic environment has its own regime, contained in several statutes. The **2.07** first consolidating act, the Water Act 1989, was rapidly superseded by the privatization of the water industry and it was split into two distinct areas. The Water Resources Act 1991 contains the main controls over water pollution and the responsibilities that the Environment Agency inherited from the National Rivers Authority for conserving water resources, ensuring that water quality objectives are met, and issuing discharge consents. The Water Industry Act 1991 (WIA 1991) deals with sewerage services, trade effluent, and the supply of water. Both of these Acts came into force on 1 December 1991, although it should be noted

---

[12] The IPPC regime was set out in the Pollution Prevention and Control Act 1999, and the Regulations made under that Act—see Chapter 6 further. There was a long transitional period, so that Part 1 of the EPA 1990 only became part of legal history in 2007. It seems that there are a large number of opportunities to get caught out amongst this administrative confusion.

[13] See the Environmental Permitting (England and Wales) Regulations 2007 (SI 2007/3538), which are themselves made under the Pollution Prevention and Control Act 1999, and came into force in April 2008. They repeal significant Sections of Part II of the EPA 1990.

[14] See the Environmental Permitting Regulations 2007, and Chapters 6 and 7 further.

[15] It should be noted that in the enthusiasm to place contaminated land in the EPA 1990, this has produced very awkward drafting. The new Part IIA starts with 78A and runs to a Section 78YC, whilst missing out 78I, 78O, and 78Y on the way—obviously in order to avoid confusion.

[16] The contained use of GMOs is still covered by the health and safety legislation and Regulations made under the Health and Safety Act 1974.

[17] EPA 1990, s 152 and the Crop Residues (Burning) Regulations 1993 (SI 1993/1366). There is no such provision in Scotland.

that they do not apply to Scotland, where the water industry was never privatized. These two 1991 Acts were amended by the Water Act 2003,[18] in particular to change the abstraction and impounding licence regime, and to introduce better water resource management. The Water Act 2003 also saw the establishment of 'Of Wat' as an independent regulatory authority.[19]

Environment Act 1995

2.08 In 1995, Parliament took the opportunity to introduce two unified regulatory bodies, the Environment Agency and the Scottish Environment Protection Agency. Provision was also made for national air quality and waste strategies, the introduction of the European concept of the 'producer responsibility for waste', an overhaul of mineral planning permissions, the provision of uniform powers for inspectors appointed by the pollution control authorities, and even hedgerow protection.

2.09 Parliament also took the opportunity in this Act to make amendments to the other Acts covering the environment. The gradual way in which these amendments have been brought into effect has disguised the substantial changes which have been made.

Public health laws

2.10 Many of the measures discussed in this book are concerned with the protection of human health. But concerns about public health extend beyond controls over air or water pollution, sewerage, waste management, and the law of nuisance—all of which have come to be seen as aspects of environmental law. There are specific statutory regimes which deal with food safety,[20] housing conditions,[21] building

---

[18] Note that various functions of the Secretary of State that were introduced or amended by the 2003 Act are devolved to the National Assembly for Wales. Section 100 of the 2003 Act amends the National Assembly for Wales (Transfer of Functions) Order 1999 to take into account the new provisions.

[19] The short name of 'Ofwat' has remained unchanged, but it now stands for the Water Services Regulation Authority, who are the regulatory authority established under the Water Act 2003, and not the Director General of Water Services (who was established under the WIA 1991). His functions were transferred to the new authority on 1 April 2006.

[20] Whilst the Food Safety Act 1990 (as amended) still sets out the framework for controlling the purity of food and regulates food premises, this is another area heavily dependent on European Union law. The enforcement of the regulations on food standards is primarily the responsibility of the environmental health officers of the local authorities. The Food Standards Agency (<http://www.food.gov.uk>) is the independent Government department set up by the Food Standards Act 2000 to protect the public's health and consumer interests in relation to food.

[21] In addition to the law of landlord and tenant, local authorities have powers under the Housing Act 1985 (as amended) to deal with housing standards, including slum clearance and overcrowding.

control,[22] and the control of communicable diseases.[23] Whilst environmental law does have its origins in the public health laws of the nineteenth century, it is now sufficiently distinct to exclude these other public health regimes, even though there is considerable scope for overlap between them.

Health and safety at work

Although a discussion of this topic lies outside the scope of this book, it is impor- **2.11** tant to bear in mind that many environmental problems are work-related. The health and safety of the workers of a company will inevitably involve not exposing them to the risks associated with environmental hazards. Under the Health and Safety at Work etc Act 1974 and its regulations, and the Factory Acts, a comprehensive system has been established in order to secure the health, safety, and welfare of people at work,[24] and to protect others against a risk to their health or safety arising from people at work.[25] The Health and Safety Executive (HSE) and local authorities share responsibility for its enforcement.[26] In effect, these powers complement the powers discussed in this book.[27]

---

[22]   See the Building Act 1984, and the Building Regulations made under it. The controls extend to services, facilities, drainage, sanitary provision, means of access, provisions for the disabled, and fire precautions. The Act includes powers to deal with dangerous and defective buildings. The regulations have been extended to cover the energy efficiency of buildings. The regulations apply to most new buildings and many alterations of existing buildings in England and Wales, whether domestic, commercial, or industrial.

[23]   See the Public Health (Control of Disease) Act 1984. On 1 April 2005, the Health Protection Agency (HPA) (<http://www.hpa.gov.uk>) was established as a non-departmental public body, replacing the HPA special health authority and the National Radiological Protection Board (NRPB). Radiation protection is now part of its health protection remit. The functions of the Agency are 'to protect the community (or any part of the community) against infectious diseases and other dangers to health' (Health Protection Agency Act 2004).

[24]   In particular, an employee's exposure to hazardous substances must either be prevented or adequately controlled, under the Control of Substances Hazardous to Health Regulations 2002 (COSHH Regulations), and the regulations on specific substances (eg asbestos, lead, radioactive material, explosives).

[25]   See ss 3 and 4 of the 1974 Act—which can include the public: eg *R v Board of Trustees of the Science Museum* [1993] 1 WLR 1171, CA, where harmful bacteria were present in the vicinity of the building from a faulty air conditioning system.

[26]   Local Authorities are the principal enforcing authority in retailing, wholesale distribution, warehousing, hotel and catering premises, offices, and the consumer/leisure industries—see the Health and Safety (Enforcing Authority) Regulations 1989(SI 1903).

[27]   For instance, no condition can be imposed on an IPC or LAAPC authorization for the purpose of securing the health and safety of persons at work only. The Environmental Permitting Guidance recommends that the Agency should take the Health and Safety Act requirements into account when setting permit conditions, and ensure that environmental permitting and Health and Safety requirements do not impose conflicting obligations (para A.1.11).

Alternatives to regulation

2.12   The regulatory system has often been criticized for lacking positive incentives for people to improve their behaviour to the benefit of the environment, and for relying too much on a 'command and control' approach.[28] Indeed, the UK, along with other countries, has used financial measures to supplement the regulatory systems, which were endorsed in the seminal White Paper *This Common Inheritance*.[29] The European Union's Sixth Action Programme[30] seeks to encourage the use of a range of measures in addition to the use of legislation and its effective implementation and enforcement. These strategic approaches include the integration of environment protection requirements into other Community policies and the promotion of sustainable production and consumption patterns through the use of a blend of instruments, including market based and economic instruments.

2.13   These alternatives to regulation remain an important part of the background to the legislation. Their ambit is wide.[31] At their simplest, this can involve increasing the level of charges which any applicant must pay to obtain a permit.[32] At a more complex level, the taxation system can be used to discourage certain types of activity (of which the Landfill Tax is the most elaborate creation)[33], tradable permit systems can be created, and changes can be made to government funding[34],

---

[28]   A useful review of the arguments, with accompanying extracts, is provided in Chapter 11 of *Environmental Protection, Law and Policy: Text and Materials* by Holder and Lee (Cambridge, 2007).

[29]   See Annex B of the White Paper, Cmd 1200 (1990), on the use of 'economic instruments'.

[30]   Environmental Action Programme 2002–12 (adopted as a Decision, 1600/2002/EC, on 22 July 2002). It sets out the framework for environmental policy-making in the European Union for this period.

[31]   The European Environment Agency and the OECD have set up a database on instruments used for environmental policy and natural resources management to provide information on environmentally related taxes, fees and charges, tradable permit systems, deposit refund systems, environmentally motivated subsidies, and voluntary approaches used in environmental policy in OECD Member countries, EEA member countries, and countries otherwise co-operating with EEA (see <www2.oecd.org/ecoinst/queries/>).

[32]   The level of charges are justified on the 'polluter pays principle', but they could also be used to influence the market.

[33]   See the Finance Act 1996 (as amended); it is the responsibility of the Treasury, and HM Customs and Excise are the regulatory authority. The tax was originally set at £7 per tonne, or £2 for less polluting matter such as inert wastes, and has been raised since—as of 1 April 2008 the standard rate of landfill tax is £32 per tonne, and the lower rate is £2.50. However, it has had the unintended environmental consequence of subsidizing the least sustainable approach to remediation, in effect of 'dig and dump'. There are therefore proposals to replace it with increased incentives by way of land remediation tax relief, which could include relief for on-site treatment costs (see 'Tax incentives for development of brownfield land: a consultation response' (December 2007, HM Treasury)). Simple measures have also been used—hence there is a differential in the tax levied on unleaded as opposed to leaded petrol in the UK Budget (and there is now a minimum tax requirement under Directive 2003/96).

[34]   Recycling credits are payable by the Waste Disposal Authority for all controlled waste which is not sent for disposal (EPA 1992 s 52). These payments may be made to individuals, but are largely made to the Waste Collection Authorities.

procurement[35], and subsidies.[36] The use of tradable permits has been seen as a more efficient way of meeting environmental objectives than the use of taxes and charges. The scheme for greenhouse gas emission allowance trading within the European Union was introduced in 2003, pursuant to Directive 2003/87/EC,[37] and the UK, like all Member States, has drawn up a National Allocation Plan indicating the allowances that will be allocated to the relevant installations.[38] This applies in addition to the UK climate change levy.[39]

Another alternative to regulation is the use of voluntary agreements with particular landowners or industries, such as have been used in the management of Sites of Special Scientific Interest (SSSIs)[40] and farming in Environmentally Sensitive Areas. The voluntary participation of companies in environmental audits and eco-management schemes has been endorsed by the EU.[41] Voluntary agreement, and consensus, has also been important in the implementation of policy. **2.14**

---

[35] There have been a series of voluntary restrictions on government procurement decisions, which have had to be accommodated within the European rules on public procurement (see further 'Making the Market Work for the Environment: Acceptance of (Some) "Green" Contract Award Criteria in Public Procurement' [2003] JEL 15 175).

[36] One awaits the further reforms to the huge farming subsidies under the European Common Agricultural Programme (CAP). As has been acknowledged, CAP imposes substantial costs on consumers and taxpayers but is inefficient in delivering support to farmers and promoting an attractive rural environment. Indeed much of the CAP still has a negative impact on the environment (see 'A Vision for the Common Agricultural Policy' December 2005, Defra and HM Treasury).

[37] The Greenhouse Gas Emissions Trading Scheme Regulations 2003 (SI 2003 No. 3311) provide the framework for the trading scheme for the purpose of implementing Directive 2003/87/EC. These Regulations control emissions of carbon dioxide from any of the listed activities set out in Schedule 1 of those Regulations. The scheme puts a price on carbon by the allocation and trading of allowances.

[38] The rules in the UK's National Allocation Plan on carbon dioxide emissions have been unsuccessfully challenged (*Cemex UK Cement Ltd v Defra, DTI and others* [2006] EWHC 3207 (Admin), (2007) Env LR 21—there was no reason for treating Cemex's commissioning difficulties at its particular installation any differently from other difficulties such as management or maintenance problems). They cannot be tailored to the individual circumstances of any particular installation, not least because this could result in discrimination to other installations or sectors.

[39] This is a tax on energy use by business and the public sector, off-set by a cut in national insurance tax (pursuant to the Finance Act 2000), see further Benjamin J. Richardson and Kiri L. Chanwai, 'The UK's Climate Change Levy: Is It Working?' [2003] JEL 15: 39–58. Domestic and transport fuel is not covered, and electricity generated from renewable energy is exempt.

[40] See the Chapter on Nature Conservation further. The past lack of coercive measures in this area was the subject of much criticism. Parliament has now chosen to introduce more stringent measures by amending the Wildlife and Countryside Act 1981 (under the Countryside and Rights of Way Act 2000).

[41] Since 2001, the EU Eco-Management and Audit Scheme (EMAS) has been open to all the economic sectors, including public and private services (pursuant to Regulation (EC) No 761/2001). It was introduced in 1995 and was originally restricted to companies in industrial sectors (under Council Regulation (EEC) No 1836/93). See further <http://ec.europa.eu/environment/emas/index_en.htm>—the objective is for the company to establish environmental policies, programmes, and management systems, evaluate its performance, and provide the information on its performance to the public.

For instance, the division of responsibilities amongst the various producers of packaging waste[42] was the subject of prior consultation and agreement between the government and the relevant industries.

2.15 In this broad context, the law seems like one instrument in the process of ensuring environmental protection. But, attractive as these options are in comparison to the confrontational approach inherent in regulation and enforcement, it must be remembered that the regulatory mechanisms remain necessary to set the required standards, to enable precautionary approaches to be required, and to support the political legitimacy of the solutions.[43]

C. The Different Jurisdictions of the UK

England and Wales

2.16 This book concentrates on environmental law in England and Wales. The legal history of the two countries has been inseparable for centuries. There has been one legal system for England and Wales since 1535 [44] and since then the people of the two countries have been subject to the same laws and court system.[45] Environmental matters are dealt with through the normal civil and criminal courts. Despite the strong support for a separate Environmental Court, given the importance of many of the issues involved and their specialist nature, there seems to be little prospect that one will be created.[46]

2.17 When the appellate jurisdiction of the House of Lords is replaced by the newly-created 'Supreme Court of the UK', in 2009, the current Supreme Court of England and Wales will be renamed the 'Senior Court' of England and Wales.[47]

---

[42] Environment Act 1995 ss 93–95, and the Producer Responsibility Obligations (Packaging Waste) Regs 1997/648, in order to implement the EC Packaging and Packaging Waste Directive 94/62/EC. Nevertheless, the regime itself still depends upon the command and control approach—relying upon registration and monitoring, and penal sanctions for non-compliance.

[43] See Macrory, 'Regulating in a Risky Environment' (2001) Current Legal Problems 619.

[44] Under the Laws in Wales Act 1535. Indeed, in Acts passed before July 1967 the word 'England' is taken to include a reference to 'Wales' (Interpretation Act 1978, ss 22, 23)—see *Halsbury's Laws of England*, volume 8(2) for a general overview of the continuing vagaries of the UK Constitution.

[45] Note that there is a High Court registry in Cardiff, and the government published proposals in 2007 for a full-time division of the Administrative Court to sit in Cardiff.

[46] Lord Woolf has remained an advocate of such a court—see Lord Woolf *The Pursuit of Justice* (OUP, 2008) which reprints his Garner lecture from 2001, 'Are the Judiciary Environmentally Myopic ?' and a lecture to UNEP from 2004 made by Prof. Malcolm Grant in *Environmental Court Project: Final Report (2000)*, see commentary of Tromans in [2001] 13 JEL 423. This also was recommended in a wide-ranging report on environmental tribunals, R Macrory and M Wood *Modernising Environmental Justice: Regulation and the Role of an Environmental Tribunal* (2003) Centre for Law and the Environment, UCL.

[47] See the Constitutional Reform Act 2005, which transfers the appellate jurisdiction of the House of Lords and the devolution jurisdiction of the Judicial Committee of the Privy

However, it has become important to make some jurisdictional distinctions between the two countries following the setting up of the National Assembly for Wales in 1999,[48] and the Government of Wales Act 2006 that transferred the Assembly's executive functions to the Welsh Ministers. The Assembly has the power to make its own Welsh rules and regulations,[49] and is under a duty to make a scheme setting out how it proposes, in the exercise of its functions, to promote sustainable development.[50] There is scope for Welsh legislation to diverge from its English counterpart,[51] as most of the statutory instruments are now enacted separately for each country, including in the areas of planning,[52] local government, agriculture, transport, housing, and environmental services. The National Assembly has already taken a lead on sustainable development and has introduced more restrictive rules on Genetically Modified Organisms (GMOs) than in England. There is also the noticeable difference that the Welsh and English languages have equal status in the courts in Wales and in all public bodies that provide services in Wales.[53] This formal devolution of power follows on from the practical distinction that used to exist when these areas were dealt with by the Secretary of State for Wales and the Welsh Office separately from the main Whitehall departments.

Council to the Supreme Court. The Act also reformed the office of Lord Chancellor, established the Lord Chief Justice as head of the judiciary of England and Wales and President of the Courts of England and Wales. It also creates a Judicial Appointments Commission, an Office of Judicial Complaints, and a Judicial Appointments and Conduct Ombudsman.

[48] Most of the functions of the Secretary of State for Wales and the Welsh Office were devolved to the Assembly under the Government of Wales Act 1998. The National Assembly of Wales (Transfer of Functions) Order (SI 1999/672) covered over 300 Acts of Parliament, and a host of private Acts and statutory instruments which needed to be altered. One large anomaly, which did not use to matter, is that the responsibilities for the water industry and rivers are cross-border—given that the river basins involved do not follow the political boundaries.

[49] Note that the Government of Wales Act 2006 (which came into force in May 2007) conferred on the Assembly the power to promulgate 'Assembly measures', that are the equivalent of an Act of Parliament in relation to specified matters in devolved fields.

[50] Government of Wales Act 1998 s 121. This legal duty is unique in the UK, and the Assembly must publish an annual review on progress and consider reviewing it in the year following each ordinary election.

[51] See further Victoria Jenkins, 'Environmental Law in Wales' [2005] 17 JEL 207, which studies the environmental laws passed by the Assembly during its first term. She considers that, after an initial period of caution, some greater differences are now emerging in the regulatory approaches being adopted, despite the common objectives. That trend is only likely to continue further.

[52] The powers of the Secretary of State under the Town and Country Planning Act 1990 in Wales were transferred to the Welsh Assembly under the Government of Wales Act 1998. The Planning Inspectorate and Welsh Historic Monuments act as executive agencies of the Welsh Ministers. Note that, unlike in England, there is now a national spatial plan for Wales (the 'Wales Spatial Plan 2004') to which local planning authorities must have regard when preparing their development plans (s 60, Planning and Compulsory Purchase Act 2004, although it is not part of the 'development plan' itself for the purposes of the statutory tests).

[53] Welsh Language Act 1993.

Scotland

2.18   Within the UK, the difference between the legal jurisdictions governing England and Wales on the one hand and Scotland on the other has always been maintained. The separate legal system of Scotland was preserved by the Act of Union 1707. The only shared court is the House of Lords, sitting as a civil court, and the two legal traditions do meet at this highest level. The highest civil court in Scotland is the Court of Session,[54] which complements the civil jurisdiction of the Sheriff Court. But the House of Lords does not have any appellate function over Scottish criminal law and procedure, where the only appeal court is the High Court of Justiciary which sits in Edinburgh.[55] The use of Scottish cases in English and Welsh courts should be approached with caution. Some landmark cases—such as *Donoghue v Stevenson*[56]—are Scottish in origin, and can be applied in both jurisdictions. Conversely, the familiar common law rule in *Rylands v Fletcher* has never applied in Scotland[57] and there is a difference of approach regarding judicial review.[58] The Scottish legal tradition is still closer to that of continental European jurisdictions, although it has never been codified. The Scottish law of property, family law, succession, and the law of obligations reflects this influence. Other more commercial areas, such as company law and revenue law, are similar in both jurisdictions.

2.19   Under the Scotland Act 1998, the Scottish Parliament has assumed legislative power for all Scottish matters, including local government, planning,[59] and environment matters. There is a Scottish Executive that has taken over most of the functions of the Secretary of State for Scotland. However, the reservation of international and EU relations to Westminster, together with the concordats and understandings agreed between the UK and Scottish governments, do mean that

---

[54] The Outer House of the Court of Session deals with first instance cases, and the Inner House (with three judges) usually sits as an appeal court.

[55] The superior criminal court at first instance is also the High Court of Justiciary, when it is sitting on circuit with a single judge. All other criminal cases are dealt with by the Sheriff Court, which may hear cases summarily (sitting alone) or on indictment (with a jury of 15). There are no lay magistrates.

[56] [1932] AC 562. As regards statute law, an English court ought to follow the unanimous judgments of the higher Scottish courts, where the question relates to the same statute (see *Halsbury's Laws of England*, Volume 26, para 585).

[57] So, in *Graham and Graham v Rechem* [1996] Env LR 158, the doctrine could not be applied to the damage caused by the escape of emissions from an incinerator, as the case was governed by Scottish law. See the Chapter on Common Law Liability further.

[58] For instance, *West v Secretary of State for Scotland* (1992) SLT 636, Court of Session, contrasts with the public and private law distinction made in *O'Reilly v Mackman* [1983] 2 AC 237, HL. The Court of Session, like the High Court, has exclusive jurisdiction over judicial review matters.

[59] The broad principles of the town and country planning system are the same as in England, including the requirement for environmental assessment, but the relevant legislation is the Town and Country Planning (Scotland) Act 1997 and separate policy guidance notes apply. There are National Planning Guidelines, and Planning Advice Notes and Circulars.

there are important practical limitations on Scottish environmental policy-making and legislation.[60]

A separate statutory agency was created under the Environment Act 1995 for **2.20** Scotland, the Scottish Environment Protection Agency (SEPA). In April 1996, it took over the responsibilities of HM Industrial Pollution Inspectorate, the Hazardous Waste Inspectorate, and all of the River Purification Authorities, and also the local authorities' responsibilities for waste regulation and all industrial air pollution under Part I of the EPA 1990. Its pollution control powers are the same as the Environment Agency, except that SEPA has control over all Pollution Prevention and Control (PPC) installations and does not share responsibility with the local authorities. One notable difference from the Agency is that SEPA has no prosecution powers. It must refer all cases to the Procurator Fiscal, who will decide whether or not criminal proceedings will be in the public interest. Local authorities remain responsible for the powers under the Clean Air Act 1993 and for the statutory nuisance regime, and for flood control.

Environmental law in Scotland has almost kept pace with developments south of **2.21** the border, while not mirroring them.[61] For instance, Environmental Permitting has not been introduced in Scotland, so the Integrated Pollution Prevention and Control and waste management licensing have not been combined. There is also a structural difference in the approach to water resources, as the water industry in Scotland was never privatized. Responsibility for water and sewerage services remains a public function, and is in the hands of the three water authorities. SEPA itself has taken over the responsibilities of the former River Purification Boards and the three island councils who were acting as River Purification Authorities.

Northern Ireland

While the Department of the Environment in Northern Ireland has existed since **2.22** 1999, the devolution of powers to the Northern Ireland Assembly and Executive has had to wait until 8 May 2007. There is a Minister for the Department, responsible for policy, and most of the day-to-day work is done by a government agency,

---

[60] See further—G Little, 'Scottish devolution and environmental law' [2000] JEL 12 155–174, for an overview. The division of responsibilities under the devolved power arrangements is sensitive to the overall UK political settlement, and there will continue to be a need for *realpolitick* rather than high theory.

[61] The annual *Pollution Control Handbook* produced by Environmental Protection UK (formerly known as the National Society for Clean Air) provides a useful sector-by-sector analysis, and notes where the regimes in Northern Ireland and Scotland differ from the rest of the UK. The legislation can be found online at <http://www.statutelaw.gov.uk>, and in Garner's *Environmental Law* (Butterworths), and the *Scottish Planning Encyclopaedia* (WG Greens, 1998). The Scottish equivalent of *Halsbury* is Stair's *Encyclopaedia of the Laws of Scotland*.

the Northern Ireland Environment Agency.[62] Given the geographical context, it is notable that issues including the environment, agriculture, and development have been identified for cross-border co-operation between existing government departments and other bodies in Northern Ireland and Ireland. The statute law of Northern Ireland is very similar to that in England and Wales, and it is generally adapted from it through delegated legislation. The Northern Ireland court system is separate from the rest of the country, and decisions of the Court of Appeal or the Court of Sessions are merely persuasive.[63] However, the highest appellate court remains the House of Lords. When the appellate jurisdiction of the House of Lords is replaced by the newly-created 'Supreme Court of the UK', the current 'Supreme Court of Judicature of Northern Ireland' will be renamed the 'Court of Judicature of Northern Ireland.'[64]

2.23   However, the legislation on the environment in Northern Ireland has been slow in comparison to developments in the rest of the UK, and even to those of the European Union. In their 1998 comprehensive overview of the situation, Morrow and Turner stated that Northern Ireland had 'become a byword for environmental inertia and a case study of worst practice in the implementation of EC law'.[65] By 2006, Turner[66] was able to note that in the previous four years there had been a significant effort on environmental law reform, which had led to a clearing of the EU legislative backlog. This was spurred by a combination of the threat of fines before the European Court of Justice and the restoration of devolution. There is still some way to go.

---

[62]   The agency was formerly known as the Environment & Heritage Service, and it was rebranded and relaunched under this new name on 1 July 2008—see further its website <http://www.ni-envi ronment.gov.uk>. Although there has been lobbying for the creation of a stand-alone environmental protection agency for Northern Ireland, there are currently no plans to create one.

[63]   Similarly the decision of the High Court in 'An application by Seaport Investments Limited and others' [2007] NIQB 62 is only persuasive, although it is the first UK case on the requirements for an environmental assessment under the SEA Directive.

[64]   See the Constitutional Reform Act 2005; note that it is also intended that the Lord Chief Justice of Northern Ireland is to be established as the head of the judiciary under the Justice (Northern Ireland) Act 2002, as amended by the Constitutional Reform Act 2005, and as President of all the relevant Courts of Northern Ireland.

[65]   See Morrow and Turner, 'The More Things Change, the More they Stay the Same? Environmental Law, Policy and Funding in Northern Ireland' [1998] 1 JEL 41. The annual *Pollution Control Handbook* produced by the NSCA provides a useful sector-by-sector analysis, and notes where the regimes in Northern Ireland differ from the rest of the UK.

[66]   See Sharon Turner, 'Transforming Environmental Governance in Northern Ireland. Part One: The Process of Policy Renewal' [2006] 18 JEL 55; her further article 'Transforming Environmental Governance in Northern Ireland. Part Two: The Case of Environmental Regulation' [2006] 18 JEL 245 calls for a 'seismic structural and cultural change' so that Northern Ireland can become a modern society organized in accordance with the principles of sustainable development.

The Influence of Other Common Law Jurisdictions

Just as the common law has spread around large parts of the globe, the different **2.24**
countries in which it has taken root provide a variety of possible examples of how
to tackle familiar environmental problems within the common law framework.
These examples can be of use in analysing legal problems within the UK, by way
of analogy, even with the growing dominance of European Union law. From time
to time, in environmental cases, the English courts have had cited to them, and
sometimes have considered, cases from countries such as the United States,
Canada, Australia,[67] New Zealand, Hong Kong, and Ireland.[68] The usefulness of
such foreign law is limited, since the jurisdictions of even these countries have
adopted different statutes and have begun to use different interpretations of the
direction which the common law should take. Even New Zealand, with its close
ties to the UK, has chosen to develop its own strand of the common law, as was
acknowledged by the Privy Council in *Invercargill City Council v Hamlin*.[69] New
Zealand also has its own comprehensive Resource Management Act 1991, which
uses an integrated approach and its own definition of 'sustainable management'.[70]
Similar caveats would apply to relying upon case law from the Indian legal system
before the UK courts, which is based on its own national legislation and the right
to a clean environment in the Indian Constitution.[71]

---

[67] Likewise, the Commonwealth looks to the UK case law—eg Papworth, 'The offence of
Causing Water Pollution: a New South Wales perspective' [1997] 1 JEL 59, where *Alphacell v
Woodward* was considered. The state of New South Wales is also home to the integrated Land and
Environment Court, established in 1980, which combines both planning and environmental juris-
dictions as well as criminal and civil jurisdictions—for a somewhat downbeat assessment of its role
see Patricia Ryan, 'Court of Hope and False Expectations: Land and Environment Court 21 Years
On' [2002] 14 JEL 301.

[68] For a general overview see Yvonne Scannell, *Environmental and Planning Law in Ireland*
(Round Hall Press, 1994). The Irish courts still rely upon familiar common law cases, but separate
case law has been developed on the Irish statutes. So, the Irish courts agree that fault is needed to
establish a case in nuisance against a hazardous use of land such as an incinerator, in *Hanrahan v
Merck, Sharpe & Dohme* [1988] IRLM 629, but they were also asked to consider whether the Irish
Constitution reversed the burden of proof in such cases.

[69] [1996] AC 624, AC; the Privy Council declined to overrule the New Zealand Court of
Appeal's rejection of the House of Lords decision in *Murphy v Brentwood*.

[70] See further Benjamin Richardson, 'Economic Instruments and Sustainable Management in
New Zealand' [1998] 1 JEL 21.

[71] The Indian Supreme Court has had to do considerable work to address the severe shortcomings of the environmental regulators in India, in response to public interest environmental cases
based on existing legislative requirements (by the likes of serial public interest litigators such as
M.C. Mehta). Commentators have however worried about the effect the Court's activism has had
on India's institutional balance. See Lavanya Rajamani, 'Public Interest Environmental Litigation in
India: Exploring Issues of Access, Participation, Equity, Effectiveness and Sustainability' [2007] 19
JEL 293, and Shubhankar Dam and Vivek Tewary, 'Polluting Environment, Polluting Constitution:
Is a 'Polluted' Constitution Worse than a Polluted Environment?' [2005] 17 JEL 383. See also the
Indian 'case study' in Chapter 10, *Human Rights Approaches to Environmental Protection*, eds Alan
Boyle and Michael Anderson (OUP, 1997).

2.25 It is perhaps inevitable that concerns about pollution of the environment in the USA should strike a chord on this side of the Atlantic. We share a common language, economic system, and legal tradition. Indeed, many environmental problems were first brought to public attention in the USA—the toxic waste dump at Love Canal in 1978, or the publication of Rachel Carson's *Silent Spring*[72] in the 1960s, are perhaps better known than the equivalent examples in the UK. In the United States, the protection of the environment is a matter of both state and federal interest. There has been substantial legislation passed by the US Congress since the 1970s. The Environmental Protection Agency (the EPA) is the main federal agency with responsibility for the protection of the environment.[73] It has broad-ranging powers to implement, monitor, and enforce environmental Regulations, and, unlike in the UK, it has the main role in establishing uniform environmental standards. Many of the environmental statutes include citizen suit provisions, which allow 'any person'[74] to commence a civil action against the alleged violator or the administrative body which has failed to act. As a result of this well-established regulatory framework, the United States is rich in jurisprudence on environmental law. But the United States is a country with multiple legal voices and the English lawyer must avoid the temptation to pick and choose those US cases which support a particular line of argument and to gloss over the wealth of equally authoritative case law which might not.[75] That having been said, when concerns over the habitat of a rare fish are able to halt the construction of a large, government-funded dam project,[76] or a secured creditor is found responsible

---

[72] *Silent Spring* (London: Penguin, 1963)—concerning the pernicious effects on the environment of the indiscriminate use of insecticides and pesticides.

[73] It was created in 1970, and brought together most of the federal government's disparate regulatory agencies on the environment. It is split into 10 regional offices. The UK has adopted a similar unified idea in setting up the Environment Agency in 1996. However, many of the UK controls are still left in the hands of central government—such as the setting of standards.

[74] eg Clean Air Act 1970, 42 USC 7604. The standard provision allows the plaintiff to obtain an injunction, declaratory relief, and possibly an order for the defendant to remedy the harm. For a useful analysis of the seminal US case on the standing to bring an environmental action—*Friends of the Earth Incorporated v Laidlaw Environmental Services* [2000] 120 S Ct 693, see JG Miller, 'Case law analysis. The standing of citizens to enforce against violations of environmental statutes in the United States' [2000] 12 JEL 370 and C Hilson, 'Case law analysis. Laidlaw: some observations from the UK/EU' [2000] 12 JEL 381.

[75] The cases must be interpreted in their proper context. Firstly, the common law tradition of the United States has been subject to a specific set of constitutional rights for over 200 years. Secondly, the United States is a country with multiple legal voices—there may be only one US Supreme Court, but the rest of the federal judicial system is split into thirteen circuits, of equal authority to each other and with their own regional courts of appeal. In addition to the federal legal system, each of the states has its own exclusive jurisdiction, constitution, legislature, and court system. There are useful parallels to be drawn from US law on environmental insurance issues, see Fogleman, *Environmental Liabilities and Insurance in England and the United States* (Witherbys, 2005).

[76] *Tennessee Valley Authority v Hill* (1978) 437 US 153, Supreme Court. An unknown species of perch, the snail darter, was discovered whilst the dam was being built. The explicit provisions of the Endangered Species Act 1973 provided absolute protection for the fish. An injunction was granted, although the dam was ultimately built. The parallels with *R v Secretary of State for the Environment, ex*

for the contamination of land by its client company's activities,[77] or the EPA is forced to regulate emissions of carbon dioxide from cars,[78] English environmental lawyers have much that they can learn from the US courts.

D. The Responsible Public Authorities

The role of central government

There is no single government department that deals with the range of environ-   **2.26**
mental issues mentioned in this book. The main responsibilities for environmental matters, as of 2008, have been given to the Secretary of State for the Environment, Food and Rural Affairs,[79] which now also incorporates the agricultural brief.[80] But the responsibility for Town and Country Planning in England lies with the Secretary of State for Communities, Local Government and Regions, who has her own sustainability agenda.[81] There is a separate Secretary of State for Transport, and the experiment of amalgamating the transport department with the environmental or the planning departments has been abandoned.[82]

---

p RSPB [1997] Env LR 431, HL, are obvious, where the expansion of Sheerness docks threatened a migratory birds' habitat—save for the fact that the RSPB never asked for an injunction—see Chapter 4 further at para 4.35.

[77] *United States v Fleet Factors Corp* (1990) 901 F 2d 1550, United States Court of Appeals, Eleventh Circuit—the creditors' involvement in the management of the bankrupt company was sufficient in theory to impose liability under CERCLA as the owner or operator. The Court did take a purposive approach in interpreting the legislation—particularly in construing the creditor's statutory exemption very narrowly—which a UK court probably would not have done. One practical response has been for US lenders to 'walk away' from such sites, and not to foreclose.

[78] *Massachusetts, et al v Environmental Protection Agency*, 549 U.S. [2007]; 127 S Ct 1438 (reversing 415 F.3d 50, D.C. Cir. 2005). This was an action by 12 States and several environmental organizations to compel the EPA to regulate greenhouse gas emissions (including carbon dioxide) from cars, arguing that the EPA was required to regulate emissions under the Clean Air Act, greenhouse gas emissions, as they are air pollutants which 'may reasonably be anticipated to endanger public health or welfare'. The issue of standing was resolved by the fact that even incremental changes (here, in sea levels) can be harmful. As a 5:4 decision of the US Supreme Court, the issue remains controversial.

[79] See the Defra website generally, at <http://www.defra.gov.uk>. It was created in 2001.

[80] The Ministry of Agriculture, Fisheries and Food (MAFF) had retained its functions for food, the licensing of pesticides, as well as responsibility for flood defence and fisheries, marine pollution outside 'controlled waters', and for the disposal and discharge of radioactive wastes from licensed nuclear sites.

[81] The Department for Communities and Local Government ('CLG') was created on 5 May 2006 with the remit to promote community cohesion and equality, as well as having responsibility for housing, urban regeneration, planning and local government. See the Department's website, at <http://www.communities.gov.uk>. Political fashion has dictated that the word 'Department' has been dropped (as of 2008). Previously, planning had been the responsibility of the now-defunct Office of the Deputy Prime Minister ('ODPM'), and the 'First Secretary of State'.

[82] The Department of the Environment and the Department of Transport were merged in May 1997, to form the Department for Environment, Transport and the Regions, and it was also responsible for planning and local government matters. It was largely replaced by the Office of the Deputy

Other departments have also retained specific functions within their control. The Department for Business, Enterprise and Regulatory Reform (formerly the Department of Trade and Industry)[83] has general responsibility for the electricity industry, oil and gas, mining, and pipelines. In addition, as a result of internal reorganization, these Departments now operate in England through separate regional offices which can act in the name of all these Secretary of States. In Wales, the Welsh Assembly Government is responsible for waste regulation, planning control, fisheries, and flood defence in Wales.

Central government guidance

2.27 It is characteristic of environmental law that, in addition to the principal Acts and Regulations, there is a considerable body of government policy. The UK Government and Devolved Administrations of Wales, Scotland, and Northern Ireland launched a Strategic Framework '*One Future—Different Paths*' on 7 March 2005. This emphasized five key, shared, UK principles of sustainable development—'Living within Environmental Limits', 'Ensuring a Strong, Healthy and Just Society', 'Achieving a Sustainable Economy', 'Using Sound Science Responsibly', and 'Promoting Good Governance'. It was stated that for a policy to be sustainable, it must respect all five principles.[84] At the same time, the UK Government published its new strategy for sustainable development—'*Securing The Future*'[85]—to take account of developments since the 1999 Strategy, both domestically and internationally, as well as devolution. There are four priority areas outlined in the Strategy: sustainable consumption and production, climate change and energy, natural resource protection and enhancing the environment, and creating sustainable communities and a fairer world. The lead Department is Defra, which chairs a Programme Board to oversee delivery of the Strategy, as the intention is that all UK Departments share responsibility for making sustainable development a reality.[86] The Strategy includes strengthening the Sustainable Development Commission and asking it to report on all of the Government's progress on sustainable development. The principles in the UK's Sustainable Development Strategy are:

- taking a long-term perspective;
- putting people at the centre;

Prime Minister after the 2001 election, when the Department of Transport was also recreated. The ODPM was replaced in May 2006 by the DCLG.

[83] See the DBERR website generally, <http://www.berr.gov.uk>, in particular the Energy Section.

[84] See <http://www.sustainable-development.gov.uk/what/principles.htm>

[85] Published on 7 March 2005 on behalf of the UK as a whole, including the devolved administrations. Available at <http://www.sustainable development.gov.uk/publications/uk-strategy/index.htm>

[86] For an overview see Andrea Ross, 'The UK Approach to Delivering Sustainable Development in Government: A Case Study in Joined-Up Working' [2005] 17 JEL 27. See also her article 'Why Legislate for Sustainable Development? An examination of Sustainable Development in UK and Scottish and Statutes' [2008] 20 JEL 35.

- taking account of the full range of costs and benefits;

- respecting environmental limits;

- the precautionary principle;

- using scientific knowledge;

- transparency, information, participation, and access to justice; and

- preventing pollution as far as is possible, and making the polluter pay for damage done by pollution.

The National Assembly for Wales is the only national government body to be **2.28** under a duty to promote sustainable development in the exercise of its functions.[87] It is also required to make a Scheme setting out how it proposes to implement the duty. The Assembly's Sustainable Development Scheme, 'Learning to Live Differently' was adopted by the Assembly Plenary in November 2000,[88] and has been followed by the revised Scheme called, appropriately, 'Starting To Live Differently'. The Welsh Assembly Government published its own 'Environment Strategy for Wales' in May 2006, which sets out the strategic direction for the next 20 years.[89] It is intended to explain the issues and to set out the environmental outcomes they want to achieve with the associated indicators and timelines for delivery. An Environment Strategy Action Plan has also been published, which contains the details of the specific action that will be taken to deliver the outcomes in the Environment Strategy, in addition to the current legislative obligations and policies, which it intends to be reviewed and updated annually.[90]

There have been annual reports on the progress made on the UK on its published **2.29** strategy ever since the 1990 White Paper entitled *This Common Inheritance*.[91] One innovation since then has been to try and quantify the progress that is being made on these issues by the use of Indicators. They are also intended to help people understand what the rather vague notion of 'sustainable development' means globally, nationally, locally, and for them as individuals. A new set of national indicators were outlined in the UK Government Sustainable Development Strategy in March 2005. The baseline assessment date for all the

---

[87] Under the Government of Wales Act 1998 s 121.

[88] In defining 'sustainable development' within the Scheme, the Assembly has adopted the *Brundtland* wording, that it will promote development which meets the needs of the present without compromising the ability of future generations to meet their own needs.

[89] The Strategy has five main environmental themes: addressing climate change; sustainable resource use; distinctive biodiversity, landscapes and seascapes; our local environment; and environmental hazards.

[90] The first review was the 'Environment Strategy for Wales: Report on Progress—September 2007' (see the Environment Strategy for Wales web pages at <http//:new.wales.gov.uk>).

[91] This was an environmental strategy (Cm 1200), which has been subsumed since then in the White Papers on Sustainable Development (1994, 1999, and 2002). Indicators were introduced in 1994.

indicators, for which data were available, was June 2005. There are 68 national indicators supporting the Strategy, including measures of everyday concern such as health, housing, jobs, crime, education, and our environment. A subset of 20 indicators are also 'UK Framework Indicators', shared by UK Government and the devolved administrations in Scotland, Wales, and Northern Ireland. These may be useful policy tools, and will keep the 'bean counters' happy, but one wonders if the strong caveat to their use, voiced in 1990, has really been overcome:

> Attempting to bring together all the policies which affect the environment is not and cannot be an exact scientific process. There is no anatomical or mechanistic relationship between them all. We cannot calibrate with precision the effect of this or that policy switch or modification on all the other related parts of the whole. To try to reduce all these issues to a table of figures is neither helpful nor honest: these are three-dimensional problems in a fast-changing world. So we are not dealing with a science, but with an area where political judgment will properly have a central role, constrained by the impertinent but implacable realities of the world.[92]

2.30 The discretion given to the public authorities by the environmental statutes is wide enough to comprehend the publication of policy statements that set out the considerations that will guide their decisions. The courts accept that policy statements do fulfil a useful role, as they promote certainty, uniformity, and even-handed justice in administrative decision-making.[93] The courts have accepted that policy statements can be taken into account not only from obvious sources such as White Papers, Circulars, Policy Guidance Notes, and previous decisions,[94] but also from less obvious sources such as written parliamentary answers[95] and even an after-dinner speech.[96]

2.31 At the national level, in addition to the national 'Strategies' on sustainable development, air quality,[97] water, energy, and waste, there are General Guidance Notes, Waste Management Papers, Planning Policy Statements, and Circulars. This is in addition to the guidance issued by the regulatory authorities themselves in the form

---

[92] Para 1.36, *This Common Inheritance*. It does perhaps help that there is a legal requirement to report, which might otherwise have let bad publicity be avoided (see Andrea Ross, 'Why Legislate for Sustainable Development? An examination of Sustainable Development in UK and Scottish and Statutes' [2008] 20 JEL 35 for a discussion of the current requirements—the introduction of these sort of procedural requirements may mean that there is a better chance to hold the government to account in the courts).

[93] See *Tesco Stores Ltd v Secretary of State for the Environment* (1995) 80 P&CR 184 HL, in particular Lord Steyn, where the status of the Secretary of State's policy on planning obligations was crucial to whether or not his decision to refuse a very valuable planning permission was lawful.

[94] *North Wiltshire DC v Secretary of State for the Environment and Clover* [1992] JPL 955.

[95] *R v Secretary of State for the Environment, ex p Surrey Heath BC* (1987) 56 P&CR 250.

[96] *Dimsdale Developments (South East) Ltd v Secretary of State for the Environment and Hounslow LBC* [1986] JPL 276.

[97] The UK Government and the devolved administrations published the latest Air Quality Strategy for England, Scotland, Wales, and Northern Ireland, 17 July 2007 (Cmd paper No 7169). It includes the air quality standards and objectives to be achieved.

of Process Guidance Notes, papers on Water Quality, Water Protection Areas, Nitrate Sensitive Areas, and the like. Fine tuning has been achieved through Good Practice Guides, advisory handbooks, and design bulletins, which provide a level of detail that is inappropriate to a statement of general policy. These policy documents are available direct from the authorities, on their internet sites, and from HM Stationery Office. They are intended both to guide the regulatory authorities, and to inform those whom they regulate on what procedure and what considerations will be relevant. They are material considerations in any regulatory decision, although an applicant may sometimes wish to go further than arguing about the application of policy and argue that the circular or guidance does not accurately reflect the law.[98]

The crown and the royal prerogative

The UK government is still treated differently in law when it exercises its preroga- **2.32** tive powers as 'the Crown'. The Crown includes not only the departments of state, such as the Ministry of Defence, but also official bodies such as the Crown Estate and the police. At the moment, actions by the government on Crown land, such as Ministry of Defence properties, are not subject to the formal environmental controls discussed in this book. As a matter of general principle, the Crown is not bound by the provisions of a statute unless the statute states that it will be, either by express words or by necessary implication.[99] Nor can the Crown be prosecuted.[100] An injunction can only be granted against officers of the Crown in limited circumstances.[101] It is possible to challenge the exercise of royal prerogative by way of judicial review,[102] and this will be considered in the light of any Acts of Parliament that exist in a similar area. Complaints can also be made to the Parliamentary Commissioner for Administration about maladministration.[103]

---

[98] In *Gillick v West Norfolk AHA* [1986] 1 AC 112, HL, Mrs Gillick challenged a 'memorandum of guidance' which purported to advise on family planning clinics. In reviewing the authorities, Lord Bridge ([1986] 1 AC 112, at 193G) acknowledged that: 'if a government department, in a field of administration in which it exercises responsibility, promulgates in a public document, albeit non-statutory in form, advice which is erroneous in law, then the court, in proceedings in appropriate form... has jurisdiction to correct the error of law by an appropriate declaration'. The consultation process may also be open to challenge for procedural unfairness—see In *R (oao Greenpeace Ltd) v Secretary of State for Trade and Industry*, discussed below.

[99] *Lord Advocate v Dumbarton District Council* [1990] 2 AC 580, HL.

[100] For instance, it would not be possible to prosecute the Highway Agency as it is an executive agency of the Department for Transport, unlike the Environment Agency which exists as a non-departmental public body in its own right.

[101] *M v Home Office*; sub nom *M, Re* [1993] 3 WLR 433, HL (contempt proceedings over handling of asylum seeker); *R v Secretary of State for Transport, ex p Factortame* [1990] 2 AC 85 (act contrary to EEC law). A declaration can be granted in lieu: s 21(1)(a), Crown Proceedings Act 1947.

[102] *CCSU* [1985] AC 374; the royal prerogative cannot give rise to new powers, and it cannot exist where a statute deals with the same matter (*Attorney-General v De Keyser's Royal Hotel Ltd* [1920] AC 508). The remedy of mandamus is only available when a Crown servant is exercising a statutory power (*Padfield v MAFF* [1968] AC 997).

[103] Parliamentary Commissioner Act 1967, as amended by the Parliamentary and Health Commissioners Act 1987. The scrutiny extends to ministerial acts, and over 100 departments

2.33 Crown immunity continues to have real effects, and does allow government departments to avoid some of the controls that would normally apply. This immunity was
apparent during the foot and mouth crisis in 2001, when the Secretary of State for
the Environment, Food and Rural Affairs was held to be entitled to dispose of the
remains of infected cattle by burial rather than by incineration as was normal.[104] In
some areas, there has been a distinct erosion of this legal immunity. For instance,
Crown immunity has been removed from NHS Hospitals, so that hospital incinerators are now subject to the same regulatory system as other incinerators.[105] The
Crown has some limited responsibilities under the principal Water Acts, following
the amendments made by the Environment Act 1995.[106] The Town and Country
Planning Act 1990 now applies to Crown land, with some reservations[107].

The local authorities

2.34 Many important functions and duties of environmental regulation are still carried
out at local government level. It is the district council, or unitary authority, who is
responsible for local air pollution control under the Environmental Permitting
provisions (formerly contained in Part I of the EPA 1990), for all statutory nuisances
under Part III of the EPA 1990, litter, hazardous substances consent, and for
public health measures. They also have the main duties for contaminated land under
Part IIA of the EPA 1990. Their particular roles in each of these fields are discussed

---

acting on behalf of the Crown (Sch 2 of the Parliamentary Commissioner Act1967), as well as to
refusals of access to information which should be made available under the Code of Practice on
Government Information. Complaints must be made through Members of Parliament—who
may themselves provide a useful ally.

[104] *Robert Feakins v Secretary of State for the Environment, Food and Rural Affairs* [2002] EWHC
2574 (Admin), which held that the Animal By-Products Order 1999 (SI 1999/646) did not bind
the Crown. Some 4,750 carcasses had been burnt on open pyres on the claimant's land, from his
own and neighbouring farms. It was reluctantly accepted by the government that the residue needed
to be removed to licensed landfill sites. Ultimately, at the Court of Appeal (2004) 1 WLR 1761,
the Secretary of State relied on the derogation option provided by European Regulations (Council
Regulation 999/2001/EC) to avoid incineration, even though there was no national legislation
implementing this. A normal operator would not have been able to act in this way.

[105] Therefore there would be a different result today in *London Borough of Hillingdon v Secretary
of State for the Environment and Hillingdon Hospital NHS Trust and Others* 30/7/99 (NHS Trust
incinerator), when Forbes J. accepted that the hospital incinerator benefited from Crown immunity
and was therefore immune from enforcement at common law and under the Town and Country
Planning Act 1990.

[106] Sch 21, paras 1 and 2, to introduce a new s 221 of the Water Industry Act 1991, and s 222
of the Water Resources Act 1991. However, the Crown cannot be found criminally liable, although
the High Court may declare that any particular act or omission is unlawful. S 222 of the Water
Resources Act 1991 was brought into force under SI 1997/1626, subject to transitional provisions.

[107] Part 7 of the Planning and Compulsory Purchase Act 2004 amended the Town and
Country Planning Act 1990 so that the 1990 Act binds the Crown. See also the Town and Country
Planning (Application of Subordinate Legislation to the Crown) Order 2006, and Department for
Communities and Local Government Circular 02/2006 'Crown Application of the Planning Acts'
for further explanation.

in the relevant chapters. The environmental health and trading standards departments of the local authorities also enforce some of the legislation relating to health
and safety, food safety, pesticides,[108] as well as the storage of explosives and petroleum
licensing.[109] The Town and Country Planning regime is administered by the local
councils, subject to the supervision of the relevant Secretary of State or Welsh Minister,
who determine appeals and retain considerable powers of direction and guidance.
The primary responsibility lies with the district council, or unitary authority, although
matters such as minerals and waste planning remain county council matters.[110] In
London, the Mayor of London has been given broad supervisory powers, including
the environment, which allow some independent action and that need to be taken
into account by the London Borough Councils and the City of London.[111]

In addition to their specific legislative roles, local authorities in England and Wales   **2.35**
have now been given a wide discretionary power to do anything they consider
likely to promote or improve the economic, social, or environmental well-being
of their area, including local action to promote the sustainable development of
their areas by delivering the actions and improvements identified in the community strategy.[112] They can also act in the courts on behalf of the public. Under
Section 222 of the Local Government Act 1972, they may undertake any legal
proceedings that are for 'the promotion or protection of the interests of the inhabitants of their area'. This includes the power to seek an injunction to enforce

---

[108] Under the Food and Environment Protection Act 1985 and the Control of Pesticides
Regulations 1986 in respect of the use of pesticides in domestic premises; the Health and Safety
Executive are otherwise responsible for regulating pesticides.

[109] The Petroleum Licensing Authorities are the authorities with responsibility for enforcement
of the Petroleum Consolidation Act 1928, and the Petroleum Consolidation Act (Enforcement)
Regulations 1979. This is normally the county council, although in London it is the London Fire
Brigade.

[110] See further *Cross on Local Government*, and see the Chapter on Planning and Pollution
Control further.

[111] See the Greater London Authority Acts 1999 and 2007. There are limits to this supervisory
power—his direction requiring a waste disposal authority to provide a new disposal site was quashed
in *R (on the application of Enfield London Borough Council) v Mayor of London* [2007] EWHC
1795 (Admin). The 1999 Act requires the Mayor to produce a number of strategies including the
Climate Change and Energy Strategy for London, Transport, the London Development Agency, the
London Biodiversity Action Plan, municipal waste management, air quality and culture. Note that
the Secretary of State retains his power to issue regional planning guidance, and has the sole power
to call-in applications and to decide appeals.

[112] Part I of the Local Government Act 2001, which came into force on 18 October 2000. This is
intended to avoid narrow legalistic debates about the statutory limits to their discretion. Examples of
the kind of action that can be taken are set out in s 2(4) of the Act, including incurring expenditure,
providing staff, goods or services to any person, entering into partnership arrangements, and carrying
out the functions of other bodies. The power cannot be used to raise money or to circumvent any prohibitions, restrictions or limitations contained on the face of legislation (s 3). The local authority will
need to have regard to statutory guidance and to its own community strategy. The Secretary of State
also has a reserve power to prevent local authorities from exercising the power to take specific actions.

obedience to the criminal law within their district. [113] Port Health Authorities have similar powers to local authorities in relation to public health, waste disposal, and the control of pollution.[114] The accountability of public bodies has also been affected by the increased contractualization of central and local government services to the private sector.[115] Most of this contractualization has been compulsory, and the environmental functions of public bodies have not been an exception to this process—such as in the creation of arm's-length waste disposal companies by local authorities under Part II of the EPA 1990.

Other public bodies and executive agencies

2.36   The traditional model of parliamentary government has been complicated by the rise of executive agencies within national departments and the creation of numerous 'non-departmental public bodies'. Any Executive Agency continues to act as the servant of central government, acting in the name of the Secretary of State, while maintaining a de facto autonomy. So, the Highways Agency is in law no more than an agent of the Secretary of State for Transport. The Planning Inspectorate, which also hears environmental appeals, is also an example of such an agency. The exception is the 'non-departmental public body', better known by the popular term 'QUANGO'.[116] These have been created by Parliament and have their own powers and duties, and exist as separate legal entities. But they often remain subject to considerable central government influence and interference. The Environment Agency is such a body. Its role is central to many of the regimes discussed in this book, and it is discussed in detail in this chapter.

2.37   There are a number of other public agencies that have a role to play in environmental issues but which were not included within the Environment Agency. The HSE still deals with health and safety at work, the storage of hazardous substances, and major accident hazards. Similarly, the Drinking Water Inspectorate remains part of Defra, although it is the Chief Inspector of Drinking Water who handles any relevant prosecutions.[117] The division of labour is even more marked in the

---

[113]   eg *Stoke-on-Trent CC v B&Q (Retail)* [1984] AC 754 (restraining Sunday trading), *City of London Corpn v Bovis Construction Ltd* [1992] 3 All ER 697 (building works as a public nuisance). The question is then whether, in the circumstances, criminal proceedings were likely to prove ineffective in achieving the public interest purposes for which the legislation in question had been enacted. But it should not be stretched too far (*Guildford Borough Council v Hein* [2005] EWCA Civ 979 – no right to retain dogs following cruelty charges).

[114]   See The Public Health (Control of Diseases) Act 1984.

[115]   The problems of the traditional legal framework in coping with the privatization of public services is discussed in Mark Freedland, 'Governing by Contract and Public Law' [1994] PL 86.

[116]   The acronym for 'quasi-autonomous non-governmental organisation', which has unflattering connotations.

[117]   DWI investigates all drinking water quality incidents, and since the Water Act 2003 it can take forward prosecutions in the name of the Chief Inspector of Drinking Water. See <http://www.dwi.gov.uk>.

area of conservation policy, even though the Agency is itself under a duty to take nature conservation considerations into account in all its activities. As discussed in Chapter 11, the different national Nature Conservancy Councils have the main responsibility for this area,[118] including Natural England, which has assumed the combined roles of English Nature with parts of the Countryside Agency and the Rural Development Service[119]. Although it is not a statutory body, the Waste Management Industry Training and Advisory Board (WAMITAB)[120] plays a public role and would be susceptible to judicial review, in a similar way to the Advertising Standards Authority.[121]

Statutory undertakers

There are a number of legal bodies that are authorized by particular statutes[122] to provide public services or utilities. These bodies used to be mainly public bodies, but there are now a large number of private companies that benefit from these powers, with the privatization of the majority of the statutory undertakers in the water, gas, electricity, and telecommunications utilities sector. In addition, the Coal Authority and Railtrack retain certain regulatory functions in their respective areas. Since privatization of the water industry in 1989, discharges into the sewers have been the responsibility of 'sewerage undertakers', who are currently the ten privatized water authorities. They are also responsible for the supply of water, in addition to the 29 other private water companies. Their role under the Water Industry Act 1991, and the considerable public powers and duties they are given, is discussed in the Chapter on the Water Industry. The privatized utilities are also subject to considerable scrutiny and control from the utility regulators, who can determine pricing and investment levels. The regulation of the water industry is in the hands of the Water Services Regulation Authority (Ofwat), under the Water

2.38

---

[118] Note that the Joint Nature Conservancy Council delivers the UK and international responsibilities of the four country nature conservation agencies: the Countryside Council for Wales, Natural England, Scottish Natural Heritage, and the Council for Nature Conservation and the Countryside (in Northern Ireland).

[119] It was established as an independent statutory Non Departmental Public Policy Body by the Natural Environment and Rural Communities Act 2006.

[120] WAMITAB is a company limited by guarantee which was founded by the Institute of Wastes Management, the National Association of Waste Disposal Contractors, and the Road Haulage Association. In 1990, the Department of the Environment entered into agreement with the Board to develop and supervise the necessary Certificates of Technical Competence (COTC). These certificates are then recognized for the purposes of determining whether a person is a 'fit and proper person' to hold a waste management licence under Part II of the EPA 1990. The first COTC was issued in 1996 and approximately 6600 COTCs had been issued by 2007 (see <http://www.wamitab.org.uk>).

[121] See *R v Panel on Takeovers and Mergers, ex p Datafin Plc* [1987] QB 815 and *R v Advertising Standards Authority, ex p Insurance Services plc* [1990] 2 Admin LR 77. This is in distinction to a body such as the Insurance Ombudsman Bureau, where the source of power is contractual and the jurisdiction is voluntary.

[122] The statutory undertakers are also given certain dispensations from planning control when carrying out development related to their operations: see the Town and Country Planning (General Permitted Development) Order 1995 (SI 1995/418).

Industry Act 1991.[123] The implications for public accountability remain unclear. In so far as they are carrying out public functions, as opposed to contractual arrangements, they are susceptible to judicial review by the courts. In most other respects, 'accountability' is now provided through the regulatory office,[124] or by the operation of market choice and the competitive pressures it brings, rather than through the assertion of an individual's constitutional legal rights in the courts.

The Royal Commission on Environmental Pollution

2.39   The relevant Royal Commission which deals with environmental matters is a standing commission, funded by the Department of the Environment. Its members are appointed by the Prime Minister. The Commission seeks to make a balanced assessment of the topics it investigates, looking at scientific, social, and economic matters as well as the legal issues involved. Its more recent reports have covered such matters as the Incineration of Waste, Transport and the Environment, the Sustainable Use of Soil, and Environmental Planning[125] and its study on 'Adapting the UK to Climate Change' is due to be published in 2009. None of the reports and recommendations prepared by the Commission establish national policy, however influential they may be. It is the convention that the government will publish its response to the proposals, which can then lend these reports considerable weight, particularly as material considerations in any discretionary determination. As a public body exercising power delegated by prerogative power,

---

[123]   The Water Services Regulation Authority (Ofwat) describes itself as 'the economic regulator of the water and sewerage industry in England and Wales', whose role is to seek value for consumers. Note that the short name of 'Ofwat' has remained unchanged, but it now stands for the regulatory authority established under the Water Act 2003, and not the Director General of Water Services. His functions were transferred to the new authority on 1 April 2006.

[124]   Indeed, the House of Lords considered that the complaint mechanism to OfWat (where there are no provisions for the recovery of legal costs) was an adequate substitute for the right to bring a nuisance action for sewage flooding from inadequate sewer systems into people's homes—*Marcic v Thames Water Utilities Limited* [2004] AC 42, HL. As was said, 'the cause of action in nuisance asserted by Mr Marcic is inconsistent with the statutory scheme. Mr Marcic's claim is expressed in various ways but in practical terms it always comes down to this: Thames Water ought to build more sewers' (per Lord Nicholls at para [34]). But note that the Claimants in *Hanifa Dobson and Others v Thames Water Utilities Ltd (OfWAT as Intervenors)* [2007] EWHC 2021 (TCC) were not precluded from bringing a claim based on nuisance involving negligence, negligence, or negligence under the Human Rights Act 1998 where, as a matter of fact and degree, the exercise of adjudicating on that cause of action was not inconsistent with the statutory process under the Water Resources Act 1991.

[125]   See <http://www.rcep.org.uk> further, where copies of all the reports are available. They are also officially published—for instance, the Sustainable Use of Soil (19th, Cm 3165, Feb 1996), Environmental Planning (Cm 5459, March 2002), The Urban Environment (Cm 7009, March 2007). The RCEP's 'Short Reports' are not part of the official series, and there is no obligation on the government to respond to them (although it has chosen to respond to the one on Biomass—'Biomass as a renewable energy source' published by RCEP in May 2004. The government responses are available on Defra's website (<http://www.defra.gov.uk>).

it is in theory capable of being amenable to judicial review.[126] It was established by Royal Warrant in 1970 with the following terms of reference:

> To advise on matters, both national and international, concerning the pollution of the environment; on the adequacy of research in this field; and the future possibilities of danger to the environment.

The Royal Commission itself has stated that: **2.40**

> We do not have the competence or the resources to act as environmental ombuds-man, dealing with appeals against local or central government decisions about spe-cific cases of alleged damage to the environment where there are already channels through which such appeals may be made; what we are able to do is to give advice on the general principles which should guide Parliament and public opinion.[127]

Other research bodies

The oldest body on the environment which has official standing is the National   **2.41**
Environment Research Council, which was established by Royal Charter in 1965. It provides independent advice and provides grants or training and research.[128] The government has also established a number of research bodies. Some are intended to bring together the relevant interest groups. The Government Advisory Committee on Business and the Environment was established in 1991 to report generally to Ministers. The Sustainable Development Commission[129] has a higher public profile, and its stated role is to act as the Government's independent watch-dog on its progress on sustainable development. It reports to the Prime Minister, the First Ministers of Scotland and Wales, and to the First Minister and Deputy First Minister of Northern Ireland. Although the Commission's influence and authority is only derived from its agreement with each of these government bod-ies, it has sought to take an independent line and to stimulate a wider debate about specific issues—for instance, by promoting tidal power, and opposing the case for new nuclear power generation. One international body which has had a consider-able influence on environmental standards is the World Health Organization (WHO), although its guidelines are better debated between experts than between

---

[126] *Council for Civil Service Unions v Minister for the Civil Service* [1985] AC 374. Moreover, advice and recommendations from public bodies to others contained in documents which them-selves have no direct legal force are susceptible to judicial review. See *R v Secretary of State, ex p Greenwich LBC* The Times 17 May 1989; *R v Deputy Governor, Parkhurst Prison* [1992] 1 AC 58.

[127] First Report, published in February 1971, Cm 4585. See also the booklet 'Royal Commission on Environmental Pollution, a guide to the commission and its work' (1996).

[128] See <http://www.nerc.ac.uk> further. Its research centres include the British Antarctic Survey and the British Geological Survey.

[129] See <http://www.sd-commission.org.uk>. It was founded by the Government in 2000, and has acted (in its words) as a 'critical friend'. Its role was expanded to take on a watchdog role as part of the UK Government's sustainable development strategy, 'Securing Our Future' (Cm 6467, March 2005). The SDC replaced the Government Panel on Sustainable Development and the discussion forum known as the 'Round Table on Sustainable Development', which was set up in January 1994 in the wake of the Rio Summit.

lawyers. It has published non-binding guideline standards for air quality,[130] which provide useful guidelines in the absence of any national standards. Its 'Guidelines for Community Noise'[131] document is often cited in noise nuisance cases.

E. The Environment Agency

The establishment of the Agency

2.42 The Environment Agency is the non-departmental public body responsible for a range of pollution prevention and control duties, water resources, and conservation issues in England and Wales, as well as flood defence, fisheries,[132] and some navigation responsibilities. Its Welsh name is 'Asiantaeth yr Amgylchedd',[133] but there is no distinction between the powers which it has in the two countries. It was established by the Environment Act 1995. Its direct responsibilities are wide-ranging, and it is also responsible for advising central government and local authorities. The Environment Agency's remit covers the whole of England and Wales; about 15 million hectares of land, 36,000 kilometres of river, and 5,000 kilometres of coastline, including 2 million hectares of coastal waters. The Agency inspects and monitors sites to check that they are complying with their environmental permits. In 2004/2005 it reported that it had made 79,221 visits to waste and PPC sites, 12,721 visits to sites with water abstraction licences, and 2,795 visits to groundwater abstractions. One wonders if the logo adopted by the Agency merely depicts a member of staff surrounded by a cloud of paperwork.

2.43 The creation of the Agency in 1995[134] fulfilled a long-standing commitment by central government to create a unified environmental regulatory body for England and Wales. A similar unified body for Scotland was set up at the

---

[130] The WHO has published 1985 Guidelines for Drinking Water and 1987 Air Quality Guidelines for Europe. The European Union has produced its own drinking water standards, which are now part of UK law, and has proposed that the WHO air quality standards should become mandatory.

[131] The Guidelines are available online at <http://www.ruidos.org/Noise/WHO_Noise_guidelines_contents.html>. This document is the outcome of the consensus deliberations in 1999 of the WHO Expert Task Force. WHO 'Guidelines' for Community Noise are exactly that, and any individual case must be judged on its merits—noise measurements below WHO guidelines may be considered a statutory nuisance, conversely, noise measurements above WHO do not necessarily prove that a statutory nuisance exists.

[132] This is one of the most visible parts of the Agency's work. Fishing for salmon, trout, freshwater fish, and eels in England and Wales requires a licence from the Environment Agency. Failure to have a licence is an offence, as is fishing in the close season. The Agency has Fisheries Enforcement Officers who patrol waterways targeting illegal fishing activity.

[133] Fortunately the term 'the Agency' is then used throughout the 1995 Act to denote both names (s 1(1)). Whilst it is a 'Non-Departmental Public Body' of the Department for Environment, Food and Rural Affairs, it is now appropriate to refer to it as 'an Assembly-Sponsored Public Body' of the National Assembly for Wales.

[134] It was set up as a legal entity on 8 August 1995, and then took over its duties from 1 April 1996.

same time. This substantially reduces the number of different public bodies with which businesses and members of the public have to deal, as well as creating cross-disciplinary staff teams within the one authority. It took over the functions of a number of bodies, namely Her Majesty's Inspectorate of Pollution, the National Rivers Authority, the Waste Regulations Authorities, and some parts of the Department of the Environment.[135] It has proved to be a successful idea, and the Agency has emerged relatively well from the government's wider review of the functions and structure of Government regulators in 2005. The Hampton Review[136] recommended the consolidation of regulators into seven thematic bodies, including an 'expanded Environment Agency'. It has also responded positively to the government's 'Better Regulation' initiative.

The legal structure of the Agency

The Agency is only empowered by the 1995 Act to carry out certain specific duties **2.44** and functions, and it can only do so in the manner set out in the Act. It is a body corporate consisting of eight to fifteen members, and it is these members (the Board) who carry out the Agency's functions and must take all its decisions.[137] The Board can then delegate its powers to its chief executive and staff.[138] The Agency has some element of accountability to Parliament, as the chief executive of the Agency can be summoned to appear before parliamentary select committees, like the Permanent Secretaries of government departments. The Agency is required to submit an annual report on its activities, and its audited accounts to Parliament[139] and to publish them.

---

[135] The property, rights, and liabilities of the predecessor bodies, as well as many of their staff, were transferred to the new authority under the provisions of the 1995 Act. At one time, it was thought that other functions such as those of the Drinking Water Inspectorate, the air pollution powers of the local authorities, as well as the functions of the HSE might be included in the new Agency, but these were omitted.

[136] 'Reducing Administrative Burdens: effective inspections and enforcement', Phillip Hampton, (March 2005, HM Treasury).

[137] Environment Act 1995, S 1 and Sch 1. The one exception is land drainage, where it is the local land drainage boards which have responsibility for all the land drainage functions except for issuing levies, making drainage charges, and borrowing money (see the Water Resources Act 1991 s 106). The old land drainage committees have been replaced, see ss 14–19 and Schs 4 and 5 of the Environment Act 1995.

[138] See Sch 1, para 6, that any act may be done by a member, officer, employee, committee, or subcommittee authorized by the Agency (ie the Board) to do so. The Board has delegated some of its regulatory functions. As any local government lawyer knows, proper delegation schemes are essential in order to avoid challenges to the public bodies' actions. Interestingly, the chief executive, at the time of the Agency's creation, was also made a member of the Board, but this is not a statutory requirement.

[139] The Annual Report is presented to Parliament pursuant to ss 46 and 52 of the Environment Act 1995. See for instance the Environment, Food and Rural Affairs Committee's report on the Environment Agency (seventh report, session 2005–6, HC Paper 780–1), and the Government's response (December 2007, Defra website).

2.45 Central government retains a considerable degree of control over the Agency. The Secretary of State is responsible for the appointment of the Chairman and the members of the Board, with one member appointed by the National Assembly for Wales, and the appointment of the chief executive also needs their approval. The Secretary of State and the Welsh Government retain their powers to intervene and give the Agency directions,[140] and it is they who approve its budget, pay the Government grant to the Agency and approve of its regulatory and charging regimes, and who establish the policy framework within which the Agency is required to operate. Conversely, the Agency does not have Crown immunity,[141] except in the limited instances where it is acting in the Minister's name.[142] It is envisaged that these arrangements will cover such areas as local air quality, assessing the impact of new and existing chemicals, and monitoring.[143] The working relationship between the Agency and its sponsoring department will remain crucial to the success of its work, and there will perhaps continue to be inevitable policy and financial tensions. The Agency is a large public body, employing about 13,000 staff and with a budget of about £1 billion, for which it must account to central government[144]. In comparison, the relevant government ministers in Defra, the main sponsoring department, have direct control over about 16,000 staff and a budget of £3.5 billion[145]. Political accountability remains an issue, and it is not a foregone conclusion that agencies like this should be independent. For instance, in rejecting the idea of an independent Environment Agency for Northern Ireland in 2008, Northern Ireland's environment minister said that her party 'took the role of environmental governance too seriously to externalize the organization into an outside agency'.[146]

---

[140] Under s 40, these directions can be general or specific.

[141] S 1(5) of the 1995 Act. So the Environment Agency was able to be prosecuted and fined £7,500 when a contractor building a flow-monitoring station on the river inadvertently leaked building waste into the River Exe in Somerset in September 2005. The pollution was the most serious 'level one' type and killed 300 fish. (Report on BBC News website, <http://news.bbc.co.uk, 2006/05/17>).

[142] However, s 38 of the 1995 Act allows any Minister to agree with the Agency that it should exercise some of his functions.

[143] For instance, the Secretary of State agreed with the Environment Agency that the information under the Sewerage Undertakers (Pollution Inventory) Direction 2004 should be furnished to the Agency acting on behalf of the Secretary of State (in exercise of the powers conferred on her by s 202 of the Water Industry Act 1991 to request information).

[144] In 2006/7, about £603m of the operational budget of around £1 billion was given in grant from the Agency's sponsoring Government Departments, but they also supervise the legal controls on how much the Agency can collect in fees.

[145] Figures for 2006–7. There are about 8,200 in the main department and the remainder are in related bodies under Defra (Press Release, 39/08, Sickness Absence Statistics); the budget was announced as part of the 2007 Pre-Budget Report and Comprehensive Spending Review, Press Release 357/07).

[146] See <http://www.planningportal.gov.uk>, report 29 May 2008, 'Northern Ireland minister rejects call for independent environment agency', comments of Arlene Foster MLA. She added: 'I am opposed to the setting up of yet more quangos where unelected people take decisions on behalf

The regional structure of the Agency

Much of the Agency's work is done from regional offices, whose boundaries were **2.46** decided by ministers in 1995. The regions are Wales, North West, North East, Midlands, Anglian, South West, Thames, and Southern. The different duties of the Agency have led to two sets of boundaries, despite the arguments in favour of following purely environmental criteria. For water management, the boundaries between regions follow the catchment areas. For pollution control purposes, although much of the boundary will be the same as the catchment area, they in fact follow the county council boundaries, and have only been altered where the local districts' boundary offers a better 'match' with the catchment area. There is an element of local accountability and consultation for the Agency's actions. In each English region, the Agency is required to maintain an Environment Protection Advisory Committee (EPAC), a Fisheries Advisory Committee, and one or more Flood Defence Committees.[147] In Wales, there are three statutory committees to advise Environment Agency Wales, and the Flood Risk Management Committee is also an executive committee.[148] Whilst this local accountability is an improvement on the situation which occurred before 1995 in some respects,[149] it does not of course reach the same level of accountability that is provided through the local authorities in each area.

The specific responsibilities inherited by the Environment Agency

The Agency is responsible for Environmental Permitting (formerly covered by the **2.47** IPPC and IPC regimes), radioactive substances control, waste regulation, major

---

of the people of Northern Ireland. I, along with my Executive colleagues will make the decisions that will be scrutinized by this House and by the [Assembly's] Environment Committee'. Foster still promised there would be 'clear blue water' between the role of the core department as policy maker and legislator and the role of the executive agency as 'protector, regulator and enforcer'.

[147] Environment Act 1995, ss 11–19. Again, the Secretary of State appoints the chairmen of the committees (s 12 and Sch 3 on REPACs). With the exception of the flood defence committee (see Chapter 9 further), they do not have executive responsibility, and the Agency must only consider any representations made by these committees with regard to the exercise of its functions in the region.

[148] The three committees are the Environment Protection Advisory Committee (EPAC), the Fisheries, Ecology and Recreation Advisory Committee (FERAC), and the Flood Risk Management Committee. The Flood Risk Management Committee is an executive committee that delivers flood risk management in Wales and is responsible for a £30m budget (there are 18 members; 8 appointed by Welsh Assembly Government, 8 appointed by the Welsh Local Government Association, and 2 appointed by Environment Agency Wales). Note that the Advisory Committee set up by s 11 of the Environment Act 1995 for advising the Secretary of State (and then the National Assembly) with respect to matters affecting, or otherwise connected with, the carrying out in Wales of the Environment Agency's functions, was abolished in 2002 (The Advisory Committee for Wales (Environment Agency) Abolition Order 2002 (Welsh SI 2002/784 (W.85)). The National Assembly will inform itself directly in relation to those matters.

[149] The National Rivers Authority used to have a Welsh advisory committee (Water Resources Act 1991, s 6), and there were regional river advisory committees (s 7). Waste management used to be a local authority matter, an element which has now been lost. There were also some non-statutory advisory bodies for waste. However, Her Majesty's Inspectorate of Pollution work was solely a matter for central government.

contaminated land sites, and the control of pollution of water. In addition, it is responsible for all of the functions previously handled by the National Rivers Authority. These included those related to the management and quality of water resources, but also the wider functions relating to flood defences, fisheries, navigation, and river conservation. The disparate nature of the Agency's powers does reflect the piecemeal history of the creation of its predecessor bodies. In particular, until 1 April 1996, there were a number of different agencies, split according to their sphere of control.

Her Majesty's Inspectorate of Pollution (HMIP)

2.48 HMIP was responsible for IPC, radioactive substances, discharges of special category trade effluent, and the spreading of sewage sludge on agricultural land. All of these functions were transferred to the Agency. The national Air Quality strategy introduced by the 1995 Act, for which the Agency is responsible, is a new power. The earliest such inspectorate was the Alkali Inspectorate (under the Alkali Act 1863), which became HM Industrial Air Pollution Inspectorate in 1983.From the time of the Control of Pollution Act 1974 until 1987, the inspectorate was part of the HSE, but it then reverted back to the Department of the Environment in 1987, when it was combined with the smaller Hazardous Waste Inspectorate to create HMIP. It remained as a government agency until the transfer to the new Agency.

The National Rivers Authority (NRA)

2.49 The NRA was a statutory body responsible for the protection of the quality of water, the management of water resources, land drainage, flood defence, the control of discharges into 'controlled waters', the licensing of water abstraction, and the duty to conserve and enhance amenity, and to promote recreation. It was created under the Water Act 1989, when the old water authorities were privatized and their regulatory functions were passed to the NRA. These privatized water companies remain. Previously, the role of regulator and provider had been combined. The ten regional water authorities were themselves created under the Water Act 1973, when they replaced the rivers authorities. The rivers authorities were themselves in turn a statutory creation, under the Water Resources Act 1963, and replaced the rivers boards which covered most of the country by then. The NRA was formally abolished by the 1995 Act, and all of its wide responsibilities were, perhaps surprisingly, transferred to the new Agency and remain with them.

Waste and the waste regulation authorities

2.50 Responsibilities for waste used to be locally-based. The county councils were the waste regulation authority for both waste planning and waste management licensing, and the unitary authorities carried out the same functions in urban areas. The 1995 Act saw these functions transferred to the national level. This centralization has extended to producing a national waste strategy, which will replace the local authorities' waste plans.[150] The London Waste Regulation Authority has been formally abolished, and the combined Waste Disposal Authorities in Merseyside and in Manchester have lost their powers. Waste itself will still be collected under arrangements made by the Waste Collection Authority (normally the district council), who will deliver the waste where the Waste Disposal Authority (still the county council) directs. The collection and disposal functions of the local authorities are intended to be transferred to LAWDCs[151]—arm's-length companies which compete by tender with the private sector.

Statutory controls over the handling of waste are a recent innovation, and there **2.51** have been a number of public bodies responsible for it. Although planning permission was required for waste disposal sites from the beginning of the planning control regime (under the Town and Country Planning Act 1947), the first specific control was only introduced under the Deposit of Poisonous Waste Act 1972. A comprehensive system for disposal licensing was only introduced by the Control of Pollution Act 1974 (CoPA 1974), which came into force on 14 June 1976. Prior to CoPA 1974, waste disposal itself was a local authority function under the Public Health Act 1936. This imposed duties and powers with regard to the removal of 'house refuse' and 'trade refuse' on the 'local authority', who also had the power to provide 'places for the deposit of refuse'.[152] The 'local authority' for these functions was the council of the borough, urban district, or rural district, although this was transferred to the county councils in 1974 under local government reorganization. The national waste strategy, the producers' responsibility for packaging waste, and the contaminated land regime are all new powers which were introduced by the 1995 Act, and for which the Agency has significant responsibility.

The Environment Agency's principal aim and objectives

In addition to the powers conferred on the Agency by the specific statutory regimes **2.52** for which it is responsible, the Environment Act 1995 seeks to lay down a 'principal aim' for the Agency to pursue as well as setting out a number of general functions with regard to each area of responsibility. These functions are expressed in a number of different ways in the 1995 Act, ranging from those which are mandatory duties to those which are merely desirable considerations to be taken into account in the exercise of the Agency's discretion. Although the aim may be to integrate all of these factors into the decision-making process of the Agency and the Secretaries of State, the question as to the weight to be attached to each consideration is

---

[150] EA 1995, s 92 introduces a new s 44A into the EPA 1990. Existing adopted waste plans will continue to have effect until the national plan is produced (para 16, Sch 23 of the EA 1995).

[151] The statutory acronym for local authority waste disposal companies—see Part II of the EPA 1990.

[152] Ibid, ss 72, 73, and 76(1)(b).

decidedly unclear. These aims, objectives, and duties are different from those which were given to its predecessor bodies. They must still be read together with the individual purposes and objectives of the different statutory regimes. In addition, much of the European legislation that provides the framework for UK environmental law is expressed to have its own objectives.[153] Much is therefore left to the Agency, in the exercise of its discretion, to determine. Underlying this determination is the pursuit of the 'principal aim', which seeks to attain the objective of sustainable development.

The principal aim of the Agency

2.53 Despite the central role given to the Agency's 'principal aim', this is not some clearly defined statement of intent. The Agency has not been enjoined, in discharging its functions, to achieve sustainable development—as it might have been. Instead, the aim is hedged about with limitations, and depends for its very substance on changeable government policy guidance. The 1995 Act states in Section 4(1) that:

> It shall be the principal aim of the Agency (subject to and in accordance with the provisions of this Act or any other enactment and taking into account any likely costs) in discharging its functions so to protect or enhance the environment, taken as a whole, as to make the contribution towards attaining the objective of achieving sustainable development mentioned in sub-section (3) below.

2.54 The content of 'the contribution' is to be determined by guidance from the relevant Minister and the Welsh Assembly Government, taking into account the Agency's responsibilities and resources, as set out in subsection 4(3). This statutory guidance is itself to be the subject of parliamentary scrutiny, and subject to the negative resolution procedure. Indeed, the introduction of parliamentary scrutiny was seen as an important safeguard, as the original Bill had only required the Ministers to give their own guidance to the Agency, thereby affording them wide discretion. The 1995 Act itself makes no further attempt, perhaps wisely, to define 'sustainable development'[154] or what the contribution is to be.[155] The Minister and the Welsh Assembly Government are also given a separate power to

---

[153] For instance, the implementation in UK law of the Waste Directive 91/156/EEC includes imposing 'relevant objectives' on the waste regulation authorities (now under the Environmental Permitting regime). Objectives also appear in the EPA 1990 s 44A and Sch 2A in relation to the national waste strategy.

[154] The explanatory document appended to the statutory guidance does contain a summary of the relevant principles, and cross-refers to the UK Strategy on Sustainable Development (Jan 1994, Cm 2426). See Chapter 3, para 3.09, further on the problems of defining the limits of sustainable development even at the international level.

[155] See Jewell and Steele, 'UK Regulatory Reform and the Pursuit of "Sustainable Development": The Environment Act 1995' (1996) 8 JEL 283, which traces the effect of the 'principal aim' on the regulatory framework set up by the Act.

issue general guidance to the Agency on the 'objectives' they consider it appropriate for the Agency to pursue, under subsection 4(2). But the Agency is only required to 'have regard to' both sets of guidance in discharging its functions. The guidance under both subsections 4(2) and 4(3) is intended to have specific parliamentary authority. Formal guidance was first issued by the then Department of the Environment and the Welsh Office in November 1996, and set before Parliament. As this was in the days before devolution, there was one single document for both countries. This was replaced in 2002, and there is now separate guidance for England and for Wales. The objectives that Ministers and the Welsh Assembly Government[156] have set for the Agency, to be applied when discharging its functions and developing its corporate strategy, are:[157]

> Protect or enhance the environment, taken as a whole, in a way which takes account (so far as is consistent with the Agency's legal obligations) of economic and social considerations, so as to make the contribution towards achieving sustainable development which the Secretary of State considers appropriate, as set out in this guidance. [158]
>
> Adopt an integrated approach to environmental protection and enhancement, which considers impacts of substances and activities on all environmental media, on natural resources, and where appropriate on human health.
>
> Discharge the Agency's functions in an economical, efficient, and effective manner and to organize its activities in ways that reflect good management practice and provide value for money.
>
> Meet high standards of professionalism (based on sound science, information, and analysis of the environment and of processes which affect it), transparency, consistency, and environmental performance.
>
> Conduct its affairs in an open and transparent manner in full compliance with the requirements of all relevant statutory provisions and codes of practice relating to the freedom of, and public access to, environmental and other information and to make such information broadly available subject to legislative constraints.

---

[156] The objectives for Wales are set out in a separate document, but are almost the same word for word—see para 4.1 of 'The Environment Agency's Objectives and Contribution to Sustainable Development in Wales: Statutory Guidance from the National Assembly for Wales' (Welsh Assembly Government, 2002).

[157] See para 4.1 of 'The Environment Agency's Objectives and Contribution to Sustainable Development: Statutory Guidance' (Dec 2002; available at <http://www.defra.gov.uk/environment/ea/sustain/index.htm>), which replaced 'The Environment Agency and Sustainable Development' (Nov 1996; DoE, MAFF, and the Welsh Office). The guidance was intended to last for at least five years.

[158] See Section 3 of the Statutory Guidance.

Ensure that regulated individuals and organizations comply with relevant legislation.

Develop in conjunction with Government a risk-based, proportionate, consistent, efficient, and cost-effective approach to the regulatory process; follow better regulation principles; and evaluate and, where necessary, improve the operation of regulation.

Provide timely and high quality advice to Government, grounded in the Agency's technical expertise and operational knowledge including, where appropriate, in relation to the development and implementation of Government policy and strategy, the implementation of international, European, and domestic legislation, and in European Union negotiations.

Reflecting on and building upon the principles of public accountability, develop a close and responsive partnership with the public, local authorities and other representatives of local communities, regional chambers and other regional bodies, other public bodies, and regulated organizations, and adopt effective procedures to manage these relationships.

Collect data of appropriate quality and prepare and disseminate information in a timely fashion for monitoring and reporting on all areas of Agency responsibility.

Monitor and produce periodic reports on the state of the environment, in collaboration with others as appropriate.

Undertake research necessary to support the Agency's functions and the delivery of its objectives, in a manner which is consistent with and complementary to the Government's research programme and takes account of research undertaken by others.

The Environment Agency's general functions

General functions with respect to pollution control

2.55 The general functions of the Agency are set out under the next few sections of the Act after the principal aim and objectives. Firstly, under Section 5, all the pollution control powers of the Agency are to be exercised 'for the purpose of preventing or minimizing, or remedying or mitigating the effects of, pollution of the environment'. This echoes the requirements with regard to IPC under Section 4(2) of the EPA 1990 and the definition of what constitutes Best Available Technology Not Entailing Excessive Costs (BATNEEC) in Section 7, but it now applies across all the regimes. The Agency must also compile information on pollution of the environment and follow developments in pollution technology and techniques. The following sections of the Act set out a number of further duties which the Agency must consider even in exercising its pollution control functions.

General provisions with respect to water

Section 6 contains a more general duty with regard to water. The Agency must **2.56**
promote the conservation and enhancement of inland and coastal waters and of
land associated with such waters, the conservation of flora and fauna that are
dependent on an aquatic environment, and the use of such waters and land for
recreational purposes. But it is only required to do so 'to such extent as it considers
desirable'. There is also a duty to conserve, redistribute, and augment water
resources, and to secure their proper use, but again only 'as it may from time to
time consider . . . necessary or expedient' (albeit subject to any ministerial direction). The only specific duty is imposed by Section 6(6) to maintain, improve, and
develop fisheries.

General environmental and recreational duties

Section 7 imposes these general duties on both the Agency and Ministers. They **2.57**
are under a duty, when formulating or considering proposals, to ensure that the
powers are exercised to 'further the conservation and enhancement of natural
beauty and the conservation of flora, fauna, and geological or physiographical
features of special interest'. The only exception made to this general duty in
Section 7(1)(a) is for pollution control, where there is only a duty 'to have regard
to the desirability' of conserving or enhancing these features. No such exception
is made for the duties in Section 7(1)(c), in considering a proposal relating to any
function of the Agency, 'to have regard to the desirability' of protecting and conserving buildings and sites of interest, 'to take into account' any effect on the
beauty and amenity of any rural or urban area, and even 'to have regard to' any
effect on 'the economic and social well-being of local communities in rural areas'.
Section 7(2) goes on to add duties to have regard to maintaining public access to
places of natural beauty and the availability of visiting sites of interest. Both subsections apply even when the Agency is dealing with water or sewerage undertakers.[159] In addition, Section 8 requires the Agency to consult with the Nature
Conservancy Councils, the National Park Authorities, and the Broads Authority
where any works may damage sites that are of special interest to these bodies.

The Agency will have to take account of any advice from Natural England when deal- **2.58**
ing with applications that affect any protected nature conservation areas,[160] and it is
also under its own duty to conserve biodiversity,[161] following the implementation

---

[159] S 7(3) and s 7(4) deals with Agency works which may obstruct navigation.

[160] As discussed in the Chapter on nature conservation; note that the Countryside and Rights
of Way Act 2000 has significantly revised the law on the notification, variation, management and
denotification of SSSIs, and there are more significant penalties for those who illegally damage
SSSIs. There is also additional protection given to European Sites and European Protected Species.

[161] Biological diversity, or 'biodiversity', is defined in the United Nations Environmental
Programme Convention on Biological Diversity as 'the variability among living organisms from
all sources including, inter alia, terrestrial, marine and other aquatic ecosystems and the ecological

of Section 40 of the Natural Environment and Rural Communities Act 2006. This requires that every 'public authority',[162] including the Agency, 'must, in exercising its functions, have regard, so far as is consistent with the proper exercise of those functions, to the purpose of conserving biodiversity'.[163] Perhaps controversially, 'conserving biodiversity' in this context includes, in relation to a living organism or type of habitat, not just restoring a population or habitat but also enhancing it.[164] This will require more than purely preventative measures to be considered. As the duty is to 'have regard' to this purpose, it is only one of many factors that the Agency must consider when deciding whether to, and how to, exercise its functions. For example, while the Agency would have regard to the purpose of conserving biodiversity in deciding whether and under what conditions to grant a licence to abstract water, this duty does not displace the other relevant factors, such as protected rights and river flows.

Incidental powers

2.59 Like other public bodies, the Agency is a creature of statute which can only do that which Parliament has authorized it to do. Again, like other public bodies, the Agency has been given incidental powers. Under Section 37, it has the power to do anything which in its opinion may facilitate the carrying out of its functions, and to acquire and dispose of land. The section also confers a specific right to institute criminal proceedings, but not civil proceedings. In Parliament, it was stated that this was implicit in the incidental powers, and it has been argued and accepted that this includes a general right to seek an injunction.[165] There is also a

---

complexes of which they are a part; this includes diversity within species, between species and of ecosystems'.

[162] 'Public authority' is defined further in the Natural Environment and Rural Communities Act 2006, s 40(4), and includes local authorities, local planning authorities, and statutory undertakers. 'Statutory undertaker' is defined as a person who is or is deemed to be a statutory undertaker for the purposes of any provision of Part 11 of the Town and Country Planning Act 1990.

[163] S 40, Natural Environment and Rural Communities Act 2006, which extends to all public authorities the duty that was previously only imposed on Ministers, government departments and the National Assembly for Wales under Section 74 of the Countryside and Rights of Way Act 2000 (to have regard to biodiversity as far as is consistent with the proper exercise of their functions). See also the Defra guidance—Guidance for Local Authorities on Implementing the Biodiversity Duty. It came into force in October 2006.

[164] Natural Environment and Rural Communities Act 2006, s 40(3). Note however that it is only Ministers, government departments, and the National Assembly for Wales who are obliged to have particular regard to the United Nations Environmental Programme Convention on Biological Diversity 1992 (s 40(2)).

[165] Viscount Ullswater, *Hansard*, HL vol 562, col 1035; for the argument that injunctions can be sought see Tromans, *Current Law Annotated Statutes, Environment Act 1995* (25, Sweet & Maxwell), at 25–99. This argument ignores the similarity with the incidental powers granted to local authorities under the Local Government Act 1972, s 111 where the case law is clear that the powers granted must be incidental to a main function, and the Section does not grant wide discretionary powers—for which s 222 of the 1972 Act was passed.

wide power to provide advice and assistance on any matter in which the Agency has skill or experience to any person.[166] Whilst the Agency has the power to provide information to the public free of charge, it is more likely to use its powers to require payment. The Agency can also agree with any person to provide advice or assistance in relation to an environmental licence at a charge, separately from the charging schemes which will be levied on each formal application. This sort of partnership would, of course, be in accordance with its statutory objectives.

Environment Agency guidance

In addition to the Agency's Enforcement and Prosecution Policy, which is dis-   **2.60**
cussed further below, there is now an extensive range of guidance documents produced by the Agency, which discuss the application process and enforcement options available to the Agency's officers within any specific function. These do not have any formal legal status, although they do assist in ensuring a more consistent approach is taken by each regional office, and in explaining the likely approach that will be taken to any issues.[167] The Agency has also continued its predecessors' policy of entering into memorandums of understanding with other public bodies, such as the HSE, with whose work their responsibilities may overlap. There are only a few statutory Codes of Practice,[168] and most Codes of Practice are simply statements of good practice.[169]

The Agency has produced a Customer Charter to assist the people it deals with.   **2.61**
Although the Charter is non-statutory, it is a Citizen's Charter, and a breach of its requirements may be prima facie evidence of maladministration.[170] Apart from the commitment to answer 90% of telephone calls within 15 seconds during

---

[166] Environment Act 1995, s 37(3)–(8); without this specific power the Agency, as with any other public body, could not require payment for its advice (*R v Richmond upon Thames LBC, ex p McCarthy and Stone* [1992] 2 AC 48, HL). Note that the 'principal aim' widens the Agency's interests, in theory, to any aspect of sustainable development—social, economic, or environmental.

[167] Many of these are published and available on the Agency's website, such as the range of Pollution Prevention Guidance Notes (PPGs) which are targeted at a particular industrial sector or activity and give advice on the law and good environmental practice. There are also internal functional guidelines, which undergo frequent review.

[168] See the Water (Prevention of Pollution) (Code of Practice) Order 1998 (SI 1998/3084), which approved the Code of Good Agricultural Practice for the Protection of Water, also known as 'The Water Code Revised 1998' (issued by the Minister of Agriculture, Fisheries and Food and the Secretary of State for Wales) and is relevant to the Agency's powers under the Water Resources Act 1991; and the Water and Sewerage (Conservation, Access and Recreation) (Code of Practice) Order 2000 (SI 2000/477), which gives practical guidance to water and sewerage undertakers and the Agency relating to their environmental and recreational duties under the Water Industry Act 1991. The Secretary of State is required to take it into account when considering the exercise of the powers under the WIA 1991 in relation to water or sewerage undertakers.

[169] For instance, the Agency's published Code of Practice 'Managing Japanese knotweed on development sites'(2006) is not a statutory code.

[170] Customer Charter leaflet, 'What can you expect from us?' (<http://www.environment-agency.gov.uk, 2008>). Maladministration is a matter for the Ombudsman (see further below).

working hours, the Charter also sets out the Agency's indicative timetables for processing the different types of applications. For instance, whilst a navigation licence should take ten working days, an application to modify or transfer of a waste management licence should take two months and a full application for a waste management licence should take four months, assuming that the application is filled in properly and includes all the information needed including the fee where appropriate. For more complicated cases, the Agency will seek to agree an extension beyond the stated times (although there is no power to do so for land drainage consents, where the two months given is statutory). The Charter also states that the Agency will attend all navigation, fisheries, or pollution incidents, which it believes are likely to have a major effect on the environment, within two hours (four hours outside normal hours). It also commits them to giving feedback whenever they are told about an incident, to let the person who reported it know what the problem was and what the Agency has done to fix it.

The financial constraints on decisions made by the Environment Agency

2.62 One of the significant restrictions on how the Agency chooses to discharge its functions is that it is required to take into account the likely costs of its actions. This general requirement under Section 4, with regard to achieving its principal aim, is taken a step further under Section 39 of the 1995 Act. This requires the Agency, both when it considers whether to exercise its powers, and then how to exercise them, to take into account the likely costs and benefits. This should ensure that the Agency's actions are proportionate in economic terms to the environmental aim to be achieved, and in accordance with the precautionary principle. The statutory duty will not apply in all cases. It does not apply to the Agency's duties, only to its powers,[171] so that the Agency cannot refuse to act on the grounds of costs in these matters. So, the Agency will not be bound by Section 39 when considering whether or not to prosecute in any given case, but Section 39 will affect decisions regarding remediation. Equally, while the Agency must rely upon water quality targets when deciding on a discharge consent, it can take account of the likely costs when setting any conditions on the consent that go beyond the minimum requirements to protect water quality. Even if the duty applies, it is not a simple exercise to take it into account. The Section itself is ambiguous. It states that the duty only applies to the extent to which it is reasonable for the Agency to take it into account, in view either of the nature or purpose of the particular power, or of the particular circumstances of the case. Moreover, the scope of any assessment of the 'likely costs and benefits' in any given set of circumstances

---

[171] EA 1995, s 39(2), a distinction which the draftsman had to emphasize with the word 'nevertheless'.

is difficult to define. The relevant 'costs' are broadly defined as including the costs to any person, or organizations, and the costs to the environment.[172]

It is part of the Statutory Guidance to the Agency that it should develop approaches **2.63** that deliver environmental requirements and goals without imposing excessive costs (in relation to the benefits gained) on regulated organizations.[173] It is certainly the case that many costs and benefits, in particular in relation to the environment, are inherently difficult to quantify, especially in monetary terms. The government has at least provided some general guide to the available literature on risk assessment and economic and policy appraisal.[174] The Agency will consider these sources, as well as issues such as the precautionary principle, the impact on the carrying capacity of the environment, the long-term implications, and the benefits for society as a whole. As has been noted:[175]

> Cost-benefit analysis ('CBA') involves expressing as many costs and benefits as possible in terms of the monetary or other value placed on them by society, and deriving the net benefit. This is a very general technique, but it has stringent information requirements. A particular area of difficulty is choice of a discount rate which may discriminate unduly against long-term options.
>
> In many CBAs there will be effects that cannot be given a monetary value and there will sometimes be key environmental assets which cannot readily be valued. Where there is no market for an environmental good, techniques for monetary valuation exist that measure people's preferences. These techniques need to be used with caution, as the values they produce may not always be robust for their intended (or unintended) uses. There is always a danger with valuation techniques of placing too much emphasis on those attributes that can be measured at the expense of those that cannot. Such approaches to trade-off often require the specialist advice of environmental economists. They are summarized in HM Treasury's 'Green Book', *Appraisal and Evaluation in Central Government*[176].

While there is no statutory obligation on the Agency to ensure that the benefits do **2.64** outweigh the costs in any given case, a failure to consider this would be prima facie evidence that the Agency had acted unreasonably. By way of comparison, the

---

[172] Ibid, s 56(1) definition, but 'benefits' is not defined. The 'environment' (defined as having here the same meaning as under Part 1 of the EPA 1990), is arguably not limited to the UK's environment, particularly given the global context of some of the statutory objectives.

[173] para 3.10, Statutory Guidance (2002). But the Statutory Guidance acknowledges that the requirement to take account of economic and social considerations has to be seen in the context of the specific activity the Agency is engaged in, as it may have only a limited discretion under the statutory powers and duties relevant to that activity.

[174] In particular, 'Guidelines for Environmental Risk Assessment and Management' (August 2000, published by the DETR, jointly with the Environment Agency and the Institute for Environment and Health), and see the Defra website further on 'Economics and Analysis'.

[175] See the discussion of cost benefit analysis in Chapter 8, Options appraisal and decision-making, 'Guidelines for Environmental Risk Assessment and Management' (DETR, 2000).

[176] *Appraisal and Evaluation in Central Government: Treasury Guidance, London, UK*, (HM Treasury, 1997), which deals with risk and environmental impacts as aspects of the general appraisal framework for projects, programmes, and policies.

policy requirement for a cost/benefit analysis, which local planning authorities are advised to do before deciding whether the service of a Stop Notice is 'expedient', has often been challenged by defendants.[177]

F. Prosecution and Enforcement of Environmental Offences

2.65 The criminal offences set out in the environmental acts cover both those who accidentally pollute the environment, and those who operate a process in breach of an authorization. In the latter case, the Environment Agency prefers to work in co-operation with those whom it regulates, so that it may be more appropriate to use an administrative notice. These are described in the chapters dealing with each regulatory regime. These notices allow the regulator to require an operator to take certain steps or carry out certain works on a case-by-case basis. In serious situations, the Agency can shut the process down, using a prohibition notice. A failure to comply with one of these notices is then a criminal offence. Indeed, although there will be an opportunity to appeal against these notices, this may not be enough to avoid criminal sanction.[178]

2.66 If someone has committed an offence, the regulators have formidable prosecution powers. In addition, if a company has committed an offence, there are also several ways in which an officer of the company, say a manager, can be personally liable as well as the company. Individuals, unlike companies, can then serve prison sentences. In many instances, it may also be possible to mount a private prosecution of a polluter. But it is by no means certain that an offender will be prosecuted. The regulators have considerable discretion in deciding whether or not to prosecute. The Environment Agency's own Enforcement and Prosecution Policy is based on the five principles, of proportionality in applying the law and securing compliance, consistency of approach, the targeting of enforcement action, and transparency in the way it chooses to act. Ultimately, the Agency will decide whether to prosecute if there is sufficient evidence and if it is in the public interest to do so. The breach may lead just to the issue of a warning letter, the service of one of the array of administrative notices, or a formal caution. It is only where the circumstances warrant it that prosecution proceedings will be implemented without prior warning or recourse to alternative sanctions. Therefore, although many of the offences are written as if they are ones of strict liability, the defendant's intent and the foreseeability of the incident itself will still be relevant in all cases.

---

[177] Town and Country Planning Act 1990, s 183 and DoE Circular 21/91, Annex 3; see Shona E Emmett, 'Stop Notices and Cost Benefit Assessment' [1996] JPL 3. But note that there is more pressure in this situation on a planning authority as, unlike the Agency, they can be liable to pay compensation if the Stop Notice is quashed (s 186).

[178] So, for permit holders, in 2005–6 the Agency issued 50 enforcement notices and took 56 successful prosecutions (the Annual Report).

Regulatory reform and risk-based regulation

'Better Regulation' initiatives have emerged from both the UK and the EU with **2.67** regard to the broad issue of how and when the state regulates private behaviour. The regulation of any behaviour that might give rise to negative environmental impacts is just one part of this wider picture. The 2002 Statutory Guidance states that the Agency must have regard to the UK Cabinet Office's five principles of 'good' regulation: transparency, accountability, proportionality, consistency, and targeting.[179] The Environment Agency itself has added to this list the issues of substantive effectiveness, cost-effectiveness (for government, regulators, and the regulated), coherence, fairness, practicability, and effective stakeholder involvement.[180] The 2002 Statutory Guidance to the Agency further states under 'Better Regulation' that any enforcement action by the Agency should be proportionate to the risk, and alternatives to formal enforcement action should be considered.[181] Where the Agency has discretion as to the manner in which it implements regulatory regimes or requirements, it should have due regard to the impact on competition in markets. It should provide adequate and timely guidance to regulated companies on any new duties contained in new legislation. The Government's Better Regulation programme now includes a Statutory Code of Practice for Regulators in England[182].

There is a risk that 'better regulation' simply means less regulation and control and **2.68** lower environmental standards, pursued in the name of saving costs and improving economic performance. On the other hand, it could lead to better pre-legislative screening of new proposals, better impact assessments, and the simplification of the existing mass of regulations. In the UK, this has already led to some reforms of environmental law, in water abstraction under the provisions of the Water Act 2003 and the consolidation of the PPC and waste regimes in the environmental permitting rules. It is also likely to affect the proposed reform of regulatory penalties and the implementation of the EU Environmental Liability Directive.

---

[179] See 'Regulation—Less is More: Reducing Burdens, Improving Outcomes' (March 2005); website at <http://www.brc.gov.uk>. These principles were first set out by the Better Regulation Task Force in the *Principles of Good Regulation* (Cabinet Office, October 2000), which is the citation given in the Agency's Objectives in the 2002 Statutory Guidance (at para 5.1).

[180] See *Delivering for the Environment: A 21st Century Approach to Regulation* (Environment Agency for England and Wales, 2003). It has found support for this approach in the European Commission Communications, *European Governance: Better lawmaking* (COM (2002) 275 final) and *Action Plan Simplifying and improving the regulatory environment* (COM 2002 (278) final).

[181] See the Agency's 2002 Statutory Guidance (cited above for England and Wales), para 5.1.

[182] The Agency has to take account of the Statutory Code of Practice for Regulators (December 2007, BERR), issued under the Legislative and Regulatory Reform Act 2006 and which was approved by Parliament in accordance with s 23 of the Act. It does not apply to Wales. The Agency must have regard to this when determining any general policy or principles about the exercise of the relevant functions, and when setting standards or giving general guidance about other regulatory functions (s 22 of the 2006 Act). They can depart from any provision of the Code if they conclude that the provision is either not relevant or is outweighed by another relevant consideration.

2.69   The Agency itself has adopted a commitment to a risk-based approach to Regulation, and it has given this the overall name of 'Modern Regulation'.[183] This means that the Agency will not apply its powers uniformly, and that it can use its limited resources in a more focused way on those areas where it thinks that it can make the most difference. It will target those operators who are seen as having the worst environmental records, and it will try to reduce the regulatory burden on those who are seen as being in compliance. The intention is also to ensure that environmental standards will improve across the board by providing financial incentives to companies to improve their environmental performance, and by encouraging the market for environmental goods and services.[184] How the policy works out in practice remains to be seen, as part of the approach is based on trusting that the operators remain compliant and that corporate social responsibility will encourage businesses to go beyond the minimum necessary to comply with the law.

2.70   If the Regulatory Enforcement and Sanctions Bill 2008 becomes law, the Environment Agency, and other regulators such as Natural England, may be able to use civil penalties and undertakings as an alternative to prosecution. The Bill incorporates most of the recommendations of the *Macrory Report*.[185] Part 1 of the Bill also proposes the creation of a Local Better Regulation Office as a statutory body to co-ordinate the regulatory actions of local authorities, particularly in trading standards, licensing, and environmental health services. It is notable that Raymond W. Mushal, from his perspective as Senior Counsel with the Environmental Crimes Section of the United States Department of Justice, has noted that if the UK does start to use the different levels of enforcement, then it is critical that a healthy balance is established and maintained between them, and that criminal law should not be allowed to become a rarity but must be considered the engine that drives enforcement.[186]

---

[183]   See *A Guide to Modern Regulation: Getting Better Results*; see also *Delivering for the Environment, A 21st Century Approach to Regulation* (Environment Agency, available online).

[184]   The role of environmental regulation in stimulating the market for environmental goods and services, driving innovation, and reducing business risk was discussed in *The Contribution of Good Environmental Regulation to Competitiveness: Paper by the Network of Heads of European Environment Protection Agencies* (2005), see <http://www.environmentagency.gov.uk/commondata/acrobat/prague_1229630.pdf>

[185]   *Regulatory Justice: Making Sanctions Effective* (Better Regulation Executive, November 2006, available on the government website <http://www.berr.gov.uk>). For those who want to follow the history of the Bill's proposals see Grekos, 'Review of Civil and Administrative Penalties for Environmental Offences: Background and Development Update Paper' [2008] JPL 463.

[186]   Mushal, 'Reflections upon American Environmental Enforcement Experience as it may Relate to Post-Hampton Developments in England and Wales' [2007] 19 JEL 201. Most modern Federal laws provide three levels of enforcement. The lowest level allows the Environmental Protection Agency to impose monetary penalties direct on violators. The next environmental response level is a civil judicial action involving the courts, while the final and highest in terms of severity is a criminal prosecution. As he says, 'no regulatory system is of any value unless it is vigorously enforced' and that 'without a commitment to aggressive enforcement, any system is just so many words'.

Prosecutions

Parliament has allocated prosecution powers to a series of prosecution authorities. **2.71**
The most important prosecution authorities for the purposes of the environment
are the Environment Agency and local county or unitary authorities in England
and county boroughs in Wales. However, in many instances, it may also be possible to mount a private prosecution of a polluter.[187] Where an offence is not an
individual grievance but involves a matter of public policy and utility, any person
has a general right and power to prosecute unless the statute creating the offence
contains some restriction or regulation limiting the right to a particular person or
body. Thus for most modern environmental legislation, including the EA 1995,
the right exists for individuals to instigate 'private' prosecutions. This right allows
pressure groups to 'focus' the attention of prosecution authorities and, in default,
to bring prosecutions where it is felt that the statutory authorities have failed
properly to exercise their duties. There are some safeguards, in that the CPS can
take over any prosecution, including private prosecutions.[188] It can also use the
general power to decide to discontinue a prosecution that has been started inappropriately.[189] There have been few private prosecutions for environmental matters in recent years.[190]

The environment agency as prosecutor

For the most important and serious breaches of environment law the prosecuting **2.72**
authority is the Environment Agency. The Agency has issued a policy document
that gives an indication of the policy it will adopt in deciding whether to prosecute
or not. The document serves the same purpose as the *Code for Crown Prosecutors*
in that it is a public declaration upon which the Agency will exercise its functions.
The publication of the document must be seen in the light of the criticism that the
Agency and its predecessor were subject to for many years, that it was too close to
the industry it was meant to regulate. The Agency, it was said, avoided confrontation

---

[187] See *R (on the application of Ewing) v Kenneth George Davis* [2007] EWHC 1730 (Admin),
Mitting J—confirming that a member of the public had the right to prosecute for any offence said
to have been committed against a provision of a public general act. In *Ewing*, the private prosecutor
was not involved in the dispute and was unaffected by the offensive behaviour alleged.

[188] The CPS has a discretion to take over proceedings in any case (including ones brought by the
Agency) under the Prosecution of Offences Act 1985 s 6(2). Note that if a case has been investigated
by the police, the CPS has a statutory duty under Prosecution of Offences Act 1985 s 3(2)(a) to take
over proceedings instituted by or on behalf of the police.

[189] Prosecution of Offences Act 1985 s 23.

[190] This decline was noted by Damian Carney in 'Environmental interest groups and private
prosecutions: a critical analysis 'ELM (2007) Vol.19 No.6 Pages 291–299. Apart from the disincen-
tives presented by costs and the evidential hurdles, he notes that publicity plays a major factor in the
decision to take an action and that there has been greater activism by public agencies. This may be an
indicator that the system is working better. See also Parpworth 'Enforcing environmental laws: the
role of the private prosecution' [2007] JPL 327, which supports its continued role as an enforcement
tool, but only as a last resort.

and dispute with industry, even when such was necessary. Such criticisms continue, as they appear to adopt a high threshold for bringing a prosecution.[191] This is perhaps 'provocative' and the Agency's record can be justified in the light of the enforcement policy and the actual severity of the incidents concerned (using their Common Incident Classification Scheme).

2.73 The Environment Agency differs from the Crown Prosecution Service as a prosecuting authority in that it acts as policeman, detective, and prosecuting authority. Parliament, in setting up the Crown Prosecution Service, signalled the need for the prosecution authority to be distanced from, and independent of, the police who were collecting the evidence. No such separation of powers exists as a matter of law within the Environment Agency. This being so, it is important that any decision to prosecute taken by the Environment Agency is made against a background of a rational, transparent, and consistent prosecution policy. A challenge can be made at the criminal court by the defendant to the decision to prosecute as part of an abuse of process submission, although this will be difficult to prove.[192] On the other hand, a decision of the Agency not to prosecute in a certain matter may be reviewable in the High Court on an application for judicial review, if the applicant is able to establish that the decision was reached because of some unlawful policy, or contrary to the stated policy, or otherwise perversely.[193]

The decision to prosecute for an environmental offence

2.74 It is by no means certain that an offender will be prosecuted. The regulators have considerable discretion in deciding whether or not to prosecute. The Environment Agency's own *Enforcement and Prosecution Policy* is based on the five principles, of proportionality in applying the law and securing compliance, consistency of approach, the targeting of enforcement action, and transparency in the way it

---

[191] See Ogus and Abbot, 'Sanctions for pollution: Do we have the right regime?' [2002] 14 JEL 281. The reply from the Agency lawyers described this as 'provocative' and defended the Agency's record—see Rick Navarro and David Stott, 'A brief comment—sanctions for pollution' [2002] 14 JEL 299. Certainly, the Agency does seem to have a more positive success rate than that of the CPS for general criminal cases, which does either suggest that more borderline prosecutions are not being pursued or that the Agency's range of other enforcement powers are being used in such cases. Different considerations do apply to these specialist areas. Lovat in 'Regulating IPC in Scotland: A study of enforcement practice' [2004] JEL 49, reports on a small study done on the views of the enforcement officers in Scotland. She makes the point that only 2% of all IPC offences in England and Wales led to a prosecution in 1998–9, and there were no prosecutions in Scotland between 1995–9.

[192] The jurisdiction of the lower courts to stay proceedings is very limited indeed and to be exercised with the very greatest caution. The Divisional Court has made it clear that it is not for the court to decide whether a prosecution was wise and well-advised or unwise and ill-advised (*Environment Agency v Stanford* [1999] Env LR 286).

[193] See *R v DPP, ex p C* [1995] 1 Cr App R 136. To date, there has been no similar challenge made to the Agency.

chooses to act. Ultimately, the Agency will decide whether to prosecute if there is sufficient evidence and if it is in the public interest to do so. The breach may lead just to the issue of a warning letter, the service of one of the array of administrative notices, or a formal caution. It is only where the circumstances warrant it that prosecution proceedings will be implemented without prior warning or recourse to alternative sanctions. Therefore, although many of the offences are written as if they are ones of strict liability, the defendant's intent and the foreseeability of the incident itself will still be relevant in all cases.

The Agency's enforcement and prosecution policy

The Agency has issued a policy document entitled, *Enforcement and Prosecution Policy* (November 1998), which sets out the general principles which the Agency intends to follow in relation to all enforcement and prosecution matters. The policy note, in so far as it is relevant to prosecutions, is divided into nine sections: **2.75**

1. The purpose of prosecution. The use of the criminal process to institute a prosecution is stated by the Agency to be an important part of its enforcement role. It aims to punish wrongdoing, to avoid a recurrence, and to act as a deterrent to others. Where the circumstances warrant it, prosecution without prior warning or recourse to alternative sanctions will be pursued. The Agency recognizes that the institution of a prosecution is a serious matter that should only be taken after full consideration of the implications and consequences. The policy note specifically indicates that regard will be had to the *Code for Crown Prosecutors* in taking decisions about prosecution. This produces a confusing array of potential policy statements and means that the Agency policy document cannot be considered as freestanding. The contents of the *Code for Crown Prosecutors* are considered below.

2. Sufficiency of evidence. A prosecution will not be commenced or continued by the Agency unless it is satisfied that there is sufficient, admissible, and reliable evidence that the offence has been committed and that there is a realistic prospect of conviction. If the case does not pass this evidential test, it will not go ahead, no matter how important or serious it may be. Where there is sufficient evidence a prosecution will not be commenced or continued unless it is in the public interest to do so. Public interest factors that can affect the decision to prosecute usually depend on the seriousness of the offence or the circumstances of the offender. These tests mirror, though not completely, those applied by the *Code for Crown Prosecutors*, which are considered below.

3. Public interest factors. In deciding whether or not to prosecute, the Agency will have regard to the following factors:
    (a)   the environmental effect of the offence,
    (b)   the foreseeability of the offence or the circumstances leading to it,
    (c)   the intent of the offender, individually and/or corporately,
    (d)   the history of offending,

(e)   the attitude of the offender,

(f)   the deterrent effect of a prosecution, on the offender and on others,

(g)   the personal circumstances of the offender.

These factors are not exhaustive and whether or not a factor applies in any given case will depend on all of the circumstances of the case. The Agency makes it clear that deciding on the public interest is not simply a matter of adding up a number of factors on each side. An overall assessment will be made.[194]

4.   Companies and individuals. The Agency states its policy on corporate responsibility with bluntness. Criminal proceedings will be taken against those persons responsible for the offence. Where a company is involved, it will be usual practice to prosecute the company where the offence resulted from the company's activities. However, in addition the Agency will consider any part played in the offence by the officers of the company including directors, managers, and the company secretary. Action may also be taken against such officers where it can be shown that the offence was committed with their consent, was due to their negligence, or that they 'turned a blind eye' to the offence or the circumstances leading to it.[195] In appropriate cases, the Agency will consider seeking disqualification of directors under the Companies Act. This provision is an important one. Individuals, unlike companies, can then serve prison sentences. It should also ensure that, in appropriate circumstances, guilty parties cannot hide behind the veil of limited liability. A director consents to the action of a company when he is 'well aware of what is going on and agrees to it'.[196] A director connives where 'he is equally aware of what is going on but his agreement is tacit, not actively encouraging what happens but letting it continue and saying nothing about it'.[197] Neglect connotes a 'failure to perform a duty which the person knows or ought to know he has'. A duty may in certain circumstances be capable of delegation. Each case turns on its own circumstances in this regard.[198]

---

[194]   There will therefore be variations across the Agency regions, depending on who is making the assessment. It is striking that the Environment Agency Wales reported in 2006–7 that it took 108 prosecutions, all of which were considered to be 'successful', for a total of fines of £276,200, and with 83 cautions (EAW, Annual Report). This suggests that they have continued the questionable 100% success rate, which means that important borderline cases are not being pursued in Wales. On the other hand, they may simply not be publicizing their failures.

[195]   By EPA 1990 s 157 (and equivalent provisions in the other Acts), where an offence under any provision of the Act committed by a body corporate is proved to have been committed with the consent or connivance of, or to have been attributable to any neglect on the part of, any director, manager, secretary, or other similar officer of the body corporate or a person who was purporting to act in any such capacity, he as well as the body corporate shall be guilty of that offence.

[196]   *Huckerby v Elliot* [1970] 1 All ER 189.

[197]   *Huckerby v Elliot*, supra.

[198]   *City Equitable Fire Insurance Co* [1925] Ch 407.

5. Choice of court. The choice of court in which an offence is tried can be of fundamental importance. The powers of the Crown Court in serious cases far outstrip those of the magistrates' court. In the most serious of cases, the Crown Court has now shown itself willing to impose severe financial penalties. In cases of sufficient gravity, for example serious environmental damage over a wide area, consideration will be given to requesting the magistrates to refer the matter to the Crown Court. Particular regard will be given to the sufficiency of the sentencing powers of the magistrates in making such requests.

6. Penalties. As part of its prosecution policy, the Agency states that it will continue to raise the awareness of the courts to the gravity of many environmental offences and will encourage them to make full use of their powers. Indeed, the Agency has often expressed its frustration at the low level of penalty and of the approach of the courts, which is in effect not to treat environmental crime as real crime. [199] This trend continues. The Agency openly stated in its overview of pollution incidents:[200]

> We take enforcement action against companies that cause serious pollution incidents. Our successful prosecutions against companies in 2006 totalled over £3.5 million in fines that averaged £11,800 per business (compared to a total of £2.7 million and an average £8,600 in 2005). We successfully prosecuted 380 individuals; including 29 company directors in 2006. Six directors were fined £5,000 or more and five received other penalties, including two custodial sentences totalling 14 months.

> This is an unusual feature to be found in a policy document on sentencing. It has no parallel in the *Code for Crown Prosecutors*. In other areas of criminal law in England and Wales, the prosecuting authority plays no active role in seeking to influence the sentencing exercise. It is submitted that although a prosecuting authority can assist the sentencing court by reminding it of its statutory powers, it is wrong in principle for the prosecuting authority actively to seek particular sentences or to seek to ensure a particular level of sentence is imposed. That is a matter for the court. This provision of the prosecution policy is no doubt borne of the frustration felt by many within the Agency with the low level of penalty that environmental offences seem to attract. It is important,

---

[199] In a press release of September 1998, entitled 'Courts' Fines Fail to Match Tough Action Against Polluters By the Environment Agency', the Agency proudly announced that whilst nearly 600 pollution related incidents had been taken to court by it in 1997–1998, the average level of fine for chemical pollutants stood at only £2,000 per tonne. 'Fines of a few thousand pounds are no deterrent to multi-million pound companies—we want fines that reflect the seriousness of the crime' we were told by the Agency's Chief Executive.

[200] *Pollution Incidents—An Overview* (Environmental Facts and Figures, Environment Agency website, 2008). Of the 161 companies that were fined over £5,000, nearly half were prosecuted for either illegal waste activities or breaches of waste regulations. Most of the rest were fined for water pollution.

however, that the role of the Agency as an impartial prosecutor and officer of the court is not contaminated in any way.

7. Presumption of prosecution. Where there is sufficient evidence, the Agency will normally prosecute in any of the following circumstances:

    (a) incidents or breaches which have significant consequences for the environment or which have the potential for such consequences;[201]

    (b) the carrying out of operations without a relevant licence—the Agency sees the strict maintenance of any licensing regime as a prerequisite to proper regulation;

    (c) excessive or persistent breaches of regulatory requirements in relation to the same licence or site;

    (d) failure to comply or to comply adequately with formal remedial requirements—the Agency is not prepared to ignore remedial requirements: it takes the view that to do so would at the very least be unfair to those who take action to comply;

    (e) reckless disregard for management or quality standards—it is, we are told, in the interest of all, that irresponsible operators are brought into compliance or cease operations

    (f) failure to supply information without reasonable excuse or knowingly or recklessly supplying false information;

    (g) obstruction of Agency staff in the carrying out of their powers;

    (h) impersonating Agency staff.

8. Alternatives to prosecution. In cases where prosecution is not the most appropriate course of action, the alternatives of a caution or warning will be considered, the choice depending on the factors set out above. A caution is defined by the Agency as appropriate where there is a written acceptance by the offender that he or she has committed the offence, and may only be used where a prosecution could otherwise properly have been brought. A caution will be brought to a court's attention if the offender is convicted of a subsequent offence. A warning is a written notification that, in the Agency's opinion, an offence has been committed. The Agency policy suggests that it will be recorded and may be referred to in subsequent proceedings. While its admissibility will no doubt be the subject of dispute upon the trial of a subsequent offence, it will be relevant in any sentencing exercise.

9. Working with other regulators. Where the Agency and another enforcement body both have the power to prosecute, the Agency will liaise with that other body to ensure effective co-ordination, to avoid inconsistencies, and to ensure that any proceedings instituted are for the most appropriate offence.

---

[201] See the Agency's policy on the classification of incidents, discussed below.

10. Non-formal policy. In addition to this formal policy, it is clear from prosecution practice that the Environment Agency also have regard to other matters. These are evidenced in the day-to-day decisions of the Agency to prosecute. Other relevant factors certainly include the public's expectation of a prosecution, the perceived attitude of the court, and local and geographic factors.

Categorization of incidents

The Agency responds to complaints and reported incidents of pollution.[202] It will **2.76** log each incident and categorize it according to its severity. The category assigned is intended to describe the impact of each incident on the different mediums of water, land and air:

(a) Category 1 incidents—the most serious; there will be persistent and extensive effects on quality, major damage to the ecosystem, closure of a potable abstraction, major impact on property, major impact upon amenity value, major damage to agriculture and/or commerce, and/or serious impact upon man.

(b) Category 2 incidents—significant but less severe; there will be significant effect on quality, significant damage to the ecosystem, non-routine notification of abstractors, significant impact on property, reduction in amenity value, significant damage to agriculture and/or commerce, and/or impact on man.

(c) Category 3 incidents—relatively minor; there will be minimal effect on quality, minor damage to local ecosystems, marginal effect on amenity value, minimal impact to agriculture and/or commerce.

(d) Category 4 incidents are reported where no impact has occurred for a particular media.

In 2006, 910 pollution incidents were categorized by the Agency as having had a **2.77** serious impact on the environment in England and Wales, falling within their categories 1 and 2.[203] Ninety-two of these incidents caused major environmental damage. However, while these are the figures that were given headline billing, it is notable that if one looks more widely, then there were 17,133 'minor' recorded

---

[202] As noted in the Customer Charter, *What can you expect from us?* (<http://www.environment-agency.gov.uk, 2008>), the Agency will attend all navigation, fisheries or pollution incidents, which it believes are likely to have a 'major effect' on the environment, within two hours (four hours outside normal hours).

[203] *Pollution incidents—an overview* (Environmental Facts and Figures, Environment Agency website, 2008). To satisfy the bean counters, the Agency reported that these statistics showed a fall by 8% between 2005 and 2006 from 990 to 910, the lowest number on record. There was some overlap between the 910 incidents—161 pollution incidents that had a serious impact on air quality (most were caused by fires, mainly at waste management sites), 219 pollution incidents had a serious impact on land quality, and 605 pollution incidents had a serious impact on water quality.

pollution incidents, falling into the Agency's category 3. In addition, 2,062,617 fly tipping incidents were recorded in 2005 on the central web-based database called 'Flycapture'.[204]

Other prosecution authorities and the Code for Crown Prosecutors

2.78 There is no specific policy on prosecution published on behalf of local authorities as a whole, although many of them will have their own published enforcement policy. Many authorities will have regard to local circumstances as a relevant consideration in the determination of whether to prosecute. This is an inevitable and broadly acceptable consequence of allocating prosecution to local bodies.

2.79 Most prudent local authorities have regard to the *Code for Crown Prosecutors* in making decisions whether or not to prosecute. While this is drafted specifically for the Crown Prosecution Service, it does set out the relevant general principles, that:

(a) each case is unique and must be considered on its own, but there are general principles that apply in all cases;

(b) the duty of the Crown Prosecution Service is to make sure that the right person is prosecuted for the right offence and that all relevant facts are given to the court;

(c) Crown Prosecutors must be fair, independent, and objective. They must not let their personal views of the ethnic or national origin, sex, religious beliefs, political views, or sexual preference of the offender, victim, or witness influence their decisions.

2.80 There are two stages in the decision to prosecute. The first stage is the evidential test. If the case does not pass the evidential test it must not go ahead, no matter how important or serious it may be. In order to pass the evidential test, Crown Prosecutors must be satisfied that there is enough evidence to provide a 'realistic prospect of conviction' against each defendant on each charge. A realistic prospect of conviction is an objective test. It means that a jury or bench of magistrates, properly directed in accordance with the law, is more likely than not to convict the defendant of the charge alleged. If, however, the case does pass the evidential test, prosecutors must decide whether a prosecution is needed in the public interest.

2.81 This second stage is the public interest test. In 1951 Sir Hartley (later Lord) Shawcross QC, the then Attorney-General, made the classic statement on public interest which has been supported by Attorney-Generals ever since: 'It has never

---

[204] The database is the result of a joint project between the Agency with Defra, the Welsh Assembly Government and local governments. The Agency and the local authorities have been submitting fly-tipping data to this 'Flycapture' database regularly since it went 'live' in April 2004. The most commonly dumped items were household waste—76%. Tyres and vehicle parts constituted only 2%. Between June and November 2004 cleaning up after fly-tipping cost an estimated £23 million.

been the rule in this country—I hope it never will be—that suspected criminal offences must automatically be the subject of prosecution.'[205] The public interest test involves prosecutors balancing the factors for and against a prosecution. A prosecution will usually take place unless there are public interest factors tending against prosecution which clearly outweigh those tending in favour. A list of common public interest factors that weigh against the instigation of a prosecution would include cases where:

(a)   the court is likely to impose a very small or nominal penalty,
(b)   the offence was committed as a genuine mistake or misunderstanding,
(c)   the loss or harm can be described as minor,
(d)   there has been a long delay between the commission of the offence and the potential prosecution which is not the fault of the defendant,
(e)   the defendant has put right the harm caused.

These are, of course, similar but not identical to those identified within the Agency **2.82** policy set out above that have been specially framed to have regard to environmental considerations. The Agency's policy in addition is to have regard to the *Code for Crown Prosecutors* in making decisions as whether to prosecute or not. The differences between the two policy documents are distinct enough in certain circumstances to cause real uncertainty as to where the public interest could be said to lie. In such cases, the decision to prosecute remains with the prosecuting authority but would be less transparent than is desirable.

Environmental sentencing

The circumstances of each case can of course vary infinitely and very few cases reach **2.83** the Court of Appeal. It has resisted the invitation to issue sentencing guidelines, even though this was the first ever report produced for them by the government-appointed Sentencing Advisory Panel.[206] It is the magistrates that have an enormous influence on the standards of environmental safety and environmental protection in England and Wales. This is because the vast majority of 'environmental cases' are dealt with in the magistrates' court and the majority of those cases are guilty pleas. Very few of the sentences that are passed in such cases are ever formally reported. Those that are reported, for example through ENDS or within *Garner's Environmental Bulletin*, illustrate a wide inconsistency of approach to sentencing.

---

[205] HC Debs, vol 483, col 681 (29 January 1951).
[206] *Advice to the Court of Appeal—1: Environmental Offences* (Sentencing Advisory Panel). It considered the Panel's advice in the case of *R v Milford Haven Port Authority* (2000) 2 Cr App R 423; [2000] Env LR 632, concerning the oil pollution from the 'Sea Empress', at para 25, per Lord Bingham of Cornhill LCJ. As required by s 80(2) of the Crime and Disorder Act 1998, the Court considered whether it should frame guidelines, but concluded that it could not usefully do more than draw attention to the factors relevant to sentence see eg *R v F Howe & Son* (1999) 2 All ER 249.

It was in the light of this that the Magistrate's Court Association commissioned a report on sentencing for environmental offences, and produced sentencing guidelines for magistrates.[207] The guidelines have been taken into account by the Court of Appeal, although not formally approved.[208]

2.84 Typically, the first sentencing option will be a fine. What this means is that the level of fines imposed by magistrates is one of the key factors in protecting the environment through influencing the future behaviour of companies and individuals likely to be involved in the commission of environmental offences. It is through the process of sentencing that the aspirations and objectives for promoting the environment, protecting endangered species and so forth, can crystallize from theory into practice. For most environmental offences, the financial penalty in the magistrates' court is a maximum of £20,000 on each charge. This financial penalty exceeds the usual statutory maximum[209] sentencing powers of the magistrates' court and is meant to send a clear signal about the seriousness with which Parliament views such breaches. It is also a clear recognition that the operation of a prescribed process commercially can be a profitable business. A conviction in the Crown Court on an indictment, for those environmental offences which are triable either way, tends to carry a penalty of a fine without limit and/or imprisonment for a maximum of two years. A term of imprisonment is unlikely in most offences. Such a sentence was held to be wrong in principle for offences of knowingly causing controlled waste to be deposited without the relevant licence, in view of the fact that the defendants' actions had resulted only in an unsightly display of old lorry tyres and had not had an adverse effect on the environment.[210]

2.85 The potential route to more consistency in sentencing was signalled in the analogous field of offences under the Health and Safety at Work Act in the case of *R v F Howe & Son*.[211] This judgment gives an indication to lower courts of the types of factors they should have regard to in imposing sentence, and these have

---

[207] *Fining of Companies for Environmental and Health and Safety Offences* (the Magistrate's Court Association, May 2001). The report *Costing the Earth* is a good practice guide (Magistrate's Court Association, Nov 2003), and sets out some worked examples for many different types of cases, and also includes copies of the guidelines and those on *Sentencing for Wildlife Trade and Conservation Offences*. The Guidelines draw on *R v F Howe & Son*.

[208] See *R v Anglian Water Services Ltd* [2003] The Times, Aug 18, CA (fine of £200,000 for serious local water pollution by sewage effluent was manifestly excessive).

[209] The statutory maximum is £5,000 at the time of writing. The Court will also normally award the prosecution its costs, which can include the costs of investigating the offence (*R v Associated Octel* [1996] EWCA Crim 1237), hence the Agency's tendency to publicize the fine and the costs as one figure.

[210] *R v O'Brien and Enkel* (2000) 2 Cr App R 358; (2000) Env LR 653, appeal against sentences of eight months' imprisonment.

[211] [1999] 2 All ER 249; [1999] 2 Cr App R 37.

also been accepted as being of assistance in cases of environmental pollution.[212] In the *Howe* case, the Court of Appeal recognized the absence of sentencing guidance in health and safety matters and the disquiet that had been expressed about the level of fines emanating from the courts. The Court sought to outline some of the relevant factors that should be taken into account as part of any sentencing exercise. In assessing the gravity of an offence, it would be helpful to look at how far short of the appropriate standard the defendant fell. The size of a company and its financial strength or weakness could not affect the degree of care that was required, but were relevant in considering the effect of the fine on any particular defendant. Particular aggravating factors were identified by the Court as follows. First, a failure to heed warnings. Second, deliberate profiting from a failure to take necessary action. Particular mitigating factors included prompt admission of responsibility and timely plea of guilty, steps to remedy deficiencies after they were drawn to the defendants' attention, and a good safety or compliance record. Any fine should reflect not only the seriousness of the offence but also the financial circumstances of the defendant. Difficulty was sometimes found in obtaining accurate information about a company's means. The starting point was its annual accounts. Where accounts or other financial information were deliberately not supplied, the court would be entitled to conclude that the defendant company were in a position to pay any financial penalty it was minded to impose. Where the fine for a serious matter was to be imposed on a company the Court was of the view that the fine needed to be large enough to bring that message home, not only to those who managed the company, but also to its shareholders.

The courts have been encouraging the use of '*Friskie Schedules*[213]—a schedule **2.86** drawn up by the prosecutor to set out the main aggravating and mitigating features with references to the facts of the case which will be presented. It should seek to agree this with the defendant, in order to avoid the need for a *Newton* hearing. Among the factors to look out for in the prosecution case are:

(a) The Facts:
    The Actual Degree of Environmental Harm
    The Risk that there would have been Environmental Harm

---

[212] These factors formed a large part of the basis of the MCA Guidelines in 2001 (see n. 207 above) and see now *R v Cemex Cement Ltd* [2007] EWCA Crim 1759 at para [34]. Even though this was a strict liability offence (unlike a health and safety offence), the Court of Appeal relied on *Howe*. The fine for a breach of an IPPC permit was reduced from £400,000 to £50,000—none of the aggravating features expressly mentioned in *Howe* were present, and all of the mitigating factors were. Reference was also made to *R v Clifton Steel Ltd* [2007] EWCA Crim 1537 (another health and safety case, where the failures were not deliberate, nor did they arise out of a desire to save money).

[213] The schedule enables there to be no doubt about the basis upon which the court is sentencing. It is named after the case of *R v Friskies Petcare UK Ltd* (2000) 2 Cr App R (S) 401—a health and safety case, where the judge had wrongly sentenced on the basis that the company had put profit before safety, because no such fact had been proved.

The Duration of incident and its recurrence

Previous Warnings and Advice

Previous Convictions or Cautions

(b)   Motivation: Any proven financial motive will be a serious aggravating factor.

(c)   Action Following the offence:

Any clean up, co-operation, steps to avoid future incidents: As a rule of thumb, a genuine step is probably one that has actually already cost money.

2.87   The use of fixed penalty notices is becoming an increasing feature of modern Regulation, and these powers were extended in the case of summary waste offences by the Clean Neighbourhoods and Environment Act 2005.[214] It is also possible for the prosecution to seek to use them

G. Holding Public Bodies to Account—Judicial Review

2.88   The law books are full of important court decisions holding public bodies to account, and it has proved to be an important remedy in environmental law as well.[215] The environmental statutes provide the framework within which the regulatory bodies must work. As a general principle, all public bodies which are creatures of statute can only do that which Parliament has authorized them to do, and any action by them must be justified by some positive statutory power or duty.[216] The powers and duties must also be exercised for the purpose for which Parliament is presumed to have intended them to be used.[217] The specific grounds upon which a public authority can be challenged by way of judicial review are the same for environmental law as for any other branch of judicial review, namely on the

---

[214] Local authorities and the Environment Agency have been given the power to issue fixed penalty notices (and, in the case of local authorities, to keep the receipts from such penalties) when businesses fail to produce waste transfer notes, or waste carriers fail to produce their registration details or evidence they do not need to be registered, or on those who leave waste out on the streets (local authority only).

[215] The main texts remain Wade and Forsyth, *Administrative Law* (9th edition, OUP), and De Smith, Woolf and Jowell, *Judicial Review of Administrative Action* (6th edition, Sweet & Maxwell). A useful summary of the principles and cases is provided by Fordham, *The Judicial Review Handbook* (4th edition, Hart Publishing).

[216] eg *Bromley LBC v GLC* [1983] 1 AC 768 at 813H–814B, HL; *Stockdale v Haringey LBC* (1990) 88 LGR 7; *Somerset CC v Fewings* [1995] 1 All ER 513 at 524, per Laws J (cited with approval in CA).

[217] *R v Tower Hamlets LBC, ex p Chetnik Developments Ltd* [1988] AC 858 at 872, citing Wade, *Administrative Law* (7th edn), 391. The avoidance by a public authority of the effect of statutory controls is also outside its powers (*R v Nottingham City Council, ex p Nottinghamshire County Council* [1988] RVR 151). See also the Hon Sir Robert Carnwath, 'The Reasonable Limits of Local Authority Powers' (1996) PL 244.

grounds of illegality, irrationality, and procedural impropriety.[218] Proportionality has only been accepted as a branch of irrationality.[219] It will apply as a separate ground of challenge where some European Union law is being applied, in distinction to central government action under domestic legislation.[220] While a lack of adequate reasons may leave the applicant, and other interested parties, in doubt as to whether the decision has been taken properly, the mere fact that the reasoning was not fully stated at an earlier stage does not mean that the decision itself is necessarily bad in law.[221]

Judicial review does also allow those who are not directly involved in the administrative process to challenge the decisions or actions of the regulatory bodies, or, indeed, their lack of action. So, in *R v Her Majesty's Inspectorate of Pollution, ex p Chapman*,[222] an individual objector was granted leave to challenge HMIP's interpretation of what constituted BATNEEC in allowing orimulsion fuel to be burnt at a power station. In *R (oao Greenpeace Ltd) v Secretary of State for Trade and Industry*,[223] the High Court was persuaded to quash the government's consultation on the future use of nuclear power, as it was procedurally unfair and a breach of a legitimate expectation that there would be full consultation before the mix between the different types of electricity generation was fixed. **2.89**

---

[218] The different types of ground were considered by Lord Diplock in *Council of Civil Service Unions v Minister for the Civil Service* [1985] AC 374 at 410–414, HL (the *GCHQ* case). It was also stressed that the control of executive action has evolved on a case-by-case basis, and that it will continue to do so ([1985] AC 374 at 414F, per Lord Roskill).

[219] *R v Secretary of State for the Home Department, ex p Brind* [1991] 1 All ER 720, HL (exclusion order); *R v Manchester Metropolitan University, ex p Nolan* [1994] ELR 380, DC (penalty for cheating not irrational or disproportionate).

[220] *R v Chief Constable of Sussex, ex p International Traders Ferry Ltd* The Independent, 31 January 1997, CA; *R v SoS for the Environment, ex p National & Local Government Officers' Association (NALGO)* (1993) 5 Admin LR 785, CA; see *R v SoS for Health, ex p Eastside Cheese Co.* (1999) CoD 321, CA. The Secretary of State's decision to ban the sale of cheese on public health grounds was not disproportionate, in the light of art 36 (now art 30) of the EC Treaty.

[221] See *Crake v Supplementary Benefit Commission* [1982] 1 All ER 498. For instance, in *R v Her Majesty's Inspectorate of Pollution, ex p Chapman* [1996] COD 154, DC. the applicant was left with only an academic point of law to argue after the power station revealed further information which it had previously claimed was covered by commercial confidentiality. However, there are many instances where there is a duty to give reasons—where the courts will expect that principal controversial issues are dealt with.

[222] [1996] COD 154 DC. However, once granted leave, the applicant was left with only an academic point of law after the power station then revealed further information. See also local residents' challenges in *R v Environment Agency, ex p Gibson and Leam* [1999] Env LR 73, QBD, which went to a full hearing on whether or not the Agency was correct to authorize waste solvents to be burnt as fuel in cement kilns.

[223] [2007] EWHC 311 (Admin), (2007) Env LR 29; the consultation was carried out by the Secretary of State for Trade and Industry as the matter concerned the future production of electricity in general. The court issued a declaration, rather than a quashing order, as the Secretary of State accepted that it would observe this.

2.90 Where a person does have a statutory right of appeal, the courts will expect this to have been used before they will consider interfering in the administrative process.[224] A challenge in the High Court by way of judicial review is not an alternative method of appeal against a public authority's decision, in the environmental or any other public law field. These appeals normally do not lie to the courts, but to the Secretary of State or the National Assembly for Wales.[225] He or she will appoint an inspector to hold an inquiry, the majority of which are done by way of written representations. Public inquiries are usually only held in respect of particularly difficult or controversial appeals.

2.91 It is not for the courts to re-determine the questions of fact for which the Agency or any other public authority is the decision-maker. Indeed, there is a marked reluctance to interfere in technical or economic regulatory cases, particularly where expert advice has been received. The court appears to characterize such claims as being merits-based challenges.[226] The Foot and Mouth epidemic in 2001 also revealed that the law responds badly to a policy crisis. As Tromans has pointed out, given the reforms that were later introduced under the Animal Health Act 2002,[227] it would appear that the Government was, to put it mildly, skating on very thin ice in terms of some of its practices during the 2001 cull of almost eleven million animals under the existing laws in the Animal Health Act 1981.[228] The courts did little to prevent this, no doubt because of the apparent urgency required to act and the clear political will behind the decisions that were taken.

2.92 A successful application will result in the particular decision being quashed, or the public authority being ordered to act or to refrain from acting in a certain way, but it will still be for that public authority to make the actual decision in the light of

---

[224] So, in *R v Environment Agency, ex p Petrus Oils Ltd* [1999] Env LR 732, QBD, the application for leave to apply for judicial review of the decision to revoke the authorization to operate a waste oil refinery refused not only because it had not been brought promptly but also because the applicant was currently pursuing a statutory right of appeal against the revocation notice.

[225] In England, since 1997, this has been the Secretary of State for the Environment, Transport and the Regions—better known in the past, when there was a separate department, as the Secretary of State for the Environment. In Wales, Scotland, and Northern Ireland the relevant Secretary of State has the equivalent role.

[226] eg *Levy v EA* (2002) July 30, EWHC; *see also R (oao Western Power Distribution Investments Ltd v Countryside Council for Wales* [2007] EWHC 50 (Admin)—review of the statutory criteria and evidence for designating a SSSI, as a habitat for mushrooms.

[227] The Animal Health Act 2002 extends and supplements the powers contained in the Animal Health Act 1981. The Act makes a number of amendments to the enforcement provisions of the 1981 Act (Part 3), and provides additional powers to tackle Foot and Mouth Disease (Part 1, extendable by order to other animal diseases) and to deal with Transmissible Spongiform Encephalopathies (TSEs) in sheep (Part 2).

[228] For trenchant (and accurate) legal comment, see Stephen Tromans, 'Silence of the Lambs: the foot-and-mouth crisis, its litigation and its environmental implications' [2002] 14 ELM197. The few cases where MAFF were prevented from acting by the courts were the exceptions. In this author's view, allegations of extreme urgency were used to trump the need for more time for reasonable debate.

the court's judgment. Indeed, in exceptional cases, where there is no real possibility that a decision which has been taken unlawfully would have been taken differently, the court may exercise its own discretion and decide not to quash the decision.[229] A recent example is the sorry saga of the Agency's flawed public consultation process as part of the consideration of an application by Rugby Cement Ltd to burn waste tyres at its cement plant. Although important internal reports had not been disclosed, the court declined to quash the authorization as the data were now out of date.[230] But if the authority changes its mind after the judicial review application is made, and carries out the act for which the order is sought, the applicants should at least recover their costs. A public authority, which acts fairly and with proper consideration of its statutory powers and duties, need not fear the scrutiny of the courts over its shoulder.

There are practical limits to the usefulness of judicial review as a remedy. In par- **2.93**
ticular, every applicant must be able to show that they have made their application for permission to apply promptly, and in any event within three months of the date of the decision under challenge. The courts will be reluctant to allow late challenges to proceed. The issue will also arise of whether an applicant has a genuine interest in the matter to be given standing (or 'locus standi') to challenge the decision by way of judicial review. It is a less onerous hurdle than it used to be. So an incorporated action group can have a sufficient interest to mount a challenge to a grant of planning permission that affected its members but which could not be said to affect the company itself.[231] One way to increase the likelihood that a court will grant standing to a third party, is if they have taken up the opportunity to become involved in the decision-making process at an early stage. Most administrative procedures, especially where the grant of a licence or authorization is being considered, allow members of the public to make representations that the decision maker should then take into account.

The need to ensure effective access to the courts remains a problem in the UK. **2.94**
A major hurdle is costs.[232] The potential adverse award of costs is still a real threat for an individual litigant, or for an environmental group, who embarks on judicial review.

---

[229] See *Bolton MBC v Secretary of State for the Environment and Greater Manchester Waste Disposal Authority* (1990) 61 P&CR 343, at 353 (compulsory purchase order); applied, for instance, to refuse relief in *R v Canterbury Council, ex p Springimage* [1993] 3 PLR 58 (planning permission), *R v North West Thames RHA, ex p Daniels* The Times, 22 June 1993, DC (unlawful failure to consult on hospital unit closure). See also *R v Secretary of State for the Environment, ex p Watson* The Times, 31 August 1998, CA (failure to follow GMO obligations). See Chapter 20 of deSmith further.

[230] *R (Edwards) v Environment Agency & Others* [2008] UKHL 22; the Court of Appeal had also declined to quash the decision, [2006] EWCA Civ 877; (2007) Env LR 9, whilst the trial judge disagreed with this argument, and had quashed the decision (see [2005] EWHC 657 (Admin)).

[231] *R v Leicestershire County Council and others ex p Blackfordby & Boothorpe Action Group Ltd* (2001) Env LR 2.

[232] See, for instance, Lord Justice Brooke, 'David Hall Memorial Lecture: Environmental Justice—The Cost Barrier' [2006] 18 JEL 341.

It also acts as something of a means test. The basic rule, as confirmed by the Court of Appeal in *Davey v Aylesbury DC*,[233] is that ordinarily costs 'follow the event', and that it is for the claimant in public interest challenge cases who has lost to show that some different approach should be adopted on the facts of a particular case. Clarke MR considered that the rationale in public law cases, as in others, was because, where an unsuccessful claim is brought against a public body, it imposes costs on that body which have to be met out of money diverted from the funds available to fulfil its primary public functions.[234] Clarke MR did, however, 'entirely agree'[235] with the guidelines set out by Sedley LJ in *Davey*, that even where a claimant loses, 'a claim brought partly or wholly in the public interest, albeit unsuccessful, may properly result in a restricted or no order for costs'.[236]

2.95 The extent to which current law and practice could enable the UK to fulfil its obligations under the 'access to justice' pillar of the Aarhus Convention has been considered by an eminent working party, led by an Administrative Court judge, Sir Jeremy Sullivan.[237] The Sullivan Report makes a series of case management recommendations for public interest cases that the judges can adopt immediately, given their procedural powers. It recommends a different approach should be taken to costs, public funding, remedies, and case management. The Report was

---

[233] *R (Davey) v Aylesbury Vale DC* [2007] 1 WLR 878. The particular issue before the Court of Appeal concerned the public authority's claim for preparation costs, before a claim is issued, in addition to a claim for preparing the written acknowledgment of service. Whereas it is appropriate to award costs for the latter (see *R (Ewing) v ODPM* [2005] 1 WLR 1260, so long as they are not excessive), the defendant authority will need to justify why it should recover these preparation costs (*Davey*, para 21). No costs can normally be claimed for opposing the grant of permission in open court *R (Mount Cook Land Ltd) v* [2004] 2 P & CR 405.

[234] *Davey*, at paras 21ff. Clarke MR adopted with approval the reasoning of Dyson J in *R v Lord Chancellor, Ex p Child Poverty Action Group* [1999] 1 WLR 347, 355h–356e, and quoted the final part of that passage, that: 'in considering whether, and in what circumstances, there should be a departure from the basic rule that costs follow the event in public interest challenge cases, in my view it is important to have in mind the rationale for that basic rule, and that it is for the applicants to show why, exceptionally, there should be a departure from it'.

[235] *Davey*, at para 29, referring back to Sedley LJ's guidelines at [21] with this general 'note of caution'. Sedley LJ specifically considered Art.9 of the Aarhus Convention.

[236] *Davey*, at para [21]. As Sedley LJ also said, in so far as they do raise issues of general environmental concern, it is right to bear in mind what this court said in *R (Corner House Research) v Secretary of State for Trade and Industry* [2005] 1 WLR 2600, paras 69–70: '69. We are satisfied that there are features of public law litigation which distinguish it from private law civil and family litigation . . . 70. The important difference here is that there is a public interest in the elucidation of public law by the higher courts in addition to the interests of the individual parties. One should not therefore necessarily expect identical principles to govern the incidence of costs in public law cases . . .'.

[237] *Ensuring Access to Environmental Justice—Report of the Sullivan Working Party* (May 2008). The Report covers England and Wales. The members of the working party were acting in their personal capacity, but did bring to bear their different experiences as lawyers working for the Environment Agency, the Legal Services Commission, barristers and solicitors (from a big city law firm and a public interest law firm) and NGOs (the Secretariat was provided by Friends of the Earth).

published in May 2008, and was almost immediately referred to with approval in the courts.

H. Holding Public Bodies to Account—Complaints to the Ombudsman

As an alternative to using the courts to seek redress, any member of the public 'who **2.96** claims to have sustained injustice in consequence of maladministration' by a local authority may complain to the Local Government Ombudsman.[238] In the case of central government actions, including those of the Environment Agency, these complaints must be made to the Parliamentary Commissioner for Administration.[239] The one exception is where the Agency is exercising its land drainage functions, which remains a matter for the Local Government Ombudsman.

The Local Government Ombudsman can receive complaints either directly from **2.97** the public or through the local authority concerned.[240] The Parliamentary Commissioner may only receive complaints through a Member of Parliament.[241] Although the Parliamentary Commissioner is accountable to Parliament, his decisions are susceptible to judicial review on the normal grounds.[242] There is normally a twelve-month time limit for making a complaint. As the Ombudsman cannot be compelled to investigate a complaint, the remedy provided is rather one of last resort.

The Ombudsman will not question the merits of an exercise of discretion taken **2.98** without maladministration,[243] and may not investigate certain subjects, such as legal proceedings, or commercial arrangements (except the acquisition of land).[244]

---

[238] Local Government Act 1974 Part III, as amended by the Local Government Act 1988 (Sch 3) and the Housing and Local Government Act 1989 (Schs 11, 12). All local authorities are covered, except parish councils (unless acting for the district or county council: ss 25, 34(1)).

[239] Parliamentary Commissioner Act 1967, as amended by the Parliamentary and Health Commissioners Act 1987. The scrutiny extends to ministerial acts, and over 100 departments acting on behalf of the Crown (Sch 2 of the 1967 Act), as well as to refusals of access to information which should be made available under the Code of Practice on Government Information.

[240] Local Government Act 1974, s 26(2) of the as amended. The complaint is made direct to the local Commissioner for the area; the local authority is obliged to refer the complaint (unlike an MP).

[241] Parliamentary Commissioner Act 1967, s 5(1)(a), referred with the complainant's consent.

[242] *R v Parliamentary Commissioner for Administration, ex p Dyer* [1994] 1 WLR 621, DC; *R v Parliamentary Commissioner for Administration, ex p Balchin* [1996] EGCS 166, Sedley J (compulsory purchase order for a road and compensation).

[243] S 12(3) of the 1967 Act; s 4(3) of the 1974 Act. An Ombudsman went too far when he criticized the merits of a local authority decision which it had been permissible to reach (*R v Commissioner for Local Administration, ex p Eastleigh* [1988] 1 QB 855, CA).

[244] Sch 5 of the 1974 Act; Sch 3 of the 1967 Act. The procurement of local government goods and services is also excluded.

Nor will the Ombudsman investigate cases where the person aggrieved has or had a legal remedy through the courts or a right of appeal or referral to a tribunal, although he has discretion where it would have been unreasonable to pursue that remedy.[245]

2.99 When it comes to determining the standard of competence that is expected, say when dealing with the changing requirements for contaminated land, it is appropriate for the Ombudsman to check what other public authorities have done in similar circumstances. So, a complaint of maladministration was rightly held to have been rejected when a complaint was made to the Ombudsman that a planning authority had failed to find out about the methane problem before giving planning permission for the development.[246] While, with hindsight, it might seem that the council had overlooked an obvious problem, the truth was that central government had encouraged the development of landfill sites before the methane problems had been recognized, and it was only later, after a disastrous explosion in another county, that positive steps were taken to assess and avoid the potential problems. This was too late for the complainant and others in the same position to be able to show that there had been maladministration.

2.100 The Ombudsman's findings have no legal sanction, but their effectiveness lies in the power to investigate, and report on, complaints independently. The Ombudsman will also encourage the public body to settle a matter, and to give compensation where appropriate. For instance, when a local council and the water authority failed to satisfactorily deal with a farmer's complaints about the ongoing pollution of a watercourse caused by the development of a nearby industrial estate, the Local Ombudsman found that there had been maladministration.[247] He recommended that the authorities should meet the farmer's professional costs, provide a separate water supply for his cattle, and compensate him for his time and trouble in trying to resolve the matter. This is a remedy that operators can also use. For instance, in 2008, a council was recommended to pay compensation to the owner of a waste recycling facility, sort out the planning enforcement issues, and to review its enforcement and local plan procedures.[248] The Ombudsman found that there had been maladministration and that the council had unfairly withheld business from him, and these errors caused him avoidable uncertainty, stress, anxiety, and legal costs.

---

[245] S 26(6) of the 1974 Act; s 5(2) of the 1967 Act.

[246] *R v Local Administration Commissioner, ex p Doy* (2002) Env LR 11; [2001] EWCA Admin 361–Doy had bought a house on an old landfill site, which then became difficult to sell. He had no direct remedy for his losses.

[247] The farmer received £25,926 in total—see Complaint no 89/B/240 reported at [1996] JPL 681. See also [1999] JPL 662 (unreasonable delay in enforcing against waste transfer site).

[248] Local Government Ombudsman found maladministration against Bath and North East Somerset Council, 10 April 2008 report <http://www.planningportal.gov.uk>. The recommendation was for £7,500 to be paid, in addition to reviewing its procedures.

3

INTERNATIONAL ENVIRONMENTAL LAW

A. **Introduction** 3.01
B. **International Law and the Environment** 3.02
   The relevance of international law within the UK 3.04
   Future legislation 3.05
   Interpretation of legislation 3.06
   European policy initiatives 3.09
   National policy 3.10
   Sustainable development and climate change 3.11
   Sustainable development 3.11
   Climate change 3.13
   The precautionary principle 3.18
C. **International Environmental Agreements** 3.20
   International trade and the environment 3.23

Marine pollution 3.25
Air pollution 3.26
Trans-frontier trade in waste 3.28
Nature conservation and the protection of wildlife 3.29
The Aarhus Convention and access to justice 3.31
D. **Human Rights Law and the Environment** 3.35
   International human rights law and the environment 3.35
   The European Convention on Human Rights 3.36
   Human Rights Act 1998 3.37
   The Convention rights 3.40
   Article 8 3.42
   Property rights 3.47
   Procedural rights 3.49

A. Introduction

This chapter is intended to cover the effect that international sources of law have **3.01** upon domestic law.[1] As with European Union environmental law, international environmental agreements have radically increased in scope and influence. The UK plays an active and influential role in international environmental negotiations, the outcomes of which are reflected in stated government policy and, in some areas, legislation. Global environmental issues are now very firmly on the

---

[1] See generally Birnie and Boyle, *International Law and the Environment* (OUP, 2002—the 3rd edition is due November 2008); Philippe Sands, *Principles of International Environmental Law* (Cambridge University Press; 2nd edition, 2003). For a general overview and analysis of some of the current preoccupations see the *Oxford Handbook of International Environmental Law* (OUP, 2007), eds. Bodansky, Brunnee, and Hey.

national political agenda, and at the forefront of public awareness about the environment in general. Climate change is recognized as the most serious environmental problem with the widest ranging effects facing both developed and developing countries, and there is now a mainstream scientific consensus about the causal link between greenhouse gas emissions and climate change.[2] The process of securing international consensus on action to reduce emissions is enormously complex and, unsurprisingly, slow moving.[3] As well as contributing to truly global environmental problems, nation states can affect their neighbours' environment on a much more localized scale, with potentially devastating effects.[4]

B. International Law and the Environment

3.02   It is an underlying principle of the international legal order that states have unlimited national sovereignty over their own resources and people, and that they are independent and equal with other states. International law can provide the mechanisms for negotiating, settling, and supervising actions by states. In the environmental field, multilateral agreements have been reached between states over issues such as conservation of migratory birds, marine pollution, and emissions to the atmosphere.[5] In addition, some areas of the planet lie outside the territorial limits of the states. These have been colloquially termed the 'global commons', which are also considered to include the high seas and the atmosphere—although each state would lay claim to the physical space that lies above its territory.

3.03   The most important source of international law is contained in 'treaties', which may be expressed to be Conventions, Protocols, Agreements, or just Treaties.[6] The agreements are rarely universal, and may simply be bilateral, and can take any form. It is agreements that comply with the rules under the 1969 Vienna Convention on the Law of Treaties[7] which are commonly accepted as treaties in

---

   [2] See the Intergovernmental Panel on Climate Change (IPCC) 4th Assessment Report. Synthesis report available at <http://www.ipcc.ch/pdf/assessment-report/ar4/syr/ar4_syr.pdf.> The IPCC was established in 1988 by the World Meteorological Organization and the UN Environment Programme (or UNEP, which co-ordinates United Nations environmental activities).
   [3] For a summary of the climate change negotiations under the United Nations Framework Convention see: <http://unfccc.int/2860.php>
   [4] In 2000 a partly Australian-owned gold mine at Baia Mare in Romania discharged cyanide into the Tisza River which flows through Hungary and Serbia. The European Environment Agency described it as 'the worst case scenario for the region's rivers' (ENDS 15/2/00).
   [5] See further Philippe Sands, *Principles of International Environmental Law*, op cit.
   [6] See Aust, Anthony *Modern Treaty Law and Practice* 2nd Edition (Cambridge University Press, 2007).
   [7] The Vienna Convention seeks to lay down rules for treaties concluded after 1980. Many treaties make provision for dispute resolution and arbitration. The role of international law to determine the relationships between nation states concerning the environment lies outside the scope of this work—although it is necessarily touched upon in the Chapter on Marine Pollution. An analysis

this context. But some major countries may not be parties to particular treaties, however ambitious their scope. For instance, in the case of the 1993 Lugano Convention on Civil Liability for Damages resulting from Activities Dangerous to the Environment, neither the EU nor the UK is a party to it. A treaty may also require further steps to be taken before it can come into force. Of particular practical importance may be the delay which may occur between a country signing a treaty, and the date at which it has been agreed that the treaty will itself enter into force.[8] The treaty may also be no more than a framework document, setting out the general principles and establishing the basic institutions, which will require further detailed negotiation and agreement in order to give substance to the commitments made. This is often true of environmental agreements, where the detailed scientific and technical aspects are set out in the annexes and appendices to agreements, or in later Protocols.[9] The only other accepted source of international law is the principles that can be derived from consistent state practice, referred to as 'customary international law'. This body of law is intended to reflect the general practice which is accepted by the states as law. Customary law consists of two elements, namely evidence of a substantial uniformity of practice by a substantial number of states, and opinio juris, in other words a general recognition by states that the practice is 'settled enough to amount to a binding obligation in international law'.[10] There is certainly rich scope for legal argument on the existence of such rules, both now and in the future, as the nature of state practice changes with time. It is in this way that international 'agreements', which were never given the status of a treaty, can still be said to contain some international law, if only in part. Those agreements which cannot lay claim to even this partial legal status may still have a profound influence on the future development of the law, as occurred with the non-binding agreements (including the Framework Convention on Climate Change) reached at the Earth Summit in Rio de Janeiro in 1992. The World Summit on Sustainable Development (WSSD) in Johannesburg in 2002 produced a Political Declaration[11] expressing commitments for implementing sustainable development, and a Plan of Implementation[12] intended to guide government activities. Both were heavily criticized by non-governmental organizations for failing to set out new commitments and targets,

---

of the broad effect of international law as a system regulating states is best found in the classic *Principles of Public International Law*, Brownlie (OUP, 6th edn, 2003).

[8] One of the worst examples of this delay is the 1982 UN Convention on the Law of the Sea which only came into force in 1994 with the accession of the sixtieth country. The UK ratified it in July 1997.

[9] See further Chapter 4, Sands, *Principles of International Environmental Law* (op cit).

[10] Aust, op cit page 11.

[11] <http://www.un.org/esa/sustdev/documents/WSSD_POI_PD/English/POI_PD.htm>

[12] <http://www.un.org/esa/sustdev/documents/WSSD_POI_PD/English/POIToc.htm>

and failing to provide for funding for implementation.[13] However, the European Union took the view that it could be 'satisfied' with the progress made, and emphasized a number of new targets including that of halting the loss of biodiversity by 2010, earlier agreed under the Convention on Biological Diversity[14] but finally endorsed at Johannesburg by all Heads of State and Government.

The relevance of international law within the UK

3.04   Developments in international law will have substantial indirect effects on national law, in bringing forward new legislation, assisting in its interpretation, and influencing the direction of policy. However, as a 'dualist' system, no international treaty can be given effect through the national courts unless it is enacted by Parliament into UK legislation. An individual party cannot rely directly upon the terms of a treaty or on the rules of international law. It is also firmly established that English courts will not rule upon the true meaning and effect of international instruments which apply only at the level of international law.[15] They will only become relevant when they have been expressly incorporated into English domestic law, or it becomes necessary to interpret them for the purposes of determining a person's rights or duties under domestic law. Note that the court will in any event decline to embark upon the determination of an issue if to do so would be damaging to the public interest in the field of international relations, national security, or defence. So, it was held to be beyond the remit of the Environment Agency to consider the legality of nuclear weapons under international law.[16]

Future legislation

3.05   Agreements made by the UK internationally will have a direct influence on the government's future legislation. The unusual status of European Union agreements is considered separately in Chapter 4. In the realm of marine pollution control, the UK signs treaties on the basis that they will be enacted, in their

---

[13]   Described by Tony Juniper, Friends of the Earth UK Director, as 'a betrayal of hundreds of millions of people around the world who are suffering the effects of environmental damage and poverty'. See <http://www.foe.co.uk/campaigns/corporates/news/earth_summit_4_september.html>. For a different response see the (then) EU Commissioner for Environment, Margarate Wallstrom's comments (EUROPA press release reference SPEECH/02/422) dated 25 September 2002.

[14]   <http://www.cbd.int>

[15]   See such cases as *R v Lyons* [2002] 3 WLR 1562, *J H Rayner (Mincing Lane) Limited v Department of Trade and Industry* [1990] 2 AC 418 (the International Tin Council case), *Campaign for Nuclear Disarmament v Prime Minister of the UK and others* [2002] EWHC 2777 (QB) (preliminary issues in an application for judicial review, regarding CND's application for an advisory declaration as to the true meaning of UN Resolution 1441 on Iraq).

[16]   *Marchiori v Environment Agency and others* [2002] EWCA Civ 03 (unsuccessful judicial review of the Agency's authorizations for the discharge of radioactive waste as part of the process of designing, manufacturing and decommissioning of Trident nuclear weapons); see also *Campaign for Nuclear Disarmament v Prime Minister of the UK and others* [2002] cited above.

entirety, into UK law.[17] The Environmental Protection Act 1990 itself provides a specific power, under Section 156, to the Secretary of State to make regulations in order to comply with the UK's international obligations, even where these may modify other parts of the main Act.[18] Other agreements will act as a guide to future developments in national law. In this way, measures which in fact have their origin in international initiatives are disguised as national measures.

Interpretation of legislation

International obligations may influence the court's interpretation of the national **3.06** legislation which purports to bring them into effect in national law. Again, the effect of European Union agreements on this point is considered separately in Chapter 4. Otherwise, the fact that a statute is passed to give effect to an international treaty does not, of itself, enable the treaty to be referred to, but:[19]

> it is a principle of construction of UK statutes, now too well established to call for citation of authority, that the words of the statute passed after the treaty has been signed and dealing with the subject matter of the international obligation of the UK, are to be construed, if they are reasonably capable of bearing such a meaning, as intended to carry out the obligation, and not to be inconsistent with it.

Therefore, when the law on a matter such as the transportation of hazardous waste **3.07** is considered, it is not enough to look only at the relevant regulations, namely the Trans-frontier Shipment of Waste Regulations 2007. This statutory instrument,[20] together with the complementary EC Waste Shipments Regulation,[21] should be read in the light of the Basel Convention on the Control of Transboundary Movements of Hazardous Wastes and their Disposal (1989).[22] In *R v Secretary of State for Trade and Industry ex parte Greenpeace (No.2)*[23] the High Court interpreted the provisions of the Habitats Directive in a way which appeared most

---

[17] See the Chapter on Marine Pollution further. For instance, many international maritime measures can be speedily given effect by an Order in Council, under s 128 of the Merchant Shipping Act 1995.

[18] The modifications pursuant to s 156 can be made to Part I (IPC and air pollution control), Part II (waste management), Part VI (genetically-modified organisms), and to ss 140–142 (controls over injurious substances). For instance, s 156 was one of the powers used to make the Genetically Modified Organisms (Deliberate Release) Regulations 2002 (SI 2002/2443) (in conjunction with other statutory powers) in order to implement Council Directive 2001/18/EC, and involved amendments to the main Act.

[19] *Garland v British Rail Engineering Ltd* Case 12/81 [1982] 2 All ER 402 at 415; [1983] 2 AC 751 at 771, per Lord Diplock; see also *R v Secretary of State for the Home Department, ex p Adan* [2001] 1 All ER 593 where the court took the generally-accepted meaning internationally for a provision in Asylum and Immigration Act 1996).

[20] SI 2007/171; as they were made under the general European Communities Act 1972, the primary UK legislation provides no help as an aid to interpretation.

[21] Regulation (EC) No 1013/2006 on shipments of waste—as a 'Regulation' the UK did not need to transpose it, as it should apply directly (see the chapter 4 on European Law).

[22] See further below on trans-frontier shipments of waste.

[23] [2000] Env LR 221.

consistent with international agreements on marine conservation. But the relevance of international law still depends on the manner in which the UK Parliament has chosen to implement, or limit the scope of, an international treaty. For instance, the Vienna Convention on Civil Liability for Nuclear Damage[24] allows the UK to extend such liability to include pure economic loss. This international agreement still does not entitle a litigant to recover for this type of damage in the UK courts, since there is nothing in the relevant statute—the Nuclear Installations Act 1965—which extends the concept of what constitutes 'nuclear damage' beyond physical injury or physical damage.[25]

3.08   The dispute between Ireland and the UK about the operation of a mixed oxide (MOX) plant at Sellafield illustrates how international environmental agreements, in this case UNCLOS,[26] interact with the provisions of EU environmental law. Ireland instituted dispute settlement proceedings under the Convention, which referred to:

> several measures of Community law, in particular Directives 85/337 and 90/313, Council Directive 92/3/Euratom of 3 February 1992 on the supervision and control of shipments of radioactive waste between Member States and into and out of the Community (OJ 1992 L 35, p. 24), as well as international agreements such as the Convention for the Protection of the Marine Environment of the North-East Atlantic.[27]

Consequently, the European Commission instituted proceedings before the Court of Justice. The ECJ found that Ireland's approach was contrary to Articles 292 EC and 193 EA, which oblige Member States to respect the exclusive nature of the Court's jurisdiction to resolve disputes concerning the provisions of community law mentioned. It was held that the institution of proceedings before the arbitral tribunal 'involve a manifest risk that the jurisdictional order laid down in the Treaties and, consequently, the autonomy of the Community legal system may be adversely affected',[28] despite the fact that Ireland did not ask the Tribunal to decide whether the UK had breached any provision of European Union law.[29]

European policy initiatives

3.09   International agreements are also indicative of the future direction of European legislation and policy, but in some areas, notably climate change, the EU plays a significant role in shaping international agreements, in general pushing for more

---

[24] The Vienna Convention on Civil Liability for Nuclear Damage (signed 21 May 1963).

[25] See *Blue Circle Limited v Ministry of Defence* [1997] Env LR 341.

[26] United Nations Convention on the Law of the Sea. <http://www.un.org/Depts/los/convention_agreements/convention_overview_convention.htm>

[27] Case C-459/03 *Commission v Ireland* [2006] ECR I-04635 paragraph 142 of the judgment.

[28] Ibid paragraph 154.

[29] See Cardwell and French 'Who Decides? The ECJ's judgment on jurisdiction in the *MOX plant* Dispute' [2007] 1 JEL 121–129.

stringent targets and setting itself higher targets than those agreed. Indeed, where the European Union has become a party in its own right to a treaty, or a protocol to a Convention, for example the Kyoto protocol to the UN Framework Convention on Climate Change, it has taken the lead in implementing the requirements in the Member States through European law.[30] Certainly, in so far as provisions of international law govern principles of Community law, these may be invoked in national courts.[31] It remains to be seen whether such provisions can usefully support a legal challenge to government actions which might be regarded as standing in direct conflict with stated environmental policy.[32]

National policy

The language of international environmental agreements is reflected in national   **3.10** policy at all levels of government. For example, Planning Policy Statement 1 on Sustainable Development (updated from PPG1 in 2005) describes sustainable development as 'the core principle underpinning planning'. The supplement to PPS1, on 'Planning and Climate Change' sets out the key planning objectives in reponse to climate change which are expected to form the basis of Regional Spatial Strategies. These include 'making a full contribution to delivering the Government's Climate Change Programme, and energy policies, and in doing so contribute to global sustainability'. Further, the impact of climate change on biodiversity is acknowledged: Regional Spatial Strategies should 'conserve and enhance biodiversity, recognising that the distribution of habitats and species will be affected by climate change'.[33] While principles like sustainable development and energy efficiency are written into policy, the application of policy is subject to the discretion of the decision-maker. The criticism is often made that the UK 'translates soft international law into soft policy commitments'.[34] Nevertheless, on occasion quite surprising decisions emerge, placing sustainability considerations above those which might normally be considered paramount. In *Dartmoor National Park Authority v Secretary of State for Transport, Local Government and the Regions*,[35] the Administrative Court dismissed an application to quash the decision of a planning inspector allowing a planning enforcement appeal made in respect of a number of residential shelters in woodland within a national park as

---

[30] See the European Climate Change Programme launched by the Commission in 2000 <http://ec.europa.eu/environment/climat/eccp.htm.>

[31] Indeed, in theory, it is possible that international environmental agreements concluded between the Community and non-member states can have direct effect in European law: cf *Bresciani case* (1976) ECR 129, ECJ; *Kupfberg case* (1982) ECR 3641.

[32] A particularly controversial proposal is the new coal fired power station (the UK's first for 24 years) at Kingsnorth in Kent, which is expected to receive government support.

[33] PPS1 Supplement: Planning and Climate Change, paragraph 9.

[34] Bell and McGillivray *Environmental Law* p 135 (7th edition, OUP 2008).

[35] [2003] EWHC 236 Admin.

part of a 'permaculture' project. The inspector had decided that a temporary departure from policy, which precluded residential development in the national park, was justified, in part because the project, by the Affinity of Woodland Workers Cooperative, was a worthwhile 'experiment in sustainable living'.[36]

Sustainable development and climate change

Sustainable development

3.11   The term 'sustainable development' has become one of the key principles under-lying environmental legislation and policy. The concept has been embodied in European Union legislation and policy,[37] and it is now part of the Treaty itself.[38] Since 1988, the UK has generally adopted the definition set out in the Brundtland Report *Our Common Future*,[39] as 'development which meets the needs of the present without compromising the ability of future generations to meet their own needs'. The UK Government has stated that 'there can be no quarrel with the Brundtland principles[40] as a general definition',[41] and has sought international consensus to develop a consistent approach. Taken together, the principles 'consti-tute the framework for international law in the field of sustainable development,

---

[36] Compare *South Shropshire Disrtict Council v First Secretary of State & Anor [2003] EWHC 1351(Admin)*: the Inspector's conclusion that a housing development and associated transport infrastructure within an Area of Outstanding Natural Beauty was not incompatible with local and national policies on sustainable development was a matter of judgment for him, and was not *Wednesbury* unreasonable.

[37] The 6th EU Environment Action Programme sets out measures to be taken to help imple-ment the renewed sustainable development strategy (SDS) adopted by the European Council on 15/16 June 2006.

[38] The amendments made by the Amsterdam Treaty 1997 include a new Art. 6, that 'Environmental protection requirements must be integrated into the definition and implementation of Community policies and activities referred to in article 3, in particular with a view to promoting sustainable development'. Again, the concept has been given no precise definition, although refer-ence is made in EU policy documents to the *Brundtland* Report.

[39] At p 43, World Commission on Environment and Development (OUP, 1987). The Commission was established by the UN General Assembly to consider a 'global agenda for change'. The *Brundtland Report* inspired the UN to organize the Rio Summit ('the Earth Summit') five years later. Whilst the definition might at first appear to place little emphasis on the social goals, the Report itself continues by stating that their definition of sustainable development: '. . . contains within it two key concepts:
- the concept of "needs", in particular the essential needs of the world's poor, to which overriding priority should be given; and
- the idea of limitations imposed by the state of technology and social organisation on the environment's ability to meet present and future needs.'

[40] Reviving growth and changing its quality; meeting essential needs for jobs, food, energy, water and sanitation; ensuring a sustainable level of population; conserving and enhancing the resource base; reorienting technology and managing risk; and merging environment and economics in decision-making.

[41] See the UK's response in July 1988, 'A Perspective by the UK on the Report of the World Commission on Environment and Development' (quoted in the 1994 White Paper, at para 1.14). It was followed by a 1989 report, *Sustaining Our Common Future* (DoE, 1989).

now confirmed as an international legal term by the ICJ in the Gabčikovo-Nagymaros case,[42] and as having practical legal consequences by the WTO Appellate Body in the *Shrimp/Turtle* case.[43]

The World Summit on Sustainable Development, ten years on from the Rio Earth **3.12** Summit, led to a specific undertaking to strengthen the role of the Commission on Sustainable Development in the implementation of Agenda 21. In 2005 the government published its updated strategy *Securing the Future*[44] setting the direction of the policy agenda on sustainable development and reiterating the main principles on which the strategy is to be based.[45] The principles apply to government policy in general, but also to the 'sustainability' of departments within government. A White Paper *Planning for a Sustainable Future*[46] was published in May 2007, as part of the major reforms to the planning system. DEFRA's second Sustainable Development Action Plan (SDAP) was published in November 2007 and sets out its 'new approach' to sustainable development.[47] The Sustainable Development Commission (the government's independent watchdog on sustainable development)[48] has produced its *Sustainable Development in Government Report 2007*, analysing the performance of central government operations against the the targets of the Framework for Sustainable Operations on the Government Estate (SOGE). The general statutory purpose of Natural England, the successor to English Nature, is set out as being 'to ensure that the natural environment is

---

[42] International Court of Justice: Case concerning the Gabcikovo-Nagymaros Project Judgment of 25 September 1997. For a general discussion see the collection of essays *Sustainable Development Law: Principles, Practices & Prospects* (eds. Cordonier Segger and Khalfan, OUP, 2004). These also discuss the International Law Association's New Delhi Declaration in 2002, which attempted to identify the supporting legal principles that could have direct effect, rather than the broad objective of sustainable development.

[43] Sands, op cit, p 11 and pp 254–55.

[44] *Securing the Future—Delivering the UK Sustainable Development Strategy*, HM Government, March 2005. <http://www.sus.tainable-development.gov.uk/publications/uk-strategy/index.htm>

[45] The four priorities referred to are: sustainable production and consumption; climate change and energy; natural resource protection and environmental enhancement; creating sustainable communities and a fairer world.

[46] Cm 7120 (May 2007), which was produced jointly by the DCLG, the DFT, Defra, and DTI. This White Paper sets out the wide-ranging package of reforms—with proposals to streamline the process in the town and country planning system, and improve the powers of local authorities to shape their local communities. There is also a strong emphasis on 'supporting sustainable economic development alongside work to tackle climate change in a way that is integrated with the delivery of other sustainable development objectives' (Executive Summary), which highlights the continuing potential for conflict between these interests.

[47] The DaSL (DEFRA as Sustainability Leader) Programme see <http://www.defra.gov.uk/environment/sustainable/pdf/sd-action-plan-07-09.pdf>

[48] For a useful summary of sustainable development principles in UK government see <http://www.sd-commission.org.uk/pages/aboutsd.html>

conserved, enhanced and managed for the benefit of present and future generations, thereby contributing to sustainable development'.[49]

Climate change

3.13   In the climate change arena, binding targets agreed under international conventions have been incorporated not only into national policy documents but also into draft legislation in the form of the Climate Change Bill 2008. In recent years, the UK government has engaged in a number of policy and legislative initiatives intended to reduce greenhouse gas emissions in line with specified targets derived from, and exceeding, those contained in the Kyoto Protocol to the UN Convention on Climate Change.[50] The second UK Climate Change Programme[51] was published in 2006, setting out the methods by which the domestic goal of reducing greenhouse gas ('GHG') emissions by around 60% by 2050[52] can be achieved. The report states that the UK's emissions are projected to be 23–25% below 1990 levels in 2010, around double its Kyoto target. The draft Climate Change Bill places a duty on the Secretary of State to 'ensure' that the 60% by 2050 target is met and to report to Parliament on progress.[53] The duty is not absolute, and amendments may be made to the statutory 'carbon budgets' in certain limited circumstances. This idea of requiring reports to be submitted follows a familiar auditing pattern, found in the use of sustainability indicators and also in the Climate Change and Sustainable Energy Act 2006.[54] There are no legal sanctions as such in the Bill. The biggest influence, therefore, that these legislative measures will have will be in underpinning important policy changes, and in promoting the further use of emission trading schemes, climate adaptation, waste reduction schemes and renewable transport fuel obligations. [55] This debate will continue to

---

[49]   Natural Environment and Rural Comunities Act 2006, s 2 (1).

[50]   To reduce emissions by 5.2 % below 1990 levels over the period 2008–12. The then 15 EU Member States adopted a target to reduce collective emissions by 8% over the same period.

[51]   <http://www.defra.gov.uk/environment/climatechange/uk/ukccp/pdf/ukccp06-all.pdf>

[52]   *Energy White Paper* 2007 available at <http://www.berr.gov.uk/energy/whitepaper/page 39534.html>

[53]   cl.2 (1). The 'net UK carbon account' in 2050 must be at least 60% lower than the baseline established in 1990, and 26–32% by 2020. There should be a 'carbon budget' every five years (cl.4). The Bill will also officially establish the Advisory Committee on Climate Change, which started work as a shadow committee in 2008.

[54]   Whilst the principal purpose of the 2006 Act is to enhance the UK's contribution to combating climate change, the main mechanism is that the Secretary of State must lay an annual report before Parliament on the steps taken by government department's to reduce GHG emissions, and on the level of emissions in the UK. This requirement will be replaced by those set out in the Climate Change Bill.

[55]   The government has already made one renewable transport fuel obligation Order in 2007, under the Energy Act 2004, which established the Office of the Renewable Fuels Agency. The new Bill would amend and enhance its role.

be played out at the policy level, and the Courts are very unlikely to consider that the current approach to climate change is erroneous.[56]

Emissions trading was one of the three market-based 'flexibile mechanisms' designed to combat climate change, introduced by the Kyoto Protocol.[57] The EU Emmissions Trading Scheme,[58] in place since 2005, is the first international trading scheme for carbon dioxide emissions. The scheme covers around 11,500 energy intensive installations across the EU, representing approximately 50% of carbon emissions in the region as a whole. Each Member State publishes National Allocation Plans determining the total quantity of carbon dioxide emissions to allocated to national companies, which are then asssessed by the Commission in the light of the criteria in Annex III of the Directive. The rejection by the Commission of a National Allocation Plan means that it cannot be implemented as it stands. So, while there is no stated limit on the quantity of allocatable emissions, National Allocation Plans must reflect the Annex III criteria, the first of which is that the proposed total quantity of allowances must be in line with the Member States' target for reduction of emissions under the Kyoto Protocol.[59] **3.14**

The UK Emissions Trading Scheme (ETS), which ran from 2002 to 2006, was the first economy-wide greenhouse gas trading scheme. A report commissioned by DEFRA[60] referred to: **3.15**

> some concern over the ease with which some participants met their targets and that the level of emissions additional reductions that the scheme has achieved (ie beyond the reductions that would have happened anyway) is lower than the headline figures suggest.

---

[56] Obvious as it may seem to lawyers, the case of *Dimmock v Secretary of State for Children, Schools and Families* [2007] EWHC 2288 (Admin) was not a case about climate change, but was about education law. Dimmock was funded to challenge the Education Secretary's decision to distribute former US Vice-President Al Gore's film, 'An Inconvenient Truth', to all state secondary schools in alleged contravention of the Education Act 1996. It needed to be acknowledged that the film was not simply a science film and that some of its content was 'partisan' (in the limited sense of the word used in the specific s 406 of the Education Act 1996, as 'one-sided'). It is notable that the government's position was based on complete acceptance of the 4th IPCC Report (which post-dated the film). There were nine points where Burton J decided that the film differed from the IPCC and that this should be addressed in the Guidance Notes for teachers to be sent out with the film. The judge referred to these as 'errors' in this limited sense—which was a word that was then quoted in the news often without the inverted commas. He did not quash the Education Secretary's decision.

[57] Together with Joint Implementation and the Clean Development Mechanism. See <http://unfccc.int/kyoto_protocol/mechanisms/items/1673.php>

[58] Established by Directive 2003/87/EC.

[59] For background to the 'flexible mechanisms' and the legal nature of allowances see Mace, MJ 'The Legal Nature of Emissions Reductions and EU Allowances: Issues addressed in an international workshop' [2005] JEEPL 2, 123.

[60] <http://www.defra.gov.uk/environment/climatechange/trading/uk/pdf/ukets1-4yr-appraisal.pdf>

3.16   It goes on to reiterate that:

> A key driver of the environmental benefits of any cap and trade scheme is the level of the cap. There is a strong case for ensuring that the number of allowances allocated promotes real emissions reductions.[61]

3.17   As part of the Energy White Paper in May 2007, the government announced its Carbon Reduction Commitment,[62] which applies mandatory emissions trading to cut carbon emissions from large commercial and public sector organizations. Around 10% of UK emissions will be covered from 2010. There will be no system of third party verification; participants will be expected to self-certify. From 2013 there will be a Government-imposed cap on the number of tradeable allowances within the scheme, sold annually by auction.

The precautionary principle

3.18   It has been argued that a general precautionary principle, to err on the side of safety and caution when faced with scientific uncertainty, has become a norm of customary international law.[63] Certainly, it is part of European environmental law, under Article 174(2), and it is discussed further in the next chapter. It has its origins in German law, as the 'Vorsorgeprinzip', but its application has been perhaps best encapsulated in the 1992 Rio Declaration:

> In order to protect the environment, the precautionary principle shall be widely applied by States according to their capabilities. Where there are threats of serious or irreversible damage, lack of full scientific certainty shall not be used as a reason for postponing cost-effective measures to prevent environmental degradation.[64]

3.19   The principle is referred to in a number of international conventions including the Framework Convention on Climate Change and the Convention on Biological Diversity. In the UK, it remains a guiding principle which will inform policy only, and where it has been cited to the courts it has not yet been used in the interpretation of policy.[65]

---

[61]   Ibid, 'Summary of Lessons Learnt' page 41.
[62]   Formerly the Energy Performance Commitment. The name was changed to prevent confusion with Energy Performance Certificates.
[63]   See McIntyre and Mosedale, 'The Precautionary Principle as a Norm of Customary International Law' [1997] 2 JEL 221, reviewing the wealth of academic authority and the few international cases where it has been cited. See also Fisher, Elizabeth 'Is the Precautionary Principle Justiciable ?' [2001] 3 JEL 315.
[64]   See principle 15 of the 1992 Rio Declaration on Environment and Development (cited below). This definition is used in the 1999 UK Strategy for Sustainable Development of para 4.1.
[65]   See the *Peralta* case before the ECJ, and *ex p Duddridge* before the High Court—both discussed below at para 4.51.

C. International Environmental Agreements[66]

The first meeting of the international community to discuss environmental issues **3.20** took place in Stockholm in 1972 at the United Nations Conference on the Human Environment. The aspirational principles that emerged from the meeting (the 'Stockholm Declaration'[67]) included a call for national co-operation to 'effectively control, prevent, reduce and eliminate adverse environmental effects resulting from activities conducted in all spheres, in such a way that due account is taken of the sovereignty and interests of all states'.[68] In 1992, representatives from 176 of the nation states of the world attended the 'Earth Summit' in Rio de Janeiro in 1992, known formally as the United Nations Conference on Environment and Development (UNCED).[69]

In fact, only two treaties were agreed at UNCED, the 1992 Biodiversity **3.21** Convention and the UN Framework Convention on Climate Change 1992.[70] In addition, there were three other instruments agreed: the Rio Declaration on Environment and Development (the Rio Declaration), the Statement of Principles for a Global Consensus on the Management, Conservation and Sustainable Development of all types of Forest (the Forest Principles), and Agenda 21. The UK published a series of papers on the strategy it adopted to achieve the commitments it made at Rio: *Sustainable Development—The UK Strategy*, *Climate Change—the UK Programme*, *Biodiversity—the UK Action Plan*, and *Sustainable Forestry—the UK Programme*.[71] Agenda 21 has already proved to be a catalyst for action for local government policy programmes in the UK, where it is known, appropriately, as Local Agenda 21. Both the 1972 Stockholm Declaration and the 1992 Rio Declaration are only intended to be influential statements, from which certain trends and norms may develop. They do reflect a certain consensus view, but they are not intended to be legal documents, and should be read in this light.

---

[66] The text of the main treaties is reproduced in *The Encyclopaedia of Environmental Law* (Sweet & Maxwell, 1993), Vol 1. The EU is a party to most of these treaties.

[67] The Stockholm Conference on the Human Environment, held by the United Nations in 1972. At about the same period, both the World Heritage Convention and CITES (below) were negotiated. The UN Environmental Programme (UNEP) itself soon held a convention on regional seas, and continues to organize and convene meetings to negotiate treaties on the environment.

[68] Principle 21. See Sands, Philippe op cit pp 35–40.

[69] Rio de Janeiro, UN Conference on Environment and Development (UNCED) 3–14 June 1992. The so-called Earth Summit II was held in New York in June 1997. Its formal title was 'The 19th Special Session of the General Assembly to review progress achieved in implementing Agenda 21'.

[70] Although it is expressed to be a 'framework', it needs little more in the way of detailed negotiation, and came into force on 21 March 1993.

[71] Cm 2426, 2427, 2428, and 2429 respectively. For an analysis of the UK law on forestry, particularly in the light of European and international obligations, see Colin Reid, 'British Forestry and the Environmental Agenda' [1997] 1 JEL 23.

The emphasis in the 1992 Rio Declaration on 'sustainable development' has no legal status, but it is arguable that it has become an international legal norm.[72] By contrast, principle 2 of the Rio Declaration does represent the position in international law. It essentially repeats principle 21 of the 1972 Stockholm Declaration,[73] that:

> States have in accordance with the Charter of the United Nations and the principles of international law, the sovereign right to exploit their own resources pursuant to their own environmental and developmental policies, and the responsibility to ensure that activities within their jurisdiction or control do not cause damage to the environment of other States or of areas beyond the limits of national jurisdiction.[74]

3.22 The Johannesburg Summit in 2002, focused largely on the alleviation of poverty, did not produce a statement of principles, or propose any specific actions.[75] However there may have been an inevitable shift in recent years from new agreements (the basic principles having already been established) to making existing agreements more effective and working towards better compliance.[76]

International trade and the environment

3.23 One continuing global dilemma is the proper relationship between economic development and the ecosystem in which that development will take place. The European Union continues to grapple with the issue, as discussed in Chapter 4. Internationally, there is a network of multilateral trade agreements made between various states, which can adversely affect the protection of the environment. The UK is also subject to the requirements of the General Agreement on Tariffs and Trade (the GATT, now the World Trade Organization). The main purpose of the Agreement is to remove restraints and distortions on international trade. As in the European Union, there is therefore an inevitable tension between the interests of removing all distortions and restrictions on trade between states, and the interests of individual countries to have a higher level of environmental protection than others. Having failed to achieve general agreement, states may still wish to take independent, unilateral action. Article XX of the GATT provides the agreed exceptions to the Agreement, which include the adoption by a state of measures which are 'necessary to protect human, animal or plant life or health' or which relate 'to the conservation of exhaustible natural resources if such measures are made effective in conjunction with restrictions on domestic production or

---

[72] See note 49 above.

[73] The phrase 'and developmental' policies was added to principle 21, to reflect the situation at the Rio Summit, which considered environmental and development matters together.

[74] An early example is the *Trail Smelter* arbitration, 33 AJIL 182 (1939), 35 AJIL (1941) between the USA and Canada. Canada was held to be liable for the fumes emitted from a copper smelter which affected the neighbouring US state of Washington.

[75] See notes 13 and 14 above.

[76] Birnie and Boyle, op cit page 159.

consumption'.[77] The exceptions are intended to be strictly applied, so that they do not become an indirect method of avoiding the GATT's main purpose. When the USA passed legislation which sought to protect dolphins from the intensive methods of fishing for tuna by preventing the imports of such tuna, Mexico was able to challenge this successfully through the GATT.[78] Such disputes will continue to have significant consequences for the development of any international agreements on the environment, and may even prevent them.[79]

One of the significant changes that has occurred has been in the importance placed **3.24** by international commercial banks on addressing environmental and social risk when considering financing large projects. This is in addition to the standards that had been expected by the World Bank and the EBRD. On 4 June 2003, ten leading international banks adopted 'the Equator Principles',[80] a set of voluntary environmental and social guidelines to be applied to all project finance transactions where capital costs exceed fifty-million dollars. They have been further revised in 2006, and have been adopted by some sixty banks as a de facto standard on how to assess major development projects around the world. These then find legal form through the contractual provisions that are required, as well as in more prudent lending.

Marine pollution

This topic is discussed in detail in Chapter 11, including the effect of interna- **3.25** tional treaties on the UK's law. The influence of international law is clear. Oil pollution from ships has been covered in a series of treaties, going as far back as 1969. Both the Merchant Shipping (Oil Pollution)Act 1971 and the Prevention of Oil Pollution Act 1971 are based on international treaties.[81] The UK in the past

---

[77] Article XX of GATT, paras (b) and (g). The Standards Code allows similar exceptions to be made.

[78] *The US Restrictions on the Import of Tuna* (1991) 30 ILM 1594; (1994) 33 ILM 859. See H Ward, 'Trade and Environment in the Round—and After' [1994] 6 JEL 263 further. Similar issues arise on international animal welfare agreements: see A Nollkamper, 'The Legality of Moral Crusades Disguised in Trade Laws: An Analysis of the EC "Ban" on Furs from Animals Taken by Leghold Traps' [1996] 8 JEL 237.

[79] For an analysis of the relationship between international trade rules and multilateral environmental agreements, see H Ward and L Siegele 'Corporate Social Responsibility—A Step Towards Stronger Involvement of Business in MEA implementation?' RECIEL 16 (2) 2007.

[80] See the article by Cull, 'Environmental Risk and Project Financing: The Equator Principles and Their Implications For Banks And Sponsors' (2007), Bloomberg European Business Law Journal Quarter 3, 2007, for an outline of the development of the Equator Principles, and their implications for banks and sponsors. The banks chose to model the Equator Principles on the environmental standards of the World Bank and the social policies of the International Finance Corporation (IFC).

[81] The Protocol to the 1969 International Convention relating to Intervention on the High Seas in Cases of Oil Pollution Casualties was then implemented by statutory instrument, the Merchant Shipping (Prevention of Pollution) (Intervention) Order 1980 No 1093. Likewise, Part XII of the 1982 UN Convention on the Law of the Sea, which requires states to take the

has also used the seas around the country to dump industrial waste, radioactive waste, and waste munitions. The UK was committed to ending the dumping of colliery waste by the end of 1997 and sewage sludge by 1998, whereas dredged materials will continue. In national law, the legal controls can be found in Part II of the Food and Environment Act 1985, and regulations made under the Merchant Shipping Act 1979. Land based sources are covered by Part IV of the Water Industry Act 1991 for discharges of trade effluent. Again, these national measures to some extent need to be seen in the light of the international agreements which cover the same areas.[82] The Marine Bill, intended to co-ordinate UK marine law and creating a new marine planning system together with marine conservation powers, was published in May 2008. One of of the draft provisions is a simplified process for obtaining consent for wind, wave, and tidal projects of less than 100MW output.

Air pollution

3.26 In addition to the environmental damage caused by emissions of greenhouse gases into the atmosphere, the depletion of the ozone layer, which would otherwise screen out ultraviolet rays, by substances such as chloroflourocarbons (CFCs) remains relevant. The Vienna Convention for the Protection of the Ozone Layer 1985, together with the subsequent 1987 Montreal Protocol,[83] aim to introduce a staged reduction in ozone-depleting substances. There are internationally agreed limits and targets for reduction. The EU's controls go further, in particular by introducing specific production caps, and the UK has sought to impose emission limits on the relevant chemicals under the controls in Part 1 of the EPA 1990. Regulation 2037/00 on Substances that Deplete the Ozone Layer was introduced in 2000 to take account of the more stringent controls placed on hydrofluorocarbons and methyl bromide by the Protocol in 1995 and 1997. The National Air Quality Strategy,[84] under Section 80 of the Environment Act 1995 continues to set 'objectives' for the reduction of a number of specified pollutants, however the

---

best practical means to protect and preserve the marine environment from pollution, has been given effect through an order under s 129 of the Merchant Shipping Act 1985: the Merchant Shipping (Prevention of Pollution) (Law of the Sea Convention) Order 1996 (SI 1996/282).

[82] So, the UK is a party to the London Convention on the Prevention of Marine Pollution by the Dumping of Wastes and Other Matters (the London Dumping Convention) 1972, which includes a prohibition on dumping high-level radioactive waste at sea, and the very detailed International Convention for the Prevention of Pollution from Ships (MARPOL) 1973, which covers similar matters outside this area. By contrast, the Bonn Agreement for Co-operation in Dealing with Pollution of the North Sea by Hydro-Carbons and Other Harmful Substances etc 1983 does not affect the rights and obligations of the states under international law. It is an agreement between the eight states bordering on the North Sea and the EEC, and is essentially one of co-operation.

[83] The Montreal Protocol on Substances that Deplete the Ozone Layer 1987; amended at the London Conference 1990, and in Copenhagen in 1992.

[84] The latest Air Quality Strategy was published in July 2007.

document does not contain legally binding provisions, except insofar as it repeats limit values in EU legislation. In May 2008 the EU adopted the Air Quality Directive,[85] which sets new air quality objectives for PM2.5 (fine particles) including an exposure reduction target. Under the Directive Member States are required to reduce exposure to PM2.5 in urban areas by an average of 20% by 2020, based on 2010 levels.

Air quality can also be affected at a regional and local level by emissions from **3.27** industrial, domestic, agricultural, and transport activities. The Geneva Convention on Long Range Trans-boundary Air Pollution 1979 is concerned with limiting, and gradually reducing and preventing, air pollution, including trans-boundary pollution. It is this treaty which underlies the European Union's controls on sulphur, nitrogen oxides, and volatile organic compounds. Although the Convention itself does not set any specific targets, these have been introduced by later protocols. The Espoo Convention on Environmental Impact Assessment in a Transboundary Context (1991) entered into force in the UK in January 1998.[86] It seeks to ensure that states carry out environmental assessments of projects which are likely to have significant adverse trans-boundary effects. This would extend the requirements to states outside the European Union's area.

Trans-frontier trade in waste

The trade in waste across national frontiers, sometimes of particularly toxic and **3.28** dangerous wastes, led to the Basel Convention on the Control of Transboundary Movements of Hazardous Wastes and their Disposal (1989).[87] UK action on the trans-frontier shipments of waste has been in part driven by this, but the major influence has been action taken at the level of the European Union, with a series of Regulations and Directives, many of which predate the international convention.[88]

---

[85] Directive 2008/50/EC, which merges much of the existing legislation (Framework Directive 96/62/EC, 1–3 daughter Directives 1999/30/EC, 2000/69/EC, 2002/3/EC, and Decision on Exchange of Information 97/101/EC) into a single directive.

[86] The Convention was concluded at Espoo in Finland on 25 February 1991. It is published in the Official Treaty Series as No 12 (1998; Cm 3879). Most of its obligations are already part of the environmental assessment regime under the EU Directive 85/337/EEC (see Chapter 15).

[87] This came into force on 5 May 1992, and was ratified by the EU and the UK in February 1994. There are also European agreements on the international transport of dangerous goods by road (1993) and the carriage by rail (1993).

[88] See the Transfrontier Shipment of Waste Regulations 2007 (which replaced those of 1994) and the revised EC Waste Shipments Regulation 1013/2006; see Chapter 7 on Waste Management further.

Nature conservation and the Protection of Wildlife

3.29 This topic is discussed in detail in Chapter 11 on Nature Conservation, including the effect of international treaties on the UK's law. The UK is party to a number of important international conventions on conservation. Some seek to protect the habitats of flora and fauna. The system of 'Ramsar' sites in the UK, which is given effect through Section 29 of the Wildlife and Countryside Act 1981, dates to the Ramsar Convention on Wetlands of International Importance especially as Waterfowl Habitat 1971. There are currently over 160 designated sites in the UK.[89] The UK government has made use of its powers under the Countryside Act 1968 and the Wildlife and Countryside Act 1981, to implement the Bern Convention on the Conservation of European Wildlife and Natural Habitats 1979 which aims 'to conserve wild flora and fauna and their natural habitats, especially those species and habitats whose conservation requires the cooperation of several states'.[90] Natura2000, a network of EU-wide nature protection areas, is comprised of Special Areas of Conservation (SACs) established under the Habitats Directive, and Special Protection Areas (SPAs) under the Wild Birds Directive. In 2006 the EU launched a 'Biodiversity Action Plan'[91] to meet its commitment to halt biodiversity loss by 2010.

3.30 Other international agreements have dealt with the protection of individual species. The 1973 Convention on International Trade in Endangered Species (CITES)[92] aims to preserve endangered species by prohibiting their trade or by regulating the international markets through a system of permits. Whaling is regulated through the 1946 International Convention for the Regulation of Whaling. The Bonn Convention on the Conservation of Migratory Species of Wild Animals 1979 requires the UK to protect a list of endangered migratory species. It provided the impetus for the agreement on the conservation of bats[93] and the 1992 agreement on the conservation of small cetaceans of the Baltic and North Sea.

The Aarhus Convention and access to justice

3.31 Both the EU and the UK have ratified the international Convention on access to information, public participation in decision-making, and access to justice in environmental matters, known as the Aarhus Convention.[94] The Convention is

---

[89] <http://www.jncc.gov.uk/page-1389>

[90] Articles 1 and 2; the Convention is also implemented through the provisions relating to the EC Habitats Directive 92/43/EEC.

[91] <http://ec.europa.eu/environment/nature/info/pubs/docs/brochures/bio_brochure_en.pdf>

[92] Signed in Washington DC, USA, in 1973. See the article of David M Ong [1998] 2 JEL 291, which analyses developments at the international and European levels.

[93] Ratified by the UK in September 1992, and which came into force in January 1994.

[94] The Convention was signed at Aarhus, in Denmark, in 1998. The EC has been a party to the Convention since May 2005 (following Decision 2005/370/EC). The UK ratified it in February 2005. See further <http://www.unece.org>.

the responsibility of the United Nations Economic Commission for Europe ('UN(ECE)'). Aarhus is concerned with civil and political rights and does not create a 'human right' to a safe environment.[95] The objective is set out in Article 1, that:

> In order to contribute to the protection of the right of every person of present and future generations to live in an environment adequate to his or her health and well-being, each Party shall guarantee the rights of access to information, public participation in decision-making, and access to justice in environmental matters in accordance with the provisions of this Convention.

The Convention is broadly worded, and allows a wide margin of discretion to **3.32** each signatory state in the way in which it is implemented. We do have the advantage of an UN(ECE) Implementation Guide,[96] which discusses the detail of the three pillars set out in the Aarhus Convention. These 'pillars' elaborate Principle 10 of the 1992 Rio Declaration,[97] which stresses the need for public participation in environmental decision-making:

1) The first pillar establishes rules and requirements for governments to disclose information about the state of the environment, and the factors, policies, and activities that influence it (the 'access to environmental information' pillar).[98]

---

[95] The distinction between some generalized right to a healthy environment, and substantive legal rights has been highlighted by the UK itself. The UK upon signing the Convention (signed by the UK on 25 June 1998, but still not ratified) declared: 'The UK understands the references in article 1 and the seventh preambular paragraph of this Convention to the "right" of every person "to live in an environment adequate to his or her health and well-being" to express an aspiration which motivated the negotiation of this Convention and which is shared fully by the UK. The legal rights which each Party undertakes to guarantee under article 1 are limited to the rights of access to information, public participation in decision-making and access to justice in environmental matters in accordance with the provisions of this Convention.'

[96] Guide published by the Economic Commission for Europe of the United Nations (UN, 2000), but it 'does not purport to be an official interpretation of the Convention' (Foreword by the UN Secretary-General, 5th para). Nor does it have the same legal force as one of the travaux preparatoires, which would have informed the actual wording of the Convention. Given its official source, it will nevertheless be seen by the courts as persuasive. The document is a well-written guide to the Convention, and is the result of a project whose steering committee has a long and distinguished list of members, many of whom were involved in drafting the convention.

[97] As stated by Kofi Annan (Secretary-General of the United Nations): 'Although regional in scope, the significance of the Aarhus Convention is global. It is by far the most impressive elaboration of principle 10 of the Rio Declaration, which stresses the need for citizen's participation in environmental issues and for access to information on the environment held by public authorities. As such it is the most ambitious venture in the area of "environmental democracy" so far undertaken under the auspices of the United Nations.' (Aarhus website)

[98] Arts. 4 and 5. This is the right of everyone to receive environmental information that is held by public authorities. This includes information on the state of the environment, on the policies or measures taken, and on the state of human health and safety where this can be affected by the state of the environment. Applicants are entitled to obtain this information within one month of the request and without having to say why they require it. In addition, public authorities are obliged, under the Convention, to actively disseminate environmental information in their possession.

2) The second pillar addresses how the public and public interest groups can participate in decision-making on policies and projects with an anticipated environmental impact (the 'public participation in environmental decision-making' pillar).[99] 'Public Participation' is not a phrase that is defined in the Convention. Clearly, the intention is to have timely, adequate, and effective participation—the Convention lays down requirements concerning notification, timing, relevant information, commenting, response, and communication. The Convention also deems that public associations and non-governmental organizations performing administrative functions under national law, shall have an interest.[100]

3) The third pillar deals with the right of the public and public interest groups to seek judicial remedy for non-compliance by governments and corporations with the legal obligations established by the first two pillars (the 'access to justice' pillar).[101] Importantly, the procedures must provide 'adequate and effective remedies, including injunctive relief as appropriate, and be fair, equitable, timely and not prohibitively expensive'.[102]

3.33 The European Union has taken an active role in implementing the Aarhus Convention. In 2003, it adopted two Directives concerning the first and second 'pillars' of the Aarhus Convention—Directive 2003/4/EC on public access to environmental information[103] and the Public Participation Directive 2003/35/EC providing for public participation in respect of the drawing up of certain plans and programmes relating to the environment.[104] The Proposal for a Directive on access to justice in environmental matters remains on the table

---

[99] Arts. 6–8. This is the right to participate in environmental decision-making. Arrangements must be made by public authorities to enable the public affected and also environmental non-governmental organizations to comment on proposals or plans and programmes, for these comments to be taken into due account in the decision-making process and for the information to be provided on the final decision and the reasons for it. The UN(ECE) Implementation Guide refers to the 'ladder' of participation (para 85), for the different levels of decision-making, from direct participation to the right to be informed only. Members of the public have most power with respect to local matters and a diminished role when the issues become more complex and affect larger numbers of people—when the politicians and public authorities must bear responsibility.

[100] See Article 2 definitions.

[101] Art.9. Everyone must have access to a review procedure before a court of law or another independent and impartial body established by law.

[102] Art.9(4). This is the perhaps the most controversial provision when it comes to the UK—see Chapter 2 further.

[103] This repealed Council Directive 90/313/EEC. Both Directives 2003/4/EEC and 2003/35/EEC also contain provisions on access to justice.

[104] This also made amendments to the provisions on public participation and access to justice Council Directives 85/337/EEC (EIA) and 96/61/EC (IPPC). Provision has also been made for better public participation in environmental decision-making in a number of other environmental directives, such as the SEA Directive 2001/42/EC and the Water Framework Directive 2000/60/EC.

(see COM(2003) 624). The European Union has also applied the provisions of the Aarhus Convention to the Community institutions and bodies.[105]

The UK has taken a more complacent view of the need to reform its procedures, **3.34** although it is a supporter of the Convention. It did introduce new Environmental Information Regulations in 2003. As for public participation, it considers that each new decision-making process has full provision for public participation— such as in the drafting of each local authority's Community Strategy. It has not, so far, considered that further action is needed on the 'access to justice' pillar. The UK is already under Article 226 infraction proceedings for not transposing the Public Participation Directive into national law. Effective measures are needed at the national level. The October 2007 report[106] commissioned by the EU Commission ranked the UK amongst the bottom five EU countries on access to environmental justice.

D. Human Rights Law and the Environment

International human rights law and the environment

Although the international conferences on the environment contain many decla- **3.35** rations and principles concerning the quality of the environment which should be provided, there is still no specific 'human right' for individuals to a safe environment. Some authors have argued that international law already recognizes a human right to a decent, viable, or healthy environment, but most remain sceptical.[107] The first principle set out in the Rio Declaration is that 'human beings . . . have the right to a healthy and productive life in harmony with nature'. Such a collective right relies upon government action, rather than conferring rights upon individuals. The most that can currently be said is that environmental rights can be indirectly derived from the existing individual rights to life, health, and property. The UK is a party to the International Covenant on Civil and

---

[105] See Regulation (EC) No 1367/2006 (which applied from 17 July 2007). This 'Aarhus Regulation' covers not only the institutions, but also bodies, offices, or agencies established by, or on the basis of the EC Treaty, which need to adapt their internal procedures and practice to the provisions of the Regulation. Regarding access to environmental information, the Aarhus Regulation extends Regulation (EC) No 1049/2001 regarding public access to European Parliament, Council, and Commission documents to all Community institutions and bodies. The Commission has adopted two Decisions to implement further the detailed rules of the Regulation.

[106] The Report was entitled *Measures on Access to Justice in Environmental Matters (Article 9(3))* (October 2007; available at: <http://ec.europa.eu/environment/aarhus/study_access.htm>). See also the critical report *Civil Law Aspects of Environmental Justice* (2003) Environmental Law Foundation.

[107] See the discussion in Birnie and Boyle, at 190ff. The international dimension is also covered in Sands, op cit page 294 onwards.

Political Rights.[108] The Covenant is the responsibility of the UN Human Rights Committee, to whom the states report. However, there is no court and no developed case law which would assist in its interpretation.

The European Convention on Human Rights

3.36 The UK is also a party to the European Convention on Human Rights and Fundamental Freedoms (the European Convention).[109] The European Convention contains rights and freedoms which are guaranteed by the contracting states against the misuse of their legislative, executive, and judicial powers. It was signed in Rome in 1950 by the Member States of the Council of Europe, as distinct from the much smaller European Union. All 47 Member States of the Council of Europe are parties to the Convention and its protocols, although not all the protocols have been ratified by the states.[110] Of course, it is perhaps the very existence of the European Court of Human Rights, and its growing body of case law, which has had the greatest influence on the development and application in the various countries of the rights and freedoms guaranteed under the Convention. The European Court remains the court of last resort, and is the ultimate authority on the interpretation of the European Convention.[111] The Court sits in Chambers of 7 judges or, in exceptional cases, as a Grand Chamber of 17 judges. The Committee of Ministers of the Council of Europe supervises the execution of the Court's judgments.

Human Rights Act 1998

3.37 The UK is obliged to ensure that the rights and freedoms under the European Convention on Human Rights are guaranteed in domestic law, and that effective remedies are provided before the national authorities for any breaches of its provisions. However, this is a good example of where an international obligation has had to await national legislation before the UK courts will apply it. For over

---

[108] New York, 19 December 1966; TS 6 (1977); Cmd 6702. The UK is not a party to the Optional Protocol. The Covenant came into force on 23 March 1976. There is no article which protects the right to property, equivalent to Art. 1 of Protocol 1 of the European Convention. Art. 17 does provide that there should be no arbitrary or unlawful interference with a person's privacy, family, home, or correspondence.

[109] Rome, 4 November 1950; TS 71 (1953); Cmd 8969. See generally, Jacobs and White: *The European Convention on Human Rights* (4th edition, OUP, 2006).

[110] The UK still has not ratified protocols 4, 7, and 12.

[111] The European Court is based in Strasbourg, and provides an excellent website, which includes a full library of its cases (see <http://www.echr.coe.int>) Unlike the European Court of Justice, there are only two official languages—English and French. The mechanism for upholding the Convention was simplified by Protocol 11 from 1 November 1998—the Commission and the Court were combined into a single, full-time court, which examines the admissibility and merits of applications submitted to it, and the Council of Ministers are no longer involved in the procedure before a decision is made. The whole Court is composed of an equal number of judges to that of the States who are party to the Convention. There is therefore one UK judge.

45 years the European Convention remained an international treaty obligation which could not be enforced by the domestic courts. It is only since the UK Government gave effect to the European Convention in domestic law, by the Human Rights Act 1998, that this is an area which the domestic courts have had to consider directly.

The Human Rights Act 1998 ('HRA 1998')[112] has made it unlawful for any 'pub- **3.38** lic authority',[113] court, or tribunal to act in a way which is incompatible with a Convention right. Any existing legislation must also be interpreted 'so far as it is possible to do so' in accordance with the Convention.[114] It is also possible for the courts to declare secondary legislation, such as rules, orders, and regulations, to be unlawful in the light of the Human Rights convention. However, while the courts can re-interpret all statues, they cannot overturn statutes—they can only to make a declaration of incompatibility.[115]

The relevant public authorities must consider how their actions affect those whom **3.39** they regulate as well as how they might affect the individual rights of the public. The HRA 1998 leaves the individual to assert his or her rights through the existing powers and procedures of the courts.[116] He or she will be able to do this either by an application for judicial review,[117] or by way of defence in any action in which a public authority attempts to use a law which is inconsistent with the

---

[112] The Human Rights Act 1998 was brought into force on 2 October 2000—the relevant SI is SI 2000/1851 (for the main part of the Act). Note that the Government of Wales Act 1998, s 107(1), came into force on 1 April 1999.

[113] S 6, HRA 1998. 'Public authority' includes the Agency. It also includes any person exercising functions which are functions of a public nature—eg Railtrack, telecom companies, registered care homes—but not when they are exercising functions of a private nature (!). This can also include companies set up by local authorities which exercise the council's role *Hampshire CC v Beer (t/a Hammer Trout Farm)* (2003) 21/7/2003, CA (running a farmer's market). See further Prof Dawn Oliver, 'Functions of a public nature under the Human Rights Act' (2004) P.L. Summer 329, on s 6(3)b) of the Human Rights Act 1998, concerning 'functions of a public nature'.

[114] S 3(1), HRA 1998. eg Coroners Courts—R *(on the application of Middleton) v HM Coroner for the Western District of Somerset and Anor* (2004) 11/3/2004, HL, where it was held that a change of statutory interpretation, authorized by the Human Rights Act 1998 s 3, was required to honour the international obligations of the UK expressed in the European Convention (here, Article 2, as the case concerned a death in custody).

[115] S 4, with an expedited Parliamentary scheme for amendment (s 11). This is a complex constitutional compromise. It is therefore likely to encourage the courts to use the statutory interpretation rule as widely as possible in order to try and avoid raising a s 4 at all. Note that the *Alconbury* case started with a Declaration of Incompatibility in the High Court (subsequently reversed by the higher courts).

[116] The Government does not consider that it has created any new remedies under the Act. It has deliberately excluded Article 13 (the right to an effective remedy) from applying, and stated that the Act does not 'incorporate' the European Convention into UK law.

[117] But note that the right to bring a case, as an alleged 'victim' of a violation (s 7(1) of the 1998 Act), is more restrictive than the tests for standing in judicial review. The European Convention also relies on an applicant being a 'victim' (hence the failure of applicants living 1,000 km from the nuclear test sites in *Tauira and others v France* [1995] DR 83-B112).

European Convention against a citizen. The 1998 Act does not provide for private individuals to rely on the rights in private actions against other individuals. It does provide a limited additional right to claim damages against the public authority.[118]

The Convention rights

3.40 As there are no 'environmental rights' under the European Convention, its effect is more general.[119] It is most likely that cases relevant to the environment will come within Article 8 (the right to respect for private and family life, home, and correspondence) or Article 1 of the First Protocol (the right to property). Procedural rights are also important, so that the way in which the authorities carry out environmental regulation may at times amount to a violation of Articles 6(1) (the right to a fair and independent hearing) and 13 (the right to an effective national remedy). The considerable jurisprudence which exists regarding Article 10, which covers the right to freedom of expression, and the right to send and receive information and ideas, would also cover access to environmental information.[120] Article 14 protects individuals against discrimination in the way in which the other rights under the European Convention are applied.[121]

3.41 On the other hand, there are no absolute rights under these Articles. Environmental considerations can be held to be sufficient justification for interference with an individual's Convention rights. In the case of *Wilson v Wychavon District Council*[122], the Court of Appeal found that although Section 183(4) of the Town and Country Planning Act 1990 did indirectly discriminate against gypsies, it could be objectively

---

[118] S 8, HRA 1998. However, as in the European Court, the English courts have held that damages are not recoverable as of right for a violation of the Convention Rights (*Anufrijeva v Southwark LBC* [2003] EWCA Civ 1406). The main concern is to bring the infringement to an end, and compensation is a secondary issue. However, some large claims have been allowed even by the European Court (eg *Pine Valley Developments v Ireland*, although this is exceptional). The English courts will look for comparables in the awards made by the Criminal Injuries Compensation Board and the Local Government Ombudsman.

[119] This is a point that has been made from the beginning of the HRA 1998—for instance, the April 1998 edition of the JPL contained three articles on the European Convention and its effect on planning and environmental law (Corner, Upton, and Kitson: [1998] JPL 301, 315, 321)—the first of many. For a relatively-upbeat assessment see Morrow, 'The Rights Question: the Initial Impact of the Human Rights Act on Domestic Law Relating to the Environment' [2005] JPL 1010, even though she accepts that individual rights in the environment are not fully and adequately addressed at the moment and looks forward to a time when these develop under the Convention regime.

[120] Eg as was argued in *Guerra v Italy* (1998) 4 BHRC 63, ECHR (failure to inform the public about chemical factory hazards and emergency procedures). But there is no legal presumption of openness with regard to all forms of public inquiry. Article 10 was not engaged by the decision to hold a closed public inquiry into Foot and Mouth—*Persey and others v SoS EFRA* [2002] EWHC 371 (Admin).

[121] Whilst *Buckley* is a good example of such an argument (for 'gypsies'), a more general example is provided by the *Pine Valley Developments and others v Ireland* [1992] 14 EHRR 319 case (individual developer treated differently).

[122] *Regina (Wilson) v Wychavon District Council and Another* [2007] 2 WLR 798.

justified by the legitimate aim of protecting the environment[123] and so was not incompatible with Article 14.[124] In a similar vein, the designation of Tree Preservation Orders[125] or nature conservation areas,[126] which severely restrict an individual's property rights, are justifiable in the wider public interest.

Article 8

Convention rights are relied upon in a wide variety of cases. In planning and envi-   **3.42**
ronmental matters, Article 8(1)[127] rights are frequently alleged to be engaged, as environmental pollution may affect an individual's well-being, and prevent them from enjoying their homes and affect their private and family life. In the terms of the Convention, the European Court has stated[128] that such a situation could be analysed as a positive duty on the State to take reasonable and appropriate steps to secure the individual's rights. It could also be said that the 'interference by a public authority' had to be justified in the terms set out in Article 8(2), that it is in accordance with the law and is necessary in a democratic society in the interests of national security, public safety, or the economic well-being of the country, for the prevention of disorder or crime, for the protection of health or morals, or for the protection of the rights and freedoms of others. In both analyses, the European Court of Human Rights stated that regard must be had to balancing the interests of the individual and the community as a whole, and that there was a certain 'margin of appreciation' for the state.

This balance was identified in the case of *Lopez Ostria*,[129] where the European   **3.43**
Court of Human Rights decided that there was a violation of the European Convention when a person and her family had to live in very difficult conditions next to a waste treatment plant, which the authorities allowed to operate without a licence, and which emitted 'gas fumes, pestilential smells, and contamination'.

---

[123] In this case, the finding that the change of use of a building to a dwelling would usually result in less harm than the stationing of a residential caravan.

[124] Article 14 EHCR 'The enjoyment of the rights and freedoms set forth in this Convention shall be secured without discrimination on any ground such as sex, race, colour, language, religion, political or other opinion, national or social origin, association with a national minority, property, birth or other status.'

[125] *R (Brennon) v Bromsgrove District Council* [2003] EWHC 752 (Admin).

[126] See n139 below.

[127] Article 8(1) ECHR 'Everyone has the right to respect for his private and family life, his home and his correspondence'. However, this is not an absolute right, and it is qualified by Article 8(2).

[128] *Lopez Ostria v Spain*, 8 July 1992, application no 16798/90; [1995] 20 EHRR 277. This is a reasoning that has then been referred to in all subsequent cases of a similar nature.

[129] *Lopez Ostria v Spain*, 8 July 1992, application no 16798/90; [1995] 20 EHRR 277. Note that the Court considered that it fell short of seriously endangering her health, and the European Court held that this did not amount to degrading treatment within the meaning of Article 3. It is perhaps not surprising that the invidious effects of pollution would be difficult to analyse in terms of Article 3, whose primary purpose is to protect the individual from torture, inhuman treatment, or punishment.

It was held that the Spanish state had not struck a fair balance in Mrs Lopez Ostria's case, and it also ordered compensation to be paid. The court applied *Lopez Ostria* in the *Guerra*[130] case, where a state's failure to inform local inhabitants of the risks from a chemicals factory, so that they might assess whether or not they would wish to continue to live near it, did not respect their private and family life and was in violation of Article 8. The balance between the interests of the individual and of the community, and the margin of appreciation allowed to national authorities to strike this balance, also proved crucial in *Buckley v UK*,[131] where the European Court held that the UK had not violated a gypsy family's rights under Article 8 when a local authority sought to enforce planning controls.

3.44 The issue of the extent of Article 8 was re-considered in 2002 in *Hatton and others v UK*,[132] which saw the Grand Chamber of the European Court (by twelve votes to five) overturn the earlier decision of one of its Chambers that the level of night-flying from Heathrow was in breach of residents' Article 8 rights. The case marked something of a turning-point in the development of human rights law, as the majority on the Court explicitly backed away from granting environmental rights any special status, and acknowledged the wide margin of appreciation available to the Member States. Whilst there were some powerful dissenting voices in *Hatton*,[133] the majority view has remained the appropriate approach to take. The central question is whether or not interference with such rights is proportionate. In *Hatton*, it was decided that the UK had struck a fair balance between Article 8 rights and the economic benefits associated with aircraft landing at night at Heathrow Airport. In the case of *Fadeyeva*,[134] the European Court decided that,

---

[130] *Guerra v Italy* [1998] 4 BHRC 63. The Court also awarded each applicant compensation.

[131] [1996] JPL 1018.

[132] (2003) 37 EHRR 28, especially paras 122 and 128.

[133] In the view of four of the judges, who dissented, 'the close connection between human-rights protection and the urgent need for a decontamination of the environment leads us to perceive health as the most basic human need and as pre-eminent. After all, as in this case, what do human rights pertaining to the privacy of the home mean if day and night, constantly or intermittently, it reverberates with the roar of aircraft engines?' (introduction to Dissenting Opinion). After analysing a body of case law, including previous decisions on the interference with Article 8 rights by aircraft noise, the dissenting Opinion states that 'in principle, the general reference to the economic well-being of the country is not sufficient to justify the failure of the State to safeguard an applicant's rights under Article 8' (para 16). See also case commentary of Hart and Wheeler, 'Night Flights and Strasbourg's Retreat from Environmental Human Rights' [2004] 16 J Environmental Law 100, supporting the dissenting voices. As they say, the Court appeared to strain both to distinguish and to limit the previous decisions in *Lopez Ostria* and *Guerra* (see the para 120), in trying to say that they were predicated on non-compliance.

[134] The ECHR case of *Fadeyeva v Russia* (55723/00) [2007] EHRR 10 is another example of a case of non-compliance—not only should the applicant have been re-housed outside the buffer zone around a steel mill, but the emissions from the steel mill also exceeded the safe limits established by domestic legislation. The Court held, unanimously, that there had been a violation of Article 8 (and awarded 6,000 euros for her non-pecuniary damage). The Court accepted the evidence that there had been actual detriment to the applicant's health and well-being, which had reached a level sufficient to bring it within the scope of Article 8.

despite the wide margin of appreciation left to the respondent State, Russia had failed to strike a fair balance between the interests of the community and the applicant's effective enjoyment of her right to respect for her home and her private life in the way in which a steel mill had been allowed to operate.

The underlying principle is that national authorities have a very wide ranging dis-   **3.45**
cretion in how competing interests are to be balanced. In the *Marcic*[135] case, which concerned flooding from foul water sewers into the claimant's property, the House of Lords rejected the claim that the claimant's Article 8 rights had been violated. The claimant could have made use of a statutory scheme to compel the water utility company, by way of an enforcement order, to remedy the inadequate drainage, but he did not do so. The question for the court was whether the statutory scheme struck a fair balance between the interests of persons whose homes and property were affected and the interests of customers and the general public. Reference was made to the Grand Chamber decision in *Hatton*, particularly to the emphasis on the 'fundamentally subsidiary nature of the Convention' and the conclusion that 'the role of the domestic policy maker should be given special weight'.[136]

A restrictive view has also been taken on who can be a 'victim'. A person can have   **3.46**
their rights affected by actions carried out on a neighbouring piece of land, so that the civil rights of Mrs Ortenberg were affected when her house was adjacent to new development.[137] On the other side of the line, are such cases as *Balmer-Schafroth*,[138] and the UK cases of *Furness*[139] and *Vetterlein*[140] where, on the evidence, the grant of permission was not directly decisive of the claimant's rights.

---

[135] [2003] UKHL 66. The Court of Appeal, [2002] EWCA Civ 64, had held that a statutory sewerage undertaker is liable for the flooding damage to premises caused by overflows from the public sewerage system—both in nuisance and under the Human Rights Act 1998, as a breach of Mr Marcic's rights to respect for his home under Article 8 and his right to enjoyment of his possession under Article 1 to the First Protocol. The HL held that the claimant did not have a common law action in nuisance against the defendant as to allow such an action would set at nought the comprehensive statutory scheme laid down in the Water Industry Act 1991. The claim under the Human Rights Act 1998 was also held to be ill-founded and the statutory scheme complied with the European Convention on Human Rights.

[136] See paragraph 41 of the Judgment.

[137] *Ortenberg v Austria* [1995] 19 EHRR 524, para 28.

[138] *Balmer-Schafroth v Switzerland* [Sept 1997]—the ECHR rejected a case brought by villagers living in the containment zone surrounding a nuclear power plant, on the grounds that they had failed to demonstrate that any specific right of theirs was at stake when the State granted an extension to operate the station. This case was followed in *Athanassaoglou v Switzerland* [2000] 2 April—another application for a nuclear power station licence. The court held that the 'victims' had not claimed any loss, economic or otherwise, for which they intended to seek compensation—they only alleged a general danger. Whilst the case was decisive of the application to extend the power station, the outcome of the procedure for approval did not determine any civil right (such as life, physical integrity and property) of the applicants.

[139] *R (on the application of Furness and Guildford BC v Environment Agency and Thames Water Services Ltd (Interested Party)* (2002) 17/12, QBD (Turner J)

[140] *R (on the application of Vetterlein) v Hampshire County Council* [2002] JPL 289, Sullivan J (see in particular paras 62 to 67).

In *Vetterlein*, it was noted that a breach of WHO guidelines, which were not mandatory, did not automatically mean that there would be serious pollution, let alone a significant danger to public health. The court considered that the objections were no more than a generalized concern as to the increases in emissions and were insufficient to engage Article 8. Nor will a quantifiable loss of value to landowners caused by neighbouring developers constitute a separate basis for alleging a breach of Convention rights. The Court of Appeal in the *Lough*[141] case rejected the claimant's argument that the effects of a proposed development were sufficient to engage his Article 8 rights. More direct impacts on amenity are expected. In *Geoffrey Wallace Andrews v Reading Borough Council*,[142] the claimant successfully argued that the increase in noise resulting from a road traffic scheme put in place by the council had substantially interfered with his Article 8 rights, and that he should be compensated for the cost of installing double glazing. The authority had been entitled to take the view that the public benefit of the scheme outweighed the detrimental impact upon the claimant and his neighbours. However, the authority's margin of appreciation was not so great as to permit the claimant to remain uncompensated.

Property rights

3.47 The general principle in Article 1 of Protocol 1 of the European Convention is that an individual has the right to the peaceful enjoyment of his property. 'Possessions' are defined widely and include possessions of economic value such as waste disposal licences, rights to extract water, and most legal interests in goods and land.[143] But, even judged in the light of this general principle, the article does allow the deprivation of possessions subject to conditions, and the control of the use of property by the state in the public interest.[144] In doubtful cases, the court has gone on to consider the correct balance in any event, such as whether there was an expectation of a certain level of compensation or of an approval of a new licence.[145] Whilst the deprivation of property without compensation is likely to be

---

[141] *David Lough and Others v First Secretary of State and Bankside Developments* (2004) 1 WLR 2557.

[142] [2005] EWHC 256.

[143] So it has been held to include an expectation that navigation rights are continued (*Josie Rowland v Environment Agency* [2003] TLR 20/1/2004, CA), the rights of minority shareholdings (*In the matter of Waste Recycling Group PLC* [2003] 28/7/03, Ch.D.).

[144] *Sporrong and Lonnroth* (1982) 5 EHRR 35, at para 61; see also *James* 21 February 1986, Series A No 52, 24; and see *S v France* (1990) 65 DR 250, discussed in Corner [1998] JPL 301 at 309. In *R v SoS for Health ex p Eastside Cheese Co.* [1999] CoD 321, the CA considered the ban of the sale of cheese, for which there was no compensation, to be in the general interest and not in violation of this Article.

[145] eg *R (oao NFU and others) v Secretary of State for the EFRA and Secretary of State for Wales* [2003] 6/3/2003, Forbes J (compensation). In *R (aoa AMVAC) v Secretary of State EFRA* [2001] EWHC Admin 1011, the court considered that a pesticide approval was not determinative of property rights (under P1-1) but if it was, then a fair balance had been struck.

justifiable only in exceptional circumstances,[146] compensation is much less likely to be a necessary requirement where a control of the use of property is imposed— given the balance to be struck.

This does mean in general that where a state authority deprives an individual of a **3.48** valuable licence, [147] such as a discharge consent, it is unlikely that this would constitute a violation of Article 1 of the First Protocol. On the other hand, there have been cases where the court has held that the individual has had to bear an excessive burden which has upset the fair balance which should be struck between the requirements of the public interest and the right to peaceful enjoyment of one's possessions.[148] There will come a stage when the level of control which is imposed will be tantamount to a deprivation of property.[149] This is a debate that may yet need to be revisited in detail once water abstraction licences become more restrictive.

Procedural rights

The Convention sets out an important statement regarding the procedural stand- **3.49** ards that are to be expected in Article 6(1), that everyone is entitled to a fair and public hearing within a reasonable time by an independent and impartial tribunal established by law in the determination of their civil rights and obligations and of an criminal charge against him. This can potentially affect all environmental cases, as the determination of an environmental application is the determination of a civil right, [150] as is the right to the peaceful enjoyment of one's possessions

---

[146] Under the Convention, there is no mention of compensation in Article 1 (P1-1). However, it is implied into the article, by a slightly unusual route, explained in detail in *Lithgow and others v UK* [1986], see para 119–121.

[147] For instance, the European Court has held that a liquor licence could be withdrawn in the public interest—*Tre Traktorer Aktiebohg* 7 July 1989, Series A No 159. A licence is no more than a discretionary entitlement and not an absolute right.

[148] In *Matos & Silva LDA v Portugal* [1997] 24 EHRR 573, the Court held that the setting up of a nature reserve had seriously affected the applicant company's land and business interests, in violation of Art. 1 of Protocol 1; the length of the proceedings had also been unreasonable, in violation of Art. 6(1). The Court did accept that the measures pursued the public interest relied on by the Government, that is to say town and country planning for the purposes of protecting the environment—at para 88.

[149] So, in *Sporrong and Lonnroth v Sweden* [1982], the ECHR held that the applicants' property rights had been violated when the local Council had continually extended the life of some expropriation permits but had never carried out the expropriation. The permits had been finally cancelled, but had prevented the applicants from selling or using their land for 23 years and 8 years respectively. The Court held that their ownership had been 'rendered precarious' by these actions. Although a measure of interference was justifiable, the Council had upset the fair balance between the individual's rights and the general interests of the community.

[150] This principle was accepted in the planning case of *Bryan v UK* [1996] JPL 386, The case concerned whether the system of appeals to a government-appointed inspector provided a fair and independent hearing. It was accepted that right of appeal to the Secretary of State is not sufficient, even with the number of procedural safeguards which the inspectors are bound to follow. See Crowe,

and property. The refusal of a licence, or its alteration or enforcement, will require proper procedural safeguards. In the area of planning cases, and by analogy environmental cases, it is accepted that the whole process must be considered, including the scope of the right to appeal to the High Court, as was confirmed by the House of Lords in *Alconbury*.[151] Greater care will be needed where the administrative decision-maker relies on findings of fact, as in enforcement proceedings, as opposed to making decisions based purely on policy grounds.[152] The same view has been taken in respect of similar areas, such as the procedures for designating a nature conservation area.[153]

'Lessons from *Bryan*' [1996] JPL 359. In addition, where the grant of planning permission directly affects a third party's property, then he or she will be protected by Article 6(1)—*Ortenberg v Austria* [1994] 19 EHRR 524. However, the proceeedings in question must be determinative of the rights in question, and a tenuous effect or consequence will be insufficient to engage these procedural rights—*Balmer-Schafroth v Switzerland* [1998] 25 EHRR 598, ECHR, where the Court held that the applicant did not have a genuine and serious 'dispute' about the danger posed by the nuclear power station.

[151] *Alconbury and others v Secretary of State for the Environment, Transport and the Regions* [2001] 2 WLR 1389, which applies even where the Secretary of State is both the policy-maker and the decision-taker. The final chapter on the case was in the ECtHR: *Holding and Barnes*, in fact the lead claimant in *Alconbury*, lost their challenge in Strasbourg—*Holding and Barnes PLC v UK* (Application No.2352/02, 12 March 2002). The ECHR relied heavily on *Bryan v UK* in deciding that the claim was inadmissible as it was 'manifestly ill-founded'. The Secretary of State can even deal with an application in which the government might be said to have a financial interest.

[152] See the distinctions drawn between different types of administrative decision in *Friends Provident*, [2002] 1 WLR 1450, para 89; and see the statements of Lord Hoffmann on enforcement cases in *Alconbury* at paras 90, 95, and 117.

[153] See *R (on the application of Aggregate Industries UK Ltd) v English Nature and Secretary of State for the Environment, Food and Rural Affairs* [2002] EWHC 1515 (Admin), where it was accepted that the oral hearing before the Council of English Nature, followed by the possibility of judicial revew, was sufficient—even though the Council was not an independent and impartial tribunal. See also *Fisher and another v English Nature* [2004] EWCA Civ 663, and *R (on the application of Trailer & Marina (Leven) Ltd v Secretary of State for the Environment Food and Rural Affairs and English Nature* [2005] 1 WLR 1267 (which also raised property right issues, under Protocol 1 Art.1).

4

EUROPEAN ENVIRONMENTAL LAW

A. **Introduction**	4.01		B. **The Implementation of**	
The structure of the European			**European Law in the UK**	4.43
Community and its institutions	4.02		The constitutional status of	
The European court of justice	4.06		European law	4.43
The ECJ and the purposive			The need for national courts to	
approach	4.09		refer questions to the ECJ	
The ECJ and proportionality	4.12		under Article 234	4.47
The current framework and aims			The use of the principles of	
of European environmental			European law in the UK	
policy	4.13		courts	4.49
The precautionary principle	4.17		The precautionary principle	4.51
European policy documents on the			The 'polluter pays' principle	4.53
environment	4.18		Environmental liability	4.54
Action programmes	4.18		C. **European Remedies for**	
Communications	4.21		**Individual Litigants**	4.56
The different types of European			Individual remedies—Judicial	
environmental legislation	4.24		review	4.58
Regulations	4.25		Individual remedies—Damages	
Directives	4.26		against the state	4.63
Directives and the doctrine of			Individual remedies—Defence in	
'direct effect'	4.30		criminal proceedings	4.69
Decisions, recommendations, and			Infraction proceedings against	
opinions	4.40		the UK	4.72
The European Union and human			Challenging community	
rights	4.41		legislation—Direct actions	4.73

A. Introduction

Whereas the European Union's jurisprudence was originally restricted to pursuing **4.01** the free movement of goods, capital, services, and people, it is now acknowledged that the protection of the environment is one of its essential objectives.[1] These changes have been reflected in the amendments made to the original Treaties by

---

[1] The EC Treaty refers to a 'high level of protection and improvement of the quality of the environment'.

the Single European Act 1986, the Maastricht Treaty 1992, and the Amsterdam Treaty 1997.[2] Although environmental protection is just one of a number of EC objectives, Article 6 of the Treaty provides that 'environmental protection require- ments must be integrated into the definition and implementation of the Community policies and activities'. Since the last edition of this book, European environmental legislation has grown exponentially in subject matter and in impact. There are few areas of environmental law in England and Wales which are not the subject of European legislation in some form. The institutions of the European Community, in particular the Commission, establish the pace and direc- tion of European environmental policy. Beyond Europe, the Community takes an increasingly prominent role in international environmental decision-making (for example, under the United Nations Framework Convention on Climate Change) both by contracting into targets at international level, and in translating those tar- gets into Europe-wide environmental policy and legislation.[3]

The Structure of the European Community and its institutions

4.02   The institutions of the European Community have law-making powers of their own, by which the sovereign rights of Member States are to some degree subordi- nate[4]. The beginnings of community law lie in the European Commission, which drafts proposals for presentation to the European Parliament and the Council of the European Union, which hold have joint responsibility for passing laws. The European Court of Justice is tasked with ensuring that community law is uni- formly interpreted and applied in each Member State. It is not possible to chal- lenge the validity of community law in the domestic courts; As the ECJ has said, it would 'imperil the very foundations of the Community' to allow this to hap- pen.[5] The one exception is human rights law, which is still separate from the

---

[2]   The Nice Treaty 2001 did not affect the environmental measures. There may be further amend- ments made by the Lisbon Treaty (December 2007), if it is ratified by all the Member States. It would re-number the Treaty provisions yet again. There would also be Qualified Majority voting, further changes to the Commission and added powers for the Parliament. However, this may suffer the same inconclusive fate as the failed Constitutional Treaty (June 2004).

[3]   For a list of areas of co-operation with 'third countries' and international conventions see <http://europa.eu/scadplus/leg/en/s15011.htm>. Note that it is intended to amend the Treaty of Rome to include the objective of 'promoting measures at international level to deal with regional or world-wide problems, *and in particular combating climate change*'. This would be part of the objec- tives in the newly-renumbered Article 191 (ex-Article 174), if the Lisbon Treaty is ratified.

[4]   See Wyatt and Dashwood *European Union Law* (5th edition Sweet & Maxwell, 2006) pp 82–84 and pp 97–110 on the principle of subsidiarity.

[5]   *Simmenthal* C–106/77 (1978) above. The Italian Constitutional Court had decided that all constitutional matters were for it to decide, and that an Italian law which had been passed in contra- diction to two EC regulations still prevailed in Italy. The ECJ stated that the regulations were directly applicable, and overruled the Italian court.

EC Treaty.[6] The ECJ has exclusive competence over the interpretation of European Community law, and its task is to interpret the Treaties.[7]

The European Council's power to adopt legislation is normally conditional upon **4.03** the submission of proposals by the European Commission. The European Commission is the Community's own executive arm, and a separate Directorate-General (known as DG Environment since 1999) initiates and defines new legislation on the environment but does not have exclusive competence in areas affecting the environment. The European Commission, as well as proposing legislation, may bring direct action against a Member State if it considers that it has breached an obligation under the Treaty (Article 226 EC).

On environmental matters the European Parliament plays an equal role in deci- **4.04** sion-making to that of the Council of Europe, under the 'co-decision' procedure introduced by the 1992 Maastricht Treaty and strengthened by the Treaty of Amsterdam in 1999. The Commission sends proposals for new legislation to both Parliament and the Council; if these bodies cannot reach agreement, the proposal is brought before a Conciliation Committee, made up of an equal number of members from both bodies. The final agreement of the two institutions is essential if the text is to be adopted as law. Parliament may still reject, by an absolute majority of its members, a text adopted by the Conciliation Committee.[8] The Parliamentary Committee on 'Environment, Public Health and Consumer Safety' (ENVI), while not having the power of veto, considers Commission proposals and draws up reports to be presented to the Plenary Assembly.

The European Environment Agency, established in October 1993 under **4.05** Regulation 1210/90, is tasked with gathering information and data on the state of the European Environment. The EEA has no enforcement powers of its own but provides scientific and technical information on environmental matters to the EU institutions, member states, and civil society.

Membership of the EEA is also open to countries that are not Member States of the European Union. The Agency currently has 32 member countries: the 27 EU

---

[6] The ECJ has acknowledged the jurisdiction of both the Italian courts (*Frontini v Ministero delle Finanze* (1974) 2 CMLR 372, and German courts (*Internationale Handelsgesellschaft v EVGF* 11/70 (1970) ECR 1125; (1972) CMLR 255) to determine these questions. Nevertheless, respect for fundamental rights forms an integral part of the general principles of EC law.

[7] The Member States have submitted to its exclusive jurisdiction to hear disputes concerning the EC Treaty under Art. 292. It is based in Luxembourg, and with the accession of the three new Member States in 1995, there are now 15 judges, and 9 Advocates General (8 after 2000, as part of the accession process). Its powers are set out in the Treaty under Arts. 221–241 (ex Arts. 165–184). The Statute of the Court of Justice is laid down in a separate Protocol, and its rules of procedure are subject to the unanimous approval of the Council (Art. 188).

[8] For an illustration of the co-decision procedure, see <http://www.europarl.europa.eu/parliament/public/staticDisplay.do?id=46&pageRank=4&language=EN.>

Member States together with Iceland, Liechtenstein, Norway, Switzerland, and Turkey. Five west Balkan countries have also applied for membership. Although the EEA has no power to police the implementation of European Community law on the environment, a body known as IMPEL—an Implementation Network set up by the European Commission with representatives from each Member State—develops best practice and monitoring standards for the implementation of Community law.

The European Court of justice

4.06 The Court of Justice, as the supreme judicial institution of the Union, retains competence for other judicial actions on fundamental questions for the Community order and carries out this mission by way of questions referred by the national jurisdictions for a preliminary ruling. However, the Treaty provides that the Statute may empower the Court of First Instance with preliminary competence in certain areas.

4.07 In order to assist the ECJ in its role, the Court of First Instance (CFI) was established in 1988 under Article 168a (now Article 225), and there is a right of appeal to the ECJ on points of law.[9] The Treaty of Nice, which entered into force on 1 February 2003 following ratification by the then 15 Member States, made a number of changes to the judicial system of the European Union. The Treaty establishes the division of jurisdiction between these two bodies but specifies that it may be adjusted by their respective Statutes (Article 225 EC). The Court of First instance is now competent for all direct actions, in particular proceedings for annulment (Article 230 EC), for failure to act (Article 232 EC), and for damage (Article 235 EC), with the exception of those allocated to a judicial chamber and those which the Statute reserves for the Court of Justice.[10]

4.08 The body of environmental case law from the European Court of Justice has grown in proportion to the amount of legislation generated by the Community institutions. In the absence of explicit guidance about how to interpret its task, the Court has a wide discretion as to how the Treaties and the subordinate legislation should be interpreted. Its only duty under the EC treaty is to 'ensure that in the interpretation and application of this treaty the law is observed'.[11]Lawyers trained in the common law tradition should beware basing their arguments upon the interpretation of a particular word in European legislation—not only is a more

---

[9] Article 58, Protocol on the Statute of the Court of Justice and the Court of First Instance, Treaty of Nice.

[10] <http://europa.eu/scadplus/nice_treaty/legal_en.htm.>

[11] Art. 220. There are no official *travaux préparatoires* for the Treaty provisions, which could be used in interpretation, and all the negotiations were conducted in secrecy. The Preamble and Part 1 provide some guidance to interpreting the articles of the EC Treaty.

purposive approach used, but all the different languages of the legislation are equally valid.[12] In a case where there is divergence between the different language versions of the legislation, the provision can be interpreted by reference to the purpose and general scheme of the rules of which it forms part.[13] The basic principles of Community environmental policy referred to in Article 174(2) of the Treaty—the precautionary principle, preventative action, rectification of damage at source, and 'polluter pays'—have informed the basis of the ECJ's rulings on environmental matters. This is not to say that a consistent approach has always been adopted, indeed in some areas—notably the precautionary principle[14]—the ECJ has until relatively recently held back from making explicit statements about how the principle should be applied.

The ECJ and the purposive approach

The European Court of Justice has generally adopted an approach to legislative **4.09** interpretation that places a high value on the environment.[15] Even before the existence of an explicit legal basis on which to develop environmental legislation, the ECJ demonstrated a flexible approach towards environmental considerations when set against the objective of economic integration. In the *ADBHU* case[16] the ECJ was asked to decide whether a Community Directive regulating the disposal of waste oils was compatible with the free trade and competition rules established by the Treaty of Rome. The ECJ ruled that the principles of freedom of trade, competition, and movement of goods were not absolute, but rather 'subject to certain limits justified by the objectives of general interest pursued by the Community, provided that the rights in question are not substantively impaired'. In effect, the Court declared environmental protection to be an essential objective

---

[12] See Kramer, *The EC Treaty and Environmental Law* (3rd edn, Sweet & Maxwell, 1998), Chapter 2, for clear examples of this in the wording of Art. 174 itself. In *Mayer Parry Recycling Ltd v The Environment Agency* (1999) Env LR 489, Carnwath J was referred to the French and Italian texts of the Waste Framework Directive for the background to the use of the word 'discard'. Note that the Court of Appeal in *Attorney-General's Reference (No.5 of 2000)* (2001) EWCA Crim 1077 decided that Carnwath J's approach had been wrong, and inconsistent with the general purpose of the Directive. See also *Arco Chemie Nederland (2000)* joined cases C-418-97 and C-419-97 on the meaning of 'discard', to which the Court of Appeal referred.

[13] So, in *Aannemersbedrijf PKKraaijveld BV and Others v Gedeputeerde Staten van Zuid-Holland* ('the Dutch dykes' case) (C–72/95) (1997) Env LR 265, distinctions could be drawn in the Environmental Assessment Directive between the versions of 'canalization and flood-relief works' in English and Finnish, where the terms employed denote the idea of flooding, as opposed to the German, Greek, Spanish, French, Italian, Dutch, and Portuguese, or the Danish and Swedish, which do not.

[14] Case T-13/99 *Pfizer Animal Health SA v Council of the European Union, 2002 ECR II-3305.*

[15] For a comprehensive analysis of recent ECJ case law on environmental matters see Macrory, Richard *Regulation, Enforcement and Governance in Environmental Law* Cameron May (2007) pp 441–476.

[16] Case 240/83 *Association de défense des brûleurs d'huiles usagés (ADBHU)* (1985) ECR 531.

of the Community, without an explicit legal basis to do so, and without reference to any other legal provisions (eg international environmental law).[17]

4.10 Where the ECJ has led the way in adopting a purposive approach to the interpretation of Community law, domestic courts have followed. For example, in considering the question of whether a project should be subject to an Environmental Impact Assessment,[18] domestic courts originally took the view that this was matter of fact and degree for the planning authority to decide.[19] Subsequently, the ECJ determined that the purpose of the Directive should not be undermined by giving unlimited discretion to Member States to decide whether projects would have 'significant effects' on the environment.[20]

4.11 The purposive approach has been adopted by domestic courts across a range of issues. In *Berkeley*[21] the House of Lords considered whether, in the absence of an environmental statement as required by Schedule 3 to Directive 85/337, there had still been substantial compliance with its provisions. The Court found that despite the detailed consideration given to the application for planning permission, and the detailed information available at public inquiry, the 'cornerstone' of the EIA regime is the 'environmental statement', without which the public's right to be involved in the decision-making process was substantially hindered. On the issue of substantial compliance, Lord Hoffman found that: 'the point about the environmental statement contemplated by the Directive is that it constitutes a single and accessible compilation'. Despite the high level of discretion given to Member States about how this information should be gathered and presented, it was not sufficient to 'treat a disparate collection of documents produced by parties other than the developer and traceable only by a person with a good deal of energy and persistence, as satisfying the requirement to make (the relevant information) available to the public'.

The ECJ and proportionality

4.12 The principle of 'proportionality' is also central to the ECJ's rulings: laws must not go beyond what is necessary to achieve the desired objectives, and take the least restrictive form in terms of impact on trade freedoms. When considering whether environmental protection measures lead to discrimination contrary to Article 28 EC (prohibition of quantitative restrictions on imports of goods between member states), the ECJ has, in a number of decisions,[22] upheld national

---

[17] For a critical summary of ECJ environmental law-making see Francis Jacobs, 'The Role of the European Court of Justice in the Protection of the Environment' [2006] JEL 18 185–205.

[18] Under the Environmental Assessment Directive 85/337.

[19] See *R v Swale BC ex parte RSPB (1991) 1 PLR 6*.

[20] Case 72/95 note 13 above.

[21] *Berkeley v Secretary of State for the Environment and Others 81 P & CR 492*.

[22] *'Walloon Waste'* C-203/96 (1998) ECR I-4075; *'Dusseldorp' Case* C-389/96 (1998) ECR I-4473; *PreussenElektra Case* C-379/98 (2001) ECR I-2099.

measures which protect the environment but are nevertheless discriminatory under Article 28. In the view of Francis Jacobs, formerly Advocate General of the European Court of Justice, 'environmental protection is (...) more likely than not to prevail over free trade considerations when the Community legislature performs the balancing act between both values. Articles 174–176 of the Treaty grant the Community powers to define its own environmental policy and therefore its own standard.'[23] In the *Danish Bottles*[24] case the ECJ ruled that impediments to free trade under Article 28 can be justified on the basis of environmental protection, even though Article 30 (which qualifies the free trade provision under Article 28) does not specifically refer to environmental protection.[25]

The current framework and aims of European environmental policy

The Treaty sets out the objectives and principles upon which the environmental **4.13** policies of the European Community will be based in Articles 174, 175, and 176.[26] This provides the basis for their interpretation, in addition to the general principles of European law.

Under Article 174(1):

> Community policy on the environment shall contribute to the pursuit of the following objectives:
> —preserving, protecting and improving the quality of the environment;
> —protecting human health;
> —prudent and rational utilisation of natural resources;
> —promoting measures at international level to deal with regional or worldwide environmental problems.

Article 174(2) then sets out important underlying themes of the policy on the **4.14** environment:

> Community policy on the environment shall aim at a high level of protection, taking into account the diversity of situations in the various regions of the Community. It shall be based on the precautionary principle and on the principles that preventive action should be taken, that environmental damage should as a priority be rectified at source and that the polluter should pay. 5 The Treaty further sets out, under Article 174(3), the matters which must be taken into account when the Community environmental policy is prepared:
> —available scientific and technical data;
> —environmental conditions in the various regions of the Community;
> —the potential benefits and costs of action or lack of action;

---

23 Note 16 above.
24 Case C-302/86 *Commission v Denmark (1988) ECR 4607.*
25 Article 30 refers to the 'protection of health and life of humans, animals or plants'.
26 Before the renumbering under Art. 12 of the Amsterdam Treaty 1997 these articles were 130R, 130S, and 130T respectively, under Title XVI. The title number has also been altered to Title XIX.

—the economic and social development of the Community as a whole and the balanced development of its regions.

4.15 Environmental legislation is introduced by the European institutions under Article 175. Article 176 also acknowledges the right of a Member State to maintain or introduce more stringent protective measures of its own environment,[27] where this is justified by scientific evidence.[28] Admittedly, these more restrictive measures are only allowed to be permanent so long as they are compatible with the EC Treaty as a whole.[29] Despite this, the use of these other articles of the Treaty will persist. In particular, Article 95 is also used where the main aim of the legislation is to ensure the free movement of goods. Measures directed at environmental protection may also be introduced under Treaty articles relating to transport and agriculture. Although in the past

4.16 Articles 175 and 95 required the use of different voting procedures, and the European Parliament had a greater power of veto under Article 95, the EC Treaty now provides that both are governed by the same co-decision procedure under Article 251, introduced by the Treaty of Amsterdam, which came into effect on 1 May 1999. Under this procedure the European Council adopts a common position on a proposal by qualified majority voting whereby the votes of Member States are weighted in accordance with their populations. Where the European Parliament indicates that it intends to reject the common position by a majority, or amends the common position by a majority in the way that the Council does not accept, a conciliation committee consisting of members of both bodies is set up, so that the Council can explain its position. If Parliament subsequently refuses to accept the common position by an absolute majority, the proposal is not adopted. Some environmental decisions still require unanimity from the Council before adoption under Article 175 2 (b). These are decisions relating to town and country planning, the quantitative management of water resources affecting their availability, and land use (with the exception of waste management).

---

[27] The Single European Act also qualified Art. 100 under a new Art.100A to allow Member States to apply higher national standards than imposed by EC law so long as they did not interfere with the common market—this became known in Denmark as the 'environmental guarantee' (since many measures would not be introduced under Art.130). It was repeated in the Amsterdam Treaty 1997 (under amended Arts. 100A and 130R(2), now Arts. 95 and 174).

[28] See Krämer, Ludwig *EC Environmental Law* (6th Edition Sweet & Maxwell) pp 126–132.

[29] A principle seen in such cases as *R v London Borough Transport Committee, ex p Freight Transport Association Ltd* [1991] RTR 13, CA; [1991] 1 WLR 828, HL—lorry silencer ban in London was held not to be compatible with the less strict standards under Directive 70/157/EEC (the HL reversed the CA, but not on this point); *Commission v Belgium* C–376/90 (1992) ECR I–6153, ECJ (protection against radiation—dose limits were minimum levels). For a full analysis of rights under Article 176 see Krämer, Ludwig op cit page 126.

The precautionary principle

Article 174 (2) of the EC Treaty requires that community policy on the environ- **4.17**
ment 'shall be based on the precautionary principle'. The European Court of
Justice did not explicitly set out the scope and application of the principle until
the *Pfizer*[30] decision in 2002, which dealt with the risk to human health associated
with antibiotics in animal feed. The court found that:

> in a situation in which the precautionary principle is applied, which by definition
> coincides with a situation in which there is scientific uncertainty, a risk assessment
> cannot be required to provide community institutions with conclusive scientific evi-
> dence of the reality of the risk and the seriousness of the potential adverse effects were
> that risk to become a reality.[31]

Yet, although conclusive scientific evidence is not required, 'a preventative measure cannot properly be based on a purely hypothetical approach to the risk,
founded on mere conjecture which has not been scientifically verified'. The burden of proof lay with the Commission; the standard of proof was met if a proper
assessment of risk was carried out, and as a result of that there were 'sufficient scientific indications' to conclude on an objective scientific basis that there was a risk
to human health. As one commentator has said, the difficulty is that by leaving the
realm of rational certainty, precaution necessarily gives rise to controversy and its
practical application to conflict.[32]

European policy documents on the environment

Action programmes

On the strategic level, the European Union has adopted a series of general Action **4.18**
Programmes, setting out the priority objectives for the environment. These have
been used to create an environmental strategy to sit alongside the Community's
economic aims. The Council now has the power to adopt the Action Programmes
under Article 175(3), after consulting the Economic and Social Committee. The
Council is then empowered to adopt the necessary measures to implement these
programmes. Pursuant to Article 175(3) the adoption of programmes constitutes
a legally binding 'decision'. The sixth community action programme was adopted

---

[30] Note 14 above.
[31] See paragraphs 142–143 of the Judgment.
[32] de Sadeleer, *Environmental Principles* (OUP, 2002) at p 91, in introducing the discussion of
the precautionary principle. As he states, whilst prevention is based on the concept of certain risk,
the new paradigm is distinguished by the intrusion of uncertainty—and that 'the question is no
longer merely how to prevent assessable, calculable, and certain risks, but rather how to anticipate
risks suggested by possibility, contingency, plausibility, probability'. de Sadeleer's book focuses on
the three main principles of the Polluter Pays, the Principle of Prevention (such as setting thresholds
and requiring BAT and EIA), and the Precautionary Principle, from an international perspective.

under such a decision.[33] As a result, its contents may be regarded as a source of law, and a guide to the interpretation of Treaty articles.

4.19   There have been six Action Programmes since 1973.[34] The Third Action Programme in 1983[35] marked a shift away from the concern that the different national policies on controlling pollution were distorting competition towards the protection of health and the sensible management of natural resources. The Fourth Action Programme in 1987[36] reflected the changes made by the Single European Act 1986, as well as acknowledging the contribution which the protection of the environment can make to improving the economy and creating jobs. The Fifth Action Programme was 'adopted'[37] in 1992 and was intended to address the principles of sustainable development. The Sixth Action Programme was formally adopted in 2002 and sets out the European Community's environmental objectives to 2012. The Programme identifies four main areas of action: tackling climate change, nature and biodiversity, environment and health, and sustainable use of natural resources and management of wastes. Interestingly, the Sixth EAP does not propose new quantifiable targets or related timetables, despite the lack of such targets having been identified as a weak point in the Fifth EAP.

4.20   The Sixth EAP contains seven 'thematic strategies' which address air pollution,[38] the marine environment,[39] the prevention and recycling of waste,[40] sustainable use of resources,[41] urban environment,[42] soil,[43] and pesticides.[44] The Sixth EAP

---

[33]   Decision No. 1600/2002 O J L242/1.

[34]   The First Action Programme, Declaration 1973, OJ C112, covered 1973–1976, and addressed urgent pollution problems. It introduced the principle that the polluter pays. The Second Action Programme, Resolution 1977, OJ C139, covered 1977–1981. Research programmes have provided the necessary information for the formulation of policies and Community legislation. There is also now a proposal for a Community Action Programme in the related area of public health and pollution related diseases (COM (97) 266—final).

[35]   Resolution 1983, OJ C46, covering 1982–1986.

[36]   Resolution 1987, OJ C328, covering 1987–1992.

[37]   The 'Fifth Action Programme' was in fact never formally adopted under Art. 130S(3). It is not, strictly speaking, an 'Action Programme' which sets legally binding objectives, but only a framework and a guide (13 June 1997, Department of Trade and Industry note). Decision 2179/98/EC on updating the programme at least has some legal force. This legal nicety did not appear to matter in practice.

[38]   COM (2005) 446, with a proposal for an *Ambient Air Quality Directive* (COM(2005) 447) September 2005.

[39]   COM (2005) 504, with a proposal for a Directive establishing a framework for Community Action in the field of marine environmental policy (COM 2005 (505).

[40]   COM (2005) 666, with a proposal for revising the Waste Framework Directive (COM (2005) 667) December 2005.

[41]   COM (2005) 670 December 2005.

[42]   COM (2005) 718 January 2006.

[43]   COM (2006) 231, with a proposal for a Framework Directive on soil protection September 2006.

[44]   COM (2006) 372, with a proposal for a Directive to establish a framework for Community action towards a sustainable use of pesticides (COM (2006) 373.

has been the subject of some criticism from the non-governmental sector due to the perceived lack of defined qualitative, and quantitative, targets.[45] However, in contrast to the preceding action programmes, the Sixth EAP is the result of the formal co-decision process provided for in the EC Treaty under Article 130, proposed by the Commission and adopted by a formal act of the European Council and Parliament. An important principle set out in the Sixth EAP is known as the 'substitution principle', explicitly applied to chemicals but arguably of much broader application. It states 'chemicals that are dangerous should be replaced by safer chemicals or safer alternative technologies not entailing the use of chemicals, with the aim of reducing risks to man and the environment'.[46] The REACH Regulation,[47] which entered into force on 1 June 2007, requires the progressive substitution of the most dangerous chemicals when suitable alternatives have been identified.

Communications

The European Commission sets out its proposals for action in Communications ('COM' documents).[48] These policy statements set out the possible direction of future European law, in some cases making very specific proposals for meeting environmental targets, for example in the reduction of greenhouse gas emissions. Firm proposals are prepared as White Papers, but the European Commission makes use of its 'Green Papers' in order to consult on future policy on specific areas. There is no difference between the two in legal terms as neither are binding. A Communication document dated 10 January 2007 sets out the Commissions proposals for keeping climate change to manageable levels and options post 2012, when Kyoto targets expire. The European Parliament adopted a resolution in response, focusing on two major objectives: limitation of the average global temperature increase to 2 °C above pre-industrialization levels, and adoption of a greenhouse gas emission reduction target for all industrialized countries of 30% in comparison with 1990 levels by 2020. Parliament also urged the inclusion of aviation and maritime transport in the negotiations over the post-2012 phase.[49] **4.21**

On 29 June 2007 the Commission published a Green Paper on Adapting to Climate Change in Europe, unequivocally setting out that a 'swift transition to a **4.22**

---

[45] *Institute for European Environmental Policy (IEEP) Report 'Drowning in Process? The Implementation of the EU's 6th Environmental Action Programme'* <http://www.eeb.org/activities/env_action_programmes/IEEPFinalReport6EAP-April2006.pdf>

[46] Decision 1600/2002, recital 25 and Art. 7.1.

[47] EC 1907/2006 (Registration, Evaluation, Authorisation and Restriction of Chemical Substances).

[48] A database of current COM documents is available under the 'Register of Commission Documents' at <http://ec.europa.eu/transparency/regdoc/recherche.cfm?CL=e>. At the time of writing there are more than 300 proposals relating to environmental matters.

[49] See adopted text P6_TA(2007)0038 available at <http://www.europarl.europa.eu>

global low carbon economy is the central pillar of the EU's integrated climate change and energy policy in order to reach the EU's objective of keeping global average temperature increase below 2 °C compared to pre-industrial levels'. The Paper points out that there are several Community policy areas that will be affected by climate change, ranging from building methods to climate-resilient crops, and poses a number of key questions, including how EU policy on public health should take climate change into account, in particular how companies and citizens can be encouraged to participate in 'adaptation actions'. A stakeholder consultation in preparation for a White Paper was held in May 2008; one interesting potential development is European Advisory Group on adaptation to climate change, suggested in the Green Paper and met with approval by stakeholders.[50]

4.23   In 2000 the Commission published a White Paper on *Environmental Liability*[51] proposing that Member States should be under a duty to ensure restoration of damage to biodiversity damage and decontamination, as distinct from what is referred to as 'traditional damage'—individual physical injury and economic loss. The driving principle of the proposed measures was that the restoration of damaged natural resources should be an administrative task at the national level.[52] In June 2008 the European Commission announced its intention to refer nine Member States (including the United Kingdom) to the European Court of Justice for failing to transpose the Environmental Liability Directive.[53]

The different types of European environmental legislation

4.24   In theory, the articles of the EC Treaty can have direct effect in UK law. But none of the three articles in Title XIX on the Environment are worded so that they could have direct effect, unlike other articles in the Treaty such as Article 28. Therefore, the main source of environmental law is the secondary legislation made under Article 249 (ex-Article 189). This allows the European Community institutions to issue regulations, directives, decisions, recommendations, and opinions. Articles 174, 175, and 176 will assist in their subsequent interpretation by the courts. The preamble to each instrument is also an essential guide to

---

[50]   For the results of the stakeholder consultation see <http://ec.europa.eu/environment/climat/adaptation/pdf/consultation_summary.pdf>

[51]   COM (2000) 66 final, 9 February 2000.

[52]   For a discussion of the background to the Environmental Liability Directive see Winter, Jans, McRory, and Krämer 'Weighing up the Environmental Liability Directive' [2008] JEL 20(2) 163–191.

[53]   Environment Commissioner, Stavros Dimas describes the Directive as 'one of the most significant pieces of EU environmental law of the last few years. More than a year after the deadline it is high time these nine Member States transposed it, nor least to create the necessary legal security for operators carrying out activities falling under the directive and to avoid distortions in its implementation (. . .) for instance, in the case of damage affecting more than one Member State.' European Commission Press Release IP/08/1025 dated 26 June 2008.

its interpretation. Under Article 253 (ex-Article 190), the preamble must state the reasons on which it is based and refer to 'any proposals or opinions which were required to be obtained' from other European institutions.

Regulations

Regulations are binding in their entirety in all Member States under Article 249 **4.25** (ex-Article 189), and are intended to be directly applicable in UK law. As the ECJ has said, 'they are an integral part of, and take precedence in the legal order applicable in the territory of each of the member states'.[54] In environmental matters, Community legislation is more usually made in the form of Directives, simply because Regulations are binding in their entirety. Regulations do not set out the sanctions which apply if they are breached; penalties for a breach are laid down by Member States.[55] One of the more intensively regulated areas is the treatment and disposal of waste, in particular hazardous waste. Examples include the Landfill Regulations,[56] which transpose the Landfill Directive 99/31EC, and the Hazardous Waste Regulations,[57] replacing the 1996 Special Waste Regulations that originally transposed the EU Hazardous Waste Directive 91/698/EEC.

Directives

Although directives are stated to be binding on Member States, as to the result to **4.26** be achieved, the actual form of the legislation and the methods to be adopted to achieve the intended result is left to each Member State to choose.[58] Therefore, the form in which a directive will be applied by the UK courts will appear to be a statutory instrument or Act like any other. But they must be interpreted in the light of European law, which may go much further than the normal canons of statutory construction. The concept of 'indirect effect' of directives, first introduced in the context of the Equal Treatment Directive,[59] has been developed by the European Court of Justice into a doctrine that requires national courts to interpret particular implementing provisions in a way which conforms with EC law. Arguably the doctrine is developing further, by requiring national courts to

---

[54] In *Amministrazione delle Finanze dello State v Simmenthal SpA* C–106/77 [1978] ECR I–629 at 643. Even so, this is put beyond doubt for the UK courts by s 2(1) of the ECA 1972. Regulations take effect immediately on the 20th day after their publication, or on the date specified in them.

[55] See Kramer, Ludwig, op cit pp56–57. So, even when Regulations are of direct application, it will still be necessary for the UK Parliament to identify what the nature of any offence will be (*Defra v ASDA Stores Ltd* [2002] The Times, June 27, 2002, DC).

[56] SI 2002/1599.

[57] SI 2005/894.

[58] Art. 189. Directives are transposed into UK law under s 2(3) of the ECA 1972. See further on the implementation of the environmental directives in Member States, Hattan, Elizabeth 'Implementation of EU Environmental Law' [2003] JEL 15(3) 273.

[59] Case 14/83 (1984) ECR 1981.

consider how domestic provisions as a whole can be applied consistently with Community law.[60]

4.27 A directive may also have 'direct effect', in whole or in part, even though the Member State has failed to transpose the directive correctly or at all into domestic law within the time allowed. The treatment of these concepts by the courts is discussed in more detail below. Part of the uncertainty which surrounds directives is inherent in their transitional nature. The directive will only come into force in a Member State on a stated date, normally three years after it is adopted, which itself will be several years after the issue was first raised in discussion between the Member States. The ECJ has held that a Member State must refrain from taking any measures which would be liable seriously to compromise the result prescribed in a directive during this transitional period. [61] In the *ATRAL* judgment, the ECJ confirmed that national laws adopted during the period allowed for the transposition of a Directive, which are liable seriously to compromise the achievement of the result prescribed by the Directive, are to be disapplied.[62]

4.28 Directives do allow the European Community to legislate on areas without the need to specify how each Member State should implement the rules. However, it is well established that while the provisions of a Directive do not need to be repeated verbatim in national legislation, and a general legal context may be adequate, that context must guarantee the application of the Directive in a sufficiently precise and unambiguous manner[63]. In 2004 the European Court of Justice found[64] that the United Kingdom had failed properly to transpose the requirements of the 'Habitats Directive' 92/43/EEC. The Commission alleged that the United Kingdom wrongly adopted a general clause for the purpose of 'filling in the gaps' in the legislation designed to transpose the Directive, and that in order to be certain of their rights and obligations, individuals had to refer to the provisions of the Directive, thus undermining legal certainty in the national context. The ECJ found that 'implementation' of the Habitats Directive by conferring powers on conservation bodies and imposing on them a requirement to undertake their functions so as to comply with the provisions of the Directive,

---

[60] For an analysis of the development of the doctrine, see Drake, Sara 'Twenty years after Von Colson: the impact of "indirect effect" on the protection of the individual's community rights' [2005] ELRev 30(3) 329–348.

[61] *Inter-Environnement Wallonie ABSL v Region Wallonie* (C-129/96) [1998] 1 All ER (EC) 155, ECJ (1997) ECR I–7411—on an Art. 177 reference. During the period before the amendments to Directive 75/442 had to be transposed into national law, the Belgian Government had purported to exempt certain hazardous industrial operations from the need for a waste management permit. Member States must not take measures 'liable seriously to compromise the result prescribed'.

[62] Case C-14/02 ATRAL (2003) ECR-I4431.

[63] Cas C-58/02 Commission v Spain (2004) ECR-I621, see also the classic case *Andrea Francovich and Others v Italy* C-6/90 and C-9/90 [1991] ECR I-5357.

[64] Case C-6/04 *Commission v United Kingdom (Re Conservation of Natural Habitats Directive)* [2005] ECR I-9017.

was inadequate. The Court held that faithful transposition of a Directive is particularly important where the adoption of conservation measures is the common responsibility of all Member States, and threats to the natural environment are often trans-boundary in nature. This decision has highlighted the difficulties inherent in the transposition of Directives; if the approach adopted by the UK in transposing the Habitats Directive was inappropriate, alternative transposition 'techniques'—such as transposing measures word-for-word even though some may overlap with existing national provisions—may be equally problematic.[65]

Directives may also contain provisions which allow Member States to determine **4.29** the details of how certain processes will be achieved. For example, the Environmental Impact Assessment Directive obliges Member States to ensure that 'the public concerned' is given the opportunity to express an opinion about a proposed project before development consent is granted. Article 6 (3) provides that the 'detailed arrangements' for this consultation process are to be left to Member States. In Ireland, the introduction of a new 'administrative fee' payable by the public, and by environmental non-governmental organizations, when making submissions or observations regarding an application for planning permission, was the subject of Article 226 proceedings by the European Commission.[66] The question for the Court was whether the discretion under Article 6 (3) was wide enough to permit a Member State to participate in environmental decision-making, subject to the payment of a fee. The Court found that Member States could impose a 'participation fee' as long as 'it is not such as to constitute an obstacle to the exercise of the rights of participation conferred by Article 6 of the Directive'; on the facts of this particular case the Court found that the fees (20 and 45 Euros) could not be regarded as constituting an obstacle to participation. The Court did not consider when a fee might become an obstacle. Interestingly, the implementation guide to the Aarhus Convention provides that although 'free access' to participation procedures should not be taken to mean that the State should subsidize all the associated costs, the State should not impose financial constraints on members of the public who wish to participate. The extent of Member State's discretion to levy fees has yet to be set against the Aarhus Convention provisions. [67]

Directives and the doctrine of 'direct effect'

The doctrine of 'direct effect' allows individuals to rely upon any rights or obliga- **4.30** tions which are conferred on them by a directive in the national courts, even

---

[65] For a full discussion of the issue see Colin T Reid and Michael Woods, 'Implementing EC Conservation Law', [2006] JEL18 135–160.

[66] Case C-216/05 *Commission v Ireland* Judgment (2006) ECR I-10787.

[67] See Ryall, Áine 'EIA and Public Participation: Determining the Limits of Member State Discretion', [2007] JEL 19 247–257.

though the directive was not transposed within the time allowed, or was transposed incorrectly. The ECJ has therefore gone a step further than the Treaty provisions and has developed this doctrine of 'direct effect', effectively a doctrine of estoppel, so that Member States cannot escape their obligations by failing to implement directives. It is a powerful statement of the supremacy of European law, and has now become the 'norm rather than the exception'.[68] In the ECJ's view, it would be incompatible with the binding effect attributed to a directive by Article 249 to exclude, in principle, the possibility that the obligation which it imposes may be invoked by those concerned.[69]

4.31 There will still be many instances when the doctrine of direct effect cannot be used. Firstly, the date for Member States to implement the directive must have passed. This question of timing has already proved to be important when new European Community measures are introduced that affect large-scale building projects. Many of these projects take many years to plan and implement, and are already in the pipeline, so to speak, when the European Community law may introduce new requirements. Some would argue that the project should then comply with the new standards, even if this would lead to serious delays.

4.32 The doctrine can only be invoked against the Member State itself, or the so-called 'emanations of the state'. The ECJ set out a working definition of an 'emanation of the state' in *Foster v British Gas plc*:[70]

> . . . a body, whatever its legal form, which has been responsible, pursuant to a measure adopted by the state, for providing a public service under the control of the state and has for that purpose special powers beyond those which result from the normal rules applicable in relations between individuals is included among the bodies against which the provisions of a Directive capable of having direct effect may be relied upon.

4.33 These 'emanations of the state' are therefore under the same obligations as central government or the national courts to apply the provisions of a directive. The reference to 'a body, whatever its legal form' is potentially significant, as private subjects may in some cases be regarded as a public entity.[71] The issue recently came

---

[68] Hartley, *The Foundations of European Community Law*, (6th edition, OUP 2007) Chapter 7 at p 205. Of course, uncertainty about the rights of the individual will persist until the Directive is properly implemented.

[69] See C-41/74 *Van Duyn v Home Office* [1974] ECR 1337 at 1348. The principle of 'effet utile' was applied. See also C-26/62 *Van Gend en Loos v Nederlandse Tarief Commissie* (1963) ECR 1.

[70] C-188/89 (1991) 1 QB 405, ECJ at 427 (para 20); (1990) 2 CMLR 833. See also *Auer v Ministère Public* [1983] ECR 2727, ECJ—a case on the professional organization of veterinary surgeons responsible for recognizing professional qualifications.

[71] Case C-157/02 *Reiser Internationale Transporte GMBH v Asfinag Autobahnen Und Schnellstrassen Finanzierungs-Aktiengesellschaft* [2004] ECR I-1477 (road hauliers could rely on directly effective provisions against a private company levying road tolls on behalf of the State).

before the European Court of Justice again in the case of *Farrell*[72]; the definition set out in *Foster* was repeated but the Court side-stepped the question of whether the Motor Insurers' Bureau of Ireland could be treated as an emanation of the state, as the national court had not provided sufficient information regarding the MIBI, taking account of the *Foster* test. However the Court reiterated that if the national court decides that the Directive cannot be relied on against the MIBI, it will nevertheless be bound to apply domestic law 'so far as possible' in accordance with the purpose of the Directive.[73]There are some useful decisions in both the ECJ and the UK courts which have held that local or regional authorities,[74] the Forestry Commissioners,[75] even constitutionally independent bodies such as the police,[76] were all emanations of the state. The ECJ has also held that it is irrelevant for the purposes of direct effect whether the state acts in a public or a private role, such as an employer[77]will come within the definition. South West Water Services Limited has been held to be an emanation of the state for employment law purposes.[78] But the same company has denied that it is covered by the Environmental Information Regulations 1992, which cover 'any body with public responsibilities for the environment'.[79] Prior to privatization, the Court of Appeal held that the water company was not an agency of the government, for the purposes of a potential award of exemplary damages.[80]

Not all directives are capable of having direct effect, by virtue of their drafting. In **4.34** order for the doctrine to be invoked, the litigant must show that the terms of the

---

[72] Case C-365/05 *Farrell v Minister for the Environment (Ireland) and Motor Insurers' Bureau of Ireland (MIBI)* [2007] ECR I-03067.

[73] Paragraph 42 of the Judgment. See also the Opinion of Advocate General Sixt-Hackl dated 5 October 2006, which concludes that the MIBI may be treated as an emanation of the state because it is authorized by the state to carry out a public function (paragraph 72).

[74] *Fratelli Costanzo SpA v Comune di Milano* (C-103/88) [1989] CMLR 239, ECJ; this includes bodies such as the London BoroughTransport Committee, see ex p *Freight Trade Association* (1991) 3 All ER 915, HL.

[75] *Petition of Kincardine and Deeside District Council* (1992) 4 JEL 289, (1993) Env LR 151, Lord Coulsfield.

[76] *Johnston v Chief Constable of the Royal Ulster Constabulary* C-222/84 [1987] QB 129, ECJ.

[77] See *Marshall v Southampton and South West Hampshire Health Authority* C-152/84 [1986] 2 WLR 780 and *Johnson* (C-222/84). This is a distinction which is still relevant in UK administrative law—see *Wade*, (7th edition, OUP 2003) p 801.

[78] *Griffin and Others v South West Water Services Ltd* [1995] IRLR 15, QBD, another employment law case.

[79] See ENDS Report no 241, Feb 1995, p 9. They may be correct in this context, even if this rather defeats the purpose of the EC Directive 90/313, 'Freedom of Access to Information on the Environment', which the Regulations implement.

[80] In *AB v South Western Water Services Ltd* [1931] 1 All ER 609 (the Camelford drinking water case).The CA made the point that the Plaintiff's argument that the company was an 'emanation of the state' in European law was a rule arising in a different context.

See Wennerås, Pål *The Enforcement of EC Environmental Law (OUP)* at page 45 for a discussion of the concept in the context of environmental law.

particular directive are sufficiently clear and unambiguous, unconditional, and do not depend on further action being taken by the Community or the Member State.[81] The directive can have direct effect in relation to only part of it.[82] Pål Wennerås notes that 'least problematic are directives that require Member States to achieve precisely circumscribed results. Chief among these are directives containing numerically defined obligations (which) may come in the form of technical requirements for the operation of various types of industrial plants,[83] emissions limits values, or quality limit values'.[84] Yet enforcement is not straightforward, because of the difficulties inherent in verifying whether particular targets have in fact been achieved.

4.35   The implementation of framework directives is also potentially problematic. In *Comitato di Coordinamento per la Difesa della Cava v Regione Lombardia*[85], the ECJ held that Article 4 of the 'framework' Directive on Waste, 75/442/EEC, to dispose of waste without endangering human health or harming the environment, did not have direct effect. The article only sets out objectives and indicates a programme which a Member State should follow, rather than requiring the adoption of specific measures. This was followed by the *San Rocco*[86] case. The ECJ held that, although Article 4 was not sufficiently clear to found a breach of the Directive without additional breaches of more precise requirements, if failure by a Member State to take the 'necessary measures' to comply with Article 4 continued for a long period of time without action, the Member State may have exceeded the discretion conferred on it. Wennerås draws attention to the case of *Pera Galini*, identified as a positive development, where on similar facts four years was considered to be a 'protracted period of time' and accordingly the Court found that the requirements of the Directive had been breached.[87] The UK courts have used the doctrine of direct effect in a number of cases in the area of environmental law. Directives 70/157/EEC and 71/320/EEC on noise and emissions from vehicles were held to have direct effect in *ex p Freight Transport Association*.[88] More recently Directive 85/337/EEC has been used by a private individual to compel a local authority to conduct an environmental impact assessment.[89]

---

[81]   See Wennerås, op cit, pp 15–44

[82]   C–380/87 *Enichem Base v Commune di Cinisello Balsamo* [1989] ECR 2491; (1991) 1 CMLR 313. The mayor of an Italian authority had banned non-biodegradable plastic bags, but had failed to remit the draft of the ban to the Commission.

[83]   E.g. 89/369/EEC and 89/42/EEC (air pollution (municipal waste incineration plants)).

[84]   Wennerås, op cit pp 38–39.

[85]   Case 236/92 (1994) ECR I-485.

[86]   Case C-365/97 *Commission v Italy (1999)* ECR I-7773.

[87]   Case C-420/02 *Commission v Greece (2005)* ECR I-11175. See Wennerås, Pal, op cit, page 42.

[88]   (1991) 1 WLR 828.

[89]   See *Wells*, note 101 below.

The doctrine has limited 'horizontal' effect, so that, as a general principle, it cannot **4.36** create obligations between individual parties or companies. This is a logical result of the reason behind the doctrine, that the obligations in the directive are undertaken by the Member State, and not by individuals. By way of example, Article 5 (1) of the Environmental Liability Directive requires operators to take preventative measures in the event of the 'imminent threat' of environmental damage. Yet in the absence of any national implementing provisions, the obligation placed on operators by the Directive cannot serve as a legal basis for national authorities to require them to take necessary preventative measures. [90]

In *ex parte Huddleston* [91] the Court of Appeal identified the distinction between **4.37** imposing legal obligations on an individual thus restricting his freedoms as against another individual (impermissible horizontal direct effect) and placing conditions on that individual's entitlement to secure a benefit from the state. The case concerned failure by the local authority to determine an application to reactivate an old mining permission under Section 22 of the Planning and Compensation Act 1991, resulting in deemed approval of the application. The provision was contrary to the (not properly transposed) Directive 85/337 on Environmental Impact Assessment. The Court of Appeal found that the appellant, a local resident, was in fact seeking to give vertical effect to the Directive as against the state (the local authority), rather than the mining company. The fact that the company would suffer some detriment was held to be a 'condition' imposed on an entitlement to a benefit from the state, as opposed to restricting its freedoms as against those of another individual. In *R v Somerset County Council* [92] the Administrative Court rejected the argument that it should seek to achieve the purpose of Directive 85/337 by refusing to allow the imposition of conditions on a minerals planning permission without an environmental impact assessment, where the authority had themselves failed to carry out the assessment. The purposive approach could not be used to place an obligation on a private individual by giving the Directive direct effect. This series of sometimes inconsistent cases is discussed in detail in the Chapter on Environmental Impact Assessment.

Nevertheless, it is suggested that the ECJ has greatly expanded the legal scope for **4.38** national environmental litigation to call on unimplemented EC Law, developing a line of case law concentrating on the effectiveness of directives, without explicitly considering whether they are capable of direct effect. [93] In the *Kraaijeveld* case

---

[90] See Winter, Jans, McRory, and Krämer 'Weighing up the EC Environmental Liability Directive' [2008] JEL 20(2) 163–191.

[91] *R v Durham County Council, Sherburn Stone and Secretary of State for the Environment, ex parte Huddleston* [2000] 1 WLR 1484.

[92] (2000) Env LR 582.

[93] Lee, Maria *EU Environmental Law, Challenges, Change and Decision Making* (Modern Studies in European Law, Hart 2005) vol 6 pp 63–66.

involving the application of the EIA Directive, the ECJ held that where a Community measure imposes a clear obligation on a Member State, national courts must be able to use that provision to review the legality of the Member State's exercise of discretion.[94] Maria Lee concludes that 'the line of cases following *Kraaijeveld* does not raise the question of rights for individuals, but concentrates on effectiveness' and notes a move away from a focus on impact on the individual to a focus on the impact of Community law.[95]

4.39   This progression is, arguably, reflected in *R (Wells) v Secretary of State for Transport, Local Government and the Regions*[96] (although the Court did not rely on the *Kraaijeveld* decision) where the European Court of Justice considered whether an individual can rely on the EIA Directive to challenge a grant of development consent; the UK Government argued that this would result in an inverse direct effect, depriving the owners of the development site (a quarry) of their rights. The ECJ held that the obligation under the Directive to carry out an Environmental Impact Assessment was 'not directly linked to the performance of any obligation which would fall, pursuant to Directive 85/337, on the quarry owners'. The fact that mining operations would have to be halted to await the results of an EIA assessment, while resulting in adverse consequences for the operator, stemmed from the fact that the national authority had failed to fulfil its obligations under the Directive. There was no 'direct link' between the rights of third parties, and the obligations of the permit holder under the non-implemented Directive. It appears that, following *Wells*, where European law confers rights on the public, individuals may bring proceedings to enforce those rights even if an adverse effect on other individuals is the result.[97]

Decisions, recommendations, and opinions

4.40   A decision is only binding under European law on those Member States to whom it is addressed. A decision which is not challenged in a direct action before the ECJ by its addressee within the limitation period becomes definitive.[98] The National Allocation Plans determining the quantity of carbon dioxide emissions that Member States grant to their companies under the second phase of the EU Emissions Trading Scheme (2008–12) were addressed to Member States by way

---

[94]   Case C-72/95 *Aanemersebedriff PK Kraaijeveld BV v Gedeputeerde Staten van Zuid-Holland* [1996] ECR I-5403.

[95]   Lee, Maria op cit page 63.

[96]   Case C-201/02 (2004) ECR 000.

[97]   See Harwood, Richard, analysis of *R (Wells) v Secretary of State for Transport, Local Government and the Regions,* [2004] 16(2) 275.

[98]   See *TWD Textilwerke Degendorf GmbH v Germany* C-188/92, ECJ FC, 9 March 1994 (1994) ECR I–833. A later challenge to the decision by way of an Art. 234 (ex Art. 177) reference from a national court cannot be made.

of Commission Decisions. Decisions are also the method by which the European Union formally adopts international treaties.[99] Recommendations and opinions have no binding effect.

The European Union and Human Rights

All the Member States of the European Union are signatories of the European **4.41** Convention on Human Rights. But it is not possible for the European Union, or any of the other European Union institutions, to be a signatory in their own right to the European Convention under the current legal structure of the union.[100] Nor is there any general power in the European Union treaties to enact rules on human rights. The European Court of Justice will continue to defer to the European Court of Human Rights on the interpretation of the European Convention. The scope of these rights to assist in protecting the environment is discussed in the International chapter. They will be relevant to the way in which European environmental law is applied. The ECJ has been developing its own case law on 'fundamental rights', as part of the general legal rules common to all Member States. The Amsterdam Treaty has reaffirmed this commitment to 'fundamental rights'.[101] The rights enshrined in the European Convention of Human Rights, just as in the constitutions of the Member States, do provide guidelines which should be followed within the framework of Community law.[102]

The Charter on Fundamental Rights[103] provides that 'a high level of protection **4.42** and the improvement of the quality of the environment must be integrated into the policies of the Union and ensured in accordance with the principle of sustainable development', echoing Article 6 of the EC Treaty. The Charter is not yet a binding part of EC law, and although it would be given legal force by the amendments

---

[99] Such as the two Council Decisions which accompanied Regulation 259/93/EEC on the control of shipments of waste: Council Decisions 93/98—concluding the Basel Convention on behalf of the Community (OJ L39/1)—and 93/114, Protocol to the Convention between Germany, Czechoslovakia, and the EEC on the International Commission for the Protection of the Elbe (OJ L45/25). The list of wastes pursuant to Art. 1(a) of Directive 75/442/EEC was also made in the form of a Decision, 94/3/EC.

[100] Advisory Opinion of the ECJ 2/94, 28 March 1996, 'Accession by the Community to the European Convention on Human Rights'; see also Hartley, *The Foundations of EC Law*, (OUP 2003) pp 132–139. All that the 1997 Amsterdam Treaty has done is to reaffirm the commitment to 'fundamental rights' (by amending Art. F of the Treaty of European Union), and to provide for some form of sanctions against a Member State which is in breach of these principles (with a view to enlarging the Union to include new countries).

[101] The Amsterdam Treaty has further amended and strengthened Art. F of the 1992 Treaty of European Union signed at Maastricht (now Art. 6 EU).

[102] See Case C-112/80 *Schmidberger v Austria* (2003) ECR I-5659 on the relationship between the free trade provisions under the EC Treaty and the right to free expression under the Convention. The Court found that Austria had not breached the Treaty by failing to ban a motorway protest.

[103] Charter on Fundamental Rights (2000) OJ C364/1 Art 37. The Charter was signed at the Nice Summit in December 2000.

made by the Lisbon Treaty[104] the prospect of this is far from uncontroversial. There is at present no explicit right to a clean environment in Community law, although several Member States' constitutions do contain this provision. It is suggested that not much is won by the insertion of such a right, as the achievement of a clean environment depends entirely on concrete political, infrastructural, and administrative action.[105]

B. The Implementation of European Law in the UK

The constitutional status of European law

4.43 It is the conceit of English jurisprudence that European law only takes effect in the UK if it is incorporated into national law directly. The mechanism is provided under the European Communities Act 1972 (the ECA 1972), whereby an Order in Council or a regulation may be made 'for the purpose of implementing any Community obligation of the UK, or enabling any such obligation to be implemented, or of enabling any rights enjoyed or to be enjoyed by the UK under or by virtue of the Treaties to be exercised'.[106] Directives are transposed into UK law in the form of statutory instruments. This dualist approach to international treaties is in contrast to the monist approach of most of the other Member States, where the European measures take effect directly. It is not a distinction that carries any weight before the ECJ, where every Member State is under the same obligation to 'take all appropriate measures, whether general or particular, to ensure fulfilment of the obligations arising out of this Treaty or resulting from action taken by institutions of the Community', and to 'abstain from any measure which could jeopardise the attainment of the objectives of the Treaty'.[107]

4.44 Under the European Communities Act 1972, all Acts of Parliament and subordinate legislation, which may appear to be purely domestic in their scope, must still be read subject to the 'rights, powers, liabilities, obligations and restrictions from time to time created or arising by or under the treaties, and all such remedies and procedures from time to time provided for by or under the treaties'.[108] There are

---

[104] Art.6 of the TEU, as amended by the Lisbon Treaty (if ratified). This should have little effect in the UK, as Protocol 7 of the Lisbon Treaty states that the Charter will not create rights that are not already recognized in the UK. The Charter was signed at Strasbourg, December 2007. It would have been part of the EU Constitution (which was not ratified).

[105] See Krämer, op cit page 450.

[106] Regulations and Orders are subject to an affirmative resolution or annulment in Parliament: s 2 and Sch 2 of the ECA 1972. The Single European Act 1986 was enacted by the European Communities (Amendment) Act 1986; the Maastricht Treaty and the Amsterdam Treaty by the European Community (Amendment) Acts of 1993 and 1998.

[107] Art. 10 (ex Art. 5) of the EC Treaty.

[108] S 2(1) of the ECA 1972.

three 'treaties' which are relevant to the 'European Union', as it must now be called.[109] In addition to the main Treaty of Rome 1957 (the EC Treaty), there are the Treaties which established the European Coal and Steel Community (ECSC) and the European Atomic Energy Community (EURATOM). The national Courts have accepted this new constitutional source of national law from an early stage.[110] In the words of Lord Denning, European Community law will remain supreme unless 'Parliament deliberately passes an Act with the intention of repudiating the Treaty or any provision in it or intentionally of acting inconsistently with it and says so in express terms'.[111]

Nevertheless, there continues to be a 'notorious and persistent' implementation **4.45** deficit in EC environmental law.[112] Proper implementation has become a strategic priority under the Sixth Environment Action Plan. Maria Lee cites the example of the UK's difficulties in implementing the Landfill Directive: the construction of new waste incinerators is integral to compliance with obligations under the Directive, but in practical terms the siting of new incinerators, and the almost inevitable degree of local of opposition, makes for a slow and politically sensitive process.

The European Commission has no inspectors monitoring the implementation of **4.46** Community Law, and relies to a great extent on information coming from members of the public, outside the Community administration system. Members of the public are able to make a complaint to the Commission in writing, simply setting out the breach of Community law and asking the commission to intervene. A register is kept of all complaints, but complainants have no direct rights if the Commission fails to examine a particular complaint.

The need for national courts to refer questions to the ECJ under Article 234

If there is any doubt about the correct interpretation of European law, the matter **4.47** may need to be referred by the court to the ECJ under Article 234 (ex-Article 177). This must be taken as a preliminary point, before the case can be determined. The national court itself must decide whether a decision on the question

---

[109] This was one of the symbolic changes of name made under the Treaty of European Union, signed at Maastricht in 1992. The Treaty of Rome itself became the 'EC Treaty', rather than the EEC Treaty, and the Council of Ministers became the European Council. Maastricht also saw the introduction of two spheres of co-operation in foreign policy and in the fields of justice and home affairs, which are separate from the three existing treaties.

[110] See *Esso Petroleum v Kingswood Motors* [1974] QB 142, Bridge J. Cases such as *ex p Factortame (No 2)*, HL (below) can be seen as merely part of this trend.

[111] *McCarthys Ltd v Smith* [1979] 3 All ER 325 at 329.

[112] Lee, Maria op cit p.49.

of European Community law[113] is 'necessary to enable it to give judgment'.[114] The reference can be made at any time in the proceedings, so that there could be a reference from the county court or any tribunal acting in a judicial capacity—although it is doubtful that this includes an inspector sitting at a public inquiry. The final court which determines the matter must consider the question.[115] The questions will be framed by the court, and need to be specific rather than hypothetical.[116] Guidance on references is available from the ECJ.[117] References to the ECJ are made on a wide range of environmental subjects but not with great frequency.[118] In 2007 the Administrative Court referred the question[119] of whether accidentally leaked sewage was 'waste' within the meaning of Article 1 (a) of Directive 75/442 (the Waste Framework Directive). The ECJ found the fact that the escape of sewage was accidental, did not prevent it from being 'discarded' and hence from being 'waste' under the framework directive. The word 'discard' had to be interpreted broadly, and in accordance with the purpose of the legislation.

4.48   The national court is not obliged to refer a question to the ECJ which is considers to be ill-founded. It is not unusual for the court, having considered the arguments in a single case, to refer some questions and not others.[120] However, if a court fails to make a reference for a preliminary ruling in circumstances where this should have been done, the Member State may be liable for damages to an individual arising from the resulting breach of community law.[121] Moreover, the ECJ has recently confirmed that a court of last instance cannot rule on the validity of the

---

[113] Preliminary questions can concern '(a) the interpretation of the Treaty; (b) the validity and interpretation of acts of the institutions of the community; (c) the interpretation of the statutes of bodies established by an act of the Council, where those statutes so provide' (Art. 234). The ECJ will not decide on the specific facts of the case or on the compatibility of the national law in question (unlike an Art. 226 (ex Art. 169) case).

[114] See *HP Bulmer v J Bollinger SA* [1974] Ch 401, CA; *Customs and Excise Commissioners v Samex* (1983) 1 All ER 1042; *R v Pharmaceutical Society of Great Britain, ex p Association of Pharmaceutical Importers (API)* [1987] 3 CMLR 951. The point must also be reasonably conclusive of the case, and on an issue which has not already been decided by the ECJ (in the sense that it is not 'acte claire'). If the point is neither difficult nor important, a reference itself may amount to a denial of justice. In *R v Pharmaceutical Society*, the court made its own decision, despite the potential pitfalls of the different methods of interpretation, texts, and language of European law.

[115] This is so even if it is a magistrates' court (*Costa v ENEL* 6/64 (1964) ECR 585).

[116] See *Criminal Proceedings against Saddick* (C-458/93) (1995) All ER (EC) 664, ECJ, and *Criminal Proceedings against Grau Gomis* (C-458/93) (1995) All ER (EC) 668, ECJ.

[117] See the Practice Direction (Article 177) Procedure (1997) All ER (EC) 1, ECJ and the Practice Direction for the English and Welsh courts: [1999] 1 WLR 260.

[118] Wennerås, op cit p 171: of approximately 225 preliminary rulings issued annually by the ECJ, less than 5% concern EC environmental law 'and many of these are driven by commercial rather than environmental interests'.

[119] *R (Thames Water Utilities Ltd) v South East London Division*, Bromley Magistrates' Court (Environment Agency, interested party) (Case C-252/05).

[120] *R (oao SPCMA SA and Others) v Secretary of State for Environment, Food and Rural Affairs* [2007] EWHC 2610 (Admin).

[121] See the Opinion of Advocate General Léger in *Traghetti del Mediterraneo SpA v Repubblica Italiana* Case C-173/03 at paragraphs 65–66.

provisions of a regulation, even if the ECJ has already decided that analogous provisions in another comparable regulation are invalid.[122]

The use of the principles of European law in the UK courts

Perhaps the most difficult general principle of European law for an English lawyer **4.49** is the different approach taken to interpretation. This problem was identified at an early stage by Lord Denning, who stated with regard to the EC Treaty, that it:[123]

> . . . lays down general principles. It expresses its aims and purposes. All in sentences of moderate length and commendable style. But it lacks precision. It uses words and phrases without defining what they mean. An English lawyer would look for an interpretation clause, but he would look in vain. There is none. All the way through the Treaty there are gaps and lacunae. These have to be filled in by the judges, or by Regulations and directives. It is the European way . . . likewise the Regulations and directives.

In addition to the principles set out in the Treaties,[124] the ECJ has developed vari- **4.50** ous fundamental principles of interpretation.[125] The reception of these principles into the common law is still an incomplete process. The principle of 'proportionality'[126] is not as a separate head of review in the UK courts. When it was considered by the House of Lords in *R v Home Secretary, ex p Brind*,[127] the court held that it was just a part of 'Wednesbury unreasonableness', rather than a heading in its own right. This does not accord with the concept of proportionality used by the ECJ. More recently, in *Alconbury Developments Limited*,[128] Lord Slynn of Hadley considered the two heads of review and stated that:

> the difference in practice is not as great as is sometimes supposed. The cautious approach of the Court of Justice in applying the principle is shown inter alia by the margin of appreciation it accords to the institutions of the community making economic assessments. I consider that even without reference to the 1998 (Human Rights) Act the time has come to recognise that this principle is part of English

---

[122] Case C-461/03 *Gaston Schul* (2006) ECR I-10513.

[123] *Bulmer Ltd v Bollinger SA* [1974] Ch 401 at 425. For a comparative analysis, and the tension between a literal and a purposive approach, see the case note at (1997) 1 JEL 168 by JDC Harte to the ECJ's decision in *R v SoS for the Environment, ex p RSPB*. See also McIntyre, Owen 'The All-consuming definition of "waste" and the end of the "contaminated land" debate?' Van de Walle and Others [2005] JEL 17 109.

[124] Article 174 (2.2) EC sets out the precautionary, preventive and 'polluter pays' principles.

[125] See Hartley, *The Foundations of European Community Law* (6th edition, OUP), Chapter 5, 'General Principles of Law'.

[126] Used for instance in the *Danish Bottles* case, *Commission v Denmark* C–302/86 [1989] 54 CMLR 619. See more recently Case C–320/03 *Commission v Austria* where the Court found that a total ban on lorries over 7.5 tonnes on a particular stretch of motorway *could* have been justified by environmental concerns, but in this case the measure taken was too radical and not proportionate; the Member State should have investigated a less restrictive measure.

[127] [1991] 1 AC 696, [1991] 1 All ER 720, HL.

[128] [2001] UKHL 23.

domestic law. Trying to keep the Wednesbury principle and proportionality in separate compartments seems to me to be unnecessary and confusing[129].

The precautionary principle

4.51 It cannot be said that the basic principles of environmental law set out in Article 174(2) will be applicable in the UK courts. This follows the *Peralta* case,[130] in which the ECJ held that Article 174R confines itself to describing the general objectives of the Community and could not override the national legislation in question. As regards the UK courts, the High Court has held that the 'precautionary principle' informs policy only, and should not be used in its interpretation.[131] This remains the position.[132] The issue arises with some regularity in claims for judicial review against grants of planning permission for mobile phone masts.[133] Although Planning Policy Guidance 8 (Telecommunications) dated 2001 provides that 'health considerations and public concern can in principle be material considerations in determining applications for planning permission',[134] this is qualified by the statement that 'the planning system is not the place for determining health safeguards'. The implication is that although the decision-maker may give consideration to what weight to attach to public health concerns, in the absence of clear evidence about impact on health (ie, where the precautionary principle might, on the ECJ approach, apply) very little weight can in fact be given. In a recent decision of the European Court of Human Rights, the court found that in the absence of conclusive scientific evidence, it had to be assumed that a mobile phone base station posed no health risks if radiation remained within the relevant guideline limits.[135]

---

[129] Paragraph 51 of the judgment.

[130] C-379/92 *Peralta* (1994) ECR I–3453, applied in C-284/95 *Safety Hi-tech Srl v S&T Srl* [1998] 14 July, ECJ and C-341/95 (validity of regulation 3093/94/EC on substances depleting the ozone layer).

[131] *R v SoS for Trade and Industry, ex p Duddridge* [1995] Env LR 131, QBD (complaint that the Secretary of State's decision allowed underground high voltage cables to pass too near to a house). The principle requires a more active stance than the simple prevention of harm. Again, no Art. 177 reference was made. Nicholas de Sadeleer comments that the case would probably have been differently decided if the underlying Directive had itself referred to the need to take a precautionary approach—in which case the court would have been obliged to consider it (*Environmental Principles*, OUP 2002 139).

[132] This current lack of judicial interest is not for want of academic discussion that it should be used—see Elizabeth Fisher, 'Is the Precautionary Principle Justiciable'? [2001] 13 JEL 315 and also 'The Precautionary Principle in the Twentieth Century: Late Lessons From Early Warnings'[2003] 15 JEL 104.

[133] *Harris v First Secretary of State and Others* [2007] EWHC 1847; *T-Mobile UK Ltd and Others v First Secretary of State and another* [2004] EWCA Civ 1763.

[134] At paragraphs 29 and 30.

[135] *Hans Gaida v Germany* (Application No. 9355/03 European Court of Human Rights 3/7/2007).

By contrast, PPS23 on Planning and Pollution Control places significant weight **4.52** on the precautionary principle. It refers to the Interdepartmental Liaison Group on Risk Assessment (ILGRA) 2002 paper's[136] 'important points' including the recommendation that 'the precautionary principle should be invoked when the level of scientific uncertainty about the consequences or likelihood of the risk is such that the best available scientific advice cannot assess the risk with sufficient confidence to inform decision-making'. In *Villa Ria Trading*[137] the Administrative Court noted that this advice was linked to the 1992 Rio Declaration on Environment and Development which states that 'lack of all scientific certainty shall not be used as a reason for postponing cost-effective measures to prevent environmental degradation'. Judge Gilbart stated that in his view, PPS23 advice on invoking the precautionary principle 'does not prevent the imposition of a condition in cases where there are reasonable grounds for suspecting that there may be contamination that needs further investigation'.

The 'polluter pays' principle

The decision has been taken by both the European Union[138] and the UK, as a **4.53** matter of principle, that the costs associated with preventing pollution, and minimizing its impact on the environment, should be borne by those responsible for it—this has become known as the 'polluter pays' principle. The costs should not be borne by the general public in whose name the controls are imposed. Therefore, operators of polluting processes are expected not only to pay for the clean-up or remediation of pollution, but also to bear the costs of any required improvements to meet increasing public standards. Moreover, those who apply for licences and authorizations have been required to pay ever-higher charges, in order to cover the administrative costs of regulators. The 'polluter pays' principle also has an economic logic, as at its heart there is the notion that this allows for the optimal allocation of limited resources. Whilst the principle may be accepted, the extent to which any polluter does in fact pay for the pollution caused is debatable and will always depend upon effective enforcement by the relevant regulators. The 'polluter pays' principle underpinned amendments made in 1995 to the Environmental Protection Act 1990.[139] In *R (National Grid Gas Plc) v Environment Agency*[140] the House of Lords decided that the costs of remediation should be

---

[136] *'The Precautionary Principle: Policy and Application'* see <http://www.hse.gov.uk/aboutus/meetings/ilgra/pppa.htm>

[137] [2006] EWHC 3326 (Admin).

[138] The European Community first mentioned the 'polluter pays' principle in its First Action Programme on the Environment (1973–77), and it has been carried through into the text of the main Treaties.

[139] Section 78(F) 'Determination of appropriate person to bear responsibility for remediation'.

[140] [2007] UKHL 30.

borne by the person causing the pollution, and not any 'innocent' successor in title. The UK will soon have to grapple with the need to ensure that there is full cost recovery for water services in accordance with the 'polluter pays' principle.[141]

Environmental liability

4.54 The Environmental Liability Directive is specifically based on the 'polluter pays' principle, and provides a common framework for preventing and remedying environmental damage.[142] This should have been transposed by April 2007, although it is now likely to be transposed by the UK in December 2008.[143] In the view of Fogleman, who has tracked the slow progress of this proposal throughout, English environmental law will change radically in the relevant areas once this happens.[144] Draft Regulations have been published for consultation,[145] which are intended to supplement existing legislation such as the Environmental Protection Act 1990, the Water Resources Act 1991, or the Wildlife and Countryside Act 1981 and the Control of Major Accident Hazards Regulations 1999.

4.55 The Environmental Liability Regulations are limited to particular types of 'environmental damage'[146] linked to rivers, habitats and species, and land contamination. They will introduce some areas of new liability, such as for land contamination caused by organisms and micro-organisms, and liability for damage to species and habitats outside the European protected sites (even in the absence of a prosecution). There will be a duty on the competent authorities to require that remedial measures are taken—in a similar vein to the duty to take action regarding statutory

---

[141] See Article 9 of the Water Framework Directive (2000/60/EC). However, the Directive does not contain any definition of costs, especially environmental and resource costs. For an analysis of the requirements of Article 9 in the light of the earlier intentions for more stringent definitions see Herwig Unnerstall, 'The Principle of Full Cost Recovery in the EU-Water Framework Directive—Genesis and Content' [2007] 19 JEL 29.

[142] Directive 2004/35/EC, which has had a long history of negotiation—the European Commission first adopted a White Paper on Environmental Liability on 9 February 2000.

[143] The European Commission has launched infraction proceedings against 9 Member States, including the UK, for their failure to implement the Environmental Liability Directive (Press Release, IP/08/1025, dated 26 June 2008). It does mean that companies are already at risk of liability.

[144] See Fogleman, 'The Environmental Liability Directive and its Impacts on English Environmental Law' [2006] JPL 1443.

[145] The draft Environmental Damage (Prevention and Remediation) Regulations 2008. There are different versions for (England) and (Wales). The UK has decided to pursue the minimum transposition of the Directive's requirements, with the exception of extending liability to cover all SSSIs. In Wales, it has also been decided to allow no permit or 'state of art' defences for damage caused by GMOs (this was option (iii) of the consultation—and was rejected in England). Consultation in England and Wales occurred in February to May 2008.

[146] The Directive does not cover all types of damage to the environment. The 'environmental damage' that it covers is defined as significant 'damage to protected species and natural habitats or in a site of special scientific interest', 'damage to water', and 'land damage' only (see Art. 2 further). However, 'complementary' and 'compensatory' remediation is required, as well as 'primary' remediation for any relevant cases of damage to species and protected natural habitats and water damage.

nuisances—and, conversely, there is a duty placed on operators to report any environmental damage and to take corrective steps. Liability will be strict liability in respect of any 'environmental damage' caused by a specified range of 'occupational activities' (described in Annex III of the ELD), and will be fault-based in respect of environmental damage to protected species and natural habitats from all other occupational activities. The Regulations do provide for appeals and for some defences against remedial costs, such as when the event causing the damage was expressly authorized by certain specified permits.[147] It is anticipated that the main businesses that will be affected are the agriculture, manufacturing, waste, and water industries, across Europe.

C. European Remedies for Individual Litigants

The principle of supremacy of Community law means that wherever there is a **4.56** conflict with national law, Community law takes precedence.[148] Certainly, it is the duty of the national courts to ensure that the legal rights of individuals under European law are effectively protected.[149] The ECJ has encouraged national courts to set aside national legislative provisions which might prevent Community rules having full effect.[150] But it is for the national courts to determine how to apply their own rules, so long as the protection of Community rights is no less favourable than that of domestic rights. This includes such matters as limitation periods,[151] often a difficult issue in claims for environmental damage. It is not intended that European law should create remedies other than those available under national law, although the creative possibilities inherent in the common law system when faced with a European dilemma were shown in *ex parte Factortame (No 2)*.[152] In the context of the Working Time Directive[153] 93/104/EEC, the ECJ has extended the principle of consistent interpretation to impose a wide-ranging obligation on the national court to examine not only implementing legislation,

---

[147] The main temporal limit is that the Directive only applies to damage occurring after the Directive should have been implemented—30 April 2007 (see Arts. 17 and 19).

[148] *Van Gend en Loos v Netherlandse Tarief Commissie* Case 26/62 [1963] ECR; *Costa v ENEL* Case 6/64 [1964] ECR 585.

[149] C-179/84 *Bozetti v Invenizzi SpA* [1985] ECR I–2301.

[150] *Simmenthal* (C-106/77 above), paras 20, 21.

[151] These are acknowledged to be necessary in the interests of legal certainty: see *Comet BV v Produktchap voor Siergewassen* C-45/76 [1976] ECR I–2043, so long as the time limits are reasonable.

[152] [1991] 1 AC 603 at 658. It was only possible for the court to grant the injunction against the Crown as there were directly enforceable European rights, as there is no such power to do so under s 31 of the Supreme Court Act 1981.

[153] Case C-397/01, *Pfeiffer* (2004) ECR I-8835.

but other legislation or national law that could achieve the purpose of the directive.[154]

4.57   The adoption of the Aarhus Convention,[155] which entered into force in October 2001, and to which the United Kingdom became a full party in May 2005, has introduced new provisions on public participation and access to justice in environmental matters. Secondary EU legislation must be interpreted as far as possible in conformity with international agreements such as the Convention. Where this cannot be achieved, it may be possible for individuals to invoke the Convention provisions directly, if they are found to be directly effective.[156] In a successful claim for judicial review by Greenpeace, of the UK government's failure to carry out a full public consultation, as it had indicated it would do, before adopting a policy to support new nuclear build. Mr Justice Sullivan found that:

> Given the importance of the decision under challenge—whether new nuclear build should now be supported— it is difficult to see how a promise of anything less than the 'the fullest public consultation' would have been consisted with the government's obligations under the Aarhus Convention.[157]

Individual remedies—Judicial review

4.58   The primary mechanism for an individual to challenge the actions of the UK government or public bodies in the UK courts is by way of judicial review. There is a specific ground for review under the Rules of the Supreme Court for a 'failure correctly to comply with Community law'.[158] Of course, judicial review is not an alternative method of appeal against a decision, and the High Court can only order a decision to be quashed, an act to be prohibited or a decision to be made, or a declaration or injunction. Damages will only be awarded in addition to one of these remedies, if the application includes a private law claim.[159] The court would normally grant relief if there has been some illegality, procedural impropriety, or irrationality,[160] although it retains a discretion not to grant relief in the circumstances of the particular case.

---

[154] See Sawyer, Katrine 'The principle of 'interpretation conforme': How far can or should national courts go when interpreting national legislation consistently with European Community law?', [2007] Statute Law Review 28(3) 165–181.

[155] Convention on Access to Information, Public Participation in Decision-Making and Access to Justice in Environmental Matters (Aarhus, Denmark, 25 June 1998).

[156] Wennerås, op cit, page 92.

[157] *R (on the application of Greenpeace Ltd) v Secretary of State for Trade and Industry* [2007] EWHC 311 (Admin).

[158] RSC Ord 53 r3(2)a(ii). For a general discussion see Neil King QC, 'Interpretation and Application of European Environmental Law in Recent Decisions of the European and National Courts' [2007] JPL 522; and Richard Gordon QC, 'Using EC Law in Environmental Judicial Review' [2007] JPL 826.

[159] S 31(4) of the Supreme Court Act 1981.

[160] *Council of Civil Service Unions v Minister for the Civil Service* [1985] AC 374, HL per Lord Diplock (the GCHQ case).

There are several special considerations that apply when a government act is challenged under European law. First, as a practical matter, the matter may need to be referred by the court itself to the ECJ as a preliminary point, under Article 234, as discussed above. Since the case will be stayed until the ECJ has given its ruling, it may be possible to obtain interim relief against the other party.[161] An interim injunction which would have the effect of disapplying apparently authentic national legislation will be exceptional.[162] There must be a serious doubt as to the validity of the national measure, damages must be an inadequate measure, and the interest of the applicant must outweigh the public interest.[163] The difficulties of seeking interim relief even against administrative decisions were clearly demonstrated in *R v Secretary of State for the Environment, ex p RSPB*[164] by the House of Lords. The Secretary of State had decided to exclude the Lappel Bank from the Medway Estuary special protection area, designated according to Directive 79/409/EEC on the conservation of wild birds. The Lappel Bank was to be used for the extension of Sheerness Docks, and those economic considerations were deemed to outweigh its nature conservation value. The RSPB sought a declaration that this was contrary to the Directive, and the House of Lords decided to refer the matter to the ECJ for a preliminary ruling on the proper interpretation of the Directive.[165] The RSPB sought an interim declaration, which would have had the effect of stopping any further irreversible development pending the ruling. The House of Lords refused to grant this, as it was tantamount to an interim injunction and the RSPB were not prepared to given an undertaking in damages. In the event the Court found for the RSPB, but by the time the ruling was made the site had already been developed into a car park. Article 9(4) of the Aarhus Convention, ratified by the UK in February 2005, now requires Member States to

4.59

---

[161] The interim relief is for the national court to grant, as the ECJ only has the power to do so on Art. 230 (ex Art. 173) cases. The High Court declined to grant Mayer Parry interim relief pending the determination of the reference, either in the form of a declaration or an injunction. (*R v Environment Agency ex parte Mayer Parry Recycling Ltd (No.2)* [2001] Env LR 35.

[162] See *ex p Factortame (No 2)* (1991) 1 AC 603 at 672, 673C, 674B per Lord Goff. These principles were applied in considering a statutory instrument in *R v HM Treasury,* ex p *British Telecommunications,* The Times, 2 December 1993, CA (Interim application, pending Art. 177 reference). BT were refused interim relief despite having a strong arguable case and an inability to recover damages. See also *Kirklees BC v Wickes Building Supplies Ltd* [1993] AC 227, HL, where the local authority obtained an interlocutory injunction for a breach of the Sunday trading laws, despite the Art. 177 reference.

[163] *Factortame (No 2)*, and see *Zuckerfabrik Suderdithmarschen* C-143/88 and C-92/89 (1991) ECR I-415. In *R v MAFF ex p Monsanto plc* [1999] 2 WLR 599 interim relief was refused.

[164] The Times, 10 February 1995, HL. The declaration sought was that 'the Secretary of State acts unlawfully if . . . he fails to act' in a certain way. This was tantamount to a mandatory order, and seems to have been a procedural attempt to avoid the consequences of seeking an injunction. The case was the latest step in the RSPB's challenge to Sheerness Docks' expansion. In *R v Swale BC, ex p RSPB* (below, n 131), their challenge to the planning permission failed on procedural grounds.

[165] The ECJ held that there had been a breach—see *R v Secretary of State for the Environment, ex p RSPB* ('the Lappel Bank') (C–44/95) (1996) 3 CMLR 411, ECJ.

provide 'adequate and effective remedies, including injunctive relief as appropriate'.

4.60 If it is alleged solely that the UK is in breach of a Directive, the question will be whether the decision is lawful in terms of European Community law and not whether the public authorities have acted reasonably.[166] So the High Court was able to hold that the attempt to redefine the limits of the Humber Estuary for the purposes of the Urban Waste Water Treatment Directive 91/271/EEC in order to reduce the treatment costs required was unlawful.[167] However applications for judicial review may particularize grounds in addition to breach of a Directive. In *Rockware Glass Ltd v Chester City Council*[168] the Administrative Court granted an application for judicial review of a decision by Chester City Council on the ground that it had failed properly to interpret and apply Directive 96/61 on Integrated Pollution Prevention and Control, partly by imposing emission limits which were not achievable. Additional grounds alleged that the authority took into account irrelevant considerations, failed to take into account material considerations, and had acted ultra vires and irrationally. This case illustrates how 'traditional' judicial review grounds may overlap with the ground that a Directive has been breached. On the issue of time limits, the Court of Appeal decided that there was no reason to disregard or modify the provisions of domestic law because the issues in the case included the validity of Community measures.[169]

4.61 Different considerations may apply when the Member State is in breach of a 'secondary obligation' to rectify an existing breach of a Directive. In *ex p Friends of the Earth Ltd*,[170] the Court of Appeal did accept that the secondary obligation on the UK was to rectify its breach of the Drinking Water Directive as soon as possible rather than merely as soon as practicable. Considerations of practicability did enter into the equation of what was possible and no principle of European or domestic law required the court to ignore the practicalities. In contrast, when the ECJ had held that the UK was in breach of its obligations under the Drinking

---

[166] *R v Ministry for Agriculture, Fisheries and Food, ex p Bell Lines* [1984] 2 CMLR 502; equally *Commission v Greece* [1992] I-2509, C-45/91, (local opposition was no justification); *Commission v Italy* Cases 30-34/81 [1981] ECR 3379; *Commission v Belgium* C-134/86 [1987] ECR I-2415.

[167] *R v Secretary of State for the Environment, ex p Kingston-upon-Hull City Council* [1996] Env. LR 248, QBD, deciding that the treatment costs were not a relevant consideration.

[168] [2005] EWHC 2250 (Admin).

[169] *R v London Borough of Hammersmith and Fulham* [2000] Env LR 549.

[170] *R v Secretary of State for the Environment, ex p Friends of the Earth Ltd* [1996] Env LR 198, CA. The Secretary of State's decision to rely upon detailed undertakings from the water companies in order to comply with the Directive was upheld. It was also important that his statutory enforcement powers could still be exercised. This case has yet to be reassessed. The ECJ held that this system breached EC Law—*Commission v UK* C-340/96 The Times, 30 April 1999.

Water Directive, the court had rejected the UK's argument that its failure was justified as it had taken all practicable steps to secure compliance.[171]

The types of relief available are more extensive for breaches of European law. It is **4.62** possible to obtain an injunction, even an interim injunction, against the Crown.[172] This may even lead to apparently authentic legislation being unenforceable. It has also proved possible for one government agency to obtain locus standi for a declaration that the government is in breach of its European obligations.[173] There is also the difficult question of whether the Member State is obliged to pay individuals damages for its failure to implement European law. There is a body of opinion that the remedies available do not extend far enough if they do not compensate an individual for his loss caused by a breach of European law. In *Hedley Lomas*, Advocate General Leger considered that a declaratory judgment in judicial review proceedings did not amount to effective judicial protection of the individual's rights under Community law.[174] Indeed, considering that relief may be denied without a consideration of the merits if the application is not made promptly,[175] judicial review as currently exercised by the UK courts may itself be ineffective protection particularly in the light of Article 9(4) of the Aarhus Convention. Where it may be inferred that national procedural rules are specifically designed to prevent or reduce claims based on Community law, the ECJ will require disapplication of the rules.[176]

Individual remedies—Damages against the State

In principle, an individual can seek damages against a public body in the English **4.63** courts for a breach of statutory duty.[177] Initially, successful claims under European

---

[171] *Commission v UK* C-337/89 [1992] ECR I-6103, for breach of Directive 80/778/EEC. The UK had failed to fulfil its obligations to ensure that the quality of water supplied in 28 supply zones conformed with the requirements concerning nitrates.

[172] *Factortame (No 2)* [1991] 1 AC 603, HL.

[173] *R v SoS for Employment, ex p EOC* [1994] 1 All ER 910. The EOC had locus standi, given their statutory duty and public law role. This principle could cover all local authorities, using the power to litigate in the interests of the inhabitants of their area (s 222 Local Government Act 1972): see Jamie Woolley, 'The Enforcement of EC Environmental Law and the Role of Local Government' in *Protecting the European Environment: Enforcing EC Environmental Law*, ed Han Somsen (Blackstone Press, 1996).

[174] ECJ Opinion on C-5/94 on 20 June 1995 (note 15 above).

[175] It must be made 'promptly and in any event within three months' of the decision: RSC Ord 53, r 4 and s 31(6) of the Supreme Court Act 1981. There must be a 'good reason' for extending time.

[176] For a full discussion of the ECJ's approach to time limits see Wennerås, op cit at page 96. with reference to Case 309/85 *Barra* (1988) ECR 355 and Case C-62/00 *Marks & Spencer* (2002) ECR I-6325.

[177] Eg *Garden Cottage Foods v Milk Marketing Board* [1984] AC 130 (Art. 86; the application for an interim injunction failed, as damages would be an adequate remedy).

law were limited to misfeasance in public office.[178] The landmark ECJ decision has been *Francovich and Bonifaci v Italy*,[179] which requires the national courts to consider awarding damages to individuals caused by a state's breach of community law. In *Francovich*, the State had failed to implement a directive which would have granted specific rights to employees when their employer becomes insolvent. In the case of environmental obligations, the national legislature has a wide discretion to choose how to implement Community law. The ECJ has considered this point in *Brasserie du Pêcheur*,[180] holding that individuals who have suffered loss were entitled to reparation where the rule of community law breached was intended to confer rights on them, the breach itself was 'sufficiently serious',[181] and there was a direct causal link between the breach and the damage sustained by the individuals.

4.64   The claim for compensation does not depend on showing fault going beyond that of a serious breach of European law. It is for the national courts to find the facts and decide how to characterize the breaches of Community law.

4.65   The national laws on liability should then be applied, including, if appropriate, exemplary damages.[182] Therefore, it is probable that *Francovich* damages would not be awarded where there was no actual harm caused. The conditions laid down for making such claims in the national courts should not be less favourable than those relating to domestic cases, or framed in such a way as in practice to make it impossible or excessively difficult to obtain reparation. Although it must be clear

---

[178]   *Bourgoin SA v MAFF* [1986] QB 716, CA (a case on Art. 30), where the claim for a breach of statutory duty was refused. Misfeasance will always be a difficult claim to prove. In *Kirklees BC v Wickes Building Supplies Ltd* [1993] AC 227, HL at 281D, Lord Goff doubted whether *Bourgoin* was still valid in the light of *Francovich* (below).

[179]   *Francovich and Bonifaci v Italy* Cases C-6/90, C-9/90 (1991) ECR I-5357. The UK has apparently settled a £34,000 *Francovich* claim for a breach of the Equal Treatment Directive (following the *Marshall* decision). As a settlement, the UK avoided the need to admit liability (Legal Times, September 1995, 1).

[180]   See the combined cases *Brasserie du Pêcheur SA v Germany; R v Secretary of State for Transport, ex p Factortame (No 4)* (C-46/93 and C-48/93); (1996) ECR I-1029. The Member State must have 'manifestly and gravely disregarded the limits on its powers'. Although it was for the national courts to decide, the ECJ did suggest that in both cases a sufficiently serious breach had occurred. On any view, it would be sufficiently serious if a breach persists despite a judgment finding that there had been an infringement, or the breach was contrary to settled case law.

[181]   So in *R v HM Treasury, ex p British Telecommunications plc* (C-392/93) (1996) The Times, 16 April, ECJ, (1996) ECR I-1631, the failure to transpose a directive correctly was held not to be a sufficiently serious breach. This is intended to reflect the liability which applies to the acts and omissions of the Community itself where it has a wide discretion, under Art. 288 (ex Art. 215) (limiting damages to where there has been a grave and manifest breach of the Community's powers). Art. 288 is considered in more detail below, under European institutions.

[182]   For instance, *R v Secretary of State for the Environment, ex p Factortame (No 5)* The Times, 3, November, HL, where the UK Government was found liable to pay damages for its discrimination on the grounds of nationality against Spanish fishermen. Notably, in *R v Ministry of Agriculture Fisheries and Food, ex p Hedley Lomas (Ireland) Ltd* (C-5/94) The Times, 6 June 1996, ECJ, [1997] QB 139.

that the Member State is in breach of Community law, the ECJ also made it clear that the claim for damages cannot be limited to the damage sustained after the court's finding that there had been an infringement.

In *Dori v Recreb*,[183] it was emphasized that this possible right to an action for dam-   **4.66** ages will be against the Member State itself, and not against the offending company or individual. Nor should the claim be made against an 'emanation of the state' for damages, as it is the Member State which is liable in such circumstances.[184] It might be possible to claim damages against the UK for its breaches of the directives on drinking and bathing water standards. There is no doubt that the UK is in breach of its obligations under European law.[185] If an individual could show that they had suffered loss or damage as a result of the failure to meet the European standards, the individual could sue the UK. This might extend also to breaches of the Access to Environmental Information Directive.[186] The Court of Appeal has opened the door to just such a claim by an individual under the Shellfish Directive in *Bowden v South West Water Services Limited*.[187] It held that it was arguable that the Directive conferred rights on individuals such as the plaintiff, who was a shellfishermen. The ECJ's judgment in *Crehan*[188] is viewed by some as an indication that national courts are under an obligation to provide a remedy for individuals who have suffered loss arising from a breach of Art.81 EC (unfair trading conditions), and, further, that this is capable of being extended in principle to parties suffering loss as a result of a breach by another individual, of any horizontal and directly effective provision.[189] However the implications for environmental litigants are uncertain.

---

[183] *Faccini Dori (Paola) v Recreb* C-91/92 (1995) All ER (EC) 1; The Times, 4 August 1994.

[184] See *Kirklees BC v Wickes Building Supplies Ltd* [1993] AC 227 at 282F–G per Lord Goff, relying on *Francovich* at paras 33–37. It would apparently be wrong that the council should find itself liable for damages as a result of performing its statutory duty under national law. The liability is that of the Member State whatever agency of the State has caused the breach of the EC obligations: *Commission v Belgium* C-77/69 (1970) ECR 237.

[185] *Commission v UK* C337/89 (drinking water) [1992] ECR I-6103, which was indeed the first ECJ decision against the UK on an environmental issue; *Commission v UK* C-56/90 (Blackpool beaches case) [1993] ECR I-4109.

[186] See, for instance, *Guerra v Italy* [1998] 4 BHRC 63, where the Italian state had withheld information from local inhabitants about the hazards posed by a chemical factory. The European Court of Human Rights awarded compensation for non-pecuniary loss (see para 22.38 further).

[187] [1999] Env LR 438, CA. The plaintiff claimed that his shellfish business had suffered because of pollution damage caused by the sewage company's discharges. The claims against the Government, the Director General of Water Services, and the Environment Agency had been struck out as unarguable, but the Court of Appeal restored certain aspects. However, it did confirm that the Bathing Water and Urban Wastewater Treatment Directives did not confer rights on fishermen. The breaches of these Directives would only be relevant to the claim in public nuisance.

[188] *Bernard Crehan v (1) Inntrepreneur Pub Company (CPC) (2) Brewman Group Limited* [2004] EWCA Civ 637.

[189] Drake, Sara 'Twenty Years after Von Colson: the impact of "indirect effect" on the protection of the individual's community rights', [2005] ELRev 30(3) 329–348.

4.67 There is some indication that national courts may be willing to apply *Francovich* damages to purely domestic situations. Marie-Pierre Granger's analysis[190] of the national applications of this decision cites the Court of Appeal's judgment in *Factortame,*[191] referring to the 'hint' that *Francovich* may be extended to national situations:

> now that it (state liability for a legislative act) is undoubtedly available in circumstances which contain a community element, it may be right on some future occasions to re-examine that tradition (according to which compensation for damages caused by the legislature are not compensated).

4.68 Following the ECJ decision in *Köbler v Republic of Austria* [192] it is possible for individual litigants to obtain reparation if their rights are affected by an infringement of Community law by a national court adjudicating at the last instance. The breach must be sufficiently serious, and there must be a causal link between the breach of obligation and the loss or damage sustained. The liability of Member States for judicial breaches of community law is not restricted to instances of intentional fault or serious misconduct by the national court, if such a limitation were to lead to the exclusion of the Member States' liability in other cases where a manifest infringement of the applicable law had occurred.[193] The point has recently been considered for the first time in a United Kingdom court,[194] in the context of failure to direct an EIA before granting outline planning permission. The basis of the complaint was that the decision had been made by a person without delegated authority; it was common ground that the EIA Directive had been properly implemented. Even though Plender J accepted that the High Court and Court of Appeal judgments disposing of the judicial review proceedings made statements which were "inconsistent with the law as it was later interpreted by the ECJ in *Commission v United Kingdom*[195], he found that there was no "manifest error" creating liability under the *Köbler* principles, which was "reserved for exceptional cases". The Court emphasized that EC law is in a process of continual development, and inconsistencies between national decisions and subsequent ECJ judgments can be expected to arise.

---

[190] Granger, Marie-Pierre F. 'National Applications of Francovich and the construction of a European administrative ius commune', [2007] ELRev 32(2) 157–198 p 188.

[191] *R v Secretary of State for Transport ex parte Factortame Ltd (No. 5) CA.*

[192] Case C-224/01 (2003) ECR I-10239.

[193] Case C-173/03 *Traghetti del Mediterraneo SpA v Repubblica Italiana* [2006] ECR I-05177 see paragraph 46.

[194] *Stephen Cooper v HM Attorney General* [2008] EWHC 2178.

[195] Case C-508/3 [2006] ECR I 3969.

Individual remedies—Defence in criminal proceedings

European law can provide a defence to a charge in criminal proceedings.[196] The **4.69** ECJ has held that the Italian Government could not rely upon a directive, which had not been fully transposed, in order to prosecute an individual for discharging cadmium into the aquatic environment without prior authorization.[197] In a prosecution regarding the transport of animals to the Continent, the UK Order was construed in accordance with the Directive it implemented.[198] Where the validity of European regulations is clear, there is no necessity to refer the issue to the ECJ.[199] Where European law is unclear, the court will be obliged to consider whether it should refer the matter to the ECJ under Article 234, as occurred in *R v Henn and Darby*.[200] But when a statute is being challenged before the ECJ, an authority can still seek to prosecute a defendant under that statute.[201]

In 2002 the European Commission proposed a new Directive on the protection **4.70** of the environment through criminal law. Initially, the Council adopted instead an initiative for a Framework Decision but following challenge by the Commission and annulment of the Framework Decision by the ECJ, a new proposal for a Directive (which will go through the co-decision procedure) was put forward. The rationale behind the new Directive is given as follows:

> The proposal will provide for a minimum standard at Community level for the definition of serious environmental criminal offences, a similar scope of liability for legal persons as well as levels of penalties for particularly serious environmental crimes. This will ensure that serious cases of environmental crime are dealt with in a similar manner in all Member States and that perpetrators cannot take benefit from the existing differences in national legislation. It will also facilitate cooperation between Member States in cross-border cases.[202]

The new Directive, if adopted, may go some way towards reducing the 'imple- **4.71** mentation gap' in environmental crime at the national level.

---

[196] *Pubblico Ministero v Ratti* C-148/78 [1979] ECR I-1629. Ratti was prosecuted although he alleged that he had packaged his goods according to the directives. The ECJ held that he could rely only on the first packaging directive, whose deadline for implementation had passed. See also *Van den Burg* (C-169/89) note 161 below, where the shop had been convicted of selling a protected bird.

[197] Criminal Proceedings against *Luciano Arcaro* (C-168/95) [1997] All ER (EC) 82, ECJ, [1996] ECR I-4707, applying *Marleasing*. The national decree was based on Directives 76/464/EEC and 83/513/EEC on the discharge of dangerous substances into the aquatic environment.

[198] *Ken Lane Transport v North Yorkshire County Council*, The Times, 22 May 1995, DC; [1995] 1 WLR 1416.

[199] See *R v Searle*, The Times, 27 February 1995, CA.

[200] [1981] AC 850; the reference should not be made until all the facts have been heard, as the jury may acquit on the facts. See also *R v Plymouth Justices, ex p Rogers* [1982] QB 863.

[201] *R v Lincoln Justices, ex p Wickes Building Supplies*, The Times, 6 August 1993, CA (Sunday trading prosecutions).

[202] EUROPA Press release reference MEMO/07/50 (<http://www.europa.eu>).

Infraction proceedings against the UK

4.72 The preceding discussion has considered how an individual may use European law in the national courts to challenge the actions of public bodies. However, an individual cannot take proceedings in the ECJ to ensure the same result. They can only complain to the Commission, and hope to persuade it to take on the case. The Commission is under a duty to ensure that the provisions of the EC Treaty and the measures taken under it are applied.[203] It does have powers of investigation, but these are very limited in the environmental field.[204] The Member States are also obliged to report on their compliance with the directives to the Commission.[205] If the Commission considers that a Member State has failed to fulfil an obligation under the Treaty, it can take proceedings against the Member State directly to the ECJ, under Article 226 (ex-Article 169).[206] The Commission must have first given the Member State an opportunity to submit its observations on the matter and so infringement procedures frequently do not get beyond the preliminary stage.[207] If the Commission does issue a Reasoned Opinion, the Member State has another opportunity to comply. It is only after a failure to comply at this stage that proceedings will be begun. The Commission can also request the ECJ to use its powers to suspend the effect of actions where it considers that the circumstances of the case require it, under Article 242, and to order any necessary interim measures to be taken under Article 243.[208] It may in practice be difficult to

---

[203] Art. 211 EC.

[204] Essentially limited to requests for information—unlike the powers of inspection available in competition matters or the distribution of EC funds generally, and in agriculture, fisheries, and slaughterhouses.

[205] Directive 911/692/EEC has harmonized the reporting of the implementation of environmental directives.

[206] For instance *Commission v France* C-38/99 (failure to transpose Directive 79/409/EEC on the conservation of wild birds—national authority not empowered to lay down closing dates for hunting which vary according to species, without evidence that staggering the closing dates does not impede complete protection of the species liable to be affected); *Commission v Hellenic Republic* C-103/00 (failure to fulfil obligations under the Habitats Directice 92/43/EEC—failure to adopt requisite measures to implement an effective system of strict protection for the sea turtle on Zakinthos).

[207] For instance, the Commission has launched infraction proceedings against nine Member States, including the UK, for their failure to implement the Environmental Liability Directive (Press Release, IP/08/1025, dated 26 June 2008). This was in the form of a 'Reasoned Opinion' (second and final written warning) to each Member States, which sets out the reasons why it considers there to have been an infringement of EU law and calls upon the Member State to comply within a specified period, normally two months. Initially, the Commission sent a 'Letter of Formal Notice' (first written warning) to the 23 Member State then concerned, requesting them to submit observations, on 1 June 2007.

[208] Under Art. 83 of the ECJ's Rules of Procedure, the application must state the circumstances for the urgency, and a prima facie case. Delay can be fatal: *Commission v Germany* C-57/89R [1989] ECR 2849 (Leybucht dyke project irreversibly affecting bird sanctuary, started in 1986, application in 1989). A successful instance, with a strong prima facie case to suspend the financial levy, was C-195/90R (1990) ECR I-2715.

persuade the ECJ to suspend the original decision, except in cases where any damage might be irreversible.[209] If the Member State does not comply with the ECJ judgment a further case can be brought, in which the Commission could seek a heavy fine as an additional sanction.[210] Similar preliminary stages apply to cases brought by one Member State against another under Article 227 (ex-Article 170), which, in addition to the political nature of such an action, means that few cases are ever brought under this article.[211]

Challenging community legislation—Direct actions

Should a litigant wish to challenge Community legislation itself, proceedings may **4.73** be commenced in the ECJ.[212] The legality of the acts or omissions of the European Community can be challenged on the grounds of lack of competence, an infringement of an essential procedural requirement, or an infringement of the Treaty or any law relating to its application, or a misuse of its powers.[213] It is only possible to challenge a regulation, directive, or decision at the ECJ within two months.[214]

However, there is a substantial procedural hurdle for individual parties. Challenges **4.74** can be made by a Member State, the European Parliament, the Commission, and the Council as of right. Individual parties can only make a challenge if they can show that either the instrument was addressed to them or that, although the legislation is addressed to a third party, they are directly and individually concerned with the legislation.[215] This effectively limits challenges by individuals to decisions, which will be clearly addressed to the individual parties concerned. Clearly, regulations and directives do affect the public as a whole. But, in order for an individual party to challenge a regulation, it would be necessary to show that, although it is in the form of a regulation, it is in substance a decision. This is a legal and

---

[209] See Wennerås, op cit at page 245 and reference to the *Paraquat* case (T-229/04 *Sweden v Commission*) (2004) OJ C106/24 as an example of the circumstances (risk to human and animal health) in which interim relief might be granted.

[210] Art. 228. Again, the Commission will issue a first written warning ('Letter of Formal Notice') and then a second and final written warning ('Reasoned Opinion'). The potential fine was introduced by Maastricht in order to bolster the infraction proceedings. However, it is a politically sensitive weapon and it would still take a decision by all of the 20 Commissioners to seek such a remedy.

[211] A rare instance is *France v UK* [1979] ECR 2923 (fishing net mesh sizes).

[212] Under Arts. 230–232 of the Treaty, for a review of an act or omission of the EC Council or Commission other than recommendations and opinions. If the action is well founded, the ECJ can declare the act to be void (Art. 174).

[213] See Hartley, op cit, chapter 11.

[214] Under Art. 230(3). So it will be impossible to seek to challenge the EC legislation at a later date, even collaterally. However, those who are not directly and individually concerned who then obtain an Art. 234 reference may benefit from the national time limits applicable.

[215] Art. 173. It has been given a narrow interpretation. See C-25/62 *Plaumann v Commnision* [1963] ECR 95 and more recently the Court of First Instance in Case T-177/01 *Jego-Quere (2002)* ECR II-2365 which provides summary of ECJ decisions on the question.

objective definition, and individual litigants have even failed even when it was possible to name all those members of a class who might be affected at any one time.[216] In the *Greenpeace* judgment regarding the provision of financial assistance by the European Commission for the construction of power stations on the Canary Islands, the ECJ upheld the Court of First Instance finding that 'an association formed for the protection of the collective interests of a category of persons could not be considered to be directly and individually concerned (. . .) by a measure affecting the general interests of that category'.[217] In other words, their interests were the same as those of any other persons in the same category. The ECJ also considered that the construction of the power stations, not the provision of financial assistance, was liable to affect the applicants' environmental rights. Therefore, they were not "directly and individually concerned" by the provision of the funds.[218] In 2002, Advocate General Jacobs invited the ECJ to overturn the *Greenpeace* judgment on the basis that the narrow approach to standing effectively excluded claims by individuals and associations[219], however this was rejected.

4.75 Public rights in the environmental sphere have been bolstered to some degree by the (as yet partial)[220] implementation of the Aarhus Convention. Under Article 9(3)[221] members of the public are to have 'access to administrative or judicial procedures to challenge acts or omissions by private and public authorities, which contravene provisions of its national law relating to the environment'. Non-governmental organizations can request Community institutions to conduct an internal review of their acts and omissions under Article 11; the outcome can be judicially reviewed. The internal review procedure, because it is addressed to the NGO, secures its standing and the problem of a 'lack of individual concern'

---

[216] For instance, that there are only 30 sugar beet producers in the EC: *Zuckerfabrik Wadenstedt GmBh v Council* Case 6/68 (1968) ECR 409. In retrospect, the class may be clear (*International Fruit Company NV v Commission* Cases 41-44/70 (1971) ECR 411). Recently, *Campo Ebro Industrial SA v Commission* T-472/93 (1995) ECR II-421, CFI, *locus* was refused to challenge a regulation on sugar prices in Spain, despite the fact the company was the only producer of isoglucose in Spain.

[217] C-321/95 *Greenpeace and Others v Commission* [1998] ECR-I-1651. See Wennerås, op cit pp 217–26 for an analysis of the case law on standing.

[218] See Sands, Philippe *Rethinking Environmental Rights – climate change, conservation and the European Court of Justice* (2008) 20 ELM 117 for an explanation of the significance of the *Greenpeace* judgment and a critique of the ECJ's approach to standing compared to that of the United States Supreme Court in *Massachusetts and Others v the United States Environmental Protection Agency*, 127 S. Ct. 1438 (2007).

[219] Opinion of A-G Jacobs (21 March 2002) 2002 ECR I-6677, Case C-50/00P *Union de Pequenos Agricultores v Council* (25 July 2002). See case comment by Granger, Marie-Pierre (2003) Enviro LR 5.1(45).

[220] See <http://www.http://ec.europa.eu/environment/aarhus/> for a summary of adoption and implementation of the first two 'pillars' of the Convention (access to information and public participation), and information about the proposed Directive on access to justice.

[221] Implemented by Regulation EC 1367/2006.

can—at least in theory—thereby be resolved. [222] However in a recent decision the Court of First Instance dismissed an action by WWF to annul a regulation setting quotas for the fishing of cod, partly on the basis that members of the North Sea Regional Advisory Council, of which it is one, are not a 'closed and identifiable group of persons . . . having a personal and identifiable interest'. The Court found that in the absence of procedural rights explicitly guaranteed to the applicant by community legislation, it would be contrary to Article 230 EC to permit it, simply on the basis of a point of view that it formulated in the course of the procedure leading to the adopted of the disputed measure, to bring an action against that measure.[223] WWF were therefore not permitted to challenge the European Council's allocation of cod quotas, a decision which might be seen as perpetuating the hurdles to participation which the Aarhus Convention was intended to remedy.

---

[222] For a detailed critical analysis of the impact of Regulation EC 1367/2006 see Wennerås, op cit pp.226–49.

[223] Case T-91/07 *WWF v Council of the European Union*, Order of 2 June 2008. See particularly paragraph 7.

5

ENVIRONMENTAL INFORMATION

A. **The Royal Commission on**		
Environmental Protection	5.01	
Introduction	5.01	
Public apprehension	5.12	
The public interest	5.13	
Progress—The change of climate	5.15	
B. **Nuclear Waste**	5.19	
The Royal Society	5.20	
C. **Environmental Information—**		
General Provisions	5.22	
Introduction	5.22	
The Environmental Information		
Regulations	5.23	
Code of practice and historical		
records	5.36	
Appeals and enforcement	5.38	
The Local Government (Access to		
Information) Act 1985	5.40	
D. **Environmental Information about**		
Land	5.50	
Town and country planning	5.50	
Environmental impact	5.59	
Appeals Under the Town and Country		
Planning Acts	5.80	

Waste	5.84
Contamination	5.93
Registers of contaminated land	5.98
E. **Information about Air Pollution**	5.121
F. **Information about Water**	5.125
The registers	5.125
The content of the registers	5.126
Integrated pollution control	
publicity	5.134
Gathering information	5.138
Publicity	5.148
G. **Information about Radioactivity**	5.153
Nuclear installations	5.153
Other premises	5.158
H. **Information on Miscellaneous**	
Matters	5.163
I. **The Powers of Inspectors**	5.165
Environment Agency inspectors	5.165
Obstruction of inspectors	5.167
Powers of entry	5.169
Emergencies	5.174
Immunity of inspectors	5.175

A. The Royal Commission on Environmental Protection

Introduction

The history of the development of the law and practice of environmental information **5.01** began with polluters, actual or potential, exhibiting hostility, or at least reluctance, to divulge anything about what they were doing. The attitude now is acceptance, sometimes grudging, that the public must be told enough to inform them of the outlines of the risks to which they may be subject. Thinking has changed radically since the days of the Alkali Inspectorate in the nineteenth century, when virtually nothing was made public, to the more liberal regime which now obtains. Even so, the contemporary literature on the subject is replete with complaint about the unwillingness, or worse, of businesses whose products might be thought to be environmentally harmful to publicize information about what they do, and of the inability or reluctance of regulatory agencies to make the polluters come clean, in every sense of the expression.[1]

5.02　This stance is explained and justified, at least in part, by the history of environmental regulation, and the traditional attitudes of the chemical industry, where recognition of the importance of environmental information and the requirement to provide it first began. The publicity put out by environmental pressure groups tends to blame industrialists and regulators for all the environmental misfortunes to which humanity is subject.[2] However, the truth is not so simple. The tenth Report of the Royal Commission on Environmental Protection, *Tackling Pollution—Experience and Prospects*,[3] for instance, spent much time and effort considering the problem of stubble burning by farmers.

5.03　A dry summer in 1983 had led to a succession of incidents, some of them road accidents involving loss of life, and many were caused by the failure of farmers to observe a Code of Practice which the National Farmer's Union had drawn up.[4] The fact that the NFU had taken the trouble to draw up and publish the Code of Practice testified that the leaders of the agricultural industry had acted responsibly, and that irresponsible individuals rather than the farming industry as a whole were to blame for the unfortunate, and in some cases tragic, events. Its concern about stubble burning led the Royal Commission to recommend that government should bring forward legislation imposing an outright ban on the practice. This was soon done, and now the burning of stubble is no more than a distant memory in the UK.

5.04　The Commission went on to recognize that there was much to praise, as well as much to criticize, in the attitudes of industry and government over the years. Historically, industry had been prone to justify its withholding environmental information by putting forward the argument that to make available details of its manufacturing processes and/or the wastes which they produced was commercially sensitive and amounted to the breaking of trade secrets. The Royal Commission gave this short shrift. It wrote:

---

[1] Examples of the more indignant are Bell and Ball, *Environmental Law*, (6th edn OUP, 2005); Bakkenist, *Environmental Information Law, Policy and Experience*, (Cameron May, 1994) .

[2] Two of the more plangent are Bell and Ball, *Environmental Law*; and Bakkenist, *Environmental Information Law and Experience* although they cannot be described as pressure groups.

[3] HMSO 1984, Cmnd 9419.

[4] Ibid, para 2.9.

In practice, incidents in which companies have obtained valuable information about a competitor from records of an environmental agency appear to be very few, notwithstanding the greater accessibility of such information in many countries such as the U.S.A. and Canada. Apart from the now notorious case of the inadvertent disclosure by the U.S. Environment Protection Agency of the formula of a successful Monsanto weedkiller, the CBI knew of only one example.[5]

The critique of the resistance to the publication of environmental information **5.05** did not end there. In subsequent comments the Royal Commission demolished other objections which had been advanced.

Modern techniques of chemical analysis are such that it would be a relatively simple matter for a competitor to discover the composition of an emission or discharge by taking a sample at the point where it left private premises . . . We therefore conclude that only on exceptional occasions would otherwise inaccessible trade secrets be revealed from the information that regulatory authorities are entitled to receive by statute.[6]

This should have disposed once and for all of the contention that business confidentiality in some way entitles industry to keep its environmental information to itself. As will be seen, however, that was to prove not to be the case.

Industrialists and businessmen had thrown up other objections to the disclosure **5.06** of environmental information. It was said that the public was not capable of understanding the technical material which would inevitably have to be made public, with two possible consequences. First, that the misunderstandings which would occur would cause unnecessary and unwarranted alarm; and secondly, that the disaffected would deliberately misrepresent the effects and results of industrial processes, and might embark on mischievous and vexatious litigation against polluters, real or imagined.

Again, the Commission's response was crisp and largely dismissive: **5.07**

While we do not necessarily see all pollution issues in the clear-cut terms in which it is the nature of pressure groups to present them, we have seen much evidence of a growing professionalism in many voluntary organisations. . . and with it an ability to evaluate and present technical and scientific reports which compare favourably with those of officially sponsored researchers. In our view, to deny access to data on the grounds that 'the public' is not competent to make 'correct' use of them is neither a tenable nor an acceptable proposition.

A notable omission from that commentary, however, is any attempt to deal with **5.08** the argument that the public, or sections of it, might fail to resist the temptation deliberately to misrepresent or otherwise misuse the information made public either directly or through the agency of regulatory bodies.

---

[5] See n 3 above, paras 2.43–2.45.
[6] Ibid, para 2.44.

5.09 Subsequent experience has shown the fears of industry not to have been entirely misplaced, and the failure of the Royal Commission to deal with the point is testimony to the argument's force.

5.10 Those opposed to the notion that information on environmental matters should be disclosed claimed, as enemies of public disclosure have since time immemorial, that the administrative costs would be prohibitive, or at least unreasonably high. The Commission attacked this proposition with characteristic pith and wit. It said:[7]

> Certainly, experience in the local government field has shown that 'public participation'—often consisting of little more than the one-way provision of information at meagrely attended public meetings—can be an unrewarding ritual for those with the task of organising it. However, the essential requirement is that information should be *available*, not that it should be forcibly fed to the public. . . If the requirement to allow public access is taken account of in designing the method by which records are compiled, and if best use is made of modern information technology, we see no reason why reasonable public access cannot be maintained without incurring burdensome administrative costs.

5.11 If those words were true in the early 1980s, the huge improvements in the storage and retrieval of information which have taken place since must surely have reinforced that conclusion many times over.

Public apprehension

5.12 There were other compelling reasons which justified making environmental information public. One was the obverse of that put forward by industry—that the public would be unnecessarily frightened by being given information which it did not, or did not fully, understand. In the Royal Commission's words: 'Secrecy—particularly the half-kept secret—fuels fear. In our visits and discussions we have noted instances where quite unnecessary concern has been caused by people's inability to obtain information on the nature of a discharge or waste material'.[8] As will be seen later, this has been an important factor in the difficulties faced by the nuclear industry almost throughout its existence.

The public interest

5.13 Finally, there was the thorny question of national security and the so-called 'public interest'. This attracted a balanced approach. On this Parliament itself has been,

---

[7] Ibid, para 2.47. Emphasis added.
[8] Ibid, para 2.52. The admonition contained at the end of that extract might have been read and remembered with profit by those concerned with the outbreaks of Creutzfeld-Jacob's disease and E coli in 1996 and 1997, and with the exposure of fighting personnel to organo-phosphates during the Gulf War.

as the Commission pointed out, inconsistent in its approach. As might have been expected, the Report came down in favour of the least possible use of the 'public interest' objection to the recording and publication of information. It concluded:

> Section 42 of the Control of Pollution Act (1974) enables the Secretary of State to exempt from publicity information about discharges (into waters and watercourses) which he is satisfied would be 'contrary to the public interest'. Perhaps surprisingly, there is no explicit equivalent provision applying to information about air pollution under section 79 (of the Clean Air Act then in force) or other forms of pollution (such as solid waste disposal). . . we think it important, however, that in applying section 42 and developing the wider principles of public information which we have advocated, Ministers and other pollution control authorities should strictly confine their interpretation of 'public interest' to 'national security' and in particular should not withhold information merely because it might cause embarrassment.[9]

It is far from certain that this recommendation has been followed scrupulously **5.14** during the period since it was put forward. The only embarrassment which could ordinarily arise from the publication of information about wastes and discharges is that caused by the considerations which the Royal Commission had analysed and, for the most part, rejected. Instances where 'national security', in the strict sense of the phrase, could be involved must be rare indeed.

Progress—The change of climate

So far the conclusions reached in the Report seem to be one-sided and largely criti- **5.15** cal of industry and regulatory agencies. Overall, however, the Commission concluded that the picture was less sombre. It found:

> . . . there have in fact been a number of moves in the direction of greater openness— some of them autonomous, others stimulated by external requirements. For one thing, the climate of opinion has changed. There is a growing acceptance on the part of industry and pollution control authorities of the need to share information with the public. . . .. The public for its part, as a result of growing interest by pressure groups and the media, is increasingly better informed on pollution issues. The sanctity of official data has become increasingly open to challenge.[10]

And a very good thing too, as most would agree. Furthermore, the Commission **5.16** was less critical than some might have wished of the allegedly cosy relationship between polluters and regulators, and of the shortcomings attributed to a system which did not invariably compel disclosure. On this, it concluded:

> Because our regulatory agencies do not always act in an adversarial way, it does not necessarily mean that there is a corrupting 'cosiness'. On the other hand, evidence can be found (from the United States of America and elsewhere) of the reverse being

---

[9] Ibid, para 2.68.
[10] Ibid, para 2.54.

true; and that reinforces our belief that there should be appropriate safeguards which place limits on what can be shielded from public view and discourage the kind of attitude (refusal to disclose information). . . not because of a strong desire to conceal information but simply because a statutory right does exist and some managements believe in exercising that right.[11]

5.17 That said, the parting word on the topic was a repeated appeal for the maximum disclosure, subject to as few exceptions as practicable.

> We consider that the aim of policy should be the progressive removal of existing discrepancies (in the law governing disclosure) so that in the long run the public will be entitled to the fullest possible amount of information on all forms of environmental pollution, with the onus placed on the polluter to substantiate a claim or exceptional treatment. Accordingly we *recommend* that a guiding principle behind all legislative and administrative controls relating to environmental pollution should be a presumption in favour of unrestricted access for the public to information which the pollution authorities obtain or receive by virtue of their statutory powers, with provision for secrecy only in those circumstances where a genuine case for it can be substantiated.[12]

5.18 It is instructive to test the efficacy of subsequent legislation and practice, described in the rest of this chapter, by reference to those principles.

B. Nuclear Waste

5.19 The Royal Commission did not change the climate of opinion overnight. One example illustrates that this was so. As is widely known, UK Nirex Ltd is charged with the unenviable task of finding a way or ways of disposing of the nuclear waste produced in the UK. Far from retreating into some sort of corporate bunker, the company established its own independent committee of outside experts, who were retained to advise it on all aspects of its work. Additionally, the company commissioned an independent report from the Royal Society, reviewing the progress made in tackling the scientific aspects of assessing the likely long-term performance of a so-called 'deep repository', which is in essence an underground tomb, far below the earth's surface, in which nuclear waste could be safely stored, for periods which to the lay mind amount to infinity.

The Royal Society

5.20 The Royal Society's Report, published in 1994, examined, among other things, the way in which Nirex had made its work public and had submitted it to the important process of 'peer review', this being the critical examination of the

---

[11] Ibid, para 2.71.
[12] Ibid, para 2.77. Emphasis added.

research and findings by other qualified scientists, meaning not merely those who were directly engaged in work on matters nuclear. On this aspect, in spite of the obvious anxiety of Nirex to ensure that its activities were subjected to independent outside scrutiny, the Report was less than congratulatory. In it, the study group of distinguished consultants and academics concluded:

> The success of the Nirex programme depends on public attitudes. It is well-known. . . that ignorance tends to widen the gap between perceptions of risk and the scientifically calculable levels of risk. Where the public have reason to suspect a 'conspiracy to suppress public knowledge' of studies of safety of radioactive waste disposal, their own anxieties may well be enhanced by concerns expressed by responsible scientists who are not privy to much of the work of Nirex. We were forcibly struck during this study by the extent to which some scientific reports of Nirex are protected from wider scrutiny by being classified 'commercial'—in confidence'. This applies particularly to reports dealing with PCPAs ('Post Closure Performance Assessments', these being analyses of the extent to which the proposed repository would succeed in preventing the nuclear waste from escaping into the surrounding geosphere and into the atmosphere during the active life of the materials involved) for Sellafield. . .. we were given few details of specific assumptions, did not have access to the databases of parameter values for models, and were given no detailed results of PCPA calculations. . ... We are reassured that Nirex increasingly recognise the need for greater openness in their scientific policy, as evidenced for example by the appointment of an independent review panel (as noted above). . . and by Nirex's initiative in approaching the Royal Society for the present study. Nevertheless, there is a need for a higher degree of exposure of Nirex's development of PCPAs for Sellafield, particularly to the scientific community beyond the group of people professionally involved in nuclear and radioactive waste matters. . . Ideally, each major stage of development of PCPAs should be open to scrutiny, so that advance to the next stage can be built upon confidence that all valid interpretations of the evidence have been adequately considered. Adherence by Nirex to this principle will help to mitigate potential future problems.[13]

It is, perhaps, unfair to draw attention to such criticisms of a single company, **5.21** which is no doubt one of many. However, they highlight the ambivalence which runs through the philosophy of the dissemination of facts and findings about environmental pollution. On the one hand, there is obvious readiness to subject some (perhaps carefully chosen) parts of a company's activity to independent criticism. On the other, the willingness is nullified by the inability or unwillingness to make public material which is critical to the making of informed judgements about the activities in question. This ambivalence is a leitmotiv which recurs throughout any account of the law and practice of environmental information.

---

[13] *Disposal of Radioactive Wastes in Deep Repositories* (Royal Society, 1994), 4.

C. Environmental Information—General Provisions

Introduction

5.22 Two enactments, one public general Act and one statutory instrument, regulate the keeping and provision of environmental information in general. The statutory instrument, the Environmental Information Regulations 2004,[14] applies universally. Since it was made under powers conferred by the European Communities Act 1972, pursuant to a Directive of the Commission of the European Union,[15] the Regulations tend to deal in generalities, seldom condescending to the particular or precise. It is therefore possible that they will have little practical effect, at least in a country where the common law still survives. Their usefulness is likely to be further diminished by the wide range of exceptions to their application, considered more fully below.

The Environmental Information Regulations

5.23 The Regulations apply to all public authorities holding environmental information, other than judicial or legislative bodies. They also apply to information produced by the authority, or held by it or on its behalf.[16]

5.24 Information to which the Regulations apply must be made available to the general public progressively and, from 1 January 2005 onwards, electronically. Information acquired before that date may be held in non-electronic form.[17]

5.25 The fundamental obligation on public authorities is to make information available on request, as soon as possible and in any event not later than 20 working days after the receipt of the request.[18] The information must be up to date, accurate, and comparable so far as the authority believes.[19]

5.26 Where it can, the authority must, if the applicant so requests, disclose where the information can be found, and the processes of analysis and sampling used in compiling it.[20] However, the general duty to disclose is qualified by many exceptions.

5.27 First, the authority need not disclose the data of which the applicant is the subject. This is curious, since the applicant might be thought to be the individual most closely concerned with that information, even though this might not interest

---

[14] SI 2004/3391.
[15] On Freedom of Access to Environmental Information (90/313).
[16] Regulation 3.
[17] Regulation 4.
[18] Regulation 5(1) and (2).
[19] Regulation 5(3).
[20] Regulation 5(5).

anyone else. The explanation may lie in the rights given under the Freedom of Information Act 2000.

Second, personal data of which the applicant is not the subject may not be dis- **5.28** closed where they are held on a database or in a filing system and disclosure would infringe the 'data protection principles' of legitimacy and fairness enshrined in the Data Protection Act 1998.[21] Where the data protection principles would be infringed the authority may avoid disclosure merely by declining to confirm or deny its existence or whether it holds it, even if it holds the information.[22]

Third, information may not be disclosed if it is not in the public interest to do so.[23] **5.29**

Fourth, there is no duty of disclosure where the request is manifestly unreasona- **5.30** ble; if it is too widely formulated, in which case the authority must ask for more particulars and assist the applicant in providing them; if the information requested is incomplete; if internal documents would have to be disclosed; if disclosure would adversely affect international relations or national security; if it would adversely affect the course of justice or a disciplinary inquiry; if it would affect intellectual property rights; except in the case of emissions, if it would impair the confidentiality of public authority proceedings protected by law; or commercial confidentiality; if it would affect the interests of the person the subject of the data where these were supplied voluntarily; or where the environment would be put at risk (as, for instance, if the location of the nest of a rare bird were disclosed).[24]

If information is disclosed, this must be done in the format requested by the appli- **5.31** cant, unless this cannot reasonably be done, or if the material is available in another format. The authority must explain why the format requested is not available.[25]

If the authority considers that the material cannot be made available within 20 **5.32** days it may comply with the request within 40 working days. It must then notify the applicant of the extension of time for compliance within the original 20 day period.[26]

A reasonable charge may be made for supplying the information, but not for **5.33** allowing access to it or examination of the data.[27]

---

[21] Regulation 13; DPA 1998 s 4, Scheds 1 and 2.
[22] Regulation 13(5).
[23] Regulation 13(3).
[24] Regulation 12(4), (5).
[25] Regulation 6.
[26] Regulation 7.
[27] Regulation 8.

5.34 If the authority does not have the information requested but believes that another public body does, it must transfer the request to the latter, and must inform the applicant. [28]

5.35 If there is a refusal to disclose, this must be in writing and be issued within 20 days of the request, specifying the reasons for refusal. The applicant must be informed of his right to make further representations on the matter.[29] Ministers may certify that disclosure would affect national security or would not be in the public interest. [30]

Code of practice and historical records

5.36 The Secretary of State is empowered to issue a Code of Practice in consultation with the Information Commissioner. The Secretary of State issued guidance under the now repealed Environmental Information Regulations 1992, which summarized their effect in layman's language.[31] No Code has been issued under the 2004 Regulations.

5.37 If historic records are involved, the responsible authority in England and Wales must consult the Lord Chancellor, and in Northern Ireland the Northern Ireland Minister. [32]

Appeals and enforcement

5.38 Appeals against decisions under the Regulations lie to the Information Tribunal.[33]

5.39 The enforcement provisions are the same as those of the Freedom of Information Act 2000.[34] It is an offence to alter information held by an authority with intent to prevent disclosure.[35] The offence is sufficiently serious for the consent of the Information Commissioner or the DPP to be necessary before proceedings can be brought.[36]

---

[28] Regulation 10.
[29] Regulation 14.
[30] Regulation 15.
[31] Regulation 16; Freedom of Access to Information on the Environment. (DOE) 1992.
[32] Regulation 17.
[33] Part V of the 2000Act (ss 57–61) deals with appeals. Rules governing the procedure of the Tribunal are contained in Sched. 6 to the Data Protection Act 1998 (as amended). On appeal the Tribunal can consider whether the notice in question is lawful and/or whether the Information Commissioner, in serving the notice in question, has correctly exercised his/her discretion. It can also review any of the Commisioner's findings of fact.
[34] Regulation 18.
[35] Regulation 19(1).
[36] Regulation 19(4).

The Local Government (Access to Information) Act 1985

Less wide reaching, but still important, are the requirements of the Local **5.40**
Government (Access to Information) Act 1985. As the title indicates, the Act is
concerned only with information held by local authorities and their officers, and
its scope has accordingly diminished with the transfer of functions from local
authorities to the Environment Agency under the Environment Act 1995. Even
so, the potential for obtaining information by using the procedures laid down
remains. Technically, the Act of 1985 inserted additional sections into the Local
Government Act 1972, after Section 106 of the latter. Therefore, references are to
the new sections of the Act of 1972.

The fundamental requirement is that meetings of local authorities, and of their **5.41**
committees and subcommittees, shall be open to the public, unless there is a reason to exclude it as prescribed by the Act.[37] The time for giving advance notice of
council and committee meetings has been extended from three days to five.[38]

There are three grounds on which the public may be excluded from a meeting. **5.42**
First, because the business to be conducted would involve the disclosure of confidential information furnished to the council by a government department on
terms that disclosure to the public is forbidden. Secondly, where disclosure has
been prohibited by an order of the court or by statute. Thirdly, the council may
exclude the public by passing a resolution that an item of business to be transacted
would involve disclosure of exempt information as defined in the Act.[39]

'Exempt information' covers many categories, not all of which relate to environ- **5.43**
mental matters. For example, there are types of information concerning council
employees and tenants which could hardly ever impinge on the environment. On
the other hand, there is no obligation to disclose information about expenditure
to be incurred by the council under any contract for the acquisition or disposal of
property or the supply of goods or services; nor instructions to counsel or counsel's advice in respect of any matter with which the authority is concerned, whether
or not litigation is contemplated; nor need the council disclose information about
any enforcement action or criminal proceedings which it is minded to take.[40]
These classes of exemption are, plainly, so wide that they can embrace many
aspects of environmental law, from prosecutions under the Clean Air Acts, to
repair of fractured local authority sewers, and many other vicissitudes besides.

---

[37] Local Government Act 1972, s 100A.
[38] Local Authorities (Access to Meetings and Documents)(Period of Notice)(England) Order
2002. SI 2002/715.
[39] Ibid, s 100A(2) and (3).
[40] Ibid, s 100I.

5.44   The corollary of the right to attend meetings of local authorities and their committees, and possibly more far-reaching, is the right of access to documents. The 1985 Act confers such a right, entitling the public to inspect copies of the agenda for meetings of councils and their committee and subcommittees, and, probably more relevantly, to inspect copies of any report made to the elected members for the purposes of the meeting.[41]

5.45   As might be expected, there are wide-ranging exceptions to the general principle. Where the appropriate officer of the authority thinks that the whole or any part of a report is likely not to be open to the public for any reason previously discussed, he may exclude from any report which is made to the authority or one of its committees the relevant passage. As is clear, this invests officers with wide powers of censorship, which may in practice be unreviewable. It will be within the officer's discretion to decide whether the report or part of it is or is not likely to be privileged from production to the public as a whole. The exercise of that discretion is, almost certainly, reviewable only by way of judicial review. As importantly, skilful editing could make it impossible to tell whether the whole or any part of a document has been concealed from the public gaze.

5.46   Parliament has placed much trust in the integrity of local government officers and in that of the elected members to whom officers are responsible. The temptation to err on the side of non-disclosure is reduced by the requirement that any document or part thereof which is withheld from publication must be identified by being marked 'Not for publication', and the reason for the claim must also be stated in writing on the copy of the report.[42]

5.47   There are similar obligations to make available to the public minutes of local authority meetings, lists of background papers supplementary to officers' reports, and at least one copy of each such paper.[43] By way of sanction, infringement of the obligations to make material available to the public is a criminal offence, punishable summarily.[44]

5.48   Although these provisions and the obligations which they impose are welcome, the limits on their scope and application are obvious. In practice, they do not appear to have achieved much in the way of creating public confidence in the stewardship of local authorities (or, for that matter, of central government) over the environment. If the amount of protest over public works, such as road and airport development schemes, is any guide, the extent of public concern, and its intensity, is, if anything, growing rather than diminishing.

---

[41]   Ibid, s 100B(1).
[42]   Ibid, s 100B(5).
[43]   Ibid, ss 100C and 100D.
[44]   Ibid, s 100H.

These general provisions apart, there are many specific statutory obligations **5.49** and duties imposed by delegated legislation which demand that landowners, developers, and others make public their intentions or past dealings with the environment. These fall most conveniently into a sort of Aristotelian categorization— obligations relating to land; to air, including fire, which for these purposes means incineration; and to water.

D. Environmental Information about Land

Town and Country Planning

One of the more striking, and probably the most commonly met, field in which **5.50** the treatment of land can impact on the environment is in the field of town and country planning. Curiously, the early town and country planning legislation made no provision for publicizing proposals to develop land. It was even possible for a prospective developer to apply for permission to develop another person's land, without the latter's knowledge. These omissions attracted criticism from the Committee on Administrative Tribunals and Enquiries (sic) (the Franks Committee) which commented:

> We regard this as unsatisfactory and recommend that owners of land and others to whom notice of a proposal to acquire land must be given under the acquisition of land procedure (such as tenants and agricultural tenants) should be informed of any third party application for planning permission in respect of that land and allowed to state their views. They should also be informed of the decision of the local planning authority and of the lodging of any appeal against that decision. This change is particularly desirable in the case of agricultural holdings since the grant of planning permission removes such statutory protection as the tenant otherwise enjoys against a notice to quit.[45]

The obvious good sense and fairness of those comments has been reflected in all **5.51** subsequent planning legislation.

Under the current legislation, the applicant for planning permission must notify **5.52** the freeholder, any tenant with more than seven years of the tenancy still to run, every agricultural tenant, and every owner of mineral rights in land in respect of which he is applying for planning permission.[46] The notice must either be given directly, or, where the owner, tenant, or owner of mineral rights cannot be found, notices must be put in a local paper circulating in the area, and by posting

---

[45] Report of the Committee on Administrative Tribunals and Enquiries, July 1957, Cm 218, para 384.
[46] Town and Country Planning Act 1990, s 65(2), (8).

a conspicuous advertisement somewhere in the parish or community in which the land is located.[47] In practice, the advertisement will almost always be displayed on the site itself.

5.53 A certificate must accompany the application for planning permission, stating that the applicant has observed the appropriate formalities.[48] It is a criminal offence to fail to comply with these requirements by issuing a certificate which purports to state that the formalities have been observed and which contains a statement known by the applicant to be false or misleading in a material particular. It is also an offence to issue such a certificate recklessly, that is, without giving thought to the accuracy of the statement or being indifferent to the issue whether the certificate is accurate or not.[49] The effect of an inaccurate certificate has been examined by the courts many times over the years, with varying results. As the law now stands, it seems that in deciding whether an inaccurate certificate invalidates the application, regard must be had to all the circumstances, including the nature of the irregularity, the identity of the applicant, the lapse of time, and the effect on the public and other parties. Errors in a certificate will not necessarily invalidate it.[50] Where, however, an applicant failed to notify the owner of the land and completed a false certificate, the latter was invalid.[51]

5.54 Each planning authority must keep a register of planning applications. This must be in two parts. The first consists of a copy of every planning application. The second is a permanent record of each application and the decision made upon it.[52] The register must be kept at the local planning authority's principal office, and be open for inspection at all reasonable hours.[53]

5.55 Certain categories of development, deemed to be especially sensitive or controversial, require special publicity. In the past, this embraced what was called 'bad neighbour development', such as public conveniences and dance halls. This classification has now been replaced by the concept of development which is sufficiently

---

[47] Town and Country Planning General Development Procedure Order 1995, Arts. 1(2) and 6.

[48] Ibid, Art. 7.

[49] Town and Country Planning Act 1990, s 65(6). As to recklessness, see *R v Caldwell* [1982] AC 341.

[50] *Main v Swansea Corporation* [1984] 49 P&CR 26.

[51] *R(Pridmore) v SalisburyDC and Another* [2004] EWHC (Admin) 2511.

[52] Town and Country Planning Act 1990, s 69; Town and Country Planning General Development Procedure Order 1995, Art. 25.

[53] Town and Country Planning Act 1990, s 69(5). In practice, this has meant that the public may examine the register during the hours during which planning authorities' offices are open for business. The Ramblers' Association has apparently complained that this is not long enough, and that the charges for copying entries in the register are too high (see Bakkenist, quoted in n1 above, at 151). It is not clear whether local government officers should have to work overtime, at the expense of council tax payers and ratepayers, and finance copying of records, in order to meet the convenience and financial demands of members of the Ramblers' Association.

important to be accompanied by an environmental statement, and which does not accord with the provisions of the relevant development plan, or would affect a footpath or bridleway.[54]

Such potentially controversial proposals must not only be publicized by way of advertisement in a local newspaper, but must also be the subject of an advertisement placed on or near the application site for not less than 21 days.[55] Other 'major developments' are also subject to special requirements as to publicity. **5.56**

For this purpose, 'major development' means the winning or working of minerals or the deposit of mineral waste; the carrying out of building or engineering operations for the purpose of or making a material change of use to the deposit of waste, or storing, treating, or processing it; the building of 10 or more dwellings, or the development of 0.5 hectares (1.2 acres approximately) of land residentially; the erection of any building with a floor space area of 1,000 square metres or more (about 13,500 square feet); and development of any kind on a site of 1 hectare (2.4 acres) or more. **5.57**

Development within these categories must be advertised by the display of site notices and by advertisement in a local newspaper, and additionally, must be notified to every adjoining owner and occupier.[56] **5.58**

Environmental impact

Obligations to publicize planning applications on these lines are of long standing and have become familiar. By contrast, a radical and dramatic change in publicity requirements was introduced by the Town and Country Planning (Assessment of Environmental Impact) Regulations 1988.[57] These were superseded by the Town and Country Planning Environmental Impact Assessment) Regulations 1999.[58] **5.59**

In essence the EIA Regulations require an applicant for planning permission for any of the prescribed categories to submit an exhaustive analysis of the environmental consequences of his proposals with the application. The categories are listed in Schedules 1 and 2 to the Regulations. Development falling within Schedule 1 must be accompanied by an environmental statement in any event. Development within Schedule 2 requires a statement if it would be likely to have **5.60**

---

[54] Town and Country Planning General Development Procedure Order 1995, Art. 8. As to environmental assessments and statements, see below.

[55] Ibid, Art. 8(3).

[56] Ibid, Art. 8(4) and (5).

[57] SI 1988/1199. Hereafter referred to for the sake of brevity as the 'EIA Regulations', that is, 'Environmental Impact Assessment' Regulations.

[58] SI 1999/293.

significant effects on the environment by virtue of matters such as its size, nature, and location.[59]

5.61 Schedule 1 developments are those with self-evident implications for the environment. They are: oil refineries; thermal and nuclear power stations; installations for the permanent storage of radioactive waste, such as that proposed at Sellafield by Nirex Ltd, and for preliminary investigation of which (not, contrary to contemporary press and other reports, a 'nuclear dump') planning permission was refused by the Secretary of State in 1997; works for the initial melting of cast iron or steel; asbestos works; chemical works in which petroleum products, sulphuric acid, nitric acid, hydrofluorides, chlorine, or fluorine are manufactured; motorways, long distance railways, and airports with runways with a minimum length of more than 2,100 metres (about 1 1/3 miles); ports and canals; incinerators and plants for the chemical treatment of special waste as defined in the Control of Pollution (Special Waste) Regulations 1981 (discussed elsewhere); and landfill sites for special waste as defined; large groundwater abstraction and recharge schemes; large water waste treatment plants; extraction of petroleum and natural gas; large dams; large pipelines; intensive pig and poultry rearing plants; pulp and paper production plants; large quarries; and petrol or chemical storage depots.

5.62 Schedule 2 developments are very many more in number, and, if anything, range even more widely. Several types of agricultural development will qualify, provided they meet the stipulations as to the potential effect on the environment. These are: water management, such as the installation of equipment for water abstractions or the creation of reservoirs; poultry and pig rearing; salmon hatcheries and farms (but not, perhaps surprisingly, similar developments for the production of trout or other fish or crustaceans); and the reclamation of land from the sea.

5.63 The extraction and treatment of a wide variety of products may also fall within Schedule 2. Examples include peat, coal, petroleum and natural gas, ores, bituminous shale, opencast mining of any mineral, such as ironstone or gypsum, and certain types of factory, such as cement works. In addition, drilling for water, drilling for geothermal purposes, and the storage of nuclear waste may qualify for inclusion in the Schedule.

5.64 Almost any development connected with the energy industry may, it seems, also be Schedule 2 development. One would expect that nuclear and fossil fuel installations, including tank farms, would qualify, as they do. So too do hydroelectric installations and wind farms.

---

[59] Ibid, reg 2(1). As described below, there is provision for resolving differences of opinion generated by the imprecision of the definition of Schedule 2 development.

Most facilities connected with the manufacture or processing of metals and glass **5.65** fall within the Schedule. Iron and steelworks, foundries, forges, smelting works, motor vehicle and aircraft factories, railway works, and shipyards are obvious candidates for inclusion in the Schedule. More obscurely, swaging by explosives and the sintering of metallic ores also qualify.[60]

In the minerals and chemical industries, coke, cement, asbestos, glass, smelting **5.66** and ceramics manufacture, all production of chemicals which does not fall within Schedule 1 qualify, provided the minimum size of installation is proposed.

The production of pesticides and pharmaceutical products, paints, varnishes, **5.67** elastomers, and peroxides are included.

Food production may also be caught, as exemplified by the inclusion of the manu- **5.68** facture of vegetable or animal oils or fats; of dairy products, confectionery, or syrup, fish meal or fish oil, and sugar; likewise brewing or malting; and abattoirs. Again, as might be anticipated, the textile, leather, wood, rubber, and paper industries qualify, as shown by the inclusion of, for example, wool scouring factories, paper, pulp, and board works, and factories where fibres are dyed, and leather is tanned or dressed.

Finally, Schedule 2 comprises a range of developments, heterogeneous and more **5.69** or less unpredictable. There is a range of infrastructure projects. They vary from building industrial estates and motorway service areas to the installation of a chairlift or cable car; from canalization to constructing a yacht marina or a motorway service area; and from a holiday village or hotel complex to a test bench for engines, turbines, or reactors. Lastly and ingloriously, there are knackers' yards.

The basis of the EIA Regulations is that a planning application which has to be **5.70** accompanied by an environmental statement may not be approved by a local planning authority or the Secretary of State for the Environment unless the required environmental information included in the statement has been taken into consideration. The applicant may submit a statement with his application, or the planning authority may decide by means of a 'screening opinion' that the application is an EIA application.[61]

In case of uncertainty whether any application falls within the EIA Regulations at **5.71** all, and, if so, which Schedule applies, the prospective applicant for planning permission may seek a determination by way of a 'scoping opinion' from the local

---

[60] According to the *Shorter Oxford Dictionary*, 'swaging' involves bending or shaping metals; while 'sintering' achieves the deposit of incrustation of deposits on the surface of rocks or other substances.
[61] Regulation 4.

planning authority, with, effectively, a right of appeal to the Secretary of State against an unacceptable determination, or failure to give a decision.[62]

5.72 The regulations ensure wide publicity for the existence and content of environmental impact assessments supporting planning applications. This applies whether the statement is submitted with the application or later.[63] Multiple copies of the statement must be supplied to the local planning authority at the application stage, and to the Secretary of State in case of an appeal, so that consultation can take place with interested bodies and parties.[64] The applicant must also make copies available for inspection by the general public.[65]

5.73 Copies of the documents generated in connection with an EIA application, and details of any decision by the Secretary of State's decision and the direction given in consequence must be placed on the planning register, and will in this way become available to the public.[66]

5.74 If the applicant for permission and the local planning authority disagree as to whether an environmental statement is needed at all, in which case the application for planning permission will not have been supported by the statement, the applicant has two, and only two, alternatives. He may accept the planning authority's view and provide a statement, or he may seek a screening direction from the Secretary of State. If he does neither within three weeks, the authority is deemed to have refused planning permission, but there is, for obvious reasons, no right of appeal to the Secretary of State under Section 78 of the Town and Country Planning Act 1990. This prevents the applicant bypassing the procedure which determines whether an environmental statement is needed.[67]

5.75 On the other hand, if an application arrives before the Secretary of State which he considers to require an environmental statement, but which is not accompanied by one, he may require the applicant to supply a statement, and is under no duty to determine the planning application unless and until the statement is received.[68]

5.76 The contents of an environmental statement are prescribed by Schedule 4. It must describe the proposed development, the site, and the nature, design, and size of the proposals, including the production processes.

---

[62] Regulation 10.
[63] Regulations 13 and 14.
[64] Regulations 13 and 16.
[65] Regulation 17.
[66] Regulations 20 and 21.
[67] Regulations 7 and 9.
[68] Regulation 8.

It must also set out the factual data necessary to identify the main effects on the **5.77** environment which are likely to arise. These will include an estimate of the residues and emissions, and an outline of the alternatives considered and rejected, with reasons. There must also be an assessment of all the direct and indirect effects of the proposal on the environment, with proposals for reducing or where possible offsetting those effects.

In the interests of the general public there must also be a summary of the state- **5.78** ment in non-technical language, and an indication of the difficulties in compiling the relevant information.

In most cases, it will be apparent at the outline planning application stage whether **5.79** or not an environmental statement is needed. In some instances it may only become clear later that there will be significant impacts on the environment, in which case a statement may have to be submitted in support of an application for approval of reserved matters.[69]

Appeals under the Town and Country Planning Acts

No less important in disseminating information about town and country plan- **5.80** ning proposals is the appeals procedure. The same publicity has to be given to an appeal as to a planning application, and, where a local planning authority has not carried out its duties as to publicizing the classes of development which need special treatment under the Town and Country Planning General Development Procedure Order 1995 at the application stage, it must make the omission good if the applicant appeals or the Secretary of State calls the application in for his own decision.[70]

Once an appeal has been validly lodged, either the applicant (who alone is entitled **5.81** to appeal against a refusal of planning permission or failure to give notice of a decision) or the local planning authority, has the right to insist that the appeal shall be conducted by way of an inquiry.[71] In practice relatively few appeals go to inquiry, the majority (about 85%) being dealt with by way of written representation or informal hearing. If either of the latter procedures is adopted, third parties and the general public will have only a limited right to participate in the proceedings, which will be conducted by the main parties. However, the requirement that publicity must be given to the appeal should at least ensure that those with an interest

---

[69] *R v Bromley LBC ex.p Barker* [2006] 3 WLR 1209 (HL).
[70] Town and Country Planning General Development Procedure Order 1995, Art. 9.
[71] Town and Country Planning Act 1990, s 79(2).

in the matter can make their views known to the Inspector who conducts the appeal by letter.[72]

5.82 By contrast, if the appeal is conducted by way of inquiry, the opportunity for public involvement is for practical purposes unlimited. While the appellant, the local planning authority, and statutory consultees[73] are entitled to appear, call evidence, and address the Inspector as of right, others may do so only to the extent allowed by the Inspector. He may also, in theory at least, refuse to permit the giving of evidence, cross-examination, and the presentation of other material, including making speeches, which he considers to be irrelevant or repetitious.[74]

5.83 This does not in practice prevent anyone and everyone who wishes to take part in an inquiry from saying what they wish as often as suits them, and no matter how many times it may have been said before, since Inspectors are, understandably, reluctant to prevent the citizenry playing its full part in the inquiry process. In the circumstances, the appeals procedure gives the general public the best opportunity of influencing the planning process, and of ventilating concern about the environmental effects of development proposals. This is because Inspectors and the Secretary of State are less likely to be influenced by local and parochial factors than members of local planning authorities.

Waste

5.84 The elaborate statutory code which regulates the production, movement, treatment, and disposal of waste under Part II of the Environmental Protection Act 1990 is dealt with fully elsewhere. For present purposes it is enough to discuss the provisions for keeping records and for making such records available to the public which the code lays down.

5.85 Under the Act of 1990, two distinct types of register must be maintained. First, waste regulation authorities (now the Environment Agency, by virtue of the Environment Act 1995) and all persons who import, export, produce, keep, treat, or dispose of waste or who deliver waste which is inherently dangerous or difficult to treat ('special waste'), must keep records and make them available to the Environment Agency.[75]

---

[72] In England, the Inspectorate is at Room 3/01 Kite Wing, Temple Quay House, 2 The Square, Temple Quay, Bristol BS1 6PN; in Wales, at Crown Buildings, Cathays Park, Cardiff CF10 3NQ. In the age of information technology, contact can be made by facsimile or e-mail.

[73] As to whom, see the Town and Country Planning (Inquiries Procedure) Rules 2000, SI 2000/1624, and the Town and Country Planning (Determination of Appeals by Inspectors) (Inquiries Procedure Rules) 2000, SI 2000/1625.

[74] Ibid, rr 14 and 15 respectively.

[75] EPA 1990, s 62(2)(e). For the precise definition of special waste, see Chapter 7.

Second, the Environment Agency has a duty to maintain a register containing **5.86**
details of licences which it has granted, or which were granted by waste regulation
authorities before 1 April 1996; of applications for licences before the Agency;
applications for the modification of licences; notices which have been issued
which modify, revoke, or suspend licences; other details which affect the terms or
validity of licences; convictions of licence holders; directions given by the Secretary
of State for the Environment; and any other matters prescribed for the purpose by
the Secretary of State.[76] The Secretary of State has exercised this latter power in the
Waste Management Licensing Regulations 1994.[77]

These matters consist of a long list of particulars which must be included in the **5.87**
public registers kept by waste regulation authorities (or, as now, the Environment
Agency), and a rather shorter list of types of information which must be excluded
or removed from the register. Particulars of current or recently current waste management licences together with associated working plans must be included. The
paradoxically named 'recently current' licences are those which have expired
within twelve months of the relevant date, and the phrase has a similar meaning
where it appears elsewhere in the Regulations.[78]

Current and recently current applications for new licences, and for transfer or **5.88**
modification of existing licences, must be recorded, together with details of supporting documents, written representations which have been considered, decisions of the Secretary of State on appeal, decisions rejecting licence applications,
and of emergencies resulting in the postponement of references under Section 37
of the Environment Protection Act 1990.

There is obvious danger that the volume of information which must be included **5.89**
in a register will be such that it will overwhelm both those charged with maintaining the register and those wishing to use it. This conclusion is reinforced by considering the other material which has to be included; details of modifications,
revocation, and suspension of licences, and of requirements imposed on licence
holders; even notices of appeal against decisions of the Agency.

The register must also include details of convictions of licence holders under Part II **5.90**
of the 1990 Act; reports produced under that Part of the Act, and of correspondence relating to river purification; monitoring information; directions given by
the Secretary of State relating to such matters as variation, suspension, or modification of licences, supervision of licensed activity, waste disposal plans, removal of
fly-tipped or other illegally deposited waste, or the removal of entries from the register; details of special waste production, including amounts and type; applications to

---

[76] Ibid, s 64.
[77] SI 1994/1056.
[78] Ibid, reg 10(1)(a) and 10(4).

surrender licences with the supporting documentation and the material thrown up by the application; Inspectors' reports; the date of any inspection made following the exercise of powers of entry, the information obtained, and the action taken; even whether or not the conditions attached to a waste management licence have been complied with where information is excluded from the register because of commercial confidentiality or for some other reason.[79] All must be included.

5.91 The size and complexity of the register are awe-inspiring, and raise the question whether its usefulness will be impaired as a result. This state of affairs is not improved by the requirement which the Regulations impose on each waste collection authority to record details of waste management licences relating to the treatment, keeping, or disposal of controlled waste, together with notices relating to the modification, suspension, or revocation of them.[80]

5.92 As already noted, the list of relaxations of the duty to keep information is shorter. There is no obligation to keep records of information relating to prosecutions, actual or prospective.[81] The Environment Agency and waste collection authorities are also not required to keep monitoring information for more than four years, or to keep records of superseded information for more than four years after it has ceased to be relevant.[82] No doubt this lightening of the burden will be much welcomed by the relevant authorities and those regulated by them.

Contamination

5.93 As is pointed out elsewhere, the code relating to the prevention and decontamination (called 'remediation' in the relevant statutory provisions) of land is now enshrined in Part IIA of the Environmental Protection Act 1990, as amended by the Environment Act 1995. The substantive provisions of that code are not material for present purposes, and are also dealt with elsewhere. Information about contaminated land is obtainable by means of a system of registration, not unlike that relating to waste, which has already been described. This too is dealt with in Part IIA of the 1990 Act.

5.94 The Secretary of State has made the Contaminated Land Regulations 2006,[83] which control, among other things, the publicity required for contaminated land.

On lodging an appeal to the Secretary of State against a remediation notice the appellant must serve copies of the notice on the enforcing authority, on any person named in the notice as an 'appropriate person' (a term of art, the meaning of

---

[79] Ibid, reg 10(1).
[80] Ibid, reg 10(3).
[81] Ibid, reg 11(1).
[82] Ibid, reg 11(2).
[83] SI 2006/1380.

which is described in Chapter 13), on the owner of all or part of the land to which the notice relates, and on any person who is not named as an appropriate person in the remediation notice, but so identified in the notice of appeal.[84]

If a hearing or inquiry is held into the appeal the parties directly affected are enti- **5.95** tled to be heard, as is any other person whom the Inspector conducting the proceedings permits. Permission must not be unreasonably withheld.[85]

The Secretary of State must notify the appellant of his decision on the appeal, and **5.96** send a copy of the notice to any person on whom the appellant was required to serve notice of the appeal.[86]

Similar requirements for publicity apply where the Secretary of State modifies a **5.97** remediation notice so as to make it less favourable to an appellant or any appropriate person.[87]

Registers of contaminated land

The obligation to maintain registers rests on enforcing authorities—local authori- **5.98** ties where the land is 'ordinarily' contaminated, and the Environment Agency in respect of special sites.[88] The authority must maintain at its principal office, if it is a local authority, or at an area office if it is the Environment Agency, a register.

The register must contain details concerning: remediation notices; statements **5.99** and declarations which it has issued and appeals against them; charging notices requiring payment of expenses which it has incurred in carrying out remediation works and appeals against them; notices served in respect of special sites; notices claiming what has been done by way of remediation in relation to contaminated or special sites served by the recipients of remediation notices; notices ending the designation of any land as a special site; and of convictions for offences committed in relation to contaminated land.[89]

In addition, the register must contain a description of the harm to controlled **5.100** waters which caused the land to be designated as contaminated; the contaminating substances; the current use; and what each appropriate person has to do by way of remediation; and the date of the remediation notice.[90]

However, it should be noted that the entry in the register of notices given by the **5.101** recipients of remediation notices or statements does no more than record the fact

---

[84] Regulation 8.
[85] Regulation 9.
[86] Regulation 10.
[87] Regulation 11.
[88] EPA 1990, s 78A(9).
[89] Ibid, s 78R(1); Regulation 13.
[90] Ibid; Schedule 3 to the Regulations.

that such notices have been given, and that the representations contained in them have been made. There is no guarantee or representation by the enforcing authority that the assertions are correct, or that further enforcement action will not necessarily be taken against the recipient of the enforcing authority's notice or statement.[91]

5.102 Where the enforcing authority makes an entry in its register in respect of land which is in the area of another authority—as, for example, where the Environment Agency does so in respect of a special site, or where a local authority takes action in respect of contaminated land which lies within the jurisdiction of another local authority but is thought to be spreading contamination—then the authority within whose area the land lies must be informed.[92]

5.103 The local authority which receives notification from another enforcing authority in the circumstances described must make the appropriate entry in its own register.[93] If information is excluded from the register because it is commercially confidential, then the existence of that information must be recorded in the register (although not, of course, anything more about it).[94] This provision was inserted in an attempt to alleviate any blighting of contaminated land which might be created by the mere fact that it was the subject of an entry in a contaminated land register kept under the Act. However, one may question whether a record of the fact that the owner of allegedly contaminated land has protested about its designation as such, or claims to have taken steps to improve matters, would have much ameliorative effect in practice.

5.104 Importantly, each registering authority is under a duty to ensure that its register is available for inspection at all reasonable times, free of charge, and that copies of entries may be made on payment of a reasonable charge.[95]

5.105 Historically there has been controversy as to the application in practice of these injunctions. Pressure groups have tried to argue, in effect, that the duty to make registers available at all reasonable times means that this should be at times which their members find convenient, and not necessarily during conventional office hours. Likewise, it has been asserted that a 'reasonable' charge is one which the person paying finds reasonable. Neither proposition has yet been tested in the courts, but it would be surprising if these contentions found favour there.

---

[91] Ibid, s 78R(3).
[92] Ibid, s 78R(4) and (5).
[93] Ibid, s 78R(6).
[94] Ibid, s 78R(7).
[95] Ibid, s 78R(8).

Another potential source of dispute is the concession which Parliament has made, **5.106** that the registers may be kept in any form.[96] Given the very large amounts of information which are bound to end up on the contaminated land registers, there are obvious advantages in the use of modern information technology as a means of storing and retrieving it. It remains to be seen whether interest groups will complain that they are prejudiced because of their inability to make use of sophisticated retrieval systems.

Enforcing authorities will need to proceed with care, however. Judicial authority **5.107** has established that, at least for the purposes of the town and country planning legislation, local planning authorities are obliged to make information available not only to applicants for planning permission but also to third parties in time for the material to be properly considered, and to give enough time for a mature response to be formulated.

An application to resume working of a long-disused quarry was made to a plan- **5.108** ning authority, and brought predictable opposition from local residents and community organizations. The latter had a statutory right to see and respond to the documents submitted by the quarry operator in support of its application. After an initial refusal and considerable pressure the planning authority supplied the documents to the residents five days before a committee was due to consider their reaction to the application, and twelve days before the deadline for taking a decision on the application expired. With great difficulty, the residents, through their advisers, prepared and lodged a response to the application but, due, it was said, to lack of time, the officers did not lay this material before their elected members. Instead, they purported to summarize the effect of the objections, stating only that these did not change the views already put by the officers, which were in essence adverse to the objectors' case.

It is not surprising that the High Court quashed the decision of the planning **5.109** authority on the ground that there had been failure to give an adequate opportunity to make representations, and failure properly to consider those representations which had been made. Technically, there had been a breach of the audi alteram partem principle, and failure to take account of a material consideration.[97]

While it is always dangerous to apply rules laid down for the purposes of one area **5.110** of statutory control to those of another, the regulation of land use planning and that of environmental protection are sufficiently similar and closely integrated to

---

[96] Ibid, s 78R(9).
[97] The latter amounting to breach of the *Wednesbury* principles (see *Associated Provincial Picture Houses v Wednesbury Corporation* [1948] 1 KB 223). The case was *R v Rochdale MBC, ex p Brown* [1997] Env LR 100.

make it likely that the same approach would be adopted to the keeping of registers of contaminated land or, for that matter, of other registers required by the environmental protection legislation.

5.111 Moreover, as information technology becomes progressively more sophisticated and easy to use, authorities will almost certainly find it increasingly difficult to explain failure to provide the public with information to which it is entitled. Conversely, the proliferation of information networks may open up a world where any owner of a personal computer can have access to a register of environmental or other information at any time.[98]

5.112 As with other registers of environmental information, there is a prohibition on including in a register any information which, in the opinion of the Secretary of State, would be contrary to the interests of national security.[99] This exemption could give rise to argument as to the effect of any direction given by the Secretary of State giving effect to this exception to the general rule. There is an obvious analogy to certificates of public interest immunity and claims of privilege which have long been litigated in the courts and which it is not appropriate to discuss here.[100]

5.113 A person who wishes to claim that information which might otherwise appear on a register should not do so because its presence there would be contrary to the interests of national security may give notice to the Secretary of State of his claim. At the same time he must notify the enforcing authority that he has done so, whereupon no information which is the subject of the notice to the Secretary of State is to be put on the register until the Secretary of State has given his ruling.[101]

5.114 The Secretary of State has power to direct enforcing authorities that specific items of information, or descriptions of information which are to be referred to him for determination, shall be excluded from contaminated land registers, and, naturally, no information which falls within the latter category may be put on a register until he has ruled that it may appear there. For obvious reasons, enforcing authorities are also required to notify the Secretary of State of any information which they exclude from a register because of a direction which he has given.[102]

---

[98] Whether this is to be regarded as a desirable objective is perhaps a matter for debate.

[99] EPA 1990, s 78S(1).

[100] The long battle between the subject and the executive over what was once 'Crown privilege', now public interest immunity, is covered in all works on administrative law. On past form, it would cause no surprise were the Secretary of State, initially at least, to assert that any ruling by him was wholly immune from challenge, and that no reasons to justify it or documents to support it need be vouchsafed, in the interests of the efficient functioning of the public service.

[101] EPA 1990, s 78S(4).

[102] Ibid, s 78S(3) and (4).

A second exemption from the obligation to record material on contaminated land **5.115**
registers arises where issues of commercial confidentiality are involved. Such
information may only appear on a register if the individual or the person carrying
on the business to which the information relates gives his agreement.[103] However,
this exemption can be conferred only if the enforcing authority or Secretary of
State so directs. For this purpose information is commercially confidential if its
being contained in the register would prejudice to an unreasonable degree the
commercial interests of an individual.[104]

In most cases the procedure to be followed will begin with a claim by the individ- **5.116**
ual or the business concerned that the information supplied is confidential as
defined. It will then be the duty of the authority to decide whether the information appears to fall within the section, and if so, to inform the supplier that it is
proposed to include the information in the register, and to give an opportunity to
make representations justifying any objection to the inclusion.[105]

While the section formally provides that the initial decision is that of the enforcing **5.117**
authority, in practice authorities are unlikely to be alive to factors which make
industrial processes or other commercial activities sensitive. The wise individual or
business will therefore take the initiative by alerting the authority to the possibility
of a claim of confidentiality when the information is supplied in the first place.

If the authority determines that the information is not confidential, the supplier **5.118**
may appeal against that determination to the Secretary of State within 21 days,
and no entry is made in the register pending the determination of the appeal.[106]
The appeal may be by way of written representations or, if either party wishes, by
private hearing. Again, for obvious reasons, there is no provision for appeal by way
of public inquiry.[107] If information is determined to be confidential it is treated as
such and excluded from the register for an initial period of four years, but the supplier may apply at the end of that period to the enforcing authority for an extension of the exclusion period. In that event the procedure of determination and
appeal will apply again.[108]

Publicity for the state of land contamination over the country as a whole may be **5.119**
achieved by the publication of reports by the Environment Agency, with equivalent provisions for Scotland. The Agency is under a duty to publish reports from
time to time, or as directed by the Secretary of State, on the state of contaminated

---

[103] Ibid, s 78T(1).
[104] Ibid, s 78T(10).
[105] Ibid, 78T(2).
[106] Ibid, s 78T(3).
[107] Ibid, s 78T(4).
[108] Ibid, s 78T(8).

land in England and Wales. It may require a local authority to supply information needed to prepare the report, and which the local authority might reasonably have been expected to obtain.

5.120 Surprisingly perhaps, there is no period stipulated during which the Agency reports have to be prepared, and no requirement as to their frequency; nor is there any sanction imposed for failure to prepare a report or for failure by a local authority to supply information if required to do so.[109] The intention must have been that discharge of these functions will be enforced in the last resort by action for judicial review by way of mandamus.

E. Information about Air Pollution

5.121 Contamination of land will not, of course, occur only by reason of the processes which attract the operation of Part IIA of the Environmental Protection Act 1990. Another source of pollution, which has given rise to consistent and growing public disquiet, is contamination through pesticides; this could potentially cause pollution of the air, and there has been widespread concern that some can be transmitted directly to man, even though there may be little or no lasting pollution of the atmosphere or the earth.

5.122 The use of pesticides is controlled by the Control of Pesticides Regulations 1986,[110] made under powers conferred by the Food and Environment Protection Act 1985. The substance of the Regulations need not be considered in any detail here. They regulate the advertising, sale, supply, storage, and use of pesticides. All these activities are subject to the consent of the Minister of Agriculture, who may impose conditions upon the applicant. Unusually, the Regulations enable, without requiring, the Minister to make available to any person on request, upon conditions which may be determined, an evaluation of the pesticide to which the approval was given, or, where conditions were imposed on the approval, the conditions were amended.[111]

5.123 The definition of an evaluation is that it need only be in writing, and have been examined by the Minister in the course of his appraisal of the pesticide to which approval was sought. The Regulations do not specify by whom the evaluation need have been made, nor do they require that the Minister shall have given weight to it. Significantly, also, there is no obligation on the Minister to make the

---

[109] Ibid, s 78U.
[110] SI 1986/1510.
[111] Ibid, reg 8.

evaluation available. The right to information is therefore strictly limited, but may, in some circumstances, be of help to a member of the public.

Even so, the use which can be made of the evaluation, and of any other material **5.124** which may be disclosed under the Regulations, is also limited. The person receiving the information may not publish it without the Minister's consent, and may not in any event make any commercial use of what has been disclosed.[112] This would, no doubt, preclude the use of the information in order to compete commercially with the party who had made it available to the Minister. It is less clear whether, for example, a party who claimed that his land or animals, kept for commercial purposes, had been damaged by pesticides would be able to make use of the evaluation and other material in support of that claim. This is no fanciful example, since the Control of Pesticides Regulations impose stringent controls over the height at which aircraft spraying pesticides may fly, distinguishing between occupied buildings, children's playgrounds, sports grounds, and buildings containing livestock, on the one hand, and other classes of land and buildings on the other.[113] The inference, supported by practical experience, is that the use of pesticides is sufficiently dangerous to carry a risk to health and property, and that persons whose health or property have been affected in circumstances which raise suspicion that pesticides might be the cause, will be minded to take legal action against the manufacturer or the person who applied the pesticide in question.

F. Information about Water

The registers

The primary source of control over the provision and publication of information **5.125** about the condition of inland waters and watercourses is the Water Resources Act 1991. As with many other codes of environmental protection, the tool used to protect the quality of water and watercourses is the register. The Environment Agency is required to keep registers relating to notices of water quality objectives or other notices which it has served under Section 83 of the Water Resources Act, which would include notices varying the objectives which the Secretary of State has specified.[114] The registers will also record applications for discharge consents under the Act, and records of effluent samples taken by the Agency for the

---

[112] Ibid, reg 8(4). Those who espouse the conspiracy theory of government will find ample opportunity for ministerial cover-up in these restrictions on the availability of information and the use which can be made of it.

[113] Ibid, Sch 4.

[114] WRA 1991, s 190(1).

purposes of any of the water pollution provisions of the Act.[115] As might be expected, the register must also contain details of information produced by analysis of the samples, and of the results of analysing samples of water or effluent taken by persons other than the Agency. This could impose heavy burdens on those charged with compiling the registers, since the potential takers of samples are legion; the list would include all water companies, and almost anyone with an interest in maintaining the purity of waters, from owners of fishing rights and fish farmers to rowing club coaches concerned that their crews shall not be poisoned if their boats should sink, and windsurfers with similar anxieties for themselves. Applications for variation of discharge consents must be recorded in the registers, as must enforcement notices requiring compliance with the terms of discharge consents, and details of convictions of people failing to comply with conditions attached to discharge consents. The registers must also give details of appeals against the refusal of discharge consents and of revocations of consents, and of other appeals, works notices, and convictions under the Act. The list ends with two virtually limitless categories of information—the register must contain details of information obtained or supplied in pursuance of conditions of discharge consents, and of such other matters relating to the quality of water or pollution of water as the Secretary of State may prescribe.[116]

The content of the registers

5.126 The previous regime was replaced and strengthened by the Control of Pollution (Applications, Appeals, and Registers) Regulations 1996.[117] The Regulations set out two fundamental objectives; first, that the information shall be recorded in such a way that it can be related to an identifiable place and is widely publicized, and second, that the information shall appear on the register for an initial period of five years, and thereafter shall be kept as long as necessary to the exercise of the Environment Agency's functions in respect of water pollution.[118]

5.127 The first objective is secured by a requirement that applications for discharge consents must be advertised in local papers and in the *London Gazette* for 28 days before any decision is taken. The Environment Agency may dispense with the need for advertisement on the grounds of national security, or where it considers that there will be no appreciable effect on controlled waters.[119]

---

[115] Ibid. The substantive provisions as to water pollution and its prevention are considered elsewhere.

[116] Ibid.

[117] SI, 1996/ 2971.

[118] Ibid, reg 3.

[119] Regulations 2–4.

Widespread consultation is mandatory. All local authorities, water undertakers, **5.128** responsible Ministers, harbour authorities, and fisheries committees must be consulted.[120]

If there is an appeal against a refusal of consent the appellant must notify the **5.129** Environment Agency, which in turn must inform any person likely to have an interest in the outcome, and any person who made representations at the application stage.[121] These parties are entitled to appear and be heard if there is a hearing into the appeal, and must be given a copy of the decision.[122]

The Regulations are otherwise concerned to spell out the details of the informa- **5.130** tion to be included in the registers which the Environment Agency keeps. Thus entries in the register of notices relating to water quality objectives served under Section 105 of the Water Resources Act 1991 must include the date of the notice, the waters to which the notice relates, the classification applicable to those waters, and the date specified in relation to that classification.

Where the entry concerns a notice served by the Secretary of State in respect of water quality objectives, the proposal made by him must be recorded, and the period for making objections or representations must be stated.[123] With appropriate amendments, the same details must be given of applications for discharge and other consents, of the consents themselves, and of the conditions subject to which the consents were granted. In addition the name of the applicant for consent must appear in the register, and the date on which it came into force.[124]

The importance attached to the ability to discover where the entry in question **5.131** applies appears in the requirements as to the details of samples of effluent and water. There is, accordingly, an express duty on the Agency to include an entry showing where the sample was taken, and, as might be expected, a requirement to enter the results of the analysis of any sample taken.[125]

Registers kept under the 1996 Regulations must also contain comprehensive **5.132** records of all relevant matters relating to discharge consents. This duty falls on the Environment Agency.[126]

---

[120] Regulation 5.
[121] Regulations 9 and 10.
[122] Regulations 12 and 13.
[123] Ibid, reg 4.
[124] Ibid, regs 5 and 6.
[125] Ibid, reg 7. There is an additional requirement that entries shall appear in the register promptly. The Environment Agency must enter the results of its own analyses within two months of the date when the sample was taken, and must enter the results of other analyses within 28 days of receiving the results. Other particulars relating to samples must be entered as soon as possible.
[126] Regulation 15.

5.133 Where the Agency requires works to be carried out in order to avoid the threat of potential pollution of waters, there are similar rights of appeal with the same publicity requirements as apply to appeals in respect of discharge consents. The registers kept by the Agency must contain similar details of the proceedings.[127]

Integrated pollution control publicity

5.134 This is now regulated by the Pollution Prevention and Control Act 1999 and the Pollution Prevention and Control Regulations 2000.[128] Information and publicity are covered by Regulations 28–31.

5.135 The Secretary of State has power to require the Environment Agency, any local authority or any person, as the case may be, to report to him on the discharge of their functions and to provide information as directed by him in a notice.[129]

5.136 Each regulator (either the Agency or a local authority) must keep a register containing the information prescribed in Schedule 2 to the Regulations.[130] The registers must contain particulars of the documentation relating to applications for and the issue of permits under the Act, of convictions for and cautions given for offences, monitoring information, waste management and incineration, and fees paid in connection with these matters.

5.137 As with discharge consents for inland waters, monitoring information is to be removed after a prescribed period (in this instance, four years) after entry on the register, or after it has been superseded by later material.[131] Details of convictions and cautions are removed after five years.[132]

Gathering information

5.138 Partly in order to enable the Environment Agency to compile the registers required by the Water Resources Act 1991, and partly in order to assist in the task of ensuring that waters and groundwater are not polluted, the Agency and the responsible Ministers have wide powers to demand information, advice, and assistance from the public at large.

5.139 Understandably, but perhaps superfluously, the Environment Agency is invested with a duty to give the Secretary of State all advice and assistance which appears to it to be appropriate for facilitating the discharge of his functions in respect of

---

[127] Anti-Pollution Works Regulations 1999. SI 1999/1006.
[128] SI 2000/1973.
[129] Regulation 28.
[130] Regulation 29.
[131] Schedule 9, paragraph 4.
[132] Ibid, paragraph 5.

water pollution.[133] A more wide-reaching provision empowers the Environment Agency and either the Secretary of State or the Minister of Agriculture to serve notice on any person requiring the supply of information reasonably required for the purpose of carrying out any of their functions relating to water pollution under the Act.[134]

This power is not altogether unprecedented. There have long been powers to req- **5.140** uisition information as to the ownership of and interests in land as a preliminary to the taking of enforcement action under the town and country planning legislation. However, the power to demand the provision of information for the purposes of the discharge of any function under a far-reaching Act of Parliament is unusual. Although the Water Resources Act made provision for the Secretary of State or the Minister of Agriculture to restrict the categories of information which might be required under the Act, and to determine the form in which the information was to be supplied, these powers have not been exercised. Within the framework of the legislation, therefore, the power to require the supply of information is unlimited.[135]

In the usual way, the Act makes it a criminal offence to fail to supply information **5.141** which may be demanded, with a statutory maximum fine on summary conviction, and an unlimited fine or a maximum of two years' imprisonment on conviction on indictment.[136] The breadth of the powers given to the regulatory authorities suggests that Parliament attaches great importance to the maintenance and improvement of the quality of waters and groundwater. This should cause no surprise in the light of recent history, and in particular of the prominence given to reports of water pollution both at sea and inland.

The existence of the power to require the provision of information is a reminder **5.142** of the principle that the dissemination of information about the environment is a bilateral process, involving obligations upon the subject as much as on regulatory bodies which have a duty to keep registers and to make their contents available to the public.

A decision of the Court of Appeal under Part II of the Environmental Protection **5.143** Act 1990 clarifying the obligations which rest upon a person to provide factual information under that statute, may be applicable to requisitions under other parts of the environmental protection legislation as a whole.

Part II of the Act of 1990 regulates the treatment and disposal of waste, including **5.144** clinical waste originating in hospitals and similar institutions. Inspectors employed

---

[133] WRA 1991, s 202(1).
[134] Ibid, s 202(2).
[135] Ibid, s 202(3).
[136] Ibid, s 202(4).

by the relevant local authority became aware of the presence of lorry trailers and roll-on roll-off containers containing clinical waste, such as human tissue, blood, body fluids, drugs, syringes, swabs, and placenta on land let to a waste disposal company and, on separate occasions, of lorry trailers in a transport cafe car park and of a warehouse let to the same company, all of which were full of plastic bags and boxes also containing the same kind of waste. In all there was about 100 tons of the waste, none of which was, naturally, the subject of a waste disposal licence of any kind. These facts amounted to clear and flagrant breaches of the code of waste regulation and disposal laid down in Part II of the 1990 Act.

5.145 The authority incurred expense in removing the waste, and was concerned to discover where the waste had come from, whether there were other places where the waste had been dumped, and to identify anyone who had been involved in moving it. (There was obvious danger to the health of such persons.) The authority therefore served requisitions for information on all these matters, which the company refused or failed to answer. The explanation or excuse was that answering the requisitions might incriminate it, and that the power to issue requisitions could in any event only be used against the holders of licences issued under the Act. The Court of Appeal had little difficulty in rejecting these contentions, because the power in Part II of the Act of 1990, like that in Section 202 of the Water Resources Act 1991, may be exercised against 'any person'. That, the court held, meant what it said, and it also ruled that there is no privilege against self-incrimination in answering requisitions, which may be issued whatever the circumstances.[137]

5.146 The good sense of that decision is clear. It would defeat the underlying objective of the legislation, which is the protection of the public and the environment from the dangers inherent in waste, and in particular in fly-tipping, to have held otherwise. If a polluter, no matter how unmeritorious, could escape the obligation to supply information needed by a regulator merely because he had neglected or refused to bring himself within the system by obtaining a waste licence, the law would obviously be defective. Moreover, the task of the authority would be made much more difficult than it already was if the polluter could deprive it of the opportunity to glean much-needed information merely because he might bring a well-deserved prosecution upon himself.

5.147 It is likely that the same approach would be followed in the event of the provisions of the Water Resources Act being tested in the same way. The judgment has been criticized for removing the right to silence in the same way that persons suspected of serious frauds and of certain drugs offences have no right to escape from incriminating themselves by refusing to answer questions. Whether this was the

---

[137] *R v Hertfordshire County Council, ex p Green Environmental Industries and another* [1997] Env LR 114.

conscious intention or not is a matter of conjecture; arguably, the potential for harm is, in different ways, as great in all three cases, and the grant of wide powers of inquisition to the Environment Agency can be justified on this ground alone.

Publicity

As well as having a duty to collect and record information the Environment **5.148** Agency is also under a duty to disseminate it. It must provide water undertakers with all information relating to their functions as may be reasonably requested.[138] The obligation applies to information about the quality of controlled waters or any other waters, and about any incident in which poisonous, noxious, or polluting matter has entered waters, whether controlled or not.[139] The information must be provided free of charge, and take such form as the undertaker may reasonably require. The water undertakers have a reciprocal duty to supply information which the Environment Agency reasonably requires for the purposes of any of its functions. The Secretary of State can enforce performance of their duties by water authorities; the Environment Agency having no power to do so.[140]

There is a general exclusion from the duty to disclose information obtained under **5.149** the Water Resources Act where commercial confidentiality is involved. The consent of an individual or manager of a business must be given for the disclosure of such information, subject to a long list of exceptions.[141]

Most are concerned with information obtained by bodies or individuals for the **5.150** purposes of the discharge of their functions under the Water Resources Act or the Water Industry Act 1991. By this token, information obtained by the Environment Agency, the Secretary of State, the Minister of Agriculture, the Director General of Water Services, the Monopolies Commission, a local authority, water and sewerage undertakers, and Inspectors appointed under the two statutes is not exempt from disclosure. The same is true of financial information supplied under the Acts, for the purposes of the Financial Services Act 1986 and, in cases of insolvency, under the Insolvency Act 1986, and of information required in order to enable the Comptroller and Auditor General to carry out his auditing and advisory functions.

Material relevant to civil or criminal proceedings is also not protected from disclo- **5.151** sure.[142] Furthermore, the Environment Agency, the Director General of Water Services, customer service committees, and the Monopolies Commission are free

---

[138] WRA 1991, s 203(1).
[139] Ibid, s 203(6).
[140] Ibid, s 203(3)–(5).
[141] Ibid, s 204(1).
[142] Ibid, s 204(2).

to include information in their reports even though it might otherwise be regarded as commercially confidential.[143]

5.152 The duties of disclosure and of confidentiality are enforceable by the sanction of criminal prosecution in the event of infringement, or for making false or reckless statements for the purposes of the Act.[144] Although the latter offences might be thought to be akin to perjury, the statute recognizes that most will not be made under oath, and the penalty, even for conviction on indictment, is a fine, with no provision for imprisonment.[145]

G. Information about Radioactivity

Nuclear installations

5.153 Nuclear power requires special consideration, since it is capable of affecting land, the atmosphere, water, and human health. That said, the requirements for publicity and the keeping of records of radioactive processes and applications follow the form of most other environmental information procedures.

5.154 Under the Nuclear Installations Act 1965, the responsible Minister, being the Secretary of State for Trade and Industry, must keep a list of every site in respect of which a nuclear site licence has been granted, authorizing the use of radioactive material. The list must include a map or maps showing the position and limits of the site, and must be available for inspection by the public. The Secretary of State must publish the arrangements made for public inspection of the list. The duty to keep the record is much more extensive than that imposed by other parts of the environmental protection legislation—the entry must remain in the list until thirty years after the last licence permitting nuclear activity on the site has expired.[146]

5.155 Another indication of the importance attached to mishaps or more serious events involving nuclear power appears in the rules governing the registration requirements in the event of a nuclear occurrence. Where an occurrence which might involve damage to persons or property takes place, and is attributable wholly or in part to radioactive materials, the Minister concerned may make an order providing for details of any person who was within a prescribed area at the time of the

---

[143] Ibid, s 204(4). The Secretary of State has power to extend the categories of exempted matters by order subject to negative resolution of the House of Commons (ibid, s 204(5)).

[144] Ibid, s 206 and s 205(6).

[145] This may be contrasted with convictions for perjury, where the Court of Appeal has indicated that, in all but the rarest cases, the guilty may expect a sentence of immediate imprisonment (see *R v Hall* [1982] 4 Cr App R 153).

[146] Nuclear Installations Act 1965, s 6.

incident to be recorded. The order must be made by statutory instrument and laid before Parliament, showing that the information is not to be treated as a mere piece of routine information gathering.

The intention seems to have been that Parliament shall be informed about all persons who might have been exposed to radiation, and that there shall be records kept about them so that the state of their health and their later histories can be verified. The duty to record information about dangerous incidents involving radioactivity goes further. Where an incident creating a risk of injury to health or damage to property occurs on a licensed nuclear site or in the course of carriage of nuclear matter where there is a duty to prevent the happening of such an event, the licensee or carrier must report the occurrence to the Health and Safety Executive.[147] It is an offence to fail to report the matter. **5.156**

An inspector may be directed to make a report on the occurrence, and this may be published to the extent that it is not inconsistent with the demands of national security to do so. To that end, the Secretary of State may direct that an inquiry shall be held, and this must be held in public unless the requirements of national security make it expedient to hold all or part of the inquiry in private.[148] **5.157**

Other premises

The Nuclear Installations Act 1965 applies not only to premises where one might imagine that very large amounts of radioactive material are kept and used. The law goes further, and requires all users and all premises where radioactive materials are kept to be registered and made the subject of some publicity. **5.158**

No person is entitled to keep, use, or to cause or permit any radioactive material to be kept or used on any premises unless he is registered, exempt from registration, or the material is mobile radioactive apparatus (such as an X-ray machine) which itself is registered or exempt from registration under the Radioactive Substances Act 1993.[149] This means that all laboratories and hospitals which use radioactive substances will need to be registered under the Act. **5.159**

Registration is achieved by applying to the Environment Agency, specifying the premises concerned, the undertaking which uses the premises, a description of the radioactive material which will be kept or used on the premises, and the way in which it will be used.[150] The Agency must send a copy of the application to every local authority within whose area the premises are located, and, at least by necessary **5.160**

---

[147] Ibid, s 22(1) and (2). Nuclear Installations (Dangerous Occurrences) Regulations 1965, SI 1965/1824.
[148] Ibid, s 22(4) and (5).
[149] Ibid, s 6.
[150] Ibid, s 7.

implication, take account of any representations on the application which the authority may choose to make.[151] The Agency may grant or refuse the application, or, if it fails to give notice of its decision within the prescribed period of two months, the applicant may treat it as refused. In that event there is a right of appeal to the Secretary of State.[152]

5.161 If it authorizes the use of radioactive material the Agency may impose conditions including requirements as to alterations to any part of the premises, or in respect of any apparatus, equipment, or appliance used there. The conditions may also require the operator to supply information as to the removal of radioactive material, or prohibit the sale or supply of that material from the premises unless prescribed labels or other marks are displayed on it.[153]

5.162 When the Environment Agency registers a person in respect of any premises it must supply him with a certificate containing all material particulars of the registration, and send a copy of the certificate to the local authority for the area where the premises are located.[154] The exemptions from the need to register under the Radioactive Substances Act are limited in scope. Premises where a nuclear site licence is in force are exempt, the reason being to avoid duplication of control.[155] The de minimis principle exempts those concerned with the keeping, use, and manufacture of clocks and watches (which have radioactive dials if they are luminous) from the need to register.[156] The Secretary of State has further powers to exempt classes of premises and categories of radioactive material from registration. He has exercised this power to cover a wide range of esoteric and infrequently met activities and types of radioactive material.[157]

H. Information on Miscellaneous Matters

5.163 For the sake of completeness, it is necessary to record that there are a number of other fields of activity where information is required to be made available, either by way of the provision of environmental impact assessments in support of

---

[151] Ibid, s 7(3).
[152] Ibid, s 7(4) and s 26. One cannot be optimistic about the chances of success on appeal against the refusal of a body as closely linked to government as the Environment Agency to grant a licence.
[153] Ibid, s 7(6).
[154] Ibid, s 7(8).
[155] Ibid, s 8(1).
[156] Ibid, s 7(3) and (4).
[157] Ibid, s 8(6). The exemption orders made under previous legislation cover an eclectic range of activities. They include exhibitions (SI 1962/2645); phosphatic substances and rare earths (SI 1962/2648); smoke detectors (SI 1980/953); and gaseous tritium light devices (SI 1985/104). The list is not exhaustive. A comprehensive catalogue can be found in the loose-leaf publications which deal with this field, and which require regular updating, as the examples given above demonstrate.

applications for planning permission, or because registration provisions, similar to those already described, have been brought into effect. The obligation to carry out environmental impact assessments arises where application is made for afforestation;[158] salmon farming in marine waters;[159] major highways;[160] harbour works;[161] and electricity and pipeline works.[162]

Concern to limit pollution of water has brought about the existence of a miscellany of registers of activities which could bear upon this issue. Registers of discharge consents have already been described. There is a register of licences granted to dump waste at sea;[163] of samples of drinking water;[164] of private water supplies;[165] trade effluents;[166] and of works undertaken by the former National Rivers Authority or the Environment Agency.[167] In addition information must be supplied to English Nature where boreholes more than 50 feet deep are sunk.[168] There are registers of sewage and water undertakers, and of ships which might be tempted to discharge wastes into the seas round the coasts of the UK, or become grounded, allowing their cargoes to escape.[169] In short there is little activity which could affect the integrity of inland and coastal waters which goes unrecorded in one or more of the registers which abound up and down the land. **5.164**

I. The Powers of Inspectors

Environment Agency inspectors

Much of this chapter has been devoted to the duties which devolve upon regulatory authorities. This, however, needs to be kept in perspective. The obligations which the statutes place upon the subject are as onerous, and some might call them oppressive.[170] The Environment Act 1995 gave inspectors appointed by the **5.165**

---

[158] SI 1988/1207.
[159] SI 1988/1218.
[160] SI 1988/1241.
[161] SI 1988/1336; SI 1989/434.
[162] SI 1990/442.
[163] Food and Environmental Protection Act 1985. The licences most frequently granted were for the dumping of sewage sludge, a practice which is now proscribed by international treaty.
[164] Water Supply (Water Quality) Regulations 1989, SI 1989/1147, amended by SI 1989/1384.
[165] Private Water Supply Regulations 1991, SI 1991/2790.
[166] Water Industry Act 1991, s 204.
[167] WRA 1991, s 191.
[168] WRA 1991, s 198.
[169] Water Industry Act 1991, s 195; Registrar General of Shipping and Seamen.
[170] 'Stunning' was the adjective used by two commentators—see Upton and Harwood (1996) JPL 623.

Secretary of State and the Environment Agency powers which would be the envy of many a secret police service. Those powers may be exercised in order to determine whether any provision of the 'pollution control enactments' is being or has been complied with; to perform any pollution control function; and to determine how such functions should be performed.[171]

5.166   There is, in brief, little or nothing in the field of environmental protection to which the powers of inspectors do not reach. Their powers are restricted to the extent that they must abide by the Codes of Practice laid down for the police under the Police and Criminal Evidence Act 1984. These give guidance as to the exercise of powers to stop and search (not available to environmental inspectors); searches of premises and seizure of property; detention, treatment, and questioning of suspects, including the administration of cautions; identification parades; and tape recording of interviews.

Obstruction of inspectors

5.167   It is an offence intentionally to obstruct an inspector in the exercise or performance of his functions.[172] Intentional or wilful obstruction means doing deliberate actions with the intention of bringing about a state of affairs which makes it more difficult for the inspector to carry out his duties. Where a waste regulation authority had requested permission to take samples from boreholes and the operator of the site filled them in before samples could be taken, it was convicted of obstructing the inspector in question.[173]

5.168   The defendant need not go so far as to obstruct an inspector in order to commit an offence. It will suffice if he fails, without reasonable excuse, to comply with any requirement imposed under Section 108 of the Environment Act, to provide facilities or assistance or information, or to permit any inspection which is reasonably required by an inspector, or prevents any other person from appearing before or answering an inspector's questions.[174] There must be doubt over the question whether failure to offer a desk at which to work or the use of a telephone would make the defendant liable to conviction for the offence of failing to provide facilities for an inspector.

Powers of entry

5.169   Inspectors have wide powers of entry. They may enter at any 'reasonable time', which will not necessarily be confined to the usual working hours, especially in

---

[171]   EA 1995, s 108(1).
[172]   Ibid, s 110(1).
[173]   *Hills v Ellis* [1983] QB 680; *Polymeric Treatments Ltd v Walsall MBC* [1993] Env LR 427.
[174]   EA 1995, s 110(2).

the event of an emergency. There is express provision for the giving of seven days' notice before entering on residential premises, or if the inspector wishes to take so-called 'heavy equipment' onto the premises in question.[175] By necessary implication, therefore, no notice is required of the intention to enter commercial or industrial premises, and the inspector may arrive without warning.

No doubt this was what Parliament intended, since surprise is of the essence of **5.170** enforcement in a field where many might be tempted to cut corners. The inspector may exercise his right of entry in the company of a police constable if there is reason to believe that there may be a serious obstruction in the execution of his duty and, once on the premises, the constable has the usual powers of the police under the Police and Criminal Evidence Act.

Having gained access to premises the inspector may make such investigations and **5.171** examinations as are reasonable in the circumstances; for this purpose he may direct that any part shall remain undisturbed for as long as may be necessary, and may take measurements, photographs, and recordings.[176] He may also take samples, or cause samples to be taken (refusal to do so would presumably fall foul of the injunction against refusal to provide facilities for the inspector, or would amount to obstructing him) of any article or substance found on the premises, or of the air, land, or water in the vicinity.[177] This power is needed in order to discover whether an escape of polluting material might have taken place.

Once he has examined the premises and taken samples, the inspector has power to **5.172** interview any person whom he has reasonable cause to believe to be able to give any information relevant to any examination or investigation.[178] Just as there is no privilege against self-incrimination in response to requisitions issued by a waste regulation authority, so there is no such privilege available to the suspect who is confronted by an inspector. The latter may require any person, whom he has reason to believe to be able to help him, to answer such questions as he thinks fit to ask, and to sign a declaration as to the truth of the answers.

It is an offence to prevent any person from answering an inspector's questions, and **5.173** so the legal adviser who advises silence does so at his peril. By way of consolation, Parliament has provided that documents are protected by legal professional privilege, although there is some doubt whether this extends to oral answers to questions put by an inspector, since these are not expressly mentioned in the Environment Act. However, it is clear that commercial confidentiality is no

---

[175] Ibid, s 108(6).
[176] Ibid, s 108(4).
[177] Ibid.
[178] Ibid, s 108(4)(j).

protection from inquiry by inspectors, in contrast to many other types of information, as is pointed out above.[179]

Emergencies

5.174 In an emergency the powers of an inspector are more dictatorial still. An emergency exists where the inspector thinks that there is immediate risk of serious pollution of the environment or serious harm to human health, or where there is likely to be danger to life or health.[180] He must also be of opinion that immediate entry to premises is necessary in order to deal with the emergency. He then has power to seize articles or substances which he believes to be an immediate cause of danger of serious pollution or serious harm to human health, and to destroy them or render them harmless by some other means.[181] In this instance alone is the inspector required to justify his actions by the making of a written report, both to the occupier of the premises and to the owner of the article or substance which has been dealt with.

Immunity of inspectors

5.175 As if to emphasize the wide powers of environmental inspectors, they are immune from both civil and criminal proceedings, no matter what their conduct, provided they can satisfy the court that they acted in good faith and that they had reasonable grounds for having done what they did.[182] The lot of an inspector is one which many a mere police constable might very well envy.

---

[179] Ibid, s 108(13).
[180] Ibid, s 108(15).
[181] Ibid, s 109.
[182] Ibid, Sch 18 para 6(4).

Part II

THE UK REGULATORY FRAMEWORK

6

ENVIRONMENTAL PERMITTING AND INTEGRATED POLLUTION CONTROL

A. Introduction	6.01	
A short history of industrial pollution control and its future	6.01	
The current system	6.04	
B. Part A(1) Installations and Mobile Plant	6.08	
The regulatory bodies	6.08	
The 'regulator'	6.08	
The Secretary of State	6.09	
The regulation of facilities	6.10	
The person	6.10	
The subject matter of IPPC: 'regulated facilities' and 'activities'	6.11	
Regulated facilities	6.11	
Activities	6.20	
The interpretation of IPPC categorizations	6.25	
The limits of IPPC	6.27	
Insignificant processes and low level activities	6.27	
Waste management	6.30	
Mobile plant	6.36	
Noise	6.38	
Radioactivity and GMOs	6.39	
The changeover from the 2000 Regulations to the 2007 Regulations— transitional provisions	6.40	
The regulator's exercise of its functions	6.41	
A(1) Installations and mobile plant	6.41	
Best available technique ('BAT')	6.56	
Waste operations	6.65	
Landfill installations	6.70	
Waste motor vehicles	6.72	
Waste electrical and electronic equipment	6.73	

Waste incineration	6.74	
Solvent emissions installations and plant	6.77	
Combustion plants, asbestos, titanium dioxide, and petrol vapour recovery	6.78	
C. The Environmental Permit Procedure	6.79	
The application	6.79	
Operator competence	6.90	
Charges	6.95	
Alternative forms of application	6.96	
The staged application	6.96	
Composite applications	6.99	
Consultation and public participation	6.103	
Public consultees	6.103	
Other European Member States	6.108	
Timing of application, including novel applications and where planning permission is required	6.109	
The determining body	6.113	
Generally	6.113	
The manner of exercising	6.114	
The framework for the decision	6.114	
The permit— specific requirements	6.120	
The permit— the conditions	6.122	
The permit— standard rules	6.129	
Conflicts between permits	6.136	
The time limits for determination of an application	6.137	
The effect of a grant	6.139	
Determination by the Secretary of State	6.140	

D. Review, Variation, Transfer, Revocation, Remediation, and Surrender of Environmental Permits 6.144

Review and inspection 6.144
Variations of environmental permits 6.147
Transfer of environmental permits 6.153
Revocation of environmental permits 6.156
Remediation 6.158
Surrender of environmental permits 6.160

E. Appeals 6.167
The right of appeal 6.167
The date for appealing 6.169
The effect of an appeal 6.171
Appeal procedure 6.172
Making the appeal 6.172
Notification 6.175
Other procedural requirements 6.176
Hearings 6.177
Written representations 6.181
Call in and recovery of cases 6.183
The decision 6.184
Costs 6.185
Further appeals 6.186

F. Enforcement of Environmental Permit Regime 6.188
Introduction 6.188
The Environment Agency's enforcement policy 6.189
The enforcing authority's investigative powers 6.190
Prohibitory notices 6.194
Enforcement notices 6.194
Suspension notices 6.196
Landfill closure notices 6.199
Direct action 6.200
Offences 6.201
The Agency's prosecution policy 6.202
Corporate offences 6.208
Operating a regulated facility without or in contravention of an environmental permit or prohibitory notices 6.209

Other offences 6.215
Offences under the environment Act 1995 6.222
Court orders 6.226
Statutory orders 6.226
Crown immunity 6.235

G. Local Authority Control of Installations and Mobile Plant 6.236
Local authority control—general matters 6.236
The role of the local authority in LAPPC and LA-IPPC 6.237

H. The Responsibilities of the Local Authority 6.242
Part A(2) Installations and mobile plant 6.243
Part B Installations and mobile plant 6.244
Waste operations 6.253
Contaminated land 6.254
Determination of LAPPC and LA-IPPC applications 6.255
The authorization framework 6.256
LA-IPPC (Part A(2)) 6.267
LAPPC (Part B) 6.276
Water consent issues 6.277
Transfer, variation, review, and revocation 6.278
Enforcement 6.283

I. Registers 6.286
The information on the public register 6.286
Form and content of registers 6.293
The exclusion from the public register of information affecting national security 6.295
The exclusion of confidential information from the public register 6.298
The result of exclusion from the public register 6.306

A. Introduction

A short history of industrial pollution control and its future

Formal air pollution control legislation was developed in the time of the Industrial **6.01**
Revolution. Following public complaints and government inquiries, the Alkali &
Works Act 1863 introduced the first set of pollution controls. The Alkali Act 1874
required that the Best Practicable Means should be used to prevent the escape of
noxious or offence gases. The various Acts were consolidated in the Alkali &c
Works Regulation Act 1906, which linked together schedules of prescribed works
with schedules that listed noxious and offensive gases. That regime was in part
replaced by regulations made under the Health and Safety at Work Act 1974. The
system relied upon annual registration (until 1989), the use of best practicable
means, and the possibility of improvement and prohibition notices as well as
prosecution. However, it was a system that only controlled particular mediums. A
different concept—an integrated system of pollution control—was first proposed
by the Royal Commission for Environmental Pollution in a 1976 Report.[1] The
idea, however, was only introduced in the Environmental Protection Act 1990
(the EPA 1990). Integrated pollution control is different from its predecessor system, but is, as will be seen, rooted in those earlier Acts. It is that concept, a fully
integrated system, which Europe has attempted to adopt by means of the Integrated
Pollution Prevention Control (IPPC) system. The process of ensuring an integrated and standardized system was continued by the enactment of the Pollution
Prevention and Control Act 1999. This framework Act replaced the
relevant parts of the EPA 1990; its terms were then implemented through
the Pollution Prevention and Control (England and Wales) Regulations 2000.
These regulations were themselves replaced by the Environmental Permitting
(England and Wales) Regulations 2007 ('the 2007 Regulations'). The main difference between the two sets of regulations was the increase in the number of operations covered by the system; essentially the integrated system was extended to
include a significant number of waste operations. It sought, additionally, to bring
the domestic system into line with the European legislative framework, primarily
the IPPC Directive.

A second phase of the Environmental Permit regime ('EPP2') is envisaged. This **6.02**
would extend the 'EPP1' system by intergrating and streamlining futher reforms.
It may include:

- water discharge consenting,
- groundwater authorization,

---

[1] Air Pollution Control: an Integrated Approach.

- water abstraction and impoundment,
- radioactive substances regulation,
- some other waste carriers and brokers.

6.03 The IPPC Directive was 'codified' in early 2008. A proposal to amend the IPPC Directive to combine it with six other EU Directives was tabled at the end of 2007.[2] This proposal is currently the subject of negotiation, and while amendments may result, they are not expected to come into force for several years.

The current system

6.04 The 2007 Regulations divide the control of potentially polluting industrial operations into essentially two parts. On the one hand, the significant industrial activities (known as Part A(1) operations) are governed by the Environment Agency ('the Agency'), and, on the other, the less significant operations (known as Part A(2) operations) and installations controlled because of their potential air emissions alone (known as Part B operations) are governed (generally) by the local authority within which the operation is undertaken[3]. Waste operations are included in one or more of these classes, depending upon their significance. Each of the classes of operation are described in Schedule 1 to the Regulations. Certain waste operations (essentially those which meet certain sustainability criteria) are exempted from permit application requirements, although they require registration.[4]

6.05 The 2007 Regulations set out a comprehensive system of control for Part A(1), A(2) and B operations. Operations may be carried out by way of fixed installations and/or mobile plant and the 2007 Regulations control (to a lesser degree for mobile plant) each of these mechanisms. An operator of such plant is required to apply for an environmental permit. Whether a permit is to be granted and, if so, what conditions the operations will be subject to, will be determined by the Agency or the local authority having regard to specific environmental protection objectives (primarily to minimize the risk of pollution to the environment) as well as the requirements of a number of different European directives.[5]

6.06 The regulations give the Environment Agency and local authorities largely the same powers for dealing with applications, reviewing permits, and enforcing breaches of their terms.

6.07 There is a comprehensive set of guidance to support the 2007 Regulations. The primary guidance, at the time of writing, included the *Environmental Permitting Core Guidance* (the 'Core Guidance') for all regulators and operators (2008),

---

[2] <http://ec.europa.eu/environment/ippc/pdf/recast/dir_2007_844_en.pdf>
[3] Subject to certain caveats dealt with below.
[4] Other operations are entirely exempted, as to which see below.
[5] These are dealt with in more detail further below.

the *Environmental Permitting Guidance The IPPC Directive Part A(1) Installations and Part A(1) Mobile Plant* (the 'EA Guidance') (2008) and the *General Guidance Manual on Policy and Procedures for A2 and Part B Installations (Local authority Integrated Pollution Prevention and Control (LA-IPPC) and Local authority Pollution Prevention and Control (LAPPC)*, ('the 'GG Manual') (Revised April 2008). Reference is made below to relevant parts of this guidance. It constitutes statutory guidance to local authority regulators.[6]

B. Part A(1) Installations and Mobile Plant

The regulatory bodies

The 'regulator'

The Agency is the 'regulator' for Part A(1) processes and waste operations (albeit **6.08** with some exceptions).[7] The Secretary of State may, however, direct that a local authority should exercise such Agency functions (and for such period of time) as is specified in the direction,[8] such a direction must be published on the Secretary of State's website.

The Secretary of State[9]

The Secretary of State possesses a range of overarching reserve powers to promote **6.09** the proper operation of the system; directions may be issued by the Secretary of State that certain classes of application should be referred to him.[10] They can be used to give a direction that a local authority is to carry out the Agency's functions in order that there is a single regulator of a site. Although Defra has an overarching responsibilty for issuing guidance, because of the role of the Secretary of State in appeals Defra will not intervene in individual cases, although it may facilitiate discussions between local authorities and businesses where this is practicable and does not compromise the appellate role.[11]

---

[6] Regulation 64, 2007 Regulations.
  [7] Regulation 32(1), 2007 Regulations. (Waste operations which are carried out as part of those processes regulated by local authorities are regulated by the local authority).
  [8] Regulation 33(1), 2007 Regulations. He cannot however direct a local authority to exercise the Agency's functions for a waste operation (unless it is part of an installation or a mobile plant).
  [9] The term 'Secretary of State' is used in this chapter to refer to the 'appropriate authority'. The Secretary of State is only the 'appropriate authority' for England. In Wales the appropriate authority is the Welsh Ministers.
  [10] Regulation 62, 2007 Regulations; in such circumstances, the applicant is given the opportunity of appearing before the Secretary of State.
  [11] GG Manual, paragraph 33.15.

The regulation of facilities

The person

6.10 Subject to the transitional provisions from the previous regime,[12] no person may operate a regulated facility except under, and to the extent authorized, by an environmental permit.[13]

The subject matter of IPPC: 'regulated facilities' and 'activities'

6.11 **Regulated facilities** IPPC controls 'regulated facilities'. Regulated facilities are, an 'installation', 'mobile plant other than waste mobile plant', 'mobile plant', and 'a waste operation not carried on at an installation or by means of mobile plant'. Each of these requires further explanation.

6.12 An 'installation' means a 'stationary technical unit where one or more activities are carried on', and 'any other location on the same site[14] where any other directly associated activities are carried on which have a technical connection with the activities carried out in the stationary technical unit and could have an effect on pollution'.[15]

6.13 The 'first limb' of the definition is that the plant or machinery must be a 'technical unit' and it must be stationary. The phrase 'stationary technical unit' has not been defined in either the Regulations, the 1999 Act, or the originating EC Directive. There has, however, been judicial consideration of the phrase in *R (on the application of Anti-Waste Ltd) v Environment Agency* [2007] EWCA Civ 1377. In the context of a whether an old landfill cell should be regarded as part of a 'stationary technical unit' comprised of an active landfill which was sited next to the old landfill site, the Court found that the identification of a 'stationary technical unit' 'can be done by identifying a space in which the scheduled activity

---

[12] See paragraph 6.40 below.

[13] Regulation 11(1), 2007 Regulations.

[14] Two sets of premises which are a half mile apart and connected by a pipeline could not be said to be on the 'same site': *United Utilities Plc v Environment Agency* [2006] Env LR 42.

[15] Regulation 2(1), 2007 Regulations. Guidance on what an 'installation' is at EA Guidance at paragraph 2.5 and following and for local authorities in the GG Manual at Annex III. This includes specific case study examples. The Commission has also recently published informal guidance on the meaning of installation, *Guidance on Interpration of 'Installation' and 'Operator' for the Purposes of the IPPC Directive*, available at <htp://ec.europa.eu/environment/ippc/pft/installation_guidance.pdf>. The Commission guidance suggests a slightly different structural appropach than has so far been the approach adopted in England and Wales. However the Commission guidance also acknowledges that the approach described here may also meet the Directive requirements and may be chosen by member states. Guidance is also given on what a 'directly associated activity' is for SED activities. It is an activity which has a technical connection with the SED activity, is carried on the same site as the SED activity and could have an effect on the discharge of volatile organic compounds into the environment. (Paragraph 2.6, EA Guidance). See paragraph 6.77 below.

can be carried out independently as a functionally self-contained operation'
(paragraph 27).

It appears that this approach derived from the submission of the claimant (see para- **6.14**
graph 21) that a unit is a 'technical unit if it is functionally self-contained'. The
Environment Agency has issued its own guidance on the meaning of 'installation' for
the purposes of the 2000 Regulations. It appears that this was considered in the *Anti-
Waste* case in which it was pointed out in that case (paragraph 20) that while such
Guidance may assist in understanding the Regulations, it was for the court to con-
strue the Regulations. The Agency's guidance has derived from an earlier guide produced by the DETR (as it then was), *IPPC: A Practical Guide*. The Practical Guide
followed the view taken by the Court that a 'technical unit can be taken to mean
something which is functionally self contained in the sense that the unit—which may
consist of one component or a number of components functioning together—can
carry out the Schedule 1 activity or activities on its own'. The current EA Guidance[16]
indicate that there are three circumstances when, two or more units should be
regarded as a single technical unit; that is, if they carry out successive steps in one
integrated industrial activity; or one of the listed activities is a directly associated activity of the other; or both units are served by the same directly associated activity.[17]

In addition, three criteria are proposed for the second limb of the definition—the **6.15**
activity must be directly associated with the stationary technical unit; the activity
must have a technical connection with the stationary technical unit; and the
activity must be capable of having an effect on emissions.

The first criterion requires that the activity serve the stationary technical unit, not **6.16**
vice-versa. The EA guidance states that if an activity, such as operating a landfill,
serves a stationary technical unit carrying out a listed activity and some other
industrial unit(s) on a different site or carrying out non-listed activities, then the
activity will only be directly associated with the stationary technical unit if that
unit is the principal user of the activity.[18]

The second criterion is 'technical connection'. The EA guidance suggests there are **6.17**
four types of directly associated activities which may be said to have a technical
connection with a stationary technical unit: input activities concerned with the
storage and treatment of inputs into the stationary technical unit; intermediate
activities concerned with the storage and treatment of intermediate products;[19]

---

[16] EA Guidance, paragraph 2.13.
[17] EA Guidance, paragraph 2.11.
[18] EA Guidance, paragraph 2.13.
[19] The example is given of where a stationary technical unit consists of a number of sub-units
with the product of one sub-unit being stored or treated prior to being passed on to the next sub-unit
in the production chain.

output activities concerned with the treatment of waste (or other emissions like manure) from the stationary technical unit; or output activities concerned with the finishing, packaging, and storage of the product from the stationary technical unit.[20] While often there will also be a physical connection (such as a conveyor belt) the EA Guidance emphasizes that this does not have to be the case.[21]

6.18 The third criterion will cover both activities which have an effect on emissions and pollution from the listed activities with which they are associated and activities which have such an effect in their own right.[22]

6.19 It is to be noted that references to an installation include references to part of an installation.[23]

6.20 **Activities** The type of activity carried on in a regulated facility defines whether it is controlled centrally by the Agency or by the relevant local authority. An 'activity' is itself defined by reference to activities included in Schedule 1 to the Regulations. In substance, therefore, an installation is controlled by the Act if it has certain 'activities' carried on within it which are identified by reference to the categories contained in Schedule 1 to the Regulations.

6.21 The IPPC system divides the activities controlled by it into seven chapters[24] (essentially, energy related activities (Chapter 1), metal processing (Chapter 2), mineral industry activities (Chapter 3), chemical industry activities (Chapter 4), waste related activities (Chapter 5), miscellaneous industrial activities (Chapter 6), and SED (solvent emissions directive) activities (Chapter 7)).

6.22 These chapters are subdivided into particular sections relating to specific types of activity under the general type contained in each chapter. For example, section 1.2 of Chapter 1 (energy related activities) deals with gasification, liquefaction, and refining activities.

6.23 These particular sections are themselves divided into 3 parts: Part A(1), Part A(2), and (generally) Part B activities. Again, looking at Chapter 1, and section 1.2, Part A(1) activities includes refining gas where that is likely to involve the use of 1,000 or more tonnes of gas in any period of 12 months, while Part A(2) includes refining gas which involves the use of less than that amount. It should be noted that not all sections of Part 2 include A(2) activities.[25] A Part B process under section 1.2 includes such matters as the storage of petrol in stationary storage tanks at a terminal.

---

[20] EA Guidance, paragraph 2.14.
[21] EA Guidance, paragraph 2.15.
[22] EA Guidance, paragraph 2.16.
[23] Regulation 2(1), 2007 Regulations.
[24] Of Part 2 of Schedule 1 to the 2007 Regulations.
[25] See, for example, section 3.2 of Chapter 3 dealing with Activities involving asbestos.

Part A(1) processes are the most significant processes which have the greatest **6.24** capacity to cause pollution. It is these activities, in the main, which are subject to central control by the Environment Agency.[26]

The interpretation of IPPC categorizations

The 2007 Regulations provide interpretation provisions to deal with the **6.25** complexity of most industrial sites. These provisions err on the side of caution and make potentially mixed uses subject to central control:[27]

- where an activity falls within a description in Part A(1) and a description in Part A(2), the activity must be regarded as falling only within that description which fits it most aptly;

- where an activity falls within a description in Part A(1) and a description in Part B that activity must be regarded as falling only within the description in Part A(1);

- where an activity falls within a description in Part A(2) and a description in Part B[28] that activity must be regarded as falling only within the description in Part A(2).

The Regulations also make provision for determining whether an activity falls **6.26** under Part A(1) or Part A(2) where the differentiation between them in a relevant section of a chapter is made by reference to capacity thresholds.[29] If an operator carries out the same type of activity in different parts of the same stationary technical unit or in different stationary technical units on the same site, the capacity of each part of each unit must be added together and the total capacity attributed to each part. It is for operators to determine what the relevant production capacity is in each case, and therefore to which regulator they should submit their applications. Regulators may offer advice on this issue, and also assess whether an operator's assessment of capacity is reasonable. This may involve considering if, for example, the installation could be run properly at that rate, or alternatively looking at the design capacity.[30] In some circumstances the maximum production capacity must be used.[31]

---

[26] Regulation 32(1) of the 2007 Regulations. Note that the Environment Agency can have control over what is to be attached to an A(2) installation permit: see below at 6.240.

[27] See paragraph 2 of Schedule 1, 2007 Regulations.

[28] Subject to an exception in relation to Solvent Emissions Directive activities.

[29] Paragraph 4 of Schedule 1, 2007 Regulations.

[30] Paragraph 2.26, EA Guidance.

[31] Eg for 'finished food production capacity'. See further paragraph 2.27, EA Guidance and paragraph (d), Section 6.8, Part 2, Schedule 1 of the 2007 Regulations.

The limits of IPPC

Insignificant processes and low level activities

6.27   The Regulations make clear that an activity identified as such under Part A(1), Part A(2), or Part B does not cease to be regarded as such an activity merely because it is in fact operated under the relevant threshold, unless the permit itself ceases to have effect.[32]

6.28   However, if an activity which could otherwise be regarded as a Part B activity cannot result in the release in to the air of certain substances[33] or there is no likelihood that it will result in the release into the air of such substances except in quantities incapable of causing pollution, they will be excepted from that categorization.

6.29   Certain specified activities which would ordinarily come under the control of the IPPC regime are excepted from control.[34] These include activities in a working museum for demonstration purposes, activities carried out in a school for educational purposes, and activities carried on as a domestic activity in a private dwelling.

Waste management

6.30   As a generality, waste management facilities will be caught by the environmental permitting regime. However, certain types of waste management activity are excluded from control. 'Excluded waste operations' and 'exempt waste operations' are not regulated facilities for the purposes of the 2007 Regulations.

6.31   'Excluded waste operations' include a number of activities which are controlled by other mechanisms, such as those which have a licence under Part II of the Food and Environmental Protection Act 1985 (that is, for the deposit or incineration of substances at sea), those operating under a consent for the disposal of liquid waste under Part III of the Waster Resources Act 1991, disposal operations of agricultural waste under an authorization under Regulation 18 of the Groundwater Regulations 1998, and the disposal or recovery of waste which is not to be treated as industrial waste or commercial waste under the Controlled Waste Regulations 1992.

6.32   The 'exempt waste operation' seeks to exclude those waste operations which are consistent with the European Union's aim to encourage sustainable waste management as set out in the Waste Framework Directive[35] if it satisfies a certain

---

[32] Paragraph 5 of Schedule 1, 2007 Regulations.
[33] Those substances include sulphur oxides, nitrogen oxides, oxides of carbon, organic compounds, and asbestos.
[34] Paragraph 3 of Part 1 of Schedule 1, 2007 Regulations.
[35] Directive 2006/12/EC.

number of criteria.[36] First, the activity must be one of a number of specified waste operations identified in Part 1 of Schedule 3 to the Regulations. These comprise, in essence, those operations which are capable in principle of being carried out without harm to the environment. Second, it must, in the main, be registered in relation to the waste operation with the 'exemption registration authority'[37] and in respect of certain other types of activity, must also be subject to a notification procedure[38] to the exemption registration authority in addition to being registered,[39] and may be subject to a condition that it be carried on by the occupier of the land in question or with the consent of the occupier or by a person who is entitled to do the operation on the land. Third, the type and quantity of waste submitted to the waste operation and the method of disposal or recovery are consistent with the need to attain the objectives of Article 4(1) of the Waste Framework Directive. These objectives are essentially to ensure that waste is recovered or disposed of without endangering human health and without using processes or methods which could harm the environment.[40]

Additionally, the disposal or recovery of household waste from a domestic property within the curtilage of that property by a person (other than an establishment or undertaking as defined under the Waste Management Directive[41]) is not a regulated facility.[42]   **6.33**

It should be noted that while a particular waste operation may not be covered by the 2007 Regulations (as a result of being an exempt waste operation), there is an overarching duty on the operator to ensure that (if they deal with controlled waste) they shall not treat, keep, or dispose of such waste in a manner likely to cause pollution of the environment or harm to human health.[43]   **6.34**

---

[36] Regulation 5, 2007 Regulations.

[37] This differs according to the nature of the operation carried on but, generally, means the Agency: paragraph 2 of Schedule 2 to the Regulations. The exemption registration authority is under a duty to maintain a register (see paragraph 4 of Schedule 2 to the Regulations), to carry out periodic inspections (see paragraph 13) and to remove entries from the register in certain circumstances (see paragraph 5).

[38] There are notification requirements which are more onerous for certain activities. See, for example, the position in relation to scrap metal and waste motor vehicles and see paragraph 8(2) of Schedule 2 to the Regulations.

[39] See paragraph 2(3) and paragraph 8 of Schedule 2 to the Regulations.

[40] It is to be noted, however, that a waste operation which involves hazardous waste or which involves the storage or treatement of waste electrical and electronic equipment as defined by Directive 2002/96/EC (the WEEE Directive).

[41] Directive 2006/12/EC.

[42] Regulation 8(3) of the 2007 Regulations.

[43] See Section 33(1)(c) of the 2007 Regulations and note the further exceptions to that requirement in Section 33(1B), Environmental Protection Act 1990.

6.35 If the activity is to continue for longer than a year, a renewal notice must be submitted before 12 months have past since the last notification.[44] The regulator can also refuse to register a notifiable exemption. There is no right of appeal against this decision but the regulator must provide reasons. The decision must be taken 25 working days following receipt of notification although it is possible to agree a longer period.[45] There are also specific registration activities for specific activities,[46] and specific record keeping requirements.[47]

Mobile plant

6.36 Mobile plant and waste mobile plant are also covered by IPPC, as are waste operations not carried on at an installation or by means of mobile plant.[48] Mobile plant is defined[49] as plant which is not an installation, which is used to carry on an activity or waste operation, and, where not used to carry on a Part A activity, is designed to move or be moved.[50]

6.37 Waste mobile plant is defined as plant which is used to carry on a waste operation (that is, the recovery or disposal of waste) and is not 'Part A mobile plant' or 'Part B mobile plant'(that is, plant used to carry out a Part A activity or a Part B activity).[51]

Noise

6.38 Noise is controlled.[52]

Radioactivity and GMOs

6.39 The control of pollution by radioactive substances and genetically modified organisms is excluded.[53]

The changeover from the 2000 Regulations to the 2007 Regulations—transitional provisions

6.40 Except where the permit is the subject of a transitional application, a PPC permit became an environmental permit on the coming into force of the 2007 Regulations (that is, 6 April 2008).[54] Additionally, an application for a PPC permit which was

---

[44] Paragraph 10, Schedule 2, 2007 Regulations.
[45] Paragraph 11, Schedule 2, 2007 Regulations; Core Guidance paragraph 14.9
[46] Paragraphs 45(1) and 45(3) of Part 2, and paragraph 6, Schedule 2, 2007 Regulations.
[47] Paragraph 12, Schedule 2, 2007 Regulations.
[48] See Regulation 8, 2007 Regulations.
[49] See Regulation 2(1), 2007 Regulations.
[50] See Regulation 2(1), 2007 Regulations.
[51] See Regulation 3(3), 2007 Regulations.
[52] See Regulation 2(1) of the 2007 Regulations as to the definition of 'pollution'.
[53] Schedule 1 to the 2007 Regulations does not include such activities.
[54] Regulation 69(1), 2007 Regulations.

outstanding when the Regulations came into force would become an environ-mental permit when it is determined.[55] The determination of an application for the grant of a PPC permit which was outstanding at the time that the 2007 Regulations came into force will be determined in accordance with the 2000 Regulations.[56]

The regulator's exercise of its functions

A(1) Installations and mobile plant

The Agency is required, when carrying out the majority of its functions under the Act and the Regulations[57] to take into account and apply the specific objectives and requirements of the IPPC Directive. In particular the Regulations require the regulators to exercise their functions to achieve the basic purpose set out in Article 1 of the IPPC Directive. That purpose is to achieve 'a high level of protec-tion of the environment taken as a whole by, in particular, preventing or, where that is not practicable, reducing emissions into the air, water and land'. The rele-vant provisions are contained in Schedule 7 to the Regulations. They comprise the following:[58]   **6.41**

When exercising its relevant functions,[59] the Agency must ensure that:[60]   **6.42**

- all appropriate preventive measures are taken against pollution in particular through application of the best available techniques;
- no significant pollution is caused;
- waste production is avoided;
- energy is used efficiently;
- the necessary measures are taken to prevent accidents and limit their consequences;
- the necessary measures are taken upon definite cessation of activities to avoid any pollution risk and return the site of operation to a satisfactory state.

Permit conditions may be imposed to reflect the general principles set out above.[61]   **6.43**

---

[55] Regulation 70(1), 2007 Regulations.

[56] Regulation 72(1), 2007 Regulations.

[57] Including the grant, variation, suspension, and revocation of permits and service of any sus-pension and enforcement notices: Regulation 9, 2007 Regulations.

[58] See paragraph 5, Schedule 7, 2007 Regulations.

[59] See Regulation 9, 2007 Regulations.

[60] See paragraph 5(1)(a), Schedule 7, 2007 Regulations and Article 3 of the IPPC Directive. Guidance for local authorities is given in the GG Manual.

[61] EA Guidance, paragraph 3.9.

6.44 The Agency is required[62] to ensure that a permit shall include all measures necessary for compliance with Articles 3 and 10 of the IPPC Directive[63] to achieve a high level of protection of the environment as a whole by means of protection of the air, water, and land. The scope of the Directive is very wide and its purpose very broad, and it must be construed accordingly.[64] Additionally, it is the central aim of the Directive which must be achieved. Accordingly, it is to be noted that simply because an air quality standard in any general area is met with an installation, it does not follow that the best available techniques have been achieved in its operation. The IPPC Directive makes it a requirement to seek 'as far as possible' the reduction of emissions and gases.[65]

6.45 The Agency shall take into account any relevant information provided under an Environmental Assessment when considering whether to grant a permit.[66]

6.46 The permit shall include emission limit values[67] for pollutants likely to be emitted from the installation concerned in significant quantities,[68] including the aim of minimizing long-distance and trans-boundary pollution,[69] having regard to their nature and their potential to transfer pollution from one medium to another. If necessary, the permit shall include appropriate requirements ensuring protection of the soil and groundwater and measures concerning the management of waste generated by the installation. The Agency may, when ensuring that there are appropriate limit values, supplement those values by parameters or technical measures,[70] and the permit must specify monitoring requirements, and the methodology, frequency, and evaluation procedures, requiring regular submission of reports to the regulator to check compliance.[71] Such measures and values shall be based on the best available technique, without prescribing the use of any technique or specific technology, but taking into account the technical characteristics of the installation concerned, its geographical location and the local environmental conditions (except in the case of mobile plant).[72]

---

[62] See paragraph 5(1)(b), Schedule 7, 2007 Regulations and Article 9(1)–(6) of the IPPC Directive.

[63] See the commentary on paragraph 5(1)(c) and (a), Schedule 7, 2007 Regulations in this section.

[64] *R (on the application of Edwards) v Environment Agency* [2008] UKHL 22, para. 70.

[65] *R (on the application of Rockware Glass Ltd) v Chester CC* [2005] EWHC 2250.

[66] See paragraph 5(1)(b), Schedule 7, 2007 Regulations and Article 9(2), IPPC Directive.

[67] An emission limit value is itself defined in Article 2(6) of the IPPC Directive.

[68] And in particular those specified in Annex III to the IPPC Directive.

[69] EA Guidance, paragraph 3.12

[70] See paragraph 5(1)(b), Schedule 7, 2007 Regulations and Article 9(3), IPPC Directive.

[71] See paragraph 5(1)(b), Schedule 7 and Article 9(5), IPPC Directive EA Guidance, paragraph 3.12.

[72] See paragraph 5(1)(b), Schedule 7 and Article 9(4), IPPC Directive.

The permit should address what steps are appropriate both before and after opera-   **6.47**
tion, which may include site monitoring and remediation.[73] The permit is also
required to contain measures relating to conditions other than normal operating
conditions,[74] for example during start-up, malfunction, leaks, or temporary stop-
pages.[75] The permit must require the operator to inform the regulator without
delay of an incident or accident that may cause pollution.[76]

The Agency is also required, where an environmental quality standard[77] requires   **6.48**
stricter conditions than those achievable by the use of the best available techniques, to impose additional measures.[78] The Agency must also take account of
other relevant legislation when determining permit conditions for an installation.
The EA Guidance suggests that in 'most' cases the requirements of other legislation are minimum obligations and any stricter conditions that may result from
IPPC requirements have to be imposed.[79]

The Agency must ensure (except in the case of Part A mobile plant[80]) that the   **6.49**
operator informs the competent authorities of any changes planned in the operation of the installation and to ensure that no substantial change in the operation
of the installation is made without a permit.[81] In circumstances, where there is to
be a substantial change, the Agency must review the Environmental Permit.[82]
It must also take the necessary measures to ensure the operator regularly informs
the competent authority of the results of monitoring of releases without delay.[83]

Substantial change means 'a change in operation which, in the regulator's opin-   **6.50**
ion, may have significant negative effects on human beings or the environment'.[84]
A 'change in operation' means 'a change in the nature or functioning, or an extension, of an installation, which may have consequences for the environment'. It can
therefore entail either technical alterations or modifications in operational or

---

[73] EA Guidance, paragraph 3.12.
[74] See paragraph 5(1)(b), Schedule 7 and Article 9(6), IPPC Directive.
[75] EA Guidance, paragraph 3.12.
[76] EA Guidance, paragraph 3.12.
[77] That is, a standard set out in community legislation. Further guidance is given at EA Guidance,
paragraphs 3.46–3.59. Note that national requirements, where stricter than the European standard, do not carry the same absolute legal obligation. The EA Guidance suggests that some national
standards—such as operational water quality EQS—should always be observed.
[78] See paragraph 5(1)(c), Schedule 7, 2007 Regulations and Article 10, IPPC Directive.
[79] EA Guidance, paragraph 3.16; this accords with the views expressed by the Court of Appeal
in the *Rockware* case.
[80] See paragraph 5(2)(e), Schedule 7, 2007 Regulations.
[81] See paragraph 5(1)(d), Schedule 7, 2007 Regulations and Article 12(1), IPPC Directive.
[82] Paragraph 7, Schedule 7, 2007 Regulations.
[83] See paragraph 5(1)(e), Schedule 7, 2007 Regulations and Article 14, IPPC Directive.
[84] Paragraph 5(5) of Schedule 5, 2007 Regulations.

management practices. Guidance on what is a 'substantial change' is given in the EA Guidance at paragraph 4.21 and following.[85]

6.51 The facts of the case will sometimes be decisive as to whether a change is a 'substantial change'. All the impacts of a proposed change must be considered, rather than just the net environmental effect. Such judgments should take account not only of releases of polluting substances, but also other pollutants (heat, noise, and vibrations) as well as alternative types of potential impacts such as increased waste production, energy consumption, or the risk of accidents.[86]

6.52 Some changes bring net benefits but may have constituent negative effects—for example changing a fuel may reduce some reductions but increase other emissions. If any potential negative effect is identified, the regulator must judge whether this is 'significant'. This should be assessed having regard to:

- the extent of the potential impact (including geographical area and size of the affected population);
- any effects on specifically protected areas, species, or other assets of particular significance;
- the trans-boundary nature of the impact;
- the magnitude and complexity of the impact;
- the probability of the impact;
- the duration, frequency, and reversibility of the impact.[87]

6.53 Substantial changes include any change in operation which in itself meets the thresholds, if any, set out in Part 2 of Schedule 1, any change in operation of an incineration or co-incineration plant for non-hazardous wate which would involve the incineration or co-incineration of hazardous waste.[88]

6.54 Changes in release of polluting substances are the most likely cause of substantial changes. Regulators should consider changes in:

- The substances released. If a new substance is to be released, consideration should be given to whether this would have a significant negative effect. However, if this new release is coupled with a reduction in a release of another substance,

---

[85] Similar guidance is also given to local authorities in the GG Manual at Annex III. The GG Manual emphasizes that in general the majority of substantial changes are expected to arise at Part A(1) installations. Part A(2) installations are generally smaller in scale and, as a result, are less likely to undergo a change which may cause a significant negative effect. For Part B installations the IPPC Directive definition only applies in relation to the purpose of preventing/reducing emissions into the air. The GG Manual emphasizes that it is not acceptable for operators to simply state that 'no complaints have been received'. A lack of complaints does not necessarily imply that there is no problem.

[86] EA Guidance, paragraph 4.23.

[87] EA Guidance, paragraph 4.24.

[88] EA Guidance. Paragraph 4.22,

then it is appropriate to consider the similarity of effects between the two in seeing whether the change is substantial.

- The level of releases of any particular substances. The test of significance should not be based on the relative increases in release from the site but on the absolute effect those releases will have on the evironment. The example is given of a small factory which seeks to triple its capacity, but that this would only constitute a substantial change if the resulting increases might have a significant negative effect.

- The nature of releases of any particular substance. This could include changes in temperature, pressure, viscosity, appearance, phase, size, and shape of particle, colour, and density.[89]

The judgment is one for the regulator to make. Regulators should be able to demonstrate that their decisions are reasonable based on the facts of the case and the standard of common sense.[90]   **6.55**

Best available technique ('BAT')

As will be clear from the above, the application of best available techniques is put   **6.56** at the heart of the matters to be taken into account by the Agency when undertaking its functions. The European definition has been incorporated into the legislation. It provides:

- 'Best available techniques' shall mean the most effective and advanced stage in the development of activities and their methods of operation which indicate the practical suitability of particular techniques for providing in principle the basis for emission limit values designed to prevent and, where that is not practicable, generally to reduce emissions and the impact on the environment as a whole.

- 'Techniques' shall include both the technology used and the way in which the installation is designed, built, maintained, operated, and decommissioned.

- 'Available' techniques shall mean those developed on a scale which allows implementation in the relevant industrial sector, under economically and technically viable conditions, taking into consideration the costs and advantages, whether or not the techniques are used or produced inside the Member State in question, as long as they are reasonably accessible to the operator.

- 'Best' shall mean most effective in achieving a high general level of protection of the environment as a whole.[91]

---

[89] EA Guidance, paragraph 4.25.
[90] EA Guidance, paragraph 4.26.
[91] Article 2(11), IPPC Directive.

6.57 In determining the BAT, special consideration should be given to the following matters,[92] bearing in mind the likely costs and benefits of a measure and the principles of precaution and prevention:

- the use of low-waste technology;[93]
- the use of less hazardous substances;
- the furthering of recovery and recycling of substances generated and used in the process and of waste, where appropriate;
- comparable processes, facilities, or methods of operation which have been tried with success on an industrial scale;[94]
- technological advances and changes in scientific knowledge and understanding;[95]
- the nature, effects, and volume of the emissions concerned;[96]
- the commissioning dates for new or existing installations;[97]
- the length of time needed to introduce the best available technique;[98]
- the consumption and nature of raw materials (including water) used in the process and their energy efficiency;[99]
- the need to prevent or reduce to a minimum the overall impact of the emissions on the environment and the risks to it;
- the need to prevent accidents and to minimize the consequences for the environment;[100]

---

[92] Article IV, IPPC Directive.

[93] The EA Guidance (paragraph 3.28) emphasizes that waste assessment should cover the amount of waste produced, the possibility of preventing it, recovering it or disposing of it safely. In certain cases it may be preferable to permit a slightly higher level of releases if this greatly reduces the volume of waste, especially if the waste is particularly hazardous. However, pollution should not be simply transferred from one medium to another. The main goal is to identify techniques that minimize all types of waste and releases at source. See also the GG Manual at paragraph 12.18.

[94] Also applies to LAPPC.

[95] Also applies to LAPPC.

[96] Also applies to LAPPC.

[97] Also applies to LAPPC.

[98] Also applies to LAPPC.

[99] Note also that care should be taken that pollution abatement technologies do not use excessive energy compared with the emission reductions they achieve. The EA Guidance emphasizes that installations in a Climate Change Agreement ('CCA') or participating in the EU-Emissions Trading Scheme ('EU-ETS') may have particular incentives in respect of energy efficiency which may be reflected in the assessment of options. Care should be taken that pollution abatement technologies do not use excessive energy compared with the emission reductions they achieve The GG Manual (paragraph 12.18) emphasizes that consideration should be given to options that use fewer resources, or those using materials less likely to produce hazards. The environmental consequences of the abstraction of water should also be considered. Annex XVI of the GG Manual deals with energy efficiency requirements under the Climate Change Levy.

[100] The EA Guidance (paragraph 3.28) emphasizes that consideration should not be limited to looking at normal operations, but also at the possibility of unintentional releases. See also GG Manual, paragraph 2.18.

- site restoration;[101]
- the information published by the Commission gathered through an exchange of information between Member States of the Community[102] or information published by international organizations.

Once the options have been identified there should be an assessment of their sig- **6.58**
nificant environmental effects, both direct and indirect. Account should in particular be taken of the above factors, to help rank the techniques. The main focus of the assessment will be on the effects of releases. The assessment should identify and quantify the effects. Most attention should be paid to large-scale releases and releases of the most hazardous pollutants. Any releases at levels so low they are unlikely to have significant effects need not be assessed[103]. Annex III of the IPPC Directive provides an indicative list, although a notable emission is carbon dioxide and the environmental assessment must consider carbon dioxide emissions.[104] Emissions of heat, vibration, and noise should also be considered, if relevant.

In ranking technologies, judgments will need to be made about the relative sig- **6.59**
nificance of different environmental effects. Guidance is given on certain basic parameters which may help to reach a conclusion. As such comparisons will often be inexact, in ranking options all assumptions, calculations, and conclusions must be open to examination and using simple numerical analysis to compare or aggregate different environmental effects should generally be avoided, except where there are recognized ways of doing this. Individual effects within options should be assessed quantitatively where possible. However, the overall assessment and comparison of options should normally include significant qualitative elements. Expert judgment should be used alongside the particular constraints of the appraisal system, so that common sense conclusions are reached.[105]

Where there is a choice, the technique that is best overall will be the BAT unless it **6.60**
is not an 'available' technique. There are two key aspects to the availability test. The first is the balance of costs and advantages. The economic assessment should include operating costs, capital costs, and any costs savings.[106] The lack of profitability of a particular business should not affect the assessment, if a particular technique is BAT within a certain sector. It is recognized that there may be some

---

[101] EA Guidance, paragraph 3.28. Consideration should be given to whether options risk polluting the site, including planning ahead for decommissioning and site restoration upon closure. For example, siting pipelines and storage tanks above ground makes leaks easier to detect and removal of pollution risks more straightforward. See also GG Manual, paragraph 2.18.

[102] Pursuant to Article 16(2) of the 2007 Regulations.

[103] Paragraph 3.23–3.24, EA Guidance.

[104] EA Guidance, paragraph 3.25.

[105] EA Guidance, paragraph 3.29.

[106] EA Guidance, paragraph 3.30.

cases in which the balance is different because of particular local environmental or technical circumstances. But it would not be right to authorize lower standards or delay the implementation of a BAT solely because an operator argued for this on the basis of its own financial position. Conversely, a regulator should not impose stricter standards than BAT simply because an operator can afford to pay more.[107] The second is whether the operator can obtain the technique. The EA guidance emphasizes that this does not mean that the technique has to be in general use. Nor does it mean that there has to be a competitive market for it. Nor does it matter if the technique is from outside the EU. It means that it has been developed or proven as a pilot, provided that the industry could then confidently introduce it.[108]

6.61 The Commission has published BAT Reference documents ('BREFs') for 30 sectors. They are not binding, but regulators are required to take account of them. The EA produces domestic guidance for individual sectors within the UK, which contains clear, indicative standards and timetables for upgrading existing installations. Operators should take account of all relevant guidance when preparing their applications and justify any proposed departures. New installations will usually be expected to comply with the indicative BATs. Further guidance is available in the EA Guidance.[109]

6.62 The wording of an appropriate BAT condition is suggested:

> The best available techniques shall be used to prevent or, where that is not practicable, reduce emissions from the (installation)(mobile plant) in relation to any aspect of the operation of the (installation)(mobile plant) which is not regulated by any other condition of this permit.[110]

6.63 Guidance emphasizes that the BAT covers both the plant in the installation and how it is used. Operation of the installation includes its management, management system, staff numbers, training, personnel competences, working methods, maintenance, records, and monitoring of any releases.[111] This means that an operator must have not only adequate technical controls on polluting releases but also ensure that operating staff are properly trained and adhere to such procedures. Permits should require the operator to keep records of such training and procedures for inspection. External certification is also encouraged, where appropriate. Use of appropriate environmental management systems may impact the level of fee that is payable in particular instances.

6.64 Further guidance is given to Local Authorities on BAT.[112]

---

[107] EA Guidance, paragraph 3.31.
[108] EA Guidance, paragraph 3.18.
[109] Paragraph 3.32–3.45, EA Guidance.
[110] GG Manual, paragraph 1.10.
[111] GG Manual, paragraph 11.6
[112] See further at paragraph (6.252 and 6.259) below.

Waste operations

A slightly different set of objectives, restrictions, and standards must be taken into **6.65** account or achieved when considering waste operations. As waste operations controlled under the 2007 Regulations will either be Part A(1), Part A(2), or Part B operations, the primary requirements will apply. These requirements are supplemented by the following aspects.

Following the submission of an application, an Environmental Permit must not be **6.66** granted in relation to a relevant waste operation if use of the site for carrying out that operation requires a planning permission and no such permission is in force.

The Agency must exercise its functions for the purposes of implementing Article **6.67** 4 of the Waste Framework Directive which requires that:[113]

- necessary measures are taken to ensure that waste is recovered or disposed of without endangering human health and without using processes or methods which could harm the environment, and in particular:
  - without risk to water, air, or soil, or to plants or animals;
  - without causing a nuisance through noise or odours;
  - without adversely affecting the countryside or places of special interest; and,
  - that necessary measures to prohibit the abandonment, dumping, or uncontrolled disposal of waste are taken.

The Agency is also required to ensure that records under Article 14 of the Directive **6.68** are kept and made available to the regulator on request.

In relation to the disposal of waste, the Agency must exercise its functions for the **6.69** purposes of implementing Article 5 of the Waste Framework Directive,[114] any waste management plan, and to ensure that requirements of Article 9(1) of the Waste Framework Directive are met.[115]

Landfill installations

Particular responsibilities have also been set down for landfill installations covered **6.70** by the 2007 Regulations.[116] The Agency must ensure that every application for an

---

[113] Paragraph 3, Schedule 9, 2007 Regulations; and see the general requirements of paragraph 3(1), Schedule 20, 2007 Regulations.

[114] See also paragraph 4 of Schedule 20, 2007 Regulations.

[115] ie, those in the second paragraph of Article 9(1). See Paragraph 4, Schedule 9, 2007 Regulations.

[116] Except for landfills which ceased accepting waste before 16 July 2001 (paragraph 1(b), Schedule 10, 2007 Regulations and except in relation to operations excluded from the scope of Directive 99/31/EC under Article 3(2), which includes inert waste suitable for redevelopment or infilling work; the spreading of sludges for fertilization and the deposit of non-hazardous dredging sludges alongside small waterways from where they have been dredged out.

environmental permit includes the information required by Article 7 of the Directive 99/31/EC ('the Landfill Directive'). The information is:

- the identity of the applicant and of the operator when they are different entities;
- the description of the types and total quantity of waste to be deposited;
- the proposed capacity of the disposal site;
- the description of the site, including its hydro-geological and geological characteristics;
- the proposed methods for pollution prevention and abatement;
- the proposed operation, monitoring, and control plan;
- the proposed plan for the closure and after-care procedures;
- any information provided under environmental impact assessment;
- the financial security by the applicant.[117]

6.71 The Agency is also required to exercise its functions in order to ensure the following objectives are met:

- That each landfill is classified into one of the following classes:
  - landfill for hazardous waste,
  - landfill for non-hazardous waste,
  - landfill for inert waste.[118]

- That measures are taken to ensure that certain wastes are not accepted in a landfill, including liquid waste, flammable waste, and clinical waste.[119]

- That only certain wastes are to be accepted in landfill, including only waste that has been subject to treatment, that only certain hazardous waste be assigned to a hazardous landfill, that inert waste landfill sites shall be used only for inert waste.[120]

- That certain requirements of the permit are specified. For example that the management of the site is in the hands of a natural person, that necessary measures are taken to prevent accidents and limit their consequences, and that adequate provision is made to ensure that the obligations (including after-care provisions) are followed.[121] In addition the permit should specify the defined types and quantities of waste, the requirements for the landfill preparations, landfilling operations and monitoring and control procedures, and to place on the applicant the responsibility to report at least annually to the competent authority on the types and quantities of waste disposed of and on the results of the monitoring programme.[122]

---

[117] See also Article 8(iv) of the Landfill Directive.
[118] Paragraph 5(1)(a), Schedule 10, 2007 Regulations and Article 4, Landfill Directive.
[119] Paragraph 5(1)(b), Schedule 10, 2007 Regulations and Article 5, Landfill Directive.
[120] Paragraph 5(1)(c), Schedule 10, 2007 Regulations and Article 6, Landfill Directive.
[121] Paragraph 5(1)(d), Schedule 10, 2007 Regulations and Article 8, Landfill Directive.
[122] Paragraph 5(1)(e), Schedule 10, 2007 Regulations and Article 9, Landfill Directive.

- That all of the costs involved in the setting up and operation of a landfill site, including as far as possible the cost of the financial security, and the estimated costs of the closure and after-care of the site for a period of at least 30 years, are covered by the price to be charged by the operator for the disposal of any type of waste in that site.[123]

- That, prior to accepting the waste at the landfill site, before or at the time of delivery, the holder or the operator can show, by means of the appropriate documentation, that the waste in question can be accepted at that site according to the conditions set in the permit. This will include the operator following certain reception procedures.[124]

- That control and monitoring procedures in the operational phase are set down. They include the following aspects:
  - the operator shall carry out a control and monitoring programme;
  - the operator shall notify the competent authority of any significant adverse environmental effects revealed by the control and monitoring procedures.[125]

- In relation to closure and after-care procedures, the Agency shall take certain additional measures in order that, in accordance, where appropriate, with the permit:
  - a landfill or part of it may only be considered as definitely closed after the competent authority has carried out a final on-site inspection;
  - after a landfill has been definitely closed, the operator shall be responsible for its maintenance, monitoring, and control in the after-care phase for as long as may be required by the competent authority, taking into account the time during which the landfill could present hazards.[126]

- The Agency is also required[127] to ensure compliance with certain parts of European Council decision 2003/33/EC. (Criteria and procedures for the acceptance of waste at landfills). Consequently, the Agency is required to:[128]
  - introduce a procedure to determine the acceptability of waste at landfills;[129]

---

[123] Paragraph 5(1)(f), Schedule 10, 2007 Regulations and Article 10, Landfill Directive.

[124] Paragraph 5(1)(g), Schedule 10, 2007 Regulations and Article 11, Landfill Directive.

[125] Paragraph 5(1)(h), Schedule 10, 2007 Regulations and Article 12, Landfill Directive.

[126] Paragraph 5(1)(i), Schedule 10, 2007 Regulations and Article 13, Landfill Directive. Note also that compliance with Article 14 is required so that existing landfills will be brought under control over a phased period: paragraph 5(1)(j), Schedule 10, 2007 Regulations.

[127] Paragraph 5(3), Schedule 10, 2007 Regulations.

[128] Subject to particular interpretative limitations set out in paragraphs 7–9 of Schedule 10, 2007 Regulations.

[129] Article 2 of the Decision.

- ensure that waste is accepted at a landfill only if it fulfils certain specified acceptance criteria;[130]
- use specific sampling and testing methods[131] to determining the acceptability of waste at landfills.

Waste motor vehicles

6.72 In addition to the overarching Environmental Permitting objectives, the Agency must exercise its functions to ensure compliance with Article 6(1) of Directive 2000/53/EC (the 'End-of-Life Vehicles Directive'). This requires the Agency to take measures to ensure that:[132]

- All end-of-life vehicles are stored (even temporarily) and treated without endangering human health and without harming the environment, and in particular:
  - without risk to water, air, soil, and plants and animals,
  - without causing a nuisance through noise or odours,
  - without adversely affecting the countryside or places of special interest.

- Any establishment or undertaking carrying out treatment operations obtains a permit from, or is registered with, the Agency.

- Any establishment or undertaking carrying out treatment operations fulfils at least the following obligations:
  - end-of-life vehicles shall be stripped before further treatment or other equivalent arrangements are made in order to reduce any adverse impact on the environment;
  - hazardous materials and components shall be removed and segregated in a selective way so as not to contaminate subsequent shredder waste from end-of-life vehicles;
  - stripping operations and storage shall be carried out in such a way as to ensure the suitability of vehicle components for reuse and recovery, and in particular for recycling;
  - treatment operations for depollution of end-of-life vehicles as referred to in Annex I(3) shall be carried out as soon as possible;
  - the permit or registration includes all conditions necessary for compliance with those requirements.

---

[130] Contained in the Annex to the Decision.
[131] Contained in Section 3 of the Annex to the Decision.
[132] Paragraph 3(1), Schedule 11, 2007 Regulations.

Waste electrical and electronic equipment

Waste electrical and electronic equipment is within the scope of Directive **6.73**
2002/96/EC (the 'WEEE Directive') and is also to be dealt with by the Agency
having regard to additional objectives. The Agency is required to ensure, in carrying out its functions in relation to installations or plant which deals with such
equipment, that:[133]

- Systems are set up to provide for the treatment of equipment using best available treatment, recovery, and recycling techniques. As a minimum, such systems
should include the requirement to remove all fluids and a selective treatment in
accordance with Annex II to this Directive.

- Operators carrying out treatment operations obtain a permit from the competent authorities.

- Operators carrying out treatment operations store and treat equipment in compliance with the technical requirements set out in Annex III of the Directive.[134]

- Operators which carry out treatment operations are encouraged to introduce
certified environmental management systems.

Waste incineration

In order to meet the requirements of Directive 2000/76/EC (the 'Waste **6.74**
Incineration Directive'), the Agency must ensure that every application for an
Environmental Permit for a waste incineration installation[135] includes a descrip-
tion of the measures which are envisaged to guarantee that:[136]

- The plant is designed, equipped, and will be operated in such a manner that
the requirements of the Waste Incineration Directive are met, taking into
account the categories of waste to be incinerated.

- The heat generated during the incineration and co-incineration process is
recovered as far as practicable.

- The residues will be minimized in their amount and harmfulness and recycled
where appropriate.

- The disposal of the residues which cannot be prevented, reduced, or recycled
will be carried out in conformity with national and Community legislation.

---

[133] Paragraph 3(1), Schedule 12, 2007 Regulations and Article 6(1), WEEE Directive.
[134] Which includes requirements for the way that particular installations/plant should be constructed and operated.
[135] That is, that part of an installation or mobile plant in which the incineration of waste falling
within certain parts of Section 5.1 of Part 2 of Schedule 2 (see paragraph 2(1), Schedule 13, 2007
Regulations).
[136] Paragraph 3, Schedule 13, 2007 Regulations.

6.75 In addition, the Agency must ensure that, in exercising its functions, a number of particular objectives are achieved,[137] including the control of the delivery and reception of waste, appropriate operating conditions, air emission limit values, water discharges from the cleaning of exhaust gases, the control of residues, monitoring and measuring provisions, and measures for dealing with abnormal operating conditions.[138]

6.76 Guidance on the Waste Directive is available as one of the set of explanatory guidance notes on the directives implemented through the 2007 Regulations[139].

Solvent emissions installations and plant

6.77 When dealing with SED installations or plant, the Agency must apply certain parts of the Directive 1999/13/EC (the 'Solvent Emissions Directive'). It must exercise its functions to ensure, in addition to the general requirements contained in the 2007 Regulations, that a number of aspects of the Solvent Emissions Directive are complied with;[140] they include ensuring that:

- All installations comply with specified emission limit values in waste gases and the fugitive emission values.

- An exchange of information between Member States and the activities concerned on the use of organic substances and their potential substitutes takes place.

- An installation supplies the Agency once a year or on request with data that enables the Agency to verify compliance with this Directive.

- Channels to which abatement equipment is connected, and which at the final point of discharge emit more than an average of 10 kg/h of total organic carbon, are monitored continuously for compliance.

- Either continuous or periodic measurements are carried out.

- Following a substantial change, compliance with requirements shall be re-verified.

- If it is found that the requirements of this Directive have been breached, the operator informs the Agency and takes measures to ensure that compliance is restored within the shortest possible time; and, in cases of non-compliance causing immediate danger to human health and as long as compliance is not restored, operation of the activity is suspended.

---

[137] Paragraph 4, Schedule 13, 2007 Regulations.
[138] See articles 4–13, Schedule 13, 2007 Regulations.
[139] It is available at <http://www.defra.gov.uk/environment/epp/documents/wid-guidance.pdf>
[140] See paragraph 3, Schedule 14, 2007 Regulations.

Combustion plants, asbestos, titanium dioxide, and petrol vapour recovery

In addition to the major installations already considered, the 2007 Regulations **6.78**
ensure that the provisions of particular European directives are complied with in
the Agency's actions.[141]

C. The Environmental Permit Procedure

The application

An application for an Environmental Permit must be made on the form provided **6.79**
by the regulator[142] and include the information specified on the form. Pre-application discussions are encouraged. The operator is expected to have read the published guidance before entering into such discussions. The regulator must not be
expected to provide advice in pre-application discussions that might prejudice its
determination of an application.[143] These discussions can clarify whether a permit
is likely to be needed, or the regulator may give general advice on how to prepare
their applications. Other parties may be invited to join these discussions, for
example a public consultee.[144] Operators should bear in mind that, especially for
controversial cases, good engagement with local or national interested parties
at the pre-application stage can be beneficial to all sides.[145]

The Agency must ensure, in relation to Part A installations and mobile plant, that **6.80**
descriptions of the following are included in an application:[146]

- the installation and its activities;
- the raw and auxiliary materials, other substances and the energy used in or generated by the installation;
- the sources of emissions from the installation;
- the conditions of the site of the installation (although not applicable in the case
  of mobile plant and a SED activity);

---

[141] See Schedules 15, 16 and 17, 2007 Regulations.
[142] See Schedule 5, 2007 Regulations. The Core Guidance provides that the form should be clear
and simple to understand, identify any administrative and technical information required, require
the information required by any relevant Directive(s), require where relevant the assessment of the
potential impact on the environment and human health, require, where relevant, a level of detail
proportionate to the environmental risk and be sufficiently comprehensive to enable operators to
submit complete applications. Core Guidance, paragraph 5.3.
[143] Core Guidance, paragraph 4.6.
[144] Core Guidance, paragraph 4.7.
[145] Core Guidance, paragraph 4.8
[146] See paragraph 4, Schedule 7, 2007 Regulations.

- the nature and quanitities of foreseeable emissions from the installation into each medium as well as identification of significant effects of the emissions on the environment;

- the proposed techonology and other techiques for preventing or, where that is not possible, reducing emissions from the installation;

- where necessary, measures for the prevention and recovery of waste generated by the installation;

- further measures planned to comply with the requirement to ensure that all appropriate preventive measures are taken against pollution in particular through application of the best available techniques, that no significant pollution is caused, that waste production is avoided,[147] the energy is used efficiently, that the necessary measures are taken to prevent accidents and limit their consequences,[148] and that the necessary measures are taken upon cessation of activities to avoid any pollution risk and return the site of operation to a satisfactory state. The main alternatives, if any, studied by the applicant should be provided in outline and a non-technical summary of the details of the application.

6.81 A fee is prescribed under a charging scheme; the charging scheme produced by the Agency prescribes a number of fee tiers which reflects the complexity of the regulated facility which is the subject of an application.

6.82 While the Agency is entitled to ask for further information,[149] an applicant would be well advised to take considerable efforts over the formulation of the application as it would be better to enhance the immediate chances of success rather than have to undertake an appeal.

---

[147] The GG Manual emphasizes the importance of waste minimization. The sector guidance notes evisage that generally permit conditions will require the operator to record materials usage and waste generation to establish internal benchmarks and to carry out a waste minimization audit at least as frequently as a permit review to account for process changes, new technical understanding and appreciation of environmental risks. If no audit has been carried out within the previous two years before an application is made, the operator should compile one within 18 months of issue of the permit, with the methodology used and an action plan for optimizing the use of raw materials submitted within two months of completion of the audit. Specific improvements resulting from the recommendations should then be carried out within a timescale approved by the local authority. Further guidance is given in Chapter 21 of the GG Manual.

[148] The GG Manual emphasizes that applications for a permit should identify the main accident hazards and potential consequences; the risk of these occuring; and the steps to be taken to reduce the risks, together with contingency plans to tackle accidents that do occur and their pollution consequences. Paragraph 20.3. The Control of Major Accident Hazard Regulations (COMAH) SI 1999/743 may also apply in appropriate cases. Most of the sector guidance notices also contain a specific framework for analysing appropriate accident risks.

[149] Paragraph 4, Schedule 5, 2007 Regulations.

The Core Guidance gives examples of information operators may wish to include **6.83** in their applications, where relevant. These include:[150]

- Environmental Impact Assessments;
- documents relating to an installation's regulation under the Control of Major Accident Hazards Regulations ('COMAH');[151]
- prior investigations for compliance with the Groundwater Regulations;[152]
- externally certified environmental management systems;
- site reports prepared for planning purposes.

The Core Guidance emphasizes that the regulator should satisfy itself that the **6.84** operator's assessment of the risk is sufficiently robust. In particular, any assumptions that the operator has made about its proposals must be clearly justified. The regulator must assess the application and the adequacy of the impact assessment including whether the control measures proposed by the operator are appropriate for mitigating the risks and their potential impact.[153] Separate guidance has been produced for environmental risk assessments, *Guidelines for Environmental Risk Assessment and Management—Revised Departmental Guidance*[154] and regulators are encouraged to make reference where appropriate to that guidance.[155]

The Core Guidance provides that the regulator should only require further informa- **6.85** tion where that information is 'essential' to allow the application to be determined. Any request for information should meet at least one of the following criteria. The information must be necessary to assess whether the proposal meets any Directive or other requirements, or to determine the appropriate permit conditions to impose.[156] This further information might, for example, comprise information to understand sufficiently the environmental impact or risk posed, or information to understand sufficiently the proposed operation.[157] Where a further information notice is required, the Core Guidance provides that it must be served as soon as possible in the determination process. The notice must clearly specify what information the regulator requires, why it needs that information, and when it must be supplied by. A reasonable period should be given for the applicant to provide the information.

---

[150] Core Guidance, paragraph 4.9. Operators should make clear which parts of any attachments are relevant to their environmental permit applications and should demonstrate how they relate to the relevant Directive requirements.

[151] The Control of Major Accident Hazards Regulations 1999, SI 1999/743.

[152] The Groundwater (England and Wales) Regulations 1998, SI 1998/2746.

[153] Core Guidance, paragraph 6.3.

[154] Department of the Environment, Transport and the Regions, Environment Agency and the Institute for Environment and Health, 2000

[155] Core Guidance paragraph 6.4.

[156] Core Guidance, paragraph 5.16.

[157] Core Guidance, paragraph 5.17.

6.86 The applicant must provide the information specified and an omission either in the range or detail may lead the regulator to consider that the applicant has failed to provide the information, and decide that the application should not be continued with. If the regulator intends to deem the application withdrawn, before doing so it must review its decision to require further information and then may serve a notice stating that the application is deemed to have been withdrawn.[158] The Core Guidance provides that where a regulator intends to do this, it should normally offer the operator a final opportunity to supply the information and a face-to-face meeting.[159] There is a right of appeal against a deemed withdrawal.

6.87 The application must be 'duly-made'. A regulator may conclude that an application is not duly made when, for example, it has not been submitted on the correct form; it is for an activity that falls outside the scope of the Regulations; it has been sent to the wrong regulator; the necessary fee has not been paid; or it has not adequately addressed a key point in the application form.[160] If there is more than one operator of an installation, all of the operators must make an application otherwise the application is not duly made.[161] The regulator should use normal standards of reasonableness and common sense when assessing whether an application was duly made. Local authorities are given specific guidance as to 'reasonableness' where sector guidance notes have not been published when the application for an existing LA-IPPC is made, or where Defra has indicated that there is a strong likelihood that the 2007 Regulations will be amended so as to transfer a particular category of installation from one Part of the Regulations to another.[162]

6.88 A regulator may also accept changes to a duly-made application where it considers it appropriate.

6.89 An applicant may withdraw an application before it is determined. If it is withdrawn, however, the applicant is not entitled to the return of any fee which accompanied it.[163]

Operator competence

6.90 The regulator must consider operator competence when assessing an application for an Environmental Permit or an application to transfer (in whole or in part) an Environmental Permit. The regulator must not issue or transfer an environmental permit if it considers that the operator will not operate the facility in accordance

---

[158] Core Guidance, paragraph 5.20.
[159] Core Guidance, paragraph 5.21.
[160] Core Guidance, paragraph 5.4.
[161] Core Guidance, paragraph 5.5.
[162] GG Manual, paragraph 4.29. See also AQ4(03) on duly-made applications (special cases). The underlying principles are still relevant.
[163] Paragraph 3, Schedule 5, 2007 Regulations.

with the permit.[164] The regulator might doubt that the operator could or is likely to comply if the operator's management system or technical or financial competence is inadequate, or if the operator has a poor record of compliance with previous regulatory requirements.[165] Regulators can impose permit conditions to ensure that standards are maintained throughout the regulated facility's life. The regulator may consider reassessing the competence of the operator if the permit conditions are not complied with. Comptence can be reassessed at any time and, if not satisfied, the regulator can revoke the permit.[166]

The nature of the required management system will depend upon the complexity **6.91** of the regulated facility. Complex regulated facilities are 'encouraged' to put in place a formal environmental management system ('EMS') externally certified to ISO 14001 or other European equivalent, and to register for the EU's Eco Management and Audit Scheme, EMAS. These standards require that the management system include safeguards for legal compliance and a commitment to continuous improvement of environmental performance. EMAS also requires organizations to produce an independently validated public report about their environmental performance. Where relevant, the Core Guidance emphasizes that performance should be benchmarked against European legislation. The Core Guidance also emphasizes that lower fees and charges may apply if an organization has implemented an EMS, as they may achieve a better Operator and Pollution Risk Appraisal scheme score under the risk rating scheme run by the Environment Agency. For simpler facilities, operators can consider whether a scheme such as BS8555 is more appropriate. Regulators should encourage an EMS where appropriate.[167]

Operators should be technically competent to operate their facility. An operator's **6.92** wider management system should contain mechanisms for assessing and maintaining technical competence. The development of industry-led competence schemes is 'strongly encouraged' and advice from the relevant Sector Skills Council should be sought in development. All schemes should be agreed with the regulator and the Government and based on accredited qualifications where these exist.[168] Additional guidance is given for waste operations.[169]

The operator of any regulated facility should be financially capable of complying **6.93** with the Environmental Permit. Specific provisions apply to landfill facilities. For other facilities, regulators should only explicitly consider financial solvency where

---

[164] Paragraph 13, Schedule 5, 2007 Regulations.
[165] Core Guidance, paragraph 8.4.
[166] Core Guidance, paragraph 8.21.
[167] Core Guidance, paragraphs 8.6–8.8.
[168] Core Guidance, paragraph 8.9–8.10.
[169] Core Guidance, paragraph 8.11–8.12.

running costs are high relative to the profitability of the activity or if the regulator has any other reason to doubt the financial viability of the activity.[170] Guidance given to local authorities suggests a credit reference check (with the authorization of the operator) or provision of alternative evidence. If alternative evidence is provided, the guidance states that it must be 'credible', such as a letter from a financial institution showing that the applicant has sufficient funds or loans available.[171]

6.94   The regulator may consider whether the operator or any 'relevant person' has been convicted of a relevant offence. A relevant offence is 'any conviction for an offence relating to the environment or environmetnal regulation'.[172] A 'relevant person' is the operator or the director, manager, secretary, or other similar officer of an operator (when it is a corporate body) and a partner in a limited liability partnership, who has either been convicted of a relevant offence or who held a position in another corporate body or partnership when it was convicted of a relevant offence. Refusal will 'normally' be appropriate for offences that demonstrate a deliberate disregard for the environment or for environmental regulation, for example, where there have been repeated convictions or deliberately making false or misleading statements.[173] The regulator must take into account the terms of the Rehabilitation of Offenders Act 1974. However, this only applies where an individual has been convicted of an offence. Where a person is a corporate body, the regulator should have regard to whether the conviction would normally have been spent if it had been committed by an individual and should normally treat the corporate body the same way.[174] The regulator may still grant or transfer a permit, or allow a permit to continue in force, even though a relevant person has been convicted of an offence.[175]

Charges

6.95   There are two related but separate charging arrangements for the Environment Agency[176] (approved by the Secretary of State) and where the local authority is the regulator (set by the Secretary of State).[177] Charges vary at different regulatory stages and between installations and sectors. Applications normally incur charges which must be paid. If the regulator judges that the application is not duly made, the charge will usually be returned. Regulators must allow for different charges for different categories of variation application to allow for the different amounts

---

[170] Core Guidance, paragraphs 8.19–8.20.
[171] GG Manual, paragraph 11.34.
[172] Core Guidance, paragraph 8.13.
[173] Core Guidance, paragraph 8.16.
[174] Core Guidance, paragraph 8.17.
[175] Core Guidance, paragraph 8.18.
[176] Under s 41 of the Environment Act 1995.
[177] Regulation 65, 2007 Regulations.

of effort the regulator must put in to determining the application, the potential environmental impact or risk, and the necessary degree of public participation.[178] Operators must also pay subsistence charges to support the regulator's ongoing costs, such as for checking, monitoring data, or compliance assessment. If an operator fails to pay a subsistence charge, the regulator may revoke the permit.[179]

Alternative forms of application

The staged application

An application may be staged where it is novel and involves complex installations, **6.96** with long lead times and multiple design and construction phases and is therefore difficult to determine properly at the design stage. It is likely that only a small number of operators will apply in this way.[180]

Guidance to local authorities anticipates that both parties will normally discuss **6.97** and agree if an application is to be treated in this way and a plan agreed.[181] In that case, the information will be submitted in stages, with each stage fully consulted on, and the general time-limits will not apply as the actual time taken for the application will depend on the number of stages involved and their complexity. An operator may submit the first stage either when they have selected the primary process or (and the guidance anticipates that this may be more common) when they have finished an outline of the process design. The operator will then give the regulator further stages of the application as they work up a more detailed proposal. Each submission will also be placed on the public register and will be open to consultation in the usual way.

The regulator will finally determine the *entire* application. The regulator and pub- **6.98** lic consultees must be provided with a complete, consolidated application rather than a set of separate submissions from each stage. Note that the regulator cannot predetermine the final outcome and must take account of any new information that emerges from a final consultation. Using a staged procedure is therefore explicitly not a guarantee that the application will be granted. However guidance indicates that the chances of refusal at the end of a staged application proceess will be small, as much of the application will have already been subject to public consultation. Possible objections and technical problems are more likely to emerge at an early stage.

---

[178] Core Guidance, paragraph 11.4.
[179] Regulation 65(5), see also Regulation 31(3), 2007 Regulations, and Core Guidance, paragraph 11.5.
[180] EA Guidance, paragraph 4.13.
[181] GG Manual paragraphs 4.14–4.18.

Composite applications

6.99 A single permit may authorize[182] the operation by the same operator (a) on the same site of more than one regulated facility other than a Part B installation or Part B mobile plant; (b) on the same site, more than one Part B installation; (c) more than one mobile plant; and (d) more than one 'standard facility'.[183] The regulator must be the same. By the same token, if there are multiple permits which authorize the operation of mobile plant by the same operator, or the operation of standard facilities, or the operation of regulated facilities on the same site by the same operator, the Agency may replace the environmental permits with a consolidated environmental permit.[184] A mobile plant may not be combined with any other category of regulated facility under a single permit, nor may LAPPC installations be combined with any other category of regulated facility.[185]

6.100 The Secretary of State can make a direction under Regulation 33 to a local authority to carry out the Agency's functions. A local authority cannot be directed to exercise the Agency's functions for a waste operation (unless part of an installation or a mobile plant). Any such direction must be published on the relevant website(s)[186] and any person affected notified. It is envisaged that these powers are likely to be used mainly where there are regulated facilities on the same site but with different regulators. It is thought this is most likely to arise where there is a waste operation taking place as part of a Part A(2) or Part B installation.[187] It is not possible to have a single permit with more than one regulator, so a direction to change regulators would allow a single permit for the site.[188] The operator or the regulators may make a written request for a direction in such cases. Where a single regulator is determined, this may result in a whole-site permit being drawn up. However, where a single permit is not possible because of the different provisions relating to Part A installations and waste operations as compared to Part B installations, there may be a single regulator but more than one Environmental Permit.[189]

6.101 The aim is to allocate regulatory responsibility to the regulator of the major activity on the site. Each case will be considered by the Secretary of State on its own merits, but will be guided by the following criteria:[190]

---

[182] Regulation 17, 2007 Regulations. Guidance for local authorities is given in the GG Manual at paragraph 2.13 and following.
[183] See below for the 'standard facility'.
[184] Regulation 18, 2007 Regulations.
[185] GG Manual, paragraph 2.18.
[186] Core Guidance, paragraph 3.9.
[187] Core Guidance, paragraph 3.12.
[188] Core Guidance, paragraph 3.10.
[189] Core Guidance, paragraph 3.15.
[190] Core Guidance, paragraph 3.13.

- Where both regulators and the operator seek a direction, the Secretary of State will issue it unless they are aware of any regulatory or environmental protection reason not to do so.

- Where there is disagreement amongst the three parties, the Secretary of State will need to be persuaded that there are sound regulatory or environmental protection reasons why regulation by a single regulator would be inappropriate.

- In considering the underlying principle that regulatory responsibility should be allocated based on the major activity on the site, and to favour the regulator who regulates that activity, the Secretary of State will consider:[191]

  - whether the 'minor' activity has disproportionate potential environmental impacts;
  - whether the 'minor' activity gives rise to particular technical or other complexities;
  - consistency with the way the other similar sites in the sector are regulated;
  - consistency with the way similar sites run by the same operator are regulated;
  - the views of the parties on the above criteria.

Further guidance is given in the GG Manual. Local authorities should consider **6.102** the following factors in determining whether the facilities are on the same site:

- Proximity; there should not be a simple 'cut-off' distance, since some industrial complexes cover very large areas but still can be regarded as one site for permitting purposes.

- Coherence of a site, such as a single fenced area, or sharing security or emergency systems.

- Management systems; the extent to which the regulated facilities share a common management system is a relevant consideration.[192]

Consultation and public participation

Public consultees

What was previously known as the statutory consultee is no longer a recognized **6.103** category of consultee in the context of Environmental Permit applications. The Agency is required to consult persons who 'in the regulator's opinion is affected by, is likely to be affected by, or has an interest in, an application'.[193] Consequently

---

[191] Core Guidance, paragraph 3.14.
[192] GG Manual, paragraph 2.16.
[193] Paragraph 5, Schedule 5, 2007 Regulations.

the need to consult any particular person is determined by the Agency. However, once it is decided that a person falls within the definition of a public consultee it must consult them (generally within 30 days of receipt of a duly made application[194]), taking steps it considers appropriate to inform them of the application and the place and times that its public register can be inspected free of charge. It should invite the consultees to make representations on the application and specify to the public consultees the address and the period within which the representations must be made.[195]

6.104 The public must be given an early and effective opportunity to participate in the permitting process. This applies to permits for new installations, substantial changes in the operation of an installation, and certain updating of a permit or permit conditions for an installation. The procedure provides that the public shall be informed, early in the procedure for the taking of a decision or, at the latest, as soon as the information can reasonably be provided, of:[196]

- the application for a new permit or the proposal for updating a permit or a permit's conditions;
- if applicable, the fact that a decision is subject to national or trans-boundary environmental impact assessment or consultations between member states;
- details of the regulator and other bodies from whom relevant information can be obtained or questions submitted, and the relevant time schedule;
- the nature of possible decisions or, where there is one, the draft decision;
- where applicable, the details relating to a proposal for the updating of a permit or permit conditions;
- an indication of the times and places where, or means by which, the relevant information will be made available;
- details of the arrangements for public participation and consultation;
- within appropriate time-frames, the main reports and advice issued to the Agency when the public were first consulted, and any other information which is relevant and only becomes available after the public were first consulted, should also be made available.

6.105 'National consultees' include: Primary Care Trusts, the Food Standards Agency, the Welsh Assembly Government, the Sewerage Undertaker, Natural England, Countryside Council for Wales, Scottish Natural Heritage, the Harbour Authorities, Local Fisheries Committees and the Environment Agency.[197]

---

[194] See paragraph 7, Schedule 5, 2007 Regulations.
[195] Paragraph 6, Schedule 5, 2007 Regulations.
[196] Annex V of the IPPD Directive, see paragraph 6 of Schedule 7 to the 2007 Regulations.
[197] Annex IV, GG Manual.

The GG Manual emphasizes that it is envisaged that newspaper advertisements **6.106** will only be required if the application is likely to give rise to local controversy or that the impacts will be felt in an area larger than the immediate vicinity and that a newspaper advertisement would be the best way of alerting potentially interested people.[198] Authorities should consider other methods and only if they have reasons to believe them inadequate should they opt for a newspaper advertisement. Other methods that might be appropriate are:

- letters sent to local residents and interested people;
- placing material on the authority's website;
- site notices (such as those used for planning applications);
- email notifications (including assembling databases of those wishing to be notified of future applications of different sorts);
- notices in public places such as a library.

In addition, a person whose land may be affected by a condition imposed under **6.107** Regulation 15 (requiring access by the operator onto the land) whether by being an occupier, owner, or lessee and who would be required to grant rights if the proposed condition were included in the Environmental Permit must be served with a notice. There is an overarching requirement to comply with the terms of Article 15 of the IPPC Directive.[199]

Other European member states

Where the Secretary of State is aware that the operation of certain installations[200] **6.108** (whether by way of a fresh application or a regulator initiated variation) is likely to have significant negative effects on the environment of another Member State, the Secretary of State shall forward particulars of the application to that Member State for consultation.[201] The Secretary of State may act independently, on a regulator's advice, or following a request from another Member State. It is likely that such consultation will be rare as England and Wales do not share any land borders with other Member States.[202]

Timing of application, including novel applications and where planning permission is required

Operators should normally make an application when they have drawn up full **6.109** designs but before construction work commences (whether on a new regulated facility or when making changes to an existing one). Where facilities are not

---

[198] Paragraphs 9.8–9.10, GG Manual.
[199] Paragraph 6, Schedule 7, 2007 Regulations. See also the compensation previsions in Schedule 5, Part 2, 2007 Regulations (paragraph 6.126 below).
[200] That is, those listed in Annex I to Directive (EC) 96/61.
[201] Paragraph 10, Schedule 5, 2007 Regulations.
[202] EA Guidance, paragraph 4.27 and 4.28.

particularly complex or novel, the operator should usually be able to submit an application at the design stage containing all information the regulator needs. If, in the course of construction or commissioning, the operator wants to make any changes which mean that the permit conditions have to be varied, the operator may apply for this in the normal way.[203]

6.110 There is, however, nothing in the Regulations to stop an operator from beginning construction before a permit has been issued. The risk is that regulators may not agree with the design and infrastructure put in place. Thus, to avoid expensive delays and re-work, the Core Guidance emphasizes that it is in the operator's interest to submit applications at the design stage as any investment or construction work that an operator carries out before they have been granted an Environmental Permit will be at their own risk and will in no way affect the regulator's decision.[204]

6.111 If an operator is planning an innovative process for which there is no relevant guidance, the operator should, in consultation with the regulator, assemble details of the processes, including the potential environmental impact, before making an application. The regulator must consider the predicted environmental outcome rather than focusing on the novel nature of the process when determining the application.[205] Where there is a long lead time and multiple design and construction phrases, the regulator and operator may agree to a staged application procedure (discussed at paragraph 6.95–6.98 above). The Core Guidance considers that this is only likely to be needed for a small number of Part A(1) installations.[206]

6.112 If a regulated facility also needs planning permission, the Core Guidance recommends that the operator should make both applications in parallel whenever possible. This will allow the pollution control regulator to start its formal consideration early on, thus allowing it to have a more informed input to the planning process.[207] For certain waste operations, however, planning permission must be in force if it is required before an Environmental Permit can be granted.[208]

The determining body

Generally

6.113 The application for an Environmental Permit relating to Part A(1) installations will be adjudicated upon by the Agency.

---

[203] Core Guidance, paragraph 4.10.

[204] Core Guidance, paragraph 4.11.

[205] Core Guidance, paragraph 4.12.

[206] Core Guidance, paragraph 4.13.

[207] Core Guidance, paragraph 4.14. GG Manual Chapter 5 gives further guidance. See also Planning Policy Statement 23 and for Wales, Planning Policy Wales Chapter 13.

[208] Paragraph 2, Schedule 9, 2007 Regulations.

The manner of exercising

The framework for the decision

The Agency must either grant or refuse a duly-made application.[209] Reasons must **6.114** be given and the applicant or opeation notified of the right to appeal* However, the Agency is required to refuse the application[210] if it considers that the applicant will not be the operator of the regulated facility or if the facility will not be operated in accordance with the environmental permit.[211] This also applies if the application is for a variation or transfer application.

Other examples of where the regulator may also refuse the application are if it **6.115** believes that the environmental impact would be unacceptable, or the information provided by the operator does not provide a reasonable basis to determine the permit conditions (taking into account any responses to requests for further information), or if the requirements of relevant European Directives cannot be met.[212]

The factors to be taken into account, as well as the objectives and aims to be **6.116** achieved when assessing permits, are set out in Schedule 7 to the Regulations; this has been dealt with above.[213]

In addition, when determining an application, the Agency has an overarching **6.117** requirement to achieve a high level of protection of the environment taken as a whole by, in particular, preventing or, where that is not practicable, reducing emissions in the air, water, and land.[214]In order to ensure the Agency is best placed to achieve this aim, it is required, to follow developments in best available techniques.[215]

The Agency has a broad discretion in determining the application. It may, in **6.118** particular, add such conditions as it sees fit.[216]

Notification of the decision on any application must be made to the applicant or **6.119** operator (and a Member State, if it has been consulted) as soon as practicable, along with notification of the rights of appeal[217].

---

[209] Paragraph 12, Schedule 5, 2007 Regulations.
* Paragraph 17, Schedule 5, 2007 Regulations. Appeals are discussed in Section E below.
[210] The same requirement is applicable to transfers.
[211] Paragraph 1, Part 1, Schedule 5, 2007 Regulations; see the guidance at paragraph 6.90 above.
[212] Core Guidance, paragraph 6.7
[213] See paragraph 6.101 above.
[214] Paragraph 3, Schedule 7, 2007 Regulations.
[215] Paragraph 8, Schedule 7, 2007 Regulations. See paragraph 6.56 and following, 6.252 and 6.259.
[216] Paragraph 12(2), Schedule 5, 2007 Regulations.
[217] Paragraph 17, Schedule 5, 2007 Regulations.

The permit—specific requirements

6.120   The permit must specify every installation to which it relates, specify the person authorized to operate the i nstallation (whether an individual, partnership, or company, and who has control over the operation of the installation) and include a map, plan, or other description of the site showing the geographical extent of the installation.[218]

6.121   The permit is also required to include emission limit values for pollutants (and, in particular, for those included in Annex III of the IPPC Directive[219]). The emission limit values will either be those set down as a Community emissions limit value or, in the absence of such a value, the values contained in other directives (specified in Annex II of the IPPC Directive).

The permit—the conditions

6.122   It has already been seen how the Agency has a wide power to impose conditions and, in concluding whether a permit should be granted, is required to take into account a number of its community obligations.

6.123   Conditions should be enforceable, clear, relevant, and workable.[220] Permit conditions may be conditions stipulating outcomes, or standards to mitigate hazards or risks, or conditions addressing particular legislative requirements. Conditions may also set out steps to be taken during, prior to, or after the operation of the regulated facility.[221] A condition must be imposed requiring notification without delay in the event of any incident or accident significantly affecting the environment.[222]

6.124   To be enforceable, conditions should state their objective, so that the operator can understand what is required.[223] If measurements are required periodically, the frequency should be stated; and the discharge point of a release limit should be specified. Time-limits should be given for meeting any tighter emission limits. Local authority regulators in particular must be careful that conditions are not included if they are solely to deliver other regulatory functions, such as health and safety or planning.[224] The term 'forthwith' should be avoided.[225] Guidance on drafting permit conditions is given in the GG Manual at paragraph 3.3 and chapter 13.

---

[218] Regulation 14, 2007 Regulations.
[219] See paragraph 5(1)(b), Schedule 7, 2007 Regulations, Article 9 and Annex III of the IPPC Directive.
[220] GG Manual, paragraph 13.5.
[221] Core Guidance, paragraph 6.12.
[222] IPPC Directive, Article 14. The GG Manual suggests the following wording: 'the authority must be notified without delay of any incident or accident significantly affecting the environment'.
[223] Core Guidance, paragraph 6.10.
[224] GG Manual, paragraph 13.10.
[225] GG Manual, paragraph 13.18–13.20.

In addition, the Agency is given a specific power to impose a condition which may **6.125** require the operator to carry out works or do other things in relation to land which he is not entitled to do without obtaining the consent of another person. If an environmental permit contains such a condition, the person whose consent is required must grant the operator such rights as are necessary to enable the operator to comply with the conditions.[226]

There are, however, a number of safeguards relating to this. First, as we have seen, **6.126** there is a specific consultation requirement if such a condition is proposed.[227] Second, if the condition is imposed, compensation is payable. As a generality, compensation is payable for loss and damage of a number of descriptions:-

(A) depreciation in the value of any relevant interest to which the grantor is entitled which results from the grant of the rights;

(B) depreciation in the value of any other interest in land to which the grantor is entitled which results from the exercise of the rights;

(C) loss or damage, in relation to any relevant interest to which the grantor is entitled, which—

    (i) is attributable to the grant of the rights or the exercise of them,

    (ii) does not consist of depreciation in the value of that interest, and

    (iii) is loss or damage for which he would have been entitled to compensation by way of compensation for disturbance, if that interest had been acquired compulsorily—

        (a) under the Acquisition of Land Act 1981; and

        (b) in pursuance of a notice to treat served on the date on which the rights were granted;

(D) damage to, or injurious affection of, any interest in land to which the grantor is entitled which—

    (i) is not a relevant interest, and

    (ii) results from the grant of the rights or the exercise of them;

(E) loss in respect of work carried out by or on behalf of the grantor which is rendered abortive by the grant of the rights or the exercise of them, including expenditure incurred in the preparation of plan or other similar preparatory matters.

The compensation will also include an amount equal to the reasonable valuation **6.127** and legal expenses[228] of the person.

The compensation arises on the date of the grant of the rights, or when, following **6.128** an appeal which was made against the conditions attached to the Environmental

---

[226] Regulation 15, 2007 Regulations.
[227] See above, paragraph 6.107.
[228] Paragraph 23, Schedule 5, 2007 Regulations.

Permit, the appeal is refused.[229] An application for compensation must be made within twelve months of the date on which the entitlement to compensation arises or within six months of date on which the rights are first exercised.[230] The means by which the heads of loss and damage are calculated, is to be undertaken in accordance with Section 5 of the Land Compensation Act 1961 so far as applicable.[231] There are specific limits to the compensation. For example, no account is to be taken of any enhancement of the value of an interest in land by reason of any building erected, work done, or improvement or alteration made on land which was done which was not reasonably necessary and which was undertaken with a view to obtaining compensation or increased compensation. There are specific provisions relating to the payment of compensation to a mortagee to ensure that the mortgagee is fairly compensated for its interests in the property in question.[232] Interest is also payable.[233]

The permit—standard rules

6.129 The 2007 Regulations have sought to speed up and reduce the cost of the permitting of controlled processes by way of a standard rule procedure.

6.130 The Agency may prepare (following consultation) standard rules for the regulated facilities that are described in the rules (known as 'standard facilities).[234] The standard rules must be published on the Agency's website. At the time of writing, such standard rules are at consultation draft stage but deal with a number of common facilities.[235]

6.131 Once published, an operator of such a standard facility may request that the environmental permit includes the relevant rules as conditions of the permit. The generic assessments of risk for standard facilities should be made available to applicants to assist them in determining whether their activity is within the scope of the standard rules, and, if they apply for a standard permit, in the adoption of suitable control measures to meet those rules.[236] If the applicant requests that the the standard rules apply, there is no right of appeal against those conditions or rules.[237]

---

[229] Paragraph 23, Schedule 5, 2007 Regulations.
[230] Paragraph 24, Schedule 5, 2007 Regulations.
[231] Paragraph 24, Schedule 5, 2007 Regulations.
[232] Paragraphs 25 and 26, Schedule 5, 2007 Regulations.
[233] Paragraph 27, Schedule 5, 2007 Regulations.
[234] Regulation 26(1) and (2), 2007 Regulations.
[235] For example, certain types of waste transfer stations and amenity sites and vehicle depollution sites.
[236] Core Guidance, paragraph 7.10.
[237] Regulation 27(3), 2007 Regulations.

One important difference from other regulated facilities is that any additional **6.132** site-specific assessment of risk is not necessary for a standard facility. Thus, regulated facilities that require a location-specific assessment of impact and risk are not suitable for standard rules.[238]

Public consultation on applications for individual standard facilities is not **6.133** required, other than for Part A installations.[239] This is because consultation has or will take place in the development of the rules.

The Agency is entitled to revise the rules, following consultation (unless it is only **6.134** a minor administrative change); when the revised rules are published, they become conditions of the Environmental Permit. An operator of a facility that is affected must normally be notified of the changes three months in advance of the publication.[240] Operators not wishing to operate under the revised rules can apply for a variation to their permit before the rules take effect.[241]

The Agency may also revoke standard rules (again, following consultation). If the **6.135** Agency takes that step, it is required to vary the permit to remove the standard rules and include such alternative conditions as it considers appropriate. The revoked rules continue to have effect until such a variation takes place.[242]

Conflicts between permits

In the event that there are two Environmental Permits operating on the site of **6.136** regulated facility, one of which is for mobile plant and the other not, and there is an inconsistency between the requirements of the two permits, the requirements of the non-mobile plant permit will take precedence.[243]

The time limits for determination of an application

The regulator should acknowledge duly-made applications and identify the date **6.137** it expects to determine the application. The general time limt is four months from receipt of the application.[244] The GG Manual emphasizes that time starts running from the date an application is received, not the date on which the application is assessed to have been duly-made.[245] However, shorter time limits apply if the application is to transfer a permit (two months), or to surrender a permit (three months), or if it is an application for a mobile plant or for a permit for a standard

---

[238] Core Guidance, paragraph 7.11.
[239] Paragraph 5(1)(b) Part 1, Schedule 5, 2007 Regulations and Core Guidance paragraph 7.14.
[240] See Regulation 28, 2007 Regulations.
[241] Core Guidance, paragraph 7.17.
[242] Regulation 30(3), 2007 Regulations.
[243] Regulation 16, 2007 Regulations.
[244] Paragraph 15(2), Schedule 5, 2007 Regulations.
[245] GG Manual, paragraph 6.5.

facility other than a Part A installation (three months), or if it is an application to vary a permit, other than where public participation is required (three months). It is open to the regulator and the applicant to agree a longer period if this is necessary.[246] However, in calculating that period, a number of periods are to be ignored: if the Agency serves a notice requiring further information or a period provided for representations from persons who may be affected by a proposed condition under Regulation 15.[247] The period also does not start to run if consultation with other Member States is required given the likely cross-boundary effects that may occur. Note also that the determination periods can lengthen if a decision is required as to whether information is commercially sensitive or for national security reasons.[248]

6.138 The Acknowledgment should explain how, if the application is not determined on time, the applicant can notify the regulator that it considers the application to have been refused and so allow an appeal against that refusal.[249] This allows the applicant to appeal against the determination.

The effect of a grant

6.139 Once granted, an environmental permit continues in force until it is revoked in whole, it is surrendered, or it is replaced with a consolidated permit.

Determination by the Secretary of State

6.140 The Secretary of State can require any application to be sent to him for determination.[250]

6.141 The Core Guidance emphasizes that this is an 'exceptional step'. It is likely to be taken only if the application involves issues of more than local importance—for example, if the application:[251]

- is of substantial regional or national significance;
- is of substantial regional or national controversy;
- may involve issues of national security of foreign governments.

6.142 If this is the case, any decision would be made solely on those grounds, with no consideration of the substantive merits of the application itself.[252]

---

[246] Core Guidance, paragraph 5.11.
[247] See above at 6.85.
[248] See below at 6.295–6.305.
[249] Paragraph 15 of Schedule 5 to the 2007 Regulations.
[250] Regulation 62, 2007 Regulations.
[251] Core Guidance, paragraph 5.45.
[252] Core Guidance, paragraph 5.45.

The Secretary of State will try to deal with such applications promptly. The regu- **6.143** lator must consult as normal but should send representations to the Secretary of State. The Secretary of State may choose to arrange a hearing and will normally do so if the regulator or the operator asks for one. The Secretary of State may then direct the regulator to grant a permit, stating which conditions should be included, or refuse the permit.[253]

D. Review, Variation, Transfer, Revocation, Remediation, and Surrender of Environmental Permits

Review and inspection

In order to ensure that permits are kept up to date and relevant and to ensure that **6.144** the operators of regulated facilities comply with the requirement of the Environmental Permit, the Agency is placed under a duty to regularly review permits and make periodic inspections of regulated facilities.[254] The EA Guidance indicates that this means a permit review is required when:

- The installation causes such significant pollution that revised or additional emission limit values are needed. This might occur if new evidence emerges in relation to one emission, whether or not currently included in the permit.[255] The scope of permit review in these circumstances should be limited to the pollutant(s) of concern and to the features of the installation giving rise to the pollution.

- Substantial changes in BAT make it possible to reduce emissions significantly without excessive costs; though note that a permit review is not required if the revision is made necessary solely by changes to environmental quality standards which must be incorporated in the permit, so such changes can be brought about by a permit variation, or operators must switch to other technologies for safety reasons.

The EA Guidance indicates that this inspection process can include reviewing **6.145** information from the operator as well as carrying out independent monitoring, site inspections, in-depth audits, and other compliance-related work.[256] Permit reviews are required to check whether permit conditions continue to reflect appropriate standards and remain adequate in light of experience and new knowledge.[257]

---

[253] Core Guidance, paragraph 5.46.
[254] Regulation 34(2), 2007 Regulations. There is also a duty on the exemption registration authority to carry out periodic inspections of exempt waste operations in paragraph 13, Schedule 2, 2007 Regulations.
[255] EA Guidance, paragraph 4.11.
[256] Core Guidance, paragraph 10.5.
[257] Core Guidance, paragraph 10.32.

The EU has produced a Recommendation on minimum criteria for environmental inspections.[258] While, formally, this Recommendation is not required to be implemented in the UK, it represents good practice.[259] The GG Manual emphasizes that local authorities should draw up inspection plans, keep inspection records, and disseminate information about inspections.

6.146 The Environment Agency will determine when to carry out reviews having regard to its experience of regulating the various sectors. Local authorities may be guided in making their decisions by advice from the Secretary of State. Regulators should inform operators at the start of a review so that they are able to input into the review process.[260]

Variations of environmental permits

6.147 A variation may occur either through an application or by the Agency acting on its own initiative.[261] A variation cannot, however, reduce the extent of the site of a regulated facility (except in the case of Part B installations).[262] A variation is most likely to be requested by the Agency in response to the findings of a permit review, because conditions are needed to deal with new matters or where a compliance assessment has identified a need to vary the conditions.[263] A variation may also be necessary for other reasons, such as a new environmental quality standard,[264] or if the Environment Agency has requested a variation on releases to water from a Part A installation.[265]

6.148 The various requirements of an initial application for a permit (see paragraphs 6.79 and following above) apply to variation applications. There are two basic situations; where public participation is required and where it is not. Public participation is required where there is a substantial change and the regulator may require consultation in other cases.[266] In these cases, the regulator will notify the operator of its decision and the consultation will proceed as if it were a substantial change.

---

[258] This is available at <http://eur-lex.europa.eu/LexUriServ/LexUriServ.do?uri+CELEX:32001 H0331:EN:HTML>

[259] GG Manual, paragraph 27.09.

[260] Core Guidance, paragraph 10.33. Note that the regulator must review conditions every four years under the Groundwater Regulations. Further guidance is given on this at paragraph 10.33 of the Core Guidance.

[261] Regulation 20(1), 2007 Regulations.

[262] A variation cannot reduce the area covered by the permit if the permit required consideration of the condition of the land. As this is not required for Part B activities (regulated for emissions to air only) this restriction does not apply to them: Regulation 20(2) and 20(3), 2007 Regulations.

[263] Core Guidance, paragraph 10.28.

[264] Core Guidance, paragraph 10.29.

[265] Regulation 58, 2007 Regulations. A specimen notice is given at Annex XI of the GG Manual.

[266] Core Guidance, paragraph 5.34. See further at paragraph 6.103 and following.

The following further differences exist.   **6.149**

If the Agency is to initiate a variation, it is required to take the steps it considers appro-   **6.150**
priate to inform the public consultees (ie those who in the Agency's opinion are likely
to be affected by the application), to inform the operator of the consultation, the
variation it proposes, and any fee that may be charged for such purposes.[267]

Any variation which is made on an application must be in consequence of the   **6.151**
variation, transfer, or partial surrender (as the case may be),[268] a variation outside
the terms of, or unrelated to, the variation, transfer, or partial surrender cannot be
made. When the restriction does apply, an operator wishing to reduce the area of
the site of the regulated facility must apply for partial surrender.[269]

A decision to vary a permit must specify the variation and the date it is to take   **6.152**
effect.[270]

Transfer of environmental permits

The Agency may transfer an environmental permit in whole or in part from the   **6.153**
operator on the joint application of the operator and the other person. In a similar
way to variation applications, an application for a transfer is governed by the provisions of Schedule 5 and, consequently the matters dealt with at paragraph
6.417–6.152 above apply to such applications. The key determinant is usually
the test of operator competence. It is envisaged that transfer will be allowed if the
proposed transferee will be the operator of the installation and will operate the
installation in accordance with the permit.[271]

Where the Agency grants an application for the transfer of an Environmental   **6.154**
Permit (whether in whole or in part) the determination must specify the date
agreed between the regulator and the applicant that is to take effect.[272]

Where an envorcement notice is in force in respect of an environmental permit,   **6.155**
and the permit is transferred to another person, the duty to comply with the
enforcement notice is also transferred to the other person to the extent that it
relates to the permit or part transferred.[273]

---

[267] Paragraph 8, Schedule 5, 2007 Regulations.
[268] Paragraph 12(3), Schedule 5, 2007 Regulations.
[269] Core Guidance, paragraph 5.32.
[270] Paragraph 18(2), Schedule 5, 2007 Regulations.
[271] GG Manual, paragraph 25.3. Further guidance is given to Local Authorities in the GG
Manual at Chapter 25.
[272] Paragraph 18(3), Schedule 5, 2007 Regulations.
[273] Regulation 21(3), 2007 Regulations.

Revocation of environmental permits

6.156 A general power is given to the Agency to revoke the Environmental Permit in whole or in part.[274] The Agency, when it decides to revoke an Environmental Permit, must notify the operator, giving the reasons for the revocation, and, in the case of a partial revocation, the extent to which the environmental permit is being revoked and any variation to be made to the conditions of the permit; the revocation date must also be specified, which must be not less than 20 working days from the date on which the notice is served.[275] The Environmental Permit ceases to have effect from that date, unless the notice is withdrawn.[276] If the notice is appealed, the revocation does not take effect until the appeal is determined—or withdrawn.[277] If the regulator revokes the Environmental Permit in part, it has the power to vary the permit conditions to the extent that it considers necessary to take account of that revocation.[278] Any post-operation requirements, such as site restoration, may remain in force.[279]

6.157 After deciding to revoke, the Agency may consider that certain steps should be taken by the operator to avoid a pollution risk resulting from the operation of the regulated facility or to return the site of the regulated facility to a satisfactory state.[280]In such circumstances, unless the Environmental Permit already makes provision for such steps, the notice must specify what additional steps should be taken. If the notice makes such a provision, the steps will be treated as conditions for the purposes of applications for variations, the service of enforcment notices, and the offence of failing to comply with a regulation.[281]

Remediation

6.158 If a regulated facility gives rise to a risk of serious pollution, a regulator may arrange for the risk to be removed. If an operator commits an offence that causes serious pollution, the regulator may arrange for steps to be taken to remedy pollution at the operator's expense. The operator must be notified before the steps are taken.[282]

6.159 Site protection must be addressed through the life of a permit. The Guidance emphasizes that restoration of the site at closure cannot justify an operator

---

[274] Regulation 22(1), 2007 Regulations.
[275] Regulation 22(3), 2007 Regulations.
[276] Regulation 22(4), 2007 Regulations.
[277] Regulation 31(9), 2007 Regulations.
[278] Regulation 22(2), 2007 Regulations.
[279] Regulation 22, 2007 Regulations.
[280] Regulation 23, 2007 Regulations.
[281] Under Regulation 38(1)(b) 2007 Regulations; see Regulation 23(6)(c), 2007 Regulations.
[282] Regulation 57, 2007 Regulations.

contaminating the site during the operation of the facility. It is not usually desirable to wait until the facility closes before removing contamination or remedying harm.

Surrender of environmental permits

As a matter of principle, an operator is entitled to surrender an environmental **6.160** permit, whether in whole or in part, by way of an application.[283] Some regulated facilities may simply notify the regulator[284] but others must make an application.[285] It is possible to surrender part of the permit. Where there is a partial surrender, the regulator may need to vary the permit conditions to reflect this.[286] Note that a partial surrender is the only way to reduce the extent of the site of the regulated facility (unless a Part B installation or mobile plant).

The nature of the application, the consultation procedures, and determination **6.161** process follow the Environmental Permit application procedures dealt with already. The application must be granted if the Agency is satisfied that the necessary measures have been taken to avoid a pollution risk resulting from the operation of the regulated facility and the site of the regulated facility has been returned to a satisfactory state, having regard to the state of the site before the facility was put into operation. If the regulator is not satisfied, it has to give notice of its determination stating that the application has been refused.

The requirement to avoid any pollution risk must be interpreted in a proportion- **6.162** ate way. In practical terms, operators should tackle the risks of any pollution that could occur, unless they are so small that further action is not justified.[287] Other than in exceptional circumstances operators should remove any contamination and return the site to the original condition. Where an operator can 'robustly' demonstrate that it is unsustainable or not practical to do this, then the contamination should be removed as far as possible.[288] Landfill sites can obviously not be returned to the previous state.

The regulator will normally attribute any additional contamination of the site **6.163** since the site has been in operation to the operation of the facility, unless the regulator is convinced that the operator cannot reasonably be held responsible for it.

---

[283] Regulation 25, 2007 Regulations.

[284] This is restricted to environmental permits for Part B installations and for mobile plant. (Regulation 24 and Regulation 25, 2007 Regulations). There is no requirement to consider the condition of the land prior to surrender of a Part B installation. Similarly with a mobile plant as it does not have a geographical site associated with it, but permit conditions for mobile plans may be in place to ensure protection of the land on which they operate.

[285] Regulation 24 and 25, 2007 Regulations.

[286] Regulation 25, 2007 Regulations. See also paragraph 5.44 of the Core Guidance.

[287] Core Guidance, paragraph 6.22.

[288] Core Guidance, paragraph 6.31.

The regulator should not hold the operator responsible for contamination on the site if it occurred before the Environmental Permit was issued under the Regulations for a new facility, or before the PPC permit was issued for a facility previously regulated under the PPC Regulations, or before the issue of waste management licence under previous regimes.[289]

6.164 The 'satisfactory state' test[290] may be significantly stricter than the 'suitable for use' test in the contaminated land regime. While 'suitable for use' is appropriate for pre-existing contamination, the Guidance emphasizes that it is not the right test for the preventative environmental permitting regime. When applying to surrender a permit, applicants are therefore advised to consider whether they might be required to carry out remediation under Part 2A of the contaminated land regime, and thus whether it would be more cost effective to undertake operations for both purposes at the same time.[291] The return of the site to a satisfactory state should include: the removal of any residual waste deposits (though clearly not for landfill facilities); removing as far as is practical any contamination to the site to return the site to the original condition; and, where removal is not practical, treating or immobilizing the contamination, remedying any harm the contamination may have caused, and mitigating the effects.[292]

6.165 Note that an operator should seek surrender of the permit so as to end regulation when a regulated facility closes but is not compelled to do so.[293] Surrender of the permit will end regulation under environmental permitting and the requirement to pay the associated annual charges.

6.166 A landfill Environmental Permit may also be surrendered.[294] Where that is done, however, then for as long as the Agency considers that a landfill is likely to cause a hazard to the environment, the operator of the site shall be responsible for monitoring and analysing landfill gas and leachate from the site and the groundwater regime in the vicinity of the site.[295]

---

[289] Namely the EPA 1990 or under Part 1 of the Control of Pollution Act 1974, Core Guidance, paragraph 6.28.

[290] See Chapter 12.

[291] Core Guidance, paragraph 6.31.

[292] Core Guidance, paragraph 6.33.

[293] Core Guidance, paragraph 6.19.

[294] A landfill facility should not apply to surrender the permit until after the appropriate period of aftercare.

[295] Paragraph 11, Schedule 10, 2007 Regulations and Article 13(d) of the Landfill Directive.

E. Appeals

The right of appeal

A right of appeal is available to a person who has applied for the grant of an **6.167** Environmental Permit, its variation, transfer (whether in whole or in part), or surrender (in whole or in part), and it has been refused by the Agency. A right of appeal is also available to the following classes of person:[296]

- who is aggrieved by an Environmental Permit condition imposed when a permit is granted, varied, or transferred;
- who is aggrieved by a deemed withdrawal when further information requested by the authority is not forthcoming;
- who is aggrieved by a decision not to authorize the closure procedure in the Landfill Directive;
- on whom a revocation notice, enforcement notice, suspension notice, or landfill closure notice is served.[297]

The right of appeal will not, however, apply where any of these decisions **6.168** implements a direction of the Secretary of State.

The date for appealing

The dates for appealing are:[298]   **6.169**

- in the case of a revocation notice, before the notice takes effect;
- in the case of a deemed withdrawal of a duly-made application for a failure to supply further information as requested, within 15 working days of the date of the relevant notice[299]—in the case of an appeal in relation to confidentiality, within 15 working days after the local authority has given its determination;[300]
- within two months from the date of the notification or notice in relation to a variation notification or suspension, enforcement, or landfill closure notice;
- in any other case not later than six months from the date of the decision or deemed decision. The GG Manual indicates this would include, for example:
  - refusal or a deemed refusal to grant a permit,
  - refusal of an application to vary a permit,

---

[296] Regulation 31, 2007 Regulations.

[297] Unless, in the case of a revocation notice or suspension notice, it is because of a failure to pay a prescribed charge in respect of the Environmental Permit: Regulation 31(3), 2007 Regulations.

[298] Paragraph 3, Schedule 6, 2007 Regulations.

[299] For deemed withdrawal notices see paragraph 4(2) of Schedule 5 of the 2007 Regulations.

[300] Regulation 53(1), 2007 Regulations.

- if an operator disagrees with a condition imposed on a grant of a permit application or with a condition imposed on variation, transfer, or surrender,
- refusal of an application to transfer a permit,
- refusal of an application to surrender a permit.

6.170 The Secretary of State has the right to allow the notice of appeal to be given after the expiry of the specified periods in relation to the deemed withdrawal of a duly-made application and in relation to a variation notification, a suspension notice, an enforcement notice, or a landfill closure notice. There is no provision to extend time in the case of revocation notices or where the time for the appeal is six months.[301]

The effect of an appeal

6.171 An appeal does not have the effect of suspending the decision or notice in question, unless the appeal is against a revocation notice. In that case the revocation does not take effect until the final determination or withdrawal of an appeal.[302]

Appeal procedure

Making the appeal

6.172 There are no charges for appealing and there is no statutory requirement to submit an appeal form. The Regulations provide that notice of the appeal should be sent to the Secretary of State. A copy should also be sent to the enforcing authority.[303] The notice must be accompanied by certain additional documents, including:

- a statement of the grounds of appeal;
- any relevant application;
- a copy of any relevant Environmental Permit;
- any relevant correspondence between the appellant and the regulator;
- any decision or notice which is the subject matter of the appeal; and
- a statement indicating whether the appellant wishes the appeal to be in the form of a hearing or by way of written representations.[304] The GG Manual emphasizes that appellants should state whether any of the information enclosed with the appeal has been the subject of a successful application for commercial confidentiality and provide relevant details, as unless such information is provided all documents submitted will be open to inspection.[305]

---

[301] Paragraph 3(2), Schedule 6, 2007 Regulations.
[302] Regulation 31(8) and (9), 2007 Regulations.
[303] Paragraph 2(1), Schedule 6, 2007 Regulations.
[304] Paragraph 2(2), Schedule 6, 2007 Regulations.
[305] Paragraph 30.9, GG Manual.

However an appeal form and guidance for environmental permitting has been **6.173** prepared and is available on the Planning Inspectorate's website.[306] A failure to follow the procedure set out in that guidance may lead to adverse cost implications.

The appellant may withdraw the appeal by notifying the Secretary of State in writ- **6.174** ing. The appellant must also send a copy of that notification to the enforcing authority/regulator.[307] If the appeal is withdrawn, notice will be given to every person who was given a notice of the appeal.[308]

Notification

Upon receipt of a notice of appeal, the regulator must within ten working days **6.175** give written notice of that notice to any person who in the regulator's opinion is affected by, or is likely to be affected by, or has an interest in, the subject matter of the appeal.[309] The notice must give a description of the subject matter of the appeal and state that representations in writing may be made to the Secretary of State within 15 working days from the date of the notice.[310]

Other procedural requirements

Within ten working days of sending such a notification notice, the regulator will **6.176** notify the Secretary of State of those persons to whom the notice was sent and the date on which the notice was sent.[311]

Hearings

A hearing must be held if the appellant or regulator requests. In other cases the **6.177** Secretary of State has discretion to proceed by way of hearing or written representations.[312]

The appellant, the regulator, and any person who has made representations to the **6.178** regulator within the statutory time period, has a right to be heard at the hearing.[313] However, the person appointed to conduct the hearing should not unreasonably withhold permission to allow any other person to be heard at the hearing.[314]

---

[306] <http://www.planninginspectorate.gov.uk/pins/environment/environment/index.htm.>
[307] Paragraph 2(3), Schedule 6, 2007 Regulations.
[308] Paragraph 4(4), Schedule 6, 2007 Regulations.
[309] Paragraph 4(1), Schedule 6, 2007 Regulations.
[310] Paragraph 4(2), Schedule 6, 2007 Regulations.
[311] Paragraph 4(3), Schedule 6, 2007 Regulations.
[312] Paragraph 5(1), Schedule 6, 2007 Regulations.
[313] Paragraph 5(3), Schedule 6, 2007 Regulations.
[314] Paragraph 5(4), Schedule 6, 2007 Regulations.

6.179   Section 250 of the Local Government Act 1972, Subsections (2)–(5) apply to hearings before an appointed person.[315] After the hearing, the appointed person must make a report in writing to the Secretary of State which must include his conclusions and his recommendations, or his reasons for not making a recommendation.[316]

6.180   The Secretary of State must notify the appellant in writing of his determination of the appeal and provide a copy of the appointed person's report. He must also send those documents to the regulator. Any persons who made representations to the appointed authority or made representations at the hearing must also be sent a copy of the determination.[317] There is no requirement to send a copy of the appointed person's report to those who made representations, other than the appellant and the regulator, but copies of decision letters can be obtained at a small charge from the Planning Inspectorate.[318]

Written representations

6.181   The written representations procedure will require substantially less organization than a hearing or inquiry. Using the analogy of planning appeals, at the present time it would be a quicker method for obtaining a decision.

6.182   Where the appeal is to be dealt with by written representations, the authority will be given 28 days (from first receiving notice of the appeal) in which to submit written representations to the Planning Inspectorate. The operator will then be given 17 days (starting from the date of the authority's representations) to make further representations. Any representations must bear the date on which they were submitted to the Planning Inspectorate and must be copied to the other party. In addition the Planning Inspectorate will send both parties' copies of any representations made by third parties and will allow them at least 14 days in which to make representations on them.[319]

Call in and recovery of cases

6.183   The Secretary of State has the power to recover individual appeal cases to himself.

The decision

6.184   When determining the appeal, the Secretary of State has the same powers as the regulator had when making the decision.[320] The Secretary of State may quash or

---

[315] Paragraph 5(6), Schedule 6, 2007 Regulations.
[316] Paragraph 5(5), Schedule 6, 2007 Regulations.
[317] Paragraph 6, Schedule 6, 2007 Regulations.
[318] Requests can be made by email—DL.Library@pins.gis.gov.uk.
[319] Paragraph 30.16, GG Manual.
[320] Regulation 31(5), 2007 Regulations.

affirm the notice and if it affirms the notice, may make such modifications as it thinks fit.[321]

Costs

The parties will usually bear their own costs but if a hearing or inquiry is held as **6.185** part of the appeal process they may apply for costs. Costs may be awarded if it can be shown that a party behaved unreasonably and put the other party to unnecessary cost. Following such an application, the decision-maker will act in the spirit of DOE Circular 8/93—The Award of Costs in Planning and Other Proceedings. The certified costs of a person summoned to appear to give evidence may also be recovered.[322]

Further appeals

There is no further statutory right of appeal. However, an appeal from the deci- **6.186** sion of the Secretary of State will lie to the High Court by way of judicial review. If a determination is quashed by a court, the Secretary of State must:[323]

* send to all those who must be notified of its original determination a statement of the matters on which further representations are invited;
* give those persons 20 working days of the date of the statement as an opportunity to make written representations;
* may, as it thinks fit, cause a hearing to be held or re-opened.

There is therefore no right for the appellant to request a hearing in such a case but **6.187** all other provisions apply if a hearing is held.[324] A copy of the determination from a re-determination of an appeal must be sent to the regulator and to any person who made representations whether in writing or at a hearing. The regulator must also be sent a copy of the report by the appointed person.[325]

F. Enforcement of Environmental Permit Regime

Introduction

A range of enforcement options are provided for under the 2007 Regulations **6.188** to ensure compliance with the authorizations and permits granted under the 1999 Act. Broadly, four options are open to it: the service of prohibitory notices; criminal prosecution; injunctive proceedings; and direct action.

---

[321] Regulation 31 (6), 2007 Regulations.
[322] Paragraph 5(6), Schedule 6, 2007 Regulations; S 250 of the Local Government Act 1972.
[323] Paragraph 7(1), Schedule 6, 2007 Regulations.
[324] Paragraph 7(1)(c) and 7(2), Schedule 6, 2007 Regulations.
[325] Paragraph 7(3), Schedule 6, 2007 Regulations.

The Environment Agency's enforcement policy

6.189　The Agency applies the same general guidance indicating the approach it will take towards enforcing the Environmental Permitting regime as it did under the previous IPPC system. The Agency will seek to apply the following general principles:[326]

- The extent of the enforcement action will, where applicable, be related to the risks of environmental harm and the seriousness of the breach of the law.[327] An environmental risk may be inconsequential and so not worth enforcing against or it may be so serious that it cannot be accepted irrespective of the economic consequences.

- The principle of consistency—taking a similar approach in similar circumstances to achieve similar ends—is to be applied. It is not clear, however, how such a principle would be applied on a national basis. The Agency recognizes that a decision to enforce may differ in the circumstances of each particular case. The Agency will take account of the scale of the environmental impact, the attitude and actions of the management of the company, and the history of previous incidents or breaches.[328]

- The Agency seeks to be transparent in its dealings. It aims to help the consent holder to understand what is expected of them and what they should expect from the Agency.

- Finally, the Agency will target its enforcement action against deliberate or organized crime.

- Action will be focused upon those who are directly responsible for the risk and who are best placed to control it.

- The Agency will prioritize its regulatory effort and it will seek to respond to complaints from the public about regulated activities.[329]

The enforcing authority's investigative powers

6.190　An officer of the enforcing authority (or regulator) may be authorized by it to carry out a comprehensive range of powers if it is considered necessary either for determining whether the provisions of Part 1 of the EPA 1990 are being (or have been) complied with, for performing a pollution control function, or for determining whether and, if so, how such a function should be performed.[330]

---

[326] This guidance is taken from the Environment Agency's policy document, *The Environment Agency Enforcement and Prosecution Policy*, November 1998, Version 1. ('The Enforcement Policy')
[327] The Encrcement Policy para11. [Available at: <http://www.environment-agency.gov.uk/business/1745440/112913/ ?version=1&lang=_e>]
[328] The Enforcement Policy, para 13.
[329] The Enforcement Policy, paras 16–18.
[330] S 108(1), EA 1995.

The powers which the authorized person is entitled to exercise are wide-ranging, **6.191** and include the following:[331]

- to enter a premises which the person believes it is necessary for him to enter;

- to make such examination and investigations as he may consider necessary;

- to direct that any premises which he has power to enter shall be left undisturbed for as long as is necessary for the purpose of any examination or investigation;

- to take measurements, photographs, or samples;

- to cause an article or substance found on a premises he is entitled to enter to be destroyed if it appears to him to have caused or to be likely to cause pollution of the environment or harm to human health, or take possession of it and retain it for the purposes of examination or to prevent tampering before examination or for the purposes of using it as evidence in proceedings. The authorized person must consult persons having duties on the premises where the article or substance is to be dismantled or otherwise dealt with for the purposes of ascertaining what dangers there may be in doing anything proposed to be done by the authorized person;[332]

- to ask questions of persons who the authorized person believed can give information which the authorized person thinks fit;

- to require the production of records which are required to be kept for the purposes of the IPC regime.

Where, under those powers, the authorized person proposes to enter any residen- **6.192** tial premises or to take heavy equipment on to any premises, then, unless it is an emergency, the entry must only be made[333] after the expiration of seven days' notice and either with the consent of the occupant of the premises or a warrant from a magistrate.[334]

Where an authorized person has reasonable cause to believe that an article or sub- **6.193** stance is a cause of imminent danger of serious pollution of the environment or serious harm to human health, he may seize it and cause it to be rendered harmless.[335]

---

[331] S.108(4), EA 1995.

[332] S.108(11), EA 1995.

[333] S.108(6), EA 1995.

[334] Schedule 18, EA 1995; see also the further provisions for a warrant relating to where entry has been or is likely to be refused and the use of force may be necessary.

[335] S.109, EA 1995.

Prohibitory notices

Enforcement notices

6.194 If the Agency considers that an operator has contravened, is contravening, or is likely to contravene an environmental permit condition, the regulator may serve an enforcement notice on him.[336] The notice must state the Agency's view that an operator has contravened, is contravening, or likely to contravene a permit, specify the matters which constitute the contravention or make the contravention likely, specify the steps that must be taken to remedy the contravention or to ensure that the likely contravention does not occur; and specify the period within which those steps must be taken. The steps that may be specified in a notice include steps to make the operation of a regulated facility comply with the environmental permit conditions, and to remedy the effects of pollution caused by the contravention.

6.195 The Environment Agency has also indicated that, in the event that the inspector intends to issue an enforcement notice, it will, unless immediate action is necessary, give the consent holder an opportunity to make representations within 10 days of receiving notice that the Agency intends to issue an enforcement notice.

Suspension notices

6.196 The suspension notice deals with more serious issues than the enforcement notice. In the event that the regulator considers that the operation of a regulated facility under an Environmental Permit involves a risk of serious pollution, it may serve a suspension notice on the operator.[337] On the service of a suspension notice the Environmental Permit ceases to have effect to the extent stated in the notice[338]. The Core Guidance emphasizes that a suspension notice should allow activities to continue unless their cessation is necessary to address the risk of pollution. While the suspension notice is in force, additional restrictions may be necessary for any activities that are allowed to continue. If this is the case, the suspension notice must set out these additional steps.[339] It is to be noted that the suspension notice is forward looking; it deals with where there is a risk of serious pollution, not where one has occurred. It would only be in circumstances where the risk was ongoing that the notice could be used. It has a protective rather than a punative purpose. There need be no contravention of any condition as a precondition to service of the notice.[340]

---

[336] Regulation 36, 2007 Regulations.
[337] Regulation 37(1), 2007 Regulations.
[338] Regulation 37(4), 2007 Regulations.
[339] Core Guidance, paragraph 10.13.
[340] Regulation 37(2), 2007 Regulations.

As for the enforcment notice, the suspension notice must comply with certain **6.197** mandatory requirements. It must state the Agency's view that there is a risk of serious pollution, specify what the risk is, what steps must be taken to remove that risk, and the period within which the steps must be taken. It must state that the environmental permit ceases to have effect to the extent specified in the notice until the notice is withdrawn; and if the environmental permit continues to authorize an operation, state any steps (in addition to those specified in the steps) which are to be taken when carrying on that remaining operation.[341]

The notice may be withdrawn at any point by the Agency and must be withdrawn **6.198** if the steps specified in the notice have been taken.[342]

Landfill closure notices

A closure notice is capable of being issued in relation to landfills.[343] It must give **6.199** the reasons for requiring initiation of the closure procedure, specify the steps the operator is required to take to initiate the procedure; and the period within which they must be taken.[344] The regulator may withdraw a closure notice at any time. The issue of a closure notice does not, however, relieve the operator of a liability under the conditions of the Environmental Permit.

Direct action

If the Agency is of the view that the operation of an installation or mobile plant under **6.200** a permit involves a risk of serious pollution, it may arrange for steps to be taken to remove that risk.[345] Additionally, if an offence under Regulation 38(1)(a)–(c) has been committed,[346] the Agency may arrange for steps to be taken to remedy the effects of that pollution; five days' notice must be given to the operator if the Agency undertakes to take action under that power.[347] The costs of taking action under either power are recoverable from the operator unless the operator shows that there was no risk of serious pollution or it is shown that the costs were unnecessarily incurred.[348]

---

[341] Regulation 37(3), 2007 Regulations.
[342] Regulations 37(5), 2007 Regulations.
[343] Paragraph 10 and 5(1)(h), Schedule 10, 2007 Regulations.
[344] Paragraph 10(1)–(2), Schedule 10, 2007 Regulations.
[345] Regulation 57(1), 2007 Regulations.
[346] As to which see below at paragraphs 6.209–6.212.
[347] See Regulation 57(2)–(3), 2007 Regulations.
[348] Regulation 57(3), 2007 Regulations.

Offences

6.201   The 2007 Regulations set out a comprehensive framework of offences to ensure compliance with its terms.

The Agency's prosecution policy

6.202   The Agency has not produced a separate enforcement and prosecution policy for the Environmental Permit system. The Agency applies the same general guidance which it used under the previous IPPC system.[349] The major points are as follows.

6.203   Account will be taken of the Government's Concordat[350] and Cabinet Office Enforcement Code[351] and the Attorney-General's Code for Crown Prosecutors when deciding whether to prosecute.[352] Where an environmental permitting regulator and another enforcement body both have the power to prosecute in respect of the same subject matter, they should liaise to avoid inconsistency and make sure that any proceedings are for the most appropriate offence.[353] In addition, the following particular factors will be taken into account: the environmental effect of the offence; its foreseeability or the foreseeability of the circumstances leading to it; the intention of the offender (whether individual or corporate); the conviction history of the offender; the attitude of the offender; the deterrent effect of a prosecution (on the offender and on others); and the personal circumstances of the offender. The Magistrates' Association have also produced a comprehensive information toolkit and sentencing guidance covering many environmental offences.[354]

6.204   Normally, the Agency will prosecute (rather than use other enforcement techniques) where:

- the offence concerns breaches or incidents which have significant consequences for the environment or which have the potential for such consequences;
- operations are carried out without the relevant licence;
- regulatory requirements are persistently breached;
- there has been a failure to comply with formal remedial requirements;
- there has been a reckless disregard for management or quality standards;
- there has been a failure to supply information without reasonable excuse or knowingly or recklessly supplying false or misleading information;

---

[349] The Enforcement Policy.
[350] Available at<http://bre.berr.gov.uk/regulation/reform/enforcement_concordat/enforcement_background.asp>
[351] Ibid.
[352] <http://www.cps.gov.uk/publications/docs/code2004english.pdf >
[353] Core Guidance, paragraph 10.19.
[354] "Costing the Earth, Guidance for Sentencers", available on the Magistrates' Association website, <http://www.magistrates-association.org.uk.>

- agency staff have been obstructed in carrying out their powers; and
- agency staff have been impersonated.

While, generally, the Agency will seek to prosecute a company where one is **6.205** involved, the Agency will consider prosecuting the directors (and seeking their disqualification) where it can be shown that the offence was committed either with their consent, their neglect, or their 'wilful ignorance'.[355]

Note that the Regulations contain an important safeguard for operators, the 'emer- **6.206** gency defence'.[356] This provides a defence where the operator shows that the acts are done in an emergency to avoid danger to human health, all reasonable steps are taken to minimize pollution, and the regulator is informed promptly. The Guidance emphasizes that emergencies ought to be relatively rare occurrences.[357]

Lastly, enforcement can be appropriate where there are no complaints. The **6.207** absence of perceptible emissions or of complaints should not be taken to mean that a process is necessarily operating satisfactorily nor is it an indicator that less regulatory effort is required (except where odour is the only pollutant being controlled). The system was set up to go beyond the statutory nuisance regime.[358]

Corporate offences

An offence of a company shown to have been committed with the consent or **6.208** connivance of an officer or attributable to any neglect on the officer's part, the officer is liable in addition to the company.[359]

Operating a regulated facility without or in contravention of an environmental permit or prohibitory notices

The primary offences under the Regulations relate to carrying on of operations **6.209** either without a permit, in contravention of one, or in breach of any prohibitory notice served by the Agency.

It is an offence to contravene, or knowingly cause or knowingly permit the con- **6.210** travention of, Regulation 12. Regulation 12 provides that no person may operate a regulated facility except under or to the extent authorized by an Environmental Permit.[360]

---

[355] The Enforcement Policy, para 24.
[356] Regulation 40, 2007 Regulations.
[357] Core Guidance, paragraph 10.19.
[358] See AQ1(02) and the GG Mannual, paragraph 28.37.
[359] Regulation 41, 2007 Regulations.
[360] Regulation 38(1)(a), 2007 Regulations.

6.211 It is an offence to fail to comply with or to contravene an environmental permit condition.[361]

6.212 It is an offence to fail to comply with the requirements of an enforcement notice, a suspension notice, or a landfill closure notice.[362]

6.213 These offences are punishable, on summary conviction, to a fine not exceeding £50,000 or imprisonment for a term not exceeding 12 months, or to both; or, on conviction on indictment to an unlimited fine or imprisonment for a term not exceeding 5 years, or to both.[363]

6.214 It is to be noted that, if an offence committed by a person under this regulation is due to the act or default of some other person, that other person is also deemed to be guilty of the offence.[364]

Other offences

6.215 While the other provisions will not, it would seem, be of general application, they are nevertheless of importance. They attempt to provide a comprehensive structure of criminal control for the maintenance of the pollution control system. However, these less serious offences require the proving of a confusing array of elements.

6.216 It is an offence to fail to comply with a notice under Regulation 60(2) for the provision of information, without reasonable excuse.[365]

6.217 It is an offence to make a statement which the person knows to be false or misleading in a material particular, or recklessly to make a statement which is false or misleading in a material particular, where the statement is made:

- in purported compliance with a requirement to provide information imposed by or under a provision of these Regulations, or

- for the purpose of obtaining the grant of an Environmental Permit to himself or another person, or the variation, transfer in whole or in part, or surrender in whole or in part of an Environmental Permit.[366]

6.218 It is an offence to intentionally make a false entry in a record required to be kept under an Environmental Permit condition.[367]

---

[361] Regulation 38(1)(b), 2007 Regulations.
[362] Regulation 38(1)(c), 2007 Regulations.
[363] Regulation 39(1), 2007 Regulations, unless the offences were committed before the commencement of Section 154(1) of Criminal Justice Act 2003, in which case the fine at summary level is £20,000 and 6 months' imprisonment.
[364] Regulation 38(3), 2007 Regulations.
[365] Regulation 38(1)(d), 2007 Regulations.
[366] Regulation 38(1)(e), 2007 Regulations.
[367] Regulation 38(1)(f), 2007 Regulations.

It is an offence for a person, with intent to deceive: **6.219**

- to forge or use a document issued or authorized to be issued or required for any purpose under an environmental permit condition, or
- to make or have in his possession a document so closely resembling such a document as to be likely to deceive.[368]

It is an offence for an establishment or undertaking to fail, if it is carrying on a noti- **6.220**
fiable exempt waste operation and wishes to dispose of or recover a greater quantity of waste than that notified, not to give notice under paragraph 9 of Schedule 2.[369]

It is an offence to fail to keep certain specified records for a period of two years and **6.221**
to fail to make them available to the exemption registration authority on request. It is also an offence for an establishment or undertaking which carries out exempt waste operations to intentionally make a false entry in a record required to be kept under paragraph 12(3) of Schedule 2 to the 2007 Regulations.

Offences under the Environment Act 1995

It is an offence for a person intentionally to obstruct an authorized person in the **6.222**
exercise of his powers or duties.[370] Those powers and duties have already been specified above.

A person guilty of the offence of obstructing an authorized person in the execu- **6.223**
tion of the powers under Section 109 will be liable, on summary conviction, to a fine not exceeding the statutory maximum (currently £5,000[371]) or, on conviction on indictment, to a fine or imprisonment for a term not exceeding two years.[372]

The following are also made offences: **6.224**

- failing to comply with any requirement imposed under Section 108 of the Environment Act 1995;
- failing to provide facilities or assistance or any information or to permit an inspection reasonably required by the authorized person;
- preventing any person from appearing before an authorized person or answering any question to which an authorized person may require an answer;
- falsely pretending to be an authorized person.

A person found guilty of any of those offences will be liable on summary convic- **6.225**
tion to a fine not exceeding level 5 on the standard scale.[373]

---

[368] Regulation 38(1)(d), 2007 Regulations.
[369] Regulation 38(2)(a), 2007 Regulations.
[370] S. 110(1), EA 1995.
[371] S. 37, Criminal Justice Act 1982.
[372] S. 110(4), EA 1995.
[373] S. 110(5), EA 1995.

Court orders

Statutory orders

6.226 Where a person is convicted of an offence of either:

- operating a process without an environmental permit or in breach of such an environmental permit (that is, under Regulation 38(1)(a));
- failing to comply with or contravening an environmental permit condition (Regulation 38(1)(b));
- failing to comply with an enforcement notice, suspension notice, or landfill closure notice (under Regulation 38(1) (c));

6.227 Then, where it appears to the court that certain matters arising from such failure or breach are ones that are in his power to remedy, it may order him to take steps to remedy those matters in addition to or instead of any punishment imposed under Regulation 39.[374] In making such an order the court should specify a time limit for compliance with the order. There is, however, a certain amount of flexibility built into the section. The time for complying with any such order may be extended, or even further extended following an application, so long as the application is made before the time as originally fixed or extended.[375]

6.228 This provision is not without ambiguity. The section refers to 'where a person is convicted of an offence under Regulation 38(1)(a), (b) or (c) in respect of a matter which appears to the court to be a matter which it is in (the convicted person's) power to remedy'. It would appear, if only because a Court's actions must be compatible with the Human Rights Act 1998, that a Court would be practically limited to matters which the defendant could remedy.

6.229 The position of the enforcing authority under the provisions of this section is also unclear. Generally, a prosecuting body should not attempt to influence any sentence of the court. However, the body would have to indicate the existence of Regulation 44 and, presumably, it will be the only body that will be in a position to assist the court as to whether any remedial steps could be taken. It would seem that any dispute arising between the defendant and the prosecuting body would have to be resolved by way of a *Newton* hearing.[376]

6.230 Failure to comply with the order would amount to a contempt of court.

---

[374] Regulation 44, 2007 Regulations.
[375] Regulation 44(3), 2007 Regulations.
[376] See *R v Newton* [1982] 4 Cr App R (S); following conviction on a guilty plea, where the court is uncertain as to the basis of sentence and the defendant's version of events is substantially at odds with that of the Crown, the Crown is allowed to cross-examine the defendant on his version.

If the regulator is of the opinion that proceedings for an offence under Regulation **6.231**
38(1)(c) (failing to comply with an enforcement notice, a suspension notice,
or a landfill closure notice) would afford an ineffectual remedy, it may take
proceedings in the High Court to secure compliance with that notice.[377]
The enforcing authority would be most likely to apply for an injunction. The
principles behind injunctions are dealt with in detail in Chapter 2 (The Structure
of Environmental Legislation and Regulation) above.

Such a power will be of particular use in cases of urgency or where it could be **6.232**
shown that criminal proceedings would be unlikely to achieve compliance with
the notice. The approach of the High Court seems, however, to be more extreme
than that.

Rather, there is an onus upon the enforcing authority to demonstrate its reasons **6.233**
for believing that criminal proceedings in the magistrates' court would be ineffectual. The court seems to have considered that it would be inappropriate to grant
an injunction until it could be demonstrated that nothing short of an injunction
would restrain the defendant. The *American Cyanamid* principles would also
apply in respect of an interim injunction.

Note also that AQ7(06) suggests that notices relating to significant cases and **6.234**
successful prosecutions are given more publicity. The guidance to local authorities
suggests that knowledge at national level of the extent and details of enforcement
action will serve as an important reminder to all operators of the potential pitfalls of
non-compliance with the regulatory requirements and as a means of enforcement
experience sharing. [378]

Crown immunity

The 2007 Regulations generally bind the Crown, but the Crown is immune **6.235**
from criminal prosecution under the Act and no enforcement action may be
taken in the High Court to secure compliance with an enforcement notice, suspension notice, or landfill closure notice.[379] However, on the application of the
enforcing authority an unlawful act or omission may be declared to be so by
the court.[380] The purpose of this provision seems to be that the Crown would
normally, on a declaration being ordered by the court, act to remedy its unlaw-
fulness. A person in the service of the Crown can be prosecuted.[381] The regulations also make particular provision for service on certain Crown operators.[382]

---

[377] Regulation 42, 2007 Regulations.
[378] GG Manual, paragraph 11.28 and Annex XII.
[379] Regulation 11 and paragraph 4(1), Schedule 2, 2007 Regulations.
[380] Paragraph 4(2)(a), Schedule 2, 2007 Regulations.
[381] Paragraph 2(2)(b), Schedule 4, 2007 Regulations.
[382] Paragraph 4, Schedule 4, 2007 Regulations.

The Secretary of State may also certify that in the interests of national security particular powers of entry must not be used in relation to particular Crown premises.[383]

G. Local Authority Control of Installations and Mobile Plant

Local authority control—general matters

6.236 Local authorities are given control of two elements of the environmental permitting scheme: Part B (also referred to as 'LAPPC') and Part A(2) installations (also referred to as 'LA-IPPC'). Part A(2) installations consist of those facilities of lesser significance than Part A(1) installations but which have the potential to cause environmental impacts on media other than air. Part B installations are, in general terms, those which were formerly controlled by the local authority under the Environmental Protection Act 1990.

The role of the local authority in LAPPC and LA-IPPC

6.237 In general, the functions in relation to a Part A(2) or a Part B installation are exercisable by the local authority in whose area the installation is or will be operated.[384] Where, however, Part A(2) or Part B operation is mobile plant, then, if the operator has his principal place of business in England and Wales, the functions in relation to such plant are exercisable by the local authority in whose area the place of business is. If, however, the operator's principal place of business is outside England and Wales, the local authority which granted the permit or, if no permit has been granted, the local authority in whose area the plant is first operated (or intended to be operated) will exercise the functions of the regulator under the 2007 Regulations.

6.238 Since these installations are, in the main, less potentially polluting either because of the inherent qualities of the operation or because of the quantities of material handled, the Agency is not usually concerned with them.

6.239 The Secretary of State may direct the Agency to exercise any local authority functions and for such a period as specified in the direction.[385] A local authority can also be directed to exercise most, but not all, of the Agency functions. It is anticipated that

---

[383] Paragraph 3, Schedule 4, 2007 Regulations.

[384] Regulation 32(2), 2007 Regulations.

[385] Regulation 33(1), 2007 Regulations. Discussed above at paragraph 6.08-6.09, 6.100. Local authorities are expected to provide the Agency with all appropriate papers and agree other necessary handover arrangements as soon as possible and usually within 15 working days of a direction: GG Manual, paragraph 2.46. The Agency has agreed to do the same.

this power will be used to aid simpler regulation.[386] In some situations it may be that there is a single regulator but more than one permit, for example where there are different provisions relating to Part A installations and waste operations as compared to Part B installations where a single permit is not appropriate. To simplify transition into the new regime, regulated facilities will remain regulated by their existing regulators in the absence of a direction, although operators and/or regulators may apply for such a direction.[387]

As a matter of good practice, however, local authorities are recommended to co-operate with the Agency in carrying out their functions,[388] the Agency should be made a consultee on all LA-IPPC applications,[389] Operational contact should be established when either body becomes aware of an application or pending application in accordance with the protocol 'Arrangements to implement the requirements of the IPPC Directive', one of the protocols in the Memorandum of Understanding between the Environment Agency and the Local Government Association.[390] Further detailed guidance is given in chapter 22 of the GG Manual. **6.240**

The Local Authority is also responsible for inspection and the Manual provides appropriate guidance.[391] **6.241**

H. The Responsibilities of the Local Authority

The responsibilities of local authorities are generally identical or similar to those of the Agency. This is to be expected as the 2007 Regulations generally place the relevant obligation on the 'regulator'. Reference should be made to the relevant sections above as approriate. This section therefore only summarizes key points and identifies major areas of difference. As for the Agency, local authorities must also in all cases take account of other relevant legislation. Specific guidance is given for local authorites, the 'GG Manual'. **6.242**

---

[386] GG Manual, paragraph 2.22. .

[387] GG Manual, paragraph 2.23. The criteria the Secretary of State will consider are given at paragraphs 2.25–2.26 of the GG Guidance. Applications should be addressed to Defra, Nobel House, 17 Smith Square, London SW1P 3JR or for Wales to the Welsh Assembly Government, Cathays Park, Cardiff CF10 3NQ. Guidance on applications is given at paragraph 2.28 of the GG Manual. See also above 6.100.

[388] Section 22, the GG Manual.

[389] Paragraph 22.7, the GG Manual.

[390] Available on the Local Government Association website, <http://www.lga.gov.uk/Publication. asp?!Section=0&id+A7823B67>; on the Environment Agency website; and in the Chartered Institute of Environmental Health's PPC Management Guide, September 2004.

[391] GG Manual, Chapter 27.

Part A(2) Installations and mobile plant

6.243 The requirements and objectives which are to be achieved by the Agency in respect of Part A(1) installations are applied equally to the local authority dealing with Part A(2) installations.[392]

Part B Installations and mobile plant

6.244 Part B Installations are treated slightly differently. The local authority is required to carry out its functions in a similar manner to the Agency.

6.245 It must exercise its functions for the purpose of preventing or, where that is not practicable, reducing emissions in to the air;[393] this is less wide ranging than is the case for Part A(1) installations and plant.

6.246 Generally, the requirements of Article 6(1) of the IPPC Directive are to be met in relation to the information required to be included for an Environmental Permit.[394]

6.247 When exercising its relevant functions,[395] the local authority has a more limited responsibility than the Agency. It must ensure that all appropriate preventative measures are taken against pollution in particular through application of the best available techniques and that no significant pollution is caused.[396] Note that while all 12 BAT considerations listed in the Directive apply to LA-IPPC, some do not apply to LAPPC.[397]

6.248 The local authority is required[398] to ensure that a permit shall include all measures necessary for compliance with Articles 3(a) and (b) and 10 of the IPPC Directive[399] for the purpose of preventing or, where that is not practicable, reducing emissions into the air. The Local Authority shall take into account any relevant information provided under an Environmental Assessment when considering whether to grant a permit.[400]

6.249 The permit granted by the local authority shall include emission limit values[401] for pollutants likely to be emitted from the installation concerned in significant

---

[392] See Part B above.

[393] Paragraph 3, Schedule 8, 2007 Regulations.

[394] Subject to some specific exceptions.

[395] See Regulation 9, 2007 Regulations.

[396] Paragraph 5(1)(a), Schedule 8, 2007 Regulations and Article 3, IPPC Directive.

[397] See paragraph 6.57 above, and further, Annex VIII of the GG Manual.

[398] See paragraph 5(1)(b) and paragraph 5(2)(b), Schedule 8, 2007 Regulations and Article 9(1)–(4) of the IPPC Directive.

[399] See the commentary on paragraph 5(1)(c) and (a), Schedule 8, 2007 Regulations in this section.

[400] See paragraph 5(1)(b), Schedule 8, 2007 Regulations and Article 9(2), IPPC Directive.

[401] An emission limit value is itself defined in Article 2(6) of the IPPC Directive.

quantities,[402] having regard to their nature and their potential to transfer pollution from one medium to another. If necessary, the permit shall include appropriate requirements ensuring protection of the soil and groundwater and measures concerning the management of waste generated by the installation. The regulator may, when ensuring that there are appropriate limit values, supplement those values by parameters or technical measures,[403] such measures and values shall be based on the best available technique, without prescribing the use of any technique or specific techonology, but taking into account the technical characteristics of the installation concerned, its geographical location, and the local environmental conditions (except in the case of mobile plant).[404]

The local authority is also required, where an environmental quality standard[405] **6.250** requires stricter conditions than those achievable by the use of the best available techniques, to impose additional measures.[406]

The local authority must ensure (except in the case of Part A(2) mobile plant[407]) that **6.251** the operator informs the competent authorities of any changes planned in the operation of the installation; and must also ensure that no substantial change[408] in the operation of the installation is made without a permit.[409] In circumstances, where there is to be a substantial change, the local authority must (like the Agency) review the Environmental Permit.[410] There is no requirement, however, for the local authority to take the necessary measures to ensure the operator regularly informs the competent authority of the results of monitoring of releases without delay.[411]

The application of best available techniques has a central place in the local author- **6.252** ity administration process,[412] the same European definitions apply to the local authority functions albeit with modifications to reflect the more limited local authority role.[413] Again, like the Agency, the local authority is required to follow developments in best available techniques.[414]

---

[402] And in particular those specified in Annex III to the IPPC Directive, except that in relation to those under the heading 'WATER' (see paragraph 5(2)(f), Schedule 8, 2007 Regulations).

[403] See paragraph 5(1)(b), Schedule 8, 2007 Regulations and Article 9(3), IPPC Directive.

[404] See paragraph 5(1)(b), Schedule 8 and Article 9(4), IPPC Directive.

[405] That is, a standard set out in community legislation.

[406] See paragraph 5(1)(c), Schedule 8, 2007 Regulations and Article 10, IPPC Directive. Discussed above at paragraph 6.48.

[407] See paragraph 5(2)(e), Schedule 8, 2007 Regulations.

[408] Defined as 'a change in operation which, in the opinion of the (Agency), may have significant effects on human beings or the environment': Article 2(9), IPPC Directive. Discussed above at 6.49–6.55.

[409] See paragraph 5(1)(d), Schedule 7, 2007 Regulations and Article 12(1), IPPC Directive.

[410] Paragraph 6, Schedule 8, 2007 Regulations.

[411] Given the absence of similar provision in Schedule 8 to paragraph 5(1)(e), Schedule 7, 2007 Regulations and Article 14, IPPC Directive.

[412] See paragraph 6.56 and following above for details relating to this issue.

[413] ie the requirement to have regard to paragraphs 4–8 of Annex IV when understanding the meaning of best available techniques.

[414] See paragraph 7(1), Schedule 8, 2007 Regulations.

Waste operations

6.253 The additional requirements and objectives sought to be achieved by the Agency in relation to waste operations apply equally to the local authority.[415]

Contaminated land

6.254 Specific guidance is also given on the overlap with the contaminated land regime, which may apply where they are either the regulator or when consulted on A1 installations.[416] Note that if an authority finds that an LA-IPPC site is polluted after it has come under a permit, it may not seek remedial action under Part IIA of the EPA 1990 if enforcement action under the 2007 Regulations is possible.[417] Normally the LA-IPPC regime's requirements will be of a higher standard. However, if the site was heavily polluted with material before LA-IPPC operations, which for some reason was not remediated before the LA-IPPC operation began, then it may still be remediated under the Part IIA regime after closure.

Determination of LAPPC and LA-IPPC applications

6.255 Essentially, the local authority regime for LAPPC and LA-IPPC is the same as the Part A(1) scheme. There are, however, a number of differences under each regime which should be noted, in particular that for LAPPC (Part B) applications the public participation directive does not apply, certain installations have different time periods, the principle of proportionality is likely to be particularly relevant, and the health and safety regulatory framework is different.

The authorization framework

6.256 The application process and decision-making procedures largely follow the system to be employed by the Agency.[418] Local authorities are strongly encouraged to allow application forms to be submitted electronically. To avoid a very prescriptive form resulting in excessive provision of information, Defra has recommended that applications require certain basic information in a prescribed format but permit operators to provide the remaining information in a way that suits the operator but cross-referenced to the form, to avoid a greater burden than is necessary on industry and authorities. Specific guidance has been issued to Local Authorities in the GG Manual, which also provides a 'good practice checklist' for Local Authorities to measure their effectiveness and efficiency in delivering their

---

[415] See paragraph 6.65 and following above.
[416] GG Manual, paragraph 18.47. (See also Chapter 12 on Contaminated Land).
[417] GG Manual, paragraph 18.49–18.52.
[418] Specific guidance is given in the GG Manual.

LA-IPPC and LAPPC service.[419] A separate fee charging scheme has been produced for LAPPC and LA-IPPC schemes.[420]

Pre-application discussions should take place between the operator and the author- **6.257** ity in order to discuss any conditions the authority proposes to include. Such discussions must not imply any advance agreement to the outcome of any application, nor should the authority be expected to provide free consultancy advice.[421] Local authorities are recommended to send draft permits to operators for comment before issuing any formal document.[422] The content of an application must comply with the terms of Schedule 2, paragraph 5 of the 2007 Regulations.[423] However, the guidance makes clear that, although sufficient information may be provided to comply with these provisions, the local authority may still require (and be entitled to require) further information.[424] It should not, however, use the procedure for asking for further information[425] to unnecessarily delay an application; nor should it be used for obtaining information which is peripheral to the main issues.[426]

The consultation process is determined by the same framework governing Part **6.258** A(1) facilities. As to who should be consulted, however, local authorities are given some guidance by Defra; they differ slightly between Part B and Part A(2) installations.[427]

The level of detail required in any application should be proportionate to the size **6.259** and scale of the installation, and the amount of information required in relation to specific particular information is that which is 'fit for purpose'. It is essential that the application is sufficiently detailed, with sufficient supporting maps and diagrams, to allow an authority to examine all elements of the activities and installation for which a permit is sought. In some situations a supporting report could comprise a paragraph or two, whereas in others a lengthy document may be required. For LA-IPPC applications, additional factors to be taken into account include whether the proposed abatement techniques or operational procedures differ from that specified within the BREF[428] or sector guidance (SG) notes,[429] or whether the installation is located in or near any sensitive locations, or where

---

[419] GG Manual, Chapter 32.
[420] Availabile from the Defra website.
[421] GG Manual, paragraph 4.19 which gives further guidance.
[422] GG Manual, page 37.
[423] See paragraph 6.79 and following above.
[424] GG Manual, paragraph 4.29.
[425] ie under paragraph 4 of Schedule 5, 2007 Regulations.
[426] GG Manual, paragraph 6.12.
[427] GG Manual, paragraph 9.16.
[428] See paragraph 6.266 below.
[429] At the time of writing, Sector Guidance Notes included:
IPPC SG1—Secretary of State's Guidance for the Particleboard, Oriented Strand Board and Dry Process Fibreboard Sector (September 2006).

there is or could be an environmental quality standard breach. For Part B applications, that second element applies where there is an emission into air, and there should be consideration of any proposal to deviate from any process guidance (PG) note.[430]

IPPC SG2—Secretary of State's Guidance for the A2 Glassmaking Sector (revised 31 October 2006).

IPPC SG3—Secretary of State's Guidance for the A(2) Ferrous Foundries Sector (January 2006).

IPPC SG4—Secretary of State's Guidance for A(2) Activities in the Non-ferrous Metals Sector (January 2006).

IPPC SG5—Secretary of State's Guidance for the A2 Galvanising Sector (September 2006).

IPPC SG6—Secretary of State's Guidance for the A2 Surface Treatment Using Organic Solvents Sector (March 2008).

IPPC SG7—Secretary of State's Guidance for the A2 Ceramics Sector including Heavy Clay, Refractories, Calcining Clay and Whiteware (September 2007).

IPPC SG8—Secretary of State's Guidance for the A2 Rendering Sector (October 2004).

IPPC SG9—Secretary of State's Guidance for A2 Roadstone Coating, Mineral and Other Processes that Burn Recovered Fuel Oil (April 2005).

IPPC SG10—Secretary of State's Guidance for the A2 Animal carcass incineration with capacity of less than 1 tonne per hour.

[430] GG Manual, paragraph 4.21—4.23. Process Guidance Notes are issued which give BAT guidance for Part B installations and activities. At the time of writing, these are:

Animal and Vegetable Processing sectors

PG6/27(05)—Vegetable matter drying processes

PG 6/5 (05)—Maggot breeding

PG 6/12 (05)—Sausage casings

PG 6/19 (05)—Fish meal processing

PG 6/24a (05)—Wet pet food manufacture

PG 6/26 (05)—Animal feed compound

PG 6/30 (Jan 06)—Mushroom Substrate Manufacture

PG 6/36 (Jan 06)—Tobacco Processes

Combustion and Incineration

PG 1/3 (95)—Boilers and Furnaces, 20-50 MW Net Rated Thermal Input (non-consolidated unofficial version with additional guidance AQ23 (04))

PG 1/4 (95)—Gas Turbines, 20-50 MW Net Thermal Input (non consolidated unofficial version with additional guidance AQ24 (04))

PG1/1 (04)—Waste Oil and Recovered Oil Burners less than 0.4MW

PG1/02 (05)—Waste Oil or Recovered Oil Burners, 0.4-3 MW Net Rated Thermal Input

PG1/05 (95)—Compression Ignition Engines, 20-50 MW Net Rated Thermal Input

PG1/12 (04)—Combustion of Fuel Manufactured from or comprised from Solid Waste in Appliances

PG5/2 (04)—Crematoria

Amendment to PG5/2 (04)—Cremation Temperature—21 November 2006

PG5/3 (04)—Animal Carcass Incineration

Minerals sector

PG 3/01 (04)—Blending, Packing, Loading, Unloading and Use of Bulk Cement

PG 3/02 (04)—Manufacture of Heavy Clay Goods and Refractory Goods

PG 3/04 (04)—Lead Glass, Glass Frit and Enamel Frit Manufacturing Processes

PG 3/05 (04)—Coal, Coke, Coal Product and Petroleum Coke

PG 3/06 (04)—Polishing or Etching Glass or Glass Products using Hydrofluoric Acid

PG 3/07 (04)—Exfoliation of Vermiculite and Expansion of Perlite

PG 3/08 (04)—Quarry Processes

PG 3/12 (04)—Plaster Processes

PG 3/13 (04)—Asbestos Processes (non consolidated with additional guidance AQ15(04))

PG 3/14 (04)—Lime Processes

PG 3/15a (04)—Roadstone Coating Processes

PG 3/15b (04)—Mineral Drying and Cooling

PG 3/16 (04)—Mobile Crushing and Screening

PG 3/17 (04)—China and Ball Clay Processes including the Spray Drying of Ceramics

PG 6/02 (04)—Manufacture of Timber and Wood-Based Products

PG 6/29 (04)—Di-isocyanate Proceses

Metals sector

PG2/01 (04)—Furnaces for the Extraction of Non-Ferrous Metal from Scrap

PG2/02 (04)—Hot Dip Galvanizing Processes

PG2/03 (04)—Electrical, Crucible and Reverberatory Furnaces

PG2/04 (04)—Iron, Steel and Non-Ferrous Metal Foundry Processes

PG2/05 (04)—Hot and Cold Blast Cupolas, and Rotary Furnaces

PG2/06a (04)—Processes Melting and Producing Aluminium and its Alloys

PG2/06b (04)—Processes Melting and Producing Magnesium and its Alloys

PG2/07 (04)—Zinc and Zinc Alloy Processes

PG2/08 (04)—Copper and Copper Alloy Processes

PG2/09 (04)—Metal Decontamination Processes

PG4/01 (04)—Surface Treatment of Metal Processes

PG6/35 (96)—Metal and other Thermal Spraying Processes (unofficial version)

Organic chemicals sector

PG4/02 (05)—Fibre re-enforced plastics

Petroleum, gas odorizing and powder coating sector

1/13 (04)—Storage, Unloading and Loading Petrol at Terminals

1/14 (04)—Unloading of Petrol into Storage at Petrol Stations

1/15 (04)—Odorizing Natural Gas and Liquified Petroleum Gas

6/9 (04)—Manufacture of Coating Powder

6/31 (04)—Powder Coating including Sherardizing and Vitreous Enamelling Dry

6/42 (04)—Bitumen and Tar Processes

Solvents sector

AQ6 (04)—Signposting Note for solvents notes

6/03 (04)—Chemical treatment of timber and wood-based products

6/07 (04)—Printing and coating of metal packaging

6/08 (04)—Textile and fabric coating and finishing

6/13 (04)—Coil coating

6/14 (04)—Film coating

6/15 (04)—Coating in drum manufacturing and reconditioning

6/16 (04)—Printing

6/17 (04)—Printing of flexible packaging

6/18 (04)—Paper Coating

6/20 (04)—Paint application in vehicle manufacturing

6/22 (04)—Leather finishing

6/23 (04)—Coating of metal and plastic

6/25 (04)—Vegetable oil extraction and fat and oil refining

6/28 (04)—Rubber

6/32 (04)—Adhesive coating including footwear manufacturing

6/33 (04)—Wood coating

6/34a (06)—Original Coating of Road Vehicles and Trailers—revised October 2006

6/34b (06)—Respraying of Road Vehicles—revised October 2006

AQ note amending PG6/35 (96) on Metal and Other Thermal Spraying Processes

6/40 (04)—Coating and recoating of aircraft and aircraft components

6/41 (04)—Coating and recoating of rail vehicles

6.260 Sector Guidance Notes and Additional Guidance Notes[431] are published to give guidance on the application of the best available techniques. Where such guidance notes are available, it may often be adequate to rely on those notes as

---

6/43 (04)—Formulation and finishing of pharmaceutical products
6/44 (04)—Manufacture of coating materials
6/45 (04)—Surface cleaning
6/46 (04)—Dry cleaning
[431] At the time of writing, excluding those published in the GG Manual, the Additional Guidance Notes included:
2008
AQ06 (08): Regulation of biodiesel production.
AQ05 (08): Petrol vapour recovery at service stations: explanatory notes on the use of orifice vent devices, pressure vacuum relief valves and applications for stage II.
AQ04 (08): Defra / TSA Dry Cleaning Spreadsheet
AQ03 (08): HAZRED guidance
AQ02 (08): Dry Cleaners: Whether pump out or rake out AQ01 (08): Categories of process regulated by different local authorities (by PG and SG note)
2007
AQ21(07): Enforcing Compliance with the Solvent Emissions Directive
AQ20 (07): Zinc and ammonia releases from galvanizing installations
AQ19 (07): Cremation Standards in the Event of Mass Fatalities
AQ18 (07): Paints Directive and vehicle refinish installations
AQ17 (07): roadstone coating plant (Document first made available in July 2007, amended August 2007)
AQ14 (07): dry cleaning—SLEAT Code of Practice
AQ12 (07): sulphur content of liquid fuels regulations
AQ10 (07): crematoria: burden sharing update
AQ8 (07): review of waste management licensing exemptions
AQ6 (07): limited review of PGs 3/14, 3/15a, 3/15b and 3/17
AQ4 (07): waste management licensing exemptions: interface with LAPPC and statutory nuisance
AQ2 (07): sulphur content of liquid fuels
AQ2 (07): fuel switching
2006
AQ21 (06): chimney height calculation helpline
AQ20 (06): Contact details of the Defra Local Authority Industrial Pollution Control Policy Team and associated other contacts details
AQ19 (06): amendment to PG5/2 (04) cremation temperature AQ17 (06): Small Waste Oil Burners and the Waste Incineration Directive
AQ10 (06): PG 6/46 (04): Spillage Trays and Bunds at Dry Cleaning Installations (PDF 40 KB)
AQ 9 (06): Crematoria: change in calculation for burden sharing
AQ 8 (06): The Buncefield Explosion + PG1/13(04)
AQ 4 (06): Roadstone Coating Plant—Use of Waste Oil
AQ 1 (06): Amendment to PG6/35(96): Metal and Other Thermal Spraying Processes
2005
AQ24(05): Crematoria—burden sharing
AQ16(05): Calculation of solvent consumption for dry cleaners
AQ12(05): PG5/2(04): Well-maintained cremators
AQ7(05): Additional Guidance for installations using waste oil
AQ6(05): A(2) incineration activities: used cooking oil
AQ1(05): Control of Mercury Emissions from Crematoria
2004
AQ32(04): Small service stations
AQ30(04): SED Determination of Compliance with Reduction Scheme

a baseline for what is BAT although each case will be case-specific, having regard to the specific facts of each case, including the precise size and configuration of the installation and activities, the actual production process used, and the location of the installation.[432]

LA-IPPC (Part A(2))

The position is similar under the LAIPPC regime. Generally, the local authority **6.261** regulator will look to act in accordance with the same principles as are applicable under IPPC in respect of Part A(1) installations.

If it is decided to grant an application, reasons must be given, in the same manner **6.262** as the Agency is required.[433] In straightforward cases, it is sufficient to state, by way of reasons, that any particular condition has been inserted because it represents, in the authority's view, best available techniques.

As for Part A(1) installations, a local authority is required to refuse an application **6.263** if the applicant will not be the operator of the installation or will not operate the facility in accordance with the permit.[434]

The implementation of Best Available Techniques in the determination of appli- **6.264** cations is, of course, central to the permit process. When assessing an application, the authority will look to ensure that BAT will be achieved in both the technical controls on polluting releases, but also to staffing, record keeping, and monitoring.[435] The process guidance notes produced for particular sectors are still relevant to consideration of applications.[436]

AQ25(04): Wood Coating, PG 6/33(04)
AQ24(04): Amendments of PG 1/4(95) Gas Turbines, 20-50 MW Net Thermal Input
AQ23(04): Amendments of PG 1/3(95) Boilers and Furnaces, 20-50 MW Net Rated Thermal Input
AQ21(04): Printing Processes (PG6/16(04))
AQ16(04): Performance Standards for enquiries
AQ15(04): Amendment to PG3/13(95): Asbestos Processes
AQ10(04): Addendum to SG7:SOS's guidance for the A2 Ceramics sector including heavy clay, refractories, calcining clay, and whiteware
AQ4(04): Classification of animal feed compounding, vegetable matter drying and pet food manufacturing
AQ3(04): Environmental Management Systems (EMS)
2003
AQ7(03): Link Authorities
AQ3(03): Animal Rendering Processes
[432] GG Manual, paragraph 12.12.
[433] See paragraph 6.114 above.
[434] Paragraph 13, Schedule 5, 2007 Regulations.
[435] Paragraph 11.8, the GG Manual.
[436] Paragraph 11.14, the GG Manual.

6.265 The achievement of BAT for Part B installations is, as has been dealt with already, restricted to emissions to the air.

6.266 In addition, the European Commission publishes BAT Reference documents (BREF notes) which will be absorbed into sector guidance notes.[437]

6.267 Two tests that authorities have been asked to consider are:

- What is the balance of costs and advantages? A technique may be rejected as BAT if its costs would far outweigh its environmental benefits.

- Can the operator obtain the technique? This does not mean that the technique has to be in general use; it need only need to have been developed and proved as a pilot, provided the industry can confidently introduce it.[438]

6.268 A general condition requiring an operator to use BAT is still capable of being imposed and is recommended at the detailed level of plant design.[439]

6.269 The basic approach to determine BAT is to identify options, assess their environmental effects, and consider the economics of implementation and use; principles of precaution and prevention are also relevant factors.[440] The environmental assessment of options should take into account a number of factors, including:[441]

- consumption and nature of raw materials;
- energy efficiency;
- waste issues;
- accidents;
- site restoration.

6.270 When undertaking the economic assessment of each option, the best techniques will be BAT unless economic considerations mean that they are unavailable.[442] An objective approach should be taken. The lack of profitability of a particular business should not affect whether a particular process is the BAT for an installation.[443] It is to be borne in mind, however, that, simply because a guidance note sets down particular emission levels, these may not amount to BAT for a particular process and it is possible for the regulator to require a less or more stringent requirement.[444]

---

[437] GG Manual, paragraph 12.24, the BREF notes can be found at <http://eippcb.jrc.es/>

[438] GG Manual, paragraph 12.9.

[439] GG Manual, paragraph 12.10, it is to be noted that the implied duty to use BAT will continue when it becomes an environmental permit; specific wording is given in the GG Manual, paragraph 12.11.

[440] GG Manual, paragraph 12.14, the GG Manual; detailed guidance as to the application of BAT is provided in Section 12 of the guidance.

[441] GG Manual, paragraph 12.18.

[442] GG Manual, paragraph 12.20.

[443] GG Manual, paragraph 12.21.

[444] *R v Daventry District Council, ex parte Thornby Farms Ltd* [2003] QB 503.

New developments in techniques after a guidance note is published should also be taken into account. Where there is no domestic guidance, operators and regulators should refer to the relevant BREF notes. Where there is no guidance, BAT should be assessed on other sources of data, including previous regulatory regimes.[445] One example where local circumstance may mean that BAT is not appropriate is where upgrading an existing installation to new installation standards where it operates very close to the new standard, but is using different plant or processes than envisaged in the guidance. Replacing the old plant with the new techniques may produce only a small decrease in releases, but a disproportionate increase in costs. Another example may be where there is a forthcoming planned closure of an installation. In such cases the change may not be appropriate.[446]

In addition to BAT, the guidance on applications indicates that LA-IPPC installa- **6.271** tions should be required as part of their permit conditions (and in order for a permit to be issued) to meet certain baseline standards of energy efficiency.[447] In addition, given the duty of local authorities to carry out a review and assessment of local air quality under Part IV of the Environment Act 1995, the authority may, if there are breaches of air quality standards or objectives which are attributable to a particular operator, review the conditions of that operator, depending upon the significance of the contribution.[448] While national domestic Environmental Quality Standards do not have the same binding legal effect as EC Environmental Quality Standards, national EQS relating to protecting the aquatic environment should always be observed.[449]

When considering the effect of a proposal on noise and vibration, conditions **6.272** should be attached to a permission which achieves the noise protection achievable under Part III of the Environmental Protection Act 1990 (ie the noise abatement system).[450] Detailed guidance is also given in relation to odour control.[451] While, in many cases, process-related condition might assist, an odour boundary condition might be warranted where the potential odour is particularly offensive.[452]

Specific guidance is also given to local authorities when regulating LA-IPPC **6.273** installations only for the determination of BAT for energy efficiency and the Climate Change Levy and the UK Emissions Trading Scheme.[453]

---

[445] GG Manual, paragraph 12.24–12.27.
[446] GG Manual, paragraph 12.30 and 12.31.
[447] GG Manual, paragraph 14.9.
[448] GG Manual, paragraph 15.7.
[449] GG Manual, paragraph 15.13.
[450] GG Manual, paragraph 16.1.
[451] GG Manual, chapter 17.
[452] GG Manual, paragraph 17.8 – 17.9.
[453] GG Manual, chapter 14.

6.274   Standard rules may be used the local authority in authorizing facilities. They are to be set down by the Secretary of State.[454]

6.275   Further discussion on BAT is given above.[455]

LAPPC (Part B)

6.276   The process of determination under the Part B is the same as LA-IPPC; although the scope of the issues for consideration is narrower under LAPPC (ie dealing with air), the local authority's main guidance for local authorities is largely equally applicable.[456]

Water consent issues

6.277   The Environment Agency must be consulted by the relevant local authority for all LA-IPPC applications, so that the Agency can decide whether to exercise its functions under Regulation 58 of the 2007 Regulations. In response to such consultation, the Agency should be expected to supply the information relating to water consent issues and if necessary a suitably worded condition or conditions. If the discharge is to a sewer, operators must apply to the sewerage undertaker for a trade effluent consent. The sewerage undertaker is obliged to consult the Agency if the new or altered trade effluent discharge could alter the effect of the treated sewage discharge on its receiving water. Detailed consideration of this process is outside the scope of this chapter. However, when determining emission limit values for discharges to sewer from an LA-IPPC installation, the reduction in pollution provided by the sewage plant should be taken into account, so that an equivalent level of protection of the environment as a whole is guaranteed and that taking such treatment into account does not lead to higher levels of pollution. In many cases the sewerage undertaker's trade effluent consent and the requirements needed to protect the ultimate receiving water are closely aligned. Where there is a complex effluent that requires additional controls to protect the environment, the Agency may request the authority in its response to consultation to include requirements on the trade effluent to sewer within the Environmental Permit.[457] Local authorities are responsible for enforcing conditions relating to water discharge like any other permit condition, although the Agency may provide some support. If an appeal is made in relation to water discharge conditions, authorities should copy relevant documents to the Agency as well as to the Secretary of State.[458]

---

[454] Regulation 26, 2007 Regulations.

[455] See paragraph 6.56 and following above.

[456] Paragraphs 4.26 and 7.1 of the GG Manual provide further guidance. All the notes are to be found at <http://www.defra.gov.uk/environment/ppc>.

[457] GG Manual, paragraph 10.14–10.21.

[458] GG Manual, paragraph 10.25.

Transfer, variation, review, and revocation

The provisions relating to the transfer, variation, and revocation of authorizations **6.278**
are effectively the same as in the Part (A1) regime. Under the LAIPPC regime,
generally the same provisions apply. There is, however, no requirement for the
operator to apply to surrender a Part B installation permit.[459] The operator is only
under a requirement to notify the local authority regulator.[460]

Detailed guidance is given for local authorities when considering site assessment **6.279**
and restoration and surrender of permits, including as to the scope of reports and
when intrusive sampling should be required.[461]

A local authority may revoke an Environmental Permit in whole or in part.[462] **6.280**
Having done so, it may require the operator to take steps to avoid pollution risk
resulting from the operation or to return the site to a satisfactory state.[463]

The powers to require avoidance of pollution or reinstatement do not exist for **6.281**
Part B Installations or Part B mobile plant.[464]

Permits must be reviewed periodically by the regulator.[465] It is to be noted that **6.282**
detailed guidance is given on the inspection of regulated permitted installations in
Chapter 27 of the GG Manual, including recommended minimum levels of
inspections for high, medium, and low risk installations and guidance on how to
assess the risk individual installations pose; and guidance on the use of continuous
emission monitoring and manual stack emission monitoring.

Enforcement

The enforcement provisions (and appeals from decisions under those provisions), **6.283**
criminal penalties, and (in general) civil court action are also available to the
local authority. Specific guidance is included on what a local authority's
approach to enforcement should be.[466]In essence, the action should be proportionate to the risks posed to the environment and the seriousness of any breach
of the law.

In addition, guidance has also been issued on how local authorities should check **6.284**
for unregulated installations. This is an integral part of the regulatory function of
local authority officers. While the list of recommended information sources is not

---

[459] Regulation 24, 2007 Regulations.
[460] Ibid.
[461] For LA-IPPC permits see GG Manual, chapter 18; for LAPCC permits see chapter 19.
[462] Regulation 22(1) 2007 Regulations.
[463] Regulation 23(1) 2007 Regulations.
[464] Regulation 23(2), 2007 Regulations.
[465] Specific guidance for local authorities is given in chapter 26 of the GG Manual. See paragraphs
6.144–6.146 above.
[466] See the GG Manual, Section 28.

definitive, it includes: local knowledge, tours around the area, use of students, use of planning authorities and planning applications, environmental business forums, liaison with health and safety/trading standards colleagues, use of Yellow Pages or equivalent, previously revoked authorized processes, targeted visits to all industrial estates, adverts placed in the local trade press by local authorities to highlight new legislation, Internet searches, trade and specialist trade directories, local newspaper and job adverts for local companies, business rate information, the Environment Agency and other government departments, and use of Companies House database. If an authority becomes aware of an unregulated installation in a particular sector and believes there may be others in that sector, it should advise Defra or the WAG who will investigate and issue guidance to all authorities if appropriate.[467] The charging scheme has also been amended to increase the application fees for those applying late, with the aim of funding authorities' work of checking for unregulated installations.[468]

6.285   Annex XII of the GG Manual includes a table listing all LA-IPPC and LAPCC offences since 2001/2. Fines ranged from £475 (premises operating without authorization) to £46,000 (emission of persistent fumes from cold blast cupola). It also gives a list of media contacts for alerting the media about successful prosecutions.

I. Registers

The information on the public register

6.286   It is the duty of the enforcing authorities, whether the Environment Agency or the local authority, to maintain a register of information on, essentially, a prescribed process.[469] It should include (inter alia) information on applications for grants, variations, transfers, or surrenders of environmental permits; environmental permits granted by that authority; enforcement, suspension, landfill closure notices, and any information given in compliance with such a notice; notices withdrawing notices; revocations; and appeals.

6.287   Schedule 19 further requires the public register to contain copies of 'all' representations made in respect of an application for an environmental permit, or in respect of an appeal,[470] all monitoring information obtained by the regulation as a result of its own monitoring, by virtue of any environmental permit condition

---

[467] GG Manual, chapter 32, paragraphs 31.11–32.15.
[468] GG Manual, paragraph 32.16.
[469] Regulation 46(1), 2007 Regulations.
[470] The regulator may omit a representation from its public register at the request of the person making the representation, but it must then include in the public register a statement that

or as a result of a notice under Regulation 16 of the 2007 Regulations, and all other information given to the regulator in compliance with an environmental permit condition, enforcement, suspension, or landfill closure notice, or Regulation 60. Every report published by the regulator relating to an assessment of the environmental consequences of the operation of the installation must also be included.[471] The public register must also contain a list identifying all waste incineration installations[472] which have a capacity of less than 2 tonnes per hour and are the subject of an environmental permit containing conditions which give effect to the Waste Incineration Directive.[473] A public register must also contain details of any conviction or formal caution for a relevant offence,[474] but a public register is not required to contain information relating to criminal proceedings, or anything which is the subject matter of criminal proceedings, until those proceedings are finally disposed of.[475] Note that spent convictions must be removed in line with statutory requirements[476] and the 2007 Regulations provide that a formal caution must be removed from the public register five years after it was given.[477]

The public register must also contain details of all fees and charges paid to the **6.288** local authority pursuant to a scheme under Regulation 65, and the total expenditure of the authority in exercising its functions under these Regulations in respect of permits granted by the authority.[478]

Once information is no longer relevant for public participation it need not be **6.289** kept on the public register.[479] However, although unnecessary information may have been removed from the register, information may still be available from the regulator either through the publication scheme or in response to information requests under Freedom of Information or Access to Environmental Information requests.[480]

---

a representation was made and was the subject of such a request. Paragraph 1(3), Regulation 19, 2007 Regulations.

[471] For a full list of what the public register should contain see paragraph 1 of Schedule 19, 2007 Regulations.

[472] 'Waste incineration installation' has the meaning given in Schedule 13 of the 2007 Regulations.

[473] Schedule 19, paragraph 1(2), 2007 Regulations.

[474] Schedule 19, paragraph 1(2), 2007 Regulations.

[475] Regulation 46(2), 2007 Regulations.

[476] Rehabilitation of Offenders Act 1974. Authorities should have systems in place to ensure this is done.

[477] Regulation 19(3), 2007 Regulations

[478] Paragraph 1(2)(c), Regulation 19, 2007 Regulations. Guidance is given in Chapter 23 of the GG Manual and at Annex X of the GG Manual. Cost accounting is required to show that money levied from business under the statutory charging scheme is generally devoted to this function. It is regarded as an important element of a best value approach.

[479] Regulation 19 (2), 2007 Regulations.

[480] Freedom of Information and the Environmental Information Regulations are discussed in Chapter 5. See also Core Guidance, paragraph 13.12.

6.290 The public registers must also hold information on Part A(1) installations and mobile plants in their areas, which are regulated by the Environment Agency (with the exception of port health authorities). The Environment Agency must supply the authority with the appropriate information[481] and intends to do this by supplying local authorities with a web link to use or pass on to any enquirers.

6.291 Port Health Authorities are not required to keep details of Environment Agency permitted installations within their areas. Each local authority whose areas adjoins that of a port health authority must include in its register information concerning Environment Agency permitted installations within the area of the port health authority.[482]

6.292 It is the duty of the particular enforcing authority to secure that the public registers which are maintained by them are available, at all reasonable times, for inspection by the public free of charge.[483] Members of the public do not have to give a reason for viewing the register. There is no obligation to publicize the existence of the public register but authorities are encouraged to do so, for example on their websites.

Form and content of registers

6.293 The public registers are not, however, required to be kept in any particular form.[484] They may be electronic. If the register is electronic, regulators should make sure they provide help for members of the public who are unfamiliar with the technology.[485] GG Manual states that 'a well-managed register will have a clear index and highlight, for example, the non-technical summaries of applications'.

6.294 Confidential information and information affecting national security is withheld from the public register (see further below). Many authorities hold a separate working file and a public register file. New guidance has been issued because it is considered that most information would have to be released under a Freedom of Information (FOI) or Access to Environmental Information requests (EIR).[486] New guidance suggests three methods by which local authorites may choose to organize their information:

1) One file is kept. File pages are marked to show whether they contain Schedule 19 information or information which is not required to be included on the public

---

[481] Regulation 46(4), 2007 Regulations.
[482] Regulation 46(5), 2007 Regulations.
[483] Regulation 46(8)(a), 2007 Regulations. Note also the duty to provide the public with the facility of obtaining copies of the entries on the register, on payment of reasonable charges: Regulation 46(8)(b), 2007 Regulations.
[484] Regulation 46(9), 2007 Regulations.
[485] Core Guidance, paragraph 13.8.
[486] See Chapter 5.

register. This is likely to be more workable if kept in electronic format so that the different categories of information can be readily identified and separated if inspection is requested.

2) One file is kept including all the Schedule 19 information and a separate detachable folder containing non-public register information is inserted in it. (This removes the need to hold duplicate papers on two separate files.)

3) One file is kept which contains all information other than (a) information withheld for commercial confidentially or national security and (b) any non-register information that the authority considers is likely to be refused if a request was made under FOI or EIR. The guidance emphasizes that a risk assessment may be needed in the third case as the authority might open itself up to a challenge for disclosing non-register information that could possibly have benefited from a valid exemption from disclosure under FOI or EIR.

The exclusion from the public register of information affecting national security

6.295 No information which would normally go onto the public register will be included if, in the opinion of the Secretary of State, that information or a specified description of information would be contrary to the interests of national security.[487] The Secretary of State may make directions as to what should be excluded from the public register or that a specified description of information should be referred to him for his determination before it is included on the register.[488] The GG Manual states that operators should make such applications directly to either the Secretary of State or the Welsh Ministers and should be marked 'application under the Environmental Permitting Regulations'[489]. If an enforcing authority does exclude information as a result of a direction by the Secretary of State (presumably a general direction), it must notify him or her that it has done so.[490]

6.296 The Act also allows any other person to protect information on the ground of national security by notifying the Secretary of State. If that procedure is undertaken, the person must notify the enforcing authority of his actions. Thereafter, none of the specified information will be put on the public register unless the appropriate authority determines that it may be included.[491]

---

[487] Regulation 47(1), 2007 Regulations.

[488] Regulation 47(3), 2007 Regulations.

[489] The address is: Secretary of State for Environment, Food and Rural Affairs, Nobel House, 17 Smith Square, London SW1P 3JR or The Welsh Ministers, Welsh Assembly Government, Carthays Park, Cardiff, CF10 3NQ

[490] Regulation 47(2), 2007 Regulations.

[491] Regulation 47(4), 2007 Regulations. The notice must specify the information and indicate its apparent nature.

6.297   If the particular information is in an application for an authorization or variation, and is of a nature that would adversely affect national security, then the regulator must not inform the public consultees unless the appropriate authority directs that it must do so.[492]

The exclusion of confidential information from the public register

6.298   Similar provisions are made in respect of confidential information. No information relating to the affairs of an individual or business shall be included in a register, without the consent of the individual or the person carrying on the business, if the information is commercially or industrially confidential[493] unless the Secretary of State directs the regulation that the information must be included on the public register. No such direction may be given unless the Secretary of State considers that the public interest in including such information outweighs the public interest in maintaining its confidentiality.[494]

6.299   Information is confidential if it is 'information that is commercially or industrially confidential in relation to any person'.[495] However, information is not to be considered commercially confidential unless it is determined to be so by the enforcing authority. The Guidance emphasizes that the operator must provide 'clear justification' for each item it wishes to be kept from the register. It will not be enough merely to assert commercial prejudice. The operator must provide substantiation that the confidentially is provided by law to protect a legitimate economic interest.[496]

6.300   A specific procedure must then be gone through to determine whether it is commercially confidential and should be excluded.[497] If the regulator fails to give notice of its determination within the period required, the regulator is deemed to have determined that the information must be included on the register.[498] The regulator must give reasons for its decision in the notice of determination and must not include the information on the public register until 15 working days have expired after it gave notice of its determination. There is a right of appeal to the Secretary of State.[499] If a notice of appeal is not given then after the period for appeal has expired the regulator must then include the information on the public

---

[492] Schedule 5, paragraph 6(2), 2007 Regulations.
[493] Regulation 48, 2007 Regulations.
[494] Regulation 56, 2007 Regulations.
[495] Regulation 45, 2007 Regulations.
[496] Core Guidance, paragraph 13.20.
[497] Regulations 50–51, 2007 Regulations.
[498] Regulation 52, 2007 Regulations.
[499] Regulation 53, 2007 Regulations.

register.[500] If a notice of appeal is given, the information must not be included until the appeal is determined.[501]

The appeal to the Secretary of State must be in writing, include a statement of the grounds of appeal, and be copied to the regulator. The appellant must state whether he wants the appeal to be by way of hearing or written representations.[502] There is a right to a hearing if the appellant so requests.[503] The appeal regulations then apply, except that a person who has made representations to the regulator other than the appellant is not entitled to be heard at the hearing.[504]Provision is made for notifications relating to the exclusion of information which is commercially confidential. The provisions generally follow those referred to above over matters affecting national security.[505] Thus the consultees referred to must not be consulted unless the consultee is a public authority and the information is necessary for the exercise of its functions or a sewerage undertaker and the information relates to the release of any substance into a sewer vested in that undertaker.[506]

6.301

The 2007 Regulations provide that there is a presumption in favour of including the information on the public register.[507] Information will only be excluded that is commercial or industrial information, whose confidentiality is provided by law to protect a legitimate public interest and where, taking into account all the circumstances, the public interest in maintaining the confidentiality of the information outweighs the public interest in including it on the register.[508]

6.302

There is an inter-relationship between decisions as to commercial confidentiality under the Regulations and FOI and EIR requests. The GG Manual indicates that they are considered to 'broadly complement' each other. It is recommended that in any given case regard is had not only to the specific provisions of the 2007 Regulations but also consider whether the information would be released or withheld in response to an EIR or FOI information request.[509] In particular, the EIR exceptions are more limited where the information to be disclosed relates to information on emissions.[510] Note that in this case the Regulations provide that 'to the

6.303

---

[500] Regulation 52, 2007 Regulations.
[501] Regulation 53(4), 2007 Regulations.
[502] Regulation 53(2), 2007 Regulations.
[503] Regulation 53(4), 2007 Regulations.
[504] Regulation 53(5), 2007 Regulations.
[505] See further above.
[506] Paragraph 6(3), Schedule 5, 2007 Regulations.
[507] Regulation 51(2)(b), 2007 Regulations.
[508] Core Guidance, paragraph 13.25.
[509] Paragraph 8.13,
[510] See Chapter 5.

extent that information relates to emissions the regulator must determine to include it on the public register'.[511]

6.304 If the regulator determines that the information is commercially confidential, the minimum amount of information necessary should be kept off the register. Other information should not be excluded unless the information is not reasonably capable of being separated from the confidential information.[512]

6.305 If monitoring information is omitted from the public register on the basis of commercial or industrial confidentiality, the regulator must include in the public register a statement indicating whether or not there has been compliance with any environmental permit condition related to that monitoring information and requiring compliance with emission limit values.[513]

The result of exclusion from the public register

6.306 Information which has been excluded from a register shall be treated as ceasing to be commercially confidential after four years (or such shorter period as specified in the final confidentiality decision).[514] However, the person who furnished it may give notice to the authority before the expiry of that period for the information to remain excluded from the register on the ground that it is still commercially confidential. The same appeal procedures then apply and any determination may be appealed against.[515] It is recommended that the regulator should write and inform operators that the end of the time-period is approaching, allowing sufficient time for re-application. However, operators should not rely on the regulator providing this service.[516]

---

[511] Regulation 51(3), 2007 Regulations.
[512] Regulation 51(4), 2007 Regulations.
[513] Regulation 19(4), 2007 Regulations.
[514] Regulation 55(1), 2007 Regulations.
[515] Regulation 55(2), 2007 Regulations.
[516] Core Guidance, paragraph 13.34.

7

WASTE MANAGEMENT

A. **Introduction**	7.01	
B. **Waste—The Definitions**	7.05	
Controlled waste	7.09	
The Controlled Waste Regulations—household waste	7.16	
Removal of household waste	7.23	
Holiday houses and caravans	7.29	
Recyclable and non-recyclable waste	7.31	
Schools, colleges, and racing stables	7.33	
Miscellaneous waste and removal charges	7.35	
Industrial waste	7.37	
Sewage	7.40	
Clinical waste	7.42	
Waste from aircraft, vehicles, and vessels	7.44	
Offensive waste	7.45	
Oil, solvents, and scrap metal	7.47	
Commercial waste	7.48	
Exemption for public bodies	7.51	
C. **Special Waste**	7.53	
Special waste—compounds	7.60	
Explosives	7.62	
Directive waste	7.63	
Hazardous waste	7.70	
Specific types of waste	7.76	
Packaging	7.77	
Motor vehicles	7.78	
D. **A National Strategy for Waste**	7.85	
Introduction	7.85	
The strategy	7.86	
The import and export of waste	7.88	
Rationing landfill	7.89	
Strategy	7.93	

E. **Waste Management—The Duty of Care**	7.95	
Introduction	7.95	
Persons under the duty of care	7.96	
Exemptions from the duty of care	7.105	
F. **Waste Licensing**	7.110	
The previous regime	7.110	
The present regime	7.111	
G. **Enforcement**	7.122	
Introduction	7.122	
The machinery of enforcement	7.123	
Registers	7.128	
H. **Obtaining a Waste Management Licence**	7.131	
Introduction—the deposit of controlled waste	7.131	
'Causing or permitting'	7.133	
Pollution of the environment and harm to health	7.136	
Defences	7.139	
Household waste	7.143	
Exemptions for incineration and burning	7.164	
Miscellaneous exemptions	7.167	
Fly-tipping	7.168	
The right to a licence	7.170	
The relationship to town and country planning	7.173	
The functions of the Environment Agency	7.174	
Fitness to hold a licence	7.177	
Conditions of a licence	7.188	
Appeals	7.193	
I. **The Duty of Care**	7.197	
Introduction	7.197	
Transfer notes	7.201	
The Code of Practice	7.203	

Carriers	7.207		Mobile plant licences	7.234
Breach of the duty of care	7.209		Closed landfill sites	7.235
Variation, transfer, surrender,		J.	**Waste Collection and Disposal**	7.236
and revocation of licences	7.211		Collection	7.236
Transfers	7.217		Disposal	7.246
Revocation	7.225		Landfill	7.257
Surrender	7.229			

A. Introduction

7.01 In recent years the thinking of government and many others about waste has changed radically. The traditional belief that unwanted material can appropriately be disposed of by releasing it into the air or water, or by putting it into or onto the land, has had to be drastically revised. Of the numerous examples which might be given, two of the more dramatic concern the dumping of sewage sludge in the sea, and the burying of household refuse in the earth ('landfill'). The former has now been outlawed in Europe, and it is becoming increasingly clear that the days of the latter are numbered.

7.02 The Environmental Protection Act 1990, as amended by the Environment Act 1995, reflects this changed approach. It defines waste at almost wearisome length, and provides for the drawing up of a national strategy to minimize the creation of it, and for its recycling where possible. The Act of 1990 also created a system of licensing virtually every person who has dealings with waste, and of the premises where the waste is kept, treated, or consigned. This is backed up with criminal sanctions for breach of the licensing restrictions.

7.03 The Act also introduced the unprecedented notion, that anyone dealing with waste remains responsible for it even after he has parted with it. This 'duty of care' requires that the waste must be passed to a properly qualified and licensed transferee, or deposited at a place and in a way which guarantees that it will not harm the environment or human health. These are the themes of this chapter.

7.04 The fundamental and first questions raised by the topic of Waste Management concern definitions. Before one can embark on a sensible study of the regime which Parliament has imposed on producers, transporters, and others concerned with waste, it is important to discover what waste is, and who is responsible for it as a manager. Neither question receives as simple an answer as might be expected, since Parliament and Ministers have laid down complex definitions of both.

B. Waste—The Definitions

Any discussion of the meaning of the word 'waste' has to begin with the statutory **7.05**
definitions, of which there are several. Some, but by no means all, are to be found
in Section 75 of the main statutory provision which deals with the subject, that is,
the Environmental Protection Act 1990 (EPA, 1990). Section 75(2) defines
'waste' as:

A. any substance which constitutes a scrap material or an effluent or other
   unwanted surplus substance arising from the application of any process, and
B. any substance or article which requires to be disposed of as being broken, worn
   out, contaminated or otherwise spoiled; but does not include ... An explosive...

The fundamental question which Section 75(2) poses is whether the identity of **7.06**
the person who has no use for the substance, or who requires to dispose of it, is
material to the issue of whether the substance qualifies as waste. The courts have
had to face this issue more than once, largely because of the ingenuity of landowners, industrialists, and others wishing to escape the consequences of their being
found to be handling waste within the definition of the EPA 1990.

The point arose in *Kent CC v Queenborough Rolling Mill Co* (1990) 89 LGR 306. **7.07**
A pottery company had used broken china, pottery, china clay, chalk, and ballast
to provide hardstanding on which to store materials on its land. Although the
defendant company had a use for the surplus material, the trial court rejected the
defence that it did not, as a result, amount to waste for the purposes of the Control
of Pollution Act 1974 (CoPA 1974). On appeal, the High Court reaffirmed the
view that the use to which the defendant company wished to devote the material
was irrelevant. The relevant factor, it was held, was the intention of the owner at
the time when the fill was removed from its original resting place.

The Court of Appeal affirmed this approach in *A-G's Reference (No.5 of 2000)*. **7.08**
Until the point comes to the House of Lords, it must be taken as established that
material discarded by one person, even if to be re-used immediately, becomes
waste.[1]

---

[1] [2002] Env LR 139. The logic of the outcome is not immediately apparent. It seems that a child
who grows out of its shirt and hands it down to a younger sibling is a waste producer; and the manager of any High Street charity shop deals in waste. However, the House of Lords has held that an
intermediate waste water treatment plant needs a permit, even though final treatment and disposal
take place elsewhere (*United Water Utilities v Environment Agency*, The Times 26 October 2007).
This is consistent with the view of the Court of Appeal as to the definition of waste.

Controlled waste

7.09 The difficulty and complexity inherent in defining what is 'waste' does not, how-ever, end there. The EPA 1990, Section 75, introduces a number of different types of waste onto the legislative scene—no fewer than four categories are involved. First, and in the context of waste management very importantly, there is 'con-trolled waste'. This embraces household, industrial, and commercial waste (see Section 75(4)). Each of these receives its own definition in Section 75.

7.10 By Section 75(5) 'household waste' means waste from dwellings (including flats), caravans, university colleges and halls of residence, schools, hospitals, and nursing homes.

7.11 By Section 75(6) 'industrial waste' is waste from a factory as defined in the Factories Act 1961, which includes a wide variety of premises since the definition of a 'fac-tory' extends over ten subsections and covers more than two pages of print. It also includes premises which the layman would not immediately classify as factories. Examples are film studios, laundries, slaughterhouses, and premises where nets are made or mended incidentally to the fishing industry. It is consistent with this that sewage escaping by accident from the pipes of a statutory undertaken is industrial, and therefore, controlled waste.[2]

7.12 To this long list Section 75(6) adds waste from premises such as bus depots, gas works, electricity generating stations, water and sewage works, (although sewage itself is not within the definition of industrial waste), and waste from other prem-ises connected with the provision of public utility services, including telecommu-nications. It is consistent with this that sewage escaping by accident from the pipes of a statutory undertaker is industrial, and, therefore, controlled waste.

7.13 'Commercial waste' is that which comes from trade premises other than factories, dwellings, mines, quarries, or farms (see Section 75(7)). It seems, therefore, that waste produced by offices, sports halls and stadia, theatres, concert halls, cinemas, hotels, restaurants, public houses, and rave parties is all 'commercial waste' as defined. The fourth category, namely radioactive waste, is discussed elsewhere.

7.14 Section 75(8) of the EPA 1990 contains an important power, which authorizes the Secretary of State for the Environment to make regulations prescribing types of waste which shall or shall not, as the case may be, be treated as falling within any of the four classes of waste discussed above. This power has been exercised by the making of the Controlled Waste Regulations 1992 (SI 1992/588). The primary function of these is to particularize and amplify the definitions of the first three categories of waste prescribed by the EPA 1990, that is, 'household', industrial', and 'commercial'. Additionally, the Controlled Waste Regulations create new

---

[2] See *R (Thomas Water Utilities Ltd) v Bromley Magistrates' Court*, Environment Agency, interested party The Times 26 August 2008.

categories of waste, regulate the system of charging for the collection and disposal of different types of waste, amend some of the licensing provisions of the EPA 1990, and amend previous regulations. Any attempt to understand the Controlled Waste Regulations is hampered by the need to cross-refer to numerous other enactments and pieces of delegated legislation. The Controlled Waste Regulations and their schedules occupy no more than eight pages of text, in the course of which they incorporate by reference no fewer than twenty-five other statutes or statutory instruments.

The List of Wastes (England) Regulations 2005 SI 2005/895 classify wastes by **7.15** category and their potential toxicity, and are as near exhaustive as they may be.

The Controlled Waste Regulations—household waste

The first function of the Controlled Waste Regulations is to prescribe that house- **7.16** hold waste is to include waste from a variety of premises which are not domestic (see Regulation 2(1) and Schedule 1). These premises are: places of religious worship and churches in Scotland; premises occupied wholly or mainly for charitable purposes by a charity, which would include charity shops and, perhaps, administrative offices, although this raises complicated issues of rating and charity law which are outside the scope of this work; land belonging to or used in connection with domestic property, a caravan, or residential home, thereby, as was no doubt intended, constituting grass cuttings and other garden waste and household waste; a private garage with a floor area of up to 25 square metres, whatever the purpose for which it is used, or a private garage, of whatever size, used wholly or mainly for the accommodation of a private motor vehicle.

The Regulations go on to prescribe a miscellany of premises whose waste is to be **7.17** treated as being household waste. Some are readily identifiable as producing waste which is for all practical purposes household waste. These include private storage premises, camp sites, and houseboats.

Others, however, are far from domestic in the amount or, in some cases, the type **7.18** of waste which they produce. They include prisons and other penal institutions, halls and other premises used for public meetings, royal palaces, and waste arising from the discharge by a local authority (but not, it seems, the Secretary of State for the Environment and Transport or the Highways Agency) of its duty to clear highways of litter. Waste from a prison or a royal palace, whether or not its type is much the same as ordinary domestic waste, is likely to be more similar in volume to that produced by, say, a hotel or a large sporting event like a Test Match or the Wimbledon lawn tennis championships. Yet the latter are deemed to generate commercial waste. The distinction does not seem to be justified by the fact that prisons or royal palaces are not run for profit. As is well known, there are privately owned and commercially operated prisons. Furthermore, a commercial meeting hall run for profit is decreed by the Regulations to produce household waste.

The justification for the differences in the types of waste must therefore remain a matter of speculation.

7.19 By contrast, Regulation 3 of the Controlled Waste Regulations stipulates that three categories of waste are not household waste for the purposes of the EPA 1990 Section 33(2), even though they may come from dwellings or premises otherwise to be treated as domestic. This means that they cannot be treated, kept, or disposed of except with and in accordance with the terms of a waste disposal licence. These classes of waste are: mineral or synthetic oil or grease; asbestos; and clinical waste.

7.20 The latter is compendiously defined by Regulation 1 as human or animal tissue, blood or other body fluids or excretions, drugs and other pharmaceutical products, swabs, dressings, syringes, needles and other sharp instruments, which would include knives, and other wastes arising from medical, nursing, dental, veterinary, pharmaceutical or similar practice, treatment, teaching, or research, or the collection of blood for transfusion. The only qualification to those wide definitions is that waste becomes clinical waste only if it may prove hazardous or cause infection to any person who comes into contact with it. This would mean that a pad of cotton wool used to mop up a nosebleed or a sticking plaster taken off a minor cut do not qualify as clinical waste, unless, of course, the blood was infected in some way. In ordinary circumstances, however, one would not rationally expect that such innocuous wastes could be hazardous or infect anyone. On the other hand, clinical waste requires special treatment, as will be seen.

7.21 Prima facie, also, domestic sewage is clinical waste, although most householders who keep sewage in a septic tank would be surprised to discover that they needed a waste disposal licence. As discussed elsewhere, they do not, although the contractor who empties the tank will need one.

7.22 It must be supposed that the Regulations demand that the three types of waste which they take outside the scope of household waste do so because they are taken to be especially harmful to health or liable to contaminate the environment if not strictly controlled. Given also that they are most difficult to dispose of, the responsibility of the producer is made proportionately greater.

Removal of household waste

7.23 The second main function of the Regulations is to control the system of charging for the removal of household waste from the premises, whether strictly to be regarded as dwellings or not, where that waste originates. Schedule 2 to the Regulations lists those types of household waste for which a collection charge may be made. Understandably, the Secretary of State for the Environment has been guided by considerations of size, weight, difficulty of eventual disposal, and quantity in deciding which types of waste shall render the producer liable to be charged for collection of his rubbish.

Thus, a collection authority may make a charge for removing any article of waste **7.24** which weighs more than 25 kilograms. Broken-down refrigerators and other white goods will probably fall into this category, as was no doubt intended. The collection authority may also charge for the removal of any article which cannot be fitted into what Regulation 2 describes as:

> . . . a receptacle for household waste provided in accordance with section 46 (of the EPA 1990); or. . . a cylindrical container 750 millimetres in diameter and 1 metre in length.

This, it may be discerned, is what used to be called a dustbin.

Garden waste, an expression used in the Controlled Waste Regulations, but not **7.25** defined there or elsewhere, may also be subject to a charge for removal. One can only surmise that the phrase includes such materials as grass cuttings, weeds, and thinnings from trees and shrubs. Whether the authorities intend that it shall include non-vegetable matter, such as unwanted plaster gnomes and birdbaths, remains to be seen.

A removal charge may also be made for clinical waste coming from domestic prop- **7.26** erty, a caravan, or moored vessel used wholly for the purposes of living accommodation. The regulations do not state for how long the vessel has to be moored for its clinical waste to be subject to a removal charge, nor do they address the maritime problem of how clinical waste from an unmoored vessel is to be treated. One may take it that the intention was to make the occupiers of houseboats liable to charges for removal of their clinical waste, while ignoring the question of who should pay for the removal of clinical waste from other vessels.

Waste from a residential hostel, residential home, university college or hall of **7.27** residence, faculty building, or even sports ground is also household waste liable to a collection charge. The liability also extends to waste from a school or other educational establishment, a nurses' home or a nursing home, and, it seems, waste from a hospital other than clinical waste.

Premises which produce both clinical and domestic waste, such as a hospital, **7.28** nursing home, or an old peoples' home, or perhaps even a private house where a resident, such as a diabetic, has to use syringes or needles regularly, are, under the Regulations, required to store their waste by category and pay for the collection of clinical waste, or risk the consequences, described below.[3]

---

[3] Controlled Waste Regulations, Sch 2 para 10; EPA 1990, s 47.

Holiday houses and caravans

7.29   The next type of waste which may attract a removal charge is that produced by a self-catering holiday dwelling or caravan, or a caravan which can only be occupied for part of the year, such as a caravan licensed for occupation only during the summer months.[4] By contrast, a boarding house or bed and breakfast establishment where the owners live and provide meals and accommodation, it seems, does not lose its domestic status, and creates household waste which does not render the operator liable to a removal charge.

7.30   The distinction has no evident logic, since a boarding house may be expected to produce much more waste than one self-catering holiday flat, chalet, or caravan, and there is no necessary added geographical or other difficulty in collecting refuse from a self-catering flat rather than from a boarding house which is next door in the same street. Not surprisingly, a charge may be made for removing a dead domestic pet, but the Regulations do not distinguish between a hamster and a horse, even though the latter may be as much loved and a family pet as the former.

Recyclable and non-recyclable waste

7.31   Paragraph 8 of Schedule 3 to the Waste Collection Regulations enables the collection authority (of which more elsewhere) to charge for the removal of waste which the occupier of domestic premises is forbidden to put into a receptacle for household waste (or dustbin, according to taste) by virtue of a notice served under the EPA 1990, Section 46, by the authority. This gives rise to difficulty. Section 46 empowers the authority to stipulate that, for example, recyclable waste shall be put into one dustbin, and all other waste into another. It is clear that, in theory at least, the collection authority might be able to charge for the removal of, say, non-recyclable waste, since this would not be permitted to go into a dustbin prescribed for recyclable waste. Section 46, however, does not, on the face of it, enable the authority to forbid the placing of household waste in a dustbin at all. The result is that the householder will always be entitled to put his rubbish into a dustbin or compartment of a dustbin, provided he sorts it in accordance with directions given by the waste collection authority.

7.32   In that event, there may be no circumstances in which a householder could be forbidden to put household waste into a dustbin, and paragraph 8 of Schedule 3 to the Waste Collection Regulations may never apply. It may be that the Secretary of State misunderstood the EPA 1990 which, it must be remembered, he promoted on behalf of the Government, or perhaps he was content that collection authorities should not have powers to preclude householders from putting waste of

---

[4] Controlled Waste Regulations, Sch 2 paras 6, 13.

certain kinds into any dustbin, leaving the authorities with the obligation to collect, free of charge, waste which they might not wish to collect at all.

Schools, colleges, and racing stables

Litter collected from open land owned by 'designated educational institutions' (in **7.33** effect, their playing fields) such as schools or colleges is liable to a collection charge, as is waste from premises which are only partly domestic.[5] This would apply to a shop with living accommodation above it, or to racing stables where the staff accommodation is an integral part of the premises—a state of affairs which in practice is relatively common.

The Regulations go on to prescribe two relatively noxious types of waste for which **7.34** a collection authority is entitled to make a removal charge. These are mineral or synthetic oil or grease; and asbestos.[6]

Miscellaneous waste and removal charges

Finally, there is a heterogeneous group of household wastes which may be liable to **7.35** a removal charge. They have little in common. Some might be thought to give rise to difficulty because of the quantities involved. But this cannot be true of all. For example, a collection authority may charge for removing waste from shops or offices on camp sites or from premises occupied by charities. Yet the waste from an office at a holiday caravan site or from a charity shop is unlikely to bulk large, although both types of waste are liable to a collection charge.

Although a charity may have to pay for the collection of waste from its shops, if it **7.36** is religious there can be no charge for collecting waste from a place used by it for religious worship, such as a church, chapel, or synagogue. Prisons and other penal institutions may have to pay for collection of their waste, in common with public meeting halls and royal palaces.[7] Again, it is not immediately apparent that the latter have anything in common with charity shops or offices on caravan sites.

Industrial waste

Schedule 3 to the Controlled Waste Regulations lists at considerable length those **7.37** wastes which are to be treated as industrial waste. Their range and diversity are wide. First, there is waste generated by a variety of commercial premises. These are garages, boatyards and marinas, and aircraft hangars, where, in each case, vehicles, vessels, and aircraft are maintained. Laboratories and workshops where the work is not carried on by employees or undertaken for commercial gain also produce

---

[5] See ibid, Sch 2 para 9; EPA 1990, s 89(1)(f).
[6] Ibid, Sch 2 paras 11 and 12.
[7] Ibid, Sch 2 paras 16, 17, and 18.

industrial waste, so that a laboratory where a university or even a private individual carries on academic research must be a producer of industrial waste, perhaps surprisingly.

7.38   By way of exception, a laboratory or workshop concerned primarily with computer operations or copying documents by photography or lithography is not taken to produce industrial waste, by Schedule 3, paragraph 3. It must, therefore, generate commercial waste instead.

7.39   Waste from factories as defined by the Factories Act 1971, considered above, where the work is undertaken by employees and/or for commercial gain, is, as has been noted already, industrial waste in any event. Predictably perhaps, wastes from approved scientific research associations, for example the Medical Research Council and the Animal Health Trust, and from dredging or tunnelling operations constitute industrial waste under paragraphs 5 and 6 of Schedule 3 to the Regulations.

Sewage

7.40   Paragraph 7 of Schedule 3 regulates the keeping and disposal of sewage. Sewage emanating from a dwelling is not in any case subject to regulation under the EPA 1990 Part II (see the EPA, Section 34(2)). Hence, as foreshadowed above, there is no obligation on a householder to subject himself to the licensing and other provisions of the EPA 1990 if the sewage from the house is kept in a septic tank.[8]

7.41   However, once the sewage has been removed from the domestic premises, usually, in practice, by a commercial waste disposal contractor, paragraph 7 of Schedule 3 to the Controlled Waste Regulations decrees that it becomes industrial waste. The same result is reached if the sewage is dealt with other than by transfer to a privy, cesspool, or septic tank. The only exceptions to this rule are those laid down in Regulation 7. These apply to the following wastes: sludge from domestic premises which is taken to a sewage treatment works and dealt with there; and sludge spread on agricultural land. The latter exemption is likely to become increasingly academic as the use of farmland for the disposal of sewage sludge becomes more outmoded, and the amount of available farmland diminishes progressively.

Clinical waste

7.42   Paragraph 8 of Schedule 3 to the Regulations is concerned with clinical waste. Paragraph 8(a) excludes from the definition of industrial waste clinical waste which is produced by a dwelling, caravan, residential home, or houseboat. Clinical waste

---

[8] Ibid, Sch 3 para 7.

which originates from such premises, it will be recalled, is household waste, but is still liable to a collection charge.[9]

By contrast, clinical waste collected by agreement from open land to which the **7.43** public has access as of right is industrial waste.[10] The practical application of this is not immediately apparent. The categories of open land to which the public has access as of right are relatively limited—they will include some public parks and common land and, probably, highways of all kinds—but little else. The readiness of individuals or organizations to collect clinical waste from such land may be queried, as may the frequency with which such waste is to be found there, with the possible exception of animal excretions. Perhaps, however, that is what the draftsman had in mind.

Waste from aircraft, vehicles, and vessels

Any waste arising from an aircraft, vehicle, or vessel which is not occupied for **7.44** domestic purposes is to be treated as industrial waste.[11] The distinction between a vessel not occupied for domestic purposes and one so occupied is easy to perceive, for the houseboat is frequently found in harbours and on rivers and canals. Similarly, there are buses and vans, both purpose-built and converted, which might be occupied for domestic purposes, if that phrase is taken to mean permanently occupied rather than used for recreation. On the other hand, the number of aircraft occupied for domestic purposes must be small indeed. Old or unwanted parts of vessels which are not household waste are also industrial waste, by virtue of paragraph 10 of Schedule 3 of the Controlled Waste Regulations.

Offensive waste

There follows a catalogue of more or less offensive types of waste. Of these, the **7.45** first is leachate from a deposit of waste or rubbish tip (see Controlled Waste Regulations, Schedule 3, paragraph 12). It is understandable that this should be classified as industrial waste, since the pollution problems created by leachates from domestic refuse tips and agricultural wastes are well known and sometimes serious. Other potentially polluting wastes are listed as industrial wastes in paragraph 13 of Schedule 3. These wastes may arise from a miscellany of premises, but have the common characteristic that they are capable of causing harm.

The premises in question are those where the activities carried on are: mixing or **7.46** selling paints (although why the latter should be thought to be environmentally sensitive is open to question—the wastes from a shop selling artists' materials

---

[9] Ibid, Sch 2 para 4.
[10] Ibid, Sch 3 para 8.
[11] Ibid, Sch 3 para 9.

are unlikely to differ from those of any other shop); sign writing, of which the same comment might be made; laundering or dry cleaning, where the wastes are more evidently potential pollutants; developing photographic film or photographic printing; selling petroleum products, including petrol, kerosene, heating oil, and similar substances; and selling pesticides, herbicides, and fungicides. All these are, no doubt, designated as industrial waste because of their capacity to pollute.

Oil, solvents, and scrap metal

7.47 By paragraph 15 of Schedule 3, waste oil, solvents, and, after 1 April 1993, scrap metal are industrial wastes. The Schedule ends by designating a variety of substances as industrial wastes. These are: wastes from kennels and catteries where animals are boarded, stables, or premises where animals are exhibited; waste arising from the discharge by the Secretary of State of his duty to keep motorways and special roads free of litter; any waste, of whatever kind, imported into Great Britain. The reason for the apparently xenophobic provision was not stated in the Regulations but is dealt with elsewhere in the legislation, as described below.

Commercial waste

7.48 The classes of waste which Schedule 4 to the Controlled Waste Regulations requires to be treated as commercial have no obvious common characteristics. They are wastes produced by a miscellany of premises, some constituting businesses conducted with a view to profit, and others not, while some defy all classification.

7.49 As one might expect, waste from offices, showrooms, and hotels is commercial waste.[12] So too is waste from a hereditament which is partly residential and partly used for a trade or business.[13] The justification for this is no doubt that waste generated by all the component parts of the premises may be placed in one container, and it is in the public interest that the occupiers should be placed under the more onerous obligations which attach to commercial waste. Paragraph 4 of Schedule 4 resurrects the notion of the private garage which is not used to accommodate a motor vehicle, but which still gives rise to waste. This obscure building, which might presumably accommodate a DIY enthusiast, likewise produces commercial waste.

7.50 By paragraph 5 of Schedule 4, waste arising in premises occupied by a club, society, or other association conducted for the benefit of the members is commercial waste. Plainly, this will include members' clubs, and, probably, the premises of clubs associated with political parties. However, there are areas of uncertainty. For instance, what is the function of a learned or cultural society, assuming that it does

---

[12] Ibid, Sch 4 paras 1 and 2.
[13] Ibid, para 3.

not enjoy charitable status (waste from premises occupied by a charity and used for charitable purposes is, it will be remembered, household waste)?[14] Is such a body conducted for the benefit of its members, or does it benefit the larger body of people who may profit from its publications or lectures given by or to its members? And what of the amateur dramatic and operatic society which puts on public performances from time to time, or the local art group which holds public exhibitions? These are likely to be conducted for the benefit of their members for the purposes of paragraph 5 of Schedule 4, but the point is not wholly free from doubt.

Exemption for public bodies

Paragraph 6 of Schedule 4 lists certain public bodies whose functions are such that **7.51** they are taken to produce commercial rather than household or industrial waste. These are: courts of law and central government departments; local authorities; bodies or individuals with functions prescribed by statute, of which the National Trust and Trinity House are examples, as are quasi-autonomous non-governmental organizations (QUANGOS). Waste from a market or fair, or that collected from a highway by a local authority under the CoPA 1974 falls into the same category.

Schedule 4 to the Control of Pollution Regulations ends with an enigma. By para- **7.52** graph 7, waste from a tent pitched on land other than a camp site is to be treated as commercial waste. It is unclear to what waste this refers. Is it designed to apply to travelling circuses and their big tops, or to the settlements of so-called New Age Travellers, or to the solitary mountaineer who pitches his tent overnight at the foot of a rock face, and if so, to which of them? Or to all three? Nothing in the EPA 1990 or the Regulations even suggests the answer to these questions. In the circumstances, the only safe assumption is that all tents pitched on land other than camp sites produce commercial waste, although whether this has any practical relevance is open to question. People who produce waste in such circumstances are likely to know little and care less for the operation of the EPA 1990, and the ability of the regulatory authorities to compel them to abide by the legislation is even more dubious.

C. Special Waste

Next, it is necessary to consider wastes which are regarded as especially noxious, **7.53** either because they are unusually toxic, or explosive. Their potential has been recognized since the late 1970s. In 1974 Parliament passed the CoPA 1974. Section 17 required the Secretary of State for the Environment to make special provision for

---

[14] Ibid, Sch 1, para 2.

the disposal, storage, recording, and regulation, by the criminal law if necessary, of wastes which he considered to be dangerous or difficult to dispose of. That duty was not discharged for some years.

7.54 In 1978, the then EEC Commission issued a Directive (78/3/19) on toxic and dangerous wastes. This demanded a response from the United Kingdom government, and resulted in the Control of Pollution (Special Waste) Regulations 1980 (SI 1980/1709). Section 62 of the EPA 1990 imposes a duty on the Secretary of State which is similar but not identical to that laid down by Section 17 of the CoPA 1974. Section 62 requires the Secretary of State to provide for the treatment, keeping, or disposal of waste which he considers so dangerous or difficult to keep or dispose of that it demands special provision ('special waste'). No regulations have been made under Section 62, so the law remains as provided by the 1980 Regulations.

7.55 By Regulation 2 of the 1980 Regulations, 'special waste' must in any event be one of the kinds listed in Schedule 1 to the Regulations, discussed below. In addition, it must meet one of the three tests which the Regulations prescribe, in Schedule 1 paragraph 1. First, it may be 'dangerous to life', in that a single dose of not more than five cubic centimetres, if ingested by a child of not more than 20 kilograms' body weight, would be likely to cause death or serious damage to tissue; or exposure to it for fifteen minutes would be likely to cause serious damage to the tissue of a human being, adult or child, by inhalation, skin or eye contact.[15]

7.56 An elaborate series of tests laid down by Schedule 1, Part II, paragraph 2 to the Regulations governs the assessment of the likely effects of ingestion for the purpose of deciding whether waste is dangerous to life for the purposes of paragraph 1. Regard must be had, for example, to different types of information in a strict order of precedence in carrying out the assessment. The most important is information about the effect of oral ingestion, that is, eating, of the relevant substance by children. The order of precedence descends through information about the effects upon adults of their eating the substance, down to information about the effects of analogous chemicals. The 'five cubic centimetre' test applies to any part of a consignment of mixed waste.[16]

7.57 The second category of special waste is that listed in Schedule 1 Part I to the Regulations, and which has a flash point of 21 °C or less, determined in accordance with a British Standard. In layman's language of course, this is waste which is potentially explosive or inflammable.

---

[15] Control of Pollution (Special Waste) Regulations 1980, Sch 1 Part II, para 1.
[16] Ibid, para 4.

Third, there is waste which is a medicinal product only available on prescription **7.58**
from a doctor.[17] Once more, and for clear reasons, it is easy to see why a medicine
sufficiently powerful to be only available on prescription from a doctor needs
special handling, treatment, and regulation once it becomes a waste as defined.

Schedule 1 to the Regulations makes rebarbative reading to anyone other than a **7.59**
highly qualified and knowledgeable chemist. In places it is so technical that the
layman must have recourse to the *Oxford English Dictionary* if he is to understand
it, since many of the substances listed are not mentioned in the *Shorter Oxford
Dictionary*. The special wastes are listed in the Schedule broadly, but not strictly,
in alphabetical order, and fall into four main groups—metallic compounds, non-
metallic compounds, substances requiring special treatment because of their
origin rather than their composition, and those which may be or become explosive. Anyone not familiar with the technicalities of the chemistry of the world
of wastes needs at least to be aware of the areas where Schedule 1 to the Special
Waste Regulations may apply.

Special waste—compounds

The largest group is that containing the metallic compounds. They include anti- **7.60**
mony, barium, beryllium, cadmium, copper, hexavalent chromium compounds
('hexavalent' meaning that the chromium is capable of reacting with six atoms of,
for instance, hydrogen, presumably to be determined, eventually, by chemical
analysis), cyanides, lead, mercury, nickel, silver, thallium, vanadium (which is
used in some dyes), and zinc.

The non-metallic substances are arsenic, all chemical forms of asbestos, boron, **7.61**
inorganic and organic halogen containing compounds such as chlorine, flourine,
iodine, and cyanogens (a halogen being a substance which forms a salt on coming
into contact with a metal), sulphur compounds, phosphorus and its compounds,
selenium, and tellurium. Biocides and phytopharmaceutical substances connected
with the growth of plants are also special wastes. Because some of these substances,
selenium and tellurium, for example, are rarely found, they are the more likely to
turn into traps for the uninformed or the unwary. The substances designated as
special wastes merely because of their origins and irrespective of their content and
chemical make-up are laboratory chemicals, and pharmaceutical and veterinary
compounds. These call for little comment, since in designating them as special
wastes the Secretary of State clearly preferred being safe to being sorry.

---

[17] Ibid, reg 2.

Explosives

7.62 Finally, there are the explosives, actual or potential. These are hydrocarbons and their oxygen, nitrogen, and sulphur compounds, of which petrol, acetylene, and benzine are examples. Other special wastes of this group are peroxides, chlorates, perchlorates, and azides (the latter, apparently, being one of the components of rocket fuel), and, possibly, heterocyclic organic compounds, these being made up of rings of atoms of more than one kind. It is necessary to include this catalogue in a legal textbook so that those dealing with waste and their advisers shall at least know when to be on their guard.

Directive waste

7.63 Parliament and Ministers having between them enacted the elaborate code defining waste which has been considered above, the government then found itself compelled to create a further category of waste. This step was, it seems, made necessary by the issue by the Commission of the EEC of two Directives, numbers 91/156/EEC and 91/692/EEC. These amended an earlier Directive, 75/442/EEC. United Kingdom law had to be made to comply with the 1991 Directives, and the Secretary of State took the opportunity to do so when he made the Waste Management Licensing Regulations 1994 (SI 1994/1056).

7.64 As their title suggests the Regulations were concerned primarily with the granting and regulation of the need to obtain waste management licences. Almost, one might think, as an afterthought, the Regulations, in Schedule 4, introduced the new category of 'Directive waste'.

7.65 Paragraph 9 of Schedule 4 declares, uncompromisingly, that Part II of the EPA 1990 shall have effect subject to the modification that any reference to waste shall include a reference to Directive waste. Part II of the Schedule lists sixteen categories of Directive waste, which correspond to the categories prescribed by the Directive. Because the Schedule reflects the approach of the Directive, it takes a form which seems odd to the eyes of the UK lawyer, in that it does not define classes of waste either exhaustively or inclusively, but gives examples of the products which the class of waste is intended to include. This could present difficulties of construction for UK courts, which the European Court of Justice may have to solve. As with special wastes, waste managers and their advisers, and, of course, regulatory bodies, will need to know the areas of activity which are liable to give rise to Directive wastes, so as to be forewarned of the responsibilities which may arise.

7.66 The classes of Directive wastes are: production or consumption residues; off-specification products; products which have passed their 'date for appropriate use', by which seems to be meant their useful life; materials which have been spilt, lost, or undergone mishap, and materials contaminated as the result of the accident. This provision reflects the determination of those concerned to see that waste remains the responsibility of someone, even if, for example, the loss or mishap is entirely accidental and the fault of no one.

The catalogue goes on to include materials which have been contaminated or **7.67** soiled as the result of deliberate actions, such as cleaning or packing containers, and the residues which they produce; unusable parts—the examples given are reject batteries and exhausted catalysts; and substances which no longer perform satisfactorily. The Regulations give as examples: contaminated acids and solvents; residues of industrial and pollution abatement processes such as slags and scrubber sludges and baghouse dusts; machining or finishing residues, and those arising from the extraction and processing of raw materials. These are, for example, lathe turnings, mining residues and oil field slops; adulterated materials such as contaminated oils; any material whose use has been banned by law; discards from farming activity, households, offices, and commercial premises; contaminated materials resulting from remedial action with respect to land.

Lastly and compendiously, the list embraces any materials not contained in the **7.68** above categories. This last class must, presumably, apply only to materials which pass some sort of test which qualifies them to be regarded as waste; otherwise every substance of any kind would have to be treated as Directive waste and be subject to control under Part II of the EPA 1990.

It is not clear that the introduction into UK law of the concept of Directive waste **7.69** adds anything to the substantive content of Part II of the EPA 1990. All the substances identified in the Waste Management Licensing Regulations can be fitted into one or other of the categories of waste other than Directive waste. Merely to provide that Part II is to be read as if waste includes Directive waste does no more than make a distinction without a difference.

Hazardous waste

The Hazardous Waste (England and Wales) Regulations 2005 SI 205/894 intro- **7.70** duce a further regime of control over waste. The wastes are defined at length in Schedules 1–3 to the Regulations.

The fundamental object of the Regulations is to require the supervision of **7.71** premises where hazardous waste as defined is produced or from which it is removed. Notice of these activities must be given to the relevant regulatory agency (in England the Environment Agency, in Wales the National Assembly).[18] There is a long list of exemptions for premises such as offices, shops, farms, and surgeries.[19]

---

[18] Ibid, reg 21(1), 56–60.
[19] Ibid, reg 23.

7.72 The Secretary of State is given wide powers to classify as non-hazardous wastes which would otherwise be hazardous.[20] Asbestos and radioactive wastes fall within the Regulations;[21] agricultural, mine, and quarry wastes do not.[22]

7.73 Specific regulations cover multiple collections from different premises, and for ships' and pipeline wastes.[23] Even so, the same basic code of control governs these wastes.

7.74 Emergencies and grave dangers receive special treatment. The obligations on producers are relaxed in these circumstances, provided they take reasonable and lawful steps to avert or mitigate the emergency or danger and notify the regulatory authority.[24]

7.75 It is a defence to a prosecution to show that reasonably practical steps were taken to minimize threats to the public and to the environment.[25]

Specific types of waste

7.76 With time, as experience of the waste control regime has progressed, it has been found necessary to provide expressly for types of waste thought to have been especially troublesome. Two of these, both of which have received adverse publicity are packaging and motor vehicles.

Packaging

7.77 Although not strictly material to this Chapter, the Packaging (Essential Requirements) Regulations 2003, SI 2003/1941 are calculated to limit the amount of packaging in which goods are exposed for sale. The hoped for effect will be to reduce the amount of waste needing treatment or disposal to landfill.

Motor vehicles

7.78 The End of Life Vehicles Regulations 2003, SI 2003/2635 and End of Life Vehicles (Producer Responsibility) Regulations 2005, SI 2005/263 have titles which almost speak for themselves. They are designed to ensure that during and at the end of their lives vehicles cause as little damage to the environment as possible. An 'end of life' vehicle is defined as one which is waste.[26]

---

[20] Ibid, regs 8–10.
[21] Ibid, regs 13 and 15.
[22] bid, regs 16 and 17.
[23] bid, regs 38–41.
[24] Ibid, reg 62.
[25] Ibid, reg 66.
[26] Ibid, reg 2.

Manufacturers (described as 'producers') of motor vehicles must ensure that their **7.79**
products do not contain heavy metals.[27] Producers must keep, and when required
produce, records showing of what materials the vehicles are made, and that the
materials are suitable.[28] Enforcement is by means of compliance notices requiring
the manufacturer to explain itself in cases where the requirements have been
infringed.[29]

A defence of due diligence is available.[30] **7.80**

Manufacturers must apply for registration and take responsibility for the vehicles **7.81**
which they make as from 1 May 2005.[31] That responsibility is to provide facilities
for collection, treatment, and disposal of all end of life vehicles in 2006 and each
succeeding year.[32] Collection facilities must be reasonably accessible to any person
wishing to return an end of life vehicle to the manufacturer.[33]

Progressively more stringent targets for re-use, recovery, and recycling are to be **7.82**
introduced between the year 2006 and 2015.[34]

When a vehicle has reached the end of its useful life it must be delivered to an **7.83**
authorized and licensed treatment plant.[35] When the site operator has destroyed
the vehicle he must issue a certificate of destruction, for which he may not charge
the last owner or holder.[36] The intention is to reduce the temptation to owners to
fly-tip decrepit vehicles.

There are detailed administrative and consequential provisions, regulating such **7.84**
matters as registration of treatment facilities, amendments to the system of recovery and re-use, certification and registration of manufacturers. All are backed
by criminal sanctions.[37]

D. A National Strategy for Waste

Introduction

Originally, the EPA 1990 provided for the administration of waste disposal **7.85**
and regulation under the Act to be undertaken by individual local authorities,

---

[27] Ibid, regs 6, 14–20.
[28] Ibid, reg 7.
[29] Ibid, regs 9, 21.
[30] Ibid, reg 12.
[31] Ibid, regs 10, 12.
[32] Ibid, reg 11.
[33] Ibid, reg 17.
[34] Ibid, reg 18.
[35] Ibid, reg 12.
[36] Ibid, reg 48; Regulations 27 and 29.
[37] Ibid, reg 23.

normally county councils in England and Wales. However, the underlying philosophy of the Environment Act 1995 was that these functions, together with the policing of most anti-pollution legislation, should be integrated. The change was imposed by Article 7 of the EC Directive 75/442/EEC ('The Waste Framework Directive'). This led to the creation of a single national environmental control body, the Environment Agency. It also entailed the removal from local authorities of their waste management policy making powers, and the transfer of them to central government.

The strategy

7.86 Section 44A of the EPA 1990 (inserted by Section 92 of the Environment Act 1995) obliges the Secretary of State to prepare a statement containing his policies for the recovery and disposal of waste in England and Wales as soon as possible. In so doing he must consult the Environment Agency, bodies appearing to represent the interests of local government and industry, and other appropriate bodies (Section 44A(5)). Section 44A(6) envisages that the Environment Agency will undertake a nationwide survey of the kinds and quantities of waste to which the Secretary of State will have to address himself. The policy statement is to be called 'the strategy'.

7.87 In December 1995 the then Government published a consultation draft of the strategy, *Making Waste Work—A Strategy for Sustainable Waste Management in England and Wales* (HMSO Cm 3040). In essence, the policy was, first, to secure reductions in the amount of waste produced. Thereafter, waste was, wherever possible, to be recycled. Where that was not possible (or, no doubt, sustainable) waste management practices were to be adopted which minimized the risk of pollution and harm to human health. In particular the strategy aims to reduce the proportion of controlled waste going to landfill sites, and to recover an increased amount of municipal waste.

The import and export of waste

7.88 The Transfrontier Shipment of Waste Regulations 1994 (SI 1994/1137), Regulation 11, require the Secretary of State to prepare a strategy for the import and export of waste to and from the UK. He discharged the duty by publishing the *UK Management Plan for Exports and Imports of Waste* (HMSO). This is based on policy of national self-sufficiency. The Regulations invest the Environment Agency, as successor to the former waste regulation authorities, with wide powers to control the import and export of wastes. The aim is to ensure that the eventual destination is a suitable place run by a responsible and competent person, and that the carrier or carriers are similarly qualified.

Rationing landfill

These aims have been refined and extended by the Waste and Emissions Trading **7.89** Act 2003. The underlying object, inspired by European Council Directive 1999/21 EC, is to reduce the amounts of biodegradable waste, such as food, garden waste, and paper sent to landfill. The machinery by which this is achieved is the rationing of the quantities of biodegradable waste sent to landfill by reference to a series of annual targets for the UK as a whole, and for England, Scotland, Wales and Northern Ireland individually.[38] The Secretary of State is to specify by regulation the amount of biodegradable municipal waste sent to landfill. The system is based on three types of year—a scheme year, being any year beginning on 1 April between 2005 and 2119;[39] a target year, that is, the scheme years 2009–10, 2012–13, and 2019–20;[40] and a non-target year.[41]

The Secretary of State has power to ration the amounts of landfill for both target **7.90** and non-target years.[42] Each regulatory authority in England, Scotland, Wales, and Northern Ireland must allocate its share of the landfill to each waste disposal authority within its country and publish the allocation.

Each allocating authority may make regulations allowing waste disposal authori- **7.91** ties to borrow allowances from a different scheme year—in other words, they may use up allowances in advance, but may not bank or carry forward allowances for use later.[43] Disposal authorities may also, if regulations yet to be made permit, trade their allowances with each other during each scheme year.[44]

There are penal sanctions for breach of these requirements, which includes exceed- **7.92** ing the maximum annual allowance.[45] Proper records must be kept, both by waste disposal authorities and landfill operators.[46]

Strategy

Each allocating authority must have a strategy for reducing the amount of biode- **7.93** gradable waste within its area.[47] The methods of reduction must include recycling, composting, biogas production, and materials and energy recovery.[48]

---

[38] Sections 1–3.
[39] Sections 1–2.
[40] Ibid.
[41] Section 4.
[42] Section 6.
[43] Ibid.
[44] Section 7.
[45] Sections 8 and 9.
[46] Sections 10–13.
[47] Sections 17–20.
[48] Sections 17–20.

7.94 Supplementary provisions authorize the Secretary of State and, in Wales, the National Assembly, to require local authorities to have waste management strategies.[49] The Act does not prescribe the content of these strategies, but it may be assumed that they will identify sites and prescribe the methods of management and disposal to be adopted at each site. In England, the Secretary of State may exempt waste disposal authorities from the duty to draw up strategies.[50]

E. Waste Management—The Duty of Care

Introduction

7.95 Section 34(1) of the EPA 1990 imposes a duty of care, more fully considered below, on a variety of persons who become responsible in one way or another for waste. In practice, it is almost impossible to have anything to do with waste and escape the duty of care, except in two sets of circumstances. The first arises under Section 34(2), which absolves the occupier of domestic property from any duty of care in respect of household waste produced on that property. Secondly, there are the exemptions conferred by the Waste Management Licensing Regulations, which have already been examined in so far as they define Directive waste, and are more fully dealt with below.

Persons under the duty of care

7.96 A person who imports waste is subject to the duty of care, and is deemed to be concerned in its management.[51] Paradoxically, the exporter of waste is not, merely by reason of that activity, taken to be concerned with its management, although he may become involved because he deals with it in other ways. Understandably and predictably, the producer of waste is also under the duty of care imposed by the EPA 1990.[52] The producer's role, like that of the importer, is not defined in the EPA 1990 or elsewhere, and it is very likely that the courts will decide as matters of fact and degree in the circumstances of each case whether an individual or body is an importer or producer. The same will probably be true of the third class of person subject to the duty of care, that is, a person who 'keeps' waste, since this word, too, is not defined in the EPA 1990 or elsewhere. Plainly, however, 'keeping' has to be distinguished from the deposit or disposal of controlled waste, since the Act regulates both of these activities. The most common, although by no means the only meaning of the word 'keep' is 'to continue to have, hold or possess'.[53]

---

[49] Sections 29 and 30.
[50] Section 33.
[51] EPA 1990, s 34(1).
[52] Ibid.
[53] *Shorter Oxford English Dictionary*, third edition.

So the producer or user, if the latter is not a contradiction in terms when applied to waste, who merely retains it without taking active steps to transfer or otherwise dispose of it, probably keeps it for the purposes of the EPA 1990. This is to be expected, since the underlying object of the Act is to ensure that at all times there is at least one person responsible for the safety of the public and the prevention of harm due to waste. The Department of the Environment is of the same view, as appears from its Circular on the Waste Management Licensing Regulations, at Annex 1, paragraph 1.5.

Next, and importantly, the EPA 1990 imposes a duty of care on a person who **7.97** 'treats' waste.[54] The Act, by Section 29(6), provides that waste is 'treated' when it is subjected to any process, including rendering it reusable or reclaiming substances from it, and 'recycle' is to be construed accordingly. This means, presumably, that rendering waste reusable or reclaiming substances from it amounts to recycling for the purposes of the EPA 1990. In turn, Section 1(5) defines 'process' in very wide language. It embraces any industrial or commercial activity carried on in Great Britain, whether on premises or by means of mobile plant, which is capable of causing pollution of the environment.

As yet, there has been no occasion to consider whether it is possible to escape the **7.98** consequences of the EPA 1990 Part II by conducting a process on a vessel, since 'premises', at least in ordinary language, means land or buildings. On the other hand, 'mobile plant' is defined by Section 1(6) of the Act to mean plant designed to be moved, whether by road or otherwise, and in the event the courts would probably be able to hold that a vessel designed to treat waste was mobile plant for the purposes of the EPA 1990.

Another query raised by the statutory definition of 'processes' is whether Parliament **7.99** intended that activities carried on for even the briefest of times should fall outside the definition. There is no reason to suppose that this was so, and there are good grounds for taking the opposite view. Even a momentary escape of a virulent poison or a brief but violent explosion could do great harm to the environment, and it is unlikely that the intention behind the EPA 1990 was to allow any process to escape the regulatory code which it imposes. Little assistance is therefore to be found, in construing Section 34 of the Act, in judicial decisions on the meaning of the word 'process' where used in other legislation, such as taxing statutes.[55]

The next, and another important category of person who is subject to the EPA **7.100** 1990 duty of care, consists of those who 'dispose' of waste. Section 29(6) provides that 'disposal' includes disposal by way of deposit in or on land. This does not appear to exclude disposal into water, not lakes, or at sea, for example. It is to be

---

[54] EPA 1990, s 34(1).
[55] As, eg, in *Vibroplant v Holland (Inspector of Taxes)* [1982] 126 SJ 182.

expected that disposal into water would be subject to the EPA 1990 controls, especially since dumping at sea has long been the subject of great, even international, controversy. In the circumstances, it is strange that Parliament should not have provided expressly for disposal at sea or in inland water.

7.101 There has been doubt in the past whether temporary deposit could amount to disposal, at least for the purposes of the CoPA 1974. It now appears to be established that even a temporary deposit constitutes disposal.[56] Again, this reflects what seems to have been Parliament's intention, since by a process of reasoning similar to that described above, even a brief period of deposit of a noxious waste is capable of producing great environmental harm.

7.102 Finally, Section 34 of the EPA 1990 imposes the statutory duty of care on a broker who has control of controlled waste. That duty is discussed more fully hereafter. The precise functions of a waste broker are not made clear by the Act, nor does it stipulate what acts amount to taking or relinquishing control of the waste. In the mid-nineteenth century, of course in a context which differs greatly from that envisaged by the EPA 1990, the court held that a broker is a person who arranges bargains between merchants and tradesmen in return for a fee or reward.[57]

7.103 As ever, caution must be exercised in applying old decisions to new cases, but as the code of environmental law comes to be developed, it is conceivable that a similar approach will be taken to the function of waste broker. It is clear, however, that the additional element of control must be present before the duty of care applies to a broker.

7.104 There remain to be examined the exemptions from the duty of care which the Waste Management Licensing Regulations confer.[58]

Exemptions from the duty of care

7.105 Strictly, regulation 16 of the Waste Management Licensing Regulations 1994 does no more than exclude persons undertaking activities regulated under statutes other than the EPA 1990 from the need to obtain a licence under Section 33 of the Act. The effect, however, is to take those persons outside the realm of management of waste, and consequently to absolve them from the duty of care imposed by the statute. It is therefore convenient to deal with the exemptions here.

7.106 The first category of exemption relates to recovery or disposal of waste designated by the Environmental Protection (Prescribed Processes and Substances) Regulations 1991.[59] These are more fully dealt with elsewhere. Briefly, they are

---

[56] See *R v Metropolitan Stipendiary Magistrate*, ex p *London WRA*, The Times, 14 January 1993.
[57] *Milford v Hughes* [1846] 16 M&W 174.
[58] SI 1994/1056.
[59] SI 1991/ 472, Sch 1, Part A, as amended by SI 1991/836 and SI 1992/514.

gasification, carbonization, and combustion in large incinerators. The EPA 1990 envisaged that HMIP and, thereafter, the Environment Agency would exercise control over these activities.

Secondly, there are activities authorized by way of integrated pollution control **7.107** under Part I of the EPA 1990, which result in the release of substances into the air, and which are prescribed in Section 5.1, Part A of Chapter 5 of Schedule 1 to the Environmental Protection (Prescribed Substances) Regulations 1991. Broadly, these activities are the incineration of chemicals and plastics, heavy metals such as cadmium, lead, and mercury, potentially dangerous wastes such as chlorine, phosphorus, and sulphur, animal remains, and the burning out of waste from containers used for the transport or storage of chemicals.

The third exempted activity is the disposal of liquid waste where this is consented **7.108** under the Water Resources Act 1991, which regulates the abstraction of water from watercourses and boreholes, or under the CoPA 1974, which is concerned with discharges into sewers.

Finally, there is exemption where the person is licensed to deposit waste in the sea **7.109** or to incinerate it at sea under the Food and Environment Protection Act 1985. However, none of these exemptions apply where the waste in question is to be disposed of by way of deposit in or on land.

F. Waste Licensing

The previous regime

Once it has been determined, first, that a substance is waste and subject to statu- **7.110** tory control, and second, that the waste is being dealt with in a way which renders the dealer subject to control, it then becomes necessary to identify the authorities which exercise the regulatory functions. Before the EPA 1990 became law, control exercised by central government through HMIP or the proposed Environment Agency could be ignored. The concern was with regulation by local authorities or other agencies. However, the Environment Act 1995 has provided that the licensing functions of local authorities shall be transferred to the Environment Agency. This now exercises the licensing and other functions of local authorities throughout England and Wales.

The present regime

The Environment Agency has various functions under the EPA 1990. First, and **7.111** probably foremost, it grants or withholds waste management licences under Section 35 of the Act. Its powers and duties are described in detail hereafter. It is enough for the moment to note that the treatment, keeping, and disposal of controlled waste on land or the treatment or disposal of such waste by means of specified mobile plant may only be undertaken by a person holding and in accordance with a waste management licence.[60]

7.112 Therefore, there are two types of waste management licence with which the Environment Agency may be concerned—a site licence, which authorizes the treatment, keeping, or disposal of waste in or on land; and a mobile plant licence, whose scope and function are self-evident.

7.113 It will cause no surprise that the Secretary of State has wide powers to supervise and intervene in the exercise of the functions of the Environment Agency. He may provide as to the conditions which may or may not be included in a licence.[61] He may also give directions to the Environment Agency as to the conditions which it may or may not include in any waste management licence.[62] He may, lastly, give guidance to the Environmental Agency as to how it shall exercise its waste management licensing functions.[63] In each instance, the Agency must give effect to the directions which it receives, and have regard to the guidance given to it. This reflects the strict control of local by central government which has been a conspicuous feature of the administrative landscape in recent years.

7.114 The second main, and almost as important, function of the Environment Agency is to police and supervise the discharge by waste handlers of the duty of care which Section 34 of the EPA 1990 imposes upon them. This duty is so important that it requires separate and specific discussion. However, the duty cannot arise until the person who owes it begins to import, carry, keep, treat, or dispose of controlled waste.[64] Since this cannot be done lawfully without a licence, it is logical to postpone examination of the duty of care until after the procedure for obtaining a licence has been described. This chapter follows that course.

7.115 Thirdly, the Environment Agency has the duty to inspect land and, if necessary, obtain information from a person who wishes to surrender a site licence authorizing the keeping, treatment, or disposal of waste on land.[65] The duty arises because, as will be seen, under the EPA 1990 the holder of a site licence cannot absolve himself from liability for the condition of the site merely by closing it down or, perhaps, by going bankrupt. This is a fundamental aspect of the duty of care already mentioned.

7.116 Fourthly, the Agency is obliged to supervise the conduct of a waste management licence holder while that licence is in force. It must ensure that the activities which

---

[60] EPA 1990, s 35(1).
[61] Ibid, s 35(6).
[62] Ibid, s 35(7).
[63] Ibid, s 35(8).
[64] Ibid, s 34(1).
[65] Ibid, s 39(4).

the licence authorizes do not pollute the environment, harm human health, or become seriously detrimental to the locality. The Agency must also ensure that the holder complies with the conditions of the licence.[66] If it considers it likely that the licence holder will pollute water, it will follow the lead given by the former National Rivers Authority, which has in recent years shown itself vigilant and ready to prosecute those who pollute waters.[67] Thus the duty to consult will almost certainly produce more than a mere exchange of paper between licensing authorities.

In this context any officer of the Environment Agency has the draconian power to carry out work on land, plant, or equipment. The Agency may recover the cost from the licence holder.[68] The policing powers include the ability to require the occupier of land to remove waste which has been unlawfully deposited, and to take such steps as may be necessary to eliminate or reduce the consequences of the unlawful deposit; to prosecute for failure to comply with the requirements; to remove the unlawfully deposited waste and recover the cost of so doing from the occupier of the land (unless the latter can persuade a magistrates' court on appeal against the original notice that he did not deposit nor knowingly cause or permit the deposit).[69] **7.117**

Unusually, the Environment Agency becomes the owner of the waste which it removes, and can deal with it accordingly.[70] This provision seems to be designed to meet the case where there is no occupier of the land where the unlawful deposit occurred, where the occupier cannot be found or where the occupier has satisfied the magistrates that he was not responsible, directly or indirectly, for the unlawful deposit. Then, apparently, the Agency is free to recover its costs, if it can, by selling the waste to someone who can find a use for it. **7.118**

In addition to exercising control and enforcement functions, the Environment Agency is bound to concern itself with forward planning. It must investigate the arrangements needed to treat and dispose of controlled waste in its areas so as to prevent or minimize pollution of the environment and damage to health and, having done so, must decide what arrangements to make; these must be embodied in a plan, which must then be kept under review and modified if necessary.[71] **7.119**

In the plan, the Environment Agency must set out the kinds and quantities of controlled waste which it expects to be in its area during the plan period, the controlled wastes which it expects to be exported during that period, those **7.120**

---

[66] Ibid, s 42(1).
[67] Ibid, s 42(2).
[68] Ibid, s 42(3) and (4).
[69] Ibid, s 59.
[70] Ibid, s 59(9).
[71] Ibid, s 50.

which will be disposed there at the same time, and the methods and priorities for disposal and treatment of controlled waste which the Agency considers should be adopted during the period of the plan. Costs and benefits of the arrangements and any modification of them are to be taken into account.[72]

7.121 The Agency is subject to central government control and is under a duty to consult the National Rivers Authority.[73] Since the Agency now exercises the functions of the former NRA, the duty must now be to have regard to the matters which that body had to take into account. The EPA 1990 stresses the importance which Ministers attach to recycling by expressly providing that the Environment Agency must consider what arrangements can reasonably be expected to be made for recycling waste, and what to include in their plans for that purpose.[74] These functions are dealt with more fully at the end of this chapter.

G. Enforcement

Introduction

7.122 Plainly, a fundamental role in the management of waste is the ability of regulatory authorities to enforce the requirement that waste shall only be tipped lawfully, and to require that waste unlawfully tipped shall be properly handled. This was a major factor in the thinking which led Parliament to create the statutory duty of care under the EPA 1990. Accordingly, the Act gives the Environment Agency powers which enable it to require that unlawfully tipped waste shall be removed.[75] The mechanism is familiar, and derives from the Public Health Acts passed in the nineteenth century.

The machinery of enforcement

7.123 As noted above, the Environment Agency may, by notice served on the occupier of land, require him to remove the waste from the land and/or to eliminate or reduce the consequences of the deposit. Parliament has thereby provisionally imposed the burden of dealing with all waste on the occupier of land, whether or not he is responsible for the unauthorized deposit (or 'fly-tipping'). There is a right of appeal to a magistrates' court, which has power to quash the requirements of the notice if satisfied that the appellant neither deposited nor knowingly caused or permitted the deposit, or if there is a material defect in the notice.[76] In any other

---

[72] Ibid, s 50(3).
[73] Ibid, s 50(5).
[74] Ibid, s 50(7).
[75] Ibid, s 59.
[76] Ibid, s 59(2) and (3).

case the court may modify the requirement of the notice or dismiss the appeal. Thus the innocent occupier who wakes up one morning to find a fly-tip on his land has a defence to the requirements of a notice under Section 59 of the EPA 1990, but if he is or becomes a party to the tipping he is liable to control under the Act. The effect of the notice is suspended pending an appeal.[77]

Failure to comply with the requirements of a notice without reasonable excuse is **7.124** a criminal offence, and, as is now commonplace, the Environment Agency may, additionally, do what the occupier was required to do by the notice and recover the cost from him.[78] The Environment Agency has similar powers in respect of waste tipped on land without first serving a notice if it appears that either it is necessary to remove the waste in order to remove or prevent pollution of land, water, or air, or harm to human health; or where there is no occupier of the land in question; or where the occupier neither made nor knowingly caused or permitted the deposit. In any event the innocent occupier cannot be made to pay the costs of removing or otherwise dealing with the waste.[79]

By contrast, the person who tipped or knowingly caused or permitted the **7.125** deposit can be made liable for the costs—if he can be found. The policing powers of the Environment Agency are extended by the imposition upon it of a duty to inspect all areas of England and Wales from time to time to detect whether any land in respect of which no site licence is in force is in such a condition, because of the presence there, or the emission of gases or discharge of fluids caused by deposits of controlled waste, that it may pollute the environment or harm human health.[80]

Once more, the Environment Agency may do works or take such other steps as **7.126** appear to it to be reasonable to avoid pollution or harm to human health. The cost is recoverable by the Environment Agency from the owner rather than the occupier of the land, except such cost as the owner can show was incurred unreasonably.[81] In fixing the cost which it decides to recover from the landowner the Environment Agency must have regard to any hardship which he might suffer from the expense incurred.[82]

By contrast to the fly-tipping provisions already discussed, the owner cannot **7.127** apparently resist paying the cleaning-up costs on the ground that he was not responsible for the deposit, and had no knowledge of it. At first sight, therefore,

---

[77] Ibid, s 59(4).
[78] Ibid, s 59(8).
[79] Ibid, s 59(7).
[80] Ibid, s 61(1). The side note to s 61 shows that it is intended to provide for the regulation of disused landfills.
[81] Ibid, s 61(8).
[82] Ibid, s 61(10).

it seems likely that the Environment Agency will choose to act under this section rather than the one concerned with fly-tipping. The relationship between the two has yet to be worked out by the courts. On the other hand, there is no doubt that the fly-tipping powers are not apt where a licensed tip has been closed, and there is a need to enforce against the landowner.

Registers

7.128   The remaining duties of the Agency are concerned with paper, in various forms. They must keep registers of all matters relating to licences which they issue; of appeals against their decisions; of convictions of licence holders; and of occasions on which they have taken action to enforce compliance with the conditions of a licence or to remedy the condition of a deposit which might pollute the environment or harm human health.[83]

7.129   The main exception to this requirement is that no information whose inclusion in the register would be contrary to the interests of national security is to appear there.[84] The Secretary of State is the judge of this.

7.130   The Environment Agency must publish reports for each financial year. The report has to set out the information contained in the register, and must appear within six months of the end of the year in question.[85]

H. Obtaining a Waste Management Licence

Introduction—the deposit of controlled waste

7.131   The system of waste management rests on a simple but solid foundation. Section 33(1) and (6) of the EPA 1990 makes it a criminal offence to deposit controlled waste, or knowingly to cause or permit the deposit of controlled waste in or on land, except in accordance with a waste management licence authorizing that deposit. Similarly, it is an offence to treat, keep, or dispose of controlled waste, or knowingly to cause or permit these activities, without or in breach of a waste disposal licence.[86]

7.132   'Dispose', in this context, includes, but is not limited to, the disposal by way of deposit on land, and 'treat' means subjecting the waste to any process, including making it reusable or reclaiming substances from it.[87] As has already been noted,

---

[83] Ibid, s 64.
[84] Ibid, s 65.
[85] Ibid, s 67.
[86] Ibid, s 33(1)(b).
[87] Ibid, s 29(6).

and as one would expect, an unlicensed temporary deposit of waste can amount to the commission of a criminal offence under Section 33 of the EPA 1990.

'Causing or permitting'

The concept of 'knowingly causing or permitting' is by no means novel. The **7.133** expression has frequently been considered by the courts in a variety of different contexts. It is by now well established that to 'permit' is looser and vaguer than to 'cause', which involves the giving of an express or positive instruction or mandate, while 'permit' embraces either an express or an implied consent.[88]

EPA re-enacts, for all practical purposes, the relevant provisions of the CoPA **7.134** 1974. Under that Act, it has been held that the offence of knowingly permitting the deposit of controlled waste is one of strict liability, in that the employer or principal of a business may be criminally liable, even though the deposit was due to the act or omission of an employee which may have been done without the employer's knowledge or even contrary to his orders.

It followed that, when controlled waste had been deposited without being covered **7.135** with earth as required by the waste disposal licence, the prosecutor, in order to secure a conviction, had to prove only that the waste was controlled waste, that it had been deposited, and that in fact the deposit was not in accordance with the requirements of the licence.[89]

Pollution of the environment and harm to health

The EPA 1990 creates a third offence. Even though treatment of or keeping waste, **7.136** or a deposit, may be authorized by a licence and effected in accordance with its terms, if the result is likely to cause pollution of the environment or harm to human health, then this is a criminal offence.[90] Both 'pollution of the environment' and 'harm to human health' are terms of art.

The former means pollution by the escape into any environmental medium of **7.137** substances or articles emanating from the waste and capable of causing harm to man or any living organism, from land or fixed plant on or in which controlled waste is treated, kept, deposited, or disposed of.[91]

The latter is widely defined to mean harm to the health of living organisms, other **7.138** interference with ecological systems of which living organisms form part, or

---

[88] See *McLeod v Buchanan* [1940] 2 All ER 179.
[89] See *Ashcroft v Cambro Waste Products* [1981] 3 All ER 699.
[90] EPA 1990, s 33(1)(c).
[91] Ibid, s 29(3).

offence to any of the senses of man or harm to his property.[92] Little, it will be observed, escapes the net in which the ignorant or incompetent can be trapped.

Defences

7.139 There are three defences to a charge of dealing with waste in contravention of Section 33 of the EPA 1990. By Section 33(7), a defendant can escape conviction, first, if he proves that he took all reasonable precautions and exercised all due diligence to avoid the commission of the offence. As yet it is unclear what distinguishes reasonable precautions from due diligence. A possible meaning is that setting up a reasonably safe system of operation amounts to taking reasonable precautions: taking reasonable steps to see that the system is followed at all times is due diligence. In each case, it will be a question of fact whether the defence has been established.

7.140 Secondly, it is a defence to prove that the defendant acted under instructions from his employer and neither knew nor had reason to suppose that he had contravened Section 33(1).

7.141 Third, he may escape conviction if he can show that the alleged contravention was done in an emergency in order to avoid danger to the public, and that as soon as reasonably practicable he informed the Environment Agency within whose area the treatment or disposal of the waste took place.

7.142 By analogy with offences under the Health and Safety at Work Acts, the burden of establishing the existence of the defence lies on the defendant—a rare exception to the general rule that the burden of proof remains on the prosecution throughout. If the analogy is pursued by the courts, the standard of proof resting on the defence will be that which applies in civil cases, that is, on the balance of probabilities rather than beyond reasonable doubt.

Household waste

7.143 The EPA 1990 excludes from the operation of the licensing system household waste which is treated, kept, or disposed of within the curtilage of the dwelling where it originated, and cases prescribed in regulations made by the Secretary of State.[93] In making the regulations the Secretary of State must have regard to the expediency of excluding from waste management control deposits which are small enough or so temporary, treated, or disposed of in ways which are so innocuous as not to harm the environment, cause damage to human health, or are regulated in other ways.[94]

---

[92] Ibid, s 29(6).
[93] Ibid, s 33(2) and (3).
[94] Ibid, s 33(4).

The Secretary of State has made the Waste Management Licensing Regulations **7.144** 1994 (SI 1994/1056) which create further exclusions. The majority of the exempt categories are exempt without qualification. A minority, however, listed in Regulation 17(2), are exempt only if carried on by or with the consent of the occupier of the land, or the person carrying on the exempt activity is otherwise entitled to do so. An example might be that the right had been acquired by prescription, or perhaps by usage, as can occur with commoners' rights. None of the exemptions, moreover, applies to special waste, unless otherwise stated.[95]

All the exempt categories of activity have to be carried on in such a way that the **7.145** type and quantity of waste, and the method of disposal and recovery, are consistent with the need to avoid endangering human health, harming the environment, causing risk to water, air, soil, plants, or animals, causing nuisance through noise or odours, or adversely affecting the countryside or places of special interest.[96]

Schedule 3 to the Waste Management Licensing Regulations is long, compli- **7.146** cated, and tedious to read. Nevertheless, its importance to persons handling waste is paramount, since it lists many activities which are exempt from licensing controls. Paragraph 1 of Schedule 3 exempts the reuse of waste glass in the manufacture and production of other glass products.

There follow, in order, several categories of undertaking. They are the operation, **7.147** loading, or unloading of a blast furnace with a capacity of up to 25 tonnes for the production of iron, steel, or non-ferrous metals, or a scrap metal furnace authorized under the integrated pollution control provisions of the EPA 1990, Part I; and the storage at a place other than a scrap metal dealer's place of business of scrap metal intended to be treated in an exempt blast furnace.

The second category consists of the burning as a fuel of straw, poultry litter, wood, **7.148** waste oil, solid fuel manufactured from waste under an authorization granted under the integrated pollution control provisions, or tyres, and the secure storage of the waste before it is burnt at the place where it is to be burnt or, for up to twelve months, where it is produced. In this context, 'secure' means that all reasonable precautions have been taken to ensure that the waste cannot escape and that members of the public are unable to gain access to it.[97]

Thirdly, there are the cleaning, washing, spraying, coating, or storage of waste **7.149** packaging or containers for reuse, subject to a maximum of 1,000 tonnes in any seven-day period, to the total amount stored not exceeding 1,000 tonnes, and no more than 1 tonne of metal containers used for the transport or storage of chemicals being dealt with in any seven-day period.

---

[95] Waste Management Licensing Regulations, Reg 17(3).
[96] Ibid, reg 17(4), Sch 4 para 4(1)(a).
[97] Ibid, reg 17(5).

7.150 Fourthly, there are various types of incineration. These are: burning waste in an incinerator with a net rated input of less than 0.4 megawatts, that is, at relatively low temperatures, and the secure, in the sense already considered, storage of the waste prior to burning; burning waste oil as a fuel in the engine of an aircraft, hovercraft, motor vehicle, railway engine, ship, or other vessel up to a maximum of 2,500 litres of oil per hour.

7.151 The fifth category embraces secure storage and spreading a variety of wastes on agricultural land, operational land of a railway, internal drainage board, or the Environment Agency; on land in forest or woodland; and on a park, garden, roadside verge, landscaped area, sports or recreation ground, churchyard or cemetery. The exempted wastes are soil, compost, wood, bark, other plant matter, food, drink or materials resulting from the preparation of food or drink, blood and gut contents from abattoirs, lime and lime sludge, gypsum, paper sludge, waste paper, and de-inked paper pulp, dredgings from inland waters, textile waste, septic tank sludge, sludge from biological treatment plants, hair, and effluent treatment sludge from tanneries.

7.152 In each case there is a maximum spreading limit of 250 tonnes per hectare in any twelve-month period, or 5,000 tonnes of waste per hectare from dredgings, and the exemption is subject to the Environment Agency being notified of particulars of the spreading. The related activity of keeping in secure storage on agricultural land of sludge to be used in accordance with the Sludge (Use in Agriculture) Regulations 1989, and spreading of sludge on other land if this results in ecological improvement and does not unduly pollute the soil in the sense defined by the 1989 Regulations is also exempt.

7.153 Likewise, spreading soil, rock, ash, sludge, dredgings from inland waters, or builders' waste in connection with a planning permission for the reclamation or improvement of the land, provided it results in benefit to agriculture or ecological improvement, and provided the land is incapable of reasonably beneficial use without reclamation or improvement, and subject to a maximum of 20,000 cubic metres of waste per hectare being spread.

7.154 Recovery within a sewage or water treatment works of sludge, subject to a total of 10,000 cubic metres of sludge being brought to the sewage works from elsewhere in any one year, and to no more than 10,000 tonnes of sludge being dealt with at a water treatment works in the same period is also exempt.

7.155 Thus far, although the materials exempted from the licensing system have little in common, it is possible to discern the links between them, in that, with a few possible exceptions, all are either innocuous or controlled under legislation other than the EPA 1990. However, in some instances—spreading abattoir products on agricultural land is an obvious one—the justification is less easy to see, since at least two of the senses, these being sight and smell, are readily offended by this activity.

The next category of exempt activity is intended to encourage the reuse of waste. **7.156** This is the storage, baling, sorting, shredding, or crushing of a range of wastes, provided these activities are undertaken with a view to recovering or reusing the material, and in each case subject to a maximum amount of the material coming to the place where it is dealt with in any one week.

The wastes are paper, cardboard, plastic, glass, cans, foil, and food or drink car- **7.157** tons. The encouragement of the reuse of waste is reflected in the exemption from licensing of composting biodegradable wastes (horse manure, for example) for the purpose of cultivating mushrooms or other purposes, subject to a maximum of 10,000 cubic metres at any time for mushroom cultivation, and 1,000 cubic metres for other purposes.

The same object justifies the exemption given to the manufacture of building **7.158** products or soil from building or civil engineering waste, and the storage and subsequent manufacture of finished goods from waste metal, plastic, glass, ceramics, rubber, textiles, wood, paper, or cardboard. Paradoxically, the beneficial reuse of waste without treatment is also exempt if no further treatment or disposal of the waste is involved. In those circumstances, one would hardly suppose that the material was waste at all.

Provided the ultimate intention is to reuse them, solvents, refrigerants, and halons **7.159** may be stored in a secure place without a licence, even though they may be special wastes, provided they are stored separately, for not more than 12 months, and subject to a maximum of 5 cubic metres of solvents, and 18 tonnes of refrigerants and halons being so stored. The refrigerants exempted in this way are specifically listed, but are likely to be of interest only to those directly involved in the refrigeration industry.[98]

As might be expected, Schedule 3 exempts the storage and laundering of waste **7.160** textiles with a view to their recovery or reuse, and the chipping or shredding of plant matter including tree bark.

The waste produced by dredging inland waters and cutting weeds there receives **7.161** particular attention. It is outside the licensing system if the mud or weeds are deposited on the bank or towpath of the water in question, or if they are placed on any bank or towpath and used for the benefit of agriculture or ecological improvement, and provided that on any one day no more than 50 tonnes of waste for each metre of bank or towpath is deposited. This seems to allow the deposit of the waste in one place, rather than spreading it evenly along the bank or towpath, and also to permit the deposit of unlimited amounts of waste, provided the daily

---

[98] The list appears at Sch 3, para 17(2).

limit is respected. The waste may also be screened or dewatered without attracting the need for a licence, and whatever its ultimate destination.

7.162   The exemption does not apply to the deposit of waste in a container or lagoon (understandably, since the potential for concentration is evident).

7.163   Baling, compacting, crushing, shredding, or pulverizing waste at the place where it is produced, and preliminary storage, and the storage by the manufacturer, distributor, or retailer of returned goods, for limited periods, likewise achieve exemption.[99]

Exemptions for incineration and burning

7.164   Schedule 3 pays particular attention to incineration and burning. No licence is needed for the incineration of waste in an incinerator authorized under integrated pollution control, nor for burning in the open air under strictly controlled conditions. Up to 10 tonnes of wood, bark, or other plant matter may be burnt on the land where it is produced in any one day, by the establishment or undertaking which produces it, but only where the land is of a kind specified. This is operational land of a railway, tramway, internal drainage board, or the National Rivers Authority, or a forest, park, garden, verge, sports or recreation ground, churchyard, or cemetery.

7.165   Waste produced elsewhere than on site by demolition work also qualifies for exemption if it is burnt in the prescribed circumstances.[100]

7.166   Similar control is imposed on the disposal of sanitary waste. Up to 25 litres may be discharged from a railway train onto the track, and up to 5 cubic metres within any twelve months may be buried on the premises where it originated.[101]

Miscellaneous exemptions

7.167   The other categories exempted by Schedule 3 are miscellaneous and more or less specialized. They call for no more than brief mention. They include wastes from peat working; spent ballast on railway or tramway operational land; borehole waste where drilling has been undertaken with planning permission; the temporary storage of garbage from merchant ships and tank washings; the burial of dead domestic pets on the premises where they lived; storage of waste samples for research purposes or where treatment of the waste is regulated otherwise than by management licence (for example, where the waste is radioactive and regulated under the Radioactive Substances Acts); waste medicines returned to pharmacies;

---

[99] Ibid, paras 27 and 28.
[100] Ibid, para 30. For example, the material burnt must be wood or other plant matter, and there is an upper limit to the amount which may be burnt in any 24-hour period of 10 tonnes.
[101] Sch 3 to the Regulations, para 31.

the temporary storage of wastes, including special wastes, at the premises where they were produced pending collection, provided that special wastes may be stored for no more than twelve months and are subject to volume controls; and temporary exemptions for lawful waste operations carried on before 1994, when Part II of the EPA 1990 came into effect.[102]

Fly-tipping

Parliament's concern with one specific type of waste disposal is evidenced by the special treatment which it received in the EPA 1990.[103] This is fly-tipping. **7.168**

Where waste is carried in and deposited from a motor vehicle, the person who controls or is in a position to control that vehicle is taken to have knowingly caused the waste to be deposited. This is so, whether or not the potential defendant gave instructions for the tipping to be carried out. This reflects two notable features of fly-tipping. First, there is its prevalence. Second, by its nature, it is difficult to detect the offender. The EPA 1990 therefore transfers responsibility for ensuring that waste is not fly-tipped onto the individual who is relatively easy to find and fix with responsibility, even though he or she might be personally blameless. As will be seen, this approach runs all through Part II of the Act. **7.169**

The right to a licence

A waste management licence can be granted only to a limited number of categories of applicant. If the licence is to relate to land, the occupier of that land may alone obtain a licence, called a 'site licence'. **7.170**

If the licence is to cover mobile plant (a 'mobile plant licence'), the only qualified applicant is the proposed operator.[104] If a site licence is required the application is made to the Environment Agency for the area in which the land is located. Where the requirement is for a mobile plant licence, the Environment Agency is again the appropriate recipient.[105] **7.171**

Although the EPA 1990 empowers the Secretary of State to prescribe the form in which an application for a licence shall be made, he has done no more than require that the application shall be in writing.[106] The Environment Agency will draw up its own application forms, in the same way as local planning authorities have done for many years. The application must be accompanied by the prescribed fee. **7.172**

---

[102] Sch 3, paras 32 et seq.
[103] At s 33(5).
[104] EPA 1990, s 35(2).
[105] Ibid, s 36(1).
[106] Waste Management Licensing Regulations, Reg 2(1).

This will be done in accordance with a scheme made by the Secretary of State and the Treasury jointly.[107]

The relationship to town and country planning

7.173   Before he applies for a site licence, the applicant should satisfy himself that planning permission has been granted for the proposed use, or alternatively that no planning permission was required and that an established use certificate or certificate of lawful existing use or development is in force.[108] It is not enough that the use of the land may be immune from enforcement action unless the appropriate certificate exists. In practice, the Environment Agency will no doubt require that a copy of the relevant permission or certificate is submitted with the application.

The functions of the Environment Agency

7.174   The powers and duties of the Environment Agency, once the application for a licence has been duly made, that is, with all the formalities observed, are closely defined. It must consult bodies concerned with such matters as nature conservation. It must also consider, although it is not bound to follow, any representations which those bodies make.[109] However, if there is a difference of opinion, the matter may be referred to the Secretary of State. The decision of the latter is final.[110]

7.175   The Environment Agency is also required to consult appropriate nature conservation bodies where any part of the land to be used under a site licence has been notified as a site of special scientific interest under the Wildlife and Countryside Act 1981. While the Agency is obliged to consider these representations it is not bound by them.[111]

7.176   Having carried out its consultations, the Environment Agency is obliged to grant the licence unless one of four conditions is satisfied. These are: (1) the applicant is not a 'fit and proper person' to hold a licence; (2) the licence must be refused for the purpose of preventing pollution of the environment; (3) the licence must be refused for the purpose of preventing harm to human health; (4) the licence must be refused for the purpose of preventing serious detriment to the amenities of the locality, unless there is a planning permission in force which authorizes the proposed use.[112]

---

[107] EPA 1990, s 41.
[108] Ibid, s 36(2).
[109] Ibid, s 36(4).
[110] Ibid, s 36(5).
[111] Ibid, s 36(7).
[112] Ibid, s 36(3).

Fitness to hold a licence

The notion of a 'fit and proper person' is developed and elaborated in Section 74 **7.177** of the EPA 1990. There are three sets of circumstances which can disqualify a person from being fit and proper to hold a licence.[113]

First, he or she may have been convicted of a relevant offence, by which is meant **7.178** either that he has been convicted of an offence committed in his capacity as the holder of a licence, or as the employee or business partner of such a holder,

Second, he or she may have been a director, manager, secretary, or similar officer **7.179** of a company which has been convicted of a relevant offence.

Third, where the proposed holder of the licence is itself a body corporate, where **7.180** one of the senior officers has personally been convicted of a relevant offence, or was a senior officer of another company similarly convicted.

These definitions leave open the question of what amounts to a relevant offence. **7.181** The answer lies in Regulation 3 of the Waste Management Licensing Regulations 1994. The convictions which amount to relevant offences are all connected with pollution. They are infringements of the Public Health Acts, the CoPA 1974 and regulations made under it, primary and delegated legislation concerning refuse and its disposal, the Water Acts, and the Clean Air Act 1993.

Draconian though those provisions are, the Environment Agency may treat a per- **7.182** son convicted of a relevant offence as fit and proper if it considers it appropriate to do so in any particular case.[114] The factors which influence the decision are apparently the identity of the offender—for instance, a licence holder who is convicted because of the act or default of an employee may be treated more leniently than the employee; the nature and gravity of the offence, and the consequences for pollution or human health of the infringement; the number of relevant offences; and the expiry of time since they were committed. An individual whose conviction is spent under the Rehabilitation of Offenders Act 1974 could legitimately expect that the authority would disregard the conviction, and in practice the same might be true of a company, although the concept of spent convictions does not apply to it.

A person, which may be a company, may also not be fit and proper if the manage- **7.183** ment of the activities which it is proposed to undertake will not be in the hands of a technically competent person.[115] Technical competence is regulated by Regulation 4 of the Waste Management Licensing Regulations 1994. In essence, this identifies the certificate issued by the Waste Management Industry Training

---

[113] Ibid, s 74(3).
[114] Ibid, s 74(4).
[115] Ibid, s 74(3)(b).

and Advisory Board which must be held by each person employed at a range of waste management facilities. The latter are landfill sites, incinerators, waste treatment plants, transfer stations, and civic amenity sites.

7.184 The details of the certificate in question are set out in Table 1 of Regulation 4(1). Scrap metal dealers' and car breakers' yards are exempt.[116]

7.185 The third factor which renders a person not fit and proper for the purposes of Section 74 of the Act is if he, as licence holder or proposed licence holder, has not made financial provision adequate to discharge the obligations which the licence imposes, and either has no intention of making such provision or is in no position to do so.[117] This reason for disqualification from the status of fit and proper person is vitally important since, as will be seen, the financial burdens imposed as the result of the duty of care to which every waste management licence holder is subject can be onerous.

7.186 The remaining grounds which may entitle the Environment Agency to refuse to grant a licence do not call for lengthy comment. The concepts of pollution of the environment and harm to human health have already been described in the context of the definition of waste in its various manifestations.

7.187 Section 36(3)(c) of the EPA 1990, which entitles the Agency to refuse to grant a licence where there will be serious detriment to the amenities of the locality, but only where there is no planning permission in force, is a valuable guide to the difference in the responsibilities of planning authorities and the Environment Agency. For these purposes, planning permission is in force only where there has been a positive decision by a local planning authority or the Secretary of State on appeal to grant planning permission, taken after 30 April 1994.[118] That date is significant because on 1 May 1994 the waste management licensing provisions of the EPA 1990 came into force, as did the EC Framework Directive on Waste (75/442/EEC). From then on, planning authorities are expressly required to have regard to detriment to amenity when considering applications for planning permission. No such obligation existed before.

Conditions of a licence

7.188 The Environment Agency has power to grant a licence subject to such terms and conditions as it deems appropriate, and these may relate to the activities which the licence authorizes, or the precautions to be taken and the works to be carried out in connection with those activities. The requirements imposed by the licence may ensure preclusive precautions to be carried out before the licensed activities begin

---

[116] Waste Management Licensing Regulations, Reg 4(2).
[117] EPA 1990, s 74(3)(c).
[118] Waste Management Licensing Regulations, Sch 4, para 9(7).

and post-operational remedial and safety requirements.[119] This power is consistent with the obligations imposed by the statutory duty of care, described below, and the obligation which in practice falls on the applicant for the licence to show that he has the financial ability to comply with its requirements, which has already been described.

The discretion vested in the Environment Agency is not unfettered. It is by **7.189** now well-established law that the exercise of a statutory discretion, which would include the power to attach conditions to a waste management licence, must be exercised so as to further the aims and objectives of the statute which confers the power.[120] It must therefore be expected that, should the point arise, the courts would hold that the conditions which can properly be attached to a waste management licence must be directed at the factors which the Agency is bound to take into account when considering the grant of a licence. These are: the fitness of the licence holder, the need to protect the environment from pollution and the public from damage to its health, and the need, where pre-1994 planning permissions are in force, to prevent serious detriment to the amenities of the locality.[121]

In all cases, the Agency must issue its decision within four months of receiving **7.190** the application, otherwise it is deemed to have refused it.[122]

Special provisions, set out in Regulations 14 and 15 of the Waste Management **7.191** Licensing Regulations 1994, apply to licences authorizing the regeneration of waste oils and disposal or tipping which might lead to a discharge into groundwater of the substances disposed of or tipped. A licence to regenerate waste oil must contain conditions preventing the oil from becoming a toxic or dangerous waste, containing PCBs or PCTs, or from being mixed with them.

Disposal or tipping which might eventually lead to the pollution of groundwater **7.192** is subject to stringent controls governing the information to be submitted to the Environment Agency before the licence is issued, monitoring and surveillance of the groundwater while the activities authorized by the licence are carried on, and the imposition of conditions attached to the licence. These must ensure that the groundwater is not contaminated.

---

[119] EPA 1990, s 35(3).
[120] See *Padfield v Minister of Agriculture* [1968] AC 997 (milk-marketing scheme); *Newbury DC v SOS* [1981] AC 578 (planning conditions).
[121] EPA 1990, s 36(3).
[122] Ibid, s 36(9).

Appeals

7.193 Where an application for a licence is refused, where it is granted subject to conditions which are unsatisfactory to the applicant, or where no decision is published within the four-month prescribed period, there is a right of appeal to the Secretary of State.[123] Similarly, there is right of appeal against subsequent decisions affecting the licence, such as its suspension or revocation.[124] The appeal against refusal to grant a licence, or the conditions attached to a licence, must be brought within six months of the decision complained of, or of the expiry of the four-month period, by giving written notice to the Secretary of State.[125] The notice of appeal must be accompanied by the prescribed documents, including relevant correspondence and other documents, and an indication whether the appellant wishes the appeal to take the form of a hearing or to proceed by written representations, as is his right.[126] The Secretary of State may then refer any matter raised by the appeal to a person appointed by him for the purpose, who will in practice be the Inspector who conducts the hearing of the appeal, or inspects the land or plant where the appeal is by written representation. The Inspector may, if the Secretary of State so decides, determine the appeal.[127]

7.194 The effect of appealing varies with the nature of the appeal. In most instances this will have the result that the decision against which the appeal is lodged is suspended. Thus a refusal to grant a licence will remain in force, as will the conditions attached to a licence which has been granted, and the decision to modify or revoke a licence will also remain in abeyance.[128] By contrast, a modification of the conditions of a licence, its revocation or suspension, remain effective pending the determination of the appeal, no doubt as a deterrent to the bringing of frivolous and cynical time-wasting appeals.[129]

7.195 However, an authority which decides to modify conditions or revoke a licence does so at its peril, since the Secretary of State may order that the holder of a modified or former holder of a revoked licence may recover compensation for any loss sustained where the authority has resolved that the decision should take effect immediately in order to prevent or minimize pollution or harm to human health.[130]

---

[123] Ibid, s 43(1).
[124] Ibid.
[125] Waste Management Licensing Regulations, Regs 6 and 7.
[126] Ibid, Reg 6(2).
[127] EPA 1990, s 43(2).
[128] Ibid, s 43(4).
[129] Ibid, s 43(5) and (6).
[130] Ibid, s 43(7).

The Secretary of State must notify his decision in writing, and, where there has **7.196** been a hearing, provide the appellant with a copy of the Inspector's report.[131] This, of course, does no more than reflect the long-established principles embodied in successive Tribunals and Inquiries Acts, and render the decision liable to scrutiny by the courts either by way of appeal under the statute or by way of judicial review under the Rules of the Supreme Court, Order 54.

I. The Duty of Care

Introduction

The principle which underlies the duty of care is that no one who deals with waste **7.197** can absolve himself of his responsibility to avoid pollution, harm to health, or the unlicensed deposit of waste simply by passing the problem to someone else. Thus, Section 34(1) of the EPA 1990 requires any person who imports, produces, carries, keeps, disposes of, or controls waste as a broker to take reasonable steps to prevent the contravention of Section 33, discussed above, by any other person. In addition, he must take reasonable measures to prevent the escape of waste from his own control and that of others. He must transfer it only to an authorized person, or to a person for 'authorized transport purposes'.

An authorized person is a waste collection authority; the holder of a waste man- **7.198** agement licence or a disposal licence under the CoPA 1974; a person exempted by the Waste Management Licensing Regulations 1994, already discussed; a carrier of waste registered under the EPA 1990 or exempted by regulations made under that Act; and a waste disposal authority in Scotland.[132]

Authorized transport purposes are the movement of controlled waste from one **7.199** place to another within the same premises; the transport of controlled waste imported from abroad which has not been landed to a destination within Great Britain—presumably this is intended to cover only waste imported by sea or air, since the concept of transporting waste which has not been landed is hardly appropriate for waste imported by road; and the export of controlled waste by air or sea, but not by road.[133]

The person dealing with waste must take reasonable steps to secure that he trans- **7.200** fers a written description of the waste such as to enable others to discharge their duty to prevent the escape of waste and to comply with the requirements

---

[131] Waste Management Licensing Regulations, Reg 9.
[132] EPA 1990, s 34(3).
[133] Ibid, s 34(4).

of Section 33. The Secretary of State has power to prescribe how this duty shall be discharged.[134]

Transfer notes

7.201   That power led to the making of the Environmental Protection (Duty of Care) Regulations 1991 (SI 1991/2839). These require that the transferor and the transferee shall both complete and sign a transfer note. The note must record the identity and quantity of the waste, and whether it is loose or in a container; if in a container, the kind; the time and place of the transfer; the name and address of both parties; whether the transferor is a producer or importer of waste; if the transfer is for authorized transport purposes, which purpose is involved; and the authority by which both parties are entitled to deal with the waste.

7.202   The Regulations also require that copies of the transfer note shall be kept by each party for two years, and that they must furnish copies on seven days' notice to the Environment Agency.

The Code of Practice

7.203   The Secretary of State must issue, and has issued, a Code of Practice giving guidance on how to discharge the duty of care. The Code is admissible in evidence in civil or criminal legal proceedings, and is to be taken into account by the court in determining any question which may arise, although breach of the Code is not automatically a breach of the duty of care.[135] Its status is therefore the same as that of the Highway Code in motoring cases.

7.204   In effect the Code recommends the application of sceptical common sense to all transactions involving waste, this being the way in which the Secretary of State foresees that dealers in waste will be able to show that they have taken reasonable measures in any given case.

7.205   A few examples give the flavour of the advice in the Code of Practice. Waste producers are advised to become suspicious if a carrier's lorries return to the site where the waste was produced much sooner than could be expected if they were taking the waste to a destination which had previously been identified. So, also, a carrier should be alert if the transfer note which he has completed states that the waste which he is to transport is paint, and a drum begins to leak a clear fluid. (In this instance the producer or importer will probably be guilty of at least two breaches of the duty of care. He will have failed to prevent the escape of the waste, and will also have failed to provide the carrier with a written description of the

---

[134] Ibid, s 34(5).
[135] Ibid, s 34(7) and (10).

waste such as to enable him to avoid breaking the requirements of a waste management licence.)

Another example given in the Code draws attention to the duty of the waste man-   **7.206**
ager who receives the waste for disposal to satisfy himself that it matches the
description which he has been given, and that it is of a type which he is competent
to handle. The best practice of the most sophisticated disposal site managers is to
have a team of scientists working in laboratories who will analyse each consignment, or make spot checks on wastes which arrive as part of a long series of
consignments.

Carriers

It is noteworthy that waste carriers are subject to particularly strict regulation.   **7.207**
First, their heavy goods vehicles are licensed under the system prescribed by the
Transport Act 1968. Next, those who carry dangerous wastes are subject to the
control imposed by the Dangerous Substances (Conveyance by Road in Road
Tankers and Tank Containers) Regulations 1981 (SI 1981/1059). This set up the
system of warning signs carried by lorries which are a familiar sight on the roads
of the UK. Thirdly, the Controlled Waste (Registration of Carriers and Seizure of
Vehicles) Regulations 1991 (SI 1991/1624) lay down a comprehensive system
of registration for waste carriers. Paradoxically, the Environment Agency may
refuse to register a carrier on the ground that he has been convicted of an offence
connected with waste management,[136] but at the same time is required to enter
the particulars of every conviction of a person whom it registers as a carrier on
the list of carriers.[137]

It should also not be overlooked that the import and export of waste are   **7.208**
regulated by the Transfrontier Shipment of Waste Regulations 1994 (SI
1994/1137), discussed in the context of the National Strategy for Waste, above.

Breach of the duty of care

Failure to discharge the duty of care is a criminal offence, punishable with a fine,   **7.209**
and triable either in the magistrates' court or the Crown Court.[138] Failure to
comply with the Carriage of Waste and Seizure of Vehicles Regulations (as to
which see above) is similarly a criminal offence, carrying the same penalties.

There is no direct consequence which affects the civil liability of the offender   **7.210**
for loss or damage arising from the breach of the duty, although a conviction

---

[136] Controlled Waste (Regulation of Carriers and Seizure of Vehicles) Regulations 1991,
SI 1991/1624, Reg 5(1).
[137] Ibid, Reg 6(1)(f).
[138] EPA 1990, s 34(6).

would no doubt have considerable evidential weight in civil proceedings following the breach. By contrast, the deposit of waste without a licence or in breach of the conditions of a licence which causes damage expressly renders the offender liable for the damage without prejudice to liability under the ordinary law of negligence, nuisance, or trespass. The only exceptions to this rule are, first, where the damage arose wholly because of the fault of the victim, and, secondly, where he voluntarily accepted the risk of the damage being caused.[139] This would cover the case of a trespasser on a site or item of mobile plant who ignores warning notices and fencing and suffers injury from coming into contact with hazardous waste.

Variation, transfer, surrender, and revocation of licences

7.211 The theme which runs through the law regulating the ownership and dealing with the waste management licence during its life, is that responsibility for proper handling of the waste shall always be vested in an identifiable party with the financial means to discharge the statutory duty of care.

7.212 The licence may be varied, but only subject to the control and approval of the Environment Agency. The Agency may vary the licence on its own initiative, or on application by the licence holder, to the extent which it holds is desirable, without requiring unreasonable expense on the part of the holder. The modification may only be made to the extent required to ensure that the operation of the licence does not infringe the three basic rules of the EPA 1990, these being the avoidance of pollution of the environment, harm to human health, and serious damage to the amenities of the locality.[140] The Environment Agency is, however, under a duty to vary licences so as to make them conform to those three principles.

7.213 Additionally, the Environment Agency is obliged to vary the licence so as to make it comply with the requirements of the Waste Management Licensing Regulations 1994, which cover the regeneration of waste oils or disposal and tipping which might affect groundwater, and which have been considered above.

7.214 The prescribed consultations must be undertaken when the Environment Agency proposes to vary a licence in the same way as they are when an application for a licence is made, except that the Environment Agency may postpone consultations if it thinks it appropriate to do so in an emergency. The Environment Agency is also, curiously, not required to consider representations made by an authority which it has consulted if it considers that the variation or modification which is about to be made will not affect the consultee.[141] This is potentially fertile ground

---

[139] Ibid, s 73(6).
[140] Ibid, s 37(1) and (2).
[141] Ibid, s 37(5).

for litigation by way of judicial review, since a body which has taken the trouble to respond to consultation by the Environment Agency will, presumably, have formed the opinion that it will be affected by the operation of the licence as proposed to be varied. In the ordinary course of events a specialist environmental regulatory body is likely to be better able to assess the consequences of the operation of a licence than even the most knowledgeable and enlightened local authority.

If the licence holder has applied for a variation of the licence and has not received a decision within two months of making the application, the Environment Agency is deemed to have rejected the application and there is a right of appeal to the Secretary of State under the EPA 1990, Section 43.[142] While the appeal is pending the decision whether or not to vary the licence is ineffective, unless the Environment Agency has stated in its notice of decision that the decision was necessary for the purpose of preventing or minimizing pollution of the environment or harm to human health. In that event the decision stands until the Secretary of State or an Inspector determines the appeal, subject to the Environment Agency being liable to pay compensation to the licence holder if it is held that it was unreasonable to put its decision into immediate effect by issuing the appropriate statement with the notice of decision.   **7.215**

The amount of compensation is determined by arbitration.[143] There is no guidance as to the principles which must be applied in assessing the compensation, but the obvious rule is that it should reflect the loss sustained by the licence holder as the result of the Environment Agency decision coming into immediate effect rather than being suspended until the appeal was determined.   **7.216**

Transfers

The increased rigour of the licensing system as compared with its predecessor under the CoPA 1974 is exemplified by the formalities which have to be observed before the licence holder can transfer the licence to another person or organization. The EPA 1990 expressly provides that a licence may be transferred whether or not it has been partly revoked or suspended, as described hereafter.   **7.217**

Both the licence holder and the proposed transferee must apply jointly to the Environment Agency for the transfer.[144] In accordance with the Waste Licensing Regulations 1994 the application must be in writing, and must be accompanied by the appropriate fee and a considerable amount of information, designed to enable the Environment Agency to satisfy itself that the site or mobile plant, as the case may be, will continue to be operated in accordance with the requirements   **7.218**

---

[142] Ibid, s 37(6).
[143] Ibid, s 43(4), (6), (7).
[144] Ibid, s 40(1) and (2).

of the Act.[145] The identity of the licence holder and the proposed transferee and their agents if any must be given, together with their addresses and the numbers of their telephones, telexes, and faxes. (As yet, there is no obligation to supply an electronic mail address, although it will cause no surprise if this omission is rectified in a future revision of the Regulations.)

7.219 Details of the senior management of a proposed transferee which is a limited company, and of the partners of a partnership, must be supplied. Details of relevant convictions must be revealed, and the technical competence of the intended site manager or person in charge of mobile plant established, by production of the appropriate certificate or documentary evidence of the person's status which makes it unnecessary for him to hold a certificate of competence. This has been described in the context of applications for the grant of licences, and is the same.

7.220 Importantly also, the financial arrangements made or to be made by the would-be transferee for the discharge of the obligations imposed by the licence have to be submitted. The applicants for transfer may also lodge any other information which they wish the Environment Agency to take into account.

7.221 If the Environment Agency is satisfied that the transferee is a fit and proper person for the purposes of the EPA 1990, it must carry out a transfer of the licence. It has no discretion in the matter. This is done by endorsing the licence with the name and particulars of the transferee, and the date, to be agreed with the applicants, on which the transfer is to take effect.[146] Again, the agency is deemed to have refused the transfer if it has not issued a decision within two months of receiving the application, and the applicants may appeal to the Secretary of State.[147] Pending the outcome of the appeal, the decision, actual or notional, to refuse to permit the transfer stands.[148]

7.222 During its lifetime, a licence may be suspended if it appears to the Environment Agency that the licence holder has ceased to be a fit and proper person as defined; that the management of the site or the mobile plant has ceased to be in the hands of a technically competent person; or that serious pollution of the environment or serious harm to human health has resulted from or is about to occur in consequence of activities covered by the licence. The suspension may relate to the whole of the licence, or to some of the activities which it authorizes.[149]

7.223 The effect is that the licence no longer authorizes the activities to which it relates, or such of them as the Environment Agency specifies. The licence holder and

---

[145] Ibid.
[146] Ibid, s 40(4) and(5).
[147] Ibid, s 40(6).
[148] Ibid, s 43(4) and (5), by operation of the principle *expressio unius est exclusio alterius*.
[149] Ibid, s 38(6).

others will therefore commit offences if they continue to deal with waste while the licence is suspended.

Associated with the suspension, the Environment Agency has power to require **7.224** the licence holder to take such measures as it considers necessary to deal with or avert environmental pollution or harm to human health.[150] It is a criminal offence to fail to comply with the requirements of the Environment Agency, and, as with other infringements of the EPA 1990, the penalties are more severe if the offence involves special waste.[151]

Revocation

The power to revoke a licence is exercisable in much the same circumstances as the **7.225** power to suspend. If it appears to the Environment Agency that the holder has been convicted of a relevant offence and has consequently ceased to be a fit and proper person, or that the continuation of the waste management activities which the licence authorizes would pollute the environment, harm human health, or be seriously detrimental to the amenities of the locality, it may revoke the licence.

Before doing so, however, the Agency must also consider whether modification of **7.226** the licence would avoid the pollution, harm, or detriment to amenity causing concern. If it appears that modification will not suffice, the power to revoke may be exercised.[152]

The licence may also be revoked if the person managing the site or mobile plant is **7.227** not technically competent. In that event the Environment Agency need not direct its mind to the possibility of modification, but may revoke the licence to the extent specified in the licence.[153] In other cases the Agency has a choice—it may revoke the licence in whole or in part.[154]

If the licence holder appeals against revocation the Environment Agency's deci- **7.228** sion is ineffective, unless it states in the notice of revocation that its action was necessary to prevent or minimize pollution or harm to health. In that event the revocation takes immediate effect, with the proviso that the Agency is liable to compensate the licence holder if the Secretary of State eventually decides that it acted unreasonably in causing the revocation to take effect immediately.[155]

---

[150] Ibid, s 38(9).
[151] Ibid, s 38(10) and (11).
[152] Ibid, s 38(1) and (3).
[153] Ibid, s 38(2) and (3).
[154] Ibid, s 38(4).
[155] Ibid, s 43.

Surrender

7.229   The principle which forbids a licence holder from walking away from his obligations under the licence is clearly shown by the procedure for surrendering a licence.
This cannot be achieved by the unilateral decision of the holder of a site licence,
for the Environment Agency must accept the surrender for it to be effective.[156]
Further, the Agency has to be supplied with sufficient information with the application for it to be able to satisfy itself that the site will be no threat to the environment or human health.

7.230   The Waste Management Licensing Regulations 1994 prescribe in detail the information which must be supplied with the application for the surrender of a site
licence.[157] The location of the site and the identity and details of the licence
holder must be set out in the way which will be familiar. The holder must also
give the Agency details of the geology and hydrogeology of the site, the engineering works carried out in order to prevent pollution of the environment or harm to
human health, the type or types of waste tipped, the amounts, and the location
within the site where the tipping took place.

7.231   Where appropriate, that is, where the site is a landfill or lagoon, monitoring
data on the quality of the surface water and groundwater, the production gas or
leachate, and the physical stability of the land must be given. These requirements, more than any others, show the extent of the obligations to which a site
licence holder is subject throughout the life of a tip which he undertakes to operate, and thereafter.

7.232   On receipt of an application for surrender of a site licence, the Environment
Agency is obliged to inspect the land and may require the licence holder to furnish
further information or evidence.[158] Next it must decide whether it is likely or not
that the condition of the land will cause pollution of the environment or harm to
human health as the result of its having been used for the treatment, keeping, or
disposal of waste.[159] If, and only if, the Agency forms the view that the condition
of the land is such that pollution or harm to health are unlikely to occur, it must
accept the surrender of the licence. Otherwise, it must refuse to do so.

7.233   The licence holder may appeal to the Secretary of State against a rejection of the
application to surrender. If no decision is issued within three months of the

---

[156] Ibid, s 39(1). However, the decision of the High Court in *Re Wilmott Trading (No 2)*, The
Times, 16 June 1999 seems to throw doubt on this principle. There it was held, with the support
of the Environment Agency and the Crown, that a waste management licence is not property, and
does not vest in the Crown as bona vacantia when a company holding a licence is dissolved. This
conundrum will need to be more fully considered in future.

[157] Waste Management Licensing Regulations, Reg 2 and Sch 1.

[158] EPA 1990, s 39(4).

[159] Ibid, s 39(5).

Environment Agency receiving it the rejection is ineffective, and the licence remains in force. This means, of course, that the licence holder continues to be bound by the conditions attached to it. Where, on the other hand, the Environment Agency accepts the surrender, it issues a 'certificate of completion', stating that it is satisfied with the condition of the site. The licence thereupon ceases to have effect.[160]

Mobile plant licences

The EPA 1990 is almost silent on the subject of the surrender of mobile plant **7.234** licences. By necessary implication, it seems, the elaborate precautions which have to be taken in respect of site licences do not apply. The holder may surrender his licence unilaterally, and provided that he does not abandon the plant so as to infringe the general prohibition on the unlicensed deposit of waste, or break the duty of care, that will be an end of the matter.

Closed landfill sites

The EPA 1990 conferred powers on waste regulation authorities which obliged **7.235** them to inspect the closed landfill sites within their areas, with a view to discovering whether landfill gas or leachates might be a potential cause of pollution of the environment or threat to human health. If it found any such sites, the authority might be required to do the work or take other steps reasonably necessary to avoid the pollution or harm. The costs might then be recovered from the owner of the land (assuming always that the owner could be found).[161] However, the provisions under which these powers could have been exercised were never brought into force, and in 1994 the government announced that it intended to replace them with special arrangements for monitoring and controlling closed landfill sites which came within the definition of contaminated land. The Environment Act 1995 equates closed landfill sites with other sorts of contaminated land. The system of remediation notices in respect of contaminated land and the rights of appeal against them are described elsewhere, and need not be repeated here.

J. Waste Collection and Disposal

Collection

In general, waste is collected in England and Wales by district councils or unitary **7.236** authorities. Each collection authority is under a duty to arrange for the collection of household waste within its area, other than from places which are so isolated or

---

[160] Ibid, s 39(6), (7), and (9).
[161] Ibid, s 61.

inaccessible that the cost of collection would be unreasonably high, or where the authority is satisfied that the person controlling the waste has made or can be expected to make adequate arrangements for its disposal.[162]

7.237   Except in cases prescribed in Schedule 2 to the Controlled Waste Regulations 1992,[163] no charge may be made for the collection of household waste, but in those cases the collection authority may make a reasonable charge for the collection, and is not bound to collect the waste until specifically asked to do so.[164] The prescribed exceptions cover items which are too heavy to be taken away on the conventional dustcart, too large to fit into a dustbin of the prescribed size (750 millimetres in diameter and 1 metre in length, it will be remembered), or of a kind which requires special treatment or handling.

7.238   These categories include garden waste, dead domestic pets, clinical waste, mineral or synthetic oil, and asbestos. Where there is a non-domestic element in the premises which generate the waste, this may also render the producer liable to pay for the removal under Schedule 2 to the Controlled Waste Regulations. A residential home, college hall of residence or school boarding house, premises or a caravan provided as self-catering holiday accommodation, prisons, public meeting halls, and royal palaces are examples of the genre.

7.239   The collection authority must make arrangements for emptying, free of charge, privies serving private dwellings within its area, and must also arrange for the removal of the contents of cesspools serving private dwellings. A charge may be made for this service if the authority considers it appropriate.[165]

7.240   The waste collection authority has the power, but not a duty, to provide dustbins, or receptacles of a kind and number specified, as the EPA 1990 describes them, and where these are provided, the householder must place his waste in the receptacle or receptacles provided.[166] This would, for example, empower the authority to require bottles or paper to be put into a dustbin designated for the purpose, a power which has been increasingly used as the policy of recycling as much waste as possible continues to be followed and intensified. The authority may also prescribe the places where the dustbins are to be placed for emptying, the material which may be put into them ('no hot ashes' being a familiar legend on plastic dustbins), whether they are to be provided free of charge or not, and whether the occupier is to provide them.

---

[162] Ibid, s 45(1).
[163] SI 1992/588.
[164] EPA 1990, s 45(3).
[165] Ibid, s 45(5).
[166] Ibid, s 46(1) and (2).

Failure to abide by any requirement is a criminal offence. There is right of appeal **7.241** to a magistrates' court against a requirement to place waste in specified receptacles on the ground that the requirement is unreasonable.[167]

The arrangements for collecting commercial and industrial waste are different, **7.242** and each is dealt with in its own specific way. The collection authority is bound to collect commercial waste from premises if the occupier requests it to do so, but the person making the request is liable to pay a reasonable charge for the service, unless the authority considers it inappropriate to levy a charge.[168]

There is, by contrast, no obligation to collect industrial waste, although the **7.243** authority may do so, subject to its obtaining the consent of the waste disposal authority for the area. It must make a reasonable charge for collecting industrial waste, and has no discretion to waive it.[169] By distinction from its duties in respect of household waste, the collection authority is not obliged to provide receptacles for commercial or industrial waste, but may do so and is obliged to make a reasonable charge.[170] The authority has powers to prescribe the numbers and types of receptacle, and may require the occupier to provide receptacles at premises where commercial or industrial waste likely to cause a nuisance or detriment to the amenities of the locality, if not kept in appropriate receptacles, is situated.

There are rights of appeal to a magistrates' court similar to those available in **7.244** respect of household waste. The appeal must be lodged within 21 days of service of the notice.[171] As with household waste, failure to comply with a requirement of the authority as to the provision and type of receptacle is a summary offence.[172]

Having collected the waste, of whatever kind, the collection authority is bound to **7.245** consider ways of recycling, by way of separating, baling, or otherwise packaging the waste. To this end it must prepare a plan setting out the arrangements which it has made or proposes to make for recycling. The arrangements must be kept under review, and the plan modified if necessary.[173] The plan must contain information as to the kinds and quantities of waste which the authority expects to collect and to buy, the arrangements which it expects to make with waste disposal contractors (of whom more below), the kinds and amounts of waste which it expects to recycle, the plant and equipment which it expects to provide for the purpose of recycling, and the financial costs and savings anticipated.[174] The plan

---

[167] Ibid, s 46(3)–(9).
[168] Ibid, s 45(2) and (4).
[169] Ibid.
[170] Ibid, s 47.
[171] Ibid, s 47(2) and (9).
[172] Ibid, s 47(6).
[173] Ibid, s 49.
[174] Ibid, s 49(3).

must be submitted to the Secretary of State for his comments and, if necessary, direction as to its content, and must be given adequate publicity.[175]

Disposal

7.246 The collection authority must deliver waste which is not to be recycled to destinations directed by the waste disposal authority for the area.[176] The disposal authority retains ultimate control over the destination of all waste collected, since the collection authority is bound to give notice of any arrangements which it makes for recycling, and the disposal authority may object to any proposed arrangement between the collection authority and a waste disposal contractor. The latter is then precluded from entering the arrangement.[177]

7.247 The general powers of waste collection authorities are completed by the provision which enables them to make their plant and equipment for the sorting of waste available to other persons, including the general public. This authorizes the provision of bottle, newspaper, and can banks, among other things.[178]

7.248 Waste disposal authorities have the same duties in respect of waste disposal arrangements and plans as waste collection authorities for their sphere of operations. Their obligations are made more complicated, however, by the involvement of waste disposal contractors in the process.[179] It has been government policy for some years that waste disposal functions shall be open to competition in a free market. With this policy in mind, Parliament has required waste disposal authorities which existed on 31 May 1991 either to make arrangements with the private sector or persons other than themselves for the keeping, collection, treatment, or disposal of waste, or to form a waste disposal company.[180]

7.249 If a disposal authority fails to take either course, the Secretary of State is under a duty to direct the authority to set up a waste disposal company, and to transfer the functions identified above ('the relevant part of the undertaking') to the new company.[181] The company, known by the acronym as a LAWDC ('local authority waste disposal company') must be an 'arm's length company' within the meaning of Section 68 of the Local Government and Housing Act 1989.[182] This means that, although the company may remain under the financial control of the authority, directors must be appointed for a fixed term, and not more than one-fifth of them may have been members or officers of the authority. Additionally, the

---

[175] Ibid, s 49(4) and (5).
[176] Ibid, s 48(1).
[177] Ibid, s 48(3)–(5).
[178] Ibid, s 48(6) and (8).
[179] Ibid, s 50(1).
[180] Ibid, s 32.
[181] Ibid, s 32(2).
[182] Ibid, Sch 2 para 5.

company must give the best consideration reasonably obtainable for any land which it occupies and in which the authority has an interest. The authority may not make grants in any way related to the company's financial results, although it may lend money for the purposes of the company acquiring fixed assets or working capital, but not otherwise.

The waste disposal authority must draw up a scheme for transferring property, rights, and liabilities to the LAWDC. Thereafter the LAWDC is free, and will be encouraged by central government, to tender for waste contracts from other disposal authorities or from the private sector.[183]   **7.250**

When awarding its contracts the authority is expressly directed to avoid undue discrimination in favour of one kind of waste disposal contractor over other kinds. This principle will be infringed if the authority invites tenders from contractors only one of whom (its own LAWDC) can undertake the contract because it alone owned the land required if the terms of the proposed contract were to be met. The disposal authority's plan must set out the arrangements to be made with waste disposal contractors, be they LAWDCs or private sector entrepreneurs, for the treatment or disposal of waste.[184] Otherwise the plan must contain the same material with respect to disposal as the plan of a collection authority. Again, recycling is to be given priority where reasonably practicable.[185]   **7.251**

Waste disposal authorities have a twofold duty, as opposed to powers. First, they must, self-evidently, arrange for the disposal of waste collected within their areas. Less obviously, however, they are required to arrange for places to be provided at which residents of the area may deposit household waste, and also arrange for the disposal of the waste so deposited. This, then, is another route by which bottle banks and civic amenity sites may be made available. The authority may only discharge the duty by way of an arrangement with a waste disposal contractor.[186]   **7.252**

The sites provided in this way must be reasonably accessible to the citizenry, be open at reasonable times, including at least one period on the Saturday, or what the EPA 1990 quaintly calls the following day of each week (presumably a Sunday), and be free of charge to residents of the authority's area.[187] One may speculate as to the system by which staff at a site might check whether a person arriving to tip waste is or is not a resident of the area, and as to the results if the staff were to try to levy a charge on non-residents.   **7.253**

---

[183] Ibid, Sch 2 Part II.
[184] Ibid, s 50(1).
[185] Ibid, s 50(4).
[186] Ibid, s 51(1).
[187] Ibid, s 51(2).

7.254 The EPA 1990 provides for adjustment of the finances of collection and disposal authorities, calculated by reference to the extent to which each relieves the other of functional and financial obligations. Thus, a disposal authority must pay to a collection authority amounts equivalent to the net saving made by the former in respect of waste which the collection authority recycles. Conversely, a collection authority is bound to pay to a disposal authority the amount of the net saving on expenditure brought about by the exercise of the disposal authority's functions. A very successful bottle bank or civic amenity site might therefore reap rewards for the disposal authority at the expense of the collection authority.[188] Similar adjustments may be made by way of payment to other persons, such as waste disposal contractors, who relieve disposal authorities of their obligations by collecting waste for recycling. Such payments are discretionary rather than obligatory.[189]

7.255 As might be expected, the EPA 1990 invests waste regulation and waste collection authorities with powers to require the occupier to remove waste from land where it has been unlawfully deposited without a licence, by fly-tipping or otherwise. The cost may be recovered from the occupier of the land, unless he satisfies a magistrates' court that he neither deposited nor knowingly caused the deposit, or that the notice requiring the waste to be removed was defective.[190]

7.256 It is a summary offence to fail to comply with the notice. Alternatively, the authority may remove the waste itself and recover the cost of doing so from the occupier if there is one and he can be found, or, perhaps more implausibly, from the person who deposited, knowingly caused, or permitted the deposit. If the authority removes the waste it becomes the owner and can deal with it accordingly.[191] Ordinarily, it could be expected that ownership of the waste would prove to be no more than a poisoned chalice, although in the right conditions reclaiming it might no doubt give some financial solace to the council tax payers and ratepayers.

Landfill

7.257 UK legislation gives effect to the continuing concern of the European Commission that the use of landfill as a means of waste disposal shall cease. It also reflects the inescapable fact that the amount of landfill available within the UK is limited, and nearing its end. The Landfill (England and Wales) Regulations 2002, SI 2002/1559 implement Directive 99/31 EC.

---

[188] Ibid.
[189] Ibid, s 52(3).
[190] Ibid, s 59.
[191] Ibid, s 59(4)–(9).

The Regulations create a system of landfill permits. Landfill falls into one of three **7.258** categories—hazardous waste; non-hazardous waste; and inert.[192] Hazardous waste is defined by reference to the Hazardous Waste Regulations 2005, described above.[193]

Non-hazardous waste, naturally, is waste which is not hazardous; inert waste is **7.259** waste which does not react with other substances and has no significant tendency to leach or otherwise pollute surface or groundwater.[194]

Landfill permits must specify the type and quantity of waste to be placed in the **7.260** relevant site, and impose conditions on the preparation, deposit, monitoring and safety of the waste.[195] Only permitted wastes may be accepted.[196] Some types of waste are exempt from the need for a permit. These are sludges, including non-hazardous dredgings; building waste used for restoration and filling-in. Sites which have been closed require no permits, depending on the deposits there. Any site closed before 16 July 2001 enjoys exemption, as do agricultural and quarry waste sites closed before 15 May 2006.[197]

Operators must ensure that their charges cover the costs of setting up and operat- **7.261** ing their sites, and the after-care.[198] This provision abolished the charges imposed under earlier agreements.[199]

The Environment Agency supervises the opening of sites, their operation during **7.262** their life, and their closure and after-care.[200]

Breach of the Regulations is a criminal offence, punishable with a fine of £10,000 **7.263** and/or imprisonment for up to 6 months on summary conviction; or with an unlimited fine and/or up to 5 years' imprisonment on conviction on indictment.[201]

Wide principles regulate the procedure for acceptance of waste. It may only be **7.264** accepted if this would not result in unacceptable emissions or endanger human health.[202] Hazardous waste as defined may be accepted at a non-hazardous waste site only if it is stable and not susceptible to leaching.[203] Full records must be kept

---

[192] Regulation 7(1).
[193] Page, supra.
[194] Regulation 7(2)–(3).
[195] Regulation 8(1)–(2).
[196] Regulation 9.
[197] Regulation 4.
[198] Regulation 11.
[199] *3C Waste Ltd v Mersey Waste Holdings Ltd* [2006] EWHC 2598 (Comm).
[200] Regulations 13,14, & 15.
[201] Regulation 17.
[202] Schedule 1, paragraph 1.
[203] Schedule 1, paragraph 3.

of the characteristics of all wastes received, including their sources, composition, appearance, and likely behaviour.[204]

7.265 All waste must be tested regularly.[205]

7.266 Part 3 of Schedule 1 to the Regulations sets out detailed criteria identifying the types of waste which may be accepted at each of the three types of landfill. This exercise covers 12 pages of text, and is necessarily technical. The tests which must be met can be illustrated by examples. Thus, at inert waste sites only waste glass based fibrous matter without organic binders or chloride containing less than 800 milligrams per kilogram of dry substances are among the wastes which may be accepted.[206]

7.267 At non-hazardous waste sites chlorides containing up to 15,000 milligrams per kilogram of dry substance are permissible.[207] At hazardous waste sites more contamination is allowed—up to 25,000 milligrams of chloride per kilogram of dry substance.[208] There are special criteria for gypsum and asbestos wastes.[209]

7.268 Schedule 2 governs the location, design, and layout of sites. For the most part the requirements embody common sense. Sites must be located with regard to the likelihood of flooding, avalanches and risks to groundwater, among other things. Leachate and rainwater must be collected and treated. There must be suitable geological barriers and liners, and there must be provision for landfill gases, smells, dust, noise and fires.[210]

7.269 Monitoring and records are covered by Schedule 3. Sampling must be carried out.[211] The site topography and settlement of the fill must be monitored.[212]

7.270 Schedule 4 contains transitional provisions.

7.271 In addition to stricter regulation of landfill sites, the use of them has been progressively discouraged. This is the rationale behind the Landfill (Scheme Year and Maximum Landfill Amount) Regulations 2004, (SI 2004/1936). These impose upper limits on the amounts of landfill which may be used for the UK as a whole, and for England, Wales, Scotland, and Northern Ireland, in any one year. These limits apply to each successive year from 2010 to 2020.

---

[204] Schedule 1, paragraph 5.
[205] Regulation 6.
[206] Schedule 1, paragraphs 10 and 11.
[207] Schedule 1, paragraph 14.
[208] Schedule 1, paragraph 17.
[209] Sschedule 1, paragraphs 15 and 16.
[210] Ibid, Regulations 2, 3, and 5.
[211] Ibid, Regulations 4 and 5.
[212] Ibid, Regulation 1.

This regime was refined and reinforced by the Landfill Allowances and Trading **7.272** Scheme (England) Regulations 2004, SI 2004/3212. The Regulations empower the Secretary of State to allocate to each waste disposal authority an allowance or ration of landfill towards the total for England laid down by SI 2004/1936, above.[213]

Where an authority does not use up its allocation for any one year it may carry **7.273** over up to 5% to the following year, unless that year is a target year (these being 2010, 2013, and 2020).[214] An authority may borrow up to 5% of its annual allowance or sell the same percentage to another.[215]

If he considers that there is a danger of the national total ration of landfill being **7.274** exceeded the Secretary of State may suspend these arrangements.[216] The resolve to reduce the amount of waste going to landfill is ever greater.

---

[213] Regulation 5.
[214] Regulation 6.
[215] Regulations 7 and 8.
[216] Regulation 9.

8

RADIOACTIVE AND HAZARDOUS SUBSTANCES, AND GENETICALLY MODIFIED ORGANISMS

A. **Introduction**	8.01	
B. **Radioactive Substances**	8.02	
Introduction	8.02	
Nuclear installations	8.06	
Nuclear installations—licensing	8.07	
Conditions of a licence	8.11	
The currency of the licence	8.12	
Surrender and revocation	8.17	
Compensation for breach of duty under the NIA	8.18	
Restrictions on the right to compensation	8.20	
Jurisdiction over claims to compensation	8.28	
Additional sanctions	8.34	
Radioactivity and congenital disease	8.36	
C. **Radioactive Materials and Waste**	8.38	
Introduction	8.38	
Exemptions from registration	8.41	
Registration procedure	8.43	
Appeals	8.45	
Mobile radioactive apparatus	8.47	
Cancellation and variation of registration	8.49	
Radioactive waste	8.50	
Enforcement	8.56	
Transport of radioactive material	8.61	
D. **Hazardous Substances— The Planning (Hazardous Substances) Act 1990**	8.65	
Introduction	8.65	
Definitions	8.67	
Keeping hazardous substances	8.70	

Exemptions from consent	8.72	
Deemed consent	8.77	
Applying for hazardous substances consent—hazardous substances authorities	8.80	
Consultation	8.84	
Determining the application	8.86	
Appeals	8.90	
Amendment and termination of consents	8.91	
Revocation and modification of consents	8.97	
Compensation	8.100	
The powers of the Secretary of State	8.105	
Enforcement of hazardous substances control	8.110	
Hazardous substances contravention notices	8.117	
Appeals against contravention notices	8.121	
Other sanctions against breaches of control	8.129	
Miscellaneous provisions	8.132	
Accidents involving hazardous substances	8.140	
Lead shot	8.149	
PCBs	8.151	
E. **Genetically Modified Organisms**	8.154	
Introduction	8.154	
The uses of genetic modification	8.157	
GMOs—the definition	8.160	
GMOs—the system of control	8.172	

Importation, acquisition, release, and marketing of GMOs	8.176	GMOs—miscellaneous provisions	8.200
		GMOs—health and safety at work	8.202
Notification	8.182	Containment of GMOs	8.203
Policing the control of GMOs	8.187	Release and marketing of GMOs	8.210
Sanctions	8.195	Traceability and labelling of GMOs	8.212

A. Introduction

8.01 The three areas of law which this chapter covers have little in common except that they deal with technologies of which the general public knows little and of which many are most apprehensive. Each is thought, rightly or wrongly, to be, potentially at least, very dangerous. The political reaction to public opinion has been to impose strict controls on the use of radioactive and dangerous materials, and to require regulation by government of the making and use of genetically modified organisms. The three systems of control are examined and described here.

B. Radioactive Substances

Introduction

8.02 Understanding the law which governs the production, transport, storage, and disposal of radioactive substances requires some knowledge of the science which governs the life and properties of these materials. Regrettably, general understanding of this has been bedevilled by a combination of misleading propaganda put out by interest groups, whose concern for truth has sometimes been subordinated to their desire for publicity, and reporting by mass media which has erred on the side of sensationalism rather than objectivity.

8.03 Without exception, impartial commentators on the safety and efficiency of nuclear sites and installations have concluded that the fears and criticisms advanced by the more extreme objectors are exaggerated and alarmist.[1] The understandable fears engendered by the horrific events at Hiroshima and Nagasaki were not allayed by the outbreak of a potentially catastrophic fire at BNFL's Windscale plant in 1957, relatively soon after the public became aware of the existence of nuclear power. More recently, the disastrous fire at the Chernobyl reactor has

---

[1] See, eg, the Report of Sir Roger Parker to the Secretary of State for the Environment of the Inquiry into BNFL's proposed THORP (Thermal Oxide Reprocessing Plant) at Sellafield: London HMSO 1987, para 2.1: 'It is . . . clear that many of the anxieties which are felt are without foundation and spring from a fear of anything nuclear, no doubt partly due to the fact that the Hiroshima and Nagasaki bombs with their devastating effects were the opening events in the development of nuclear power.'

helped to fuel the fears of the uninformed, and given ammunition to those who prey upon them. The fact that the plant was used at the time for the manufacture of weapons will have done nothing to reassure the laity as to the safety of nuclear power.

However, it is well to see the context in which radioactivity has to be considered. **8.04** Eighty-seven per cent of all the radioactivity to which the ordinary person is exposed in the course of one year comes from natural causes—these include cosmic rays, to which one is exposed every time one flies in an aeroplane, the gas radon which is found everywhere, and is concentrated in Cornwall and the Aberdeen area in the UK, and in food. Of the remaining 13%, 12% is received from medical sources as X-rays and radiation therapy of diverse kinds. The remaining 1% comes from various sources, including the fallout from nuclear weapons testing (0.4%). Less than 0.1% is derived from discharges from nuclear installations.[2]

The Windscale fire, which caused an escape of radioactive material and led to the **8.05** government having to pay substantial compensation to farmers and others,[3] resulted eventually, and with the intervention of the Vienna Convention on Civil Liability for Nuclear Damage,[4] in the passage of the Nuclear Installations Act 1965. This was the earliest piece of legislation regulating the use of nuclear power which remains in force today.

Nuclear installations

Partly as a response to the Windscale fire, and partly to discharge the government's **8.06** obligations under the Vienna Convention,[5] Parliament passed the Nuclear Installations Act 1965 (NIA). This has two primary functions: first, to provide for the licensing of nuclear reactors and other installations designed to store, process, or dispose of nuclear fuel; and second to give persons suffering loss or damage as the result of nuclear occurrences a (limited) right to compensation.

Nuclear installations—licensing

Perhaps understandably, the foundation of the licensing system for nuclear **8.07** installations is that there is an absolute prohibition on installation or operating any nuclear reactor (other than one comprised in a means of transport such as a ship). There is a similar prohibition on carrying on any process preparatory or ancillary to the production of nuclear energy which involves or is capable of causing the emission of ionizing radiations. Thirdly, no person may store, process, or dispose

---

[2] See *Living with Radiation* (National Radiological Protection Board, 4th edn, 1989). For a fuller introduction to and discussion of the science and philosophy of nuclear power, see the Sixth Report of the Royal Commission on Environmental Pollution, 1976 (Cm 6618).
[3] See Cm 302, HMSO, 1957.
[4] Vienna, 21 May 1963; Cm 2333.
[5] See n 4 above.

of nuclear fuel or other irradiated matter, other than in accordance with a valid licence issued by the Environment Agency (previously the Health and Safety Executive).[6] Additionally, and perhaps unnecessarily, the Secretary of State for Energy (in respect of England, Wales, and Northern Ireland) and the Secretary of State for Scotland have prescribed that installations which carry on processes involving plutonium and/or enriched uranium shall also be subject to licensing.[7]

8.08 The significance of plutonium is that it is, first, highly toxic if inhaled (although not if eaten); and, secondly, that it is an important ingredient in the manufacture of atomic weapons. Uranium, and particularly its isotope uranium 235 (235 being the sum of the protons and neutrons in the nucleus of an atom of the material), is highly fissile, and therefore crucial to the generation of nuclear power.[8] It is also, and for the same reason, important to the manufacture of weapons. So potentially dangerous are these two substances that, even where a licence is in force, no person other than the Atomic Energy Authority (AEA) may extract plutonium or uranium from irradiated matter, or treat uranium so as to increase the amount of uranium 235 contained in it (the process known as 'enrichment'), without a permit issued by AEA or the appropriate government department.[9]

8.09 It is a criminal offence either to operate a nuclear installation without a licence, or to deal with plutonium or uranium without a valid permit. Where a permit is issued, the relevant Minister may prescribe that the Official Secrets Act applies to the premises of the permit holder, and restrict access thereto except to police officers, authorized inspectors, and government officials.

8.10 Only a body corporate may be given a nuclear licence, which may cover two or more installations, provided that these are in the vicinity of each other.[10] 'In the vicinity' is not defined for these purposes, but would no doubt cover complexes such as BNFL's Sellafield plant, where there are a number of installations, including a nuclear power station (Calder Hall), thermal oxide reprocessing plant (THORP), and a store for radioactive wastes. If so directed by the Environment Agency, the applicant must notify public bodies such as local authorities and water undertakers, which might have an interest in ensuring that the activity carried on in the premises does not affect their areas of responsibility.[11]

---

[6] NIA, s 1(1), (2).

[7] Nuclear Installations Regulations 1971, SI 1971/1823, reg 3.

[8] See the Sixth Report of the Royal Commission on Protection of the Environment, n 2 above, paras 66 and 86; *Living with Radiation*, n 3 above, Ch 2.

[9] NIA, s 2.

[10] Ibid, s 2(1B), Sch 1.

[11] Ibid, s 3(1) and (2).

Conditions of a licence

The NIA, understandably, is directed at ensuring that nuclear installations are **8.11** operated safely and efficiently, and therefore contains detailed provisions governing the conditions which may be attached to a licence. These are to be those considered to be desirable in the interests of safety, both in normal circumstances and in the event of accident or other emergency.[12] In particular, conditions may require that the licensee maintains an efficient system for detecting and recording ionizing radiations emitted or discharged; for regulating the design, siting, construction, installation, operation, and maintenance of plant or other equipment; providing for preventing and dealing with emergencies or accidents; and for regulating the discharge of any substance on the licensed site.[13]

The currency of the licence

Once the licence has been granted, and while it remains in force, the Environment **8.12** Agency is obliged to consider any representations made by trade unions which might affect the exercise of its licensing powers.[14] The licensee must keep on display on the site copies of the conditions attached to the licence, presumably, among other reasons, so that trade union representatives may inform themselves from time to time as to whether those conditions are being observed.[15]

Failure to display the conditions or to comply with them renders the licensee, and **8.13** any person having duties on the site (in effect, those employed there) who commits the contravention, liable to a fine or imprisonment.[16]

While the licence remains in force, its existence must be entered on a list of licensed **8.14** nuclear sites to be kept by the Minister. The entry must remain on this list until 30 years after the licence has been revoked or surrendered, as to which see below.[17] While the licence is in force, the licensee must secure that no 'occurrence' (not defined for the purposes of this section, and only partially defined for other sections of the NIA, as to which see below) results in injury to the person or damage to property caused by radioactive nuclear matter, or by a combination of such matter and toxic, explosive, or other hazardous properties (expressions which are also not defined), or by ionizing radiation emitted from non-nuclear matter, or from waste, whether nuclear or not.[18]

---

[12] Ibid, s 4(1).
[13] Ibid.
[14] Ibid, s 4(4). It is perhaps surprising that this provision survived the election of successive governments who might have been thought to be unsympathetic to the views of trade unions on this, as on other matters.
[15] Ibid, s 4(5).
[16] Ibid, s 4(6). The offences are triable either summarily or on indictment; for the level of fines and imprisonment, see below.
[17] Ibid, s 6.
[18] Ibid, s 7(1).

8.15   It is not clear whether the duty is more than the normal common law duty to take reasonable care to ensure that no harm to person or property occurs, although it seems probable that the duty is absolute. It has, however, been held that Section 7 does not require the licensee of a nuclear site to act as the insurer against all injury or damage which may emanate from a licensed site.[19] Further, the section requires only that the licensee shall take steps to secure that no physical injury or damage occurs. It is not liable where radioactive dust has been deposited on premises and led to a reduction in their market value, causing economic loss. By contrast, where there is physical impact on the claimant's premises as the result of the escape of radioactive material the licensee is liable.[20]

8.16   The AEA is subject to a similar duty and liabilities, as is the Crown, in respect of any site occupied by a government department.[21] The latter provision is no doubt intended to cover premises such as those where research into atomic weapons is conducted, and where they are manufactured or tested by the Ministry of Defence.

Surrender and revocation

8.17   At any time the licensee may surrender, or the Environment Agency may revoke, a nuclear site licence.[22] Thereupon, the licensee must deliver the licence in accordance with any direction of the Environment Agency, and must keep notices posted on the site indicating its limits and take any other steps as the Agency may direct for warning of or preventing the risk of injury from radiation.[23] The notices must be displayed during the period of responsibility of the licensee, that is, until the Environment Agency gives notice that it is of opinion that the danger from radiation has ended, or until a new licence is issued for the whole or part of the site to the original licensee or to some other person.[24] Failure to display the required notices

---

[19]   *Re Friends of the Earth* [1988] JPL 93. One of a series of largely unsuccessful actions brought by bodies opposed to the use of nuclear energy in attempts to block the implementation of planning permissions or other consents which had been granted following vigorous opposition (in this instance, Sizewell B PWR nuclear power station). As to the others, see below.

[20]   *Merlin v British Nuclear Fuels* [1990] 3 All ER711. The reasoning behind the decision was that even though there might be an increased risk to health because of radioactive contamination of the plaintiffs' house, it was impossible to say whose risk was to be compensatable, or at what level of contamination compensation for breach of the duty would be payable (see [1990] 3 All ER at 721). That case was distinguished in *Blue Circle Industries v MOD* [1998] 3All ER 355. There escape of plutonium from AWE Aldermaston (not revealed for four years) had contaminated the claimant's land and required the removal of large amounts of topsoil to remove the contamination. A proposed sale of the land fell through and damages were recovered. Presumably the nuclear dust in *Merlin's Case* could have been removed without altering the fabric. See also *Magnhard v UKAEA* ENDS Reports No.344 page 58.

[21]   NIA, ss 8 and 9.

[22]   Ibid, s 5(1).

[23]   Ibid, s 7(2).

[24]   Ibid, s 7(3).

is a criminal offence, punishable summarily with a fine or, in the case of a second or subsequent offence, on indictment with a fine or imprisonment.[25]

Compensation for breach of duty under the NIA

If the holder of a nuclear site licence, the AEA, or the Crown is in breach of the **8.18** duty to secure safety to person or property under Sections 7, 8, or 9 of the NIA, or a foreign operator whose country is a party to the Vienna Convention fails to take steps to secure the safety of its radioactive materials during carriage to or from that operator's site under Section 10 of the NIA,[26] then compensation is payable wherever the injury or damage occurred.[27] Understandably, if the injury or damage is due partly to radiation and partly to other causes (say, to explosion or exposure to toxins) the victim's right to compensation is unaffected, although no claim to double damages may arise.[28]

It seems that even a licensee may have a right to compensation if another party **8.19** agreed to compensate it, or if the injury or damage was the result of an intentional act or omission.[29] The right to claim compensation is, however, subject to numerous restrictions and limitations. These must now be considered.

Restrictions on the right to compensation

First, an occurrence involving irradiated material being transported from a **8.20** licensed site within the UK, and which occurred wholly within the territorial limits of one signatory state to the Vienna Convention other than the UK, or any occurrence causing injury or damage within the territorial limits of a country which is not a party to the Vienna Convention, is exempt from liability.[30] By an exception to the exception, the victim of injury or damage falling within the two categories identified above may claim compensation if the injury or damage was sustained on an aircraft or ship registered in the UK.[31]

Injury or damage caused by the carriage of radioactive material from a site outside **8.21** the countries which have signed the Vienna Convention to a foreign operator's site by agreement with the latter, and which is not on a site in the UK which is licensed under the NIA is not the subject of compensation unless the agreement expressly so provides.[32]

---

[25] For the levels see ibid, s 7(4).
[26] See n 4 above.
[27] Ibid, s 12(1).
[28] Ibid, s 12(2).
[29] Ibid, s 12(3A). However, the subsection is drafted in such convoluted and elliptical fashion that it is hard to be sure that it has any meaning.
[30] Ibid, s 13(1).
[31] Ibid, s 13(2).
[32] Ibid, s 13(3).

8.22   Injury or damage due to acts of war are likewise outside the scope of compensation, although the consequences of natural disasters are not.[33] Liability in respect
of the latter may arise even though the disaster could not reasonably have been
foreseen, a provision which reinforces the conclusion that liability under Section
12 of the NIA is absolute, subject to the limitations already discussed.[34]

8.23   Section 13(5) of the NIA provides for cases involving a person who may not have
caused the injury or damage sustained as the result of a nuclear occurrence, but
where the local law of a country which has not signed the Vienna Convention, or
the provisions of a treaty regulating liability for the carriage of goods by air or road
which has been incorporated into English law by statute, renders that person liable for compensation. In such cases the party who paid the compensation is treated
as having a claim under Section 12 of the NIA, and may press it wherever the
injury or damage was sustained. However, he may not claim more than the amount
for which he was held liable, and is in any event limited to the maximum laid
down by Section 16 of the NIA, discussed below.[35]

8.24   A curious provision means that the claim of any party is to be reduced by the fault
of the claimant to the extent, but only to the extent, that the injury or loss was
attributable to any act of the claimant committed with intention of causing harm
to any person or property or with reckless disregard to the consequences.[36] This
will exclude claims for injury sustained by terrorists who blow themselves up with
nuclear weapons, and, no doubt, protesters or other trespassers on nuclear installations. It is not clear, however, why Parliament placed such tight restrictions on
the exemption of nuclear site operators from the consequences of the acts of disaffected malefactors. It might have been expected that any contributory negligence or
malignant intent would relieve the operator from liability, by analogy with the relief
given against the results of acts of war.

8.25   A further limitation on the right to claim compensation is that a breach of duty in
respect of irradiated material does not give rise to any lien or action in rem in
respect of any ship or aircraft, even though the claim for financial compensation
under Section 16 of the NIA may not have been settled.[37]

8.26   Another limit on the right to compensation arises from the statutory limitation
period prescribed by Section 15 of the NIA. This recognizes the delay, well known
to scientists, which may elapse before the consequences of exposure to radiation
become apparent. Therefore, the claim must be brought within 30 years of the

---

[33]   Ibid, s 13(4).
[34]   Ibid.
[35]   Ibid, s 13(5), (5A).
[36]   Ibid, s 13(6).
[37]   Ibid, s 14.

occurrence giving rise to the claim, or the last of a series of occurrences or the end of a continuing occurrence.[38] Where the occurrence followed the theft, loss, jettison, or abandonment of nuclear matter, the occurrence which occasioned the claim must have taken place within twenty years of the theft or other event.[39]

An important limitation on the right to claim compensation concerns the amount **8.27** for which an operator may be liable in respect of any one occurrence. The upper limit for the total liability of a site operator is £140,000,000, and that for a licensee is £10,000,000.[40] The liability is further restricted where a foreign operator has caused the injury or damage in question. In effect, such an operator is not liable to any extent greater than that to which he would have been subject under the law of his own country.[41] Claims made where the culpable party is not liable to pay (as, for example, against an exempt foreign operator or carrier), those made more than 10 years after the occurrence of which complaint is made, or more than 20 years after the theft, loss, jettison, or abandonment of nuclear matter, or which exceed the upper limit in respect of funds made available to meet the UK's treaty obligations in respect of occurrences arising out of the carriage of nuclear material, are all to be made either to the Secretary of State for Trade and Industry or the appropriate government department.[42] Disputes as to the liability for or the amount of compensation are determined by the High Court.[43]

Jurisdiction over claims to compensation

As the Chernobyl disaster made very clear, escapes of nuclear material can have **8.28** international repercussions. Section 17 of the NIA recognizes this by providing for cases where there might be doubt as to which country's courts have jurisdiction over claims for injury or damage from radioactivity, instances where liability is shared, and for foreign judgments. The Secretary of State for Trade and Industry may issue certificates to the effect that a claim or question falls to be determined by the court of another party to the Vienna Convention or other treaty relating to liability for nuclear occurrences, in which case the certificate is conclusive evidence that the courts of the state so certified have jurisdiction, and the claim in the UK court must be set aside.[44]

---

[38] Ibid, s 15(1).

[39] Ibid, s 15(2).

[40] Ibid, s 16(1); Nuclear Installations (Increase in Operators' Limits of Liability) Order 1994, SI 1994/909.

[41] NIA, s 16(2).

[42] Ibid, s 16(3). For instance, a claim in respect of a site occupied by the Crown would be made to the department which operated the site.

[43] Ibid, s 16(4). In Northern Ireland the High Court of Justice and in Scotland the Court of Session are the equivalent tribunals.

[44] Ibid, s 17(1) and (2).

8.29 Where two or more persons are found liable for injury or damage, then for the purposes of proceedings in UK courts, including the enforcing of foreign judgments, all are jointly and severally liable, except that the AEA or the Crown are not liable to more than the amount for which either was initially liable in the case of a licensee. A foreign operator is similarly not liable for more than the amount for which he is responsible under foreign law.[45]

8.30 Where a judgment has been given in a foreign court and is enforceable in the UK in pursuance of an international treaty it may, as one would expect, be enforced. By contrast, even where the injury or damage may have been the subject of an international treaty to which the UK is a party, but the judgment was given in the courts of a country not party to the treaty and the judgment debt is not awarded pursuant to the international conventions on the carriage of goods by air or on land to which the UK is a party, this will be a defence to proceedings for recovery of the debt.[46] It will be seen that, in general, it is possible to maintain claims in respect of injury or damage caused by nuclear occurrences in countries which are parties to treaties which the UK has signed, but not otherwise. However, even a successful claimant before a UK court cannot issue execution against the property of a foreign government.[47]

8.31 Since virtually all activity involving radioactive materials is undertaken by the Crown or on behalf of government, it is not surprising that Parliament has provided that it shall make available enough money to meet all claims made within ten years of the relevant occurrence ('the relevant period'),[48] up to a maximum of £300,000,000 in special drawing rights.[49] On the other hand, the licensee of a nuclear site must make its own arrangements for insurance or other means of meeting claims against it, up to the £10,000,000 limit prescribed by Section 16(1) of the NIA.[50] Failure to comply with this requirement is a criminal offence, punishable with a fine at the rate prescribed under the Magistrates' Courts Act 1980 or three months' imprisonment on summary conviction, or by an unlimited fine or two years' imprisonment on indictment.[51]

8.32 Government is able to keep itself informed about the extent to which nuclear licensees face claims, since each must notify the Secretary of State once it appears that claims lodged against it total £6,000,000, or three-fifths of the amount of

---

[45] Ibid, s 17(3).
[46] Ibid, s 17(5).
[47] Ibid, s 17(6).
[48] See ibid, s 15(2).
[49] Ibid, s 18(1) and (2).
[50] Ibid, s 19(1).
[51] Ibid, s 19(5).

maximum liability prescribed for the time being.[52] For obvious reasons, government has to be informed of any occurrence involving irradiated material which takes place on a licensed site or during the carriage of such material where a person is under a duty imposed by the Act.

Where the occurrence involves the emission of ionizing radiation, which might **8.33** cause death or serious injury to health, the breaking open of a container in which nuclear matter is being carried, or an explosion or fire likely to affect the safe working of a nuclear installation, then the matter must be reported as quickly as possible to the Secretary of State, the local authority for the area, and to the Chief Constable for the area.[53] Again, failure to give the notice is an offence, punishable with relatively small fines and short periods of imprisonment.[54]

Additional sanctions

Although the penalties imposed on nuclear operators and licensees appear, at first **8.34** sight, to be relatively lenient, there are other sanctions available to ensure compliance with the requirements of safety at nuclear installations. Where a body corporate is convicted of an offence under the Act, and a director, manager, secretary, or other senior officer of the company is proved to have consented to, connived at, or been guilty of neglect in connection with the offence, he or she is liable to the same penalties.

Where the offence is heinous, as, for example, producing atomic energy without **8.35** a licence, there is no limit on the fine which may be imposed.[55] That said, there is no recorded occasion on which an offence against the Act has been committed, so the question of penalties may and will, it is hoped, be academic.

Radioactivity and congenital disease

There is some, although controversial, evidence that radiation may cause muta- **8.36** tions and genetic aberrations in humans. Experiments on mice have induced hereditary damage in mice, although there is no statistically significant increase in hereditary defects in the children of the survivors of the Hiroshima and Nagasaki bombings.[56]

Recognizing the risk of radiation to unborn children, Parliament passed the **8.37** Congenital Disabilities (Civil Liability) Act 1976. This enacts that anything which affects the ability of a man or a woman to have a normal healthy child, or

---

[52] Ibid, s 20(1).
[53] Ibid, s 22; Nuclear Installations (Dangerous Occurrences) Regulations 1965, SI 1965/1824.
[54] NIA, s 22(2).
[55] Ibid, s 25(1) and (2).
[56] *Living with Radiation*, supra, Ch 4.

which affects a pregnant woman in such a way that her child is born with disabilities which would not otherwise have been present, is an injury for the purposes of the Nuclear Installations Act 1965.[57] The provisions of that Act therefore apply to claims in respect of hereditary defects. 'Disabilities' are widely defined, and include not only physical deformity, disease, or abnormality, but also predisposition to physical or mental defect in future. This is so whether or not the predisposition is susceptible of immediate prognosis or not.[58] Loss of expectation of life is, however, not compensatable under the Act.[59]

C. Radioactive Materials and Waste

Introduction

8.38 As has been seen, installations where radioactive materials are used are subject to control under the Nuclear Installations Act 1965. That system is complemented by the Radioactive Substances Act 1993 (RSA). This prohibits the keeping or use for the purposes of any undertaking of radioactive material, or material which might reasonably be believed to be radioactive.[60] The prohibition does not apply where the person using the material is registered under the RSA, where he is exempt, or where the material is apparatus which is registered under other provisions of the Act.[61]

8.39 'Radioactive material' receives a complicated definition.[62] In essence it is material which contains one of eight elements identified in Schedule 1 of the Act, the radioactivity of which, measured in becquerels, exceeds a specified minimum; or a substance possessing radioactivity due to nuclear fission or another process by which it was subjected to ionizing radiation (which therefore includes nuclear waste), including contamination by nuclear waste. A becquerel (abbreviated to Bq) is the standard international unit of radioactivity equal to one radioactive transformation per second. Although the Secretary of State for the Environment has power to prescribe levels of radioactivity below which a substance is not to be treated as radioactive, and to vary the list of elements in Schedule 1 to the Act,[63] he has not exercised either power.

---

[57] Congenital Disabilities (Civil Liability) Act 1976, s 3(2).
[58] Ibid, s 4(1).
[59] Ibid, s 4(4).
[60] RSA s 6(1).
[61] Ibid. There are, for example, exemptions for instruments used for testing for radioactivity in the Radioactive Substances (Testing Instruments) Etc. Order 2006 SI 2006/1500.
[62] Ibid, s 1(1).
[63] Ibid, s 1(4) and (5).

An application for registration under the RSA is made to the Environment Agency **8.40** under Section 7 of the Act.[64] The application must specify the premises to which it relates, the undertaking for the purposes of which the premises are used, and the radioactive material which will be kept or used on the premises, together with the maximum quantity likely to be there at any one time. Additionally, the application must specify the way in which radioactive material is proposed to be used on the premises.[65]

Exemptions from registration

There is no need to apply for registration of a premises for which a nuclear site **8.41** licence is in force, or if the licensee's period of responsibility under such a licence (as to which see above) has not ended.[66] The Environment Agency may, however, attach conditions to an existing nuclear site licence to the same effect as those which it may impose on registration of premises under the RSA.[67]

All persons are exempted from registration in respect of the keeping and use of **8.42** clocks or watches (their luminous dials being radioactive) except those concerned with premises where such timepieces are manufactured or repaired.[68] The Secretary of State has power to confer further exemptions by statutory instrument, as noted above. However, there are various orders made under earlier legislation, now repealed, which confer exemption from the need to register under the RSA[69] and which remain in force.

Registration procedure

The Environment Agency must consult all the local authorities in whose areas the **8.43** premises are located. Having done so it may grant the application unconditionally, register the premises in respect of one or more specified types of radioactive material, or register part of the premises or particularized apparatus or equipment. It may also impose conditions requiring that it be notified of the removal of radioactive material from the premises to another place. It can also regulate the labelling of radioactive material which is sold so that it is identified as radioactive and/or stating what the material is. Additionally, it can impose any other conditions which it thinks appropriate.

---

[64] Ibid, s 7(1).
[65] Ibid, s 7(2).
[66] Ibid, s 8(1).
[67] Ibid, s 8(2).
[68] Ibid, s 8(4) and (5).
[69] For the sake of brevity, these can be identified as having for the most part been made in 1962. The first has the SI No 2645, and the last SI No 2712. 1963 SIs Nos 1832 and 1836; SI 1967/1797; SI 1980/953; SI 1985/1049; 1986/1002; and 1990/2512 also exempt a wide variety of materials and activities from registration. These range from uranium and thorium compounds to hospitals.

8.44   The Environment Agency may refuse to register, and, if it fails to determine the application within the prescribed period, the applicant may treat this as a refusal. So far this sanction has proved ineffective, since the Secretary of State has not pre-scribed a period within which the Environment Agency must act.[70]

Appeals

8.45   If the Environment Agency refuses an application for registration or for authori-zation to dispose of or accumulate radioactive waste (as to which more below), or if it imposes limitations or conditions on a grant of authorization or registration the person directly concerned, that is, the applicant, may appeal to the Secretary of State.[71] There is, however, no right of appeal against decisions of or notices served by Ministers.[72] The appeal must be in writing, and must be made within two months of the decision or notice of which the complaint is made. It must be accompanied by copies of the application and the decision, copies of relevant cor-respondence, a full statement of the appellant's case, and an indication whether the appellant wishes there to be a hearing or is content to proceed by way of writ-ten representations.[73]

8.46   If there is a hearing before an inspector appointed by the Secretary of State, the inspector must report in writing with his conclusions and recommendations, or reasons for not making recommendations. The Secretary of State must notify the appellant of his decision on the appeal with his reasons in writing.[74] The similarity to the inquiries procedure under the Town and Country Planning Act is obvious. The Regulations do not expressly provide for a right of appeal to the High Court on a point of law against the decision of the Secretary of State under the Tribunals and Inquiries Acts.

Mobile radioactive apparatus

8.47   The code of control for radioactive apparatus is in principle virtually indistin-guishable from that which governs radioactive installations. There is an absolute prohibition on the use of such apparatus for any purpose in the absence of regis-tration under the RSA. The regulatory code applies to activities involving the use of apparatus for testing the characteristics of substances or articles, or for releasing radioactive material into the environment or into organisms.[75] This would cover, among other things, chest X-ray machines and apparatus used to discover faults

---

[70]   RSA, s 7.
[71]   Ibid, s 26(1) and (5).
[72]   Ibid, s 26(3) and (4).
[73]   Radioactive Substances (Appeals) Regulations 1990, SI 1990/2504.
[74]   Ibid.
[75]   RSA, s 8.

in engines or other machinery. Much the same machinery of application, consultation, appeal against refusal to register or registration subject to conditions, and registration, operates as in the case of nuclear installations.[76]

As with other provisions of the RSA, the Secretary of State has not made regulations **8.48** exempting mobile apparatus, other than testing instruments, from registration under the powers which the Act gives him, but earlier statutory instruments remain in force.[77]

Cancellation and variation of registration

While any person is registered as a user of radioactive material or of mobile **8.49** radioactive apparatus, the Environment Agency may vary or cancel the registration, by attaching conditions or limitations where none has previously been imposed, or by varying conditions or limitations. He must notify the holder of the registration, who has the same rights of appeal as an original applicant.[78]

Radioactive waste

The same fundamental regime controls the disposal and accumulation (that is, **8.50** storage, pending disposal) of waste as that to which nuclear material users and operators of mobile plant are subject. Accordingly, the familiar procedure of application to the Environment Agency, consultation, and decision by him, followed by appeal, if appropriate, to the Secretary of State, applies.[79] The RSA confers exemption from the need for registration where the waste is accumulated on a nuclear installation site, where the waste consists of clocks or watches, or where the Secretary of State excludes waste from the registration provisions by statutory instrument.[80]

The history of the disposal of radioactive waste has been punctuated by the **8.51** unremitting opposition of interest groups, hostile to the use of nuclear power, to attempts to solve the problem. In the event, the courts have had to consider the meaning and effect of these sections more than most other provisions of the legislation which relates to nuclear power. It is now clear that the Environment Agency or the Secretary of State, when deciding whether to authorize the disposal

---

[76] Ibid, ss 10 and 11.

[77] These exempt electronic valves and testing instruments from registration (see SI 1967/1797; and SI 1985/1049).

[78] Ibid, ss 12 and 26(1).

[79] Ibid, ss 13, 14, 18, and 26.

[80] Ibid, ss 14(3), 15(1), and 15(2). Pursuant to the latter powers the Secretary of State and his predecessors have exempted a wide variety of substances from the need to register. These include Geological Specimens (SI 1962/2712); Smoke Detectors (SI 1980/953); Gaseous Tritium Light Devices (SI 1985/1048); and other arcana.

or accumulation of radioactive waste under Section 16 of the RSA, must consider whether the disposal or accumulation, as the case may be, is justified, that is, whether the benefits of the proposal outweigh the disadvantages inherent in the fact that all escapes of radioactivity, no matter how small, are potentially injurious to health.

8.52 Further, even though there might be widespread opposition to a proposal to build a thermal oxide reprocessing plant (THORP) to deal with nuclear waste, the Secretary of State is not bound to hold a public inquiry into an application for authorization, provided he concludes, without being irrational or unreasonable, that he has sufficient material to enable him to take a decision that no inquiry is necessary. Nor need he necessarily take into account the costs incurred before he has to consider the question ('sunk costs').[81]

8.53 The Environment Agency has power to revoke or vary an authorization to dispose of or accumulate nuclear waste. This, the High Court has held, empowered the former Chief Inspector of nuclear installations to relax or tighten the conditions attached to an authorization, but not to widen its general scope, for instance, by extending the types of waste included in the original authorization.[82]

8.54 Where the Environment Agency or the appropriate Minister considers that the disposal of radioactive waste to which an application for authorization relates is likely to require special precautions to be taken by a local authority, water company, or other public body, it or he must consult with the body concerned before granting the authorization. This might apply, for example, where an underground repository for nuclear waste could possibly pollute groundwater which was to be taken for human consumption. In such a case there might well be a requirement imposed on the authorization by way of condition that stringent monitoring or other safety precautions should be taken. This would throw up the need to consult with the authorities affected.

---

[81] *R v Secretary of State, ex p Greenpeace and Another*[1994] 4 All ER 352. One of a flurry of challenges to the various permits which preceded the opening of the THORP at Sellafield. The flurry became almost a blizzard when there was a proposal to establish a MOX (mixed oxide) plant which would enable the reprocessed waste to be used as fuel for reactors, but with similar lack of success for the objectors. *R (Friends of the Earth) v Secretary of State* [2002] Env LR 612, CA; see also *Marchioni v EA* [2002]. It is not for the court or the EA to question the legal validity of the Trident missile programme when deciding whether to licence the disposal of waste from the missiles.

[82] *R v Pollution Inspectorate, ex p Greenpeace (No 2)* [1994] 4 All ER 329. In this case Greenpeace was described judicially, before the events concerning the Brent Spar oil platform, as responsible and respected, and for those reasons, among others, as having sufficient locus standi to challenge the decision of HMIP to vary BNFL's authorization to discharge radioactive waste from Sellafield.

A body which is consulted under this provision may charge the cost of taking the **8.55** precautions upon the holder of the authorization, provided that it is empowered to do so by a condition attached to the authorization.[83]

Enforcement

The policing of the use of nuclear materials under the RSA is effected in two **8.56** ways. First, a person registered to use nuclear materials or radioactive apparatus, or the holder of an authorization in respect of nuclear waste, must publicize and keep records relating to the activities carried on.

Secondly, the Environment Agency has enforcement powers. Copies of a certificate **8.57** of registration or of an authorization, as the case may be, must be displayed on the relevant premises, so that people working there can conveniently read them.[84] Operators who fall within the ambit of the RSA must also keep records for such periods as the Environment Agency or the Minister may direct including the time after the permitted activities have come to an end.[85] Failure to comply with either requirement is an offence.[86]

The Environment Agency's enforcement powers may be exercised in respect of a **8.58** failure, actual or anticipated, to comply with a condition or limitation attached to a registration or authorization. In such an event, it may serve an enforcement notice setting out its opinion, specifying the matters constituting the failure to comply with the condition or limitation, or those making it likely that such a failure will occur, and stating the steps required to remedy the matters complained of. Failure to comply with an enforcement notice is a criminal offence, which Parliament evidently regards as serious, since the penalty on summary conviction is a fine of £20,000 or six months' imprisonment, and an unlimited fine or five years' imprisonment on conviction on indictment.[87]

Even where the operator is complying with the requirements of his registration or **8.59** authorization in full, the Environment Agency, the relevant Minister, or in default the Secretary of State, may serve a prohibition notice, where the keeping or use of radioactive material or mobile apparatus, or the disposal or accumulation of radioactive waste are thought to involve imminent risk of pollution of the environment or harm to human health. The notice must set out the opinion of the person who serves it, state the matters said to give rise to the relevant risk, and what must be done to remove that risk. Importantly, the notice suspends the registration or

---

[83] RSA, s 18.
[84] Ibid, s 19.
[85] Ibid, s 20.
[86] Ibid, s 33.
[87] Ibid, ss 21 and 32.

authorization until the notice is withdrawn wholly or to the extent which it specifies.

8.60 Failure to comply with a prohibition notice carries the same heavy penalties, as does non-compliance with an enforcement notice.[88] There are the same rights of appeal against enforcement and prohibition notices as against refusals or conditional grants of registration and authorization.[89]

Transport of radioactive material

8.61 Responsive to widespread public apprehension about the risk of accidents occurring during the movement of radioactive material around the world, and inside the UK in particular, Parliament and Ministers have made special provision for regulating the carriage of radioactive material by whatever means. The underlying provision is Section 11 of the NIA. This imposes a duty on any person on whose behalf radioactive material other than excepted material is carried within the territorial limits of the UK to secure that no occurrence involving the nuclear matter causes injury to the person or damage to property other than that of the responsible party. This general provision is amplified and refined by the Radioactive Material (Road Transport) Regulations 2002,[90] made under the Radioactive Material (Road Transport) Act 1991. These regulate the personnel who may travel in a vehicle transporting radioactive materials; the keeping of records; placarding of the vehicles in question; packaging, even down to the colour of the cover (yellow and white) and the typeface (black); the parts of the vehicle in which drivers and others may travel (no person may ride in the compartment where the nuclear material is kept); the duties of drivers, including an obligation to stay with the vehicles unless the radiation is at a low level and to observe stringent parking requirements; and notification of the police and the carrier in case of loss or damage of the nuclear materials or other emergency.

8.62 There are exemptions from the Regulations in respect of harmless consignments, and, for example, the watches worn by drivers and others, and the luminous dials of the vehicle itself. In 1975 the Department of Transport issued a Code of Practice for the Carriage of Radioactive Materials by Road. This is required reading for all engaged in such activities.

8.63 Trans-frontier shipment of radioactive waste is regulated by the Transfrontier Shipment of Radioactive Waste Regulations 1993.[91] These regulations, made by the Secretary of State under the European Communities Act 1972, invest the

---

[88] Ibid, ss 22 and 33.
[89] Ibid, s 26(2).
[90] SI 2002/1735.
[91] SI 1993/3031.

Environment Agency with licensing powers over shipments of radioactive material between Member States of the European Union, and into and out of the states of the Union. There is the familiar right of appeal to the Secretary of State against the Environment Agency's decisions.

A series of accidents which occurred to trains transporting nuclear waste has led **8.64** to the making of the Carriage of Radioactive Material by Rail Regulations 1996, SI 1996/2090.

D. Hazardous Substances—The Planning (Hazardous Substances) Act 1990

Introduction

Historically, the regulation of hazardous substances was seen as part of the town **8.65** and country planning code, although it never sat happily within the framework of the Town and Country Planning Acts.[92] In time, the fundamental difference between land use planning and the control of dangerous materials was borne in upon government, and the radical overhaul of the land use planning and environmental legislation which took place in 1990 included the enactment of the Planning (Hazardous Substances) Act 1990 (HSA), which establishes a separate code of regulation for hazardous substances.

As its title suggests, the Planning (Hazardous Substances) Act 1990 has marked **8.66** similarities to the Town and Country Planning Acts. It lays down a system of control and enforcement over the keeping and use of potentially dangerous material, which closely resembles, but is distinct from, the now familiar planning legislation.

Definitions

The first, and self-evident question to be asked when one addresses the control of **8.67** hazardous substances, is 'What is a hazardous substance for the purposes of the HSA?' The Act itself is silent on this. For an answer one must go to Schedule 1 to the Planning (Hazardous Substances) Regulations 1992,[93] made by the Secretary of State under Section 40 of the HSA. The Schedule lists no fewer than 71 substances which are to be treated as hazardous. Their names will mean little to anyone with less than a university degree in chemistry—for, instance, number 57, '3,3,6,6,9,9-Hexamethyll.2.4.5-tetroxacyclononane (>75%)' is unlikely to strike a chord of recognition in many.

---

[92] See Housing and Planning Act 1986.
[93] SI 1992/656.

8.68 The substances fall into three categories—toxic; highly reactive and explosive; and flammable. The quality of each substance which renders it liable to control under the HSA is specified against each.[94] This varies widely. For example, up to 1,000 tonnes of ammonium nitrate based products manufactured chemically for use as fertilizers (number 40) may be kept or used without attracting the provisions of the HSA, while no more than 1 kilogram of 2,3,7,8-Tetrachlorodibenzo-p-dioxin (TCDD) (number 34) may be accumulated without control under the Act.

8.69 Even the definitions in Part D of Schedule 1, which purports to make the Schedule comprehensible by dealing with interpretation, are extremely technical, and many require detailed scientific knowledge before they can be understood. The unwary who grapple with this Schedule unaided do so at their peril.

Keeping hazardous substances

8.70 The fundamental concept which underlies the HSA is that hazardous substances consent is needed where a hazardous substance is present on land in amounts exceeding those prescribed under the Hazardous Substances Regulations.[95] Accumulation of hazardous substances on land without consent is a criminal offence, punishable on summary conviction by a fine of up to £20,000, and by an unlimited fine on conviction on indictment.[96]

8.71 As might be expected, there are exceptions to the general rule requiring that hazardous substances consent shall be obtained for the presence of those substances on land. (For these purposes 'land' has the same meaning as in the Town and Country Planning Act 1990, and so means any corporeal hereditament.)[97]

Exemptions from consent

8.72 Even the exemption from the need for consent by reference to the amount of the substance is not straightforward. The controlled quantity must not be exceeded both on the land where it is kept, and also when that land is taken together with other land controlled by the same person and within 500 metres of the site, or in or on a structure or building within 500 metres.[98] In addition, there is no need for consent if the substance is temporarily present on land while it is being transported from one place to another, provided it is not unloaded.[99]

---

[94] Ibid, Sch 1 col 2.
[95] HSA, s 4(1).
[96] Ibid, s 23(1), (4). The criminal and other sanctions for breach of hazardous substances control are considered more fully below.
[97] Ibid, s 39(2); Town and Country Planning Act 1990, s 336(1).
[98] HSA, s 4(2).
[99] Ibid, s 4(3).

The Secretary of State also has power to make regulations prescribing that land of **8.73** any description may be exempt from the requirement of consent, or that the circumstances in which the substances are kept make it unnecessary to obtain consent.[100]

Finally, there is the important exception which arises from, in the jargon of envi- **8.74** ronmental legislation, 'established presence'. This is a concept designed to cater for the transitional period immediately after the HSA came into force on 1 June 1992. Where a hazardous substance was present on land at any time between 30 May 1991 and 1 June 1992 ('the establishment period'), a claim to hazardous substances consent may be made.[101]

Thus, consent is required even where land may have been used for keeping haz- **8.75** ardous substances for many years, but, subject to the stipulations of the HSA, the consent may be demanded as of right where the use pre-dated the coming into force of the Act on 1 June 1992. The claim had to have been made within the transitional period of six months from 1 June 1992, and in the form prescribed by the Secretary of State.[102] The hazardous substances authority (as to which see below) had a duty to determine the application for deemed consent within two weeks of receiving it, otherwise consent was deemed to have been granted, subject to two qualifications. First, if the substance was of a kind, and kept in such quantities that the keeper was required to notify the Health and Safety Executive of his activities under the Health and Safety at Work Act 1974, and the Notification of Installations Handling Hazardous Substances Regulations 1982,[103] the necessary notice must have been given.

The substances concerned were listed in Schedule 1 to the Notification Regulations, **8.76** which, though shorter, is likely to give as much trouble to the non-scientist as Schedule 1 to the Hazardous Substances Regulations 1992. Broadly, the substances listed are those with a propensity to poison, burn, or blow up those who come into contact with them. The second qualification is that the quantity of a hazardous substance as defined for the purposes of the HSA must have been present in more than the prescribed quantity at some time during the establishment period, otherwise there is no right to deemed consent.[104] If, for any reason, the hazardous substances authority considered that the claim for deemed consent

---

[100] Ibid, s 4(4). Surprisingly, since he made the Hazardous Substances Regulations in 1992, the Secretary of State did not take that opportunity to exercise his prescriptive powers under s 4. He has never exercised them.
[101] HSA, s 11(1).
[102] HSA, s 11(2). The details of the requirements for an application are set out in reg 14 of the Hazardous Substances Regulations 1992 (SI 1992/656), referred to above.
[103] SI No 1357.
[104] HSA, s 11(3)–(5).

was invalid, it was bound to notify the applicant within the two-week period, and state the reasons for its opinion.[105] The procedure for appealing against an unacceptable decision is considered below.

Deemed consent

8.77 A deemed hazardous substances consent is automatically subject to a variety of conditions. First, the maximum amount of the substance which may be present on the site and on other land or structure, or within a building controlled by the applicant within 500 metres of the site, may not exceed the established quantity, this being the amount notified before 1 June 1992 under the Notification Regulations (as to which see above), or twice the quantity notified under those Regulations before 30 May 1991, or, where no notification was needed, 50% more than the maximum quantity present on the site between 30 May 1991 and 1 June 1992.[106]

8.78 The Secretary of State has also prescribed rigorous technical conditions as to the temperature of vessels in which substances are to be stored pursuant to deemed consents, the location of such vessels, and the regulation of moveable containers and the amounts of substances stored in them.[107] Where a government department authorizes development carried out by a local authority or statutory undertakers, and this involves the presence of hazardous substances which give rise to a need for a hazardous substance consent, the department may also give that consent.

8.79 The same applies to orders made by the Secretary of State under the Transport and Works Act 1992, which for the most part replaces the procedure by way of private Act of Parliament.[108]

Applying for hazardous substances consent—hazardous substances authorities

8.80 An application for hazardous substances consent, or any kind, is made to the hazardous substances authority for the area in which the land in question lies. In general, this will be the district council (metropolitan or non-metropolitan) in England, in Wales the county or county borough council, and in London the London Borough Council.[109] However, where the land is in a non-metropolitan

---

[105] Ibid, s 11(6).
[106] Ibid, s 11(7), (8).
[107] Ibid, s (7)(b); Hazardous Substances Regulations 1992, Sch 3.
[108] HSA, s 112.
[109] Ibid, s 1.

county and is in a National Park administered by a planning board, the board is the hazardous substances authority.

If the land is used for mineral working or the disposal of refuse or waste in England, **8.81** or where there is no planning board for the National Park (as, for example, in the Yorkshire Dales and the Yorkshire Moors National Parks) the authority is the county council. The Broads Authority is the hazardous substances authority for the Norfolk Broads, as are all urban development corporations, housing action trusts, and the Urban Regeneration Agency for their respective areas.[110]

An application for express consent has to be made in accordance with Regulations **8.82** 5–13 in Part 3 of the Hazardous Substances Regulations 1992. The formalities closely resemble those of the town and country planning code, without mirroring them exactly. The application must be made on the prescribed form, and be accompanied by a plan or plans on the scale which the Regulations stipulate.[111]

The applicant must publish notice of the making of the application in a local **8.83** newspaper, and post the notice on the land, unless he has no right of access to it, and has taken, unsuccessfully, reasonable steps to acquire such right of access. He must send a copy of a certificate of compliance with the publicity requirements with the application, and if he is not the owner of the land must notify all the owners. A copy of the application must be available for inspection in the locality of the application. These steps must be taken within 21 days before the application is submitted to the authority.[112]

Consultation

Having received the application and satisfied itself of its validity, and of that of the **8.84** accompanying certificates and other documents, the authority must undertake extensive consultations. The statutory consultees include the Health and Safety Executive, the National Rivers Authority (both predecessors of the Environment Agency), the fire and civil defence authorities, statutory undertakers, the adjoining local authority if the site is within two kilometres of the boundary of the hazardous substances authority's administrative area, and, if a site of special scientific interest is involved, the appropriate Conservancy or Countryside Council.[113]

That list is not exhaustive, but indicates the Secretary of State's resolve that any **8.85** body which might conceivably be interested in the outcome of the application shall have the opportunity to express a view.

---

[110] Ibid, s 3.
[111] Reg 5.
[112] Regs 6, 7, and 8.
[113] Reg 10.

Determining the application

8.86 Having allowed the time for the making of representations on the application to elapse, and after carrying out the necessary consultations, the hazardous substances authority has three choices. It may refer the application to the Secretary of State; it may seek to agree with the applicant an extension of time for deciding the application beyond the eight weeks within which its decision must otherwise be taken; or it may proceed to determine the application.[114] If it takes the latter course, it again has three options. First, it may grant consent unconditionally, a choice which few hazardous substances authorities are likely to make if they model their policies on those of planning authorities.

8.87 Second, it may grant consent subject to conditions. The HSA expressly stipulates certain matters to which conditions may be directed, which are how, where, and when any substance to which the consent relates may be used; a requirement that the substance shall be permanently removed on or before a stipulated date, or before the end of a specified period. Additionally, and by analogy with the Town and Country Planning Acts, it is likely that, if required to do so, the courts would hold that conditions must fairly and reasonably relate to the consent granted, must be relevant to the policy of the HSA, that is, the protection of persons working at the consented site and of the public, and must not be perverse.[115]

8.88 The HSA imposes an express duty to state the reasons for granting consent subject to conditions clearly and precisely, a requirement which has only relatively recently been imposed on local planning authorities.[116] In addition to notifying the applicant of the decision, the authority must also inform the Environment Agency, the London Borough, or county council for the area if that authority is not the hazardous substances authority, any consultee who made representations about the application, and any owners of the land who made representations.[117] There is a similar obligation on the authority to notify the applicant, with the reasons, where the Secretary of State directs that the application shall be referred to him instead of being decided by the authority, and to offer the applicant the opportunity to make representations at an inquiry.[118]

8.89 Third, consent may be refused outright.

---

[114] HSA, s 11(1)–(3).

[115] HSA, s 10. See, eg, *Pyx Granite v MHLG* [1960] AC 260; *Newbury DC v SOS* [1981] AC 578.

[116] It is unclear whether the inference is that planning authorities are free to state their reasons obscurely and at length.

[117] HSA, s 11(4) and (5).

[118] Ibid, s 12.

Appeals

On receipt of the authority's decision, the applicant has six months in which to **8.90** appeal to the Secretary of State if he is aggrieved by it. He must appeal by completing the form obtainable from the Department of the Environment, and by sending with the form copies of the application, the notices and certificates which accompanied it, the correspondence about the application with the hazardous substances authority, and the decision notice. In addition he must send copies of the certificate stating that he is the owner of the land or that he has notified the owner of the making of the application. He must also notify the authority by sending it a copy of the appeal form and certificate.[119]

Amendment and termination of consents

At any stage during the life of a hazardous substances consent, any party, whether **8.91** or not it owns the land or was the applicant for the original consent, may apply to the authority to remove a condition subject to which the consent was granted. It seems that it is not possible to apply simply to vary a consent (by, for example, changing the quantity of the hazardous substance which may be brought onto the land). It follows that a third party has the power potentially to affect the rights and criminal liabilities of the landowner and the person operating the installation which makes use of hazardous substances, without the permission of either. Their only safeguard is the right of the owner and occupier to be notified of the making of the application, in the same way as if it were an application for a fresh consent.[120]

When faced with such an application the authority has no power to decide whether **8.92** the consent should be continued or should have been granted in the first place, it may only have regard to the condition or conditions subject to which the consent was granted or should be continued.[121] If the consent was granted for the presence on land of more than one substance, the authority may not take account of conditions other than those which regulate the presence of the substance which is the subject of the application. If more than one consent exists in respect of the land, the authority may have regard only to the consent which is the subject of the application.

On those bases, it may determine either that the consent should be granted subject **8.93** to conditions different from those to which it was originally granted, or may decide that it should be granted unconditionally. Otherwise it must refuse the application.[122]

---

[119] Ibid, s 13.
[120] Ibid, s 13(1); Hazardous Substances Regulations 1992, regs 6 and 7.
[121] HSA, s 13(2), (3).
[122] Ibid, s 13(3)–(7).

8.94 If there is a change in the control of part of the land which has the benefit of a hazardous substance consent (in the same way as planning permission enures for the benefit of the land concerned), the consent is automatically revoked, unless application has been made to the authority before the change in control occurs.[123] This contrasts with the status of a planning permission, which enures for the benefit of the land concerned unless expressly otherwise provided in the permission itself. It is therefore important to apply for the continuation before the control changes.

8.95 The requirement to obtain continuation of the consent where only part rather than the whole of the land becomes subject to changed control seems to be directed at preventing uncontrolled subdivision of consented land. Although the HSA does not define 'control' for the purposes of these provisions, on the ordinary meaning of English it seems more likely that Parliament had in mind a change in the ultimate direction of the enterprise, rather than the replacement of one relatively modest functionary, such as a manager or foreman, by another.

8.96 The formalities to be observed when the application is made are very similar to those which regulate applications for original consents, and demand that the same information shall be supplied to the authority.[124]

Revocation and modification of consents

8.97 The authority has a general power to revoke or modify consents, to the extent which it considers expedient, and having regard to material considerations.[125] If a consent is revoked or modified by the exercise of this power, the authority is liable to compensate persons affected by it. Specifically, the authority may revoke a consent if it has for practical purposes been abandoned, that is, if the use of the land to which a consent relates has changed materially for the purposes of the Town and Country Planning Acts, or if a planning permission for operational development of the land has been granted and implemented in whole or in part.

8.98 Similarly, if the consent applies to one substance only, which has not been present on the land in the quantity permitted or in a greater quantity, or if it relates to more than one substance, and none has been present in amounts equal to or exceeding the controlled quantity, then the consent is taken to have been abandoned, and the authority may revoke it. In any of these four cases, no compensation is payable, however.[126] Any order made under Section 14 must specify the grounds on which it is made, and must be confirmed by the Secretary of State before it can take effect.

---

[123] Ibid, s 17(1).
[124] Hazardous Substances Regulations 1992, reg 5(3), Sch 2.
[125] HSA, s 14(1), (16)(1).
[126] Ibid, s 14(2), 16(1).

Notice of the making of the order must be served on the owner and the person **8.99** other than an owner appearing to be in control of all or part of the land. If the authority is of the opinion that any other person will be affected by the order it must serve that person with notice of the making of the application as well. In accordance with the general law, a body corporate is a person for these and all other purposes of the HSA. Any person served with notice of the order has the right to appear at an inquiry before an Inspector appointed by the Secretary of State before the order is confirmed.[127]

Compensation

In those instances where compensation is payable, any person who has suffered **8.100** damage by reason of depreciation in the value of an interest which he holds in the land in consequence of the order, or of the value of minerals on or in it, or a person who is disturbed in the enjoyment of the land or minerals lying there, is entitled to compensation. The latter provision would, as was no doubt intended, confer a right to compensation to the operator of an enterprise involving the storage or handling of hazardous substances who occupied the land under a licence, perhaps paying royalties or some other licence fee to the landowner.

A person who carries out works in compliance with the order is entitled to com- **8.101** pensation from the hazardous substances authority in respect of expenses reasonably incurred. This seems to make the authority liable to compensate a contractor engaged by the owner or operator of the land. However, if that is the effect of this provision, the outcome is less startling than might at first appear. If there were no such liability to compensate a contractor, it might be difficult to find anyone prepared to carry out the work needed in order to secure compliance with a revocation or modification order, especially if the owner or operator of the land were bankrupt or untraceable (this having been a major problem associated with waste disposal and storage sites, as is described elsewhere). The knowledge that he could look to the authority for his expenses, including perhaps a profit element, might be thought to embolden even the most timorous contractor into undertaking the work.[128]

Compensation is to be assessed by the Lands Tribunal in case of a dispute, in **8.102** accordance with the rules governing the assessment of compensation on compulsory purchase. This, in general, involves assessing the diminution in the open market value of the land, assuming a willing buyer and a willing seller. The details of this are, however, outside the scope of this book.[129]

---

[127] Ibid, s 15.
[128] Ibid, s 16.
[129] Ibid, s 16(5). Town and Country Planning Act 1990, ss 17 and 18. Land Compensation Act 1961, s 5.

8.103 There is special provision for the compensation payable where a hazardous substances authority revokes or modifies a consent following an application for its continuation where the control of part of the land has changed. The details of the procedure are discussed above.

8.104 Somewhat unsatisfactorily, the HSA provides that in such instances compensation is payable to the person in control of the whole of the land before that control became subdivided.[130] The statute is silent as to the procedure to be followed, the basis on which compensation is to be calculated, and the way in which disputes as to compensation are to be resolved. It therefore remains to be seen how the courts will make good these omissions should this become necessary. The obvious solution would be for the Lands Tribunal to decide disputed cases of compensation in accordance with the rules which apply in other cases of revocation or modification. Nonetheless, the technical justification in law for this solution is not immediately apparent.

The powers of the Secretary of State

8.105 These are, on the whole, what might be expected, given that he has supervisory powers over the administration of the legislation by hazardous substances authorities. The powers reflect, with some distortions, those which he possesses over planning authorities under the Town and Country Planning Acts. The Secretary of State may give directions requiring an authority to refer an application for hazardous substances consent or for continuation of a consent to him rather than determining it itself. This is identical to the power to 'call in' under the planning legislation. The HSA enables the direction to be given either to a particular authority or to authorities generally, or to an individual application, or to specified classes of applications.

8.106 In spite of having taken powers from Parliament to do so, the Secretary of State has not made any general direction under the HSA, and seems content to use his powers to make directions in respect of individual applications. Where he makes a direction, he must give the applicant or the authority, if either wishes, the opportunity to appear at an inquiry before an Inspector and to make its views known before he takes any decision.[131]

8.107 The HSA provides that the Secretary of State's decision on a matter referred to him is final. That is, however, misleading, since there is a statutory right of appeal to the High Court on the grounds that his decision was not within the powers of the HSA, or that the relevant procedural requirements have not been complied

---

[130] HSA, s 18.
[131] Ibid, s 20.

with (the grammar is that of the statute).[132] The right is available equally to the authority as it is to an applicant. Again, the statutory right of appeal is for practical purposes the same as that available to a party aggrieved by a decision of the Secretary of State under the Town and Country Planning Acts.

The powers of the High Court on appeal resemble those which it possesses under **8.108** the planning legislation. It may suspend the operation of the Secretary of State's decision by interim order (a power exercised sparingly under the Planning Acts), or quash the decision if satisfied that it was not within the powers of the HSA or that there was failure to comply with the requirements of the Act or of the Tribunals and Inquiries Acts 1958 and 1971, which regulate the conduct of inquiries held under, among other things, the HSA, and that the failure prejudiced the interests of the applicant.

It would be unwise to be misled by the proposition, which appears from time to **8.109** time in the HSA, that the decision of the Secretary of State is final, since failure or refusal by him to take a decision whether to give a direction or to determine an appeal relating to a hazardous substances consent may be challenged by judicial review by way of mandamus.[133] This topic is dealt with more fully elsewhere.

Enforcement of hazardous substances control

It has already been noted, briefly, that keeping or using hazardous substances in **8.110** breach of the regulatory system laid down by the HSA is a criminal offence. The sanctions to which those who infringe the canons of the Act are exposed need closer examination. A person may commit an offence, and is an 'appropriate person' under the HSA in one of three instances.

First, and obviously, if a quantity of a hazardous substance which exceeds the con- **8.111** trolled quantity prescribed by the Regulations has been present on the land and there is no consent at all, there is an offence. Secondly, if the amount of the substance exceeds the maximum permitted by any consent in force in respect of the land, an offence will also be committed. Thirdly, failure to comply with a condition attached to a consent carries criminal liability.

Where the offence arises because the amount of the substance exceeds the legal **8.112** limit, the person knowingly causing the substance to be present, or who allows it to be present, or who controls the land, is the 'appropriate person', and is guilty of the offence. Where, by contrast, there is a breach of condition, only the persons knowingly causing or allowing the breach are guilty.[134] The penalties for commission of an offence have been described above.

---

[132] Ibid; see also s 22(1) and (2).
[133] Ibid, s 22.
[134] Ibid, s 23(2), (3).

8.113 It is a defence for a person accused of one of the above offences to prove that he took all reasonable precautions and exercised all due diligence to avoid committing the offence. The difference between these components of the defence is not clear—on one view of the statute the two appear to be indistinguishable. It may be, however, that taking reasonable precautions imports the notion that a reasonably safe system of working is established, while the exercise of due diligence involves ensuring that the system is followed.

8.114 There is a second defence—that the commission of the offence could only have been avoided by taking action involving a breach of statutory duty. This might, for example, entail risks to the employees or the public in breach of the Health and Safety at Work Act, which is outside the scope of this chapter.

8.115 A third possible defence, where the charge is that the permitted amount of the substance in question had been exceeded, is that the defendant did not know, and had no reason to believe, that the amount of the substance on the land was excessive.

8.116 Likewise, if he can show that he did not know, and had no reason to believe, that there had been a breach of a condition attached to the consent, this will be a defence. In considering the question of the size of the fine which it decides to impose, the court must have regard to the financial benefit which accrued to the convicted person or which appears likely to accrue in consequence of the offence.[135]

Hazardous substances contravention notices

8.117 By way of addition and alternative to criminal prosecution for contravention of hazardous substances control, the HSA gives the hazardous substances authority enforcement powers modelled on and virtually the same as those invested in a planning authority in case of a breach of planning control. It is not clear why it was thought necessary to duplicate the sanctions available, unless the notion of unauthorized keeping or use of hazardous substances is so heinous that a battery of remedies should be on hand in order to intimidate potential offenders. On the other hand, it is possible that there was thought to be a need to provide a remedy for breaches of control, as well as punishing them.

8.118 Where it appears to a hazardous substances authority that there has been a breach of hazardous substances control, it may serve a contravention notice alleging that the control has been contravened, and requiring such steps as it considers appropriate to remedy the contravention, in whole or in part. The notice is to be served only if the authority thinks it expedient to do so, there being no statutory

---

[135] Ibid, s 23(4)–(7).

obligation to take action, even in the event of a manifest and flagrant breach of control.[136] However, the authority is expressly prohibited from serving a hazardous substances contravention notice where it appears that the contravention of control can be avoided only by taking action which would amount to a breach of statutory duty.[137]

As with a town and country planning enforcement notice, a contravention notice **8.119** must be served on the owner of the land, any other person who appears to be in control of that land, and on any other person prescribed by the Secretary of State. He has prescribed, not as crisply as he might have, all persons appearing to the authority to have an interest in the land which is materially affected by the notice.[138] The notice must also identify the land to which it relates, by reference to a plan or otherwise; specify a date not less than 28 days from the date of service as the date on which it is to take effect; and the steps required to be taken in order to remedy the alleged breach of hazardous substances control and the period following the date of service of the notice within which each step is to be taken.

The notice may, if the authority thinks it expedient, require that the substance **8.120** which is the subject of the notice shall be removed from the land. If it does so, the authority may also require that the consent shall cease to have effect at the end of a period specified in the notice, or that the consent shall cease to have effect in respect of specified substances where more than one substance is the subject of the consent.[139] The notice must also state the reasons for it being issued, and inform the recipients of their rights of appeal.[140]

Appeals against contravention notices

The rights of appeal are identical to those available to those persons who are the **8.121** objects of enforcement action under the Town and Country Planning Acts.[141] So, the appellant may claim that hazardous substances consent should be granted for the matters which are the substance of the contravention notice; that the alleged contravention has not occurred; that if it did occur it was not a contravention of control; that the notice was not served as required by the HSA; that the requirements of the notice exceeded what was necessary to remedy the contravention of which complaint was made; and that the time for compliance with the notice was too short.[142]

---

[136] Ibid, s 24(1).
[137] Ibid, s 24(3).
[138] Hazardous Substances Regulations 1992, reg 17(2).
[139] HSA, s 24(5), (6), and (7).
[140] Hazardous Substances Regulations 1992, reg 17(3).
[141] Ibid, regs 18 and 19.
[142] Town and Country Planning Act 1990, s 174, as applied to HSA.

8.122 The procedure for appeal is governed by the Planning (Hazardous Substances) Regulations 1992, Schedule 4, Parts 1–5. In essence, these reproduce the relevant provisions of the Town and Country Planning Act 1990, amended to take account of the details of the system of hazardous substance control.

8.123 Notice of appeal must be given in writing, which may be delivered direct to the appropriate office of the Department of the Environment, or the Welsh Office, as the case may be, or by posting in time for it to arrive in the ordinary course of post before the expiry of the 28 day period at the end of which the notice takes effect. Importantly, the notice of appeal must be accompanied by a copy of the contravention notice, and by a statement of the grounds on which the appeal is made, and also the appellant's submissions in relation to each ground of appeal. Failure to set out those submissions in respect of each of more than one ground of appeal will entitle the Secretary of State to determine the appeal without considering any ground which is not supported by a statement of submissions.

8.124 If either the appellant or the authority requests it, the Secretary of State must hold an inquiry before an Inspector appointed by him. He need not, however, provide for an inquiry to be held if he proposes to dismiss an appeal on the ground that consent ought not to be granted or that a condition attached to a consent ought not to be discharged, or where he proposes to allow an appeal on the ground that the matters alleged to amount to a contravention of hazardous substances control, have not occurred.[143]

8.125 It is a matter for speculation how the Secretary of State could, normally at least, form even a provisional view on either issue without first fully informing himself by way of an inquiry about the facts and circumstances surrounding the dispute between the parties. It seems likely, therefore, that the power to dispense with an inquiry will be, or ought to be, used sparingly.

8.126 The powers of the Secretary of State are the same as he possesses when determining an appeal against a planning enforcement notice. He may correct any defect, error, or misdescription in the notice or may vary its terms, provided in each case that he is satisfied that the amendment will not cause injustice either to the appellant or the authority. He may, of course, either quash the notice or uphold it, with or without amendment. This power carries with it the ability to discharge any condition subject to which the consent was originally granted, and to substitute another condition in its place. In short, the Secretary of State has all the powers of a hazardous substances authority to whom an application for consent has been made in the first place. This includes authority to require payment of the requisite fee stipulated by virtue of Section 26A of the HSA.[144]

---

[143] Hazardous Substances Regulations, Sch 4, Part 5.
[144] Ibid.

The decision of the Secretary of State in relation to a grant of consent or other **8.127** determination of an appeal is final, subject only to the statutory right of appeal to the High Court on a point of law.[145] Leave to appeal against such a decision must be obtained from a single judge, this being a safeguard against the waste of the court's time similar to that brought about by unmeritorious appellants whose only wish was to prolong the time during which they could carry on activities in contravention of town and country planning control.

In this respect, an appeal on a point of law against a decision of the Secretary of **8.128** State in respect of a contravention notice is very like an application for judicial review, although the latter remedy will not be available to a party aggrieved by such a decision.

Other sanctions against breaches of control

Still more sanctions can be used against a recalcitrant owner or operator who tries **8.129** to defy a contravention notice which has taken effect, with or without an appeal to the Secretary of State (the notice will have not taken effect until that appeal has been determined either by the Secretary of State himself, or by the courts on appeal from him).

The authority may enter on the land, take the steps required by the notice to **8.130** remedy the contravention, and recover the cost from the owner. In such a case the owner is to be taken to have incurred the expense on behalf of the person who actually carried out the contravention of control, and the latter is bound to reimburse the owner accordingly.[146] Obstructing a person seeking to exercise the power to enter and carry out works to secure compliance with the notice is a criminal offence, and the expenses incurred may be made a charge on the land. It is a further criminal offence to fail to comply with a contravention notice which is in force, and on a second or subsequent conviction the defendant may be guilty of offences in respect of any period of time following the first conviction.[147]

Finally, the HSA confers a residual power on the authority to obtain an injunction **8.131** if it considers it necessary or expedient for any actual or apprehended contravention of hazardous substances control. Both the High Court or any county court have power to grant injunctions in such cases, and they may be granted against persons whose identity is unknown.[148] This completes the catalogue of the formidable arsenal of remedies available to authorities wishing to prevent breach of the law regulating hazardous substances.

---

[145] Ibid, reg 22.
[146] Ibid, Sch 4, Part 5.
[147] Ibid.
[148] HSA, s 26AA.

Miscellaneous provisions

8.132 The Secretary of State may grant temporary exemption from the need to comply with hazardous substances control if it appears to him either that a community is being or is likely to be deprived of an essential service or commodity, or if the presence of a hazardous substance as set out in his direction is necessary for the provision of such a service or commodity. The direction granting exemption may be withdrawn at any time, and in any event expires three months after it is made, unless extended by the Secretary of State by a further direction. The obvious occasion for the exercise of the power is that it will be used in emergencies, although this is not to be taken as the only reason for invoking it.[149]

8.133 By analogy with the town and country planning legislation, hazardous substances authorities must keep registers of applications for consents, of consents which have effect, of the revocations and modifications made to them, and of directions made by the Secretary of State granting temporary exemptions from control.[150]

8.134 The HSA expressly preserves the system of control laid down by the Health and Safety at Work Act 1974, and of prohibition or improvement notices made under it. If a hazardous substance consent or contravention notice purports to allow or require anything to be done which contravenes the 1974 Act, the latter prevails, and the consent or contravention notice is to that extent void. The predominance of the Health and Safety at Work Act is emphasized by the provision that if the Health and Safety Executive advises the hazardous substances authority that all or part of a consent or notice is void because it conflicts with the 1974 Act, the authority must revoke it, or modify it in accordance with the advice.[151]

8.135 The HSA makes special provision for extending hazardous substances control to the land of hazardous substances authorities and the Crown, in the case of the latter both while it is held by the Crown, and in anticipation of its being sold. The main distinction is that none of the sanctions available in cases of breach of control are available against the Crown, even though the regulatory discipline applies to Crown land.[152]

8.136 The interests of the Church Commissioners in ecclesiastical property are recognized in Section 34 of the HSA. The Commissioners must be served with notices where enforcement action is taken in respect of church lands, and compensation payable under the HSA is payable to them.

---

[149] Ibid, s 27.
[150] Ibid, s 28. The complicated rules which govern the content of registers are contained in the Hazardous Substances Regulations 1992, reg 23.
[151] HSA, s 29.
[152] Ibid, ss 30–32.

Lastly, the HSA contains a number of provisions designed to ensure that even the **8.137** most contumacious owner or occupier of land cannot prevent investigation of his activities. Anyone authorized by an authority or the Secretary of State may enter land at any reasonable time for the purpose of surveying it in connection with an application for hazardous substances consent or a proposal to issue a contravention notice or for ascertaining whether a contravention of control amounting to an offence has taken place.

An officer of the Inland Revenue Valuation Office ('the District Valuer') or of an **8.138** authority may enter for the purpose of survey in connection with a claim for compensation, and a person authorized by the Secretary of State or an authority may also enter in order to discover whether a contravention notice has been complied with or not.[153]

Where there is power to enter land for these purposes, and admission to the land **8.139** has been refused, or refusal is anticipated, or the case is urgent, a justice of the peace may issue a warrant to enter the land on it being shown by sworn evidence in writing that these conditions are met. Entry may be effected on one occasion only and must take place within one month of the issue of the warrant, and at a reasonable hour, unless in case of urgency. Resistance to execution of the warrant is a criminal offence. In short, Parliament, in providing for eternal vigilance over the keeping and use of hazardous substances, left nothing to chance.[154]

Accidents involving hazardous substances

The tendency to impose ever stricter controls on dangerous activities is exemplified **8.140** by the Control of Major Accidents Regulations 1999.[155] These apply to establishments where toxic, polluting, explosive or flammable substances are kept in prescribed quantities.[156] Where the materials are kept in larger quantities the controls are correspondingly stricter. In laboratories and academic research premises the controls are less onerous. [157]

A major accident is one where uncontrolled emissions, fire or explosion occurs, **8.141** leading to serious damage to human health or the environment. [158] The operators of all relevant premises must develop major accident prevention policies and record them. The policy must identify the major hazards which may arise, and specify the personnel responsible for dealing with them. Operating and emergency

---

[153] Ibid, s 36.
[154] Ibid, ss 36A, and 26B.
[155] SI 1999/743.
[156] Regulation 3; Sched. 1
[157] Ibid.
[158] Sched. 2.

procedures must be devised and staff trained appropriately. Performance and developments in technology must be kept under review.[159]

8.142 All operators must notify the 'competent authority', that is, the Health and Safety Executive and the Environment Agency of the address of the premises, the operator and the person in charge, the substances kept, and the potential risks.[160]

8.143 Any increase in the amount of substances kept or change in their identity or the procedures adopted must also be notified.[161]

8.144 Additionally, operators of factories and similar premises must prepare and lodge with the competent authority safety reports showing that equipment and procedures are safe, and that major hazards have been identified and emergency procedures devised.[162] Reports must be reviewed whenever there are changes to the operation, or technical developments, and in any case after five years.[163] On and off-site emergency plans are required and are also subject to review.[164]

8.145 In order to protect the public, operators must supply to schools, hospitals, and other public institutions within a protection zone designated by the competent authority information about the safety measures set up. The information must be available to the general public permanently.[165]

8.146 The information must contain the name and address of the operator, identify the person giving the information, explain what is going on the factory, and specify the potential hazards. It must also advise the public what to do if there is a major accident. Commercial confidentially, national security, and personal privacy may justify withholding information.[166]

8.147 The competent authority has power to require an operator to show that proper safety measures are operative, and major accidents must be reported.[167] Where necessary the competent authority may prohibit an establishment or part of it from coming into operation, and must prohibit this where the safety measures are 'seriously deficient' (an expression not defined).[168]

8.148 The competent authority must set up a system of annual inspection of factories and other establishments, and also of major incidents.[169] It must also notify the

---

[159] Ibid.
[160] Reg 1; reg 6; Schedule 3.
[161] Reg 6.
[162] Reg 6.
[163] Reg 7; Sched.4.
[164] Reg 8–11.
[165] Reg 14.
[166] Sched 6.
[167] Reg 15.
[168] Regs 17 and 18.
[169] Reg 19.

European Commission of any major accident, together with an analysis of the causes.[170]

Lead shot

If major incidents are at one end of the spectrum of man-made environmental crises, the Environmental Protection (Restriction on Use of Lead Shot) (England) Regulations[171] are at the other. **8.149**

These prohibit the use of lead shot in guns fired below high tide mark in a long list of SSSIs set out in Schedule 1 (ranging from Blenheim Park to Wraysbury Gravel Pits). They also forbid the use of lead shot fired at coot, ducks, geese, swans, and moorhens.[172] **8.150**

PCBs

The dangers of polychlorinated biphenyls and kindred substances have been known for decades and legislation to guard against them has been in force for at least 20 years. The aim now is to eliminate their use altogether. They have historically been used in the manufacture of, for example, fluorescent lights and refrigerators. There is positive evidence that they are carcinogenic in animals and possibly, though not demonstrably, in humans. They are also potentially harmful to human immune and reproductive systems. They can be ingested in food and breast milk, and factory workers can be exposed to them.[173] **8.151**

These considerations lie behind the Environmental Protection (Disposal of PCBs and other Dangerous Substances) Regulations 2000.[174] Apart from PCBs, the Regulations apply to terphenyls, methane compounds, and mixtures containing these substances.[175] It is illegal to hold equipment contaminated by the prohibited substances after July 2000, except by registered holders and businesses concerned with decontamination or the disposal of contaminated equipment.[176] **8.152**

Registered holders may hold contaminated equipment for the purposes of decontamination, PCBs themselves for the purpose of analysis, transformers holding small amounts of PCBs and equipment intended to be replaced before July 2008.[177] There is provision for registration of holders and appeals against refusal **8.153**

---

[170] Reg 21.
[171] SI 1999/2170
[172] Reg 3; Sched 2.
[173] US Environmental Protection Agency website.
[174] SI 2000/1043.
[175] Reg 2.
[176] Reg 3.
[177] Reg 4.

to register and for records of contaminated equipment. All breaches of the regulations are enforceable by criminal prosecution.[178]

E. Genetically Modified Organisms

Introduction

8.154　Genetic engineering and modification involve scientific techniques and experimentation which are at the outer edges of human knowledge. The legal practitioner needs to know the rudiments of the science, if only so that he can be aware that his client is engaged in or embarking on an area of activity where the law that regulates the engineering or modification of genes may apply or be relevant.

8.155　The idea of altering or improving the genetic characteristics of plants and animals in order to improve their looks, performance, or both, is far from novel. Gardeners have bred hybrid roses for generations, and the sanguine or gullible have for centuries paid enormous sums of money for thoroughbred racehorses in the hope that they or their progeny will run far faster than the rest.[179] With the discovery of the double helix pattern of the arrangement of genes in DNA (deoxyribonucleic acid) by Crick and Watson in the 1950s the foundation was laid for the modern science of genetic modification.

8.156　The discovery in the 1970s that ribbons of DNA could be cut and stitched end to end produced the result that scientists were able to remove a gene from one organism and reposition it in the same organism, or alternatively insert it into a wholly different creature, where it could replicate. This, it transpired, could be achieved in days or weeks rather than the years during which traditional breeding techniques have traditionally operated (it is noteworthy that the record time for the Epsom Derby set in 1936 was not broken until 1995).

The uses of genetic modification

8.157　The practical applications of genetic modification are numerous and varied. In the field of medicine, vaccines, drugs, and diagnostic aids have been produced by the use of genetically modified organisms (GMOs). GMOs have been used to breed pest resistant plants, short-stemmed cereals which are not flattened by heavy rain and which can therefore be more easily harvested, and plants which are resistant to herbicides and which can therefore be sprayed with weedkillers which affect only the target weeds.

---

[178]　Regs 6, 7, 8, and 13.
[179]　See Hilaire Belloc, More Peers, 'Lord Hippo'.

Other uses include the control of oil spills, water purification, and degrading **8.158** chemicals in toxic waste. The obverse is that GMOs have the potential for use as biological agents in war or by terrorists. Many GMOs are also pathogenic, that is, capable of producing disease if they merely escape without falling into the wrong hands. The need for regulation of those GMOs which have so far been discovered or made is therefore demonstrable, without taking account of those which may be produced in future.[180]

This necessarily short and oversimplified description of genetic engineering and **8.159** the ways in which GMOs are produced should enable the layman to be on his guard if issues as to their creation, keeping, transport, sale, or release into the environment should arise.

GMOs—the definition

Because of the potential dangers associated with the escape or deliberate release of **8.160** GMOs, Part VI of the EPA 1990 is primarily directed at preventing or minimizing damage to the environment which might arise from either cause.[181] To this end, the definitions in the EPA 1990 and the subordinate legislation made under it cast the net wide.

'Organism' means, for practical purposes, any living creature, no matter how big **8.161** or how small, other than a human being or a human embryo. It also includes any article consisting of or including 'biological matter', that is, tissue, cells, genes, or other genetic material of any kind, which is capable of replication or transferring genetic material. This is true whether or not the organism occurs naturally or is produced artificially, or whether it has ever been part of a whole organism.[182]

An organism is genetically modified if either its genes or other genetic material are **8.162** inherited or otherwise genetically derived from genes or other genetic material, or if its genes have been modified by means of an artificial technique prescribed by the Secretary of State (for the Environment).[183] The Secretary of State has prescribed several techniques for this purpose. To anyone other than a specialist biologist their meaning and significance are obscure. They are set out in full in Section 106 of the Act and in Regulation 3 of the Genetically Modified Organisms

---

[180] This summary is taken from the 13th Annual Report of the Royal Commission on Environmental Pollution, 1989, Cm 720. There are additional concerns identified there, namely that GMOs can reproduce and multiply spontaneously with knock-on effects. For instance, widespread growth of insect-resistant plants might lead to the evolution of insects resistant to the toxins produced by the modified plant.

[181] EPA, s 106(1).

[182] Ibid, s 106(2) and (3).

[183] Ibid, s 106(4).

(Deliberate Release) Regulations 2002.[184] In brief, the techniques amount to a variety of ways in which molecules of nucleic acid, and specifically DNA, can be introduced into a host organism, such as a virus, microbial plasmid, or other vector system which can be a transmitting agent of heritable genetic material prepared or manufactured elsewhere.

8.163 An example given in the regulation is in vitro fertilization using recombinant DNA, although this is but one of many, most of which will be unfamiliar to the layman. The powers of the Secretary of State are very wide, since they enable him to specify any technique for modifying genes which in his opinion would produce organisms which ought to be treated as having been genetically modified. The only restriction on these powers appears to be that he may not specify techniques which involve no more than the giving of assistance to naturally occurring means of reproduction.[185]

8.164 The expression 'Genetically Modified Organism' naturally calls for close definition. It means 'any acellular, unicellular, or multicellular entity other than humans or human embryos, and includes any article or substance consisting of or including biological matter'. The latter includes tissue, cells, sub-cellular matter, and genes, whether naturally or artificially produced. An organism is genetically modified for the purposes of the Act if any of its genes are modified by an artificial technique prescribed by the Secretary of State, or inherited or otherwise derived through any number of replications.[186]

8.165 As has been observed, a main aim of Part VI of the EPA 1990 is the minimization or removal of damage to the environment. As happens elsewhere in the Act, the concept receives detailed statutory elaboration. The environment is defined, with Aristotelian overtones, as consisting of land, air, water, or any of these.[187]

8.166 The concept of damage is widely defined. 'Damage' means the presence in the environment of one or more GMOs which is or are capable of causing harm to living organisms (including man) which the environment, as defined, supports.[188] It is apparent, therefore, that actual damage is not an element in the activation of Part VI of the EPA 1990. The mere potential for damage will be enough. This notion is reinforced by the approach of the Act to defining 'harm' and the capacity to cause it.

---

[184] SI 2002/2443.

[185] EPA, s 106(5).

[186] See EPA 1990, s 106.

[187] Ibid, s 107(2). By contrast to the Town and Country Planning legislation, the EPA 1990 does not address the possibility that one, such as water, might overlie another, such as land. The reason may well be that potential damage to any one of the three media will be enough to activate the provisions of Part VI.

[188] EPA, s 107(3).

GMOs are to be regarded as capable of causing harm if they, or one of them, are **8.167** present in such numbers that they are or that one of them is individually capable of causing harm, whether or not such harm in fact materializes. GMOs are also to be regarded as capable of causing harm if they are able to produce descendants which themselves are capable of causing harm, even though the parent organisms may be wholly innocuous. 'Harm' means harm to the health of humans, including offence to any of the five senses, or harm to property, harm to other living organisms, or to the ecological systems of which they form part.

The Secretary of State has power to prescribe categories of GMOs which are to be **8.168** regarded as for practical purposes harmless, either by reference to their capacity for causing harm, or by reference to the harm which they may bring about. He has prescribed two types of GMO as appropriate to be disregarded, provided that they are released or marketed (concepts which are discussed below) in accordance with and with the authority of a consent granted by the Secretary of State under Section 111 of the EPA 1990, which is also discussed below, or released with the written consent of the competent Minister or authority of a Member State of the EU in accordance with the Deliberate Release Directive of the Commission.

The categories are GMOs which control the number or activity or both of any **8.169** organisms, and GMOs which control toxic waste.[189]

It is necessary to note the definition of 'control'. This is important, because of the **8.170** emphasis in the EPA 1990 on the control over and prohibition of release or escape of GMOs. Organisms of any kind (whether they are GMOs or not) are deemed to be under the control of a person where they are contained by a physical, chemical, or biological barrier, or a combination of the three, used to ensure that the organisms or their descendants do not enter the environment, or for ensuring that the organisms or their descendants which may enter the environment are harmless when they do so.[190]

Linked with this are the definitions of 'release' and 'escape'. A person releases an **8.171** organism if he causes or permits it to cease to be under his control. The organism escapes if it ceases to be under his control without his causing or permitting the release.[191]

---

[189] Ibid, s 107(8); Genetically Modified Organisms (Deliberate Release) Regulations 2002, SI 2002/2443, reg 4.
[190] EPA, s 107(9).
[191] Ibid, s 107(10). This subsection, since it seems to do no more than spell out at some length mere propositions of common sense, might be thought to be superfluous.

GMOs—the system of control

8.172 In theory at least, the EPA 1990 appears to contemplate two separate and complementary codes of control over the import, acquisition, release, and marketing of GMOs. In practice, and as the law now stands, there is only one. However, the first system requires that any person who imports, acquires, releases, or markets any GMO must first carry out an assessment of the risks of damage to the environment inherent in the nature of the organism or in the way in which he proposes to deal with it. The risk is that of damage to the environment.

8.173 The operator must also notify the Secretary of State of his intentions with respect to the GMO and provide such information as may be required, in cases where the Secretary of State so prescribes.[192] In fact, for reasons which will become apparent, the Secretary of State has not made any regulation under this section of the EPA 1990, so the provision is for all practical purposes a dead letter.

8.174 This conclusion is reinforced by the provision that no obligation arises either to undertake a risk assessment or to give notice to the Secretary of State where his consent to an activity is necessary under Section 111 of the Act, discussed below. For similar reasons, the general duty to take reasonable steps to identify the risks of damage to the environment as a result of the importation or acquisition of GMOs, and the prohibition on the import, acquisition, or release of GMOs where there is a risk of damage to the environment, is at present equally academic.[193]

8.175 Were this system of control to be in force, the Secretary of State would have power to serve prohibition notices where he had reason to believe that the import, acquisition, release, marketing, or keeping of any GMO would involve a risk of damage to the environment. Service of a prohibition notice would require the recipient to dispose of the GMO in question as quickly and safely as practicable, or to deal with it in the way specified in the notice.[194] There is no right of appeal against a prohibition notice, which must, for the present at least, be regarded as a weapon to be held in reserve by the Secretary of State in case the alternative system of control should prove inadequate. That system now requires consideration.

Importation, acquisition, release, and marketing of GMOs

8.176 The main thrust of the regime by which activity involving GMOs is supervised is the requirement that the consent of the Secretary of State is needed for the import, acquisition, release, or marketing of the organisms in cases or circumstances prescribed.[195] On its face, this might appear to contemplate a limited power of control

---

[192] Ibid, s 108(1).
[193] See EPA, s 109.
[194] Ibid, s 110.
[195] Ibid, s 111(1).

by the Secretary of State. However, he has taken the opportunity to declare that his consent will be needed in any case or circumstance other than the release of an 'approved product'. Yet, an approved product is one marketed in accordance with a consent which he has granted. In brief, by this circular route, the Secretary of State has assumed control over all activities involving GMOs.[196]

By the same token, the Secretary of State's consent is needed to keep GMOs which **8.177** have been imported or acquired. The applicant for consent needs to be aware of the heavy burden of providing information which lies upon him. Any application for consent must, as is conventional, be made in writing. It must set out not only the name and address of the applicant, but also the names and qualifications of the scientist and every other person involved in the release of the organism in question. A full description of the scientific properties of the organism is required, and a statement of the techniques involved in handling, identifying, and detecting them.

The applicant must also describe the locations at which the organism will be **8.178** released, and give information about the natural predators, the prey, competitors, symbions, and hosts. Full details of all the possible pathological, ecological, and physiological traits are also required.[197] The obligations of the applicant are not ended even if he manages to comply with the extensive requirements as to notification in his application. The Secretary of State may require him to supply further information within a prescribed period, and may refuse to determine the application if the applicant fails to comply with the requirement. If the applicant becomes aware of further information which could affect the risk of harm to the environment due to the release or marketing of the organism, and that information is available before the application has been determined, he must notify the Secretary of State.[198]

While the Secretary of State has power to exempt individuals or classes of person **8.179** from the need for consent, he has exercised that power very sparingly. He has exempted persons who were marketing a product which was not an approved product before 1 February 1993 in the UK. In view of the definition of 'approved product', considered above, it is doubtful if this exemption has any effect in practice.[199]

The Secretary of State has wide powers to impose conditions on the grant of **8.180** consent. First, he has a general power to attach such conditions as he thinks fit to

---

[196] Genetically Modified Organisms (Deliberate Release) Regulations 2002, Regs 5 & 2.

[197] Ibid, Part II and Sch 1. The requirements of the Regulations set out in the text are no more than examples, intended to show the scope and range of the information which must be supplied. Recourse must be made to the Regulations themselves before an application is made.

[198] EPA, s 111(6) and (7).

[199] Deliberate Release Regulations 2002, supra, reg 11.

any consent.[200] This formula has been long established under the town and country planning legislation, and has been the subject of extensive judicial comment. Although there has been no judge-made law as yet under the EPA 1990, it is likely that the same tests will be applied to conditions imposed on grants of consent to market or import GMOs as have governed the validity of conditions attached to planning permissions.

8.181 These tests are three in number. First, the condition must advance the purposes of the legislation in which it is contained; it may not be imposed for purposes outside the Act in question. Second, it must fairly and reasonably relate to the permission or consent granted. And, third, it must not be so unreasonable that no reasonable authorizing body could have imposed it.[201]

Notification

8.182 Secondly, and without prejudice to the general power described above, the Secretary of State may require by condition that he shall be given notice of any fact, or he may prohibit or restrict the keeping, releasing, or marketing of any GMO in specified cases or circumstances. Where a condition requires the person enjoying a consent to cease keeping any GMO, he must dispose of it either as required by the condition, or if there is no such requirement, as quickly and safely as practicable.[202]

8.183 Every consent includes implied conditions that the holder shall take all reasonable steps to keep himself informed by reference to all the circumstances as to the risk of harm to the environment arising as a result of the importation or acquisition of the GMO in question; and that he must notify the Secretary of State if at any time it appears that the risks were more serious than appeared to be the case when the consent was granted. It is clear, therefore, that consent holders must keep themselves abreast of developments in the research into and understanding of the GMOs with which they are concerned.

8.184 The holder's responsibilities do not end there. Additional implied conditions require that he must take all reasonable steps to keep himself informed of any damage to the environment caused by his keeping the GMOs or any future damage which may arise if he continues to do so; he must notify the Secretary of State if it ever appears that the risks were more serious than was originally apparent; and must use BATNEEC for keeping the GMOs under control and for preventing damage to the environment if he continues to keep them.

---

[200] EPA, s 112(1).
[201] See, among other authorities, *Newbury DC v SOS* [1981] AC 578. The extensive and subtle jurisprudence which governs the validity of planning conditions can be found in the specialist works on that subject.
[202] EPA, s 112(2).

With appropriate amendments the same burdens are imposed on the holders of **8.185** consents to the release or marketing of GMOs.[203] The duty to keep abreast of scientific progress in the field is reinforced by further implied conditions which require consent holders of all kinds to keep themselves informed of developments in techniques designed to minimize the risks of damage to the environment, and to notify the Secretary of State of any better techniques which may be discovered. This reflects the facts that genetic engineering is a fast developing science, and that relatively little is known about its potential for good or ill.[204]

The EPA 1990 contains nothing which gives a right of appeal against the exercise **8.186** by the Secretary of State of his condition-making powers. The only redress open to the aggrieved consent holder, or to a person refused consent, will therefore, presumably, be to apply for judicial review. As with applications for planning permission, the Secretary of State may make a scheme for charging applicants for consent and the holders of consents. The fees may be sufficient to defray the costs of this discharge of his functions under Part VI of the EPA 1990, but may not exceed those costs.[205]

Policing the control of GMOs

The Secretary of State has power to appoint suitably qualified people to act as **8.187** inspectors for the purpose of carrying Part VI of the EPA 1990 into effect. In practice these inspectors are likely to be members of or attached to the Environment Agency, although no appointments have as yet apparently been made.

The inspectors have powers to enter and inspect premises where they have reason **8.188** to believe that GMOs are kept or have been kept; from which they have reason to believe that GMOs have been released or have escaped; or where they have reason to believe that harmful GMOs may be; or where there is evidence that damage to the environment has been caused by GMOs. The powers are not, however, exercisable in respect of premises used wholly or mainly for domestic purposes (an expression not defined in the Act, and which will have to be applied by the courts by reference to the facts of each case).

The powers extend further than mere entry and inspection. In addition, the **8.189** inspectors may carry out tests; order that all or part of the premises shall be left undisturbed for so long as is reasonably necessary to carry out the tests which may be thought desirable; dismantle and test any equipment or other thing which appears to contain or to have contained GMOs, if necessary to the point of destruction, but not otherwise; seize and retain for the purposes of examining,

---

[203] EPA, s 112(2), (3), (4), and (5).
[204] Ibid, s 112(7).
[205] Ibid, s 113.

preventing interference until the examination has been completed, or eventually producing in evidence in legal proceedings anything which appears to be a GMO, or to contain or include GMOs; and require any person whom they have reasonable cause to believe to be able to provide information to answer questions which the inspectors think fit to ask and later to sign a declaration as to the truth of the answers.

8.190 The safeguards on the exercise of these powers are limited. Equipment may only be dismantled or tested in the presence of a person having responsibilities in respect of premises if that person makes a request to this effect, and after consultation with such persons as the inspector thinks appropriate for the purpose of discovering what dangers, if any, may be involved in the action which he proposes to undertake. This seems to recognize that the inspectors cannot or will not be fully informed about the precise properties of the GMOs with which they will be dealing.

8.191 The power to seize goods or materials can be exercised only if the inspector leaves a notice with particulars of what he has seized with a responsible person at the premises, or displayed in a conspicuous notice fixed there. If part of a batch is seized, the inspector must, if practicable, take a sample, and leave part of the sample with a responsible person at the premises. No answer given in response to a demand for information is admissible in evidence in legal proceedings. It must be inferred that the inspector's power to interrogate is intended to enable him to find out facts rather than assemble evidence against anyone concerned with the use of GMOs. That conclusion is strengthened by the fact that the inspectors have no power to compel the production of documentary material which would be protected by legal professional privilege.[206]

8.192 However, there are other powers which enable inspectors to assemble evidence admissible in legal proceedings. The Secretary of State, who will no doubt act on the advice of and in concert with the inspectors, may give written notice requiring any person, whether he is the holder of a consent or not, and who appears to be involved in importing, acquiring, keeping, release, or marketing of GMOs, to be about to become involved, or to have been involved, to furnish information about any aspect of those activities.[207]

8.193 The Act does not specifically provide that information so supplied shall not be admissible in legal proceedings. Provided therefore, that the requirements of the general law as to admissibility have been met, there seems to be no reason why such information should be inadmissible. Inspectors also have an important residual power, exercisable where they have entered premises and found there anything

---

[206] Ibid, s 115.
[207] Ibid, s 116.

which they have reason to believe to be or include a GMO or GMOs, and which is a cause of imminent danger to the environment. In that event the organism may be seized and rendered harmless either by destruction, or by bringing it under proper control, or otherwise. If it is practicable and safe to do so, the inspector must take a sample of the thing or batch in question, and give a responsible person at the premises a portion of the sample, suitably identified.

Having exercised his powers, the inspector must 'as soon as may be' write a report **8.194** setting out what he did and why, and give one copy to a responsible person at the premises and, unless that person is the owner of the site, serve the owner with another copy of the report. If reasonable enquiries fail to uncover the owner, the responsible person at the premises must be served with the owner's copy.[208]

Sanctions

The EPA 1990 provides that every failure to comply with the requirements of Part **8.195** VI is a criminal offence. So too is the provision of false information when required to give information by an inspector or the Secretary of State, forging a consent, and even falsely pretending to be an inspector. The Act distinguishes between a more serious category of offence, punishable on summary conviction with a fine of up to £20,000 or six months' imprisonment, or both (or an unlimited fine and five years' imprisonment on conviction on indictment), and the less serious, punishable with the statutory maximum fine or six months' imprisonment on summary conviction (or an unlimited fine and two years' imprisonment on conviction on indictment).

The most serious offences are those of using or otherwise dealing with GMOs **8.196** without consent or in breach of the conditions of a consent (contrary to Section 111); failure to carry out risk assessments and to use BATNEEC, contrary to Section 109; and contravention of a prohibition notice served under Section 118.

It is a defence to a charge connected with a consent, or the lack of it, or a prohibi- **8.197** tion notice to show that the defendant took all reasonable precautions and exercised all due diligence to avoid the commission of the offence.[209] Continued failure to carry out a risk assessment after one conviction is a continuing offence carrying a daily financial penalty. The gravity of offences against Part VI of the

---

[208] Ibid, s 117.

[209] If the EPA 1990 is to be construed in the same way as statutes regulating the carriage of goods by sea (an assumption which may prove not to be well founded), then exercising due diligence is for practical purposes the same as taking reasonable care. A principal may be liable vicariously for the negligence of an employee of an independent contractor (see *Riverstone Meat v Lancashire Shipping* [1961] AC 807). However, it would not be surprising if the operator of premises involving GMOs were held liable for the negligence of an independent contractor, given the potential for damage and harm in the event of misuse or accident.

EPA 1990 is emphasized by the provision which restricts prosecutions to cases where the Director of Public Prosecutions has consented to this course.[210]

8.198   Where a defendant faces a charge of failing to use BATNEEC in respect of dealings with a GMO, the burden of proof lies on him to show that there was no better available technique available to him. The burden, by analogy with similar provisions in the Health and Safety at Work Acts, is likely to be held to be to the civil standard of proof, that is, on the balance of probability, rather than beyond reasonable doubt. If a condition in a consent requires an entry to be made in a record to the effect that any other condition has been complied with, and the entry has not been made, this is admissible evidence of the fact that the condition has not been observed.[211]

8.199   The courts are given a relatively unusual power to order a person convicted of an offence connected with risk assessment, a consent or lack of it, or a prohibition notice, to take steps, to be specified in the order, to remedy the consequences of the act or omission leading to the conviction. This power is exercisable in addition to the power to fine or imprison. Lest this should prove ineffective, for whatever reason, the Secretary of State may himself arrange for the remedying of any harm caused by the commission of an offence connected with these matters, and may recover the cost of the steps taken from the convicted person.[212]

GMOs—miscellaneous provisions

8.200   The Secretary of State must keep a register of notices, applications, information supplied to him, consents granted, and convictions under Part VI. The details of these matters which must be recorded are extensive. The register is open to inspection by the public free of charge, and for copying on payment of reasonable charges.

8.201   The register is not to contain information if the Secretary of State considers that this would be contrary to the interests of national security, if inclusion might result in damage to the environment, or if it is commercially confidential. Information falling into the last category will only be excluded if the person supplying it specifically applies for it to be excluded from the register. Even if the application is granted, the privilege conferred lapses after four years, and a fresh application for exclusion has to be made.[213]

GMOs—health and safety at work

8.202   Although they fall outside the scope of this work, persons dealing with GMOs are subject to a separate regulatory code designed to protect employees and others, as

---

[210]   EPA, s 118.
[211]   Ibid, s 119.
[212]   Ibid, ss 120 and 121.
[213]   Ibid, ss 122 and 123.

opposed to the environment at large, from harm caused by the organisms. Regulations made under the Health and Safety at Work Act 1974 require risk assessments and notification of activity similar to those described above. The existence of this system of control should, therefore, not be overlooked.[214]

Containment of GMOs

As their name suggests, the Regulations noted above,[215] are concerned to ensure that GMOs are securely contained during the course of development, research and storage before release to the environment or marketing. The object is to protect humans from risks to health, and to protect the environment from harm.[216] **8.203**

The Health and Safety at Work Act 1974 is extended to cover schools and universities and those attending them.[217] All activity involving genetic modification must be accompanied by a risk assessment, both where micro-organisms and other organisms are involved.[218] The assessment must be reviewed and the results of the review notified to the Secretary of State and the Minister for the Environment, Food and Rural Affairs.[219] **8.204**

When premises are first used for the purposes of genetic modification the operator must notify the Ministers, and can only begin work once the notice has been acknowledged.[220] **8.205**

The risks to be identified are grouped into four classes, from no or negligible risk (Class 1) to high (Class 4). All activity involving risk in Classes 1 and 2 must be notified before work begins, and emergency plans prepared.[221] **8.206**

The Ministers and their Scottish equivalents are required to examine all notifications and to ensure that they comply with the Regulations.[222] They must keep a register of notifications, excluding material which affects national security. [223] The Health and Safety Executive has power to request additional information from applicants and to embargo the proposed activity until that information is provided.[224] **8.207**

---

[214] For the details, see the Genetically Modified Organisms (Contained Use) Regulations 2000, SI 2000/2831.
[215] See n 189.
[216] Regulation 3.
[217] Regulations 4 and 5.
[218] Regulations 6and7.
[219] Regulation 8.
[220] Regulation 9.
[221] Regulations 10 and 11.
[222] Regulation 14.
[223] Regulations 24 and 24A.
[224] Regulation 14(3) and (4).

8.208   Operators must appoint safety committees and must also isolate buildings where necessary with airlocks, negative air pressure systems, and disinfectant, depending on the level of risk.[225] Emergency plans must be drawn up, and any accidents reported to the Ministers.[226]

8.209   There are rights of appeal against refusal to allow proposed activities; against requirements to provide containment measures to which the applicant takes exception; and against similar instructions issued by the Ministers. However, appeal is to the Secretary of State, meaning, since he is a constituent of the competent authority, that the prospects of success on appeal are likely to be limited.[227]

Release and marketing of GMOs

8.210   Some provisions of the Genetically Modified Organisms (Deliberate Release) Regulations 2002[228] have been noted above. Additionally, the Regulations establish a system regulating the release and marketing of GMOs by factories, laboratories, universities, and schools and apply when these establishments create or use them.[229]

8.211   Likewise, the duties of operators, teachers, and researchers are much the same as those imposed by the Contained Use Regulations 2000, discussed above. It is therefore not necessary to rehearse them in detail.

Traceability and labelling of GMOs

8.212   The European Commission has laid down rules which govern the labelling and tracking of GMOs.[230] The Genetically Modified Organisms (Traceability and Labelling) Regulations 2004 incorporate these rules into English law.[231]

8.213   Incorrect labelling of products containing GMOs, misuse of such products, failure to keep and transmit accurate information about them, and to keep proper records are all prohibited.[232] Local and port authorities are charged with the duty of enforcing compliance with the Regulations.[233] They may appoint inspectors with powers of entry.[234] They may also demand information about the content of products containing GMOs which are placed on the market.[235]

---

[225] Regulation 16; Schedule 8.
[226] Regulations 20 and 21.
[227] Regulation 29.
[228] SI 2002/2443.
[229] Regulation 14.
[230] Regulation (EC) No. 1830/2003(3).
[231] SI 2004/2412.
[232] Schedule to the Regulations.
[233] Regulation 3.
[234] Regulations 4 and 5.
[235] Regulation 6.

9

WATER RESOURCES

A. **Water Resources—An Introduction** 9.01
  The main Acts 9.01
  European law 9.04
  The public authorities 9.06
  The Environment Agency and its
    duties and powers 9.07
    The Agency's relationship with
      the water industry 9.12
B. **Water Resources Management** 9.15
  The strategic policy framework 9.15
    Water Framework Directive 9.16
  River Basin Management Plans 9.18
    The potential to set minimum
      acceptable flows 9.21
  Groundwater 9.22
    Oil Storage 9.25
    Nitrate vulnerability zones 9.28
  Abstraction licensing 9.32
    The requirement for an abstraction
      licence 9.33
    General exemption for
      small quantities 9.34
    Potential enforcement and offences 9.35
    Restriction on who can apply for an
      abstraction licence 9.37
    Types of abstraction licence 9.38
    The application process for an
      abstraction licence 9.41
    The Secretary of State's role in
      abstraction licencing 9.45
    Appeals regarding an abstraction
      licence 9.46
    The contents of an abstraction
      licence 9.47
    Other abstraction licence exemptions 9.49
  Damage from abstraction 9.50
  Impounding licences 9.51
  Modification and revocation of licences 9.55

  Agency proposals to revoke or modify 9.56
  Modifications on the application
    of the owner of fishing rights 9.57
  Water rights trading 9.59
    Charges for licences 9.60
    Compensation provisions 9.61
C. **Drought** 9.62
  Ordinary drought order 9.63
  Emergency drought order 9.67
    Restricting the use of water 9.69
    Effect on Inland Navigations 9.70
    Power to carry out works 9.71
    Compensation 9.72
  Drought Permits 9.73
  Offences 9.76
  Drought Plans 9.77
D. **Control of Pollution of**
   Water Resources 9.78
  Water quality 9.78
  Water pollution offences 9.81
    The common elements of
      Section 85 offences 9.87
    Controlled waters 9.89
    Causing or knowingly permitting—
      acts and omissions 9.90
  Causing 9.93
  Liability due to an act or default 9.98
    Poisonous, noxious, or
      polluting matter 9.100
    Waste matter 9.102
    Trade effluent or sewage effluent 9.103
    Entry or discharge 9.106
    A prohibition imposed under
      Section 86 9.107
  Statutory defences 9.108
    Discharge consents 9.109
    Emergency 9.115
    Vessels 9.119

Crown immunity	9.120	Riparian owners	9.132
Highway authorities	9.121	Regional flood defence	
Abandoned mines	9.122	committees	9.133
Anti-pollution works notices	9.125	Internal drainage boards	9.134
E. Land Drainage and Flood Control	9.128	Drainage powers	9.137
Introduction	9.128	Standards of flood defence	9.143
Flood controls	9.129	Financial provisions	9.144

A. Water Resources—An Introduction

The main Acts

9.01 The Water Resources Act 1991 and the Water Industry Act 1991 contain the main regulatory powers over the supply of water and its protection. These Acts have consolidated all the legislation covering water pollution which had previously been spread over about 20 Acts.[1] These regimes heavily regulate an individual's common law rights and responsibilities in this area.[2]

9.02 This chapter focuses on 'controlled waters'. This is defined as including all territorial waters, estuaries, rivers, streams, and groundwater, and those lakes and ponds which discharge into a watercourse.[3] In addition to the general duty to maintain and improve water quality, the Environment Agency has the power to licence water abstraction and impoundment, control water in times of drought, and to control discharges into controlled waters. The discharge consents deal only with the point of discharge, and do not regulate the whole process. The offences under Section 85 of the Water Resources Act 1991 for causing or knowingly permitting water pollution have proved to be an effective weapon. There have been some high-profile cases, which are of wide application.

9.03 The Water Resources Act 1991 and the Water Industry Act 1991 also mark an important division of responsibilities. After the privatization of the water industry in 1989, the control of rivers was separated from the water and sewerage services. This latter area is now covered by the Water Industry Act 1991, and is therefore discussed separately in the following chapter. The privatized water companies act

---

[1] The Water Act 1989 had only amended Part II of the Control of Pollution Act 1974 which had brought together the river pollution Acts: the Public Health Acts of 1848 and 1875, which controlled the supply of water and the provision of sewers, and the Rivers Pollution Prevention Act 1876.

[2] A good overview of the common law in this area is *Wisdom's Law of Watercourses* (now in its 5th edition, authored by William Howarth, March 1992, Shaw & Sons Ltd). Although it is now out of date in terms of the regulatory developments in this area, much of the common law on water and riparian rights does indeed have well-established and deep roots. For a detailed explanation of the convoluted English legal history of water and riparian rights, see Getzler, *A History of Water Rights at Common Law* (OUP, 2004).

[3] S 104 of the Water Resources Act 1991 (WRA 1991).

as statutory undertakers, with certain statutory powers and duties, to provide the water supplies. Although the same company may be involved, there is a separate set of statutory bodies who are appointed as the sewerage undertakers, responsible for the sewers and sewerage treatment systems. While there is a general right to communicate with public sewers to discharge foul water and surface water, the occupier of any trade premises needs a consent from the sewerage undertaker to discharge trade effluent to a sewer. As a result, most discharges are made to the sewers, connected to treatment works, and only then to controlled waters.

European law

The laws emanating from the European Union have played a major part in recent   **9.04** developments on improving the quality of water. The EC produced its first main Directive on water pollution in 1976 (76/464/EEC)[4], which sets out the substances which are considered harmful to water, and various subsidiary directives have been produced.[5] The EC has led the way on protecting Groundwater (Directive 80/68/EEC), setting quality standards for Bathing Water (Directive 76/160/EEC), Drinking Water (Directives 75/440/EEC and 80/778/EEC), Freshwater Fish (Directive 78/659/EEC) and Shellfish (Directive 79/923/EEC), Urban Wastewater Treatment (Directive 91/271/EEC), and Nitrate Pollution (Directive 91/676/EEC).

These controls have now been brought together in the *Water Framework Directive*   **9.05** (2000/60/EC). This will require significant changes over the next 15 years to European law, including replacing many of the old directives. Its main aims are to prevent further deterioration of water resources, protect and enhance aquatic eco-systems and wetlands, promote sustainable development, and mitigate the effect of floods and droughts. These changes will also find their way through to UK law. The UK was required to transpose the Water Framework Directive by December 2003, and this was done by the Water Environment (Water Framework Directive) (England and Wales) Regulations 2003. The detailed controls will start

---

[4] This Directive became known as a 'framework' Directive, although its official title is Council Directive of 4 May 1976 on pollution caused by certain dangerous substances discharged into the aquatic environment of the Community (76/464/EEC). Its objective was to regulate potential aquatic pollution by the thousands of chemicals already produced in Europe at that time, and it initially included controls over discharges to groundwater as well (which then became covered by a specific directive). The 'candidate list I' set out in the Commission's Communication dated 22 June 1982 under Art. 6 of 76/464/EEC has already been replaced by the 'List of priority substances' in 2000/60/EC (see Art. 22).

[5] Five directives were made, based on Article 6 of Directive 76/464/EEC, in order to set specific emission limit values and quality objectives for 18 of the List 1 substances—they were also referred to as 'daughter' directives. They include controls on discharges of mercury, cadmium, and hexachlorocyclohexane. It is intended to replace them with a single 'daughter' Directive to the Water Framework Directive.

from about 2009. The aim is to achieve 'good status' for all inland and coastal waters by 2015. River Basin Management Plans will be mandatory.

The public authorities

9.06 There are close links between the public bodies that are responsible for water resources. Defra is responsible for water policy in England, not only for matters relating to its supply and resources, but also in relation to the regulatory systems for the water environment and the water industry. These include the policies for drinking water quality, the quality of water in rivers, lakes, estuaries, coastal and marine waters, sewage treatment, and for reservoir safety.[6] The Welsh Assembly Government carries out the same functions in Wales. These are the main sponsoring departments for the Environment Agency, which is responsible for local control and enforcement regarding the maintenance of water quality, water resources, and flood defence in England and Wales. The Drinking Water Inspectorate regulates the quality of drinking water,[7] and Ofwat (the Water Services Regulation Authority)[8] is responsible for the economic regulation of the water industry. Water UK is the representative trade body for all of the UK water and wastewater service suppliers.[9] The Water Industry is discussed further in the following chapter. There is also an independent Consumer Council for Water which represents consumers and can assist in sorting out complaints.[10]

The Environment Agency and its duties and powers

9.07 The main guardian of our rivers and waterways since 1 April 1996[11] has been the Environment Agency or, in Welsh, *Asiantaeth yr Amgylchedd*. The functions of the National Rivers Authority (NRA) under the Water Resources Act 1991 and the Land Drainage Act 1991 were taken over by the Agency as part of the move to an integrated system of environmental regulation that was the cornerstone of the Environment Act 1995.

---

[6] See the Defra website further, <http://www.defra.gov.uk>. As discussed in Chapter 2, Defra was created in 2001, and combines Environment Food and Rural Affairs.

[7] DWI investigates all drinking water quality incidents in England and Wales, and since the Water Act 2003 it can take forward prosecutions in the name of the Chief Inspector of Drinking Water. DWI remains part of Defra. See <http://www.dwi.gov.uk> further.

[8] See <www.ofwat.gov.uk> further. The name of 'Ofwat' has remained unchanged, from the days when the Director General of Water Services was responsible for this role under the Water Industry Act 1991. His functions were transferred to the new authority on 1 April 2006, under the provisions of the Water Act 2003.

[9] Water UK (<http://www.water.org.uk>) represents the trade at national and European level.

[10] Set up under s 27A of the WRA 1991 (as inserted by the Water Act 2003). It started work in 2005, and replaced the Customer Service Committees and the Ofwat National Consumer Council (which was known as 'WaterVoice'). See <http://www.ccwater.org.uk.>

[11] Environment Act 1995 ('EA 1995'), s 2 and s 56, which establishes the 'transfer date'.

The general powers and duties of the Agency and the duty to take into account the **9.08** likely costs and benefits have been discussed in Chapter 2. In addition to the principal aim of the Agency with regard to the promotion of sustainable development,[12] the Agency has the express duty generally to promote the conservation and enhancement of the natural beauty and amenity of inland and coastal waters and of land associated with such waters, the conservation of flora and fauna which are dependent on the aquatic environment, and the use of such waters and land for recreational purposes.[13] The Agency need only carry out that duty, however, 'to such extent as it considers desirable',[14] although the discretion so left to it should presumably be exercised consistently with its principal aim and objectives.

The pollution control powers and functions that the Agency took over from the **9.09** NRA[15] are to be exercisable for the purpose of preventing or minimizing or remedying or mitigating the effects of pollution of the environment.[16] The Agency is also charged with the more specific duties of:

(1) taking such steps as it may consider necessary or expedient for conserving, redistributing, or otherwise augmenting water resources in England and Wales and of securing the proper use of those resources;[17]

(2) exercising a general supervision over all matters relating to flood defence;[18] and

(3) maintaining, improving, and developing salmon fisheries, trout fisheries, freshwater fisheries and eel fisheries.[19]

Such duties are to be exercised within territorial limits which ensure no overlap **9.10** with the relevant Scottish authorities. These duties with respect to water are also expressly subject to the general environmental and recreational duties of the Agency set out in Section 7 of the EA 1995, and to the biodiversity duty.

There are two Codes that are relevant to the Agency's powers under the Water **9.11** Resources Act 1991. The Code of Good Agricultural Practice for the Protection of Water, also known as 'The Water Code Revised 1998' [20] is relevant to farmers

---

[12] EA 1995, s 4. See Chapter 2 further. The aim is to protect or enhance the environment taken as a whole as to make the contribution towards attaining the objective of achieving sustainable development which the Government thinks it should make, which is set out in the Statutory Guidance to the Agency.

[13] EA 1995, s 6.

[14] EA 1995, s 6(1).

[15] EA 1995, s 5(5) and see WRA 1991, ss 161–161D Part III.

[16] EA 1995, s 5(1).

[17] Ibid, s 6(2). See further below on the relationship with the water industry.

[18] Ibid, s 6(4). See further below.

[19] Ibid, s 6(6).

[20] It was approved by the Water (Prevention of Pollution) (Code of Practice) Order 1998 (SI 1998/3084), and was issued by the Minister of Agriculture, Fisheries and Food and the Secretary of State for Wales.

and seeks to promote practices to avoid or minimize pollution. The Agency is required to take into account whether there has been, or is likely to be, any contravention of an approved code of practice in determining whether to impose a prohibition on a discharge consent[21] or to use any powers which may be conferred on it by regulations under Section 92 of the WRA 1991. The Water and Sewerage (Conservation, Access and Recreation) Code of Practice[22] gives practical guidance to water and sewerage undertakers and the Agency relating to their environmental and recreational duties under the Water Industry Act 1991.

The Agency's relationship with the water industry

9.12 When carrying out any of its functions the Agency is under a duty to have particular regard to the duties imposed by the Water Industry Act 1991 on any water undertaker or sewerage undertaker likely to be affected by the exercise of the power in question.[23] So the Agency has to bear in mind the implications of its decisions and actions for water supply and sewage treatment but ultimately the Agency's other aims, objectives, and duties, for example, in relation to the protection of the environment, may have to take precedence. Ministers have to take account of this duty on the Agency when exercising their powers in relation to the environment and particularly the water environment.[24]

9.13 One important manifestation of this duty to have regard to the needs of the water and sewerage undertakers is that the Agency, when making its decisions on any related discharges or consents, must take account of the costs that have to be incurred by the water undertakers. The Agency may not be able to require improvements to be made as quickly as might otherwise be required. The investment and price limits are set by Ofwat, and these reflect the assumptions that have to be made about what the companies need to spend to meet their capital expenditure programmes and to finance their operations.[25] While Ofwat is responsible for setting price limits, the Government determines the policies that may affect the factors that they use to determine the price limits, and the Agency is only a consultee in this process. Defra's contribution to each periodic Price Review includes a Statement of Obligations to water and sewerage

---

[21] These powers are given under WRA 1991, s 86(1).

[22] It was approved by the Water and Sewerage (Conservation, Access and Recreation) (Code of Practice) Order 2000 (SI 2000/477). There was a similar code for the NRA dating from 1989.

[23] WRA 1991, s 15(1).

[24] Ibid, s 15(2).

[25] The 2004 periodic review (PR08) started officially on 15 October 2002 and ended in December 2004 when OFWAT set price limits for the period 2005–2009. The periodic review (PR09) was launched by Ofwat in 2007 and will end in November 2009, when Ofwat will set the price limits for 2010–2015.

undertakers,[26] and the statutory Social and Environmental Guidance to Ofwat. The Guidance sets out the key areas of social and environmental policy to which the Government expects Ofwat to contribute to. As required under the Water Industry Act 1991 (as amended by the Water Act 2003), the revised draft Guidance has to be laid before Parliament.[27] Welsh Ministers issue separate statutory Guidance in respect of Ofwat's activities in appointment areas wholly or mainly in Wales. Ofwat will take these into account when it reviews the water undertakers' business plans and assesses their future revenue needs.

The Water Act 2003 does require the water companies to further water conserva- **9.14** tion.[28] They must also develop and publish water resources management plans and drought plans.[29] This is in addition to the obligation on the water undertakers to develop water resources for the purpose of performing their general duty to develop and maintain an efficient and economical water supply in their areas and to ensure that all such arrangements have been made for providing supplies of water to premises and for making water supplies available to people who want them.[30] The Agency is also under a duty to take all such action as it may from time to time consider to be necessary or expedient for the purpose of conserving, redistributing, or otherwise augmenting water resources in England and Wales and of securing the proper use of those resources.[31] One way the Agency can carry out its duty is to enter into arrangements with water undertakers to secure the proper management or operation of those waters, reservoirs, and works that the undertakers use to carry out their obligations to maintain water supplies. The undertaker's obligations under such an arrangement can be enforced by the Secretary of State by use of enforcement orders under Section 18 of the Water Industry Act 1991.

---

[26] The Statement of Obligations (21 December 2007) is in effect a checklist of the statutory obligations which apply to the water industry. It is organized into chapters on climate change, supply–demand balance and water resources, drinking water quality, the water environment, and other miscellaneous provisions.

[27] The draft Statutory Social and Environmental Guidance to Ofwat was issued for consultation on 7 February 2008 (which ended in June 2008), and was then laid before Parliament.

[28] WIA 1991, s 3(2)(a), as amended by the Water Act 2003, s 82; the duty has not been extended beyond the water industry. In the case of public bodies, they must only 'consider' how to conserve water supplied to their premises, Water Act 2003, s 83. Central government must take steps to encourage the conservation of water, and is then responsible for monitoring and reporting on the progress made in this area (s 81).

[29] WIA 1991, ss 37A to 37D and ss 39B and 39C (as inserted by the Water Act 2003, s 62–64).

[30] Water Industry Act 1991, s 37, and EA 1995, s 6(2).

[31] EA 1995, s 6(2).

B. Water Resources Management

The strategic policy framework

9.15   The legal and policy framework for managing water in England and Wales is being re-assessed. A new water strategy for England, *Future Water*, was launched by Defra in 2008.[32] In Wales, it is dealt with as part of the national Environment Strategy.[33] The government has acknowledged that securing and maintaining water supplies is vital to the prosperity of the country and to the health of people and the environment.[34] It has taken the view that, in some areas, current supplies are already unsustainable and this situation was exacerbated by the drought in South East England between 2004 and 2006. These pressures are also going to get worse as the climate changes, the economy grows, and population increases. It considered that, combined with the need to reduce CO2 emissions from the water industry and from the use of hot water in homes, this means that the UK must find ways of improving efficiency, and of reducing demand and wastage. The emphasis therefore in *Future Water* is on the sustainable delivery of secure water supplies, an improved and protected water environment, fair, affordable and cost-reflective water charges, reduced greenhouse gas emissions from the water sector, and a more sustainable and effective management of surface water.

Water Framework Directive

9.16   The Water Framework Directive ('WFD')[35] represents the most substantial piece of EU water legislation to date and is the result of about 18 years of discussion and debate[36]. It came into force on 22 December 2000, and was transposed into UK law in January 2004 (the 'WFD Regulations').[37] The essential aim is that the UK,

---

[32] *Future Water*, Defra, 7 February 2008.

[33] The *Environment Strategy for Wales*, published on 17 May 2006.

[34] See the Ministerial statement made by the Secretary of State when launching the national strategy, *Future Water*, 7 February 2008.

[35] The 'Directive 2000/60/EC of the European Parliament and of the Council establishing a framework for the Community action in the field of water policy', which is commonly referred to as the Water Framework Directive (or, even shorter as 'WFD') even in the European Union. It was adopted on 23 October 2000.

[36] The need for comprehensive water legislation was identified by the European Council in 1988. It then took nearly ten years before the European Commission could finally publish its first proposals in February 1997, and this was then followed by a complicated decision-making process under the 'co-decision' procedures between the European Parliament and the European Council.

[37] The Water Environment (Water Framework Directive) (England and Wales) Regulations 2003 (SI 2003/3242), which came into force on 2 January 2004. These Regulations were made jointly with the National Assembly for Wales. Separate provision has had to be made in the north-west of England, as the Northumbria River Basin District includes a small part of Scotland (for Northumbrians, and for those who collect curios, see The Water Environment (Water Framework Directive) (Northumbria River Basin District) Regulations 2003.

like the other Member States, must aim to reach 'good'[38] chemical and ecological status in their rivers, lakes, estuaries, coastal waters, and groundwaters by 2015. This will require the promotion of the sustainable use of water, a reduction of pollution of water, especially by any 'priority' and 'priority hazardous' substances, and the continuing reduction of groundwater pollution. A 'priority list' of substances posing a threat to or via the aquatic environment has already been established at the European level as part of the WFD.[39] This list includes the 'priority hazardous' substances which are considered to pose the greatest threat. While considerable research and analysis is still required to establish the quality objectives under the WFD,[40] it does mark a further step away from the traditional reactive approach to water pollution problems.

The WFD also sets out requirements for the European Commission to propose **9.17**
further Directives to protect against water pollution, in the form of 'daughter directives'. The Groundwater Directive (2006/118/EC) is the first of these to be adopted, and a further 'daughter directive' has been proposed in relation to the pollution of surface water by pollutants on a list of priority substances.[41]

River Basin Management Plans

The WFD Regulations require the creation of a formal strategic planning pro- **9.18**
cess for the purposes of managing, protecting, and improving the quality of water resources. This has to be done for each river basin district.[42] It is intended that

---

[38] There are five categories in the WFD: high, good, moderate, poor, and bad (Annex V). 'High status' is defined as the biological, chemical, and morphological conditions associated with no or very low human pressure. It is the 'reference condition', by which the other categories are assessed— 'Good status' means 'slight' deviation from this, 'moderate status' means 'moderate' deviation, etc.

[39] There are currently 33 substances on this priority list, which was agreed in 2001 (under Decision 2455/2001/EC). It is likely that the list will be reviewed regularly.

[40] For substantial reservations about the criteria adopted by the WFD and the underlying basis for any ecological valuation, see William Howarth, 'The Progression Towards Ecological Quality Standards' [2005] 18 JEL 3. In particular, as he says, the criterion used for high-status ecosystems generate counter-intuitive consequences when applied in the context of an extensively developed country such as the UK. In particular, the ambiguity of the concept of 'naturalness' and the degree of symbiosis between human and non-human components of ecosystems seem to be neglected or underestimated. These criteria are now, however, the current legal requirements.

[41] A European Commission proposal for a 'daughter' Directive on the priority substances was published in July 2006 (COM(2006)397 final). It includes environmental quality standards for the concentrations of the 33 priority substances (and eight other pollutants) in surface water bodies. The proposal is also being promoted as part of the Commission's Better Regulation initiative, as it would replace five of the old 'daughter' directives (which supplemented Directive 76/464/EEC).

[42] These districts and their boundaries are identified by Regulation 4 of the WFD Regulations 2003. The general responsibility for ensuring that the WFD is given effect remains with central government, although much of the work is being done by the Agency. This means the Secretary of State in relation to river basin districts in England, and the National Assembly for Wales in relation to such districts in Wales, and both of them together in relation to such districts that are partly in England and partly in Wales.

there will be a River Basin Management Plan ('RBMP'), which will establish the environmental objectives and programmes of improvement measures for each district.[43] The draft Plan will be subject to public consultation, as well as the approval by central government, before it is adopted by the Agency. The Agency also has the power to prepare supplementary plans, for specific areas or types of water in the district, and these do not require the approval by central government.[44]

9.19 The importance of these RBMPs is not to be underestimated. The Secretary of State, the Welsh Assembly, the Agency, and other public bodies are then required to have regard to the River Basin Management Plan, and to any supplementary plans, in exercising their functions in relation to the river basin district.[45] Once they are adopted, these documents will set the agenda for the foreseeable future, and the draft versions will gather increasing weight as material considerations as their adoption process progresses. At the moment there are only generic environmental objectives set out in the WFD in each district, and these will be given further precision at the national level. In particular, further to the generic European definition of ecological status,[46] the RBMP will set out what is considered to be 'good ecological status' for that district which the Directive itself does not seek to define. The RBMP must also include the information specified in the relevant provisions of the Directive, including on full cost recovery for water services.[47]

9.20 The initial stages of preparing the RBMP have required the Agency to carry out detailed analysis of the characteristics of each river basin district and to conduct a review of the impact of human activity on the status of surface water and groundwater in each of the river basin districts.[48] The Agency must also monitor the status of water quality and prepare and maintain a register of the 'protected areas'

---

[43] WFD Regulations 2003, regs 10–15. The plan will detail how the ecological status, quantitative status, chemical status, and protected area objectives are to be reached within the required timescale.

[44] Reg 16; there must still be public consultation on any supplementary plan.

[45] Reg17; the WFD Regulations contain a specific list of relevant legislation, ranging from the general (such as the Environment Act 1995, and the European Communities Act 1972) to the specific (Salmon and Freshwater Fisheries Act 1975, Part 2A of the Environmental Protection Act 1990 etc).

[46] 'Ecological status' is defined as 'an expression of the quality of the structure and functioning of aquatic ecosystems associated with surface waters, classified in accordance with Annex V [of the WFD]' (reg 2(2) of the 2003 Regulations, which repeats the definition in the WFD).

[47] The relevant provisions of the WFD are Article 9(2) and (4) (recovery of the costs of water services), Annex II, point 1.3(vi) (exclusion of elements from the assessment of ecological status), Annex V points 1.3 and 1.3.4 (confidence and precision in monitoring surface water), point 2.4.1 (confidence and precision in monitoring groundwater) and points 2.4.5 and 2.5 (presentation of monitoring results for groundwater), and Annex VII, Part A (elements to be covered in river basin management plans).

[48] Reg 5 of the 2003 Regulations; this is in accordance with Annex II to the Directive regarding the characterization, etc of waters. This first had to be done by 22 December 2004, and the results

for each river basin district[49]—which includes drinking water reservoirs, any areas of water identified or designated for the conservation of habitats or species directly depending on water, or for the protection of economically-significant aquatic species, designated recreational bodies of water, and Nitrate Vulnerable Zones ('NVZs'). The central government departments have carried out an economic analysis.[50] The Agency must by such date as central government may direct prepare and submit to them a river basin management plan for each river basin district.[51] Whilst there is a phased introduction for the plans, they must all be published by 22 December 2009, and then reviewed every six years thereafter.

The potential to set minimum acceptable flows

The Agency has the power to submit to the Secretary of State for his approval a **9.21** statement which provides for the 'minimum acceptable flow' for any particular inland waters.[52] That flow is determined by the Agency's view of the minimum flow needed for safeguarding public health and for meeting (in respect of both quantity and quality) the water requirements of agriculture, industry, water supply, navigation, fisheries, and land drainage from those and any other waters affected. The statement has to set out how the flow is to be measured. The Agency must consult widely with interested parties before it prepares the statement in relation to any particular waters. The difficulty of reconciling all these concerns probably explains why these provisions have never been used, although the Agency does look at what is an acceptable remaining flow further down river whenever they grant a licence allowing the abstraction of water from a source.

Groundwater

The Groundwater Regulations 1998[53] were introduced by the UK to implement **9.22** the requirements of the Groundwater Directive (80/68/EEC). This aims to protect groundwater from pollution by controlling discharges and disposals of certain dangerous substances to groundwater. The Groundwater Directive is to be repealed by the Water Framework Directive in 2013. There will be amended regulations produced by the UK before then in order to implement both the Water Framework

---

must be periodically reviewed and updated (initially by 22 December 2013 and thereafter every six years). An economic review is also required (reg 6).

[49] Reg 8 of the 2003 Regulations. The first deadline for this was 22 December 2004. The 'protected areas' are also defined here.

[50] Reg 6.

[51] Reg 11 of the 2003 Regulations.

[52] WRA 1991, s 21.

[53] SI 1998/2746; they supplement the Waste Management Licensing Regulations 1994 reg 15 and existing water pollution legislation.

Directive and its 'daughter' Directive on the protection of groundwater.[54] This new
Groundwater Directive (2006/118/EC) is itself commonly referred to as the
'Groundwater Daughter Directive'. The Groundwater Daughter Directive must
be transposed by 2009,[55] and its requirements will therefore apply alongside the
1980 Groundwater Directive until December 2013. The objective under the WFD
for groundwater is to meet 'good chemical status' by 2015, and to prevent or limit
the input of pollutants to groundwater. As the Groundwater Daughter Directive
was adopted later than was expected under the agreed WFD timetable, the Secretary
of State and National Assembly for Wales have used their powers to direct the
Agency to identify interim criteria for what constitutes 'good groundwater status'
and 'trend identification and reversal'.[56]

9.23   At the moment, the Groundwater Regulations 1998 only apply to certain listed
substances, and the intention is to prevent the direct or indirect discharge of list
I substances into groundwater and to control pollution resulting from the direct
or indirect discharge of list II substances.[57] The Regulations exclude radioactive
substances, domestic effluent from isolated dwellings, small quantities and concentrations of list I or II substances, and activities for which a waste management
licence is required.[58] These restrictions on listed substances will be expanded
by the provisions that will be made under the Groundwater Daughter Directive,
so that all substances that are liable to cause pollution are covered. This would
include, for example, nitrates. At the moment, the listed substances are divided
into two lists:

• List 1 substances: these are the most toxic substances, and must be prevented
  from entering groundwater. They can be disposed of in the ground, under a
  permit, but they must not reach the groundwater. These include pesticides,
  sheep dip, solvents, hydrocarbons, mercury, cadmium, and cyanide.

• List 2 substances: these are the less dangerous substances. While they can be
  discharged to groundwater under a permit, they must not cause any pollution.
  This will affect the discharge of sewage, trade effluent, and most wastes.

---

[54] Consultation on the necessary amendments to the Groundwater Regulations was carried out
in May 2008.
[55] The UK has until January 2009 to transpose the Directive, and the consultation documents
regarding this were published in May 2008. The Directive GwD fulfils the requirement of the WFD
for 'measures to prevent and control groundwater pollution' (Art.17). In particular, it includes
criteria for assessing good groundwater chemical status, for identifying pollution trends, and for
establishing starting points for trend reversal.
[56] The Groundwater (Water Framework Directive) Direction 2006, for the implementation of Article 17(4) of Directive 2000/60/EC. It was made under their powers in s 40(2) of the
Environment Act 1995, in March 2006. These criteria will then be applied through the amended
Regulations.
[57] Regulations 3 to 13.
[58] Regulation 2.

Substances in this list include some heavy metals and ammonia (which is present in sewage effluent), phosphorus and its compounds.

The Agency has published maps of the groundwater protection zones which it will rely upon when it is consulted on any proposal. The protection of groundwater, especially freshwater aquifers, from potential sources of pollution is an important planning consideration.

9.24

Oil Storage

The Groundwater Regulations 1998 contain powers to control underground tanks, including those used to store oil. Separate regulations have also now been introduced in England to control the installation and maintenance of above-ground oil tanks (hereafter the 'Oil Storage Regulations').[59] There are currently no similar regulations for Wales.[60] The Oil Storage Regulations cover all types of oil, except waste mineral oil,[61] and apply to the storage of more than 200 litres of oil,[62] or 3,500 litres in the case of domestic premises.[63] There is no definition of what constitutes a tank that is 'in-use', or of what constitutes 'storage', within the Oil Storage Regulations. For the purposes of these Regulations, the Environment Agency has stated that it will look at site specific details; consider the risk on site; and check what measures are being taken to help reduce potential incidents.[64] The Oil Storage Regulations do not apply to the storage of any oil on farms if the oil is for use in connection with agriculture within the meaning of the Agriculture Act 1947. There are, however, separate regulations[65] that cover the storage of oil used for heating or power on agricultural premises such as those

9.25

---

[59] The Control of Pollution (Oil Storage)(England) Regulations 2001.

[60] By contrast, in Scotland the Water Environment (Oil Storage) (Scotland) Regulations 2006 apply. These Scottish regulations impose different requirements to the England regulations. There are currently no similar regulations for Northern Ireland.

[61] So it would include petrol, diesel, bio-diesel, vegetable (new and waste), synthetic and mineral oils. Waste mineral oil is covered by the Waste Management Licensing Regulations. In the case of flammable liquids, such as petrol, additional health and safety requirements may also apply. The actual storage of the petroleum itself is controlled by the Petroleum (Consolidation) Act 1928 (as amended), and a licence is needed from the petroleum licensing authority (usually the Fire Service or County Council Trading Standards Department).

[62] The regulations cover the size of container. As the Agency's FAQs states, sites with an oil tank of 1,000 litres capacity that only ever has 199 litres of oil stored would have to comply.

[63] An exemption is provided for oil which is used for domestic premises, where the oil storage container has a capacity of 3,500 litres or less. But the Building Regulations (Approved Document J) will apply to all new or replacement oil storage tanks regardless of their capacity.

[64] See the Agency's website for *Frequently Asked Questions on the Control of Pollution (Oil Storage) (England) 2001'* (as updated March 2007).

[65] The Silage, Slurry and Agricultural Fuel Oil Regulations 1991 ('SSAFO').

used for horticulture, fruit growing, seed growing, market gardens, and nursery grounds. Crown land is essentially exempt from them[66].

9.26   The Oil Storage Regulations applied to the construction of all new tanks from 1 March 2003, and have been phased in with respect to existing oil tanks.[67] The main requirement is that oil shall be stored in a container which is of sufficient strength and structural integrity to ensure that it is unlikely to burst or leak in its ordinary use, and that the container must be situated within a secondary containment system.[68] There are no legal requirements for maintenance within the Oil Storage Regulations.[69]

9.27   The Agency will in most cases seek voluntary compliance with these regulations, or serve an Anti-Pollution Works Notice, requiring that the storage facilities are brought up to the required standards. It is a summary offence to fail to comply, with a fine of up to £5,000. It is a standard Agency condition on any licence, permit or authorization that any oil stores on a site should comply with the Oil Storage Regulations, although sometimes more stringent measures may be required under the relevant regime.

Nitrate vulnerability zones

9.28   The designation of areas as Nitrate Vulnerable Zones (or NVZs) has been as a direct result of European Union legislation. The EC Nitrates Directive (91/676/EEC) aims to reduce nitrate pollution from agriculture and to prevent further pollution arising. It requires Member States to establish an Action Programme of control measures designed to reduce nitrate loss from agricultural practices and to apply it throughout the country or in designated areas which are vulnerable to nitrate pollution. These controls, and the general control over water pollution, are the only means available to control nutrient pollution, particularly as the European Court of Justice has held that slurry does not come within the legal definition of waste.[70]

9.29   The first attempt of the government to designate NVZs was heavily criticized as it limited to them to about 8% of the land area of England and Wales, as it only

---

[66] The Agency can serve a notice requiring improvements on Crown land, and WRA 1991, s 222(2) allows the Agency to seek a declaration in the High Court when a Crown body commits an offence.

[67] The controls applied in 2003 for those tanks at 'significant risk', and in 2005 for all tanks.

[68] Reg. 2; the secondary containment system must have a capacity of not less than 110% of the container's storage capacity or, if there is more than one container within the system, of not less than 110% of the largest container's storage capacity or 25% of their aggregate storage capacity, whichever is the greater. Reg 3 places further requirements on fixed tanks, and Reg 4 on mobile bowsers.

[69] However there is guidance in Pollution Prevention Guidance Note 2, Above Ground Oil Storage.

[70] *Commission of the European Communities v Kingdom of Spain, Intervener: United Kingdom* Case C-416/02, [2005] ECR I-7487 (arising for a dispute about a cattle farm).

designated NVZs for the protection of drinking water sources, rather than for all surface and ground waters.[71] This led to infraction proceedings and the UK losing a case in the European Court of Justice on this failure to implement the Directive.[72]

As a result of this, further areas were designated as NVZs in October 2002[73] which now cover about 55% of England and Wales.

The same Action Programme[74] of measures that applied in the original NVZs entered into force within these additional NVZs in December 2002. The Action Programme comprises controls on the use of fertilizers and manures by farmers. The designation of land as an NVZ has three main implications with financial consequences for farmers. In summary these are (a) the requirement, where sandy or shallow soils predominate, to have available sufficient storage for slurries to enable the closed period to be met; (b) restrictions on the amount of organic nitrogen that can be applied to land; and (c) the requirement for every farm within the designated area to keep additional farm and field records.   **9.30**

The Environment Agency is responsible for enforcement in England. The regulations provide for possible prosecution of farmers in breach of Action Programme measures. However, past experience of the Agency has been that around 80% of farmers are found to be in compliance and the vast majority of breaches have been for failure to keep adequate records. This is therefore an area where the Agency has indicated that it intends to apply a risk-based approach to targeting enforcement efforts.   **9.31**

Abstraction licensing

The main power enjoyed by the Agency to assist in conserving water resources is its ability to restrict the abstraction of water from inland waterways and underground strata and to control the obstruction and impedance of the flow of inland waters. Substantial changes to the rules on Abstraction Licensing in the WRA 1991 were introduced on 1 April 2006,[75] and it is intended that the removal of   **9.32**

---

[71] See the Protection of Water Against Agricultural Nitrate Pollution (England and Wales) Regulations 1996 (SI 1996/888).

[72] Case C-69/99 *European Commission v United Kingdom* [2000] ECR I 10979.

[73] The Nitrate Vulnerable Zones (Additional Designations) (England) (No. 2) Regulations 2002 (SI 2002/2614).

[74] See the Action Programme for Nitrate Vulnerable Zones (England and Wales) Regulations 1998 (SI 1998/1202); note that the Protection of Water Against Agricultural Nitrate Pollution (England and Wales) (Amendment) Regulations 2006 (SI 2006/1289) have applied the requirements for public participation (under Article 2 of Directive 2003/35/EC) to Action Plans.

[75] See the Water Act 2003 (Commencement No. 6, Transitional Provisions and Savings) Order 2006 (SI 2006/984 C.30)—the transitional provisions include converting certain licences to transfer licences, and ensure that combined abstraction and impoundment licences are replaced by separate licences by the Agency.

the main exemptions from the licensing system will take place in April 2009. There will then be a comprehensive set of controls in place, which will allow the Agency to manage the use of water to meet the needs of society and the needs of the environment. Whilst the consultation on these changes, regarding such matters as time limits and catchment-wide strategies, dates back to 1999,[76] the reforms have had to wait for new legislation and the changes made by the Water Act 2003 have been brought into force gradually. The administration for making applications is intended to be simpler, and the 2003 reforms have reduced the barriers to the trading of water rights between licence holders.

The requirement for an abstraction licence

9.33 The restriction is on abstraction of water from any source of supply.[77] 'Abstraction' means doing anything to remove water from the source of supply, whether temporarily or permanently, including where the water is transferred to another source of supply.[78] 'Source of Supply' means any inland waters or any underground strata containing water.[79] 'Inland waters' are widely defined as meaning the whole or any part of any river, stream, or other watercourse whether natural or artificial and whether tidal or not, any lake or pond natural or artificial, any reservoir or dock, and any channel, creek, bay, estuary, or arm of the sea.[80] 'Underground strata' do not include man-made works in such strata such as pipes or sewers but water is included where it is contained in a well or borehole or similar works and excavations where the water enters from the underground strata.[81] 'Discrete waters', that is self-contained bodies of water such as lakes, ponds, or reservoirs, or self-contained groups of such bodies of water which do not discharge into any other inland waters, are not subject to the controls.[82]

General exemption for small quantities

9.34 As a general rule, a licence is needed if someone takes more than 20 cubic metres[83] (4,400 UK gallons) of water per day from a river, stream, or canal. This deregulatory change is estimated to have taken 20,000 of the previous 48,000 licences out of the licensing requirements altogether, as the previous limit under Section 27 of the WRA 1991 was only for 5 cubic metres of water unless it was for domestic

---

[76] The reforms followed the government's review of this area in *Taking Water Responsibly* (1999).
[77] Ibid, s 24.
[78] Ibid, s 221(1).
[79] Ibid, s 221.
[80] Ibid, s 221.
[81] Ibid, s 221(3).
[82] Ibid, s 221(1).
[83] WRA 1991, s 27 (as substituted by the Water Act 2003). The average water usage by a single UK household is 150 litres a day (unmetered households) or 135l in metered households (OfWat data as at 13.12.2005 on Domestic Water Consumption, reported on <http://www.sustainable-development.go.uk>).

or agricultural use. In order to be exempt, the abstraction must not form part of a continuous operation, or of a series of operations, by which more than an aggregate of 20 cubic metres is abstracted during the day. The Secretary of State retains the power to vary this threshold for particular areas.[84] It is also possible that compulsory registration of these exemptions may be introduced in a particular area.[85]

Potential enforcement and offences

These regulatory controls are supported by the criminal law. It is an offence, except **9.35** in pursuance of a licence granted by the Agency and in accordance with the terms of that licence either to abstract water from any source of supply, or to cause or permit anyone else to abstract water.[86] Similarly it is a criminal offence to do any specified works or to install machinery to abstract water from underground strata unless the abstraction is authorized by a licence and the works or machinery are constructed or installed in accordance with the terms of the licence.[87] The magistrates may impose a fine up to £20,000 upon conviction for such an offence and the Crown Court has unlimited powers to impose a fine.[88]

The Agency now has the power to issue an enforcement notice if significant **9.36** environmental damage is caused by an unlawful abstraction or impounding, or an activity that contravenes the conditions of a licence. The enforcement notice can require the cessation of the breach, or of the failure to comply, and the carrying out of specified works or operations to remedy or mitigate the effects. The contents of an enforcement notice in relation to a breach of a restriction on the abstraction or impounding of water are prescribed by the Water Resources (Abstraction and Impounding) Regulations 2006.[89] It is an offence to fail to comply with an enforcement notice,[90] and the Agency can take further steps

---

[84] WRA 1991, s 27A. The Agency would have to apply (or can be directed to apply) to the Secretary of State or the Welsh Assembly Government for an Order setting a different threshold. This may be greater or less than the normal figure of 20 cubic metres in a specified area, inland waters or class of underground strata. If the threshold is reduced, and no licence can be obtained, compensation will be payable for any loss or damage caused.

[85] WRA 1991, s 39B (as inserted by the Water Act 2003); the Agency has the power to apply to the Secretary of State or National Assembly of Wales for an Order which designates an area for compulsory registration of any exempt protected rights. If the Order is made, only the registered exempt abstractions will keep their protected right status.

[86] Ibid, s 24(1) and (4).

[87] Ibid, s 24(2), (3), and (4).

[88] Ibid, s 24(5). The previous statutory limit on a fine in the magistrates was raised from £5,000 by the Water Act 2003.

[89] See Part 4; this applies the procedures in the Anti-Pollution Works Regulations 1999 (SI 1999/1006) to appeals which may be brought against enforcement, works and conservation notices (regs. 28 and 30).

[90] The person is then liable, on summary conviction, to a fine not exceeding £20,000 or, on conviction on indictment, to a fine (WRA 1991, s 25C, as inserted by the Water Act 2003, s 30).

to secure compliance.[91] Furthermore, it is intended that from July 2012, the Agency will also be able to limit or remove someone's permanent licence without compensation if they are causing serious damage to the environment.[92]

Restriction on who can apply for an abstraction licence

9.37   Only a person who occupies the land contiguous to the waters concerned or who will, when the licence is granted, have access to the land can apply for a licence. [93] If the abstraction is to be from underground strata a person is only entitled to apply for a licence if he occupies or will occupy the land of which the strata form part or land containing an excavation filled by water from those strata. So, in effect, a statutory abstraction licence can only permit that which the owner or occupier of land already enjoys under common law.

Types of an abstraction licence

9.38   An abstractor will require a licence in order to abstract any quantity of water which is above the licensing threshold and which is not otherwise exempt. Following the reforms made by the Water Act 2003, there are three types of abstraction licence available:[94]

A.   **'Temporary licences'**: these can be granted for water abstraction for any purpose, for any period of 28 days or less. They have no protected rights status.

B.   **'Transfer licences'**: these can be granted for water abstraction to transfer water from one supply source to another, so long as there will be no intervening use. They do not have protected rights status. Such a licence might be required by a navigation authority, or internal drainage district, or to transfer water within the same source for dewatering activities.

C.   **'Full licences'**: these are the standard water abstraction licence for any other licensable use. They do have protected rights status.

9.39   Many of the abstraction licences that were in existence before the Water Act 2003 are unaffected by the changes that it makes, and they will be deemed to be 'full licences' under the new system. However, where an abstraction is no longer

---

[91]   The Agency may carry out the works itself at the expense of the person on whom the enforcement notice is served, if the person fails to comply with the notice (s 25C(3)). It may take proceedings in the High Court to secure compliance with the notice if it is of the opinion that proceedings for an offence would afford an ineffectual remedy (s 25C(4)).

[92]   See the Water Act 2003, s 27 (which came in force on 1 April 2004); this applies when a licence to abstract water is revoked or varied 'on or after 15 July 2012' in pursuance of a direction under the WRA s 54 or s 56.

[93]   Ibid, s 35. It is enough to show that the applicant has entered into negotiations to acquire an interest in land which would give the right to occupy or that compulsory purchase has been initiated which would give the applicant that right (s 35(4)).

[94]   WRA 1991, s 24A, as inserted by Water Act 2003.

required to be licensed because of the introduction of the new minimum threshold, then the licence ceases to have effect for that abstraction.[95]

A licence can be transferred between an existing and proposed new licence holder.[96] **9.40**
They will both need to sign up to the transfer of a licence, and the licensed volumes may be split between two or more parties. It will be up to the parties involved to agree on the apportionment, and for the Environment Agency to authorize the licences. It remains a condition for allowing a transfer that the transferee has a right of access to the abstraction point. Licences are considered to be part of the estate of a deceased holder, and of the property of a bankrupt, and they will vest accordingly.[97]

The application process for an abstraction licence

The Water Resources (Abstraction and Impounding) Regulations 2006[98] specify **9.41**
the new procedural requirements in respect of the licensing of abstraction and impounding of water in England and Wales. All applications for an abstraction licence or an impounding licence must be made to the Agency, using the form issued by the Agency.[99] The Regulations also require the Agency to acknowledge receipt of an application, and provide the applicant with specified information.[100]
The application normally has to be publicized.[101] The Agency normally has four months to make a decision,[102] unless it has formally requested further information, and it will serve notice of its decision on an applicant or refer the matter to the Secretary of State, or (as the case may be) to the National Assembly for Wales. Any appeal must be made within 28 days.[103] When the Agency requires a licence itself, it must follow similar procedures and requirements.[104]

---

[95] Water Act 2003, s 102. The rights will still be protected.

[96] WRA 1991, ss 59A, 59C and 59D (as inserted by the Water Act 2003).

[97] S 59B, but both full and transfer licences will lapse after 15 months if the EA is not informed of the vesting by the person in whom the licence vests.

[98] SI 2006/641—these replace the Water Resources (Licences) Regulations 1965, which have remained in force under the WRA 1991.

[99] Reg 4; the applicant must provide all the information, including maps and reports, as the Agency 'reasonably requires in order to determine it' (reg 3). This does mean that the Agency can ask the applicant to commission and pay for all the relevant expert reports.

[100] Reg 8. Note that special provisions apply where the application relates to abstraction or impounding in a National Park or the Broads (reg 9).

[101] Ibid, s 37; reg 6 prescribes the manner in which notice of such applications must be published, while reg 7 provides exceptions to the requirement to advertise if the application is essentially for a repeat licence in the same terms. The Regulations also prescribe the information that must be contained on the register of abstraction and impounding licences (reg 34).

[102] Reg 10; however, it is allowed only 28 days to determine temporary licences, and three months where it is an application that does not need to be publicized (ie an application for a repeat licence).

[103] Reg 12, and be in the form specified in reg 13.

[104] Part 3 of, and Schedule 2 to, the Regulations make modifications to the WRA 1991 as it applies to abstraction or impounding by the Agency.

9.42 The Agency may either grant a licence 'containing such provisions as the Agency considers appropriate' or 'if it considers it necessary or expedient to do so, may refuse to grant a licence'.[105] The Agency will consider the written representations received in response to the publicity for the application, and it must consider the reasonable requirements of the applicant[106] and, in the case of new licences, the existing rights and privileges.[107] These are protected rights[108] from which the Agency is not entitled to derogate in granting a licence without the consent of the person entitled to the right. If it does grant such a licence it is a valid licence but the owner of the protected rights may bring an action for damages against the Agency for breach of statutory duty.[109]

9.43 The Agency must also consider the river flow and the effect the abstraction would have on that flow. As there are still no 'minimum acceptable flows' that have been determined, the Agency must have regard to the matters which it would consider in determining such a flow, namely the existing flow, the character of the inland waters, any water quality objectives established under the WRA 1991, the minimum flow needed for safeguarding the public health, and the requirements of navigation, fisheries, and land drainage.[110] Much of this analysis is now contained in the Catchment Abstraction Management Strategy (CAMS)[111] which have been prepared by the Agency. CAMS is described by them as the vehicle for reviewing time-limited licences, determining whether they should be renewed and on what terms. The Agency will use the relevant CAMS to determine whether a catchment is one where it considers that 'no water is available', or that it is 'over licensed'. They also make water resources allocation public to help to show how the needs of abstractors and the aquatic environment are balanced.

---

[105] WRA 1991, s 38(2)(a) and (b).

[106] Ibid, s 38(3)(a) and (b).

[107] Ibid, s 39. The rights in question are those of the owners of contiguous land exempted from control (and who have protected rights), and abstraction in accordance with an abstraction licence (s 48(1)). However, the Agency no longer has to consider existing protected rights when dealing with an application to renew a licence on the same terms and conditions.

[108] The definition of a 'Protected Right' has been changed by the Water Act 2003. It is now that 'protected right means a right to abstract, which someone has by virtue of the small abstractions exemptions defined in the Water Act 2003 or by virtue of having an abstraction licence. The right protected is the quantity that can be abstracted up to that allowed by the exemption or the terms of the licence.'

[109] Ibid, s 60.

[110] Ibid, s 21(4) and (5).

[111] In April 2001 the Agency published Managing Water Abstraction: The Catchment Abstraction Management Strategy Process (updated July 2002). Each CAMS area document should be read in conjunction with this. It has not been a simple task. Initially, there were 129 CAMS to be produced for England and Wales, and there will be 101 CAMS by 2014 following the review of CAMS boundaries by the Agency.

The Agency must give reasons for its decisions.[112] It is intended that the Agency's **9.44** decisions for the refusal of an application for an authorization or where an abstraction authorization has been granted in the face of significant opposition should be published on the Internet.[113] As of 2008, there is only one decision statement, relating to Thames Water Utilities Ltd's application to renew a variation to the 'base licence' at the Axford Pumping Station, Axford, Wiltshire which supplied public water. The decision illustrates the wide range of factors that now have to be taken into account, from the immediate concerns such as the effect on the water resources, quantity and quality of water in the River Kennet, and the effect of any fisheries, to the wider issues of ecology and conservation, flooding, archaeology, recreation and amenity, and the social and economic welfare of rural communities. As for costs and benefits, it was considered that there were no significant costs to Thames Water Utilities Ltd, and an environmental benefit to the River Kennet. The Agency decided not to grant the variation requested for an increase to the daily peak rate, but did grant a variation to the base licence to allow an increased annual volume for which the applicant had demonstrated a 'reasonable need'. It also imposed a time limit of 2011 so that the licence would be reviewed again in accordance with the CAMS common end date for that catchment.[114]

The Secretary of State's role in abstraction licencing

The Secretary of State has a supervisory role. He can either 'call in' a particular **9.45** application for a licence so that it is determined by him,[115] or an appeal can be made to him from a decision to refuse a licence or to impose onerous conditions or other requirements or because a decision has not been made within the prescribed time. Unlike under the planning system, the Secretary of State does not himself grant the relevant authorization but will direct the Agency to grant the licence on such terms as he specifies in his direction.[116] Unlike the Agency, the Secretary of State is entitled to direct that a licence be issued which would authorize an abstraction which derogates from existing protected rights without

---

[112] WRA 1991, s 195A (as inserted by s 51 of the Water Act 2003).

[113] The publishing of decision statements on the Internet originated from the Environment Agency's response to the Governments paper *Taking Water Responsibly*.

[114] The summary of reasons given by the Agency were that Thames Water had not demonstrated need for its proposed variation, that the proposed variation was not environmentally sustainable, and that the licence that was issued set out the appropriate balance between the operational considerations of Thames Water and the environmental considerations affecting the River Kennet. It was no doubt relevant that the relevant water resources management unit in the Kennet and Pang CAMS was assessed as being 'Over abstracted'.

[115] WRA 1991, s 41. The Secretary of State can give a direction to the Agency either calling in a particular application for determination by him or specifying a class of applications which are to be determined by him. It is likely to be a rare occurrence.

[116] Ibid, s 42(5).

the consent of the owner of those rights. The owner of those rights may, however, make a claim for damages against the Agency in those circumstances.[117]

Appeals regarding an abstraction licence

9.46 An applicant for a licence may appeal to the Secretary of State if 'dissatisfied with the decision of the Agency' or if the Agency fails to determine the application or to notify the applicant of a call in.[118] Most appeals can be deal with by written representations, but a local inquiry or a hearing must be held if the applicant or the Agency insists.[119] The Secretary of State can allow or dismiss the appeal or vary any part of the decision appealed against even if that part of the decision was not expressly appealed against. He can direct the Agency to revoke a licence.[120] Again, in determining the appeal, he must consider the same matters as the Agency would have to have taken into account at first instance but he is not subject to the same restriction against derogating from existing protected rights. As in Town and Country Planning, the Secretary of State's decisions in the exercise of his supervisory role are final and cannot be questioned in any court of law other than by way of a statutory challenge in the High Court.[121] The grounds are the usual limited grounds of the decision not being within the powers of the Act or of failure to comply with the relevant procedural requirements resulting in substantial prejudice. Only the Agency or a relevant applicant or appellant or licence holder may apply to the High Court to challenge the decision. Consultees have no such entitlement.

The contents of an abstraction licence

9.47 Every abstraction licence is required to: [122]

(1) specify how much water is authorized to be abstracted from that particular source of supply during a specified period or periods;
(2) specify a method for measuring or assessing the quantity abstracted;
(3) make provision for determining by measurement or assessment how much water is to be taken to have been abstracted during any such period;

---

[117] Ibid, s 60(3).

[118] Ibid, s 43(1). Note that the Water Resources (Abstraction and Impoundment) Regulations 2006 only allow 28 days to make an appeal (reg 12) from the date of the decision (or from the date when there should have been a decision).

[119] There are no formal procedural rules, but the Planning Inspectorate will follow the spirit of the similar rules for the relevant type of planning appeal. See, further, the PINS guidance note obtainable from the environmental appeals team at <http://www.planning-inspectorate.gov.uk>

[120] WRA 1991, s 44(6).

[121] Ibid, s 69.

[122] Ibid, s 46(2)–(5).

(4) indicate the means by which the water is to be abstracted either by specifying the works, machinery, or apparatus to be used or by setting down requirements that the works, machinery, or apparatus must meet;

(5) specify the land on which the water is to be abstracted except in the case of licences granted to the Agency or a water or sewerage undertaker or other supplier of water;

(6) specify the purposes for which the water is to be used, and the Agency may also wish to specify the land on which the water can be used;

(7) state whether the licence is to remain in force until revoked or is to expire at some time specified in the licence;

(8) name the licence holder, although there is nothing to prevent the licence holder from himself authorizing someone else (such as another farmer using the licence holder's land under an agreement between the two farmers) to abstract the water. Only the named licence holder can be liable to criminal prosecution for breach of a licence condition.

Different periods of abstraction, different points of abstraction, different means **9.48** of abstraction, and different purposes for abstraction may all be dealt with in one licence.[123] A licence holder may hold more than one licence authorizing abstraction at different points or by different means from the same source of supply.[124] However, it is now a legal requirement to put a start and an end date on all new abstraction licences, so that they are time-limited. The Agency has been adopting a policy of relating this to the end date of the relevant Catchment Abstraction Management Strategy.

Other abstraction licence exemptions

In addition to the right to abstract small quantities of water without a licence, **9.49** there were a number of exceptions to this regime of control over abstractions and impounding works in the WRA 1991. These exemptions from the requirement to have a licence will become more limited when the amendments made by the Water Act 2003 are brought into force:

(1) *Navigation, Harbour and Conservancy Authorities.* These are bodies which have the duties or powers given to them by relevant enactments respectively to work and control any canal or other inland navigation, to control harbours, and to conserve the navigation of a tidal water. Under the previous regime, all transfers of water from one area of inland water to another by them for the purposes of their functions were exempt from licence control. The amendments made by the Water Act 2003 will limit these exemptions

---

[123] Ibid, s 46(6).
[124] Ibid, s 46(7).

once the provisions are brought into force, so that a transfer licence is likely to be required.[125] The construction or alteration of impounding works by these authorities will remain exempt from licensing if the works do not have any effect beyond the authority's water system.[126]

(2) *Right to Abstract for Agriculture and Drainage Purposes.* Previously, there was no restriction on abstraction for land drainage purposes,[127] including for the protection of land against erosion or encroachment from inland waters or from the sea. Land Drainage will generally remain exempt, but licences will now be required for the use by agricultural operations of trickle irrigation and land drainage,[128] once the relevant provisions of the Water Act 2003 are brought into force.

(3) There was an exemption for abstractions that were necessary to prevent *interference with any mining, quarrying, engineering, building, or other operations* or to prevent damage to works resulting from such operations.[129] Abstractions for dewatering mines, quarries, or engineering excavations will now generally require a licence (usually a temporary or transfer licence).[130] An emergency can be exempt, so long as notice is given within five days. However, where it is intended to construct or extend a well, borehole, or other works in order to abstract groundwater so as to protect underground works, prior notification of those works must be given to the Agency.[131] That gives the Agency the opportunity to serve a conservation notice requiring reasonable measures to be taken to conserve groundwater which in the Agency's opinion will not interfere with the protection of the underground works. The recipient of such a notice can appeal against it on the basis that the measures required are not reasonable or that the measures would interfere with the protection of the underground works.

(4) *Water used on a vessel.* Machinery may be used on a vessel to abstract water for use on that or any other vessel.[132]

---

[125] WRA 1991, s 26 (as substituted by s 5 of the Water Act 2003, from a date to be appointed). Transfers wholly within a water system operated by these authorities (eg wholly within a network of canal pounds and canal locks) would not require a licence.

[126] Ibid, s 26(2).

[127] Ibid, s 29(1).

[128] WRA 1991, s 29 (as amended). The exemption is removed from farming practices such as a warping (to leave silt deposits on land) and trickle irrigation. These activities could previously be controlled by the Agency issuing a Conservation Notice (WRA 1991, s 30 which has been repealed).

[129] The original version of WRA 1991, s 29(2).

[130] S 29 (as amended by the Water Act 2003).

[131] WRA 1991, ss 199 and 199A (as amended by s 8, of the Water Act 2003) require an operator to give prior notice to the EA of mining operations affecting water resources (these repeat the provisions of the former WRA 1991, ss 30 and 31).

[132] Ibid, s 32 (1).

(5) *Fire-fighting Purposes.* Abstraction of water for fire-fighting or for testing or training in the use of fire-fighting equipment is exempted from the restriction.[133]

(6) *Groundwater Exploration.* Abstraction in the course of groundwater exploration and evaluation is exempted provided it has the consent of the Agency and is in accordance with the conditions attached to that consent.[134]

(7) *Excepting Order.* The Secretary of State may by order except any one or more sources of supply from the restriction on abstraction.[135] The Agency or a navigation authority, harbour authority, or conservancy authority may apply for such an order on the grounds that the restriction is not needed in relation to the source or sources of supply concerned. The Secretary of State can take the initiative and direct the Agency to apply. Conversely, the Secretary of State or National Assembly of Wales may make an Order to cancel those exemptions and introduce licensing to these areas.

Damage from abstraction

Following the implementation of the new Section 48A of the WRA 1991 on 1 **9.50** April 2005, all abstractors have a statutory duty not to let their abstraction cause loss or damage to others.[136] Except as provided for in Section 48A, no other claim may be made in civil proceedings by a person against an abstractor, although this does not prevent or affect a claim for negligence or breach of contract.[137] The court may not grant an injunction against the abstractor under Section 48A if that would risk interrupting the supply of water to the public, or would put public health or safety at risk.

Impounding licences

The other area of control is over 'impounding works'.[138] These are dams, weirs, or **9.51** other works in any inland waters which impound, that is impede, the flow of water, and also any works which divert the flow in connection with the construction

---

[133] Ibid, s 32(2).

[134] Ibid, s 32(3).

[135] Ibid, ss 33 and 33A (as inserted).

[136] WRA 1991, s 48A was inserted by the Water Act 2003. This provision therefore only relates to loss or damage incurred after the commencement date (1 April 2005) and removes the licence holder's existing defence provided by the abstraction licence.

[137] S 48A(6); however, at common law, the landowner has the right to abstract water flowing beneath his land regardless of the consequences to his neighbours and it cannot be said that he owes a duty of care in doing so (see *Stephens v Anglian Water Authority* [1987] 1 WLR 1381, CA (and the authorities discussed therein).

[138] Ibid, s 25.

or alteration of such a dam or weir.[139] Again discrete waters are not subject to this control.

9.52   It is a criminal offence to begin or cause or permit another person to begin such works without a licence and, where a licence is held, to do such works not in accordance with its terms and requirements.[140] The courts have the same powers to fine on conviction. The application has to be made on the form prescribed by the Water Resources (Abstraction and Impounding) Regulations 2006, and the application process follows the same procedures as abstraction licensing as discussed above.

9.53   The Water Act 2003 has now ensured that Impounding licences will be needed for the life of any such works. Section 2 of the 2003 Act amends Section 25 of the WRA 1991 so that impounding licences (whether issued before or after 1 April 2006)[141] will remain in force for the lifetime of the works. This enables the Agency to modify the conditions on the licence if it is necessary to ensure that the impounding works do not cause damage to the environment. The Agency's duty to revoke an impounding licence at the request of the holder has also been amended, and the revocation of an impounding licence can now be made conditional on the removal of the works or restoration of the site to the Agency's satisfaction.[142]

9.54   Section 4 of the Water Act 2003 provides the Agency with a power to serve a works notice on the relevant person (normally the owner) to carry out remedial works on an existing impoundment that is causing environmental damage. Failure to comply with the notice is an offence. The Agency has also been given power over impounding works that are unlicensed, either because their construction pre-dated the licensing regime or a licence has been revoked.[143] This enables it to take action regarding works that are, or in the future may, cause environmental problems. There is a 21-day time-limit for serving a notice of appeal against a notice requiring existing, unlicensed impounding works to be licensed.[144]

Modification and revocation of licences

9.55   A licence holder can apply to the Agency to revoke his licence and the Agency must then to do so,[145] and this is a simple way of ending any continuing

---

[139]   Ibid, s 25(8).

[140]   Ibid, s 25(2).

[141]   This is the date the amendments came into force—SI 2006/984.

[142]   WRA 1991, s 51 (as amended by s 21 of the Water Act 2003). This decision can be appealed to the Secretary of State or the National Assembly (s 51(1C–1G)).

[143]   Water Act 2003 ss 3–4; this is a stand-alone power, and has not been added into the body of the WRA 1991.

[144]   Reg 33; this also applies, with suitable modification, the appeals provisions under the Anti-Pollution Works Regulations 1999 to any such appeal.

[145]   WRA 1991, s 51(1).

obligations under the licence. A licence holder can also apply to the Agency to vary the licence. The Agency then treats that application in the same way as a new application for a licence, except that if the variation sought is simply a reduction in the quantity of water to be abstracted then there is no need to publicize the application in the same way as a fresh application.[146]

Agency proposals to revoke or modify

Abstraction licences can be revoked if they are not used for four years (down from seven years), without the payment of compensation.[147] The Agency can also take the initiative and formulate proposals to revoke or vary a licence. In formulating such proposals, the Agency has to have in mind its general environmental and recreational duties. The proposals will be notified to the holder and any relevant navigation authority, harbour authority, or conservancy authority and publicized.[148] If the licence holder objects, the proposals are referred to the Secretary of State[149] who then considers the proposals, the objection, and any written representations.[150] Again the Secretary of State can decide to hold an inquiry or a hearing but he must hold one or the other if the licence holder so requires. If the licence holder does not object within the time prescribed, the Agency can go on to revoke the licence or vary its terms in accordance with its proposals. In keeping with his general supervisory role, the Secretary of State also has the power to take the initiative (either because of representations to him or otherwise) and direct the Agency to formulate proposals to revoke a licence or vary its terms.[151] The same procedure will be followed. **9.56**

Modifications on the application of the owner of fishing rights

An owner of fishing rights[152] who considers that an abstraction licence has interfered with his fishing can apply to the Secretary of State for the revocation or variation of that licence.[153] **9.57**

Compensation may then be payable for any loss or damage caused. If the Secretary of State determines on such an application that the grounds for so varying **9.58**

---

[146] Ibid, s 51(2), (3), (4).

[147] S 61(4) (as amended by the Water Act 2003); The Agency has stated that it will not use this power in cases where any period of non-use is part of the agreed need for a licence—for instance it is a licence for emergency supply or for periods when irrigation is not required.

[148] The procedure for publishing notices of proposals by the Agency to modify a licence are prescribed by Reg. 31.

[149] WRA 1991, s 53(4).

[150] Ibid, s 54.

[151] Ibid, s 52(2).

[152] Defined in s 55(5) as a right to fish which constitutes or is included in an interest of land or which is given by an exclusive licence granted for valuable consideration.

[153] Ibid, s 55.

or revoking the licence have been established but that nevertheless the licence should not be varied or revoked, then the owner of the fishing rights is entitled to compensation.[154] Questions of disputed compensation are again dealt with by the Lands Tribunal.

Water rights trading

9.59 While it is possible to buy someone's land with an abstraction licence, and to apply to the Agency to transfer the rights, it has now become possible to transfer rights to abstract water from one person to another, for some or all of the water covered by an existing abstraction licence. It involves the trading of rights only, not the trading of actual water, and the transferred rights will need to be set out in a new abstraction licence. This is intended to help with the situation that is likely to arise in the future where no new licences are available in an area, and so it will become possible to buy the rights to abstract water held under someone else's licence. Therefore any trade will involve an application to vary or revoke a licence and an application for a new licence. It will be for the trader to find a trading partner and to agree what water rights will be traded within the same river catchment or groundwater area. Potential traders are encouraged to contact the Agency to find out whether a trade is possible, and to avoid unexpected costs or delays in getting their approval for the new licence[155]. The applications should be determined within three months (four months if advertising is needed).

Charges for licences

9.60 The Agency will charge for the regulation of water abstraction licences. There is a fixed application charge,[156] and an annual subsistence charge[157] which is payable by everyone who holds a licence to abstract or impound water. Where the holder fails to pay the charges due in respect of his licence, the Agency may in accordance with the procedures prescribed in the Environmental Licences (Suspension and Revocation) Regulations 1996 suspend or revoke the licence.[158]

---

[154] Ibid, s 62(3). This applies unless the Agency sets in train the compulsory acquisition of the rights from him within six months of the certificate.

[155] The Agency has produced a basic leaflet *Accessing Water Resources: A guide to water rights trading* (March 2007).

[156] The Scheme of Abstraction Charges is made each year by the Agency under the powers vested in it under the Environment Act 1995, ss 41 and 42. There is a minimum annual charge, currently £25. The application charge is £135 for 2008/9.

[157] The subsistence charge is calculated by reference to the annual licensed volume, the source, season, and loss rate. There is also a Standard Unit Charge (SUC) depending on the region in which the abstraction is authorized to be made, and an Environmental Improvement Unit Charge (EIUC) to recover the costs of compensation payments in the region.

[158] The regulations are made under s 41(6) and (10) of the Environment Act 1995.

Compensation provisions

A licence holder may carry out work which is rendered abortive by the subsequent **9.61** revocation or variation of his licence, or he may suffer loss or damage directly attributable to that revocation or variation. In such cases he will be entitled to compensation from the Agency provided the revocation or variation was at the direction of the Secretary of State.[159] If the modification was on the initiative of the Agency, no compensation is payable because the holder could have required the matter to be referred to the Secretary of State under Section 53. Expenditure preparatory to any works can be included within a claim, but otherwise no compensation is payable for any work done before the licence was granted or for any loss or damage arising out of anything that happened before the grant. No compensation is payable if no water had been abstracted in the four years before the notice of the proposals to revoke or vary the licence was served on the holder.[160] Any question of disputed compensation is to be referred to and determined by the Lands Tribunal in accordance with its normal rules, subject to any necessary modifications. Where compensation is payable by the Agency because it was complying with a direction of the Secretary of State, he may—but does not have to—indemnify the Agency.[161]

C. Drought

The normal use of water during periods of drought can be changed by the making **9.62** of a formal order. Ever since the long hot summer of 1976, and the exceptional drought that resulted, the Secretary of State has had the power to make Drought Orders (including emergency orders).[162] The Agency has also been given the power under reforms introduced by the Environment Act 1995 to issue Drought Permits to allow additional sources of water to be used and to restrict the supply and use of water. There is a formal public procedure that must be followed before these measures can be used, which will allow objections to be made and considered. Indeed, these measures may often be considered together at the same public hearing. For instance, in December 2003, the Agency issued two drought permits to a water company to allow it to pump water from Lake Windermere and

---

[159] WRA 1991, s 61 (as amended by the Water Act 2003).
[160] Ibid, s 61(4) (as amended). It was previously seven years.
[161] Ibid, s 63.
[162] Water Resources Act 1991 Part II Chapter III, ss 73 to 81, as amended by the Environment Act 1995. The procedure for making an order is set out in Schedule 8 of the WRA 1991. Drought Orders were first introduced by the Drought Act 1976. Further information can be found in the joint publication *Drought Orders and Drought Permits* produced by Defra, the Welsh Assembly Government and the Environment Agency, the current version of which is dated July 2005.

Ullswater in order to maintain stocks in its reservoirs and the Secretary of State also agreed to make the United Utilities Water plc (Ullswater) (Drought) Order 2003.[163] It was also considered appropriate that these measures were taken in the winter, in advance of the anticipated drought arising in the following summer. Not only was a public local inquiry held, but the Environment Agency was also asked to undertake an assessment of the Order's impact under the requirements of the Habitats Regulations, in consultation with English Nature.

Ordinary drought order

9.63 An 'ordinary drought order' will remove restrictions on taking water from specified sources of supply, and under specified conditions. It will take the form of a statutory instrument. The procedure has to be initiated by an application to the Secretary of State by either the Environment Agency or by a water undertaker who claims that there is serious water supply shortage.[164] The application must be publicized, notice of it must be served on local authorities and on other bodies and persons potentially affected by the order, and the notice must tell them that they may object to the application. If objection is made a local inquiry or hearing must be held unless the order needs to be made urgently to enable the deficiency in supplies to be effectively met.[165] The authorizations, prohibitions, limitations, suspensions, or modifications in such orders last for a maximum of six months unless extended by the Secretary of State to a maximum of one year.[166]

9.64 The formal test that the Secretary of State will consider before he makes an ordinary drought order[167] is that he must be satisfied that because of 'an exceptional shortage of rain', there exists or is threatened either (1) a serious deficiency of supplies of water in any area; or (2) such a deficiency in the flow or level of water in any inland waters that there is a serious threat to any flora or fauna which depend on those waters. This second ground cannot be relied upon by a water undertaker.[168]

---

[163] SI 2003/3341; the Drought Order lasted for just over three months and allowed the utility company to construct and maintain a temporary weir across the river flowing from Ullswater and to reduce the normal specified rates of flow in the river. United Utilities reported that, due to an increase in rainfall during the winter, the reservoirs refilled adequately and the company found that it did not need to use the permits or order (United Utilities 'Corporate Responsibility Report, Our Impacts 04, Resource Use and Efficiency').

[164] WRA 1991, s 74.

[165] Ibid, Sch 8 para 2.

[166] Ibid, s 74(3), (4).

[167] Ibid, s 73(1). He has a wide discretion—the power is that he 'may' make such provision by order 'as appears to him to be expedient with a view to meeting the deficiency'.

[168] Ibid, s 73(3)(b).

Although most orders to date have been sought by the water companies, the Act **9.65**
deals firstly with the situation where the Agency applies for an order. Such an
order made may: [169]

(1) authorize the Agency to take water from any source specified in the order
    subject to any conditions or restrictions in the order;
(2) authorize the Agency to discharge water to any place specified in the order
    subject to conditions or restrictions in the order;
(3) authorize the Agency to prohibit or limit the taking of any water (including
    by a water undertaker) from a specified source if the Agency is satisfied that
    such taking of water seriously affects the supplies available to it or to any other
    person;
(4) suspend or modify any existing restriction or obligation to which the Agency,
    a water or sewerage undertaker, or any other person is subject, in respect of:
    a. the taking of water from any source;
    b. the discharge of water;
    c. the supply of water in terms of quantity, pressure, quality, means of supply,
       or otherwise; or
    d. any treatment of water;
(5) authorize the Agency to suspend or modify any effluent discharge consent.

Where a water undertaker applies for an order,[170] the order may contain the same **9.66**
provisions as where the application is made by the Agency save that the authority
is given to the undertaker itself to take or discharge water, taking water by the
Agency itself may be restricted, and the undertaker may be authorized to prohibit
or limit the use of water for any specified purpose within a range of purposes
directed by the Secretary of State.[171]

Emergency drought order

An 'emergency drought order'[172] enables water companies to restrict the use of **9.67**
water and to supply water by stand pipes or water tanks. Again the initiative for
such orders must come from an application by the Agency or a water undertaker.
The same procedures apply. These orders can only be made when the Secretary of
State is satisfied that because of the exceptional shortage of rain there is such an
existing or threatened serious deficiency of water that the economic or social

---

[169] Ibid, s 74(1).
[170] Ibid, s 74(2).
[171] The Drought Direction, made by the Secretary of State on 18 April 1991 under the old s 131
of the Water Act 1989 (general drought orders), lists the non-essential uses of water which can be
banned under a drought order and goes further than a hosepipe ban.
[172] WRA 1991, s 75.

well-being of people in the area is likely to be threatened.[173] No such applications have been made in recent years.

9.68 These emergency orders may contain any of the provisions that an ordinary drought order may contain except that they may authorize a water undertaker to restrict the use of water for any purpose the undertaker thinks fit and are not limited to the purposes directed by the Secretary. More importantly, the emergency order may authorize the undertaker to set up water tanks or stand pipes and to supply water by those means.[174] The Secretary of State may give directions as to how these powers are to be exercised and he is empowered to enforce such directions against water and sewerage undertakers by enforcement orders under Section 18 of the Water Industry Act 1991. The provisions of these orders have a shorter life span of three months, with a maximum of five months if they are extended by the Secretary of State.[175]

Restricting the use of water

9.69 The Water Resources Act, under Section 57, provides the Agency with the power to impose a temporary restriction on the abstraction of water for spray irrigation during exceptional shortages of rain or other emergencies. A Drought Order can also authorize a water undertaker to prohibit or limit the use of water. When it does so the undertaker is empowered to apply the restriction to all consumers, or to particular types of consumers, or to a particular consumer—presumably when that consumer is a very heavy user of water or where the source is particularly sensitive.[176] The consumers must have the restriction brought to their attention either by a notice published in the local paper or by individual notification. The restriction then comes into effect 72 hours later.

Effect on Inland Navigations

9.70 Drought orders may include provisions which aim to ensure that in so far as possible any effects of the order on canals and navigable rivers is kept to a minimum.[177]

Power to carry out works

9.71 Drought orders may authorize any works needed to perform any duty imposed or exercise any power conferred by the order,[178] and can grant a right of entry to do so. Twenty-four hours' notice must be given before any land is entered to do

---

[173] Ibid, s 73(2).
[174] Ibid, s 75(2)(c).
[175] Ibid, s 75(3), (4).
[176] Ibid, s 76(1)(a).
[177] Ibid, s 77(1).
[178] Ibid, s 78.

the works. Planning permission for the works is given by the Town and Country Planning (General Permitted Development) Order 1995, Schedule II, Part 17, Class E(f).

Compensation

Provision is made by Schedule 9 of the WRA 1991 for payment of compensation by the applicant for an order where loss or damage is suffered by any person as a result of the exercise of powers conferred by that order. **9.72**

Drought Permits

The system of drought permits was introduced by the Environment Act 1995 and it enables the Environment Agency itself to free water undertakers from restrictions on taking water from specified sources.[179] It may be expected to be a quicker and cheaper response to the problems of drought than the procedure for drought orders made by the Secretary of State. The procedural provisions and the provisions as to compensation in relation to drought orders also apply to these permits. **9.73**

The water undertaker will have to apply to the Agency for a permit. The Agency can only issue one if it is satisfied that, because of an exceptional shortage of rain, a serious deficiency of supplies of water in the area exists or is threatened. The permit lasts for six months unless it is extended by the Agency to a maximum of one year. The permit can authorize the water undertaker to take water from a specified source subject to appropriate conditions or restrictions, and it can suspend or modify any existing restrictions on the taking of water from any source. **9.74**

If the permit relates to a source which supplies water to a canal or navigable river the navigation authority has to consent to the taking of water or to the removal of the restriction on the taking of water. **9.75**

Offences

It is an offence to take or use water contrary to the terms of a drought order or permit, or to discharge water otherwise than in accordance with the terms of an order or permit.[180] It is also an offence to fail to provide and maintain the measuring apparatus required by an order or permit and to fail to allow inspection of the apparatus or relevant records. It is a defence to show that all reasonable precautions were taken and all due diligence was exercised to avoid committing such an offence. **9.76**

---

[179] Ibid, s 79 A.
[180] Ibid, s 80. The penalties are a fine up to the statutory maximum in the magistrates' court and unlimited in the Crown Court (s 80(4)).

Drought Plans

9.77 It is now a requirement that the water companies prepare Drought Plans to ensure the security of the public water supply in periods of water shortage, caused by exceptionally low rainfall. These were initially voluntary plans, but are now set out in legislation following the amendments made by the Water Act 2003.[181] The first drought plans were published on the water companies' websites in 2007, and included such measures as campaigns to encourage reduced consumption by the public, hosepipe bans, enhanced leakage control, and pressure reduction. They will therefore be material considerations in any application for a drought order or permit.

D. Control of Pollution of Water Resources

Water quality

9.78 It is the duty of the Secretary of State, the National Assembly of Wales and of the Agency to exercise their powers under the water pollution provisions of the WRA 1991 in such a way as to ensure as far as practicable that the water quality objectives in respect of the relevant waters are achieved at all times.[182] There are a number of European Directives that have defined the acceptable water quality for particular purposes, and these have been transposed into UK law. These are being reviewed with the aim of simplifying them, in the name of Better Regulation, as part of the work under the Water Framework Directive. They currently concern the quality of surface water intended for abstraction for drinking water,[183] the concentrations of dangerous substances found in them,[184] their use as bathing waters,[185] their

---

[181] Water Industry Act 1991, ss 39B–39C (as inserted by the Water Act 2003), and the Drought Plan Regulations 2005 (SI 2005/1905) and the Drought Plan Directions (September 2005). At the 'Water Summit' called by the government in 1997, Ministers had obtained a voluntary commitment from water companies to produce drought contingency plans.

[182] WRA 1991, s 84.

[183] Directive 75/440/EEC (repealed and replaced by the Water Framework Directive from 22 December 2007); this was partly implemented by the Surface Water (Classification) Regulations 1989 (SI 1989/1148), but these were revoked and the whole Directive was transposed by the Surface Waters (Abstraction for Drinking Water)(Classification) Regulations 1996, SI 1996/2001 as amended by SI 2000/3184 and SI 2001/3911.

[184] Surface Water (Dangerous Substances) (Classification) Regulation s 1989, SI 1989/2286, 1992, SI 1992/327, and 1997, SI 1997/2560 and SI 1998/389.

[185] Directive 76/160/EEC (which is intended to be repealed on 31 December 2014, once the Directive 2006/7/EC has been implemented); this is implemented by the Bathing Waters (Classification) Regulations 1991 (SI 1991/1597) as amended by Environment Act 1995 s 120(1), Sch 22, para 233(1) and modified in relation to England by Bathing Waters (Classification) (England) Regulations 2003, SI 2003/1238.

qualities as river ecosystems,[186] their ability to support fish life,[187] and concerning the classification of coastal or brackish waters for their ability to support shellfish.[188]

The statutory mechanism for setting these objectives is to be found in the Water **9.79** Resources Act 1991, Sections 82–84. The first step is for the Secretary of State by regulation to set out a system for classifying controlled waters according to quality criteria themselves defined in the Regulations.[189] Then, for the purpose of maintaining and improving the quality of controlled waters, he or she will serve a notice on the Agency specifying the classification and the date by which and after which the relevant waters have to comply with that classification.[190] He must publicize it in a way he considers appropriate to bring it to the attention of those likely to be affected. The notice must allow at least three months for objections and representations. He must consider those matters and then either proceed with the proposal in its original terms or he can modify it.[191] Once the water quality objectives have been established, they can be reviewed after five years or when and if the Agency asks for a review.[192] The provisions for publicity apply to a review.

While water quality standards are now led by the requirements of European Union **9.80** law, the provisions of the Water Resources Act 1991 were the result of the Government's intention set out in *This Common Inheritance*[193] to set water quality objectives by law on a consistent basis to cover all types of water courses. Before the creation of the new private sector water companies and the National Rivers Authority by the Water Act 1989, individual water authorities had set water quality objectives on an informal basis. These objectives varied from area to area. Rivers and canals were classified in accordance with a non-statutory scheme suggested by the National Water Council which classified them into categories with quality being related to actual or intended use, ranging from class 1A ('water of high quality suitable for potable supply abstractions; game or other high

---

[186] Surface Waters (River Ecosystems) (Classification) Regulations 1994 (SI 1994/1057) as amended by Environment Act 1995 s 120(1), Sch 22, para 233(1)

[187] The Freshwater Fish Directive (78/659/EEC), implemented by the Surface Waters (Fish Life) (Classification) Regulations 1997 (SI 1997/1331), amended in 2003 (SI 2003/1053). The Directive is due to be repealed in 2013 by the Water Framework Directive. The UK designated further areas after the European Commission issued an Article 226 Reasoned Opinion in 2002 for the UK's failure to comply with the Freshwater Fish Directive.

[188] The original Shellfish Waters Directive (79/923/EC) was repealed by the codified Shellfish Waters Directive (2006/113/EC), which itself is due to be repealed in 2013 by the Water Framework Directive. The original Directive was implemented by the Surface Waters (Shellfish) (Classification) Regulations 1997 (SI 1997/1332).

[189] WRA 1991, s 82.

[190] Ibid, s 83.

[191] Ibid, s 83(4).

[192] Ibid, s 83(3).

[193] September 1990, Cm 1200.

class fisheries; high amenity value') to class 4 ('waters which are grossly polluted and are likely to cause nuisance').

Water pollution offences

9.81   Section 85 of the WRA 1991 creates a series of offences of polluting controlled waters. The power to prosecute for these offences is a very important weapon in the Agency's armoury and one that is used frequently and with tenacity. A success-ful prosecution is usually followed by a press release by the Agency explaining the nature of the offence and the penalty imposed—no doubt as an encouragement to others to be even more vigilant against the risks of water pollution. The Agency reported that sewage was the most common pollutant of controlled waters, and was found at 16% of serious incidents in 2006.[194] This is not surprising given that the sewage and water industry accounted for almost a quarter of serious (category 1 and 2) water pollution incidents. Farming and other industry caused 11% and 12% of serious water pollution incidents respectively. When it comes to dealing with the Agency over a potential prosecution, careful attention should be paid to the Agency's Code of Practice on Enforcement and Prosecution.[195]

9.82   The power to prosecute is not, however, reserved to the Agency. Private individu-als may prosecute for these offences and the environmental campaigning group Greenpeace successfully prosecuted an American chemical company in respect of discharges from its plant in Cumbria.[196] It has even led to the Environment Agency being prosecuted for the actions of its sub-contractors for this offence.[197]

9.83   A person contravenes Section 85(1) if he causes or knowingly permits:

(1)   any poisonous, noxious, or polluting matter, or any waste matter[198] to enter any controlled waters;

---

[194] *Pollution Incidents—An Overview* (Environmental Facts and Figures, Environment Agency website, 2008). However, the bald statistics are a little unreliable, as the Agency found that it was unable to find the source of pollution of nearly half of all serious incidents.

[195] See the discussion of this in Chapter 2.

[196] Private prosecution the 1989 Water Act of Albright & Wilson (September 1991). They were fined £2,000 for exceeding the limits in the discharge consent granted to its surfactants and phos-phoric acid plant at Marchon, Cumbria. Greenpeace had taken samples from the discharge pipe in the Irish Sea.

[197] The private prosecution was brought by a local landowner, Ian Cook, after a sub-contrac-tor employed by the Environment Agency to build a flow-monitoring station on the River Exe, in Somerset, inadvertently leaked toxic building waste into the main river. The Environment Agency was fined £7,500, its subcontractor was fined £27,500, and they were ordered to pay the costs of £2,932 between them (BBC News, published 17 May 2006).

[198] Note that the word 'solid' has been deleted, and 'waste', in the term 'waste matter', has been specifically linked into the definition of waste set out in European law and in the UK's waste man-agement regime. See the discussion of 'waste matter' further below.

(2) any matter, other than trade effluent or sewage effluent, to enter controlled waters by being discharged from a drain in contravention of a prohibition imposed under Section 86;

(3) any trade effluent or sewage effluent to be discharged:
    (a) into any controlled waters; or
    (b) from land in England and Wales, through a pipe, into the sea outside the seaward limits of controlled waters;

(4) any trade effluent or sewage effluent to be discharged, in contravention of any prohibition imposed under Section 86, from any building or from any fixed plant:
    (a) onto or into any land; or
    (b) into any waters of a lake or pond which are not inland freshwaters;

(5) any matter whatever to enter any inland freshwaters so as to tend to impede the proper flow of the waters in a manner leading, or likely to lead, to a substantial aggravation of:
    (a) pollution due to other causes; or
    (b) the consequences of such pollution.

Section 85(6) creates the further offence of contravening the conditions of any **9.84** consent given under that Chapter of the Act and 'contravening' includes failing to comply with the conditions.[199] This is an important provision. In 2005–6, 39 successful prosecutions were brought regarding breaches of water quality discharge consents, with fines totalling £189,650, and one enforcement notice was served by the Agency.[200]

The maximum penalties for these Section 85 offences are, on summary convic- **9.85** tion, imprisonment up to a maximum term of three months or a fine up to £20,000 or both and, on conviction on indictment, imprisonment for a term not exceeding two years or an unlimited fine or both. As discussed in Chapter 2, the normal sentence will be a fine. In 2003, the courts considered that a fine of £200,000 was manifestly excessive for a pollution incident when there had been a discharge of sewage effluent into a river,[201] particularly when compared to the total fines imposed in 2001 in the case of *R v Yorkshire Water Services Ltd.*[202] Even though it was a serious local case, and a fail-safe system should have been in place, the court took account of the company's prompt remedial action, its guilty plea, and the steps taken by it to prevent a recurrence. The fine was reduced to £60,000. The case is also notable for the more lenient approach taken by the Court of

---

[199] Ibid, s 221.
[200] Table 1: Prosecutions, fines and enforcement notices served by the Agency, *Pollution Incidents—An Overview* (Environmental Facts and Figures, Environment Agency website, 2008).
[201] *R v Anglian Water Services Ltd* [2003] EWCA Crim 2243.
[202] [2001] EWCA Crim 2635.

Appeal to the number of the defendant company's 64 similar previous convictions for sewage pollution. Unlike the crown court judge, they considered that they were not of great significance in light of the scale of their operations.

9.86 The courts do have the powers to impose severe fines. In respect of the widespread pollution caused by the oil tanker, the *Sea Empress*,[203] when it was grounded outside Milford Haven, the crown court judge regarded it to be a very serious case calling for a substantial penalty. He imposed a fine of £4 million, with costs. The Court of Appeal did consider that this was excessive, and reduced the fine to £750,000. It held that the judge had failed to give effect to the agreed basis of the port authority's plea of guilty, to give full credit for the guilty plea, and to consider the possible impact of a £4 million fine on the port authority's ability to perform its public functions, on its financial position and prospects, and the potential blight on the economy of the local area. It was accepted that the fine should recognize the seriousness of such disasters and the need to ensure the highest levels of vigilance.

The common elements of Section 85 offences

9.87 Section 85 creates offences of strict liability. On one view, these are offences which 'are not criminal in any real sense, but acts which in the public interest are prohibited under a penalty'.[204] However, this view has not prevailed. In considering the nature of the liability under Section 85(1) in the *Sea Empress* case, Lord Bingham CJ has stated:[205]

> Parliament creates an offence of strict liability because it regards the doing or not doing of a particular thing as itself so undesirable as to merit the imposition of criminal punishment on anyone who does or does not do that thing irrespective of that party's knowledge, state of mind, belief or intention. This involves a departure from the prevailing cannons of the criminal law because of the importance which is attached to achieving the result which Parliament seeks to achieve.

9.88 This therefore means that the defendant is left with few options in mounting a defence, however inadvertent it may seem that the cause of the pollution may be.

---

[203] *R v Milford Haven Port Authority* [2000] 2 Cr App R 423; [2000] Env LR 632. The Crown Court decision, when the fine of £4million was imposed (in addition to the £825,000 costs award), is reported at [1999] 1 Lloyd's Rep 673, (David Steel J). The total cost of the cleanup operation along the Pembrokeshire coast was estimated to be approximately £60 million.

[204] See *Alphacell Limited v Woodward* [1972] AC 824 at 648, comments at the end of Lord Salmon's judgment. The relevant words of the offence under the Rivers (Prevention of Pollution) Act 1951 were 'if he causes or knowingly permits to enter a stream any poisonous, noxious or polluting matter'. Lord Salmon did however acknowledge that 'It is of the utmost public importance that our rivers should not be polluted. The risk of pollution, particularly from the vast and increasing number of riparian industries, is very great.'

[205] *Environment Agency v Milford Haven Port Authority* (the *Sea Empress* case), [2000] 2 Cr App R (S) 423 at 432.

Points that would in other instances provide a good defence can then only be raised by way of mitigation. This is no doubt why considerable attention is paid to checking whether the prosecution has proved all the elements of the offence.

Controlled waters

Section 104 of the WRA 1991 defines the 'controlled waters' to which these pollution controls apply. These include: **9.89**

(1) relevant territorial waters, that is to say waters which extend seaward for three miles from the baselines from which the breadth of the territorial sea adjacent to England and Wales is measured;

(2) coastal waters, that is any water within the area extending landward from those baselines as far as the high tide limit or up to the freshwater limit of rivers; maps of freshwater limits are specified on maps deposited with the Agency;[206]

(3) inland freshwaters, that is any relevant lake or pond or any relevant river or watercourse which is above the freshwater limit; a relevant lake or pond is essentially one that is not landlocked and a relevant river or watercourse is one that is not a public sewer;

(4) groundwaters, that is any waters contained in underground strata.

Causing or knowingly permitting—acts and omissions

The distinction between 'causing' and 'knowingly permitting' is in essence a distinction between acts and omissions. These two limbs of Section 2(1)(a) of the Rivers (Prevention of Pollution) Act 1951, which was in the same terms as Section 85(1) of the WRA 1991, were analysed by Lord Wilberforce in *Alphacell v Woodward* [1972] AC 824 at 834 in these words: **9.90**

> The subsection evidently contemplates two things—*causing*, which must involve some active operation or chain of operations involving as a result the pollution of the stream; *knowingly permitting*, which involves a failure to prevent the pollution, which failure, however, must be accompanied by knowledge.

So if the charge is 'causing', the prosecution have to prove that the pollution was caused by something which the defendant did, rather than merely failed to prevent. But the notion of 'causing' is present in both limbs: under the first limb what the defendant did must have caused the pollution, and under the second limb his omission must have caused it. The distinction in Section 85(1) between acts and omissions is due to the fact that Parliament added the requirement of knowledge when the cause of the pollution is an omission. The defendant must be proved to have known that the pollution was entering the waters; it would not seem necessary that he knew the nature of the polluting matter. The defendant   **9.91**

---

[206] WRA 1991, s 192.

must, however, have the power to prevent the pollution and know he has the power to prevent the pollution to satisfy 'knowingly permitting'.

9.92 Liability under the first limb therefore requires that the defendant must have done something. It is not, however, necessary for the prosecution to prove that the defendant's positive act was the *immediate* cause of the pollution. There is no such requirement in the section. The earlier cases[207] which appeared to add that further requirement have now been disapproved.[208] In *Empress Cars*[209] Lord Hoffman explained that these cases:

> take far too restrictive a view of the requirement that the defendant must have done something. They seem to require that his positive act should in some sense have been the *immediate* cause of the escape. But the Act contains no such requirement. It only requires a finding that something which the defendant did caused the pollution . . . . Maintaining lagoons of effluent or operating the municipal sewage system is doing something.

Causing

9.93 The courts have repeatedly said that the notion of 'causing' is one of common sense but, noticing how often magistrates have attempted to apply common sense to this issue and found themselves reversed by the Divisional Court for error of law, Lord Hoffman in *Empress Cars* set out to provide the necessary guidance.[210] The first point he emphasized was that common-sense answers to questions of causation will differ according to the purpose for which the question is asked. He gave as an example a careless motorist who leaves his radio in his car; a thief breaks the quarter-light, enters the car, and steals it. If the thief is on trial, so that the question is whether he is criminally responsible, then the obvious answer is that the thief caused the damage. In the context of an inquiry into the owner's blameworthiness under a non-legal, common-sense duty to take reasonable

---

[207] *Price v Cromack* [1975] 1 WLR 988, the defendant maintained two lagoons on his land into which he agreed that the owners of adjoining land could discharge effluent. The lagoons developed leaks which allowed the effluent to escape into the river. Lord Widgery CJ held that the defendant was entitled to be acquitted because there was no 'positive act' on his part. The effluent came onto the land by gravity and found its way into the river by gravity 'with no act on his part whatever' [1975] 1 WLR 988 at 994. In *Wychavon District Council v National Rivers Authority* [1993] 1 WLR 125, the council maintained the sewage system as agent for the statutory water authority. Raw sewage was received into the sewers which were operated, maintained, and repaired by them. One of the sewers became blocked and sewage flowed into the storm water drainage system and then into the river. The Court held that the council had not done any positive act which caused the pollution. If it had known of the blockage it might have been guilty of 'knowingly permitting' the pollution but it was not liable for causing it.

[208] By the Court of Appeal in *Attorney General's Reference (No 1 of 1994)* [1995] 1 WLR 599 and by the House of Lords in *National Rivers Authority v Yorkshire Water Services* [1995] 1 AC 444 and in *Empress Car Company (Abertillery) Ltd v National Rivers Authority* [1999] 2 AC 22.

[209] *Empress Car Co (Abertillery) Ltd v NRA (now The Environment Agency)* [1999] 2 AC 22.

[210] [1999] 2 AC 22 at 29.

care of one's own possessions, one would say that his carelessness caused the loss of the radio.

Furthermore, there may be different answers to questions about causation when attributing responsibility to different people under the same rule. So in *National Rivers Authority v Yorkshire Water Services Ltd*, the defendant was a sewerage undertaker which received sewage, treated it, and then discharged the treated liquid into the river. It was held to have caused pollution when a solvent called iso-octanol, which some unknown person had discharged into the sewer, passed through the treatment works and into the river.[211] On the other hand if the person who had poured the solvent down the drain was prosecuted then he too would have been held to have caused the pollution. It is therefore wrong in the case of a prosecution under Section 85 to ask 'What caused the pollution?' There may be a number of correct answers to a question put in those terms. The only question which has to be asked for the purposes of Section 85(1) is 'Did the defendant cause the pollution?'. The fact that for different purposes or even for the same purpose one could also say that someone or something else caused the pollution is not inconsistent with the defendant having caused it.

9.94

The fact is that one cannot give a common-sense answer to a question of causation for the purpose of attributing responsibility under some rule without knowing the purpose and scope of the rule. In the case of the duty imposed by Section 85(1), the liability imposed by the subsection is strict: it does not require mens rea in the sense of intention or negligence. Strict liability is imposed in the interests of protecting controlled waters from pollution. Therefore, Lord Hoffman held in *Empress Cars* that because liability is strict in order to achieve this purpose, it includes liability for certain deliberate acts of third parties and for natural events. So he held that the case of *Impress (Worcester) Ltd v Rees* [1971] 2 All ER 357 was wrongly decided because the Divisional Court had reasoned that the defendant was entitled to be acquitted simply because the escape of fuel oil from a tank into a river was caused by the deliberate act of a stranger opening a valve.

9.95

Nevertheless, Section 85(1) does not create an absolute liability in the sense that all that has to be shown is that polluting matter escaped from the defendant's land, irrespective of how this happened. It is still necessary to prove that the defendant caused the pollution. Lord Hoffman, therefore, sought to identify the principle by which some acts of third parties or some natural events negative the causal connection for the purposes of Section 85(1) and others do not. He rejected foreseeability as the principle. Liability under Section 85(1) is strict and not based on

9.96

---

[211] The *Yorkshire Water Services Ltd* case is also notable for the result, as the company was found 'not guilty', even though it had caused the pollution, because it was able to successfully rely on the defence available to statutory undertakers in what is now WRA 1991, s 87(2).

negligence in which foreseeability is an ingredient. The question whether the defendant ought reasonably to have foreseen what happened is not relevant. The question remains whether the defendant caused the pollution and foreseeability is not the criterion for determining whether a person caused something or not. People often cause things which they could not have foreseen. Lord Hoffman decided that the only common-sense distinction is between acts and events which, although not necessarily foreseeable in the particular case, are in the generality a normal and familiar fact of life, and acts or events which are abnormal and extraordinary. Leaky pipes and lagoons, even vandalism, are normal facts of life even though the particular defendant could not reasonably have foreseen that it would happen to him. So if the defendant did something which produced a situation in which the polluting matter could escape but a necessary condition of the actual escape which happened was the act of a third party or a natural event, justices must consider whether the act or event should be regarded as a normal fact of life or something extraordinary. If it was in the general run of things a matter of ordinary occurrence, it will not negate the causal effect of the defendant's acts, even if it was not foreseeable that it would happen to that particular defendant or take that particular form. If it can be regarded as something extraordinary, it is open to justices to hold that the defendant did not cause the pollution. The distinction between ordinary and extraordinary is one of fact and degree to which the justices must apply their common sense and knowledge of what happens in the area. So in the *Empress Cars* case it was held that the defendant had been rightly convicted when a person unknown had opened the unlocked tap on an oil tank and the contents of the tank had run into a drum to which the tank was connected by a connection pipe, overflowed into the yard, and passed down the drain into the River Ebbw Fach. On those facts there was ample evidence on which the Crown Court was entitled to find that the company had caused the pollution.

9.97 The complexities of who can be held responsible during the management of an incident can depend on the contractual arrangements that have been made. In *Environment Agency v BIFFA Waste Services and another*,[212] the contractors who were instructed to organize the tankering away of the leaking sewage and also the tanker company were acquitted where it had not been established that they had any more responsibility than to carry out the specific measures that they had been instructed to carry out.

---

[212] [2006] EWHC 1102 (Admin). The court held that additional pollution was caused when the person in charge of the site failed to make arrangements for further tankering.

Liability due to an act or default

The potential liability for pollution of controlled waters reaches beyond those **9.98** persons or companies who are immediately responsible for it. As discussed above, although it was alleged that it was vandals who had caused the escape of diesel in the *Empress Cars* case, their actions were not deemed to be 'extraordinary' and the company was held to be guilty. But the liability goes further than that. The WRA 1991 makes specific provision in Section 217(3) of the WRA that:

> . . . where the commission by any person of an offence under the water pollution provisions of this Act is due to the act or default of some other person, that other person may be charged with and convicted of the offence whether or not proceedings for the offence are taken against the first-mentioned person.

This can be an appropriate charge, combined with Section 85(1), where a land- **9.99** owner permits someone else to carry out an operation on his land which gives rise to a risk of pollution and pollution is caused. This responsibility was considered by the courts when Express Dairies Ltd was prosecuted by the Environment Agency.[213] Express Dairies Ltd allowed another company to load and unload milk at its depot. The company spilt the contents of some milk churns. The Court held that if a landowner, such as Express, is going to permit an operation on his land which gives rise to a risk of pollution, then in order not to fall foul of Section 85(1) he must carry out a risk assessment and respond to what that assessment reveals. Otherwise if pollution does occur it may be impossible for him to say that the offence committed by those using his land was not due to one or more of his acts or defaults.

Poisonous, noxious, or polluting matter

There is no statutory definition in the WRA 1991 of these terms and so they bear **9.100** their ordinary meaning.[214] It is the nature of the matter which is relevant and not the effect that the entry of the matter has on the quality of the receiving waters. So it seems that the offence would be committed if poisonous, noxious, or polluting matter entered controlled waters even where the receiving waters were so polluted already that the newly introduced matter did not make the overall quality of the waters worse. It is the potential effect which appears relevant to liability rather

---

[213] *Express Ltd v Environment Agency* [2004] EWHC 1710 (Admin); for a case law analysis see Carolyn Abbot, 'Water Pollution and Acts of Third Parties' [2005] 18 JEL 119. As she says, it is arguable that the decision in the *Express Ltd* case should be seen as an application of the principle in *Sea Empress*, so that Express Dairies were guilty of an offence under Section 85(1) regardless of Section 217(3).

[214] See *R v Dovermoss* [1995] 159 JP 448 CA, which held that 'pollute' should bear its ordinary dictionary meaning and that the OED defined polluting as 'to make physically impure, foul or filthy; to dirty, stain, taint, defoul'. One of the grounds of appeal had been that, as the ammonia levels were lower than those permitted by the regulations, and there was no harmful effect on animal or plant life, then the company had not committed an offence under Section 85(1).

than any actual harm caused, although of course the extent of any actual harm would be relevant to the appropriate penalty imposed.

9.101 Given the importance of the amenity value of controlled waters, it is likely that matter would be considered polluting if it could make the waters less pleasant to look at, for example by discolouration. This was the approach taken by the court in *Express Ltd v Environment Agency* [2004][215] where the spillage of cream had entered the nearby stream. The court held that 'polluting matter' does not need to be either poisonous or noxious, as it is sufficient if it stains or taints the water, and that the magistrates were entitled to conclude that the cream that had been released into the controlled waters had the potential for harm. Such an approach would also be consistent with the meaning given to 'pollution of the environment' in the EPA 1990, Section 29, which includes offence to man's senses. However, the fact that a spillage has caused no actual harm to the watercourse will be a relevant factor in the decision on what enforcement action should be taken. On the other hand, it has been held that no offence was caused under Section 85 Water Resources Act 1991 when lorries drove through a river and stirred up the silt from the river bed.[216] Even if this made the water cloudy, it did not involve introducing anything into the water which was not there before.

Waste matter

9.102 For the purposes of Section 85, the 'waste matter' to which this section refers does not also have to have the qualities of being poisonous, noxious, or polluting. An important amendment has recently been made to the section as it originally referred to 'any solid waste matter'. This ambiguous phrase has been now tidied up. The word 'solid' has been deleted, and the definition of 'waste', in the term 'waste matter', has been specifically linked into the definition of waste set out in European law and in the UK's waste management regime. [217] A new Section 85(7) defines it as including anything that is waste for the purposes of Directive 2006/12/EC.[218] Whether matter is waste will therefore depend on the intention of the holder of the waste and whether they are discarding it, and there is a rich body of case law on this point.[219] Directive 2006/12/EC is the directive that consolidates the previous directives that dealt with waste management, although it does exclude certain types of waste from its scope. The new Section 85(7) of the WRA 1991

---

[215] *Express Ltd v Environment Agency* [2004] EWHC 1710 (Admin), also discussed above.

[216] *National Rivers Authority v BIFFA Waste Services Ltd* [1996] Env LR 227.

[217] The relevant amendments were made as part of the consequential amendments in the Environmental Permitting (England and Wales) Regulations 2007 (SI 2007/3528) — see reg 73 and Sch 21, Pt 1, para 21, as from 6 April 2008.

[218] The only waste matter excluded is the 'waste' excluded from the scope of Directive 2006/12/EC by Article 2(1) of that Directive (see s 85(7)).

[219] See Chapter 7 on waste management further.

repeats these exclusions,[220] so that it will be important to ensure that any water pollution caused by waste waters or agricultural waste are defined in terms of their poisonous, noxious, or polluting qualities and not as waste matter.

Trade effluent or sewage effluent

'Effluent' is defined in Section 221 as meaning any liquid including particles of **9.103** matter or other substances in suspension in the liquid. 'Trade effluent' is defined by Section 221 as including any effluent discharged from premises used for carrying on any trade or industry. It does not include surface water, or water from roofs, nor domestic sewage. Premises used for agricultural purposes, or for fish farming, or for scientific research are to be considered as premises used for carrying on a trade whether the activities are for profit or not.

'Sewage effluent' includes any effluent from the sewage disposal or sewerage works **9.104** of a sewerage undertaker. Again surface water is not included. Note that it is also possible to prosecute an escape of sewage as a waste offence under Part II of the EPA 1990.[221]

For the purposes of the offences under Section 85(3) and (4), the sewerage under- **9.105** taker is responsible for the discharge of sewage effluent from his sewer or works where he was bound either unconditionally or subject to conditions which were observed to receive the relevant matter into the sewer or works even though he would not have caused or knowingly permitted the discharge on the application of the normal principles.[222] Conversely it is a defence for a sewerage undertaker to show that even though there has been a contravention of the conditions of a discharge consent, the contravention was because of a discharge by some other person into the sewer which the undertaker was not bound to receive and the

---

[220] Article 2(1) of Directive 2006/12/EC states that the following shall be excluded from the scope of the Directive: (a) gaseous effluents emitted into the atmosphere; and (b) where they are already covered by other legislation: (i) radioactive waste; (ii) waste resulting from prospecting, extraction, treatment and storage of mineral resources and the working of quarries; (iii) animal carcases and the following agricultural waste: faecal matter and other natural, non-dangerous substances used in farming; (iv) waste waters, with the exception of waste in liquid form; (v) decommissioned explosives.

[221] *R (Thames Water Utilities Ltd) v Bromley Magistrates' Court* (Case C-252/05) [2007] 1 WLR 1945, ECJ. In the prosecution proceedings under the EPA 1990, s 33 in the magistrates' court, the water company raised the question whether sewage which had escaped could be 'waste' within Directive 75/442. The magistrates referred the question to the ECJ which held that it could, and the fact that it was spilled accidentally did not prevent it from being 'discarded' and therefore waste.

[222] WRA 1991, s 87(1A); where there is an agreement under s 110A between sewerage undertakers, then sub-sections 87(1b) and (1c) deem that it is 'the sending undertaker' that is then responsible. Sections 87(1)(1A)(1B)(1C) were substituted for the original s 87(1) by the Competition and Service (Utilities) Act 1992, s 46(1)(3) in May 1992.

undertaker could not reasonably have been expected to prevent the discharge into the sewer.[223] This defence is available in respect of all the Section 85 offences.[224]

Entry or discharge

9.106 It has been held by a magistrate's court[225] that there is a distinction between the 'entry' of matter to waters and its 'discharge' into those waters in that discharge implies a release through a pipe or some other controlled release. So the defendant was not guilty of an offence under Section 85(3) where trade effluent had percolated through the ground from the defendant's premises into the controlled waters. It was held that the effluent had *entered* the waters but had not been *discharged* into the waters. This interpretation does seem to accord with the ordinary meaning of 'discharge' and Section 85(2) does refer to entry 'by being discharged from a drain or sewer' which supports this interpretation.

A prohibition imposed under Section 86

9.107 This Section empowers the Agency to serve a notice on a person prohibiting him from making or continuing a discharge or attaching conditions to the making or continuing of the discharge. The Section also contains a power to prescribe by regulation certain substances or particular concentrations of substances whose discharge is then prohibited, but no relevant regulations have been made. The prohibition does not take effect until three months after the notice is served unless the Agency considers that there is an emergency which justifies the prohibition coming into force earlier. The recipient of the notice can, however, extend the three-month period by making an application for a discharge consent and the notice then does not bite until that application is finally disposed of.[226] Once a prohibition takes effect the offences under Section 85(2) and (4) are committed when the defendant causes or knowingly permits the entry or discharge. Even on a charge of 'knowingly permitting' it does not appear necessary for the prosecution to prove that the defendant knew of the prohibition or of any relevant condition whose non-observance is relied on. In the context of waste disposal it has been held that the prosecution simply have to prove knowledge of the deposit of the waste not that the deposit was in contravention of a condition in the waste management licence.[227]

---

[223] Ibid, s 87(2).
[224] *NRA v Yorkshire Water Services* [1995] 1 AC 444.
[225] *National Rivers Authority v Coal Products Ltd* ENDS December 1993, Vol 227, p 45.
[226] WRA 1991, s 86(6).
[227] *Ashcroft v Cambro Waste Management* [1981] 1 WLR 1349.

Statutory defences

A person is not guilty of an offence under Section 85 if the entry occurs or the   **9.108**
discharge is made 'under and in accordance with, or as a result of any act or
omission under and in accordance with' various statutory consents, licences,
and authorizations. These are:

(1) a discharge consent given under the WRA 1991; see further below;
(2) a permit granted under the Environmental Permitting (England and Wales)
     Regulations 2007, except insofar as the permit authorizes a Part B activity
     within the meaning of those Regulations.[228] These provisions essentially rep-
     licate the previous exclusions under s 88(1) for discharges made in accordance
     with an IPPC permit and a waste management licence. The defence regarding
     a waste management licence was employed successfully by Coal Products
     Limited in their prosecution by the NRA before the Chesterfield Magistrates[229]
     when they argued that the tars which had percolated into the river had come
     from the tip or lagoon on their site subject to a disposal licence under the
     1974 Act. Presumably the magistrates were satisfied that the entry of the pol-
     luting matter into the river was under and in accordance with the licence
     or was as a result of an act or omission under and in accordance with
     the licence. As both the Agency and the local authority can grant such
     authorizations, this defence does rely on the one regulatory hand knowing
     what the other regulatory hand is doing in controlling discharges to control-
     led waters from the regulated activities;
(4) a licence to deposit substances and articles at sea under the Food and
     Environment Act 1985;
(5) Section 163 of the WRA 1991, that is, discharges made for works purposes
     by the Agency, or Section 165 of the Water Industry Act 1991, that is, such
     discharges by a water undertaker;
(6) any local statutory provision or order which expressly confers power to
     discharge effluent into water; or
(7) any prescribed enactment.

Discharge consents

The power to control water pollution by the issue and enforcement of discharge   **9.109**
consents is central to the performance by the Agency of its duty under Section 84
to ensure so far as practicable that the water quality objectives for any waters are
achieved. Section 88(2) of the WRA 1991 introduces Schedule 10 of the Act

---

[228] See the amended s 88(1)(c). The necessary amendments and repeals were made by the
Environment Permitting (England and Wales) Regulations 2007 (SI 2007/3528) from 6 April
2008, subject to savings.
[229] *National Rivers Authority v Coal Products Ltd* ENDS December 1993, Vol 227, p 45.

where the procedures for applying for consents are set out. The Control of Pollution (Applications, Appeals, and Registers) Regulations 1996[230] further specify the procedures. The procedures follow the normal pattern of application, publicity, consultation, and determination. The Agency has four months in which to make a determination unless a longer period is agreed, after which the application is deemed to have been refused and an appeal may be made to the Secretary of State or the National Assembly of Wales.[231] The Secretary of State and the National Assembly of Wales have the power to call in an application for their determination.[232] Where a consent is granted it is subject to such conditions as the Agency thinks fit and may include conditions covering the places where the discharges may be made and the design of the outlets, the nature, composition, temperature, volume, and rate of discharge and the periods when the discharge may be made, the treatment of the discharges to minimize polluting effects, sampling procedures and measuring procedures, the recording of results, and the making of returns to the Agency.[233]

9.110 The Agency also has power to issue a consent unilaterally without any application having been made to it where effluent or other matter has been discharged into controlled waters or where there has been a discharge in contravention of a prohibition under Section 86.[234] If it thinks that a repetition is likely, the Agency can serve on the discharger an instrument in writing giving consent to future discharges subject to specified conditions. The position for the future is then certain and any prosecution can be founded on the simple contravention of the conditions of the discharge consent under Section 85(6).

9.111 The Agency may review consents but not within four years of their grant[235] because each consent has to specify a minimum four-year period in which no variation or revocation will take place. When the Agency does review a consent it can revoke it or modify its conditions or impose conditions on a previously unconditional consent.

9.112 The Secretary of State has the power to direct the Agency to do any of those things either in order to meet a community or international obligation or for the protection of public health or of flora or fauna dependent on an aquatic environment or following any representations made to him.[236] Compensation may be payable

---

[230] SI 1996/2971, as amended by SI 1999/1006 and modified by SI 1998/1649.
[231] WRA 1991, Sch 10 para 3(2).
[232] Ibid, Sch 10 para 5.
[233] Ibid, Sch 10 para 3(4). They must also exercise their powers and duties so as to ensure that discharges into controlled waters comply with the requirements of the Urban Waste Water Treatment (England and Wales) Regulations 1994 (SI 1994/2841, as amended by SI 2003/1788).
[234] WRA 1991, Sch 10 para 6.
[235] Ibid, Sch 10 paras 7 and 8.
[236] Ibid, Sch 10 para 7(4).

in respect of any loss or damage suffered as a result of the Agency complying with such a direction for early modification on the basis of protection of public health or of flora or fauna unless the direction was a result of an unforeseeable change in circumstances.[237]

As already indicated, Section 85(6) creates the offence of contravening the conditions of a discharge consent; 'contravention' includes a failure to comply.[238] Even where a particular discharge breaches more than one condition of the consent, only one offence is committed for each discharge.[239] A developer of an industrial estate has been held liable for an offence under Section 85(6) where it retained ownership of the surface water drainage system but where its tenant made the contravening discharge. The Court of Appeal held that the prosecution did not have to prove that the defendant performed the positive act of discharge: the Act contemplated workable constraints and intended that the regime of consents would be comprehensive. The developer was entitled to the benefits of the consent and so was also subject to the burden of its conditions.[240] **9.113**

There would seem to be little scope for challenge to the unreasonableness or validity of a condition in a prosecution brought for its alleged contravention. In *R v Enttrick Trout Company* [1994] Env LR 165, the defence sought to mount such a challenge on the basis that the condition in question which limited the quantity of trade effluent discharged was invalid because it had not been imposed for a permissible purpose, namely the prevention of pollution, and because it was unnecessary as the discharge did not pollute the river. The Court of Appeal held that such a defence could not be run in a criminal prosecution because the defence were seeking to argue procedural invalidity which had to rely on evidence and argument which the criminal court was not properly placed to deal with. Such arguments could only be run by judicial review. Since this decision, the Court of Appeal in *R v Wicks*,[241] in the context of an enforcement notice issued in respect of a breach of planning control, decided that there is no proper distinction between substantive and procedural invalidity and that any argument on invalidity can only be run by judicial review or statutory challenge where available. There is therefore likely to be even less scope for the collateral challenge to a condition attached to a discharge consent than was allowed in the *Enttrick Trout* case. **9.114**

---

237 Ibid, Sch 10 para 7(5).
238 Ibid, s 221(1).
239 *Severn Trent River Authority v Express Food Group* [1989] 153 JP 126.
240 *Taylor Woodrow Property Management Ltd v NRA* [1995] Env LR 52.
241 [1998] AC 92, HL.

Emergency

9.115 It is a defence to a charge under Section 85 that the entry or discharge in question was caused or permitted or made in an emergency in order to avoid danger to life or health.[242] The defence is subject to the requirements—which would have to be established by the defendant on the balance of probabilities—first, that he had taken all such steps as were reasonably practicable in the circumstances for minimizing the extent of the entry or discharge and of its polluting effects and, secondly, that he furnished particulars of the incident to the Agency as soon as reasonably practicable after the entry occurred.

9.116 Although the danger is not expressed to be to *human* life or health, it seems unlikely a court would accept danger to animal or plant life or health as being a sufficient emergency to justify a contravening discharge or entry.

9.117 As the entry has to be caused or permitted or discharge made *in order* to avoid danger, it seems likely that the defendant's knowledge or belief as to the state of emergency will be relevant in establishing the defence. If a defendant genuinely believed he would have to discharge the matter in question in order to save life, it is submitted the defence would be made out even if with hindsight it appeared that that belief was wrong—provided the other requirements for the defence were met.

9.118 The defence can apply at a late stage in the chain of causation. In *Express Dairies Distribution v Environment Agency,*[243] the court acquitted the company on the basis of Section 89(1) when the driver of a milk tanker had had to pull over onto the hard shoulder of a motorway, following a blow out of one of its tyres. The delivery pipe on the tanker was also broken by the accident, and this caused a large quantity of milk to leak into controlled waters. The court considered that the blow out was not an extraordinary event and that everything else had followed from that, so that there had been no break in the chain of causation. However, the driver's decision to pull over because of the tyre blowout had been done to avoid danger to life or health.

Vessels

9.119 It is not an offence under Section 85 to cause or permit a discharge of trade or sewage effluent from a vessel[244] but any of the other offences under Section 85, notably causing or knowingly permitting poisonous, noxious, or polluting matter to enter controlled waters may be committed from a vessel. The Agency's

---

[242] WRA 1991, s 89(1).

[243] *Express Dairies Distribution v Environment Agency* [2003] EWHC 448 (Admin); (2004) 1 WLR 579.

[244] WRA 1991, s 89(2).

bye-law-making powers under Schedule 25 of the WRA 1991 are used to deal with sewage discharges from vessels.

Crown immunity

Government Departments and other parts of the Crown cannot be prosecuted for **9.120** any contravention of any provision made by or under the WRA 1991, even though the provisions of the Act do bind the Crown.[245] The most that the Agency can do is to apply to the High Court for a declaration that there has been an unlawful act or omission of the Crown which constitutes such a contravention.

Highway authorities

Highway authorities have a duty to maintain highways and that includes keeping **9.121** them properly drained.[246] To carry out that duty they have the power to lay drains and to discharge water from those drains into inland or tidal waters.[247] Therefore, a highway authority will only be guilty of an offence under Section 85 if the Agency has exercised its power under Section 86 to prohibit the discharge. Note that the Highways Agency, which is responsible for the national road network, falls into a separate category. It is part of the Department for Transport, and acts in the name of the Secretary of State and not as an independent body.

Abandoned mines

There is a great potential for pollution from contaminated water from mines. **9.122** Serious incidents of river pollution have occurred after coal and tin mines have closed. Water accumulates underground and becomes contaminated and highly acidic. Mine operators have to pump underground workings to maintain working conditions and they have to be careful to avoid committing the offences under Section 85. But once the mine closes, pumping ceases and control over the contaminated water may end. The long predicted demise of many entire coal fields and the more surprising closure of many modern mines have made this an acute problem.

Nevertheless, the view has been taken that protection should be given to landown- **9.123** ers who may never have been responsible for mining at all and who may have bought the land without being aware that it was undermined. So a defence to the offences under Section 85 is provided by Section 89(3) for a person who merely *permits* water from an abandoned mine or an abandoned part of a mine to enter controlled waters. So a landowner is not guilty if he simply allows the position to

---

[245] Ibid, s 222—note that the text of the original s 222 was amended by the Environment Act 1995, Sch.21, para 2.

[246] Highways Act 1980, s 41.

[247] Ibid, s 100.

continue where, for example, old mine shafts on his land are discharging polluted water into controlled waters or where contaminated water from an old mine on another person's land is flowing across his land and into a river.

9.124 However, the defence was withdrawn as from the 31 December 1999 in respect of owners and former operators of abandoned mines.[248]

Anti-pollution works notices

9.125 The Agency has the power to enter onto land and carry out works to prevent the entry of polluting matters into controlled waters, to remove any such matters or remedy their effect, or to restore the controlled waters. The Agency can then recover its costs. These powers were granted to it under Section 161 of the 1991 Act. In 1999, new powers were added to the 1991 Act, under the amendments made by the Environment Act 1995. The Agency was given the power to compel owners and occupiers to clean up land and water in order to avoid water pollution, under Section 161A of the 1991 Act.

9.126 The Works Notice under s 161A can be served on the person who caused or knowingly permitted any poisonous, noxious, or polluting matter to be present at the place from which it is likely to enter controlled waters, or to be present in the controlled waters. The notice can be appealed, although there is a short window of 21 days in which to do so.[249] This power does sometimes overlap with the powers under the contaminated land regime,[250] and it is only a matter of policy that the contaminated land regime should take priority. Such a notice can only be issued after the Agency has consulted with the affected persons.[251] It is a criminal offence for the recipient to fail to comply with the Notice within the specified time.[252] The Agency may also enter their land and 'may do what that person was required to do and may recover from him any costs or expenses reasonably incurred by the Agency in doing it'.[253]

9.127 There is an express statutory provision that any person whose consent is required 'shall' grant such rights in relation to any land as will enable the person on whom the notice is served to comply with the requirements,[254] and compensation is payable to them for this.[255] While this right could be the basis for seeking an injunction to compel access to be given, the 1991 Act does not provide for any

---

[248] WRA 1991, s 89(3A).

[249] See the Anti-Pollution Works Regulations 1999, SI 1999/1006.

[250] See Chapter 12 further, and the provision for serving Remediation Notices where significant harm is likely to occur to controlled waters.

[251] WRA 1991, ss 161A(4) and 161B(3) (as amended).

[252] Ibid, s 161D.

[253] Ibid, s 161D(3).

[254] Ibid, s 161B.

[255] The Anti-Pollution Works Regulations 1991, reg 7.

sanctions where a third party refuses to grant consent for any works that are required under such a notice. The burden is still on the recipients to ensure that any consents are forthcoming. This burden is the same burden that would apply if the works required, say, planning permission.

E. Land Drainage and Flood Control

Introduction

A distinct and self-contained regulatory regime governing the management of inland waterways and the prevention of flooding is established by the Land Drainage Act 1991.[256] This is an almost exclusively administrative piece of legislation, and, as the long title of the Act reveals, consolidates earlier statutes, notably the Land Drainage Act 1930. It deals with the constitution, membership, and functions of the bodies responsible for drainage, that is, principally, drainage boards and local authorities. A second and important subject is the control of the flow of watercourses and ditches, mainly by regulating the extent to which they can be obstructed, and by providing for their maintenance. Most of the rest of the Act is concerned with the financing of and expenditure by drainage boards and other drainage authorities. As will be seen, these provisions are of a kind which is familiar in most spheres of public administration.

9.128

Flood controls

Central Government has overall policy responsibility for flood and coastal erosion risk, and it provides most of the necessary funds to the Environment Agency and the other flood and coastal defence authorities for flood management work. The Environment Agency has been tasked with exercising a 'general supervision' over all matters relating to flood defence in relation to England and Wales,[257] in addition to its principal aim with regard to the promotion of sustainable development.[258] The Agency also has a crucial consultation role in the planning regime when new development is proposed in areas of flood risk.[259] The Agency has had

9.129

---

[256] 1991, c 59. and in local Land Drainage Bye-laws. For a comprehensive overview see Howarth *Flood Defence Law* (2002, Shaw and Sons).

[257] Environment Act 1995 s 6(4); this is subject to WRA 1991, s 106 (obligation to carry out flood defence functions through committees).

[258] EA 1995, s 4. See Chapter 2 further. The aim is to protect or enhance the environment taken as a whole as to make the contribution towards attaining the objective of achieving sustainable development which the Government thinks it should make, which is set out in the Statutory Guidance to the Agency.

[259] See Chapter 14 further; general policy on this in England is set out in the Planning Policy Statement 25 ('PPS 25'), and in Wales in TAN 15 Development and Flood Risk (2004). These now set out a sequential test (rather than just a precautionary approach) for developing sites, and protect all 'functional flood plains' from everything but exceptional development.

to adapt its policies and processes in order to anticipate the impacts of climate change in flood risk management, and allowance must now be made for this in any flood risk assessment.[260]

9.130 The Agency is partly responsible for sea defences[261] and is also the land drainage authority for any 'main rivers' which are defined as 'a watercourse vested in, or under the control of, a drainage body'.[262] These 'main rivers' are designated as such on main river maps, and are generally the larger arterial watercourses. All other rivers and watercourses are 'ordinary watercourses' and are the responsibility either of the Internal Drainage Boards (in areas known as Internal Drainage Districts) or of the local authority. This does mean that the Agency only has the powers to carry out flood defence works on main rivers, and that it only has a supervisory role over other watercourses (including giving land drainage consent). It has however been agreed that the Agency should take over responsibility for the management of these 'critical ordinary watercourses'[263] from the local authorities and internal drainage boards.

9.131 At the moment, there are perhaps too many public organizations involved in the provision of flood defence. The National Audit Office has reported that the extent of joined-up working required to protect those at risk represented 'a massive challenge'.[264] Further changes to the funding and organization of flood management may follow in 2009 when the Government intends to publish a draft Floods

---

[260] But note that, as of 2008, the Environment Agency's Flood Map and Flood Zones do not take account of climate change impacts—they were drafted before this policy presumption was accepted.

[261] The Agency shares this role with the maritime local authorities, who look after coast protection (prevention of coastal erosion) and may also undertake sea defence works. Coast protection is the responsibiliy of 'coast protection authorities', which are district or unitary councils (the Coast Protection Act 1949).

[262] Land Draining Act 1991 s 72 (as amended). The original text of the LDA 1991 referred to the National Rivers Authority, and these references have been replaced by the Environment Agency (pursuant to the consequential amendments made by the Environment Act 1995, Schedule 22).

[263] This a category of 'ordinary watercourses' which the Agency and other authorities agree are critical because of their potential to put large numbers of people and property at risk from flooding.

[264] The National Audit Office reported on 'Inland Flood Defence' (March 2001). In 2001, it reported that in addition to the Agency and central governmment, there were 235 Internal Drainage Boards, 9 Regional and 11 Local Flood Defence Committees, and all the local authorities involved. It reviewed the matter again in 'Building and maintaining river and coastal flood defences in England' (June 2007). Since 2001, general conditions of assets had not improved significantly, with 50 percent of linear defences and 61 percent of flood defence structures in good condition or better in 2007—compared to 64 per cent and 57 per cent respectively at the time of the NAO's previous 2001 report.

and Water Bill.[265] The European Union is also proposing a Directive to ensure that there is a concerted EU action programme for flood protection.[266]

Riparian owners

The primary responsibility for all watercourses rests with the private landowners, as the riparian owners. It is accepted at common law that an occupier of land is entitled to prevent river flood waters coming onto his land, and that he will not then be liable in nuisance if damage was thereby caused to someone else's property.[267] This protection against a 'common enemy' is not unlimited, as an occupier must act reasonably. Furthermore, if private defences are constructed and they are not properly maintained, a person flooded as a result could have a claim in negligence or nuisance against their owner. Their responsibilities also include accepting natural flows from upstream, and maintaining the system to allow water to pass on without obstruction. Any obstructions affecting the flow must also be removed by them. There is something of a general misconception that the Agency and the local Council are also responsible for this work, whereas they only have permissive powers to act, for instance to mitigate the effects of flooding. Works on any watercourse require Land Drainage Consent from the Environment Agency, and may also require planning permission from the Local Planning Authority.

9.132

Regional flood defence committees

The Agency's actual flood defence functions are carried out by the Regional Flood Defence Committees (RFDCs), as its agent.[268] Following the reforms made by the Water Act 2003, there are now 11 regional committees in place of the 20

9.133

---

[265] This proposed Bill is in response to the review 'Learning lessons from the 2007 floods—Full Report' (June 2008), known as the Pitt Report, and and the Government's Water Strategy, *Future Water*. This may include giving the Agency greater overall powers. The Government agreed with Pitt's Interim Report, published in December 2007, which stated that flooding legislation should be updated and streamlined under a single unifying Act of Parliament that addressed all sources of flooding, clarified the responsibilities and facilitated flood risk management.

[266] The European Commission published a proposal for a Directive on the assessment and managment of floods (COM(2006) 15 final). The draft EC Floods Directive would require the UK to carry out a preliminary flood risk assessment for each river basin district, and to prepare flood risk maps and flood risk management plans. This follows the Commission's Communication on flood risk management (COM(2004) 472 final, July 2004).

[267] See *Arscott and Others v Coal Authority and Another* [2005] Env LR 6, CA. The Coal Board had deposited spoil on recreation grounds that were frequently susceptible to flooding in 1972–1975. The River Taff overflowed in October 1998, and the raised levels caused the flooding of A's property. No negligence could be shown. Nor was this a contravention of the European Convention on Human Rights 1950 (specifically Article 8 and Protocol 1, Article 1).

[268] Enviroment Act 1995 ss 14–19. These Committees are made up of Ministry appointees and local councillors. They therefore provide some local accountability.

regional and local flood defence committees in England.[269] It is the RFDC that will determine the local flood defence policy, determine each year the Agency's three-year business plan and approve its programme of work for the following year, and determine the local levy on council tax. They are empowered to provide flood warning systems,[270] and to make bye-laws for flood defence purposes.[271] Their powers include maintaining, improving, or constructing drainage works for the purpose of defence against sea water or tidal water anywhere in their area, including the territorial sea beyond low-water mark.[272]

Internal drainage boards

9.134 Part I of the Land Drainage Act 1991 establishes internal drainage districts, these being areas which will derive benefit from drainage operations, or avoid danger because of those operations.[273] Each internal drainage district is the responsibility of an internal drainage board.[274] The boards are bodies corporate, elected by a curiously old-fashioned looking system, which enfranchises the occupiers or owners of land within the internal drainage district, and gives them voting powers which increase with the rateable value of the property in question.[275] The activities of internal drainage boards are subject to general supervision by the Environment Agency, as successor to the National Rivers Authority.[276] Thus, the Agency has powers to review the boundaries of internal drainage districts, to amalgamate the whole or parts of different drainage districts, to abolish them and set up new ones, amend their constitutions, and even to amend local Acts of Parliament which deal with drainage matters.[277] If the Environment Agency petitions him, the relevant Minister may make the Agency the internal drainage board for any drainage district.[278] The Agency has general supervisory powers over internal drainage

---

[269] The Water Act 2003 provided for the abolition of local committees and their replacement by regional committees—it inserted a new s 18A into the WRA 1991, and amended Schedule 4 (by s 66 and 68 of the Water Act 2003)—eg the Anglian Regional Flood Defence Committee (Abolition) Order 2004 abolished the Anglian Regional Flood Defence Committee, and the five local flood defence districts within its area, and created three single-tier regional flood defence committees. Funding arrangements were also changed so that the Environment Agency now receives a single grant-in-aid from the Department for Environment, Food and Rural Affairs to allocate to the committees.

[270] Water Resources Act 1991 s 166.

[271] Ibid, Sch 25, para 5.

[272] Ibid, ss 2, 165.

[273] Land Drainage Act 1991, s 1(1).

[274] Ibid, s 1(2).

[275] Ibid, s 1(3) and Sch 1. This is reminiscent more of Old Sarum than the era of the new millennium.

[276] Ibid, s 2 and passim.

[277] Ibid, ss 2 and 3.

[278] Ibid, ss 4 and 72(1). In England, this responsibility now lies with Defra, and in Wales, it is the National Assembly of Wales.

boards, including the power to give directions guiding them as to the exercise of their functions. Its consent is also needed if a drainage board wishes to carry out drainage works which affect the interests of another board, or result in the discharge of water into a main river.[279]

Additionally, the Environment Agency has default powers in cases where drainage boards fail to exercise their land drainage powers adequately, and may also direct that a local authority can exercise default powers in place of a drainage board. In cases of dispute as to whether default powers should be conferred the matter is resolved by the relevant Minister, if necessary after a public local inquiry.[280] **9.135**

Finally, internal drainage boards are constrained in two further respects. In an interesting precursor to the controversy over the 'right to roam', they, together with the Environment Agency and the Ministers, must have regard at all times to the needs of the environment and recreation, including the desirability of preserving (though not of extending) the public freedom of access to areas of woodland, mountains, moor, heath, down, cliff, foreshore, and buildings or sites of archaeological, architectural, or historic interest.[281] Secondly, where Natural England, the Countryside Council for Wales, the National Parks Authority, or the Boards Authority consider that their interests are affected by the activities of a drainage board, they may give notice to that effect, in which case the board must consult the notifying body before carrying out any works which might affect those interests.[282] **9.136**

Drainage powers

Drainage boards, local authorities, and the Environment Agency have the powers which it might be expected they would possess. These are to maintain existing works, meaning watercourses and dams, sluices, weirs, locks, and other drainage works; to improve them, that is, by deepening, widening, straightening watercourses, and removing or altering weirs, dams, sluices, and other works. Again predictably, the powers include power to construct new works.[283] An inevitable **9.137**

---

[279] Ibid, s 7. The concept of a 'main river' leads to an egregious example of the parliamentary draftsman's art. The interpretation section of the Land Drainage Act refers the seeker after the law to the definition of 'main river' in the WRA 1991. The phrase is not mentioned at all in the general interpretation section of this statute, and the reader eventually tracks it down in s 113, which is the interpretation section of Part IV. There, the draftsman vouchsafes the less than helpful insight that a 'main river' is one shown as such on a main river map, without specifying what that is, or where it can be found. This dispels any doubt which might have lingered, that statutes are drafted for the convenience of the draftsman, not for those affected by them.

[280] Land Drainage Act 1991, ss 9 and 10.

[281] Ibid, s 61A; this section replaces the lesser duty that was set out in the old s 12 of the LDA 1991 (which was repealed by the Land Drainage Act 1994, s 2).

[282] Ibid, s 61C; this section replaces the similar duty set out in the old s 13 of the LDA 1991 (which was repealed by the Land Drainage Act 1994, s 2).

[283] Ibid, s 14.

concomitant of those powers is that they produce spoil, especially where dredging leads to the removal of mud or silt from the bed of a watercourse. This may be deposited without payment on the bank or on land sufficiently close to the watercourse to enable the spoil to be deposited by mechanical means in one operation.[284] The Act does not help with the meaning of this. The better meaning seems to be that one swing of the jib of a crane would meet the demand of the Act, while one journey by a tipper would not, since this would involve two operations, namely that of loading into the tipper and later moving the latter.[285] If the deposit of spoil inflicts injury on any person, this latter is entitled to compensation.[286]

9.138 The Act provides specifically for areas too small to warrant their own drainage board. Such areas may be made the subject of individual action by the Environment Agency or local authorities authorized by it. Where that action is taken the owners of the land to which the scheme relates are liable for the costs, up to a maximum of £50 per hectare of their holdings.[287] This shows that these actions are to be essentially minor works.

9.139 Internal drainage boards are given a variety of other powers to enable them to carry out their basic functions. They may enter into arrangements with navigation and conservancy authorities, with private individuals, or with corporate bodies for the carrying out of drainage works, and the discharge of obligations imposed by custom, tenure, prescription, or otherwise for the repair of watercourses, bridges, drains and culverts, and other artificial drainage works.[288]

9.140 A fundamental element in the efficient drainage of land is the operation of the rivers, canals, ditches, and culverts carrying the water which would otherwise cause floods. Accordingly, the Land Drainage Act 1991 makes it unlawful to obstruct the flow of a watercourse or culvert without the consent of the drainage board.[289] Anyone wanting to erect a mill, dam, weir, or other obstruction, or to build or alter a culvert, may apply for permission to do so to the relevant drainage board, which must not unreasonably withhold consent, and is deemed to have granted consent if it has not expressly refused it within two months of the application.[290]

---

[284] Ibid, s 15.

[285] The history of this provision is interesting. In *Jones v Mersey River Board* [1958] 1 QB 143, the Court of Appeal decided that the 'bank' of a watercourse was no more than the land required to contain the water. The Land Drainage Act 1930 was later amended so as to introduce the notion of the single mechanical operation, although this was not defined. The parliamentary draftsman strikes again.

[286] Land Drainage Act 1991, s 15(4).

[287] Ibid, s 18.

[288] Ibid, ss 18–21.

[289] Ibid, s 23.

[290] Ibid. This reverses the procedure under the Town and Country Planning Acts, where permission is deemed to have been refused in default of a decision. There is argument as to which approach is preferable.

Disputes are to be referred to arbitration by a Civil Engineer; any unauthorized obstruction may be the subject of an abatement notice, failure to comply with which is a criminal offence. Drainage boards have further powers to take steps to remove the obstruction at the expense of the offender.[291]

The obverse is that drainage boards, local authorities, and the Environment Agency have powers to secure the removal of obstructions to watercourses. Where the proper flow of water is impeded, they may, by notice served on the person controlling the part of the watercourse where the obstruction occurs, the owner or occupier of the riparian land, or the person causing the obstruction, require its removal. However, the consent of the owner and occupier of the land must be obtained where a person other than the owner or occupier is served with a notice.[292] There is then a right of appeal to a magistrates' court, which must be exercised within 21 days. The grounds of appeal are conventional—that the notice was not justified; that the notice is defective; that there has been unreasonable refusal to approve alternative works; that the time for compliance was too short; that it would have been equitable to serve the notice on someone else; and that some other person ought to contribute to the costs of compliance.[293] **9.141**

Ditches receive special treatment under the Act. A 'ditch' includes a culvert, but not a watercourse vested in or controlled by a drainage board. Ditches are the responsibility of Agricultural Lands Tribunals, who may order riparian owners and occupiers and persons with responsibility for them to maintain and dredge ditches, and to protect them. There is no right of appeal against any such order, and if it is not obeyed the relevant Minister or a drainage board authorized by him may carry out the work and recover the cost from the persons named in the order. However, the board must leave the land as secure against trespass as it found it, and must pay compensation, to be assessed by the Lands Tribunal, for damage caused which was unconnected with the authorized works.[294] The Agricultural Lands Tribunal has similar powers in respect of the carrying out of work to ditches on the application of any owner or occupier of land which drains to a ditch. The Tribunal may authorize the applicant to enter on another person's land and carry out the work specified, at the applicant's expense, and subject to the same conditions as apply to drainage boards.[295] **9.142**

---

[291] Ibid, s 24.
[292] Ibid, s 25.
[293] Ibid, s 27.
[294] Ibid, ss 28 and 29.
[295] Ibid, s 30.

Standards of flood defence

9.143 Most flood defences are publicly owned, so that the Agency is responsible for defence against flooding from main rivers and either the internal drainage boards or the local authorities are responsible for other watercourses. The standard of protection varies across the country according to local geography and local priorities, and the authorities are not under a statutory duty to provide these defences, nor indeed flood warnings. This does mean that, contrary to what might be expected, there will be no liability if they fail to exercise these powers. The only duty is to not to add to the damages which that person would have suffered had the authority done nothing.[296] One of the areas where this may yet be sorely tested is the government policy of 'managed retreat' in the case of sea defences, in those places where it is not economic to maintain existing sea walls.

Financial provisions

9.144 Historically, awards made under statute could impose obligations to carry out drainage work, or could exempt from obligations. The Land Drainage Act 1991 empowers the relevant Minister to vary those awards on the application of the Environment Agency. The Agency or internal drainage boards may similarly commute obligations or exemptions imposed by tenure, custom, prescription, or otherwise.[297] Where such variation or commutation occurs, the Environment Agency is to determine the compensation payable to anyone losing an exemption from the obligation to carry out drainage works. The amount is to be the capitalized value of the annual cost of the work from which the claimant was exempt. A person aggrieved by the Agency's award may have the matter referred to arbitration by a civil engineer.[298]

9.145 Internal drainage boards are financed by the levy of drainage rates. An internal drainage district may be divided for the purpose of levying differential drainage rates. The purpose was no doubt to reflect differences in the cost of draining low-lying areas as compared with more easily treated lands.[299] Thus a specified percentage of the occupiers of land within an area may petition the drainage

---

[296] See *East Suffolk Rivers Catchment Board v Kent* [1940] AC 74, where the catchment board took an excessive time to repair breaches in the sea wall (178 days rather than a probable 14 days). The landowner failed to recover for the additional flood damage as the Board was only exercising a power. However, a failure to maintain an artificial channel such as a highway drain can lead to liability (*Bybrook Barn Centre Ltd v Kent County Council* [2001] BLR 55—but no duty to enlarge it). *Capital Counties plc v Hampshire County Council* [1997] QB 1004, CA, is one of the rare examples where the fire authority was held to be liable for its actions which had added to the damage caused by a fire.

[297] Land Drainage Act 1991, ss 32 and 33.

[298] Ibid, s 34.

[299] Ibid, Part IV, Chapter I.

board to apportion the drainage expenses of its area.[300] With the same object in mind, the board itself may subdivide its district and levy differential drainage rates in respect of each part.[301]

The Act provides, in Chapter II of Part IV, for the levying of drainage rates by **9.146** machinery which is based on the general rating code, and which differs from it only in detail. Discussion of this is not appropriate or relevant here.

---

[300] Ibid, ss 37 and 73(2).
[301] Ibid, s 38.

10

THE WATER INDUSTRY

A. **Organization of the Water Industry** 10.02
    Historical background 10.02
    The privatized water industry 10.09
      Water and sewerage undertakers 10.09
      Licensed water suppliers 10.11
      The Secretary of State and the
          Authority 10.12
      The Council 10.14
      Local authorities 10.15
B. **General Duties Under the WIA** 10.16
    Section 2—General service duties
      of the Secretary of State/NAW
      and the Authority 10.17
    Sections 3 and 4—General environmental
      and recreational duties of the
      Secretary of State/NAW, the
      Authority, and undertakers 10.19
C. **Appointment of Water and**
    Sewerage Undertakers 10.25
    Introduction 10.25
    Conditions of appointment 10.28
    Modification of conditions 10.32
      Modification with agreement of the
        undertaker and the Authority 10.33
      Modification following reference to
        the Competition Commission 10.34
      Modification under the Enterprise
        Act 2002 10.39
    Variation and termination of
      appointments 10.40
    Mergers and disposal of land 10.44
      Mergers 10.44
      Disposal of protected land 10.46
D. **Water Undertakers** 10.49
    General duty on water undertakers
      under Section 37 10.50
    Regulations 10.52
    Duties of water undertakers in
      relation to domestic supply 10.57

    Duty on water undertaker to provide
      and maintain domestic supplies 10.58
    Demand for a domestic supply 10.61
    Enforcement 10.63
    Duty on water undertaker to provide
      a new water main for domestic
      purposes 10.65
    Enforcement 10.68
    Duty of water undertaker to provide
      connection to water main for
      domestic purposes 10.69
    Enforcement 10.74
    Duty on water undertaker to maintain
      constancy and pressure of domestic
      supplies 10.75
    Enforcement 10.79
    Duties of water undertakers with
      regard to non-domestic supplies 10.80
    Duty of water undertakers to
        maintain existing non-domestic
      supplies 10.80
    Requests to water undertakers for
      new non-domestic supplies 10.81
    Fire hydrants 10.84
    Cleansing sewers etc 10.85
    Bulk supplies 10.86
    Disconnections 10.89
    Obligations on water undertakers
      in respect of the quality of
      domestic supply 10.95
    Duty on water undertakers and
      licensed water suppliers under
      Section 68 10.95
    Water unfit for human consumption 10.102
    Quality of non-domestic supply 10.105
    Contamination, waste and droughts 10.106
    Contamination and waste 10.106
    Hosepipe bans 10.108
    Drought orders 10.109

Water resources management plans	10.110
Drought plans	10.111
E. Licensed Water Suppliers	10.112
Rights conferred by a water supply licence	10.116
F. Water Supply Functions of Local Authorities	10.122
G. Sewerage Undertakers	10.127
General duty	10.128
Regulations	10.131
Drainage of premises	10.136
Right of occupiers/owners of premises to utilize undertaker's sewerage system	10.136
New connections to existing sewers	10.139
Requisitions of new sewers for domestic purposes	10.143
Sewers to premises erected before 1995	10.146
Other powers with respect to the sewerage system	10.148
Compensation following exercise of powers under Sections 101A–116	10.152
Trade Effluent	10.153
Introduction	10.153
Discharge consent under Section 119	10.159
Variation of discharge consents	10.162
Agreements under Section 129	10.165
Special category effluent	10.168
Reference to the Environment Agency	10.169
Review by Environment Agency	10.171
Procedure	10.173
Processes regulated under Section 2 of the Pollution Prevention and Control Act 1999	10.175
Treatment	10.176
Discharges of treated sewage	10.181
H. Sewerage Functions of Local Authorities	10.182
I. Undertakers' Works etc	10.184
Powers to lay pipes in streets and private land	10.184
Pipe laying in streets	10.187
Pipe laying in private land	10.189
Discharges by water undertakers in the course of pipe laying	10.191
Restrictions on interference with other water-related infrastructure	10.193
Compensation for pipe laying in private land	10.194

Code of Practice and complaints	10.195
Compulsory purchase of land by water and sewerage undertakers	10.198
Compulsory works orders of water undertakers	10.199
Adoption of apparatus	10.200
Water undertakers—agreements to adopt domestic water mains etc at a future date	10.201
Sewerage undertakers—adoption of existing apparatus at insistence of undertaker	10.208
Sewerage undertakers—adoption of proposed apparatus at insistence of owner	10.209
The mining code	10.211
Maps of underground apparatus	10.214
Right of landowners to require removal of undertaker's apparatus	10.217
J. Powers of Entry of Water and Sewerage Undertakers	10.219
K. Charges	10.222
Charges schemes and agreements	10.222
Metered supply of water	10.227
L. Enforcement	10.230
Introduction	10.230
Enforcement orders	10.232
Duties enforceable under Section 18 and responsibility for enforcement	10.233
Obligation to make enforcement order	10.236
Final and provisional enforcement orders	10.237
Procedure for confirming provisional enforcement orders and making final enforcement orders	10.242
Compliance with enforcement orders	10.244
Financial penalties	10.245
Special administration orders	10.250
Power to require information in connection with enforcement action	10.253
M. Complaints Against Undertakers and Licensed Water Suppliers	10.255
N. Review and Information Provided by the Secretary of State and the Authority	10.259
Review and reports	10.259
Information	10.260

This chapter considers the law now contained in the Water Industry Act 1991, as **10.01** amended. It starts with a brief historical account of the provision of water and sewerage services and then considers the functions of water and sewerage undertakers today.

A. Organization of the Water Industry

Historical background

Water and sewerage services were originally provided by undertakers (usually a **10.02** water company, a local authority, or a joint board or committee of local authorities) created by local Acts and performing general duties under the Public Health Acts 1875–1936. The result was a multitude of different undertakers, numbering some 200 by the 1970s. Control of rivers was dealt with separately, latterly by river boards established under the Water Resources Act 1963.

Substantial reorganization was effected by the Water Act 1973. This established **10.03** ten water authorities responsible for all functions relating to water treatment and supply, sewerage and sewage disposal, rivers, land drainage, flood defence, pollution control, and inland fisheries. Twenty-eight statutory water companies, with responsibility for water supplies in certain areas, were also retained. The functions of local authorities were drastically reduced, although they continued to play a significant role in the provision of sewerage services through agency agreements with water authorities.

The Water Act 1973 did not provide for detailed regulatory control. The **10.04** Secretary of State for the Environment had power to give directions to water authorities, and also a range of default powers. However, there were no detailed mechanisms for exercising these powers, nor for enforcing the duties of the authorities.

The results of the 1973 reforms were not satisfactory. Public sector water authori- **10.05** ties suffered from underfunding. The improvement of water quality, which became important as a result of several EEC Directives (notably 80/778 on drinking water), was not adequately addressed.

Privatization of the water industry was affected by the Water Act 1989. This again **10.06** separated water and sewerage services from control of rivers. The assets of water authorities were transferred to private companies appointed as undertakers with responsibility for the provision of water and sewerage services. An entirely new regulatory system was established.

The Water Act 1989 was consolidated in the Water Industry Act 1991 ('WIA'), now **10.07** the principal Act governing the water industry. The 1991 Act has subsequently been modified by the Competition and Service (Utilities) Act 1992, the Environment Act 1995, the Water Industry Act 1999, and the Water Act 2003.

10.08 The 28 statutory water companies continue to exist: the 1989 Act provided that these should be appointed as water undertakers in their areas. The powers and corporate structure of the statutory water companies are now governed by the Statutory Water Companies Act 1991.

The privatized water industry

Water and sewerage undertakers

10.09 Responsibility for the provision of water and sewerage services is now vested in 'water and sewerage undertakers', namely the 28 statutory water companies and privately owned 'water services companies' appointed as undertakers in the areas formerly covered by the ten water authorities.

10.10 Parts III and IV of the WIA deal separately with provision of water and sewerage services. Detailed standards of performance are imposed by regulations made under the Act, and by conditions in the Instrument of Appointment of each undertaker. Obligations imposed by statute and conditions are enforced by the Secretary of State for Environment Food and Rural Affairs ('the Secretary of State') and the Water Services Regulation Authority ('the Authority').

Licensed water suppliers

10.11 In an endeavour to promote competition in the water industry, provision was made in 2005 to allow companies other than water undertakers to supply treated water to non-household premises taking at least 50 megalitres of water annually, using the network of water undertakers. Such a supply has to be permitted by a 'water supply licence' granted by the Authority and such suppliers are known as 'licensed water suppliers'. The WIA imposes some statutory duties on licensed water suppliers. Further obligations are imposed by conditions in water supply licences. The enforcement powers of the Secretary of State and the Authority under the WIA are available against licensed water suppliers.

The Secretary of State and the Authority

10.12 The industry is regulated by the Secretary of State and the Water Services Regulation Authority. The latter replaced the Office of Water Services in 2006 (Section 1A). The Secretary of State and the Authority are themselves subject to general service and environmental duties imposed by Sections 2–4 of the WIA.

10.13 In Wales most of the responsibilities of the Secretary of State have been transferred to the National Assembly for Wales ('NAW').

The Council

An independent Consumer Council for Water ('the Council') exists to protect **10.14** customer interests. This was established in 2005 to replace the Customer Service Committees set up on privatization (Section 27A). The Council is separate from the Authority, unlike the Customer Service Committees, which were part of OFWAT. The Council's principal role is to obtain and keep under review information on customer matters, to provide information and advice to public authorities, undertakers, and consumers, and to investigate complaints. A series of regional committees advise the Council and carry out such other functions as the Council determines. The Council has no enforcement powers.

Local authorities

The role of local authorities in the water industry is now slight, being confined **10.15** principally to investigating and reporting on the activities of appointed companies. Local authorities retain a significant role in policing private water supplies and have certain powers against appointed companies in respect of insufficient water supplies. They also retain the power, under Section 97, to enter into agency agreements with sewerage undertakers.

B. General duties under the WIA

All regulation under the WIA takes place within the framework of general service **10.16** duties binding on the Secretary of State/NAW and the Authority and general environmental duties binding on the Secretary of State/NAW, the Authority and appointed companies. These are found in Sections 2–4, and reflect Parliament's general aspirations for the privatized water industry.

Section 2—General service duties of the Secretary of State/NAW and the Authority

Four general duties to ensure the efficient provision of water and sewerage services **10.17** are imposed on the Secretary of State/NAW and the Authority by Section 2(2a). These are that all other powers and duties for the regulation of undertakers must be exercised in the manner he/it considers best calculated:

- to further the 'consumer objective' (namely to protect the interests of consumers, where ever appropriate by promoting effective competition between those engaged in the provision of water and sewerage services. Particular regard must be had to the interests of vulnerable groups.[1]

---

[1] Water Industry Act 1991, s 2(2C).

- to secure that the functions of a water and sewerage undertaker are properly carried out;

- to secure that companies appointed as undertakers can finance the proper carrying out of those functions (in particular by securing reasonable returns on their capital); and

- to secure that the activities of licensed water suppliers are properly carried out.

10.18   Five secondary duties are imposed by Section 2(3). These are to promote efficiency and economy by water and sewerage undertakers, to ensure there is no undue preference or discrimination in fixing of water and sewerage charges, to secure that the interests of consumers are protected in the application of the proceeds of the sale of land, to secure that the interests of consumers are protected when an appointed company acts other than in the exercise of its functions as undertaker, and to promote sustainable development. These duties are 'subject to' the four duties in Section 2(2a).

Sections 3 and 4—General environmental and recreational duties of the Secretary of State/NAW, the Authority, and undertakers

10.19   General environmental and recreational duties are imposed by Section 3 on the Secretary of State/NAW, the Authority, and all undertakers. These duties apply whenever such a person/body is 'formulating or considering any proposals' relating to the functions of an undertaker. As with Section 2, there are primary and secondary requirements.

10.20   The three primary duties, set out in Section 3(2), are:

- That any powers connected with the proposal must be exercised 'so as to further the conservation and enhancement' of the 'natural beauty and the conservation of flora, fauna and geological or physiographical features of special interest' and, in the case of appointed companies, to further water conservation. This obligation only applies to the extent that it is consistent with the general duties of the Secretary of State/NAW and the Authority under Section 2, and with the purposes of any enactment relating to the functions of the undertaker.

- To have regard to 'the desirability of protecting and conserving buildings, sites and objects of archaeological, architectural or historic interest'.

- To take into account 'any effect which the proposals would have on the beauty or amenity of any rural or urban area' or on any of the features mentioned in the above obligations.

The three secondary requirements, set out in Section 3(3), are to take into account: **10.21**

- the desirability of preserving for the public any freedom of access to areas of woodland, mountains, moors, heath, down, cliff or foreshore, and other places of natural beauty;
- the desirability of maintaining public access to any building, site or object of archaeological, architectural or historic interest; and
- the effect that the proposals would have on public access to such an area or feature.

Sections 3(5) and 4 impose other duties on undertakers alone. Section 3(5) relates   **10.22** to making available for recreational purposes any water or nearby land over which the undertaker has rights. Section 4 relates to land notified to an undertaker as being of special interest by Natural England or the Countryside Council for Wales, a National Park Authority, or the Broads Authority. If the undertaker wishes to carry out works that might injure such land it must first consult with the authority concerned.

All the obligations on undertakers under Sections 3 and 4 are enforceable by the   **10.23** Secretary of State/NAW under Section 18 (see paras 10.232–10.254).

Under Section 5 the Secretary of State/NAW may approve codes of practice which   **10.24** give guidance to undertakers on their duties under Sections 3 and 4. Pursuant to this duty the *Code of Practice on Conservation, Recreation and Access* was approved in 2000. Contravention of a code of practice does not of itself involve any breach of Sections 3 or 4. Nor does it give rise to civil or criminal liability. However, the Secretary of State/NAW has to take breaches of a code of practice into account in deciding when and how to exercise his/its powers, including enforcement powers, under the Act.

C. Appointment of Water and Sewerage Undertakers

Introduction

A company may be appointed as a water or sewerage undertaker for a defined   **10.25** area.[2] The areas of water and sewerage undertakers do not have to be co-extensive.

The power to make new appointments and to terminate existing appointments is   **10.26** exercisable by the Secretary of State/NAW or by the Authority (with the Secretary of State's authorization).[3]

---

[2] Ibid, s 6(2).
[3] Ibid, s 6(1).

10.27 The Secretary of State/NAW are under a duty to ensure that all areas of England and Wales have water and sewerage undertakers at all times.[4] Appointments covering the whole of England and Wales were made on privatization: new appointments only have to be made when an existing company is replaced or the area it serves is reduced.

Conditions of appointment

10.28 Detailed conditions are imposed in all appointments and extend the scope of regulatory control, particularly with regard to price structure and customer relations.

10.29 The Secretary of State/NAW/Authority can impose such conditions as appear to be requisite having regard to the duties imposed under Sections 2 and 3. The Act expressly contemplates conditions:

- relating to the circumstances in which the company can be replaced as undertaker;[5]
- requiring payments to the Secretary of State;[6] and
- requiring the company to comply with any direction given by the Authority, or making the doing of specified acts subject to the consent of the Authority.[7]

10.30 Conditions do not have to be connected with the supply of water or sewerage services or the exercise of any of the powers or duties of water or sewerage undertakers.[8]

10.31 A Model Instrument of Appointment, containing model conditions, has been published.

Modification of conditions

10.32 Conditions in an appointment can lay down a procedure for their own modification. Where such a procedure is not available, the Authority can modify conditions in three circumstances.

Modification with agreement of the undertaker and the Authority

10.33 A condition can be modified under Section 13(1) with the consent of the undertaker and the Authority. Such modification requires certain procedural steps to be followed and the Secretary of State can veto:

- the proposed modification of a condition relating to the replacement of the company as undertaker;

---

[4] Ibid, s 7(1).
[5] Ibid, s 7(4)(c).
[6] Ibid, s 11(1).
[7] Ibid, s 12(1).
[8] Ibid, s 11(2).

- the proposed modification of a condition stated in the appointment to be incapable of modification and relating to the disposal of the company's protected land; and

- a proposed modification which can only be made by the Secretary of State under Section 16 following a reference to the Competition Commission.[9]

Modification following reference to the Competition Commission

A condition can be modified following a reference to the Competition Commission **10.34** by the Authority under Section 14. Such a reference asks the Commission to investigate whether any matter relating to the functions of a particular appointed company operates against the public interest and, if so, whether the injury to the public interest could be remedied by modifying conditions in the company's appointment.[10] In considering whether any matter operates against the public interest, the Commission must have regard to the matters covered by the general duties of the Secretary of State/Authority imposed by Sections 2 and 3.[11]

The Commission has a range of investigative powers for the purpose of dealing **10.35** with such a reference.[12]

The Commission's report must give definite conclusions on the questions put to **10.36** it and may specify any modifications to conditions that would prevent the injury to the public interest.[13] If the Commission recommends modifications, the Authority must make such modifications as appear to it to be requisite for the purpose of remedying or preventing the injury to the public interest identified in the report.[14] These need not be those recommended by the Commission. Before making any modification, the Authority must give notice of the proposed modification, with its reasons, and invite representations.[15]

The Commission can veto a modification proposed by the Authority if the pro- **10.37** posed modification does not appear to the Commission to be requisite for the purpose of remedying the adverse effects specified in its report (Section 16A(3)). If the Commission exercises this power it must itself make such modification as appears to it to be requisite.[16]

The Authority cannot, under this procedure, modify any condition which deals **10.38** with the replacement of the company as undertaker or the disposal of the company's

---

[9]   Ibid, s 13(4) and (5).
[10] Ibid, s 16(1).
[11] Ibid, s 14(6).
[12] Ibid, s 14B.
[13] Ibid, s 15(1).
[14] Ibid, s 16(1).
[15] Ibid, s 16(2).
[16] Ibid, s 16A(4).

protected land if such condition is stated in the appointment to be incapable of modification.[17]

Modification under the Enterprise Act 2002

10.39   Finally, the Office of Fair Trading, the Competition Commission, or the Secretary of State can modify conditions in the course of making certain orders under the Enterprise Act 2002.[18] This power is exercisable by the Secretary of State in Wales.

Variation and termination of appointments

10.40   The power to terminate an appointment or to vary the area covered by an appointment is exercisable by the Secretary of State/NAW or the Authority (with the consent or authorization of the Secretary of State/NAW) in four circumstances identified in Section 7. These are:

- Where the company consents.[19] This provision would be applicable where, for example, the special administrator (see below) of an appointed company consents to the appointment of a replacement company.

- Where the change relates to an area in which there are no premises served by the existing appointee.[20] This allows for 'inset' appointments, often on greenfield development sites, and is designed to encourage competition between undertakers.

- Where the change relates to a part of the company's area in which premises are/are likely to be supplied with at least 50 megalitres (250 megalitres in Wales) of water in any period of twelve months and the customer concerned consents.[21] This is designed to enable inset appointments to be made for large individual users of water. Any money spent on, or committed to, the provision of a water supply to such premises by an existing appointee must be taken into account by the Secretary of State/NAW/Authority in deciding whether to permit an inset appointment of this type.[22]

- Where the variation/new appointment is made in accordance with conditions in the original appointment.[23]

---

[17]   Ibid, s 16(5).
[18]   Ibid, s 17.
[19]   Ibid, s 7(4)(a).
[20]   Ibid, s 7(4)(b).
[21]   Ibid, s 7(4)(bb) and (5).
[22]   Ibid, s 9(3).
[23]   Ibid, s 7(4)(c).

In order to ensure the continued provision of water and sewerage services, no ter- **10.41**
mination or variation comes into effect until a replacement undertaker is
appointed.[24]

An aspirant company can apply for an appointment/variation under which it will **10.42**
replace an existing undertaker using the procedure set out in Section 8. The applicant must give notice of the application to the existing undertaker, the Environment
Agency and every local authority in the relevant area. If the Secretary of State/
NAW or the Authority is minded to make the appointment/variation, public
notice of the proposal must be given and representations and objections invited.
Section 8(7) provides for regulations to be made governing the making of applications: no regulations have yet been made.

A variation/new appointment will almost certainly require a transfer of assets from **10.43**
the old to the new appointee. This requires a scheme of transfer under Schedule 2.
Such a scheme must be drawn up by the existing undertaker with the consent of the
new appointee and approved by the Secretary of State/NAW/Authority. The
Secretary of State/NAW/Authority is under a duty to ensure, so far as is consistent
with his/its duties under Sections 2 and 3, that the interests of the shareholders
and creditors of the existing appointee are not unfairly prejudiced.[25]

Mergers and disposal of land

Mergers

Competition in the water industry consists only in the comparisons that can be **10.44**
made between the performance of undertakers operating in different areas and
depends on there being a sufficient number of separately owned water companies.
Accordingly the Office of Fair Trading must make a merger reference to the
Competition Commission whenever any merger of undertakers is proposed,[26]
subject to financial restrictions to allow small mergers.[27] References are investigated by the Competition Commission under the Enterprise Act 2002, the main
purpose being to determine whether the merger could prejudice the ability of the
Authority to make comparisons between different water enterprises. The
Commission does not need to act if it considers that the benefits of the merger
outweigh any such prejudice.

The Commission has certain investigative powers even after a merger has taken **10.45**
place.

---

[24] Ibid, s 7(3).
[25] Ibid, s 9(4).
[26] Ibid, s 32.
[27] Ibid, s 33.

Disposal of protected land

10.46 The old water authorities held extensive areas of land, including many country-side areas, and there was concern that privatized utilities might be tempted to sell or to restrict access to this. The duties under Sections 3 and 4 were in part designed to address these concerns. In addition, restrictions are imposed on the disposal of land by undertakers.

10.47 These restrictions, contained in Section 156, apply to all land transferred to the undertaker on privatization and all land acquired in connection with water or sewerage functions since ('protected land').[28] An undertaker can only dispose of protected land or any right over such land, with the consent of the Secretary of State/NAW or under a general authorization from him/it.[29] The Secretary of State/NAW has the power to impose conditions on such consents. Where the land is in a National Park, the Broads, an Area of Outstanding Natural Beauty (AONB), or is a Site of Special Scientific Interest (SSSI). Conditions can require:

- that consultation with Natural England/the Countryside Commission for Wales should take place;
- that the undertaker should enter into a management agreement under the Wildlife and Countryside Act 1981 or a covenant relating to access to or to the use or management of the land; and
- that the undertaker should offer the land, on such terms as may be specified, to a named body.

10.48 The general environmental duties imposed by Section 3 apply to an undertaker when it is proposing to dispose of protected land in a National Park, the Broads, or an AONB or SSSI, but not to other protected land.[30] They also apply to all actions by the Secretary of State/NAW under Section 156.

D. Water Undertakers

10.49 The statutory duties of water undertakers take the form of a general obligation, amplified in regulations, and a series of specific statutory functions relating to connections to the public water system and the maintenance of supplies.

---

[28] Ibid, s 219(1).
[29] Ibid, s 156.
[30] Ibid, s 156(7).

General duty on water undertakers under Section 37

The general obligation of a water undertaker, imposed by Section 37, is to: **10.50**

> 'develop and maintain an efficient and economical system of water supply within its
> area and to ensure that all such arrangements have been made:
> (a) for providing supplies of water to premises in that area, and for making such sup-
>   plies available to persons who demand them; and
> (b) for maintaining, improving, and extending the water undertaker's water mains
>   and other pipes as are necessary for securing that the undertaker is and continues
>   to be able to meet its obligations under [Sections 37–93 of the Act].'

Breach of Section 37 is enforceable under Section 18 by the Secretary of State/NAW   **10.51**
or by the Authority (with the authorization of the Secretary of State/NAW).[31]

Regulations

This duty is supplemented by regulations of two types. The first type, made under   **10.52**
Section 38(1), imposes precise operational standards and links the Section 37
duty to the performance of other statutory obligations. Breach of any such standard or obligation counts as a breach of Section 37.

Regulations of the second type, made under Section 38(2), prescribe standards of   **10.53**
performance for the provision of water supplies to be achieved in individual cases.
The current regulations are the Water Supply and Sewerage Services (Customer
Service Standards) Regulations 1993, 1996, and 2000. These standards are not
tied to the Section 37 duty. Instead provision is made for the payment of compensation in the event of breach.

New regulations of either type can be made in two ways. The first involves an   **10.54**
application from the Authority to the Secretary of State/NAW. The Authority
must carry out research into the views of a representative sample of persons likely
to be affected. A copy of the application must be served on the relevant undertakers, and an opportunity for representations or objections given. The Secretary of
State/NAW can only make regulations which differ from those set out in the
application if such proposed modifications have been notified to the Authority
and any undertakers affected.[32]

Second, the Secretary of State/NAW can make regulations of his/its own accord   **10.55**
when he/it considers that they would contribute towards the attainment of policies on public health or the environment or that there are exceptional reasons in
the public interest for regulations to be made.[33] The Secretary of State/NAW must
first carry out research into the views of a representative sample of persons likely

---

[31] Ibid, s 37(2).
[32] Ibid, s 39(1)–(3).
[33] Ibid, s 39(4).

to be affected.[34] He/it must give notice of the proposed regulations and consider any representations or objections received.[35]

10.56   A degree of public scrutiny of undertakers' performance under Section 38 regulations is achieved by the publicity provisions in Sections 38A and 39A. Under section 39A each water undertaker must inform its customers, in such manner as the Authority directs, of the standards applicable to it under s 38(1)(b) and of its performance measured against those standards. Under Section 38A the Authority is also under a duty to collect information about the payment of compensation by undertakers under Section 38(2) regulations and about the overall levels of performance. It can require undertakers to provide information for this purpose. It must publish, at least once a year, such of this information as it considers appropriate.

Duties of water undertakers in relation to domestic supply

10.57   Following the pattern of earlier legislation, the WIA imposes strict duties on water undertakers to provide and maintain domestic water supplies. Undertakers are under a duty to maintain domestic supplies to premises already connected to the public water supply system and to provide new supplies for domestic purposes. This may require the provision of a new water main.

Duty on water undertaker to provide and maintain domestic supplies

10.58   Section 52 imposes a duty on water undertakers (i) to provide a supply of water sufficient for domestic purposes to premises already connected to a main by a service pipe and (ii) to maintain the connection with the main.

10.59   'Domestic purposes' are defined by Section 218 as the drinking, washing, cooking, central heating, and sanitary purposes for which water supplied to premises is used. 'Premises' have been held to cover a boarding house[36] and a school,[37] but not toilets at a railway station.[38]

10.60   The duty is only owed in respect of premises actually supplied before 1 September 1989 or in respect of which a demand for a domestic water supply (see below) has been made[39] but does not apply if, since 1 September 1989 or the date of the making of the demand, the undertaker has exercised its disconnection powers. The duty only applies to buildings or parts of buildings, and thus is not owed to caravans etc.[40] The building must be connected to one of the undertaker's mains

---

[34]   Ibid, s 39(7).
[35]   Ibid, s 39(5).
[36]   *Pidgeon v Great Yarmouth Waterworks Co* [1902] 1 KB 310.
[37]   *SW Suburban Waterworks Co v St Marylebone Union* [1904] 2 KB 174.
[38]   *MWB v London, Brighton and South Coast Rly* [1910] 2 KB 890.
[39]   Water Industry Act 1991, s 52(2).
[40]   Ibid, s 52(3).

and satisfy certain qualifications relating to the way in which the connection was made.

Demand for a domestic supply

Where a domestic supply is not presently provided to a building that is connected   **10.61**
to the undertaker's mains, a demand for such a supply can be made by the occupier or the owner. Subject to the qualfications set out below the undertaker is
obliged to provide the supply.

Where the demand is made by the owner he must agree to pay the undertaker's   **10.62**
charges.[41] Where the demand for a supply is made following a disconnection for
failure to pay charges, the undertaker can require the person making the demand
to pay the unpaid charges and the costs of the disconnection before the supply is
restored. The undertaker can also require that a cistern should be installed/main-
tained, that the fittings used in the premises should not contravene Section 74
regulations, and that any notice served under Section 75 requiring steps to
prevent contamination or waste should be complied with.

Enforcement

The domestic supply duty is owed to those persons responsible for paying charges   **10.63**
in respect of the supply.[42] Such person can sue the undertaker for any loss or damage caused as a result of breach of the duty. It is a defence for the undertaker to
show that it took all reasonable measures and exercised all due diligence to avoid
the breach.[43] Failure to comply with a demand for a domestic supply in respect
of particular premises is not enforceable under Section 18 by the Secretary of
State/NAW/Authority.

Where a local authority considers that the insufficiency of supply to any premises   **10.64**
may endanger life or health, it may require the water undertaker to provide an
alternative supply.[44]

Duty on water undertaker to provide a new water main for domestic purposes

The construction of a new water main to provide water sufficient for domestic   **10.65**
purposes can be secured by the service of a requisition under Section 41. A requisition can be served by the owner/occupier of a building or a proposed building (or
any part of a building or proposed building) or by a local authority.

---

[41] Ibid, s 52(5).
[42] Ibid, ss 54(1) and 93(1).
[43] Ibid, s 54(2).
[44] Ibid, s 78.Ð

10.66   Upon service of such a requisition, the undertaker is obliged to provide the main, provided that any financial conditions imposed under Section 42 are met. A requisition can require a main that goes beyond the undertaker's current infrastructure plans. Section 42 entitles the undertaker to require the requisitioner to give reasonable undertakings to meet the cost of providing the main over a twelve-year period. The undertaker can also require security to be provided (unless the requisitioner is a local authority). The cost will include that of any new tanks, service reservoirs, and pumping stations required, and the cost of increasing the capacity of existing mains requisitioned in the previous twelve years.[45]

10.67   The water undertaker must lay the main within three months of the 'relevant day'. This is the later of: the day on which the financial requirements of Section 42 are met, and the day on which the places of connection of the service pipe from the premises to the main are determined. The three-month period can be extended by agreement, or, in default of agreement, by the Authority. Likewise, the route of the new main and the place of connection are determined by agreement or in default of agreement, by the Authority.[46]

Enforcement

10.68   The duty to provide the main is owed to the requisitioner. He can sue for loss or damage caused by breach of the duty. It is a defence for the undertaker to show that it took all reasonable steps and exercised all due diligence to avoid the breach.[47] Failure to comply with a requisition in respect of particular premises is not enforceable under Section 18 by the Secretary of State/NAW/Authority.

Duty of water undertaker to provide connection to water main for domestic purposes

10.69   In a situation where the necessary water mains already exist, the owner or occupier of premises (again a building or part of a building, or the site of a proposed building or part of a building) can, by service of a notice under Section 45, require an undertaker to connect a service pipe to the premises from an existing water main, for the purposes of providing a domestic water supply. The undertaker is thereupon obliged to make the connection and to carry out certain ancillary works[48] within a specified time[49] provided that any conditions imposed under Sections 47–50 are satisfied.

---

[45]   Ibid, s 43(4) and (5).
[46]   Ibid, s 44.
[47]   Ibid, s 41(3) and (4).
[48]   See Ibid, s 46.
[49]   Ibid, s 51.

A Section 45 notice must be accompanied by such information as the undertaker **10.70** requires. If this is not provided the undertaker can, in certain circumstances, delay the carrying out of the works required by the notice. The undertaker can impose conditions relating to a variety of specified matters by serving a counter-notice within 14 days of the service of the connection notice.

The obligation does not arise if the main concerned is a trunk main or a main used **10.71** solely for non-domestic supplies.[50]

The undertaker is entitled to recover the expenses reasonably incurred in carrying **10.72** out the relevant works from the person who served the notice.[51] The Authority determines disputes about whether expenses have been reasonably incurred.[52]

In addition to the costs of providing the connection, undertakers may incur costs **10.73** in increasing the capacity of existing mains to enable them to accommodate the additional flows. Prior to the 1989 Act such costs were met out of the general charges paid by all customers. Now, under Section 146(2), undertakers are given power to levy charges for making new domestic connections to cover these.

Enforcement

A person who has served a Section 42 notice can sue the undertaker for loss or **10.74** damage caused by failure to provide the connection etc. In such proceedings it is a defence for the undertaker to show that it took all reasonable steps and exercised all due diligence to avoid the breach.[53] Failure to comply with a connection notice in respect of particular premises is not enforceable under Section 18 by the Secretary of State/NAW/Authority.

Duty on water undertaker to maintain constancy and pressure of domestic supplies

Section 65 imposes a duty on water undertakers to ensure that water used for **10.75** domestic supplies and fire hydrants is laid on constantly and at such pressure as will cause the water to reach the top storey of the highest building in the under-taker's area, provided that this is not higher than the height to which the water will flow by gravitation from the service reservoir or tank from which the supply is taken.

The duties of constancy and pressure of supply only relate to water in the under- **10.76** taker's mains and pipes—they do not apply once the water has passed over the boundary of the consumer's premises or through the stopcock. The obligation is

---

[50] Ibid, s 45(2).
[51] Ibid, s 45(6).
[52] Ibid, s 45(6A).
[53] Ibid, s 45(4) and (5).

not breached if constancy or pressure is reduced during the carrying out of necessary works.

10.77 The Secretary of State/NAW can modify these requirements by statutory instrument, following an application by the Authority or the relevant undertaker.

10.78 Undertakers have power under Section 66 to require works to be carried out to maintain water pressure and to prevent water from running to waste.

Enforcement

10.79 The obligations of undertakers under Section 65 are enforceable by the Authority under Section 18. In addition, breach of the obligations is a criminal offence. In such criminal proceedings it is a defence for the undertaker to show that it took all reasonable steps and exercised all due diligence to avoid breaching the duty.

Duties of water undertakers with regard to non-domestic supplies

Duty of water undertakers to maintain existing non-domestic supplies

10.80 There is no right to demand a supply of water for non-domestic purposes or to serve premises that are not a building. However where such premises are already supplied with water, a water undertaker is only permitted to disconnect the supply in the defined circumstances set out below. It is a criminal offence to disconnect any premises except in the cirumstances set out in the WIA or any other enactment.[54]

Requests to water undertakers for new non-domestic supplies

10.81 While the owner of premises can make a request for the provision of a non-domestic supply under Section 55 to the water undertaker for the area (and in some circumstances to another water undertaker), the undertaker is only obliged to provide the supply sought on such terms and conditions as are fixed by agreement, or, in default of agreement, by the Authority, according to what appears to it to be reasonable.[55] The undertaker can refuse to provide a supply if the measures required would involve unreasonable expenditure or if they would otherwise put at risk its ability to meet existing or probable future supply obligations.[56] In assessing whether expenditure would be unreasonable, account must be taken of present domestic and non-domestic supply obligations and probable future domestic supply obligations. The undertaker is also entitled to refuse to provide the supply if the water fittings to be used contravene Section 74 regulations.[57] The Authority decides on disputes about the applicability of these exceptions.[58]

---

[54] Ibid, s 63(3).
[55] Ibid, s 56(1).
[56] Ibid, s 55(3).
[57] Ibid, s 55(4).
[58] Ibid, s 56(2).

For the purpose of resolving any dispute about whether a Section 55 supply should **10.82** be provided, and, if so, on what terms, it is for the undertaker to show that it should not have to provide the supply.[59]

Charges for a non-domestic supply of water should be fixed by a charges scheme **10.83** made under Section 143. If there is no such scheme and the undertaker and the owner cannot agree on the charges, they must be determined by the Authority. In making such determination the Authority must have regard to the desirability of the undertaker recovering the expenses incurred in providing the supply and securing a reasonable return on its capital.[60]

Fire hydrants

Section 57 imposes a duty on water undertakers to fix fire hydrants in convenient **10.84** locations at the request of the fire authority and to allow water to be taken from these for the purpose of extinguishing fires. Owners of factories and other places of business can request the installation, at their expense, of fire hydrants near to their premises.[61] This duty is Enforceable by the Secretary of State/NAW under Section 18.[62]

Cleansing sewers etc

Section 59 imposes a duty on water undertakers, at the request of a sewerage **10.85** undertaker, highway authority, or local authority, to provide water for cleansing sewers, drains, and highways and for supplying public pumps, baths, or wash-houses, on such terms and conditions as are reasonable. The duty under Section 59 is enforceable by the Authority under Section 18.

Bulk supplies

Water undertakers can supply water to each other by agreement. Further, the **10.86** Authority can order one undertaker to provide a 'supply of water in bulk' to another water undertaker or to a company which has applied to be appointed as a water undertaker, if it appears that such a supply cannot be secured by agreement and that this is necessary or expedient for the efficient use of water resources or the efficient supply of water.[63] In deciding whether to make such an order the Authority must take into account the desirability of facilitating competition within the water industry and enabling the supplying undertaker to recover its expenses and to meet its existing obligations and likely future obligations.

---

[59] Ibid, s 56(7).
[60] Ibid, s 56(5).
[61] Ibid, s 58.
[62] Ibid, s 57(7).
[63] Ibid, s 40(1).

10.87   If the request for such a supply is by a company that has not yet been appointed as an undertaker, the order cannot take effect until that company has been appointed.

10.88   Under Section 40A the Authority can vary a bulk supply order.

Disconnections

10.89   The undertaker's duty to maintain connections and supplies is qualified by the rights to disconnect the supply in Sections 60–63. The most significant and controversial of these is the power to disconnect for failure to pay water charges, contained in Section 61. This power is heavily constrained. The Section 61 power cannot be used in respect of premises listed in Schedule 4A. These include dwellings, houses in multiple occupation, accommodation for the elderly, hospitals, premises used for the provision of medical or dental services, residential care homes, children's homes, schools, prisons, detention centres, police stations, fire stations, and ambulance stations.

10.90   Even where the Section 61 power is available, a supply can only be disconnected if the occupier of the premises is liable to pay water charges and has failed to do so within seven days of service on him of notice requiring payment. If, within that period, the occupier serves a counter-notice disputing the liability to pay, the undertaker can only disconnect the supply if it obtains a judgment against the occupier, or the occupier has, since the date of the counter-notice, made and breached an agreement for the purposes of avoiding or settling court proceedings. The relevant code of practice goes further and requires that the undertaker should not exercise its disconnection powers before obtaining a court judgment for the arrears. The undertaker exercising these powers can recover the reasonable expenses of making the disconnection.

10.91   Under Section 60, a water undertaker can disconnect a service pipe or otherwise cut off or reduce a supply if this is reasonable for the purposes of carrying out necessary works. Reasonable notice has to be given, except in the case of emergencies. The works must be carried out with reasonable dispatch, and, where a domestic supply is interrupted for more than 24 hours, an emergency supply must be made available. This duty is owed to the relevant consumer who may sue the undertaker for loss or damage that results from any breach.

10.92   A customer can himself request that the supply to premises be disconnected by serving a notice on the undertaker that a supply of water is no longer required.[64]

---

[64]   Ibid, s 62.

Section 75 gives undertakers powers to make disconnections to prevent contamination or waste of water. **10.93**

It is a criminal offence for an undertaker to disconnect a water supply otherwise than pursuant to statutory powers.[65] **10.94**

Obligations on water undertakers in respect of the quality of domestic supply

Duty on water undertakers and licensed water suppliers under Section 68
As has been pointed out, one of the objectives of privatization was to ensure that effective measures were taken to secure compliance with EC Directives on water quality. The current Directive (98/83) is implemented by regulations made pursuant to a general duty as to water quality imposed in Section 68. **10.95**

Section 68, which applies where the supply system of an undertaker is used to supply water for domestic and food production purposes, imposes two requirements on the water undertaker: that such water must be wholesome at the time of supply and that the undertaker must ensure, so far as is reasonably practicable, that there is, in relation to each source or combination of sources of the supply, no deterioration in the quality of water so supplied.[66] The latter is designed to prevent any reduction in the quality of water where the standard is already high. **10.96**

The duty applies whether or not the water using the system is the undertaker's water. The duty is not breached if the water only becomes unwholesome after leaving the undertaker's pipes, subject to certain exceptions. **10.97**

There is a similar duty on licensed water suppliers when supplying water for domestic food production purposes under a retail authorization.[67] **10.98**

Standards of wholesomeness for the purposes of the Section 68 duty are set out in Regulations made under Section 69. The current Regulations are: **10.99**

- The Private Water Supply Regulations 1991
- The Water Supply (Water Quality) Regulations 2000
- The Water Supply (Water Quality) (Amendment) Regulations 2001
- The Water Supply (Water Quality) Regulations 2001
- The Water Supply (Water Quality) Regulations 2000 (Amendment) Regulations 2007.

These deal only with water used for non-domestic food production purposes and such domestic purposes as consist in or include cooking, drinking, food preparation, or washing. The Regulations define wholesomeness by reference **10.100**

---

[65] Ibid, s 63(3).
[66] Ibid, s 68(1).
[67] Ibid, s 68(1A).

to maximum/minimum concentrations/values for a series of chemical and microbiological parameters. In addition water must not contain any other micro-organism, parasite, or substance at such a level as to constitute a potential danger to human health and must satisfy requirements for nitrates and nitrites. Compliance is policed by the Drinking Water Inspectorate.

10.101   The duty is enforceable under Section 18 by the Secretary of State/NAW. There is no provision for an individual affected by breach of this duty to take proceedings under the WIA, although there may be civil liability under the Consumer Protection Act 1987 and in negligence for damage to property.[68]

Water unfit for human consumption

10.102   In addition to the provisions of Section 68 and the above Regulations, a criminal offence is committed under Section 70 where the supply system of the water undertaker is used to supply water to premises and the water is 'unfit for human consumption'. The offence is committed by the undertaker whose supply system is involved (the 'primary undertaker') and any employer of persons or any self-employed person who is concerned in the supply of the water.[69] This would include a licensed water supplier and its employees.

10.103   'Unfit for human consumption' is not defined in the Act.

10.104   In such proceedings it is a defence for the primary undertaker to show that it had no reasonable grounds for suspecting that the water would be used for human consumption or that it took all reasonable steps and exercised all due diligence to secure that the water was fit for human consumption on leaving its pipes.[70] Proceedings for this offence can only be instituted with the consent of the Secretary of State/NAW or the Director of Public Prosecutions.[71]

Quality of non-domestic supply

10.105   Although there is no statutory duty relating to the quality of water supplied for purposes other than domestic and food production purposes, regulations can be made by the Secretary of State/NAW setting standards for the wholesomeness of water supplied for any purpose.[72]

---

[68]   *Read v Croydon Corp* (1937) 37 LGR 53.
[69]   Water Industry Act 1991, s 70(1A).
[70]   Ibid, s 70(3).
[71]   Ibid, s 70(4).
[72]   Ibid, s 67.

Contamination, waste and droughts

Contamination and waste

Concerns about conserving water supplies and preventing contamination have **10.106** exercised the public mind in recent years. The WIA contains a variety of provisions designed to force undertakers and regulators to meet these concerns. Sections 93A–93D, inserted by the Environment Act 1995, impose on undertakers a duty to promote the efficient use of water by customers and empower the Authority to give directions on how the duty is to be discharged. Sections 71–73 create a variety of criminal offences relating to waste and misuse of water. Section 74 empowers the Secretary of State/NAW to make regulations to prevent contamination, waste, undue consumption and misuse of water, and to control water fittings used by customers. The relevant regulations are the Water Supply (Water Fittings) Regulations 1999, the Water Supply (Water Fittings) (Amendment) Regulations 1999, and the Water Supply Licence (Prescribed Water Fittings Requirements) Regulations 2005.

Provision can be made for enforcement by water undertakers, local authorities **10.107** and other prescribed persons.[73] Section 75 empowers an undertaker to serve on a consumer a notice requiring appropriate steps to be taken to prevent contamination or misuse of water and, in appropriate cases, to cut off the water supply.[74]

Hosepipe bans

If a water undertaker considers that there is a serious deficiency of water available **10.108** for distribution it can institute a ban on the watering of private gardens or the washing of cars by hosepipe under Section 76.

Drought orders

Drought orders are made under the Water Resources Act by the Secretary of State/ **10.109** NAW to regulate the taking of water by water undertakers from water sources during droughts. An order sought by an undertaker can suspend or modify its supply obligations. An undertaker can also seek an order restricting certain uses of water within its area.

Water resources management plans

Under Sections 37A–D water undertakers are obliged to prepare and maintain **10.110** water resources management plans to show how they propose to manage and develop water resources so as to be able to continue to meet their supply obligations. The plan period should be 25 years. Plans are likely to require strategic

---

[73] Ibid, s 74(3)(a).
[74] Ibid, s 75(2).

environmental assessment. Section 37B lays down procedural provisions for the formulation of such plans: these include publicity for draft plans, the opportunity to make representations, public inquiries, and the power of the Secretary of State/ NAW to direct changes to the plan. Once finalized, the plan must be reviewed by the undertaker annually.

Drought plans

10.111 Under Section 39B, water undertakers have to prepare and maintain drought plans to explain how, during periods of drought, they will discharge their duties to supply an adequate supply of wholesome water under Sections 37 and 67–69 'with as little recourse as reasonably possible to drought orders or drought permits'.[75] The procedures in Section 37B for water resources management plan apply to drought plans.

E. Licensed Water Suppliers

10.112 Arrangements to allow companies other than those appointed as undertakers to supply water using the public supply system were introduced in 2005 in order to provide additional competition to water undertakers. These suppliers are granted a licence for this purpose by the Authority and are known as licensed water suppliers. Licensed water suppliers will, in the main, serve commercial customers— they can only supply non-household premises which take at least 50 megalitres of water annually.[76] 'Non-household premises' are premises which do not provide a home. Many non-household premises will still use water for domestic purposes.

10.113 A water supply licence will allow the licensee to use an undertaker's pipes to supply water to a customer's premises (a 'retail authorization'). A 'supplementary authorization' may also allow the licensee to introduce its own water into the undertaker's system.[77]

10.114 Applications to the Authority for licences and for the variation of licences are made under Section 17F and the Water Supply Licence (Applications) Regulations 2005. Conditions can be imposed under Section 17G. Standard conditions have been published by the Secretary of State/Authority under Section 17H.

10.115 The main enforcement measures applicable to water undertakers (enforcement orders, financial penalties, and special administration orders) are available against

---

[75] Ibid, s 39B(1).
[76] Ibid, s 17(3).
[77] Ibid, s 17A(2) and (5).

licensed water suppliers. The main source of the legal obligations of a licensed water supplier will be the conditions in its licence, which are enforceable under Section 18. Relatively few of the statutory duties on water undertakers are extended to licensed water supplier, although a licensed water supplier is under a duty similar to that under Section 68 when supplying water to premises for domestic or food production purposes under a retail authorization.[78]

Rights conferred by a water supply licence

Under Section 66A a licensed water supplier with a retail authorization can require a water undertaker to provide a supply of water to the licensee's customer. The undertaker can decline the request if: **10.116**

- the supply is for land without buildings or for non-domestic purposes and would mean either that the undertaker's own supply would be at risk or that it would incur unreasonable expenditure; or
- the water fittings used contravene specified provisions of Section 74 regulations.

Where the licensee has a supplementary authorization it can require the undertaker to allow the licensee to introduce water into the undertaker's system, subject to similar exemptions.[79] **10.117**

Any dispute about the application of these exemptions can be referred by the licensee to the Authority for determination.[80] **10.118**

If no exemption is applicable, the terms of the relationship between the undertaker and the licensee will settled by agreement or, in the absence of agreement, by the Authority.[81] **10.119**

The terms must provide for payments by the licensee to the undertaker in accordance with the 'costs principle' in Section 66E, that is that the undertaker should recover from the licensee any expenses reasonably incurred in performing its obligations to the licensee and its loss of revenue 'to the extent that those sums exceed any financial benefit which the undertaker receives' as a result of the licensee supplying water to its customers. The Authority has issued guidance on such terms. **10.120**

In circumstances set out in Sections 63AA to 63AC customers can transfer from a water undertaker to a licensed water supplier. **10.121**

---

[78] Ibid, s 68(1A).
[79] Ibid, s 66B.
[80] Ibid, s 66D.
[81] Ibid, s 66D.

F. Water Supply Functions of Local Authorities

10.122 The role of local authorities with regard to water supply is now relatively limited, being essentially confined to four areas, as follows. First, under Sections 77 and 78, local authorities have a general power of supervision of water undertakers. A local authority may take steps to keep itself informed about the wholesomeness and sufficiency of water supplies to premises in its area, including private supplies.[82] It must inform a water undertaker of anything suggesting that a supply for domestic or food production purposes by the undertaker or a licensed water supplier using the undertaker's system is or is likely to become unwholesome or insufficient or a danger to health, or that the duty to prevent the deterioration of such supply is being contravened.[83] If, following such notification, the authority is not satisfied that adequate remedial action has been taken, it must inform the Secretary of State.[84] The authority has no enforcement powers of its own.

10.123 Second, under Section 79, a local authority has certain duties where it is not practicable for a water undertaker, at reasonable cost, to supply wholesome water to premises in pipes sufficient for domestic purposes. If the authority is satisfied that such insufficiency or unwholesomeness is a danger to life or health and that it is practicable at reasonable cost for the undertaker to supply the premises by means other than pipes (for example by tankers), the authority must require the undertaker to do so, for such period as it specifies.[85] Failure to comply with such a requirement is, however, only enforceable by the Authority under Section 18. The local authority must pay any water charges in respect of such supply, but can recover these from the owner/occupier of the premises concerned.

10.124 Third, Section 74 regulations (dealing with water fittings) can confer enforcement powers on local authorities.[86]

10.125 Fourth, local authorities are the principal regulatory bodies for private supplies of water. Private supplies are those provided otherwise than by an undertaker or licensed water supplier and will include water taken by riparian owners from rivers, and supplies from lakes and springs. Local authorities have wide powers under Sections 80–83 to serve notices requiring the improvement of private supplies for domestic and food production purposes. In particular they can require remedial action to be taken where such supplies are not wholesome. Standards of wholesomeness are laid down in the Private Water Supply Regulations 1991.

---

[82] Ibid, s 77(1).
[83] Ibid, s 78(1).
[84] Ibid, s 78(2).
[85] Ibid, s 79(2).
[86] Ibid, s 74(3)(a).

Such notices require to be confirmed by the Secretary of State if objections are received.[87]

Finally, one power under other legislation needs to be mentioned. Section 25 of the Building Act 1984 provides that a local authority must not give building regulations approval to plans for the construction of new houses unless they show satisfactory arrangements for the supply of wholesome water for domestic purposes from the system of an undertaker or a private supply. **10.126**

G. Sewerage Undertakers

Sewerage undertakers perform two discrete functions: the provision of sewerage services to drain buildings/land and the receipt of trade effluent from industrial premises. The WIA imposes a general duty on sewerage undertakers to provide a system of sewers and to empty and treat their contents, and provides for this to be amplified in regulations. It then makes separate provision for these two functions. **10.127**

General duty

The overriding duty of sewerage undertakers is set out in Section 94. This requires undertakers: **10.128**

> To provide, improve and extend a system of sewers (whether inside [their] area or elsewhere) and so to cleanse and maintain those sewers so as to ensure that that area is and continues to be effectually drained and
> To make effective provision for the emptying of those sewers and such further provision (whether inside [their] area or elsewhere) as is necessary from time to time for effectually dealing, by means of sewage disposal works or otherwise, with the contents of those sewers.

In performing this duty the undertaker must have regard to existing and likely future obligations to receive trade effluent into its sewers and to the need to provide for the disposal of such effluent.[88] **10.129**

These duties are enforceable under Section 18 by the Secretary of State/NAW or by the Authority (with the consent or authorization of the Secretary of State/NAW).[89] **10.130**

---

[87]   Ibid, s 81.
[88]   Ibid, s 94(2).
[89]   Ibid, s 94(3).

Regulations

10.131 As with the general duty on water undertakers, the Section 94 duty is supple-mented by regulations of two types. The first type identifies circumstances which are to be regarded as involving a breach of Section 94 by reference to other statu-tory provisions (Sections 98–117 for sewerage functions and Sections 118–141 for trade effluent functions) or to standards of performance set out in the regulations.[90]

10.132 The second type prescribes standards of performance to be achieved in individual cases.[91] These are not linked to the Section 94 duty. Instead, provision is made for the payment of compensation to persons affected by any breach. The current reg-ulations are contained in the Water Supply and Sewerage Services (Customer Service Standards) Regulations 1993 and the Water Supply and Sewerage Services (Customer Service Standards) (Amendment) Regulations 2000.

10.133 Under Section 95A the Authority is obliged to collect information about the payment of compensation and the overall levels of performance achieved by sew-erage undertakers and to publish such of this as it considers to be expedient. Under s 96A a sewerage undertaker must itself publish information, in such ways as the Authority directs, about its overall performance in relation to regulatory standards.

10.134 There are two ways in which new regulations of either type can be made. The first involves an application from the Authority to the Secretary of State/NAW. The Authority must carry out research into the views of a representative sample of persons likely to be affected. The application must set out the proposed regu-lations and must be served on the relevant undertakers, and an opportunity for representations and objections given. The Secretary of State/NAW can only make regulations which differ from those set out in the application if the proposed modifications have been notified to the Authority and any undertakers affected.[92]

10.135 Second, the Secretary of State/NAW can make regulations without an application from the Authority where he/it considers that the regulations will contribute towards the attainment of policies on public health or the environment or that there are exceptional reasons in the public interest for regulations to be made (Section 96(4)). The Secretary of State/NAW must first carry out research into the views of a representative sample of persons likely to be affected.[93] The Secretary

---

[90] Ibid, s 95(1).
[91] Ibid, s 95(2).
[92] Ibid, s 96(3).
[93] Ibid, s 39(7).

of State/NAW must give notice of the proposed regulations and consider any representations received.[94]

Drainage of premises

Right of occupiers/owners of premises to utilize undertaker's sewerage system

Section 106 gives the owner or occupier of premises and the owner of a private **10.136**
sewer which drains premises, the right to have his drains/sewers connect with the
public sewer of a sewerage undertaker and thereby to discharge foul and surface
water into that system.[95]

Although the Section 106 right is not in terms confined to drainage for domestic **10.137**
purposes, it does not extend to the discharge of liquid from a factory (other than
domestic sewage or surface water) nor to the discharge of any matter prohibited
by any enactment.[96] In this regard, Section 111(1) makes it an offence to discharge into a public sewer:

(a) Any matter likely to injure the sewer . . . To interfere with the free flow of its
    contents or to affect prejudicially the treatment and disposal of its contents;
(b) Any such chemical refuse or waste steam, or any such liquid of a temperature
    higher than 110 degrees Fahrenheit if, either alone or in combination with the
    contents of the sewer/drain, they are dangerous, a nuisance or likely to cause
    injury to health; or
(c) Any petroleum spirit or carbide of calcium.

There is also no right under Section 106 to drain foul water into a surface water **10.138**
sewer, nor, except with the undertaker's consent, to drain surface water into a
foul water sewer.[97]

New connections to existing sewers

Where premises are not already connected to a public sewer, the Section 106 right **10.139**
entitles the owner/occupier to give notice of a proposal to make a connection to a
sewer to the sewerage undertaker. The undertaker is obliged to permit the connection to be made unless within 21 days it gives notice that it considers that the
method of construction or the condition of the drain/sewer on the premises does
not satisfy its standards, or would cause the connection to be prejudicial to the
undertaker's system.[98] The undertaker cannot refuse to permit the connection

---

[94] Ibid, s 96(5).
[95] Ibid, s 106(1).
[96] Ibid, s 106(2)(a).
[97] Ibid, s 106(2)(b).
[98] Ibid, s 106(4).

for any other reason, eg because its system is inadequate to receive the new flow.[99] However, in charging the owner/occupier for the connection, the undertaker can recover the costs of increasing the capacity of the existing system.[100]

10.140 The connection can in theory be made by the owner/occupier himself. Not surprisingly, the undertaker can insist on carrying out the necessary works itself, by giving notice to this effect within 14 days of the owner/occupier's notice.[101] It is a criminal offence for the recipient of such notice to carry out the works himself. Where such notice is given, and provided that reasonable costs have been paid, or reasonable security given, the undertaker is obliged to make the connection.[102] The Authority resolves disputes about the reasonableness of requirements as to costs and security.[103]

10.141 Where the undertaker does not elect to make the connection itself, it has the right to supervise works carried out by the owner/occupier. In making the connection the owner/occupier has the same powers of breaking open streets etc as an undertaker under Sections 158 and 161(1) of the WIA 1991 (see paras 10.184–10.186).[104]

10.142 It is a criminal offence to make a connection with a public sewer otherwise than pursuant to these powers.[105] The sewerage undertaker is entitled to close any connection so made, and to recover the costs incurred from the offender.

Requisitions of new sewers for domestic purposes

10.143 The owner or occupier of premises and a local authority can require an undertaker to provide new public sewers or lateral drains to drain buildings or proposed buildings for domestic purposes. The obligation is triggered by service of a requisition under Section 98. Provided the requisitioner complies with the 'financial conditions', the undertaker must provide the sewer. The financial conditions ensure that the requisitioner gives undertakings to meet the expenses of the works over a twelve-year period or, at the requisitioner's request, to pay a single sum.

10.144 Unless the requisitioner is a public authority, the financial conditions may also require him to give security for these undertakings.

10.145 Once a requisition has been made and the financial conditions met, the undertaker is obliged to provide the new sewer/lateral drain within six months of the 'relevant day'. This is the later of: the date on which the financial conditions

---

[99] *Smeaton v Ilford Corp* [1954] Ch 450.
[100] Water Industry Act 1991, s 146(2).
[101] Ibid, s 107.
[102] Ibid, s 107(3).
[103] Ibid, s 106(4A).
[104] Ibid, s 108.
[105] Ibid, s 109.

are met and the date on which the places of connection with the relevant private drains/sewers are determined.[106] This duty is owed to the requisitioner who can sue the undertaker for loss or damage caused by a breach. It is a defence for the undertaker to show that it took all reasonable steps and exercised all due diligence to avoid the breach.[107] The obligation to comply with a requisition in respect of paricular premises is not enforceable under Section 18 by the Secretary of State/NAW/Authority.

Sewers to premises erected before 1995

An additional obligation to provide sewers has been created by Section 101A, **10.146** which was added to the WIA by the Environment Act 1995. This creates a general duty to provide sewers for domestic purposes for premises erected before 20 June 1995 which are not connected to a public sewer and where the current arrangements are likely to cause adverse effects to amenity or the environment. This is obviously directed at tackling premises drained by soakaways etc. The Secretary of State can issue guidance on the circumstances that trigger the obligation. Disputes about whether the duty arises in any particular case are resolved by the Environment Agency.[108] There is no provision for an owner/occupier to require the provision of such a sewer under Section 101A—the duty only exists if the undertaker accepts that it does, or if the Environment Agency has so determined. Enforcement of the duty under Section 101A is by the Secretary of State/ NAW or by the Authority (with the authorization or consent of the Secretary of State/NAW) under Section 18.

The costs of providing such a sewer have to be borne by the undertakers' customers **10.147** generally.

Other powers with respect to the sewerage system

Sewerage undertakers have a range of other powers designed to facilitate the provi- **10.148** sion of an effective general sewerage system. Four deserve mention. First, where a person proposes to construct a drain or sewer that, in the view of the undertaker, is likely to form part of the general sewerage system, the undertaker can impose requirements under Section 112 as to its construction. Such requirements will be designed to ensure that the new apparatus operates effectively as part of the general system. The person proposing to construct the sewer/drain can appeal against such requirements to the Authority. A failure to comply with such requirements which cause the undertaker to suffer loss or damage is actionable at the suit of the undertaker. The undertaker is liable to pay to the person constructing

---

106 Ibid, s 101.
107 Ibid, s 98(3) and (4).
108 Ibid, s 101A(7).

the drain/sewer any extra expenses reasonably incurred in complying with such requirements.

10.149 Second, an undertaker has power under Section 113 to replace private drainage systems which connect with a public sewer or a cesspool, and which, though adequate for their purposes, are not adapted to the general sewerage system of the area, or, in the undertaker's opinion, are otherwise objectionable. Such replacement must be carried out at the undertaker's expense. An owner of premises aggrieved by an undertaker's proposal can refer his grievance to the Authority.

10.150 Third, undertakers have powers under Section 114 to investigate private sewers and drains connecting with public sewers which they suspect are, or are likely to become injurious to health or a nuisance, or so defective as to admit subsoil water. This is a curious power because undertakers have no specific powers to deal with such drains if they are found to be defective. The powers under Section 113 above would not appear to be applicable. The power under Section 101A only applies if the premises are not connected to a public sewer. Only local authorities have power to take action against nuisances and to carry out works to private sewerage apparatus.

10.151 Finally, undertakers have a wide power to discontinue/prohibit the use of sewers vested in them.[109] Where such discontinuance would deprive a person of the lawful use of a sewer, the undertaker must make alternative provision. Disputes about such alternative provision are resolved by the Authority.

Compensation following exercise of powers under Sections 101A–116

10.152 The above powers carry a liability, under paragraph 4 of Schedule 12, to 'make full compensation to any person who has sustained damage. . . in relation to a matter as to which that person has not himself been in default. . .'. Disputes about the fact of damage and the amount of compensation are settled by arbitration, unless the amount claimed is under £5,000, in which case the Authority deals with the matter.

Trade effluent

Introduction

10.153 The receipt into public sewers of waste liquid from industrial processes is treated quite differently from drainage for domestic purposes. There is no right to make such discharges, and handling such discharges is an essentially commercial activity of undertakers. Of course the receipt of such discharges creates the potential for pollution and sewerage undertakers need to ensure that, when they in turn

---

[109] Ibid, s 116.

pump the contents of their sewers into controlled waters, the terms of the relevant discharge consents are met.

'Trade effluent' is defined in Section 141(1) as: **10.154**

> any liquid, either with or without particles of matter in suspension in the liquid, which is wholly or partly produced in the course of any trade or industry carried on at trade premises; and
> in relation to any trade premises,. . . any such liquid which is so produced in the course of any trade or industry carried on at those premises.

'Trade premises' mean any premises used or intended to be used for the carrying **10.155** on of any trade or industry, including agriculture, horticulture, fish farming, and scientific research or experiment. The definition effectively embraces all liquid produced in the course of commercial/industrial activity and is based on the source of the effluent rather than its content.

The Section 106 right to discharge foul and surface water into public sewers **10.156** does not cover non-domestic discharges from factories and the discharge of trade effluent is only lawful if permitted by a discharge consent under Section 119 or by an agreement under Section 129.[110] Such a consent/agreement can cover discharges of matter that would ordinarily be prohibited under Section 111(1)(a) or (b).[111]

The definition of trade effluent is deliberately wide and covers discharges contain- **10.157** ing dangerous substances. The discharge of defined types of dangerous trade efflu-ent, known as 'special category effuent', is subject to additional control by the Environment Agency (see below).

The Secretary of State/NAW has power to make regulations applying the provi- **10.158** sions dealing with trade effluent (but not special category effluent) to other discharges.[112]

Discharge consent under Section 119

Consent to discharge trade effluent can be sought by the owner or occupier **10.159** of trade premises by application to the relevant undertaker.[113] The application must specify the nature and composition of the effluent, the maximum daily discharge and the maximum rate of discharge proposed. If consent is granted, the undertaker can impose conditions governing these matters, the level of charges to be paid for receiving the discharge, the sewers into which the effluent can be discharged, the timing of discharges, the diminution or elimination of

---

[110] Ibid, s 118(4).
[111] Ibid, s 118(3).
[112] Ibid, s 139(1).
[113] Ibid, s 119(1).

any specified constituent in certain types of effluent, the temperature, acidity, and alkalinity of the effluent, and monitoring of the discharges. It is a criminal offence to breach a condition in a trade effluent consent.

10.160 In fixing charges, regard must be had to the nature, composition, and volume of the effluent, any additional expense incurred, or likely to be incurred, in connection with the reception/disposal of the effluent, and any revenue likely to be derived by the undertaker from the effluent.

10.161 If an undertaker refuses to grant the consent, the applicant can appeal to the Authority under Section 122. An appeal can also be made against a failure to determine an application within two months and against the imposition of any condition. On an appeal against a condition the Authority can review all the conditions in the consent, although the Authority cannot impose conditions as to charges if the relevant matter is covered by a charges scheme under Section 143. Where the Authority can impose conditions as to charges, it must have regard to the desirability of the undertaker recovering its expenses associated with the receipt of the discharge and securing a reasonable return on its capital.[114]

Variation of discharge consents

10.162 An important feature of the consent system is the undertaker's right, under Section 124, to vary the terms of any consent. This power is needed to enable existing consents to be brought into line with new environmental standards.

10.163 A variation can add to, remove, or change the conditions in the consent. A variation must be notified to the owner/occupier and cannot come into effect for at least two months (unless the variation relates to the paying of charges, in which case it can come into effect on any day after the giving of the notice).[115] The undertaker can appeal to the Authority against such a variation within this period, or later, with the Authority's consent. The variation is suspended until the appeal is determined, unless the variation relates to charges. The Authority has a wide discretion on such an appeal, including the power to substitute a more onerous variation.

10.164 Protection is given to the discharger by restrictions on the frequency of variations. Ordinarily no variation can be made within two years of the grant of the consent or of a previous variation, unless the owner/occupier consents. This restriction does not apply if the undertaker considers that the variation is necessary to provide proper protection for persons likely to be affected by discharges permitted under the unmodified consent.[116] A variation on this basis carries with it an

---

[114] Ibid, s 135(2).
[115] Ibid, s 126.
[116] Ibid, s 125(1).

obligation to pay compensation unless the variation is needed as a result of an unforeseen change of circumstances since the beginning of the relevant two-year period that is not attributable to other discharge consents given since the consent in question.[117] The Secretary of State has power to make regulations governing the measure of such compensation.[118]

Agreements under Section 129

Permission to discharge trade effluent can also be secured by agreement with the undertaker under Section 129. **10.165**

There is no right of appeal against a refusal to make an agreement. If an owner/occupier cannot achieve what he wants by agreement he must use the consent procedure, if necessary appealing under Section 122. An agreement is likely to be more appropriate where the owner/occupier is funding infrastructure works required for the reception or disposal of his effluent. **10.166**

The undertaker cannot vary an agreement unilaterally. **10.167**

Special category effluent

Trade effluent containing dangerous substances identified in the Trade Effluents (Prescribed Processes and Substances) Regulations of 1989–1992 is known as 'special category effluent'. Discharge of such effluent is subject to additional control. The Regulations reflect first, the so-called 'Red List' of substances regarded as so dangerous that discharges into water ought to be minimized wherever practicable and secondly EEC Directive 76/464 on pollution to the aquatic environment. **10.168**

Reference to the Environment Agency

Discharges of special category effluent are subject to the normal requirement for a consent under Section 118 or an agreement under Section 129, but such consent or agreement must accord with instructions given by the Environment Agency. Accordingly, whenever a consent is sought or an agreement is proposed, the undertaker must refer to the Environment Agency the question of whether the discharge should be permitted and, if so, on what terms.[119] This obligation does not arise if, within two months, the undertaker refuses the application for a consent.[120] **10.169**

---

[117] Ibid, s 125(2).
[118] Ibid, s 125(5).
[119] Ibid, ss 120(1) and 130(1).
[120] Ibid, s 120(2) and (3).

10.170 While the reference is being considered, the undertaker is barred from authorizing/agreeing to the discharge.[121] Failure to make a reference is a criminal offence.[122] The Environment Agency can exercise its powers of review (see below) if a discharge of special category effluent has been permitted without such a reference having been made.[123]

Review by Environment Agency

10.171 The Environment Agency has power to review consents and agreements under which special category effluent is discharged.[124] This is in addition to the undertaker's power to vary consents. On review the Agency can revoke any previous determination, consent, or agreement.

10.172 A review cannot be carried out within two years of the last determination by the Agency on a reference or review, unless the relevant consent/agreement was granted/made in defiance of the Agency's instructions given on an earlier reference/review, or, since the last determination, there has been a breach of a condition imposed by the Agency on such a reference/review.[125] In addition, more frequent reviews can be carried out if this is necessary to give effect to EU or other international obligations or for the protection of public health or of flora or fauna dependent on an aquatic environment.[126]

Procedure

10.173 The procedure on a reference and a review is the same and is set out in Section 132. The Agency must invite and consider representations from the undertaker and the owner/occupier concerned. Having considered the matter, the Agency must issue a notice stating one of three things: (i) that the discharge must be prohibited, (ii) that the discharge must be prohibited unless specified conditions are imposed or (iii) that there is no objection to the discharge and the Agency does not intend to impose any conditions. The undertaker must exercise its power to give a consent or to make an agreement in accordance with the determination. Thus the undertaker can refuse to permit a discharge that the Agency is prepared to allow, but cannot take a less restrictive approach. Breach of these requirements is a criminal offence. For the purpose of securing compliance with instructions given under Section 132 the Agency can revoke consents/agreements already granted/made by undertakers.[127]

---

[121] Ibid, ss 120(4) and 130(2).
[122] Ibid, ss 120(9) and 130(7).
[123] Ibid, ss 120(10) and 130(9).
[124] Ibid, s 127.
[125] Ibid, ss 127(2) and 131(2).
[126] Ibid, ss 127(3) and 131(3).
[127] Ibid, s 133(6).

If, following a determination by the Agency, the undertaker refuses the application for consent, fails to determine it within two months or imposes conditions, the normal rights of appeal to the Authority still apply. However, the Authority is obliged to exercise its appellate powers in accordance with the Environment Agency's determination,[128] so there is no point in appealing against a decision that merely reflects the Agency's determination.

10.174

Processes regulated under Section 2 of the Pollution Prevention and Control Act 1999

In order to avoid a duplication of regulatory control, effluent that would otherwise count as special category effluent is not so regarded if it arises from a process that requires a permit under Section 2 of the Pollution Prevention and Control Act 1999 and a permit has been sought (it does not matter that it has been granted or refused). An ordinary trade effluent discharge consent is still required for such discharges.

10.175

Treatment

Requirements for the treatment of sewage are imposed by the Urban Waste Water Treatment (England and Wales) Regulations 1994 as amended. These Regulations supplement the Section 94 duty and implement EC Directive 91/271. This Directive sets standards for sewerage systems, the treatment of sewage, and the discharge of trade effluent from treatment works.

10.176

The Regulations apply to 'urban waste water', which is defined as 'domestic waste water or the mixture of domestic waste water with industrial waste water and/or run off rain water'. 'Domestic waste water' is 'waste water from residential settlements and services which originates predominantly from the human metabolism and from household activities'. 'Industrial waste water' is 'any waste water which is discharged from premises used for carrying on any trade or industry, other than domestic waste water and rain run off water'. The definition is thus wide enough to cover practically all types of foul and surface water that an undertaker is likely to have in its sewers, as well as many types of trade effluent.

10.177

General obligations under the Regulations relate to the catchment areas of individual 'urban waste water treatment plants' or final discharge points, referred to as 'agglomerations'. The Regulations require that 'collection systems' for collecting waste water from agglomerations of various sizes (measured in terms of population) should have been provided by 31 December 2005. Such collection systems must be designed and constructed in accordance with the best technical knowledge not entailing excessive cost. Water in the collection systems must be treated

10.178

---

[128] Ibid, s 133(1).

in accordance with Regulation 5. This requires various grades of treatment depending on the size of agglomeration and the sensitivity of the receiving waters. For this purpose receiving waters have to be categorized as either sensitive or 'high natural dispersion' areas.

10.179 Specific obligations with regard to industrial waste water are imposed by Regulations 7 and 8. Regulation 7 imposes a general duty on the Secretary of State, the Authority and sewerage undertakers to exercise their trade effluent functions so as to ensure that the requirements of Schedule 4 of the Regulations are met. Schedule 4 requires that such waste water entering the undertaker's collection systems and treatment plants should be subject to pre-treatment designed to achieve certain safety and environmental objectives. Trade effluent agreements and consents should be varied so as to comply with these requirements. Consents and agreements are to be reviewed 'at regular intervals'.

10.180 Regulation 8 imposes additional obligations with regard to the treatment of biodegradable industrial waste water that does not enter urban waste water treatment plants and so is not caught by the above controls.

Discharges of treated sewage

10.181 Under Section 117 sewerage undertakers are prohibited from discharging foul water into any water course unless it has been treated. Sewerage undertakers discharging treated sewage into controlled waters will require, and have to comply with, a discharge consent under the Water Resources Act 1991. Disposal of the by-products of treatment (for example, sewage sludge) on land will require a waste management licence under the Environmental Protection Act 1990.

H. Sewerage Functions of Local Authorities

10.182 As has been mentioned, the WIA continues to allow local authorities to enter into agency agreements with sewerage undertakers to perform sewerage functions on the undertaker's behalf.[129]

10.183 In addition, local authorities have various powers with regard to the provision of sewerage services under the Building Act 1984. In particular, building regulation control will ensure that new premises are provided with adequate drainage and that new buildings are not constructed over existing sewers and drains. A local authority can also require the disconnection of disused drains, has remedial

---

[129] Water Industry Act1991, s 97.

powers where the drainage provision to a building is inadequate,[130] and can carry out repairs to drains, private sewers, water closets, pipes, and soil pipes.[131]

I. Undertakers' Works etc

Powers to lay pipes in streets and private land

Not surprisingly, water and sewerage undertakers, though now privately owned, have extensive powers to carry out works etc associated with their statutory functions. These are contained in Sections 155–192 of the WIA. These powers are expressed to be cumulative and to be 'without prejudice to any power conferred by virtue of any agreement'.[132] **10.184**

The most significant works powers of undertakers are the pipe-laying powers contained in Sections 158 and 159. These powers cover works to lay and keep 'pipes' in streets and private land and to inspect, maintain, adjust, and repair such pipes. 'Pipes' are defined as water mains, resource mains, discharge pipes, and service pipes (in the case of water undertakers) and sewers, disposal mains and lateral drains vested in sewerage undertakers or laid under Section 98 or 101B (in the case of sewerage undertakers).[133] **10.185**

These powers are likely to be sufficient for all but the most substantial infrastructure schemes and are far less cumbersome to exercise than the other compulsory powers described below. **10.186**

Pipe laying in streets

Section 158 permits water and sewerage undertakers to lay pipes in streets and to break open streets, to tunnel or bore them, to open sewers, drains, or tunnels and to remove earth and other materials for this purpose. A 'street' includes any highway, whether adopted or not. Water and sewerage undertakers also have power to carry out works in streets to ensure that water in 'relevant waterworks' is not polluted or contaminated[134] and in connection with the provision of meters.[135] 'Relevant waterworks' are waterworks containing any water which is or may be used by a water undertaker to supply premises. **10.187**

None of these provisions contain any procedural requirements. However, such works are subject to Part III of the New Roads and Street Works Act 1991 which **10.188**

---

[130] Building Act 1984, s 59.
[131] Public Health Act 1961, s 17.
[132] Water Industry Act 1991, s 192(5).
[133] Ibid, s 158(7).
[134] Ibid, s 161(1).
[135] Ibid, s 162.

requires the giving of advance notice of, and the co-ordination of works. In addition, undertakers carrying out such works are under a duty to cause as little damage as possible and must pay compensation for any loss or damage that is caused. Disputes about such compensation are settled by arbitration.[136]

Pipe laying in private land

10.189　Section 159 empowers water and sewerage undertakers to lay pipes and to carry out incidental works in private land without the consent of the owner/occupier. 'Reasonable notice' has to be given. This means not less than three months' notice for the laying of a new pipe (otherwise than in substitution for an existing pipe) and not less than 42 days' notice for an alteration to an existing pipe.[137] This apparently draconian power has been a feature of the law for many years.

10.190　Water and sewerage undertakers also have power under Section 161(2) to carry out works on private land to ensure that water in 'relevant waterworks' is not polluted or contaminated.

Discharges by water undertakers in the course of pipe laying

10.191　In the course of exercising pipe-laying powers under Sections 158, 159, 161(1), 161(2), and 163 a water undertaker may discharge water into any available watercourse.[138] This right also applies to works by water undertakers for constructing, altering, cleaning, or examining a reservoir, borehole, or other apparatus. The power is not shared by sewerage undertakers. The water undertaker is not allowed to discharge anything that harms the works or property of any railway undertaker or navigation authority or which floods or damages any highway. Where the discharge is from a pipe exceeding 229 mm in diameter the consent of the Environment Agency is required.[139]

10.192　The water undertaker is under a duty to 'take all necessary steps' to secure that the water discharged is 'as free as may be reasonably practicable' from mud or silt or solid, polluting, offensive or injurious substances, or any substance prejudicial to fish or spawn, spawning beds, or food of fish. Breach of these obligations is a criminal offence.[140] In addition, the undertaker must cause as little loss and damage as is possible and must pay compensation where loss and damage is caused. Disputes about compensation are settled by arbitration.[141]

---

[136]　Water Industry Act 1991, Sch 12, para 1.
[137]　Ibid, s 159(5).
[138]　Ibid, s 165(1).
[139]　Ibid, s 166.
[140]　Ibid, s 165(3).
[141]　Paragraph 6 of Schedule 12.

Restrictions on interference with other water-related infrastructure

Restrictions are imposed on the exercise of pipe laying powers to prevent interference **10.193** with other water-related infrastructure etc. Thus Section 186 provides that these powers do not authorize interference with certain flood defence works, land drains, irrigation works, and water courses without the consent of the persons affected. Also, any works by sewerage undertakers that would injure reservoirs, canals, watercourses, streams, or the supply, quality, or fall of water in them require the consent of the person who would ordinarily be entitled to restrain such injury. Such consent may be subject to conditions, but cannot be unreasonably withheld. Section 187 provides that works under Sections 158, 159, 161(1), 163, and 165 can only be carried out in tidal lands with the approval of the Secretary of State/NAW.

Compensation for pipe laying in private land

Compensation is payable by water or sewerage undertakers when pipes are laid in **10.194** private land. The relevant provisions, which are contained in paragraphs 2 and 3 of Schedule 12, provide for compensation for any depreciation in value of the land on which the works take place (assessed under the rules in Section 5 of the Land Compensation Act 1965), for other loss in respect of such land that would have produced disturbance compensation in the case of compulsory purchase, and for damage or injurious affection to other land. Disputes about compensation are resolved by the Lands Tribunal.

Code of Practice and complaints

Section 182 imposes a duty on water and sewerage undertakers to submit to the **10.195** Secretary of State/NAW, for his/its approval, a code of practice on the carrying out of works under these powers. If required to do so, they must also submit modifications to such a code. These obligations are enforceable by the Secretary of State under Section 18. Contravention of a code of practice does not affect the powers of the undertaker nor give rise to criminal or civil liability. It is, however, a matter to be considered by the Authority when deciding whether to make a financial award under Section 181 (see below).

Complaints about pipe laying in private land are dealt with using a special proce- **10.196** dure under Section 181. Complaints should be made in the first instance to the undertaker. If the undertaker fails to deal with the complaint, having been given a reasonable opportunity to do so, the Authority must investigate it. If the Authority finds that the undertaker has failed to consult the owner/occupier about the exercise of these powers, or has, by the unreasonable exercise of its powers, caused loss or damage, it can award up to £5,000 to a complainant. If the complainant is already entitled to compensation under another enactment (including under Schedule 12), the Authority can only make an award if it considers that it is appropriate 'to reflect the fact that it was not reasonable for the undertaker to cause the complainant to sustain the loss or damage or to be subjected to the inconvenience'.

10.197   The Authority does not have to investigate complaints which it considers to be vexatious or frivolous or which are late (ie made over 12 months, or such longer period as the Authority may allow, after the relevant matter came to the attention of the complainant).

Compulsory purchase of land by water and sewerage undertakers

10.198   The wide scope of the pipe-laying powers conferred by Sections 158 and 159 mean that, in most instances, water and sewerage undertakers will not need to acquire land in order to carry out their works. Where land does have to be acquired, a compulsory power is conferred by Section 155. This authorizes acquisition of any land required by an undertaker 'for the purposes of or in connection with the carrying out of its functions'. This includes power to create new rights, to provide for the extinguishment of existing rights and to acquire land required to be given in exchange for common land. The procedure for such acquisition is that of the Acquisition of Land Act 1981. Compensation is assessed in the ordinary way, subject to specified modifications to the Compulsory Purchase Act 1965 set out in Schedule 9 of the WIA.

Compulsory works orders of water undertakers

10.199   In addition to the compulsory purchase powers discussed above, water under-takers (but not sewerage undertakers) can seek a 'compulsory works order' under Section 167. Such an order can be made to facilitate the carrying out of building or engineering operations or the making of discharges into inland waters or underground strata. The order is made by the Secretary of State/NAW by statutory instrument, following an application from an undertaker, and grants such powers etc as are required by the undertaker for the purpose of the works/discharges. The scope of such an order is potentially very wide indeed: it can provide for the compulsory acquisition of land and interests in land, amend or repeal any local statutory provision, and apply any of the works powers that would not otherwise be available, with or without modifications. The procedure for making compulsory works orders is set out in Schedule 11.

Adoption of apparatus

10.200   The apparatus of a water or sewerage undertaker is 'vested' in the undertaker. Vesting gives the undertaker ownership of the pipe/sewer itself and the right to occupy the space taken by the sewer in the subsoil.[142] Pipes/sewers constructed by

---

[142]   See *Newcastle under Lyme Corp v Wolstanton Ltd* [1947] Ch 92.

an undertaker for the purposes of its undertaking are automatically vested in the undertaker. Pipes and sewers that are constructed privately are vested in the undertaker by a process known as 'adoption', which may be compared to the adoption of highways by a highway authority. Because adoption carries with it responsibility to maintain the pipe/sewer, it is usually in the interests of the owner to have his pipes/sewers adopted by an undertaker. There are different provisions dealing with the adoption of privately constructed water and sewerage apparatus.

Water undertakers—agreements to adopt domestic water mains etc at a future date

A water undertaker cannot allow a privately constructed mains or service pipe intended for the supply water for domestic or food production purposes to be connected to its system until the main/pipe has been adopted.[143] **10.201**

Sections 51A–E, introduced in 2002, allow developers etc who are constructing or proposing to construct water mains and service pipes for domestic purposes to the standards of the relevant water undertaker to apply for an agreement that the undertaker will adopt the pipe at a specified date in the future. **10.202**

If the undertaker refuses the application or fails to determine it within two months or imposes terms unacceptable to the applicant, there is a right of appeal to the Authority.[144] **10.203**

The applicant will have to provide, at his expense, associated infrastructure necessitated by the new mains/pipe. **10.204**

The undertaker is entitled to recover the costs of incorporating the new mains/pipe into its supply system.[145] It can require that the mains/pipe should be constructed with a higher capacity than the developer requires, at the undertaker's expense. **10.205**

These provisions do not apply to mains/pipes intended for non-domestic purposes, but there is nothing to prevent a developer and an undertaker from negotiating an agreement that such a mains/pipe should be adopted.[146] **10.206**

Such an agreement is enforceable by the owner/occupier of the premises connected to the mains/pipe. It is not enforceable under Section 18 by the Secretary of State/NAW/Authority. **10.207**

---

[143] Water Industry Act 1991, s 51D.
[144] Ibid, s 51B.
[145] Ibid, s 51C.
[146] Ibid, s 51A(2).

Sewerage undertakers—adoption of existing apparatus at insistence of undertaker

10.208 For historical reasons, many existing sewers are not vested in sewerage undertakers. Accordingly, sewerage undertakers have the right to adopt private apparatus compulsorily. The sewerage undertaker must give notice of its intention to the existing owner. The owner then has two months to make an appeal to the Authority. If there is no such appeal the undertaker can make a declaration vesting the sewer in it.[147] If an appeal is made, the Authority has the power to make such a declaration and can impose conditions, including conditions as to the payment of compensation by the sewerage undertaker. Section 102(5) contains the considerations that are relevant to an undertaker's decision to adopt. Under Section 105A the Secretary of State can make regulations requiring undertakers to prepare schemes under which they will be obliged to exercise their Section 102 powers in defined cicumstances.

Sewerage undertakers—adoption of proposed apparatus at insistence of owner

10.209 A developer constructing/proposing to construct a sewer or sewage disposal works can apply to the relevant sewerage undertaker for an agreement that it will adopt the sewer/works on completion, or at some other specified time.[148] The undertaker can require specified information to be provided with such an application. Any agreement can contain provisions relating to the construction of the sewer/works and other conditions. An appeal can be made to the Authority against the refusal of the application, the failure to determine such an application within two months, or the imposition of conditions.[149] In determining any appeal, the Authority can impose such terms as it considers to be reasonable.

10.210 An agreement of this type is enforceable by the owner or occupier of the premises served by the relevant sewer/works.[150] It is not enforceable under Section 18 by the Secretary of State/NAW/Authority.

The mining code

10.211 Important provisions governing the relationship between water and sewerage undertakers and the owners of minerals underneath undertakers' apparatus are contained in the mining code set out in Schedule 14. This is designed to obviate the need for an undertaker, when acquiring land or rights for the purpose of installing apparatus, to pay compensation for the right to support from underlying minerals until the mine owner wishes to work them.

---

[147] Ibid, s 102.
[148] Ibid, s 104.
[149] Ibid, s 105(2).
[150] Ibid, s 104(5).

The scheme of Schedule 14 is as follows: when an undertaker acquires land, **10.212** whether compulsorily or by agreement, or carries out works on land, it does not (in the absence of express provision) acquire underlying minerals. This means that the undertaker is not liable to pay compensation for such minerals, and the mine owner retains the right to extract them. However, once apparatus is installed, the mine owner cannot work to within 37 metres of it unless, not less than 30 days before the start of working, he has served notice of his intention on the undertaker. If the undertaker considers that the working would damage its apparatus, and is willing to pay appropriate compensation, it can, by service of a counter-notice, prohibit or restrict the working. The measure of compensation is the value of a right to support from the underlying minerals. If no such counter-notice is served, the mine owner can work the minerals 'by proper methods and in the usual manner of working . . . in the district in question', even if this causes damage to the undertaker's apparatus.

The mine owner retains the right to make communications through minerals **10.213** underneath the apparatus to achieve access to any minerals on the other side. If it is not possible to work such minerals, compensation for severance is payable.

Maps of underground apparatus

Under Sections 198 and 199 water and sewerage undertakers are obliged to keep **10.214** maps showing the location of all underground apparatus vested in them (and, in the case of water mains, where a vesting declaration has been made but has not yet taken effect). Such maps must be kept up to date and open to public inspection. Separate sewer maps must be kept for the area of each local authority and must be supplied to the relevant local authority.

The obligation to show apparatus does not extend to service pipes or sewers etc **10.215** laid before 1 September 1989 where the undertaker does not know or have reasonable grounds for suspecting their existence, or where it is not reasonably practicable for the undertaker to discover the course of the pipe/sewer and the undertaker has not done so.

These obligations are enforceable by the Secretary of State/NAW under **10.216** Section 18.

Right of landowners to require removal of undertaker's apparatus

Landowners have the right to secure the removal of apparatus installed in their **10.217** land in certain circumstances. This is the result of Section 185, the product of a late addition to the Water Bill with no precedent in any earlier water legislation. Section 185 provides that, where apparatus 'is for the time being kept installed . . . on, under or over any land', a person with an interest in that land or in adjacent land can, by serving notice on the undertaker, require the removal of the apparatus if this is necessary to enable that person to carry out 'improvement' of his land. 'Improvement' includes any development or change of use of the land. The undertaker must comply with such a requirement except to the extent that it is unreasonable. The undertaker is entitled to recover its expenses from the person serving the notice and can require security for these costs. A notice served under Section 185 cannot require an undertaker to alter or remove any apparatus in a street.

10.218 The duties on the undertaker under Section 185 are enforceable by the Authority under Section 18.

J. Powers of Entry of Water and Sewerage Undertakers

10.219 Undertakers have wide powers to enter premises to carry out inspections and works in connection with their functions. In particular both water and sewerage undertakers have power to enter premises to carry out surveys and tests (including the digging of boreholes) to determine whether, and if so how, works powers (ie under Sections 158, 159, 161(1), 161(2), 163, and 165) should be exercised, and for the purposes of exercising such powers.[151]

10.220 In addition there are a number of powers of entry particular to water and sewerage undertakers. Thus water undertakers can enter premises:

- to carry out tests and surveys in order to determine whether it would be appropriate for the undertaker to acquire any land or apply for a compulsory works order;[152]
- to investigate whether any disconnection power should be exercised or any works under Sections 64(4), 66(3), or 75 carried out or to exercise such power (these powers cover the provision of separate service pipes to premises, the provision/repair of cisterns to prevent wastage, the prevention of damage to persons and property from defective fittings and works to prevent contamination of water);[153]
- to monitor and record whether water supplied for domestic or food production purposes is wholesome at the time of supply;[154]
- to monitor and record the quality of water from any source used for such purposes;[155]

---

[151] Ibid, s 168.
[152] Ibid, s 169.
[153] Ibid, s 170(1).
[154] Ibid, s 170(1).
[155] Ibid, s 170(1).

- to investigate breaches of Section 72 (this prohibits acts leading to the pollution of water for human consumption or domestic or food production purposes);[156]
- to investigate whether any provision relating to water fittings or the misuse of water is being breached;[157]
- to determine whether powers conferred by regulations made under Section 74 should be exercised and to exercise such powers;
- to carry out tests, inspections, and measurements etc, permitted by regulations made under Section 74;[158]
- to ascertain whether there has been any breach of a hosepipe ban.[159]

Sewerage undertakers have a wide power to enter premises to carry out their functions under the 'relevant sewerage provisions'.[160] These cover all powers and functions in relation to sewerage services[161] and the receipt of trade effluent[162] and most works powers other than pipe-laying powers.[163] **10.221**

K. Charges

Charges schemes and agreements

The levying of charges is subject to a high level of regulatory control. The basic right of water and sewerage undertakers to fix, demand, and recover charges for the services they provide is conferred by Section 142. Charges are fixed by agreement with the customer or by a charges scheme under Section 143. The Authority must approve all charges schemes.[164] The Secretary of State/NAW can give guidance to the Authority on the granting of such approval.[165] The Secretary of State can make regulations concerning the contents of charges schemes.[166] The current regulations are the Water Industry (Charges) (Vulnerable Groups) Regulations 1999 and the Water Industry (Charges) (Vulnerable Groups) (Amendment) Regulations 2000, 2003, and 2005. **10.222**

Charges for the provision of a water supply or of sewerage services to a dwelling cannot be fixed by agreement unless the agreement was made before 1 April 2000. **10.223**

---

156 Ibid, s 170(2).
157 Ibid, s 170(3).
158 Ibid, s 170(3).
159 Ibid, s 170(4).
160 Ibid, s 171.
161 Ibid, ss 102–109, 111–116.
162 Ibid, ss 118–141.
163 Ibid, s 219.
164 Ibid, s 143(6).
165 Ibid, s 143(7).
166 Ibid, s 143A.

10.224 Any agreement for charges for the receipt of trade effluent must be contained in an agreement made under Section 129. Additionally provision for charges for the receipt of trade effluent can be fixed by the conditions of a consent.[167]

10.225 Sewerage undertakers cannot make charges for the making of a vesting declaration under Sections 102 or 103, for the drainage of a highway or for the disposal of the contents of drains or sewers used for draining highways.[168]

10.226 A water undertaker cannot make charges for the use of water taken for the purposes of extinguishing fires or for the testing of fire-fighting equipment.[169]

Metered supply of water

10.227 Historically, charges for domestic water services were often fixed by reference to the rateable value of the premises served. Such charges were abolished from 31 March 2001 and charges now have to be based on standard flat rates or on volume (ie a metered supply).

10.228 A customer can elect to be charged by volume[170] by serving a 'measured charges notice'. The water undertaker is not obliged so to charge if this is not reasonably practicable or would involve unreasonable expenditure.[171] Disputes are resolved by the Authority. The customer can revoke a measured charges notice in prescribed circumstances.[172]

10.229 There are restrictions on the right of water undertakers to imposed metered charges on domestic customers in cases where charging has not previously been by volume.[173]

L. Enforcement

Introduction

10.230 Most general duties of water and sewerage undertakers and licensed water suppliers, whether arising from statute, regulations, or the conditions of appointment/licence, are enforceable by the Secretary of State/NAW/Authority by enforcement order and financial penalties under Sections 18–22F. The most serious breaches can be dealt with by special administration orders. The only exceptions are

---

[167] Ibid, s 1221(2)(e).
[168] Ibid, s 146(4).
[169] Ibid, s 147.
[170] Ibid, s 144A.
[171] Ibid, s 144A(3).
[172] Ibid, s 144A(5).
[173] Ibid, s 144B.

duties enforceable only by criminal sanctions, and duties that are only owed to particular individuals.

The ability of third parties, including of local authorities, to take legal action **10.231** against breaches of the general obligations of undertakers is severely constrained. Section 18(8) provides that where contravention of a condition of appointment/ licence or of a statutory duty is enforceable by enforcement order, the only other remedies are those that are available 'otherwise than by virtue of its constituting such a contravention' and those for which express statutory provision is made. This probably has the effect of precluding any proceedings for judicial review for breach of the duty itself. Most of the general duties do not carry with them an express right to seek damages in the event of breach.

Enforcement orders

Section 18 provides for enforcement orders which impose mandatory require- **10.232** ments on an undertaker/licensed water supplier designed to remedy a breach. An enforcement order can be made in respect of:

- breach of a statutory duty which is expressly made enforceable under Section 18;
- breach of a condition of an appointment/licence;
- action by an undertaker which causes, contributes to causing or is likely to cause a licensed water supplier to breach a condition of its licence or a statutory duty which is enforceable under Section 18;
- action by a licensed water supplier which causes, contributes to causing, or is likely to cause an undertaker to breach a condition of its appointment or a statutory duty which is enforceable under Section 18.

Duties enforceable under Section 18 and responsibility for enforcement

A statutory duty is enforceable under Section 18 only if express statutory provi- **10.233** sion is made to this effect. Most general statutory duties are so enforceable, and most statutory duties that are owed to particular individuals are not. Conditions in appointments and water supply licences are enforceable under Section 18.

Responsibility for enforcement under Section 18 is split between the Authority **10.234** and the Secretary of State/NAW. The Authority is responsible for enforcing conditions in appointments and licences.[174] The general duty to maintain water and sewerage services under Sections 37 and 94 can be enforced by either the Secretary of State/NAW or the Authority (with the Secretary of State's consent

---

[174] Ibid, s 18(6)(b).

or authorization). Most other statutory duties are enforceable only by the Secretary of State/NAW. Those enforceable by the Authority alone are:

- Section 59 (duty to supply water for public purposes);
- Section 181(3) (provision of information following complaints about exercise of pipe-laying powers over private land);
- Section 185 (duty to remove pipes to facilitate improvement of land); and
- Section 196 (public inspection of trade effluent consents).

10.235 Regulations can create duties enforceable under Section 18, and, where they do so, will identify who is responsible for enforcement.

Obligation to make enforcement order

10.236 There is an obligation to make an enforcement order if the Secretary of State/NAW/Authority is satisfied that a relevant breach is occurring or is likely to occur.[175] This obligation is removed in five instances set out in Section 19, namely if:

- The Secretary of State/NAW/Authority is satisfied that the relevant contraventions are trivial.[176]
- The Secretary of State/NAW/Authority is satisfied that the extent to which the company is contributing to the contraventions is trivial.[177]
- The Secretary of State/NAW/Authority is satisfied that the company has given, and is complying with, an undertaking to take all appropriate steps to comply with the relevant obligation.[178] Such an undertaking is itself enforceable under Section 18 by the Secretary of State/NAW or the Authority (with the authorization of the Secretary of State/NAW) (Section 19(2)). The giving of undertakings is an important way in which undertakers can avoid enforcement action. They are designed to address situations where compliance with statutory duties or conditions involves large-scale capital expenditure.
- The Secretary of State/NAW/Authority is satisfied that the duties imposed on it by Sections 2–4 of the Act preclude the taking of such action.[179] This means, for example, that no enforcement action can be taken if the Secretary of State/NAW/Authority is satisfied that such action would prejudice the ability of the undertaker to finance the proper carrying out of its functions.
- The Authority is satisfied that the most appropriate way of proceeding is under the Competition Act 1998.[180]

---

[175] Ibid, s 18(2).
[176] Ibid, s 19(1)(a).
[177] Ibid, s 19(1)(aa).
[178] Ibid, s 19(1)(b).
[179] Ibid, s 19(1)(c).
[180] Ibid, s 19(1A).

Final and provisional enforcement orders

Enforcement orders are either 'final' or 'provisional'. Requirements in a final order **10.237** operate permanently, but a final order can only be made after certain procedural steps have been followed. A provisional enforcement order can be made immediately but its requirements can only last for a maximum of three months. If a provisional enforcement order is confirmed its requirements become permanent. Confirmation involves the same procedural steps as the making of a final enforcement order.

Enforcement action must take the form of a final enforcement order unless it **10.238** 'appears . . . that it is requisite' that a provisional enforcement order should be made, having regard to the extent to which any person may suffer loss as a result of the acts likely to be done before a final enforcement order can be made.[181] This suggests that provisional enforcement orders should only be made where serious and imminent injury is threatened.

Where a provisional enforcement order is made, the Secretary of State/NAW/ **10.239** Authority is obliged to confirm it if he/it remains satisfied that the company is in breach of the relevant obligation and that the provisions of the order 'are requisite' for the purpose of securing compliance.[182]

The Secretary of State/NAW/Authority can revoke any enforcement order that **10.240** he/it has made. In the case of a final enforcement order or a confirmed provisional enforcement order, notification requirements have to be followed.[183]

A company can only challenge an enforcement order on legal grounds, namely **10.241** that the order is not within the powers of Section 18 or that the relevant procedural steps in Section 20 have not been followed. Such challenge has to be made to the High Court within six weeks of service of the order.[184]

Procedure for confirming provisional enforcement orders and making final enforcement orders

The procedure for making final enforcement orders and for confirming provi- **10.242** sional enforcement orders is laid down in Section 20. The Secretary of State/ NAW/Authority must give notice of the proposed order, and must invite representations and objections.[185] The notice must be published, placed on the Section 195 register (see below) and served on the company concerned and, if appropriate, the Authority. The proposed order can only be modified if the company

---

[181] Ibid, s 18(2) and (3).
[182] Ibid, s 18(4).
[183] Ibid, s 20(6)–(8).
[184] Ibid, s 21.
[185] Ibid, s 20(1).

consents or if further notice is given and any further representations/objections are considered.[186] A copy of the final order/confirmed provisional order must be served on the company concerned, and publicized.[187]

10.243 Where the Secretary of State/NAW/Authority, having given notice of a proposed order, concludes that it is inappropriate to take enforcement action because one of the exceptions in Section 19 applies, he/it must give notice of this view to the company, and publish the notice. Where such a decision is taken by the Secretary of State/NAW and is based on an undertaking, a copy of the undertaking must be served on the Authority.[188]

Compliance with enforcement orders

10.244 The requirements of an enforcement order are binding on the company concerned. The Secretary of State/NAW/Authority can institute injunction proceedings to restrain actual or apprehended breaches of an order[189] and failure to comply with a final enforcement order or a confirmed provisional enforcement order is one of the grounds on which a special administration order can be sought (see below). In addition a duty to comply with an enforcement order is owed to any person who may be affected by contravention of the order and such a person can seek damages in respect of any loss or damage occasioned as a result.[190] In such proceedings it is a defence for the company to show that it took all reasonable steps and exercised all due diligence to avoid contravening the order. This defence is not available if the enforcement order relates to a breach of Section 68(1)(a) or (1A)(a) (the duty to supply wholesome water for domestic purposes).[191]

Financial penalties

10.245 Power to impose financial penalties under Sections 22A–F was introduced by the 2003 Act. The power allows the imposition of a 'fine' on an undertaker/licensed water supplier for breach of a condition or of a statutory requirements and for failure to meet prescribed standards of performance that occurs after 1 April 2005. The sanction does not involve any requirement to take remedial action and is more straightforward to impose than an enforcement order. It is possible to impose a financial penalty and to make an enforcement order in respect of the same breach.

---

[186] Ibid, s 20(3) and (4).
[187] Ibid, s 20(5).
[188] Ibid, s 19(3).
[189] Ibid, s 22(4).
[190] Ibid, s 22.
[191] Ibid, s 22(3).

Financial penalties can be imposed by the Secretary of State/NAW/Authority in **10.246** respect of:

- breach of a statutory duty enforceable under Section 18 by an undertaker or a licensed water supplier;
- action by an undertaker which has caused a licensed water supplier to breach such a duty or which has contributed to such a breach by a licensed water supplier; and
- action by a licensed water supplier which has caused an undertaker to breach such a duty or which has contributed to such a breach by an undertaker according to which it is responsible for enforcement under Section 18.

Financial penalties can be imposed by the Authority in respect of: **10.247**

- breach of a condition in an appointment or a water supply licence;
- action by an undertaker which has caused a licensed water supplier to breach a licence condition or which has contributed to such a breach by a licensed water supplier; and
- action by licensed water supplier which has caused an undertaker to breach a condition of its appointment or which has contributed to such a breach by an undertaker.

The relevant enforcing authority must give notice of its intention to impose a **10.248** penalty and consider any representations received. The undertaker can appeal against the imposition of a penalty to the High Court on specified grounds (Section 22E). There are time limits on the imposition of such penalties.[192]

The Secretary of State/NAW and the Authority must publish their policy on the **10.249** imposition of such penalties. A joint statement was published in March 2005.

Special administration orders

A special administration order is a draconian measure, designed for the most seri- **10.250** ous breaches. Such an order divests the company of its statutory responsibilities. A special administration order can be made against a company appointed as a water or sewerage undertaker or against a 'qualifying' licensed water supplier (ie a licensed water supplier with both a retail authorization and a supplementary authorization whose water is designated as a strategic supply).

A special administration order can only be made by the High Court and appoints **10.251** a special administrator to arrange for the transfer to a new appointee/licensee of the company's business while ensuring that core water/sewerage functions are carried out in the meantime. The special administrator must act in a manner

---

[192] Ibid, s 22C.

which protects the interests of the members and creditors of the company. Arrangements for the transfer of rights, liabilities, and property to the new appointee(s) are made under Schedule 2.[193]

10.252 An application for a special administration order can be made by the Secretary of State/NAW or the Authority (with the consent of the Secretary of State/NAW). The court can only grant the application in one of the circumstances set out in Section 24(2), namely:

- There is an actual or apprehended breach of any 'principal duty' of such serious-ness that it is inappropriate for the company to continue to hold its appoint-ment or licence.[194] 'Principal duty' means (in the case of an undertaker) the duties imposed by Sections 37 and 94 and (in the case of a licensed water sup-plier) any licence condition and any statutory requirement imposed by the licence. A special administration order cannot, however, be sought where notice under Section19(3) has been served in respect of the breach (ie a notice that, having considered the making of an enforcement order, or the confirmation of a provisional enforcement order, the Secretary of State/NAW/Authority has decided that he/it is precluded from proceedings with enforcement action by the terms of Section 19).

- There is an actual or apprehended breach of a final enforcement order/con-firmed provisional enforcement order of such seriousness that it is inappropri-ate for the company to continue to hold its appointment/licence.[195]

- Notice of termination of the appointment has been given in accordance with the terms of conditions in the appointment, but the undertaker is unwilling or unable to participate in arrangements (approved by the Secretary of State or the Authority) for the termination.[196]

- Action by a licensed water supplier has caused a water undertaker to breach any principal duty and that action is serious enough to make it inappropriate for the company to continue to hold its licence.[197]

- The undertaker/licensee is unable or is likely to be unable to pay its debts.[198]

- The Secretary of State for Trade and Industry has certified that, were it possible, it would be appropriate for him to petition the court for the winding up of the undertaker/licensee and it would be just and equitable for the company to be wound up.[199] The NAW does not exercise this function in Wales.

---

[193] Ibid, s 23(4).
[194] Ibid, s 24(2)(a).
[195] Ibid, s 24(2)(b).
[196] Ibid, s 24(2)(d).
[197] Ibid, s 24(2)(bb).
[198] Ibid, s 24(2)(c).
[199] Ibid, s 24(2)(d).

- The undertaker is unable/unwilling to participate in arrangements approved by the Secretary of State for the appointment of a new undertaker under Section 7(4)(c).[200] Section 7(4)(c) provides for the appointment of a new undertaker in circumstances set out in conditions in the appointment of the original undertaker.

It will be appreciated that a special administration order, by divesting a company of its business, has similarities to the winding up of a company. The Act in fact prohibits both the winding up of an appointed company or licensed water supplier (whether by court order or voluntarily) and the making of an administration order under the Insolvency Act 1986.[201]

Power to require information in connection with enforcement action

The Secretary of State/NAW and the Authority have powers to demand information in connection with their enforcement responsibilities. Under Section 203 each can serve a notice on any person requiring the provision of documents and information if it appears that an undertaker/licensed water supplier may be perpetrating a breach enforceable under Section 18.[202] Such a notice cannot require the giving of information or documents which would be privileged for the purposes of High Court proceedings.[203] **10.253**

It is an offence to fail to comply with such a notice without reasonable excuse, or intentionally to destroy or alter any document covered by such a notice. In the event of a failure to comply with such an order, the Secretary of State/NAW or the Authority can seek a High Court order requiring the default to be made good. **10.254**

M. Complaints Against Undertakers and Licensed Water Suppliers

The WIA makes fairly elaborate provision for the handling of complaints against undertakers and licensed water suppliers. The Act contemplates that the first avenue of complaint will be to the undertaker/licensee itself or to the relevant customer services committee of the Council. To deal with complaints made directly to them, undertakers are obliged to establish complaints procedures.[204] The relevant regional committee of the Council must be consulted on such procedures, **10.255**

---

[200] Section 24(2)(e).
[201] Insolvency Act 1986, Sections 25–26.
[202] Water Industry Act 1991, s 203(1).
[203] Ibid, s 203(3).
[204] Ibid, ss 86A and 116A.

which must be approved by the Authority and publicized. The Authority can order reviews of the complaints procedure and can direct that modifications should be made. These duties are enforceable under Section 18 by the Authority.[205]

10.256 If a complaint is made to the Council it must be investigated unless it appears that:

- the complaint is frivolous or vexatious;
- the matter is one which the Authority should investigate under Section 181 (works powers on private land, see below), in which case it must refer the matter to the Authority;
- it is a matter where an enforcement order or a financial penalty might be appropriate, in which case it must refer the matter to the Authority/Secretary of State/NAW;
- the subject matter of the complaint may involve the commission of a criminal offence, in which case it must refer the matter to the Secretary of State/NAW;
- the subject matter of the complaint is one which can be referred to the Authority for determination, in which case it must refer the matter to the Authority— if the complainant consents.

10.257 In addition, the Council is not required to investigate a complaint if it appears unlikely that the complaint could be resolved by action by the undertaker/licensee or the undertaker/licensee has not been given a reasonable opportunity to deal with the complaint.

10.258 If the Council investigates the complaint, it has power to require the provision of information from the undertaker under Section 27H. It can make representations to the relevant undertaker: if this does not produce a resolution, it can report to the Authority or the Secretary of State/NAW.[206] The Council has no enforcement powers of its own.

N. Review and Information Provided by the Secretary of State and the Authority

Review and reports

10.259 Under Section 27(1) the Authority is obliged to keep under review, so far as appears to it to be practicable, the activities associated with the carrying out by undertakers/licensed water suppliers of their functions. More generally, it is

---

[205] Ibid, ss 86A and 116A.
[206] Ibid, s 29(10).

under a duty to collect information on the companies themselves and on their performance as undertakers/licensed water suppliers, with a view to informing itself about matters relevant to any of its powers or duties (including, of course, enforcement powers).[207] The Secretary of State can give directions to the Authority about matters to which it should have particular regard when determining its priorities for the purposes of carrying out reviews under Section 27(1). The Secretary of State exercises this power in relation to Wales as well as England.

Information

Under Section 195 the Authority must keep a public register containing details of **10.260** all appointments of undertakers and licensed water supply licences (including terminations of appointments, variations, and modifications of conditions and all directions, consents, and determinations given under appointments), enforcement orders, revocations of enforcement orders, undertakings given under Section 19, and special administration orders.

The Secretary of State/NAW can publish such information relating to any matter **10.261** connected to the carrying out of the functions of an undertaker or a licensed water supplier by any company. The Authority can publish such information and advice for customers as appears to it to be expedient.[208]

The Secretary of State/NAW can require undertakers and licensed water suppliers **10.262** to provide information relating to the carrying out of their functions or its functions under the Act.[209] This obligation is enforceable by the Secretary of State under Section 18. The Authority has no statutory powers to require the provision of information from an undertaker (except for enforcement purposes), but the conditions of appointment invariably require the undertaker to supply information requested by the Authority.

---

[207] Ibid, s 27(2).
[208] Ibid, s 201(1) and (2).
[209] Ibid, s 202(1).

11

NATURE CONSERVATION

A. **Introduction**	11.01
B. **The Organization of Nature**	
Conservation	11.02
Governmental organizations	11.02
Central Government	11.02
Local Government	11.03
The UK Conservation Bodies	11.04
The Environment Agency	11.06
The Forestry Commission	11.07
The Crown Estate Commissioners	11.09
The Natural Environment Research	
Council (NERC)	11.10
The European Community	11.11
Non-Governmental organizations	11.12
ARG UK (Amphibian and	
Reptile Groups of the UK)	11.13
The Bat Conservation	
Trust (BCT)	11.14
Bird Life International	11.15
Botanical Society of the	
British Isles (BSBI)	11.16
British Herpetological	
Society (BHS)	11.17
British Trust for Conservation	
Volunteers (BTCV)	11.18
British Trust for Ornithology	
(BTO)	11.19
Buglife—the Invertebrate	
Conservation Trust	11.20
Butterfly Conservation	11.21
Fauna and Flora International (FFI)	11.22
Froglife	11.23
IUCN—The World Conservation	
Union (IUCN)	11.24
The Mammal Society	11.25
Marine Conservation Society	
(MCS)	11.26
National Federation of Badger	
Groups (NFBG)	11.27
The National Trust	11.28
Plantlife International	11.29
People's Trust for Endangered	
Species (PTES)	11.30
Royal Society for the Prevention	
of Cruelty to Animals	
(RSPCA)	11.31
Royal Society for the Protection	
of Birds (RSPB)	11.32
Wildfowl and Wetlands Trust	
(WWT)	11.33
The Wildlife Trusts	11.34
The Woodland Trust	11.35
World Conservation Monitoring	
Centre (WCMC)	11.36
WWF UK (World Wide Fund	
for Nature)	11.37
Other groups	11.38
C. **International Obligations**	11.40
The Convention concerning the	
protection of the World	
Cultural and Natural Heritage	
('World Heritage Sites')	11.41
The Ramsar Convention on	
wetlands of international	
importance ('The	
Ramsar Convention')	11.42
The Convention on international	
trade in endangered species	
('The CITES Convention')	11.43
The Bern Convention on the	
conservation of European	
wildlife and natural habitats	
('The Bern Convention')	11.44
The Bonn Convention on the	
conservation of migratory	
species of wild animals	11.45
EC Council Directive on the	
conservation of wild birds	
('The Birds Directive')	11.46

EC Council Directive on the assessment of the effects of certain public and private projects on the environment ('The EIA Directive')	11.47	Special Protection Areas (SPAs)		11.67
		Special Areas of Conservation (SACs)		11.68
		The Habitats Regulations		11.69
EC Council Directive on the conservation of natural habitats and of wild flora and fauna ('The Habitats Directive')	11.49	National Nature Reserves (NNRs)		11.73
		Marine Nature Reserves (MNRs)		11.77
		Sites of Special Scientific Interest (SSSIs)		11.78
		Limestone pavements		11.83
The Rio Convention on biological diversity ('The Biodiversity Convention')	11.50	Areas of Special Protection (AOSPs)		11.84
		Local Nature Reserves (LNRs)		11.85
The Convention for the Protection of the marine environment of the North-East Atlantic (OSPAR)	11.55	Sites of Nature Conservation Interest or Importance (SNCIs and SINCs)		11.86
		Environmentally Sensitive Areas (ESAs)		11.87
EC Council Directive on the environmental assessment of plans and programmes (The SEA Directive)	11.56	National Parks		11.88
		The Norfolk and Suffolk Broads		11.89
		Areas of Outstanding Natural Beauty (AONBs)		11.90
Convention on access to information, public participation in decision-making and access to justice in environmental matters ('The Aarhus Convention')	11.57	Green belts		11.91
		Country Parks		11.92
		E. Species Protection		11.93
		Introduction		11.93
		Evaluation procedures		11.94
		Conservation of birds		11.96
EC Water Framework Directive ('The Water Framework Directive')	11.58	Protection of other wild animals		11.103
		Protection of fish		11.115
D. Habitat Conservation	11.59	Protection of individual wild plants		11.118
Introduction	11.59	Trees and woodlands		11.121
Biogenetic Reserves	11.63	Important hedgerows		11.130
Biosphere Reserves	11.64	Protection of endangered species		11.133
Ramsar sites	11.65			

A. Introduction

11.01   The key to the conservation of wildlife is the protection of the habitat upon which species of fauna and flora depend; but this objective is inextricably linked with the wise use and management of the nation's land resources as a whole. In consequence, there now exists an extensive raft of UK and international legislation for protecting species and habitats together with a range of organizations whose prime concern, or as part of a wider brief, is to work for the conservation of biodiversity.[1] This chapter looks at the organization of nature conservation by way of an initial review of the main governmental and non-governmental organizations affecting the UK, followed by the primary international obligations to which this country

---

[1] See paras 12.49–11.50 below.

is subject. It then considers, in greater detail, habitat conservation and species protection under domestic law applicable primarily to England and Wales.

B. The Organization of Nature Conservation

Governmental organizations

Central Government

Although the detailed administration of nature conservation lies in the hands of **11.02** specialist bodies, the determination and direction of policy and legislation is still controlled by Central Government. Currently, in England these functions are undertaken by the Department of Communities and Local Government (CLG) and the Department for Environment, Food, and Rural Affairs (Defra).[2] Following devolution, they are discharged by the appropriate Assemblies for the remainder of the UK.[3] These also include responsibility for determining policy and pro-grammes related to nature conservation, including agri-environmental schemes such as Environmentally Sensitive Areas (ESAs).[4] Central Government is also responsible for handling conservation issues arising from major infrastructure and other projects requiring consent[5] as well at European and international levels, including the implementation of Community law and other treaty obligations.

---

[2] National guidance in England is currently provided by *Planning Policy Statement 9: Biodiversity and Geological Conservation* and accompanying ODPM Circular 6/2005/Defra Circular 01/2005 (see: <http://www.communities.gov.uk/publications/planningandbuilding/circularbiodiversity>)

[3] Under Sch 2 of the Government of Wales Act 1998 and the National Assembly of Wales (Transfer of Functions) Order (SI 1999/673) the functions of the Secretary of State for Wales, amongst other matters, in respect of planning, highways, local government, and the environment were passed to the Assembly. These are now exercised under the Government of Wales Act 2006. National Guidance is currently provided by the overarching Planning Policy Wales and TAN 5 *(Nature Conservation and Planning)* (see: <http://www.wales.gov.uk/topics/planning/policy>). Following the Scotland Act (Commencement Order (SI 1998/3178)) all the Secretary of State's pow-ers were passed to the Scottish Parliament, including planning and other land use matters, except for those which had been specifically retained by Westminster under of the Scotland Act 1998 Sch 5. Currently, natural heritage policy is found in NPPG14, soon to be replaced by SPP14 (see: <http://www.scotland.gov.uk/planning>). In the case of Northern Ireland, land use and environmental issues are still dealt with by the Department of the Environment (Northern Ireland) following the restora-tion of power to the Northern Ireland Assembly in May 2007. Current policy on planning and nature conservation is found in PPS2 (see: <http://www.planningni.gov.uk/AreaPlans_Policy/APP.htm>)

[4] Currently, for England, these are ESAs, Countryside Stewardship and the Environmental Stewardship Higher Level scheme (HLS); Wales: ESA, Tir Cymen and Tir Gofal; Scotland: ESA, Countryside Premium, Rural Stewardship and Land Management Contracts; Northern Ireland: ESA, Countryside Management.

[5] The scope of such administration includes major planning proposals as well as appeals, respec-tively under the Town and Country Planning Act 1990, as 77 and 78, together with their environ-mental effects where the project falls within one of those identified in the Town and Country Planning (Environmental Impact Assessment (England and Wales)) Regulations 1999 or the other Assessment Regulations. Practical guidance and assistance can be obtained from the Institute of Environmental Management and Assessment, Lincoln (<http://www.iema.net>), a non-profit

Although often overlooked, the Countryside Act 1968 places a general obligation upon every minister, government department, and public body, in the exercise of their statutory functions relating to land, to have regard to the desirability of conserving the natural beauty and amenity of the countryside, including the flora, fauna, and geological and physiographical features.[6]

Local Government

11.03   Local authorities are actively involved in nature conservation, primarily through their administration of the planning system.[7] While the scope of this book does not include detailed coverage of this subject it should be borne in mind that these authorities exercise considerable control over changes in land uses. The exercise of their powers has a considerable influence on how development policies and proposals affect local habitat and species resources. Cumulatively, they strongly influence the overall nature conservation picture through the formulation of development plan policies as well as through the grant or refusal of planning permission, with and without formal environmental assessment, and the subsequent protection through planning conditions and agreements. Nature conservation issues also arise from the environmental impacts from other local authority responsibilities such as coast protection, roads and highways, and waste disposal.

The UK Conservation Bodies

11.04   In England,[8] following the implementation of the Natural Environment and Rural Communities Act 2006 (NERCA 2006), one body called 'Natural England' acts as an integrated countryside and land management agency.[9] Elsewhere, these

---

making organization which undertakes technical reviews for local authorities and provides advice and guidelines for best practice in environmental assessment and auditing (see also n 36 below).

   [6] Countryside Act 1968, ss 11, 49(4).

   [7] Regional assemblies and unitary authorities currently deal with strategic policy and related planning issues. The jurisdiction of county councils and unitary authorities covers mineral and waste planning. Boroughs, districts and other local councils (for which purpose includes, also, unitary authorities) deal with development control and policy at local level.

   [8] Until April 1991 and the implementation of the reforms introduced by the Environmental Protection Act 1990 (EPA 1990), the Nature Conservancy Council acted as the single national body responsible for nature conservation throughout Great Britain, whilst the Countryside Commissions were responsible for the natural beauty of the countryside and its public enjoyment. From April 1991 until October 2006 these functions were then undertaken by the Nature Conservancy Council for England, better known as 'English Nature', the Countryside Agency (the Commission's landscape, access and recreation elements) and the Rural Development Service (Defra's environmental land management functions). As a Non-Departmental Public Body (NDPB) Natural England is theoretically independent of Government. However, the Secretary of State for Environment, Food and Rural Affairs has the legal power to issue guidance to Natural England on various matters, a constraint that was not placed on its predecessor NDPBs.

   [9] NERCA 2006, s 2(1) states: 'Natural England's general purpose is to ensure that the natural environment is conserved, enhanced and managed for the benefit of resent and future generations, thereby contributing to sustainable development'. S 2(2)(a) includes promoting nature conservation and protecting biodiversity.

functions are undertaken by the Countryside Council for Wales (CCW), Scottish Natural Heritage (SNH), and the Council for Nature Conservation and the Countryside (CNCC) in Northern Ireland. Through the Joint Nature Conservation Committee (JNCC),[10] the UK conservation bodies,[11] coordinate and promote national and international conservation issues that affect Great Britain as a whole. The JNCC advises Central Government as well as carrying out joint monitoring and research and the setting of common standards.[12] It is also charged with the making of periodic reviews and recommendations for changes to the list of protected animals and plants protected by the Wildlife and Countryside Act 1981 (WCA)[13] and commissioning and supporting research.[14] All these agencies are funded by Central Government and are subject to ministerial appointments, directions, annual reports, and accounts.

Natural England[15] and CCW[16] are the respective agencies in England and Wales **11.05** statutorily responsible for advising Central and Local Government on nature conservation and for monitoring, research, and promotion of wildlife and natural features. Both have a specific duty to conserve biodiversity.[17] Specifically, they have the power to establish, maintain, and manage nature reserves, notify and protect Sites of Special Scientific Interest (SSSIs), advise Central Government on policies affecting nature conservation and their implementation, provide advice and disseminate knowledge about nature conservation, and commission and support research. They advise upon and issue licences under the WCA and Habitats Regulations 1994 (as amended), for example, in respect of the translocation of protected species. They also act as a statutory consultee to local authorities in development plan preparation and development control. In addition, their functions extend to conserving and enhancing the natural beauty and amenity in the countryside and the encouragement of facilities for the enjoyment of the countryside[18] with due regard to the economic and social interests of rural areas including National Parks,[19] though these are administered by separate authorities.[20]

---

[10] Ibid, s 31 and Sch 4. The Committee comprises 14 members: a Chairman and five independent Members appointed by the Secretary of State (currently Defra); the Chairmen or deputy Chairmen of Natural England, CCW and SNH; the Chairman of CNCC; and one other member of each of these bodies.

[11] NERCA 2006, s 32(1).

[12] Ibid, s 34(2).

[13] WCA, ss 22(3), 24(1).

[14] NERCA 2006, s 36(2). These functions are, however, only exercised by statute by the 'GB conservations bodies' which are defined by s 32(2) as Natural England, CCW, and SNH.

[15] NERCA 2006.

[16] Established under the EPA 1990, s 128. CCW's statutory functions are set out in s 132(1).

[17] NERCA 2006, s 40.

[18] Ibid, ss 2(2)(b)–(e), 99 (Natural England); EPA s 130(2) (CCW).

[19] NPACA 1947, s 6(1); EPA, s 130(2)(a).

[20] NPACA, s 11A.

The Environment Agency

11.06   The functions of the Environment Agency (the Agency)[21] within England and Wales embrace a broad range of tasks relating to the management of water resources, control of pollution, flood control, land drainage, fisheries, and navigation. In the discharge of its functions the Agency has a duty, to such extent as it considers desirable, generally to promote the conservation and enhancement of the natural beauty and amenity of inland and coastal waters and of land associated with such waters, and the conservation of flora and fauna which are dependent on an aquatic environment, and the use of such waters and land for recreational purposes.[22] A similar general duty applies to all the other functions of the Agency,[23] which include waste management and pollution control together with the licensing of certain industrial processes. Part of the Agency's function is the monitoring of Codes of Practice with respect to environmental and recreational duties.[24] Within the remainder of the UK, the equivalent functions are undertaken, respectively, by the Scottish Environment Protection Agency (SEPA)[25] and the relevant agencies within the Departments of the Environment, and, of Agriculture and Rural Development in Northern Ireland.

The Forestry Commission

11.07   The role of the Forestry Commission in respect of nature conservation arises from its responsibility for the management of large areas of productive woodland still in public ownership and for encouraging and regulating the development of private forestry within England, Wales, and Scotland. Although the Forestry Commission's statutory duty remains to promote the interests of forestry, the development of afforestation, and the production and supply of timber and other forest products[26] it is now tempered by the requirement 'to endeavour to achieve a reasonable balance between' the foregoing objectives and 'the conservation and enhancement of natural beauty and the conservation of flora, fauna, and geological or physiographical features of special interest'.[27] For example, the Forestry Commission promotes multi-purpose forestry not just through timber production but also by conservation and recreation initiatives, which include Forest Parks, Forest Nature Reserves, or Woodland Parks.

---

[21] Since April 1996, following the reforms introduced by the Environment Act 1995 (the EA 1995) the Agency has assumed the functions previously undertaken by the National Rivers Authority (NRA) under the Water Resources Act 1991 and the Land Drainage Act 1991.

[22] EA 1995, s 6(1).

[23] Ibid, ss 7, 8 including flora, fauna, geological or physiographical features of special interest.

[24] Ibid, s 9 (following consultation with Natural England and CCW).

[25] Ibid, s 20 and Sch 6.

[26] Forestry Act 1967, s 1(2). The Commissioners are appointed by the Crown and are subject to the same administrative procedures as other governmental agencies.

[27] Ibid, s 1(3A). The application of these principles is now heightened by the Environmental Assessment (Forestry) Regulation 1998.

With the move, in recent years, towards forestry initiatives by the private sector, **11.08**
the Forestry Commission's control over private forestry is achieved, first, by a full
statutory scheme imposing a requirement for a felling licence before any significant felling is carried out[28] and, secondly, by way of grant schemes for planting.
Although no statutory restrictions exist for planting,[29] control exists in an economic context such that no major planting can now be economically viable without grant aid. The Commission's grant schemes now take account of such
considerations as habitat diversity, environmental protection, and amenity,
together with public access, in addition to commercial timber production.[30]
Furthermore, in more sensitive areas certain new planting proposals may also have
to be the subject of environmental assessment.[31]

The Crown Estate Commissioners

The Commissioners[32] are responsible for maintaining and enhancing the value of **11.09**
the Crown Estate, as an estate, as well as administering the Crown's rights in areas
of land where it retains a major interest, notably, the foreshore and seabed.[33]

The Natural Environment Research Council (NERC)

This statutory body was established by the Science and Technology Act 1965. **11.10**
NERC plays an active and important role in research, relevant to nature conservation, in the fields of earth sciences and ecology.[34] It is the parent body for the
British Antarctic Survey, the British Geological Survey, the Institute for Terrestrial
Ecology, and the Institute of Freshwater Ecology. Accordingly, it provides a major
coordinating role in the field of research into nature conservation issues but has no
legal powers of intervention or control.

---

[28] Ibid, s 9(1). See further under felling licences at para 12.133 below.
[29] TCPA, s 55(2)(e) expressly excludes 'forestry' (including afforestation) from the meaning of
'development'.
[30] For example, under the Commission's England Woodland Grant Scheme, grants are available
for the establishment of woodlands either by planting or the promotion of natural regeneration with
higher sums for broadleaves rather than for conifers. Management grants are also available.
[31] Environmental Impact Assessment (Forestry) (England and Wales) Regulations 1999.
A relevant project means one which is likely to have a significant effect on the environment and
involves initial afforestation (when this may lead to adverse ecological changes). In *R (Tree and
Wildlife Action Committee Ltd) v Forestry Commissioners* [2007] EWHC 1623 (Admin) these
Regs were considered in the context of a (successful) High Court challenge of a negative screening
opinion on the ground that the Commissioners had failed to consider the whole project which comprised not only deforestation but also the proposed development of 20 football pitches, changing
rooms and parking for 184 cars.
[32] Crown Estates Act 1961, s 1. The Commissioners are appointed by the Crown but are subject
to ministerial direction and report annually to the Monarch and to Parliament.
[33] See further n 130 below.
[34] Science and Technology Act 1965, s 1(3).

The European Community

11.11 The influence of the Community, particularly in the field of agriculture and the effects of economic concepts such as 'quotas' and 'set aside', has had as much direct effect on nature conservation, in practical terms, as its legislative directions and litigation against the UK have had in legal terms. In these latter respects, it was the need to comply with the Wild Birds Directive (79/409) ('the Birds Directive') which was one of the major factors which led to the Wildlife and Countryside Act 1981 and, more recently, that the Habitats Directive (92/43) had not been sufficiently transposed into UK national law by the Conservation (Natural Habitats etc) Regulations 1994 ('the Habitats Regulations').[35] Nature conservation issues are monitored and regulated, administratively, from Brussels through the European Commission's Environment Directorate-General, which initiates and defines new environmental legislation and ensures that agreed measures are put into practice by Member States.

Non-Governmental organizations

11.12 Set out below, in alphabetical order, are the other principal non-governmental organizations concerned with nature conservation in the UK.[36]

ARG UK (Amphibian and Reptile Groups of the UK)

11.13 Formerly known as the Herpetofauna Groups of the British Isles (HGBI), ARG UK is a network of local groups involved with the conservation of amphibians and reptiles.

The Bat Conservation Trust (BCT)

11.14 The Trust was formed in 1990 to conserve bats, their roosts, and feeding habitats and to prevent their further decline. BCT acts as a major source of information,

---

[35] In *Case C-6/04, Commission v United Kingdom* (judgement 2 October 2005) the Commission's allegation that the UK had failed to transpose adequately various provisions of the Habitats Directive 92/43/EEC was upheld by the Second Chamber of the ECJ in a number of respects. Among the breaches found by the Court was failure to transpose adequately Art. 6(3) and (4) in relation to the failure within the UK to treat development plans as a 'plan' or 'project' within the meaning of Art. 6(3), particularly given their development control significance. This has led to amendments to the Habitats Regulations requiring 'land-use plans' to be the subject of Appropriate Assessment of their implications on SPAs and SACs under the new Part 4A (Regs 85A to 85E) introduced by the Conservation (Natural Habitats & c.) (Amendment) Regulations 2007 (SI 2007/1843).

[36] For a fuller list please attempt a web search using, for example, <http://www.wildlifeinforma tion.org >or <http://www.swed.org.uk>. Readers 'attention is also drawn to the work of two practitioners' bodies. The Institute of Environmental Management and Assessment (IEMA), formed in 1990, has, as part of its initiatives to improve standards of Environmental Assessment, published 'Guidelines for Baseline Ecological Assessment' to help standardize survey and evaluation methodologies. It also undertakes appraisals of Environmental Statements and Assessments, principally for local authorities. The Institute of Ecology and Environmental Management (IEEM), formed in 1991, is, in effect, the recognized professional body for ecologists and environmental managers. It sets standards of qualifications and working practices for ecological survey and evaluation.

notably their recent publication of 'Bat Survey Guidelines 2007', as well as assisting with various conservation initiatives.

Bird life International

Formerly the International Council for Bird Preservation, this organization, **11.15**
formed in 1922, exists as a worldwide partnership of organizations working for
the conservation of birds and their habitats. As such, it has become the leading
authority on the status of the world's birds and their habitats.

Botanical Society of the British Isles (BSBI)

The BSBI was founded in 1836. An association of amateur and professional bota- **11.16**
nists, particularly in respect of flowering plants and ferns, the Society has carried
out a number of nationally recognized plant distribution surveys and published
plant atlases (most notably the New Atlas of the British and Irish Flora 2002) and
books.[37]

British Herpetological Society (BHS)

The BHS was founded in 1947 by a group of naturalists to cater for all aspects of **11.17**
interest in reptiles and amphibians. It is the accepted authority on reptile and
amphibian conservation in the UK and holds an advisory role to Natural England.

British Trust for Conservation Volunteers (BTCV)

The BTCV, formed in 1959, is the largest practical conservation charity within **11.18**
the UK. A network of 90 local offices throughout England, Wales, and Northern
Ireland organizes a wide range of environmental projects, including the creation
of new habitats together with the voluntary labour to undertake them.

British Trust for Ornithology (BTO)

The BTO, formed in 1933, exists to conduct and promote research into Britain's **11.19**
birds and their habitats. Accordingly, it is able to provide independent scientific
data through a network of members who are knowledgeable volunteer birdwatch-
ers, as well as practical involvement in conservation issues.

Buglife—the Invertebrate Conservation Trust

Buglife is a charity formed in 2002 dedicated to maintaining sustainable popula- **11.20**
tions of insects, spiders, and earthworms and other invertebrates.[38]

---

[37] See para 12.98 below.
[38] See its rapid rise to prominence in *R (Buglife— the Invertebrate Conservation Trust) v Thurrock
Thames Gateway Development Corporation and Rosemound Developments Ltd*, [2008] EWHC 475
for its unsuccessful challenge to the grant of permission for development of a distribution depot

Butterfly Conservation

11.21 Formerly known as British Butterfly Conservation, this organization was formed in 1968 with the aim of saving wild butterflies and their habitats.

Fauna and Flora International (FFI)

11.22 Formerly known as the Fauna Preservation Society and also the Fauna and Flora Preservation Society, FFI has been involved in wildlife conservation, particularly overseas, since 1903. It was instrumental in promoting the first controls of trade in threatened species, and was involved in the creation of the World Wildlife Fund and the International Union for Conservation of Nature and Natural Resources. It continues to play an active part in international conservation through its own projects on specific conservation issues.

Froglife

11.23 Froglife is a registered charity, formed in 1989, concerned with the protection and conservation of native herpetofauna in the wild.

IUCN—The World Conservation Union (IUCN)

11.24 Founded in 1948 and formerly known as the International Union for the Conservation of Nature and Natural Resources, the IUCN seeks to influence, encourage, and assist societies throughout the world to conserve nature and natural resources by bringing together states, government agencies, and non-governmental organizations, across some 125 countries. Specific action groups are formed and projects are run on particular species, biodiversity conservation, and the management of habitats.

The Mammal Society

11.25 Founded in 1954, the Society aims to promote interest in all British mammals, whether endangered or common. It undertakes a number of research projects as part of the furtherance of its aims, in consequence of which it is an important source of survey information.

Marine Conservation Society (MCS)

11.26 Formerly known as the Underwater Conservation Society, MCS was founded in 1979. Its main aim is to protect the marine environment, for both wildlife and future generations, by promoting its sustainable and environmentally sensitive management policies through which better protection can be given for marine species and habitats. It provides expert advice on these issues together with a number of publications.

---

on the site of the former power station in Thurrock on the grounds that there had been a failure to consider biodiversity issues sufficiently.

National Federation of Badger Groups (NFBG)

The NFBG is a voluntary organization, formed in 1986, to co-ordinate measures **11.27** to enhance the welfare, conservation, and protection of badgers in the UK. Through local badger protection groups, advice, surveying, and monitoring services can be provided to landowners and others concerned about badger activity. The NFBG also represents badger conservation 'interests' on the Government Advisory Board concerning 'Badgers and Bovine Tuberculosis'.

The National Trust

Although a statutory body, having been incorporated under a private Act of **11.28** Parliament in 1907,[39] the Trust remains a non-governmental organization. It owns significant landholdings, particularly in areas of great scenic beauty, in consequence of which it is a major agency in the field of active nature conservation. Its statutory constitution includes 'the permanent preservation for the benefit of the nation of lands . . . of beauty or historic interest and. . . the preservation (so far as practicable) of their natural aspect and features and animal and plant life'.[40] Certain land held by the Trust is inalienable, so is permanently held for the Trust's purposes, thereby requiring special procedures if compulsory purchase is required, for example, to construct a new road.[41] The Trust also has the powers to make bye-laws, including controls to prevent any damage or disturbance to plants or animals[42] and to make and enforce restrictive covenants even though no adjacent land is held.[43]

Plantlife International

This organization was formed in 1989. It is the only charity in the UK dedicated **11.29** exclusively to preserving wild plants and their habitats. Its goal is to stop the loss of plants in Britain and Europe and to promote wild flowers through special management programmes, acquiring land, and campaigns.

People's Trust for Endangered Species (PTES)

This charity was created in 1977 to ensure a future for endangered species through- **11.30** out the world, with a special focus on native British mammals.

---

[39] National Trust Act 1907; see also National Trust Charity Scheme Confirmation Act 1991 and National Trust Acts 1937, 1939, 1953, 1971. The National Trust for Scotland was set up by the National Trust for Scotland Order Confirmation Act 1935 and subsequent Acts 1938–1973.
[40] National Trust Act 1907, s 4(1).
[41] Acquisition of Land Act 1981, s 18.
[42] National Trust Act 1971, s 24.
[43] National Trust Act 1937, s 8.

Royal Society for the Prevention of Cruelty to Animals (RSPCA)

11.31 The RSPCA was founded in 1824 with the objectives of promoting kindness and preventing cruelty to animals. Through its 300 inspectors nationwide it inevitably becomes involved in the protection and preservation of wild animals in a practical way, for example, in its seabird recovery initiatives after marine oil spills.

Royal Society for the Protection of Birds (RSPB)

11.32 The RSPB, founded in 1889, is a charity with the specific aim of protecting wild birds and their environment, primarily by the purchase of land to create new nature reserves. It manages over 100 reserves throughout the UK, covering more than 97,000 hectares, with a diverse range of habitats. Although a non-statutory consultee its views carry great weight. It also undertakes a number of research programmes and forms part of the global partnership known as Bird Life International (see above).

Wildfowl and Wetlands Trust (WWT)

11.33 The Trust was formed in 1946 and was formerly called 'The Wildfowl Trust'. It works to save and conserve wetlands for their wildlife through programmes of research, conservation, and education, as a result of which it has gained an international reputation particularly in respect of its study of the populations, behaviour, and migration of endangered species. The WWT maintains eight centres in the UK.

The Wildlife Trusts

11.34 Formed in 1981 and known, officially, as The Royal Society for Nature Conservation (the RSNC), The Wildlife Trusts exist to protect threatened wildlife in town and country in the form of a nationwide network of local Trusts who manage some 2,000 nature reserves.[44] The RSNC is the national association of The Wildlife Trusts.

The Woodland Trust

11.35 The Trust, formed in 1972, is the largest national conservation charity concerned solely with the conservation of Britain's native trees and woodlands. It currently owns and manages some 635 woods, covering over 21,000 acres, in 59 counties in England, Wales, and Scotland, many of which have been given to the Trust to ensure their long-term future preservation and enhancement.

---

[44] See further under Sites of Nature Conservation Interest at paragraph 11.88 below.

World Conservation Monitoring Centre (WCMC)

WCMC, formerly known as the Conservation Monitoring Centre, formed in **11.36**
1982, is a joint venture between the International Union of Nature and Natural
Resources (IUCN—the World Conservation Union), the United Nations
Environment Programme (UNEP), and the World Wide Fund for Nature
(WWF). Its primary aim is to support conservation and sustainable development
through the provision of information on the world's biological diversity. Its 'Red
Data Books' are now officially recognized sources of information on the scarcity
and conservation status of all forms of species in Britain, for example, as applied
under the Hedgerows Regulations 1997.[45]

WWF UK (World Wide Fund for Nature)

WWF(UK), formerly the World Wildlife Fund, was set up in 1961. Although a **11.37**
registered charity, it is the largest international voluntary organization devoted
entirely to the care and protection of the natural living world. About one-third of
the funds of WWF(UK) is spent on funding a large range of conservation projects
throughout Britain with the other two-thirds being used to fund international
projects in the developing world and industrialized countries.

Other groups

This section of the chapter would be incomplete without mention of the growing **11.38**
number of pressure groups whose aims, less directly, embrace nature conservation. The oldest amongst these groups is the Campaign for the Protection of Rural
England (CPRE) formed in 1926. Nationally, CPRE campaigns in the cause of
rural conservation, both within and without Parliament, by seeking to influence
planning and development control policies together with the upholding of environmental interests through objections, for example, to major roads, the effects of
agriculture on the landscape, energy policy, and water strategy.

Friends of the Earth, formed in 1971, aims to change policies and practices which **11.39**
'degrade' the environment. Greenpeace (UK Office), formed in 1977, is part of an
international, independent voluntary organization which acts against 'abuse to
the natural world' by campaigning against pollution and habitat loss. It is particularly famous for its high-profile activities, for example, the occupation of the
redundant Shell Brent Spar Oil Platform.

---

[45] See, further paragraphs 12.94, 12.136 below.

C. International Obligations

11.40 The protection of certain species of fauna and flora cannot depend solely on national legislation and actions since factors, such as natural dispersion and annual migration, result in these species crossing national boundaries. Accordingly, the UK Government has formally stated that it 'attaches great importance to the various international obligations it has assumed, is determined to honour them and to encourage other countries similarly to honour theirs'.[46] Therefore, their significance should not be underestimated, particularly the EC Council Directives and the legal principle of 'direct effect'.[47] Indeed, the underlying principles of 'biodiversity',[48] following the Rio 'Earth Summit' in 1992, now apply to all aspects of nature conservation. The UK's international obligations also underlie much of the detailed legislative framework set out later in this chapter.

The Convention concerning the protection of the world cultural and natural heritage ('World Heritage Sites')

11.41 This Convention was adopted by the United Nations Educational, Scientific and Cultural Organization (UNESCO) in November 1972 and was ratified by the UK in 1984. It requires a World Heritage List to be established under the management of an inter-governmental World Heritage Committee (WHC) which, in turn, is advised by the International Council on Monuments and Sites (ICOMOS) and the World Conservation Union. Each member state makes its own nominations and is required to do all it can to ensure adequate protection is available through its own legislation. A World Heritage Site (WHS) has to be of 'outstanding universal value'. Applications are considered by ICOMOS, which advises the WHC before approval by UNESCO. Of the 25 WHSs currently within the UK, three are included for reasons of natural beauty and nature conservation rather than on archaeological or historical grounds. These are the Giant's Causeway and the Causeway Coast, St Kilda, and the Dorset and East Devon Coast[49]. The Department for Culture Media and Sport (DCMS) is responsible for the UK's general compliance and is advised by the JNCC in recognizing and managing natural sites. Nomination of sites, in England, is by DCMS and elsewhere within the UK by the respective devolved administrations.

---

[46] PPG9, para 8.

[47] See Chapter 3.

[48] See further para 11.50.

[49] Additional protection is being advanced through the Heritage Protection Bill since, at present, WHS status is only a material, albeit an important, planning consideration which will usually require EIA of a development proposal (see PPG15 (*Planning and the Historic Environment*) (1994), paras.2.22–2.2.3), although a separate statutory controls may apply eg designation as a conservation area.

The Ramsar Convention on wetlands of international importance ('The Ramsar Convention')

This Convention was adopted in Ramsar, Iran in February 1971, signed by the **11.42** UK Government in 1973, ratified in 1976, and amended (as a result of the EC Council on the Conservation of Wild Birds—the 'Birds Directive') in December 1982. The Convention requires each participating country to designate suitable wetlands within its territory, promote the conservation of designated sites (and their waterfowl) and, as far as possible, the 'wise use' of all its wetlands. The areas to which the Convention can be applied include 'marine water' to a depth of six metres at low tide, which permits wider areas to be covered than those under a designation under UK domestic law as a SSSI. Currently, there are about 80 Ramsar sites within the UK (for example, Bridgwater Bay and Malham Tarn), most of which are also Special Protection Areas (SPAs) under the Birds Directive as well as listed as SSSIs. Examples include the Dee Estuary and the North Norfolk Coast. Compliance has been achieved largely through the creation of SSSIs under Part II of the WCA, as now supplemented by the Habitats Regulations.

The Convention on international trade in endangered species ('The CITES Convention')

This Convention was signed in Washington in March 1973 and made part of **11.43** European Law by two EC Regulations (338/97 and 1808/01). They include some additional species to the CITES list and also provisions prohibiting or restricting the importation of species which are considered to be a threat to native EC flora and fauna. CITES was initially given effect in the UK by the Endangered Species (Import and Export) Act 1976.[50] It is now supplemented by the Control of Trade in Endangered Species (Enforcement) Regulations 1997[51] (known as 'COTES') which provide enforcement measures and penalties to implement Council Regulation 338/97/EC. Defra currently acts as the CITES management authority for the UK with the JNCC acting as scientific authority on animals and the Royal Botanic Gardens, Kew acting as scientific authority for plants. Enforcement is the responsibility of HM Customs and Excise and the police

The Bern Convention on the conservation of European wildlife and natural habitats ('The Bern Convention')

This Convention was agreed by the Committee Members of the Council of **11.44** Europe in June 1979 and came into force on 1 June 1982. It carries obligations to conserve wild plants, birds, and other animals with particular emphasis on

---

[50] See also section on Protection of Endangered Species, para 12.138 below.
[51] As amended by SI 2005/1674.

endangered and vulnerable species and their habitats. The provisions of the Bern Convention now underlie both the Habitats Directive as well as UK wildlife legislation. Statutory compliance has been made by Part I of the WCA.

The Bonn Convention on the conservation of migratory species of wild animals

11.45   This 1979 Convention requires the protection of certain listed endangered migratory species. It encourages separate international agreements covering particular species. Currently, there are three such agreements in force. The Agreement on the Conservation of Bats in Europe (1994) deals with the need to protect bats, particularly their feeding and roosting areas. However, it was not accepted by the UK since protection was already provided to bats under Part I of the WCA, as supplemented, now, by the Habitats Regulations. Secondly, there is the Agreement on the Conservation of Small Cetaceans of the Baltic and North Seas (ASCORBANS) (1996). Thirdly, there is the Agreement on the Conservation of African–Eurasian Migratory Waterbirds (1996). It is particularly noteworthy for its aim to cover some 40% of the earth's surface, some 60 million square kilometres, covered by the range states of the 116 migratory waterbirds the subject of the agreement.

EC Council Directive on the conservation of wild birds ('The Birds Directive')

11.46   This Directive was designated under the provisions of Directive 79/409. Article 1 of the Birds Directive provides for the protection, management, and control of all species of naturally occurring birds in their wild state within the European territory of member states (ie excluding Greenland). Articles 2 and 3 require measures to be taken to preserve sufficient diversity of habitats for all species of wild birds naturally occurring within the territories of member states in order to maintain populations at ecologically and scientifically sound levels. Article 4 requires member states to take special measures to conserve the habitat of certain particularly rare species of migratory species (for example, the whooper swan, the osprey, the corncrake, and the nightjar) as well as preventing the deliberate killing or capture of birds or damage or destruction to their nests and eggs.[52] Article 4(3) requires the Commission to co-ordinate measures to ensure that SPAs are set up, within which member states must take appropriate steps to avoid pollution or deterioration of habitats. Compliance with the provisions of the Birds Directive has largely been secured by Part I of the WCA save with regard to habitat, which is now covered by a combination of powers under Part II of the WCA, the Conservation

---

[52] Birds Directive, Art. 5.

(Natural Habitats, &c) Regulations 1994 ('the Habitats Regulations') and the Off-Shore Marine (Natural Habitats &c) Regulations 2007.[53]

EC Council Directive on the assessment of the effects of certain public and private projects on the environment ('The EIA Directive')

This was designated under the provisions of EC Council Directive 85/337. It **11.47** required environmental assessment to be carried out before the decision is taken to grant permission for certain types of project which are likely to have significant environmental effects. In England and Wales the Directive was implemented through the Town and Country Planning (Assessment of Environmental Effects) Regulations 1988. Separate Regulations, also published during 1988, have implemented the Directive in respect of other development projects such as highways, afforestation projects, land drainage improvement works, and salmon farming in marine waters.[54] In 1995 further Regulations were passed to cover projects excluded from the formal grant of planning permission as a result of 'permitted development rights' and as a result of enforcement action. However, Directive 85/337 was amended by a new Directive 97/11, which came into force on 3 March 1997. As it required implementation by member states within two years of that date, replacement Regulations were issued as the Town and Country Planning (Environmental Impact Assessment) (England and Wales) Regulations 1999 ('the EA Regulations').[55]

The EA Regulations identify two categories of project. Schedule 1 projects require **11.48** an assessment in all cases as they relate to major proposals such as crude-oil refineries, thermal power stations, motorways and other major roads, and bridges. For Schedule 2 projects, like mineral extraction, golf courses, motorway service areas,

---

[53] These Regulations, which came into force on 21 August 2007, apply in the 'offshore area' where the UK has jurisdiction beyond its territorial sea, which is broadly from 12 to 200 nautical miles from the UK coast. They protect marine species and wild birds through a number of offences that aim to prevent environmentally damaging activities in a manner consistent with the Wild Birds Directive and the Habitats Directive so follows closely the pattern of the Habitats Regulations 1994 (as amended). For example, deliberately killing or significantly disturbing a protected species (such as dolphins) is now a criminal offence. The 2007 Regulations also apply to offshore marine installations and certain ships and aircraft.

[54] Current regulations mainly date from 1999/2000; but see more recent changes eg the EIA (Agriculture) (England) (No.2) Regulations 2006. For further information, see generally: < http://www.communities.gov.uk/planningandbuilding/planning/sustainabilityenvironmental/environmentalimpactassessment/>

[55] Separate 1999 EIA Regulations apply, respectively, to Scotland (SSI199/1) and Northern Ireland (SR1999/73). Following the decisions of the ECJ (*R (Barker) v Bromley LBC and the FSS; Case C-290/03; Commission v UK; Case C-508/03*) and the House of Lords in [2006] UKHL 52 that outline planning permission and the decision approving reserved matters together constitute a multi stage 'development consent' further amendments are awaited to the EA Regulations to take full account of the need for EIA. These are also intended to cover the submission of details pursuant to an outline planning permission.

and coast protection works an assessment is not compulsory below certain size thresholds. The test is whether the project is 'likely to have significant effects on the environment by virtue of factors such as their nature, size and location'.[56] Questions of classification are essentially matters of fact and degree and not law, which the courts have held are primarily for the local planning authority to decide acting reasonably.[57] Schedule 4 of the EA Regulations requires certain specified information to be given including 'a description of the aspects of the environment likely to be significantly affected by the development, including in particular, population, flora, fauna, soil, water, air, climatic factors [. . .] landscape and the interaction between the above factors plus the mitigation measures where such adverse effects are identified. Practical Guidance is currently given in DOE Circular 2/99 ('Environmental Impact Assessment'). The EA Regulations include threshold criteria for assessing whether Schedule 2 projects are likely to have a 'significant' effect or where their location includes any part within a 'sensitive area'.[58]

EC Council Directive on the conservation of natural habitats and of wild flora and fauna ('The Habitats Directive')

11.49 This was designated under the provisions of EC Council Directive 92/43, adopted on 21 May 1992, and required national implementation by 21 May 1994. Although a number of its provisions were already covered by the National Parks and Access to the Countryside Act 1949 (NPACA) and Part II of the WCA, the UK has given effect to the Habitats Directive by the Habitats Regulations 1994,[59] and, more recently, by the Off-Shore Marine (Natural Habitats &c) Regulations 2007.[60] Article 2(1) states that the aim of the Habitats Directive is 'to contribute towards ensuring biodiversity through the conservation of natural habitats and of wild flora and fauna in the European territory of Member States'. It also requires member states to take measures 'to maintain or restore natural habitats and wild species to a favourable conservation status, natural habitats and species of wild fauna and flora of Community interest'.[61] Sites to be designated as Special Areas

---

[56] Reg 4(5) and Sch 3 provide selection criteria for screening Sch 2 development. See also DOE Circular 2/99, para 28.

[57] *R v Rochdale MBC, ex parte Tew* [2000] Env LR 1; *ex parte Milne* [2001] Env LR 22; *R (Goodman) v Lewisham LBC* [2003] EWCA Civ 140

[58] Reg 2 defines 'sensitive area' as including land subject to a SSSI, SPA or SAC designation or within a National Park or AONB. See also DOE Circular 2/99, paras 36–40 (under the heading 'Projects in environmentally sensitive locations').

[59] See The Conservation (Natural Habitats, &c.) Regulations 1994 (as amended) and The Conservation (Natural Habitats, &c.) (Northern Ireland) Regulations 1995 (as amended). The Habitats Regulations apply to the UK land area and its territorial sea (to 12 nautical miles from the coast).

[60] See n53 above.

[61] Habitats Directive, Art. 2(2).

of Conservation (SACs) had to be agreed with the Commission by June 1998,[62] leading to, in the words of Article 3(1), a 'coherent European ecological network' under the title 'Natura 2000', including those set up under the Wild Birds Directive.[63] Subsequent articles deal with the administration and management of SACs,[64] the protection of species,[65] and the like. Legal considerations affecting designation are dealt with in the next section of this chapter on Habitat Conservation under not only the sections dealing respectively with SPAs, SACs, and the Habitats Regulations but also in respect of SSSIs through which they already held protection under UK domestic law.

The Rio Convention on biological diversity ('The Biodiversity Convention')

This was an important component of the 'Earth Summit' which took place in Rio **11.50** de Janeiro in June 1992 in the context of a United Nations Conference on Environment and Development. It was attended and signed by around 150 Heads of State or Governments. It requires each contracting party to 'develop national strategies, plans or programmes for the conservation and sustainable use of biological diversity or adapt for this purpose existing strategies, plans or programmes which shall reflect, inter alia, the measures set out in this Convention relevant to the Contracting Party concerned'.

The Earth Summit also led to a number of other major agreements including the **11.51** 'Rio Declaration', a statement of principles which addressed the need to balance the protection of the environment with the need for sustainable development, 'Agenda 21', an action plan for the next century aiming to integrate environmental concerns across industry, agriculture, fisheries, energy, transport, recreation, and land use, the 'Convention on Climate Change' which committed all ratifying countries to prepare national programmes to contain greenhouse gas emissions to 1990 levels by the year 2000, and a Statement of Principles for the sustainable management of forests. Currently, a 2010 target has been set for the achievement of a 'significant reduction in the current rate of loss of biological diversity' as set at the World Summit on Sustainable Development in South Africa in 2002 and also in Sweden that same year.

'Biodiversity', the shorthand that is now used, simply means 'the variety of life **11.52** forms we see around us. It encompasses the whole range of mammals, birds, reptiles, amphibians, fish, insects and other invertebrates, plants, fungi, and

---

[62] Ibid, Art. 4(4).
[63] Ibid, Art. 3(1).
[64] Ibid, Arts 4–11.
[65] Ibid, Arts 12–16.

micro-organisms'.[66] Article 2 of the Biodiversity Convention defines the term to mean: 'The variability among living organisms from all sources including, inter alia, terrestrial, marine, and other aquatic ecosystems and the ecological complexities of which they are a part; this includes diversity within species, between species and of ecosystems.' The UK Biodiversity Action Plan (UKBAP) points out that:

> it is important to stress the linkage between species and habitats. Changing a habitat will often affect the diversity of species contained within it and conversely a change in the number and assemblage of species may affect the habitat. A crucial test of the 'health' of a local environment is reflected in the wildlife community appropriate to the area or habitat. If the rate of change or loss is markedly greater than ordinary evolutionary processes would imply, this could indicate a systematic problem to which we should pay serious attention.[67]

11.53   In effect, biodiversity is a quality of life issue since it concerns man's environment including his natural surroundings. When making decisions affecting the use of land it is intended to operate, first, on the 'precautionary principle' but also, where opportunities exist, lead to enhancement of the environment.[68]

11.54   The UKBAP was published in 1994 in response to the requirement of Article 6 of the Convention to develop national strategies for the conservation of biological diversity and the sustainable use of biological resources. The overall goal of the UKBAP is 'to conserve and enhance biological diversity within the UK and to contribute to the conservation of global diversity through all appropriate mechanisms'.[69] Conservation and enhancement of overall populations of native species, wildlife systems, and ecosystems, the increasing of public awareness, and involvement in conserving biodiversity and contributing to the conservation of biodiversity on a European and global scale were seen as three key objectives.[70] A Steering Group, envisaged in the UKBAP, reported at the end of 1995. It recommended a number of action plans to protect certain species and key habitats together with the administrative structures required to carry out these proposals. Following government endorsement in May 1996 the UK Biodiversity Group was established to oversee and co-ordinate the implementation of the UKBAP, monitor and evaluate national biodiversity targets, report on progress, and advise the Government as to how best to secure progress. In 2003 this Group was replaced

---

[66] 65 UKBAP (1994), chapter 1, para 1.10. The draft Marine Bill, published by Defra on 3 April 2008, contains various proposals which will help us to better protect marine ecosystems and stem the decline in marine biodiversity. Part 4 provides for the designation and protection of Marine Conservation Zones.

[67] Ibid, para 1.12.

[68] See, now, the express statutory duty placed on all public authorities within England and Wales under NERCA 2006 s 40(1), in the exercise of their functions, to 'have regard, so far as is consistent with the proper exercise of those functions, to the purpose of conserving biodiversity'.

[69] UKBAP, para 1.28.

[70] Ibid, para 1.28.

by the UK Biodiversity Partnership together with a Standing Committee assisted by two advisory groups, The Biodiversity Reporting and Information Group and the Biodiversity Research Advisory Group. In 2007 the revised UK lists of priority species and habitats were published.[71] The next steps are now to refine the priority actions, to which end three types of Action Plan have now been developed which set priorities for nationally and locally important habitats and wildlife with reporting on targets on a three to five year cycle.[72]

The Convention for the protection of the marine environment of the North-East Atlantic (OSPAR)

OSPAR was adopted in Paris in 1992 to provide a comprehensive and simplified **11.55** approach to addressing all sources of pollution which might affect this maritime area as well as seeking to protect the marine environment by retaining all decisions, recommendations and agreements previously adopted, in 1972, under the Convention for the Prevention of Marine Dumping from Ships and Aircraft (The Oslo Convention) and, in 1974, under the Convention for the Prevention of Marine Pollution from Land-Based Sources, including the discharge of dangerous substances from water-courses or pipelines (The Paris Convention). A Commission administers OSPAR and develops policy and international agreements, the Secretariat for which is based in the UK, which ratified OSPAR in 1998. Implementation within the UK is currently undertaken by Defra.

EC Council Directive on the environmental assessment of plans and programmes (The SEA Directive)

Directive 2001/42/EC introduced the process known as Strategic Environmental **11.56** Assessment (SEA). Its objective is to provide a high level of protection of the environment and to contribute to the integration of environmental considerations into the preparation and adoption of plans and programmes with a view to promoting sustainable development by ensuring that an environmental assessment is carried out of certain plans and programmes which are likely to have significant effects on the environment. It includes all plans and programmes which are prepared for agriculture, forestry, fisheries, energy, industry, transport, waste management, water management, telecommunications, tourism, town and country planning, or land use which set out a framework for future development consent of projects listed in Annexes I and II of Directive 85/337/EC or which, in view of

---

[71] NERCA 2006, s 41(1) (England) replacing the previous provisions under CROW 2000, s 74; NERCA 2006), s 42(1) (Wales). The UK lists contain 1,149 species and 65 habitats were listed as priorities for conservation action. Continuing reporting takes place through an on-line system called BARS (Biodiversity Action Reporting System)

[72] Species Action Plans; Habitat Action Plans and Local Action Plans. For more detailed information see: <http://www.ukbap.org.uk>

the likely effect on sites, have been determined to require an assessment under Directive 92/43/EEC.[73] Information must also be made available on the adopted plan or programme and how the environmental assessment was taken into account. The SEA Directive was transposed into English law by the Environmental Assessment of Plans and Programmes Regulations 2004 by two separate statutory instruments.[74]

Convention on access to information, public participation in decision-making and access to justice in environmental matters ('The Aarhus Convention')

11.57 Negotiated through the United Nations Economic Commission for Europe it was concluded in Aarhus, Denmark in October 1998. Both the European Community as a whole and the UK Government, separately, ratified the Aarhus Convention in 2005. Many of the provisions are already in operation in the UK through the outworking of Directive 2003/4/EC on public access to environmental information,[75] Directive 2003/35/EC on public participation in respect of the drawing up of certain plans and programmes relating to the environment.[76]

EC Water Framework Directive ('The Water Framework Directive')

11.58 Directive 2000/60/EC is the most substantial piece of water legislation ever produced by the European Commission. It is intended to act as the major driver for achieving sustainable management of water in the UK and the other Member States by requiring that all inland and coastal waters within defined river basin districts[77] must reach at least good chemical and ecological status by 2015. It also defines how this target should be achieved through the establishment of environmental objectives and ecological targets for surface waters. The intended result is a healthy water environment achieved by taking due account of environmental, economic, and social considerations. Article 14 of the Directive requires Member States to encourage the active involvement of all interested parties in its implementation, particularly public consultation which is essential during the production, review, and updating of river basin management plans which form the central

---

[73] Article 3(2).

[74] SI 2004/1633 for England; SI/1656 for Wales. See also the Environmental Assessment (Scotland) Act 2005 and the Environmental Assessment of Plans and Programmes Regulations (Northern Ireland) 2004 (SR2004/280).

[75] See eg Environmental Information Regulations 2004 (SI 2004/3391).

[76] For the current position see the most recently published Aarhus Convention Implementation Report (April 2008) downloadable from the Defra website: <http://www.defra.gov.uk/environment/internat/aarhus/index.htm>

[77] The WFD introduces the concept of integrated river basin management based on 11 River Basin Districts in England and Wales (one of which covers cross-border river basins between England and Scotland).

theme of the Directive. The WFD came into force on 22 December 2000, and was transposed into UK law in 2003.[78] It also sets out requirements for the Commission to propose further laws to protect against water pollution. In this respect, a 'daughter directive' (2006/118/EC) aimed at protecting groundwater was adopted in December 2006. Member States have until January 2009 to bring into force laws, regulations, and administrative provisions to implement the new Directive.[79] The new Directive will operate alongside 1980 Groundwater Directive until December 2013. The two Groundwater Directives adopt similar approaches to preventing goundwater pollution, but there will need to be adjustments to the existing regime to accommodate the changes brought about by both the WFD and the new Groundwater Directive. A Commission proposal for a separate daughter directive on priority substances, initially published in July 2006, is intended to include environmental quality standards for the concentrations of the priority substances in surface water bodies.[80]

D. Habitat Conservation

Introduction

The word 'habitat' is used in ecological parlance to mean the environment of a **11.59** plant or an animal. As a term, it embraces a whole range of considerations, notably vegetation, soil, and climatic factors. The word 'conservation', in this context, means the maintenance of growth and activity of plants and animals, through the natural succession of vegetation with and without some degree of management, in a particular area.[81]

In the UK, spurred on by European wildlife Directives, habitat conservation, **11.60** through legal protection, has largely been achieved through the creation and maintenance of statutory site designations of the best areas. The cornerstone of this legal protection arises from the designation of all national sites of nature conservation importance within England and Wales, in respect of which this section

---

[78] The Water Environment (Water Framework Directive) (England and Wales) Regulations 2003, SI 2003/3242; The Water Environment and Water Services (Scotland) Act 2003; The Water Environment (Water Framework Directive) Regulations (Northern Ireland) 2003. For more information see: <http://www.euwfd.com/html/water_framework_directive.html>

[79] As the WFD was later than expected, the Groundwater (Water Framework Directive) Direction 2006 was made to the Environment Agency in early 2006 enabling them to put in place interim criteria for 'good groundwater status' and 'trend identification and reversal 'pending adoption of a new groundwater directive.

[80] There are currently 33 substances on this priority list, which was agreed in 2001 (Decision 2455/2001/EC). These substances are referred to as 'priority substances', and those which are thought to pose the greatest threat are further identified as 'priority hazardous substances'. The list will be reviewed on a regular basis.

[81] More specific definitions can be found in the *Penguin Dictionary of British Natural History*.

now focuses, is now found in Part II of the WCA (as amended[82]). However, a hierarchy of designations, to reflect the degree of importance in terms of quality is to be found in the Government's land use policies for nature conservation.[83]

11.61 Continuing recognition of the UK's international obligations is reflected in the status of Ramsar Sites as the highest order of ranking, together with Biogenetic and Biosphere Reserves, after which come those sites of European importance, designated under the Birds Directive as SPAs and under the Habitats Directive as SACs, both now directly protected by UK domestic law through the Habitats Regulations. These areas are then followed by those sites and areas specifically identified and protected by UK nature conservation legislation. In order of ranking they are NNRs, Marine Nature Reserves (MNRs), SSSIs, and Local Nature Reserves (LNRs) under the NPACA and Part II of the WCA.

11.62 Habitat conservation is also assisted through countryside designations, in the context of the wider issues of landscape protection, arising from the geographical location of a particular area of interest within a National Park, the Norfolk and Suffolk Broads, or an Area of Outstanding Natural Beauty. More specific conservation issues arise from the statutory protection of Limestone Pavements and from regulation of agricultural practices in certain parts of England and Wales as Environmentally Sensitive Areas, Nitrate Sensitive Areas, and Habitat Scheme Water Fringe Areas. Finally, through the development plan process, nature conservation by way of countryside protection can arise from designation of land, for example, as Green Belt. More directly, both within and without urban and non-urban areas, there can also exist, at local level, non-statutory nature reserves, sometimes known as Sites of Nature Conservation Importance or Interest (SNCIs) or as Sites of Interest for Nature Conservation (SINCs), or as County Wildlife Sites.

Biogenetic Reserves

11.63 Biogenetic Reserves are certain heathlands and dry grasslands which have been identified under a Council of Europe Programme, dating from 1973, for the conservation of such habitats as representative examples of European flora and fauna and natural areas. They are intended to act as 'living laboratories'. Due to their importance, a number are NNRs and all are existing SSSIs. After consultation with Local Planning Authorities (LPAs), owners, and occupiers, designation has been by the relevant Secretary of State on the recommendation of the relevant conservation body.[84]

---

[82] Principally by the Countryside and Rights of Way Act 2000 and NERCA 2006.

[83] See n 2 (England) and n 3 (Wales, Scotland and Northern Ireland).

[84] The UK list of Biogenetic Reserves identifies a number of English grasslands and steppes (respectively in East Sussex, Dorset, Durham, Humberside, Hampshire, and two in Wiltshire, heathlands of which several are in England (Cornwall, Cumbria, Dorset, Suffolk, and Surrey, two are in Scotland (Kincardine and Gordon) and one in Wales (Gwynedd).

Biosphere Reserves

A Biosphere Reserve is a designation arising from a UNESCO Programme called   **11.64**
'The Man and the Biosphere'. Launched in 1970, the purpose of the designation
is to conserve examples of all major types of ecosystems and to provide sites for
integrated ecological research and environmental training activities. They are
intended to act as benchmarks or standards for the measurement of long-term
changes in the biosphere.[85] Most are based on existing NNR designations, details
of which were submitted to UNESCO by the respective Secretaries of State.

Ramsar sites

Ramsar sites continue to have no statutory basis for their designation under UK   **11.65**
domestic law. Nevertheless, they are recognized as being areas of sufficient international importance to warrant specific identification[86] and continuing recognition by this country's land-use planning system.[87] The Ramsar Convention has
required each participating country to designate suitable wetlands within its territory, promote the conservation of designated sites (and their waterfowl), and, as
far as possible, ensure the 'wise use' of all its wetlands. Selection of a site is the
responsibility of each signatory taking account of the significance of each site in
terms of its ecology, botany, zoology, limnology, or hydrology.[88] Once a wetland
has been added to the List of Wetlands of International Importance which the signatories to the Convention have undertaken to protect, the state is under an obligation to formulate and implement its planning so as to promote the conservation
of the site.[89] Sites which have been placed on the List can be reduced in size or
deleted if this is required by 'an urgent national interest' but, so far as possible,
compensation should be provided by the creation of additional nature reserves
and other protection.[90]

---

[85] The UK list identifies three Biosphere Reserves in England (Braunton Burrows NNR,
Moorehouse Upper Teesdale, and the North Norfolk Coast), one in Wales (Dyfi NNR), and nine in
Scotland (including the Isle of Rum, St Kilda, and Taynish NNRs).

[86] WCA 1981, s 37A(2) only requires Natural England and CCW, following designation, to
notify the relevant local authority in whose area the wetland is situated, every owner, the Environment
Agency, and every relevant undertaker under the WIA 1991 and every Internal Drainage Board
under the LDA 1991.

[87] See eg decision letter reported in [1997] JPL 373 concerning a concrete and piled quay and the
reclamation of 8.7 hectares of foreshore at Mostyn, Clwyd within the Dee Estuary, Wales affecting
an SPA/SSSI/Ramsar Site.

[88] Ramsar Convention, Art. 2(2).

[89] Ibid, Art. 3.

[90] Ibid, Arts 2(5) and 4(2).

11.66 Currently, there are 80 listed Ramsar sites within England[91], one of which over-laps with Scotland (Upper Solway Flats and Marshes) and 3 of which (the Dee Estuary, the Midland Meres and Mosses and the Severn Estuary) overlap with Wales, which has 7 separate listings.[92] Recent extensions have been to the Stour and Orwell Estuaries (2005) and to the Humber Estuary (2007). All Ramsar sites have SSSI designation and most also have Special Protection Area (SPA) status.[93] Protection continues to be achieved largely through the powers under Part II of the WCA in respect of SSSIs, as now supplemented by the Habitats Regulations in respect of those designated SPAs. Where such statutory designation has not taken place or is still subject to agreement with the European Commission, national policy advice[94] is that listed Ramsar sites should be considered in the same way for development control purposes as designated SPAs and SACs.

Special Protection Areas (SPAs)

11.67 SPAs are intended to protect the habitats of rare and vulnerable birds, listed in Annex I to the Birds Directive, and, for regularly occurring migratory species.[95] They form part of the Natura 2000 network under Article 3(1) of the Habitats Directive.[96] All classified and candidate SPAs have SSSI designation so are protected under Part II of the WCA as well as under the Habitats Regulations.[97]

---

[91] The JNCC website lists three locations as proposed Ramsar sites: Dungeness to Pett Level; Mersey Narrows and North Wirral Foreshore; and Upper Nene Valley Gravel Pits (as at 31 August 2007).

[92] See also the JNCC website for the full list of all UK Ramsar sites of which, as at 31 August 2007, there were 146 designated sites (covering 782,727 ha) and 7 proposed sites.

[93] At 31 March 1998 some 16 Ramsar sites did not have SPA/proposed SAC designations. The DETR Consultation Document entitled *Sites of Special Scientific Interest—Better Protection and Management* (September 1998) proposed that all Ramsar sites should have the same protection afforded to SPAs and SACs. However, the DETR (August 1999) report on the outcome of the conservation exercise was silent on this aspect.

[94] eg PPS9, para.6 for English pSPAs.

[95] The Wild Birds Directive provides no formal criteria for selecting SPAs, so the JNCC, on behalf of the UK Conservation Bodies, has published SPA Selection Guidelines for use in the UK.

[96] In the UK, the first SPAs were classified in the early to mid 1980s. In the mid-1990s, the JNCC and country agencies were requested by government to review the SPA network leading to the publication of the SPA Review (Stroud et al. 2001; 'The UK SPA network: its scope and content', JNCC). The Review, which focused largely on terrestrial SPAs, presents site accounts that sometimes differ from the classified SPA citation and Natura 2000 Standard Data Form; and JNCC advises that as the accounts are effectively lists of potential qualifying species and as such, according to government policy, give these species are fully protected in the SPA or potential SPA (pSPA). It also has led to the legal documents for many classified SPAs in the UK network now being amended to incorporate changes to qualifying species; this process will take some time to complete. Although the UK has SPAs with marine components, to date, there is only one entirely marine SPA, Carmarthen Bay (Wales), which was classified in 2003 for its non-breeding aggregations of common scoter. Work is currently underway by JNCC and the UK Conservation Bodies to identify further SPAs with marine components that will comprise a suite of entirely marine SPAs.

[97] Habitats Regulations, Reg. 10(1). This includes pSPAs under Regs10(1)(c) and 10(2). A full list of SPAs is provided on the JNCC website.

Only ecological factors may be taken into account in the identification of SPAs and their boundaries, following the decision of the European Court of Justice in the *Lappel Bank* case in June 1996.[98] However, the Habitats Regulations do not provide statutory protection for potential SPAs (pSPAs) before they have been agreed with the European Commission. In consequence, reliance has to be placed on national policy advice,[99] that pSPAs should be considered in the same way for development control purposes as if they had already been classified or designated.

Special Areas of Conservation (SACs)

SACs are intended to protect the habitats of threatened species of wildlife under **11.68** Articles 2 and 3 of the Habitats Directive.[100] Article 3 of the Habitats Directive requires the establishment of a European network of important high-quality conservation sites that will make a significant contribution to conserving the 189 habitat types and 788 species identified in Annexes I and II of the Directive (as amended). The listed habitat types and species are those considered to be most in need of conservation at a European level (excluding birds). Protection for SACs arises under the Habitats Regulations.[101] While there is no specific legal ruling on the point it appears, again, that only scientific factors may be taken into account in the identification of SACs and their boundaries.[102] However, as with pSPAs, the Habitats Regulations do not provide statutory protection for candidate SACs (cSACs), in consequence of which national policy[103] can only advise that cSACs should be considered in the same way as confirmed SACs for development control purposes.

---

[98] The leading case on designation, *R v Secretary of State for the Environment, ex parte The Royal Society for the Protection of Birds* concerning the exclusion of the Lappel Bank mudflats from the Medway Estuary and Marshes SPA and which led to a reference by the House of Lords [1997] Env LR 431 to the European Court of Justice [1997] Env LR 442, confirmed that a Member State was not authorized to take account of the economic requirements mentioned in Article 2 of the Birds Directive when designating an SPA. In that case the Port of Sheerness had planning permission to reclaim part of the Lappel Bank area in order to facilitate expansion, without which the commercial viability of the port would be inhibited which could justify the exclusion as a superior interest. The ECJ also rejected this point together with the argument of overriding public interest. See also n 153 below regarding local government administrative boundaries with the sea.

[99] eg PPS9, para.6 for English pSPAs.

[100] Habitats Regs, regs. 7 and 8. Of the Annex I habitat types, 78 are believed to occur in the UK and of the Annex II species, 43 are native to, and normally resident in, the UK.

[101] Habitats Regs, reg 10(1). This includes pSACs under reg 10(1)(c) and 10(2). In *R (Newsum) v Welsh Assembly Government* [2005] EWHC 538 (Admin) it was held that the inclusion of a site as a candidate SAC (cSAC) still fulfilled a legitimate purposes although the EC had, by that point, designated the land. Richards J also did not rule out the possibility that the power to classify as an SAC did not include the power to declassify where it was shown that a Member State had acted unlawfully in including land on a list of cSACs.

[102] See the *Lappel Bank* case at n 98. The JNCC website lists 614 designated SACs, SCIs or cSACs in the United Kingdom including cross border sites (excluding Gibraltar). In addition, there are 8 possible SACs and 1 draft offshore sites that have not yet been submitted to the European Commission.

[103] eg PPS9, para.6 for English pSPAs.

The Habitats Regulations

11.69 As the Habitats Regulations apply to SPAs and SACs, this section deals with the legislative considerations applicable to both designations which provide the additional protection given to those wild animals and plants of particular vulnerability within Europe by way of protection under the criminal law[104] and through bye-laws.[105] The system of direct protection and conservation introduced by the Habitats Regulations mirrors that in respect of SSSIs under the WCA. Conservation of the habitat of SPAs and SACs is encouraged through the use of management agreements.[106] Notification of potentially damaging operations is equally applicable to SPAs and SACs.[107] In addition, the Secretary of State can make 'special nature conservation orders' prohibiting operations which are likely to destroy or damage the flora, fauna, and the like[108] and, if required, exercise compulsory purchase powers to secure the land from further damage or threat.[109]

11.70 However, the Habitats Regulations go much further than the WCA by placing a duty upon LPAs to review all extant planning permissions or deemed permissions which are likely to have a significant effect on any existing or future SPA or SAC, either individually or in combination with other development.[110] This review, currently being applied only to classified SPAs, applies to all planning permissions, whether express or deemed, unless the development to which it relates has been completed or the permission has become time expired.[111] Where 'adverse effects' cannot be overcome either directly or through other regimes, Regulation 56 encourages the use of the, hitherto, rarely used power of revocation or modification of a permission or a discontinuance order[112] as well as voluntary restrictions

---

[104] Habitat Regulations, regs 39(1), (6), 41(1), (6) (specific wild animals), 43(1), (7) (specific wild plants), 100 (attempts). See also regs 101–101F (powers of stop and search detention and of wild life inspectors) and 103 (forfeiture by court order).

[105] Ibid, regs 28–31, 94–96 (including powers of entry and compensation).

[106] Ibid, regs 16 and 17.

[107] Ibid, regs 18–21 and n 165 below.

[108] Ibid, regs 22–27 and Sch 1. A breach of a special nature conservation order is punishable by fine both on summary conviction (level 5–maximum) or on indictment (unlimited) (reg 23(3)) and liable to a restoration order (reg 26).

[109] Ibid, regs 98 and 99 provide supplementary provisions including powers of entry.

[110] Ibid, regs 50, 51, 55, and 56. regs 64, 65, and 66 also provide that existing Special Development Orders, Simplified Planning Zones, and Enterprise Zones cease to have effect as to the (automatic) grant of planning permission. This exercise currently excludes deemed permissions under the Pipe-Lines Act 1962, the Electricity Act 1989, and the Transport and Works Act 1992 which will be the subject of future review. Habitats Regulations, regs 71–82 cover these activities. Reg 50(2) puts each review in the context of the site's nature conservation objectives.

[111] Ibid, reg 55. See also n 153 regarding the local government jurisdictional area where seaward and estuarine boundaries are involved.

[112] Town and Country Planning Act 1990, s 97 (revocation and modification notices); Ibid, s 102 (discontinuance notices). Both require confirmation by the Secretary of State and give rise to a right of compensation under the TCPA 1990, ss 107 and 115 respectively. Reg 57(1) and (3) state that such notices take effect upon service.

on the future use of land by the use of planning agreements under Section 106 of the Town and Country Planning Act 1990 (TCPA). For existing users of land, Regulation 60 is also noteworthy as it has removed permitted development rights granted before as well as after the Habitats Regulations came into force on 30 October 1994. It now requires such operations only to be undertaken with the written approval of the LPA.[113] So far as 'other regimes' are concerned, an equal duty is placed on the Environment Agency to review all IPC authorizations and waste licences under Parts I and II of the EPA 1990 and all water discharge consents under the WRA 1991. A similar duty is placed upon the relevant local authorities in respect of all Part I EPA 1990 processes requiring authorizations.[114] These provisions are also intended to apply to local authority and Crown development.

The Habitats Regulations also place severe restrictions on the grant of planning **11.71** permission[115] for any development[116] which is likely to significantly[117] affect a classified SPA or an SAC[118] and which is not directly connected with or necessary for the management of that site.[119] In such circumstances, alternative solutions must be sought. In the event that no alternative solution can be found, planning

---

[113] Reg 60 has had the effect of removing permitted development rights granted on land within (and probably adjoining) European sites where the development so authorized (eg wildfowl shooting under 'the 28 day rule'—see Town and Country Planning (General Permitted Development) Order, Sch 2, Part 4, Class B) is likely to have a significant effect unless the written approval of the local planning authority has been obtained under reg 62. Loss of permitted development rights gives rise to a claim for compensation under the TCPA 1990, s 107, which, currently, have to be met directly from local authority finances. Unauthorized development should be addressed by way of enforcement action under Part VII of the TCPA 1990 and/or by court injunction.

[114] Ibid, regs 83, 84, and 85.

[115] Ibid, regs 48, 49, and 54. All applications for planning permission, whether submitted before or after 30 October 1994 which are granted after this date are affected including matters ordinarily covered by permitted development rights (see n 99 above). Reg 48 incorporates a similar requirement to notify the Conservation Bodies to that found in the Town and Country Planning (General Development Procedure) Order 1995, art. 10(1)(u), for development affecting SSSIs.

[116] Development includes 'permitted development'.

[117] In *ADT Auctions Ltd v SSETR* [2000] JPL 115 it was held that it was implicit in the wording of reg 48(5) that the adverse effect on the integrity of the site had to be a significant effect.

[118] Habitats Regulations reg 48(1)(a). Natural England, on whom the main review burden falls (along with the CCW in Wales), consider that the phrase 'likely to have significant effect' should be applied in the same way as under DoE Circular 2/99 in respect of environmental assessments be based on the precautionary principle and relate to the significant effects on why the SPA/SAC has been designated, which can sometimes be indirect (eg disturbance, changes in flight paths or in air, soil, or water quality) and not merely concern the extent of the land take. Many potentially difficult cases, so far, have been resolved by the use of conditions (see DoE Circular 11/95) or s 106 planning obligations. In so far as there exist any publications, attention is drawn to the guidance notes that were published by English Nature for local authorities. Habitats Regulations Guidance Note HRGN 1 is concerned with regulation 48 and 'the Appropriate Assessment'. HRGN 2 deals with reviews of existing planning permissions and other consents. HRGN 3 assists with the application of the test of 'Likely Significant Effect' found in regs 20, 24, 48, and 60, whilst HRGN 4 considers the issue of permitted development rights. Otherwise, advice should be sought directly from Natural England.

[119] Ibid, reg 48(1)(b).

permission must not be granted unless the proposed development has to be carried out for imperative reasons of overriding public interest, including those of a social or economic nature.[120] Necessary compensatory measures will also be required.[121]

11.72 Currently, the practical outworking of these provisions has mainly been in the area of planning policy and development control, and, in particular following ECJ ruling in the *Waddenzee* case,[122] a subsequent ruling that the UK had inadequately implemented the Habitats Directive[123] and consequent concerns by English Nature/Natural England over the impacts of future housing developments, particularly on the Thames Basins Heaths SPA. A fundamental issue, for which some judicial guidance has now been provided,[124] has been to confirm that mitigation or avoidance measures[125] can be taken into account at the outset when the competent authority[126] is considering whether an Appropriate Assessment[127] is required.

---

[120] Ibid, reg 49(1) and (5). See eg *Humber Sea Terminal Ltd v Secretary of State for Transport* [2005] EWHC 1289 (Admin) in respect of a Harbour Revision Order. Usually, the application will be 'called-in' and determined by the Secretary of State himself (following a public inquiry).

[121] Ibid, reg 53.

[122] Case C-127/02: *Landelijke Vereniging tot Behoud van de Waddenzee v Staaatssecretaris van Landbouw, Natuurbeheer en Visserij*; (judgment 7 September 2004). It concerned the renewal of annual licences, granted for limited periods over several years, by the Dutch Secretary of State for agriculture, nature conservation and fisheries for the mechanical fishing of cockles in the Waddenzee SPA. Although the Habitats Directive does not define the terms 'plan' or 'project' the ECJ was of the opinion that a new (appropriate) assessment was required for each licence both of the possibility of carrying on that activity and of the site where it should be carried out. This approach is based both on the precautionary principle, and, upon the basis that the integrity of the site should not be adversely affected. The Court also stressed how rigorous the appropriate assessment must be as a process, and, that the activity may only be authorized where no reasonable scientific doubt remains as to the absence of effects on the integrity of the site.

[123] In *Case C-6/04, Commission v United Kingdom* (judgment 2 October 2005). See n 35 above.

[124] *R (Hart DC) v SSCLG* [2008] EWHC 1204 (Admin).

[125] Under the direction of Natural England, through its (draft) Delivery Plan, some (but not all) of the affected SE local planning authorities have been opting for enhancement of existing or the creation of new recreational areas outside the TBHSPA, known as Suitable Accessible Natural Greenspace (SANG), through a 'roof tax'(ie standard form financial payments). A similar approach has been adopted in Dorset.

[126] In the planning context, this will be either the relevant local authority or, if an appeal or a 'called-in' application the Secretary of State. However, for other forms of "plan or project" it can be, for example, the Environment Agency (see *R (Friends of the Earth) v Environment Agency* [2004] Env LR 31).

[127] Reg 48(1). The *Hart* case also confirms that the Assessment does not need to be in a particular form, as with EIA. The case of *R (Lewis) v Redcar and Cleveland BC and Persimmon Homes Teeside Limited* [2008] EWCA Civ 746 also confirms the appropriateness of the planning case officer consulting with the relevant bodies (there, Natural England and RSPB) and reporting her opinion to the Committee.

National Nature Reserves (NNRs)

NNRs are areas of national,[128] and sometimes international, importance, which **11.73** are owned or leased by a UK conservation body, or by bodies approved by them, or are managed in accordance with Nature Reserve Agreements (NrAs)[129] with landowners and occupiers.[130] Areas of foreshore and tidal waters can be included within a Reserve.[131] All NNRs have SSSI designation and are subject to compliance with the Habitats Regulations.[132]

The NPACA[133] defines the word 'nature reserve' as meaning (a) land[134] managed **11.74** solely for a conservation purpose[135] or (b) land not only managed for a conservation purpose but also for a recreational purpose[136] if the latter does not compromise the management of the former. The term 'managed', in this context, embraces a number of forms of tenure including land owned or leased by an Appropriate Conservation Body[137] or other approved body (for example, a County Wildlife Trust) as well as land held under a management agreement (NrA). Because of the need to maintain a particular regime, control tends to be achieved either through purchase of the land, leasing it (usually for 21 years or more), or entering into an NrA with the owner.[138] Such an agreement, which is enforceable against successors in title, must be consistent with the purpose of the NNR designation. It may provide for the management of the land 'in such manner, the carrying out thereon of such work and the doing thereon of such other things as may be expedient for the purposes of the agreement',[139] and so can contain both restrictive and positive elements.

---

[128] WCA 1981, s 35(1) makes national importance a mandatory requirement

[129] NPACA, s 15(2)(a) defines a 'nature reserve agreement' as an agreement falling within NERCA 2006, s 7.

[130] NPACA, s 16(1) separately deals with NNR management agreements for Scotland and Wales but in the text above the term 'NrA' is used to cover all three geographical areas for ease of reference.

[131] Ibid, s 114(1); *Evans v Godber* [1974] 1 WLR 1317.

[132] Habitat Regs, reg 3(2).

[133] NPACA, s 15(1).

[134] Land is defined by s 114(1) to include land covered by water and as respects Scotland includes salmon fishings

[135] Ibid, s 15(2) states that land is managed for a conservation purpose if it is managed for the purpose of: (a) providing under suitable conditions and control special opportunities for the study of, and research into, matters relating to the fauna and flora of Great Britain and the physical conditions in which they live, and for the study of geological and physiographical features of special interest in the area; or (b) preserving flora and fauna or geological or physiographical features of special interest in the area or for both these purposes.

[136] Ibid s 15(3) states that land is managed for a recreational purpose if it is managed for the purpose of providing opportunities for the enjoyment of nature or for open-air recreation.

[137] NPACA, s 15A(1): Natural England, SNH and CCW.

[138] Where land covered by the NrA subsequently becomes an SAC (or SPA) then the NrA stands as the management agreement for the SAC for the purposes of reg 16 of the Habitats Regulations (see, reg 17).

[139] NERECA, s 7(2)(c); NAPACA, s 16(3)(a).

Whole or part payments, both to defray management costs and as compensation for restrictions, can also be made by the Appropriate Conservation Body.[140]

11.75 However, when compared with the regime for SSSIs, there are three practical differences which the additional NNR designation can bring. First, save by the use of compulsory purchase powers,[141] NNRs require the prior consent of every owner, lessee, and occupier before a regime of management can be achieved. Secondly, NNR designation is not in perpetuity and can be reviewed at the end of the NrA and/or lease period. Thirdly, the level of compensation does not depend on future profits foregone in the interests of conservation but may be fixed in advance for a significant period of years.[142] As the level of management that can be offered, for example through nature wardens or voluntary agencies, will have been agreed beforehand, this form of designation can be more beneficial for nature conservation purposes than a SSSI, where, by reason of the limitation of the power to make management agreements under Section 15(2) of the Countryside Act 1968 (the CA 1968), only these types of agreements can currently prevail for SSSIs.

11.76 The existence of an NrA allows the appropriate nature conservation body to introduce bye-laws to protect the NNR by, amongst other matters, prohibiting or restricting pest control, the shooting of birds within and without the boundaries, and providing for licensing of any of the controlled activities;[143] though these bye-laws cannot restrict the rights of owners, lessees, or occupiers any further nor interfere with any public rights of way or with statutory undertakers. Compensation is payable if the rights of others are interfered with as a result of the introduction of them.[144]

Marine Nature Reserves (MNRs)

11.77 MNRs are designated to conserve marine flora or fauna or geological or physiographical features or to allow the study of such features.[145] The designation may be applied to any areas of land covered (continuously or intermittently) by tidal waters or to parts of the sea up to the seaward limits of territorial waters.[146]

---

[140] Ibid s 7(2)(e); Ibid s 16(3)(c).

[141] NPACA, ss 17 and 18.

[142] See, further, DOE Circular 4/83 ('Financial Guidelines for Management Agreements').

[143] NPACA, s 20(2). The restriction on shooting under s 20(2)(c) is primarily used against wildfowlers.

[144] Ibid, s 20(3).

[145] There are three designated MNRs: Lundy Island (in England), Skomer Island (in Wales) under the WCA, s 36(1) and Strangford Lough (in Northern Ireland) under the Nature Conservation and Amenity Lands (Northern Ireland) Order 1985. Elsewhere, a number of voluntary marine nature reserves (vMNRs) have been established, on a non-statutory basis, by agreements between non-governmental organizations, stakeholders and user groups.

[146] WCA, s 36(1) and Sch 12.

An MNR can be made in respect of Crown Land but only with the consent of the appropriate authority.[147] The appropriate conservation body is required to manage the MNR both to comply with its designation and under the requirements of the Habitats Regulations.[148] It also has the power[149] to make bye-laws for the protection of the MNR, subject to the consent of the Secretary of State, except where they would interfere with the bye-law-making function already vested in another authority. This power includes permit schemes; but they cannot interfere with the right of passage of any vessel other than a pleasure boat, which, in turn, cannot be excluded from all of the MNR for all of the year.[150]

Sites of Special Scientific Interest (SSSIs)

All sites of national and international nature conservation importance on land are **11.78** notified as SSSIs.[151] They are the most widespread nature conservation designation within the UK.[152] While found in urban and suburban areas as well as the countryside, the power of designation under the WCA is limited to areas of land with a seaward limit of the low water mark of ordinary neap tides in England and Wales and of spring tides in Scotland.[153]

---

[147] Ibid, s 67(2).

[148] Reg 3(2).

[149] WCA, ss37(1),(2).

[150] WCA, s 37(3).

[151] SSSI designation is applicable in England, Scotland and Wales. Originally notified under the National Parks and Access to the Countryside Act 1949, SSSIs have been renotified under the Wildlife and Countryside Act 1981. Improved provisions for the protection and management of SSSIs were introduced by the Countryside and Rights of Way Act 2000 (in England under the WCA, ss 28(1) etc and by WCA, s 27AA applying WCA ss 28–34 to Wales) and the Nature Conservation (Scotland) Act 2004. The equivalent in Northern Ireland is known as an Area of Special Scientific Interest (ASSI), the notification process for which is under the Nature Conservation and Amenity Lands (Northern Ireland) 1985. Measures to improve ASSI protection and management are contained in the Environment (Northern Ireland) Order 2002.

[152] At the time of the first edition of this Chapter (2000) it was estimated that there were over 6,000 SSSIs covering in excess of 2,000,000 hectares equivalent to 8% of the total land area of Great Britain. In proportional terms, 65% lay within England, including Greater London, 20% in Scotland, and 15% in Wales. Natural England's statistics identify 4114 SSSIs covering 1,076,971 ha. in England, CCW's statistics identify 1,018 SSSIs covering 264,773 ha in Wales, SNH's statistics identify 1455 SSSIs covering 1,039,005 ha in Scotland while 257 ASSIs covering 94,602ha are present in Northern Ireland at June 2008.

[153] The SSSI/ASSI designation may extend into intertidal areas out to the jurisdictional limit of local planning authorities, generally Mean Low Water in England and Northern Ireland; Mean Low Water of Spring Tides in Scotland. In Wales, the limit is Mean Low Water for SSSIs notified before 2002, and, for more recent notifications, the limit of Lowest Astronomical Tides (LATs), where the features of interest extend down to LAT. There is no provision for marine SSSIs/ASSIs beyond low water mark, although boundaries sometimes extend more widely within estuaries and other enclosed waters. The legal presumption is that land below the high water mark is owned by the Crown (*Attorney-General v Emerson* [1891] AC 649) unless ownership of the foreshore (between High and Low Water marks) has passed to an individual by express grant or prescription (see eg *Tito v Waddell (No 2)* [1972] AC 425; *Earl of Lonsdale v Attorney-General* [1982] 1 WLR 887; and NPACA, s 114(1) for definition of 'land'. However, the jurisdiction of a local planning authority

11.79 The objectives of the system of SSSIs are to identify sites which support habitats and species of flora and fauna of particular ecological value, to notify those responsible for them of their value, and to provide a mechanism whereby changes to that land which might harm that value can be considered by the conservation authorities before they take place, thereby offering the opportunity for a range of controls to be agreed or imposed at that stage. The relevant geological or biological features are chosen for their 'naturalness, diversity, typicalness and size' although the sole requirement is that the Appropriate Conservation Body should be 'of the opinion that any area of land is of special interest by reason of any of its flora, fauna, or geological or geographical features'.[154]

11.80 JNCC's publication *Guidelines for Selection of Biological SSSIs*[155] provides a very helpful insight into the mechanics of site selection of typical sites within subregional areas.[156] The 'opinion' of the Conservation Body is, in itself, sufficient, so long as they are of the opinion that the statutory criteria are applied.[157] In practice, the decision is made by the Chairman and Council of that Agency in consultation with their officers. This system of designation has also been found to be compliant

---

is taken as including all the land, even though it may be covered by water (eg an estuary), which is within its identified local government boundaries including every accretion from the sea, whether natural or artificial, and any part of the seashore to the low water mark (see Local Government Act 1972 s 72(1)). In some cases, seaward boundaries are fixed by local Act but generally they are delineated by reference to the limit of medium tides. LGA 1972, s 71(1) enables reviews to take place.

[154] WCA, s 28(1) (Natural England); WCA, s 27AA applying s 28(1) to CCW. Equivalent provisions operate in Scotland and Northern Ireland.

[155] Guidance first given to staff by the NCC in 1989. Volume 1 (Parts A and B) of the *Guidelines* provides the rationale for SSSIs, the operational approach, and criteria for selection. Volume 2 (Part C) gives detailed guidelines for habitats and species groups.

[156] In *R (Western Power Distribution Investments Ltd) v Countryside Council for Wales* [2007] EWHC 50 (Admin), in relation to the selection of land forming two redundant reservoirs due to its habitat for waxcap mushrooms Collins J held that although JNCC's guidance suggested that preferably the best site should be identified this did not mean that only one site should be chosen as it might be desirable to notify more than one if more than one met the statutory criteria. Whilst finding that CCW's strategy was flawed, because it prevented notification of sites that would otherwise fulfil the criteria, he considered that in the instant case CCW had not in fact applied the strategy and the decision had not been based upon anything other than a genuine opinion that the statutory criteria were satisfied. The judge also observed that resource considerations could play no part in deciding whether a site met the criteria. If it did it had to be notified. CCW had not been obliged to make exhaustive enquiries about alternative sites before reaching its decision. If there are, indeed, better sites then denotification can take place. Furthermore, the notification did not necessarily preclude development at least in part of the reservoirs.

[157] As demonstrated, for example, in *R v Nature Conservancy Council, ex p London Brick Property Limited* [1996] JPL 227. There, the subject matter of the designation was a scarce species of water beetle found at a clay pit near Peterborough, Cambridgeshire. Maintenance of the habitat was dependent upon London Brick carrying out the positive operation of pumping water out of the pit to maintain current levels, which Section 28(1) could not require it to do. Whilst accepting that the site might cease to have its special qualities, May J held that as the site was not doomed, it was not necessary for the Council to be assured that the special interest would be reasonably assured in the future.

with the European Convention on Human Rights.[158] The extent of the boundaries of the SSSI is also a matter for the Appropriate Conservation Body.[159] The overspill or 'peripheral effects' of such occurrences have led Natural England to recommend the identification of 'buffer land' over which control is required to ensure full protection of the SSSI. Given that the legal status and restrictions under the WCA can only apply to the designated area the *Guidelines* encourage the decision to be made on the ability to draw a boundary which defines the limits of the ecological influence.[160] In consequence, it is suggested that 'boundaries-of-convenience' should be adopted, such as roads, railways, fences, and ownership limits.[161] On the other hand, the presence of artificial features; especially those of a recent or highly intrusive kind (for example, hill roads, pipes, dams, pylons, snow fences, and buildings) may be a valid reason for rejecting a site due to the effect on the 'appearance of naturalness' which may be an integral quality of a wildlife area.[162] In the end, the boundaries must be fixed so that the integrity or 'wholeness' of the SSSI can be defended to the extent that a minimum standard of

---

[158] In *R (Aggregate Industries UK Ltd) v English Nature* [2002] EWHC 908 (Admin) Forbes J held that the right to a fair hearing under Article 6 was engaged by the notification and confirmation process under WCA, s 28, and, that English Nature lacked the necessary objective appearance of impartiality and independence of a 'tribunal' to satisfy Article 6, the right of judicial review sufficed to meet the guarantees of Article 6 (the right to a fair hearing). Furthermore, the judge held that English Nature's decision-making process was to do with policy and/or expediency and did not require the safeguards provided by a quasi-judicial fact-finding process such as a public local inquiry. In *R (Fisher) v English Nature* [2004] EWCA Civ 663 the Court of Appeal was asked to consider a challenge to the lawfulness of a decision by English Nature to confirm a SSSI designation in respect of 13,335.70 hectares of intensely farmed arable land, the nesting territory of the stone-curlew, a European protected species of bird in respect of whom an SPA had also been made. At appeal, the issues were whether the SSSI designation and notification procedures had been appropriate and whether there had been a breach of the appellant's rights under Article 1 of the First Protocol. The appropriateness of a SSSI designation, and, over so extensive an area was, unsurprisingly, considered by the Court, to have been addressed by English Nature in a rational and fair manner of their statutory responsibilities. Accordingly, there had been no procedural irregularity and no disproportionate impact on the appellant's Article 1 First Protocol rights. See also *Trailer & Marina(Leven) Ltd v Secretary of State for the Environment, Food and Rural Affairs* [2007] EWCA Civ 1580 where it was held that the cessation of previous compensation payments under the WCA, prior to its amendment by the Countryside and Rights of Way Act 2000 (which introduced the new ss 28–28Q) did not offend Article 1, First Protocol Rights (the right to property)

[159] In *Sweet v Secretary of State for the Environment and the Nature Conservancy Council*, [1989] JPL 927 the applicant, a farmer on the Somerset Levels, challenged the validity of an order, contending that land which was not of national importance should not be included. In rejecting that submission, Schiemann J held that the whole of the land should be viewed as a single environment, thereby entitling the Secretary of State to bring all of it within the designation; although the judge did recognize the problems which could occur where, for instance, rare animals graze on vegetation in one field, which vegetation was dependent for its continued life on an aquifer one mile away.

[160] *Guidelines*, para 5.4.

[161] Ibid, para 5.9.

[162] Ibid, para 5.11.

'special interest' can be justified.[163] In consequence, the *Guidelines* list the following factors as being most likely to influence the extent of the SSSI:[164]

(1) The amount of diversity within the categories of vegetation, flora, and fauna.
(2) The degree of overlap between categories on a site.
(3) The geographical concentration or localization of categories.
(4) The vulnerability of features to decline through continuing adverse environmental influences.
(5) The international importance of any categories, leading to a need for greater than average representation.

11.81 The notification, usually in the form of a letter together with a map of the whole site, must be sent not only to every owner and occupier of the land but also to the relevant local authority and to the Secretary of State.[165] It must also specify 'the flora, fauna, or geological or physiographical features by reason of which the land is of special interest' and 'any operations appearing to the Council (of the Conservation Agency) to be likely to damage that flora or fauna or those features'.[166] This requirement is achieved by the service of two documents in addition to the form of notification. The first is a technical account of the flora, fauna, and physical features of the site in nature conservation terms with basic supporting data. The second document lists 'operations likely to damage' (OLDs), previously termed 'potentially damaging operations' (PDOs), which must be carefully controlled or prohibited, for example, ploughing.[167] The notification procedure also has to specify a time limit (not less than three months from the giving of the notice) within which (and the manner in which) representations or objections should be made to the Council (of the Conservation Body).[168] The Council (of that Body) is under no higher duty than to 'consider any representations or objections duly made',[169] following which the Body can either withdraw or confirm the notification (with or without modifications)[170] with a cut-off date of nine months

---

[163] Ibid, para 5.13.
[164] Ibid, para 8.2.
[165] WCA, s 28(1).
[166] Ibid, s 28(4).
[167] Catch-all categories like 'recreational and other activities likely to damage or disturb features of interest' are also included though their legality is questionable in view of the need to identify specific operations under s 28(4)(b). See also *Sweet v Secretary of State for the Environment* [1989] JPL 927 and the scope of the term 'operation' in n 165 below.
[168] WCA, s 28(3).
[169] Ibid.
[170] WCA, s 28E(1) gives immediate effect to such notifications immediately upon receipt (including any modifications) unless with the written consent of Natural England or under a management agreement or scheme (s 28E(3)). A limited right of appeal to the Secretary of State/NAW is provided under s 28F(1) where consent is refused under s 28E(3)(a) by Natural England/CCW. However, this may be determined by way of a public inquiry (s 28F(10)). Compensation provisions are provided under s 28M(1). Criminal offences and fine penalties

from the date when the notification was served on the Secretary of State.[171] The notification of additional land[172] and ability to enlarge the SSSI[173] follow similar procedures. The withdrawal of a notification is made through a power to denotify.[174]

The power to control the management of land, both designated as an SSSI **11.82** and any neighbouring property,[175] lies at the heart of this system of habitat conservation.[176] In recent years the Conservation Bodies have sought, increasingly, to achieve positive management rather than simply trying to prevent damage to land.[177] It is also noteworthy that about one-third of all SSSIs are owned by voluntary conservation organizations, including the RSPB, the County Wildlife Trusts, and the National Trust. Nonetheless, the system of statutory management notices continues to underpin the control system[178] with the ultimate power of compulsory purchase if either a management agreement cannot be concluded or is breached in such a way that the land is not being managed satisfactorily.[179] Nevertheless, in terms of a Public Service Agreement target set for Defra in 2002 that 95 percent of SSSI land, by area, should be in favourable condition by 2010, at the end of March 2008, 82.7 percent of land designated as SSSIs in England was judged by Natural England to be in a 'favourable or recovering condition'.

Limestone pavements

Limestone pavements are rare landscape features, fissured by natural erosion **11.83** and found mainly in the North of England.[180] Most already had or now have

---

of a contravention under s 28E(1) (or by a statutory undertaker under s 28G) are set out in s 28P. The Court is also given the additional power to order restoration of the SSI under s 31(1).

[171] Ibid, s28(5), (6).

[172] Ibid, s28B.

[173] Ibid, s28C.

[174] Ibid, s28D.

[175] Notification of the Conservation Agencies is required under the Town and Country Planning (General Development Procedure) Order 1995, art 10(1)(u), for any development affecting a SSSI. A consultation area may extend up to a maximum of two kilometres from the boundary of the SSSI (for wetlands). Article 4 Directions (under Town and Country Planning (General Permitted Development) Order 1995), removing permitted development rights (with the consent of the Secretary of State), are also encouraged for sites of 'particular importance'. The Water Industry Act 1991, s 156 places special duties on water and sewerage undertakers when disposing of any of their protected land within a SSSI, a National Park, or the Broads (to which the Norfolk and Suffolk Broads Act 1988, s 5 applies similar notification requirements in that area).

[176] CA, s 15; WCA, s 28J. Compensation provisions are provided under s 28M(2). See also Defra's *Guidelines on Management Agreement Payments and Other Related Matters.*

[177] WCA, s 28G.

[178] Ibid, s 28J (management schemes) and under s28K (the more draconian management notice), against which a right of appeal lies under s 28L(1) but which may be determined by way of a public inquiry (s 28L(12)).

[179] Ibid, s 28N.

[180] About 3,000 hectares of limestone pavements are recorded within the UK, of which 2,400 hectares are within England, 300 hectares in Scotland, 200 hectares in Northern Ireland, and 70 hectares in Wales.

SSSI designation. Nevertheless, specific powers were sought by the former Nature Conservancy Council, and introduced by Section 34 of the WCA, to protect them from damage done by stone removal for garden rockeries. The making of a Limestone Pavement Order (LPO) is a two-stage process commencing with notification of the county planning authority by the relevant Conservation Agency followed by the decision to make the LPO, which is then confirmed by the Secretary of State.[181] The effect of designation is to prohibit the removal or disturbance of limestone,[182] other than by the express grant of planning permission.[183] No compensation is payable for land designated under an LPO. An LPO can be made in respect of Crown Land but only with the consent of the appropriate authority.[184] As limestone pavements are identified as a priority habitat in Annex I of the Habitats Directive, they are also subject to the requirements of the Habitats Regulations.[185]

Areas of Special Protection (AOSPs)

11.84 These are not the same as SPAs. The power to establish 'Areas of Special Protection' for Birds (ie Bird Sanctuaries) is given to the Secretary of State under Section 3 of the WCA, a power previously available under the Protection of Birds Act 1954.[186] It enables orders to make unlawful not only prohibited acts under Section 1 of the WCA but also additional offences of disturbing nesting wild birds and their young not already specifically protected under Section 1(5), and can prohibit entry to the whole or part of any protected area, either generally or during specified periods. Furthermore, the general exceptions given by virtue of Section 2 of the WCA do not apply where the prohibitions that can be invoked under Section 3 in respect of an AOSP are in operation.[187] However, AOSPs can only be made with the consent of all owners and occupiers of the land in question, in consequence of which they have been little used in recent years despite the advantage that they have over SSSIs, in that they can be made over areas partly of land and partly of water. For example, an order was made extending the Gibraltar Point AOSP in 1995.[188] It is also noteworthy that virtually all the orders establishing Bird Sanctuaries prior to the WCA are still in force.[189]

---

[181] WCA, s 34(1) and (2) and Sch 11.
[182] Ibid, s 34(4). The maximum fine is currently £20,000 on summary conviction.
[183] Ibid, s 34(5).
[184] Ibid, s 67(2).
[185] Reg 3(2).
[186] Wildlife Refuges are equivalent to Areas of Special Protection in Northern Ireland under the Wildlife (Northern Ireland) Order 1985.
[187] See also para 12.104 below.
[188] SI 1995/2876. The original order for Gibraltar Point, Lincs was made in 1971.
[189] There are 35 AOSPs within the United Kingdom, of which 7 are in Scotland and the remainder within England and Wales.

Local Nature Reserves (LNRs)

Under Section 21 of the NPACA local authorities are given the same powers to   **11.85**
designate and manage local nature reserves (LNRs) as the Conservation Bodies
have in relation to NNRs.[190] A LNR is a habitat 'of local significance, which can
make a useful contribution both to nature conservation and to the opportunities
for the public to see, learn about, and enjoy wildlife'.[191] The statutory provisions
are the same as for NNRs, including powers of compulsory purchase as well as
management.[192] The local authority is required to consult the relevant Conservation Agency about the establishment of the LNR, who in turn can give practical
help and, in some circumstances, grants as well as advice on bye-laws to protect
the Reserve. These should follow a model available from and will require confirmation by the Secretary of State.[193]

Sites of Nature Conservation Interest or Importance (SNCIs and SINCs)

Whilst LNRs may sometimes be identified by LPAs as 'Sites of Nature Conservation   **11.86**
Importance' (SNCIs), County Wildlife Sites (CWSs), or 'Sites of Importance for
Nature Conservation' (SINCs)[194] they are not usually the same. Accordingly, care
should be taken regarding the assumptions that should be made. In essence, the
difference lies in the fact that a LNR is a formal legal designation whereas an SNCI
is one adopted by a LPA albeit for statutory plan-making purposes,[195] in consequence of which the latter may not have the same degree of legal protection.[196] The
nature conservation value may also be of much lesser significance. Ordinarily,
as part of the necessary preparation of development plans, the relevant LPA will

---

[190] NPACA, s 21(4) states 'the foregoing parts of this Act shall apply. . . with the substitution for
references to [the Nature Conservancy Council] of references to the local authority and as if references [in ss 16(1) and 17(1)] to the national interest included references to the interests of the locality'.
Local Government Act 1972, Sch 17, para 34 enables the power to make and manage LNRs to be
exercisable at both county and local council levels including the Broads Authority (under s 111A)
and every National Park Authority (EA 1995, Sch 9, para 3). The LNR equivalent in Northern
Ireland is known as Local Authority Nature Reserves (LANRs), the current power for which is found
in the Nature Conservation and Amenity Lands (NI) Order 1985.

[191] Ibid, para A22.

[192] NPACA, s 21(4) applying ss 16 and 17.

[193] There are currently 1280 LNRs in England covering nearly 40,000 hectares of land (JNCC,
June 2008). At the time of the first edition of this chapter there were 630 LNRs covering some
29,442 hectares (Sept 1999).

[194] The term SNCI tends to be the more commonly used acronym, eg in counties such as Dorset
and Surrey, along with CWS. However, certain counties (eg Hampshire) still adopt the term Site of
Importance for Nature Conservation (SINC).

[195] Part II of the TCPA 1990 and the new Local Development Plan system under Part 2 of the
Planning and Compulsory Purchase Act 2004.

[196] ie as a material consideration to which appropriate weight will be attached depending upon
the stage at which the plan may have reached and the degree of objections to the policy in question.
See further PPG 1 (Revised) (General Policy and Principles), paras 50–56.

have commissioned survey work from a specialist environmental consultancy and/or from local wildlife trusts and conservation groups.[197] The results of this work should normally be available for consideration and discussion with planning officers in relation to any proposal which may have an effect upon the SNCI.[198]

Environmentally Sensitive Areas (ESAs)

11.87 Although not a formal habitat designation, and now being phased out, Environmentally Sensitive Areas (ESAs) remain as areas of special landscape, wildlife, or historic interest which can be protected or enhanced by supporting specific agricultural practices.[199] ESAs were authorized by Council Regulation (EEC) No. 797/85 as a voluntary scheme and designated under the Agriculture Act 1986, following consultation with the relevant conservation bodies. They were implemented by way of agreements with landowners or occupiers having an interest in the agricultural land within or partly within the ESA.[200] They specify the requirements as to agricultural practices, methods, and operations and the installation or use of equipment, the period or minimum period for which such agreements must impose such requirements, provisions for any breaches, and the rates or maximum rate of compensation payable by government.[201] From March 2005 Defra introduced a new Environmental Stewardship Scheme[202] which now supersedes ESAs and Countryside Stewardship Schemes.

National Parks

11.88 Initially, ten National Parks within England and Wales were designated in the 1950s.[203] However, this number has been recently increased by the creation of the

---

[197] TCPA 1990, ss 11 (UDPs), 30 (local plans); PPG 12, paras 4.1–4.3.

[198] Local Government (Access to Information) Act 1985 introducing ss 100A to 100I to the Local Government Act 1972 (see further Chapter 5).

[199] See Defra website for a list of English ESAs. Please also refer to the First Edition of this book (paras. 12.90 and 12.91) for two other MAFF initiatives, Nitrate Sensitive Areas (NSAs) and Habitat Scheme Water Fringe Areas (WFAs).

[200] Agriculture Act 1986, s 18(3).

[201] Ibid, s 18(4).

[202] Entry Level Stewardship is open to all farmers and landowners, is intended to provide simple and effective land management. Organic Entry Level Stewardship is open to all farmers not receiving Organic Farming Scheme payments. Higher Level Stewardship which provides targeted environmental management and capital works plans that achieve a wide range of environmental benefits across the whole farm. See also n4 above for details of other UK agri-environmental schemes

[203] Peak District, Lake District, Snowdonia, Dartmoor, Pembrokeshire Coast, North York Moors, Yorkshire Dales, Exmoor, Northumberland, and Brecon Beacons were all designated between 1951 and 1957. The National Parks (Scotland) Act 2000 enabled the establishment of National Parks in Scotland. National Parks were established in Loch Lomond and The Trossachs in 2002 and in the Cairngorms in 2003. In Northern Ireland there is currently only a Ministerial commitment to work towards the establishment of national parks in Northern Ireland, and in particular towards a Mourne National Park, the designation power for which is currently found in the Nature Conservation and Amenity Lands (NI) Order 1985.

New Forest National Park in March 2005[204] and the current designation process[205] of the South Downs National Park, which is anticipated to be concluded in 2009.[206] The statutory purpose of National Parks is to conserve and enhance their natural beauty, wildlife, and cultural heritage and to promote opportunities for public understanding and enjoyment of their special qualities.[207] The National Park system fulfils a habitat conservation role, through its administration by a special National Park Authority for each Park, which has most of the functions of a local authority.[208] In addition, specific protection is given to moor and heath over 20 years old, which has not been used for agricultural purposes, by prohibiting agricultural or forestry operations without the consent of the Park Authority.[209] The Authority also has power to make bye-laws.[210] The Secretary of State for Transport can also make orders restricting traffic on any roads in the area.[211] Special rules also apply to the disposal of certain land by water and sewerage undertakers[212] as well as giving prior notification of works.[213]

---

[204] New Forest National Park Designation (Confirmation) Order 2005.

[205] South Downs National Park (Designation) Order 2002.

[206] See: <http://www.countryside.gov.uk/LAR/Landscape/DL/new_designations/SouthDowns/index.asp>

[207] NPACA, ss 5(1) and (2) (as amended).

[208] EA 1995, ss 65 etc; see especially NPACA, s 11A and TCPA 1990, s 4A for general duties and planning functions within the boundaries of the National Park. See also *R v Northumberland National Park Authority, ex p Secretary of State for Defence* [1998] 77 P&CR 120 confirming the planning jurisdiction of the Park Authority solely within the boundaries of the National Park. Note also MPS 1 (*Planning and Minerals*) (2006), para 14 for severe restrictions on mineral extraction. Permitted development rights are restricted not only to land within but also adjoining the administrative area of the NPA by reason of the Town and Country Planning (Permitted Development) Order 1995, art 1(5) applying restrictions to Sch 2, Parts 1, 8, 17, 24, 25 and art 1(6) extending those restrictions to Sch 2, Part 6, Class A (agricultural development) and Part 7, Class A (forestry development). Grants are available under s 44 of the WCA.

[209] WCA, s 42(3) and (4), in effect, provides a procedure by which the applicant gives written notification to the NPA of the intended operation. If the NPA issues no decision within three months the work may be carried out. Alternatively, if the NPA refuses consent it remains unlawful to carry out the work for a period of 12 months from the date of notification, the purpose of the postponement being to enable the NPA to offer a management agreement to the applicant under s 39 of the WCA which, in turn, would contain compensation payments for the restrictions the NPA would wish to have imposed. An arbitration provision is provided by s 50(3) of the WCA. Unlawful conversion of the land to agriculture within the 20-year period is to be ignored (s 42(7)). Punishment is by fine, on summary conviction, to the maximum (currently £20,000), and unlimited on indictment (s 42(5)).

[210] NPACA, s 90(1). See also *R v Dyfed County Council, ex p Manson* [1995] Env LR 83 concerning an unsuccessful judicial review application to quash bye-laws made under the Act in respect of the Pembrokeshire Coast National Park.

[211] Road Traffic Regulation Act 1984, s 22.

[212] WIA 1991, s 156.

[213] WIA 1991, s 4, WRA 1991, s 17, LDA 1991, s 13.

The Norfolk and Suffolk broads

11.89 The Broads is an area comprising about 111 square miles[214] embracing 42 'broads'
of some 2,000 acres and 124 miles of navigable waterway. Due to their unique
requirements they were eventually given equal status to that of a National Park in
1988.[215] The Broads Authority[216] exercises similar functions to those of a National
Park Authority save that its general duties extend to protecting the interest of navigation in addition to conserving and enhancing the natural beauty of the Broads
and promoting its enjoyment by the public.[217] The Broads Authority's map,
reviewable every five years, identifies those areas of the Broads whose natural
beauty it is particularly important to conserve, in consultation with Natural
England and other relevant bodies.[218] A procedure, similar to that under Sections
28 and 42 of the WCA, requires prior written notice to be given to the Broads
Authority of certain potentially harmful operations in certain designated areas

---

[214] The area covers land within the valleys of the Rivers Bure, Ant, Thurne, and Yare within
Norfolk and the Waveney in the Norfolk/Suffolk border valley. The original broads were created
by peat working during the medieval ages (esp the thirteenth century), which became flooded as a
result of a rise in sea levels.

[215] Norfolk and Suffolk Broads Act 1988.

[216] Ibid, s 1. The Broads Authority (BA) consists of a total of 35 members, of which there are 18
local authority members (drawn from the two county councils (six) and two each from the six local
councils including Norwich City and Great Yarmouth Borough Councils), 15 members appointed
respectively by the Countryside Commission (two), Natural England (one), the Great Yarmouth
Port and Haven Commissioners (two), the Environment Agency (formerly the NRA) (one), and by
the Secretary of State (nine), plus two members appointed by the BA from the membership of the
Navigation Committee (separately created under s 9) (s 1(1)). The BA is financed by charges made
for navigation, grants, and by a levy imposed on the eight local authorities. It is the sole district planning authority and responsible for its own local plan (known as the 'Broads Plan'). Planning applications are submitted to the district council in whose area the proposed development lies, which passes
applications to the BA for decision (except minerals and waste applications which are determined by
the appropriate county council). Permitted development rights are restricted not only to land within
but also adjoining the administrative area of the BA by reason of the Town and Country Planning
(Permitted Development) Order 1995, art 1(5) applying restrictions to Sch 2, Parts 1, 8, 17, 24, 25
and art 1(6) extending those restrictions to Sch 2, Part 6, Class A (agricultural development) and
Part 7, Class A (forestry development).

[217] Ibid, s 4(1).

[218] Ibid, s 5(1)(a) identifies areas of grazing marsh, fen marsh, reed bed, or broad-leaved woodland. S 5(2), in effect, provides a very similar procedure to that under s 42(3) and (4) of the WCA by
which the applicant gives written notification to the BA of the intended operation. If the BA issues
no decision within three months the work may be carried out. Alternatively, if the BA refuses consent it remains unlawful to carry out the work for a period of 12 months from the date of notification, the purpose of the postponement being to enable the BA to offer a management agreement to
the applicant under s 39 of the WCA (extended by para 31(2) of Sch 3 to the WCA) which, in turn,
would contain compensation payments for the restrictions the BA would wish to have imposed. An
arbitration provision is provided by s 50(3) of the WCA. Punishment for unlawful operations is by
fine, on summary conviction, to the maximum (currently £20,000), and unlimited on indictment
(s 42(5)).

with certain default provisions if its consent is not given within three months of such notification.[219] Powers to make bye-laws are also given to the Authority.[220]

Areas of Outstanding Natural Beauty (AONBs)

As the primary objective of designating AONBs is to conserve the natural beauty **11.90** of the landscape, the effect of designation on nature conservation is purely secondary.[221] AONBs are designated by the same process as National Parks under the NPACA.[222] There are currently 37 AONBs in England and Wales.[223] Once created, Natural England and the Countryside Council for Wales must be consulted by the LPA both on the preparation of development plans and on the making of arrangements for public access to land for recreation.[224] The local authority is also given the power to withdraw permitted development rights[225] as well as to make bye-laws for any of its own land within the AONB.[226] The Secretary of State for Transport can also make orders restricting traffic on any roads in the area.[227] Special rules also apply to the disposal of certain land by water and sewerage undertakers.[228]

Green Belts

The designation and maintenance of Green Belts has been a long-established part **11.91** of the UK planning system, upheld by the courts on numerous occasions, but one which has no substantive statutory foundation.[229] Their primary function is to

---

[219] Norfolk and Suffolk Broads Act 1988, ss 6 and 24, enforceable by fine on summary conviction.

[220] Ibid, s 24.

[221] In Northern Ireland AONBs were designated under the Nature Conservation and Amenity Lands Order (Northern Ireland) 1985. In Scotland, National Scenic Areas (NSAs) are broadly equivalent to AONBs of which there are currently 40 land-based NSAs and one marine area. Relevant Scottish planning policy is set out in NPPG14. Additionally, provision is made in Scotland for Natural Heritage Areas are intended to be special large discrete areas of the countryside of outstanding natural heritage value containing a wide range of nature conservation and landscape interests where integrated management will be encouraged taking account of recreational use and wider socio-economic activities. Powers to designate NHAs are set out in the Natural Heritage (Scotland) Act 1991 though none, to date, have been designated.

[222] NPACA, s 87.

[223] England and Wales.

[224] Ibid, s 88(1).

[225] Town and Country Planning (Permitted Development) Order 1995, Art 1(5)(b) applying restrictions to Sch 2, Parts 1, 8, 17, 24, 25.

[226] NPACA, s 90(1).

[227] Road Traffic Regulation Act 1984, s 22.

[228] See n 212 above.

[229] The Metropolitan Green Belt was established by the Green Belt (London and Home Counties) Act 1938, an enactment which still remains in force. Green belt policy over development control, which effectively preserves the Metropolitan Green Belt, is applied through statutory development plans, strategically through Structure Plans, and locally through district/borough local plans. Unitary development plans apply to areas within Greater London. The same policy

maintain an area of openness (ie, free of built development) around major conurbations by checking the sprawl of large built-up areas, safeguarding the countryside from further encroachment, preventing towns from merging, to preserve the character of historic towns, and assisting in urban regeneration.[230] This policy objective has been achieved through a strict policy of planning restraint requiring boundaries, once set, to be fixed and permanent, save in exceptional circumstances, as well as recognizable.[231] As the intention is to preserve openness, both policy and case law recognize a presumption against inappropriate development save in very special circumstances.[232] Green Belts can provide opportunities for outdoor sport and recreation as well as retaining and enhancing attractive landscapes, but their primary intention is to protect the countryside.[233] Woodland, forestry, and related land management which does not rely on built development is now increasingly encouraged.[234] Accordingly, their nature conservation role is a useful though secondary function. As a result of development plan approvals, they cover about 12% of England.[235]

Country Parks

11.92 Country Parks are statutorily declared and managed by local authorities.[236] They are intended, primarily, for recreation and leisure opportunities close to population centres so do not, necessarily, have any nature conservation importance. Nevertheless, many lie within or include areas of semi-natural habitat and so can

---

framework applies elsewhere within England where Green Belts are found (eg within south-east Dorset, the West Midlands, and around Greater Manchester). DoE *Planning Policy Guidance Note PPG 2 (Green Belts)* (1995) includes a map identifying all 14 areas which, in September 1993, covered a total area of 1,555,700 hectares. Equivalent advice is found in Planning Policy Wales (2002), paras 2.6.1 etc and in Scotland in SPP21 (2006).

[230] PPG 2, paras 1.4–1.7. In essence, green belt policy identifies certain limited types of new development (eg agriculture, forestry, and certain forms of outdoor sport) which are appropriate development. Buildings must also be essential in terms of size and function (eg a clubhouse). Otherwise, very special circumstances must be established (PPG 2, paras 3.1–3.5). See also *Pehrsson v Secretary of State for the Environment* [1990] JPL 764. Reuse is permitted but again in limited circumstances, including redevelopment of major developed sites (eg large hospitals and other institutions).

[231] Ibid, paras 2.6–2.9 and *Carpets of Worth v Wyre Forest District Council*, [1992] 62 P&CR 334.

[232] Ibid, para 3.1 etc and *Pehrsson v Secretary of State for the Environment*, ante.

[233] Ibid, paras 1.4 and 1.6.

[234] Ibid, para 3.16 and Annex A, paras A1 and A2.

[235] Ibid, para 1.3 and map.

[236] In England and Wales under the Countryside Act 1968, s 7; in Scotland under the Countryside (Scotland) Act 1967; but in Northern Ireland Country Parks exist as a non-statutory designation. It should also be noted that, in addition, in Scotland, local authorities, with the approval of the Scottish Government, have the power to designate Regional Parks under the Wildlife and Countryside (Scotland) Act 1981. These are extensive areas of the countryside where existing land uses continue but are managed by agreement with the landowners to allow for public access and informal recreation and to protect local landscapes.

form a valuable network of locations at which informal recreation and the natural environment can coexist.

E. Species Protection

Introduction

Currently, Part I of the Wildlife and Countryside Act 1981 (WCA) provides the **11.93** single most important statutory protection for wildlife and plants. It puts into effect the UK's international obligations under the Bern Convention and the Wild Birds Directive. In summary, it creates a large number of offences relating to the killing and taking of wild birds, other animals, and plants and relies upon the use of Schedules to identify the categories of species which enjoy differing levels of protection. The Secretary of State is given wide powers, by way of statutory instrument, to alter the contents of these Schedules and other aspects of this legislation.[237] The GB Conservation Bodies, acting jointly through the JNCC, are specifically required to review the Schedules every five years but may amend it at any time. [238] In addition, the Habitats Regulations now give additional protection to certain wild animals and plants through the status of 'European protected species'. The Wild Mammals (Protection) Act 1996 makes it an offence to commit a wide range of cruel acts against any wild mammal with intent to inflict unnecessary suffering. Separate specific legislation is used to protect and conserve badgers, deer, seals, freshwater and marine fish, and endangered species. The protection and conservation of trees and woodland arises through the Forestry Act 1967 and

---

[237] WCA, s 22. The Schedules are divided as follows: Sch ZA1 (Birds Which Re-Use Their Nests); Sch 1: Birds Protected By Special Penalties (Part I: At All Times; Part II: During The Close Season); Sch 2: Birds Which May Be Killed Or Taken (Part I: Outside the Close Season; Part II: By Authorised Persons At All Times); Sch 3: Birds Which May Be Sold (Part I: Alive At All Times If Ringed And Bred In Captivity; Part II: Dead At All Times); Sch 4: Birds Which Must Be Registered If Kept In Captivity; Sch 5: Animals Which Are Protected; Sch 6: Animals Which May Not Be Killed Or Taken By Certain Methods; Sch 7: Protection of Certain Mammals (through amendments to certain enactments); Sch 8: Plants Which Are Protected; Sch 9 (Part I: Animals Which Are Established In The Wild; Part II: Plants [which should not be allowed to grow in the wild]). The following variations to the Schedules have been made to date:

SI 1988/288—amended Schs 5 and 8; SI 1989/906—amended Sch 5; SI 1991/367—amended Sch 5; SI 1992/320—amended Sch 9; SI 1992/2350—amended Schs 5 and 8; SI 1992/2674—amended Sch 9; SI 1992/3010—amended Schs 2 and 3; SI 1994/1151—amended Sch 4; SI 1997/226—amended Sch 9; SI 1998/878—amended Schs 5 and 8; SI 188/288—amended Schs 5 and 8; SI 2006/1382 – which introduced Sch ZA1 inserted by NERCA 2006, s 47(3); SI 2007/1843—amended Schs 5 and 8.

[238] WCA, s 24(1) (as amended).

Part VIII of the Town and Country Planning Act 1990. Important hedgerows were made the subject of separate Regulations in June 1997.[239]

Evaluation procedures

11.94 The degree of rarity of a particular animal or plant species is now classified subject to nationally recognized criteria through what is known as the 'Red Data List' system. This is a method of classifying the extinction risk and conservation status of animal and plant species across the planet developed by the International Union for the Conservation of Nature and Natural Resources (IUCN).[240] As a result of the involvement of the JNCC and other Conservation organizations, standard criteria have been applied to assess the national importance of British species, thus allowing the ecological significance of species records to be assessed.[241] The Red List system classifies listed species as Extinct (EX), Extinct in the Wild (EW), Critically Endangered (CR), Endangered (EN), Vulnerable (VU), Near Threatened (NT), Least Concern (LC), Data Deficient (DD), and Not Evaluated (NE). In evaluating bird populations, a complementary system published by the RSPB is also in use. This red list identifies birds whose population or range has rapidly declined recently or historically together with those of global conservation concern. The current list arose from initiatives taken, in 1996, by the leading non-governmental bird conservation organizations which agreed the priorities for bird conservation for the whole of the UK including the Channel Islands and the Isle of Man. The current list (for the period 2002–2007) of 247 regularly occurring species is divided into three sections: red, amber, and green. The red list species are those of greatest conservation concern and deserve urgent, effective action. Currently, 40 species are listed. Amber list species are of medium conservation concern. It includes birds whose populations are in moderate decline, rare breeders, internationally important and localized species, and those of an unfavourable conservation status in Europe. The list currently numbers 121 species. Of all other species which are monitored, some 86 are on the green list. With regard to native plants, species which are threatened are included in the Red Data List 2005. A species is listed as CR where its population comprises <50 mature individuals, as EN where its populations comprises <250 mature individuals, and as VU where its population comprises <1000 individuals or it has been recorded from five or fewer locations. Invertebrates considered to occur in 100 or fewer 10-km squares are further classified as nationally scarce (Notable), divided into Notable A (16–30 squares) and Notable B (31–100 squares).

---

[239] See Hedgerows Regulations 1997 made under the EA 1995, s 97 (paras 12.134–12.136 below).

[240] See further para 11.24 above.

[241] See, eg, the application of RDB criteria in the Hedgerow Regulations, Sch 1, Part II, paras 6(3)(B), 6(4).

Standard practices for the evaluation of ecological interest are usually applied by **11.95** reference to the criteria set out by D A Ratcliffe, in 1977, in his book *A Nature Conservation Review*[242] and as further extended by the NCC (now Natural England and its counterparts in Wales and Scotland) in 1989 through its *Guidelines for Selection of Biological SSSIs*.[243] Primary criteria used for the evaluation of a site are size, diversity, naturalness, rarity, fragility, and typicalness. Secondary criteria are considered to be recorded history, position in an ecological or geographical unit, potential value, and intrinsic appeal and are only noted if they make a special contribution to the interest in a particular area. Scales of comparison vary from the international to the context of the local area, which is usually taken as being the relevant county rather than district administrative area save where this is an urban one, for example, Greater London. However, some criteria are absolute. For example, an ancient woodland[244] is fragile, irrespective of whether it is being considered in a local or international context. Further guidance on valuing ecological receptors (species and habitats) is set out within the Institute of Ecology and Environmental Management's (IEEM) 'Guidelines for Ecological Impact Assessment' July 2006.

Conservation of birds

Part I of the WCA concerns the protection of birds and their eggs. Section 1(1) **11.96** makes it an offence for any person intentionally to do any of the following: to kill, injure, or take any wild bird; to take, damage, or destroy the nest of a wild bird while it is in use or being built; or to take or destroy the egg of any wild bird. Section 27(1) of the WCA defines a 'a wild bird' as 'any bird of a kind ordinarily resident in or a visitor to Great Britain in a wild state but does not include poultry (ie domestic fowls, geese, ducks, guinea fowl, pigeons, quails, and turkeys) nor any game bird (ie pheasant, partridge, grouse, (moor game), black (or heath) game, and ptarmigan)'. There are currently 79 species of birds listed in Part I of Schedule 1 (for example, avocets, kingfishers, and woodlarks).

---

[242] Cambridge University Press.

[243] See also para 11.78 above. Reference should also be made to the NCC's *Handbook for Phase 1 Habitat Survey: A Technique for Environmental Audit* (1989).

[244] Ancient woodland sites are those identified by Natural England as having been woodland since at least the seventeenth century and possibly longer. They are valued for their rich and characteristic flora and fauna, particularly in view of their decline in the last 50 years. Their area and distribution are documented in Ancient Woodland Inventories produced by Natural England. See also Oliver Rackham, *Ancient Woodland—Its History, Vegetation and Uses in England* (Edward Arnold, London, 1980).

11.97 Offences involving these birds attract 'special penalties',[245] as do offences committed in the close season (ie from 1 February to 31 August, for most species)[246] relating to birds on Part II of the Schedule (ie, goldeneye, greylag geese in certain parts of Scotland, and pintails). Some exceptions are permitted by Section 2 to allow the shooting of the species listed in Part I of Schedule 2 outside the close season (for example coots, mallards, and woodcocks). Part II of this Schedule permits 'killing or taking' of other species (for example crows, magpies, starlings, and woodpigeons) at all times but only by 'authorized persons', which is defined by the WCA[247] as including (a) the owner or occupier of the land on which the authorized action is taking place, or any person authorized by him, (b) any person authorized in writing by the local authority for that area, (c) any person authorized in writing by the relevant Conservation Body, the Environment Agency, statutory water undertakers, a Scottish district fisheries board, or a local fishery committee under the Sea Fisheries Regulation Act 1966 (in England and Wales). The WCA expressly excludes from the definition 'wild bird' one which is shown to have been bred in captivity.[248] On the other hand, Section 14 expressly prohibits the release or permitted escape into the wild of any animal which is of a kind not ordinarily resident in and is not a regular visitor to Great Britain in a wild state or is included in Part I of Schedule 9. Among the birds listed are included the Canada goose, the white-tailed eagle, and the ruddy duck.

11.98 The word 'take' means the capturing of a live wild bird;[249] but it does not matter whether the bird is alive or dead, in whole or in part, to be guilty of the offence of being 'in possession or control' under Section 1(2)(a) of the WCA. The offence is also committed by possessing or controlling an egg of a wild bird or part of such an egg.[250] Furthermore, anything calculated to prevent the hatching of an egg is included within the meaning of 'destroying' eggs.[251] Intentionally disturbing a wild bird, listed in Part I of Schedule 1, whilst it is building a nest or is in, on, or near a nest containing eggs or young, or the intentional disturbance of the dependent young of that bird, also constitutes an offence under Section 1(5).

11.99 With the exceptions noted below, all these offences are ones of strict liability, that is, it is unnecessary for the prosecution to prove that the accused knew that the

---

[245] A fine not exceeding level 5 on the standard scale (currently £20,000). Other offences under ss 1–8 are subject to a maximum fine of level 3 (£5,000).

[246] WCA s 2(4).

[247] Ibid, s 27(1).

[248] Ibid, s 1(6).

[249] *Robinson v Everett* [1988] Crim LR 699, which concerned possession of a stuffed and mounted golden eagle.

[250] WCA s 1(2)(b).

[251] Ibid, s 27(1) within the interpretation of the word 'destroy'.

bird is a wild bird within the WCA.[252] However, a number of statutory defences are available. Section 1(3) provides that a person in possession of the bird or egg is not guilty if he can show that that bird or egg had not been killed or taken or it had been killed or taken otherwise than in contravention of the WCA or its statutory predecessors (the Protection of Birds Acts 1954 to 1967). A defence is also available, under the same section, if it can be shown that the bird or egg had, at some earlier stage, been sold otherwise than in contravention of the WCA or its statutory predecessors. Under Section 4, the taking of a disabled bird in order to tend and release it is excluded, along with mercy killing of a seriously disabled bird with no reasonable chance of recovery, provided that, in both cases, the original injury was not the result of that person's unlawful act.[253] Acts which are the incidental result of a lawful operation and which could not reasonably have been avoided are also excluded, for example, the destruction of nests when felling woodland.[254] Further allowances are made for authorized persons if they can show that their action was necessary for the purpose of preserving public health, public safety, or air safety, or preventing the spread of disease or serious damage to livestock, crops, fruit, growing timber, or fisheries.[255] Provided the action was carried out by licence, specific exemptions are given by Section 16(1) (for example, scientific and educational purposes, taxidermy, and photography). An express exemption is also made for the gathering, for human consumption, of gannets on Sula Sgeir, gulls' eggs, and, in the case of lapwings, eggs before 15 April each year.[256] Furthermore, no offence[257] is committed if the act in question has been required by Ministers in the exercise of their powers relating to agricultural pest control or is done under the Animal Health Act 1981 or an order made under it.[258]

The power to establish 'Areas of Special Protection' for Birds (AOSPs) under Section 3 has already been considered within the section under Habitat Conservation above.[259] While some categories of wild birds are given added protection by the WCA with others protected only during a close season, all 'pest' species are, in practice, deprived of general protection; but, in all cases, the methods by which birds can be taken or killed are strictly controlled. Section 5(1) not only provides a comprehensive list of prohibited practices, the use of which attracts a 'special penalty',[260] but also the additional offence of knowingly causing or **11.100**

---

[252] *Kirkland v Robinson* [1987] Crim LR 643.
[253] WCA, s 4(2)(a), (b).
[254] Ibid, s 4(2)(c).
[255] Ibid, s 4(3).
[256] Ibid, s 16(2).
[257] Ibid, s 4(1).
[258] Agriculture Act 1947, s 98.
[259] See para 11.84 above.
[260] See n 246 above.

permitting any of the prohibited acts.[261] These include mechanical and electrical traps, poisons, stupefying drugs, birdlime, bows and crossbows, explosives, automatic and semi-automatic weapons, very large shotguns, spotlights, night sights, artificial lighting, dazzling devices, gas, smoke, chemical wetting agents, sound recordings (of birds or animals), live decoys, and mechanically propelled vehicles.[262] A statutory defence is provided[263] if it can be shown that the prohibited device or 'article' was used in the interests of public health, agriculture, forestry, fisheries, or nature conservation. Furthermore, 'authorized persons' can use cage-traps or nets to take the species listed in Part II of Schedule 2 (for example crows, magpies, and woodpigeons). They can also use nets for taking wild ducks, by means of certain forms of duck decoy, and cage-traps to take game birds solely for breeding.[264]

11.101   Section 6 regulates the sale of live or dead wild birds or their eggs. A live bird is treated as any bird, one of whose parents was a wild bird, as described.[265] The section provides that the sale, offer, or exposure for sale of any live birds (except those listed in Part I of Schedule 3, for example blackbirds, goldfinches, and yellowhammers, if ringed and bred in captivity), their eggs, or parts of their eggs (for example blown eggs) is an offence, together with the publication of any advertisements 'likely to be understood as conveying' that the person concerned buys or sells such things or intends so to do.[266] The same acts are made offences by Section 6(2), other than with regard to some game.[267] It is also an offence to exhibit live wild birds (other than ones within Part I of Schedule 3) or a live wild bird one of whose parents was wild.[268] The 'special penalty' fine applies to Schedule 1 birds in this context.[269]

11.102   In respect of captive birds, Section 7(1) requires the registration and ringing of all species listed in Schedule 4 which include, by way of example, buntings, falcons,

---

[261]   As added by the Wildlife and Countryside (Amendment) Act 1991.
[262]   'Vehicle' includes aircraft, hovercraft, and boats (s 27(1)).
[263]   WCA, s 5(4).
[264]   Ibid, s 5(5).
[265]   Ibid, s 6(3)(b). Any reference in s 6 to any bird included in Sch 3, Part I, includes any bird bred in captivity which has been ringed or marked under regulations made under this subsection, currently the Wildlife and Countryside (Ringing of Certain Birds) Regulations 1982 (SI 1982/1220).
[266]   Ibid, s 6(1).
[267]   Ibid, s 6(2) and (8) create the power to make regulations to secure that no person shall become or remain registered within certain periods of time. These are currently found in the Wildlife and Countryside (Registration to Sell etc Certain Dead Birds) (Amendment) Regulations 1982 (SI 1982/1219) (amended by SI 1991/479). The Birds (Registration Charges) Act 1997, introducing a new s 6(8A), also now gives the Secretary of State the power to charge a reasonable sum (if any) for any registration effected under the Regulations.
[268]   Ibid, s 6(3).
[269]   Ibid, s 6(4) and n 246 above.

and warblers.[270] Conviction of any offence under Part I of the WCA automatically debars the offender from keeping such birds for at least three years,[271] along with any person who 'knowingly' disposes of such a bird to him.[272] Section 8(1) requires a captive bird to be kept in a cage or receptacle of sufficient height, length, or breadth to permit it to stretch its wings freely. This provision does not apply to poultry nor the transporting of the bird, showing for public exhibition or competition (for a maximum aggregate period of 72 hours), or whilst the bird is undergoing veterinary examination.[273] Failure so to do is an offence carrying the 'special penalty'.[274] Furthermore, it is an offence for any person involved in the release of any captive bird, which term includes game birds and other birds that can be shot by 'authorized persons' (under Part II of Schedule 2), to permit such release for the purposes of being shot immediately after its liberation.[275]

Protection of other wild animals

A 'wild animal' is defined by Section 27(1) of the WCA as 'any animal (other than a bird) which is or (before it was killed or taken) was living wild'. Schedule 5 lists nearly 100 animals including adders, all species of bats, dolphins, porpoises, and whales, red squirrels, the common frog, and common toad, together with the great-crested newt, the natterjack toad, and the sand lizard. A number of these species are also protected under the Habitats Directive and the Habitats Regulations,[276] though the great-crested newt, because of its rarity in Europe (as a whole) under the Bern Convention rather than in the UK, has gained a notoriety beyond that which it perhaps deserves. By Section 27(3) any reference in Part I to an animal of any kind includes, unless the context otherwise requires, a reference to an egg, larva, pupa, or other immature stage of an animal of that kind. As certain types of beetle, butterfly, and moth are included within the Schedule the term necessarily includes the eggs of these insects.

11.103

Section 9 makes it an offence, subject to the statutory defences provided,[277] intentionally to kill, injure, or take a wild animal listed in Schedule 5[278] or to possess or control any live or dead animal (or any part of or anything derived from such animal)

11.104

---

[270] Ibid, s 7(1) gives the power to make regulations. Currently, these are the Wildlife and Countryside (Registration and Ringing of Certain Captive Birds) Regulations 1982 (SI 1982/1221). The Birds (Registration Charges) Act 1997 adds a new s 7(2A) giving the additional power to charge for such registrations.

[271] Ibid, s 7(3)—five years from conviction for a 'special penalty' offence; otherwise three years.

[272] Ibid, s 7(4).

[273] Ibid, s 8(2).

[274] Ibid, s 8(1) and n 246 above.

[275] Ibid, s 8(3).

[276] See n283 below.

[277] Ibid, s 9(1).

[278] Ibid, ss 9(3), 10.

listed in Schedule 5.[279] It is also an offence to damage, destroy, or obstruct access to any 'structure or place' which any such animal uses for shelter or protection, or to disturb it when it uses such a structure or place.[280] However, the use of a 'structure or place' for 'shelter or protection' will vary from animal to animal and particular seasons. Bat colonies typically have a number of roosts whilst amphibians require water and/or land depending on the time of year. Accordingly, these phrases must be understood as referring to habitual uses. Trade in all but two species[281] is forbidden under Section 9(5). Section 14ZA(1) also makes it a criminal offence to offer or expose for sale invasive non-native species of animals.

11.105   However, the actual degree of legal protection that is given to individual animals varies significantly. For example, the British butterflies listed in Schedule 5 are protected under all parts of Section 9(1). On the other hand, the only protection that is given, under Section 9(5), to the common frog or common toad is in the prohibition of trading in these species. Further, but still only partial, protection is given to the adder, grass snake, common lizard, and slow-worm in that they can lawfully be taken but cannot be killed, injured, or traded. The list of protected animals under Schedule 5 can best be described as 'fluid', which should be checked with the relevant devolved government body directly before any potentially unlawful action is taken.[282] It should also be borne in mind that Section 14(1) expressly prohibits the release or permitted escape into the wild of any non-native species of animal or one included in Part I of Schedule 9 (for example, the muntjac, the black rat, and the grey squirrel).

11.106   Section 10 mirrors Section 4 in setting out certain statutory exemptions to the offences under Section 9. Thus, Section 10(1) permits actions to be taken to meet ministerial requirements in respect of preventing damage to agriculture and the spread of disease, and Section 10(3) enables mercy killing of disabled animals along with acts which were 'the incidental result of a lawful operation and could not reasonably have been avoided', ie, genuine accidents (subject to the provisions of Section 10(5)). 'Authorized persons'[283] do not commit an offence when they kill or injure a wild animal to prevent serious damage to livestock, fodder, crops, timber, or to any other form of property or to fisheries.[284] However, it should be noted that Section 10(6), which has no counterpart in Section 4, disallows the statutory defence under Section 10(4) where it had become apparent, previously,

---

[279]   Ibid, s 9(2). Following *Robinson v Everett* (above) the possession of a stuffed wild animal (listed under Sch 5) or its skin would be an offence unless it could be shown that it had not been killed or sold in breach of the relevant provisions.

[280]   Ibid, s 9(4).

[281]   The freshwater pearl mussel and the mire pill beetle.

[282]   See, again n 236 above.

[283]   See n 247 above.

[284]   WCA, s 10(4).

that such action would be required to the wild animal and a licence under Section 16(3) authorizing that action had not been applied for as soon as reasonably practicable or the licence application had been refused.

Section 10(2) provides an additional defence not found in Section 4, namely, that **11.107** the damage, destruction, obstruction, or disturbance took place within a dwelling house.[285] However, Section 10(5) reduces this 'exemption' to the 'living area'[286] in the case of bats unless Natural England or the other relevant Conservation Agency has been notified of the proposed action and it has had a reasonable time to advise whether it should be carried out and, if so, the method to be used. Additional regard should also be paid to the Habitats Regulations which provide separate statutory controls for European protected species.[287]

Section 11 also mirrors Section 5 as to the prohibition of certain methods of kill- **11.108** ing or taking any wild animal, including those species of wild animals identified in Schedule 6 (for example bats, dormice, shrews, and hedgehogs). It lists, amongst other devices, the use of traps, including self-locking snares,[288] automatic and semi-automatic weapon, night sights, gas, smoke, live decoys, and any mechanically propelled vehicle in immediate pursuit for the purpose of driving, killing, or taking the animal;[289] and in this context it should be particularly borne in mind that when an offence relates to several individual species (for example the destruction of a bat colony) the maximum fine can be imposed in respect of each single animal which has been killed.[290] Again, exemptions are given to cover the interests of public health, agriculture, forestry, fisheries, or nature conservation, provided that all reasonable steps are taken to prevent injury.[291]

In addition, Section 1 of the Wild Mammals (Protection) Act 1996 makes it a **11.109** criminal offence to commit a wide range of cruel acts against any wild mammal[292] with intent to inflict unnecessary suffering. Section 2 lists a number of statutory defences including mercy killing, if the act was a lawful activity under another enactment, or if it arose from the lawful use of any poisonous or noxious substance.

---

[285] 'Dwelling house' includes a cellar (see *Grigsby v Melville* [1973] 3 All ER 455 at 462.
[286] ie within a 'house in which people actually live or which is physically capable of being used for human habitation '(see *Lewin v End* [1906] AC 299 at 304 per Lord Atkinson), so would exclude eaves, cavity walls, storage lofts, cellars, and garages.
[287] Habitats Regulations, regs 38–41B including defences.
[288] WCA, s 11(1).
[289] Ibid, s 11(2).
[290] Ibid, s 21(6).
[291] Ibid, s 11(6).
[292] 'Wild mammal' means any mammal which is not a domestic or captive animal within the meaning of the Protection of Animals Act 1911 or the Protection of Animals (Scotland) Act 1912 s 3.

Penalties include a fine and imprisonment, as well as the confiscation of any vehicle or equipment used in the commission of the offence.[293]

11.110 Certain species of animal, identified as 'European protected species' in Annex IV(a) to the Habitats Directive, also receive protection under the Habitats Regulations. Schedule 2 lists 13 species, all of which are found in Schedule 5 to the WCA. They include all species of bats, dolphins, porpoises, and whales as well as the great-crested newt, the natterjack toad, and the sand lizard. The offences identified under Regulation 39 are, essentially, the same as those under Section 9 of the WCA though, in one instance, the offence is simply one of 'deliberate disturbance'. Similar exceptions to those found in Section 10 of the WCA are given by Regulation 40; though the respective offences of disturbance and damage or destruction of a breeding site or resting place are limited simply to 'anything done within a dwelling-house'. Regulation 41 prohibits the same methods of taking or killing animals prohibited by Section 11 of the WCA in respect of certain animals listed in Schedule 3 to the Habitats Regulations. These include some species protected by the WCA (the allis shad and the vendace) but also a number which are not (for example the grayling, the mountain hare, the Atlantic salmon, and most varieties of seal, though these last two receive limited protection by other legislation).[294] Licensing powers are provided by Regulations 44 and 45. Offences are liable to a fine, on summary conviction, not exceeding level 5.[295]

11.111 Badgers are given specific protection by the Protection of Badgers Act 1992, which consolidated earlier legislation found in the Badgers Acts 1973 to 1991. As they are neither rare nor under threat the main purpose of this legislation has been to save these animals from cruelty rather than safeguarding their nature conservation status. Sections 1–5 of the 1992 Act create a number of offences, commencing with the wilful killing, injuring, or taking of a badger (including by badger tongs) or an attempt so to do.[296] Cruelty, by ill-treatment, digging (except as permitted by or under the Act), and the use of certain firearms is prohibited by Section 2(1). Interference with a badger sett,[297] intentionally or recklessly, by damaging it or any part, destroying it, obstructing access to or any entrance of the sett, causing a dog[298] to enter, or disturbing a badger while it is in occupation are all recognized

---

[293] Ss 5 and 6(1). The maximum fine is currently £5,000 per animal affected (level 5) or a term of imprisonment of six months (or both) (s 5).

[294] Salmon and Freshwater Fisheries Act 1975 and the Protection of Seals Act 1970, see below.

[295] Habitats Regulations, regs 39(6), 41(6).

[296] Protection of Badgers Act 1992, s 1(1).

[297] A 'badger sett' means any structure or place which displays signs indicating current use by a badger. The terms 'main', 'annexe', and 'outlier' are helpfully defined in the RSPCA booklet *Problems with Badgers* (1990).

[298] Protection of Badgers Act 1992, s 13(1) gives the court the power both to order the destruction or other disposal of the dog and/or disqualify the offender from having custody of a dog for such period as it thinks fit.

offences by Section 3. The sale and possession of live badgers is not permitted[299] nor the tagging, or ringing, or other marking of them.[300] In addition to a fine or imprisonment[301] the court must order forfeiture of any badger or badger skin, in respect of which the offence has been committed. It can also order the forfeiture of any weapon or article used in connection with the offence.[302]

Statutory exemptions permit mercy killing,[303] the temporary stopping up of **11.112** badger setts, or limited interference for the purposes of fox hunting,[304] and the treatment of injured animals.[305] Licences are needed where there is likely to be longer-term interference with a sett[306] or other circumstances affecting the welfare of the badgers. These licences are granted by the Conservation Bodies. For example, they are required for the purpose of implementing a planning permission[307] or the preservation or archaeological investigation of a Scheduled Ancient Monument.[308] Ministerial permission is required for agricultural or forestry operations involving water courses, flood defences, or land drainage.[309] Either body can grant a licence to interfere with a badger sett for the purpose of controlling foxes in order to protect livestock, game, or wildlife.[310] Revocation of the licence as a result of failure to comply with any condition imposed by the licence creates an offence punishable by fine.[311]

Limited protection is given to the four main species of deer (red deer, fallow deer, **11.113** roe deer, and sika deer) in England and Wales by the Deer Act 1991[312] which

---

[299] Ibid, s 4. 'Sale' includes hire, barter, and exchange (s 14).

[300] Ibid, s 5.

[301] Offences under ss 1(1) or (3), 2, or 3 carry, on summary conviction, imprisonment for a term not exceeding six months or a fine not exceeding level 5 or both for offences under ss 4, 5, or 10(8) a fine not exceeding that level.

[302] Ibid, s 12(4).

[303] Ibid, s 6.

[304] Ibid, s 8(4)–(9).

[305] Ibid.

[306] See n 297 above for definition of 'sett'.

[307] Protection of Badgers Act 1992 s 10(1)(d). Natural England requires, in the case of a development, a copy of the detailed planning permission in force, a survey of the status of any setts within the development area and their known or likely occupancy, the impact of the development on the sett(s), a scheme of appropriate mitigation works, a method statement, and confirmation of expert supervision and execution of the necessary works. Licences are usually not issued during the breeding season between 1 December and 30 June.

[308] Ibid, s 10(1)(e).

[309] Ibid, s 10(2).

[310] Ibid, s 10(3).

[311] Ibid, s 10(8) and n 301 above.

[312] As amended by he Regulatory Reform (Deer) (England and Wales) Order 2007 from 1 October 2007 which allows, for example, the use of 0.22 centre fire rifles for shooting smaller species of deer (namely muntjac and Chinese water deer), any reasonable means of humanely dispatching deer that are suffering due to illness or disease and enables licensed killing or taking of deer during the close season to prevent deterioration of the natural heritage or to preserve public health and safety.

consolidates earlier legislation and identifies a number of specific offences. In Scotland, the legislation has now been consolidated into the Deer (Scotland) Act 1996. Poaching and related activities are prohibited by Section 1 of the 1991 Act,[313] the taking or killing of deer during the close season is restricted by Section 2,[314] and at night by Section 3,[315] while the use of certain articles and weapons is prohibited by Section 4.[316] In addition, Section 5 makes it a separate offence to attempt to commit any of the offences under Sections 2–4. Exceptions are given by Section 7 for occupiers of land, similar to those found in the WCA, namely, mercy killing or to control deer as pests under ministry direction.[317] An exception is given where only killing can prevent damage to crops, vegetables, and other forms of property.[318] In addition, exemption through licensing by one of the Conservation Agencies is given by Section 8.[319] Powers of search, arrest, and seizure are given by Section 12. Penalties are specified, on summary conviction, as a fine not exceeding level 4 or a term of imprisonment of three months, or both, with each deer treated as a separate offence.[320] The court may also make an order[321] forfeiting any deer or venison, vehicle, or animal in the offender's possession at the time of the offence. Disqualification from holding a game dealer's licence[322] can also be made.

---

[313] Deer Act 1991, s 1(1) and (2) creates three offences, whilst trespassing: (i) killing or attempting to take, kill, or injure any deer; (ii) searching or pursuing any deer with the above intentions; (iii) removing the carcass of any deer. S 14(1) also makes the body corporate as well as the individual liable for the offence.

[314] Sch 1 sets out the various close seasons for each of the four species, differentiating between stags (1 May to 31 July inclusive other than Roe Deer—1 November to 31 March) and hinds (1 March to 31 October inclusive). These periods are different from those applicable to Scotland under the Deer (Scotland) Acts 1959–1982.

[315] 'Night' is defined by s 3 as the period 'between the expiry of the first hour after sunset and the beginning of the first hour before sunrise'.

[316] Traps, snares, poisoned, or stupefying bait (s 4(1)); any firearm or ammunition mentioned in Sch 2 (ie smooth bore guns, low velocity rifles, airguns, air rifles, or air pistols), any arrow, spear, or similar missile, or any missile carrying poison, stupefying drug or muscle-relaxing agent (s 4(2)). The use of a mechanically propelled vehicle (which term includes aircraft, hovercraft, and boats by s 16) for firing purposes or to drive deer is also forbidden (s 4(4)).

[317] The control of deer as pests can be exercised under the more general rules on pest control under of the Agriculture Act 1948 s 98, by which Defra can make 'pest control orders'. In this context, s 7(1) permits relaxation of shooting during the close seasons and at night.

[318] Deer Act 1991, s 7(3). The exemption is given to the occupier of the land on which the action is taken, any member of his household normally resident (acting with written authority), or any other person with written authority (s 7(4)).

[319] A licence cannot permit the use of any net, trap, stupefying drug, or muscle-relaxing agent (s 8(3)).

[320] Ibid, s 9(1) and (2). Level 4 is currently fixed at £10,000.

[321] Ibid, s 13(1).

[322] Ibid, s 10(1) prohibits the possession, sale, and purchase of venison during a close season and at any other time otherwise than to a licensed game dealer (ie licensed under the Game Act 1831 and the Game Licences Act 1860), who must keep proper records by s 11. A body corporate as well as the individual offender in its employment are both liable for these offences (s 14(1)).

The grey seal and the common seal, the only two species of British seal, are pro-   **11.114**
tected by the Conservation of Seals Act 1970.[323] Section 1 forbids their poisoning
and the use of certain types of firearm[324] while Section 3 gives the Secretary of
State power to establish sanctuary areas. Exemptions are provided by Section 9 to
permit the killing of seals as an act of mercy, or where they have damaged fishing
nets, tackle, or fish. The taking and subsequent release of injured seals is also permitted together with the 'unavoidable killing or injuring of any seal as an incidental result of lawful action'. Licences to kill seals are issued by the Secretary of State,
after consultation with the Conservation Agencies, for scientific or educational
purposes, prevention of damage to fisheries, the elimination of population sur-
pluses, and for the conservation of any flora and fauna of any designated conservation site.[325]

Protection of fish

The protection of fish that are not artificially farmed is also the subject of legal   **11.115**
regulation although the legislation in question is designed more to protect stocks
as a resource from over-exploitation. Inland fishing is subject to considerable legal
controls under both the English and Scottish legal systems.[326] In both jurisdictions, fishing within the close reason is prohibited.[327] Protection applies to salmon,
trout, and all other freshwater fish. There is also prohibition of the use of certain
implements and other methods to catch or retain fish,[328] the intentional killing or
taking of any immature or unclean fish, (ie, one about to spawn or not yet recovered from spawning) or the disturbance of them,[329] and causing or knowingly

---

[323] Identified by SI 1996/2905.

[324] Conservation of Seals Act 1970, s 1. It should be noted that s 2 sets close seasons for both
types of seal. Powers of search and seizure are given by ss 4, 5, and 6.

[325] Ibid, s 10 (as amended).

[326] The Salmon and Freshwater Fisheries Act 1975 applies to England and Wales and in Scotland
by the Salmon and Freshwater Fisheries (Consolidation) (Scotland) Act 2003. In England and
Wales, the Environment Agency is responsible for maintaining, improving, and developing salmon
fisheries under the Water Resources Act 1991, s 114.

[327] Salmon and Freshwater Fisheries Act 1975, ss 19–23 and Sch 1 restrict fishing seasons and
the sale of wild fish, including the export of salmon and trout.

[328] Ibid, s 1(1) prohibits implements including firearms, otter laths or jacks, wires and snares,
spears, gaffs, and lights. Seine or draft nets are prohibited for the catching of salmon and migratory
trout across more than three-fourths of any waters (s 3(1)). Explosives, poisons and other noxious
substances, and electrical devices are prohibited other than for scientific purposes or for the protection, improvement, and replacement of fish stocks (s 5(1) and (2)). Fixed engines (special nets),
fishing weirs, and mill dams are subject to regulation under ss 6–8. Fish passes must be made and
maintained in water frequented by salmon and migratory trout under s 9. Sluices and gratings are
regulated by ss 13 and 14 whilst boxes and cribs in fishing weirs or fishing mill dams are prohibited
by s 16(1) unless they satisfy certain requirements.

[329] Ibid, s 2(1) and (2). The offence is not committed if the fish is taken accidentally and returned to
the water with the least possible injury (s 2(3)). Wilful disturbance of spawning fish, other than in the exercise of a legal right to take materials from the water, is also an offence under s 2(4); but none of the foregoing

---

permitting the release of poisonous or polluting liquid or solid matter.[330] Fishing licences, the powers of water bailiffs, and other administrative matters are also dealt with by the 1975 Act.[331]

11.116 For marine fishing, the law is of more recent origin and largely derives from the competing economic and social interests of those states within and without the European Community and the need for fishing quotas and other protective measures. UK law, by the Sea Fisheries Regulation Act 1966 and the Sea Fish (Conservation) Act 1967 (as amended by the Sea Fish (Conservation) Act 1992), provides a management and licensing system for fishermen, their fishing boats, and those boats receiving trans-shipped fish. In addition, the Sea Fisheries (Wildlife Conservation Act) 1992, containing one substantive section, requires the Minister of Agriculture, Fisheries and Food, and the Secretaries of State concerned with the sea fishing industry[332] for the remainder of the UK, to have regard to the conservation of marine flora and fauna and to try and achieve a balance between those considerations and any others. The Environment Act 1995 (EA 1995) introduced specific environmental duties by way of amendment to both the 1966 Act and the 1967 Act in respect of 'marine environmental matters'.

11.117 The taking of shellfish is regulated to the extent that private fisheries for oysters, mussels, cockles, clams, scallops, and queens receive protection under the Sea Fisheries (Shellfish) Act 1967.[333] In addition to making provision for minimum permissible sizes of creatures to be caught,[334] a close season is prescribed for the sale of indigenous oysters.[335] A prohibition is also included for the possession or sale of edible crabs which are carrying spawn or have just cast their shells;[336] but there is no restriction on the right of the public to dig for bait on the foreshore as an ancillary right to public fishing.[337]

---

offences are committed if the act is for the purpose of artificial propagation or for some scientific purpose or the development of a private fishery with the permission of the water authority for that area (s 4(5)).

[330] Ibid, s 4(1). Ministerial approval is required by s 4(3) before a prosecution can be brought.

[331] Ibid, ss 25–27 and Sch 2 for licences; ss 28–37 for powers of administration and enforcement; and ss 38–40 for the application of the Act to works below the high water mark, the Border Rivers and the Solway Firth, and the River Severn.

[332] The scope of the Act is applied to 'the Sea Fisheries Acts', which are defined as meaning 'any enactments for the time being in force relating to sea-fishing, including any enactment relating to fishing in the sea for shellfish, salmon or migratory trout'.

[333] Sea Fisheries (Shellfish) Act 1967, ss 1–3.

[334] Sea Fisheries (Conservation) Act 1967, s 1 and eg the Under-sized Lobsters Order (SI 1993/1178).

[335] Sea Fisheries (Shellfish) Act 1967, s 16.

[336] Ibid, s 17 (but not if the crabs are being used for bait).

[337] *Anderson v Alnwick District Council* [1993] 1 WLR 1156.

Protection of individual wild plants

Statutory protection of individual wild plants is found in Section 13 of the WCA, **11.118** which makes it an offence intentionally to pick, uproot, or destroy any wild plant listed in Schedule 8. A 'wild plant' is defined by Section 27(1) as meaning 'any plant which is or (before it was picked, uprooted or destroyed) was growing wild and is of a kind which ordinarily grows in Great Britain in a wild state'. The word 'pick' means 'gather or gather any plant without uprooting it' while 'uproot' is defined as meaning 'dig up or otherwise remove the plant from the land on which it grows'. Schedule 8 includes over 150 types of different plant with such diverse names as Dickie's bladder fern, river jelly lichen, rigid apple moss, turpswort, and greater yellow-rattle.

Unless an authorized person,[338] it is also an offence intentionally to uproot any **11.119** wild plant not included in the Schedule.[339] The same offence would also be committed under Section 1 of the Theft Act 1968 as even wild plants are usually somebody's property; though it should be noted that, under Section 4(3) of the 1968 Act, a person who picks flowers, fruit, or foliage from a plant growing wild, or who picks any fungus growing wild, does not steal them unless he does so for reward or for sale or for some other commercial purpose. It is also an offence to sell, offer, possess, transport, or attempt to trade, any live or dead wild plant or any parts of it or any derivative of such plant.[340] However, it is not an offence to show that 'the act was an incidental result of a lawful operation and could not reasonably have been avoided'.[341] Finally, Section 14(2) makes it an offence to plant or otherwise cause to grow in the wild any plant which is included in Part II of Schedule 9 (for example, giant hogweed, giant kelp, and Japanese knotweed) due to their invasive and consequently harmful effects. Section 14ZA(1) also makes it a criminal offence to offer or expose for sale invasive non-native species of plants

Certain plants which have European species protection are identified in Schedule 4 **11.120** of the Habitat Regulations, which transposes this requirement of the Council Directive on Habitats (92/43) into UK law. The Schedule currently lists nine species of plants which are protected within Europe, all of which are already protected under Schedule 8 of the WCA. These include the shore dock, lady's slipper, fen orchid, and yellow marsh saxifrage. Offences are similar to but slightly wider than those under the WCA. Regulation 43(1) makes it an offence deliberately to pick, collect, cut, uproot, or destroy a wild plant of a European protected species. It is also an offence to keep, transport, sell, or exchange or offer for sale or exchange any live or dead plant of a European protected species or any part or anything

---

[338] See n 247 above.
[339] WCA, s 13(1)(b).
[340] Ibid, s 13(2).
[341] Ibid, s 13(3).

derived from it.[342] Licensing provisions, similar to those found under the WCA, are to be found in Regulations 44 and 45.

Trees and woodlands

11.121 Trees are subject to two main areas of legal protection. First, there is forestry, where conservation is achieved through direct controls regulating the planting, maintenance, and felling of trees and related grant schemes which have already been outlined above in connection with the work of the Forestry Commission.[343] Secondly, planning legislation, principally through the Town and Country Planning Act 1990 (TCPA), contains a number of special provisions which recognize the value of trees to the character and amenity of particular localities and the consequent need for their protection.

11.122 As trees are not structures nor buildings for the purposes of the development control system, planning permission is not required for their planting or their cutting down. Section 55(2)(e) of the TCPA also excludes any change of use of land to forestry or woodland from the definition of 'development'. However, Section 197 imposes a general duty on LPAs to make adequate provision for trees when planning permission is granted, including the attaching of conditions to the permission, for example for the retention of certain ones and the protection or replacement of others. In addition, this duty also involves consideration of whether to impose tree preservation orders (TPOs) on existing trees.[344]

11.123 Sections 198(1)–(3) of the TCPA currently[345] make provision for the preservation 'in the interests of amenity'[346] of trees, groups of trees, or woodlands by prohibiting

---

[342] Habitats Regulations, reg 43(2).

[343] See n 26–28 above.

[344] For specific guidance, which has the same weight as a Government Circular, see DCLG's *Tree Preservation Orders: A Guide to the Law and Good Practice* (2000), which cancelled sections VI, VII, VIII, IX, and X of DoE Circular 36/78 *Trees and Forestry*, in so far as they relate to England and also *Tree Preservation Orders: A Guide to the Law and Good Practice* (1994). See also *Robinson v East Riding of Yorkshire Council* [2002] EWCA Civ 1660 confirming the wide discretionary powers given to LPAS. The compliance of the statutory regime with the ECHR was judicially confirmed through the case of *R (Brennon) v Bromsgrove District Council* [2003] EWHC 752 (Admin).

[345] Further changes are currently being promoted, at the time of writing, through the Planning Bill (2008) which amends the TCPA by providing for the transfer of provisions from tree preservation orders into regulations ('tree preservation regulations'). For this purpose the Bill inserts seven new sections to the current TCPA. New s 202A makes general provision about the regulations. New ss 202B to 202G contain additional details about the sort of provision that may be contained in the regulations, including provision about the form and procedures to be followed where TPOs are to be confirmed, prohibited activities in relation to trees, applications for consent to carry out works to trees, powers to give consent to works subject to conditions; appeals against decisions to refuse consent; entitlement to compensation following decisions on applications for consent; and the keeping of public registers containing information on TPOs.

[346] Ie public benefit. The DCLG *Guide* advises, at para. 3.2, that: 'LPAs should be able to show that a reasonable degree of public benefit would accrue before TPOs are made or confirmed. The trees, or at least part of them, should therefore normally be visible from a public place, such as a

felling, topping, lopping, uprooting, wilful damage, or wilful destruction without the consent of the LPA, and by securing the replacement of trees. The TPO procedure for England and Wales is now found in the Town and Country Planning (Trees) Regulations 1999 ('the TPOR'). The LPA is required[347] to specify and identify the location of the trees, groups of trees, including their number, or woodlands in question together with a map at a scale sufficient to give a clear indication of their respective positions.[348] However, the LPA is not required to send a copy of the TPO to other local residents, authorities (such as parish councils) or groups; though where their interests are likely to be affected or where there is likely to be a good deal of public interest in the TPO, the LPA should consider notifying them or displaying a site notice at a convenient place in the locality.[349] The notice must set out the grounds for the making of the order, the place where it can be inspected by the public, and stating that objections and representations may be made (which must be in writing)[350] by a date being at least 28 days after the date of its service.[351] The foregoing notification provisions apply equally to the notice of confirmation.[352] The TPO itself must be substantially in the form prescribed by the TPO Regulations[353] known as the 'Model Order'. It does not normally take effect until confirmed by the LPA.[354] A right of challenge to the High Court is also given.[355] In conservation areas all trees are automatically covered by a TPO;[356] but only limited protection is afforded to these trees as it arises from the procedural requirement to give prior notification of felling proposals to the LPA, which provides them with an opportunity to object.[357]

---

road or footpath, although, exceptionally, the inclusion of other trees may be justified. The benefit may be present or future; trees may be worthy of preservation for their intrinsic beauty or for their contribution to the landscape or because they serve to screen an eyesore or future development; the value of trees may be enhanced by their scarcity; and the value of a group of trees or woodland may be collective only. Other factors, such as importance as a wildlife habitat, may be taken into account which alone would not be sufficient to warrant a TPO. In the Secretary of State's view, it would be inappropriate to make a TPO in respect of a tree which is dead, dying or dangerous.'

See also *Re Ellis and Ruislip-Northwood UDC* [1920] 1 KB 343.

[347] TPOR, reg 2(1).
[348] Ibid, reg 2(2) and (3). The map becomes part of the TPO.
[349] See the DCLG *Guide*, para. 3.28
[350] Ibid, regs 3(1), reg 4(1).
[351] Ibid, reg 3 (2).
[352] Ibid, reg 6.
[353] See 'The Schedule' to the TPOR.
[354] TCP s199(1). See also *Bellcross Co Ltd v Mid-Bedfordshire DC* [1988] 15 EG 106. However, immediate effect can be achieved, without prior confirmation, under s 201(1) by way of a provisional TPO.
[355] TCPA, s 288(1), within six weeks from the date when the order is confirmed (s 284(1)(e) and (2)(c); but the court has no power to suspend the TPO by way of interim order (s 288(5)).
[356] Ibid, s 211(1). Exemptions are provided as to certain activities by TPOR, reg 10, and in respect of trees less than 75 millimetres in diameter at a point 1.5 metres above ground level.
[357] Ibid, s 211(3), which provision also provides a statutory defence to prosecution.

11.124 Unfortunately, the TCPA contains no definition of the term 'tree'. It has been suggested that as a rough rule of thumb, in woodland at least, the term should only apply where the diameter of the trunk is greater than 7–8 inches;[358] but, generally, the test appears to have been left to common sense by the courts.[359] Cultivated fruit trees are expressly excluded from the consent requirements of TPO Regulation.[360] Woodland orders are discouraged by paragraph 41 of DOE Circular 36/78 ('Trees and Forestry') on the ground that a TPO can render essential management difficult and cumbersome. Paragraph 44 also advises that a TPO can only apply to trees and not to bushes or shrubs or to hedges as such, rather only trees within a hedge; hence the recent statutory protection introduced by Section 97 of the EA 1995.

11.125 Once a TPO has been made, consent must be applied for from the LPA, in the same way as an application for planning permission, before any work can be done to the tree other than certain recognized exemptions under Section 198(6), namely, where a tree is dying or dead or has become dangerous or an obligation is imposed by Act of Parliament or for the prevention or abatement of a nuisance.[361] It is also permissible to cut down, lop, or top a tree where that work is required to implement a detailed planning permission or a deemed permission under permitted development rights.[362, 363] The procedure for applications and appeals is curiously still found in the Schedules containing the model form of TPO. If consent is refused, made the subject of unreasonable conditions, or not determined within eight weeks then a right of appeal exists to the Secretary of State within 28 days of the LPA's decision,[364] the determination of which is dealt with by written representations but with the right to appear before an Inspector.[365] Compensation is payable in consequence of the refusal or conditional grant of consent save where

---

[358] *Kent County Council v Batchelor (No 1)* [1976] 33 P&CR 185, at 189 (per Lord Denning) and now, by logical application, TPOR, reg 10(2) dimensions—see n 356 above.

[359] See eg *Bullock v Secretary of State for the Environment* [1986] 40 P&CR 246 where Phillips J stated that a TPO could refer to anything which one would ordinarily call a tree, as opposed to bushes, shrub, or scrub. Hence, a coppice fell within the meaning of 'trees' so could be the subject of a TPO.

[360] TPOR, Schedule, para 5(1)(b) and (c) of Model Form of TPO.

[361] See also TPOR, Schedule, para 5(1) of Model Form of TPO which mainly lists identified exemptions 'in respect of statutory undertakers' works. In *Northampton Borough Council v Perrin* [2007] EWCA Civ 1353 the Court of Appeal., considering the application of section 198(6)(b) of the 1990 Act, held that alternative engineering solutions were relevant to the determination of the question whether the cutting down, uprooting, topping, or lopping of a tree was necessary for the prevention or abatement of a nuisance.

[362] Ibid, para 5(1)(d).

[363] See Part I of Sch 2 to the Model Form of TPO and adopted and modified provisions of the TCPA printed in Part II.

[364] Model Form of TPO, para 7.

[365] For clearest explanation of procedure see Part II (of Sch 2) setting out modified TCPA ss 78 and 79 procedures.

the LPA certifies that its decision is made in the interests of good forestry or that the trees (other than woodland trees) have an outstanding amenity value or where replanting is required.[366]

Under Section 210(1) of the TCPA there are two main offences which can be **11.126** committed in contravention of a TPO. First, it is an offence of strict liability to cut down, uproot, or wilfully destroy such a tree.[367] Secondly, it is an offence to wilfully damage, top, or lop a tree in such a manner as to be likely to destroy it.[368] The same offences apply to trees within conservation areas, except that it is a defence under Section 211(3) to have done such actions either with the LPA's consent or after six weeks from the date of notification of them. Exceptions are permitted where a tree is dying or dead or has become dangerous or an obligation is imposed by Act of Parliament.[369]

On summary conviction, the offender can be fined up to level 5, and on an unlim- **11.127** ited basis on indictment. In all instances, the court will have particular regard to any financial benefit which appears to have accrued to the offender as a result of the offence.[370] In addition, the LPA is entitled to seek the civil remedy of an injunction in order to prevent possible contraventions when these are known or likely to occur.[371]

Compulsory replacement of trees which have been removed in contravention **11.128** of a TPO, or where their removal was only authorized on the grounds that they were dead, dying, or had become dangerous, is a separate remedy available to the LPA under Section 206. However, it is only enforceable by way of a replanting notice under Section 207(5), against which a right of appeal lies to the Secretary of State under Section 208. Powers of execution of the necessary work and recovery of its costs are given to the LPA by Section 209. Similar provisions apply to conservation areas under Section 213 of the TCPA. Accordingly, the fundamental problem remains that these protective measures remain essentially reactive rather than being able to promote the sound management of trees.

Felling licences are required from the Forestry Commission under Section 9(2) of **11.129** the Forestry Act 1967 whenever any significant felling is proposed. This control is based on commercial factors rather than amenity considerations. It applies to the

---

[366] TCPA, ss 203 and 204 and Model Form of TPO, para 9.

[367] Ibid, s 210(1)(a); *Maidstone Borough Council v Mortimer* [1980] 3 All ER 522 and *R v Alath Construction Limited* [1991] 1 PLR 25.

[368] Ibid, s 210(1)(b). 'Wilful destruction' involves the tree being rendered useless rather than total obliteration (*Barnet London Borough Council v Eastern Electricity Board* [1973] 1 WLR 430).

[369] Ibid, s 198(6) and Model Form of TPO, Sch 2.

[370] Ibid, s 210(2) and (3).

[371] Ibid, s 214A and *Kent County Council v Batchelor (No 2)* [1978] 3 All ER 980.

felling of any trees over 8cm in diameter, 15cm in coppices, measured 1.3cm from the ground. Topping and lopping of trees, fellings in gardens, orchards, church-yards, and public open spaces are amongst the permitted exceptions.[372] Where a TPO also applies, the application goes to the Forestry Commission, who must consult with the relevant LPA. Either the TPO legislation will then be applied by the LPA or the Forestry Commission will grant, with or without conditions, or refuse the licence, which, in the latter case, will lead to the payment of com-pensation.[373] If a licence is granted there is also an obligation to restock the land unless waived by the Forestry Commission.[374] Unauthorized felling is subject to a financial penalty and the requirement to restock.[375]

Important hedgerows

11.130 Section 97 of the EA 1995 finally brought about the legislative protection of important hedgerows that had been awaited since the Government's statement of intent in the 1990 White Paper (*This Common Inheritance*). Whilst the legislation is intended to protect 'important hedgerows' its effect is simply to prevent their removal either by grubbing up or other destruction. The crucial question as to what constitute 'important hedgerows' is left, by Section 97(2) and (3), to the Hedgerows Regulations 1997. They do not apply to garden hedges.[376] They are also a separate and distinct form of control from that introduced under the Anti-Social Behaviour Act 2003 to prevent high hedges made from cypresses and other rapidly growing evergreen species.[377]

11.131 The 1997 Regulations only apply to the removal of a 'hedgerow'.[378] However, the term 'hedgerow' is not defined by the Act or by the Regulations. The accompany-ing practical guidance, currently published by Defra *The Hedgerows Regulations—a*

---

[372] Forestry Act 1967, s 9(2)–(4). Other exclusions include the felling of 'thinnings' up to 10 cms in diameter to improve growth, the felling of up to 5 cubic metres in any calendar quarter (provided that no more than 2 cubic metres are sold), or any felling to prevent or abate a nuisance or at the request of an electricity operator or to carry out development under the TCPA 1990.

[373] Ibid, ss 10–11 and the Forestry (Felling of Trees) Regulations 1979 which include a pre-scribed form (Sch 2). See s 15 for procedures where there is an overlapping TPO.

[374] Ibid, s 12.

[375] For felling without a licence, s 17 imposes a fine (level 4) on summary conviction or twice the sum which appears to the court to be the value of the tree, whichever is the higher. Ss 17A–17C, respectively, give the Commissioners power to require restocking where unauthorized felling has taken place, an appeal procedure, and enforcement powers.

[376] Hedgerows Regulations, Reg 3(3): 'within the curtilage of, or marking a boundary of the curtilage of, a dwelling-house'.

[377] See also the High Hedges (Appeals) (England) Regulations 2005.

[378] The *Hedgerows Review* (p. 14) (1998) revealed that DETR legal advice had been that the word 'hedgerow' could only be given its ordinary and natural meaning so cannot be applied to spe-cial regional or local uses of this term, thereby excluding from the operation of the 1997 Regulations 'hedge-banks', Cornish banks, and Welsh 'cloddiau'. Other traditional boundary features (eg dry stone walls and slate fences) are also not protected.

Guide To The Law And Good Practice, suggests that parties should look at a good dictionary in order to give the word its natural meaning. The consensus suggests that the term should be applied to a row of bushes forming a hedge with the trees growing in it, especially where it forms a boundary of a field, road, etc. It follows that the term excludes landscape features or corridors or ditches.[379] Application is established, first, in terms of certain measurement criteria, ie, continuous lengths of hedgerow in excess of 20m or a hedge less than 20 m in length but where, at each end, it meets another hedgerow.[380] Domestic hedgerows are expressly excluded.[381] Secondly, 'importance' is determined by establishing either that the hedgerow has to have been planted 30 years or more (before the date of the removal notice) or that it satisfies certain specified criteria concerning its archaeological, historic, or biological value. The suggested criteria set out in Schedule 1, Part II are complex. They include, for example, the marking by the hedgerow of the boundary of a pre-1850 parish or township, or of an archaeological site recorded either as a Scheduled Ancient Monument or within the County's Historic Environmental Record, or which is the habitat for a certain number of birds and animals, or contains a certain number of different species of plant identified in the Red Data Books.[382] Some practical guidance is to be found in the *Guide To The Law And Good Practice*.

A notification procedure, similar to that currently applied to other forms of permitted development,[383] requires the owner, or, in certain cases, the relevant utility operator, to notify the LPA prior to the commencement of the proposed works of removal.[384] Under the current Regulations the LPA has, unless extended by agreement, 42 calendar days (six weeks) from receipt of the notice in which to give or refuse consent for the notified work.[385] However, work can commence to remove the hedgerow if the LPA has not responded within the specified period.[386] **11.132**

---

[379] These comments are drawn from one of the few appeal decision letters published so far by the Planning Inspectorate (see T/APP/HGW/99/110 dated 29 June 1999 concerning a site near Alerford Road (A642/M1 junction), Garforth, Leeds).

[380] Hedgerows Regulations 1997, reg 3(1) applies to any hedgerow growing in or adjacent to any common land, protected land, land used for agriculture, forestry, or the keeping of horses, ponies, or donkeys.

[381] Ibid, reg 3(3), within the curtilage of, or marking a boundary of the curtilage of, a dwelling house.

[382] See further para 11.94 above.

[383] See eg Town and Country Planning (General Permitted Development) Order 1995, Sch 2 Part 6 (Agricultural buildings and operations) and Part 24 (Telecommunications).

[384] Hedgerows Regulations, Reg 5(1). A standard form of applicant's notice (referred as a 'hedgerow removal notice') is set out in Sch 4.

[385] Ibid, reg 5(6). The *Hedgerows Review* recommends that the notification period should be extended to 56 days (eight weeks) in line with the planning system, with the facility for an extension of this period by agreement between the parties.

[386] Ibid, reg 6(1) set out a list of permitted work including the substitution of an existing opening (subject to replacement), a temporary access in an emergency, carrying out of developing

The LPA's formal response should be either to issue a written notice stating that the hedgerow may be removed[387] or issue a hedgerow retention notice (HRN) within this period.[388] Provisions are also to be found within the Regulations for criminal penalties, replacements, and appeals against HRNs.[389]

Protection of endangered species

11.133   The Endangered Species (Import and Export) Act 1976 gave effect to the Convention on International Trade in Endangered Species ('The CITES Convention').[390] The 1976 Act[391] contains five Schedules listing, respectively, 'animals', 'plants', and 'items', the importation and exportation of which are restricted, and 'animals' and 'plants', the sale (etc) of which is restricted. Endangered species which are prohibited from importation include gibbons, sperm whales, certain types of parrot, and sea turtles. Plants include certain species of aloe and cacaceae. Among those species which are banned from being exported include owls, ospreys, falcons, collared doves, types of frog and mussel. Whale meat, whalebone, elephant tusks, and rhinoceros bone are among those items restricted both for import and export. Offences, which seek to prohibit imports without a licence,[392] include selling, offering or exposing for sale, or having in the defendant's possession for sale, anything imported contrary to the Act or any part or derivative from it.[393] Provision is made for a statutory defence of 'reasonable

---

permitted by a consent under the TCPA 1990, works under the LDA 1991, the WRA 1991, and the EA 1995 in respect of flood defence or land drainage, obstruction or interference with power lines, plant health, certain highway works, and for the proper management of the hedgerow.

[387]   Ibid, reg 5(1)(b)(i). The removal must be carried out in accordance with the proposal set out in the hedgerow removal notice (reg 5(1)(c)). A period of two years beginning with the date of the service of the hedgerow removal notice for the work to be carried out is provided by reg 5(1)(d).

[388]   Ibid, reg 5(1)(b)(ii). The HRN must specify each criterion (of those listed in Sch 1) which applies to the hedgerow in question unless it is a replacement hedgerow (under reg 8(4)).

[389]   Ibid, reg 7(1) sets out the criminal offences of intentionally or recklessly removing or causing or permitting somebody to remove any hedgerow the subject of the notification procedure. Conviction, by way of summary offence, is by way of a fine up to a maximum of level 5 (currently £20,000), or unlimited fine on indictment (reg 3(4)). Reg 8 gives the LPA the power to seek a replacement. Appeals to the Secretary of State for Environment, Transport and the Regions, within 28 days of the service of the HRN, are dealt with under reg 9 with the power to award costs other than in written representation cases. The power is given to the LPA to seek a restraining injunction in the civil courts under reg 11. Regs 12–14 deal with rights of entry. Reg 15 deals with hedgerows owned by the LPA to which the Regulations apply. Practical advice on appeals can be obtained from the Planning Inspectorate's website.

[390]   See para. 11.43 above

[391]   Endangered Species (Import and Export) Act 1976, as amended by s 15 of the WCA, which added Schs 4 and 5.

[392]   Ibid, s 1(1) subject to the licensing provisions under s 1(2) and (3).

[393]   Ibid, s 4(1) and (1A).

enquiries',[394] which can be satisfied by a signed certificate from the supplier that he, too, had made enquiries at the time when he came into possession of the prohibited item.[395] The 1976 Act is supplemented by the Control of Trade in Endangered Species (Enforcement) Regulations 1997[396] (known as 'COTES') which provide enforcement measures and penalties to implement Council Regulation 338/97/EC.

---

[394] Ibid, s 4(2).
[395] Ibid, s 4(3).
[396] As amended by SI 2005/1674.

12

CONTAMINATED LAND

A. Introduction	12.01		Measure would cause hardship to	
Control over development	12.03		appropriate person if required	
Building regulations	12.04		by a remediation notice	12.57
Power to abate the condition of a			Remediation	12.60
vacant site/open land which is			Test of reasonableness	12.64
seriously injuring the amenity			The 'appropriate person' for a	
of the locality	12.05		measure	12.65
Statutory nuisance	12.07		Class A and B liability groups	12.65
Water	12.11		Class A liability group	12.68
Activities regulated under the			'Person'	12.68
Environmental Permitting			'Caused'	12.69
Regulations 2007	12.15		'Knowingly permitted'	12.70
Civil liability	12.17		'To any extent referable'	12.73
B. Part IIA of the EPA	12.23		Chemical reactions etc	12.74
'Contaminated land'	12.27		Mines abandoned before	
Pollution linkage	12.31		31 December 1999	12.75
'Significant harm'	12.32		Residual liability of owner/occupier	12.76
'Significant possibility' of			Land which is only	
significant harm	12.33		contaminated land because	
Harm caused by facilities regulated			it is causing pollution of	
under the Environmental			controlled waters	12.76
Permitting Regulations	12.34		The appropriate person in the	
'Pollution of controlled waters'	12.35		case of escapes	12.77
Identification of contaminated land	12.37		Person who causes or knowingly	
Duty to inspect	12.37		permits the contaminants	
Notification and consultation	12.40		to be in the original site	12.79
Special sites	12.43		Subsequent owners of the	
Remediation started before land			original site	12.80
is designated as a special site	12.48		Owner/occupier of the second	
Termination of designation	12.50		site, where the second site	
The duty to serve a remediation			threatens harm	12.81
notice	12.51		Owner/occupier of the second	
Introduction	12.51		site where the third	
Restrictions	12.53		site threatens harm	12.82
Section 78YB—overlap with			Insolvency practitioners	12.84
other controls	12.54		Exclusion and apportionment of	
Section 78H(5)—			liability where there are several	
unreasonable cost,			appropriate persons for a	
voluntary remediation etc	12.55		particular remediation measure	12.85

Exclusion of persons within		Consultation	12.96
Class A liability group	12.88	Contents	12.100
Apportionment between remaining		Other permission	12.102
members of the Class A		Measures affecting rights of	
liability group	12.89	third parties	12.103
Exclusion of members of a		Appeals against remediation	
Class B liability group	12.90	notices	12.105
Apportionment between remaining		Offences of non-compliance	12.107
members of the Class B		Remediation by enforcing authority	12.110
liability group	12.91	Recovery of expenses	12.113
Remediation measure attributable		Charging notices	12.117
to two or more linkages	12.92	Information and reports	12.119
Limits on duly apportioned		National security	12.122
costs to be borne by		Confidential information	12.123
the appropriate person	12.95	Reports	12.128
The remediation notice	12.96	Guidance	12.129

A. Introduction

12.01 Historically, contamination of land has received much less legislative attention than pollution of the air or water. In the late 1980s, however, increased concern about the environment and wider understanding of the toxic effect of many pollutants led to considerable interest in the subject. A 1990 report on contaminated land by the House of Commons Select Committee on the Environment drew attention to this and to the absence of any clear policy on the subject. The government responded with a proposal for registers of land that had been subject to contaminative uses.[1] Concerns about the blighting effect of such a register meant that Section 143 was never brought into effect and was subsequently repealed. There followed a complete change of approach and the addition of a new Part IIA into the 1990 Act.[2] Part IIA was enacted in 1995 but only brought into effect in 2000.

12.02 Although Sections 78A–78YC of the Environmental Protection Act 1990 are the only provisions in English law dealing in terms with contaminated land, they cover only a relatively small part of the topic. They are directed at securing the cleaning up of existing contaminated sites by regulatory intervention. They do not apply if the activity causing the contamination is still taking place and is regulated under other regimes of control. They do not seek to prevent future contamination. They do not deal with civil liability for injury caused to persons or property by contaminants in land. These matters are addressed by other areas of law. In none of these is there any concept of 'contaminated land': the contamination of land is merely the circumstance that triggers the operation of the relevant liability.

---

[1] EPA 1990, s 143.
[2] EPA 1990, ss 78A–78YC.

Control over development

The presence of contaminants in land may mean that a proposed new use of the **12.03** land would be unsafe unless remediation works are carried out. Control over the redevelopment of land is a matter of planning control and one function of the planning system is to secure the carrying out of necessary remediation works before new development can take place. Guidance on the development of contaminated sites is contained in *Planning Policy Statement 23: Planning and Pollution Control* (2004). This makes the following points:

- the provisions of Part IIA focus on achieving remediation voluntarily, where possible: 'much of this will be secured through the planning system rather than through Part IIA;[3]

- the presence of contamination in a site is a material consideration for the planning authority in the formulation of development plan policies and in deciding whether to grant permission for proposed development;[4]

- responsibility for identifying contaminated land and for ensuring that remediation is undertaken to ensure that it can be developed safely rests with the developer;[5]

- the local planning authority must satisfy itself that the potential for contamination and any risks associated with it are properly addressed and that the development incorporates remediation and management measures to deal with 'unacceptable risks', including those covered by Part IIA;[6]

- where there is reason to suspect contamination of the site or where the proposed use would be particularly sensitive to contamination, the authority should normally require a desk top study of the readily available records assessing the previous uses of the site and their potential for contamination. If the potential for contamination is confirmed, further studies to assess the risks and to appraise the options for remediation should be required;[7]

- remediation achieved through the planning system (including by conditions in planning permissions) should secure the removal of unacceptable risks and make the site suitable for the new use. As a minimum, the land should not be capable of being identified as contaminated land under Part IIA after the start of the new use.[8]

---

[3] Planning Policy Statement 23: Planning and Pollution Control (2004), para 19.
[4] Ibid, para 20.
[5] Ibid, para 20.
[6] Ibid, para 23.
[7] Ibid, para 24.
[8] Ibid, para 25.

Building regulations

12.04   Regardless of the existence of any necessary planning permission, building regulations approval for building etc works will be refused if the presence of contamination will directly affect the building or its structure or the health and safety of its
occupiers. Requirement C2 of Schedule 1 of the Building Regulations 2000
requires that 'reasonable precautions shall be taken to avoid danger to health and
safety caused by substances on or in the ground covered or to be covered by the
building and any land associated with the building'. Guidance applicable to this
requirement is provided in Approved Document C on *Site Preparation and
Resistance to Moisture* 2004.

Power to abate the condition of a vacant site/open land which is seriously injuring the amenity of the locality

12.05   Under Section 215 of the Town and Country Planning Act 1990, a local planning
authority can require steps to be taken to abate the condition of a vacant site or
open land which is seriously injuring the amenity of the locality. The power is
exercised by service of a notice on the owner of the land, requiring works of abatement to be carried out. The recipient can appeal against the notice to a magistrates'
court on one of a number of specified grounds. One is that the condition of the
land is attributable to and arises 'in the ordinary course of events' from an activity
which is not in breach of planning control. This covers activities which do not
breach planning control because they are immune from enforcement action as well
as activities expressly permitted by an express grant of planning permission.

12.06   Failure to comply with a Section 215 notice is a criminal offence. In the event of
non-compliance, the local planning authority has power to enter the land and
execute the works itself.

Statutory nuisance

12.07   Under Sections 79 and 80 of the EPA 1990, local authorities are under a duty to
inspect their areas to detect statutory nuisances and to secure the abatement of any
that are found. A statutory nuisance can include premises, accumulations and
deposits which are prejudicial to health or a nuisance.[9] However, where land is in
a 'contaminated state' it cannot amount to a statutory nuisance. Land is in a 'contaminated state' where, as a result of substances in it, it is in a condition where
(a) significant harm is being caused or there is a significant possibility of such
harm being caused or (b) significant pollution of the water environment is being
caused or there is a significant possibility of such pollution being caused.[10] This is

---

[9]   EPA1990, ss 79(1)(a) and (e).
[10]   Ibid, ss 79(1A) and (1B).

intended to mirror the test for the identification of land as contaminated under Part IIA. Sites where the contamination does not reach this threshold are potentially amenable to control under the statutory nuisance regime.

Where a statutory nuisance exists, an abatement notice must be served on the **12.08** 'person responsible for the nuisance', unless the nuisance arises from a structural defect in premises or has not yet occurred, or the person responsible for the nuisance cannot be found, in which cases the notice must be served on the owner/occupier of the premises concerned. The 'person responsible' for the creation of a nuisance is the person to whose act, default or sufferance the nuisance is attributable.[11] The recipient of an abatement notice can appeal against it to a magistrates' court. Failure to comply with an abatement notice without reasonable excuse is a criminal offence. A defence of best practicable means is available in some circumstances.

A private individual aggrieved by a statutory nuisance can make a complaint to a **12.09** magistrates' court under Section 82 of the EPA. On hearing the complaint, the court can make an abatement order and impose a fine on the person responsible for the nuisance.

Under Section 76 of the Building Act 1984, a local authority can serve a notice **12.10** authorizing itself to do works of abatement if it is satisfied that proceeding under the normal abatement notice procedure would cause unreasonable delay.

Water

The Water Resources Act 1991 (WRA) makes it an offence to pollute 'controlled **12.11** waters' (ie, territorial, coastal, inland, and groundwaters). In particular, under Section 85, it is an offence to cause or knowingly permit 'any poisonous, noxious or polluting matter or any solid waste matter' to enter a controlled water. This provision could obviously be used against a site which was leaching contaminants into a waterway. It is a defence to show that the pollution arises from an activity permitted under a discharge consent or a permit under the Environmental Permitting Regulations 2007.[12]

Under Section 161 of the WRA, the Environment Agency can take action to fore- **12.12** stall the threat of pollution to controlled waters and to require remedial action to be taken where pollution has already occurred. It can also recover its expenses from those responsible for the threat.

Permission to discharge pollutants into controlled waters can be granted by a con- **12.13** sent issued by the Environment Agency under the WRA. Consents are normally

---

[11] Ibid, s 79(7).
[12] WRA1991 s 88.

granted for the discharge of effluent by commercial activities and are subject to conditions regulating the nature and quantity of the discharges made.

12.14 A remediation notice under Part IIA cannot impede or prevent the making of a discharge permitted by a discharge consent.[13]

Activities regulated under the Environmental Permitting Regulations 2007

12.15 The Environmental Permitting (England and Wales) Regulations 2007 SI 2000/3538 introduce an integrated permit system to cover matters previously regulated under the Pollution Prevention and Control Act 1999 and by waste management and waste disposal licensing. An 'environmental permit' is required for the operation of a 'regulated facility'.[14] The Regulations provide that existing waste disposal licences, PPC permits, and waste management licences should become environmental permits.[15] Enforcement can be taken if the terms of a permit are being breached or are likely to be breached.[16]

12.16 Part IIA does not apply to any significant harm or pollution of controlled waters by reason of which land would otherwise fall to be regarded as contaminated if that harm etc is attributable to the operation of a regulated facility and enforcement action under Regulations 36, 37, or 42 could be taken against it.[17] This means that if the activity is governed by a permit, enforcement action has to be taken under the 2007 Regulations and the harm in question cannot be the basis for the designation of a site as contaminated land. However if the activity requires, but does not have a permit, Part IIA can operate (an offence under Regulation 38(1)(a) will also be committed).

Civil liability

12.17 Where the contamination of land causes injury to the property of a neighbour or personal injury, the question of civil liability may arise. Such liability is almost entirely ignored by the various statutory regimes discussed above. Only in one instance is a right to seek damages expressly created, namely Section 73(6) of the EPA (damages in respect of loss or injury caused by any deposit of waste which constitutes an offence under Section 33(1) or Section 63(2) of the Act).

12.18 Whether damages can be sought for breach of any other pollution duty, will depend on it being shown that the relevant obligation is intended to benefit a particular class of persons. Given that most environmental legislation is supposed to benefit

---

[13] EPA1990, s 78YB(4).
[14] Reg 12.
[15] Reg 69.
[16] Reg 36.
[17] EPA1990, s 78YB(1).

the public at large, this test will be difficult to satisfy. Some environmental statutes expressly provide that breach of their provisions does not create civil liability.[18]

Opportunities for securing damages for injury caused by contamination are pro-   **12.19**
vided by the tort of nuisance and under the rule in *Rylands v Fletcher*.[19] A nuisance arises if the use or condition of land interferes with the reasonable enjoyment of neighbouring land or causes damage to persons or property on such land. This definition is obviously wide enough to embrace the injurious effects of contamination. Only a person with an interest in the injured land can bring an action. Damages can be sought against any person who has created the nuisance, whether or not he continues to have control of the land from which the nuisance originates. Where the nuisance is naturally occurring or arises as a result of the act of a trespasser, the owner or occupier of the land is only liable if, knowing of the nuisance, he has failed to take reasonable steps to abate it. A defendant is only liable for those kinds of injury which are reasonably foreseeable.

The rule in *Rylands v Fletcher* deals with liability arising from isolated escapes from   **12.20**
land. This applies where a defendant has brought onto his land, for his own purposes, an item or substance which is not naturally there and which is known to be likely to cause injury should it escape. If an escape occurs, the defendant is liable for injury of any foreseeable kind. It is not necessary for a plaintiff to have any interest in land. Although in previous case law there had been a tendency to regard substances associated with industrial processes as 'natural' to the land, the House of Lords in *Cambridge Water Co v Eastern Counties Leather*[20] held that the storage of substantial quantities of chemicals on land could not be so regarded. On the other hand, in *Transco v Stockport MBC*,[21] it was held that bringing water through pipes to provide a domestic water supply to a block of flats should be regarded as a natural us of land.

Liability under both nuisance and *Rylands v Fletcher* is strict. However, the require-   **12.21**
ment of foreseeability of damage means that, in cases of historic contamination, where the harmful effects of pollutants were not appreciated at the relevant time, liability will be avoided.[22]

The final relevant head of tortious liability is occupiers' liability. Under the   **12.22**
Occupier's Liability Act 1957 occupiers of land owe a 'common duty of care' to ensure that 'visitors' are safe for the purposes for which they enter the land. Where the threat to visitors arises from contamination of land, the duty will arise even though the occupier was not responsible for causing the contamination. However,

---

[18] For example WRA 1991, s 100.
[19] (1868) LR 3 HL 330.
[20] [1994] 2 AC 264.
[21] [2004] 2 AC 1.
[22] *Savage v Fairclough* [2000] Env LR 183.

the duty is unlikely to require the remediation of contamination—a warning will be sufficient to discharge the occupier's duty if it enables the visitor to be reasonably safe. In limited circumstances an occupier can owe a duty to trespassers on his land.

B. Part IIA of the EPA

12.23 Part IIA of the EPA provides for local authorities to identify 'contaminated land' and to require its remediation by service of 'remediation notices'. In specified cases, where contamination is likely to be more serious, the land has to be identified as a 'special site' and is the responsibility of the Environment Agency. Guidance issued by the Secretary of State for the Environment, Food, and Rural Affairs is an important part of the regime of Part IIA: in many instances the Act provides for it to be binding. The current guidance is contained in Defra Circular 01/2006 *Contaminated Land* (September 2006) ('the Circular').

12.24 The underlying aim of remediation is to make land suitable for its current use, or for future uses that are likely to receive planning permission, rather than to make it safe for any use.[23]

12.25 Part IIA is supplemented by the Contaminated Land (England and Wales) Regulations 2006, (SI 2006/1380) ('the Regulations').

12.26 Part IIA was extended to contamination caused by radioactivity in England by the Radioactive Contaminated Land (Modification of Enactments) (England) Regulations 2006. The implications of these regulations are considered in x–xx in this work.

'Contaminated land'

12.27 For the purposes of Part IIA land is 'contaminated' if it has been polluted by the entry into it of substances and injury of specified kinds is threatened as a result. Many sites which contain pollutants do not pose any threat of injury and so are not contaminated for the purposes of Part IIA. Section 78A(2) defines 'contaminated land' as:

> any land which appears to the local authority . . . to be in such a condition, by reason of substances in, on or under the land, that
> a. Significant harm is being caused or there is a significant possibility of such harm being caused, or
> b. Pollution of controlled waters is being or is likely to be caused.

12.28 It is proposed to replace (b) with 'significant pollution of controlled waters is being caused or there is a significant possibility of such pollution being caused', it

---

[23] Defra Circular 01/2006, Annex 1, paras 9–15.

being feared that the existing wording may lead to land being regarded as contaminated land as a result of minor pollution of controlled waters.[24]

If it appears to a local authority that two or more sites, when considered together, **12.29** fall within Section 78A(2), both/all should be treated as contaminated, whether or not each individual site would be so considered.[25]

Although the words 'appears to' in Section 78A(2) seem to import an element **12.30** of discretion, the question whether land is contaminated must be determined in accordance with guidance given by the Secretary of State/NAW (Section 78A(5)). This guidance is contained in Chapter A of Annex 3 of the Circular, the import of which is summarized below.

Pollution linkage

Local authorities are told that they must identify for each site a contaminant, a **12.31** 'receptor' (which can include controlled waters) and a 'pathway' (a route or routes through which the potential target is or could be exposed to the contaminant).[26] The identification of these elements is referred to as a 'pollutant linkage'.

'Significant harm'

Section 78A(4) defines 'harm' as 'harm to the health of living organisms or other **12.32** interference with the ecological systems of which they form part, and, in the case of man, includes harm to his property'. The Circular identifies, by means of Table A of Annex 3, the circumstances in which harm to particular receptors is to be regarded as significant for this purpose.

Type of receptor	Description of harm to that type of receptor that is to be regarded as significant harm
1 Human beings	Death, disease, serious injury, genetic mutation, birth defects, or the impairment of reproductive functions. For these purposes, disease is to be taken to mean an unhealthy condition of the body or a part of it and can include, for example, cancer, liver dysfunction, or extensive skin ailments. Mental dysfunction is included only insofar as it is attributable to the effects of a pollutant on the body of the person concerned.In this Chapter, this description of significant harm is referred to as a 'human health effect'.

(cont.)

---

[24] See Defra Circular 01/2006, Annex 2, para 6.31.
[25] EPA1990, s 78X(1).
[26] Defra Circular 01/2006, Annex 2, para 2.6.

Type of receptor	Description of harm to that type of receptor that is to be regarded as significant harm

2 Any ecological system, or living organism forming part of such a system, within a location which is:
 	
  • an area notified as an area of special scientific interest under section 28 of the Wildlife and Countryside Act 1981;
  • any land declared a national nature reserve under section 35 of that Act;
  • any area designated as a marine nature reserve under section 36 of that Act;
  • an area of special protection for birds, established under section 3 of that Act;
  • any European Site within the meaning of regulation 10 of the Conservation (Natural Habitats etc) Regulations 1994 (i.e. Special Areas of Conservation and Special Protection Areas);
  • any candidate Special Areas of Conservation or potential Special Protection Areas given equivalent protection;
  • any habitat or site afforded policy protection under paragraph 6 of PPS9 on nature conservation (i.e. candidate Special Areas of Conservation, potential Special Protection Areas and listed Ramsar sites); or
  • any nature reserve established under section 21 of the National Parks and Access to the Countryside Act 1949.
	For any protected location:
	
	  • harm which results in an irreversible adverse change, or in some other substantial adverse change, in the functioning of the ecological system within any substantial part of that location; or
	  • harm which affects any species of special interest within that location and which endangers the long-term maintenance of the population of that species at that location.
	  • In addition, in the case of a protected location which is a European Site (or a candidate Special Area of Conservation or a potential Special Protection Area), harm which is incompatible with the favourable conservation status of natural habitats at that location or species typically found there.
	
	In determining what constitutes such harm, the local authority should have regard to the advice of English Nature and to the requirements of the Conservation (Natural Habitats etc.) Regulations 1994.
	
	In this Chapter, this description of significant harm is referred to as an 'ecological system effect'.

3 Property in the form of:
 	
  • crops, including timber;
  • produce grown domestically, or on allotments, for consumption;
  • livestock;
  • other owned or domesticated animals;
  • wild animals which are the subject of shooting or fishing rights.
	For crops, a substantial diminution in yield or other substantial loss in their value resulting from death, disease or other physical damage. For domestic pets, death, serious disease, or serious physical damage. For other property in this category, a substantial loss in its value resulting from death, disease, or other serious physical damage.
	
	The local authority should regard a substantial loss in value as occurring only when a substantial proportion of the animals or crops are dead or otherwise no longer fit for their intended purpose. Food should be regarded as being no longer fit for purpose when it fails to comply with the provisions of the Food Safety Act 1990. Where a diminution in yield or loss in value is caused by a pollutant linkage, a 20% diminution or loss should be regarded as a benchmark for what constitutes a substantial diminution or loss.
	
	In this Chapter, this description of significant harm is referred to as an 'animal or crop effect'.

Type of receptor	Description of harm to that type of receptor that is to be regarded as significant harm
4 Property in the form of buildings. For this purpose, 'building' means any structure or erection, and any part of a building including any part below ground level, but does not include plant or machinery comprised in a building.	

'Significant possibility' of significant harm

Authorities are told to take into account the nature and degree of harm threat- **12.33** ened, the susceptibility of potential receptors and the likely timescale in which the harm might occur.[27] The possibility of significant harm should be regarded as significant in circumstances identified in a second table, Table B.

Descriptions of Significant Harm (As Defined in Table A)	Conditions for there Being a Significant Possibility of Significant Harm
1 Human health effects arising from: • the intake of a contaminant; or • other direct bodily contact with a contaminant.	If the amount of the pollutant in the pollutant linkage in question: • which a human receptor in that linkage might take in; or • to which such a human might otherwise be exposed, as a result of the pathway in that linkage, would represent an unacceptable intake or direct bodily contact, assessed on the basis of relevant information on the toxicological properties of that pollutant. Such an assessment should take into account: • the likely total intake of, or exposure to, the substance or substances which form the pollutant, from all sources including that from the pollutant linkage in question; • the relative contribution of the pollutant linkage in question to the likely aggregate intake of, or exposure to, the relevant substance or substances; and • the duration of intake or exposure resulting from the pollutant linkage in question. The question of whether an intake or exposure is unacceptable is independent of the number of people who might experience or be affected by that intake or exposure. Toxicological properties should be taken to include carcinogenic, mutagenic, teratogenic, pathogenic, endocrine-disrupting and other similar properties.

(cont.)

---

[27] Defra Circular 01/2006, Annex 3, para A.28.

Descriptions of Significant Harm (As Defined in Table A)	Conditions for there Being a Significant Possibility of Significant Harm
2 All other human health effects (particularly by way of explosion or fire).	If the probability, or frequency, of occurrence of significant harm of that description is unacceptable, assessed on the basis of relevant information concerning: • that type of pollutant linkage; or • that type of significant harm arising from other causes. • In making such an assessment, the local authority should take into account the levels of risk which have been judged unacceptable in other similar contexts and should give particular weight to cases where the pollutant linkage might cause significant harm which: • would be irreversible or incapable of being treated; • would affect a substantial number of people; • would result from a single incident such as a fire or an explosion; or • would be likely to result from a short-term (that is, less than 24-hour) exposure to the pollutant.
3 All ecological system effects.	If either: • significant harm of that description is more likely than not to result from the pollutant linkage in question; or • there is a reasonable possibility of significant harm of that description being caused and if that harm were to occur or would result in such a degree of damage to features of special interest at the location in question that they would be beyond any practicable possibility of restoration. Any assessment made for these purposes should take into account relevant information for that type of pollution linkage, particularly in relation to the ecotoxicological effects of the pollutant.
4 All animal and crop effects.	If significant harm of that description is more likely than not to result from the pollutant linkage in question, taking into account relevant information for that type of pollutant linkage, particularly in relation to the ecotoxicological effects of the pollutant.
5 All building effects.	If significant harm of that description is more likely than not to result from the pollutant linkage in question during the expected economic life of the building (or, in the case of a scheduled Ancient Monument, the foreseeable future), taking into account relevant information for that type of pollutant linkage.

Harm caused by facilities regulated under the Environmental Permitting Regulations

12.34 Part IIA does not apply to any harm caused by activities covered by an environmental permit in respect of which enforcement action under Regulations 36, 37, or 42 of the 2007 Regulations could be taken.[28] Such harm cannot be the basis on which land is designated as contaminated land.

---

[28] Environmental Permitting (England and Wales) Regulations 2007, r. 78YB(1).

'Pollution of controlled waters' 'Controlled waters' are all territorial, coastal, **12.35** inland, and underground waters. 'Pollution of controlled waters' means 'the entry into controlled waters of any poisonous, noxious or polluting matter, or any solid waste matter' (Section 78A(9)). It is an offence under Section 85 of the WRA 1991 to cause or knowingly permit such substances to enter controlled waters. The test of contamination in Part IIA thus covers activity that is already prohibited. There is no definition in either Act of 'poisonous, noxious or polluting matter'.

It is the entry of substances from the land into the controlled waters that counts— **12.36** authorities are told to disregard substances already present in the controlled waters.[29]

Identification of contaminated land

Duty to inspect

Section 78B imposes on every district and unitary authority a duty to 'cause its **12.37** area to be inspected' to identify contaminated land and for the purpose of deciding whether such land should be designated as a special site.

In performing this duty the local authority must act in accordance with guidance **12.38** issued by the Secretary of State.[30] The guidance is contained in Chapter B of Annex 3 of the Circular. This tells local authorities to take a strategic approach to carrying out the inspection of its area, based on a written strategy. This must be kept under review. The strategy should take into account the history and scale of industrial activity in the authority's area.[31] Designation of land as contaminated must follow a 'scientific and technical assessment'.[32]

To facilitate the process of identification, local authorities have power to enter **12.39** land to take samples and to carry out related activities.[33] If the authority thinks that land, if contaminated, would be a special site, it should endeavour to arrange for the land to be inspected by the Environment Agency.[34]

Notification and consultation

Once a local authority has identified contaminated land, it must 'give notice of **12.40** that fact' to the Environment Agency, the owner and any occupier of the land, and those initially thought to be responsible for remediation.[35] The Circular additionally

---

[29] Defra Circular 01/2006, Annex 3, para A.37.
[30] EPA1990, s 78B(2).
[31] Defra Circular 01/2006, Annex 3, paraB9–14.
[32] Defra Circular 01/2006, Annex 3, paras B44–51.
[33] EA1995, s 108.
[34] Defra Circular 01/2006, Annex 3, paras B28 and B30.
[35] EPA1990, s 78B(3).

requires the authority to prepare a 'written record of the determination' that the land is contaminated. The Circular imposes detailed requirements about the way in which such a determination is to be made and the contents of the written record.[36]

12.41 A further notice under Section 78B must be given if it subsequently transpires that different persons should bear responsibility for remediation.[37]

12.42 The identification of land as contaminated triggers the authority's duty to serve a remediation notice[38] and the associated duty to consult likely recipients and owners/occupiers of the land[39] (see paras 12.60–12.64).

Special sites

12.43 'Special sites' are contaminated sites with particularly severe problems and are the responsibility of the Environment Agency. The categories of contaminated land which must be designated as special sites are prescribed in regulations.[40] In formulating such regulations, the Secretary of State/NAW may have regard to whether land of particular types would or might cause serious harm or serious pollution of controlled waters and to whether the Environment Agency is likely to have expertise in dealing with such harm or pollution.[41] Different provision for different localities can be made.[42]

12.44 Regulations 2 and 3 provide that the following types of contaminated land will be special sites:

- land contaminated by acid tars;
- land that has been used for the purification of crude petroleum or oil extracted from petroleum, shale, or other bituminous substance (except coal);
- land that has been used for the manufacture of explosives;
- land used under an authorization for a prescribed process designated for central control (except where the process comprises solely things being done by the way of remediation);
- land used for a Part A(1) installation under an environmental permit;
- land within a nuclear site;

---

[36] Defra Circular 01/2006, Annex 3, paras B52.
[37] EPA1990, s 78B(4).
[38] Ibid, s 78E.
[39] Ibid, s 78H.
[40] Ibid, s 78C(8).
[41] Ibid, s 78C(10).
[42] Ibid, s 78C(9).

- land used for military purposes and owned or occupied by the Ministry of Defence, the Defence Council, an international headquarters or defence organization, or the service authority of a visiting force;
- land used for the manufacture, production, or disposal of chemical or biological weapons, biological agents or toxins;
- land comprising premises designated under the Atomic Weapons Establishment Act 1991;
- certain lands at Greenwich Hospital (to which s 30 of the Armed Forces Act 1996 applies);
- land which is contaminated by radioactive substances;
- land adjoining or adjacent to any of the above and which is contaminated by the escape of contaminants from such land;
- land that is polluting so badly controlled waters used or intended to be used for the supply of drinking water that treatment is required to secure compliance with the Water Supply (Water Quality) Regulations 2000 and the Private Water Supply Regulations 1991;
- land that is polluting controlled waters so badly that the Surface Waters (Dangerous Substances) Regulations 1989–1998 are breached; and
- land that is polluting specified major aquifers with pollutants identified in List 1 of the Groundwater Directive (80/68/EEC).

12.45 When a local authority is considering whether land falls within the above categories, it must request the advice of the Environment Agency and 'have regard to' any response.[43] If the authority then decides that a special site should be designated, it must notify the Environment Agency, the owner and any occupier, and each person responsible for remediation.[44] If the Environment Agency disagrees with the authority's decision, it can, within 21 days, give notice to the authority to this effect, together with its reasons. The local authority must then refer the question of designation to the Secretary of State/NAW.[45] The Secretary of State/NAW can confirm or reverse the local authority's decision.

12.46 If no reference to the Secretary of State/NAW is required by the Environment Agency, the local authority's decision that the land should be a special site has the effect of so designating it.[46] Where designation takes place in this way, the

---

[43] Ibid, s 78C(3).
[44] Ibid, s 78C(1) and (2).
[45] Ibid, s 78D(1).
[46] Ibid, s 78C(7).

Environment Agency, the owner, any occupier, and the person(s) responsible for remediation have to be notified.[47]

12.47 The Environment Agency can take the initiative in the designation of a special site by serving a notice on the relevant authority stating its view that a particular site should be so designated.[48] The authority must then consider whether the site should indeed be so designated and give notice of its decision to the Environment Agency, the owner and any occupier, and each person responsible for remediation.[49] If the authority decides not to designate the site as a special site, the Environment Agency can, using the procedure under Section 78D, require the question of designation to be referred to the Secretary of State/NAW.

12.48 **Remediation started before land is designated as a special site**   Designation as a special site can only occur if land has already been identified as contaminated land. Ordinarily the identification of land as contaminated sets in motion the procedures for the service of a remediation notice. Not surprisingly, a remediation notice cannot be served while the question of designation as a special site is being settled. Where a remediation notice has been served before the question of designation as a special site has arisen, the Environment Agency has a discretion to adopt the remediation notice. If it does so, it must notify the person responsible for remediation and the relevant local authority.[50]

12.49 If a local authority has begun to take remediation action itself under Section 78N on land which is designated as a special site, the authority can continue with its works and recover its expenses in the normal way (see paras 12.110–12.113 below).[51]

12.50 **Termination of designation**   If it appears to the Agency that land no longer requires to be designated as a special site, it may notify the Secretary of State and the relevant local authority that the designation has been terminated.[52]

The duty to serve a remediation notice

Introduction

12.51 Where land has been designated as contaminated land/a special site, the enforcing authority (the Environment Agency in the case of land is identified as a special site and the local authority in the case of other contaminated land) is under a duty, after consultation, to serve a 'remediation notice' requiring that specified measures be taken to secure the remediation of the contamination.

---

47 Ibid, s 78C(6).
48 Ibid, s 78C(4).
49 Ibid, s 78C(5).
50 Ibid, s 78Q(1).
51 Ibid, s 78Q(1).
52 Ibid, s 78Q(4).

The notice must be served on the person who will be responsible for carrying out   **12.52**
the measures (the 'appropriate person'). The measures required will determine
who is potentially capable of being an appropriate person for the purpose of the
notice.

Restrictions

Significant restrictions on the circumstances in which a remediation notice can be   **12.53**
served are imposed by Sections 78YB and 78H(5).

Section 78YB—overlap with other controls   Section 78YB is intended to ensure   **12.54**
that Part IIA does not duplicate existing regulatory control, and provides as
follows:

- *Harm arising from activities regulated by an environmental permit*   Section
  78YB(1) provides that Part IIA does not apply to harm caused by activities covered by an environmental permit in respect of which enforcement action under
  Regulations 36, 37, or 42 of the 2007 Regulations can be taken (see paras 12.34
  above).

- *Unlawful deposit of controlled waste*   Section 78YB(3) provides that, if land is or
  becomes contaminated land because of the deposit of waste, a remediation
  notice cannot be served if it appears to the enforcing authority that the deposit
  is amenable to control by a waste regulation authority or a waste collection
  authority under Section 59(1) and (7) of the EPA 1990. Under Section 59(1) a
  waste regulation authority or a waste collection authority can require the
  removal of controlled waste deposited on land otherwise than in accordance
  with a environmental permit. Under Section 59(7), such authorities can take
  direct action against such waste in certain circumstances.

- *Activity covered by a discharge consent*   Section 78YB(4) provides that a remediation notice cannot impede or prevent the making of a discharge into controlled
  waters permitted by a consent under the WRA 1991. This exception does not
  apply to past discharge consents.

Section 78H(5)—unreasonable cost, voluntary remediation etc   Section 78H(5)   **12.55**
provides that a remediation notice cannot be served if the enforcing authority is satisfied that one of four further exemptions applies. These are:

- *No reasonable measures*   That there are no remediation measures which could be
  imposed on the person concerned that are reasonable, having regard to the test
  in Section 78E(4).[53] Section 78E(4) provides that:

- 'the only things by way of remediation which the enforcing authority may do or
  require to be done ... are things which it considers reasonable, having regard to—

---

[53] Ibid, s 78H(5)(a).

- the cost which is likely to be involved; and
- the seriousness of the harm or of the pollution of the water environment in question.'

Paragraphs C.29–C.33 of Annex 3 of the Circular indicate that, in assessing whether a remediation measure is reasonable having regard to the cost likely to be involved, the benefits capable of being achieved (in terms of the reduction/mitigation of harm or pollution of controlled waters) must make it worth incurring the costs involved. The timing of the remediation works should be considered. The financial circumstances of the appropriate person are not relevant to this assessment.

- Voluntary remediation. That appropriate remediation measures are being or will be taken without the need for a remediation notice. Where the person responsible for remediation is willing to accept responsibility voluntarily, he can either do the works himself or enter into an agreement with the enforcing authority that the authority will do the works at his expense.[54] The Circular lays considerable importance on achieving remediation voluntarily.[55]

- Enforcing authority is responsible for remediation. That it appears that the person responsible for remediation is the enforcing authority itself.[56]

- Direct action. That the enforcing authority's powers to take action itself under Section 78N (see below) are exercisable.[57]

12.56 Where the first exception applies, the enforcing authority has to prepare a 'remediation declaration' setting out why it would have required measures to be taken and the grounds that have satisfied it that the steps cannot be required.[58] In the other three cases, the person or authority taking the remediation measures must prepare a 'remediation statement' giving details of the remediation action that has been or will be taken, the persons or bodies taking such action and the timescale for such action.[59] It is obviously assumed that where the authority concludes that it is itself responsible for taking remediation action (the third situation), it will in fact do so.

12.57 **Measure would cause hardship to appropriate person if required by a remediation notice** Although the financial resources of the appropriate person are not relevant to the test of reasonableness etc in Section 78E(4), Sections 78N(3)(e),

---

[54] EPA1990, s 78H(5)(b).
[55] Defra Circular 01/2006, Annex 1, paras 16–18, and Annex 2, para 6.6.
[56] Ibid, s 78H(5)(c).
[57] Ibid, s 78H(5)(d).
[58] Ibid, s 78H(6).
[59] Ibid, s 78H(7).

78P(2), and 78H(5) mean that a remediation notice cannot be served if compliance would cause hardship of defined kinds to the appropriate person.

These provisions are dealt with in detail below, but in summary their effect is as **12.58** follows. Under 78N(3) an enforcing authority has power to take direct action in certain situations. One is where the costs of the measure could not be recovered from the relevant appropriate person given the test in Section 78P(2). Section 78P(2) provides that, in deciding whether to recover such costs, the authority should consider the hardship that this would cause to the appropriate person. This test is further explained in Chapter E of Annex 3 of the Circular.

In any case where the enforcing authority has power under Section 78N to carry **12.59** out a measure itself, it is precluded from serving a remediation notice requiring that measure.[60] The hardship that would be inflicted on the appropriate person will thus prevent a measure from being required in a remediation notice—although the authority can still carry out the measure itself.[61]

Remediation

'Remediation' is widely defined. It means works for the purpose of assessing the **12.60** condition of the contaminated land/controlled waters or other nearby land, works etc to prevent, minimize, or mitigate the significant harm or pollution of the controlled waters which has caused the land to be identified as contaminated, works to restore the land/waters to their former state, and subsequent monitoring of the land/waters.[62] In determining what is to be done by way of remediation and the standard of remediation to be sought, the enforcing authority must have regard to guidance issued by the Secretary of State/NAW.[63] This guidance is set out in Part C of Annex 3 of the Circular.

Paragraph C.17 of Annex 3 indicates that remediation should make contami- **12.61** nated land suitable for its present or likely future use. Paragraph C.18 provides that the standard to be achieved for each pollution linkage is:

> . . . that which would be achieved by the use of a remediation package which forms the best practicable techniques of remediation for—
>
> - ensuring that the linkage is no longer a significant pollution linkage, by doing any one or more of the following –
> - removing or treating the pollutant;
> - breaking or removing the pathway; or
> - protecting or removing the receptor; and

---

[60] Ibid, s 78H(5).
[61] Defra Circular 1/2006, Annex 2, para 10.5.
[62] EPA1990, s 78A(7).
[63] Ibid, s 78(5).

- remedying the effect of any significant harm or pollution of controlled waters which is resulting or has already resulted from the significant pollution linkage.'

12.62 In assessing what would be the best practicable techniques, authorities should 'work on the basis of authoritative scientific and technical advice'.[64] 'Where there is established good practice for the remediation of a particular. . . linkage, the authority should assume that this represents the best practicable technique for a linkage of that type, provided that:

    A. It is satisfied that the use of that means of remediation is appropriate. . .; and

    B. the remediation actions involved would be reasonable having regard to the cost which is likely to be involved and the seriousness of the harm or pollution of controlled waters in question.'[65]

12.63 Where there is more than one pollution linkage the remediation notice must deal with each, although conflicting or overlapping requirements should be avoided.[66]

Test of reasonableness

12.64 Remediation measures must satisfy the test of reasonableness imposed by Section 78E(4) discussed at paras 12.42–12.43 above.

The 'appropriate person' for a measure

Class A and B liability groups

12.65 The 'appropriate person' is the person who, in accordance with the terms of Section 78F, is responsible for taking a particular remediation measure. Different measures in respect of the same piece of land may have different appropriate persons.

12.66 As has been seen, the essential feature of contaminated land is that substances have entered it and that significant harm or pollution of controlled waters is being caused/threatened as a result. In the first instance the appropriate person for a particular remediation measure is 'any person' who 'caused or knowingly permitted' the substance(s) to which the measure is 'to any extent referable' to be present in the land.[67] Persons who are appropriate persons for a measure on this basis are known as the 'Class A liability group' for that measure.

12.67 However, if no person falling within Section 78F(2) and (3) can be found for the measure, the appropriate person for that measure is the present owner or occupier

---

[64] Defra Circular 1/2006, Annex 3, para C.21.
[65] Ibid, para C.22.
[66] DEFRA Circular 1/2006, Annex ?, paras 6.26–9.
[67] EPA1990, s 78F(2) and (3).

of the land.[68] Such persons are known as the 'Class B liability group' for that measure. This means that, for any particular remediation measure, there will always be an appropriate person.

Class A liability group

'Person'   In *R (National Grid Gas plc) v Environment Agency*[69] it was held that the   **12.68**
reference to 'person' in Section 78F(2) was not apt to cover every person who, by statute, became the successor to the liabilities of original polluters. In that case, pollution had been caused by two private gas companies: these were amalgamated and the amalgamated company was then nationalized. The applicant was the statutory successor of the nationalized gas board and was held not to be the appropriate person for measures referable to the polluting substance. In that case it was important that the transfer scheme transferred liabilities that existed 'immediately before' the transfer: the transfers took place many years before liabilities under Part IIA were created.

'Caused'   'Caused' is a familiar term in environmental law. It has been held,   **12.69**
under Section 85 of the WRA 1991, that 'causing' involves no mental element.[70] Companies are vicariously liable for pollution caused by their employees acting in the ordinary course of their employment.[71] The Circular suggests that the term requires involvement in some active operation or series of operations, including, in appropriate cases, a failure to act.[72]

'Knowingly permitted'   The Circular suggests that a current owner of land will   **12.70**
be regarded as knowingly permitting contaminants to 'be in' his land if he is aware of their presence and fails to do something that he is able to do to remove them.[73]

It was held in *Circular Facilities (London) Ltd v Sevenoaks DC*[74] that what is   **12.71**
required is knowledge of the presence of the substance, not knowledge of its potential to cause contamination.

The Circular expresses the view that an owner/occupier will not be regarded as   **12.72**
knowingly permitting the contaminants to be in his land simply by reason of having been notified by the local authority that the land is contaminated.[75]

---

[68] EPA1990, s 78F(4).
[69] [2007] 1 WLR 1780.
[70] *NRA v Yorkshire Water Services Ltd* [1995] 1 All ER 225.
[71] *NRA v McAlpine* [1994] 4 All ER 286 and see also *Empress Car Co (Abertillery) Ltd v NRA* [1998] 1 All ER 481.
[72] Defra Circular 1/2006, Annex 2, para 9.9.
[73] Ibid, para 9.10.
[74] [2005] JPL 1624.
[75] Defra Circular 1/2006, Annex 2, para 9.13.

12.73 **'To any extent referable'**   Section 78F(3) means that, if a measure is not referable to the substance which the person caused or knowingly permitted to be in the land, that person is not an appropriate person for the measure. On the other hand a remediation measure can be treated as being referable to a substance even though the need for the measure is only partially attributable to the presence of that substance.[76]

12.74 **Chemical reactions etc**   If a person has caused or knowingly permitted a substance to be in land and the substance is subject to a chemical reaction or biological process, that person is regarded as also having caused or knowingly permitted any resulting substances to be in the land.[77]

12.75 **Mines abandoned before 31 December 1999**   Where a person permits water from a mine abandoned before 31 December 1999 to enter any controlled waters, or to reach a place where it is likely to enter controlled waters, a remediation notice cannot require him to do anything that he could not have been required to do had Section 78(2)(b) not been enacted (Section 78(2)(b) provides that land is contaminated if it causes or is likely to cause pollution of controlled waters).[78] In other words, that person can only be required to take a measure if the substances in the mine are also causing significant harm or the significant possibility of such harm, and the measure is designed to address this. Such a person may have liabilities under the WRA 1991 in respect of the pollution of the controlled waters: the purpose of this provision is to ensure that Part IIA does not impose any additional liabilities on him.

Residual liability of owner/occupier

12.76 **Land which is only contaminated land because it is causing pollution of controlled waters**   Where land is treated as contaminated because its condition causes pollution of controlled waters or the likelihood of such pollution, there is no residual liability in respect of any remediation measure which the owner/occupier could not have been required to carry out had Section 78(2)(b) not been enacted (Section 78J(2)). Like Section 78J(3) discussed above, this is to ensure that the liabilities of such an owner/occupier for the pollution controlled waters are limited to those under the WRA.

The appropriate person in the case of escapes

12.77 A feature of many contaminants is their mobility. Sites often become contaminated through the migration of contaminants from other land. Section 78K is designed to avoid the burden of remediation falling on the owner/occupier of the

---

[76] EPA1990, s 78F(10).
[77] Ibid, s 78F(9).
[78] Ibid, s 78J(3).

receiving land. It also attempts to deal with the situation where contaminants from an original site pass into a second site and thence into a third site.

The upshot of the complicated provisions of this section can be expressed as follows. **12.78**

Person who causes or knowingly permits the contaminants to be in the original **12.79** **site**   A person who causes or knowingly permits the contaminants to be in any land is taken to have caused or knowingly permitted those substances to be in any other land to which they appear to the enforcing authority to have escaped.

Subsequent owners of the original site   Where an original owner of land caused **12.80** or knowingly permitted contaminants to be in a site and the contaminants escape, a subsequent owner of the site has no liability for the effects of the escape, unless he caused or knowingly permitted the escape.[79]

Owner/occupier of the second site, where the second site threatens harm   Where **12.81**

- a person causes or knowingly permits contaminants to be in a site;
- they escape (whether directly or indirectly) into a second site; and
- remediation is required of a site (which may or may not be the second site) or controlled waters, as a result of the second site threatening harm;
- the owner/occupier of the second site is only liable if:
  (i) he caused or knowingly permitted the contaminants to be in his site; or
  (ii) he is owner/occupier of the site/waters requiring the remediation action.[80]

Owner/occupier of the second site where the third site threatens harm   Where **12.82**

- a person causes or knowingly permits contaminants to be in a site;
- they escape (whether directly or indirectly) into a third site via a second site; and
- remediation is required as a result of the third site threatening harm;
- the owner/occupier of the second site is only liable if:
  (i) he caused or knowingly permitted the contaminants to be in his site; or
  (ii) he is also the owner/occupier of the third site.[81]

These restrictions do not cut down the power of an enforcing authority to take **12.83** remediation action itself under Section 78N (see paras 12.110–12.113 below). However, the authority cannot recover the cost of such works from any owner or

---

[79] Ibid, s 78K(5)
[80] Ibid, s 78K(3).
[81] Ibid, s 78K(4).

occupier of a site if that person could not himself have been required to do the works by reason of these restrictions.[82]

Insolvency practitioners

12.84   During the passage of the Environmental Protection Bill, insolvency practitioners expressed concern that they could be liable for remediation measures by virtue of their administration of companies in receivership if those companies had been responsible for contamination. Section 78X(3) and (4) exempts receivers from personal liability for the cost of any remediation measure, save to the extent that the contamination was caused by their own acts or omissions.

Exclusion and apportionment of liability where there are several appropriate persons for a particular remediation measure

12.85   It may transpire that there are several appropriate persons for an identified remediation measure. There may be several different people who are caught by the test of 'causing or knowingly permitting' pollutants to be in the land—for example, the original polluter, the original owner who permitted the pollution, and subsequent owners who, knowing of the problem, failed to take steps to deal with it. Where residual liability is relevant, the occupier of a site may not be the same person as its owner.

12.86   Chapter D of Annex 3 lays down rules for (i) the exclusion of liability of different members of Class A and B liability groups and (ii) the apportionment of the cost of carrying out the measure if several appropriate persons remain.

12.87   In some cases a single remediation measure may be required to deal with the consequences of several pollution linkages and different groups of appropriate persons may exist in respect of each linkage. There are rules for attributing responsibility for the measure as between the groups. Once this has been done the rules for excluding liability of persons within the group and for apportioning the cost between the remaining persons apply.

Exclusion of persons within Class A liability group

12.88   Where there is more than one person in the Class A liability group for a measure, the sequential exclusions set out in paragraphs D47–D72 should be applied until only one Class A person remains. In summary the tests are as follows:

- *Test 1 (excluded activities)* This excludes anyone who is treated as having caused or knowingly permitted the pollutant to be in the land only by reason of having

---

[82]   EPA1990, s 78K(6).

carried out certain specified activities which, in the Government's view, carry limited responsibility. These activities include:

- giving or withholding financial assistance;
- carrying out action under an underwriting policy;
- providing legal, financial, engineering, scientific, or technical advice;
- creating a tenancy over the land;
- issuing a statutory permission, licence, or consent for any action or omission by reason of which someone else has caused or knowingly permitted the presence of the pollutant; and
- performing acts required in a contract with someone else who caused or knowingly permitted the pollutants to be on the land.

- *Test 2 (payments made for remediation)* This excludes a member of the Class A liability group if he has effectively paid another member of the group to carry out adequate remediation.

- *Test 3 (sold with information)* This excludes a member of the Class A liability group if he sold the land or let it on a long lease and ensured that the purchaser/tenant knew of the presence of the pollutants and had the opportunity to take this into account when agreeing the price. This exclusion only applies if the purchaser/tenant is also a Class A person and the transaction was at arm's length.

- *Test 4 (change to substances)* This excludes a member of the Class A liability group if the significant pollution linkage has only arisen because another member of the group introduced another substance which reacted with the original substance.

- *Test 5 (escaped substances)* Where land is contaminated as a result of the escape of pollutants from other land, this excludes anyone who is a member of the Class A liability group solely because he caused or knowingly permitted the substances to be present in the original site where another member of the group was responsible for their escape.

- *Test 6 (introduction of pathways or receptors)* This excludes a member of the Class A liability group if the relevant pollution linkage has only arisen because another member of the group has subsequently introduced a pathway or receptor.

Apportionment between remaining members of the Class A liability group

If, after the application of these exclusions, two or more members of the group **12.89** remain, their respective liabilities for the remediation measure are fixed in accordance with their 'relative . . . responsibility . . . for creating or continuing the risk now being caused by the significant pollution linkage'.[83] Further guidance is given in paragraphs D77–D86.

---

[83] Defra Circular 1/2006, Annex 3, Para D75.

Exclusion of members of a Class B liability group

12.90 Where, in respect of any particular linkage there are several members of the Class B liability group, the tests set out in paragraphs D88–D89 are applied. These aim to exclude any member of the Class B liability group who does not have an interest in the capital value of the land.

Apportionment between remaining members of the Class B liability group

12.91 If, after the application of these tests, two or more members of the Class B liability group remain and the remediation measures relate to a particular part of the land in question, liability is imposed on the owner/occupier of that part. Otherwise liability is apportioned according to the share of the capital value of the whole of the land held by each.[84]

Remediation measure attributable to two or more linkages

12.92 A particular remediation measure may deal with two or more pollution linkages: this can be because the same measure is required for both ('common action') or because the measure is part of the best combined scheme for the linkages ('collective action'). Where there are different pollution linkages there are likely to be different liability groups and rules in paragraphs 89–100 of Annex D deal with the attribution of responsibility for the measure between these.

12.93 In the case of common action:

- if there are two or more Class A liability groups for the linkages, they should bear the full cost equally;
- if there is no Class A liability group but two or more Class B liability groups, these should be treated as a single group and the rules for exclusion and apportionment for members of a Class B liability group applied.[85]

12.94 In the case of collective action, where there are two or more Class A liability groups, division of the costs should be based on the hypothetical costs of each element of the collective action.[86] Where there are two or more Class B liability groups, the above rule applies.

Limits on duly apportioned costs to be borne by the appropriate person

12.95 Once the enforcing authority has conducted the above exercise and apportioned the costs of each remediation measure between the non-excluded appropriate persons, it must consider whether any of those persons should be relieved of his liability for the cost of the measure. To decide this the authority must consider

---

84 Ibid, Paras D91–97.
85 Ibid, Paras D98–99.
86 Ibid, Paras D100.

whether, if it carried out the remediation measures itself, it would seek to recover that cost from that person. The recovery of costs is considered below. It will be seen that costs may not be recovered if this would cause hardship. Where the authority decides that the appropriate person would be able to claim such hardship, it cannot serve a remediation notice requiring that appropriate person to carry out/contribute to the cost of that measure.[87]

The remediation notice

Consultation

Before a remediation notice can be served, the enforcing authority must make **12.96** reasonable endeavours to consult the contemplated recipient of the notice, the owner, and any other person who appears to occupy the whole or part of the land, on the question of what measures are to be taken by way of remediation (Section 78H(1)). In addition, Section 78H(3) provides that a remediation notice cannot be served for at least three months after notification to the appropriate person(s) of the identification of the land as contaminated or of its designation as a special site. Although there is no mention of consultation taking place during this period, this is plainly what is intended.

In detail, Section 78H(3) provides as follows: **12.97**

- A remediation notice cannot be served by a local authority between the initial identification of the land as contaminated under Section 78B(1) and three months after the Section 78B(3) notice of this identification has been served on the appropriate person.[88]

- In the case of a special site, a remediation notice cannot be served between the initial identification of the land as contaminated under Section 78B(1) and three months after notice of designation as a special site by the local authority. If the Environment Agency challenges the designation as a special site, the period is extended to three months from the date of the Secretary of State's decision.[89]

- Where the initiative for designation of a special site comes from the Environment Agency, no remediation notice can be served between the initial notice from the Agency to the local authority telling it to consider the designation of the land as a special site and three months after notice of the decision of the local authority/Secretary of State.[90]

---

[87] Defra Circular 1/2006, Annex 2, Paras 10.1–9 and see paras x–xx above.
[88] EPA1990, s 78H(3)(a).
[89] Ibid, s 78H(3)(b).
[90] Ibid, s 78H(3)(c).

12.98 The consultation process is extremely important. It offers appropriate persons the opportunity to persuade the enforcing authority not to serve a remediation notice, for example by offering a negotiated settlement or by showing that the contemplated remediation steps are not reasonable, taking into account cost and the seriousness of the harm.

12.99 These time restrictions do not apply where it appears to the enforcing authority that there is an imminent danger of serious harm or of pollution of controlled waters.[91]

Contents

12.100 A remediation notice, when served, must specify the steps which have to be taken in order to achieve the remediation of the contamination and the periods within which such steps must be taken.[92] Different requirements can be imposed on different persons.[93] Where two or more appropriate persons are responsible for the same measure, the remediation notice must state the proportion of the cost of the measure that each is liable to bear.[94] Regulation 4 prescribes the contents of a remediation notice.

12.101 The service of a remediation notice must be recorded on the register maintained by the enforcing authority (see below at paras 12.119–12.127).

Other permission

12.102 Remediation may require planning permission or a permit under the Environmental Permitting Regulations.[95]

Measures affecting rights of third parties

12.103 A remediation notice can require an appropriate person to take measures which will interfere with the rights of third parties. Under Section 78G(2), a person whose consent is required for such works is obliged to grant, or join in granting such consent. Before serving a remediation notice which will require the granting of such rights, the enforcing authority must make reasonable endeavours to consult such persons.[96] This obligation does not prevent the immediate service of a remediation notice where imminent danger of serious harm is threatened.[97]

---

[91] Ibid, s 78H(4).
[92] Ibid, s 78E(1).
[93] Ibid, s 78E(2).
[94] Ibid, s 78E(2).
[95] Defra Circular 1/2006, Annex 1, paras 42 and 50.
[96] EPA1990, s 78G(3).
[97] Ibid, s 78G(4).

Persons who are compelled to grant rights etc under Section 78G are entitled to **12.104**
claim compensation from the appropriate person.[98]

Appeals against remediation notices

Under Section 78L, an appeal can be made against a remediation notice within 21 **12.105**
days to the Secretary of State/NAW by anyone on whom the notice was served. If
the Secretary of State/NAW is satisfied that the notice contains a 'material defect',
it must be quashed. Otherwise the Secretary of State/NAW has a discretion to
confirm, modify, or quash the notice and to extend the period for compliance.[99]

The procedure for making such appeals and the grounds on which appeals may be **12.106**
made, are covered in regs7–12 of the Regulations. Appeals are determined by
holding a hearing or an inquiry. It is likely that the availability of this right of
appeal will make judicial review an inappropriate avenue for challenging a remediation notice, at least at the behest of persons on whom the notice is served.

Offences of non-compliance

It is an offence for a person on whom a remediation notice has been served to fail **12.107**
to comply with its requirements without reasonable excuse.[100] Where the remediation notice is served on two or more persons and requires each to pay a specified
proportion of the costs of the works, it is also a defence for a defendant to prove
that his non-compliance arose because one or more of the other persons refused
or was not able to comply with the notice.[101]

Where the contaminated land in question is industrial, trade, or business premises, **12.108**
the maximum penalty on summary conviction is a fine of £20,000 or such larger
sum as the Secretary of State may fix.[102] In other cases the maximum fine is level 5
on the standard scale.[103] There is provision for daily fines for continued breaches
after an initial conviction.

The enforcing authority can also apply to the High Court for an injunction in **12.109**
order to secure compliance with the remediation notice if it thinks that criminal
proceedings would be an ineffectual remedy.[104]

---

[98] Ibid, s 78G(5).
[99] Ibid, s 78L(2) and (3).
[100] Ibid, s 78M (1).
[101] Ibid, s 78M(2).
[102] Ibid, s 78M(4).
[103] Ibid, s 78M(3).
[104] Ibid, s 78M(5).

Remediation by enforcing authority

12.110 Normally an enforcing authority can only secure remediation by means of a remediation notice. However, the authority can carry out remediation measures itself in six circumstances specified in Section 78N: where the authority is satisfied that any of these applies, it is prohibited from serving a remediation notice.[105] These circumstances are that:

1) The enforcing authority considers that it is necessary to take action itself to prevent imminent danger of serious harm or serious pollution of controlled waters.[106] In this case the enforcing authority can do whatever it considers appropriate by way of remediation.[107]

2) The appropriate person has made a written agreement with the enforcing authority for that authority to do, at the appropriate person's expense, works which he would otherwise be required to do. In this case the enforcing authority can do anything provided for in the agreement.[108]

3) An earlier remediation notice has been served, but the recipient has failed to comply with it. In this case the enforcing authority can do anything which the remediation notice required.[109]

4) The enforcing authority is precluded from imposing a requirement on an appropriate person by Sections 78J (pollution of controlled waters and from abandoned mines) or 78K (limits on liability in respect of escapes).[110] In this case the enforcing authority can carry out such requirements itself.

5) The enforcing authority considers that, if it were to do the remediation works itself, it would not exercise its right to recover the cost of the works from the appropriate person, or would only seek to recover a proportion of the costs (see paragraph 12.114).[111] This rather convoluted provision seems to entitle enforcing authorities to take action themselves in situations where they do not think that the appropriate person would be able to afford to carry out the necessary works.

6) After reasonable inquiry, no appropriate person in relation to the particular measure has been found.[112] In this case the enforcing authority can do whatever the appropriate person could have been required to do.

12.111 Steps taken under Section 78N must satisfy the test of reasonableness in Section 78E(4) discussed at paragraph 12.42 above.

---

[105] Ibid, s 78H(5)(d).
[106] Ibid, s 78N(3)(a).
[107] Defra Circular 1/2006, Annex 2, Paras 5.1–5.8.
[108] EPA1990, s 78N(3)(b).
[109] Ibid, s 78N(3)(c).
[110] Ibid, s 78N(3)(d).
[111] Ibid, s 78N(3)(e).
[112] Ibid, s 78N(3)(f).

The enforcing authority has no power to carry out remediation measures in **12.112** those situations where Section 78YB means that a remediation notice cannot be served (because the contaminating activity is regulated under other regimes of control.[113]

Recovery of expenses

Where an enforcing authority carries out remediation works itself under Section **12.113** 78N, it is said to be entitled to recover its costs from the relevant appropriate person unless the situation falls within 2 or 4 above.[114] The entitlement in cases falling within 5 above presumably relates to the proportion of the works.

Where the authority is entitled to recover its costs from more than one appropri- **12.114** ate person, it can recover a proportion of the expenses from each. The proportions are determined using the above mentioned rules for apportioning liability between appropriate persons.

In exercising this power the authority must consider any hardship which such **12.115** recovery may cause and the guidance set out in Section E of Annex 3 of the Circular.[115] Section E provides that, with regard to members of a Class A liability group, the authority should seek to recover its costs more readily if the person was carrying on a business when he caused or knowingly permitted the pollutants to enter the land. The authority should consider waiving or reducing the liability where (i) another person caused or knowingly permitted the contaminants to be in the land, (ii) that person cannot now be found, but (iii) if he could, he would bear the entire responsibility for remediation. The authority can also reduce or waive its claim in certain circumstances related to the rules of exclusion from liability.[116]

With regard to members of a Class B liability group, authorities should consider **12.116** waiving or reducing the liability where the costs of remediation exceed the value of the land[117] or where the owner/occupier shows that he took such steps as could reasonably have been expected to establish the presence of the pollutants before purchase, but was nevertheless unaware of their presence.[118] Where the premises are a dwelling, the authority should consider waiving part/all of the liability if the owner/occupier did not know and could not reasonably have been expected to know of the presence of pollutants when he bought the house.[119]

---

[113] Ibid, s 78N(2).
[114] Ibid, s 78P(1).
[115] Ibid, s 78P(2).
[116] Defra Circular 1/2006, Annex 3, para E.33.
[117] Ibid, para E.40.
[118] Ibid, para E.42.
[119] Ibid, para E.44.

12.117 **Charging notices**   Where costs are recoverable from an owner of contaminated land who has caused or knowingly permitted the relevant substances to be in the land, the enforcing authority can serve a 'charging notice' creating a charge on the premises to cover the costs of the works, and interest.[120]

12.118 A person served with a charging notice can appeal against it to the county court within 21 days.[121] Grounds of appeal will be prescribed by regulations: no such regulations have yet been made. On appeal the court can confirm the notice without modification, substitute a different sum, or order that the notice should have no effect.[122]

Information and reports

12.119 Under Section 78R local authorities and the Environment Agency must keep registers giving prescribed particulars of the following:

- remediation notices issued by it;
- appeals against such notices;
- remediation statements and declarations;
- appeals against charging notices;
- notices designating land as a special site;
- notices terminating the designation of a site as a special site;
- notification given by persons on whom a remediation notice has been served, or who have been required to prepare a remediation statement, stating what they claim to have done by way of remediation;
- notifications from the owner or occupier of land in respect of which a remediation notice has been served, or in respect of which a remediation statement has been prepared and published, of what he claims has been done on the land by way of remediation;
- convictions for the offence of failure to comply with a remediation notice; and
- the other matters set out in Schedule 3 of the Regulations.

12.120 Notification by any person of what he claims has been done by way of remediation does not constitute a representation by the authority maintaining the register that such works etc have in fact been done, nor as to the manner in which they may have been done.[123]

---

[120] EPA1990, s 78P(3) and (4).
[121] Ibid, s 78P(8).
[122] Ibid, s 78P(9).
[123] Ibid, s 78R(3).

The Environment Agency must supply each local authority with such entries **12.121** from its register as relate to land in the authority's area. The authority must then enter such particulars on its own register. Registers maintained by the Environment Agency and local authorities must be open to public inspection.[124]

National security

The Secretary of State/NAW has power to prevent the inclusion of information in **12.122** registers where he/it considers that such inclusion would be contrary to the interests of national security. He/it can give enforcing authorities directions specifying types of information which either must be excluded on this basis or which must be referred to him/it for determination on the question of exclusion. The Secretary of State/NAW must be notified of any information that is excluded from a register on this ground. A person who considers that information should be excluded for this reason can notify the Secretary of State/NAW to this effect. If such a notification is made, the information cannot be included on a register unless the Secretary of State/NAW so determines (see Section 78S).[125]

Confidential information

Section 78R will require the disclosure of information which is commercially confi- **12.123** dential. Section 78T provides for the exclusion of certain information of this type.

Information is regarded as commercially confidential in relation to any person if **12.124** its inclusion on the register would prejudice to an unreasonable degree his commercial interests. In assessing this, no account is taken of prejudice relating to the value of the contaminated land or to the ownership or occupation of that land.[126] If the enforcing authority/Secretary of State/NAW determines that information satisfies this test in relation to a person carrying on a business under the procedure described below, the information cannot be included on a register without that person's consent. However the Secretary of State/NAW can direct that information of specified types must be included on the register regardless of consent.[127]

Where information is excluded under Section 78T, the register must contain a **12.125** statement indicating the existence of the information.[128]

Where an enforcing authority obtains information which, in its view, might be **12.126** commercially confidential, it must notify the person concerned and give him a reasonable opportunity to object to its inclusion on the register. The enforcing

---

[124] Ibid, s 78R(4), (6), and (8).
[125] Ibid, s 78P(9).
[126] Ibid, s 78T(10) and (11).
[127] Ibid, s 78T(1).
[128] Ibid, s 78R(7).

authority must take such objections/representations into account before determining whether the information is commercially confidential. Where the authority determines that the information is not commercially confidential, the person must be given the opportunity to appeal to the Secretary of State. If an appeal is made, the information cannot be entered onto the register unless the Secretary of State dismisses the appeal or the appeal is withdrawn.[129]

12.127 Commercially confidential information which is excluded from a register is treated as ceasing to be commercially confidential four years after the original determination. The person who furnished the information may, however, apply to the enforcing authority for a determination that the information should continue to be regarded as commercially confidential and therefore excluded.[130]

Reports

12.128 Under Section 78U the Environment Agency is under a duty 'from time to time', and whenever the Secretary of State/NAW so directs, to produce and publish reports on the state of contaminated land in England and Wales. The Agency can, for the purposes of preparing such reports, require a local authority to furnish it with such information as the authority has, or may be expected to obtain, in connection with its contaminated land functions.

Guidance

12.129 The Environment Agency can give a local authority guidance on particular contaminated sites in the authority's area. The local authority must have regard to such guidance in exercising its powers and duties with regard to that land, except to the extent that such guidance is in conflict with guidance issued by the Secretary of State.[131]

12.130 The Secretary of State's power to issue guidance has been discussed above. Where this guidance is binding it has to be laid before Parliament.[132] Guidance on the following matters is binding:

- the identification of contaminated land;[133]
- the duty to inspect for contaminated land;[134]

---

[129] Ibid, s 78T(2) and (3).
[130] Ibid, s 78T(8).
[131] Ibid, s 78V(1) and (2).
[132] Ibid, s 78YA(2).
[133] Ibid, s 78A(2) and (5).
[134] Ibid, s 78B(2).

- on which of two or more potential appropriate persons should be excused from liability;[135] and

- the proportion of the costs of remediation to be borne by two or more appropriate persons.[136]

Before exercising any of his powers to give guidance, the Secretary of State must **12.131** consult the Environment Agency and such other bodies as he considers appropriate.[137]

---

[135] Ibid, s 78F(6).
[136] Ibid, s 78F(7).
[137] Ibid, s 78YA(1).

13

MISCELLANEOUS ENVIRONMENTAL CONTROLS

A. **Introduction**	13.01	
B. **Pollution of the Air**	13.02	
Alkali works	13.02	
Clean Air Acts	13.05	
The Ringelmann Chart	13.06	
Prevention measures—industrial furnaces	13.10	
Prevention measures—domestic furnaces	13.14	
Monitoring	13.15	
The height of chimneys	13.19	
Smoke control areas	13.26	
Creating a smoke control area	13.31	
Smoke control areas—Offences	13.38	
Burning unauthorized fuels	13.39	
Adaptation of existing furnaces and fireplaces	13.43	
Motor fuel and air pollution	13.49	
The lead content of petrol	13.52	
The lead content of diesel	13.54	
Cable burning	13.57	
Research into air pollution	13.58	
Records and returns	13.60	
Notices connected with research and publicity	13.65	
Mines and quarries	13.70	
Railway engines	13.71	
Vessels	13.72	
Research establishments	13.73	
The Crown	13.74	
Administration	13.75	
Corporations, occupiers of premises, and powers of entry	13.77	

Conclusion	13.78	
C. **Noise Pollution—Construction Sites**	13.79	
Control of works	13.79	
Sanctions	13.83	
Section 61 consent	13.85	
D. **Loudspeakers in Streets**	13.88	
The controls	13.88	
Relaxation of control	13.91	
Relaxation of control—Procedure	13.94	
E. **Noise Abatement Zones**	13.96	
Introduction—Declaring a noise abatement zone	13.96	
The controls	13.98	
The register of noise levels	13.101	
Reductions in noise levels	13.103	
Anti-Social behaviour	13.108	
F. **Noise from Plant or Machinery**	13.112	
G. **Aircraft Noise**	13.122	
Introduction	13.122	
Control by the Secretary of State for Transport	13.124	
Short take-off and landing (STOL) aircraft	13.133	
H. **Noise—Road Traffic**	13.137	
The mischief	13.137	
Exemptions from control	13.141	
MOT test certificates	13.143	
I. **Burglar Alarms**	13.145	
J. **Implementation of EU Directives on Noise**	13.151	

A. Introduction

13.01 This chapter is a miscellany of topics which defeat classification into any discernible pattern. It is, therefore, necessarily disjointed. Broadly, however, it covers pollution of the air, and certain specific types of noise pollution. It is likely that air pollution problems will arise more frequently in practice than difficulties produced by the noise sources which this chapter covers. The more commonly met types of noise pollution are discussed elsewhere.

B. Pollution of the Air

Alkali works

13.02 As is described in the chapter covering the history of environmental law, control of air pollution was initially introduced to meet concern about emissions from alkali producing factories. The regime introduced in the late nineteenth century and developed in the Alkali etc Works Regulation Act 1906 survived in part until replaced by the comprehensive environmental legislation of the early 1990s. A few vestigial provisions remain in force even now, primarily so that they can be replaced in their entirety by statutory instruments made under the Health and Safety at Work Act 1974. To that extent they lie outside the ambit of this book.

13.03 While the Act of 1906 regulates the emission of hydrochloric acid gas from alkali works, the main object, as will have been divined, was the protection of workers in and visitors to such works, rather than the protection of the environment in the general sense of the word. The same may be said of the surviving sections of the Health and Safety at Work Act 1974, Part I.[1]

13.04 Apart from these, what remains of the Act of 1906 is a collection of heterogeneous provisions relating to the registration of alkali works, the technical conditions under which the concentration of hydrochloric acid in gases is to be assessed, and the regulation of procedure in cases of complaint by local authorities and actions for nuisance caused by alkali works.

Clean Air Acts

13.05 The most momentous re-enactment of the earlier statutes was the updating of the clean air legislation by the Clean Air Act 1993. This relied heavily on the framework laid down by the Clean Air Act 1956, but, as will be seen, went further than its predecessor. Advances in technology and medical knowledge, perhaps mixed

---

[1] Health and Safety at Work Act 1974, ss 1 and 5.

with a dose of common sense, had made it unavoidably clear in the 1950s that many respiratory complaints, some of them even fatal, were connected with the emission of coal smoke from domestic fires and factory furnaces. The Clean Air Act 1956 reflected Parliament's concern, since Part I was devoted to the regulation of the emission of dark smoke. The Clean Air Act 1993 followed the same pattern.

The Ringelmann Chart

The Act began by prohibiting the emission of dark smoke from the chimney of any building and made it an offence to emit such smoke on any day.[2] 'Dark smoke' is a technical concept. It involves the use of a device little known outside the environmental health departments of local authorities called a Ringelmann Chart. This is a card on which a series of cross-hatched areas are shown, each darker than the last, the darkness being achieved by increasing the amount of cross-hatching. The user (normally an environmental health officer) places it between himself and the source of the smoke. He then judges the match between the colour of the smoke and the appropriate area on the chart. If the smoke is darker than shade 2 (shade 1 being white, shade 2 containing 20% of black), then it is 'dark smoke'. **13.06**

The margin of error is obviously wide and the opportunity for misrepresentation clear, facts recognized by Parliament, which provided that the court may be satisfied that smoke emitted may be dark even though there may have been no actual comparison made between the smoke and the Chart.[3] Regulations made under the Clean Air Act 1956, which remain in force, permit the emission of dark smoke from any chimney for up to ten minutes in any eight hours, or for up to fourteen minutes if soot blowing takes place, provided that no single emission exceeds four minutes, or if black smoke, that is, registering more than shade 4 on the Ringelmann Chart, lasts for more than two minutes in any half hour. **13.07**

The object seems to have been to exempt conscientious householders and others from the consequences of brief malfunctions in their domestic heating arrangements or other furnaces, and to allow for emissions occurring during warm-up periods.[4] Similar prohibitions, sanctions, and exemptions are applied to the emissions of dark smoke from industrial or trade premises.[5] **13.08**

---

[2] Clean Air Act 1993, s 1(1) and 2. An emission occurs when smoke moves above ground within the boundary of the premises. The smoke need not cross the boundary of the site. *O'Fee v Copeland BC* [1996] Env LR 66, CA.

[3] Clean Air Act 1993, s 3. One is tempted to wonder why Herr Ringelmann bothered to invent his Chart, or why it was dignified with a mention in a United Kingdom Statute.

[4] Dark Smoke (Permitted Periods) Regulations 1958, SI 1958/498.

[5] Clean Air Act 1993, s 2.

13.09 The discharge of dark smoke from vessels was exempted from control, again provided the emissions were strictly limited in time, but the exemption periods varied, according to the type of boiler responsible for sending out the smoke, and whether the vessel was under way or stationary. For example, dark smoke could legitimately be emitted from a ship with a forced draught oil-fired boiler furnace for up to ten minutes in all during any two-hour period: while the smoke from a coal-fired boiler furnace could be expelled for only ten minutes in one hour if the vessel was under way, but for twenty minutes in any one hour if she was moving.[6]

Prevention measures—industrial furnaces

13.10 It was, of course, all very well to provide criminal sanctions against those responsible for chimneys which emitted unwholesome smoke, but it was as important to take steps to secure that the emissions did not occur at all. To this end the Clean Air Act 1993 requires that any furnace other than a domestic furnace used to burn pulverized fuel, or to burn solid matter at a rate of more than 45.4 kilograms per hour, or to burn liquids or gases at a rate equivalent to 366.4 kilowatts per hour, shall be fitted with plant designed to arrest grit and dust. The local authority must approve the design of the plant, and furnaces commissioned after the Act passed into law have also to be installed in accordance with plans and specifications approved by the local authority.[7]

13.11 Although the Secretary of State for the Environment has power to make regulations varying the rates of combustion which activate the requirement to install arrestment plant, he has not exercised the power. However, he has other powers, these being to exempt prescribed classes of furnace from regulation in respect of arrestment plant.[8] The classes of furnace so exempted are: mobile furnaces providing temporary sources of power during building operations; those used for research, or for agricultural purposes; and small furnaces other than those used for the incineration of refuse, of specified construction, and designed to burn not more than 25 pounds per hour of the solid or liquid fuel by which they are powered.[9]

13.12 A further possible route to exemption is offered by local authorities. The occupier of a building may apply for exemption. If the authority gives no decision within eight weeks of receiving the application it is deemed to have given an

---

[6] Dark Smoke (Permitted Periods) (Vessels) Regulations 1958, SI 1958/878.
[7] Clean Air Act 1993, s 6(1).
[8] Ibid, s 7.
[9] Clean Air (Arrestment Plant) Regulations 1969. It will be immediately perceived that these Regulations were made, not under the Act of 1993, but under earlier legislation, this being the Clean Air Act 1968, and the Minister being the former Minister of Housing and Local Government.

unconditional exemption. Otherwise it may grant exemption if satisfied that the emission of dust and grit will not be prejudicial to health or a nuisance even though the furnace may not be fitted with grit and dust arresting plant.[10] The applicant may appeal to the Secretary of State against the authority's refusal to grant exemption.

The Secretary of State has the same wide powers as a local authority, with an addi-   **13.13**
tional obligation, not resting on the latter, to give reasons for his decision.[11] There is no specific provision for the conduct of appeals under this section, and it must therefore be inferred that neither the applicant nor the authority could, for example, insist on putting its case at an inquiry, or claim more than the right to submit written representations to the Secretary of State.

Prevention measures—domestic furnaces

Domestic furnaces are subject to a similar regulatory code. It is a criminal offence   **13.14**
to use a domestic furnace in a building which burns pulverized fuel in any quantity, or which burns other solid fuel or waste at a rate of 1.02 tonnes per hour or more, unless the furnace is provided with grit and dust arresting plant approved by the local authority. As with commercial and industrial furnaces, there is a right of appeal to the Secretary of State against a refusal to approve the plans and specifications of the plant.[12]

Monitoring

Since prevention rather than cure was the underlying objective of the Clean Air   **13.15**
Acts, the Act of 1993 contains detailed provisions requiring what is now called monitoring of emissions from furnaces and chimneys. Emissions from any furnace which burns pulverized fuel have to be monitored, as do those from furnaces burning 45.4 kilograms an hour or more of solid matter, or liquid or gaseous fluid at a rate of 366.4 kilowatts an hour or more. These requirements are enforced by the requirement that the occupier of the building containing a furnace or furnaces subject to monitoring obligations shall take and record measurements of the emission of dust, grit, and fumes, if necessary adapt the chimney serving the furnace in question, and shall provide and maintain monitoring apparatus, and make the results available to the local authority.[13]

Regulations made under the equivalent section of the Clean Air Act 1956 pre-   **13.16**
scribed that the apparatus should comply with various British Standards Institute

---

[10] Clean Air Act 1993, s 7(2) and (3).
[11] Ibid, s 7(5).
[12] Ibid, ss 8 and 9.
[13] Ibid, s 10.

procedures and requirements, that measurements should be taken in accordance with procedures recommended in scientific publications, and that records of measurements should be kept and sent to the responsible local authority in such form that the dates and amounts of the emissions are readily understood.[14] These regulations remain in force.

13.17 Supplementary powers enable the occupier of a building which contains a furnace of a size less than a relatively modest prescribed maximum to require the local authority to measure the emissions of grit, dust, and fumes. This, of course, absolves the users of small furnaces from the duty to comply with the onerous monitoring obligations to which operators of larger plant are subject.[15]

13.18 These provisions are expressly applied to furnaces which are not located inside buildings, but which are fixed to the land where they are situated, with the duties and liabilities of the occupier of a building transferred to the person who has possession of the boiler or industrial plant served by the furnace.[16] In order that a local authority may be able to police the operation of all furnaces properly, it has power to require all operators of furnaces to apply within fourteen days of the service of a written notice information about the specifications and operation of their plant, including the fuel or waste burnt in them. Failure to supply the information required, or providing information known to be false in a material particular are both criminal offences.[17]

The height of chimneys

13.19 It has been recognized for many years that air pollution can be controlled and reduced if chimneys are built to a minimum height. Accordingly, successive Clean Air Acts have contained powers which enable local authorities to regulate the height of all types of chimney built in their areas. The Clean Air Act 1993 re-enacts provisions formerly contained in the Acts of 1956 and 1968.

13.20 In principle, all furnace chimneys must be of a height approved by the local authority for the area. Any furnace which burns pulverized fuel, or more than a relatively small amount of other solid, liquid, or gaseous matter may only be operated if the local authority has approved the height of the chimney. This rule applies whether the furnace is inside a building or not.[18]

13.21 There are a few limited exemptions from this general restriction. Where the chimney was built or plans for its construction passed before 1 April 1969 the

---

[14] Clean Air (Measurement of Grit and Dust from Furnaces) Regulations 1971, SI 1971/161.
[15] Clean Air Act 1993, s 11.
[16] Ibid, s 13.
[17] Ibid, s 12.
[18] Ibid, s 14.

controls do not apply.[19] Also exempted are five categories of essentially temporary furnace. Where the furnace is a temporary replacement for another which is being repaired, rebuilt, or replaced; where it is a temporary source of power required for building or engineering works; or for investigation or research; where the furnace is used merely to bring other plant up to its operating temperature; and where it provides power or heat for the purposes of agriculture and is mobile or transportable, no approval is needed.[20]

Application for approval of the height of a chimney must be made to the local **13.22** authority for the area, which may not approve the height of the chimney unless it is satisfied that, so far as practicable, smoke, grit, dust, gases, or fumes emitted therefrom will not be prejudicial to health or a nuisance. In deciding whether this test is satisfied, the authority must have regard to the purpose of the chimney, the location and uses of nearby buildings, ground levels, and any other material considerations.[21]

Failure to determine the application within four weeks or any longer agreed period **13.23** amounts to a deemed approval without conditions or qualifications. Otherwise the authority may grant unconditional approval to the proposed height, or may attach conditions to the approval which regulate the rate or quality, or both, of the emissions. If the authority refuses to approve the height, it must state its reasons, and specify the lowest height which it would be prepared to approve, and any conditions subject to which such approval would be given.[22]

The applicant has a right of appeal to the Secretary of State against any decision of **13.24** the local authority. The only restrictions on the power of the Secretary of State on appeal are that he must give written reasons for his decision, and, like a local authority, state what height of chimney he would be prepared to approve if he dismisses the appeal.[23]

The same controls apply to the height of chimneys on dwellings, shops, and offices **13.25** outside Greater London and in outer London boroughs, these being chimneys which do not carry the exhaust products of furnaces. When plans are deposited under the Building Regulations, the authority must decide whether to approve the height of the chimney or chimneys shown on the plans by reference to the

---

[19] Ibid, Sch 5 para 7.
[20] Clean Air (Height of Chimneys) (Exemption) Regulations 1969, SI 1969/411. No regulations have been made under the Clean Air Act 1993.
[21] Clean Air Act 1993, s 15(1).
[22] Ibid, s 15(4) and (5).
[23] Ibid, s 15(8) and (9). It is a matter for regret that similar requirements have not been written into other regulatory codes, such as the Town and Country Planning Acts. An indication from the Secretary of State dismissing a planning appeal as to what he would regard as suitable development would assist planning authorities and applicants and avoid repeated appeals. In practice, however, the Secretary of State virtually never condescends to give such help.

same considerations as govern the approval of furnace chimneys. There is the same right of appeal to the Secretary of State, but neither he nor the local authority is required to state what height of chimney would be acceptable if the decision is adverse to the applicant.[24]

Smoke control areas

13.26 Parliament found it desirable to back up the licensing system for furnaces and new chimneys now established under Parts I and II of the Clean Air Act 1993 with more stringent controls, applicable to old and new furnaces and chimneys alike. This was done by the invention of the smoke control area in the Clean Air Act 1956, a concept which has been perpetuated in successive consolidating Acts.

13.27 The underlying principle of a smoke control area is a prohibition on the emission of smoke of any kind within the area. The occupier of a building from a chimney from which smoke is emitted on any day is guilty of an offence. Similarly, the person having possession of a boiler or plant within the area from the chimney of which smoke is emitted on any day is also guilty of an offence.[25]

13.28 This does not mean that householders must go cold and no industrialist or commercial operator carry on business within a smoke control area. It is a defence to any prosecution under Part III of the Act to show that the alleged emission was not caused by the use of fuel other than an authorized fuel.[26] This parliamentary ellipsis leads eventually to the conclusion that one may burn authorized fuels in fireplaces and furnaces within a smoke control area.

13.29 The authorized fuels are prescribed by the Smoke Control Areas (Authorized Fuels) Regulations 1991.[27] These were made for the purposes of the Clean Air Act 1956, and remain in force, like the other pre-1993 statutory instruments already described. Anthracite, semi-anthracite, electricity, gas, and low volatile steam coals are generically and automatically authorized fuels.[28] The Schedule to the Regulations prescribes in great detail the constituents of products made by identified fuel manufacturers which are also authorized to be burnt in smoke control areas. Two examples give the tenor of the Schedule, and the precision with which the Secretary of State defined the authorized fuels. One such fuel is 'Coalite manufactured by Coalite Products Limited at Bolsover, near Chesterfield, Derbyshire and at Grimethorpe, Yorkshire using a low temperature carbonisation process'.[29]

---

[24] Ibid, s 16.
[25] Clean Air Act 1993, s 20(1) and (2).
[26] Ibid, s 20(4).
[27] SI 1991/1282.
[28] Ibid, reg 2.
[29] Ibid, Sch 1 para 7.

It follows that coalite manufactured elsewhere than at Bolsover or Grimethorpe cannot be burnt in a smoke control area.

Even greater detail is built into the descriptions of most other commercially pro- **13.30**
duced fuels. For instance, paragraph 11 describes 'Flamelite pellets, manufactured by Alfred McAlpine Energy Limited at Rheola Works, Resolven, West Glamorgan, which—(a) comprise pre-mixed anthracite duff and filter cake combined with a fixed proportion of starch-based binder; (b) were manufactured from those constituents by a process involving extrusion and heat treatment at about 100 degrees centigrade; (c) are unmarked pellets approximately 25mm in diameter . . .', and so on. There are 20 paragraphs in the Schedule, which describe all the products which qualify as authorized fuels in as much detail as those quoted.

Creating a smoke control area

A smoke control area may come into existence in one of two ways. First, a local **13.31**
authority may declare all or any part of its district to be such an area, in which case the broad prohibition on burning unauthorized fuels comes into effect, or, as an alternative, the authority can make a smoke control order.

An order may make different provision for different parts of the smoke control **13.32**
area, and, in particular, may limit the prohibition on burning unauthorized fuels to specified classes of building in the smoke control area. In addition, the order may exempt specified buildings or classes of buildings, fireplaces or classes of fireplace, from the same prohibition.[30]

The procedure for making a smoke control order is not designed to appeal to **13.33**
those concerned with the rights of the individual. Notice of intention to make the order must be published in the *London Gazette* (hardly bedside reading for most citizens) and in a local newspaper. Notices, similar to those publicizing planning applications, must also be posted in 'conspicuous places' within the area to which the order will relate. There is no minimum number of such notices which must be posted or definition of conspicuous place, the decision being left to the authority's discretion.

In the event of anyone becoming aware of the authority's intentions, and presum- **13.34**
ing to object to them, the council is bound merely to consider the objection before making the smoke control order. No independent scrutiny of the proposal to make the order is needed, and the Secretary of State is not involved, at least formally, at any stage. The fact that there seems to have been no litigation in the 40 years since the procedure was first introduced suggests that the public accepts the desirability of reducing the emission of poisonous smoke, and is, perhaps

---

[30] Clean Air Act 1993, s 18.

understandably, unconcerned with the near dictatorial powers available to bring this about.[31]

13.35 The second way in which a smoke control order may be made is by direction of the Secretary of State. He may direct an authority to prepare and submit to him for his approval one or more smoke control orders. The power is fettered by a requirement on the Secretary of State to consult the authority before he issues the direction, and by prescription of a minimum period of six months for preparation of the order.[32]

13.36 When the order has been prepared (or subsequently modified by the authority within the prescribed period), the Secretary of State may approve the proposals unconditionally wholly or in part, with or without modifications, or may reject them. If he decides to reject the proposals wholly or in part, or if the authority fails to submit the proposals in time, the Secretary of State may declare the authority to be in default, and may direct it to make the smoke control order within a time and in a way which he specifies.[33]

13.37 Although consultation, as already described, is a fetter on the discretion of the Secretary of State's powers, the shackles are unlikely to be heavy in practice. The courts have considered the meaning of the word more than once. The essence of consultation is that the party under the duty must communicate a genuine invitation, extended with a receptive mind, to the consultee to give advice.[34]

Smoke control areas—Offences

13.38 It is automatically a criminal offence to emit smoke from a chimney of any building within a smoke control area or from a chimney which does not serve a building but is connected to a fixed boiler or industrial plant.[35] A fresh offence takes place on each day on which the emission occurs, and is punishable by a fine imposed by a magistrates' court.[36] The principal defence to a charge of emitting smoke is that the smoke was created by burning one of the authorized fuels already described.

---

[31] Ibid, Sch 1.
[32] Ibid, s 19(1).
[33] Ibid, s 19(3) and (4).
[34] See per Donaldson J in *Agricultural Training Board v Aylesbury Mushrooms Ltd* [1972] 3 All ER 280 at 284, approving a dictum of Morris J in *Rollo v Minister of Town and Country Planning* [1948] 1 All ER 13.
[35] Clean Air Act 1993, s 20(1).
[36] Ibid, s 20(2) and (5).

Burning unauthorized fuels

Even where a smoke control area has been created, unauthorized fuels may be **13.39**
burnt in fireplaces of a type prescribed by the Secretary of State, provided he is satisfied that the unauthorized fuel can be burnt without producing any smoke or a
substantial quantity of smoke.[37] He has prescribed ten types of incinerator and
boiler, manufactured by Apollo Incineration Systems Limited, Clearview Stoves,
and Farm 2000 Limited. These must be installed in accordance with the manufacturers' instructions, and may burn only the materials for which they were designed.
Thus, for example, the Clearview fireplaces, being wood burning stoves, may only
be fed with firewood which has been stacked and dried, and the Farm 2000 boilers
may only burn cereal straw.[38]

A further exemption from the controls may arise by reason of the Secretary of **13.40**
State having relaxed the prohibition on the emission of smoke in all or part of
any smoke control area. This he may do after consulting the local authority concerned, and, once the relaxation has been permitted, the authority has the responsibility of taking the steps which it considers suitable for bringing the effect
of the order for relaxation to the notice of persons affected.[39] This in practice
will mean giving sufficient notice to residents of the area in question, to occupiers
of premises other than dwellings, and to the operators of furnaces and other
industrial plant. Ordinarily, a notice of the conventional kind in the appropriate
local newspaper will probably suffice, supplemented, where necessary, by advertisements similar to those displayed under the Highways Acts and Road Traffic
legislation.

The Clean Air Act 1993 contains other provisions calculated to ensure the purity **13.41**
of the atmosphere by nipping attempts to pollute it in the bud. It makes it a separate offence to acquire any solid fuel for use in a building, a fixed boiler, or industrial plant in a smoke control area; or to sell by retail any solid fuel which the
seller proposes to deliver to a building in a smoke control area or to premises
where there is a fixed boiler or industrial plant. Self-evidently, authorized fuel is
not within the definition of 'solid fuel', so that it cannot be an offence to buy or
sell the former.[40]

With appropriate amendments, the Secretary of State has the same power to **13.42**
suspend or remove the smoke controls which give rise to these offences as he

---

[37] Ibid, s 21.
[38] Smoke Control Areas (Exempted Fireplaces) Order 1993, SI 1993/2277.
[39] Clean Air Act 1993, s 22.
[40] Ibid, s 23(1) and (2).

does in respect of the making of smoke control orders, in which case no offence will be committed.[41]

Adaptation of existing furnaces and fireplaces

13.43 As is and was obvious to Parliament, the creation of a smoke control area is capable of involving householders and others in great expense. Where their heating or power producing systems were incapable of complying with the general prohibition on the emission of smoke, existing systems would have to be adapted or removed and replaced. The Clean Air Act 1956 had addressed this, and the Clean Air Act 1993 adopted and extended those provisions.

13.44 Under the latter, the local authority can serve notice in writing on the occupier or owner of a private dwelling, requiring that the dwelling shall be adapted so as to avoid contraventions of the prohibition of smoke in the smoke control area. In this context 'adapting' means adapting or converting any fireplace; replacing a fireplace with another or with some other means of heating or cooking; altering a chimney; providing gas or electrical means of ignition, or some other special type of ignition; or carrying out operations incidental to any of the foregoing.

13.45 The general provisions of Part XII of the Public Health Act 1936, which govern the rights of appeal and enforcement of notices requiring the execution of works, apply in relation to notices requiring the adaptation of dwellings. There is, accordingly, a right of appeal to a magistrates' court on the grounds, for example, that the works required are unreasonable, or that the owner or occupier, as the case may be, should have been served rather than the recipient of the notice.[42] In particular, the authority itself has power to carry out the work required by the notice in the event of non-compliance, and may recover a maximum of three-tenths of the cost of doing so, or such lesser sum as it thinks fit, from the owner or occupier.[43] If, however, the owner or occupier or any person interested in a dwelling built before 15 August 1964 (an 'old dwelling') carries out the work of compliance with the notice, he or she may recover seven-tenths, or a larger amount if the authority thinks fit, of the cost of so doing from the local authority.[44]

13.46 Comparable benefits are available to the owners and occupiers of churches, church halls, chapels, and other premises occupied for the purposes of a charity not established or conducted for profit or other body whose main objects are charitable or otherwise concerned with the advancement of religion, education, or social welfare, even though it may not, technically, be a charity.

---

[41] Ibid, s 23(4)–(6).
[42] Ibid, ss 24(1), (2) and 27.
[43] Ibid, s 24(3).
[44] Ibid, s 25 and Sch 2.

The owners or occupiers of such buildings may, if the local authority thinks fit, be **13.47** paid the whole or any part of the expenditure which they incur in adapting their buildings so that they comply with the requirement that smoke shall not be emitted within a smoke control area.[45] Given the straitened financial plight of most local authorities, at least when asked to spend money on projects which do not directly benefit the authority itself, it is unlikely that charities or cognate bodies will succeed in getting financial help with the cost of complying with smoke control orders for the foreseeable future.

An appropriate percentage of the expense of providing a means of heating or **13.48** cooking which can be readily removed from the premises without damaging the building itself, which is, in other words, a tenant's fixture, is recoverable by an owner or occupier from the local authority, or vice versa.[46]

Motor fuel and air pollution

Although governments, whatever their political complexion, have traditionally **13.49** been reluctant to restrict the use of motor vehicles, the Clean Air legislation is an example, albeit somewhat pallid, of the recognition that pollution of the air by vehicle exhausts is a major environmental problem.

Since the 1970s Ministers have had power to prescribe the composition **13.50** and content of motor vehicle fuel, and to restrict the production, treatment, distribution, import, sale, or use of such fuel.[47] The only regulations which have been made relate to the sulphur and lead content of motor fuels, these being the only areas which have been the subject of EU Council Directives. It is an offence to market gas oil whose sulphur content exceeds 0.2% by weight, unless it is carried from outside the EU in the fuel tank of a vessel, aircraft, or motor vehicle, or is fuelling one of those means of transport from inside the EU to a third country, or is to be processed prior to final combustion, or is aviation kerosene.

Enforcement of the prohibition is policed by local authorities, who **13.51** are under a duty to sample the sulphur content of gas oil placed on the market in their areas, and to interpret the checks which they carry out in

---

[45] Ibid, s 26.
[46] Ibid, s 28.
[47] Control of Pollution Act 1974, now contained in the Clean Air Act 1993, s 30. No regulations were made under the Act of 1974 until an EEC Directive (75/716/EEC) as amended by Directive 87/2/EEC, and 85/210/EEC, as amended by 85/581/EEC required the government to take action (anticipatory in the latter cases). Regulations have been made under the Clean Air Act 1993, replacing the earlier regulations which had remained in force for the purposes of that Act. These are dealt with in the text of this chapter.

accordance with an identified British Standard (BS 2000 Part 336:1993 and ISO 8754:1992).[48]

The lead content of petrol

13.52 The lead content of motor fuel is also regulated by delegated legislation, made by the Secretary of State for Transport.[49] The regulations are highly technical, and unlikely to interest persons not directly concerned with the distribution or sale of petrol or diesel oils. In essence the year is divided into three seasons for the purposes of the regulations—summer, winter, and an intermediate period, which for the purposes of the sale of petrol extends from 1 September until 31 October in any one year, and is, in effect, what was once called autumn.[50]

13.53 During that period, it is an offence to distribute or sell petrol which, if leaded, does not comply with the so-called intermediate leaded petrol requirement, or, if unleaded, with the winter requirements. These requirements are set out in great detail in the regulations, by reference to a series of BS standards.[51] Different requirements apply to petrol distributed or sold during the winter, that is, between 1 November and the following 15 April, and to that distributed or sold during the summer, from 16 April to 31 August.

The lead content of diesel

13.54 There are similar but slightly different restrictions on the distribution and sale of diesel fuel. For these purposes there is no intermediate period, and summer extends from 16 March until 9 September in any one year, the rest of the year being winter.[52] The variations are accounted for by the differing effects on petrol and diesel oils of changes in temperature.

13.55 Fuels used for the purpose of testing or experiments in connection with the composition or content of motor fuel, or of the design and performance of motors or other articles using or intended to use such fuel where the composition and content of the fuel are relevant to the design or performance of the motor or article are exempt from the restrictions. Fuels for use in aircraft and in vehicles constructed or adapted solely for competitions or trials are similarly exempt.[53]

13.56 It is a defence to a prosecution for breach of the regulations to show that the breach was due to a mistake, to reliance on information supplied by another

---

[48] The Marketing of Gas Oil (Sulphur Content) Regulations 1994, SI 1994/2249.
[49] The Motor Fuel (Composition and Content) Regulations 1994, SI 1994/2295.
[50] Ibid, reg 6(1).
[51] Ibid, regs 5 and 6.
[52] Ibid, reg 6.
[53] Ibid, reg 8.

person, to the act or default of another person, to accident, or to any other cause beyond the defendant's control, provided he took all reasonable precautions and exercised all due diligence to avoid the breach by himself and his employees.[54] It is noticeable, however, that, even though the consequences of air pollution by burning motor vehicle fuels are well documented, and can be perceived by the senses on any hot day in a large city, the law does not as yet restrict the use of motor vehicles in large cities or elsewhere, in any meaningful way. The UK Government, it is true, launched a so-called air pollution initiative in August 1996, with high aspirations to reduce the levels of air pollution caused by vehicle emissions, but the effectiveness of this must remain a matter of conjecture, especially since the growth in road traffic continues unstoppably.

Cable burning

Part IV of the Clean Air Act ends with a peremptory section making it an offence **13.57** to burn cable with a view to recovering metal, unless the burning is part of a process which is subject to integrated pollution control (IPC) under Part I of the Environmental Protection Act 1990 (EPA 1990).[55]

Research into air pollution

Part V of the Clean Air Act 1993 is concerned with research into the causes of **13.58** air pollution, including monitoring the levels and effects of contamination of the air. Generally, it throws the burden of conducting or financing the research and monitoring onto local authorities. They are given powers to conduct research and investigation into problems of air pollution, or to contribute to the cost of such research. They may arrange to publish information on those problems, including the giving of lectures and addresses (the difference between the two not being apparent), and holding seminars and discussions. They can also prepare visual material in the shape of pictures, films, and models and hold, or pay for the holding of, exhibitions designed to inform the public, or sections of it, about air pollution problems.

An important qualification on the power to publicize information about air pol- **13.59** lution is that a local authority may not disclose trade secrets except with written permission from a party authorized to disclose the trade information. This has the effect of protecting the commercial interests of polluting industries and others, who may bring civil proceedings for breach of the duty to maintain trade secrecy. Otherwise it is a defence to both civil and criminal proceedings brought against

---

[54] Ibid, reg 8(3).
[55] Clean Air Act 1993, s 33. IPC is fully considered elsewhere in this work.

an authority, its members, or officers, to show that the information was published in compliance with the Clean Air Act.[56]

Records and returns

13.60 The power to disseminate information presupposes a power to collect information as well. That power can be exercised by the local authority serving written notice on the occupier of any premises in its area requiring the occupier to furnish by way of periodic returns or otherwise estimates or other information, including records, of emissions of pollutants and other substances from the premises other than a private dwelling or a caravan.[57]

13.61 If the processes carried on in the premises are subject to IPPC under the Pollution Prevention and Control Act 1999, the notice may not require the provision of information of a kind supplied under IPPC. In any event the notice may not require returns at intervals of less than three months, or call for information covering a period of more than one year. Unusually, the Clean Air Act lifts Crown immunity, because it empowers a local authority to serve notices in respect of Crown premises and servants of the Crown, but only to the extent defined by regulations made by the Secretary of State for the Environment. Unsurprisingly, he has availed himself freely of the power to exclude the operation of the Act over Crown lands and servants.[58]

13.62 The list of premises exempted from inquisition by local authorities contains many dozens of entries. Some have obvious links with national security. These include the Atomic Weapons Research Establishment at Aldermaston and the Microbiological Research Establishment at Porton Down, Salisbury. In other cases the connection is less clear—one instance being the MOD(PE) Stores Depot at Aston Down, Stroud, Gloucestershire.[59] Failure to comply with a notice or knowingly making a false statement in an estimate or a return is a criminal offence triable summarily.

13.63 The occupier who is required to provide information about air pollution has a right to appeal against the notice on the grounds that disclosure of the material required would unreasonably disclose a trade secret, or be contrary to the public interest, or that the information cannot be readily collected or obtained and is

---

[56] Ibid, s 34. One suspects that the right of action available to polluting industries is at least capable of abuse, in that an unscrupulous industrialist could readily intimidate a local authority anxious not to involve its rate and council tax payers in expense. The absence of reported judicial authority under this section and its predecessors in the Clean Air Act 1956 and the CoPA 1974 suggests that abuses have not existed or have been undetected.

[57] Ibid, s 36.

[58] Ibid.

[59] Control of Atmospheric Pollution (Exempted Premises) Regulations 1977, SI 1977/18.

not immediately available. The appellant must give written notice to the Secretary of State within the time given for compliance with the notice. The notice of appeal must state the grounds of the appeal, specify the facts and reasons relied on, and be accompanied by the notice complained of and any other relevant documents. There is no provision for an inquiry, although the Secretary of State may require either party to submit a further statement in writing in respect of any matter raised by the appeal if he thinks fit.[60]

In addition to obtaining information from others, a local authority may **13.64** itself enter on premises for the purpose of measuring and recording emissions, if necessary without the agreement of the owner or occupier.[61] The right of entry is exercisable only after not less than three weeks' written notice of the intention to enter has been given.[62] Again, the powers conferred by the Clean Air Act must not be exercised so as to duplicate the controls under IPC.

Notices connected with research and publicity

The exercise of local authority functions dealing with research and publicity is **13.65** strictly controlled by regulations.[63] Notices served under Section 38 of the Clean Air Act 1993 may relate to the emission of pollutants and other substances from chimneys, flues, or other outlets to the atmosphere provided the emission is of sulphur dioxide or particulate matter derived from any combustion process where the material being heated does not contribute to the emission.[64] Thus it is likely that this category of emission would include those from chimneys where metals are being smelted or refined.

On the other hand, where the material being heated contributes to the emission **13.66** of gas or particulates, any gas or particulate matter may be the subject of a notice served by a local authority. The same holds good for emissions from chimneys and flues used in connection with a non-combustion process or similar industrial activity.[65] This, presumably, would include processes which result in emissions due to the use of acids or other chemicals.

Any notice must specify the premises to which it relates, and may require the **13.67** supply of estimates of considerable quantities of information in respect of

---

[60] Clean Air Act 1993, ss 36 and 37. Control of Atmospheric Pollution (Appeals) Regulations 1977, SI 1977/17.
[61] Clean Air Act 1993, ss 35 and 56.
[62] Ibid, s 35(2).
[63] Ibid, s 37. The Control of Atmospheric Pollution (Research and Publicity) Regulations 1977, SI 1977/19.
[64] Ibid, reg 3.
[65] Ibid.

sulphur dioxide—the aggregate duration of all discharges during any specified period; the temperature in degrees Celsius; the efflux velocity in metres per second; the volume flow rates in cubic metres per hour; the height in metres above ground level at which each discharge takes place. Finally, the authority may require to be given information about the aggregate quantity of the gas discharged during the specified period, ascertained either by calculating the emission by reference to the quantity of fuel burnt or by direct measurement, if the occupier and the authority agree to this. With appropriate variations having regard to their physical characteristics, the same information may be required in respect of particulates and gases other than sulphur dioxide.[66]

13.68 The notice must be served by recorded delivery post, and proof of service may be made by producing a copy of the notice and a certificate signed by an authorized officer of the authority stating the date of service. The authority must keep a register of the information which it obtains under the Regulations and the Clean Air Act 1993.[67]

13.69 Lastly, the Secretary of State may direct local authorities to make arrangements for the provision, installation, operation, and maintenance of monitoring apparatus, and for the transmission of the information obtained in this way to him. He must first consult the authority, and any temptation to exercise the power of direction without due consideration is restrained by the requirement that he must pay for the apparatus and its installation.[68]

Mines and quarries

13.70 Part VI of the Clean Air Act 1993 covers a hotchpotch of unrelated special cases. The owners of mines or quarries which produce coal or shale must employ all practicable means for preventing combustion of refuse deposited in the spoil tips (or spoilbanks, as the side heading to the section describes them). Breach of the obligation is a criminal offence.[69]

Railway engines

13.71 Somewhat anachronistically, the Act also prohibits the emission of dark smoke as defined from a railway locomotive engine. It is an offence to emit such smoke, although the owner of the engine must use any practicable means to prevent the emission of such smoke, and commits an offence only if he fails to do so.[70]

---

[66] Ibid, reg 4.
[67] Ibid, regs 5 and 6.
[68] Clean Air Act 1993, s 39.
[69] Clean Air Act 1993, s 42. The word 'spoilbank' is described in the *Shorter Oxford Dictionary* as 'local'.
[70] Clean Air Act 1993, s 43. This is a provision now likely to be of practical importance only to steam railway enthusiasts.

Vessels

The Clean Air Act also applies to vessels in the same way as it does to buildings, **13.72** with the amendments made necessary by the characteristics peculiar to a vessel. Instead of the duties of the Act being imposed on the occupier, they rest on the master of a vessel as well as on the owner. Ships in waters not navigable by seagoing ships, such as canals and non-tidal rivers, are deemed to be within the area of the local authority which is closest to the vessel in question at the time of the offence; and the same test determines the area of the local authority for the purposes of the Act where a ship breaches it within territorial waters.[71]

Research establishments

Chimneys, furnaces, boilers, industrial plant, and premises used for the purposes **13.73** of investigation or research into air pollution may be exempted for a specified period and subject to conditions from the restrictions of the Clean Air Act and the EPA 1990. The applicant for exemption may appeal to the Secretary of State against the authority's decision.[72] There is no procedure laid down for the conduct of these exemption appeals.

The Crown

The Clean Air Act lies lightly on the Crown. Local authorities have power to **13.74** report on emissions of smoke or dark smoke, grit or dust from Crown premises to the responsible Minister, but only in cases where they think it proper to do so. In the possibly unlikely event of his receiving such a report the Minister in question must inquire into the circumstances, and, if cause for complaint is revealed, he must then take all practicable steps to prevent or minimize the emission of the smoke, grit, or dust. The Act applies to the masters of vessels owned by the Crown in the same way as it does to other vessels, but the Crown as owner of the vessels is not bound by the Act, as is normal in these cases.[73] Given the lack of precision with which the duties of the Crown are set out, it is almost inevitable that the way in which the Crown exercises its functions will one day be challenged by way of judicial review.

Administration

The administrative and miscellaneous provisions of the Clean Air Act follow **13.75** familiar lines. The Secretary of State is given power to apply the Act to fumes or

---

[71] Ibid, s 44.
[72] Ibid, s 45.
[73] Ibid, s 46.

prescribed gases in the same way as it regulates the emissions of grit and dust.[74] This power has never been exercised, and the same is true of the power to make regulations giving effect to international agreements on air pollution control.[75]

13.76   As is not uncommon, the Act makes it an offence to disclose trade secrets which have been communicated in accordance with its provisions, and provides that there shall be a daily penalty in cases of repeated or cumulative offences involving air pollution.[76] Less commonly, the Act imposes a duty on local authority officers to warn occupiers of premises, and those in possession of furnaces, plant, railway engines, and the owners or masters of vessels of their opinion that an offence involving the emission of smoke is being or has been committed. Unless the notice is given within four days of the commission of the alleged offence, the burden of showing that the notice was given rests upon the prosecution, and, if no notice is given at all, then this will be a defence to the charges.[77]

Corporations, occupiers of premises, and powers of entry

13.77   The provisions relating to offences by corporations, to the powers of the county court to authorize occupiers to carry out work where they are otherwise unable to do so without the landowner's consent, and as to powers of entry and inspection are in the usual statutory form.[78]

Conclusion

13.78   Conventional and uncontroversial though much of the Clean Air legislation may be, it has been one of the more notably successful of the environmental regulatory codes. Anyone over the age of, say, 60 who remembers the state of the atmosphere during childhood, and, especially, the great fogs of 1953, can attest its efficacy and the benefits which it has brought about. It is not without interest that it has never been found necessary to pass the Clean Air Acts in statutes containing more than about 60 sections—a marked contrast to the prolixity of most other similar codes. There may be a lesson for posterity in that.

---

[74]   Ibid, s 47.
[75]   Ibid, s 48.
[76]   Ibid, ss 49 and 50.
[77]   Ibid, s 51.
[78]   See ibid, ss 52–56. So too are the defences that an offence was committed by the act or default of a person other than the party charged, and the powers enabling local authorities to obtain information, the default powers of the Secretary of State, the power to hold local inquiries, and the joint exercise of local authority functions—see ss 57–61.

C. Noise Pollution—Construction Sites

Control of works

For reasons as yet unexplained, while most of the Control of Pollution Act 1974 **13.79** (CoPA 1974) was repealed and re-enacted in the environmental legislation passed in the early 1990s, and notably in the EPA 1990, a few of its controls remain in force. The first of these is the code regulating noise from construction sites.

The CoPA 1974 gives local authorities powers to serve a notice imposing require- **13.80** ments on the way in which certain specified works are carried out. The works in question are the erection, construction, alteration, repair, or maintenance of buildings, structures, or roads; the breaking up of or boring under roads or adjacent land in connection with the construction, inspection, maintenance, or removal of works. This, it seems, would include laying sewers or other services in connection with the erection of a new building or other construction or engineering work; work of demolition or dredging; and (superfluously, perhaps) any other work of engineering construction.[79]

The requirements may relate to the plant or machinery which may or may not be **13.81** used; the hours during which work may be carried out; the level of noise which may be emitted from the premises; and may provide for any change of circumstances. It is unclear why the last power was included in the statute, but a notice might, for example, appropriately address a change in the identity of the contractors working on the site, or a change in the plant or machinery used, whether the change resulted in more or less noise being generated.[80] There are the familiar stipulations as to the way in which notices are to be served, and as to the matters which the authority must take into account when deciding whether to serve a notice under Section 60. These are: any code of practice issued under Part III of the CoPA 1974;[81] and the need to ensure that the best practicable means are employed to minimize noise.

The authority must also have regard to the possible alternative types of plant and **13.82** machinery available to do the work which would be as effective in minimizing noise as those which the authority is minded to specify, and which would be more acceptable to the operators of the site. This, almost inevitably, requires full consultation between the authority and the operator. Lastly, the authority must

---

[79] CoPA 1974, s 60(1) and (2).
[80] Ibid, s 60(3).
[81] The Secretary of State for the Environment has issued the Control of Noise (Codes of Practice for Construction and Open Sites) Order 1984, SI 1984/1992. This approves BS 5228 Part 1: 1984 in respect of construction sites and BS 5228 Part 3: 1984 for opencast coal extraction.

consider the need to protect neighbours from the effects of noise.[82] As might be expected, there is a right of appeal against a notice to a magistrates' court.

Sanctions

13.83 It is an offence to contravene a requirement of a notice without reasonable excuse.[83] Prosecution, however, is not the only sanction available to a local authority where there are reasonable grounds for inferring that criminal process would be ineffective to prevent breaches of the notice. In such a case a local authority may be granted an injunction under Section 222 of the Local Government Act 1972.

13.84 The interaction of the two remedies was well illustrated by a case in which nationally known and respected contractors were the site managers for the construction of a multi-storey office block in the City of London, on land which adjoined an underground railway line. The construction site was across the street from a housing site. The railway authorities insisted that work over or close to the track should take place only during the three or so hours of the very early morning when the electric current driving the railway was switched off. The Corporation of the City, mindful no doubt of the interests of local residents and of its obligations under Section 60 of the CoPA 1974, served a notice prohibiting works for much longer times than those directed by the railway. Caught between the devil and the deep blue sea, the site managers caused or permitted work to be carried on at times which infringed the notice from the start of operations, and continued to do so even after 18 informations had been laid against them under Section 60, and before the criminal proceedings were heard. The effect on the residents, the court found as a fact, was devastating. In the circumstances, it is no surprise that the trial judge held that the contractors could be restrained by injunction from working outside the permitted hours without a reasonable excuse, and his decision was upheld by the Court of Appeal.[84]

Section 61 consent

13.85 An alternative way in which the contractor can obtain authority for proposed construction or engineering activities is to apply for consent to the work under Section 61 of the CoPA 1974. Under that Section, a person intending to carry out construction or other work may apply to a local authority for consent to the work. If Building Regulation consent is required in addition to consent under the CoPA 1974, the applications must be made either at the same time, or the

---

[82] CoPA 1974, s 60(4).

[83] Ibid, s 60(7) and (8). The grounds on which an appeal may be brought are listed in the Control of Noise (Appeals) Regulations 1975, SI 1975/2116, reg 5.

[84] *City of London Corporation v Bovis Construction Ltd* [1992] 3 All ER 697.

application for Building Regulation consent must precede that made under the Act of 1974.

On receipt of the application, the local authority is required to apply the same **13.86** tests as if it were considering whether to serve a notice on its own initiative, and must give its decision within 28 days. If it fails to do so or refuses consent, the applicant may appeal to a magistrates' court.[85] On the other hand, if the authority is satisfied that the application is sufficiently detailed for it to be able to give a decision, and that if the works were carried out in accordance with the application it would not serve a notice requiring noise abatement measures to be taken, then it may grant consent. Such a consent may be conditional, may be limited or qualified to allow for a change in circumstances, and may be limited in duration.[86]

It is a defence to any proceedings under Section 60 to show that the alleged con- **13.87** travention amounted to the carrying out of works in accordance with the consent, unless the allegation is one of failure to remove waste from the site. In that event a prosecution under Section 59 of the EPA 1990 may still succeed.[87]

D. Loudspeakers in Streets

The controls

It is an offence to operate a loudspeaker in a street between 9pm and 8am for any **13.88** purpose, or at any time for the purpose of advertising any entertainment, trade, or business. For the purpose of the section a 'street' is a highway or any other road, footway, square, or court open to the public for the time being.[88] An area in Petticoat Lane Market in London under a building raised on stilts, open on three sides and walled on the fourth, where traders' stalls were placed, and to which the public had access was held to be a street within the meaning of this section.[89]

Devices fitted to the inside of shop windows which send sound waves into the **13.89** street for advertising purposes are in the street. The window is within the street in a realistic and practical sense.[90]

There are naturally many exceptions to the general rule. **13.90**

---

85   CoPA 1974, s 61(6)–(7).
86   Ibid, s 61(4) and (5).
87   Ibid, s 61(8) and (9).
88   Ibid, s 52(1).
89   *Tower Hamlets LBC v Creitzman* [1984] JP 630 DC.
90   *Westminster City Council v French Connection Retail Ltd.* [2005] EWHC 933.

Relaxation of control

13.91 The Secretary of State may extend the times between which there is a total prohibition on the use of loudspeakers by order (but may not reduce them). A local authority may grant consent to the use of loudspeakers under Schedule 2 to the Noise and Statutory Nuisance Act 1993.[91] Loudspeakers operated by the emergency services, the Environment Agency, and water and sewage undertakers are exempt from the restrictions, as are those for communicating with a vessel for the purpose of directing its movement, or forming part of a public telephone system.[92]

13.92 The controls do not extend to loudspeakers in or fixed to a vehicle, and which are operated solely for the entertainment of or for communication between the driver and passenger or form part of the horn or warning instrument of the vehicle, and, importantly, provided the loudspeaker is operated so as not to give reasonable cause for annoyance.[93] For reasons which are obscure, this permits the youthful proletariat to fit its cars with horns which play snatches of music at deafening volume.

13.93 Travelling showmen may use loudspeakers in their fairgrounds with impunity, as may transport undertakings when making announcements to their passengers or employees.[94] Finally, vendors of ice cream and other perishable commodities may cry their wares through loudspeakers, but only between noon and 7pm, and provided they do not give reasonable cause for annoyance to persons in the vicinity.[95]

Relaxation of control—Procedure

13.94 As already noted, a local authority may, by positive resolution, relax the rigour of the CoPA constraints on the use of loudspeakers in streets. It may do so only in response to a written application, containing such information as the authority 'may reasonably require'. If it decides to grant the application, the fact must be published in a local paper, and the relaxation of the restrictions on the use of loudspeakers in streets will then apply in the area of the local authority.

---

[91] CoPA 1974, s 62(1A), (1B), and (3A). The Statutory Nuisance Act, considered below, authorizes relaxations on the use of loudspeakers for events like carnivals and the London Marathon.

[92] CoPA 1974, s 62(2).

[93] Ibid. The proviso that there shall be no annoyance is important, since it enables the untutored adolescent who winds down the car windows and turns up the volume to be prosecuted, but not sufficiently often.

[94] Ibid.

[95] Ibid, s 62(3).

The use of loudspeakers for electioneering or advertisement of any entertainment, **13.95** trade, or business may not be authorized, however.[96] It therefore appears that the authority may authorize the use of loudspeakers in streets during carnivals or street fairs, but not for the purpose of giving advance notice of such events.

E. Noise Abatement Zones

Introduction—Declaring a noise abatement zone

Parliament intended that local authorities should be able to take positive action **13.96** to ensure that whole areas should enjoy favourable noise climates. To this end the CoPA 1974 invests local authorities with powers to declare noise abatement zones throughout England and Wales.[97] Before doing so the authority must serve every owner, lessee, and occupier with a copy of the proposed order declaring the zone, and publish copies of the order in the *London Gazette* and a local newspaper in two successive weeks.

If there are objections to the order the authority need do no more than consider **13.97** them before it makes the order, and need not even do that if satisfied that to do so would be unnecessary having regard to the nature of the premises to which the order will relate or to the interest of the objector or objectors in the premises. Noise abatement orders may vary or revoke previous orders, and their operation may be postponed if the authority thinks fit.[98]

The controls

If a noise abatement zone has been designated, the council must measure the level **13.98** of noise emanating from premises of any class to which the order relates within the zone, and keep records of the measurements which it obtains. A copy of the record must be served on the owner and occupier of every premises where measurements were taken, and the recipient may appeal to the Secretary of State 'against the record' within 28 days.[99]

This apparently means that the right of appeal is limited to a challenge to **13.99** the accuracy or fairness of the records obtained, since the Secretary of State may do no more than give directions to the authority as to the record of the noise

---

[96] Noise and Statutory Nuisance Act 1993, s 8, Sch 2.
[97] S 63.
[98] Ibid, Sch 1. It is not clear how the exercise of concluding that it is unnecessary to consider an objection can be undertaken without first considering the objection itself, a mystery which the parliamentary draftsman has not condescended to solve.
[99] Ibid, s 64(1)–(3).

measurements after he has dealt with the appeal.[100] An appeal must be lodged by giving written notice to the Secretary of State, and sending copies of the notice, and any other relevant plans, documents, and correspondence.

13.100 The Secretary of State may then choose whether to require the appellant and the authority to set out their respective cases in writing, or to hold an inquiry. His powers in deciding the appeal are the same as those of the authority in the first instance. Lodging the appeal will have the effect of suspending the notice if the noise is caused by the performing of a duty imposed by law, as might, for example, occur if the activity was being carried out by a statutory undertaker. The notice will also be suspended if compliance with it would involve any person in expenditure, although this is, by the very nature of the compilation of a record of noise measurements, unlikely.[101]

The register of noise levels

13.101 The register of noise levels must be open to public inspection free of charge at all reasonable hours. The noise levels have to be measured and calculated in accordance with the Memorandum on Measurement and Calculation of Noise Levels. This is extremely technical, and will probably be fully understood only by scientists experienced in the field of acoustics. It gives guidance as to the points at which noise levels are to be measured, the times at which measurements are to be taken, the method of measurement (Leq in dB(A) over a stated period of time), the meters to be used, and so on. The examples given in the Memorandum suggest that the Secretary of State at least envisaged that noise abatement zones and registers would be used to control noise generated by factories and other industrial premises. The register must contain details of the premises concerned, the methods employed to calculate or measure noise levels and the equipment used, and the places, dates, and times at which measurements were taken.[102]

13.102 It is an offence for the noise level to exceed that recorded in the register, unless the local authority consents to the excess in writing. If an application for consent has not been dealt with after two months, the application is deemed to have been refused, and the applicant may appeal to the Secretary of State. If a magistrates' court convicts a person of the offence of exceeding the registered noise levels it may order the execution of works for preventing the continuing or recurring of the offence, provided it is satisfied that the offence is likely to continue or recur, and may direct the local authority to make the order instead of the court itself.[103]

---

[100] Ibid, s 64(4).
[101] Control of Noise (Appeals) Regulations 1975, SI 1975/2116.
[102] Control of Noise (Measurement and Registers) Regulations 1976, SI 1976/37.
[103] CoPA 1974, s 65.

Reductions in noise levels

A local authority has power to bring about a reduction in the noise levels produced **13.103** by buildings of the prescribed classes within noise abatement zones. In order to do so, the authority must first be satisfied that the noise levels emanating from any premises within a noise abatement zone are unacceptable having regard to the purposes for which the noise abatement order was made, secondly, that the noise levels could be reduced at reasonable cost, and, thirdly, would afford a public benefit.

If it appears that those three conditions are met, the authority may serve a notice **13.104** on the person responsible for the noise levels, requiring him to reduce the level of noise to one specified in the notice; to prevent any subsequent increase in noise level without consent from the authority; and to take such steps as may be specified to achieve those purposes. The notice is a 'noise reduction notice'. It may specify particular times or days during which the noise level is to be reduced, and may prescribe different noise levels for different times or days. The requirements of the noise reduction notice must be recorded on the noise level register.

The recipient of the notice may appeal to the magistrates' court against it within **13.105** three months. The permitted grounds of appeal are virtually the same as those open to the recipient of a notice requiring the reduction of noise on a construction site, notably, that the best practicable means have been used for preventing or counteracting the effect of the noise where it was caused in the course of a trade or business. This is additional to the usual objections to a notice on procedural grounds, or on the ground that its demands are unreasonable or excessive. Failure to comply with a noise reduction notice without reasonable excuse is an offence.[104]

A further and final power available to local authorities where a noise abatement **13.106** zone has been declared is to regulate the level of noise from buildings about to be erected or adapted within the zone, to which the noise limitation regulations will apply. In that event the owner or occupier, actual or prospective, may apply to the authority to determine the level of noise which the premises may acceptably generate. The authority may (but need not) then determine the appropriate level, and record it in the noise level register. The rights of appeal and powers of the Secretary of State on appeal are as already described.[105]

Although the powers and duties in respect of noise abatement zones appear to be **13.107** straightforward to obtain and administer, little use has been made of these functions under the CoPA 1974 since it came into force. The costs of administering the legislation have been perceived to outweigh the benefits to local communities.[106]

---

[104] Ibid, s 66: Control of Noise (Appeals) Regulations 1975, SI 1975/2116, Part III.
[105] Control of Noise (Appeals) Regulations, above, Part II.
[106] See ENDS Report No 225, October 1993.

Anti-Social behaviour

13.108 Additional powers to put an end to excessive noise arise under Part V of the Anti-Social Behaviour Act 2003. These are a response, perhaps too belated, to the emergence of the rave and other events, even when authorized, towards the end of the twentieth century.

13.109 The Act gives a local authority power to close licensed premises or those holding temporary events notices for up to 24 hours. The power may be exercised where the authority believes that noise coming from the premises is causing a public nuisance, and that closure is necessary. [107]

13.110 The aim is to prevent licensed events from causing excessive annoyance. It is a criminal offence to open the establishment during the prohibited period. [108]

13.111 The Act identifies the Chief Executive of the authority as the officer who exercises the power of closure. He may delegate this to any environmental health officer and in practice will doubtless invariably do so. [109]

F. Noise from Plant or Machinery

13.112 Similar provisions enable local authorities to control and limit the noise made by plant and machinery. The details might be found, if anywhere, in regulations made under the CoPA 1974. No doubt for reasons similar to those which applied to noise abatement zones (see note 105), no such regulations have been made. [110]

13.113 However, as technology advances, the ability of machines to impinge on the world increases in proportion. The European Union therefore issued Directive 2000/14/EC, brought into UK law by the Noise Emissions in the Environment by Equipment for Use Outdoors Regulations 2001. [111] The length of their title is not reflected in the complexity of the Regulations.

13.114 The object is to limit the noise emitted by a wide range of mechanical devices, ranging from tower cranes to lawnmowers. The Regulations do not apply to road transport vehicles, trains, trams, aeroplanes, and passenger vessels, nor to military or emergency vehicles. [112] Equipment manufactured before 3 July 2001 is also exempt. [113]

---

[107] Anti-Social Behaviour Act 2003, s 40.
[108] Ibid.
[109] Ibid, s 41.
[110] CoPA 1974, s 68.
[111] SI 2001/1701.
[112] Reg 4.
[113] Reg 5.

The basic rule prohibits the marketing of relevant equipment unless it meets the **13.115** noise levels specified in Schedule 3.[114] This does not apply to equipment to be used outside the European Community, nor to re-exported goods.[115]

Contravention of the Regulations is a criminal offence, to which there is a defence **13.116** of taking reasonable steps and exercising due diligence to avoid committing the offence. [116] Directors, managers, and other senior officers of companies may be personally liable to prosecution.[117]

The scope of the Regulations is wide. Schedule 1 lists builders' plant and equip- **13.117** ment of many kinds, and also a range of domestic garden appliances such as lawn-mowers and motor hoes. These must not emit noise exceeding the prescribed levels.[118]

Schedule 2 is less rigorous. It requires only that the permitted and guaranteed **13.118** sound level shall be marked on the equipment.[119] Examples of devices within the Schedule are leaf-blowers and collectors, scarifiers and refuse collection vehicles.

Schedule 6 prescribes the methods for measuring the noise emitted by the relevant **13.119** equipment. Schedule 13 deals with enforcement.

The Secretary of State is the enforcement authority.[120] He has power to make test **13.120** purchases and of search and seizure.[121] He may prohibit the offering for sale of equipment which he suspects may contravene the Regulations by issuing a 'sus-pension notice'.[122] There are the usual rights of appeal against the exercise of these powers to a magistrates' court.

Proceedings may be brought in respect of alleged offences at any time within **13.121** twelve months instead of the more usual six,[123] and the Secretary of State may apply to the justices for forfeiture of contravening goods with a right of appeal to the Crown Court.[124]

---

[114] Regs 7 and 8.
[115] Reg 9.
[116] Regs 18 and 20.
[117] Reg 21.
[118] Reg 6.
[119] Ibid.
[120] Ibid, Schedule 13, paragraph 1.
[121] Ibid, paragraphs 2 and 3.
[122] Ibid, paragraph 6.
[123] Ibid, paragraph 12.
[124] Ibid, paragraph 13.

G. Aircraft Noise

Introduction

13.122   Intrusive though it is and distressing though it may be, aircraft noise is a phenomenon which in law has to be supported by the earthbound majority in the interests of those who fly. The effects of aircraft noise are excluded from the controls imposed by the CoPA 1974, and the Civil Aviation Act 1982 confers a general immunity from action for trespass or nuisance in respect of flights by aircraft other than model aircraft.

13.123   The only qualifications on this general rule are that the height of the aircraft above the ground must be reasonable having regard to all the circumstances, and that the aircraft has complied with the provisions of any Air Navigation Order in force for the time being. A similar, relatively wide immunity from action exists in respect of noise caused by aircraft on aerodromes.[125]

Control by the Secretary of State for Transport

13.124   The citizen is dependent almost entirely on the Secretary of State for Transport for protection from the effects of aircraft noise near aerodromes and elsewhere. He has power to prescribe the number of occasions on which aircraft may take off or land from airports.[126] The exercise of those powers has been, historically, eventful.

13.125   The Secretary of State for Transport has the difficult duty of balancing the interests of people whose everyday (and, more especially) night life may be seriously affected by aircraft movements and the noise which they create, against those of the airline industries and their customers. As technical progress brought about decreases in the levels of aircraft noise, he tried to achieve a proper balance by introducing a scheme under the Civil Aviation Act 1982 which did not limit the number of aircraft movements at Heathrow, Gatwick, and Stansted airports, but instead introduced a mathematical quota system. This would have enabled the airport authorities and the airlines to decide for themselves what aircraft could be flown from the airports, more use of 'quieter' aircraft enabling more take-offs and landings to occur. This was held to conflict with the clear wording of the Act, which made the scheme unlawful and ultra vires.[127]

---

[125]   CoPA 1974, ss 58 and 59. Civil Aviation Act 1982, ss 76 and 77: Air Navigation Order 1989, SI 1989/2116; Air Navigation (Noise Certification) Order 1990, SI 1990/1514.

[126]   Civil Aviation Act 1982, s 78(3).

[127]   *R v Secretary of State for Transport, ex p Richmond LBC and others*, [1994] 1 All ER 577. A subsequent scheme was also quashed by way of judicial review for procedural irregularity.

Given the strictly limited protection from aircraft noise which the law affords to people living near them, it is hardly surprising that proposals to extend the runway or terminal capacity of large airports are so bitterly resisted. More recently, the Secretary of State has used his powers to make delegated legislation to lessen the impact of aircraft noise, by imposing stricter limits on the noise emitted by engines. **13.126**

The vehicle is the Aeroplane Noise Regulations 1999.[128] These impose controls on the levels of noise produced by all aircraft, whatever their size, with a watershed of 5700 kilograms.[129] The use of civil sub-sonic jet aircraft is prohibited unless the CAA certifies that they meet noise emission requirements.[130] Since Concorde ceased to fly this must apply to all civil jet aircraft. The standards required for securing certification vary with the weight of the aircraft, as noted above. **13.127**

If satisfied that the aircraft, whether jet propelled or propeller driven, meets the specified noise requirements the CAA must grant a certificate in the prescribed form.[131] **13.128**

There are miscellaneous exemptions from the effect of the Regulations. These include aircraft in the process of conversions so as to meet the required noise emission standards;[132] aircraft replacing those accidently destroyed where no comparable replacement is on the market;[133] planes of historical interest;[134] importantly, where the operator can satisfy the CAA that compliance with the Regulations would unreasonably and adversely affect its operations it can secure exemption;[135] also significantly, where refusal of registration would ground more than 10% of the jet fleet of a European Community carrier.[136] There is, finally, a sweeping up exemption for exceptional cases, for all types of aircraft.[137] **13.129**

The exemptions, plainly designed to protect the commercial interests of airlines, show the tensions which influence legislators and regulators when they are required to balance those concerns against those of the wider public whose priority is a good night's sleep. **13.130**

---

[128] SI No. 1452.
[129] Regs 4 and 5.
[130] Regs 8 and 9.
[131] Regs 15 and 16.
[132] Reg 20.
[133] Reg 21.
[134] Reg 22.
[135] Reg 23.
[136] Reg 24.
[137] Reg 13; Schedule 1.

13.131 If the CAA proposes to grant an exemption it must first inform the European Commission, and the Authority may in any case prevent an aircraft from flying if it has reason to believe that it is intended to be operated without a certificate.[138]

13.132 Contravention of the Regulations is an offence, carrying liability to a fine on summary conviction.[139]

Short take-off and landing (STOL) aircraft

13.133 Other new technological developments have made it necessary to cater specially for these types of plane. Two city airports, London and Belfast, are subject to special controls under the Aerodromes (Noise Restrictions etc.) Regulations 2003.[140] Additionally, any airport having more than 50,000 civil subsonic jet movements per calendar year is subject to control.[141]

13.134 The Secretary of State, as competent authority, may impose operating restrictions on qualifying airports, having regard to the location, design, noise climate, and economics of the airport.[142] On six months notice, he may ban movements of 'marginally compliant' aircraft, these being those which just meet certification limits prescribed in the 1999 Regulations.[143] Additionally, he may require aircraft operators to reduce the number of movements of marginally compliant aircraft.[144]

13.135 There are exemptions for aircraft from developing countries;[145] for exceptional cases;[146] and for operations involving movement for the purpose of repair or maintenance.[147]

13.136 There is a right of appeal to arbitration against decisions of the Secretary of State.[148]

H. Noise—Road Traffic

The mischief

13.137 Political rhetoric frequently contains demands for a one-clause Bill to remedy some perceived wrong or injustice. The clamour is rarely answered, yet the

---

[138] Regs 6 and 25.
[139] Regs 27 and 28.
[140] SI 2003/1742.
[141] Reg 3.
[142] Reg 6; Schedule 2.
[143] Regs 2 and 7.
[144] Ibid.
[145] Reg 8.
[146] Reg 9.
[147] Ibid.
[148] Reg 12.

legislation regulating the emission by noise from motor cycles comes close to doing so.

The Motor Cycle Noise Act 1987 is commendably brief, consisting of two Sections **13.138** and one Schedule with a mere three paragraphs. It empowers the Secretary of State for Transport, after consultation, to make regulations prescribing requirements for exhaust systems for motor cycles, or silencers and other components for such systems.

It is an offence to supply, offer or agree to supply, to expose, or have in one's pos- **13.139** session an exhaust system, silencer, or other component which does not comply with the requirements of the regulations. The Secretary of State may grant exemptions from the requirements, either generally, or by written notice given to an individual.[149]

The Motor Cycle Silencer and Exhaust Systems Regulations 1995[150] discharge **13.140** the functions conferred on the Secretary of State eight years before. No explanation has been given for the delay—it can hardly have taken that time to consult with the motor cycle industry and users' organizations.

Exemptions from control

The Regulations exhibit features of many contemporary statutory instruments, in **13.141** that they incorporate by reference European Council Directives and British Standard Specifications. This makes it impossible for anyone other than the most determined to discover what obligations apply to the construction of motor cycles or their use.

In brief, silencers and exhaust systems must be marked clearly and indelibly (and, **13.142** presumably, constructed) in accordance with three specified European Council Directives or three British Standard Specifications. There are exemptions for silencers and exhaust systems which are not for use on roads or on motor cycles made before 1985. Curiously, the controls do not bite on silencers or exhaust systems fitted to the motor cycle at the time when it is supplied to the customer or other user, whether the machine is new or second hand. The intention seems to have been to regulate only the activities of businesses which exist to fit replacement silencers and exhaust systems.

MOT test certificates

It has long been necessary for owners of road vehicles more than three years old to **13.143** obtain a test certificate demonstrating their roadworthiness. The Motor Vehicles

---

[149] Motor Cycle Noise Act 1987, s 1.
[150] SI 1995/2370.

(Approval) Regulations 2001[151] continue and fortify the restrictions on noise emissions imposed by similar regulations in 1982 and 1984.

13.144 At great length, the Regulations prescribe the standards of construction needed before the vehicle can be used on a road, of which exhaust and engine noise are only two of many.[152]

I. Burglar Alarms

13.145 In addition to the problems of loudspeakers, the Noise and Statutory Nuisance Act 1993 addresses burglar alarms, or audible intruder alarms, as they are described with what is presumably unintended ambiguity. After consulting the Chief Constable for its area, a local authority may resolve that Schedule 3 to the Act of 1993 shall apply to its area on a date specified in the resolution.

13.146 Thereafter, any person installing an audible alarm must ensure that it complies with requirements prescribed by the Secretary of State for the Environment, although no such requirements have yet been made. The fact of installation must also be made known to the council within 48 hours. The police must be notified in writing of the names, addresses, and telephone numbers of two key holders. They must be occupiers of premises other than those where the alarm has been installed, and possess keys which enable them to obtain access if the alarm should be activated. Alternatively, a company whose business consists of holding keys will suffice. The local authority must also be told the address of the police station which has been given the details of the keyholders.

13.147 Where the alarm goes off for more than one hour, giving reasonable cause for annoyance (a requirement which should not be difficult to meet), an officer of the local authority may enter the premises, without using force, in order to turn off the alarm. If he is unable to gain access even with the help of the keyholders, he may apply to a justice of the peace, who may authorize forcible entry for the purpose of turning off the alarm. The officer must then turn the alarm off and reset it if practicable, and leave the premises as secure as he found them, also if practicable.

13.148 Officers and members of the authority are not liable personally for any action taken in good faith for the purposes of the Act, other than to surcharge.[153] However, the fact that the action was taken in good faith would ordinarily raise the presumption that no surcharge was payable in any event.

---

[151] SI 2001/25.
[152] See Schedule 4.
[153] Noise and Statutory Nuisance Act 1993, s 9 and Sch 3.

Those powers have been augmented by Part 7 of the Clean Neighbourhoods and **13.149** Environment Act 2005. This enables district or London Borough councils in England, and county or county borough councils in Wales, to declare alarm notification areas within their areas.[154]

The Act makes similar provision for the nomination and notification of key- **13.150** holders as those of the Act of 1993. The main difference introduced by the Act of 2005 is that an authorized officer of the local authority may enter the alarmed premises after the alarm has rung continuously for twenty minutes, or intermittently for more than one hour. Otherwise his powers and duties are for practical purposes the same as those afforded by the earlier legislation.

J. Implementation of EU Directives on Noise

The Commission of the European Union has issued other directives dealing with **13.151** a variety of matters, which the UK Government has been obliged by the Treaty of Rome and the European Communities Act 1972 to incorporate into UK law. Nearly all regulate the noise emitted by a variety of vehicles or appliances, and will be of doubtful interest to any except the manufacturers of these devices, and environmental health officers. For the sake of completeness they are listed in the footnote below.[155]

---

[154] Ibid, s 69.
[155] Motor Cycles (Sound Level Measurement Certificates) Regulations 1980, SI 1980/765; Motor Vehicles (Type Approval for Goods Vehicles) (Great Britain) Regulations 1982, SI 1982/1271; Construction Plant and Equipment (Harmonisation of Noise Emission Standards) Regulations 1985, SI 1985/1968; Road Vehicles (Construction and Use) Regulations 1986, SI 1986/1078; Agricultural or Forestry Tractors and Tractor Components (Type Approval) Regulations 1988, SI 1988/1567; Lawnmowers (Harmonisation of Noise Emission Standards) Regulations 1992, SI 1992/168; Motor Vehicles (EC Type Approval) Regulations 1992, SI 1992/3107.

PART III

THE ROLE OF TOWN AND COUNTRY PLANNING

14

THE RELATIONSHIP BETWEEN PLANNING CONTROL AND POLLUTION CONTROL

A. Introduction	14.01	
B. The Relationship Between Planning And Pollution Controls	14.04	
The legal overlap	14.04	
Development and the requirement for environmental impact assessment	14.07	
PPS 23 and the policy approach to the overlapping controls	14.09	
The court's approach to the overlapping controls	14.12	
Sustainable development and the planning system	14.16	
C. An Outline of the Town and Country Planning Regime	14.21	
The statutory framework of town and country planning law	14.21	
The planning authorities	14.22	
The requirement to obtain planning permission	14.25	
The meaning of 'development'	14.25	
Material changes of use	14.28	
Permitted development rights	14.30	
The determination of applications for planning permission	14.32	
The statutory test and the role of the development plan	14.32	
Outline applications	14.35	
Material considerations	14.38	
Conditions	14.41	
Planning obligations	14.47	

The location and need for a development	14.50	
Risk assessment	14.52	
Public opposition as a material consideration	14.55	
Planning appeals	14.58	
Court challenges	14.59	
The role of third parties in the planning process	14.61	
Planning enforcement powers	14.63	
Special considerations and regimes	14.67	
Listed buildings and conservation areas	14.67	
Conservation areas	14.71	
Archaeology and historical monuments	14.73	
Nature conservation constraints	14.75	
Trees and hedgerows	14.77	
D. The Environment and Development Plans	14.79	
E. Planning Considerations for Specific Types of Development	14.84	
Industrial pollution and development control	14.84	
Waste management and development control	14.87	
Nuisance and the effect of planning permission	14.92	
Noise and development control	14.93	
Flood risk areas	14.97	

A. Introduction

14.01   Regardless of the need to obtain the necessary consents under the environmental legislation discussed elsewhere in this book, most new development will also require a separate planning permission under the Town and Country Planning Act 1990 (TCPA 1990). This regime is concerned with building and engineering operations carried out on anyone's land and the use to which their land is put. This chapter covers the overlap between the Environmental Acts and the town and country planning regime. While it also provides an outline of the planning regime, practitioners must rely upon the specialist texts for a full understanding of its complexities.[1] Significant amendments have also been made by the Planning and Compulsory Purchase Act 2004, in particular with regard to development plans and by the Planning Act 2008 with regard to major infrastructure projects.

14.02   The planning regime depends upon obtaining prior permission for any new development from the local planning authority (LPA). These permissions will be determined in accordance with detailed land use development plans, which cover the whole country, and in the light of government policy guidance and other material considerations. Certain aspects of the development can be controlled by conditions, but once a planning permission is implemented there are no continuing controls over the development. Many environmental problems have been exacerbated by bad planning decisions, while others have been avoided by locating new developments sensitively. Indeed, the planning regime can be used as a tool to control the location of developments in order to avoid or minimize any adverse effects on adjoining areas of land, and in order to ensure the site itself is properly restored after a particular use has ceased. There is an obvious overlap between this and the extent to which any polluting activity is authorized under the pollution control regimes, although different considerations apply.

14.03   The planning authority should be concerned with the overall effect of the development on the character of the area and on adjoining uses, rather than with the effect on the environment of potentially polluting emissions. This does not mean that there is a clear legal division between the regimes, and there is considerable scope for duplication, and possible conflict, between environmental and planning controls. Little has really changed since the 1990 White Paper *This Common Inheritance* identified the common ground between the two systems in the real world.[2]

---

[1] The main source used by practitioners is the *Encyclopaedia of Planning Law and Practice*, ed Lockhart-Mummery and others (Sweet & Maxwell, 1969), whose nine volumes cover the main legislation, statutory instruments, and policy notes. A useful practical explanation is provided by Tromans and Turrall Clarke, *Planning Law Practice and Precedents* (Sweet & Maxwell, 1991). Both are loose-leaf, and regularly updated.

[2] *This Common Inheritance—Britain's Environmental Strategy* (Cm 1200, September 1990), at para 6.39. This paragraph was considered as stating the overall government policy in *Gateshead*

Planning control is primarily concerned with the type and location of new development and changes of use. Once broad land uses have been sanctioned by the planning process, it is the job of pollution control to limit the adverse effects that operations may have on the environment. In practice there is common ground. In considering whether to grant planning permission for a particular development, a local authority must consider all the effects, including potential pollution; permission should not be granted if that might expose people to danger. A change in an industrial process may well require planning permission as well as approval under the environmental protection legislation.

B. The Relationship Between Planning and Pollution Controls

The legal overlap

Although it could be said that both planning control and pollution control **14.04** are concerned with protecting the environment, they have been created with different purposes in mind. The aim of the town and country planning system is to regulate the use and development of land,[3] while the Environmental Acts control the damaging effect on the environment of processes and activities which cause pollution.[4] There is little integration between the Environmental Acts and the Town and Country Planning Acts.[5] Neither is there a clear-cut dividing line provided in the legislation, and the courts themselves have avoided trying to fill this statutory omission. While environmental matters must be taken into account in the drafting of the land use development plans, and will be relevant to the grant or refusal of planning permission, each case must still be dealt with on its own merits.[6]

The use of planning controls is an important part of taking on anticipatory **14.05** approach to pollution control. But this anticipatory approach is also being adopted to a greater extent by the environmental regimes. Therefore, the

---

MBC v Secretary of State for the Environment and Another [1994] JEL 93. Indeed, the White Paper deals both with Town and Country issues (Part III: Land Use, Countryside, Wildlife, Towns and Cities and the Heritage) and the Pollution Control regimes (in the chapters in Part IV).

[3] *Stringer v Minister of Housing and Local Government* [1971] 1 All ER 65.

[4] Using the broad terms of Glidewell LJ in *Gateshead MBC v Secretary of State for the Environment and Another* [1995] JPL 432 at 434.

[5] One exception is in the area of waste management, see para 14.63 below and the introduction of a single consenting regime for major infrastructure projects under the Planning Act 2008.

[6] *Gateshead MBC v Secretary of State for the Environment and Another* [1994] JEL 93 at 99, per Sullivan J, that to try to draw a line is unhelpful for this very reason. The Court of Appeal agreed with the conclusions reached by Sullivan J in 'his careful and admirable judgment' [1995] Env LR 37 per Glidewell LJ.

relationship between the two sets of controls continues to evolve.[7] There is there-fore a perception that the introduction of more and more stringent and compre-hensive pollution controls is taking away the LPA's ability to consider all aspects of the development proposal. Indeed, the door may eventually close on the right of a local planning authority to treat detailed pollution control points as material to a determination under the planning regime.[8] This is the implication which can be drawn from government policy statements, but there is no legal rule to this effect, and, as will be seen, the judges have their feet firmly in that door. There should be no doubt that the environmental impact of emissions, and the need to protect the environment, are legitimate material considerations in all planning decisions.

14.06   No planning authority could lawfully adopt a policy of hiving off all consider-ation of such environmental effects in their entirety to the EPA regime. Neither would it be lawful to take no account in the planning process of the existence of such a stringent regime for preventing or mitigating environmental impacts.[9] The planning system is only part of a complex regulatory framework and it should not be forced into filling an all-encompassing role.

Development and the requirement for environmental impact assessment

14.07   As part of the planning control process, promoters of major development projects may be required to carry out an environmental impact assessment ('EIA'). This procedural requirement is intended to ensure that the effects on the environment are taken into account as early as possible in the planning and decision-making process. The assessment process will draw together the expert analysis of the different areas of the environment which are affected, and present them in such a way that the importance of the predicted effects, and the scope for mitigating them, can be properly evaluated. It does not change the weight that should be given to the environmental considerations in the planning decision. Nor does it affect the dividing line between planning controls and pollution controls. There is also now a requirement to carry out strategic environmental impact assessment of plans and programmes as a whole.[10]

---

[7] See S Tromans 'Town and Country Planning and Environmental Protection' (1991, JPL Occasional papers, Sweet & Maxwell) for a discussion of the position in 1991. The author also identifies the policy considerations regarding the overlap which were discussed in the early reports of the Royal Commission on Environmental Pollution and the 1990 White Paper, *This Common Inheritance*.

[8] This is certainly the view taken by K Mylrea, case analysis of *Gateshead* [1994] JEL 101 at 105–106. If an LPA did so in anything other than very clear cases, it could be said to have acted unreasonably in the *Wednesbury* sense.

[9] See *Gateshead MBC*, especially Sullivan J [1994] JEL 93 at 99 and Glidewell LJ [1995] Env LR 37. In *R v Bolton MBC, ex p Kirkman* [1998] JPL 787, the Court of Appeal dismissed the submission that the planning authority was in breach of its duty in allowing the details of environmental control to be handled by the Agency as unarguable.

[10] Under the Environmental Assessment of Plans and Programmes Regulations 2004, which implement the relevant EC Directive. See Chapter 15 further.

The requirement to provide an EIA, and the standard to which it should be **14.08**
carried out, has been the subject of considerable controversy. This subject is therefore addressed in detail in Chapter 15. Essentially, whether or not a project will
require an assessment will be based on the type of project, and not on the state of
the land on which the development will take place. For certain types of projects,
such as an oil refinery, a large power station, or a motorway, there must be such an
assessment, but in others, such as mineral extraction, intensive livestock farming,
and roads, an assessment will only be required if it 'would be likely to have
significant effects on the environment' by virtue of its size or location.[11] The
decision-maker cannot then grant planning permission without having first taken
the environmental information into account.[12] Although much of the information provided in an environmental assessment will be similar to that required for
an Environmental Permit, any applicant will have to go through both processes if
they apply to his proposals. The whole process of assessment will delay the project
timetable,[13] and often add considerably to the costs of a development.

PPS 23 and the policy approach to the overlapping controls

Government policy on the interaction of planning and pollution controls is now **14.09**
contained in Planning Policy Statement (PPS) 23, which replaced the former
PPG23 in 2006. As set out at paragraph 2, the Statement advises that:

1) The impact of proposed development on soil, air, or water is capable of being
   a material planning consideration. It should therefore be taken into account in
   forward planning or development control decisions.[14]
2) The planning system is important in complementing pollution control, but
   should not duplicate the latter.[15]
3) Planning authorities and other regulators therefore need to cooperate closely
   in order to ensure that potentially damaging development can co-exist with its
   neighbours.[16]

---

[11] The categories of development where an assessment will be mandatory, or only required
subject to this discretionary test, are set out in Schedule 1 and 2 respectively of the Town and
Country Planning (Environmental Impact Assessment) (England and Wales) Regulations 1999
(SI 1999/293). The new Regulations replace the 1988 Regulations, and give effect to amendments
made to the EC Directive on Environmental Assessment (85/337/EEC) by Directive 97/11/EC.

[12] Reg 3 of the 1999 Regulations.

[13] One immediate effect is that the planning authority is given 16 weeks, rather than the normal
8 weeks, to determine the application (reg 32 of the 1999 Regulations, which modifies Reg 20 of
the General Permitted Development Order 1995, SI 1995/419 (the GPDO 1995)—although this
timescale is often lengthened by agreement or by formal requests for further information.

[14] PPS 23, paragraph 8 further elaborates on para 2.

[15] Ibid, paragraph 10.

[16] Ibid, paragraph 11.

4) While past contamination may affect and/or restrain the future use of land, redevelopment may offer opportunities to deal with contamination.[17]

5) Developers and others should be alive to the possibility of contamination from natural as well as man-made sources. It is well-known, for example, that radon gas is found in some areas of the UK, and is radioactive.[18]

6) Developers should discuss known or suspected contamination problems with all the responsible authorities.[19] This proposition seems self-evident.

7) Wherever possible, developers should submit applications for planning permission and pollution control permits together, so that the entire package can be dealt with at the same time.[20]

14.10 These general principles are amplified in the Annexes to PPS 23. Annex 1 is directed at air and water quality. It reminds those concerned of the IPPC code and goes on to stress the government's concern with and policies on climate change, emphasizing that the planning system is important in helping to reach the goal of reducing carbon dioxide emissions.[21] As to water, the Annex rehearses the rules prescribed by the EU Water Framework Directive (2000/60/EC) and the need to strike a balance between the conflicting need to improve water quality and at the same time taking account of technical feasibility and cost ('derogation').[22] The Annex encourages the provision of sustainable drainage systems (SUDS), such as on-site water storage and filtration ponds or swales, rather than sewers and drains connected to treatment works.[23] This is often applied as a planning condition to new developments, whereby the system will be implemented in accordance with the scheme submitted to the planning authority for its approval.

14.11 Annex 2 to PPS 23 concerns contaminated land. It recommends the application of the principles of the regime regulating contaminated land established by Part IIA of the EPA 1990 to all development planning and control regarding this type of land, and sets out some recommended planning conditions.[24] Indeed, for land that is covered by the Part IIA regime, an exception is provided for redevelopment work. Where a developer is willing to undertake remedial action on a site, neither the Agency nor a local authority can use their powers to serve a Remediation Notice. They will be able to require that a Remediation Statement is prepared, but they can only take further action if they are not satisfied that the proposed

---

[17] Ibid, paragraph 17. After all, no one wishes to live on the site of a former rubbish tip, even if it is safe to do so.

[18] Ibid, paragraph 19.

[19] Ibid, paragraph 22.

[20] Ibid, paragraph 14.

[21] Annex 1, paragraph 1.14; Appendix 1C.

[22] Ibid, paragraph 1.19; Appendix 1D.

[23] Ibid, paragraph 1.31.

[24] Appendix 2, paragraph 2.2.

remedial measures are appropriate.[25] This is an acknowledgement that redevelopment is likely to remain the primary method by which contaminated land will be cleaned up, and the means by which the necessary funds can be generated to do the work required.

The court's approach to the overlapping controls

The courts have yet to find a comprehensive answer to this question about the   **14.12**
appropriate overlap.[26] For the moment, it seems that some duplication is unavoidable. As acknowledged in PPS 23,[27] and in the earlier case of *Gateshead MBC*,[28] the bottom line is that a planning authority can, and should, refuse planning permission if it concludes that the wider impact of potential releases on the development and use of land is unacceptable, despite the potential consideration of this point in the pollution control process. But the normal result will be that planning permission will be granted and the concerns about potential releases will be left for the pollution control authorities to determine. The point at which the concerns about pollution can be left to the pollution control regime is a matter of planning judgement. If a planning authority decides to do so, the decision is not susceptible to challenge in the courts unless it is unreasonable in the *Wednesbury* sense. These are arguments which will continue to trouble the courts—they were raised in *R v Bolton Metropolitan Council, ex p Kirkman*,[29] when a challenge was made to the grant of planning permission for another waste incinerator.

Two recently decided cases show how the law is evolving. The first concerned a   **14.13**
quarry, this being an activity which frequently raises controversy over environmental issues. [30] Following an inquiry, a planning inspector granted planning permission to extend the quarry and to use it as a landfill site. He recognized that there would be grave environmental consequences, which he sought to mitigate by imposing conditions, which required the planning authority to approve any departure from the landscape proposed or from specified mitigation measures; and for control of dust emissions. However, he left control of smell and vermin to

---

[25] EPA 1990, s 78H(5)(b). Remediation of a development site under the Part IIA regime will therefore be exceptional.

[26] PPS 23, paragraph 2.26; *Gateshead MBC v SOS*, supra.

[27] Supra.

[28] Supra, that 'if it had become clear at the inquiry that some of the discharges were bound to be unacceptable so that a refusal by HMIP to grant an authorization would be the only proper course, the Secretary of State following his own express policy should have refused planning permission'. Such clarity is rarely achieved.

[29] [1998] JPL 787, QBD and CA. Whilst *Gateshead MBC* was followed, the law regarding waste management had changed. Planning authorities must now take account of the 'relevant objectives' of the Waste Management Licensing Regulations 1994 themselves, and cannot leave this to the Agency. This is considered in more detail below, at para 15.64–15.68.

[30] *Smith v Secretary of State* [2003] 2 P&CR 11.

be exercised by the Environment Agency through IPPC. A local resident challenged the decision, on the ground that the permission did not tie the conditions
to the mitigation measures which the operator put forward. The challenge failed.
The Court of Appeal held that a planning authority, including the Secretary of
State, must ensure that it has sufficient details of the nature of the proposals and
their possible impact on the environment. This demands consideration of the significant effects rather than every possible consequence. The authority is entitled
to have regard to decisions likely to be taken by other regulators, including the
Environment Agency, but may not leave them free to re-assess the environmental
impact. This is the task of the planning authority itself, which must address all the
significant consequences and impose appropriate conditions.

14.14   The case of *Smith* leaves an important question unanswered. It does not indicate
authoritatively what may be covered by condition, and what is to be left to IPPC
(and now, Environmental Permitting). True it is, as the Court said, that quarries
are not subject to IPPC, and dust emissions could only be regulated by planning
condition.[31] This, however, raises the question why smells and vermin should not
be controlled in the same way. This dilemma will have to be resolved.

14.15   In the second case, *Hopkins*, [32] a planning inspector dismissed an appeal against
refusal to permit a concrete plant and factory on an industrial estate. The main
reason was the effects of dust on nearby residents, which were unacceptable, even
though IPPC controls would be available. The High Court dismissed the developer's argument that the inspector failed to understand that IPPC control was a
sufficient safeguard against dust nuisance. The court held that while planning
authorities are entitled to take account of IPPC, they are not as a matter of
law obliged to do so. The correct approach is for the authority to focus on the
intended use and its implications, rather than on the control of the processes and
emissions. However, it is again unclear how the two areas are to be distinguished
in practice.

Sustainable development and the planning system

14.16   The Government has set out what it refers to as its overarching planning policies
on the delivery of sustainable development through the planning system in
Planning Policy Statement 1 (PPS1).[33] This is something of a step change. It is
now stated that 'Sustainable development is the core principle underpinning
planning' and that 'At the heart of sustainable development is the simple idea of

---

[31] Paragraph 51.
[32] *Hopkins Developments Ltd v Secretary of State* [2006] EWHC Admin. 2823.
[33] Planning Policy Statement 1: Delivering Sustainable Development (February 2005); this
replaced Planning Policy Guidance Note 1: General Policies and Principles (PPG1) which was
published in February 1997. PPS 1 uses the Brundtland definition of sustainable development.

ensuring a better quality of life for everyone, now and for future generations'. PPS 1 draws on the four aims for sustainable development that were set out in the Government's 1999 strategy.[34] These are: social progress which recognizes the needs of everyone; effective protection of the environment; the prudent use of natural resources; and the maintenance of high and stable levels of economic growth and employment.

Paragraph 13 of PPS 1 sets out the 'Key principles' that should be applied to both **14.17** development plans and planning decisions. These emphasize that an integrated approach is needed, in which environmental, economic and social objectives are achieved together over time. PPS 1 also refers to a 'spatial planning approach' being at the heart of planning for sustainable development.[35] This goes beyond traditional land use planning to bring together and integrate policies for the development and use of land with other policies and programmes which influence the nature of places and how they can function. This will therefore include the LPA's Community Strategy[36] as well as such plans as the corporate plan, and urban and rural regeneration strategies, regional economic and housing strategies, community development and local transport plans.[37]

Whilst PPS 1 included the need to ensure that development plans contributed to **14.18** global sustainability by addressing the causes and potential impacts of climate change,[38] there is now a Supplement to PPS 1 on this topic.[39] Development plans should included policies which reduce energy use, reduce emissions (for example, by patterns of development which reduce the need to travel), promote the development of renewable energy resources, and take climate change impacts into account in the location and design of development. Planning authorities have been advised to have regard to this PPS as a material consideration which may

---

[34] A Better Quality of Life—A Strategy for Sustainable Development for the UK—Cm 4345, May 1999. The Planning White Paper, *Planning for a Sustainable Future* (2007, Cm 7120), has emphasized the fundamental importance of planning in delivering sustainable development in a changing global context.

[35] Paras 30–32, PPS 1. This is a frustratingly vague concept, but it is intended to shift the emphasis in the planning system, which used to consider land use issues alone, and to make planning decisions part of the overall approach.

[36] The local authority has a duty to prepare a Community Strategy, under the Local Government Act 2000, for promoting or improving the economic, social and environmental well-being of their areas, and contributing to the achievement of sustainable development in the UK. These rather vague aspirational plans have gained greater importance now that they will affect development control issues.

[37] Para 32, PPS 1. Further guidance is contained in PPS11 (Regional Spatial Strategies) and PPS12 (Local Development Frameworks).

[38] Further guidance was also given in 'The Planning Response to Climate Change—Advice on Better Practice'(ODPM, September 2004).

[39] Planning and Climate Change—Supplement to Planning Policy Statement 1 (December 2007). Note that Hurwitz, 'Planning and Climate Change: Recent Government Initiatives' [2007] JPL 1002 reviews the situation before the PPS 1 Supplement was published.

supersede the policies in their earlier development plan.[40] Where proposals are inconsistent with the Key Planning Objectives set out in this PPS, they are advised that consideration should be given as to how proposals could be amended to make them acceptable or, where this is not practicable, to whether planning permission should be refused.[41] This is complemented by the moves to improve the Building Regulations to require major reductions in carbon emissions from all new homes to get to zero carbon by 2016, and there are similar ambitions to cut carbon emissions from new non-domestic buildings. Planning conditions can be imposed to require greater improvements.[42] The Planning and Energy Act 2008 has given local planning authorities the power (but not a duty) to include planning policies in their development plans on energy use and energy efficiency.

14.19 Planning authorities have begun to include sustainable development policies in their development plans. Such policies can most appropriately be included at the strategic level, but they have also filtered down into Local Plans where detailed policies apply. Greater weight in planning decisions will now be placed on a number of issues. Some are related to transport and the need to travel, so that an emphasis is placed on providing for integrated transport, and concentrating uses which generate a large number of trips in places well served by public transport. There is also a stated preference for a sequential approach to allowing development, starting with sites within existing urban areas, and the recycling of previously used land, before considering any greenfield sites. Nature conservation issues have been given greater weight, as has the need to preserve and enhance listed buildings and conservation areas. A greater emphasis is placed on good design, not just for the short term but over the lifetime of the development.[43]

14.20 There is one clear obstacle to achieving sustainable development in the current planning system. Planning permissions may go through an elaborate examination before they are granted, including an environmental impact assessment in some cases, but there is no provision to periodically review them thereafter. A planning permission also attaches to the land, and is very rarely granted in relation to an individual person, so that anyone may benefit from them, or choose to walk away from them. Most of the pollution control regimes contain provision for the review

---

[40] Para 11, PPS 1 Supplement. But it also stresses that information sought from applicants should be proportionate to the scale of the proposed development, its likely impact on and vulnerability to climate change. The requisite information may also be made available to the planning authority through the submitted Design and Access Statement, or forms part of any environmental impact assessment or other regulatory requirement.

[41] Para 39, PPS 1 Supplement.

[42] Para 8, PPS 1 Supplement. For instance, by requiring a higher standard than the Building Regulations would impose, under the Code for Sustainable Homes: A step-change in sustainable home building practice (DCLG, December 2006), and the technical guide (March 2007). There is a 'star' system from 1 to 6.

[43] It is even stated that 'Design which fails to take the opportunities available for improving the character and quality of an area should not be accepted', and paragraphs 33–39 elaborate on this.

and variation of the authorizations which have been granted, and both the air pollution and waste management controls seek to control the surrender of the authorization. Planning permissions cannot be reviewed in this way, although there is a tendency to seek more elaborate conditions.[44] While every permission should have a condition limiting its implementation to a three-year period,[45] it will be valid for all time once it has been implemented. While a permission can be revoked in the public interest, compensation for its full value will be payable to its owner. Monitoring is seen as one way to help address this issue. As PPS 1 highlights, every LPA now has a responsibility for reporting on an annual basis concerning the extent to which its local development plan policies are being achieved, in an Annual Monitoring Report. The intention is their role is not to be restricted to plan making and development control, but must involve facilitating and promoting the implementation of good quality development.

C. An Outline of the Town and Country Planning Regime

The statutory framework of town and country planning law

The current framework of the Town and Country Planning regime dates from 1947. The Town and Country Planning Act 1947 was passed during the period of nationalization and the post-war reconstruction of Britain. Indeed, the Act effectively nationalized the private rights of every landowner to develop their land as they wished. The 1947 Act took effect at a time when there was little environmental protection legislation.[46] The main act is now the Town and Country Planning Act 1990 ('TCPA 1990'),[47] which operates in a very different regulatory climate.

14.21

---

[44] Conditions can impose requirement to monitor emissions, and to phase the development in accordance with details that need to be approved by the LPA. The review of old mineral planning permissions, under the Planning and Compensation Act 1991, s 22 is a one-off exception, where they have all had to be revisited.

[45] TCPA 1990, s 91 (as amended). This was previously five years.

[46] The regime was introduced on 1 July 1948. Water and drainage problems were covered by the Public Health (Drainage of Trade Premises) Act 1937 and the Rivers Pollution Prevention Act 1876 (the 1876 Act was soon replaced by the Rivers (Prevention of Pollution) Act 1951). The worst industrial processes were regulated under the Alkali etc Works Act 1906. The remainder could be dealt with as nuisances, under the statutory nuisance provisions of the Public Health Act 1936. The Clean Air Acts only date from 1956 and 1968. There was no legislation at all on waste until the Deposit of Poisonous Waste Act 1972, and its deposit was only properly controlled by the Control of Pollution Act 1974.

[47] It was passed along with three other planning Acts, the Planning (Listed Buildings and Conservation Areas) Act 1990, the Planning (Hazardous Substances) Act 1990, and the Planning (Consequential Provisions) Act 1990. Most of the provisions of the Acts came into force on 24 August 1990. The exception is the Planning (Hazardous Substances) Act 1990, analysed in Chapter 8, which came into force on 1 June 1992. The TCPA 1990 was intended to be a

The planning authorities

14.22   The Secretary of State[48] and the National Assembly for Wales[49] have wide-ranging powers of supervision under the TCPA 1990. All planning appeals lie to them, and they are responsible for the Planning Inspectorate.[50] They can 'call-in' any particular planning applications from the local authorities for their own decision. They can intervene in the preparation of the development plan, and the Secretary of State adopts the regional spatial strategies in England[51] and the National Assembly adopts the Wales Spatial Plan.[52] They also issue a wide range of policy documents. In England, the Department of Culture, Media, and Sport retains responsibility for designating listed buildings.[53]

14.23   In areas where there are still two tiers of local government, the local planning authority ('LPA') for most purposes, including the responsibility for granting

---

consolidating Act, and it has been amended by the Planning and Compensation Act 1991, and supplemented by the Environment Act 1995 and the Pollution Prevention and Control Act 1999.

[48] Planning is the responsibility of the department for Communities and Local Government ('CLG'), which has the remit to promote community cohesion and equality, as well as having responsibility for housing, urban regeneration, planning and local government. See the Department's website, at <http://www.communities.gov.uk>. Political fashion has dictated that the word 'Department' has been dropped (as of 2008). Previously, planning had been the responsibility of the now-defunct Office of the Deputy Prime Minister ('ODPM'), and the 'First Secretary of State'.

[49] The powers of the Secretary of State under the Town and Country Planning Act 1990 were transferred to the Welsh Assembly under the Government of Wales Act 1998. The Planning and Compulsory Purchase Act 2004 makes provision for the National Assembly for Wales to prepare and publish a national spatial plan for Wales to which local planning authorities must have regard when preparing their development plans. See para 2.41, Chapter 2, for a general comment on the changing status of Welsh law. The Welsh Assembly has, effectively, stepped into the shoes of the Secretary of State for Wales—including for planning appeals and call-ins.

[50] The Planning Inspectorate acts as an Executive Agency, and is not an independent legal body. It does produce useful guidance on appeals—see their website at <http://www.planning-inspectorate.gov.uk>. It has also been given responsibility for environmental appeals.

[51] See the Planning and Compulsory Purchase Act 2004 Part 1, and the policy guidance in PPS 11 (September 2004). Since September 2004, there has been a regional spatial strategy for each English region which forms part of the statutory development plan. The Secretary of State prescribed that the previous regional planning guidance ('RPG') produced by him is the initial regional spatial strategy for each region. The regional spatial strategy sets out the Secretary of State's policies in relation to the development and use of land in the region. The Regions are defined in accordance with the Regional Development Agencies Act 1998.

[52] Planning and Compulsory Purchase Act 2004, s 60. The decision has been made that there will be only one level of development plan in Wales, at the local government level, and there are no regional spatial strategies. General guidance has been provided by *Local Development Plans Wales* (Welsh Assembly Government, 2005). The new arrangements for local development plans in Wales are set out in the Planning and Compulsory Purchase Act 2004 Part 6.

[53] Listed Buildings are afforded additional protection from unsuitable development—see paragraph 14.67 below. The Secretary of State at the Department for Culture, Media and Sport is also the decision maker for scheduled monument consent matters under the Ancient Monuments and Archaeological Areas Act 1979. The National Assembly for Wales carries out all these functions (note that 'Cadw: Welsh Historic Monuments' is only an Agency within the National Assembly for Wales, and not a separate body).

planning permissions, will be the district or borough council. The county council remains responsible for strategic planning, and fulfils the role of the local planning authority in the specific areas of waste planning and minerals. In areas with unitary authorities, which include Wales, this distinction will not apply. Special provision has been made in National Parks under the Environment Act 1995, where the National Park Authorities now have responsibility for planning. In areas covered by urban development corporations, planning powers may be temporarily passed to the Development Corporations by statutory instrument.[54] These authorities will discharge their functions through their committees, made up of locally-elected councillors, drawing on the advice and recommendations of local authority employees. In London, while the 32 London Boroughs and the City of London have control of planning within their areas, a new tier of local government with an elected Mayor and Assembly was created in 2000.[55] The Mayor is responsible for the 'Spatial Development Strategy' for London, which is part of the development plan hierarchy, and the local development plans in London have to be in 'general conformity' with it. The Strategy is part of a range of strategies produced by the Mayor which cover areas such as Transport, the London Development Agency, the London Biodiversity Action Plan, municipal waste management, air quality, and culture.[56] The Mayor also has power to direct a borough council to refuse planning permission for major planning applications, and to direct that he should act as the LPA in determining any application which is of 'potential strategic importance'.[57]

Even though there is no specific legislative requirement on LPAs to take account **14.24** of government policy guidance in deciding on planning applications, they greatly influence the planning system. They are material considerations which must be taken into account by the LPAs,[58] and if an authority decides not to follow a relevant government policy it must have clear and convincing reasons for not

---

[54] For instance, the London Docklands Development Corporation, whose planning powers were handed back to the relevant London Boroughs at the end of its ten-year life in 1998.

[55] Greater London Authority Act 1999.

[56] The relationship between the two tiers is not simple. In *Mayor of London v Enfield London Borough Council* [2008] EWCA Civ 202—the Mayor of London's direction (under the Greater London Authority Act 1999, s 356) requiring a waste disposal authority to provide a new site as a compensatory provision for the closure of a recycling site was held to be untenable once his underlying justification had been rejected by a planning inspector as part of the appeal into the redevelopment of the closed site.

[57] TCPA 1990, s 2A (inserted by the Greater London Authority Act 2007, s 31). The Town and Country Planning (Mayor of London) Order 2008 (SI 2008/580) defines what are such applications, and sets out the circumstances in which the Mayor's powers to give directions may be exercised (it replaces the previous 2000 Order). The disappointed developer can still appeal against any refusal to the Secretary of State.

[58] See *Gransden v Secretary of State* [1985] 54 P&CR 86, *R v Secretary of State, ex p Richmond LBC* [1996] 1 WLR 1460, and the discussion in *R v Bolton MBC, ex p Kirkman* [1998] JPL 787.

doing so. Wales has a large number of 'Technical Advice Notes', and only six Planning Guidance (Wales) Notes, rather than the 25 Planning Policy Guidance Notes or Statements which apply to England. There remain some differences in approach, for instance, PPG 13 (March 1994), which did much to promote the cause of sustainable transport, did not apply in Wales. In England, the Government has produced a substantial body of PPSs which set out their policies on different aspects of the planning system, and which are replacing the earlier PPGs.[59] There are now 25 PPSs or PPGs, ranging from the 'General Policy and Principles' set out in PPS 1, the Green Belt in PPG 2, housing in PPS 3, industrial and commercial development, and small firms in PPS 4, rural areas in PPS 7, to transport in PPS 13.[60] PPS 23 deals with planning and pollution control. There are also a large number of government Circulars, which are primarily concerned with explaining legislation and procedure.[61] Government policy is also set out in White Papers, Minerals Planning Guidance Notes, Regional Planning Guidance Notes, and Ministerial Statements.

The requirement to obtain planning permission

The meaning of 'development'

14.25   Section 55 of the TCPA 1990 sets out the definition of 'development' and therefore defines the limits of what requires planning permission:

> the carrying out of building, engineering, mining or other operations in, on, over, or under land, or the making of any material change in the use of any buildings or other land.

14.26   'Building operations' (Section 55(1A)) are stated to include the demolition of buildings, rebuilding, structural alterations of or additions to buildings, and other operations normally undertaken by a person carrying on business as a builder. But while this definition may seem to be fairly broad, it may be the case that a proposal will fall outside the control of the town and country planning regime.

14.27   The development or use may have been commenced before the planning system was introduced in 1948, or it may have become an established use. Not all changes in use are seen as 'material', particularly if they involve only the intensification of the level of activity of the same type of use. The legislation has also introduced a large number of permitted changes of use, and permitted development rights.

---

[59]   Planning Policy Guidance Notes.
[60]   Other PPSs (and the previous PPGs) are referred to in the text of this chapter. They are available from <http://www.communities.gov.uk>, from HMSO, and are reproduced in the *Encyclopaedia of Planning Law and Practice* (Sweet & Maxwell).
[61]   eg DoE Circular 11/95 on Planning Conditions.

In this way, there are a number of potentially polluting activities which will not require planning permission.

Material changes of use

Whilst it may be fairly obvious whether or not physical development of land has **14.28** occurred, permission is also required for any 'material change of use'.[62] The Use Classes Order 1987 provides a useful way of assessing the use of land. It divides uses into different classes and is arranged into four parts covering Shopping Area Uses, Business and Industrial Uses, Residential Uses, and Community Uses.[63] Changes of use which remain within the same Use Class will not be material,[64] and there are a number of permitted changes of use between classes.[65]

There has been a considerable relaxation of planning controls over 'bad neigh- **14.29** bour' developments. There used to be special industrial use classes under Classes B3 to B7. These have been repealed, and such uses will fall within the broad use classes. The more stringent controls placed on these type of uses are now to be found in the Environmental Acts.[66] Some uses are outside the Use Classes Order, and can loosely be referred to as 'sui generis' uses. For instance, scrapyards do not come within the business and industrial use classes,[67] and therefore will not benefit from any rights to change their use without permission.

Permitted development rights

Not all building work which amounts to development requires planning **14.30** permission from the local planning authority. In order to avoid clogging the system, the government has itself permitted certain classes of development to be

---

[62] The grant of the permission for the erection of a building may specify the purposes for which the building may be used, but if it does not, the permission shall be construed as including permission to use the building for the purpose for which it was designed (TCPA 1990, s 75(2) and (3)).

[63] Part A: Shopping Area Uses, so that Class A1 is for Shops, A2 for Financial and Professional Services, and A3 for Food and Drink; Part B: Business and Industrial Uses, so that Class B1 is for general business, which can be carried out in a residential area, and B2 is general industrial, B8 is for Storage and Distribution. Part C: Residential Uses: Class C1 for Hotels and Hostels, C2: Residential Institutions, C3: Dwelling Houses. Part D: Community Uses—Class D1 Non-residential Institutions and D2 Assembly and Leisure. See generally Circular 13/87, Change of use of Buildings and Other Land: Town and Country Planning (Use Classes) Order 1987 (WO 24/87).

[64] TCPA 1990, s 55(2)(a)—but it will need permission if the change also involves building operations.

[65] Under Part 3 of Schedule 2 of the GPDO 1995: eg from A3 to A1, from B2 (general industrial) to B1 or B8 (warehouses).

[66] This is a point foreshadowed in *This Common Inheritance—Britain's Environmental Strategy* (Cm 1200, September 1990) at para 6.40. Para 3.29 of PPG 23 is out-of-date in this respect.

[67] See the UCO 1987, art 3(6)(g). Art 3(6) specifically excludes a number of uses from the order. Waste disposal installations are also 'sui generis' (reg 35(2) of the Town and Country Planning (Environmental Impact Assessment) Regulations 1999, SI 293)—although some waste processes can claim to be general industrial uses (B2).

carried out without the express permission of the LPA. These 'permitted development' rights are set out in the Town and Country Planning (General Permitted Development) Order 1995 ('the GPDO 1995').[68] Some of these permitted development rights cover small-scale development, such as development within the curtilage of a dwelling house,[69] minor operations,[70] and temporary buildings and uses.[71] The GPDO 1995 also permits whole classes of development which relate to certain types of industry and business, all of which would otherwise require planning permission and be subject to public scrutiny.[72] Industries such as agriculture and forestry have always benefited from considerable freedom from control, even though they may be carrying out development in sensitive areas.[73] There is also a raft of permitted rights for development by local authorities, local highway authorities, drainage bodies, the Environment Agency (as the successor to the National Rivers Authority), and by statutory undertakers.[74]

14.31 Permitted development rights may be withdrawn in part or in whole by the Secretary of State, or the LPA with his approval, for specific areas.[75] Some rights are also withdrawn if the land is situated in a National Park, the Norfolk Broads, a Conservation Area, or an Area of Outstanding Natural Beauty.[76] Permitted development rights are also withdrawn for certain developments requiring environmental assessment.[77]

The determination of applications for planning permission

The statutory test and the role of the development plan

14.32 The LPA may grant planning permission, subject to such conditions as it thinks fit, or refuse planning permission. In dealing with such an application, the authority must have regard to the provisions of the development plan, so far as it

---

[68] SI 1995/418.

[69] Part 1 of Schedule 2, including such matters as the erection of a satellite dish, enlargements of under 50 cubic metres or 10 percent of a house—even though this may cause considerable concerns to the neighbouring properties.

[70] Part 2, such as the erection of a fence up to 1.8 m high.

[71] Part 4, such as temporary operations up to 28 days in duration.

[72] So, general industrial and warehouse developments benefit from the rights set out in Part 8 of Schedule 2 of the GPDO 1995.

[73] See Parts 6 and 7 of the GPDO 1995. The erection and alteration of agricultural buildings has at least been made more restrictive since amendments made in 1992 requiring prior notification to the local planning authority—who can at least then choose whether or not to interfere.

[74] See Parts 12–16 of the GPDO 1995. Special provision is made for aviation development (Part 18), mining operations (Parts 19–23), and telecommunications (Parts 24 and 25).

[75] Directions made under the GPDO 1995, art 4(1).

[76] GPDO 1995, art 1(5). Art 1(6) imposes further restrictions on land in National Parks and certain specific areas in England and Wales.

[77] GPDO 1995, art 3(1).

is material to the application, and to any other material consideration.[78] The essential statutory test is 'if, where in making any determination under the planning Acts, regard is to be had to the development plan, the determination shall be in accordance with the plan unless material considerations indicate otherwise'.[79] This has introduced a presumption in favour of permitting development proposals which are in accordance with the development plan. The authority must give its reasons for refusing or granting permission.[80]

Decision-makers must take account of all the policies in the plan, including those which indicate that the decision could be decided both ways, and decide the application in the light of the plan as a whole.[81] But this new status of the development plan has not altered the role of the courts, as the House of Lords has clearly stated:[82]   **14.33**

> Section [38(6)] has not innovated upon the principle that the court is concerned only with the legality of the decision-making process. As Lord Hoffmann observed in *Tesco Stores v Secretary of State for the Environment*;[83] 'If there is one principle of planning law more firmly settled than any other, it is that matters of planning judgment are within the exclusive province of the local planning authority or the Secretary of State[. . .].

All landowners and developers have had to become more aware of the need to take a long-term view and to influence the contents of the development plan rather than relying on the appeal process. It is no longer wise to wait and see what proposals might arise, when there are only a few chances to influence the plan. The development plan review process has also become a forum for third-party objectors and campaigners to influence the direction of policy and to oppose the development of specific proposals and sites.   **14.34**

---

[78] TCPA 1990, s 70.

[79] Planning and Compulsory Purchase Act 2004, s 38(6) (which replaced the similar test in the TCPA 1990, s 54A). The 'development plan' comprises adopted plans only, and development plans which are still in the course of preparation are only material considerations.

[80] General Development Procedure Order 1995, art 22 (as amended). The Decision Notice must contain a summary of the reasons for the grant of planning permission and a summary of the policies and proposals in the development plan which are relevant to that decision.

[81] *R (oao Cummins) v Camden LBC* [2001] EWHC Admin 1116. A breach of one policy does not necessarily show that the development is not in accordance with the development plan.

[82] *City of Edinburgh v Secretary of State for Scotland* [1997] 1 WLR 1447 at 1459 (per Lord Clyde). The House of Lords confirmed that the decision-maker's assessment of the considerations can only be challenged on the ground that it is irrational or perverse (at 1459d–g). Although the case concerned Scottish law, and the court referred to the Scottish statutory test, the English courts have applied the *City of Edinburgh* case in their cases as the same principles apply (see *R v Leominster District Council, ex p Pothecary* [1998] JPL 335, CA).

[83] [1995] 1 WLR 759 at 780.

Outline applications

14.35 It is possible to apply for planning permission for a building without providing the full details of what is proposed. Such an outline permission allows a developer to quickly establish whether the principle of the development is acceptable or not. The LPA can then grant outline planning permission, and leave various matters to be determined at a later stage. Specific legislative provision is made for outline applications which reserve the details of the siting, design, external appearance, means of access, and the landscaping of the site for later approval,[84] although this is becoming less easy to do in the face of requirements for Design and Access Statements.[85]

14.36 Certain matters can also be covered by a specific condition which allows the developer to submit details for later approval, as often happens with the landscaping or the details of the materials to be used. It may not always be possible to make such a decision on the principle without knowing a considerable amount about the details. This is often the case with potentially polluting activities, as their effect on the local environment is often the fundamental point upon which the rest of the application rests. Therefore, the LPA has the specific power to require that the outline application and one or more of the reserved matters must be considered together if they form the opinion that this is appropriate in the circumstances of any particular case.[86]

14.37 As a matter of policy, it is not usually appropriate to apply for outline permission for a development where the risk of pollution is significant.[87] At the least, full information on the environmental impact should be provided to the planning authority even though the rest of the application may be in outline. The planning authority can then impose conditions to ensure that the development takes place in a form which would not lead to significantly different environmental effects.[88]

Material considerations

14.38 The LPA has the unenviable task of taking into account all the considerations which might be material to the determination of an application. As well as the

---

[84] An application can reserve one of more of these matters for later approval (s 92 and GDPO 1995, art 3). The application for approval of the reserved matters should then be made within 3 years of the grant of the permission.

[85] Design and Access Statements.

[86] GDPO 1995, art 3—the Local Planning Authority must notify the applicant of this within one month, and request the further details they require.

[87] Therefore, in waste management applications and situations where a pollution control authorization will be necessary, a full planning application should normally be made.

[88] These conditions could include requirements to submit further environmental information, and to take any steps which then become necessary as a result. Para 77 of Circular 11/95 on Conditions also states that the conditions may incorporate the mitigation measures identified in an Environmental Statement. See Chapter 15 further.

issues highlighted in national planning policy, all the fundamental land use factors are included, such as the number, size, layout, siting, landscaping, design and external appearance of buildings, and the means of access, together with the impact on the wider landscape, the neighbourhood, and local infrastructure. What might be seen as purely private interests, such as a loss of privacy, can be relevant if they coincide with the public interest. The basic question is not whether owners of neighbouring properties would experience financial loss, but whether the proposal would unacceptably affect amenities and any existing uses of land which ought to be protected in the public interest. The question whether or not any matter is a material consideration is for the courts.[89] They have adopted the approach that no list of 'material considerations' in a planning decision can be exhaustive or comprehensive:

> In principle it seems to me that any consideration which relates to the use and development of land is capable of being a planning consideration. Whether a particular consideration falling within that broad class is material in any given case will depend on the circumstances.[90]

The difficulty then lies in what weight any particular consideration should be given in the determination, and what balance should be struck between the competing interests. The courts have tended to accept that this matter of judgement should be left to the decision-maker. **14.39**

However, the Government has highlighted a number of considerations in PPS 23 which it considers are material to potentially polluting developments—location, the impact on amenity, the assessment of the risk and impact of potential pollution on the use of other land,[91] the prevention of nuisance, the impact on roads,[92] the need for the development, any environmental or other benefits, and the feasibility of restoring the land to adequate standards. It is accepted that the planning system must focus on any potential for pollution, but only to the extent that it may affect the current and future uses of land.[93] The overlap between planning concerns and pollution control concerns has been discussed above. The weight which is likely to be attached to any particular consideration will be reduced to the extent to which it is capable of being addressed by the pollution control regimes. **14.40**

---

[89] *Bolton MBC v Secretary of State for the Environment* [1991] JPL 241. A material consideration is the same as a relevant consideration in administrative law (*Tesco Stores Limited v Secretary of State for the Environment* ([1995] 70 P&CR 184).

[90] Per Cooke J, *Stringer v Minister of Housing and Local Government* [1971] 1 All ER 65 at 77.

[91] For instance, an incinerator was refused in part because it would deter other development and investment in the vicinity, [1993] JPL 1072.

[92] The science of assessing the indirect consequences of pollution, such as from increases in road traffic, is uncertain and this is specifically not covered by PPGS23.

[93] See text box after para 1.9, paras 1.33, 3.2, and 3.3 of PPG 23.

Conditions

14.41 Section 70 of the TCPA 1990 allows the LPA to grant planning permission 'either unconditionally or subject to such conditions as they think fit'.[94] Conditions can also be imposed on land which is outside the area of the application, but which is under the control of the applicant.[95] The planning authority should consider whether suitable conditions might overcome any legitimate planning objections, and therefore allow the development to go forward.

14.42 As a matter of law, every condition must be imposed for planning purposes, be fairly and reasonably related to the development permitted, and be reasonable.[96] The DoE Circular 11/95 on Conditions goes further and advises that conditions should only be imposed where they are necessary, relevant to planning, relevant to the development to be permitted, enforceable, precise, and reasonable in all other respects.[97] It is in this respect that conditions which seek to duplicate pollution controls,[98] such as the level of emissions from developments, are likely to be quashed on appeal even though they would be lawful.

14.43 It would probably be ultra vires for planning authorities to decide to impose conditions because they lacked confidence in the effectiveness or enforcement of pollution controls, nor is it possible to justify imposing a condition just because the pollution controls are subject to review and change, as this is an inherent part of those regimes. Where the planning interests can be distinguished from the pollution control issues, conditions can be justified.

14.44 It has been standard practice for many years for planning conditions to control the levels of noise which a site can produce.[99] PPS 23 itself accepts that a condition may be needed to protect amenity or limit the hours of operation of a plant, to require the use of certain modes of transport, even to provide information which is necessary to monitor a planning matter. PPS 23 also accepts that planning conditions could be imposed to require the provision of recycling facilities at certain developments. Planning conditions are also appropriate to deal with decontamination, and the proper restoration of a site. This extends to landfill sites,

---

[94] As a matter of practice, unconditional planning permissions are a thing of the past, but the power remains to grant one. In addition, there is a standard statutory condition which will be attached to all permissions limiting the time to implement them to five years from the date they are granted, TCPA 1990, s 91.

[95] TCPA 1990, s 72(1)(a).

[96] *Newbury District Council v Secretary of State for the Environment* [1981] AC 578, HL. The planning purpose is that the condition must be connected with the use or development of land.

[97] See Circular 11/95, listed at para 14. This has been a long established part of the guidance—see the previous Circulars 22/80, at para 13, and 1/85 at para 19.

[98] PPS 23 sets out government policy on what it considers to be 'appropriate'(see also paras 22 and 23 of Circular 11/95).

[99] See the advice in PPG 24.

even though the Agency can control the circumstances under which the waste management licence is to be surrendered.

Sometimes, a development will not be acceptable unless works are carried out on **14.45** land outside the applicant's control. The courts have approved the use of a particular type of negative condition, known as the 'Grampian condition',[100] to allow permission still to be granted. The LPA can prevent the development being started or brought into use unless and until the required works are completed. This has particularly been used with regard to off-site highway and drainage works, but the principle could also be extended to environmental improvements.

Since the developer may have to rely upon another person carrying out the works, **14.46** it may mean that the development will be very difficult to implement. As a matter of policy, such a condition should not be imposed if there is no reasonable prospect of it being complied with.[101] This may mean that planning permission must be refused.

Planning obligations

Planning obligations are usually made in order to facilitate the granting of a **14.47** permission. They can be used to ensure the provision of alternative amenity land or land for a nature reserve, or to provide funds for renewable energy or to help maintain or clean up other land—none of which could be covered by planning conditions. If the planning obligation has some connection with the development, which is not de minimis, then regard should be had to it as a material consideration. The weight attached to it is then a matter for the decision-maker.[102]

Planning obligations are agreements made under Section 106 of the TCPA 1990[103] **14.48** which allow persons interested in land to restrict the use or development of their land or to provide for the payment of monies to the LPA. The obligations may be made either by agreement with the LPA or by unilateral undertaking, and are normally made conditional on a planning permission being granted and implemented. A planning obligation is best understood as being similar to a covenant binding the land of the person entering into the obligation and is

---

[100] This is named after the Scottish case of *Grampian Regional Council v City of Aberdeen* [1983] 1 WLR 1340.

[101] See para 40 of the Annex to Circular 11/95. The courts, by contrast, have held such a condition not to be automatically unreasonable and, therefore, invalid (*British Railways Board v Secretary of State for the Environment and Hounslow LBC* [1993] 3 PLR 125, HL).

[102] *Tesco Stores Limited v Secretary of State for the Environment* [1995] 70 P&CR 184, HL.

[103] S 106 of the 1990 Act was substantially recast by the provisions of the Planning and Compensation Act 1991. Those made under s 52 of the Town and Country Planning Act 1971 remain valid.

enforceable by the LPA.[104] It is a tool in the process of applying for and gaining planning permission for land. It is also a method by which a developer can provide the LPA with an assurance or 'planning gain' which will overcome an objection to the development.

14.49 The obligation also has the potential danger of being used as a means of buying planning permission by providing planning benefits. The Secretary of State has stated that, in order to avoid this, as a matter of policy, he expects that planning obligations should only be sought where they are necessary to the granting of permission, relevant to planning, and relevant to the development to be permitted. Unacceptable development should never be permitted because of unrelated benefits offered by the applicant, nor should acceptable development be refused permission simply because the applicant is unable or unwilling to offer such unrelated benefits.[105] It is likely that the system of planning obligations will be reformed, with the introduction of a Community Infrastructure Levy to provide for a standard charge to be levied on all new development in addition to any site-specific obligations.[106]

The location and need for a development

14.50 Particular facilities may need to be located in sensitive areas. In the light of the proximity principle, new waste management and disposal facilities will need to be near the source of waste. Minerals can only be extracted from where they are found in the ground. The growth of an important industry may depend on expanding an existing facility, or constructing a new one. There may be good reasons of social or economic policy, and also of environmental policy, to allow the development, but it may still pose a considerable pollution risk for an area, even if the development will be of the latest design. No one is likely to be willing to accept it on their back doorstep. The planning system is used to having to strike this balance between competing interests.

---

[104] The obligations are enforceable using civil remedies by the LPA against the person entering into the obligation, and against any person deriving title to the land from that person. S 106 agreements can be modified or discharged by agreement with the LPA or by a formal application to do so (ss 106A, 106B).

[105] See para B7 of Circular 1/97. In circumstances where it is reasonable to impose a condition or to require the developer to enter into a planning obligation 'the imposition of a condition which satisfies the policy tests of DoE Circular 11/95 is preferable because it enables a developer to appeal to the Secretary of State' (para B20). Duplication should also be avoided.

[106] This will be introduced under the provisions of the Planning Bill 2008, and the regulations made pursuant to it. The 'CIL' is likely to be levied as a specific sum per dwelling or per square metre of development, and will follow the example of the 'tariff' schemes introduced by some local planning authorities (eg City of London, Milton Keynes). It is unlikely to cover householder development. This issue has been debated for a decade—note that Sections 46–48 in the Planning and Compulsory Purchase Act 2004 (which would have replaced Section 106 of the TCPA 1990) were never implemented.

It is not yet a part of the planning regime that the developer must show that his **14.51** development is 'needed'.[107] The basic position is that if there are no sound reasons for refusing planning permission, then it should be approved even though there are other sites upon which the development could be built to better effect. However, there are many cases where the chosen site has clear environmental disadvantages, and balanced against this is that there is a proven need for the development. It may also be the case that national or local policy require alternative sites to be considered.[108] In such circumstances, it will be a material consideration that the development could be built on more suitable sites.[109]

Risk assessment

In reaching their decisions, planning authorities are warned in PPS23 that they **14.52** should not seek to substitute their interpretation of the risk assessment for that of the relevant authority, and that they should not give weight to matters which are properly the subject of the pollution control regime and which do not have land use implications. Moreover, the perception of risk, for instance of a pollution incident, should not be material to the consideration of the planning application unless the land use consequences of the perception can be demonstrated.[110] This is easier said than done, particularly when there is substantial public opposition. This has been apparent in the constant level of public concern about the rapid expansion of the mobile phone network across the country. The masts and antennae are subject to permitted development rights,[111] and the local planning authority has very limited grounds upon which to object. The continuing

---

[107] The alternative argument made by commentators that this lack of need test is too permissive in the light of growing environmental concerns remains, although it has not yet found favour (eg Tim Jewell, 'Planning Regulation and Environmental Consciousness: Some Lessons from Minerals' [1995] JPL 482). It is only where there is a limited need that the LPA may be under an obligation to carry out a comparative assessment of the planning merits of the identified rival sites, see *R (oao Chelmsford Car & Commercial Ltd) v Chelmsford Borough Council* [2005] EWHC 1705 (Admin) (social housing sites).

[108] Eg PPG 8 on Telecommunications—*Phillips v First Secretary of State* [2004] JPL 613; but the court also confirmed the general proposition that the fact that there are alternatives will in general be immaterial or of negligible weight, citing *R (Mount Cook Land Ltd) v Westminster City Council* [2003] EWCA Civ 1346.

[109] See *GLC v Secretary of State for the Environment and LDDC and another* [1986] 52 P &CR 158 CA; *Trusthouse Forte Hotels v Secretary of State for the Environment* [1986] 279 EG 680. So, the LPA was held to be under an obligation to carry out a comparative assessment of the planning merits of the two identified rival sites in *R (oao Chelmsford Car & Commercial Ltd) v Chelmsford Borough Council* [2005] EWHC 1705 (Admin) (limited need for social housing development).

[110] See PPS 23 passim.

[111] GPDO 1995, Part 24; the mast or antenna will have deemed planning permission if the LPA does not object within 56 days, and it is also remarkable how often the planning officers have missed the 56-day time limit in which to make any objection. This has even led the Local Government Ombudsman to issue a special report on the apparent maladministration— 'Telecommunications masts' (19 June 2007). See also Kemp, 'Perceived risk as a material consideration: the case of telecom developments' [2003] JPL 13.

problem has been the perceived adverse effects on people's health from the emissions. The government has issued clear policy guidance on this, supported by what it considers to be the best available scientific evidence, to ensure that the international guidelines for public exposure in respect of emissions from mobile phone masts are met. The result has been that, provided the operators can show that they have met these standards and have followed the correct application procedures and limitations, any decision to refuse permission based on public perceptions or fears of a mast's effects stands almost no chance of success.[112]

14.53 For major developments, the LPA is likely to have the relevant information made available to it through the Environmental Impact Assessment process. Concerns may arise about noise, land contamination, the discharge of effluent or leachates, possible toxic releases, and the generation of waste, and higher standards are expected in sensitive locations. The pollution control authority will also be able to advise on the extent to which it can address such considerations under its own statutory powers. This can cause a certain amount of frustration at the planning stage, as the detailed information which the pollution control authority will need to have about the design of the particular processes or abatement techniques may not be available.

14.54 A considerable amount of time may need to be spent speculating on the likely standards which the Agency might impose in the light of the need to use best available techniques or even the balance which it will strike in order to achieve the best practicable environmental option. The Agency will need to make representations on its likely view, and give evidence at the appeal stage. The planning authority must still be able to make an assessment of the likely risk of pollution from a site. In *Envirocor Waste Holdings v Secretary of State for the Environment*,[113] an inspector's appeal decision was quashed because he had not made it clear how he judged that there would be malodorous emissions from a waste transfer site which would affect the locality.

Public opposition as a material consideration

14.55 All decisions to grant planning permission are made by politicians, or at least in their name. It may become politically unacceptable for them to permit a controversial proposal, however good the objective reasons for doing so. Given the unreliability of scientific opinion, and growing public wariness, many potentially polluting developments will be controversial. The courts have had to review recent decisions where planning permission has been refused because of general fears

---

[112] See *T-Mobile (UK) Ltd, Hutchinson 3G UK and Orange v First Secretary of State and Harrogate BC* [2004] EWCA Civ 1763; [2005] Env LR 18—planning inspector's refusal to grant planning permission was quashed, to the relief of the mobile phone operators, and to the growing frustration of those who question the science.

[113] [1996] Env LR D42; see case report and comments by Tromans, [1996] JEL 354.

over the effect of the proposed development. An application for the extension of a bail hostel was refused on appeal by an inspector because there was evidence that it would exacerbate the severe problems caused to nearby residents by the existing users of the hostel. The court upheld the appeal decision, stating that justified public concerns about what it termed the 'emanations from the land', including the activities of those using the land, may be a relevant planning consideration.[114]

The Court of Appeal has quashed the Secretary of State's decision to award the **14.56** appellant's inquiry costs against a local authority because he held that the public's perceived fears were not a material planning consideration. The local authority had opposed the development of a chemical waste treatment plant because of the perceived public safety risk and the substantial public opposition to the plant.[115] The Secretary of State should have asked himself the question as to whether or not the authority's opposition was unreasonable. If their concerns had been supported by some valid evidence, with which he disagreed, an award of costs might not have been appropriate.

It was stated in the Court of Appeal that perceived fears of the public are a **14.57** planning factor which can amount (perhaps rarely) to a good reason for refusal,[116] but this probably goes too far. The emphasis on requiring justification for the fears which are expressed has long been thought to be the main control on the temptation for local authorities to refuse any controversial developments. Indeed, in *Gateshead MBC*,[117] whilst the LPA and the Inspector attached weight to the public's concerns about the uncertain effect of the air emissions, the Secretary of State gave very little weight to them in the light of the stringent, objective controls available under the EPA 1990. In this respect, the presence of the appeals system, and the potential costs sanctions for causing unnecessary appeals, are intended to prevent unnecessary refusals of permission. It does not always do so.

Planning appeals

A planning appeal can be made against the LPA's refusal of planning permission, **14.58** and against the conditions imposed on a permission.[118] Like appeals under the

---

[114] *West Midlands Probation Committee v Secretary of State for the Environment* [1998] JPL 388, CA. See also the section on Public Pressure in the Judicial Review Chapter at paras 22.48 ff.

[115] *Newport County BC v Secretary of State for Wales* [1998] JPL 377, CA (the planning permission was granted on the appeal). One of the local authority's reasons for refusal had been that 'the proposed development is perceived by the local community to be contrary to the public interest generally and to their interests in particular'.

[116] [1998] 1 PLR 47 at 55, per Aldous J. But see the criticism by the editors of the *Planning Encyclopaedia* (see Vol 2, P70.22/1/1).

[117] [1995] JPL 432, CA, discussed above.

[118] TCPA 1990, s 78. An applicant can also appeal on the ground that the LPA has failed to determine his application. An analogy can be drawn with the appeal procedures for environmental cases—see Chapter 21 further.

Environmental Acts, the appeal will be to the Secretary of State, and not to a court. In practice, most appeals are determined by an inspector, appointed by the Secretary of State, and acting under transferred powers. Although appeals have a quasi-judicial status and formality, it is a re-hearing and the inspector or the Secretary of State can decide all the issues on the appeal as if it was a fresh consideration of the application. He or she may also use their own professional expertise and knowledge in reaching their decision. The only person who has a right to appeal is the original applicant, who must do so within six months from the date of his or her receipt of the LPA's decision. It is also possible for those persons having an interest in the land to appeal against the service of an Enforcement Notice, which must be done before the date the notice comes into force.[119] Most appeals are determined by way of written representations, and even in the bigger cases there is an increasing tendency for the use of an informal hearing rather than the formality and expense of a public inquiry. The Secretary of State has the power to award costs against any party to the appeal. As a matter of policy, costs do not follow the event and will normally only be awarded where an appellant or an LPA has acted unreasonably and caused others to incur unnecessary costs.[120]

Court challenges

14.59   Unlike the Environmental Acts, the TCPA 1990 limits the right to challenge planning appeal decisions to the statutory rights of appeal available under Sections 288 and 289.[121] The decision can only be challenged on points of law. There are two grounds of challenge, that the decision was not within the powers of the Act, or that any legislative requirement has not been complied with. These narrow grounds have been held by the courts to include similar grounds to those which can be raised on a judicial review.

14.60   While the standards expected of appeal decisions are high, they are not required to deal with every single point raised in the inquiry. Proper and adequate reasons must be given, which deal with the substantial points that have been raised.[122]

---

[119] S 174; the notice will come into force after 28 days at the least from the date of its service.

[120] The power is given under the Local Government Act 1972, s 250(5) (and the TCPA 1990, s 320). The government views the award of costs as a disciplinary control to stop the appeal process being abused—see Circular 8/93 generally; costs are rarely awarded to third parties (see para 15, Annex 3). For instance, costs were awarded against a developer for persisting in an appeal when it had failed to provide adequate information on landfill gas, [1992] JPL 992.

[121] Otherwise, the validity of the decision cannot be questioned in any legal proceedings whatsoever (The TCPA 1990, ss 284, 285). This does not apply to Breach of Condition Notices.

[122] The standard of reasons must be adequate, and deal with the principal controversial issues which have been raised, see *Bolton MBC v Secretary of State for the Environment* [1995] JPL 1043, HL. The decision letter should not be read as if each sentence was part of either a statute or a conveyancing document, but read as a whole—see the points made by a former Chief Planning Inspector, Stephen Crow, in his article, 'Challenging Appeal Decisions, or the use and abuse of the "toothcomb"' [1998] JPL 419.

Under Section 288, any person aggrieved by a planning appeal decision has only six weeks within which to challenge the decision. Under Section 289, the appeal decision on an enforcement notice must be challenged within 28 days. The challenge can only be made by the appellant, or anyone with an interest in the land, or the local authority, and the leave of the court must first be obtained. If the High Court does quash the appeal decision, the matter is remitted to the Secretary of State to be re-decided. The Court has no power to substitute its own decision.

The role of third parties in the planning process

In planning cases, the first opportunity for local people and interest groups to make representations will be at the application stage. The rights of neighbours to be notified of applications have been strengthened in order to encourage this. All representations which are properly received must be taken into account by the LPA in its decision.[123] As a matter of practice, and good politics, late representations will almost always be considered. Representations can also be made on any appeal. However, the opportunity to make representations at a public inquiry will only arise if permission is refused, or the Secretary of State insists on making the decision himself, on a so-called 'call in' inquiry, or where the application is refused and the applicant appeals. Third parties do not have a right of appeal under the statutory procedures. **14.61**

An application for judicial review will be the only available remedy to them if planning permission is granted. Judicial review is also the only way for a third party to challenge the Secretary of State's decision on the appeal, following the public inquiry. This is not an opportunity for the courts to re-hear the merits of the case, so it is only legal points (such as mistake of law or the lack of an environmental assessment[124]) which will be worth pursuing at this stage. **14.62**

Planning enforcement powers

There is no legal fetter on taking enforcement action against operations which are covered by other regimes but which are in breach of planning control. Planning enforcement powers can therefore be used to complement the pollution control powers. Only the LPA has the right to take enforcement action. There is no private right to take enforcement proceedings under the TCPA 1990. **14.63**

The LPA has a similar system of notices to the pollution control authorities which it can use to control breaches. But there are slightly different names for notices **14.64**

---

[123] See the TCPA 1990, s 71 and the GDPO 1995, arts 8 and 19. The public should make their representations within 21 days of the erection of the site notice, or 14 days from the date the application is advertised.

[124] eg *Berkeley v Secretary of State for the Environment* [2001] 2 AC 603—despite also arguing the point at the public inquiry, the case was also pursued through the courts (and as far as the House of Lords).

which achieve a similar purpose. Planning Contravention Notices can be used to request information about the ownership and the current uses of land.[125] The Enforcement Notice can be used against any 'breach of planning control'. A Stop Notice allows the LPA to ban an activity almost immediately, and it may be served with or after an enforcement notice dealing with that activity.[126] A Breach of Condition Notice can be used to take enforcement action on conditions, and there are no rights of appeal.[127] The LPA also has a wide-ranging power to seek injunctions for any breach or any anticipated breach of planning control.[128] A breach of planning control is not in itself a criminal offence.[129] The criminal offence is to fail to comply with these notices, and is punishable only with a fine. Failure to comply with an injunction is a contempt of court.

14.65 The Enforcement Notice is the primary method by which the LPA will seek to enforce planning control. It may issue and serve an Enforcement Notice where it appears to it that there has been a breach of planning control and that it is 'expedient' to issue the notice having regard to the provisions of the development plan and to any other material considerations.[130] In making this decision, the availability of other enforcement powers under other regimes—such as the EPA 1990—will be relevant. The Enforcement Notice must specify the steps which the LPA requires to be taken to remedy the breach of planning control, the time period for compliance, and must set out the reasons for issuing the notice. Once the period for compliance has ended, and no appeal has been made, the Notice

---

[125] Either as a straightforward notice under the TCPA, s 330 or as a Planning Contravention Notice under s 171C.

[126] TCPA 1990, s 183. It cannot be appealed. Failure to comply with a stop notice is a criminal offence. Compensation may be payable if the stop notice or its enforcement notice is withdrawn, varied, or quashed and the activity prohibited was not in breach of planning control (s 186). A Temporary Stop Notice is now also available—Part 4 of the Planning and Compulsory Purchase Act 2004 inserted ss 171E to 171H into the TCPA 1990.

[127] TCPA 1990, s 187A. The conditions and the breach must be sufficiently precisely described in order to survive scrutiny in the magistrates' court. A breach of condition notice specifies steps to comply with a condition, giving a set period for compliance. It cannot be appealed, and a failure to comply with the conditions or do the specified steps is a summary offence, punishable with a fine. Whilst enforcement notices can be issued against breaches of conditions or limitations, this is a faster enforcement method.

[128] TCPA 1990, s 187B.

[129] However, it is a criminal offence to breach listed building or scheduled monument controls, without the need to serve notices.

[130] TCPA 1990, s 172. This applies to enforcement notices, but the same general principles apply to all enforcement action in planning. Parliament specifically rejected, in passing the Planning and Compensation Act 1991, an attempt to impose a general duty on LPAs to take enforcement action. The Secretary of State has the power if he feels it is expedient to issue an enforcement notice in respect of any land, but he may not do so without consulting the LPA. Guidance on planning enforcement is provided in PPG 18.

will have permanent effect.[131] Enforcement can, however, be a long, drawn-out process. An appeal against the enforcement notice will suspend its effect pending the outcome of the appeal.[132] Almost invariably, a decision on appeal against an enforcement notice is issued only several months after service of the notice.

A 'breach of planning control' may either be the carrying out of development **14.66** without the required planning permission, or a failure to comply with any condition or limitation subject to which a planning permission has been granted. There is an absolute time limit in which enforcement action must be taken.[133] Enforcement action in respect of any operational development or the material change of use of any building as a single dwelling house can only be taken within four years. All other breaches of planning control can only be enforced against within ten years of the beginning of the breach. Once a development is immune from enforcement, it is also possible to obtain a certificate of lawful use of development (known as a CLEUD)[134], which indeed is the way that many old waste sites have proceeded.

Special considerations and regimes

Listed buildings and conservation areas

The most stringent planning controls are those which exist to conserve and **14.67** protect the historic and cultural environment, under the Town and Country Planning (Listed Buildings and Conservation Areas) Act 1990. These controls often apply to sites in historic areas, and may have a substantial effect in terms of cost and design on the redevelopment options which are available.

The effect of major development on environmentally sensitive locations, a term **14.68** which includes historic landscapes and buildings, is also one of the factors which must be assessed in the Environmental Impact Assessment process. It has not been

---

[131] The only way for the developer to alter the effect of an enforcement notice is to apply for planning permission. The notice will cease to have effect only so far as it is inconsistent with that permission. It can only be withdrawn or its requirements relaxed by the LPA. The TCPA 1990 therefore lays down stringent requirements about the contents of the Notices and their service on the owner of the land, as well as on any other person having an interest in the land.

[132] There is great incentive to appeal, as an appeal can include an application for planning permission for the unlawful development. Moreover, it is no defence to any subsequent prosecution to argue issues that should have been raised on appeal.

[133] TCPA 1990, s 171B.

[134] The provisions relating to 'CLEUDs' were introduced in the 1991 Act to replace Established Use Certificates. The certificate determines the lawfulness of existing uses, past operational development, and any failure to comply with conditions or limitations (s 191(1)). Uses and operations are lawful if no enforcement action may then be taken in respect of them and they do not constitute a contravention of any of the requirements of any enforcement notice then in force. An applicant can seek a prospective determination by asking for a certificate of lawfulness for a proposed use or development (known as a CLOPUD!), under s 192.

necessary to revise the system in the light of increasing environmental concerns. This separate system of controls is well established, and exercises continuous control.

14.69 There are presently over 500,000 listed buildings in England and about 18,000 in Wales, which are protected under the Town and Country Planning (Listed Buildings and Conservation Areas) Act 1990 ('the Listed Buildings Act').[135] It is no surprise to find a listed structure in the middle of an old gasworks, or adjoining an old industrial site. For instance, the redevelopment of the unused railway lands near the historic stations in north London needs to take account of the listed stations, engine sheds, and gas holders. Once a building is listed, any structure or erection, and any part of the building will be protected.[136] Listed building control is independent of any requirement to obtain planning permission for development. Frequently both listed building consent and planning permission will be required, although applications will be made to the same LPA. Listed building control covers many activities, such as internal works, which are not operational development if they affect the character of the listed building. Works affecting the listed building's character of special architectural or historic interest are banned unless authorized by listed building consent or excepted under the Listed Buildings Act. It is a criminal offence to carry out works to a listed building without the necessary consent, and the offence is one of strict liability.

14.70 The system of listed building enforcement notices operates on similar lines to enforcement notices for breach of planning control.[137] In addition to the need to obtain listed building consent, in deciding whether or not to grant planning permission to a development, regard must be had to the desirability of preserving a listed building and its setting.[138] There is a policy presumption against total or substantial demolition unless it is shown that all reasonable efforts have been made to sustain the present use or to find viable new uses for the building.[139] In practice, consent to demolition is rarely given.

---

[135] Guidance on listed buildings is still provided by PPG 15, 'Planning and the Historic Environment'(1994). As a matter of policy, listed buildings are classified as Grade I (2% of all buildings), Grade II* (4%), and the remainder as Grade II. Applications for listed building consent are made under the Listed Buildings Act 1990 to the LPA (s 10). The procedure is governed by the Town and Country Planning (Listed Buildings and Conservation Areas) Regulations 1990. Like planning applications, a right of appeal lies to the Secretary of State if the application is refused, is approved subject to conditions, or is not determined (s 20). A possible ground of appeal is that the building should not be listed (s 21(3)).

[136] Note also that any object or structure within the curtilage of the building which, although not fixed to the building, forms part of the land and has done so since before 1 July 1948 will be protected (Listed Buildings Act, s 1(5)).

[137] Unlisted buildings may receive temporary protection from demolition or alteration by service of a building preservation notice (Listed Buildings Act, s 3(1), (2)).

[138] Ibid, s 66(1), Listed Buildings Act.

[139] PPG 15, para 3.17. There is some scope for arguing that the benefits to the community from the redevelopment would outweigh the loss resulting from demolition.

Conservation areas

Conservation areas are 'areas of special architectural or historic interest the **14.71** character or appearance of which it is desirable to preserve or enhance'.[140] There is no formal designation procedure and it is not part of the development plan process. When making decisions under the Planning Acts, in respect of buildings or land in a conservation area, special attention shall be paid to the desirability of preserving or enhancing the character or appearance of that area.[141]

Buildings in conservation areas which are not listed may only be demolished if **14.72** conservation area consent is obtained.[142] Permitted development rights are also restricted in conservation areas, and all trees will also be protected.

Archaeology and historical monuments

Further controls over the historic environment are provided under the Ancient **14.73** Monuments and Archaeological Areas Act 1979. Under this Act, the Secretary of State has compiled a Schedule of Ancient Monuments of national importance, which are listed (or 'scheduled') because of their 'historic, architectural, traditional, or archaeological interest'. A monument can be a building, structure, work, or its site or remains, above or below the surface. Scheduled monument consent from the Secretary of State is needed to carry out works to them, even of repair.[143] The desirability of maintaining an ancient monument and its setting is a material consideration in planning decisions, whether or not it is scheduled. The proper exploration and recording of archaeological remains has also gained increasing importance in recent years.[144]

There are some other designations which do not carry with them any additional **14.74** legal protection. If a site is listed as a World Heritage Site, or is included in English Heritage's Register of Parks and Gardens of Special Historical Interest, or the Register of Battlefields, it will not benefit from any additional controls. The status

---

[140] Listed Buildings Act. They are designated by the LPA, although the Secretary of State (and in London, English Heritage) has concurrent designation powers. Conservation area policy is contained in PPG 15, s 4. There were estimated to be about 8,000 conservation areas in England in 1994 (para 4.2, PPG 15).

[141] S 72(1).

[142] Listed Buildings Act, s 74(1). This procedure is enforced by the listed buildings provisions of the Listed Buildings Act as amended by the Town and Country Planning (Listed Buildings and Conservation Areas) Regulations 1990.

[143] The application procedure is similar to a called in application for planning permission, and the Secretary of State must hold a public inquiry or allow interested parties to be heard (see Sch 1 of the 1979 Act and the Ancient Monuments (Applications for Scheduled Monument Consent) Regulations 1981, SI 1981/1301). It is a lengthy process.

[144] Archaeology is still covered in detail in PPG 16, 'Archaeology and Planning'(1990). It is most often dealt with by way of conditions. In areas designated as Areas of Archaeological Importance, it is an offence to carry out certain specified operations without consent. It is possible to get consent to do the works (see the Ancient Monuments and Archaeological Areas Act 1979, s 33).

will be an important material consideration in any decision, but its importance may be outweighed in the planning balance by other considerations—such as the necessity of quarrying materials wherever they are found.[145]

Nature conservation constraints

14.75 It has become increasingly clear that nature conservation designations can place considerable new constraints on development. What was once a mudflat available for the expansion of Sheerness Docks suddenly is a protected site for migratory birds.[146] Government advice is set out in PPS 9 on 'Biodiversity and Geological Conservation'. There are controls on development on or near to Sites of Special Scientific Interest, or near badger setts, and the UK has been obliged under the Habitats Directive (92/43/EC) to select, register, and notify important sites for flora and fauna.

14.76 Where a development is likely to have a significant effect on such a site—even indirectly—the LPA must consider the possible effects on the site and restrict the grant of planning permission where the site would be adversely affected. It must even consider revoking old permissions on this basis. But the LPA should not refuse permission if conditions can be imposed which would prevent damaging impacts on wildlife habitats or important physical features.[147] The matter is discussed further in Chapter 12 on Nature Conservation.

Trees and hedgerows

14.77 Normally, the felling and cutting down of trees does not involve 'development' and so does not require planning permission. Only extensive works would amount to an engineering or other operation. However, the LPA is under a general duty to consider the amenity value of trees in the exercise of its planning functions, and conditions can be imposed to protect them as part of the planning permission.[148]

14.78 Specific trees can also be protected from lopping, felling, topping, uprooting, or wilful damage by tree preservation orders,[149] and trees growing in conservation areas are similarly protected.[150] For a long time, the protection of important

---

[145] eg *R v North Somerset Council, ex p Garnett* [1998] EGCS 48—quarry extended in nature conservation area and historic park.

[146] See *R v Secretary of State for the Environment, ex p RSPB*, The Times, 10 February 1995, HL and the subsequent ECJ case. See para 4.35 further.

[147] See government policy at paras 118–119 of Circular 11/95. Areas can be fenced off, and operations can be restricted to certain times of the year. See PPG 9 further.

[148] TCPA 1990, s 197.

[149] Ibid, s 198, where it is 'expedient in the interests of amenity'; enforcement provisions are provided in the Act, including prosecutions and injunctions.

[150] TCPA 1990, ss 211 and 212.

hedgerows was uncertain, but new regulations under Section 97 of the Environment Act 1995 introduced a separate requirement to obtain the local authority's approval before removal. As with many such single-issue measures, there is considerable controversy as to whether the regulations go far enough, and whether they are too cumbersome to be of much practical use.

D. The Environment and Development Plans

A detailed discussion of the development plan system must be left to the specialist **14.79** planning texts.[151] The development plan system is in a considerable state of flux. In England, the Planning and Compensation Act 2004 has introduced a system of Regional Spatial Strategies,[152] and local planning authorities are now in the course of preparing new development plans in the form of Local Development Documents.[153] In Wales, the requirement is for each LPA to produce a local development plan.[154] Given the long transition, the bedrock remains the 'saved policies' from the earlier adopted development plans. But the process of adoption will continue to change the policy framework, as any conflict between policies must be resolved in favour of the policy which is contained in the last document to be adopted.[155]

The 'development plan' for any area in England therefore now comprises a **14.80** number of different documents.[156] In Greater London, the development plan is the Mayor's spatial development strategy, and all the development plan documents (taken as a whole) which have been adopted or approved in relation to that area. For any area in the rest of England, the development plan is the regional spatial strategy for that region, and all the development plan documents (taken as

---

[151] For instance, the detailed procedures are set out in the *Encyclopaedia of Forms and Precedents*, Vols 41(3) and 41(4), Town and Country Planning (Butterworths, 5th edition, 2007 Reissue, by Upton and Charles).

[152] Part I of the 2004 Act.

[153] Part II of the 2004 Act, and the regulations made under it. The government has used the informal term 'the Local Development Framework' ('LDF'), to refer to all the local development documents ('LDDs') collectively. These are intended to be adopted in accordance with the approved Local Development Scheme ('LDS'). National policy is set out in PPS 12 'Local Development Frameworks' (revised and republished in 2008).

[154] See the Planning and Compulsory Purchase Act 2004 Part 6. The definition does not therefore include the Wales Spatial Plan. General guidance has been provided by *Local Development Plans Wales* (Welsh Assembly Government, 2005).

[155] See the Planning and Compulsory Purchase Act 2004, s 38(5). This rule also applies to the policies in any development plan 'saved' by the Planning and Compulsory Purchase Act 2004 during the transitional period (s 38(8)).

[156] See the Planning and Compulsory Purchase Act 2004 s 38. The definition of the 'development plan' in that Act as opposed to the Town and Country Planning Act 1990 takes account of the changes to the planning system made by the 2004 Act.

a whole) which have been adopted or approved in relation to that area. For an area in Wales, the development plan should ultimately be the local development plan adopted or approved in relation to that area.

14.81 The basic purpose of local development documents is that they 'must (taken as a whole) set out the authority's policies (however expressed) relating to the development and use of land in their area'.[157] The LPA must have regard in preparing the local development documents to national policies, the regional spatial strategy, and their own community strategy, amongst a list of prescribed considerations.[158] This is similar to the list that applied to the old development plans prepared under the TCPA 1990. The local development documents must also be in 'general conformity' with the regional spatial strategy or, in London, with the spatial development strategy.[159]

14.82 It is intended that the new development plans are 'spatial plans', and the LPA must carry out a sustainability appraisal of the proposals in each local development document.[160] The Sustainability Appraisal incorporates the environmental report required by European Directive 2001/42/EC, on the assessment of the effects of certain plans and programmes on the environment, known as the Strategic Environmental Assessment Directive ('the SEA Directive').[161] It is also now the LPA's duty to produce their development plans with the objective of contributing to the achievement of sustainable development.[162] The Habitats Regulations also require all planning authorities to draw up development plans to take account of policies encouraging the management of landscape features which are of major

---

[157] Planning and Compulsory Purchase Act 2004, s 17(3)—this accords with the old caselaw that it is the duty of planning authorities to formulate in their local plans all their development and land use proposals, and not to omit any of them: see *Great Portland Estates v Westminster City Council* [1985] AC 661, HL.

[158] Planning and Compulsory Purchase Act 2004, s 19(2) and the Town and Country Planning (Local Development) (England) Regulations 2004, SI 2004/2204 reg 15. The old list was at s 12(6) of the TCPA 1990 and in SI 1999/3280 reg 20(2) (both of which have been repealed).

[159] Planning and Compulsory Purchase Act 2004, s 24.

[160] S 19(5) for England and s 62(6) for Wales, Planning and Compulsory Purchase Act 2004. The appraisal must be published and must also be submitted when the local development document is submitted to the Secretary of State. The report should identify the process by which the sustainability appraisal has been carried out, the baseline information used to inform the process and the outcomes of that process.

[161] This Directive was implemented by the Environmental Assessment of Plans and Programmes Regulations 2004, SI 2004/1633, and the Environmental Assessment of Plans and Programmes (Wales) Regulations 2004 (SI 2004/1656). It applies to all development plans whose formal preparation began after July 2004, and those which were not adopted by 21 July 2006. The European Union's proposals to require strategic environmental assessment have had a long history—it was in the Commission's legislative programme since 1994, but only ever reached the stage of a discussion document (COM (96) 511).

[162] Planning and Compulsory Purchase Act 2004, s 39. The LPA must have also have regard to national policies and advice contained in any guidance issued by the Secretary of State or the National Assembly for Wales (s 39(3)).

importance for wild flora and fauna, such as river banks, hedgerows, ponds, and small woods. [163]

Minerals, because of their potential effects on the environment, are given special **14.83** treatment. They are the subject of minerals local plans, prepared by minerals planning authorities (usually county councils or National Park Authorities) under Section 37 of the TCPA 1990. In a National Park the planning authority may choose whether to deal with minerals in its local plan or to prepare a specialized minerals plan. Waste, too, may be the subject of a special local plan. Where there are still county councils, they will prepare a Waste Local Plan.[164] Alternatively, the Secretary of State may direct that waste policies are to be contained in a local plan or a minerals local plan. It will also be necessary to take account of European waste law in preparing the waste local plan, as discussed below.

E. Planning Considerations for Specific Types of Development

Industrial pollution and development control

Development proposals for installations which also fall within Environmental **14.84** Permitting will require the LPA to consider their potential environmental impact. The leading case remains that of *Gateshead MBC v Secretary of State for the Environment*,[165] which was a challenge to the grant of planning permission to a clinical waste incinerator (which was then covered by Part 1 of the EPA 1990). Lord Justice Glidewell agreed that this meant that:

> . . . the extent to which discharges from a proposed plant would necessarily or probably pollute the atmosphere and/or create an unacceptable risk of harm to human beings, animals or other organisms, was a material consideration to be taken into account when deciding to grant planning permission.

As discussed in the second section of this chapter, this does not mean that the **14.85** planning authority should substitute its own judgement for that of the other regulating authority. The point at which concerns about pollution can be left to be considered by the pollution control authorities is a matter of planning judgment. Even if it is decided to grant planning permission, this should not prevent the enforcing authority from exercising its own discretion to refuse an environmental permit where necessary. The case does provide a useful illustration of just how much information the planning authorities will require in order to

---

[163] Conservation (Natural Habitats etc) Regulations 1994 (SI 1994/2716) reg 37. The Directives are 92/43 (Habitats) and 79/409 (Wild Birds). See Chapter 12.
[164] TCPA 1990, s 38.
[165] [1995] JPL 432, CA.

make their decision. The timescale involved in gaining the permission also illustrates the desirability of avoiding the need of an appeal, and any legal challenge. Northumbria Water Group's first application was made in 1989, and the Secretary of State issued his decision letter in May 1993 (following a detailed public inquiry). The High Court and the Court of Appeal rejected the Council's arguments that the Secretary of State could not lawfully abdicate his planning responsibilities to the EPA regime and that there was no evidence on which he could be satisfied that the controls under the EPA would be adequate. The Court of Appeal delivered its judgment in May 1994, bringing to an end five years of uncertainty.

14.86 It is only where waste management matters are concerned, such as in the case of incinerators, that the planning authority is under a duty to consider the objectives of the relevant pollution control regime more specifically. This also means that the planning authority is entitled to exercise a greater control and to conduct a greater degree of investigation than would be permitted or expected in other, non-waste cases.

Waste management and development control

14.87 The development of waste management facilities has always been the subject of controversy. This is the only area where the legislation has made a specific link between the need to have planning permission and the grant of an environmental licence. Under Part II of the EPA 1990, and now the Environmental Permitting Regulations 2007, if planning permission is required for a waste management site, it must be obtained before the operator can apply for a licence.[166] This is the main stage at which the public can become involved. Indeed, it will be the only opportunity to oppose a new site because of its serious detriment to the amenities of the locality, [167] including traffic routeing.[168] The legislative scheme then assumes that the LPA will have decided that the site is appropriate in the locality. This is not quite the absolute prohibition that it might seem on the Agency redetermining

---

[166] See the Environmental Permitting Regulations 2007, Sch 9 para 2 previously set out in the EPA 1990, s 36(2); this is one of the essential requirements set out in the EPA 1990, s 36 along with the operator being a 'fit and proper person'. A similar requirement for planning permission applied under the previous waste disposal regime (CoPA 1974, s 5). For old-established sites, it will be sufficient if the site benefits from an established use certificate or CLEUD.

[167] It is only if the planning permission was granted before 1 May 1994, or the site only has an established use certificate, that the Agency may consider refusing the application for a licence 'for the purpose of preventing serious detriment to the amenities of the locality'. Indeed, there should otherwise be no reason to impose a waste management licence condition regarding local amenity (see *Attorney-General Reference (No 2 of 1988)* [1990] 1 QB 77, CA).

[168] So, in *Residents Against Waste Site Ltd v Lancashire County Council and Another* [2007] EWHC 2558 (Admin), the LPA, acting in its capacity as the waste planning authority, should have ensured that there were planning conditions on traffic routeing attached to the planning permission for a waste technology plant.

such issues, as it must also act in accordance with the 'relevant objectives' under Article 4 of the Waste Framework Directive.[169]

The LPA can deal with questions about the effect of the waste management **14.88** proposals in terms of their location and effect on amenity. Planning conditions can be imposed to limit such matters as the area to be filled, the general type of waste, the noise levels, hours of operation, and restoration and aftercare provisions.[170] If built development is intended, once the site is restored, this should be the subject of a fresh planning application. Realistic provision should be made in the development plan to allocate sites and provide criteria by which applications are to be judged for types of industry or facilities which may be detrimental to amenity and conservation matters, or a potential source of pollution, such as waste facilities. There is a wide margin of discretion for LPAs in drafting their development plans regarding the location of waste disposal sites, not only as to the detail of their provision, but also to how prescriptive the plan should be.[171] The waste management plan is not the only factor which determines the exact location of waste disposal sites. Account must be taken of PPS 10, which along with the Waste Strategy, is one of the documents that form part of the UK's waste management plans which are required by Article 7 of the EU Waste Framework Directive. The Waste Strategy 2007 sets out national standards and targets, and some key objectives. These include the aim to reduce waste, to increase its reuse and recycling, to provide more energy from waste, and to use less landfill. The Waste Strategy 2007 sets higher national targets for recycling, composting and recovery of household and municipal waste. Note that the TCPA 1990 has now been amended, so that there is no dispute that 'waste' in terms of the planning regime is defined in accordance with European law.[172]

---

[169] The effect of Art.4 is discussed below. The former provision was that the Agency could still refuse a licence if it was necessary in order to prevent 'pollution of the environment'or 'harm to human health' (EPA 1990, s 36(3)). The wide definition of 'pollution'the Environmental Permitting Regulations 2007 will also amenity issues to be considered by the Agency.

[170] The matter is discussed in more detail in Annex A of PPG 10, 'Planning and Waste Management', and in Waste Management Paper No 4. The aftercare of landfill sites and their restoration is dealt with in passing (paras. A48 and A49 of Annex A), and this is perhaps better dealt with in the waste management licence.

[171] *Wallis v Vale of Glamorgan Council* [2006], shows the difficulty in establishing that a development plan is inadequate. A criteria-based policy was used but no locations were identified. The court relied on the ECJ's guidance upon the proper approach to Article 7 in its decision in *Commune de Brain-le-Chateau and Michel Tilleut and Others v Region Wallonee* (Joined cases C-53/02 and C217/02), which was quoted by Auld LJ at paragraph 23 and 85 of his judgment in *Derbyshire Waste Ltd and Another v The Secretary of State for the Environment, Food and Rural Affairs* [2004] EWCA Civ 1508. Plans will vary, both according to their national, regional or local scale and, in the latter two cases particularly, differing constraints relating to the area, existing provision, needs and competing demands for other use of land.

[172] It 'includes anything that is waste for the purposes of Directive 2006/12/EC of the European Parliament and of the Council on waste, and that is not excluded from the scope of that Directive

14.89 National Policy on waste planning is now dealt with in PPS 10 'Planning for Sustainable Waste Management', published in 2005. PPS 10 requires the planning authorities to consider the best use for each waste stream, regional self-sufficiency, the proximity principle, and the waste hierarchy in making their decisions. The first choice of the PPS is that the amount of waste should be reduced as far as possible. The least favoured option is disposal without recovery.[173] The LPA is also under a legal duty when dealing with the recovery or disposal of waste to discharge its planning functions in accordance with the 'relevant objectives' under Article 4 of the Waste Framework Directive.[174] The same objectives apply to the Agency in the discharge of its functions under the Environmental Permitting regime (and were applied to Parts I and II of the EPA 1990). This duty will apply to development plans and to planning applications for such matters as landfill operations, incinerators, recycling or reclamation facilities, and waste-to-energy plants, and the storage of waste pending any of these operations. The relevant part of the objective under Article 4 is:

> . . . to ensure that waste is recovered or disposed of without endangering human health and without using processes or methods which would harm the environment and in particular without—

(i) risk to water, air, soil, plants or animals; or

(ii) causing nuisance through noise or odours; or

(iii) adversely affecting the countryside or places of special interest.

14.90 As regards waste disposal, there are additional objectives under Article 5 of the Waste Framework Directive. These deal with the need to establish an integrated and adequate network of installations, to ensure that the European Community and Member States become self-sufficient, and that waste is disposed of in one of the nearest appropriate installations by means of the most appropriate technologies.[175] In addition, a planning authority must not grant planning

---

by Article 2(1) of that Directive' (s 336(1), inserted as part of the consequential amendments made by the Environmental Permitting (England and Wales) Regulations 2007, SI 2007/3528 (the 'EPR 2007'), as from 6 April 2008.

[173] See Annex C, PPS 10.

[174] Every planning authority must exercise its functions in relation to waste operations (a) 'for the purposes of implementing Article 4 of the Waste Framework Directive'(2006/12/EC); and (b) when exercising a function under the plan making provisions 'for the purposes of implementing Article 3(1) of the Waste Framework Directive'(EPR 2007, reg 68 and Sch 20 para 3). But note that para 6 states that nothing in para 3 requires a planning authority to deal with a matter which the relevant pollution control authority has power to deal with. This was previously set out in reg 19 and Sch 4 of the Waste Management Licensing Regulations 1994, with reference to the earlier Waste Directive 75/44/EC.

[175] EPR 2007, reg 68 and Sch 20 para 4. This requires that every planning authority must exercise its specified functions in relation to disposal of waste (a) for the purposes of implementing Article 5 of the Waste Framework Directive (but ignoring the words 'in cooperation with other Member States where this is necessary or advisable', no doubt to avoid awkward debates), and

permission for a landfill unless it has taken the requirements regarding the location of a landfill set out in paragraph 1.1 of Annex 1 of the Landfill Directive into consideration.[176]

It was accepted by *R v Bolton MBC, ex p Kirkman*[177] that this duty to have regard **14.91** to these objectives has affected the application of the principles of the *Gateshead MBC* case to planning applications which concern waste facilities. *Kirkman* left the law on the precise dividing line between the duties of the planning and pollution control authorities in cases concerning waste disposal and recovery in some confusion. Although the courts heard extensive argument, they were only ever concerned with an application for leave to apply for judicial review, as to whether the applicant's submissions were arguable or not. In the combined cases of *Thornby Farms Ltd* and *Murray*,[178] the Court of Appeal held that, provided the objectives are always kept in mind, it is not an overriding consideration and it is therefore lawful to give greater weight to other material considerations in making the final decision whether or not to grant planning permission. Furthermore, the planning authority will not be in breach of duty in allowing the details of environmental control to be handled by the Agency. This accords with the principles set out in *Gateshead MBC*, and the Environmental Permitting Regulations 2007 themselves state that nothing requires the planning authority to deal with any matter which the relevant pollution control authority has the power to deal with.[179] This includes the issue of considering whether a particular method is the Best Practicable Environmental Option (BPEO). So, while it was accepted in the case of *Blewett*,[180] that (where there are no current regional or local waste management

---

(b) for the purposes of implementing, so far as material, any waste management plan. But note that para 6 states that nothing in para 4 requires a planning authority to deal with a matter which the relevant pollution control authority has power to deal with.

[176] EPR 2007, para 6(2). These locational requirements in the Landfill Directive include the distance from boundary to residential and recreational areas, the existence of groundwater, flooding and the cultural patrimony. The oddity of the EPR 2007 is that they do not mention para 1.2 of Annex 1—that an authorization can only be given if the requirements in para 1.1 'indicate that the landfill does not pose a serious environmental risk'. Strictly interpreted that would be a matter for the Agency, and not the planning authorities—which hardly accords with the broad purposes of the Directive.

[177] [1998] JPL 787, CA. Similarly to *Gateshead*, the Agency had decided that the proposed incinerator would be acceptable, and that any emissions could be made harmless by conditions on the authorization. At the time of *Kirkman*, there was no specific policy presumption or preference for recycling over incineration or energy recovery, so it could not be said to be unlawful not to apply such a preference.

[178] *Thornby Farms Ltd v Daventry District Council; David Murray v Derbyshire County Council* [2002] EWCA Civ 31, [2002] Env LR 687, CA. At that time, the objectives were set out in Art 4 Waste Framework Directive 75/442/EEC.

[179] See Sched 20, para 6. This is not a new provision—Waste Management Regulations 1994, Sch 4 para 2(2) provided the same.

[180] *Derbyshire Waste Ltd v Blewett and Secretary of State for the Environment, Food and Rural Affairs* [2004] EWCA Civ 1508; [2005] Env LR 15. The court accepted that the requirement for

plans) the LPA should undertake some BPEO analysis itself before granting planning permission, this was not the same as making it a pre-condition that the LPA had to conclude that the proposal was the Best Practicable Environmental Option before granting planning permission.

Nuisance and the effect of planning permission

14.92 Much depends on the exercise of the planning judgement of the LPA as to how it perceives an area should develop. The planning system is expected to control both the location of development which may give rise to pollution and the location of other development in its proximity. PPS 23 points out that whilst occupants of new developments should be protected from pollution, existing industries should not face unreasonable additional constraints.[181] For instance, the radio masts at Jodrell Bank have benefited from an exclusion zone, preventing permission being given for residential development too near to the sensitive masts.[182] It was also a material consideration in another case that a development would be near a sewage treatment works, given the inherent characteristics of the works.[183] Conversely, it is also a proper material consideration in granting permission for a new development that the law of nuisance can be used to require noise from existing developments to be reduced.[184] So, it was apparently not perverse for an LPA to grant permission for a residential estate right next door to industry, despite the possibility of future complaints.[185] But, in more extreme cases, it might be an abuse of power for the LPA to seek to change the character of the area in this way. The relevance of planning permissions in nuisance actions is considered in Chapter 16 on Common Law Liability.

Noise and development control

14.93 The prevention and control of noise both from and within a new development are relevant planning considerations.[186] While the planning system cannot deal with existing noise problems, an actual increase in activity, which produces a noise

---

BPEO in Art 8 of Directive 1999/31 was part of UK law. Whether any particular method of disposal is the BPEO, is intended to be dealt with as part of the waste management plans made pursuant to Council Directive 75/442.

[181] See paragraph 4.

[182] *Stringer v MHLG* [1970] 1 WLR 1281; see also *RMC Management Services Ltd v SSE* [1972] 222 EG 1593 (refusal of permission for concrete manufacturing plant adjacent to hi-tech factory).

[183] *Ricketts & Fletcher v Secretary of State for the Environment* [1988] JPL 768.

[184] *Fitzpatrick Developments Ltd v MHLG* [1965] 194 EG 911 (houses near a sawmill); but it would be wrong for the authority to urge the residents to take action, per Simon Brown LJ in *R v Exeter City Council, ex p J L Thomas* [1991] 1 QB 471.

[185] *R v Exeter City Council, ex p J L Thomas* [1991] 1 QB 471; but the commentary at [1990] JPL 129 at 137 suggests that it would be an abuse of power if the authority had only recently granted permission for that factory use.

[186] See *Newham LBC v SSE and East London Housing Association* [1987] 53 P&CR 98.

problem, may itself amount to development as a material change of use: an extreme example is where the Court of Appeal held that the increase in the number of dogs to 41 at a residential property was a change of use.[187]

PPG 24, 'Planning and Noise', contains a general discussion of the different **14.94** powers available, and the introduction of some non-binding residential standards. As PPG 24 makes clear, the development plans for the area should provide the framework within which the location of noise-sensitive developments can be assessed. Development should be guided to the most appropriate locations, and if it is not possible to separate land uses, it may be practicable to control or reduce noise by using conditions or planning obligations.

Conditions can range from being simple—for instance, by requiring self-closing **14.95** doors, or that the windows on a certain facade should be fixed shut—to complex ones which require noise measurements to be made.[188] Mitigation measures can involve engineering measures, changing the layout of a development, or using administrative solutions such as controlling the operating hours. It may even be justifiable to duplicate the statutory nuisance controls by imposing a planning condition requiring sound insulation to be installed, or noise to be controlled.

The justification lies in the need to safeguard amenity, which is a planning objec- **14.96** tive, and the condition would prevent the development being carried out in a way which would be likely to give rise to problems under the other legislation.[189] But the grant of planning permission will not remove the need to comply with other statutory controls. There can be duplication, and PPG 24 urges the LPA to seek to complement them.[190]

Flood risk areas

There has been a belated realization that tougher controls are needed on develop- **14.97** ment in the flood plain. The Department of Communities and Local Government has provided a separate Planning Policy Statement 25 on Development and Flood Risk ('PPS 25'). When it was produced in December 2006 it introduced distinctly tougher policy tests than had been set out in the Planning Policy Guidance note 25 which it replaced, and required allowance to be included in

---

[187] *Wallington v Secretary of State for the Environment and Montgomeryshire* [1990] JPL 278.
[188] See Annex 4 of PPG 24.
[189] *Newham London Borough v Secretary of State for the Environment* [1986] JPL 607—the High Court accepted the LPA's argument that noise disturbance was a ground for refusal on the conversion of houses into flats, which the inspector had rejected.
[190] It is not unlawful for the controls to be duplicated—in the rather unfortunate case of *R v Kennet DC, ex p Somerfield Property Co* [1999] JPL 361, QBD, the local authority agreed one set of noise controls under the statutory nuisance regime and then imposed a tougher standard on the planning permission for an extension to the existing development.

any assessments for the likely impacts of climate change. There is also a detailed practice guide to PPS 25,[191] which provides advice on the practical implementation of the policies described in PPS 25, relying upon case studies to illustrate the key principles. Both the *Planning and Climate Change—Supplement to Planning Policy Statement 1* and *PPS25* require that the spatial planning process should take account of climate change impacts in assessing these risks. In Wales, an even tougher policy approach has been taken, which requires an assessment to be made not just of the 1-in-100-year flood, but also the 1-in-1,000-year flood event.[192]

14.98 The planning authority remains the principal decision-maker regarding applications for new development. The Environment Agency's role[193] is to support the planning system by providing timely information and advice on flooding issue that is fit for purposes. At a strategic level, the Agency is a statutory consultee for the Strategic Environmental Assessments and Sustainability Appraisals of development documents, and it has the further responsibility of providing Regional Planning Bodies with advice on Regional Flood Risk Assessments and providing local planning authorities with advice on the preparation of Strategic Flood Risk Assessments for the purposes of preparing their development plans.[194] The Agency has also published flood plain maps which it will rely upon when it is consulted on any proposal. There is even an interactive map on their website. The Agency estimates that there are now 1.8 million homes and 185,000 commercial premises at risk from flooding.

14.99 The relevant policy principles[195] reflect the importance that the Government places on ensuring that development plan policies for the allocation of sites and any development control decisions avoid creating increased flood risks to people and property where possible, and manage the risks elsewhere. As regards development control decisions, the LPA is required to apply the sequential approach at a site level in order to minimize flood risk by directing the most vulnerable development to areas of lowest flood risk, and to match the vulnerability of the land use

---

[191] 'PPS 25 Development and Flood Risk Practice Guide'; A consultation draft was published in February 2007, and finally produced in June 2008.

[192] See TAN 15 (2004).

[193] Paragraphs 30 and 31 of PPS 25.

[194] PPS 25 (at paragraphs 25 to 29) makes it clear that the local planning authority should consult the Environment Agency when preparing policies in their LDDs on flood risk management and in relation to areas potentially identified as at risk of flooding. The guidance further states that sustainability appraisals prepared by the local planning authority as part of their local development framework ('LDF'), land allocations and development control policies should all be informed by a Strategic Flood Risk Assessment ('SFRA'). The *Practice Guide on PPS 25* explains the essential role the SFRA has in the evidence gathering stage of the plan preparation process, and that the SFRA will provide the evidence base for application of the Sequential Test in the land use allocation process.

[195] Decision-making principles are addressed at paragraph 7 of the PPS 25 guidance.

to the flood risk. The detailed policy guidance on the 'sequential test' utilizes 'Flood Zones' which reflect the probability of sea and river flooding.[196] Even within these Flood Zones, new development should be directed to sites at the lowest probability of flooding and the flood vulnerability of the intended use should be matched to the flood risk of the site, steering higher vulnerability uses towards parts of the site which are at lowest probability of flooding.[197]

The procedures relating to the actual grant of planning permission in areas at risk **14.100** from flooding in England have also been amended to enhance the role of the Agency.[198] The first step is that when a planning authority is determining an application for planning permission, it must consult with the Agency for:

Development, other than minor development,[199] which is to be carried out on land—

(i) in an area within Flood Zones 2 or 3;[200] or
(ii) in an area within Flood Zone 1 which has critical drainage problems and which has been notified for the purpose of this provision to the local planning authority by the Environment Agency.
(ze) Any development of land of one hectare or more.

The second step is that the local planning authority must notify the Secretary of **14.101** State of any planning application for major development where they are still

---

[196] See Annex D to PPS 25; the Annex also explains the role of SFRAs (as defined in Annex E) as the basis for the application of the Sequential Test. Paragraph D5 of Annex D to PPS 25 sets out the approach to be adopted by LPAs (or other decision makers) on the application for the Sequential Test requiring LPAs to steer new development to Flood Zone 1. Where there are no reasonably available sites within Flood Zone 1, in allocating land in LDDs or in determining applications for development should take account of the flood risk vulnerability of land uses and consider reasonably available sites Flood Zone 2, applying the Exception Test if required. Finally, this part of the guidance makes absolutely clear that only where there are no reasonably available sites in Flood Zones 1 and 2 should LPAs consider the suitability of sites in Flood Zone 3, again taking account of the flood risk vulnerability of land uses and applying the Exception Test, if required.

[197] Paragraph D6 of Annex D, of PPS 25.

[198] Article 10 (zd) and (ze), the Town and Country Planning (General Development Procedure) Order 1995 ('the GDPO')—as amended from 1 October 2006.

[199] Minor development is defined within Article 10 of the GDPO as: (i) development of an existing dwelling-house, or development within the curtilage of such a dwelling-house, for any purpose incidental to the enjoyment of the dwelling-house as such; (ii) the extension of an existing building used for non-domestic purposes where the floorspace created by the development does not exceed 250 square metres; and (iii) the alteration of an existing building where the alteration does not increase the size of the building.

[200] Flood Zone 1 is the lowest category (less than 1 in 1000 probability); Flood Zone 2 is medium probability and Flood Zone 3 is high probability. The 'functional flood plain' is Zone 3B. Flood Zones are defined in Table D.1, Annex D. The Flood Zones refer to the probability of flooding and ignore (as a matter of policy) the presence of existing defences,' because these can be breached, overtopped and may not be in existence for the lifetime of the development'(see footnote 6 to para 17, PPS 25).

minded to grant permission in a flood risk area, despite there being an outstanding objection from the Environment Agency.[201] This gives the Secretary of State the opportunity to consider whether it would be appropriate to call the application in for his determination. However, it is notable that the *PPS 25 Practice Guide* expects that there will be continuing discussions between the local planning authority, the Agency, and the applicant, in an attempt to overcome any outstanding Agency objections, so that a reference to the Secretary of State is intended to be rare.

14.102 In order to assist dealing with the large number of such consultations, the Agency has produced standing advice to local authorities,[202] which provides a checklist for any low risk planning applications where, whilst flood risk is an issue, there is no need to consult the Agency directly for a bespoke response. The Standing Advice also sets out those higher risk developments on which the Agency is a statutory consultee and will need to be consulted directly. The Standing Advice also provides advice for applicants and agents on the requirements for flood risk assessment (FRA) for both low and higher risk developments.

---

[201] The Secretary of State for Communities and Local Government has made the Town and Country Planning (Flooding)(England) Direction 2007, which came into force on 1 January 2007, and was made pursuant to the provisions of the GDPO 1995.

[202] The Standing Advice is published on the Agency's website. The Standing Advice provides, inter alia, a consultation matrix based upon the GDPO 1995 (as amended) providing guidance on what a consultation should contain. The Advice also includes the Sequential Test table, which is referred to in the Practice Guide Companion to PPS 25 (see Table 1.3) and general advice to applicants and their agents on matters relating to flood risk assessment.

15

ENVIRONMENTAL IMPACT ASSESSMENT

A. Introduction	15.01	
What is Environmental Impact Assessment?	15.05	
What is Strategic Environmental Assessment ?	15.07	
B. The Legislative Framework	15.10	
The purpose of Environmental Impact Assessment	15.10	
The implementation of the Directive in UK law	15.14	
The 1985 Environmental Assessment Directive	15.14	
The 1997 Environmental Assessment Directive	15.17	
Directive 2003 amendment	15.19	
The effect of the reforms on existing applications	15.20	
The relationship between the Directives and UK law	15.21	
C. When is Environmental Impact Assessment required?	15.22	
The 'project' to be assessed	15.22	
The general definition	15.22	
Are outline applications still possible?	15.24	
Defining the project in relation to future development	15.29	
Identifying a project as 'EIA development'	15.31	
The EIA Regulations 1999	15.32	
Schedule 1 development	15.33	
Schedule 2 development	15.34	

Exclusive thresholds	15.36	
Development in a 'sensitive area'	15.38	
Further development, changes and modifications to development projects	15.39	
Schedule 2: general selection criteria	15.41	
Government guidance on Schedule 2	15.43	
Guidance on the use of indicative criteria and thresholds	15.44	
D. Deciding Whether an Environmental Impact Assessment is Required	15.45	
The initial screening	15.45	
The environmental effects on other countries	15.51	
E. The Contents of the Environmental Statement	15.52	
The prescribed contents	15.52	
The required level of detail	15.54	
Requests for further information	15.55	
Limiting the scope of the assessment	15.57	
F. The Use of the Environmental Statement in the Consent Decision	15.59	
G. Possible Challenges	15.63	
Public participation	15.63	
The requirement to provide a non-technical summary	15.65	
Reasons for the decision	15.66	
Challenges through the courts	15.67	

A. Introduction

The process of environmental impact assessment has become an integral part **15.01** of the planning process for large-scale development projects. An assessment will automatically be required for certain types of projects, such as an oil refinery, a motorway, or a large power station. There are also a large number of other types of projects, from intensive agriculture, to mineral extraction, industrial estate development, the food industry, and flood defence works, where an assessment will be required if the particular project is likely to have significant effects on the environment. This can extend to less obvious categories of projects such as shopping centres, intensive livestock units, ski lifts, and golf courses.

15.02 The purpose of the assessment is to ensure that the effects on the environment of these important projects are taken into account as early as possible in the decision-making process. Since the requirement to carry out an assessment can also be a lengthy and expensive one, considerable controversy has arisen as to whether or not a formal assessment is legally required and, if so, to what standard. This has led the courts to comment that 'The EIA process is intended to be an aid to efficient and inclusive decision making in special cases, not an obstacle race'.[1]

15.03 The requirement to carry out an assessment has its origins in European Union law, and it is implemented in the UK by way of regulations. The requirement was introduced by the 1985 Directive 85/337/EEC on the Assessment of the Effects of Certain Public and Private Projects on the Environment ('the 1985 Environmental Assessment Directive').[2] This Directive was substantially amended by a 1997 Directive, 97/11/EC ('the 1997 Environmental Assessment Directive'), whose provisions came into force on 14 March 1999,[3] and also in 2003.[4] The main regulations are the Town and Country Planning (Environmental Impact Assessment) (England and Wales) Regulations 1999 ('the 1999 Regulations'), because most of the projects which are covered also require planning permission. This chapter therefore concentrates on these regulations. Environmental assessment is also required as part of the other development control procedures which exist in the UK, such as those for highways, pipelines, and harbour and electricity projects. The requirement to carry out an Environmental Impact Assessment is not discretionary, and it must be carried out if a project is likely to have significant effects on the environment.[5]

15.04 It is important to note that the environmental impact assessment process is not an alternative process for granting development consent. It runs in parallel with these other regimes. In the case of the planning regime, where a project does require an assessment, the 1999 Regulations impose certain procedural requirements with regard to the grant of planning permission for that project. In addition, in order

---

[1] *R (oao Jones) v Mansfield BC* [2004] Env LR 391 at para 57, per Carnwath LJ.
[2] Council Directive 85/337/EEC, OJ L 175, 5 July 1985, p 40.
[3] Council Directive 97/11/EC, OJ L 73, 14 March 1997, p 5.
[4] Council Directive 2003/35/EC.
[5] See para 12 of the DETR Circular 2/99.

to ensure that projects do not avoid the requirements, the 1999 Regulations also restrict the rights that would otherwise apply to local authority development and to developments in simplified planning zones, enterprise zones, and under any permitted development rights.[6] The timescale for making a decision is also extended as a matter of law.[7] This time period can be, and frequently is, extended further by agreement between the local planning authority (LPA) and the applicant, given the complexity of the issues that are raised. The Environmental Statement which is submitted as a result of the assessment will be a significant material consideration in determining whether or not planning permission should be granted. No permission can be granted by the LPA, or the Secretary of State, unless the 'environmental information' provided has been taken into account.[8] This information includes not only the Environmental Statement submitted by the applicant, but also any other representations which have been duly made by any other person, including members of the public, about the environmental effects of the development.[9] But, at the end of the day, even if significant effects on the environment are identified, permission may still be granted in the light of all material considerations.

What is Environmental Impact Assessment?

Formal environmental impact assessment (EIA) is a procedure for 'drawing **15.05** together in a systematic way expert quantitative analysis and qualitative assessment of a project's environmental effects, and presenting the results in a way which enables the importance of the predicted effects, and the scope for mitigating or modifying them, to be properly evaluated by the relevant decision making body before a decision is given'.[10] The Environmental Statement is the document, or the series of documents, which sets out and summarizes the results of the assessment. The developer of the project produces the Statement and it is intended that it should inform the decision-making body, statutory consultees, and the public about the effects of the proposal.

---

[6] The 1999 Regulations, (SI 1999/293 as amended), regs 22–26 Crown development no longer remains exempt from the requirements (despite para 157 of Circular 2/99)—indeed, the ECJ found the UK was in breach of its obligations under the EIA Directive (Case C-37/05, *Commission v United Kingdom* [2006] in this regard. The UK has accepted that it must apply the EIA measures to Crown development by way of legislation, and not by an administrative practice.

[7] The 1999 Regulations, reg 32(2), from the statutory eight-week period to 16 weeks—the same provision applied under the 1988 Regulations.

[8] The 1999 Regulations, reg 32(2). The same requirement was made by reg 4(2) of the 1988 Regulations. Whilst the European Directive refers to the need to obtain 'development consent' for projects, this phrase is directly interpreted as the need for planning permission in the 1999 Regulations as regards the planning regime.

[9] Ibid, reg 2(1).

[10] This is the wording from Circular 15/88, para 7—a less complete description is used in para 9 of Circular 2/99 (which replaces Circular 15/88), although it does also mention that the information should be properly understood by the public as well as the authority.

15.06 Some confusion has arisen over the legal terminology that has been used to describe the assessment process. The original UK guidance published in 1988 referred to the whole process as 'environmental assessment' (or EA). The latest amendments have now led the UK Government to use the term 'environmental impact assessment' (or EIA), which is more widely understood throughout the European Union. In addition, all development which requires an EIA will now be referred to as 'EIA development', rather than by the cumbersome (if more accurate) descriptions of 'EA Schedule 1 development' or 'EA Schedule 2 development'. The 1999 Regulations have also introduced a number of new terms. The process whereby an applicant can request the competent authority to determine whether an assessment is required for their project is now called a 'screening opinion'. If the Secretary of State is asked to make this determination, he will make a 'screening direction'. The developer can now ask the LPA for a formal 'scoping opinion' as to the information to be provided before submitting the environmental statement. These are discussed below. One difference in the terminology persists, in that the two crucial lists of the types of development for which an EIA may be required are referred to as Annexes in the Directive and Schedules in the UK Regulations.

What is Strategic Environmental Assessment ?

15.07 In a similar fashion to planning applications, the environmental consequences of certain plans and other projects will need to be assessed prior to their adoption or implementation. Those 'plans and projects' will be subject to review to ensure that they '. . . provide for a high level of protection of the environment and to contribute to the integration of environmental considerations into the preparation and adoption of plans and programmes with a view to promoting sustainable development'.[11] This requirement is now set out in the Environmental Assessment of Plans and Programmes Regulations 2004.[12] These Regulations implement Directive 2001/42/EC, commonly known as the Strategic Environmental Assessment Directive.[13] This had to be implemented in the UK by 21 July 2004, and

---

[11] Article 1, SEA Directive. Note that the agreement at Kiev of the Protocol on SEA to the Espoo Convention (May 2003) may lead to further reforms to the SEA requirements in due course.

[12] SI 1633/2004; see also the guidance on the requirements of the SEA Directive called 'A Practical Guide to the SEA Directive'(ODPM, September 2005). See further, the article by Robinson and Elvin 'The Environmental Assessment of Plans and Programmes' [2004] JPL 1028.

[13] Directive 2001/42/EC on the assessment of the effects of certain plans and projects on the environment (OJ 21.7.2001). The Commission has also produced guidance on this—'Implementation of Directive 2001/42 as to the assessment of the effects of certain plans and programs on the environment'.

although the UK Government failed to do so in time, this does not appear to have had any significant consequences in the long run.

Where an environmental assessment is required, it must be carried out during the **15.08** preparation of the plan or programme and before its adoption or submission to the legislative process.[14] The review is carried out according to similar criteria to those which are applicable to planning applications in the 1999 Regulations, such as the likely significant effects on the environment, an assessment of the measures to prevent or off-set those effects, and a description of measures to monitor the environmental effects and any mitigation measures, which is then produced in a written report.[15] While the requirements of a SEA and a Sustainability Appraisal of a development plan are distinct, it is possible to satisfy them both through a single appraisal process.[16] The strategic assessment of the plan or programme will not prejudice the later requirements for an EIA for any particular project that is subject to that plan or programme.[17]

The plans and programmes which are covered include those which are 'prepared **15.09** at national, regional or local level through a legislative procedure . . . or which are required by legislative, regulatory or administrative provisions'.[18] The SEA Directive lists plans and programmes for agriculture, forestry, fisheries, energy, industry, transport, waste management, water management, telecommunications, tourism, and town and country planning or land use, and which set the framework for Annex I and II projects.[19] This therefore includes any Development Plan, and any 'fast-track' Parliamentary proceedings for the approval of

---

[14] Article 4(1), SEA Directive. The NI case of *Seaport Investments Ltd and others v Department of the Environment for Northern Ireland* [2007] NIQB 62, confirms that there should be substantial compliance with the SEA Directive.

[15] See generally Annex 1. The requirements for assessment follow the components of those required for the EIA of projects, including the preparation of an environmental report containing the required information to identify the likely significant environmental effects of implementing the plan or programme, and a consideration of the reasonable alternatives taking into account the objectives and geographical scope of the plan or programme (Article 5). There must be consultation with the relevant authorities and with the public (Article 6), and information provided on the plan or programme adopted (Article 9).

[16] This approach has been upheld in *R (on the application of Howsmoor Developments Ltd and others) v South Gloucestershire County Council* [2008] EWHC 262 (Admin)—whilst the case confirmed that the SEA Directive did not have retrospective effect, it did look at the issue of development briefs more widely. See Chapter 14 further for a discussion of development plans.

[17] See Article 11(1), SEA Directive.

[18] Article 2(a). Appendix 1 to the ODPM's *Practical Guide* (2005) contains an extensive (indicative) list of the plans and programmes which are subject to the SEA directive. National Planning Statements or White Papers that set out national strategies for the determination of the grant of permission for major developments such as airports and energy installations are likely to come within the scope of the SEA Directive.

[19] Article 3. Minor modifications and plans for small areas will require an assessment where they are likely to have a significant environmental effect (Art. 3(3)).

major infrastructure. The only blanket exclusions are for financial and budget plans, and those serving the sole purpose of national defence and civil emergency. Other areas are more doubtful. For instance, whilst the current view is that the SEA Directive does not apply to Catchment Area Management Strategies (CAMS), it is no doubt out of an abundance of caution that the Environment Agency intends to identify the links between CAMS and SEA in all future CAMS. It will then be able to argue that there has been substantial compliance with the SEA Directive, should this ever become an issue.

B. The Legislative Framework

The purpose of Environmental Impact Assessment

15.10 Environmental Impact Assessment is aimed at providing the competent authorities with the relevant information to enable them to take a decision on a specific project in full knowledge of the project's likely significant impact on the environment. The preamble to the 1985 Environmental Assessment Directive explains that the Action Programmes of the European Communities on the environment stress:

- that the best environmental policy consists in preventing the creation of pollution or nuisances at source rather than subsequently trying to counteract their effects,

- that there is therefore a need to take effects on the environment into account at the earliest possible stage in all the technical planning and decision-making processes, and

- that therefore there is a need for procedures to be implemented to evaluate such effects.

15.11 Indeed, the preamble to the 1997 Environmental Assessment Directive describes the environmental assessment procedure as 'a fundamental instrument of environmental policy'.

15.12 The Court of Appeal has provided a useful summary of the statutory provisions and authorities in the case of *Maureen Smith*.[20] As was said in that case, the starting point is the EIA Directive to which the UK gave effect by the 1988 Regulations, and now by the 1999 Regulations. The approach remains coloured by the Directive, the purpose of which is described in the speech of Lord Hoffman

---

[20] *Maureen Smith v Secretary of State for the Environment, Transport and Regions and others* [2003] EWCA Civ 262; [2003] Env LR 32, at paras 22–33.

in *Berkeley v Secretary of State for the Environment* [21]—in essence the Directive requires not merely that the planning authority should have the necessary information, but that it should have been obtained by means of a particular public procedure, namely that of an EIA. The basic requirement is set out in Article 2(1) of the 1985 Directive. This article, as amended by the 1997 Directive,[22] states:

> Member States shall adopt all measures necessary to ensure that, before consent is given, projects likely to have significant effects on the environment by virtue, inter alia, of their nature, size or location are made subject to a requirement for development consent and an assessment with regard to their effects. These projects are defined in Article 4.

Certain classes of projects are identified as requiring a mandatory environmental assessment, under Article 4.1 and Annex I of the Directive. This list is reproduced in Schedule 1 of the UK Regulations. For other types of projects, under Article 4.2 and Annex II of the Directive, the Member States are given a discretion to determine whether their characteristics require that an assessment be carried out. The list of these projects is reproduced in Schedule 2 of the UK Regulations. The 1997 Directive, which has now been implemented in the UK, has extended the number of projects for which an assessment must be considered, and has refined the process in the light of the experience gained in the Member States. The 1997 Directive has also amended Article 2(1) to include the requirement that development consent must be obtained for the projects covered. This strengthens the process. There have been occasions in the past where a project has not needed to obtain a formal consent, even though it would require an environmental impact assessment. There was therefore no formal way in which the project could be refused consent.   **15.13**

The implementation of the Directive in UK law

The 1985 Environmental Assessment Directive

Directive 85/337/EEC required Member States to take the measures necessary to comply with its requirements within three years of its notification, by 3 July 1988.[23] The UK Government has sought to implement the Directive by regulations made under the European Communities Act 1972 in respect of the different areas affected, so that there are separate regulations for town and country   **15.14**

---

[21] [2001] 603 at 615 (as quoted in *Maureen Smith*).
[22] Article 1.1 of the 1997 Directive allegedly replaces the wording of Art 2(1) of the 1985 Directive, but the only change is the addition of the words 'a requirement for development consent and' to the existing text.
[23] Article 12.

planning,[24] intensive cultivation,[25] afforestation,[26] land drainage,[27] salmon farming,[28] highways,[29] electricity and pipelines,[30] railways and other major infrastructure projects,[31] harbours,[32] and now water management projects.[33] Parliamentary Standing Orders provide for environmental assessment of developments promoted by private and hybrid Bills, unless the Secretary of State directs that no environmental statement is required.[34] The extensive list of regulations

---

[24] The first regulations were the Town and Country Planning (Assessment of Environmental Effects) Regulations 1988 (SI 1988/1199). These were revoked with savings by Town and Country Planning (Environmental Impact Assessment) (England and Wales) Regulations 1999 (SI 1999/293) (which has also been further amended).

[25] Environmental Impact Assessment (Uncultivated Land and Semi-natural Areas) (England) Regulations 2001—separate regulations were required as 'agriculture'is normally not development for which planning permission is required. There are clear thresholds, so that unless the productivity of 'uncultivated land'was intensified above the normal level, an increase in the productiveness of such land does not come within the definition of 'intensive agricultural purposes' (reg.2(1)—see *Alford v Department for Environment, Food and Rural Affairs* [2005] EWHC 808 (Admin).

[26] Environmental Impact Assessment (Forestry) (England and Wales) Regulations 1999, SI 1999/2228 (further amended by SI 2006/3106), which revoked SI 1988/1207. A special regime is required because, by virtue of the TCPA 1990, s 55(2)(e), planning permission is not required for the use of any land for forestry and there are extensive permitted development rights for forestry-related development (under Part 7, Town and Country Planning (General Permitted Development) Order 1995, SI 1995/418, as amended).

[27] Environmental Impact Assessment (Land Drainage Improvement Works) Regulations 1999, SI 1999/1783 (further amended by SI 2005/1399 and SI 2006/618), which revoked SI 1988/1217.

[28] Environmental Impact Assessment (Fish Farming in Marine Waters) Regulations 1999, SI 1999/367 (as amended) which revoked Environmental Assessment (Salmon Farming in Marine Waters) Regulations 1988, SI 1988/1218.

[29] Highways (Environmental Impact Assessment) Regulations 2007, SI 2007/1062 (formerly the Highways (Assessment of Environmental Effects) Regulations 1988, then Highways (Assessment of Environmental Effects) Regulations 1999, SI 1999/369). The Regulations inserted a new s 105A in the Highways Act 1980—in any case where the Secretary of State for Transport has under consideration the construction of a new highway or the improvement of an existing highway, he must determine whether or not it requires an environmental assessment under the Council Directive and if so, he must publish an environmental statement.

[30] Electricity Works (Environmental Impact Assessment) (England and Wales) Regulations 2000, SI 2000/1927 (as amended); Pipe-line Works (Environmental Impact Assessment) Regulations 2000, SI 2000/1928 (as amended); Gas Transporter Pipe-line Works (Environmental Impact Assessment) Regulations 1999/1672 (as amended). These projects often obtain deemed planning permission as part of the authorization process.

[31] Transport and Works (Assessment of Environmental Effects) Regulations 1995, SI 1995/1541. The Transport and Works Act 1992 provides a statutory mechanism for large-scale projects to obtain planning permission and related consents. Previously, such projects would have required a Private Act of Parliament.

[32] Marine Works (Environmental Impact Assessment) Regulations 2007, SI 2007/1518.

[33] Water Resources (Environmental Impact Assessment) (England and Wales) Regulations 2006, SI 2006/3124. These cover water management projects for agriculture, involving the abstraction (taking) or impoundment (storage) of water—including irrigation. This can also apply to abstractions and impoundments that do not currently require an Environment Agency abstraction licence (ie for trickle irrigation), where significant environmental effects are likely.

[34] This is even though the Environmental Assessment Directive does not apply to national legislation as it is assumed that the objectives of the Directive are achieved through the legislative process (Art 1.5).

have been introduced in a rather piecemeal fashion, in a rather patch and mend approach, as further gaps in the UK's implementation of the underlying EIA Directive have emerged.

The first Circular which was published to explain the provisions of the regulations **15.15** dealing with town planning (Circular 15/88) claimed, with a hint of pride, that, unlike in some European countries: 'In the UK there is already a highly developed body of planning and pollution control legislation which is designed to ensure that the environmental and other consequences of individual proposals are fully considered before permission is given'.[35] However, despite the UK's apparent compliance with the requirements of the 1985 Directive, a number of gaps in the UK legislation have had to be plugged since then. Permitted development rights were withdrawn for developments within the Directive which had not been subject to a consent procedure applying environmental assessment.[36] The Town and Country Planning (Environmental Assessment and Unauthorized Development) Regulations 1995[37] required the submission of environmental statements before permission could be granted on an enforcement notice appeal for development falling within the Directive. These amendments had little practical significance as such development is rarely carried out under permitted development rights or without planning permission. Whilst the Transport and Works Act Rules provided for environmental statements for major infrastructure schemes covered by them, no express reference was made in the Act. The Transport and Works (Assessment of Environmental Effects) Regulations 1995[38] clarified the Act by requiring the Secretary of State to confirm that he had considered any environmental statement required by the Directive.

Compliance with the Directive is a continuing obligation, and the ECJ has **15.16** confirmed that it applies to the pre-application stage as well as any other part of a multi-stage consent process, despite the UK's previous insistence that reserved matters stages were excluded.[39] Draft Regulations were produced in 2007,[40] in the light of the ECJ's judgment in *Barker*, that the UK should provide for the

---

[35] Para 6.
[36] Town and Country Planning (General Permitted Development) Order 1995, SI 1995/418 (as amended art 3(10)); Town and Country Planning (Environmental Impact Assessment) (England and Wales) Regulations 1999, SI 1999/293 (as amended).
[37] SI 1995/2258—revoked and replaced by the 1999 Regulations (as amended).
[38] SI 1995/1541.
[39] *R v LB of Bromley ex p Barker* [2007] UKHL 52 and *R (Anderson) v Bradford MDC* [2006] EWHC 3344 (Admin).
[40] The draft Town and Country Planning (Environmental Impact Assessment) (England) (Amendment) Regulations 2007, consultation draft issued October 2007. This follows the ECJ's ruling in the combined cases of Cases C-508/03, *Commission v United Kingdom* and C-290/03 *Barker v London Borough of Brent* [2006] ECR I-3969, [2006] QB 764. A new Regulation 26B would apply the 1999 Regulations to multi-stage consents, subject to some procedural exceptions.

provision of an EIA at the reserved matters stage of a planning permission, where it emerges that there are unanticipated environmental effects. These regulations will be accompanied by further guidance.

The 1997 Environmental Assessment Directive

15.17   The 1997 Directive made significant changes to the EIA regime by amending the 1985 Directive. The main changes were to increase the number of projects that are subject to the EIA process, and to require that an individual determination be made in each case. Developers can obtain advice from the competent authorities on the required content of the environmental statement, and for a formal screening decision as to whether an assessment is required. The competent authorities must give their reasons for granting the development consent, as well as for its refusal. The Directive also introduces a formal procedure for consulting other Member States on those projects which might affect their countries.

15.18   The amendments made by the 1997 Environmental Assessment Directive were transposed into English law in respect of planning matters by the Town and Country Planning (Environmental Impact Assessment) (England and Wales) Regulations 1999 ('the 1999 Regulations').[41] The 1999 Regulations consolidated all the previous regulations, which had been used to implement the requirements of the 1985 Directive, for those projects which amounted to 'development'.[42] A new Circular was published in England, Circular 2/99 'Environmental Impact Assessment', which replaced Circular 15/88 in its entirety. Welsh Office Circular 11/99 provides similar advice for the Principality. The 1999 Regulations apply to any 'request for development consent' submitted to a competent authority from 14 March 1999.[43] Highways development, which would otherwise enjoy Crown immunity, is subject to the amended Directive by Sections 105A, 105B, and 105C of the Highways Act 1980.[44] The remaining assessment regimes were also updated to accord with the new Directive.

Directive 2003 amendment

15.19   The EIA Directive was further amended in 2003, in order to implement the Aarhus Convention on public participation.[45] The changes are intended to

---

[41] SI 1999/293.

[42] The Regulations revoked and re-enacted with the amendments are the following: SI 1988/1199, SI 1990/367, SI 1992/1494, SI 1992/2414, SI 1994/677, SI 1995/417, and SI 1995/2258.

[43] The 1999 Regulations, reg 34(2). Applications made before that date were subject to the provisions of the 1985 Directive and the old regulations.

[44] Inserted by the Highways (Assessment of Environmental Effects) Regulations 1999, SI 1999/369.

[45] Amended by Directive 2003/35/EC. The main amendments are that the public should be informed not only of any EIA proposals, but also of the supplementary information gathered in the process. Any supporting documents submitted by the developer should be made available

improve public involvement. The 1999 EIA Regulations have been amended[46] as a result, and require publicity for any further information voluntarily submitted by a developer. These provisions applied to any applications submitted on or after 15 January 2007.

The effect of the reforms on existing applications

The continuing reforms that have been made to the EIA regime mean that long-running applications may have to meet the revised standards before they can receive consent. However, this is not always the case. The reforms introduced by the 1985 Environmental Assessment Directive did not apply to projects for which an application for development consent was submitted before the date the Directive came into force. These were termed 'pipeline projects', like the Twyford Down M3 extension and the A41 Newbury Bypass,[47] where the procedures leading to consent were already under way when the Directive came into force on 3 July 1988. The same arguments arose on the 1999 amendments, to those projects which were then brought within the scope of the Directive. On the grounds of legal certainty, the important date has been taken to be the date on which the development consent procedure was initiated.[48] It is only if this procedure becomes unduly delayed, or there are significant changes made to the project, that it might be right to require that a new consent procedure should be initiated and the obligation to carry out an EIA should also be reconsidered.

15.20

The relationship between the Directives and UK law

As explained above, the UK Government sought to implement the EIA Directive by making regulations and by inserting new sections into the TCPA 1990 and the Highways Act 1980. However, there have been a number of significant cases before the British courts where it has been alleged that the UK has failed to implement the requirements of the Directive correctly. It is a general principle of

15.21

---

to the public concerned. Any public notice and decision statement must include reference to the public participation process and that there is the right to challenge the decision and what is the procedure for doing so.

[46] Amended by the Town and Country Planning (Environmental Impact Assessment) (Amendment) Regulations 2006 (SI 2006/3295) for England, and by Town and Country Planning (Environmental Impact Assessment) (Amendment) (Wales) Regulations 2006 (Welsh SI 2006/3099) for Wales. The Regulations however make no mention of the process being 'fair, equitable, timely and not prohibitively expensive'.

[47] See *Twyford Parish Council* above, *Secretary of State for Transport v Haughian CA* above and the 'Dortmund Power Station Case': C-431/92 *Commission v Germany* [1995] ECR I-2189.

[48] C-236 *Bund Naturshutz Bayern* [1994] ECR I-497 (and see para 4.25 above further). The arguments for this date were supported on the grounds of legal certainty, proportionality, and legitimate expectations. But there is an argument that a planning appeal inquiry in the UK is intended to be a fresh hearing, so that the Secretary of State or his Inspector should consider the obligation afresh, even if the original application was made before the date the Directive applied (contrary to the view of McCullough J in *Twyford Parish Council*).

European Union law that, where a Member State fails to implement a Directive correctly, the provisions of the Directive can be relied upon by an individual against the state wherever the provisions of the Directive appear, as far as their subject matter is concerned, to be unconditional and sufficiently precise.[49] There had been a difference of views in the British courts over whether the 1985 Environmental Assessment Directive, in whole or in part, had this 'direct effect' so as to enable individuals to rely on its provisions to challenge some of the controversial projects of the recent past. It is now generally assumed that the provisions of the 1985 Directive are capable of being given direct effect by the UK courts. The turning point was the decision of the European Court of Justice in October 1996 in the *Dutch Dykes* case.[50] The issue continues to arise, so that in *Barker* [51] the claimant was able to argue succcessfully that the UK had failed to implement the requirements of the Directive. A continuing theme in all cases is that 'the wording of the Directive indicates that it has a wide scope and a broad purpose'.[52]

C. When is Environmental Impact Assessment Required?

The 'project' to be assessed

The general definition

15.22 Under Article 1 of the 1985 Environmental Assessment Directive, the requirements 'apply to the assessment of the environmental effects of those public and private projects which are likely to have significant effects on the environment'. A 'project' is widely defined in Article 2 as 'the execution of construction works or of other installations or schemes and other interventions in the natural surroundings and landscape including those involving the extraction of mineral resources'.

---

[49] *Marshal* [1986] ECR 723; see further the discussion of the principle of Direct Effect in Chapter 4, European Environmental Law, at para 4.24.

[50] *Kraaijveld v Zuid-Holland* [1997] Env LR 265—on an Art 177 reference for a preliminary ruling. This change in views was seen in the case of *R v North Yorkshire County Council, ex p Brown* [1999] JPL 616, HL (registration of an old minerals permission—environmental assessment was not required by the legislation). It was a disputed issue at first instance, [1997] Env LR 391. When *ex p Brown* reached the Court of Appeal, [1998] Env LR 385, the *Dutch Dykes* decision was known and it was common ground between the parties that the Directive had direct effect. The House of Lords in the same case simply applied the Directive, giving it direct effect without expressly referring to the concept.

[51] *R v LB of Bromley ex p Barker* [2007] UKHL 52; and also in the ECJ [2006] ECR I-3969, [2006] QB 764.

[52] See the *Dutch Dykes* case [1996] ECR I-5403, ECJ, cited with approval by Lord Hoffman in *ex p Brown* [1999] JPL 616, HL.

Clearly a decision has to be made in any particular case as to what constitutes 'the **15.23** project'. In most cases, the proposal will be self-contained and its limits will be clear. But there are a number of cases where there is scope for a difference of views as to where 'the project' begins and ends. So, when a developer intends to widen an orbital motorway in different sections, would 'the project' be a particular section or would it be the whole scheme for the entire motorway? A reasonable judgment has to be formed, bearing in mind the primary obligation to ensure that, before consent is given, the decision-making body has before it an assessment of significant likely effects on the environment. Although subsidiary consents can themselves be subject to the Directive, they are unlikely to be of a sufficient scale— seen in isolation from the main scheme—to come within the criteria where an assessment is required.

Are outline applications still possible?

It will be particularly difficult for the competent authority to exercise its judgment **15.24** of what information should be provided when the project is only seeking outline consent. These types of projects are, by their very nature, not fixed in stone at the outset, and yet the authority must judge what the likely significant effects that it will have on the environment are. In some cases, a bare outline application, with no fixed details, will be lawful for the purposes of the planning regime and unlawful for the purposes of the EIA regime

This issue arose recently under the equivalent schedule of the 1988 Regulations **15.25** with regard to the outline application for a large business park in Rochdale, in two successive court cases: *R v Rochdale Metropolitan Borough Council ex p Tew and others* and *R v Rochdale Metropolitan Borough Council ex p Milne and others*.[53] The court agreed with the local objectors that whilst the application met the requirements of the planning regime, a generalized description of the development did not suffice for the purposes of the environmental assessment regime. The description had to contain sufficient detail to enable the main environmental effects and mitigation measures to be identified and assessed. The court did not rule that outline applications cannot continue to be used in these cases, but it is implicit that their usefulness had been severely limited by the need to provide adequate details to satisfy the EIA regime. In *ex p Milne* (sometimes referred to as 'Tew II'), the application survived the challenge. The developer provided the information as to the scale of the development, while reserving design to the reserved matters stage. It was held that sufficient information had now been provided so that the

---

[53] *R v Rochdale MBC ex p Tew and others* [1999] 3 PLR 74, Sullivan J and *R v Rochdale MBC ex p Milne and others* [2001] JPL 470; it is notable that the Council conceded that there had been a breach of the regulations in *R v Waveney DC ex p Bell* [2001] Env LR 465 where there were no details of the design submitted as part of the environmental statement on the bare outline planning application.

likely significant effects on the environment could be assessed. The courts have dealt with it as a matter of fact and degree.[54] The effect of these judgments is strengthened by the more detailed requirements of the 1999 Regulations. The new Circular makes it clear that all the requirements of Schedule 4 must be met, even if an outline planning application is made.[55] Even so, this still appears to take many developers by surprise, for whom the outline application has always been such a flexible friend.

15.26   One way of addressing the issue of how to assess outline permissions is to prescribe a framework within which reserved matters have to be applied for. For example, a Masterplan produced for prescriptive (rather than illustrative) purposes and to which future applications for reserved matters must be related is a method which found favour with the Court in the first *Rochdale* case.[56] The judgment of Sullivan J is especially instructive on what is or is not permissible:

> Recognising, as I do, the utility of the outline application procedure for projects such as this, I would not wish to rule out the adoption of a masterplan approach, provided the masterplan was tied, for example by the imposition of conditions, to the description of the development permitted. If illustrative floorspace or hectarage figures are given, it may be appropriate for an environmental assessment to assess the impact of a range of possible figures before describing the likely significant effects. Conditions may therefore be imposed to ensure that any permitted development keeps within those ranges.

15.27   This judicial guidance was interpreted by the developer and by the Council on the second consideration of the similar business park application so as to require a condition to be imposed on the outline planning permission, to be carried out in substantial accordance with the Masterplan.[57] This approach was accepted by the Court when a further challenge was made, in the second *Rochdale* case [58], as being a legitimate approach notwithstanding that it preserved a degree of flexibility. The key principle is that it is for the decision-maker (whether the local planning authority or the Secretary of State at inquiry) to determine whether what has been

---

[54]   See *Elmbridge BC and others v Secretary of State for the Environment, Transport and the Regions* (2000, November 10), where Richards J reluctantly had to apply *ex p* (see n 33) *Tew* and *ex p Berkeley* in deciding that the Secretary of State's grant of planning permission for a motorway service area was ultra vires the EIA regime. As in *ex p Tew*, a bare outline application with only an 'illustrative masterplan' had been submitted.

[55]   Para 58

[56]   See n 33

[57]   Condition (numbered 1.7) was that 'The development on this site shall be carried out in substantial accordance with the layout included within the Development Framework document submitted as part of the application and as shown on drawing number 97218/150 Revision A dated 22 July 1999, entitled "Masterplan with Building Layouts"'. The reason given for it was 'The layout of the proposed business park is the subject of an environmental impact assessment and any material alteration to the layout may have an impact which has not been assessed by that process'.

[58]   See n 33

provided is sufficient, or whether it preserves too much flexibility. There is no reason why 'a description of the project' for the purposes of the EIA Directive should not recognize that reality. In the case of *R v Weymouth and Portland Borough Council ex p Portland Port Limited and another*[59] the court held that the tying of the masterplan to the description of development can be achieved either through conditions or by a Section 106 Agreement.

However, where it is provided that the consent procedure involves a principal **15.28** decision and others implementing that decision which cannot extend beyond the parameters set by that decision (such as an outline planning permission), the effects that the development may have on the environment must be identified and assessed at the stage of the principal decision.[60] It is only if the effects are not identifiable until the time of the implementing decision that the assessment should be carried out at that later stage.

Indeed, in the second *Rochdale* case, Sullivan J was clear that

> . . . This does not give developers an excuse to provide inadequate descriptions of their projects. It will be for the authority responsible for issuing the development consent to decide whether it is satisfied, given the nature of the project in question, that it has 'full knowledge' of its likely significant effects on the environment. If it considers that an unnecessary degree of flexibility, and hence uncertainty as to the likely significant environmental effects, has been incorporated into the description of the development, then it can require more detail, or refuse consent.

Defining the project in relation to future development

A project or development should not be considered in isolation if 'in reality it **15.29** is properly to be regarded as an integral part of an inevitably more substantial development'. As stated in the Circular, at para 45; 'In general, each application (or request for an opinion) should be considered for EIA on its own merits. The development should be judged on the basis of what is proposed by the developer.' But, as para 46 states '. . . for the purposes of determining whether EIA is required, a particular planning application should not be considered in isolation if, in reality, it is properly to be regarded as an integral part of an inevitably more substantial development'. This issue arose in the case of *Candlish*,[61] where a challenge was made to what was described as a 'Phase 1' development of roads. The judge agreed that the question whether the development is of a category described in either

---

[59] [2001] EWHC Admin 1171. In this case, the Section 106 Agreement required an application for the approval for the development to be in accordance with the Masterplan, the design statement and the environmental statement.

[60] *R (Delena Wells) v Secretary of State* Case C-201/02 [2004] 1 CMLR. 31, ECJ, at para 52.

[61] *R (oao Candlish) v Hastings BC and Hastings* [2005] EWHC 1539, at paras 68 and 69, with reference to *R v Swale Borough Council, ex p RSPB* [1991] JPL 39. This also accorded with the comments of the Advocate–General in the *Naturschutz* case.

schedule must be answered strictly in relation to the development applied for, not any development contemplated beyond that. But he also agreed that a different approach should be taken to 'the further question arising in respect of a Schedule 2 development'—the question whether it 'would be likely to have significant effects on the environment by virtue of factors such as its nature, size or location'. That should be answered rather differently, as the proposal should not then be considered in isolation 'if in reality it is properly to be regarded as an integral part of an inevitably more substantial development'. As he also stated, 'In common sense, moreover, developers could otherwise defeat the object of the regulations by piecemeal development proposals'. The EU has provided some guidance on assessing cumulative effects, over the anticipated lifetime of the project.[62]

15.30 There will be a limit on what is considered to be reasonably linked. In *Portland Port Limited*, the Council Planning Officer's report made reference to future plans for a permanent sailing academy, the possibility of a marina, and possibly an Olympic regatta in 2012 if Britain were to host the Olympics in that year. It was submitted to the court that it was wrong to divide up the scheme into the present and the future when the future was reality rather than fantasy. Unsurprisingly, the Court held that there was no requirement to carry out an environmental assessment of future ambitions.[63]

Identifying a project as 'EIA development'

15.31 As explained above, the 1985 Environmental Assessment Directive distinguishes between projects where environmental assessment is mandatory, listed in Annex I to the Directive, and those projects where an assessment will only be required if the Member State considers that their characteristics so require, listed in Annex II. This division is maintained in the Regulations implementing the Directive in the UK. It should be borne in mind that, despite the very specific nature of the Schedules to the UK Regulations, a need for an EIA may still arise from the wording of the Directive itself. This has often been part of the submissions made by applicants who complain that a project has not been assessed.[64] The 1999 Regulations have tried to avoid this problem recurring, firstly by closely following the wording of the amended Directive itself and, secondly, by stating that the expressions used in the Regulations and in the Directive have the same meaning for the purposes of the Regulations as they do for the purposes of the Directive.[65]

---

[62] *EU Guidelines for Cumulative Effects Assessment 1999* (Hyder for EC DG XI Environment May 1999).

[63] *R v Weymouth and Portland Borough Council ex p Portland Port Limited and another* [2001] EWHC Admin 1171.

[64] Eg *Berkeley v Secretary of State*, over the definition of an 'urban development project'.

[65] Reg 2(3) of the 1999 Regulations—although, arguably, this is the law in any event (see the discussion of indirect and direct effect of European law on UK law in Chapter 4, at paras 4.22 and 4.24).

The EIA Regulations 1999

The Town and Country Planning (Environmental Impact Assessment) (England **15.32**
and Wales) Regulations 1999 ('the 1999 Regulations')[66] apply to development
for which an application for planning permission is received, or which is begun
under permitted development rights, or is subject to a planning enforcement
notice, on or after 14 March 1999. The expressions used in the regulations, such
as 'development', 'planning permission', and 'application', have the same meaning
as they do in the TCPA 1990.[67] The 1999 Regulations adopted the general term
of 'EIA development'[68] to describe all developments where an assessment is
required. EIA development is defined as development of any description mentioned in Schedule 1 to the Regulations, and of any description mentioned in
Schedule 2 which is likely to have significant effects on the environment by virtue
of factors such as its nature, size, or location. All Schedule 1 development will be
EIA development, but not all Schedule 2 development will be. There is a limited
category of 'exempt development'.[69] Guidance upon the Regulations is given, for
England, by DETR Circular 2/99 'Environmental Impact Assessment' and for
Wales by Circular 11/99.[70]

Schedule 1 development

Schedule 1 of the 1999 Regulations sets out the 20 different categories of **15.33**
development for which an environmental impact assessment must be carried out.
These repeat the wording and numbering of Annex I of the 1985 Directive, as
amended by the 1997 Directive. Six of the nine categories in the 1988 Regulations
were extended,[71] and, more importantly, eleven new categories were added. If a
project—or for planning purposes, a 'development'—exceeds the threshold set
out in the Regulations for that category of project then an assessment is required.
Therefore, a waste disposal installation for non-hazardous waste must have a capacity exceeding 100 tonnes per day before the project falls within the description in

---

[66] SI 1999/293. They consolidate the old regulations which applied to planning matters,
including the 1988 Regulations, and re-enact them in line with the new amendments (see n 27
above). These 1999 Regulations have been further amended by SI 2000/2867, SI 2006/3295, SI
2006/3099 (Wales), SI 2008/1556).

[67] The 1999 Regulations, reg 2(2).

[68] Defined in the 1999 Regulations, reg 2(1). The 1988 Regulations simply referred to Sch 1
applications or Sch 2 applications, and did not provide a general term to be used.

[69] Defined in reg 2(1), and used in the definition of Sch 1 and Sch 2 development. The exemptions are limited to projects for national defence purposes or those exceptional specific projects
for which the Secretary of State has made a direction under reg 4(4) that they are exempt (and
has followed the requirement of Art 2(3) of the 1985 Directive).

[70] Revised guidance is due, in the light of the ECJ cases where the UK regime was criticized, in
Cases C-508/03, *Commission v United Kingdom* and C-290-03 *Barker v London Borough of Brent*.

[71] Categories 3 (radioactive waste), 4 (cast-iron and steel works), 6 (integrated chemical
installations), 7 (roads—to include dual carriageways), 8 (ports and harbours), and 9 (special waste
installations—to add landfill).

paragraph 10 of Schedule 1 (for which an EIA is obligatory). By comparison, there is no minimum capacity for hazardous waste installations described in paragraph 9 (so that an EIA is obligatory for all such installations). Similarly, a Schedule 1 project must involve the abstraction of over 10 million cubic metres of groundwater annually (paragraph 11), the keeping of 60,000 hens in intensive conditions (paragraph 17(a)), or, say, developing a quarry with a surface area of over 25 hectares (paragraph 19). However, even if a project falls below the threshold for a Schedule 1 project, it will have to be considered against the criteria set out in Schedule 2 before it can be safely said that no assessment is required. It will also be necessary to consider if a modification to a Schedule 1 project should itself be made subject to an assessment, as explained below. The list of Schedule 1 projects now covers the following types of development, which are more fully described in the Regulations:

1. Crude-oil refineries and installations for the gasification and liquefaction of coal or bituminous shale.
2. Thermal power stations and other combustion installations; and nuclear power stations and other nuclear reactors.
3. Installations designed for the production, processing, or disposal of irradiated nuclear fuel or radioactive waste.[72]
4. Integrated iron, steel, and other metals works.
5. Installations dealing with asbestos.
6. Integrated chemical installations.
7. Construction of long-distance railway lines, airports, motorways, and dual carriageways.
8. Large inland waterways and ports.
9. Waste disposal installations for the incineration, chemical treatment, or landfill of hazardous waste.
10. Waste disposal installations for the incineration or chemical treatment of non-hazardous waste.
11. Groundwater abstraction or artificial groundwater recharge schemes.
12. Works for the transfer of water resources, other than piped drinking water.
13. Waste water treatment plants.
14. Extraction of petroleum and natural gas.
15. Dams and other water storage installations.
16. Pipelines for the transport of gas, oil, or chemicals.
17. Installations for the intensive rearing of poultry or pigs.

---

[72] Note that other installations for the processing and storage of radioactive waste will be caught by Sch 2—not only if they involve development but also if they require an authorization or variation of an authorization under the Radioactive Substances Act 1993 (1999 Regulations, Sch 2, para 3(g)).

18. Industrial plants for wood pulp, paper, and board.
19. Quarries, opencast mining, and peat extraction.
20. Installations for the storage of petroleum, petrochemical, or chemical products.

Schedule 2 development

Whilst Schedule 1 schemes require a mandatory assessment, not all the schemes **15.34** which are listed in Schedule 2 will automatically be 'EIA development'. An individual development, which comes within a category listed in the Schedule, will only be subject to assessment if it is considered likely to have significant effects on the environment by virtue of factors such as its nature, size, or location.[73] While the 1988 Regulations contained only a list of developments and applied this general test, the 1999 Regulations are more specific.

The list of development projects in Schedule 2 of the 1999 Regulations was **15.35** substantially amended and rewritten in comparison to the Schedule in the 1988 Regulations. The list mentions 86 types of projects broken down into 13 categories. Although the categories are not exactly similar to those set out in Annex II of the Directive, the description of the types of projects is broadly the same:

1. Agriculture[74] and 'aquaculture'.[75]
2. Extractive industry. This includes underground mining, dredging, and those quarries not covered by Schedule 1.
3. Energy industry. This includes those installations and storage facilities which fall outside Schedule 1, and even wind farms.[76]
4. Production and processing of metals.[77] This includes iron and steel works, foundries, the assembly of motor vehicles, shipyards, and the manufacture of aircraft and railway equipment.

---

[73] See the definition of what constitutes 'EIA development' in the 1999 Regulations, reg 2(1).

[74] Most agriculture is not 'development' (see Chapter 14 further). But this category can cover greenhouses, irrigation and land drainage, and intensive livestock units (see paras A1–A6 of Annex A of Circular 2/99). Separate regulations have had to be made for those agricultural projects which may have significant environmental effects, but which are not covered by the TCPA 1990.

[75] Better known as fish farming—see para 1(d) of Sch 2. The applicable threshold is that the fish farm must produce more than 100 tonnes of dead weight fish per year. Under the Circular, the same 100 tonne limit is used to indicate where an EIA is more likely and particular attention must be paid to the impacts on the hydrology and ecology of the surrounding area (Para A4 of Annex A).

[76] The exclusive threshold for wind farm developments is 2 turbines, or those structures over 15 metres (para 3(i) of Sch 2). The Circular states that an EIA is more likely if five or more turbines are involved, or more than five megawatts are generated (para A15 of Annex A of Circular 2/99). Particular attention should be paid to the visual and noise impacts.

[77] The exclusive threshold is stated to be for a new floor space which exceeds 1,000 square metres (col 2 of para 4 of Sch 2). The Circular states that an EIA is more likely if the operational

5. Mineral industry. This includes coke ovens, cement manufacture, asbestos, glass making and ceramic products.[78]
6. Chemical industry.[79]
7. Food industry.[80]
8. Textile, leather, wood, and paper industries.[81]
9. Rubber industry.[82]
10. Infrastructure projects. This category brings together a number of developments. It includes those railways, airfields, roads, harbours, waterways, pipelines, coastal works, and groundwater abstraction projects which do not fall within Schedule 1. It also includes industrial estate developments, urban development projects (including shopping centres, car parks, sports stadiums, and leisure centres), and motorway service areas.[83]
11. Other projects. This miscellany includes motor-racing tracks, non-hazardous waste disposal installations,[84] wastewater treatment plants, installations to destroy explosive substances, and even knackers' yards.
12. Tourism and leisure. This is a new category, and includes skiing developments, marinas, holiday villages, theme parks, campsites, and golf courses.[85]
13. Any change or extension of Schedule 1 or Schedule 2 development. This category was previously limited to modifications to Schedule 1 projects only. It also includes any temporary developments which would otherwise fall

---

development covers more than 10 hectares, or the development gives rise to significant discharges of waste, pollutants, or noise. The need for a consent under other environmental protection legislation is not in itself a justification for an EIA to be required (para A16, Annex A of Circular 2/99).

[78] Similar thresholds apply as apply to para 4 (see n 70 above).
[79] Similar thresholds apply as apply to para 4 (see n 70 above).
[80] Similar thresholds apply as apply to para 4 (see n 70 above).
[81] Similar thresholds apply as apply to para 4 (see n 70 above).
[82] Similar thresholds apply as apply to para 4 (see n 70 above).
[83] The exclusive threshold for these last three types is stated to be for a new area of development of 0.5 hectares (col 2 of para 10 of Sch 2). An exclusive threshold of 1 hectare applies to the other projects mentioned, although all coastal works are covered. The indicative thresholds in the Circular vary greatly and are set out at para A17–A30 of Annex A of Circular 2/99. For instance, a business park should be over 20 hectares before an EIA is likely, whilst coastal works need only be over 1 hectare.
[84] The exclusive thresholds refer to the method of disposal—no incinerators are excluded, nor any installation within 100 metres of controlled waters. Otherwise, the development area should exceed 0.5 hectares (col 2 of para 11(b) of Sch 2). The indicative thresholds in the Circular state that an EIA is more likely if the installation would have a capacity of 50,000 tonnes a year, or cover 10 hectares or more. Civic amenity sites and sites handling inert wastes are unlikely to require an EIA (para A36 of Annex A of Circular 2/99). Attention should be paid to the potential impact of discharges, emissions, and odours.
[85] The exclusive threshold is generally set at 1 hectare of new development, although 0.5 hectares applies in the case of holiday villages and theme parks. Marinas should enclose 1,000 square metres of water (col 2 or para 12 of Sch 2). Golf courses are not mentioned in the 1985 Directive, even as amended. The Secretary of State has used his power under s 71A of the TCPA 1990 to include them. New 18-hole courses are likely to require an EIA, whereas development at existing courses is unlikely to do so (para A34, Annex A of Circular 2/99).

within Schedule 1, where the development is mainly undertaken for the testing or development of new materials, and will not last for more than two years. See the discussion on modifications below.

Exclusive thresholds

The 1999 Regulations introduced the use of exclusive thresholds, and specific **15.36** criteria, which are set out in Schedule 2 itself. This Schedule takes the form of a table, where each description of a development category is set out in column 1, with the applicable minimum thresholds and the relevant criteria set out along-side in column 2. A development will not normally be an 'EIA development' if the development is below or does not meet any threshold or criterion in column 2.[86] However, these thresholds and criteria do not apply to Schedule 2 development if it is in a 'sensitive area'. In addition, in order to ensure that each case is assessed individually, all Schedule 2 projects could still require an assessment, under the general selection criteria set out in Schedule 3 of the 1999 Regulations. This use of exclusive thresholds by the UK is in accordance with European law.[87] Note that these exclusive thresholds and criteria are different from the policy thresholds and criteria set out in government guidance which are to be used in deciding whether or not the Schedule 2 development requires an EIA (which are referred to as indicative thresholds).

The Secretary of State may also direct that a particular development described in **15.37** Schedule 2 is EIA development, even if it does not meet the size thresholds or other criteria in Schedule 2 or it is not in a sensitive area.[88]

Development in a 'sensitive area'

The simplest test which can now be applied is to consider whether any part of the **15.38** Schedule 2 development to be assessed is in a 'sensitive area'. If so, there is no need to consider the exclusive thresholds and criteria set out in the schedule and an EIA is required. If the development only adjoins such an area, this test will not apply

---

[86] See the definition of 'Schedule 2 development'in the 1999 Regulations, reg 2(1). The use of exclusive thresholds goes much further than the former practice of only using indicative thresholds in the guidance to the 1988 Regulations. So, in the threshold in Schedule 2 of 1,000 cubic m of new floorspace (in relation to a change or extension to an existing cement works) was considered in *R (Horner) v Lancashire County Council and Castle Cement Ltd* [2005] EWHC 2273. Ouseley J held either that the silo had 'floorspace', albeit not in a normal sense, which was below the 1000 m2 threshold, or that alternatively it did not have any 'floorspace' so could not be above the threshold. The only solution would be to ask the Secretary of State for a direction.

[87] *Berkeley (No.3) v Secretary of State for Environment, Transport and the Regions and LB of Richmond* [2001] EWCA Civ 1012, and see W Upton 'Berkeley (No.3) The use of minimum size thresholds in Environmental Impact Assessment' [2002] 14 JEL 331.

[88] Reg 4(8). A potential application of this power is in respect of the New Forest Heritage Area which is treated by the Secretary of State as a sensitive area even though it is not within the legislative definition (DETR Circular 2/99, para 38).

and the development will have to be considered against the thresholds and criteria set out in the Regulations and the guidance. A 'sensitive area'[89] is defined for the purposes of the 1999 Regulations as:

a) a Site of Special Scientific Interest,

b) land subject to a nature conservation order,

c) land within 2km of a SSSI which has been notified to the LPA for the purpose of consultation with English Nature or the Countryside Council for Wales,

d) a National Park,

e) the Broads,

f) a World Heritage Site,

g) a scheduled ancient monument,

h) an area of outstanding natural beauty,

i) a special protection area, designated and candidate special areas of conservation, and Ramsar sites.[90]

Further development, changes and modifications to development projects

15.39   The EIA Directive does not apply to decisions which involve merely the 'detailed regulation of activities for which the principal consent, raising the substantial environmental issues, has already been given'.[91] On the other hand, it is accepted that the periodic review of an existing permission is to be treated as a new development consent.[92] A more difficult issue is raised where the existing development is modified or changed.

15.40   The modification of a development that has already been carried out is included in Schedule 2 as a possible type of development which may require a separate environmental impact assessment. This is important. The ECJ ruled in the *Dutch Dykes* case that the purpose of the Directive would be undermined if

---

[89]   Defined in the 1999 Regulations, reg 2(1).

[90]   Despite the argument in favour of automatically requiring an EIA for all developments in the areas designated under the Wild Birds Directive and the Habitats Directive, this has been rejected. This is specifically noted in para (10) of the Preamble to the 1997 Environment Assessment Directive.

[91]   [1999] JPL 616 at 621, per Lord Hoffman. Followed, without argument, in *R v Peak District National Park Authority, ex p Bleaklow Industries Ltd* [1999] EGCS 58. But see the discussion on the proper use of conditions below.

[92]   This has arisen in the case of old mineral planning permissions, considered in *R v North Yorkshire County Council, ex p Brown* [1999] JPL 616, HL. See also *Burgemeester en Wethouders van Haarlemmerliede en Spaarnwoude* C-81/96 [1999] Env LR D7, ECJ. The High Court had agreed with the council that the 1991 Act procedure was not the grant of 'development consent' [1997] Env LR 391. The Court of Appeal and the House of Lords disagreed. Whilst the imposition of conditions was not a decision that entitled the developer to proceed, he could not proceed without such determination and this was a necessary condition for his being entitled to proceed at all. This brought the determination within the concept of development consent. Without the imposition of the conditions, there might be a significant effect on the environment.

'modifications to development projects' were so construed as to enable certain works to escape the requirement of an impact assessment even though the works involved were likely to have significant effects on the environment. Under the 1999 Regulations, those modifications where part or all of the works lie within a sensitive area will require an assessment. Otherwise, paragraph 13 of Schedule 2 sets out certain limitations, so that not all changes or extensions to an existing Schedule 1 or Schedule 2 development must be considered. These limitations essentially repeat the exclusive thresholds and criteria which would apply to the main development. For instance, if less than 1,000 square metres of new floor space is added to a crude oil refinery (which itself was a Schedule 1 project) this would not normally require an assessment.[93] The change or extension is considered on its own, as to whether it is likely to have a significant effect on the environment. The criteria and thresholds are not applied to the whole of the development as it is proposed to be modified. Just because a lane of a motorway is widened, this will not require an assessment to be carried out, let alone an assessment of the whole motorway project. By adopting this approach, of isolating the matter under consideration to the change or extension alone, it should not be necessary to define the limits of the underlying 'project'. However, there will come a stage at which the change or extension should be considered as a project in its own right and considered in the normal way. The requirement to assess a change to a project is also linked to the need for development consent. So, a proposal to change the fuel used at a cement manufacturing plant to include some fuels derived from waste tyres did not require an EIA before the Agency could grant the relevant pollution consent, as it did not involve the construction of anything.[94]

Schedule 2—General selection criteria

An additional feature of the 1999 Regulations is the provision in Schedule 3 of **15.41** selection criteria for screening all Schedule 2 development. These criteria must be taken into account by the local authority or the Secretary of State in making the decision that a particular development is EIA development, to the extent to which they are relevant to that specific development.[95]

Schedule 3 of the 1999 Regulations basically repeats the relevant wording of **15.42** Annex III in the amended 1985 Directive. There are three broad criteria to be

---

[93] See sub-para (ii) of the second col of para 13 of Sch 2, which applies the threshold set out at para 6(a) (chemical industry) to changes or extensions to projects under para 1 (crude oil refineries) of Sch 1. Of course, the general criteria under Sch 3 of the 1999 Regulations will still need to be considered.

[94] *R (Edwards) v Environment Agency and Others* [2008] UKHL 22 (notable also for its consideration of public consultation requirements); whilst the introduction of tyre burning was a 'change' in the manner of operating an installation, and could constitute a 'project' within Art.1.2 of the Directive, it did not require 'development consent' (*R v Environment Agency Ex p Gibson* [1999] Env LR 73 and *R v Durham CC Ex p Lowther* [2001] EWCA Civ 781 considered).

[95] Reg 4(5).

used in assessing whether a particular project is likely to have a significant effect on the environment: the characteristics of the development, its location, and the characteristics of the potential impact. The development's characteristics include, but are not limited to, its size, its cumulative effect with other development, the use of natural resources, the production of waste, pollution, and nuisances, and the risk of accidents. The environmental sensitivity of the location includes considering the existing land use, the relative abundance, quality, and regenerative capacity of the natural resources in the area, and the 'absorption capacity' of the natural environment.[96] The potential impact is to be assessed in relation to these criteria, and in particular to the extent of the impact, its trans-frontier nature, its magnitude and complexity, its probability and its duration, frequency, and reversibility.

Government guidance on Schedule 2

15.43 Circular 2/99 seeks to provide guidance on which developments under Schedule 2 will require an assessment. It states that the basic question to be asked, which derived from Article 2.1 of the 1985 Directive, is 'Would this particular development be likely to have significant effects on the environment?'[97] The guidance indicates that an assessment will be needed in three main types of case:[98]

a) major developments which are of more than local importance;
b) developments proposed for particularly environmentally sensitive or vulnerable locations;
c) developments with unusually complex and potentially hazardous environmental effects (for example, possible complex, long-term, or irreversible impacts or release of hazardous contaminants from contaminated land).

Guidance on the use of indicative criteria and thresholds

15.44 The Circular stresses that because of the range of potential Schedule 2 projects it is not possible to lay down quantified criteria for identifying those projects which warrant assessment. However, Appendix A of the Circular sets out indicative thresholds and criteria for development in Schedule 2 to assist in determining whether EIA development is proposed. The criteria and thresholds listed in Annex A of the new Circular 2/99 are notably more cautious than those contained in the

---

[96] This absorption capacity includes paying particular attention to wetlands, coastal zones, mountains and forest parks, nature reserves, classified nature conservation sites, areas in which the European environmental quality standards have been exceeded, densely-populated areas, and landscapes of historical, cultural, or archaeological significance (as set out in Sch 3, paras 2(c)(i)–(viii)). Size cannot be the sole criterion (*Commission v Ireland* C–392/96, The Times 19 October 1999, ECJ).

[97] Para 18 of Circular 2/99.

[98] Circular 2/99, para 33. These are identical to the tests previously contained in Circular 15/88, at para 20.

original 1988 Circular. Much more care and attention will need to be spent on every application. The Circular itself states that there is no universal test and that projects must be considered on a case-by-case basis.[99] The introductory paragraph to Annex A itself stresses their indicative nature and that the location of the development is of crucial importance. The more environmentally sensitive the location, the lower will be the actual threshold at which significant effects can be said to be likely. In the *Dutch Dykes* case discussed above, the ECJ recognized that Member States could establish criteria or thresholds for Annex II projects such that all projects of a certain class would be exempted in advance from the requirement of an assessment. But the Member State would exceed the limit of its discretion and thereby be subject to control by the Court, unless all projects excluded could, when viewed as a whole, be regarded as not being likely to have significant effects on the environment. The British Government has avoided this risk by putting forward only indicative thresholds and criteria and leaving the ultimate decision to case-by-case examination. The 1997 Directive allows for both approaches and for a combination of the two.[100]

D. Deciding Whether an Environmental Impact Assessment is Required

The initial screening

In many cases, a formal environmental statement is submitted by an applicant **15.45** with a planning application without being formally requested.[101] The development will then be treated as an 'EIA development'.[102] Otherwise, the burden lies with the LPA and, in certain circumstances, the Secretary of State. They are obliged to consider whether development is 'EIA development'. If a planning application is submitted for Schedule 1 or 2 development without an environmental statement, and no 'screening opinion' or 'screening direction' has yet been made, the LPA must adopt a 'screening opinion'.[103] This is a formal statement whether or not the proposed development is EIA development. If the LPA wishes

---

[99] Para 43 of the main text of the Circular.

[100] Art 4 of the 1985 Directive as substituted by Art 1.6 of the 1997 Directive.

[101] The requirements of the Regulations will then apply (reg 4(2)(a)). The application must be stated to be for the purposes of the Regulations—otherwise the statement will not have any formal status and the planning authority will still need to determine if an assessment is required.

[102] This is subject to any contrary direction by the Secretary of State under reg 4(3). Such direction is very unlikely: rejecting a submitted environmental statement as unnecessary is likely to spark developer concern and third-party challenge.

[103] reg 7.

to delegate that decision to an officer, it must do so formally.[104] When the authority, or the Secretary of State, decides that a development is EIA development, they must clearly and precisely give their full reasons for this decision.[105] The current position in UK law is that reasons do not have to be given for refusing to direct that an EIA is required,[106] and this issue has been referred to the ECJ.[107]

15.46 The Courts have accepted that the interpretation of Schedules 1 and 2 is an issue of law, and not simply a matter of reasonable judgement.[108] On the other hand, it will be a matter of judgment whether or not the environmental effects are likely to be significant, so that localized adverse environmental effects might be insufficient in the circumstances.[109]

15.47 It is arguable that mitigation measures should not be taken into account at the screening stage, and that these are part of the environmental assessment process once it has been identified that the project is likely to have significant environmental effects.[110] The UK courts have not adopted such an approach,[111] and have so far accepted that the extent to which remedial measures can be taken into account in screening decisions depends on the facts of each individual development.

---

[104] *R v St Edmundsbury Borough Council, ex p Walton* [1999] 3 PLR 51, [1999] ELR 869. In contrast, no express delegation is needed for a junior minister or civil servant to exercise the powers of the Secretary of State (*Carltona v Commissioners of Works* [1943] 2 All ER 560).

[105] The 1999 Regulations,reg 4(6). This then allows the applicant to consider whether or not he should challenge this decision.

[106] See *R v Secretary of State for the Environment, Transport and the Regions ex p Marson* [1998] Env LR 761, CA (on an application for permission to appeal). Permission to appeal to the House of Lords was refused. This has been followed by the English Courts since then, see *R v St Edmundsbury BC Ex p Walton* [1999] Env LR 879 per Hooper J; *BAA plc v Secretary of State for Transport, Local Government and the Regions* [2002] EWHC 1920; [2003] JPL 610; *Gillespie v First Secretary of State* [2003] EWHC 8; [2003] 1 P & CR 30 A decision that a Schedule 2 development is not likely to have significant effect on the environment will still need to be recorded (reg 20).

[107] See *R (Christopher Mellor) v Secretary of State for Communities and Local Government* [2008], reference made by the CA. The Secretary of State had determined that EIA was not required on a planning application for a medium secure hospital unit in North Yorkshire.

[108] *R (Goodman) v Lewisham LBC* [2003] EWCA Civ 140. The Courts will therefore be more inclined to intervene.

[109] *R (Malster) v Ipswich Borough Council* (2002) PLCR 251 CA—although this was a decision on a permission hearing only, it was considered good law (and distinguished) in *Goodman*.

[110] See the cases of *Catt* (see n 111), and *Littlewood* [2008] EWHC—where the argument has not (yet) succeeded.

[111] *Gillespie v First Secretary of State and Bellway Urban Renewal* [2003] EWCA Civ 400, (2003) Env LR 30. The Secretary of State had considered that there was no need for an EIA, and approved the development subject to conditions to carry out a detailed site examination to establish the nature, extent and degree of the site contamination and to remediate it prior to commencement of the development. The Court of Appeal held that on considering whether an environmental impact assessment was required before planning permission could be granted, the Secretary of State did not have to ignore proposed remediation measures but could not assume that in a case of any complexity they would be successfully implemented. The Court of Appeal has backed way from this in *R (Catt) v Brighton BC* [2007] EWCA Civ 298 and adopted a more general approach.

As the government has noted,[112] this will be done with regard to: the extent of the investigation into the impact of the development and environmental problems arising from it, up to the time of the screening decision; the nature of the proposed remedial measures including uncertainties; the extent to which those have been particularized; their complexity; the prospects of their successful implementation; the prospect of adverse environmental effects in the course of the development, even if of a temporary nature; the final effect of the development. However, the LPA needs to ensure that the planning conditions designed to mitigate the likely effects of a proposed development are not used as a substitute for environmental impact assessment or to circumvent the requirements of the EIA Directive.[113]

In order to avoid any possible uncertainties and unforeseen delays, a potential **15.48** developer may ask the LPA for a 'screening opinion'.[114] This request can be made before the planning application is submitted, and the applicant is only required to provide limited details of his proposed development.[115] The authority will consider firstly whether it meets the Schedule 1 or 2 criteria and, if it is within Schedule 2, whether it is likely to have significant effects on the environment. If the authority fails to determine the request within three weeks (or any longer agreed period), or decides that it is EIA development, the potential developer may 'appeal' to the Secretary of State by requesting a 'screening direction'.[116] If a screening direction or an unchallenged screening opinion determines that proposed development is EIA development, then an environmental statement will have to be submitted with a planning application. The preparation of the statement in such circumstances can delay the submission of the planning application itself considerably. Where a developer is about to carry out development which would normally be permitted development he can seek an opinion from the LPA as to

---

[112] The 'Note on environmental impact assessment directive for local planning authorities' (published on the Defra website).

[113] The 'Note on environmental impact assessment directive for local planning authorities' (published on the Defra website), with reference to *R (oao Lebus) v South Cambridgeshire DC* [2003] 2 PLR 5. This involved development for an egg production unit to house 12,000 free range chickens. The LPA officers had concluded that the potential adverse impacts of the development would be insignificant with proper conditions and management under enforceable under Section 106 planning obligations. The Court held that 'it is not appropriate for a person charged with making a screening decision to start from the premise that although there may be significant impacts, these can be reduced to insignificance by the application of conditions of various kinds. The appropriate course in such a case is to require an environmental statement and the measures which it is said will reduce their significance.'

[114] 1999 Regulations, reg 5. The 'screening'process also existed under the 1988 Regulations (reg 5), although it was not given this name.

[115] Although an applicant should ideally provide as much information as possible, and, to make representations, he or she is only required to provide a plan sufficient to identify the land, a brief description of the nature and purpose of the development, and its possible effects on the environment (reg 5(1) and (2)).

[116] reg 5(6).

whether the development is EIA development.[117] If the information then emerges that the application does require an EIA, the LPA will not be able to change its screening opinion. The only way to address this anomaly is for the LPA, or an interested party, to request a screening direction from the Secretary of State before any decision is taken on the application.[118]

15.49   If the planning application is 'called in' by the Secretary of State, or the refusal of the planning application is appealed to him, and it appears that it may be EIA development, he must make a 'screening direction'.[119] If the matter arises during the course of a planning appeal, the Inspector will be obliged to refer the matter to the Secretary of State for such a direction. The Secretary of State also has a supervisory role, and he has the power to make a direction that Schedule 2 development is EIA development at any time in the planning process.[120]

15.50   It is open to a prospective developer to 'volunteer' an environmental statement and either expressly accept that it is submitted in accordance with the Regulations, in which case the procedure set out in the Regulations will apply to it, or leave it to the authority to decide whether formal consideration of environmental information is needed. If it decides it is and the developer agrees then again the provisions of the Regulations apply. If the authority decides a formal environmental assessment is not warranted, it must still consider the information provided by the developer in so far as it is material to its decision on the application but the formal procedures of the Regulations will not apply to the determination. If the authority decides formal consideration of environmental information is needed but the developer does not agree then again he may seek a direction from the Secretary of State on the matter.

The environmental effects on other countries

15.51   The 1997 Directive requires the UK to establish procedures to ensure that consultation is carried out with other Member States of the European Union where a development is likely to have significant effects on the environment of that country.[121] This also applies to countries outside the European Union which

---

[117] Ibid, reg 35(3).

[118] See *Fernback and others v Harrow LBC* [2001]. The Court held that a 'negative' screening opinion issued by an LPA did not determine whether an application for planning permission was 'EIA Development', but a 'positive' one by the LPA was determinative. On the other hand, an opinion by the Secretary of State, either way, is determinative.

[119] Ibid, regs 8, 9. This ought to avoid the issue of whether an environmental statement is required arising during a public inquiry (eg the Kohlerdome stadium proposal for Luton Town Football Club in 1996 where the call in inquiry was adjourned after several weeks of evidence) or after determination (eg *Berkeley v Secretary of State for the Environment* [1998] Env LR 741).

[120] Town and Country Planning (General Development Procedure) Order 1995, SI 1995/419, art 14(2) as substituted by the 1999 Regulations, reg 35(8).

[121] 1999 Regulations, regs 26–28, in order to implement Art 7 of the amended 1985 Directive. See also paras 115–118 of Circular 2/99.

have ratified the Espoo Convention, which deals with the trans-boundary effects of projects.[122] This has the potential for considerable complications. However, the decision on whether or not to consult other countries lies with the Secretary of State. As the Circular states, such cases will be 'rare in England' and Wales, so these provisions may be of little everyday relevance. For the moment, those projects which affect Scotland or Wales or England as well as the home country fall outside these provisions, but consultation with the relevant authorities in those countries will doubtless be essential.

E. The Contents of the Environmental Statement

The prescribed contents

There is no prescribed form that an Environmental Statement ('ES'), which is   **15.52** produced as a result of the requirement for Environmental Impact Assessment, must take. However, it must be contained in a single, accessible document, accompanied by a non-technical summary.[123] The Government has produced a Good Practice Guide,[124] in addition to the advice contained in Circular 2/99. As a matter of law, all that is required is that the applicant must provide an 'environmental statement' as it is defined in the Regulations. The definition contained in the 1999 Regulations[125] states that an environmental statement must 'at least' include the information referred to in Part II of Schedule 4, and some of the information referred to in Part I of Schedule 4. Part II in effect repeats the provisions of Article 5(3) of the amended Directive, namely that an ES must provide:

1. A description of the development comprising information on the site, design, and size of the development.
2. A description of the measures envisaged in order to avoid, reduce and, if possible, remedy significant adverse effects.

---

[122] The UNECE Convention on Environmental Impact Assessment in a Trans-boundary Context ('the Espoo Convention') (Cm 1645).

[123] The failure in *Berkeley v Secretary of State for the Environment* [2001] 2 AC 603, HL, was that the alleged environmental statement had to be pieced together from a number of documents emanating from different sources. This is not to say that the EIA cannot run to many volumes.

[124] *Preparation of Environmental Statements for Planning Projects that Require Environmental Assessment—A Good Practice Guide* (HMSO, 1995) remains extant. The EU has also produced some guidance.

[125] Contained in the list of general definitions in reg 2(1). The requirement is similar to that which was required under the 1988 Planning Regulations (under Sch 3), that a statement must contain the 'specified information' and might include further information on the matters listed 'by way of explanation and amplification'.

3. The data required to identify and assess the main effects which the development is likely to have on the environment.

4. An outline of the main alternatives studied by the applicant or appellant and an indication of the main reasons for his choice, taking into account the environmental effects.

5. A non-technical summary of the information provided under paragraphs 1 to 4.

15.53 In addition, the Environmental Statement must include some of the information referred to in Part I of Schedule 4. This requirement is subject to two general limitations set out in the statutory definition itself.[126] Firstly, the applicant must include such of the information as is 'reasonably required to assess the environmental effect of the development'. Secondly, the applicant is only expected to provide such information as he can be 'reasonably required to compile' having regard in particular to current knowledge and methods of assessment. This requirement lies at the heart of the assessment process, and underlies the importance of the ability of an applicant to limit the scope of the statement by first obtaining a 'scoping decision' from the authority.[127] Where the applicant requests information for the purposes of EIA from the LPA, and bodies such as the Environment Agency, English Nature, and the Countryside Agency, they must make it available to him.[128] The matters for possible inclusion in the ES under these Part I requirements in effect repeat those set out in Annex IV of the amended 1985 Directive. They are:

1. Description of the development, including in particular:
   a) a description of the physical characteristics of the whole development and the land-use requirements during the construction and operational phases;
   b) a description of the main characteristics of the production processes, for instance, nature and quantity of the materials used;
   c) An estimate, by type and quantity, of expected residues and emissions (water, air, and soil pollution; noise, vibration, light, heat, radiation, etc) resulting from the operation of the proposed development.

2. An outline of the main alternatives studied by the applicant or appellant and an indication of the main reasons for his choice, taking into account the environmental effects.[129]

---

[126] This is in accordance with the amended Art 5(1) of the 1985 Directive.

[127] Although an environmental statement is not invalid if it does not meet the requirements set out in a scoping decision, it is likely to be subject to requests for further information (as pointed out in Circular 2/99, para 95).

[128] The 1999 Regulations, reg 22. But they can make a reasonable charge for providing the information (see Circular 2/99, paras 98 and 99).

[129] This is a new addition, although the spirit of the 1985 Directive would have required the statement to mention it.

3. A description of the aspects of the environment likely to be significantly affected by the development, including, in particular, population, fauna, flora, soil, water, air, climatic factors, material assets, including the architectural and archaeological heritage, landscape, and the interrelationship between the above factors.

4. A description of the likely significant effects of the development on the environment, which should cover the direct effects and any indirect, secondary, cumulative, short, medium and long-term, permanent and temporary, positive and negative effects of the development, resulting from:
   a) the existence of the development;
   b) the use of natural resources;
   c) the emission of pollutants, the creation of nuisances, and the elimination of waste, and
   d) the description by the applicant of the forecasting methods used to assess the effects on the environment.

5. A description of the measures envisaged to prevent, reduce, and where possible offset any significant adverse effects on the environment.

6. A non-technical summary of the information provided in accordance with this part of the schedule.

7. An indication of any difficulties (technical deficiencies or lack of know-how) encountered by the applicant in compiling the required information.

The required level of detail

The requirements of this Schedule do not provide those involved with much **15.54** certainty about the level of detail that is required. Whilst there are a number of matters listed in Part II which must be provided, the bulk of the environmental statement will only cover the details of the assessment process so far as this is 'reasonably required'. The courts have decided that any challenge to the actual contents of an Environmental Statement (ES) is really a *Wednesbury* unreasonableness point.[130] Further, the Developer is only expected to assess those points which are likely to have a *significant* impact on the environment, not to assess *all* the potential impacts.[131]

Requests for further information

Where the authority or the Secretary of State consider that further information is **15.55** required, it or he can ask the developer in writing to provide it.[132] It is a formal

---

[130] *R (oao Jones) v Mansfield DC* [2003] EWCA Civ 1408, [2004] Env LR 21.

[131] See, for instance, the judgment of Sullivan J in *Tew* at 98B: '... the environmental statement does not have to describe every environmental effect, however minor, but only the "main effects" or "likely significant effects"'.

[132] Reg 19.

process, and the Circular encourages the authorities to only use their powers to request information which is necessary to complete the statement, and not to obtain clarification or non-substantial information.[133] The request must also be publicized, and the time period for making the decision may be considerably delayed.[134] The developer must provide the information, and there is no statutory mechanism by which he or she can appeal against the request. If the developer does not provide the further information under the 1999 Regulations, or if what is provided is still not considered to be adequate, the authority will refuse the planning application to which it is attached.[135] However, there is an additional power for the planning authority to require the applicant to produce evidence to verify any information in the environmental statement.[136] This is in addition to the power to request further details of reserved matters on an outline planning application.[137]

15.56 Government guidance puts the obligation to consider further information in stronger terms than the Circular,[138] that the LPA is responsible for evaluating the ES to ensure it addresses all of the relevant environmental issues and that the information is presented accurately, clearly and systematically. It should be prepared to challenge the findings of the ES if it believes they are not adequately supported by scientific evidence. If it believes that key issues are not fully addressed, or not addressed at all, it *must* request further information. The authority has to ensure that it has in its possession *all* relevant environmental information about the likely significant environmental effects of the project *before it* makes its decision whether to grant planning permission. It is too late to address the issues after planning permission has been granted.

Limiting the scope of the assessment

15.57 While the required contents set out in Schedule 4 will assist in defining what areas should be considered in general, the 1985 Directive and the 1988 Regulations

---

[133] See paras 110–112 of Circular 2/99.

[134] Reg 19(7)—the determination is delayed until 14 days after the further information requested has been sent to all persons to whom the statement was sent (or 21 days if there has been a local newspaper advertisement). This is to allow for further representations to be received.

[135] Under the 1999 Regulations, reg 3, the authority will take the lack of environmental information into account in its determination under the TCPA 1990. Note that the environmental statement cannot be considered to be invalid because of inadequate information—the authority is still under a duty to determine the application. If the LPA does delay making a decision at all, the developer can appeal against the non-determination.

[136] Reg 19(10). This request is subject to the requirements of reasonableness. The publicity requirements set out in the Regulations with regard to request for further information do not apply.

[137] Under the Town and Country Planning (General Development Procedure) Order 1995, SI 1995/419, art 3(2).

[138] The 'Note on environmental impact assessment directive for local planning authorities' (published on the Defra website).

gave little specific guidance.[139] Whilst informal discussions and consultation are encouraged, under the provisions of the 1999 Regulations, the developer can now ask the LPA for a 'scoping opinion' as to the information to be provided before submitting the environment statement.[140] This allows the developer to be clear about what the LPA considers the main effects of the development are likely to be and, therefore, the topics on which the environmental statement should focus. This request can be submitted at the same time as a request for a screening opinion, and the same information must be submitted.[141] The authority is not otherwise under an obligation to give its opinion on the scope of the proposed statement.

The authority should consult the developer and the consultation bodies.[142] If no **15.58** scoping opinion is adopted within five weeks of the request, or any longer period agreed in writing, then the developer may apply to the Secretary of State for a scoping direction.[143] But there is no right of appeal against the terms of the opinion or direction, and the opinion really only acts as a guideline. The authorities can still use their powers to request further information, both as regards the environmental statement and as regards the planning application, if necessary, and should keep the scope under review.

F. The Use of the Environmental Statement in the Consent Decision

When it comes to the decision on the application, the Environmental Statement **15.59** is only part of that process. The LPA must consider 'environmental information' which is defined as meaning 'the environmental statement, including any further information, any representations made by any body required by these Regulations to be invited to make representations, and any representations duly made by any other person about the environmental effects of the development'.[144] The bottom line is that, where an ES has been submitted,[145]

---

[139] There was encouragement for discussions about the scope of the assessment between the developer and the authority, and the booklet on Environmental Assessment provided a checklist of issues (Appendix 4 of *Environmental Assessment: A Guide to Procedures* (HMSO, 1989)).

[140] 1999 Regulations, reg 10—which implements Art 5(2) of the 1985 Directive, as amended. See also the EU Scoping Guidance.

[141] The 1999 Regulations, reg 10.

[142] These bodies are defined in reg 2(1) as those who would normally be consulted on a planning application, and must include the principal council for the area, the Countryside Commission, the Nature Conservancy Council (or the Countryside Council for Wales), and the Environment Agency.

[143] reg 10(7).

[144] As defined in reg 2(1).

[145] The EIA Regulations 1999, reg 3(2).

The relevant planning authority or the Secretary of State or an inspector shall not grant planning permission pursuant to an application to which this regulation applies unless they have first taken the environmental information into consideration, and they shall state they have done so.

15.60 The Environmental Statement is part of the decision-making process. Even if the ES is deficient in a number of respects, the LPA is not deprived of jurisdiction unless the ES is so deficient that it cannot be described as an ES as defined by the Regulations.[146] The process of publicity for the ES and public consultation gives those persons who consider that the ES is inaccurate or inadequate or incomplete an opportunity to point out those deficiencies. There must be sufficient information about the proposed development to enable any likely significant environmental effects to be identified.

15.61 Where permission is granted, the planning authority must ensure that conditions or restrictions are attached so that the scheme which is brought forward for approval at reserved matters stage does not differ significantly from that which has been approved. It was acknowledged in *Maureen Smith*[147] that it is certainly possible to leave the final details of (for example a landscaping scheme) to be clarified either in the context of a reserved matter where outline planning consent has been granted, or by virtue of a condition where full planning consent has been given. But the LPA cannot use conditions to avoid assessing the likely significant environmental effects. In *Hardy*,[148] the grant of permission was quashed as the LPA could not conclude that there would be no environmental effects until further surveys on the presence of protected bats had been done. If the LPA lacks an important piece of information in order to assess whether significant effects are likely, it cannot leave that matter to be ascertained later under a condition after planning permission has been granted. This has not changed in the light of *Barker*. As the House of Lords stated, the first recital in the EIA Directive indicates that the competent authority must take account of the effects on the environment of the project in question at the earliest possible stage in all the technical planning and decision-making processes. In the case of a Schedule 2 development the

---

[146] *R (Blewett) v Derbyshire County Council* [2004] Env LR 29, per Sullivan J at 41 and 68. The Court of Appeal dismissed the appeal against the judgment, [2004] Env LR 15, but did not have to consider the EIA points.

[147] At para 28.

[148] *R v Cornwall County Council, ex p Hardy* [2001] Env LR 473; Preliminary surveys had identified the possible presence of bats (a European protected species) and the nature conservation authorities had recommended further surveys. This point remains even where it will be possible to carry out an EIA of such matters at the reserved matters stage of the planning process. Note that part of Harrison J's reasoning in *Hardy* was based on the fact that assessing the impact on the bats could not be delayed as no EIA would then be possible (see paras 69–72).

competent authority must decide at the outset whether an EIA is needed because the development is likely to have significant effects on the environment.[149]

Whilst it is permissible for the decision-maker to contemplate the likely decisions that others will take in relation to the details of the development, such as an Environmental Permit, the decision-maker is not entitled to leave the assessment of likely impact to a future occasion simply because he contemplates that the future decision-maker will act competently. Constraints must be placed on the planning permission within which future details can be worked out, and the decision-maker must form a view about the likely details and their impact on the environment.[150] **15.62**

G. Possible Challenges

Public participation

Members of the public, including pressure groups and other organizations, can play an important part in the EIA process. As Lord Hoffman said in *Berkeley*:[151] **15.63**

> The Directive requires not merely that the planning authority should have the necessary information, but that it should have been obtained by means of a particular procedure, namely that of an EIA. And an essential element in this procedure is that what the Regulations call the 'environmental statement' by the developer should have been 'made available to the public' and that the public should have been 'given the opportunity to express an opinion' in accordance with article 6(2) of the Directive.

The competent authority cannot give development consent to the project without taking the views of the public, as well as other authorities, into account. The public must be informed of the decision taken, and, now, also of the main reasons for that decision. In order to assist this participation, the environmental statement must be publicized and the public concerned must be given an opportunity to have their views heard before the development consent is granted.[152] **15.64**

---

[149] *R v London Borough of Bromley ex p Barker* [2006] UKHL 52, at paras 22 to 24, citing *Wells* (para 51). It will be possible to justify an EIA later, if it does not become apparent until a later stage in the multi-stage consent process that the project is likely to have significant effects on the environment (as the European Court said in para 48 of its judgment). This may be because the need for an EIA was overlooked at the outline stage, or it may be because a detailed description of the proposal to the extent necessary to obtain approval of reserved matters has revealed that the development may have significant effects on the environment that were not anticipated earlier.

[150] *Maureen Smith*, para 33

[151] *Berkeley v Secretary of State for the Environment* [2001] 2 AC 603 at 615.

[152] This is a specific part of the EIA regime—see Art 6(2) and (3) of the 1985 Directive, both in its original form and as amended by the 1997 Directive.

The new Circular also states that the information provided should be properly understood by the public as well as by the competent authorities.[153] The environmental statement will either be publicized as part of the notification procedure on the planning application, or it will be separately publicized if it is submitted at a later date.[154] Copies of the statement and all other relevant decisions must be placed on the planning register along with the particulars of the planning applications.[155] The applicant must make available a reasonable number of copies of the statement, both for inspection by the public and so that they can acquire a copy at a reasonable charge.[156] This is in addition to the requirement to provide copies to the LPA and the consultation bodies. In a glorious acknowledgement of the importance of public participation, Lord Hoffman in *Berkeley*[157] stated that, under the EIA regime:

> The directly enforceable right of the citizen...is not merely a right to a fully informed decision on the substantive issue. It must have been adopted on an appropriate basis and that requires the inclusive and democratic procedure prescribed by the Directive in which the public, however misguided or wrongheaded its views may be, is given an opportunity to express its opinion on the environmental issues.[158]

The requirement to provide a non-technical summary

15.65 The Environmental Statement can become very technical and run to several large volumes of information and analysis. It is an important part of the process that the public can understand what has been submitted, in 'accessible plain English'.[159] The 1985 Directive therefore provided that a non-technical summary must be submitted as part of the Environmental Statement. The lack of a proper non-technical summary may jeopardize the ability of interested parties to respond to the consultation process and to make adequate representations to the decision-maker. Copies of the summary are part of the Environmental Statement and must be publicized as part of it. In theory, therefore, a reasonable charge could be made for providing the public with copies, although the Circular does encourage applicants to make copies available free of charge.[160]

---

[153] Para 9 of Circular 2/99.

[154] Regs 13, 14, and 16. A reasonable number of copies must be available to the public, and any charge for them must be reasonable (regs 17, 18).

[155] Reg 20(1). Where a screening or scoping decision has been made before the planning application is made (and so nothing is yet registered), these documents must be made available at the same place as the planning register and kept for two years (reg 20(2)).

[156] Regs 17 and 18, and see paras 100 and 101 of Circular 2/99.

[157] *Berkeley v Secretary of State for the Environment* [2001] 2 AC 603.

[158] These words have an echo at the ECJ as well—that "however misguided and wrongheaded the public's views may be, they must be given an opportunity to express their opinions on the environmental issues arising from a project'(Advocate-General Elmer in the case of *EC Commission v Federal Republic of Germany* (Case C-431/92) [1995] ECR I- 2819, para 35).

[159] Para 85 of Circular 2/99.

[160] Para 105 of Circular 2/99.

Reasons for the decision

As part of the reforms of the 1985 Directive, the competent authorities are required **15.66** to give their reason for the decisions they make on an EIA application. In particular, the 1999 Regulations require that the planning authority provides a statement containing the content of the decision, the conditions, 'the main reasons and considerations on which the decision is based', and a description of the main mitigation measures where necessary.[161] The decision must also be publicized, although this does not include a requirement that the whole statement is published. The LPA must inform the Secretary of State of the decision, and the public, normally by publishing a notice in a local newspaper. This is in addition to the requirement for UK planning authorities to give their reasons for refusing or granting planning permission. The 1999 EIA Circular suggests that the planning officer's report to the committee which takes the decision should normally meet the necessary requirements for the statement.[162]

Challenges through the courts

Any challenge to the validity of decisions for alleged want of compliance with the **15.67** Directive should be made by way of judicial review or as part of the statutory appeal process. While the point has a certain political impact, the courts have rightly refused to accept that the failure to provide an assessment is a proper defence to an action for possession of land which has been compulsorily acquired for the project.[163] If the court finds that there has been illegality in the decision, the court's discretion to decline to quash the decision is fairly circumscribed. Where there is an EIA point, the court has a narrow discretion to decline to quash the decision, so long as the particular breach of the regulations could not be described as trivial.[164] The error is not capable of a later cure (unlike, say, the

---

[161] Reg 21(1)(c). If the decision is taken by the Secretary of State or one of his inspectors, they must provide the LPA with this statement (reg 21(2)). The list of matters to be covered repeats that in the Directive (Art 9(1)). The old version of Art 9 of the 1985 Directive only required an authority to give its reasons 'where the Member States 'legislation so provides'.

[162] See the very brief comment at para 127 of Circular 2/99.

[163] *Secretary of State for Transport v Haughian* [1997] Env LR 59—the Court of Appeal held that even if there had been a failure to comply with the requirements of the Directive, the Crown's title to the land for the controversial Newbury Bypass (acquired by compulsory purchase order) was voidable only and was good against mere trespassers on the land.

[164] Lord Bingham observed in *Berkeley v Secretary of State for the Environment* [2001] 2 AC 603 at 608 that 'Even in a purely domestic context, the discretion of the court to do other than quash the relevant order or action where such excessive exercise of power is shown is very narrow. In the Community context, unless a violation is so negligible as to be truly de minimis and the prescribed procedure has in all essentials been followed, the discretion (if any exists) is narrower still: the duty laid on member states by Article 10 of the EC Treaty, the obligation of national courts to ensure that Community rights are fully and effectively enforced [and various particular points on the EIA Directive] . . . all point towards an order to quash as the proper response to a contravention such as

failure to publish reasons after the decision is issued). However, the substantial compliance may still be sufficient—so that it will not be sufficient to show that there has been a procedural error in the EIA process. A claimant will have to show that its interests had been substantially prejudiced by that failure.[165] Indeed, in *Edwards*,[166] the House of Lords was satisfied that it would have exercised its discretion not to quash the decision, as although there was no requirement for an EIA for the changes made to the cement works, regarding the burning of waste fuels, there had been substantial compliance in any event.

---

admittedly occurred in this case.' See eg *R v Waveney DC ex p Bell* [2001] Env LR 24, clear failure to submit a valid and complete EIA, applying *Berkeley*. A trivial example is where the decision to grant permission was taken a few hours before the consultation period closed, and no representations were received after the decision (*R (Wembley Fields Ltd) v Brent LBC* [2005] EWHC 2978 (Admin)).

[165] *Younger Homes (Northern) Ltd v (1) First Secretary of State (2) Calderdale Metropolitan District Council* (2004) 30/6/2004, CA—Y failed to show that it had been substantially prejudiced, and its challenge failed—*R (on the application of Richardson) v North Yorkshire CC* [2004] JPL 911 applied (the failure to provide a statement containing the main reasons for the decision could be remedied by placing a substitute Notice of Decision on the appropriate register), *Berkeley v Secretary of State for the Environment* [2001] 2 AC 603 distinguished.

[166] *R (Edwards) v Environment Agency and others* [2008] UKHL 22, at para 58, 72, 81.

Part IV

THE COMMON LAW

16

COMMON LAW LIABILITY FOR ENVIRONMENTAL DAMAGE

A. **Introduction**	16.01	Rights to water	16.75
B. **Nuisance**	16.04	Contractual liabilities	16.76
Introduction	16.04	H. **Civil Liability of the**	
Types of private nuisance	16.05	**Regulatory Authorities**	16.77
Nuisance by physical damage or		General considerations	16.77
encroachment	16.06	Damages for maladministration	16.78
Nuisance by interference with the		Liability in negligence	16.79
enjoyment of land	16.08	Liability for negligent operational	
Who may sue in private nuisance?	16.11	or policy decisions	16.81
Responsibility for the nuisance	16.12	Liability for negligent	
The wrongdoer	16.12	inspection and regulation	16.82
The occupier	16.13	Liability for the public	
The landlord	16.15	authority's decision not to act	16.85
The concept of the reasonable user	16.17	Nuisances created by public	
Foreseeability in nuisance	16.21	authorities	16.86
Public nuisance	16.30	I. **Causation**	16.88
Defences to nuisance	16.34	J. **Practical Considerations**	16.93
Statutory authorization	16.35	Civil litigation—the costs and risks	16.93
Prescription	16.39	Limitation of actions	16.94
Unsuccessful defences	16.41	Latent damage and limitation	
C. **The Rule in** *Rylands v Fletcher*	16.45	periods	16.97
D. **Negligence**	16.54	K. **The Measure of Damages**	16.98
Duty of care	16.55	Introduction	16.98
Foreseeability in negligence	16.59	Damages for personal injury	16.99
Breach of duty	16.62	Damage to property	16.100
The defendant's reliance on		The assessment of property	
common practice	16.65	damages	16.102
The defendant's reliance on		Damage caused to part of a	
regulatory standards	16.66	property	16.103
E. **Trespass**	16.67	Recovering the costs of repair	16.104
F. **Breach of Statutory Duty**	16.71	Damages for nuisance	16.106
The Occupiers' Liability Acts	16.71	The problem of economic losses	16.107
Breaches of general statutory duties	16.72	Loss due to hidden defects and	
G. **Liability for Breach of**		fear of future damage	16.109
Contractual or Property Rights	16.74	Damages for negligent advice	16.111
Breaches of covenants	16.74	Exemplary damages	16.112

A. Introduction

16.01 The major powers of environmental control are contained in statute law, with the common law having a subsidiary role. In *Cambridge Water Company v Eastern Counties Leather Limited*,[1] the House of Lords was presented with the opportunity to develop general principles to provide for liability in respect of environmental pollution. Lord Goff, in the leading judgment, acknowledged that the protection and preservation of the environment were now perceived as of crucial importance to the future of mankind, and that significant steps had been taken nationally and internationally to promote this. However, it was the House's view that:[2]

> It does not follow from these developments that a common law principle, such as the rule in *Rylands v Fletcher*, should be developed or rendered more strict to provide for liability in respect of such pollution. On the contrary, given that so much well-informed and carefully-structured legislation is now being put in place for this purpose, there is less need for the courts to develop a common law principle to achieve the same end, and indeed it may well be undesirable that they should do so.

16.02 With the judgment in *Transco v Stockport MBC*[3] affirming the approach in *Cambridge Water*, there is no suggestion that the House of Lords will be prepared to abandon its cautious approach to extending environmental liability at common law. It therefore remains unlikely that private law will become a tool for imposing stringent liabilities on polluters.

16.03 Since environmental protection is a matter of wider public interest, it is perhaps unsurprising that the private law has a more limited role. However, the common law still has a part to play in enabling companies and private individuals to protect their proprietary and other interests, which can be contemplated as environmental in character. A variety of tortious causes of action—nuisance, the rule in *Rylands v Fletcher*, trespass, negligence and the infringement of specific property rights, such as easements or covenants—may have relevance. All of these areas are extensively covered in specialist texts. The aim of this chapter is to provide an overview of the various causes of action, with a view to demonstrating their potential utility in enabling individuals to seek environmental protection through private law.

---

[1] [1994] 2 AC 264.
[2] Ibid at 305, per Lord Goff.
[3] [2004] 2 AC 1 at 9–10, per Lord Bingham.

B. Nuisance

Introduction

There are two types of nuisance at common law: private or public. All types of **16.04**
nuisance involve acts that interfere with the use or enjoyment of land.[4] Private
nuisance is intended to protect the proprietary interests of the claimant from
unlawful interference caused by activities carried out on, and emanating from,[5]
the defendant's land.[6] In private nuisance, the acts of the defendant on his or her
own land need not be unlawful in themselves; those activities only constitute a
nuisance when they give rise to an interference with the use or enjoyment of
neighbouring land.[7] Indeed, it is essential for the defendant to be a neighbour of
the claimant because 'a nuisance cannot arise if what has taken place affects only
the person or persons occupying the premises where the nuisance is said to have
taken place'.[8] Public nuisance will arise where the nuisance affects a sufficiently
large class of the public, and is a common law offence. Public nuisance has much
in common with private nuisance, but also has several distinguishing features,
which are considered more fully below.

Types of private nuisance

There are broadly two categories of private nuisance: (1) nuisance by physical **16.05**
damage or encroachment[9] upon the claimant's land; and (2) interference with the
use or enjoyment of the claimant's land. Each type attracts different considerations, but, depending on the circumstances of the particular case, the categories
can overlap.

Nuisance by physical damage or encroachment

With this type of nuisance, a defendant may be liable where the claimant can **16.06**
prove that physical damage or encroachment to his or her property has occurred,
and that it was caused by the acts or omissions of the defendant. The state of the

---

[4] *Read v J Lyons & Co Ltd* [1947] AC 156; see *Clerk & Lindsell on Torts* (1954), p 561 at 20–01,
where nuisance is said to be incapable of exact definition.

[5] *Bybrook Barn Garden Centre Ltd v Kent County Council* [2001] Env LR 30 at 551, per
Waller LJ.

[6] But see *Hubbard v Pitt* [1976] QB 142 and *Church of Jesus Christ of Latter Day Saints v Price*
[2004] EWHC 3245 at [152], per Beatson J, where the defendant's act of shouting offensive comments on the highway caused interference with the claimant's enjoyment of its land and was held to
constitute a private nuisance.

[7] See *Thompson-Schwab v Costaki* [1956] 1 WLR 335 at 338, citing a passage to this effect from
the 11th edition of *Clerk & Lindsell*.

[8] *National Coal Board v Neath BC* [1976] 2 All ER 478 at 482.

[9] See *Clerk & Lindsell* at 20–06, which treats nuisance by encroachment as closely related to
trespass.

land affected and the character of the neighbourhood are not relevant.[10] Accordingly, where an easement of light was obstructed, the standard of light to be expected was absolute, and no different in a Wolverhampton manufacturing district, Mayfair, or in the countryside.[11]

16.07 Damages have been recovered under this category for nuisances caused by, inter alia, oil pollution,[12] vibrations causing structural damage,[13] landslips,[14] tree roots growing into[15] or overhanging[16] the defendant's land, and tree roots causing shrinkage of clay and subsidence.[17]

Nuisance by interference with the enjoyment of land

16.08 A number of factors will need to be assessed in order to establish whether there has been an actionable nuisance under this category. No claimant can claim an absolute standard of comfort and convenience, for fear of being dismissed as 'oversensitive'.[18] A court must decide what is reasonable according to the ordinary usages of mankind living in a particular society.[19]

16.09 The claimant's expectations must also be judged in the context of the character of the neighbourhood. The old maxim, 'What would be a nuisance in Belgrave Square would not necessarily be so in Bermondsey'[20] still holds true. Any interference must be judged in 'the circumstances of the place where the thing complained of actually occurs'[21]. For instance, a plaintiff who lived in the Fleet Street of the past failed in his action for nuisance when a new printing press was started next door. However, this does not mean that claimants living in industrial areas are bound to fail:

---

[10] *St Helen's Smelting Co v Tipping* [1865] 11 HLC 642 at 650, per Lord Westbury LC.

[11] *Horton's Estate Ltd v James Beattie Ltd* [1927] 1 Ch 75 at 78.

[12] *Esso Petroleum Co Ltd v Southport Corp* [1956] AC 218.

[13] *Hoare & Co v McAlpine* [1923] 1 Ch 167 per Astbury J (piledriving), although the court considered that it could also have succeeded under *Rylands v Fletcher*.

[14] *Leakey v National Trust* [1980] QB 485.

[15] *Butler v Standard Telephones and Cables Ltd* [1940] 1 KB 399.

[16] *Lemmon v Webb* [1895] AC 1.

[17] *Hilda's Montessori Nursery Ltd v Tesco Stores Ltd* [2006] EWHC 1054 (applying *Loftus-Brigham v Ealing LBC* [2003] EWCA Civ 1490); the tree roots must on the balance of probabilities have materially contributed to the subsidence and damage.

[18] Interference with the storing of particularly sensitive paper (*Robinson v Kilvert* [1889] 41 ChD 88) did not constitute a nuisance. Cf: *McKinnon Industries Ltd v Walker* [1951] 3 DLR 577 at 581, Lord Simonds, where the effect of noxious gases on growing sensitive flowers like orchids was held to be a nuisance.

[19] *Sedleigh-Denfield v O'Callaghan* [1940] AC 880 at 903, per Lord Wright.

[20] *Sturges v Bridgman* [1879] 11 ChD 852 at 856, per Thesinger LJ (complaint about use of pestle and mortar near consulting rooms, upheld).

[21] *St Helens Smelting Co v Tipping* [1865] 11 HLC 642. See JE Penner, 'Nuisance and the Character of the Neighbourhood' [1993] 5 JEL 1.

It does not follow that because I live, say, in the manufacturing part of Sheffield I cannot complain if a steam hammer is introduced next door, and so worked as to render sleep at night almost impossible, although previously to its introduction my house was a reasonably comfortable abode, having regard to the local standard; and it would be no answer to say that the steam hammer is of the most modern approved pattern and is reasonably worked.[22]

A grant of planning permission is capable of changing the character of a neighbourhood, although this may only apply in the case of major developments.[23]

Actionable nuisances in this category include: noise from industrial installations,[24] an interference with a person's leisure activities,[25] and odours.[26] Smoke or fumes are examples of agents that may both cause damage to property, and also interfere with the claimant's enjoyment of it.[27] **16.10**

Who may sue in private nuisance?

Only those persons with a proprietary interest in the land affected may bring a claim in private nuisance. In *Hunter v Canary Wharf*,[28] the Court of Appeal had held that occupiers of a property as a home could sue in nuisance, owing to the 'substantial link' between the person enjoying the use and the land upon which he or she enjoys it.[29] However, this was overruled by the House of Lords. Those with exclusive possession, such as a freeholder or a tenant in possession, may sue, but a mere licensee may not. A reversioner may also sue in so far as any damage is done to the value of the reversion.[30] The right to sue extends to successors in title, and in cases of physical damage, this may be so even if the claimant did not own the affected land at the time it was first damaged.[31] The decision of the House reflects the essence of nuisance as a tort against land, rather than a tort against the person.[32] **16.11**

---

[22] *Rushmer v Polsue & Alfieri* [1906] Ch 234, per Cozens-Hardy LJ; specifically approved by Lord Loreburn LC [1907] Ch 121 at 123.

[23] See further below, under 'Defences to Nuisance: Statutory Authorisation'.

[24] *Halsey v Esso Petroleum* [1961] 1 WLR 683.

[25] But in *Hunter v Canary Wharf Ltd* this did not include interference with television reception; nor did it in *Bridlington Relay v Yorkshire Electricity Board* [1965] Ch 436 (radio and TV relay system).

[26] Eg *Bainbridge v Chertsey UDC* [1915] 84 LJ Ch 626 (smell from a sewage farm); *Adams v Ursell* [1913] 1 Ch 269 (odour from a fish and chip shop).

[27] Eg *Manchester Corporation v Farnworth* [1930] AC 171 (fumes from a generating station over farmland); see also *Salvin v North Brancepath Coal Co* [1874] 9 Ch App 705 (smoke from large coking plant); *Wood v Conway Corpn* [1914] 2 Ch 47 (fumes damaged trees); *Pwllbach Collier Co Ltd v Woodman* [1915] AC 634 (coal dust from a depot).

[28] [1997] AC 655.

[29] Ibid at 675.

[30] Ibid at 692; there was a powerful dissenting judgment from Lord Cooke of Thorndon, a New Zealand appellate judge, in support of the idea that the law should now recognize such a right of action.

[31] *Delaware Mansions Ltd v Westminster City Council* [2001] 1 AC 321.

[32] Ibid at 693, per Lord Goff; see also Newark, 'The Boundaries of Nuisance' 65 LQR 480.

Responsibility for the nuisance

The wrongdoer

16.12 The primary responsibility for a nuisance lies with the actual wrongdoer. Subject to any limitation period and the test of foreseeability, discussed below, the wrongdoer remains responsible for all the damage flowing from the nuisance, even though he or she might no longer be in occupation of the land and so unable to prevent it.[33]

The occupier

16.13 A subsequent occupier can become liable for a nuisance if, despite not creating it, he or she continues or adopts the nuisance. In *Sedleigh-Denfield v O'Callaghan*,[34] it was said that:

> An occupier of land 'continues' a nuisance if, with knowledge or presumed knowledge of its existence, he fails to take any reasonable means to bring it to an end, though with ample time to do so. He 'adopts' it if he makes any use of the erection, building, bank or artificial continuance which constitutes the nuisance.

16.14 If a risk of damage becomes foreseeable after a period of time, by improvement in knowledge, scientific or otherwise, the occupier will come under a duty to abate the nuisance.[35] This aspect of liability is considered further below, under 'Foreseeability in Nuisance'.

The landlord

16.15 A landlord is not normally liable for the acts of the tenant, including the creation of a nuisance to neighbouring occupiers. The tenant is in actual occupation and is therefore the appropriate person to sue. This can be particularly relevant in cases concerning contaminated land, or where a landfill site is operated under a lease. But the landlord can be liable if it is shown that he or she expressly or impliedly authorized the tenant to create the nuisance. For example, a landlord was held liable for permitting his tenant to blast for limestone on his land when the tenant used the normal methods of quarrying.[36] Similarly, a local authority landlord was

---

[33] This is so even if the land is conveyed to another—*Roswell v Prior* [1701] 12 Mod 635; *Thompson v Gibson* [1841] 7 M&W 456 (both concern permanent nuisances—the erection of a building).

[34] [1940] AC 880 at 894, per Viscount Maugham; a local authority had trespassed onto the defendant's land and placed a culvert in a ditch. They also incorrectly placed a grid across the culvert, which created a danger of flooding. The defendant became aware of the culvert but did nothing, although the risk was apparent and could have been prevented without great expense.

[35] *Anthony v Coal Authority* [2006] Env LR 17 at [129]–[133] (the risk of spontaneous combustion had not been foreseeable at the time the defendant's predecessor created spoil heaps at a tip, but the defendant became liable once it had presumed knowledge of the risk).

[36] *Harris v James* [1876] 45 LJQB 545.

held liable for noise nuisance that was the natural consequence of the activity for which the land had been let.[37]

If the landlord has covenanted to repair, or has retained control by having a power   **16.16** to repair, it has long been established that he is liable if a nuisance is caused by breach of that covenant.[38] Where a landlord knew, or ought to have known, about the existence of a nuisance prior to the grant of a tenancy, notwithstanding any covenant to repair, the landlord is liable; this is so unless he or she is excused by some further fact.[39] An assignee of the reversion who takes the assignment of the freehold with knowledge of the nuisance will be treated in the same way as the landlord.[40] Where injury results from the condition of the premises, liability may also arise in negligence.[41]

The concept of the reasonable user

Liability in nuisance is contained by the principle of the 'reasonable user', a recip-   **16.17** rocal concept intended to give effect to the notion of 'good neighbourliness'.[42] In *Cambridge Water*, Lord Goff put it as follows:

> . . . although liability for nuisance has generally been regarded as strict, at least in the case of a defendant who has been responsible for the creation of a nuisance, even so that liability has been kept under control by the principle of reasonable user – the principle of give and take between neighbouring occupiers of land . . . The effect is that, if the user is reasonable, the defendant will not be liable for consequent harm to his neighbour's enjoyment of his land; but if the user is not reasonable, the defendant will be liable, even though he may have exercised reasonable care and skill to avoid it.[43]

The Court of Appeal have illustrated this point in the context of residential prop-   **16.18** erty in *Baxter v Camden LBC*.[44] The defendant Council had converted a Victorian terraced house into flats at a time when building regulations did not require

---

[37] *Tetley v Chitty* [1986] 1 All ER 663 (go-karting); an injunction was granted and damages awarded. The situation changes when one tenant sues his landlord because another tenant's ordinary activities are disturbing him due to the state of the premises. The tenant will be deemed to take the premises as he finds them (*Baxter v Camden LBC (No 2)* [1999] 3 WLR 93). Nor can the tenant sue his landlord for a breach of the covenant of quiet enjoyment: see *Southwark LBC v Mills* combined with *Baxter* on the appeal to the HL.

[38] *Payne v Rogers* [1794] 2 HBl 350, although the tenant may be jointly liable: *St Anne's Well Brewery Co v Roberts* [1929] 140 LT 1.

[39] *Brew Bros Ltd v Snax (Ross) Ltd* [1970] 1 QB 612.

[40] *Sampson v Hodgson-Pressinger* [1981] 3 All ER 710.

[41] In *Rimmer v Liverpool City Council* [1985] QB 1, the landlord who built and designed the premises was held to be liable to those who were reasonably likely to be injured by their defective condition.

[42] *Hughes v Riley* [2006] 1 P&CR 29 at [29], per Chadwick LJ.

[43] [1994] 2 AC 264 at 299.

[44] [2001] QB 1 at 12, per Tuckey LJ.

soundproofing. Upon hearing an appeal against the trial judge's finding that the sound penetration constituted an actionable nuisance, Tuckey LJ said:

> . . . ordinary use of residential premises without more is not capable of amounting to a nuisance. Ordinary use may only give rise to a nuisance if it is unusual or unreasonable having regard to the purpose for which the premises were constructed.

16.19 It followed that, since the conversion had done nothing to change the purpose for which the house was used and there was nothing unreasonable about it, there was no actionable nuisance.

16.20 The object and the duration of the activity allegedly constituting the interference are relevant to determining whether the user is reasonable or unreasonable. For example, a builder will not be responsible for a nuisance if he uses all reasonable skill and care to avoid annoyance to his neighbour by the works of demolition or building. But there may come a time when the works are sufficiently substantial or excessively lengthy as to become unreasonable, at which point they will constitute a nuisance.[45] In *Arscott v Coal Authority*,[46] the Court of Appeal recently summarized the position as follows: '. . . it may broadly be said that a landowner will not be liable in nuisance for the consequences of what would be recognised as a natural use of his land by him, unless the quality or extent of that use by him was unreasonable'. But as the above extract from *Cambridge Water* indicates, once nuisance is established, the exercise of reasonable care and skill will not excuse the defendant.

Foreseeability in nuisance

16.21 It is now clear that liability for nuisance is not strict. Notwithstanding the control mechanism of the 'reasonable user', the concept of foreseeability has had an increasingly important role to play. The justification for requiring foreseeability is the difficulty in finding fault without it[47]. In *Cambridge Water*, Lord Goff continued:

> . . . it by no means follows that the defendant should be held liable for damage of a type which he could not reasonably foresee; and the development of the law of negligence in the past 60 years points strongly towards a requirement that such foreseeability should be a prerequisite of liability in damages for nuisance, as it is of liability in negligence.[48]

16.22 First, it must have been foreseeable to the defendant that such behaviour would inflict harm to the claimant. This must take account of the state of technical knowledge that the defendant can reasonably be expected to have had at the date the cause of action arose. Secondly, it must have been foreseeable to the defendant that the type of damage would be caused. It is not sufficient that the injury

---

[45] *Matania v National Provincial Bank Ltd* [1936] 2 All ER 633, CA (building alterations); *Metropolitan Properties Ltd v Jones* [1939] 2 All ER 202 (three weeks noise).
[46] [2005] Env LR 6 at 83, per Laws LJ.
[47] *The Wagon Mound (No. 2)* [1967] 1 AC 617 at 639, per Lord Reid.
[48] [1994] 2 AC 264 at 300.

suffered by the claimant was the direct result of the nuisance if that injury was unforeseeable.

The foreseeability of a particular type of harm can result in liability for nuisance **16.23** arising from nonfeasance, a failure to act. As already outlined, occupiers may become liable for nuisances that they did not create but of which they are presumed to have knowledge. Such a person will be liable if he or she fails to exercise reasonable diligence to discover if there is a nuisance:

> The responsibility which attaches to the occupier because he has possession and control of the property cannot logically be limited to the mere creation of the nuisance. It should extend to his conduct if, with knowledge, he leaves the nuisance on his land. The same is true if the nuisance was such that with ordinary care in the management of his property he should have realised the risk of its existence.[49]

It follows that the occupier's liability for nuisance will arise where he or she, as **16.24** Lord Wright said, 'did not without undue delay remedy it when he became aware of it, or with ordinary and reasonable care should have become aware of it'. This reaffirms that the duty arises if it was the sort of risk that should have been foreseeable.[50] Where the ignorance is reasonable, the defendant will not be liable.[51]

In recent years, the requirement of foreseeability has engendered a positive duty to **16.25** abate nuisance caused by naturally occurring phenomena. The starting point is *Leakey v National Trust*,[52] where a landslip caused damage to the plaintiff's adjoining property and the National Trust had known about the instability of their land some eight years prior to its occurrence. The Court of Appeal held that there is 'a duty to do that which is reasonable in all the circumstances, and no more than what, if anything, is reasonable, to prevent or minimise the known risk of damage or injury to one's neighbour or to his property'.[53] The *Leakey* principle therefore does not impose an absolute duty to prevent harm to a neighbour arising from natural phenomena.

In *LE Jones (Insurance Brokers) Ltd v Portsmouth City Council*,[54] a case concerning **16.26** damage caused by tree roots, Dyson LJ summarized the rationale for imposing this positive duty as follows:

> In my view, the basis for the liability of an occupier for a nuisance on his land is not his occupation as such. Rather, it is that, by virtue of his occupation, an occupier usually has it in his power to take the measures that are necessary to prevent or eliminate the nuisance. He has sufficient control over the hazard which constitutes the

---

[49] *Sedleigh-Denfield v O'Callaghan* [1940] AC 880 at 905, per Lord Wright.
[50] Eg *Cunliffe v Bankes* [1945] 1 All ER 459.
[51] Eg *Ilford UDC v Beal and Judd* [1925] 1 KB 671, a wall was built over an unknown sewer, which cracked; similarly, *Anglian Water Services v H G Thurston & Co Ltd* [1993] EGCS 162.
[52] [1980] QB 485; applying the Privy Council opinion in *Goldman v Hargrave* [1967] 1 AC 645 (lightning strike in a forest).
[53] Ibid at 524, 526 per Megaw LJ.
[54] [2003] 1 WLR 427 at 431.

nuisance for it to be reasonable to make him liable for the foreseeable consequences of his failure to exercise that control so as to remove the hazard.

16.27 In *Delaware Mansions Ltd v Westminster City Council*,[55] another tree root case, the House of Lords made it clear that liability under the *Leakey* principle will not arise until the landlord knows, or ought reasonably to know, that he or she is in breach of the duty.

16.28 When establishing what is reasonable to prevent or minimize the risk from a naturally occurring hazard, the following circumstances may be relevant: the owner's knowledge of the hazard, including the extent to which it was reasonably foreseeable,[56] the extent of the risk in terms of likelihood of its occurrence and the seriousness of the consequences; the practicability of the steps required; the cost of the work required, and the relative financial resources of the parties.[57] The relative resources of the parties might mean that the defendant merely has a duty to warn his neighbour and to offer the opportunity of carrying out the works on his or her land. However, the importance of the financial resources of the parties has since been played down by the Court of Appeal in *Abbahall Ltd v Smee*.[58] The defendant was the owner of a flying freehold through adverse possession, but her impecuniosity did not exonerate her from failing to contribute to remedying a nuisance caused by a leaking roof. It was considered unreasonable for the defendant to continue living in a leaking property which was damaging her neighbour's property, while doing nothing to contribute to the remedial costs because she had chosen to live in a property she could not afford to maintain. The defendant was therefore ordered to contribute equally to the remedial works. The standard of care expected under the *Leakey* principle is therefore of uncertain scope, but the relevant circumstances now seem to encompass whether it is reasonable to seek a contribution from the neighbouring owners.

16.29 Knowledge and foreseeability also have particular implications where pollution arises as a result of vandalism. It is a defence to show that the loss was caused by the act of a stranger or trespasser.[59] But a duty might then arise to take steps to abate the nuisance after the trespasser has created it,[60] once the defendant has or

---

[55] [2002] 1 AC 321 at 335, per Lord Cooke.
[56] This qualification was added by the Court of Appeal in *Holbeck Hall Hotel Ltd v Scarborough Borough Council* [2000] QB 836 (where a landslip was held not to have been reasonably foreseeable) and *Green v Lord Somerleyton* [2003] 1 P&CR 33 (where it was confirmed that the *Leakey* principle does apply to damage caused by naturally flowing water).
[57] See also *Anthony v Coal Authority* [2006] Env LR 17 at [133].
[58] [2003] 1 All ER 465 at 478, per Munby J; a case perhaps best not categorized under the *Leakey* principle, although the court plainly treated it as such.
[59] Eg *Cushing v Peter Walker & Sons Ltd* [1941] 2 All ER 693 (enemy action—the ultimate trespassers); *Smith v Littlewoods Organisation Ltd* [1987] 2 WLR 480 (cinema fire).
[60] *Sedleigh-Denfield v O'Callaghan* [1940] AC 880, as above.

ought to have had knowledge of its existence. In this situation, by parity of reasoning, the *Leakey* principle applies.[61] Accordingly, a plaintiff was unable to recover damages when, as a result of trespassers damaging the pipes to an upstairs flat without the landlord's knowledge, her flat was flooded with water.[62]

Public nuisance

A public nuisance arises where an activity materially affects the reasonable comfort and convenience of a sufficiently large class of the public[63]. Such a class has been analysed in general terms by Lord Denning:[64] **16.30**

> I prefer to look at the reasons for the thing and to say that a public nuisance is nuisance which is so widespread in its range or so indiscriminate in its effect that it would not be reasonable to expect one person to take proceedings on his own responsibility to put a stop to it, but that it should be taken on the responsibility of the community at large.

Whether a sufficiently large class of the public is affected will turn on the facts. For example, in *R v Goldstein*[65] the House of Lords held that the activity of posting salt as a practical joke to a friend, which leaked onto the hands of a postal worker who feared it might be anthrax, could not amount to a public nuisance since it was insufficiently public. By contrast, in *East Dorset DC v Eaglebeam*,[66] although the households affected by the noise from a motor-cross event did not comprise a whole town, a substantial number of households on the edge of Bournemouth were affected; this was held to constitute a sufficiently large class of the public to amount to a public nuisance. Public nuisance was appropriately used when the discharge of oil from a stranded tanker was likely to be carried onto the shore to the prejudice and discomfort of the public[67] and when the traffic at commercial docks disturbed the residential amenity of nearby dwellings.[68] When a local authority instituted proceedings for an injunction under Section 222 of the Local Government Act 1972, many residents were affected by the noise from construction work, so it is puzzling why the claim was not alternatively pleaded in public nuisance.[69] **16.31**

---

[61] See the discussion in *Leakey v National Trust* [1980] 1 QB 485.

[62] *King v Liverpool City Council* [1986] 1 WLR 890.

[63] See generally Spencer, 'Public Nuisance—a Critical Examination' (1989) 48 CLJ 55.

[64] *Attorney-General v PYA Quarries* [1957] 2 QB 169 at 190–191, CA (relator action for an injunction, quarry blasting).

[65] [2006] 1 AC 459.

[66] [2006] EWHC 2378 (QB) at [5]–[7]; [2007] Env LR D9.

[67] *Southport Corporation v Esso Petroleum* [1954] 2 QB 182 (possible defence of necessity).

[68] *Gillingham BC v Medway (Chatham) Dock Co Ltd* [1992] 3 All ER 923, which failed on policy grounds (see above, 'Defences to Nuisance—Statutory Authorization').

[69] See the comment by Dawn Oliver, 'The Use of High Court Injunctions to Control Noise Pollution' [1989] 1 JEL 112, concerning *Mayor and Commonalty of the City of London v Bovis*

16.32 If an individual wishes to claim in circumstances which amount to a public nuisance, he or she must show that they have suffered some special damage over and above that of the community.[70] Obstruction of the highway can often cause special damage. For example, in *Business Environment Group Ltd v Wembley Fair (Wembley) Ltd*,[71] the claimant brought a claim in, inter alia, public nuisance because it suffered financial losses when the defendant's market obstructed access to the claimant's place of business.

16.33 In *R v Goldstein*,[72] the House of Lords recently confirmed the continued status of public nuisance as a common law offence. A prosecution may be brought by the Attorney-General or a local authority. In recent times, charges have been brought in respect of the noise caused by 'acid house' parties[73]. The mens rea of the crime is established according to same principles of knowledge or presumed knowledge as apply in private nuisance.[74] The Environmental Protection Act 1990 and the Noise Act 1996 have put statutory force behind certain private and public nuisances, and created criminal offences in some cases. Such matters are dealt with in detail elsewhere in this volume.

Defences to nuisance

16.34 In addition to defences arising out of a lack of knowledge or foreseeability, the general defences to torts (necessity, contributory negligence, novus actus interveniens, volenti non fit injuria) apply equally to nuisance. Moreover, in the environmental context, the defences of authorization by statute and right acquired by prescription have greater relevance.

Statutory authorization

16.35 Where a certain activity is directed by statute, this can constitute a defence provided that the nuisance is authorized expressly or by necessary implication.[75] This depends upon proper interpretation of the relevant statute. The principle then is that the defendant will not be liable for any nuisance which he can show would be the 'inevitable result' of an operation authorized by Parliament, such as operating

---

Construction [1989] JPL 263. It would have avoided the difficulties in proceeding under s 222 based on a hybrid set of allegations of 'unlawful activity' and a criminal offence.

[70] *Allen v Gulf Oil Refinery Ltd* [1981] AC 1001; *British Celanese Ltd v AH Hunt (Capacitors) Ltd* [1969] 1 WLR 959.

[71] [2005] EWCA Civ 1230.

[72] [2006] 1 AC 459.

[73] *R v Ruffell (David)* [1992] 12 Cr App R (S) 204; *R v Shorrock (Peter)* [1994] QB 279.

[74] *R v Shorrock* at 284 (£2,500 fine), applying *Sedleigh-Denfield v O'Callaghan* [1940] AC 880 and *Attorney-General v PYA Quarries* [1957] 2 QB 169.

[75] *Geddis v Proprietors of Bann Reservoir* (1878) 3 App Cas 430.

a particular railway or an oil refinery.[76] But the defendant must continue to exercise due diligence in order to avoid liability:

> The onus of proving that the result is inevitable is on those who wish to escape liability for nuisance, but the criterion of inevitability is not what is theoretically possible but what is possible according to the state of scientific knowledge at the time, having also in view a certain common sense appreciation, which cannot be rigidly defined, of practical feasibility in view of the situation and of expense.[77]

In *Allen v Gulf Oil Refining Ltd*,[78] the House of Lords made it clear that immunity **16.36** would only be conferred to the extent of the statutory authorization. A claimant therefore still has a remedy if it can be shown that the actual nuisance, if any, exceeds that for which immunity is conferred.

Where nuisance is not expressly or impliedly authorized by a statute, the authori- **16.37** ties may often be distinguished on the narrowest of grounds.[79] In *Marcic v Thames Water Utilities Ltd*,[80] the principle of statutory authorization was extended to exclude liability for nuisance at common law where to impose such liability would be inconsistent with a statutory scheme. The claimant's garden had been repeatedly flooded by sewers maintained by the defendant undertaker. Under the Water Industry Act 1991, the defendant had no control over the volume of water entering the system, and the only way to abate the nuisance would have been to build further sewers. The 1991 Act also provided for a scheme of enforcement of the sewerage undertakers' drainage obligations. In these circumstances, the House of Lords held that the common law could not impose liability at odds with the statutory scheme because this would be contrary to the intention of Parliament. This may be compared with *Pride of Derby v British Celanese*, where a local authority that discharged sewage into a river was not excused from liability by relying upon a statutory power to extend a disposal plant that it did not exercise; indeed, its failure to do so was the basis of liability in nuisance.[81]

Direct statutory authorization should be contrasted with local authorization in **16.38** the form of planning permission, which will not constitute a defence to nuisance.

---

[76] *Allen v Gulf Oil Refinery Ltd* [1981] AC 1001 (noxious odours, noise, etc, emitted from a refinery constructed under the Gulf Oil Refining Act 1965); cf: *Metropolitan Asylum District v Hill* [1881] 6 App Cas 193 (no defence as no specified statutory location for smallpox hospital); *Tate & Lyle Ltd v GLC* [1983] 2 AC 509 (ferry terminal design which diverted silt onto P's jetty was not an inevitable part of the authorization).

[77] *Manchester Corporation v Farnworth* [1930] AC 171 at 183, per Lord Dunedin (power station authorized by statute, but failure to use reasonable diligence to prevent fumes and contamination).

[78] [1981] AC 1001 at 1014, per Lord Wilberforce.

[79] *Bybrook Barn Garden Centre Ltd v Kent County Council* [2001] Env LR 30 at 551, per Waller LJ.

[80] [2004] 2 AC 42 at 57–58.

[81] *Pride of Derby v British Celanese* [1953] Ch 149.

In *Hunter v Canary Wharf Ltd*,[82] the Court of Appeal stated that the powers and duties conferred by Parliament on planning authorities are not such that, in granting planning permission under their delegated powers, they can confer immunity in nuisance upon the works carried out in pursuance of the consent. This is so even where a statutory enterprise zone has been established. The planning authority has no jurisdiction to authorize a nuisance save, if at all, in so far as it has the statutory power to permit the change of the character of the neighbourhood,[83] as occurred in *Gillingham BC v Medway (Chatham) Dock Co Ltd*.[84] Planning permissions are relevant in judging the character of the area, but they are not decisive per se.[85] Even this power to change a neighbourhood's character has led some commentators[86] to allege that what should be a matter of legal rights, in particular the private right to property, has become merely one of administrative decision making. In *Wheeler v JJ Saunders*, Lord Justice Peter Gibson suggested that the *Gillingham* principle is confined to 'major development[s] altering the character of the neighbourhood with wide consequential effects'[87]. His Lordship continued:

> I am not prepared to accept that the principle in the *Gillingham* case must be taken to apply to every planning decision. The court should be slow to acquiesce in the extinction of private rights without compensation as a result of administrative decisions which cannot be appealed and are difficult to challenge.[88]

Prescription

16.39 There is a defence to certain types of private nuisance if it can be shown that a right to carry out the activity has been acquired as an easement by prescription. This is, of course, limited to rights that are capable of being easements.[89] This defence has no relevance to nuisances arising from malodours, noises, and vibrations since such activities are not capable of existing as easements. No question of prescription can arise until a nuisance is committed; thereafter the defendant must show

---

[82] [1997] AC 655 at 668 per Pill LJ, applying the dictum of Viscount Dunedin in *Manchester Corporation* [1930] AC 171 at 183. This point was not argued in the appeal to the House of Lords. See also *Delyn BC v Solitaire (Liverpool) Ltd* [1995] EGCS 11 (planning permission for a market did not override any other rights relating to the land, including nuisance actions or the Council's own statutory market rights).

[83] *Allen v Gulf Oil* [1979] 3 All ER 1008 at 1020 per Cumming-Bruce LJ.

[84] [1992] 3 All ER 923, Buckley J.

[85] See J Steele and T Jewell, 'Nuisance and Planning' (1993) 56 MLR 568, case comment on *Gillingham*.

[86] See the Case Analysis of Crawford at [1992] J Env L 262 at 270; Penner, 'Nuisance and the Character of the Neighbourhood', op cit.

[87] [1996] Ch 19 at 35.

[88] Ibid.

[89] See *Gale on Easements* (17th edition, Sweet and Maxwell 2002), 1–05 to 1–63.

that the user has continued for the appropriate period of prescription.[90] It follows that if the right has been exercised nec vi nec clam nec precario[91] for over 20 years, the defendant has the right to continue the activity. For example, a defendant could acquire a right to discharge surface water onto neighbouring land or to send smoke through flues into a party wall,[92] but not if this has been done secretly.[93]

No such right can be acquired to commit a public nuisance.[94] Moreover, a right **16.40** cannot be claimed if it has been exercised contrary to law.[95] Nor is it possible to acquire a prescriptive right the extent of which is indeterminate or changes constantly.[96] Both of these points are illustrated by *Hulley v Silversprings Bleaching Co*,[97] where the defendant had been discharging the factory's emissions, including bleach, into a river for over 20 years. The user was an offence under the Rivers Pollution Prevention Act 1876, and the increase in the amount of the discharges had destroyed the certainty and uniformity which was essential for the measurement of the user.

Unsuccessful defences

The fact that a claimant is aware of a known interference before he or she moves **16.41** to an area is irrelevant.[98] Accordingly, there is no defence of 'coming to the nuisance'.

It is no defence to justify the activity as a useful one, or one which is necessary in **16.42** the public interest. In *Shelfer v City of London Electric Lighting Co*[99] the point was made that:

> Neither has the circumstance that the wrongdoer is in some sense a public benefactor (*eg* a gas or water company or a sewer authority) ever been considered a sufficient reason for refusing to protect by injunction an individual whose rights are being persistently infringed.

---

[90] See the Prescription Act 1832, ss 1–2. Note that in *Halsey v Esso Petroleum* [1961] 1 WLR 683 at 702, the nuisances were all of recent origin and the prescriptive defence pleaded failed on this ground.

[91] 'Without force, stealth, or precariousness (permission)'

[92] *Attorney-General v Copeland* [1902] 1 KB 690 and *Jones v Pritchard* [1908] 1 Ch 630 respectively.

[93] See *Liverpool Corporation v Coghill* [1918] 1 Ch 307. The discharges were done at night and were also illegal.

[94] *R v Cross* [1812] 3 Camp 224.

[95] *Cargill v Gotts* [1981] 1 WLR 441 (abstraction of water without a licence).

[96] *Lemmon v Webb* [1894] 3 Ch 1 at 14, per Lindley LJ; affirmed [1895] AC 1 (overhanging tree boughs).

[97] [1922] 2 Ch 268, Eve J (the claim for damages and an injunction succeeded); see also *Scott-Whitehead v National Coal Board* [1987] 53 P&CR 263, QBD (discharge of mine water).

[98] Cf *Sturges v Bridgman*, see n 52 above.

[99] [1895] 1 Ch 287, at 316, per Lindley LJ, applied in *Kennaway*. See the discussion at paras 20–86 and 20–87 in *Clerk & Lindsell* (19th edn. Sweet & Maxwell, 2006).

16.43 *Miller v Jackson*[100] is difficult to reconcile with *Shelfer*. In allowing a cricket pitch to be used without restraint, Lord Denning held that the interests of the public at large should prevail over the plaintiff's private interest in enjoying his property without interference from errant cricket balls. It appears that such a balance may be a relevant factor in assessing the reasonableness of the user and the character of the neighbourhood, but it should not amount to a defence in itself.[101]

16.44 In addition, the question of public benefit can have a bearing on the appropriate remedy. In *Dennis v Ministry of Defence*[102] Buckley J irresistibly concluded that the extreme noise created by RAF Harriers constituted a highly intrusive nuisance. Nevertheless, the public interest required that the training of pilots should continue, and this was reflected in the remedy. Since injunctions are discretionary, the High Court permitted the nuisance to continue, but the claimant was instead awarded substantial compensation.[103] His Lordship was at pains to point out that the facts of the case were extreme and not analogous to any authorities,[104] so it might be that such an approach is unlikely to recur frequently[105].

C. The Rule in *Rylands v Fletcher*

16.45 The original form of the rule is contained in the judgment of Blackburn J in *Rylands v Fletcher:*[106]

> . . . the person who for his own purpose brings on his lands and collects and keeps there anything likely to do mischief if it escapes must keep it at his peril, and, if he does not do so, is prima facie answerable for all the damage which is a natural consequence of its escape.

16.46 In the House of Lords, Lord Cairns went on to introduce the concept of 'non-natural use', thereby creating a tort of strict liability.

---

[100] [1977] QB 966, CA (but found liable in negligence), and not followed in *Kennaway v Thompson* [1981] QB 88, CA (speedboats on a lake).

[101] Note the rationalization of Lord Denning's judgment by the writers of *Clerk & Lindsell* (19th ed) at 20–87.

[102] [2003] Env LR 34.

[103] Effectively 'Lord Cairn's Act' damages in lieu of an injunction, pursuant to the Supreme Court Act 1981, s 51.

[104] At 758.

[105] But see *Andrews v Reading Borough Council (No. 2)* [2005] EWHC 256 at [92], where Calvert-Smith J followed *Dennis* and held that a road improvement scheme of overall benefit to the public did not confer immunity from actions in nuisance (and under Art 8 ECHR) on the implementing authority.

[106] (1866) LR 1 Ex 265 at 279; affirmed, (1886) LR 3 HL 330 at 338–340.

The rule has been restricted over the years, in particular since the judgment of the   **16.47**
House of Lords in *Cambridge Water Co Ltd v Eastern Counties Leather Plc.*[107] The
defendant had in the past used a chemical, perchloroethene (PCE), to degrease
animal pelts at its tannery, located just over one mile away from a borehole operated by the plaintiff. Until 1976 small quantities of PCE had regularly spilled and
seeped through the tannery floor to the soil, and thereafter into the aquifer serving
the plaintiff's borehole. The plaintiffs had tested the water supply in 1976, and
found it to be wholesome. However, no tests were made for PCE because its presence in the public water supply was not then a matter of concern. In 1983, following UK implementation of the EEC Drinking Water Directive (80/778/EEC), it
was discovered that the quantities of PCE found in the borehole water exceeded
the prescribed limits. Their Lordships did not dispute that the defendant's use of
the land to store large quantities of chemicals was 'non-natural' or that their
'escape' would give rise to liability, even if reasonable precautions had been taken.
The issue was whether or not the rule in *Rylands v Fletcher* should be developed as
a principle of strict liability for damage caused by ultra-hazardous operations.
Lord Goff preferred to leave such a step to Parliament.[108] Moreover, the House
considered that prior to 1976 the damage was not foreseeable, so the defendant
should not be held liable. Accordingly, the rule in *Rylands v Fletcher* was treated as
'an extension of the law of nuisance to cases of isolated escapes'.[109] Foreseeability
by the defendant of the relevant type of damage is therefore a prerequisite of liability under this rule, as it is for nuisance generally.[110]

In *Transco v Stockport MBC,*[111] the House of Lords declined an invitation to abol-   **16.48**
ish the rule. The claim, concerning a significant leak of water from a pipe, failed.
The House affirmed the approach that it had taken in *Cambridge Water* of treating
the rule as 'a sub-species of nuisance'. It follows that a claim for death or personal
injury cannot be made under the rule since this does not relate to any right in or
enjoyment of land.[112] Lord Bingham appeared to go further when he held that the
rule applies only to activities that the defendant 'ought reasonably to have recognized as giving rise to an *exceptionally high* risk of danger or mischief if there
should be an escape, however unlikely'.[113]

---

[107] [1994] 2 AC 264.
[108] Likewise in *Murphy v Brentwood DC* [1991] 1 AC 398, the HL stated that the precise limits
and extent of the duty which should be imposed in the public interest on builders and local authorities were best dealt with by the legislature (eg Defective Premises Act 1972).
[109] At 306.
[110] At 302, per Lord Goff.
[111] [2004] 2 AC 1.
[112] Ibid at 10–11.
[113] Ibid at 11; emphasis added.

16.49 In some of the older authorities, liability under the rule in *Rylands v Fletcher* has been established in a wide range of circumstances including explosives,[114] sewage,[115] gas,[116] or the hydraulic transmission of water under pressure.[117] However, in the wake of *Cambridge Water* and *Transco*, in which the House of Lords sought to define the parameters of the rule more keenly, the older authorities must be treated with caution.

16.50 The controller or owner of the 'dangerous thing' is primarily liable for any damage resulting from its escape. Another occupier of the land is not liable unless he or she has authorized, expressly or by implication, the keeping or collecting to take place.[118] Under the rule in its original form, anyone who had been 'damnified' by the escape could make a claim under the rule, whether or not they were occupiers of adjoining land. However, the latter-day kinship between nuisance and the rule under *Rylands v Fletcher* must be borne in mind. In the wake of *Hunter v Canary Wharf* and *Transco*, in the future, claimants may be required to have an interest in the affected land.[119] Since claims under the rule are often made in the alternative to a claim in nuisance, for practical purposes it is likely to make little difference.

16.51 Historically, the defence of 'natural use' has been commonly pleaded. The non-natural uses in the older authorities mentioned above can be compared with those that have been held to be ordinary, natural uses of the land, such as a fire in a grate[120] and the use of gas, water, and electricity in a house, as opposed to bulk storage.[121] Natural uses have also included less obvious categories, such as the ordinary winning and working of minerals,[122] and the manufacture of electrical and electronic components on an industrial estate.[123] The position was once qualified in *Rickards v Lothian*[124] as follows:

> It must be some special use bringing with it increased danger to others and must not merely be the ordinary use of the land or such a use as is proper for the general benefit of the community.

---

[114] *Rainham Chemical Works v Belvedere Fish Guano Co* [1921] 2 AC 465.

[115] *Smeaton v Ilford Corporation* [1954] Ch 450.

[116] *Dunne v North Western Gas Board* [1964] 2 QB 806 (gas explosion, statutory duty so *Rylands* distinguished).

[117] *Charing Cross Electricity Supply Co v Hydraulic Power Co* [1914] 3 KB 772.

[118] *Rainham Chemical Works v Belvedere Fish Guano Co* [1921] 2 AC 465; *Whitmores Ltd v Stanford* [1909] 1 Ch 427.

[119] However, see *Clerk & Lindsell* at 21–15, where the author discusses this point and notes *McKenna v British Aluminium Ltd* [2002] Env LR 30, where the High Court did not strike out a claim under *Rylands v Fletcher* brought by claimants lacking an interest in the land.

[120] *Sochacki v Sas* [1947] 1 All ER 344, Goddard CJ (which escaped into the rest of the house).

[121] *Collingwood v Home & Colonial Stores Ltd* [1936] 3 All ER 700.

[122] *Rouse v Gravelworks Ltd* [1940] 1 KB 489 (natural accumulation of water also).

[123] *British Celanese Ltd v A H Hunt (Capacitors) Ltd* [1969] 1 WLR 959, Lawton J (storage of metal foil, which blew into P's property, shorting out the electricity supply; duty in nuisance and negligence also).

[124] [1913] AC 263 at 279, per Lord Moulton.

However, in *Cambridge Water*, the House was concerned that the concept of **16.52** 'natural use' of land would be inappropriately widened in order to circumscribe liability under the rule. Perhaps one of the perceived benefits of introducing a foreseeability test was that it would curtail this feared extension. Accordingly, Lord Goff did not hesitate in viewing the storage of PCE as 'an almost classic case of non-natural use'[125] Subsequently, in *Arscott v Coal Authority,*[126] Laws LJ has commented upon the diminishing importance of the distinction between natural and non-natural uses. It is therefore most unlikely that, in future, the concept of 'natural use' will expand as a defence, either on the basis of an alleged community benefit, or at all.

The rule under *Rylands v Fletcher* has had recent application in the context of **16.53** fire damage. Under the Fires Prevention (Metropolis) Act 1774, there is no common law liability for fires accidentally started. However, the 1774 Act has no application where the fire is caused by a dangerous thing.[127] In *LMS International Ltd v Styrene Packaging & Insulation Ltd.,*[128] a fire on neighbouring land was caused by a hot wire machine cutting polystyrene foam blocks. His Honour Judge Peter Coulson QC observed that the authorities relating to fire damage were not all cited to the House in *Transco,*[129] and considered that the modern form of the rule under *Rylands v Fletcher* had plain and obvious application.[130] Given that the Court of Appeal has also recently confirmed that the rule is 'alive and well'[131], it appears that *Rylands v Fletcher* continues to have some utility, albeit within the limits set out in *Cambridge Water* and *Transco*.

D. Negligence

In the context of environmental protection, the very broad area of negligence has **16.54** a limited function. With the exception of 'toxic tort' personal injury cases, negligence tends to have a gap-filling role, or, as occurred in *Cambridge Water*, may be pleaded as an alternative cause of action to nuisance. What follows is an outline of the fundamental principles, together with some examples of environmental cases where negligence has played a notable, although not necessarily successful, part.

---

125 At 309.
126 [2005] Env LR 6 at 84, per Laws LJ.
127 *Perry v Kendricks Transport Ltd* [1956] 1 WLR 85.
128 [2005] EWHC 2065.
129 Ibid at [26].
130 Ibid at [276].
131 *Arscott*, as above, at 84.

Duty of care

16.55 The central concept of the law of negligence is the duty of care. This is the first stage in determining whether the law will impose liability on a person for harm caused to another in a given situation. The three-stage test contained in *Caparo Industries Plc v Dickman*[132] is the sine qua non for establishing a duty of care:

> What emerges is that, in addition to the *foreseeability of damage*, necessary ingredients in any situation giving rise to a duty of care are that there should exist between the party owing the duty and the party to whom it is owed a relationship characterised by the law as one of '*proximity*' or '*neighbourhood*' and that situation should be one in which the court considers it *fair, just and reasonable* that the law should impose a duty of a given scope on the one party for the benefit of the other.

16.56 A careless defendant may cause harm to a claimant, but he or she will not be negligent unless it is demonstrated that the parties had the requisite proximity, that the type of damage was foreseeable, and that it is fair, just and reasonable to impose a duty of care. Lord Bridge also referred to 'the more traditional categorization of distinct recognizable situations as guides to the existence, the scope and the limits of the varied duties of care which the law imposes'.[133] There is a recent trend for this 'incremental approach' to be considered as a 'check or guide to the application of the *Caparo* tests',[134] but that is not to say that the law is closed to developing novel categories of liability.

16.57 In general, the law of negligence only imposes liability for misfeasance—the wrongful performance of an act—rather than nonfeasance in the form of 'pure omissions'.[135] However, where an individual is responsible for creating a danger or has special responsibility over another, that person may come under a duty to act by taking precautions or warning others.[136]

16.58 *Sutradhar v Natural Environment Research Council*[137] draws together the above principles in the environmental 'toxic tort' context. The British Geological Survey (BGS), a department of the defendant, had carried out research for the Bangladeshi government into the use of groundwater. The BGS tested for certain compounds, but did not test for the presence of arsenic in drinking water. The claimant suffered arsenic poisoning and brought a claim in negligence, alleging that the defendant had been under a duty to test for arsenic, or alternatively, that they should not have published a report that through silence gave the impression that

---

[132] [1990] 2 AC 605 at 617–618, per Lord Bridge; italics added.
[133] Ibid.
[134] *Islington LBC v UCL Hospital NHS Trust* [2006] PIQR P29 at 40, per Buxton LJ.
[135] *Smith v Littlewoods Organisations Ltd* [1987] 2 AC 241 at 247.
[136] Eg *Vacwell Engineering Co Ltd v BDH Chemicals Ltd* [1971] 1 QB 11 (manufacturer who knew of a dangerous feature in one of its products was under a duty to warn customers).
[137] [2007] Env LR 10.

the water was arsenic-free. The House of Lords upheld the Court of Appeal's decision to strike out the claim. First, it was held that a body's expert knowledge did not impose upon it a general duty to prevent harm to others, and it could not be held liable for a pure omission to test for arsenic. Secondly, the defendant had neither control over the supply of drinking water in Bangladesh, nor a legal duty to ensure that the water was safe. Applying the *Caparo* test, the defendant could not reasonably have foreseen that the report would be relied upon as affirming the safety of the drinking water, and it would not be fair, just, or reasonable to impose a duty of care in these circumstances.

Foreseeability in negligence

In *Cambridge Water*, at first instance the plaintiff also failed in its negligence action **16.59** because it could not show that the effect of the PCE spillages on the groundwater was foreseeable by the defendant.[138] As has long been said:

> The court must be careful to place itself in the position of the person charged with the duty and to consider what he or she should have reasonably anticipated as a natural and probable consequence of neglect, and not to give undue weight to the fact that a distressing accident has happened, or that witnesses are prone to regret, *ex post facto*, that they did not take some step which it is now realised would definitely have prevented the accident.[139]

Foreseeability will also depend on any knowledge that the defendant had, or **16.60** ought to have had, about the claimant's vulnerability. This means that a higher standard will be expected of defendants when they are aware that there are children at risk, who are too young to understand danger,[140] or when they ought to be aware of the vulnerability of certain classes of potential victims.[141]

The state of knowledge, both factual and technical, which a defendant can be **16.61** reasonably expected to have at the date when the cause of action arose is relevant to determining foreseeability. Hindsight must be avoided. In *Roe v Ministry of Health*[142], when the issue arose of whether the staff of a hospital could be expected to foresee that the contents of an ampoule would have been contaminated by phenol leaching in through a hairline crack, Lord Denning was prompted to say, 'We must not look at the 1947 accident with 1954 spectacles'. Where the state of technical knowledge is well-documented, foreseeability will be simpler to prove.

---

138 [1993] Env LR 116 at 144.
139 *Glasgow Corporation v Muir* [1943] AC 448 at 454, per Lord Thankerton.
140 Eg *Mourton v Poulter* [1930] 2 KB 183; see also *Morrell v Owen*, The Times, 14 December 1993 (disabled adults).
141 *Haley v London Electricity Board* [1965] AC 778 (a hammer left blocking an excavation was inadequate warning for the blind, and it was reasonably foreseeable that blind people would be walking along the pavement).
142 [1954] 2 QB 66.

Margereson v J W Roberts[143] was a landmark case because it was the first occasion a British court awarded mesothelioma victims compensation as a result of environmental, rather than occupational, exposure to asbestos.[144] The state of scientific information available at the time of exposure was such that the Court of Appeal was able to give a definite answer to the question of when it was reasonably foreseeable that the asbestos dust would cause the type of damage suffered by the factory's neighbours. Similarly, in *Barclays Bank plc v Fairclough Building Ltd (No 2)*, the Court of Appeal held that a contractor who undertook work on materials containing asbestos should have been aware of the serious health risks by at least 1988.[145] The coming into force of specific regulations in 1987, and the extensive publicity about asbestos, meant that a contractor was under a duty to find out about the risks before undertaking such work. However, in cases where the science is evolving, and there are large reputations and sums of money at stake, proving foreseeability is likely to be more complex.[146]

Breach of duty

16.62 The standard of care to be reached is that of the 'reasonable and prudent man'[147] in the circumstances; a defendant who, by his act or omission, fails to reach this standard is in breach of duty. A professional will be judged according to the accepted practices of a responsible body of professionals,[148] unless the accepted practice would itself not stand up to logical scrutiny.[149]

16.63 The standard will be higher if the operations undertaken are inherently dangerous,[150] as may often be the case for industries regulated under the environmental Acts. As Lord Dunedin has said, 'People must guard against reasonable probabilities, but they are not bound to guard against fantastic possibilities'.[151] This judgment may be influenced by the severity of the likely harm if it does occur. The courts have emphasized that 'those who engage in operations inherently dangerous must take precautions which are not required of persons engaged in the ordinary routine of daily life'.[152] It is also influenced by the cost of taking

---

[143] The Times, 17 April 1996.

[144] See Stephen Fietta, 'Negligence: duty of care', ICCLR 1996, 7(7), C136–138.

[145] The Times, 15 February 1995.

[146] For example, in efforts to secure compensation for industrial workers suffering from Vibration White Finger (see *Armstrong v British Coal Corporation*, The Times, 6 December 1996).

[147] *Blyth v Birmingham Waterworks* (1856) 11 Ex 781 at 784, per Baron Alderson.

[148] *Bolam v Friern Hospital Management Committee* [1957] 1 WLR 582.

[149] *Bolitho v City and Hackney Health Authority* [1998] AC 232.

[150] Eg *Beckett v Newalls Insulation Co* [1953] 1 WLR 8 (gas containers brought into a confined space on a ship under construction).

[151] *Fardon v Harcourt-Rivington* [1932] 146 LT 391 at 392.

[152] *Glasgow Corporation v Muir* [1943] AC 448 at 456, per Lord Macmillan; see also *Beckett* supra.

the necessary precautions with regard to the risk, although it has been said that the courts 'should be more concerned with what appears to be fair and reasonable than with wider utilitarian calculations'.[153]

The standard to be expected can vary if an emergency occurs, as an emergency   **16.64** may overburden available resources, leaving one person suddenly faced with doing many things at once.[154] Difficulties have arisen with the duty owed by rescuers who enter what is by definition a hazardous situation.[155] In *McFarlane v EE Caledonia*[156], the court had to consider the position of a rescue vessel which was damaged in the course of helping with the Piper Alpha oil rig fire in the North Sea. In these circumstances, a rescuer's error of judgment should rarely give rise to liability, unless they have significantly aggravated the situation.

The defendant's reliance on common practice

Adherence to common practice is strong evidence that the defendant is acting to   **16.65** the correct standard of care.[157] For example, in *Thompson v Smith Shiprepairers (North Shields) Ltd,*[158] there was general inaction in shipyards with regard to the possible dangers from industrial noise. Despite actual knowledge that shipyard employees had suffered deafness as a result of excessive noise, the risks were seen as an acceptable and inescapable feature of the industry. By 1963, there was greater awareness of the dangers and the necessary protective equipment had been available for some time. This date marked the dividing line between a reasonable policy of inaction and an unreasonable failure to take reasonably practicable action. It followed that if an employer failed to take the necessary precautions after 1963, it might be held liable in negligence. However, if the risks are unreasonable in any given circumstances, the adoption of the common practice will not be enough to avoid liability. In *Bux v Slough Metals Ltd,*[159] the employer had complied with the regulations to provide eye goggles to their foundry workers. But the employer did not insist that they should be worn, nor provide instruction as to their use. The plaintiff could pursue his claim since the regulations did not supersede the common law duty of care. Many industries have adopted safety standards which are important evidence of the general standards to be expected. Although not legally

---

[153] *Morgan Crucible v Hill Samuel* [1991] Ch 295 at 303, per Hoffman J.

[154] 'The fact that he does one of them incorrectly should not lightly be taken as negligence' *Wilsher v Essex AHA* [1987] QB 730 at 749, per Mustill LJ.

[155] If the rescuers are themselves acting under a statutory duty, then the courts will be even more reluctant to impose a standard of liability which would inhibit them in exercising their duties (see *Capital and Counties plc v Hampshire County Council* [1997] 3 WLR 331).

[156] [1994] 2 All ER 1; the claim for psychiatric damage to the bystanders on the ship, who were off-duty workers from the rig, failed on the grounds of remoteness.

[157] *Stokes v Guest, Keen and Nettlefold (Bolts and Nuts) Ltd* [1968] 1 WLR 1776 at 1783.

[158] [1984] QB 405, per Mustill J.

[159] [1973] 1 WLR 1358.

binding, the British Safety Standards have been accepted as strong evidence of the consensus of professional opinion and current experience.[160]

The defendant's reliance on regulatory standards

16.66   A defendant may be able to claim that they have statutory authorization to carry out their activity in a certain manner, or to a certain standard, at least for the relevant time when the cause of action accrued. In *Budden v BP*,[161] two infant plaintiffs alleged personal injury and sued BP and Shell Oil for damages and an injunction to restrain the defendants from adding organo-lead additives to their petrol. Even on the assumption that some physical injury had been caused, the oil companies applied to strike out the action on the ground that they had complied with the regulations enacted under the CoPA 1974, by which the Secretary of State had prescribed maximum limits for lead content. The Court of Appeal held that the manufacturers could not be negligent if the limit to which they had adhered was one which Parliament had impliedly approved and which they, therefore, were entitled to assume was consistent with the public interest. The rationale for this approach was the court's reluctance to implement its own permissible limit of universal application, which was at odds with that tacitly approved by Parliament. However, there has been some concern that *Budden* goes too far. While the limits set down in regulations should be relevant to determining the common law duty of care, regulations ought not be an automatic defence to negligence which, in effect, deprives injured persons of a cause of action.[162]

E. Trespass

16.67   Any unjustifiable intrusion onto another's land is capable of founding an action in trespass. Trespass differs from nuisance in that the interference must be direct, and there is no requirement to prove actual damage.

16.68   The mere physical presence of a person on the land of another may thus constitute a trespass.[163] Accordingly, an interim injunction may be sought in respect of an

---

[160] See *Ward v The Ritz Hotel (London) Ltd* [1992] PIQR 315 (P fell over a balcony, whose railing was lower than the British Standard; judge gave too little weight to the standard); BS 4142 on noise was relied upon in the noise nuisance case of *Tetley v Chitty* [1986] 1 All ER 663 at 666–667, per McNeill J.

[161] [1980] JPL 586; the alternative action in public nuisance was struck out at first instance.

[162] See the Case Comment to *Budden* [1980] JPL 586 at 587, with reference to the Trade Effluents Sub-Committee of the Central Water Advisory Committee in 1960; *Budden* is contrasted with riparian rights to water, which are not altered by the grant of licence to discharge polluting matter.

[163] Merely setting foot on the land of another is sufficient: *Ellis v Loftus Iron Co* (1874) LR 10 C & P 10, 12 per Coleridge CJ.

anticipated incursion on to land by environmental protestors. It is now accepted that it is not necessary for such persons to be named, provided they can be referred to by a sufficiently precise description.[164] Protestors have sought to argue that their trespass was justified in order to protect the public from harm,[165] or to prevent a breach of planning law,[166] but such arguments are generally not likely to succeed.

Further examples of trespass in an environmental context include depositing **16.69** material in or on land,[167] or entering land below its surface, for example to extract natural resources.[168] The law of trespass can also be used by a landowner or occupier when a licensee or invitee acts outside or in excess of his rights under a licence.[169] This may arise where a landfill operator has deposited unauthorized materials, for instance when putrescible waste is deposited in a site leased only for inert materials.

The damage complained of must follow so immediately from the act as to be a **16.70** direct part of the act.[170] In *Esso Petroleum Co Ltd v Southport Corporation*[171] the master of a stranded oil tanker discharged 400 tons of oil in an effort to lighten the ship. The oil was carried by the tide and polluted the foreshore. An action was brought in negligence, nuisance, and trespass. Although trespass was not argued in the House of Lords, Lords Radcliffe and Tucker did not consider that there had been a trespass, since the damage to the foreshore lacked the requisite inevitability. The general rule appears to be that when a substance such as a pollutant passes onto the land of another merely as a result of a landowner exercising his own rights on his own property, this is properly characterized as a nuisance,[172] whereas a

---

[164] See *Hampshire Waste Services Ltd v Intending trespassers upon Chineham Incinerator Site* [2003] EWHC 1738 (Ch); [2004] Env LR 9 in which Sir Andrew Morritt VC granted such an injunction against intending trespassers of unknown identity.

[165] For example *Monsanto v Tilly* [2000] Env LR 313 in which protestors destroyed genetically modified crops.

[166] For example *Mayor and Burgesses of the London Borough of Bromley v Susanna (a female)* [1999] Env LR D13 (CA) in which protestors argued that the proposed development would be contrary to planning and environmental law.

[167] See for example *Kynoch Limited v Rowlands* [1912] 1 Ch 527 (CA) (rubbish deposited on a strip of land and against a wall).

[168] A recent example of such a cause of action is the case of *Bocardo SA v Star Energy UK Onshore Ltd and another* [2008] EWHC 1756 (Ch) in which the equivalent of one million barrels of oil was extracted from reserves extending to a point almost one kilometre beneath the Surrey estate of the businessman Mohamed Al Fayed.

[169] In *Hillen v ICI (Alkali) Ltd* [1936] AC 65, once the stevedores adopted an unauthorized method of unloading, they became trespassers (although the case concerned whether there was a duty of care to them).

[170] *Esso Petroleum Co Ltd v Southport Corporation* [1954] 2 QB 182 at 195, per Denning LJ in the Court of Appeal.

[171] [1954] 2 QB 182 (CA); and [1956] AC 218 (HL).

[172] *Reynolds v Clarke* [1725] 2 Ld Ray 1399.

deliberate policy of releasing a substance such as sewage across a neighbour's land can amount either to nuisance or trespass.[173] A defendant may claim that his actions were done with the express or implied consent of the claimant, or under statutory authorization. The same considerations which apply in the case of a nuisance will then apply.

F. Breach of Statutory Duty

The Occupiers' Liability Acts

16.71 By statute, an occupier owes a duty of care in respect of the safety of those who enter his or her land, particularly if the land is in a hazardous state. Section 2(2) of the Occupiers' Liability Act 1957 imposes on the occupier of land or premises a duty to take reasonable care to see that every lawful visitor will be reasonably safe for the purpose for which the visitor has been invited or permitted there. Slippery paths are a classic breach of the duty,[174] but it could easily extend to such matters as spillages of hazardous substances. The duty exists in relation to dangers arising from the 'state of the premises or things done or omitted to be done on them',[175] and not in relation to dangers which one would reasonably expect to exist in land of a given type due to its nature.[176] The occupier can warn his visitors, but such a warning will only be sufficient if, in all the circumstances, it enables the visitor to be reasonably safe.[177] An occupier is not ordinarily responsible for a visitor's own unsafe system of work.[178] The courts have taken a broad approach to the question of who will be held responsible. An 'occupier' as used in the 1957 Act connotes a sufficient degree of control, which can include contractors.[179] A licensee or visitor may become a trespasser, who has no right of action under the 1957 Act, if he operates outside of the terms of the licence under which he is on the property.[180] The Occupiers' Liability Act 1984 imposes upon an occupier a duty to warn unlawful visitors and take reasonable steps to prevent them from being physically injured, if he has reasonable grounds to believe a danger exists on his land. The occupier should

---

[173] *Pearce v Croydon RDC* [1910] 74 JP 429.

[174] *Murphy v Bradford DC*, The Times, 11 February 1991, CA (system of warning was insufficient).

[175] S1(1).

[176] See *Tomlinson v Congleton Borough Council* [2003] UKHL 47; [2004] 1 AC 46 per Lord Hoffman at [26]–[27].

[177] S 2(4)(a).

[178] See *Ferguson v Welsh* [1987] 1 WLR 1553, HL.

[179] *AMF International Ltd v Magnet Bowling Ltd* [1968] 1 WLR 1028, QBD, applying *Wheat v E Lacon & Co Ltd* [1966] AC 552, HL.

[180] *Hillen v ICI (Alkali) Ltd* [1936] AC 65, HL (stevedore injured when dangerous unloading method used without authority). See para 17.46.

adequately fence off, or erect warning signs about, any hazards. Whether an occupier does owe a duty in each individual case will be a question of fact.[181]

Breaches of general statutory duties

Despite the policy arguments in favour of a general duty of care, there is no equivalent in environmental law to the general statutory liability which is placed on employers under the Factory Acts to provide a safe place of work.[182] Nor is it easy to imply such a duty into the Acts. Most of the environmental Acts are silent as to whether the obligations or prohibitions which are imposed are for the benefit or protection of a particular class of individuals. Even if it can be said that a particular environmental Act does confer a public right, a particular member of the public will only have a civil remedy if he suffers 'particular direct and substantial'[183] damage which is different from that which is common to all other members of the public. The courts have already held that the fact that work is carried out in breach of the Building Regulations is unlikely to be held to be sufficient to impose a duty of care in that respect.[184] It also is unlikely that a cause of action will be held to arise, for instance, from a breach of the statutory duty to use 'BATNEEC'[185] when carrying out a prescribed process under Part I of the EPA 1990. In the WRA 1991, it is made explicit that neither Section 70, with regard to abstraction licences, nor Section 100, with regard to pollution offences, confers an individual right of action for a breach of the statutory duty involved. **16.72**

A few environmental statutes do expressly provide for civil liability to be imposed on persons as a result of breaches of their statutory duties. There is absolute civil liability imposed under the Nuclear Installations Act 1965, Sections 7 to 10. Sections 153 and 154 of the Merchant Shipping Act 1995 impose strict liability on the owners of oil tankers in relation to damage caused by oil spills. Water companies are liable for any escape of water from one of their pipes, under Section 209 of the WIA 1991. Under the EPA 1990, Section 73(6), a claim in damages can be made for any loss caused by an unlawful deposit of controlled waste, which has been deposited in breach of Sections 33(1) or 63(2). The liability of public authorities for a breach of their statutory duties is considered separately below. **16.73**

---

[181] *White v St Albans City and District Council*, The Times, 12 March 1990, CA—trench on fenced-off land; see also *Ratcliff v McConnell* [1999] 1 WLR 670, CA (no duty to a particular trespasser to warn of danger of diving into a swimming pool).

[182] See, for example, *Larner v British Steel* [1993] 4 All ER 102, CA in relation to the duty contained in the Factories Act 1961, s 29(1).

[183] The words of Brett J in *Benjamin v Storr* [1874] LR 9 CP 400, 407.

[184] Supported by Lord Wilberforce in *Anns*, but not by the Court of Appeal (obiter) in *Murphy*.

[185] Best Available Techniques Not Entailing Excessive Cost—see EPA 1990, s 7.

G. Liability for Breach of Contractual or Property Rights

Breaches of covenants

16.74 Companies and private individuals may be able to protect their interests by bringing an action for a breach of covenant. This might arise, for instance, where a neighbour's land use is in breach of a restrictive covenant placed on his land or where a neighbour has interfered with easements across his land. The use of covenants is an important way in which landlords and tenants can protect their rights during the lifetime of the lease. If a covenant is broken during the life of the lease, the normal rule will be that the landlord or tenant should be put in the same position in which he would have been if there had been no breach of covenant by the other party.[186] When the tenant surrenders the demised premises to the landlord, there are often outstanding liabilities under the lease. It is a fairly standard clause that the premises should be yielded up in accordance with the covenants. If the tenant has breached his covenant to keep the premises in repair, the landlord is prevented by statute from recovering more than the amount (if any) by which the value of the reversion has been diminished.[187] If, however, there has been a breach of a covenant to carry out works such as restoring a landfill site,[188] there will be no such statutory limit and the normal common law rules will apply. The normal approach is to award the diminution in value caused to the relevant party's interest in the land.[189]

Rights to water

16.75 The owners and occupiers of land which adjoins a watercourse have riparian rights to use the water subject to the reasonable and ordinary use of others. They do not own the water as such, but there is a right to a regular flow of water without sensible alteration in its character.[190] An action may lie in trespass if the purity of the water is affected.[191] The grant of a licence to discharge polluting matter into a river

---

[186] See *Woodfall's Law of Landlord and Tenant*, para 11.034 and *Livingstone v The Rawyards Coal Company* (1879–80) LR 5 App Cas 25 (HL). It should further be noted that specific performance will only be granted where damages would be an inadequate remedy.

[187] The Landlord and Tenant Act 1927, s 18(1) prescribes this upper limit on the tenant's liabilities, although the common law rules for the calculation of damages continue to apply.

[188] Note that a covenant requiring 'infilling and restoration of the quarry to agriculture' is a positive covenant, and relief cannot be sought under the Law of Property Act 1925 s 84: *Bedwell Park Quarry Company v Hertfordshire County Council* [1993] JPL 349, CA (waste disposal site and planning agreement under, TCPA 1971, s 52).

[189] See further the section on Damages below.

[190] *Scott-Whitehead v National Coal Board* [1987] 53 P&CR 263, QBD; and see generally the classic text, W Howarth, *Wisdom's Law of Watercourses* (5th ed. Shaw and Sons, 1992).

[191] *Jones v Llanrwst UDC* [1911] 1 Ch 393; *John Young & Co v Bankier Distillery Co* (1893) AC 691 (HL) (mine water discharged into stream used by distillery).

according to certain regulatory standards should in no way alter the common law rights of a riparian owner to sue the licence holder if damage is caused.[192] The sophisticated system of regulation of discharges to water, and the use of statutory standards, were introduced with the purpose of maintaining and restoring the wholesomeness of rivers, whereas the common law is concerned with the maintenance and protection of the proprietary rights of riparian owners. Any interference with 'percolating water'[193] will be dealt with according to the normal rules of tort law. The argument that there is a separate right of action in such cases, based on strict liability, was rejected by the House of Lords when they overruled the Court of Appeal's decision in the *Cambridge Water Company* case.[194]

Contractual liabilities

It has become an important feature of company acquisitions, and of property transactions, to take account of the potential environmental liabilities.[195] This is reflected not only in the prolonged pre-contractual measures which may be necessary—such as conducting an environmental audit to ensure due diligence—but also in the terms of the contract. The key point is to establish in any contract the baseline liabilities of both sides at the date of the acquisition, which should ensure the minimum of future dispute. Any purchaser should also be wary of assuming responsibility for any past liabilities. Although the regulators will first pursue people who have caused any pollution, ultimately the current owner or occupier of the relevant land can be held responsible. Indeed, a buyer might prefer to buy only part of the property or take a lease of the property, in order to limit his responsibilities. One technique has been to grant 'piecrust'[196] leases, in the hope that anything under the land will not then be the tenant's responsibility.[197] In a company acquisition, it might be advantageous only to transfer the assets of a company, rather than acquiring its shares and taking over all its existing criminal and civil liabilities.

16.76

---

[192] The issue of relying on statutory standards as a defence to a nuisance is discussed at para 17.44 above.

[193] *Ballard v Tomlinson* [1885] LR 29 ChD 115—as 'a natural right incident to the ownership of . . . land'. The House of Lords re-analysed the right in *Cambridge Water*, as part of a person's use or enjoyment of his or her land.

[194] [1994] 2 AC 264, at 296C–G. The water company's right to abstraction was acknowledged, but the right of action lay in nuisance, for interference with the use or enjoyment of their land, and in negligence.

[195] See further Brian Greenwood, 'The Environmental Transaction' [1996] JPL Occasional Series—which highlights the need to take account of most of the regimes discussed in this book.

[196] That is to say, a lease of only the land's surface.

[197] This remains an untested technique to avoid statutory responsibility—the relevant regimes may impose liability for any hazardous materials which are 'in, on or under' the land (eg the contaminated land regime).

H. Civil Liability Of Regulatory Authorities

General considerations

16.77 In principle, the liability of a public authority and its officers in tort should be the same as that of a private person. The authority will be held liable for the acts of its own officers, when they are acting within the scope of their responsibilities to it.[198] But the courts have taken the view that, due to the nature of a public body's statutory powers and duties, the scope of its liability may be limited.[199] The courts will not be willing to impose a duty of care on a public authority if this would be inconsistent with, or tend to discourage them from, the due performance of their statutory duties.[200] This applies with particular force to the environmental Acts. Therefore, it will not always be possible to recover compensation when a regulator causes loss and damage to an individual or a company, even if they do so carelessly.

Damages for maladministration

16.78 English law still does not recognize a general right to damages where there has been maladministration by a public authority.[201] There may come a time when this is a right recognized in the English courts, particularly under the influence of European law[202] and the introduction of claims against public authorities who have breached an individual's human rights.[203] For the moment, it is necessary to make a claim under a recognized principle of civil liability. It is not enough to allege simply that there is a cause of action in tort because there has been some unlawful conduct by a public body.[204] There is a separate tort of 'misfeasance in public office', where there has been a deliberate or malicious abuse of power or

---

[198] A vexed area for the employees, given that they may not be covered by contractual indemnity where they act ultra vires (see *Burgoine v Waltham Forest LBC* [1997] BCC 347). Employees can claim against their negligent employers if they suffer injury or loss in the course of their work under the normal rules of negligence (see for example *White v Chief Constable of South Yorkshire Police* [1999] 2 AC 455 (HL) per Lord Hoffman at 506.)

[199] See *Stovin v Wise* [1996] AC 923 (HL) at 946 per Lord Hoffman.

[200] See *Welton v North Cornwall DC* [1997] 1 WLR 570, CA.

[201] For instance, in *R v Knowsley MBC, ex p Maguire*, The Times, 26 June 1992, Schiemann J (failure to licence hackney carriages; no general right to damages for maladministration).

[202] European Union cases such as *Francovich* and *Brasserie du Pêcheur* allow an individual to seek damages against the member state for breaches of their European obligations (see further the chapter on European law, paras 4.38 ff).

[203] Under the Human Rights Act 1998, there is a right to claim damages for a violation of the European Convention of Human Rights (see para 22.35).

[204] *Dunlop v Woollahra Municipal Council* [1982] AC 158, PC.

deliberate maladministration.[205] Otherwise, at the moment, only the Local Government Ombudsman will be interested in a claim for compensation for maladministration.[206]

Liability in negligence

In most cases the careless exercise of a statutory function, in the absence of negli-   **16.79**
gence, will not be sufficient to found a cause of action.[207] Although no statute can be expected to authorize a public authority to carry out its work negligently,[208] it might still be difficult for a claimant successfully to sue an authority in negligence. In *X (minors) v Bedfordshire CC and others*,[209] the House of Lords re-emphasized that the plaintiff has to show that the circumstances are such as to raise a duty of care at common law. Even if the authority carelessly carries out a statutory power or duty, and causes harm to a third party, that third party still needs to satisfy the tests in *Caparo Industries plc v Dickman*.[210] Novel categories are likely to be developed incrementally and only by analogy with the existing categories of cases where public authorities have been held liable. In particular, the policy consideration of whether or not it is just and reasonable to impose a duty of care on a defendant has great weight where public authorities are concerned. A duty of care has been denied with regard to the particular way the police,[211] or the rescue services such as the fire brigade,[212] or coastguard,[213] carried out an operation. However, the courts have become wary of allowing authorities to benefit from

---

[205] See Wade and Forsyth, *Administrative Law* (9th edn, OUP, 2004) further. A public authority can be vicariously liable for the acts of its officers which amount to misfeasance (see *Racz v Home Office* [1994] 2 AC 45, HL). For the tort of misfeasance in public office see *Smith v East Elloe RDC* [1956] AC 736.

[206] See para 22.11 further—the Ombudsman can recommend that some compensation is paid by the public authority.

[207] See X (minors) v Bedfordshire CC and others [1995] 2 AC 633, HL.

[208] See *Wade* at 771 ff.

[209] [1995] 2 AC 633, HL.

[210] [1990] 2 AC 605; principles for bringing an action in negligence were set out in *Curran v Northern Ireland Co-ownership Housing Association Ltd* [1987] AC 718 at 727–728, per Lord Bridge.

[211] *Hill v Chief Constable of West Yorkshire* [1989] AC 53, HL; but a duty can arise where the police take over a situation and act foolishly (*Knightley v Johns* [1982] 1 WLR 349).

[212] See the combined cases in *Capital and Counties Plc v Hampshire CC* [1997] 3 WLR 331, CA; and earlier cases such as *John Munroe (Acrylics) Ltd v London Fire and Civil Defence Authority and others*, The Times, 22 May 1996, Rougier J. Yet in *Crown River Cruises Ltd v Kimbolton Fireworks Ltd and London Fire and Civil Defence Authority*, The Times, 6 March 1996, the authority was held 75 percent liable—just as one fire brigade was held liable in *Capital Counties Plc*. Indeed, the general exclusion of liability to the public at large in *Capital and Counties plc* can be distinguished once an emergency service accepts a specific call from an individual—see *Kent v Griffiths (No.3)* [2001] QB 36, CA (failure of ambulance to respond to 999 call).

[213] *Skinner v Secretary of State for Transport*, The Times, 3 January 1996, QBD; *OLL Ltd v Secretary of State for Transport* [1997] 3 All ER 897, QBD.

a blanket immunity.[214] The Court of Appeal in *Lam v Brennan (t/a Namesakes of Torbay) and Torbay Borough Council*[215] held that the town and country planning regime provides a regulatory scheme for the benefit of the public at large and therefore a private right of action for breach of statutory duty would not arise in relation to the grant of planning permission or the failure to enforce planning controls. However, subsequently in *Kane v New Forest DC (No.1)*[216] it was held that *Lam* did not operate so as to give a local planning authority a blanket immunity from liability if it permits the construction of a foreseeably dangerous footpath in exercising its statutory functions. Similarly, the House of Lords in *Phelps v Hillingdon LBC*[217] doubted *X (minors)* in holding that there was no justification for a blanket immunity for education workers exercising their statutory functions.

16.80 Where an environmental Act provides a statutory right of appeal against an adverse decision or action, as most do, the courts are likely to hold that it is not just and reasonable to impose a common law duty of care as well.[218] Therefore, if the Environment Agency were to handle a waste management licence application negligently, the applicant's best remedy will probably lie in an appeal.[219] But if an Act does not provide a statutory remedy, it will be necessary to look at the Act's construction to determine whether it was intended to confer a private right on members of a class of the public.[220] For instance, in *Read v Croydon Corporation*,[221] the court did hold that the specific statutory duty to provide wholesome water was a duty intended to protect individuals such as the plaintiffs. But in *Capital and Counties Plc v Hampshire CC*,[222] the statutory duty on the fire brigade to take all reasonable measures to ensure that there was an adequate water supply for firefighting was held not to confer a private law right on individuals, but was merely part of its general administrative functions.

---

[214] Following *Osman v United Kingdom* 29 EHRR 245 as interpreted in *Barrett v Enfield London Borough Council* [2001] 2 AC 550, HL.

[215] [1998] PLCR 30, CA.

[216] [2001] EWCA Civ 878; [2002] 1 WLR 312 at 317 per Simon Brown LJ.

[217] [2001] 2 AC 619.

[218] *Jones v Department of Employment* [1989] 1 QB 1 (social security benefits).

[219] Cf *R v Hounslow LBC, ex p Williamson* [1996] EGCS 27, QBD. If no appeal is made, it may also be impossible to establish causation. The applicant had turned down the opportunity to appeal the local planning authority's view that a particular permission was needed.

[220] See *R v Deputy Governor of Parkhurst Prison, ex p Hague* [1992] 1 AC 58, cited by Lord Hoffman in *Stovin v Wise* (below).

[221] [1938] 4 All ER 631 (typhus epidemic)—concerning s 31 of the Water Act 1945 (now s 68(1) of the WIA 1991). Note that the provision of a statutory penalty for a breach of the duty was not held to be an exclusive remedy.

[222] [1997] 3 WLR 331, CA—the third case brought by *Church of Jesus Christ of Latter Day Saints (GB) v West Yorkshire FCDA* included a claim for a breach of statutory duty after the fire brigade could not find an adequate supply of water to fight the fire.

Liability for negligent operational or policy decisions

A useful analytical distinction can still be drawn between operational and policy **16.81** matters.[223] Operational matters, such as driving a vehicle, providing a safe system of work, and checking a register are capable of giving rise to a duty of care on a public body.[224] Policy matters, particularly involving a discretion, will generally not. As the part played by broad discretionary considerations grows, the less readily a common law duty will be imposed. There is no clear-cut distinction, although cases concerning matters such as the allocation of scarce resources and the distribution of risks are altogether unsuitable for actions in negligence.[225] Although the demarcation between policy and operational decisions has been described as 'thin and obscure'[226], it can be illustrated by the decision in *Rigby v Chief Constable of Nottinghamshire*.[227] In that case, the Chief Constable was not held liable in negligence for choosing a particular type of CS gas device, but he was held liable for the operational failure to have fire-fighting equipment available when the CS gas was fired into a shop setting it on fire. Similar questions may arise with the Environment Agency's decisions, particularly given their duty under Section 39 of the EA 1995 to take account of the likely costs and benefits of their actions. Where the statute only imposes general duties on an authority, which lack specific content, it is unlikely that a breach will be held to provide a cause of action. For instance, the court held that there was no private law action if the Minister for Education failed 'to promote the education of the people of England and Wales'.[228] The same approach is likely to be taken on the similar wording of the various general duties placed on the Environment Agency.

Liability for negligent inspection and regulation

As a matter of policy the courts are unlikely to hold that a duty of care arises where **16.82** an authority is carrying out its inspection and enforcement duties, or is offering an informal advisory service as part of its duties.[229] The Court of Appeal in *Welton v North Cornwall District Council*[230] has held that liability will be excluded on policy grounds if it is inconsistent with, or has the tendency to discourage, the due performance of the authority's duties. This has been confirmed in

---

[223] See for example *Barrett v Enfield LBC* [2001] 2 AC 550, HL.

[224] Eg *Coats Paton (Retail) Ltd v Birmingham Corporation* (1971) 69 LGR 356.

[225] See the dicta of Lord Woolf MR in *Kent v Griffiths (No. 3)* [2001] QB 36, CA, at [47].

[226] *Lavis v Kent County Council* [1994] 90 LGR 416, CA, per Steyn LJ.

[227] [1985] 1 WLR 1242.

[228] *Watt v Kesteven CC* [1955] 1 QB 408; see also *R v SS for Social Services, ex p Hincks* [1973] 123 SJ 436 (provision of an 'efficient and comprehensive' health service).

[229] Eg that planning permission would be given: *Tidman v Reading BC*, The Times, 10 November 1994, Buxton J; see also *Strable v Dartford BC* [1984] JPL 329; *Ryeford Homes v Sevenoaks DC*, The Times, 15 February 1989; *R v Hounslow LBC, ex p Williamson* [1996] EGCS 27.

[230] [1997] 1 WLR 570; *Independent*, 17 July 1996, CA.

Harris v Evans and another,[231] where the advice given by a health and safety inspector to a local authority was alleged to have been negligent. It was held to be implicit in the system of improvement and prohibition notices that this might cause economic loss or damage to those who were subject to them, and the Act itself provided the remedies for this, by way of appeal.

16.83 However in exceptional cases the court will impose liability for careless inspection or advice. There must be something more than the performance (negligent or otherwise) of the statutory function to establish such an assumption of responsibility.[232] *Welton v North Cornwall District Council* [233] is an example of such an exceptional set of circumstances. The council's environmental health officer had insisted that if certain works were not carried out, he would close the business down. In fact, the works were unnecessary, and the inspector was found to have given negligent advice, acted outside both his statutory powers and the informal enforcement policy of the council, and known that the plaintiffs would rely upon his advice without independent inquiry. The Court of Appeal held that the facts fell within *Hedley Byrne*, and that there were no policy reasons for excluding liability. Similarly, where it is reasonable for an applicant to rely upon representations made by a senior member of the local authority's staff, and he is then prevented from continuing the works he had commenced as a result of the representations, a duty of care may arise.[234]

16.84 It is also possible that liability for negligent inspection will attach if the case involves personal injury, or damage to other property. *Murphy v Brentwood District Council*[235] leaves this possibility open. For example, the building regulation authority could be liable if a member of the public is injured due to the authority's failure to ensure that a new building has proper foundations.[236] The local authority has sufficient powers to supervise and control the construction of the building, and the purpose of those powers is to protect the future occupants and users from

---

[231] [1998] 1 WLR 1285, CA.

[232] See *Lam v Brennan (t/a Namesakes of Torbay) and Torbay Borough Council* [1998] PLCR 30, CA, at 50 per Potter LJ. The plaintiff had sought to plead his cause of action on the basis of 'assumption of responsibility', as well as on the basis of a breach of statutory duty.

[233] [1997] 1 WLR 570; *Independent*, 17 July 1996, CA.

[234] See *Lambert v West Devon BC* [1997] JPL 735 (the applicant was told that his planning application had been approved)—again, a *Hedley Byrne* type of duty arose. Even after *Welton*, these types of cases should still give rise to liability.

[235] [1991] 1 AC 398, HL (negligent approval of building plans). The liability of public bodies for economic loss to third parties was severely restricted—see the section on economic loss below further. The law in New Zealand has taken the opposite path (see *Invercargill City Council v Hamlin* [1996] AC 624, PC).

[236] *Anns v Merton LBC* [1978] AC 728—although overruled by *Murphy* on economic loss, it remains good authority for this proposition; see also *Dutton v Bognor Regis UDC* [1972] 1 QB 373 (house foundations).

harm. In *Scott-Whitehead v National Coal Board*,[237] the local water authority were held to be liable in negligence when they failed to warn riparian owners downstream about the effects of mine water pollution of the river, which was clearly able to damage the plaintiff's crops. The owners of the mine, the National Coal Board, were not found liable. It was reasonable for them to rely upon the water authority to warn others, since the authority knew when, and at what level of water, the river might be affected by the discharges, and they also knew the identity of all those who were licensed to abstract water from the river. An authority was also held liable for failing to warn water customers that the supply of water through their old lead pipes might cause health problems.[238] Equally, the Environment Agency would also be liable for failing to take reasonable steps to prevent further pollution once it is informed of an incident.

Liability for the public authority's decision not to act

The liability of public bodies for a failure to act was considered by the House of Lords in *Stovin v Wise*.[239] All their Lordships agreed that the circumstances giving rise to liability were limited.[240] Lord Hoffmann gave the reasoned judgment for the three majority Law Lords. He held that the minimum preconditions for liability were that (i) it would in the circumstances have been irrational not to have exercised the power, so there was in effect a public law duty to act; and (ii) there are exceptional grounds for holding that the policy of the statute requires compensation to persons who suffer loss because the power was not exercised.[241] The House of Lords has since stated as a matter of principle that it is difficult to imagine a case in which a common law duty can be founded purely on a benefit which a public body has a public law duty to provide.[242]

16.85

---

[237] [1987] 53 P&CR 263, QBD.

[238] *Barnes v Irwell Valley Water Board* [1939] 1 KB 21, CA (no breach of statutory duty to supply wholesome water in their own pipes); *Read v Croydon Corporation* [1938] 4 All ER 631 (typhoid).

[239] [1996] 3 WLR 388, per Lord Hoffman. Note that it was only a 3:2 decision. The highway authority had a power to remove obstructions, and had known that one existed which obstructed visibility at a junction. A motor cyclist was injured in an accident at the junction and the authority was joined as a defendant.

[240] The minority judgment was given by Lord Nicholls, with Lord Slynn agreeing: there must be a failure to act as a reasonable authority would do (in *Wednesbury* terms) and the existence of special circumstances imposing a concurrent common law liability. On the construction of the Highways Act, the minority considered that a duty did arise.

[241] Lord Hoffmann left open the question whether *Anns* was wrong to distinguish *East Suffolk Rivers Catchment Board v Kent* [1941] AC 74, which had laid down that 'where a statutory authority is entrusted with a mere power it cannot be made liable for any damage sustained by a member of the public by reason of a failure to exercise that power' (Lord Romer at 102). The Board was not liable for the excessive time taken to repair a sea wall, even though the land had remained flooded for 178 days rather than 14 days. Certainly, it might be decided differently today—contrast *Curran v Northern Ireland Co-Ownership Housing Association Ltd* (see above).

[242] *Gorringe v Calderdale Metropolitan Borough Council* [2004] UKHL 15; [2004] 1 WLR 1057. See per Lord Hoffman at [32].

Nuisances created by public authorities

16.86 The liability for a nuisance created by publicly-authorized work will depend on whether or not the authority was acting under a duty or power. An authority is restricted by its statutory duties and powers in the way that it can act, so that it can be authorized to do something which necessarily involves committing a tort.[243] Whilst *Stovin* was concerned with liability in negligence, a public authority can be liable, on similar principles, in nuisance.[244] The classic dicta are contained in *Department of Transport v North West Water.*[245] A water main had burst, causing damage to the plaintiff's highway. The water company had not been negligent, but the relevant Act did impose a general liability on them for nuisance. The court held that, in the absence of negligence, a body is not liable for a nuisance which is attributable to the exercise by it of a duty imposed on it by statute. Since the judge held that the burst water main had occurred only as a result of the water company's duty to supply water under pressure, the action failed. Liability in nuisance may be more readily imposed where the authority has chosen to exercise its powers, rather than just acting under a duty, when it causes a nuisance.[246]

16.87 The distinction between a public authority's liability in nuisance when it is acting pursuant to a duty rather than a power can be seen in the responsibilities of sewerage undertakers. A sewerage undertaker must discharge certain of its functions so as not to create a nuisance.[247] It is not under a similar constraint when exercising its power to inspect, maintain, and repair. It must only take such reasonable steps to check the pipes and to take reasonable care in cleaning and maintaining them.[248] Whilst the private owner of a sewer would be liable under the rule in *Rylands v Fletcher* if there were an escape of sewage, therefore, the rule does not apply to the statutory undertaker unless it has acted negligently.[249] This matter was discussed

---

[243] This is similar to the situation in *Allen v Gulf Oil Refining Ltd* [1981] AC 1001. Since there was statutory authority to build and operate an oil refinery, the company could not be held liable for anything which was an inevitable consequence of that authorization. The availability of statutory authority as a defence is discussed above, at para 17.23.

[244] *Pride of Derby and Derbyshire Angling Association v British Celanese Ltd* [1953] Ch 149.

[245] [1984] AC 336, in which the House of Lords approved the dicta of Webster J [1983] 3 WLR 105 at 109.

[246] Although, again, the authority must be expressly liable for a nuisance under the terms of the statute. See *Clerk & Lindsell*, at para 20–77, which prefers the interpretation that the statute must expressly make the authority liable for nuisance rather than just by implication—as suggested in *North West Water*.

[247] Under the WIA 1991, s 117(6), with regard to its functions under ss 102–105, 112, 115, and 116 (but not s 94(1)). Local Acts may contain similar duties.

[248] *Bateman v Poplar District Board of Works* [1887] 37 ChD 272; *Cox v Paddington Vestry* [1891] 64 LT 586 (failure to take steps in the knowledge that pipes were leaky).

[249] *Smeaton v Ilford Corporation; Pride of Derby; Dunne v North Western Gas Board* [1964] 2 QB 806 (both gas and water).

in *Dear v Thames Water and others*.[250] The plaintiff's house had suffered from periodic flooding from a private culvert and stream and escapes of sewage from the manhole covers of a sewer. The plaintiff claimed in negligence for the failure to carry out the statutory duties and for allowing a nuisance to continue. The culvert was the responsibility of the riparian owners, whilst the stream was the responsibility of the National Rivers Authority. They had become inadequate to cope with the flooding as a result of further building development in the area. But the court held that there had been no negligence, and that the plaintiff had failed to establish a duty of care. The claim in nuisance also failed, as the authority had taken over a sewerage and drainage system which had become inadequate for reasons outside of their control. Even though *Dear* can be seen as a case confined to its own facts, the possibility of a cause of action in nuisance in similar circumstances remains.

I. Causation

One of the major obstacles to successfully proving an environmental claim is proving that the defendant caused the loss or damage suffered by the claimant. In essence, the court must be satisfied that 'but for' the acts or omissions of the defendant, the claimant would not have suffered the loss or damage. It follows that if the loss would have occurred in the absence of the defendant's unlawful conduct, he cannot be held liable.[251]   **16.88**

However, in certain circumstances a defendant can be held liable even if his conduct was only *one* cause of the loss, rather than the sole or even predominant cause. In *Bonnington Castings v Wardlaw*,[252] an employee who was exposed to silica dust at his workplace contracted pneumoconiosis. Some of the dust had entered the work atmosphere as a result of the employer's negligence, but the main cause of the dust was not due to its negligence. The House of Lords held that the plaintiff had to show that the defendant's conduct had caused or 'materially contributed' to the damage. The defendant in *Bonnington Castings* was held liable for the full extent of the loss, but where the size of the defendant's material contribution is known, his liability will not extend beyond that proportion.[253] Following *Fairchild v Glenhaven Funeral Services Limited*,[254] where multiple defendants are   **16.89**

---

[250] (1993) 33 Con LR 43; (1994) 4 Water Law 116, Peter Bowsher J, QC (OR).

[251] See *Barnett v Chelsea and Kensington Hospital Management Committee* [1960] 1 AC 428; or *Robinson v Post Office* [1974] 2 All ER 737.

[252] [1956] AC 613. The liabilities of employers towards their employees, under the health and safety legislation, and other statutory duties, lie outside this book.

[253] See for example *Holtby v Brigham Cowan (Hull) Ltd* [2000] 3 All ER 421.

[254] [2002] HL; [2003] 1 AC 32.

each in breach of a similar duty such that it is impossible to demonstrate which one caused the damage, it is considered unjust as a matter of policy to deny the claimant compensation. Thus in exceptional circumstances, the normal rules of causation may be relaxed on policy grounds.

16.90 Where pollution has occurred as a result of a number of concurrent acts, liability is imposed on each person who contributed to causing the damage or loss.[255] Where the defendants have acted in concert, joint liability will attach. However, where they have not acted together, the question for the court is whether the damage can be treated as divisible or not. If the damage is not divisible, the defendants will be treated as joint tortfeasors, and each will be liable for the whole damage. If it can be divided, then the defendants will only be liable for each part attributable to them.[256] The court may of course apportion loss under the Civil Liability (Contribution) Act 1978 where more than one person is liable for 'the same damage'. It is in this way that the law can give redress when the loss is caused by a cocktail of chemicals or causes.

16.91 Causation may also be difficult to prove because certain aspects of environmental science are in their infancy. For instance, electromagnetic radiation is not well understood. Hence, the challenge in *ex p Duddridge*[257] had to be made on the precautionary approach, rather than on established science. Conversely, incidents such as fish mortality are well understood, and can be predicted from the release of certain chemicals.

16.92 The burden that the claimant has to discharge is the ordinary standard of proof in civil cases, the balance of probabilities,[258] but this can involve disproving other likely causes. In *Reay and Hope v BNFL*,[259] the plaintiffs alleged that the exposure of an employee of British Nuclear Fuels to radiation had affected the health of his wife and child. The child had contracted leukaemia, which hereditary disposition was alleged to have been caused by the radiation. The only evidence was the statistical link between the father's exposure to radioactive plutonium emissions at the plant and the development of the leukaemia. French J found that the defendant's

---

[255] See *Thorpe v Brumfit* [1873] 8 Ch App 650; *Lambton v Mellish* [1894] 3 Ch 163; *Blair v Deakin* [1887] 57 LT 522; *Pride of Derby and Derbyshire Angling Association Limited and another v British Celanese Limited and others* [1952] 1 All ER 1326.

[256] Denning LJ has suggested, obiter, in *Roe v Ministry of Housing* [1954] 2 QB 66, that once the plaintiff has established that either A or B were negligent, it is then for the defendants to explain the facts if only one is to be held liable.

[257] *R v Secretary of State for Trade, ex p Duddridge* [1995] Env LR 151, see the precautionary principle further (at para 3.11). A claim for compensation in tort would almost certainly have failed.

[258] *Bonnington Castings* (supra) overruled *Vyner v Waldenburg Brothers* [1946] KB 50, which had held that the onus was on the employer to show that a breach of safety regulations had not caused the accident. The standard was the same for breaches of statutory duty as for common law.

[259] [1994] Water Law 22–23; 5 Med LR 1.

alternative theories of how the damage was caused were no less plausible than the plaintiff's, and the claim failed.

J. Practical Considerations

Civil Litigation—the costs and risks

An extreme example of the formidable practical problems which can be involved **16.93** in bringing a successful civil case in an untried area of environmental liability is the case of *Graham and Graham v ReChem International Ltd.*[260] The defendant company, who had operated a hazardous waste incinerator, were sued in negligence and nuisance by local farmers for the damage caused to their cattle. The incinerator itself had closed in 1984, and the case only came to court in October 1993. The case then lasted for 896 hours in court, spread over 198 days. Eighty lay witnesses were called, as well as 21 expert witnesses on such issues as veterinary toxicology, agricultural accountancy, incinerator design, the mechanisms of dioxin formation, pollution dispersion and deposition, the analysis of trace organics, and meteorology. The defendant company's costs have been estimated at £4.5 million, and the cost to the Legal Aid Board at £1.5 million. The case failed on the issue of causation, as there were other, more plausible explanations which existed for the cattle's injuries. Although one should not expect that most cases will involve such complications, any claimant who embarks on civil litigation must be aware of its risks.

Limitation of actions

One of the continuing problems for cases concerning pollution is determining **16.94** when the damage occurred. With a gradual accumulation of a contaminant, there may be no single point in time at which it can be said that the damage was caused. This can have important limitation consequences for the bringing of an action.

Under the Limitation Act 1980, Parliament has established a limit on the period **16.95** within which actions must be brought.[261] The six-year time limit for bringing a claim for breach of contract runs from the date of the breach and not from the date at which the damage is caused. For contracts under seal and obligations under a statute,[262] which are treated as 'specialties', a time limit of twelve years applies.

---

[260] [1996] Env LR 158. Although it probably made no difference to the result, the parties agreed that the rule in *Rylands v Fletcher* did not apply as the case was governed by Scottish law.

[261] A claim is brought when the claim form is issued, rather than when it is served on the defendant (see *Thompson v Brown* [1981] 1 WLR 744, per Lord Diplock at 752. His Lordship talks of issuing a 'writ or other originating process'.)

[262] Eg *Collin v Duke of Westminster* [1985] QB 581.

An action in tort must be brought within six years from the date at which the right of action accrues. In the case of a tort which is actionable per se, for example trespass, the right of action accrues when the tort is committed. In other cases, the general rule is that the right of action accrues when damage is sustained, and not when the claimant becomes aware of the damage. There is an overriding time limit of fifteen years from the date of the negligent act to which the damage is in part or in whole attributable.[263] Where personal injury is involved, and it is alleged that there has been negligence, nuisance, or a breach of statutory duty, an action must be brought within three years from the date when the right of action accrued or, if later, from the date of the claimant's knowledge (Sections 11, 14). This will apply even if the cause of action has not accrued or the extended period allowed for latent damage claims has started.

16.96 The time limit can be extended by the court's exercise of its discretion under Section 33 with regard to personal injury cases. The court will have regard to the circumstances of the case and the factors listed in Section 33(3).[264] Section 32 is also relevant to environmental cases. If a fact relevant to the claimant's action has been deliberately concealed from him by the defendant, the period for bringing an action will not begin to run until he has discovered the concealment or could with reasonable diligence have done so. It is further provided under Section 32(2) that a deliberate breach of a duty in circumstances where it is unlikely to be discovered for some time amounts to a deliberate concealment of the facts involved in the breach of that duty.[265] So, where an operator has deliberately deposited hazardous waste in a landfill site licensed only to take inert wastes, which is an offence under the waste management regime, the time period for bringing an action will be delayed until it is discovered.[266] Each fresh damage may lead to a fresh cause of action, as in subsidence damage,[267] or an escape of sewage from a sewer.[268] This can lead to a continuing state of dispute between the parties. Where unlawfully deposited material is left on land, there is a continuing trespass from day to day for as long as the material is left there.[269]

---

[263] Limitation Act 1980, s 14B, inserted by the Latent Damage Act 1986. This does not apply to personal injuries cases to which the Limitation Act 1980, s 11 applies.

[264] See for example *Nash v Eli Lily* [1993] 1 WLR 782 CA (mass product claim, question of when the plaintiff should have had knowledge of a significant injury).

[265] The House of Lords in *Cave v Robinson Jarvis & Rolf* [2002] UKHL 18; [2003] 1 AC 384 held that s 32(2) only covers situations in which the defendant knows he is committing a breach of duty, or intends to do so.

[266] Similarly *King v Victor Parsons & Co* [1973] 1 WLR 29, CA (contractual warranty; concealment that the defendant knew that house built on an unstable landfill site).

[267] See *Crumbie v Wallsend Local Board* [1891] 1 QB 503.

[268] *Ryeford Homes v Sevenoaks DC* [1988] 16 Con LR 75 at 80.

[269] For example *Holmes v Wilson* [1839] 10 A & E 503.

Difficulties may arise when a latent defect causes damage. Due to the inability to **16.97** recover for economic loss in most instances, the action will only accrue from the date the physical damage is caused. This should work in the claimant's favour. In *Nitrigin Eireann Teoranta v Inco Alloy Ltd*,[270] a claimant company had bought and installed a pipe in its chemical factory which had been negligently manufactured. Attempts were made to repair the pipe when it started cracking in 1983, but, despite this, the pipe ruptured the next year and the gas which escaped caused a major explosion. The claim was brought in 1990, and the limitation point was taken as a preliminary issue. The court decided that the date when the cause of action accrued in negligence was when the physical damage occurred, in 1984, and not from the date of the earlier cracking which had only caused economic loss. However, a claimant must beware being barred in such situations where the economic loss does give rise to a cause of action.[271]

K. The Measure of Damages

Introduction

The courts do not award compensation for damage caused to 'the environment' **16.98** per se. The normal remedy which the courts can offer an aggrieved claimant is monetary compensation for his own injuries and losses.[272] The correct measure of damages in any case is intended to be the sum of money which puts the injured party in the position in which he would have been but for the defendant's conduct. Damages will be awarded for every kind of injury or damage caused, and for the consequential loss and expense so long as these are not too remote.[273] However, economic losses remain difficult to recover (see below). Claimants are also under a duty to mitigate their losses, so that they will not recover damages if they have aggravated or prolonged their injuries through their own actions. Damages are normally assessed on a once and for all basis, so as to include past and future losses. If there is a possibility of some future loss occurring, such as further deterioration

---

[270] [1992] 1 WLR 498, May J.

[271] For instance, the House of Lords case of *Pirelli General Cable Works Ltd v Oscar Faber and Partners* [1983] 2 AC 1. Similar facts to *Nitrigin* arose, but the plaintiff's claim was time-barred as it was against the consulting engineer who designed the pipes. The limitation period ran from the date when the pipes had cracked, and not from when the cracks could reasonably have been discovered.

[272] Injunctions are not available in negligence claims (see *Miller v Jackson* [1977] QB 966 at 980), but they are an important remedy in nuisance actions.

[273] Remoteness of damage, and the type and scale of the consequential losses which can be recovered, are vexed topics—and will vary from case to case. They are likely to be significant areas of dispute in a complex environmental case.

or the late onset of an illness, this needs to be taken into account and compensated accordingly. However, if there is a continuing wrong such as a nuisance, this problem does not arise.

Damages for personal injury

16.99 In the case of personal injury, an award of damages can only ever be by way of compensation. In an environmental case, the general damages which can be awarded for personal injuries in a negligence action will be assessed following the usual principles. These principles are extensively covered in the main texts.[274] A proper assessment of the loss is not a simple task, but there are numerous reported cases on the quantum of damages for particular types of injuries, and these provide a guide to the likely range of general damages.[275] The element of predictability brought by such precedents as to a court's likely award can assist in persuading parties to settle cases. Further damages for other expenses and financial losses which have been incurred will be a matter of arithmetic, but there is still a large degree of judgment involved in assessing appropriate damages for pain, suffering, and loss of amenity, as well as the likelihood of future losses. The claimant will want the level of damages to include the possible loss of earnings in the future, including the loss of opportunities for career development. The extent of a claimant's injuries often only becomes clear after the passage of several years, but the task of the court is to assess the chances and risks at the date of the trial. While it is possible to apply for provisional damages,[276] the courts still prefer to deal with matters in one final award. For instance, future medical cost will be assessed as a future loss, using a multiplier for the likely number of years for which it will be needed. There have been continuous efforts to persuade the courts to extend the category of persons who can claim for this further, but the courts have essentially made a policy decision to limit the class of person who can recover.

Damage to property

16.100 When damage is caused to a person's property, compensation will normally only cover physical damage to the property which diminishes its value. As dust is an inevitable incident of urban living, and a reasonable amount of cleaning can be expected by householders, the amount of dust created must be excessive before

---

[274] See *Kemp & Kemp* (Sweet & Maxwell 2008); *McGregor on Damages* (Sweet & Maxwell 2007). The main heads of damages will be for the loss of earnings, pain and suffering, and loss of enjoyment of life.

[275] Cases on quantum are summarized in texts such as *Kemp & Kemp*, the Judicial Studies Board's own *Guidelines for the Assessment of General Damages in Personal Injury Cases* (OUP 2008), and in the monthly digests in Current Law and Halsburys Law Review.

[276] Under of the Supreme Court Act 1981, s 32A.

it will give rise to damages.[277] The same requirements would apply to assessing the effects from chemical spillages, as in the *Cambridge Water Co* case, or to escapes of methane gas.[278] The one exception is trespass, but the absence of any actual loss will only lead to an award of only nominal damages.[279]

It is possible to take a broad interpretation of where the line should be drawn as to **16.101** what constitutes physical damage. The question of whether or not any physical damage has occurred will be affected by the requirements of any statutory regulatory system. Where the contaminated parts of a ship were hosed down with soda to neutralize a leak of hydrochloric acid, and then washed down with fresh water to satisfy the port authorities that the ship was in an acceptable condition, there was held to have been sufficient physical damage to found a case in negligence.[280] In the *Cambridge Water Co* case,[281] the damage was caused because the water from the borehole was no longer wholesome according to the new European Union standards, rather than because it was in fact proved to be dangerous to human health. In *Blue Circle Industries Plc v Ministry of Defence*,[282] damage was held to have been caused because the radioactive contamination of some marshland was at a level which was above the regulatory levels set under the Radioactive Substances Act 1960 and HMIP insisted that it was cleaned up, even though it did not pose any threat to health.

The assessment of property damages

Where physical damage has occurred, the normal principle of assessment to be **16.102** applied is the difference in value of the affected property before and after the act. For a landlord, the relevant value would be the difference in the ordinary letting value, whereas a farmer might claim the lost yield from his damaged fields.[283] In *Blue Circle Industries*,[284] a case concerning land contamination, the principal part of the damages awarded was for the lost opportunity of a sale. The court held that the right approach was to arrive at a figure reflecting the difference between the plaintiff's position as it would have been without contamination and as it in fact

---

[277] See *Hunter v Canary Wharf Ltd* [1996] 1 All ER 482 at 499, CA.

[278] See *Gresten v Municipality of MC* [1974] 41 DLR (3rd) 646, Ontario High Court; *Eckersley v Binnie & Partners* 18 February [1988] 18 Con LR 1, CA (natural methane caused explosion—question over consultant's state of knowledge).

[279] Eg *National Provident Institution v Avon County Council* [1992] EGCS 56, ChD.

[280] *Re The Orjula* [1995] 2 Lloyd's Rep 395, Mance J.

[281] [1994] 2 AC 264 at 294g per Lord Goff—see para 16.17 further.

[282] [1999] Ch 289, CA—discussed further below.

[283] *Swordheath Properties v Tabet* [1979] 1 All ER 240 and *Scott-Whitehead v National Coal Board* [1987] 53 P&CR 263, QBD, respectively.

[284] [1999] Ch 289, CA—the damages awarded exceeded £5 million. The plaintiff had sued the Ministry for damages and costs founded on the statutory cause of action in the Nuclear Industries Act 1965, s 12. The court held that the compensation payable under the Act was governed by ordinary common law principles.

turned out, and then to reduce the resulting figure by a percentage reflecting the uncertainty of the sale. Where the property affected is a claimant's home, the court may award additional damages to reflect the 'insult' of the trespass.[285]

Damage caused to part of a property

16.103 The defendant may argue that the injury which has been caused has only affected a small area of the claimant's property, and so cannot be used to found a claim in respect of the remainder of the property. The courts have held that it is a question of fact whether the property has been physically changed, such question being asked in relation to the property as a whole. In many cases, contamination of a small part of a large estate could be dismissed as 'de minimis', but it depends on the nature of the contamination. In *Blue Circle Industries*,[286] the escape was small and only affected an area of unused marshland on the plaintiff's 137-acre estate, but it was an escape of a particularly hazardous material, plutonium, and this was far from 'de minimis'. Damages were awarded for the loss of value of the estate as a whole. In *St Helens Smelting Co v Tipping*,[287] the estate in question, only part of which was affected by the defendant's factory fumes, extended over 1,300 acres.

Recovering the costs of repair

16.104 Where the claimant is able to establish that he has a reasonable intention to rebuild the damaged property, and that his is an exceptional case, the proper measure may be the actual cost of reinstating the building to its former state.[288] It was reasonable in *Radford v de Froberville*[289] to restore a wall, but in *Tito v Waddell (No. 2)*[290] the plaintiff was unable to recover for the full cost of covenanted restoration works, after an island had been ravaged by mining. In such contractual claims, the terms of the covenant may determine what damages should be awarded for its breach, rather than what might be the most sensible solution to the current problem.[291]

---

[285] *Davies v Ilieff* [2000] WL 33201551, per Mr B Livesey QC (sitting in the Chancery Division) at page 23. Such damages should reflect the insult and distress caused but remain in a 'moderate compass'.

[286] (1998) 76 P&CR 251, Ch D, confirmed in the Court of Appeal, the key point was that it was reasonably foreseeable that the contamination would affect both the use and value of more than the marshland.

[287] (1865) 11 HLC 642.

[288] *Ward v Cannock Chase DC* [1986] Ch 546 (the house had a particular value to the plaintiff); *Dodd Properties (Kent) v Canterbury City Council* [1980] 1 WLR 433 (building work damaged garage); the cost was found to be unreasonable in *Farmer Giles v Wessex Water Authority* [1990] 1 EGLR 177, CA, and *Skandia Property (UK) Ltd v Thames Water Utilities Ltd*, The Times, 7 Sept, CA.

[289] [1977] 1 WLR 1262.

[290] [1977] Ch 106.

[291] *Dean v Ainley* [1988] 1 WLR 1729, CA, at 1737. *Radford* was approved and applied.

In the *Cambridge Water Co* case,[292] damages would have been assessed with refer- **16.105**
ence to the cost of acquiring an alternative borehole and building a new pumping
station to provide the necessary drinking water, given that the option of installing
cleansing equipment at the original borehole was prohibitive. If, following repair,
a property remains less valuable or useful or some other financial loss is caused,
compensation should further be payable in respect of that additional loss.[293] In
Blue Circle Industries,[294] the plaintiff recovered the costs payable for the actual
removal of the contaminated material. But the court also held that it was clearly
foreseeable that the radioactive contamination would have an adverse effect on
the marketing of the estate and would diminish its value. The plaintiff's additional claim, based on the lost opportunity of a sale, was accepted in principle.

Damages for nuisance

In a nuisance case, the normal principles for assessing damages will apply. In addi- **16.106**
tion, whilst an injunction is often applied for by the claimant, the court may also
use its equitable discretion to award damages in lieu of an injunction.[295] But where
there has been an interference with the enjoyment of the property, the courts are
faced with a more difficult task. First, allowance must be made for the activities
which the defendant could have lawfully carried out. In *Andreae v Selfridge &
Co*,[296] it was made clear that the court must be careful not to penalize the defendant company by throwing into the scales against it losses caused by operations
which it was legitimately entitled to carry out. It could be made liable only in
respect of matters in relation to which it had crossed the permissible line. Although
it is difficult to put a financial value on concepts such as inconvenience or loss of
amenity, this does not mean that such damages cannot be awarded.[297] One
approach has been to assess the damage for loss of amenity by analogy with

---

[292] [1994] 2 AC 264 at 294. Although, by the time of the HL hearing, cleansing technology had
improved sufficiently to be used—which might have changed the amount of the loss.

[293] See *Payton v Brooks* [1974] RTR 169; *Louis v Sadiq* (1997) 74 P&CR 324, CA.

[294] *Ministry of Defence v Blue Circle Industries Plc* [1999] Ch 289, distinguishing *Merlin v British
Nuclear Fuels plc* [1990] 2 QB 557.

[295] See the 'good working rule' in *Shelfer v City of London Electric Lighting Co (No. 1)* [1895] 1
Ch 287, CA, at 322 per A L Smith LJ that damages in substitution for an injunction may be given
if the injury to the plaintiff's legal rights is small, can be adequately compensated by a small money
payment, and the case is one in which it would be oppressive to the defendant to grant an injunction; and see *Kennaway v Thompson* [1981] QB 88. The Court of Appeal distinguished *Shelfer* in
Gafford v Graham (1999) 77 P&CR 73, CA, where the plaintiff had previously expressed his willingness to accept damages. The appropriate basis for awarding damages remains the sum which the
plaintiff might reasonably have demanded as a quid pro quo for relaxing the relevant restrictions in
perpetuity.

[296] [1938] Ch 1, CA, Sir Wilfrid Greene MR (award of £4,500 damages reduced to £1,000).

[297] See *Ruxley Electronics and Construction Ltd v Forsyth* [1996] AC 344, HL, per Lord Mustill
at 360–361, and per Lord Lloyd of Berwick at 374—cited with approval in *Hunter v Canary Wharf
Ltd* [1997] AC 655, HL, per Lord Lloyd of Berwick at 696e and per Lord Hoffman at 706e.

compensation for an equivalent personal injury. In *Bone v Seale*[298] the effect of nuisance from an unpleasant smell was compared with the likely award in personal injury for a temporary loss of smell. Damages for the discomfort caused when a plaintiff was forced to live in a damaged and overcrowded property were awarded in *Ward v Cannock Chase*,[299] up until the time the premises were reinstated. In *Halsey*,[300] the plaintiff was awarded £200 in 1961 for the 'very considerable discomfort' suffered from the smells, acidic deposits, oily smuts, the noise from the boilers, and traffic generated by the nearby oil refinery. It should be remembered, however, that following *Hunter v Canary Wharf*[301] damages in nuisance can only be awarded to the claimant for the injury to his land and his enjoyment of that land, and not for his personal injury.

The problem of economic losses

16.107 Claimants may incur losses which do not involve any damage to their persons or to their physical property, and which only affect their financial interests. For instance, a large number of people might be affected when a river is polluted with toxic chemicals following a negligent spillage, but both the category of successful claimants and the amount which they might recover in compensation will be limited. As a matter of policy, the English courts continue to limit the possibility of recovery for what they consider is essentially economic loss rather than physical damage. Given that most economic arrangements are made voluntarily, with an opportunity to balance the risks and responsibilities which might arise, the courts may well hold that it is not fair, just, or reasonable to impose a duty of care[302] in a particular case.

16.108 Even if the courts do hold that a claimant does have a cause of action, the courts will not award compensation in tort for what they consider to be

---

[298] [1975] 1 WLR 797 at 803–804 (offensive smell from pig farm, discomfort for 12 years). This analogy was doubted by Lord Lloyd of Berwick in *Hunter v Canary Wharf*, supra, and specifically rejected by Lord Hoffman. But the analogy still provides a useful yardstick.

[299] [1986] Ch 546 at 579 (but the additional anxiety and distress caused was not a type of damage foreseeable as a consequence of the original negligence).

[300] Supra (public nuisance); but it is a variable calculation—in *Emms v Polya* [1973] 227 EG 1659, Plowman J awarded £350 for one year's disruption from a neighbour's building works.

[301] [1997] AC 655, HL. See for example the dicta of Lord Goff at 692. Of course, the plaintiff may sue in negligence for personal injury.

[302] See *Greater Nottingham Co-operative Society v Cementation Piling & Foundations Ltd* [1989] 1 QB 71, CA (no duty of care on a subcontractor to avoid economic loss where there was a contractual warranty to carry out the works with reasonable skill and care); *Hill Samuel Bank Ltd v Frederick Brand Partnership* [1994] 10 Const LJ 72 (no duty of care where the architects and engineers had given collateral warranties to a purchaser that they would carry out the work as agreed with the developer).

'purely economic loss'.[303] Economic loss will however be recoverable if it is a foreseeable consequence of physical damage which has been caused by the defendant. Thus it is often possible to avoid complicated arguments about pure economic loss if it can be shown that the defendant has caused some physical change to a claimant's property which has rendered it less valuable or usable.[304] But it may not be easy to prove that there has been physical damage in an environmental case. In *Merlin v British Nuclear Fuels plc*,[305] the High Court held that it was too far-fetched to extend the concept of damage for injury to property to cover the presence of radionuclides in the air space within the walls of a house, which therefore rendered it less valuable as a family home. The diminished value of the house caused by the radiation levels was dismissed as pure economic loss which did not come within the claim which was limited to 'damage . . . to property' recoverable under the Nuclear Installations Act 1965.[306] The courts may yet be persuaded that tangible damage has been caused as our scientific understanding of the long-term effects of pollution on the human environment, and on a person's property, increases.

Loss due to hidden defects and fear of future damage

'Economic loss' may occur in situations where there is no apparent damage to a **16.109** piece of property and the claimant has to spend money on its repair due to some latent defect. If the defect is discovered before it causes any damage, the loss sustained by the owner who has to repair or demolish it in order to avoid a potential source of danger to a third party is purely an economic loss.[307] Where the loss is so characterized, it will only be recoverable where there is a special relationship between the parties akin to a contractual one, such as in *Hedley Byrne & Co Ltd v Heller & Partners Ltd*.[308] The situation is apparently different if the defective product or property causes actual damage to another piece of property which

---

[303] See eg *Simaan Contracting Co v Pilkington Ltd* [1988] 1 QB 758, at 781 per Bingham LJ; *Murphy v Brentwood DC* [1991] 1 AC 398, at 475 per Lord Bridge.

[304] For instance, as occurred in *Ministry of Defence v Blue Circle Industries Plc* [1999] Ch 289.

[305] [1990] 2 QB 557 at 570, per Gatehouse J. The court held that there was no *Hedley Byrne* relationship between the operators of the Sellafield nuclear plant and the plaintiffs who were local residents. The case may be limited to the interpretation of the compensation payable under the Act.

[306] Although in the Scottish case of *Magnohard Ltd v United Kingdom Atomic Energy Authority* [2004] SC 247 at 272 Lady Paton in distinguishing *Merlin* expressed reservations about the restriction of the definition of 'damage to property' to purely physical damage. In so doing the learned Judge made reference both to dicta in *Ministry of Defence v Blue Circle Industries Plc* [1999] Ch 289 and dicta of Pill LJ in the Court of Appeal in *Hunter v Canary Wharf Ltd* [1997] AC 655 at 676.

[307] *Murphy v Brentwood* [1990] 2 All ER 908, HL, applying the reasoning of Lord Bridge in *D & F Estates Ltd v Church Commissioners* [1989] AC 117.

[308] [1964] AC 465 (the action failed as the advisors had specifically added a disclaimer to their advice).

then itself requires repair. If the other property is functionally distinct from the defective property, then there is no bar on recovery for the cost of its repair.[309]

16.110 A claimant will not normally recover damages where there has been a depreciation in the value of his property due only to the fear of future damage.[310] The inquiry into damages must be directed to the effects of the physical damage which have occurred rather than the fear of possible future damage.[311] If a landowner can show that some physical damage has occurred, the fear of future damage may then be reflected in the diminution in the value of the land which has suffered physical damage. As a matter of expert valuation evidence, it is accepted that contaminated land may often be subject to a continuing 'stigma' because of its previous contamination, even if it has been successfully cleaned up.[312]

Damages for negligent advice

16.111 In many instances, it will be necessary to rely upon advice and guidance from environmental specialists, but it will not always be possible to recover for the financial losses which might occur when the advice turns out to be incorrect. Since liability for the provision of information or services has been held to be governed by the assumption of responsibility between the parties,[313] it is important to determine the scope of the instructions which have been given and accepted. Relationships which can give rise to liability are not limited to contractual or fiduciary relationships, but include those which 'are "equivalent to contract" in that there has been an assumption of responsibility in circumstances in which, but for the absence of consideration, there would have been a contract'.[314] This would appear to limit the scope of this exception, so that a professional who provides a careless report to

---

[309] *D & F Estates v Church Commissioners* [1989] 1 AC 177—also referred to as the complex structure theory. Thus, in *Murphy v Brentwood*, Lord Bridge drew a distinction between the situations where a defective boiler explodes, damaging a building, and where the inadequate foundations of a building cause it to crack and the whole structure is seen to be defective. There is also a statutory exception for dwelling houses: where the builder or other worker has taken on work in connection with a dwelling house, s 1 of the Defective Premises Act 1972 imposes a duty to carry out the work professionally and so that the dwelling is fit for habitation.

[310] See *Shuttleworth v Vancouver Hospital* [1927] 2 DLR 573 (fear of infection from isolation hospital); *Murphy v Brentwood*.

[311] See *West Leigh Colliery v Tunnicliffe* [1908] AC 27; *Hooper v Rogers* [1975] Ch 43, at 47.

[312] See Royal Institute of Chartered Surveyors' Guidance on the point, in their annual Appraisal and Valuation Manual; but note that the CA had to reduce the property's value in *Blue Circle Industries* (supra) as all the experts had included an element for the general stigma.

[313] *Henderson v Merrett Syndicates Ltd* [1995] 2 AC 145, per Lord Goff; *Spring v Guardian Assurance plc* [1995] 2 AC 296; and *Hedley Byrne & Co Ltd v Heller & Partners Ltd* [1964] AC 465 (eg per Lord Reid at pp. 483, 486 and 487).

[314] *Hedley Byrne & Co Ltd v Heller & Partners Ltd* [1964] AC 465 at 528, per Lord Devlin. The actual contractual background will be relevant (see *Henderson v Merrett Syndicates Ltd* [1995] 2 AC 145; *Pacific Associates Inc v Baxter* [1990] 1 QB 993).

a company is only liable for any loss caused to the company, and to those to whom he or she knows that the report is required to be shown. The crucial issue is the purpose for which the report is made. One could imagine such a situation arising with reports on a contaminated site, or existing industrial premises, where the developer makes no independent assessment, and it later emerges that the land has been purchased at an overvalue.[315] In some cases, it may be reasonable to assume that a claimant will take steps to assure himself of certain facts independently.[316] In the case of a negligent valuation, the courts have awarded the difference between the price paid and that which would have been paid if the plaintiff had been properly advised.[317] In addition, damages for the physical consequences of the breach, such as physical discomfort, may be awarded, but not for the mental distress caused.[318]

Exemplary damages

At times, pollution incidents may involve gross negligence and have very serious **16.112** consequences. But however outrageous the defendant's conduct is, it is unlikely that exemplary damages, which are essentially punitive, will be awarded. *Rookes v Barnard (No. 1)*[319] established two categories where a court can consider awarding exemplary damages, both of which are capable of having some application in the environmental field. The first is where there has been oppressive, arbitrary, or unconstitutional conduct by government servants.[320] Lord Devlin in *Rookes* expressly excluded oppressive action by private corporations or individuals from this category.[321] Secondly, exemplary damages can be awarded where there has been some deliberate and wilful conduct, which has been calculated by the defendant to make a profit which may well exceed any damages that he might

---

[315] For instance, in *Lidl Properties v Clarke Bond Partnership* [1998] Env LR 662 (OR) it was held that consultants' negligent advice was capable of giving rise to a potential liability for economic loss in relation to a remediation scheme for contaminated land. On the facts, negligence was not made out, and the loss was not caused by the advice in any event.

[316] Eg *Dillingham Construction v Downs* [1972] 13 Build LR 97 (builder relied upon employers' assurance that certain work could be done).

[317] *Perry v Sidney Phillips & Son* [1982] 1 WLR 1297, CA—which can be characterized as a recovery of an overpayment rather than for a loss of value.

[318] *Watts v Morrow* [1991] 4 All ER 937, CA—a moderate award of £750 was made, rather than the first instance judge's £4,000 for distress and inconvenience caused by the negligent survey.

[319] [1964] AC 1129, HL; and see *Broome v Cassell & Co* [1972] AC 1027, HL.

[320] For example a police officer forging a signature on a document purporting to withdraw a complaint of theft (*Kuddus v Chief Constable of Leicestershire* [2001] UKHL 29; [2002] 2 AC 122); also wrongful arrest by the police (*Hodden v Chief Constable of Lancashire* [1987] QB 380, CA).

[321] [1964] AC 1129 at 1226. Whereas an individual may be more powerful than another, 'the servants of the government are also the servants of the people and the use of their power must always be subordinate to their duty of service'.

have to pay.[322] In *Kuddus v Chief Constable of Leicestershire*, Lord Scott of Foscote expressed [323] a preference that the anomolous remedy of exemplary damages in civil cases should not be available in cases of negligence, nuisance, strict liability, and also breach of statutory duty except where the statute in question authorized the remedy.

---

[322] In *Broome v Cassell & Co* [1972] AC 1027, libellous material was calculated to boost the profits made from a book; also where a landlord unlawfully evicts his tenant (*Guppys (Bridport) Ltd v Brookling* [1983] 14 HLR 1; *Drane v Evangelou* [1978] 1 WLR 455, CA).

[323] [2001] UKHL 29; [2002] 2 AC 122 at 159.

INDEX

abuse of process
  Environment Agency 2.73
access to justice 2.94–2.95
  Aarhus Convention 2.95, 3.31–3.34, 4.57, 4.59,
    4.62, 4.75, 11.57
air pollution
  alkali works 6.01, 13.02–13.04
  Clean Air Acts 1.74–1.75, 13.05, 13.70–13.78
    cable burning 13.57
    chimneys, height of 13.19–13.25
    dark smoke: Ringelmann Chart 13.06–13.09
    entry, powers of 13.64, 13.77
    monitoring of emissions 13.15–13.18, 13.69
    motor fuel 13.49–13.56
    prevention measures: domestic and industrial
      furnaces 13.10–13.14
    records and returns 13.60–13.64
    research into air pollution 13.58–13.59
    research and publicity, notices connected
      with 13.65–13.68
    smoke control areas 13.26–13.48
  Control of Pollution Act 1974 1.84
  Industrial Revolution 6.01
  international law 3.26–3.27
  pesticides
    information on 5.121–5.124
aircraft
  fuel 13.50, 13.55
  noise pollution 13.114, 13.122–13.136
  waste 7.44
ancient monuments and
    archaeology 14.73–14.74, 15.38
anti-social behaviour 13.108–13.111
appeals
  air pollution
    Clean Air Act 1993 13.12, 13.14, 13.24,
      13.45, 13.63, 13.73
  contaminated land
    register: commercial confidentiality 5.118,
      12.126
    remediation notices 5.94–5.97,
      12.105–12.106
    special sites 12.45
    works of abatement 12.05
  environmental impact assessments 5.71,
    5.74, 15.67

environmental information 5.38, 5.80–5.83
  register: confidential information 6.300–6.301,
    6.306
hazardous substances 8.90, 8.107–8.108,
  8.120–8.128
land drainage 9.141
nature conservation
  tree preservation orders 11.123, 11.125, 11.128
noise pollution 13.82, 13.86, 13.98–13.100,
  13.102, 13.105, 13.120, 13.121
permits, environmental 6.119, 6.277
  date for appealing 6.169–6.170
  effect of appeal 6.156, 6.171
  procedure 6.172–6.187
  register: confidential information 6.300–6.301,
    6.306
  right of appeal 6.86, 6.131, 6.167–6.168
planning 5.80–5.83, 14.58–14.62, 14.65
radioactive substances 8.45–8.46, 8.49, 8.50,
  8.60, 8.63
waste management 7.241, 7.244
  licenses 7.193–7.196, 7.215, 7.228, 7.233
water industry
  sewerage 10.148, 10.161, 10.163, 10.174,
    10.209, 10.241, 10.248
  water 10.203, 10.241, 10.248
water pollution
  anti-pollution works notices 9.126
water resources
  abstracting licences 9.41, 9.46, 9.49
  impounding licences 9.54
archaeology and ancient monuments 14.73–14.74,
  15.38
Areas of Outstanding Natural Beauty (AONBs)
  10.47, 10.48, 11.90, 14.31, 15.38
asbestos 16.61
  waste management 7.19, 7.22, 7.34, 7.72, 7.267

badgers 11.111–11.112, 14.75
best available technique (BAT)
  permits, environmental 6.46, 6.48, 6.56–6.64,
    6.117, 14.54
  local authorities 6.247, 6.252, 6.260,
    6.264–6.275
biodiversity 2.58, 3.03, 3.10, 4.23, 9.10, 11.05
  Rio Earth Summit 11.50–11.54

Broads/Broads Authority 9.136, 10.22, 10.47, 10.48, 11.89
  environmental impact assessments 15.38
  planning 14.31
burglar alarms 13.145–13.150

causation 12.69
  civil liability 16.88–16.92
charities
  smoke control areas 13.46–13.47
  waste 7.16, 7.35, 7.36, 7.50
civil liability *see* **common law**
climate change 3.13–3.17, 4.21–4.22, 9.129
  planning 14.10, 14.18, 14.97
climate change levy 2.13
clubs for benefit of members
  waste 7.50
common law
  causation 16.88–16.92
  company acquisitions 16.76
  contract, breach of 9.50
  covenants, breach of 16.74
  damages 16.98
    economic losses 16.107–16.110
    exemplary 16.112
    negligent advice 16.111
    nuisance 16.106
    personal injury 16.99
    property, damage to 16.100–16.105
  influence of other common law
     jurisdictions 2.24–2.25
  introduction 16.01–16.03
  negligence 16.54
    advice 16.111
    breach of duty 16.62–16.66
    duty of care 16.55–16.58
    flood waters, river 9.132
    foreseeability 16.59–16.61
    regulatory authorities 16.79–16.85
    waste management 7.210
    water abstraction 9.50
    water quality 10.101
  nuisance 16.04
    contaminated land 12.19, 12.21
    damages 16.106
    defences 16.34–16.44
    flood waters, river 9.132
    foreseeability 16.21–16.29
    planning permission and 14.92
    private 16.04, 16.05–16.11, 16.39
    public 16.04, 16.30–16.33, 16.40
    reasonable user 16.17–16.20
    regulatory authorities 16.86–16.87
    responsibility for 16.12–16.16

    statutory 1.22–1.24, 12.07–12.10
    waste management 7.210
  occupiers' liability 12.22, 16.71
  practical considerations
    costs and risks 16.93
    limitation periods 16.94–16.97
  property, purchase of 16.76
  regulatory authorities 16.77
    maladministration 16.78
    negligence 16.79–16.85
    nuisances 16.86–16.87
  Rylands v Fletcher, rule in 16.45–16.53
    contaminated land 12.19, 12.20, 12.21
  statutory duty, breach of 12.17–12.18,
    16.72–16.73
  occupiers' liability 12.22, 16.71
  trespass 7.210, 16.67–16.70, 16.75
companies
  acquisitions of 16.76
  Clean Air Act 1993 13.77
  corporate social responsibility 2.69
  environmental offences 2.66, 2.75, 2.85, 6.205
    permits and past 6.94
    waste management licences and past 7.180,
      7.182
  vicarious liability 12.69
  water industry
    winding up 10.252
compensation
  contaminated land: remediation 12.104
  damages
    European law, breach of 4.48, 4.62, 4.63–4.68
    judicial review 4.58, 4.62
  damages, measure of 16.98
    damage to property 16.100–16.105
    economic losses 16.107–16.110
    exemplary 16.112
    negligent advice 16.111
    nuisance 16.106
    personal injury 16.99
  hazardous substances 8.136, 8.138
    consents 8.97, 8.98, 8.100–8.104
  land drainage 9.137, 9.144
  nature conservation 11.76, 11.125
  nuclear installations 8.18–8.19
    jurisdiction 8.28–8.33
    radioactivity and congenital disease 8.36–8.37
    restrictions 8.20–8.27
  permits, environmental 6.126–6.128
  planning permission 14.20
  waste management licences 7.195,
    7.215–7.216, 7.228
  water industry 10.53, 10.56, 10.132, 10.152,
    10.164, 10.196, 10.244

compulsory purchase 10.198
  mining code 10.211, 10.212, 10.213
  works 10.188, 10.192, 10.194
water pollution
  anti-pollution works notices 9.127
  discharge consents 9.112
water resources
  abstraction licences 9.58, 9.61
  drought orders 9.72
Competition Commission
  water industry 10.34–10.39, 10.44–10.45
confidentiality, commercial
  air pollution 13.59, 13.63, 13.76
  contaminated land 5.115–5.118,
    12.123–12.127
  generally 5.30
  genetically modified organisms 8.201
  permits, environmental 6.298–6.306
conservation
  areas 14.71–14.72
  nature *see* **nature conservation**
consumer protection 10.101
contaminated land
  building regulations 12.04
  civil liability 12.17–12.22
  closed landfill sites 7.235
  control over development 12.03
  guidance 12.129–12.130
  introduction 12.01–12.02
  nuisance, statutory 12.07–12.10
  open land 12.05–12.06
  permits, environmental 6.254, 12.15–12.16,
    12.34, 12.54, 12.102
    surrender of 6.164
  redevelopment 14.11
  registers 5.93, 5.98–5.105, 12.119–12.121
    commercial confidentiality 5.115–5.118,
      12.123–12.127
    form 5.106
    national security 5.112–5.114, 12.122
    time to consider information/
      respond 5.107–5.111
  remediation *see* **contaminated land: Part IIA**
    of EPA
  reports by Environment Agency on 5.119–5.120,
    12.128
  vacant sites 12.05–12.06
  waste authorities 12.54
  water pollution 12.11–12.13, 12.54
    anti-pollution works notices 9.126
contaminated land: Part IIA of EPA 12.23–12.26
  charging notices 12.117–12.118
  identification of 12.37–12.42
  information 5.93–5.120, 12.119–12.128

limits on duly apportioned costs 12.57–12.59,
    12.95, 12.115–12.116
  meaning of 12.27–12.36
  reasonableness test 12.55, 12.64, 12.111
  remediation 12.63–12.64
    by enforcing authority 12.110–12.116
    causation 12.69
    escapes 12.77–12.83
    insolvency practitioners 12.84
    meaning of 12.60
    special site designation 12.48–12.49
    standard of 12.61–12.62
  remediation notice
    appeals against 5.94–5.97, 12.105–12.106
    consultation before service of 12.96–12.99
    contents 12.100
    developers 14.11
    duty to serve 12.51–12.59
    offences of non-compliance 12.107–12.109
    other permissions 12.102
    register 12.101
    third party rights 12.103
  reports 5.119–5.120, 12.128
  remediation: appropriate persons 12.65–12.84
    apportionment of liability where
      several 12.85–12.87, 12.89, 12.91
    exclusion of liability where several 12.85–12.88,
      12.90
    two or more pollution linkages 12.92–12.94
  special sites 12.43–12.50
contract, breach of 9.50
cost-benefit analysis 2.63–2.64
costs 16.93
  appeals
    permits, environmental 6.173, 6.185
    planning 14.58
  judicial review 2.94
covenants, breach of 16.74
credit reference checks 6.93
criminal proceedings
  offences *see* **environmental offences**
  proposed Directive 4.70–4.71
Crown
  Clean Air Act 1993 13.61, 13.74
  Crown Estate Commissioners 11.09
  hazardous substances 8.135
  immunity 2.32–2.33, 6.235
    Environment Agency 2.45
    Water Resources Act 1991 9.120
  nature conservation 11.70, 11.77, 11.83
  oil storage 9.25

damages *see* **compensation**
data protection 5.28

declarations
  EU law, breach of 4.59, 4.62
deer 11.113
directors of companies 2.75, 6.205
drought orders, permits and plans 9.62–9.77,
    10.109, 10.111

electrical and electronic equipment
  waste 6.73
emissions trading 2.13, 3.14–3.17
end-of-life vehicles 6.72, 7.78–7.84
enforcement of environmental offences 2.65–2.66
  decision to prosecute 2.74
    Code for Crown Prosecutors 2.75, 2.79–2.82,
      6.203
    Environment Agency 2.74–2.77, 2.82,
      6.202–6.207, 9.81
    local authorities 2.78–2.79, 6.283
  environmental information 5.38
  prosecutions 2.71–2.73
    Environment Agency 2.72–2.73
    private 9.82
  reform and risk-based regulation 2.67–2.70, 9.31
  sentencing *see* **sentencing**
England and Wales
  environmental law in 2.16–2.17, 2.26
Environment Agency
  aim and objectives, principal 2.52–2.54
  civil liability *see under* public authorities
  contaminated land 12.11–12.14, 12.23, 12.43,
    12.45, 12.47, 12.48, 12.50, 12.97
    guidance 12.129, 12.131
    register 5.98–5.118, 12.119–12.127
    reports on 5.119–5.120, 12.128
  Customer Charter 2.61
  drought orders and permits 9.62–9.76
  effluent, discharge of special category 10.169,
    10.170–10.172, 10.173
  enforcement 2.65, 2.72–2.73, 9.81
    Agency as prosecutor 2.71, 2.72–2.73
    categorization of incidents 2.76–2.77
    civil penalties and undertakings 2.70
    decision to prosecute 2.66, 2.74–2.77, 2.82
    reform and risk-based regulation 2.67,
      2.69, 2.70
  environmental permitting *see* **permits,
    environmental**
  establishment of 2.42–2.43
  financial constraints 2.62–2.64
  flood control and land drainage 9.129, 9.130,
    9.132, 9.134, 9.135, 9.136, 9.137, 9.138,
    9.141, 9.143, 9.144
  general functions

  general environmental and recreational
    duties 2.57–2.58
  guidance 2.60–2.61
  incidental powers 2.59
  pollution control 2.55
  water 2.56, 9.02, 9.07–9.14, 12.12–12.14
  international law and 3.04
  landfill 7.262
  legal structure 2.44–2.45
  loudspeakers 13.91
  nature conservation 11.06, 11.70
  permits *see* **permits, environmental**
  planning system 14.54, 14.98, 14.100, 14.101,
    14.102
  radioactive materials and waste 8.40, 8.41, 8.43,
    8.44, 8.50, 8.53, 8.54, 8.57, 8.58, 8.59, 8.63
    nuclear installations 8.07, 8.10, 8.12, 8.17
  regional structure 2.46
  registers
    contaminated land 5.98–5.118,
      12.119–12.127
    information requisitions: no right to
      silence 5.144–5.147
    radioactivity 5.158–5.162
    waste 5.85–5.92
    waste management licenses 7.128–7.130
    water 5.125–5.152, 5.164
  responsibilities inherited by 2.47–2.51
  waste management 7.85, 7.86, 7.88, 7.106
    licensing *see* licensing *under* **waste management**
    permits *see* permits *under* **waste management**
  water 2.56, 9.02, 9.07–9.14, 12.12–12.14
    drought orders and permits 9.62–9.76
    flood control and land drainage 9.129, 9.130,
      9.132, 9.134, 9.135, 9.136, 9.137, 9.138,
      9.141, 9.143, 9.144
Environmental Court 2.16
environmental impact assessments (EIAs)
  challenges, possible 15.63–15.67
  contents of 5.76–5.78, 15.52–15.58
  definition of 'project' 15.22–15.23
    future development 15.29–15.30
    outline applications 15.24–15.28
  Espoo Convention 3.27, 15.51
  generally 5.59, 5.70–5.75, 5.79, 5.163, 14.07–
    14.08, 14.68, 15.01–15.05
  implementation of Directive 15.14–15.16, 15.21
    1997 amendment 15.17–15.18
    2003 amendment 15.19
    direct effect 15.21
    reforms and existing applications 15.20
  nature conservation 11.47–11.48
  other countries 3.27, 15.15

public participation 5.72, 5.78, 15.63–15.66
purpose of 15.10–15.13
requirement for 15.22–15.32
  decision 15.45–15.51
  further development and changes to
    projects 15.39–15.40
  Schedule 1 developments 5.60, 5.61, 15.32,
    15.33
  Schedule 2 developments 5.60, 5.62–5.69,
    15.32, 15.34–15.35, 15.36, 15.37,
    15.41–15.44
  sensitive areas 15.36, 15.38
  thresholds, exclusive 15.36–15.37
scoping direction 15.58
scoping opinion 5.71, 15.06, 15.57–15.58
screening direction 5.74, 15.06, 15.45,
  15.48, 15.49
screening opinion 5.70, 15.06, 15.45,
  15.47, 15.48
statutory interpretation
  purposive approach 4.10, 4.11
strategic environmental assessment (SEA) 11.56,
  14.07, 14.82, 14.98, 15.07–15.09
terminology 15.06
use of: consent decision 15.59–15.62
environmental information *see* **information,**
  environmental
environmental management system (EMS) 6.91
environmental offences
administrative notices 2.65
air pollution
  Clean Air Act 1993 13.14, 13.18, 13.27–
    13.28, 13.38, 13.41, 13.50, 13.53, 13.56,
    13.62, 13.70, 13.71, 13.76
contaminated land
  remediation notices 12.107–12.108
  works of abatement 12.06
end-of-life vehicles 7.84
enforcement *see* **enforcement of environmental**
  offences
European law
  defence 4.69
  proposed Directive 4.70–4.71
genetically modified organisms 8.195–8.199
hazardous substances 8.70, 8.110–8.116, 8.130,
  8.139
  PCBs 8.153
information 5.39
  disclosure and confidentiality 5.152
  failure to supply 5.47, 5.141
landfill 7.92, 7.263
listed buildings 14.69
nature conservation

birds 11.96–11.102
  endangered species 11.133
  hedgerows 11.132
  other wild animals 11.103–11.114
  tree preservation orders 11.126–11.127,
    11.129
  wild plants, individual 11.118–11.120
noise pollution 13.83, 13.88, 13.102, 13.105,
  13.110, 13.116, 13.132, 13.139
permits, environmental 6.208–6.225, 6.285
planning control 5.53, 14.64
radioactive substances 5.156, 8.57, 8.58, 8.60
  nuclear installations 5.156, 8.09, 8.13, 8.17,
    8.31, 8.33, 8.34–8.35
right to silence, no
  requisitions for information 5.144–5.147
waste management 7.124, 7.131–7.142, 7.209,
  7.223, 7.224, 7.241, 7.244, 7.256, 9.107
water industry
  sewerage 10.140, 10.142, 10.170, 10.254
  water 10.79, 10.80, 10.94, 10.254
water pollution
  anti-pollution works notices 9.126
  section 85 offences *see under* **water pollution**
water resources
  abstraction 9.35, 9.36
  drought orders and permits 9.76
  impounding 9.52, 9.54
  oil storage 9.27
Equator Principles 3.24
European Convention on Human Rights
European Union 4.41
generally 3.36
Human Rights Act 1998 3.37–3.39, 6.228
rights 3.40–3.41
  Art 6: procedural rights 3.79, 11.80
  Art 8: privacy 3.42–3.46
  Protocol 1, Art 1: property rights 3.47–3.48,
    11.80
Sites of Special Scientific Interest (SSSIs) 11.80
European Environment Agency (EEA) 4.05
European law
audits 2.14
criminal offences
  proposed Directive 4.70–4.71
emissions trading scheme 2.13
environmental assessment 15.14, 15.17,
  15.19, 15.21
implementation in UK
  constitutional status of European
    law 4.43–4.46, 15.21
  EIA Directive 15.14–15.20
  Environmental Liability Directive 4.54–4.55

European law (*cont.*)

implementation in UK (*cont.*)

polluter pays principle 2.27, 4.53, 4.54

precautionary principle 2.27, 2.62, 2.63, 3.19, 4.51–4.52

proportionality 2.88, 4.50

reference to ECJ under Art 234 4.47–4.48, 4.59, 4.69

use of European law principles 4.49–4.55

international law and 3.08, 3.09, 4.57

Aarhus Convention 3.33

air pollution 3.26, 3.27

judicial breaches of 4.68

nature conservation 11.11, 11.46–11.49, 11.56, 11.58

noise 13.113, 13.151

precautionary principle 3.18–3.19, 4.08, 4.17

UK 2.27, 2.62, 2.63, 3.19, 4.51–4.52

remedies 4.56–4.57

challenges to EU legislation: direct actions 4.73–4.75

individuals: damages against State 4.48, 4.62, 4.63–4.68

individuals: defence 4.69–4.71

individuals: judicial review 4.58–4.62

infraction proceedings against Member States 4.72

strategic environmental assessments 15.07, 15.09

waste management

trans-frontier trade in 3.28

water 9.04–9.05, 9.16–9.17, 9.22

European Union

Court of First Instance (CFI) 4.06, 4.07

Eco Management and Audit Scheme (EMAS) 6.91

environmental law *see* **European law**

European Court of Justice (ECJ) 4.02, 4.06–4.08

challenges to EU legislation: direct actions 4.73–4.75

infraction proceedings against Member States 4.72

proportionality 4.12

purposive approach 4.09–4.11

reference to: Art 234 4.47–4.48

human rights 4.02, 4.41–4.42

objectives 4.01, 4.09

policy documents

action programmes 2.12, 4.18–4.20, 9.131

communications 4.21–4.23

policy framework and aims 4.13–4.16

precautionary principle 3.18, 4.08, 4.17

role 4.01

structure and institutions 4.02–4.05

substitution principle 4.20

types of legislation 4.24

decisions, recommendations and opinions 4.40

directives 4.26–4.29

directives and 'direct effect' 4.30–4.39, 15.21

regulations 4.25

voting procedures 4.16

World Summit on Sustainable Development (2002) 3.03

fishing rights

abstraction licences 9.57

protection of fish 11.115–11.117

flood control

drainage

financial provisions 9.144–9.146

internal drainage boards 9.134–9.136

powers 9.137–9.142

introduction 9.128

pipe laying and 10.193

planning 14.97–14.102

regional flood defence committees 9.133

responsible bodies 9.129–9.131

riparian owners 9.132

standards of flood defence 9.143

fly-tipping 2.77, 5.146, 7.123, 7.127, 7.168–7.169, 7.255

Forestry Commission 11.07–11.08, 11.129

Franks Committee 5.50

freedom of information 5.27, 6.294

see also **information, environmental**

'*Friskie Schedules*' 2.86

genetically modified organisms (GMOs)

environmental permits 6.39

health and safety at work 8.202, 8.204

system of control 8.172–8.175

containment of 8.203–8.209

definitions 8.160–8.171

importation, acquisition, release and marketing of 8.176–8.181

notification 8.182–8.186

policing 8.187–8.194

register 8.200–8.201

release and marketing of 8.210–8.211

sanctions 8.195–8.199

traceability and labelling 8.212–8.213

Wales 2.17

Green Belts 11.91

habitats *see* **nature conservation**

Hampton Review 2.43

hazardous substances

accidents 8.140–8.148

appeals 8.90, 8.107–8.108, 8.120–8.128

consent 8.70–8.71
    amendment and termination of 8.91–8.96
    appeals 8.90
    applications 8.80–8.83
    compensation 8.97, 8.98, 8.100–8.104
    consultation 8.84–8.85
    deemed 8.74–8.79
    determination of application 8.86–8.89
    exemptions from 8.72–8.76
    revocation and modification of 8.97–8.99
contravention notices 8.117–8.120
    appeals 8.120–8.128
    other sanctions 8.129–8.131
criminal offences 8.70, 8.110–8.116, 8.130,
    8.139, 8.153
definitions 8.67–8.69
enter land, power to 8.137–8.139
introduction 8.65–8.66
landfill 7.258, 7.264, 7.267
lead shot 8.149–8.150
miscellaneous provisions 8.132–8.139
PCBs 8.151–8.153
registers 8.133
Secretary of State, powers of 8.105–8.109, 8.126
health and safety at work 2.11, 2.85, 13.02, 13.03
    genetically modified organisms 8.202, 8.204
    hazardous substances 8.134, 8.142
hedgerows, important 11.130–11.132, 14.78
High Court
    hazardous substances 8.107–8.108,
        8.127–8.128, 8.131
    nature conservation
        trees 11.123
    radioactive substances 8.27, 8.46, 8.53
    water industry 10.241, 10.248, 10.251, 10.254
    water resources
        abstracting licences 9.46
    see also injunctions; judicial review
highway authorities
    water pollution 9.121
    water undertakers 10.85
history of environmental law
    cholera epidemic of 1831 1.02–1.06
    integrated approach: modern
        legislation 1.85–1.90
    introduction 1.01
    modern developments 1.67–1.84
    Public Health Act 1848 1.07–1.13
    Public Health Act 1875 1.14–1.30
    town and country planning 1.53–1.66,
        1.70, 1.88
    unfit housing 1.38–1.41
        Housing Act 1890 1.42–1.52
    water pollution 1.31–1.37

HMIP (Her Majesty's Inspectorate of
    Pollution) 2.48
hospitals 2.33
    waste 7.10.7.28
        clinical 7.19–7.20, 7.28
housing
    unfit 1.38–1.41
        Housing Act 1890 1.42–1.52
human rights
    ECHR see European Convention on Human
        Rights
    European Union 4.02, 4.41–4.42
    international law 3.35
    permits, environmental 6.228

India 2.24
information, environmental
    Aarhus Convention 3.31–3.34, 11.57
    air pollution 13.58–13.59, 13.68
        pesticides 5.121–5.124
    general provisions 5.22
        appeals 5.38
        Code of Practice 5.36
        enforcement 5.39
        historical records 5.37
        Local Government (Access to Information)
            Act 1985 5.40–5.49
        regulations 5.23–5.35
    genetically modified organisms 8.200–8.201
    hazardous substances 8.133, 8.145–8.146
    Inspectors
        immunity of 5.175
        obstruction of 5.167–5.168
        powers of 5.165–5.166
        powers of entry 5.169–5.173
        powers where emergency 5.174
    land: contamination 5.93–5.120,
        12.119–12.128
    land: town and country planning 5.50–5.58
        appeals 5.80–5.83
        environmental impact assessments 5.59–5.79,
            15.63–15.66
    land: waste 5.19–5.21, 5.84–5.92
    miscellaneous matters 5.163–5.164
    nuclear waste 5.19
        Royal Society 5.20–5.21
    permits, environmental 6.97, 6.286–6.306
    public interest 5.13–5.14, 5.29, 5.35
    radioactivity
        nuclear installations 5.153–5.157
        nuclear waste 5.19–5.21
        other premises 5.158–5.162
    right to silence, no
        requisitions for information 5.144–5.147

information, environmental (*cont.*)
  Royal Commission on Environmental
      Pollution 5.01–5.11
    progress 5.15–5.18
    public apprehension 5.12
    public interest 5.13–5.14
  sewerage undertakers 10.133, 10.214–10.216,
      10.253–10.254, 10.259–10.262
  water 5.125–5.133, 5.164
    gathering information 5.138–5.147
    integrated pollution control
        publicity 5.134–5.137
    publicity 5.148–5.152
    undertakers/licensed water suppliers 10.56,
        10.214–10.216, 10.253–10.254,
        10.259–10.262
injunctions
  contaminated land
    remediation notices 12.109
  Crown 2.32, 4.62
  Environment Agency
    power to seek 2.59
  European law, breach of 4.59, 4.62
  hazardous substances 8.131
  interim 4.59, 4.62, 6.233, 16.68
  nature conservation
    tree preservation orders 11.127
  noise pollution 13.83, 13.84
  permits, environmental 6.231–6.233
  planning control 14.64
  trespass 16.68
  water abstraction 9.50
  water industry 10.244
  water pollution
    anti-pollution works notices 9.127
insolvency practitioners 12.84
Inspectors
  immunity of 5.175
  obstruction of 5.167–5.168
  powers of 5.165–5.166
  powers of entry 5.169–5.173
  powers where emergency 5.174
international law
  agreements 3.03, 3.20–3.22
    Aarhus Convention 2.95, 3.31–3.34, 4.29,
        4.57, 4.59, 4.62, 4.75, 11.57
    air pollution 3.26–3.27
    international trade and
        environment 3.23–3.24
    marine pollution 3.25
    nature conservation/protection of
        wildlife 3.29–3.30, 11.40–11.45,
        11.50–11.55
    trans-frontier trade in waste 3.28

  climate change 3.13–3.17
  customary law 3.03, 3.18
  European Union
    decisions 4.40
    international agreements 3.08, 3.09
    policy initiatives 3.09
  human rights law 3.35
  introduction 3.01
  national policy 3.10
  national sovereignty 3.02
  precautionary principle 3.18–3.19
  relevance within UK 3.04
    future legislation 3.05
    interpretation of legislation 3.06–3.08
  sources of 3.03
  sustainable development 3.11–3.12, 3.21

judicial review
  Aarhus Convention 4.62
  access to information
    local authorities 5.45
  costs 2.94
  Crown 2.32, 13.74
  damages 4.58, 4.62
  Environment Agency
    decision not to prosecute 2.73
    reports on contaminated land 5.120
  environmental impact assessments 15.67
  generally 2.88–2.95
  genetically modified organisms 8.186
  grounds 2.88, 4.58
    EU law, failure to comply with 4.58–4.62
  hazardous substances
    consent 8.109
    contravention notices 8.128
  locus standi 2.89, 2.93
  merits-based challenges 2.91
  Parliamentary Commissioner for
      Administration 2.97
  permits, environmental 6.186
  planning decisions 14.62
  Royal Commission on Environmental
      Pollution 2.39
  statutory undertakers 2.38
  time limits 2.93, 4.62
  waste management
    licences 7.196, 7.214
    Waste Management Industry Training and
        Advisory Board (WAMITAB) 2.37

land drainage
  abstraction licences 9.49
  drainage, powers 9.137–9.142
  financial provisions 9.144–9.145

flood controls 9.129–9.133, 9.143, 10.193
  planning: flood risk areas 14.97–14.102
internal drainage boards 9.130, 9.134–9.136
introduction 9.128
landfill 7.01
  closed sites 7.235
  generally 7.257–7.274
  permits, environmental 6.70–6.71
    closure notices 6.199
    surrenders 6.166
  planning 14.44, 14.90
  rationing 7.89–7.92
  tax 2.13
leases
  covenants, breach of 16.74
  'piecrust' 16.76
limitation periods
  EU and domestic law 4.56
  generally 16.94–16.97
  nuclear installations
    compensation 8.26, 8.27
listed buildings 14.19, 14.67–14.70
local authorities
  access to information 5.40–5.49
  air pollution: Clean Air Act 1993
    entry, power of 13.64
    monitoring of emissions 13.17, 13.18, 13.69
    motor fuel 13.51
    prevention 13.12, 13.19, 13.22
    research and publicity 13.58, 13.59, 13.60,
      13.65, 13.68
    smoke control areas 13.31, 13.40, 13.44,
      13.45, 13.47, 13.48
  building regulations approval
    plans for new houses 10.126, 10.183
  contaminated land 12.23, 12.129
    powers and duties *see* **contaminated land**
    registers 5.93, 5.98–5.118, 12.119–12.127
  enforcement 2.71, 2.78–2.79
    Code for Prosecutors 2.79–2.81
  permits, environmental 6.234, 6.283–6.285
  nature conservation 11.03, 11.70, 11.85, 11.92
  noise pollution 1.83
    powers and duties *see* **noise pollution**
  permits, environmental 6.04–6.07, 6.08, 6.09,
    6.236–6.242
    appeals 6.277
    applications 6.87, 6.99, 6.100–6.102
    best available technique 6.247, 6.252, 6.260,
      6.264–6.275
    charges 6.95, 6.256
    conditions 6.124
    contaminated land 6.254
    determination 6.255–6.276

enforcement 6.234, 6.283–6.285
    Environment Agency 6.277
    Part A(2) (LA-IPPC) installations 6.04, 6.23,
      6.25, 6.26, 6.27, 6.87, 6.100, 6.236,
      6.240, 6.243, 6.247, 6.251, 6.254, 6.255,
      6.256, 6.258, 6.259, 6.261–6.264,
      6.266–6.275, 6.277, 6.278, 6.285
    Part B (LAPPC) installations 6.04, 6.23, 6.25,
      6.27, 6.28, 6.99, 6.100, 6.147, 6.160,
      6.236, 6.244–6.252, 6.255, 6.256, 6.258,
      6.259, 6.265, 6.276, 6.278, 6.281, 6.285
    reviews and inspections 6.145, 6.146, 6.282
    substantial changes 6.251
    transfer, variation and revocation 6.147,
      6.278–6.281
    unregulated installations 6.284
    waste operations 6.04, 6.100, 6.253
    water consent issues 6.277
  planning 14.23
    powers and duties *see* **town and country**
      planning
  registers
    clean air 13.68
    contaminated land 5.98–5.118,
      12.119–12.127
    integrated pollution control
      publicity 5.134–5.137
    noise levels 13.101, 13.104
    planning 5.54, 5.73, 15.64
  role of 2.34–2.35, 7.85, 7.110
  sewerage 10.15, 10.150, 10.182–10.183, 10.214,
    10.231
  statutory nuisance 12.07, 12.10
  waste, commercial 7.51
  water supply 10.15, 10.85, 10.107, 10.122–
    10.126, 10.231
Local Better Regulation Office 2.70
London 2.34, 2.50, 13.25, 13.84, 13.88
  aircraft noise 13.125, 13.133
  planning 14.23, 14.69, 14.80, 14.81

maladministration 16.78
Manchester 2.50
marine pollution 3.25, 11.55, 16.73
Merseyside 2.50
Mexico 3.23
minerals local plans 14.83
mines
  abandoned
    contaminated land 12.75
    water pollution 9.122–9.124
  Clean Air Act 1993 13.70
  water and sewerage undertakers 10.211–10.213
mobile phone masts 14.52

motor fuel 13.49–13.56
motor vehicles
  noise pollution 13.137–13.144
  waste 6.72, 7.78–7.84

national indicators 2.29
National Parks 11.05
  environmental impact assessments 15.38
  establishment of 1.71–1.72
  generally 11.88
  land drainage 9.136
  planning 14.23, 14.31, 14.83
  water industry 10.22, 10.47, 10.48, 11.88
National Rivers Authority 2.49, 7.116, 7.121,
  7.164, 8.84, 9.07
national security
  Clean Air Act 1993 13.62
  contaminated land 5.112–5.114, 12.122
  generally 5.13–5.14, 5.30
  genetically modified organisms 8.201
  nuclear installations 5.156, 5.157
  permits, environmental 6.235, 6.294,
    6.295–6.297
  waste management licences 7.129
National Trust 7.51, 11.28, 11.82
Natural England 2.37, 11.72, 11.82, 11.89
  enforcement 2.70
  Environment Agency and 2.58
  land drainage 9.136
  purpose of 3.12, 11.04, 11.05
  water industry 10.22
Natural Environment Research Council
  (NERC) 11.10
nature conservation
  European Union 11.11, 11.40
    Birds Directive 11.46, 11.49
    EIA Directive 11.47–11.48
    Habitats Directive 11.49, 14.75
    SEA Directive 11.56
    Water Framework Directive 11.58
  habitats 11.59–11.62, 14.82
    Areas of Outstanding Natural Beauty (AONBs)
      10.47, 10.48, 11.90, 14.31, 15.38
    Areas of Special Protection (AOSPs) 11.84
    biogenetic reserves 11.63
    biosphere reserves 11.64
    Broads/Broads Authority 9.136, 10.22, 10.47,
      10.48, 11.89, 14.31, 15.38
    Country Parks 11.92
    Environmentally Sensitive Areas (ESAs) 11.87
    Green Belts 11.91
    limestone pavements 11.83
    Local Nature Reserves (LNRs) 11.85
    Marine Nature Reserves (MNRs) 11.77

  National Nature Reserves (NNRs) 11.63,
    11.73–11.76
  National Parks *see* **National Parks**
  Ramsar sites 11.65–11.66, 15.38
  Sites of Nature Conservation Importance
    (SNICs and SINCs) 11.86
  Special Areas of Conservation (SACs) 11.49,
    11.68–11.72, 15.38
  Special Protection Areas (SPAs) 11.42, 11.66,
    11.67, 11.69–11.72, 15.38
  SSSIs *see* **Sites of Special Scientific Interest**
  international law 3.29–3.30, 11.40
    Aarhus Convention 2.95, 3.31–3.34, 4.57,
      4.59, 4.62, 4.75, 11.57
    biodiversity 11.50–11.54
    endangered species, trade in 11.43
    marine environment: OSPAR 11.55
    migratory species 11.45
    wetlands 11.42, 11.65
    wildlife and natural habitats: Bern
      Convention 11.44
    World Heritage Sites 11.41
  introduction 11.01
  organization of
    European Union 11.11
    government 11.02–11.10
    non-governmental organizations 11.12–11.39
  planning 11.70, 11.71, 11.72, 11.121–11.128,
    14.19, 14.75–14.78, 14.82, 15.38
  species protection 11.93
    birds 11.96–11.102
    endangered 11.133
    evaluation procedures 11.94–11.95
    fish 11.115–11.117
    hedgerows, important 11.130–11.132, 14.78
    other wild animals 11.103–11.114
    trees and woodland 11.121–11.129, 14.72,
      14.77–14.78
    wild plants, individual 11.118–11.120
  waste management
    licensing 7.175
negligence 16.54
  advice 16.111
  breach of duty 16.62–16.66
  duty of care 16.55–16.58
  flood waters, river 9.132
  foreseeability 16.59–16.61
  regulatory authorities 16.79–16.85
  waste management 7.210
  water abstraction 9.50
  water quality 10.101
New Zealand 2.24
nitrate vulnerability zones (NVZs) 9.20, 9.28–9.31
noise pollution 1.83

aircraft 13.114, 13.122–13.136
  burglar alarms 13.145–13.150
  construction sites 13.79–13.87
  environmental permits 6.38
  EU Directives 13.151
  loudspeakers in street 13.88–13.95
  noise abatement zones 13.96–13.111
  planning considerations 14.44, 14.93–14.96
  plant and machinery 13.112–13.121
  road traffic 13.137–13.144
non-governmental organizations 4.75
  nature conservation 11.12–11.39
Northern Ireland
  aircraft noise
    Belfast 13.133
  Areas of Special Scientific Interest (ASSIs) 11.78
  biodegradable waste 7.93
  environmental law in 2.22–2.23, 2.45
  landfill 7.89–7.92, 7.271
  nature conservation 11.06
    Council for Nature Conservation and the
      Countryside (CNCC) 11.04
nuclear installations
  compensation for breach of duty under NIA
    8.18–8.19
    jurisdiction 8.28–8.33
    radioactivity and congenital disease 8.36–8.37
    restrictions 8.20–8.27
  criminal offences 8.09, 8.13, 8.17, 8.31, 8.33,
    8.34–8.35
  information 5.153–5.157
  introduction 8.02–8.06
  licensing 8.07–8.10
    conditions 8.11, 8.12, 8.41
    currency of licence 8.12–8.16
    duty under NIA 8.14–8.15
    surrender and revocation 8.17
  nuclear waste 8.50–8.55
    environmental information 5.19–5.21
  statutory duty, breach of 16.73
nuisance
  contaminated land 12.19, 12.21
  damages 16.106
  defences 16.34–16.44
  flood waters, river 9.132
  foreseeability 16.21–16.29
  planning permission and 14.92, 16.38
  private 16.04, 16.05–16.11, 16.39
  public 16.04, 16.30–16.33, 16.40
  reasonable user 16.17–16.20
  regulatory authorities 16.86–16.87
  responsibility for 16.12–16.16
  statutory 1.22–1.24, 12.07–12.10
  waste management 7.210

occupiers' liability
  contaminated land 12.22
  duty of care 16.71
Office of Fair Trading
  water industry 10.39, 10.44
OfWat (Water Services Regulation Authority)
  establishment of 2.07
  responsibilities 2.38, 9.06, 9.13
oil storage 9.25–9.27
oil tankers 16.73
Ombudsman
  complaints to 2.32, 2.96–2.100, 16.78

PCBs (polychlorinated biphenyls) 8.151–8.153
permits, environmental
  activities/operations covered *see* **regulated**
    industrial operations
  appeals 6.119, 6.277
    date for appealing 6.169–6.170
    effect of 6.156, 6.171
    procedure 6.172–6.187
    register: confidential information 6.300–6.301,
      6.306
    right 6.86, 6.131, 6.167–6.168
  applications 6.79–6.89
    alternative forms of 6.96–6.102
    charges 6.81, 6.89, 6.95
    consultation and public participation 6.97,
      6.103–6.108, 6.133, 6.134, 6.135
    innovative processes planned 6.111
    mobile plant 6.80, 6.99
    operator competence 6.90–6.94
    Part A installations 6.80, 6.133, 6.137
    Part A(1) installations 6.111
    Part A(2) (LA-IPPC) 6.87, 6.100
    Part B (LAPPC) installations 6.99, 6.100
    planning permission 6.112, 14.84–14.85
    timing 6.109–6.112
  categorizations 6.04–6.05
    interpretation of 6.25–6.26
  charges 6.81, 6.89, 6.95, 6.165, 6.256
  compensation 6.126–6.128
  conflicts between 6.136
  contaminated land 6.164, 6.254, 12.15–12.16,
    12.34, 12.54, 12.102
  determination 6.114–6.119
    effect of grant 6.139
    local authorities 6.255–6.276
    Part A(1) installations 6.113
    permit: conditions 6.122–6.128
    permit: specific requirements 6.120–6.121
    permit: standard rules 6.129–6.135
    Secretary of State 6.140–6.143
    time limits 6.124, 6.128, 6.137–6.138

permits, environmental (*cont.*)
  effect of grant 6.139
  effluent, special category 10.175
  enforcement 6.188
    court orders 6.226–6.230
    Crown immunity 6.235
    direct action 6.200
    Environment Agency: general principles 6.189
    Environment Agency: prosecution
        policy 6.202–6.207
    High Court 6.231–6.233
    investigative powers 6.190–6.193
    landfill closure notices 6.199
    local authorities 6.234, 6.283–6.285
    offences 6.201, 6.208–6.225
    prohibitory notices 6.194–6.198
    publicity 6.234
  industrial pollution control
    current system 6.04–6.07
    future 6.02–6.03
    history 6.01
  limits/exclusions
    GMOs 6.39
    insignificant processes and low level
        activities 6.27–6.29
    mobile plant 6.36–6.37
    radioactivity 6.39
    waste management 6.30–6.35
  local authorities *see under* **local authorities**
  noise 6.38
  operations covered *see* **regulated industrial
        operations**
  planning 6.112, 14.84–14.86
  register 6.97, 6.286–6.292
    confidential information 6.298–6.306
    form and content 6.293–6.294
    national security 6.294, 6.295–6.297
  regulator's exercise of functions 6.41–6.48,
        6.236–6.254
    best available technique (BAT) 6.46, 6.48,
        6.56–6.64, 6.117, 6.247, 6.252, 6.260,
        6.264–6.275, 14.54
    combustion plants, asbestos, titanium dioxide
        and petrol vapour recovery 6.78
    environmental quality standard 6.48
    general principles 6.42
    landfill installations 6.70–6.71
    solvent emissions installations and plant 6.77
    substantial changes 6.49–6.55, 6.251
    waste electrical and electronic equipment 6.73
    waste incineration 6.74–6.76
    waste motor vehicles 6.72
    waste operations 6.65–6.69, 6.253
    water consent issues 6.277
  regulatory bodies 6.08–6.09
    composite applications 6.99–6.102
    Environment Agency 6.04, 6.06, 6.08, 6.24,
        6.239–6.240
  remediation 6.158–6.159
  requirement for 6.10
  review and inspection 6.144–6.146, 6.282
  revocation of 6.156–6.157, 6.278, 6.280
  Secretary of State 6.08, 6.09, 6.100–6.101,
        6.140–6.143
  surrender of 6.160–6.166, 6.279
    mobile plant 6.160
    Part B (LAPPC) installation 6.160, 6.278
  time limits 6.97, 6.103, 6.124, 6.128, 6.137–
        6.138, 6.156
    appeals 6.169, 6.170, 6.175, 6.176, 6.182,
        6.186
    enforcement 6.192, 6.195, 6.200
  transfer of 6.153–6.155, 6.278
  transitional provisions 6.40, 6.239
  variation of 6.147–6.152, 6.278
    Part A installations 6.147
    Part B (LAPPC) installations 6.147
  water pollution 9.108
pesticides 5.121–5.124
planning control *see* **town and country planning**
polluter pays principle
  European Union 4.08, 4.53, 4.54
  UK 2.27, 4.53, 4.54
    charges for permits 2.13
pollution
  air *see* **air pollution**
  marine 3.25, 11.55, 16.73
  noise *see* **noise pollution**
  planning and pollution controls, relationship
        between *see under* **town and country
        planning**
  water *see* **water pollution**
precautionary principle
  European law 3.18, 4.08, 4.17
  international law 3.18–3.19
  UK guiding principle 3.19, 4.51–4.52
    Environment Agency 2.62, 2.63
    Sustainable Development Strategy 2.27
private prosecutions 2.71
producer responsibility for waste
  introduction of concept of 2.08
property rights
  rights to water 16.75
proportionality
  European Court of Justice 4.12
  permits, environmental 6.162, 6.255, 6.259, 6.283
  UK courts 2.88, 4.50
    judicial review 2.88

public authorities
central government, role of 2.26, 7.85
  guidance 2.27–2.31
  national indicators 2.29
  nature conservation 11.02
civil liability 16.77
  maladministration 16.78
  negligence 16.79–16.85
  nuisance 16.86–16.87
local authorities *see* **local authorities**
other public bodies and executive
    agencies 2.36–2.37
  Environment Agency *see* **Environment Agency**
  Royal Commission 2.39–2.40
  statutory undertakers 2.38
other research bodies 2.41
waste, commercial 7.51
water 9.06
public health laws 2.10
public participation procedures
Aarhus Convention 3.31–3.34, 4.29, 4.57, 11.57
environmental impact assessments 5.72, 5.78,
  15.63–15.66
permits, environmental 6.104, 6.106, 6.148,
  6.255
see also **information, environmental**

quarries 14.13–14.14
Clean Air Act 1993 13.70
planning 14.74

radioactive substances
appeals 8.45–8.46, 8.49, 8.50, 8.60, 8.63
criminal offences 5.156, 8.57, 8.58, 8.60
  nuclear installations 5.156, 8.09, 8.13, 8.17,
    8.31, 8.33, 8.34–8.35
enforcement 8.56–8.60
environmental permits 6.39
groundwater 9.23
information
  nuclear installations 5.153–5.157
  nuclear waste 5.19–5.21
  other premises 5.158–5.162
installations *see* **nuclear installations**
introduction 8.02–8.05, 12.26
mobile apparatus 8.47–8.48, 8.49
planning and pollution controls: radon gas 14.09
radioactive material: registration 8.38
  appeals 8.45–8.46, 8.49
  applications 8.40
  cancellation and variation 8.49
  definition 8.39
  exemptions 8.41–8.42
  procedure 8.43–8.44

radioactive waste 5.19–5.21, 7.72, 7.167,
  8.50–8.55
transport of radioactive material 8.61–8.64
**regulated industrial operations (environmental
  permits)**
categorizations 6.04–6.05
  interpretation of 6.25–6.26
GMOs 6.39
limits/exclusions
  GMOs 6.39
  insignificant processes and low level
    activities 6.27–6.29
  mobile plant 6.36–6.37
  radioactivity 6.39
  waste management 6.30–6.37
noise 6.38
permits *see* **permits, environmental**
radioactivity 6.39
subject matter 6.11
  activities 6.20–6.24
  installation 6.12–6.19
  mobile plant 6.36–6.37
  Part A(1) activities 6.23, 6.24
  Part A(2) activities 6.23
  Part B activities 6.23
  regulated facilities 6.11–6.19
  waste operations 6.01, 6.04, 6.11, 6.30–6.37
regulatory framework
alternatives to regulation 2.12–2.15
health and safety at work 2.11
public health laws 2.10
statutes
  Environment Act 1995 2.08–2.09
  Environmental Protection Act 1990 2.06
  Water Acts 1991 2.07
religious worship, places of
smoke control areas 13.46–13.47
waste 7.16, 7.36
remedies
Aarhus Convention 4.59
compensation *see* **compensation**
declarations 4.59, 4.62
European law 4.56–4.57
  challenges to EU legislation: direct
    actions 4.73–4.75
  individuals: damages against State 4.48, 4.62,
    4.63–4.68
  individuals: defence 4.69–4.71
  individuals: judicial review 4.58–4.62
  infraction proceedings against Member
    States 4.72
injunctions *see* **injunctions**
judicial review *see* **judicial review**
research establishments 7.39, 13.73

risk assessments
  floods 9.129
  planning authorities 14.52–14.54
  water pollution 9.99
risk-based regulation 2.67–2.69
Royal Commission on Environmental Pollution
  environmental information 5.01–5.18
  generally 2.39–2.40
  integrated system of pollution control 6.01
Rylands v Fletcher, rule in 16.45–16.53
  contaminated land 12.19, 12.20, 12.21

Scotland
  biodegradable waste 7.93
  environmental law in 2.18–2.21
  landfill 7.89–7.92, 7.271
  nature conservation 11.78, 11.115
    Scottish Natural Heritage (SNH) 11.04
  Scottish Environment Protection
    Agency (SEPA) 2.20, 2.21, 11.06
  water industry 2.07, 2.21
seals 11.114
sentencing 2.83–2.86
  contaminated land
    remediation notices 12.108
  fixed penalty notices 2.87
  genetically modified organisms 8.195
  hazardous substances 8.70
  landfill 7.263
  permits, environmental 6.213, 6.223, 6.225,
    6.285
  radioactive substances 8.58
    nuclear installations 8.31
  water pollution
    section 85 offences 9.85–9.86
  water resources
    abstraction 9.35
    oil storage 9.27
sewerage undertakers
  apparatus
    adoption of 10.200, 10.208–10.210
    landowners and removal of 10.217–10.218
    maps of underground 10.214–10.215
  appointment of 10.25–10.43
  charges 10.159–10.160, 10.222–10.225
  complaints against 10.196–10.197,
    10.255–10.258
  compulsory purchase of land 10.198
  duties 10.127
    drainage of premises 10.136–10.152
    general 10.128–10.130
    general environmental and
      recreational 10.19–10.24
    regulations 10.131–10.135

enforcement
  financial penalties 10.245–10.249
  information, power to require 10.253–10.254
  orders 10.232–10.244
  special administration orders 10.250–10.253
  entry, powers of 10.219, 10.221
  information 10.133, 10.214–10.216,
    10.253–10.254, 10.259–10.262
  introduction 2.38, 9.03, 9.11, 9.12–9.13,
    10.09–10.10
  local authorities 10.15, 10.150, 10.182–10.183,
    10.214, 10.231
  loudspeakers 13.91
  mergers 10.44–10.45
  mining code 10.211–10.213
  permits, environmental 6.277
  protected land, disposal of 10.46–10.48, 11.88
  reviews 10.259
  section 85 offences 9.105
  trade effluent 10.153–10.167
    special category 10.168–10.175
  treatment of sewage 10.176–10.180
    discharges of treated sewage 10.181
  waste, controlled 7.12, 7.40–7.41, 9.104
  water undertakers 10.85
  works 10.184, 11.88
    code of practice 10.195
    compensation 10.188, 10.194
    pipe laying 10.185–10.190, 10.193–10.197
    pollution prevention 10.187, 10.190
Sites of Special Scientific Interest (SSSIs) 2.14,
  11.78, 14.75
  agencies 11.05
  biogenetic reserves 11.63
  environmental impact assessments 15.38
  limestone pavements 11.83
  management of land 11.75, 11.82
  National Nature Reserves 11.73
  notification 11.81
  objectives 11.79
  site selection 11.80
  Special Protection Areas 11.67
  undertakers: disposal of protected
    land 10.47, 10.48
  voluntary agreements 2.14
  wetlands 11.42, 11.66
solvent emissions installations and plant 6.77
Special Areas of Conservation (SACs) 11.49,
  11.68–11.72, 15.38
Special Protection Areas (SPAs) 11.42, 11.66,
  11.67, 11.69–11.72, 15.38
statutory duty, breach of
  civil liability 12.17–12.18, 16.72–16.73
  occupiers' liability 12.22, 16.71

statutory interpretation
  international obligations and 3.06–3.07
  purposive approach 4.08, 4.09–4.11
statutory nuisance
  contaminated land 12.07–12.10
  creation of 1.22–1.24
statutory undertakers 2.38
  sewerage *see* **sewerage undertakers**
  water *see* **water undertakers**
strategic environmental assessment (SEA) 11.56,
  14.07, 14.82, 14.98, 15.07–15.09
substitution principle 4.20
Sullivan Report 2.95
sustainable development 3.03, 3.11–3.12, 3.21
  planning policies 14.16–14.20
    sustainable drainage systems 14.10
  Sustainable Development Commission 2.41

taxation
  climate change levy 2.13
  landfill tax 2.13
tenants
  covenants, breach of 16.74
time limits
  advance notice: meetings of local authorities 5.41
  air pollution
    Clean Air Act 1993 13.12, 13.18, 13.23,
      13.35, 13.64, 13.76
  contaminated land 12.45, 12.97, 12.99, 12.118
    register: commercial confidentiality 5.118
  environmental impact assessments 5.74
  EU legislation
    challenge to 4.73
    domestic legislation and 4.56, 4.60
  hazardous substances 8.75, 8.83, 8.86, 8.90,
    8.119, 8.123, 8.132, 8.139
  information 5.25, 5.32, 5.35
  judicial review 2.93, 4.62
  land drainage 9.140, 9.141
  limitation periods 4.56, 8.26, 8.27, 16.94–16.97
  nature conservation
    hedgerows 11.132
    Sites of Special Scientific Interest (SSSIs) 11.80
    tree protection orders (TPOs) 11.123, 11.125
  noise pollution 13.86, 13.98, 13.102, 13.121,
    13.134
  nuclear installations
    compensation 8.26, 8.27
  Ombudsman 2.97
  permits, environmental 6.97, 6.103, 6.124,
    6.128, 6.137–6.138, 6.156
    appeals 6.169, 6.170, 6.175, 6.176, 6.182, 6.186
    enforcement 6.192, 6.195, 6.200
    waste management 6.35

  planning 14.20
    appeals 14.60
    enforcement 14.66
  radioactive substances 8.26, 8.27
    appeals 8.45
  waste management 7.244
    licensing 7.190, 7.193, 7.215, 7.221, 7.233
  water industry
    sewerage undertakers 10.139, 10.145, 10.161,
      10.163, 10.164, 10.174, 10.189, 10.197,
      10.208, 10.209, 10.212, 10.241, 10.248
    water undertakers 10.67, 10.70, 10.90,
      10.102–10.104, 10.106, 10.189, 10.197,
      10.203, 10.212, 10.241, 10.248
  water pollution
    anti-pollution works notices 9.126
    discharge consents 9.109, 9.111
    section 86 prohibition 9.107
  water resources
    abstraction licences 9.41, 9.44, 9.49, 9.59
    drought orders 9.63, 9.71
    impounding licences 9.54
    quality, water 9.79
    river basin management plans 9.20
town and country planning
  appeals 5.80–5.83, 14.58–14.62, 14.65
  central government 2.26, 14.09–14.11, 14.22,
    14.24
  cost-benefit analysis 2.64
  determination of applications
    conditions 14.41–14.46
    location and need for
      development 14.50–14.51
    material considerations 14.38–14.40,
      14.55–14.57
    outline applications 14.35–14.37,
      15.24–15.28
    planning obligations 14.47–14.49
    risk assessment 14.52–14.54
    statutory test 14.32–14.34
  enforcement powers 14.63–14.66
  environment and development
    plans 14.79–14.83
  Green Belts 11.91
  history of 1.53–1.66, 1.70, 1.88
  nature conservation 11.70, 11.71, 11.72, 14.19,
    14.75–14.78, 14.82, 15.38
    trees 11.121–11.128
  nuisance and planning permission 14.92, 16.38
  planning applications
    amenity, detriment to 7.187
    environmental impact *see* **environmental**
      impact assessments
    notification 5.50–5.53

town and country planning (*cont.*)
  planning applications (*cont.*)
    outline 14.35–14.37, 15.24–15.28
    register 5.54, 5.73, 15.64
    special publicity 5.55–5.58
    third parties 5.107–5.109, 14.61
    time to consider information/
       respond 5.107–5.109
  planning and pollution controls 14.01–14.03
    courts, approach of 14.12–14.15
    EIAs *see* **environmental impact assessments**
    legal overlap 14.04–14.06
    policy approach: PPS 23 14.09–14.11, 14.40,
       14.44, 14.52, 14.92
    sustainable development 14.16–14.20
  requirement to obtain planning
       permission 14.25–14.31
  special regimes
    archaeology and historical
       monuments 14.73–14.74
    conservation areas 14.71–14.72
    hedgerows 14.78
    listed buildings 14.67–14.70
    nature conservation constraints 14.75–14.76
    trees 14.77–14.78
  specific types of development
    environmental permits 6.112, 14.84–14.86
    flood risk areas 14.97–14.102
    noise 14.93–14.96
    nuisance 14.92
    waste management 7.173, 7.187, 14.86–14.91
  statutory framework 14.21
    planning authorities 2.34, 14.22–14.24
  waste management 14.83, 14.86–14.91
    licensing 7.173, 7.187, 14.87
tradable permits 2.13
trains 13.114
  railway engines 13.71
trees and woodlands
  planning 14.72, 14.77–14.78
  protection of 11.121–11.129
trespass 7.210, 16.67–16.70, 16.75

UNESCO 11.41, 11.64
United States 2.25, 3.23

vessels
  Clean Air Acts
    1993 Act 13.72, 13.74
    dark smoke 13.09
  fuel 13.50
  Marine Nature Reserves (MNRs) 11.77
  noise pollution 13.91, 13.114
  waste 7.44, 7.167

    clinical waste 7.26, 7.42
  water pollution 9.119
vicarious liability 12.69
voluntary agreements 2.14

Wales
  appeals 2.90
  biodegradable waste 7.93
  Countryside Council for Wales 9.136, 10.22,
    11.04, 11.05
  Environment Agency 2.45, 2.46, 2.54
  environmental law in 2.16–2.17, 2.26, 2.28
  landfill 7.89–7.92, 7.271
  oil storage 9.25
  planning policy and guidance 14.24, 14.79, 14.97
  water 9.06, 9.15
waste management
  1970s legislation 1.76–1.82, 2.51
  appeals 7.241, 7.244
    licensing 7.193–7.196, 7.215, 7.228, 7.233
  asbestos 7.19, 7.22, 7.34, 7.72, 7.267
  brokers, waste 7.102–7.103
  caravans 7.10, 7.26, 7.29–7.30
  civil liability 7.210
  clinical waste 7.19–7.22, 7.26, 7.28, 7.42–7.43
  collection 7.236–7.245
    disposal 7.246–7.256
  commercial 7.13, 7.14, 7.48–7.52
    collection 7.242, 7.243, 7.244
  definitions 7.05–7.08
    clinical 7.20–7.21
    commercial 7.13, 7.14, 7.48–7.52
    controlled waste 7.09–7.15
    garden waste 7.25
    household 7.10, 7.14, 7.16–7.22, 7.42
    industrial 7.11–7.12, 7.14, 7.37–7.47
    receptacle for household waste 7.24
    slurry 9.28
  disposal 7.246–7.256
    bottle banks and civic amenity
       sites 7.252–7.253
    company: LAWDC 7.248–7.251
  duty of care 7.95, 7.114, 7.115, 7.197–7.199,
    7.211
    breach of 7.209–7.210
    carriers 7.207–7.208
    code of practice 7.203–7.206
    exemptions from 7.104–7.109
    persons under 7.96–7.103
    transfer notes 7.200–7.202
  enforcement 7.122–7.130
  exports 7.88, 7.96, 7.199, 7.208
  fly-tipping 2.77, 5.146, 7.123, 7.127,
    7.168–7.169, 7.255

holiday houses 7.29–7.30
household waste 7.10, 7.14, 7.16–7.22, 7.95
    charging for removal 7.23–7.36, 7.42
    collection 7.236–7.241
    exclusion from licensing 7.143
imports 7.47, 7.88, 7.96, 7.199, 7.208
industrial 7.11–7.12, 7.14, 7.37–7.47
    collection 7.243, 7.244
international law 3.28
introduction 7.01–7.04
landfill *see* **landfill**
licensing 7.110–7.121, 9.23, 10.181
    appeals 7.193–7.196, 7.215, 7.228, 7.233
    applications 7.172
    compensation 7.195, 7.215–7.216, 7.228
    conditions 7.188–7.192
    exemptions 7.143–7.167
    fitness to hold a license 7.177–7.187
    functions of Environment
        Agency 7.174–7.176
    offences 7.131–7.142, 9.107
    planning permission 7.173, 7.187,
        14.86–14.91
    revocation 7.225–7.228
    right to a licence 7.170–7.171
    surrenders 7.229–7.234
    suspension 7.222–7.224
    transfers 7.217–7.221
    variation 7.211–7.216
motor vehicles 6.72, 7.78–7.84
nuclear waste 5.19–5.21, 7.72, 7.167, 8.50–8.55
offences 7.124, 7.131–7.142, 7.209, 7.223,
    7.224, 7.241, 7.244, 7.256, 9.107
oil or grease 7.19, 7.22, 7.34
packaging waste 2.14
permits, environmental
    electrical and electronic equipment 6.73
    incineration 6.74–6.76
    motor vehicles 6.72
    waste mobile plant 6.36–6.37
    waste operations 6.01, 6.04, 6.11, 6.30–6.37,
        6.65–6.69, 6.100, 6.253
    waste gases 6.77
planning 7.173, 7.187, 14.86–14.91
    waste local plan 14.83
radioactive waste 5.19–5.21, 7.72, 7.167,
    8.50–8.55
recycling 7.31–7.32, 7.240, 7.245
registers 5.84–5.92, 5.164
    incineration installations 6.287
    information requisitions: no right to
        silence 5.144–5.147
septic tanks 7.21, 7.40, 7.41
sewage 7.12, 7.40–7.41, 9.104

special waste 7.53–7.59, 7.76, 7.144,
    7.167, 7.224
    compounds 7.60–7.61
    Directive waste 7.63–7.69
    explosives 7.62
    hazardous 7.70–7.75
    motor vehicles 7.78–7.84
    packaging 7.77
statutory duty, breach of 16.73
strategy, national 7.85–7.94, 14.88–14.91
structure of regulation 2.50–2.51
trans-frontier trade 3.28
vessels, moored and unmoored 7.26
Waste Management Industry Training and
        Advisory Board (WAMITAB) 2.37
water pollution
    sewage 9.104
    waste matter 9.102
water industry
    Consumer Council for Water 10.14
    duties under WIA, general 10.16–10.24
    Environment Agency and 9.12–9.14
    introduction 9.03
    licensed water suppliers 10.11, 10.112–10.121
        complaints against 10.255–10.258
        enforcement 10.230, 10.232–10.254
        information 10.259–10.262
        quality, water 10.98, 10.102
        reviews 10.259
    local authorities
        sewerage 10.15, 10.150, 10.182–10.183,
            10.214, 10.231
        water 10.15, 10.85, 10.107, 10.122–10.126,
            10.231
    organization of 10.02–10.15
    private supplies 10.125
    undertakers *see* **sewerage undertakers; water
        undertakers**
water pollution
    anti-pollution works notices 9.125–9.127, 12.12
    Environment Agency
        duties and powers 9.09–9.11, 12.12–12.14
    groundwater 9.22–9.31
    historical background
        Rivers Pollution Prevention Act 1876
            1.31–1.37
    quality, water 9.78–9.80, 10.95–10.105
    rights to water 16.75
    section 85 offences 9.02, 9.81–9.86, 12.11
        act or default of another 9.98–9.99
        acts and omissions 9.90–9.92
        causation 9.93–9.97
        controlled waters 9.89
        entry or discharge 9.106

water pollution (*cont.*)

section 85 offences (*cont.*)

poisonous, noxious or polluting
matter 9.100–9.101

strict liability 9.87–9.88, 9.95

trade or sewage effluent 9.103–9.105

waste matter 9.102

section 85 offences: statutory defences 9.108,
9.119–9.121

abandoned mines 9.122–9.124

discharge consents 9.109–9.114, 10.181,
12.11, 12.13–12.14

emergency 9.115–9.118

section 86 prohibition 9.107

water resources

abstraction licences 9.32–9.33

appeals 9.41, 9.46, 9.49

application process 9.41–9.44

charges 9.60

compensation 9.58, 9.61

contents of 9.47–9.48

damage from abstraction 9.50

enforcement and offences 9.35–9.36

exemptions 9.34, 9.49

modification and revocation 9.55–9.58

restriction on applicants 9.37

Secretary of State's role 9.45

transfer of 9.40

types of 9.38–9.39

water rights trading 9.59

drought

offences 9.76

orders 9.62–9.72, 9.76, 9.77, 10.109

permits 9.73–9.75, 9.76, 9.77

plans 9.77, 10.111

Environment Agency

duties and powers 2.56, 9.02, 9.07–9.14

groundwater 9.22–9.24, 9.49

nitrate vulnerability zones 9.20, 9.28–9.31

oil storage 9.25–9.27

impounding licences 9.51–9.54

introduction 9.01–9.14

land drainage and flood control 9.128–9.146,
10.193

planning: flood risk areas 14.97–14.102

pollution *see* **water pollution**

quality, water 9.78–9.80, 10.95–10.105

registers 5.125, 5.164

content of 5.126–5.133

gathering information 5.138–5.147

integrated pollution control
publicity 5.134–5.137

publicity 5.148–5.152

rights to water 16.75

river basin management plans 9.18–9.20

minimum acceptable flows 9.21

strategic policy framework 9.15

Water Framework Directive 9.16–9.17, 11.58

waste disposal 7.100, 7.108, 7.109, 7.213

water undertakers

apparatus

adoption of 10.200–10.207

landowners and removal of 10.217–10.218

maps of underground 10.214–10.215

appointment of 10.25–10.43

charges 10.222–10.223, 10.226–10.229

complaints against 10.196–10.197,
10.255–10.258

compulsory purchase of land 10.198, 10.199

contamination, prevention of 10.106–10.107

disconnections 10.89–10.94

drought orders, permits and plans 9.62–9.77,
10.109, 10.111

duties 10.49

domestic supplies 10.57–10.79, 10.95–10.104

general 10.50–10.51

general environmental and
recreational 10.19–10.24

non-domestic supplies 10.80–10.88, 10.105

regulations 10.52–10.56

enforcement 10.230–10.231

domestic supplies 10.63–10.64, 10.68, 10.74,
10.79, 10.101–10.104, 10.244

financial penalties 10.245–10.249

information, power to require 10.253–10.254

orders 10.232–10.244

special administration orders 10.250–10.253

entry, powers of 10.219–10.220

hosepipe bans 10.108

information 10.56, 10.214–10.216,
10.253–10.254, 10.259–10.262

introduction 2.38, 9.03, 9.11, 9.12–9.14,
10.09–10.10

licensed water suppliers and 10.113,
10.116–10.121

local authorities 10.15, 10.85, 10.107,
10.122–10.126, 10.231

loudspeakers 13.91

management plans, water resources 10.110

mergers 10.44–10.45

mining code 10.211–10.213

protected land, disposal of 10.46–10.48, 11.88

quality 9.78–9.80

domestic supplies 10.95–10.104

non-domestic supply 10.105

reviews 10.259

statutory duty, breach of 16.73
waste, prevention of 10.106–10.107
works 10.184, 11.88
   code of practice 10.195
   compensation 10.188, 10.192, 10.194

compulsory orders 10.199
pipe laying 10.185–10.197
pollution prevention 10.187, 10.190
wildlife *see* **nature conservation**
World Health Organization (WHO) 2.41, 3.46